THE BOOK
OF THE STATES
1982-1983

VOLUME 24

THE COUNCIL OF
STATE GOVERNMENTS

THE COUNCIL OF STATE GOVERNMENTS

LEXINGTON, KENTUCKY

THE COUNCIL OF STATE GOVERNMENTS

The Council is a joint agency of all state governments—created, supported, and directed by them. It conducts research on state programs and problems; maintains an information service available to state agencies, officials, and legislators; issues a variety of publications; assists in state-federal liaison; promotes regional and state-local cooperation; and provides staff for affiliated organizations.

HEADQUARTERS OFFICE
Iron Works Pike, P.O. Box 11910, Lexington, Kentucky 40578

EASTERN OFFICE
1500 Broadway, 18th Floor, New York, New York 10036

MIDWESTERN OFFICE
203 North Wabash Avenue, Chicago, Illinois 60601

SOUTHERN OFFICE
3384 Peachtree Road, NE, Atlanta, Georgia 30326

WESTERN OFFICE
165 Post Street, 5th Floor, San Francisco, California 94108

WASHINGTON OFFICE
444 North Capitol Street, Washington, D.C. 20001

ISBN 0-87292-025-9
Printed in the United States of America
Price: $35.00

FOREWORD

For the twenty-fourth time since The Council of State Governments was founded, we present a new edition of *The Book of the States*. The increasing complexity and importance of state government can be measured by the amount of information in this book; more than 50 articles and nearly 300 tables. With the help of state government officials, university scholars and federal administrators we have gathered facts, figures and interpretations on nearly every aspect of state government activity. A strong theme of change dominates this edition, as author after author points out the momentous potential of changes in the federal system and the impact of rapidly changing revenues and funding.

This edition emphasizes the preceding two years, and where possible, extends coverage to early 1982. The legislative, executive and judicial branches of state government are surveyed, as well as intergovernmental affairs and all the major activities of the states. Volume 24 of *The Book of the States* will be supplemented during the next two years by volumes on legislators and state elected officials, state legislative leadership and committees, and state administrative officials.

The Council of State Governments gratefully acknowledges the help of all those who contributed to this book.

Lexington, Kentucky
April 1982

Frank H. Bailey
Executive Director

THE BOOK OF THE STATES

IS PUBLISHED BIENNIALLY BY
THE COUNCIL OF STATE GOVERNMENTS
IRON WORKS PIKE, P.O. BOX 11910
LEXINGTON, KENTUCKY 40578

Editing
Jack L. Gardner, Editor
L. Edward Purcell, Executive Editor

Research and Information Development
Karen Haller
Mary Caufield Breeding
Carolyn Kenton

Composition
Linda Bowman, Compositor and Editorial Assistant

Production
Susan Morrisette, Editorial and Production Assistant

Proofreading
Rosemary Staley
John Cornett
Sandra Wood
Robert Treadway

CONTENTS

85913

Section VI. ADMINISTRATION

1. Administrative Activities

2. Employment

Section VII. FINANCES

1. Revenue, Expenditure and Debt

2. Taxation

3. State Financial Administration

Section VIII. MAJOR STATE SERVICES

1. Education

2. Transportation

3. Health and Human Services

4. Safety and Public Protection

LIST OF TABLES

SECTION III. THE GOVERNORS AND THE EXECUTIVE BRANCH

Section IV. THE LEGISLATURES

Section V. THE JUDICIARY

Section VI. ADMINISTRATION

1. Administrative Activities

2. Employment

Section VII. FINANCES

1. Revenue, Expenditure and Debt

2. Taxation

3. State Financial Administration

Section VIII. MAJOR STATE SERVICES

1. Education

Section IX. The State Pages

xiv

INTRODUCTION

WITH THE PUBLICATION OF THIS VOLUME, The Council of State Governments marks the fiftieth anniversary of its formal organization in 1933. In that year, the American Legislators' Association met in Harrisburg, Pennsylvania, and the organization's president, former Colorado Senator Henry Toll, presented for adoption the articles of organization for The Council of State Governments. Toll, who was immediately designated the Council's first executive director, had worked since the early 1920s toward such a national organization embracing all aspects of state government.

Toll was an energetic and innovative organizer. Deciding that a roster of the nation's more than 7,000 state legislators was needed, he collected the names and published them in the first number of a monthly leaflet, *The American Legislator.*

So began a tradition. A need was filled by research and eventual publication of information of interest and importance to all the states. From these beginnings, the Council has grown, prospered and changed, but has adhered to its tradition—changed only in scope and degree.

In 1935, the Council published the first volume of *The Book of the States*, and other activities, still typical of the Council, began in the same year: the Council began to coordinate the Commissions for Interstate Cooperation and became the secretariat for the newly formed National Association of Attorneys General and the National Association of Secretaries of State. The Council's Chicago headquarters had begun in 1930 to operate on a regional level with the appointment of a regional director for the Midwest, and in 1935, the regional aspect grew with establishment of an office in New York to serve Northeastern states.

In 1938, Toll returned to his Denver law practice, and Frank Bane began a 20-year tenure as executive director. Under Bane's direction, the Council widened its activities on both the national and regional levels. The first information and inquiry service was established in 1938, which continues today as one of the basic services of the Council. In the same year, the Council opened a federal-state liaison office in Washington, D.C. During World War II, the Council helped coordinate state councils of defense, and in 1941, published the first volume of *Suggested State Legislation*, a project (now in its forty-first edition) that grew out of the drafting of national defense legislation for the states. In 1942, the Council's Western regional office in San Francisco was opened. Shortly after the war, the National Legislative Conference was formed in association with the Council, joining a growing number of such interstate organizations.

In 1958, Bane left the Council to become the first chairman of the Advisory Commission on Intergovernmental Relations. He was succeeded by Brevard Crihfield, a 14-year veteran of the Council staff. That same year the Council's periodical, *State Government*, became a quarterly, and a new monthly news magazine, *State Government News*, began publication. The Southern regional office in Atlanta opened in 1959. Secretariat services continued to expand during the late 1960s with the addition of the National Conference of Lieutenant Governors. In 1969, the headquarters office moved to Lexington, Kentucky, and the Chicago office became the regional center for the Midwest.

The organizational framework of the Council underwent significant changes during the 1970s. The membership of the governing board was broadened in a series of steps, to eventually include all 50 state governors and a legislator for each state. The executive committee became more active between annual meetings of the governing board and was expanded to include more members from affiliated organizations. In the mid-1970s, state legislators and governors reorganized themselves into more politically active associations and established independent headquarters. The Council of State Governments, however, reaffirmed its role as a non-partisan service organization.

In 1977, Herbert L. Wiltsee, long-time head of the Council's Southern regional office, became executive director, followed in 1978 by William J. Page Jr., former head of Florida's Department of Health and Rehabilitative Services. During these years, the Council expanded research and state management services activities and worked on several special projects under federal and private grants. In 1979, representatives of the National Association of State Auditors, Comptrollers and Treasurers joined CSG's executive committee, as members of a newly formed affiliate organization.

In 1981, Frank H. Bailey became the sixth and current executive director.

As American institutions go, one of 50 years is almost ancient, but the day-to-day activities of The Council of State Governments, as it passes this milestone, reveal a vigor mixed with reassuring continuity. While he might be mildly surprised by the number of employees or the breadth and depth of research and service, Henry Toll would doubtless be pleased with the Council's 1983 activities: gathering and distributing ideas and information from and to the states in order to aid cooperation, improve operations and strengthen their places in the American system.

The current federal focus on a separation of state-federal responsibilities has meant a renewed interest in the states. The Council is uniquely qualified to aid the states in the 1980s through its representation of a broad group of state decision-makers on the national and regional levels.

Section I
INTERGOVERNMENTAL AFFAIRS
1. Interstate Organizations

THE COUNCIL OF STATE GOVERNMENTS

THE COUNCIL OF STATE GOVERNMENTS is a non-profit, state-supported and directed service organization of all 50 states. Formally organized in 1933, the Council collects and distributes information, promotes interstate cooperation and works to improve state administration and management. For 50 years, the mission of the Council has remained firm—to strengthen the operations of states and their roles in the American federal system.

The Council's four regional offices, the headquarters and the Washington, D.C., liaison office collect, analyze and distribute state government information nationwide. Thousands of reports and surveys are collected by the Council, and, after analysis, made available to state officials. This includes response to hundreds of individual inquiries each month for state government information and tabular aggregation of all state responses on a particular issue. In many cases, after a thorough examination of an issue, the Council will recommend possible action on a specific program or problem. Information is distributed through regional and national conferences, training programs and publications.

The Council's basic premise is that the states themselves are a primary source of ideas, and so it serves as a conduit for the flow of information. The diversity of the 50 states has always been a fertile source of innovative solutions to the problems of state governments.

Offices of the Council

From its earliest years, directors of The Council of State Governments have understood the need for regional operations in coordination with a central office. When the Council's first national headquarters opened in Chicago in the early 1930s, a regional director was selected to work with the Council's executive director and charged with the specific duty of serving the Midwestern states.

Three more regional offices have been added during the intervening years. In 1935, the New York office was created to serve the Northeastern states. Soon after, an office was established in San Francisco for Western states, and in 1959, the Atlanta office began to serve Southern states. When the Council's headquarters office moved to Lexington, Kentucky, in 1969, the Chicago office became the regional center for the Midwest. Earlier, in 1938, a state-federal liaison office had been opened in Washington, D.C.

The issues and activities for each regional office are selected by a regional executive committee, comprised of state officials from that region.

Prepared by Jennifer Stoffel, Public Information Officer, The Council of State Governments.

Finances and Direction

The states and U.S. territories and commonwealths contribute to the Council's financial support. In addition, the Council administers federal and private-foundation grants that support research and information projects that align with the states' interests.

Overall direction of the Council's staff and activities comes from a governing board consisting of all the nation's governors and, typically, two legislators from each state and jurisdiction. By tradition, the president of the Council is a governor, and the chairman is a state legislator. Members of the governing board include representatives from the national organizations of lieutenant governors, attorneys general, chief justices, and state auditors, comptrollers and treasurers.

From this broadly based governing body of approximately 175 elected state officials, an executive committee of about one-fifth that number is selected to manage the business affairs of the Council between annual governing board meetings. The annual meeting directs Council activities and provides a forum for discussion of substantive state issues.

In 1979, the governing board of The Council of State Governments adopted amendments to its articles of organization which were designed to further enhance the regional concept. These changes provided a stronger role for regional state officials in the selection of regional office directors and forming regional budgets. The executive committee selects an executive director who is in charge of the Council's national and Washington offices. A final budget coordination procedure, outlined in the amended articles, places decision-making authority in a 13-member budget committee, representing both national and regional perspectives.

Activities of the Council

The Council of State Governments is based on the premise that the states themselves are the best sources of innovations, ideas and information, and its activities reflect this belief.

In Lexington, the States Information Center (SIC), a personal, direct-access inquiry and referral service, fields questions from state officials. By quickly locating statistical information, providing in-depth information through documents available for loan, and identifying appropriate experts on a given issue, the SIC unit replies to over 5,000 requests a year. In addition, the SIC library maintains 17,000 documents including Council and other organizational studies and an extensive collection of state government department and agency reports.

The Council also publishes a variety of materials about state government, including periodicals, directories, research reports, and a comprehensive reference guide, *The Book of the States*. Published biennially, *The Book of the States* has been revised and expanded over the years to reflect state government reorganization and to respond to the states' information needs. It is supplemented with three directories that include names, addresses and telephone numbers for the states' legislators, principal staffs, statewide elected officials and major administrative officials.

An annual edition of *Suggested State Legislation* has been published since 1941, providing a source of legislative ideas and drafting assistance. The draft acts to be included in each edition are selected by a committee of legislators and other state officials.

The Council also publishes a variety of periodicals: *State Government News*, published monthly, reports on noteworthy developments plus annual summaries of legislative action in the states; *State Government*, published since 1930, is a quarterly journal of state affairs providing a forum for the discussion of governmental problems, state innovative trends and issues; *State Government Research Checklist*, published six times a year, is an inventory of current state survey and research reports, as well as a guide to state government information sources and trends.

CSG also develops, produces and distributes audio-visual training and informational materials. Packages are presented in a variety of forms including slides, audiotapes, videotapes and films. These training packages are oriented to state government and can be modified to match an agency's needs and methods of operation.

The Washington, D.C. office of the Council serves as liaison with Congress, White House staff, federal agencies and public interest groups by monitoring and analyzing federal policy, legislation and regulations for state officials and Council offices. The office staff also advance state interests and Council policy positions at the federal level. In 1981, a reform, proposed by CSG in its "Blueprint for Regulatory Reform," had far-reaching impact. This proposal to place the burden of proof for demonstrating state non-compliance with federal regulations on the federal executive branch rather than on state education agencies was incorporated in the education block grant section of the federal budget reconciliation bill.

The Council's commitment to keeping the states informed and aware of innovations in state programs, improvements in state administration and solutions to state problems is the impetus behind the development of a range of policy and management services to state governments. The services range from one-on-one consultations to technical assistance projects to comprehensive management studies. A few of the policy and management activities follow:

- The Innovations Program studies and reports on significant innovations in state government.
- The Interstate Consulting Service, an adjunct to the Innovations Program, is a method by which states can provide each other with expertise.
- The Productivity Research Center monitors state projects aimed at improving productivity.
- The Executive, Management and Employee Development Program is designed to develop training support and materials for state government personnel and to maintain an information exchange of training and management development materials.
- The Council's work in state accounting has resulted in a set of preferred accounting practices which have begun to have an impact on bond ratings.
- The Environmental Resources and Development Program conducts policy research and information services in order to improve the states' capability to manage natural resources.
- The Licensure Information System can retrieve state laws from all states concerning licensing of over 40 health occupations and professions, and the exchange of information on other specific issues is provided through the newly created Clearinghouse on Licensing, Enforcement and Regulation.
- The Reapportionment Service monitors state plans and is a source of information on state activity and judicial criteria.

The Council also provides staff and secretariat services for several national organizations of state officials. The Council works with 33 affiliated and cooperating associations. The seven affiliate organizations are the National Conference of State Legislatures (NCSL), the Conference of Chief Justices, the National Conference of Lieutenant Governors (NCLG), the National Association of State Purchasing Officials (NASPO), the Conference of State

Court Administrators, the National Association of State Auditors, Comptrollers and Treasurers (NASACT), and the National Association of Attorneys General (NAAG). In addition, the Council provides staff support to the National Association of State Personnel Executives, the National Conference of State General Services Officers, the National Association for State Information Systems (NASIS), and the Clearinghouse on Licensing, Enforcement and Regulation.

5

REGIONAL CONFERENCE OFFICIALS OF THE COUNCIL OF STATE GOVERNMENTS

EASTERN CONFERENCE

Speaker Pro Tem Marshall French, New Hampshire, *Chairman*
Representative W. Paul White, Massachusetts, *Vice-Chairman*
Representative Timothy Moynihan, Connecticut, *Immediate Past Chairman*

CONNECTICUT
Sen. Audrey P. Beck
Rep. Irving Stolberg
Deputy Speaker Robert Frankel
Rep. Kevin P. Johnston
Rep. David Lavine

DELAWARE
Thomas Carper, State Treasurer
Pres. Pro Tem Richard S. Cordrey
Speaker Charles L. Hebner
Nancy Olsen, Exec. Asst. to the Lt. Gov.

MAINE
Sen. Thomas R. Perkins
Rep. G. William Diamond

MASSACHUSETTS
Sen. Joseph B. Walsh
Joseph Lawless, Dir. of Research, Office of the Speaker

NEW JERSEY
Sen. Pres. Carmen Orechio
Assemblyman Willie Brown
Speaker Alan Karcher
Robert Smartt, Deputy Director, New Jersey General Assembly

NEW YORK
Sen. Hugh T. Farley
Sen. John J. Marchi
Sen. Linda Winikow
Speaker Stanley J. Fink

PENNSYLVANIA
Sen. Michael O'Pake
Rep. R. Harry Bittle
Rep. George Pott

RHODE ISLAND
Gov. J. Joseph Garrahy
Sen. Rocco A. Quattrocchi
Speaker Matthew J. Smith
Arthur Markos, Deputy Dir., Governor's Special Development Office

VERMONT
Lt. Gov. Madeleine M. Kunin
Sen. William T. Doyle
Rep. Chester M. Taft

VIRGIN ISLANDS
Sen. Vice-Pres. Gilbert A. Sprauve

COMMITTEES AND CHAIRMEN
Energy—Rep. David Lavine, Connecticut
Fiscal Affairs and Government Operations—Rep. Irving Stolberg, Connecticut
Human Resources—(Vacancy)
Task Force on Environment—Rep. R. Harry Bittle, Pennsylvania
Special Task Force on Economic Affairs—Rep. George Pott, Pennsylvania
Legislative-Executive Staff Task Force —
   Robert Smartt, Deputy Dir., New Jersey General Assembly
   Nancy Olsen, Exec. Asst. to the Lt. Gov.

MIDWESTERN CONFERENCE

Sen. Pres. Fred A. Risser, Wisconsin, *Chairman*
Rep. Harold P. Dyck, Kansas, *Vice Chairman*

ILLINOIS
Sen. Pres. Philip J. Rock

INDIANA
Rep. Doris Dorbecker
Rep. John J. Thomas (ex officio)

IOWA
Sen. Calvin O. Hultman

KANSAS
Sen. Pres. Ross O. Doyen

MICHIGAN
Sen. Doug Ross

MINNESOTA
Rep. James I. Rice

MISSOURI
Sen. Pres. Pro Tem Norman L. Merrell

NEBRASKA
Sen. Robert L. Clark

NORTH DAKOTA
Rep. Roy Hausauer

OHIO
Sen. Pres. Paul E. Gillmor

SOUTH DAKOTA
Sen. James B. Dunn
Speaker Pro Tem Jerome B. Lammers (Alternate)

WISCONSIN
Thomas Peltin, Exec. Dir., Interstate Cooperation
  Commission (Alternate)

TASK FORCES AND CHAIRMEN
Agricultural Transportation—Rep. Walter J.
  Roorda, Indiana
Business Development—Sen. Fred A. Kerr, Kansas
Education—Rep. Carl M. Johnson, Minnesota;
Energy—Sen. Hubert H. Humphrey III, Minnesota;
Legislative Oversight—Sen. Pres. Pro Tem Mary
  McClure, South Dakota
Taxation—Rep. James D. Braden, Kansas

MIDWESTERN GOVERNORS' CONFERENCE

Gov. John Carlin, Kansas, *Chairman*
Gov. Lee S. Dreyfus, Wisconsin, *Vice Chairman*

LEAD GOVERNORS
Energy—Gov. Albert H. Quie, Minnesota
Capital Formation—Gov. James R. Thompson,
  Illinois
Water Management—Gov. William G. Milliken,
  Michigan

SOUTHERN LEGISLATIVE CONFERENCE

House Maj. Ldr. John E. Miller, Arkansas, *Chairman*
Sen. Pres. Michael H. O'Keefe, Louisiana, *Chairman-Elect*
Rep. T. W. Edwards Jr., South Carolina, *Vice Chairman*
Rep. Mark D. O'Brien, Kentucky, *Past Chairman*

ALABAMA
Lt. Gov. George McMillan Jr.
Pres. Pro Tem. Finis E. St. John III (Alternate)
Speaker Pro Tem Richard S. Manley
Speaker Joe C. McCorquodale (Alternate)

ARKANSAS
Sen. William D. Moore Jr.
Rep. Ray S. Smith Jr.
Speaker Lloyd C. McCuiston Jr. (Alternate)
Rep. John M. Lipton (Alternate)

FLORIDA
Speaker Ralph Haben
Speaker Pro Tem Barry Kuten (Alternate)
Rep. Wayne Hollingsworth (Alternate)

GEORGIA
Sen. Render Hill
Sen. Joseph Kennedy (Alternate)
Speaker Thomas B. Murphy
Rep. Ward Edwards (Alternate)

KENTUCKY
Pres. Pro Tem Joseph W. Prather

LOUISIANA
Sen. Pres. Pro Tem Samuel B. Nunez Jr. (Alternate)
Speaker John J. Hainkel Jr.
Speaker Pro Tem Frank P. Simoneaux (Alternate)

MARYLAND
Sen. Pres. James Clark Jr.
Sen. Harry J. McGuirk (Alternate)
Speaker Benjamin L. Cardin
Speaker Pro Tem Daniel J. Minnick Jr. (Alternate)

MISSISSIPPI
Sen. Ollie Mohammed
Rep. Kenneth O. Williams

NORTH CAROLINA
Sen. Pres. Pro Tem W. Craig Lawing
Sen. Kenneth C. Royall Jr. (Alternate)
Speaker Liston B. Ramsey

OKLAHOMA
Sen. Pres. Pro Tem Marvin York
Sen. Ernest Martin (Alternate)
Speaker Daniel D. Draper Jr.
Rep. Vernon Dunn (Alternate)

PUERTO RICO
Sen. Luis A. Ferre
Sen. Jose M. Ramos-Barroso (Alternate)
Rep. Jose Granados-Navedo
Rep. Severo E. Colberg (Alternate)

SOUTH CAROLINA
Sen. Pres. Pro Tem L. Marion Gressette
Sen. Rembert Dennis (Alternate)
Speaker Raymon Schwartz Jr.
Speaker Pro Tem Michael R. Daniel (Alternate)

TENNESSEE
Lt. Gov. John S. Wilder
Speaker Ned R. McWherter
Rep. John T. Bragg (Alternate)

TEXAS
Sen. John Traeger
Sen. Ray Farabee (Alternate)
Speaker Bill Clayton
Rep. Pete Laney (Alternate)

VIRGINIA
Pres. Pro Tem Edward E. Willey
Sen. Hunter B. Andrews (Alternate)
Speaker A. L. Philpott
Del. J. William O'Brien Jr. (Alternate)

WEST VIRGINIA
Sen. Carl E. Gainer
Sen. Pres. Warren R. McGraw (Alternate)
Del. W. Marion Shiflet
Speaker Clyde M. See Jr. (Alternate)

COMMITTEES AND CHAIRMEN

Agriculture and Rural Development—Rep. Charles R. Moore, Arkansas

Consumer Protection—Sen. William D. Moore Jr., Arkansas

Criminal Justice—Sen. Riley C. Darnell, Tennessee

Energy—Rep. Bob Argo, Georgia

Environmental Quality and Natural Resources— Sen. Perrin Purvis, Mississippi

Federal Preemption—Rep. Kenneth O. Williams, Mississippi

Fiscal Affairs and Government Operations— Sen. Ted Little, Alabama

Human Resources and Urban Affairs—Rep. Charles Mann, Georgia

Transportation—Sen. Robert Crook, Mississippi

SOUTHERN GOVERNORS' ASSOCIATION

Gov. Richard W. Riley, South Carolina,
Chairman
Gov. William P. Clements Jr., Texas,
Vice Chairman

LEAD GOVERNORS

Agriculture—Gov. James B. Hunt Jr., North Carolina

Criminal Justice and Public Safety—Gov. Christopher S. Bond, Missouri

Economic Development—Gov. William Winter, Mississippi

Education—Gov. Harry R. Hughes, Maryland

Energy and Environment—Gov. John Y. Brown Jr., Kentucky

Human Resources—Gov. Bob Graham, Florida

Transportation—Gov. William P. Clements Jr., Texas

INTERGOVERNMENTAL AFFAIRS

WESTERN CONFERENCE

Sen. Cary Peterson, Utah, *Chairman*
Speaker Pro Tem Russ Donley, Wyoming, *Chair-Elect*
Sen. Sam Guess, Washington, *Vice Chairman*
Sen. Keith Ashworth, Nevada, *Past Chairman*

ALASKA
Sen. Robert H. Ziegler

ARIZONA
Sen. James Mack
Rep. Sam A. McConnell Jr.
Rep. James J. Sossaman (Alternate)

CALIFORNIA
Sen. Pres. Pro Tem David A. Roberti
Assemblyman Michael Roos

COLORADO
Speaker Carl B. Bledsoe

IDAHO
Sen. James E. Risch
Sen. Mike Mitchell
Rep. Walter E. Little

MONTANA
Sen. Pat M. Goodover
Speaker Robert L. Marks
Rep. John Vincent

NEVADA
Sen. Pres. Pro Tem James I. Gibson
Sen. Norman D. Glaser
Sen. Lawrence Jacobsen
Speaker Robert R. Barengo

NEW MEXICO
Sen. Alex G. Martinez
Rep. James A. Caudell
Rep. Dan Berry
Rep. Leo Catanach

OREGON
Sen. Pres. Pro Tem Cliff Trow
Rep. Gretchen Kafoury
Rep. Ben "Kip" Lombard
Rep. Max Rijken
Rep. William Grannell

UTAH
Sen. Pres. Miles "Cap" Ferry
Sen. Ivan Matheson
Sen. Wilford Black
Speaker Norman H. Bangerter

WASHINGTON
Sen. John D. Jones
Rep. Gary A. Nelson

WYOMING
Sen. L. Donald Northrup
Rep. Bob Burnett
Rep. Harry B. Tipton (Alternate)

COMMITTEES AND CHAIRMEN
Corrections—Sen. Mike Mitchell, Idaho
Energy Conservation and Renewable
    Resources—Rep. John Vincent, Montana
Energy and Minerals Development—Rep. Dan Berry,
    New Mexico
Hazardous Materials—Sen. Lawrence Jacobsen,
    Nevada
Human Resources—Sen. Sam Guess, Washington
International Trade—Rep. Max Rijken, Oregon
Public Lands—Sen. Ivan Matheson, Utah
Transportation—Sen. Wilford Black, Utah
Water Policy—Rep. Ben "Kip" Lombard, Oregon

WESTERN GOVERNORS' CONFERENCE

Gov. Ed Herschler, Wyoming, *Chairman*
Gov. Victor Atiyeh, Oregon, *Vice Chairman*

PROPOSALS OF THE COMMITTEE ON SUGGESTED STATE LEGISLATION

1981 Suggested State Legislation

Proposals Accompanied by Draft Legislation

Alimony and Child Support Act
Awards of Custody Act
Adoptive Information Act
Birth Certificates for Foreign-Born Adoptees Act
Displaced Homemakers Act
Minors' Consent to Donate Blood Act
Blood Test Act
Conversion of Group Health Insurance Act
Clinical Laboratory Billing Information Act
Domestic Violence Act
Prohibition of Rebates for Patient Referrals Act
Fraudulent Use of Birth Certificates Act
Computer Crime Act
Financial Transaction Card Crime Act
Motion Picture Fair Competition Act
Office of Consumer Advocate Act
Art Consignment Act
911 Emergency Telephone Number Act
State Audit Acts
  Auditor Revenue Act

Grant Audit Funding Act
Auditor Access to Records Act
Duties of Agencies with Regard to
  Audit Reports Act
Set-Off Debt Collection Act
Local Government Borrowing Supervision and
  Assistance Act
Commercial Redevelopment Districts Act
Industrial and Commercial Redevelopment Act
Small Business and Local Development Corporation
  Capital Loan Program Act
Business Regulation and Licensing System Act
Business Regulation and Licensing Act
Mobile Home Park Bill of Rights Act
Alternative Mortgage Act
Federal Land Acquisition Act
Act to Remove Barriers to Coordinating
  Human Service Transportation
Act to Remove Legal Impediments to
  Ridesharing Arrangements
Humane Slaughter Act—Amendments

Statements without Accompanying Draft Legislation

Revisions in the Uniform Vehicle Code—Statement

Uniform Real Estate Time-Share Act

1982 Suggested State Legislation

Proposals Accompanied by Draft Legislation

Abandoned Railway Reopening
  Trust Agreements Act
Energy Credit Program Act
Forms Management Center Act
Hazardous Waste Site Approval and Selection
Public Lands Act
Insurance Policy Language Simplification Act
Plain Language Consumer Contracts Act
Gasoline Price Posting Act
Mandatory Sprinkler Systems Act
Litter Control and Recycling Act
Prevention and Control of Local Government
  Financial Emergencies Act
Indexation of Income Tax for Inflation Act
Small Business Equity Corporation and Small
  Business Investment Acts
Cooperative Economic Development Act
Capital Budgeting and Planning Act
Neighborhood Assistance Act

Restitution and Pre-trial Intervention Act
Regulation of Precious Metal Dealers Act
Standards for Speed-Measuring Instruments Act
Trafficking in Controlled Substances Act
Protection of Public Employees Act
Incentive Pay for State Employees Act
Reduced Worktime Program Act
Shared Work Unemployment Compensation Act
Community Resource Act
Equal Access to Public Facilities Act
Crowd Control Act
Second Medical Opinion Act
Shelters for Victims of Domestic Violence Act
Retardation Prevention and Community Services Act
Subsidy Program for Qualified Parents Act
Rights of Nursing Home Residents Act
Educational Policy Planning Act
Liens on Personal Property in
  Self-Service Storage Act

AFFILIATED AND COOPERATING ORGANIZATIONS

The Articles of Organization of The Council of State Governments recognize two forms of association with the Council by groups of state officials—affiliated and cooperating. The Council presently recognizes 33 such groups—seven affiliated and 26 cooperating.

For organizations affiliated with the Council, the state services agency is authorized to provide financial assistance and secretariat and other staff services.

The seven affiliated organizations of the Council are the:

National Conference of State Legislatures,
Conference of Chief Justices,
National Association of Attorneys General,
National Conference of Lieutenant Governors,
National Association of State Purchasing Officials,
Conference of State Court Administrators,
National Association of State Auditors, Comptrollers and Treasurers.

The Council's Articles of Organization also permit its executive committee to recognize other groups and associations of state officials as cooperating organizations and maintain continuing cooperative arrangements with such organizations.

The cooperating organizations include the:

National Conference of Commissioners on Uniform State Laws,
Parole and Probation Compact Administrators' Association,
Association of Juvenile Compact Administrators,
Interstate Conference on Water Problems,
National Association of State Mental Health Program Directors,
Adjutants General Association of the United States,
National Conference on Uniform Reciprocal Enforcement of Support,
Association of State and Interstate Water Pollution Control Administrators,
National Association of State Boating Law Administrators,
National Association of State Civil Defense Directors,
Association of State Correctional Administrators,
National Association of State Units on Aging,
National Association of Extradition Officials,
National Association of State Juvenile Delinquency Program Administrators,
State Personnel Administrators Association,
Council of State Administrators of Vocational Rehabilitation,
National Association for State Information Systems,
National Association of Regulatory Utility Commissioners,
Coastal States Organization,
Federation of Tax Administrators,
National Association of Tax Administrators,
Conference of State Sanitary Engineers,
National Conference of States on Building Codes and Standards,
National Association of State Departments of Agriculture,
National Conference of State Criminal Justice Planning Administrators, and
National Conference of State General Services Officers.

SELECTED ORGANIZATIONS SERVING
STATE AND LOCAL GOVERNMENT OFFICIALS

Academy for State and Local Government, 400 North Capitol Street, NW, Suite 390, Washington, D.C. 20001. (202) 638-1445

Advisory Commission on Intergovernmental Relations, 1111-20th Street, NW, Suite 2000, Washington, D.C. 20575. (202) 653-5640

American Association of State Highway and Transportation Officials, 444 North Capitol Street, Washington, D.C. 20001. (202) 624-5800

American Judicature Society, 200 West Monroe, Suite 1606, Chicago, Illinois 60606. (312) 558-6900

American Planning Association, 1313 East 60th Street, Chicago, Illinois 60637. (312) 947-2560

American Public Health Association, 1015-15th Street, NW, Washington, D.C. 20005. (202) 789-5600

American Public Welfare Association, 1125-15th Street, NW, Suite 300, Washington, D.C. 20005. (202) 393-7550

American Public Works Association, 1313 East 60th Street, Chicago, Illinois 60637. (312) 947-2520

American Society for Public Administration, 1225 Connecticut Avenue, NW, Washington, D.C. 20036. (202) 785-3255

Association of Government Accountants, 727 South 23rd Street, Suite 100, Arlington, Virginia 22202. (703) 684-6931

Association of State and Territorial Health Officials, 1015-15th Street, NW, Suite 404, Washington, D.C. 20005. (202) 789-1044

Building Officials and Code Administrators International, 17926 South Halsted Street, Homewood, Illinois 60430. (312) 799-2300

Conference of Chief Justices, 300 Newport Avenue, Williamsburg, Virginia 23185. (804) 253-2000

Conference of State Court Administrators, 300 Newport Avenue, Williamsburg, Virginia 23185. (804) 253-2000

Council of State Community Affairs Agencies, 444 North Capitol Street, Washington, D.C. 20001. (202) 624-5850

Council of State Governments, Iron Works Pike, P.O. Box 11910, Lexington, Kentucky 40578. (606) 252-2291

Council of State Planning Agencies, 444 North Capitol Street, Suite 291, Washington, D.C. 20001. (202) 624-5386

Education Commission of the States, 300 Lincoln Tower Building, 1860 Lincoln Street, Denver, Colorado 80295. (303) 861-4917

Federation of Tax Administrators, 444 North Capitol Street, Washington, D.C. 20001. (202) 624-5890

International Association of Chiefs of Police, 11 Firstfield Road, Gaithersburg, Maryland 20878. (301) 948-0922

International City Management Association, 1400 Connecticut Avenue, NW, Washington, D.C. 20036. (202) 828-3600

International Personnel Management Association, 1850 K Street, NW, Suite 870, Washington, D.C. 20006. (202) 833-5860

Interstate Conference of Employment Security Agencies, 444 North Capitol Street, NW, Suite 126, Washington, D.C. 20001. (202) 628-5588

Municipal Finance Officers Association of U.S. and Canada, 180 North Michigan Avenue, Chicago, Illinois 60601. (312) 977-9700

National Association for State Information Systems, Iron Works Pike, P.O. Box 11910, Lexington, Kentucky 40578. (606) 252-2291

National Association of Attorneys General, Iron Works Pike, P.O. Box 11910, Lexington, Kentucky 40578. (606) 252-2291

National Association of Conservation Districts, 1025 Vermont Avenue, NW, Washington, D.C. 20005. (202) 347-5995

National Association of Counties, 1735 New York Avenue, NW, Washington, D.C. 20006. (202) 783-5113

National Association of Insurance Commissioners, 350 Bishops Way, Brookfield, Wisconsin 53005. (414) 784-9540

National Association of Regulatory Utility Commissioners, 1102 ICC Building, P.O. Box 684, Washington, D.C. 20044. (202) 628-7324

National Association of State Auditors, Comptrollers, and Treasurers, Iron Works Pike, P.O. Box 11910, Lexington, Kentucky 40578. (606) 252-2291

National Association of State Boards of Education, 444 North Capitol Street, NW, Suite 526, Washington, D.C. 20001. (202) 624-5844

National Association of State Budget Officers, 444 North Capitol Street, Washington, D.C. 20001. (202) 624-5382

National Association of State Departments of Agriculture, 1616 H Street, NW, Washington, D.C. 20006. (202) 628-1566

National Association of State Mental Health Program Directors, 1001 Third Street, SW, Suite 114, Washington, D.C. 20024. (202) 554-7807

National Association of State Purchasing Officials, Iron Works Pike, P.O. Box 11910, Lexington, Kentucky 40578. (606) 252-2291

National Association of Tax Administrators, 444 North Capitol Street, Washington, D.C. 20001. (202) 624-5890

National Center for State Courts, 300 Newport Avenue, Williamsburg, Virginia 23185. (804) 253-2000

National Conference of Commissioners on Uniform State Laws, 645 North Michigan Avenue, Chicago, Illinois 60611. (312) 321-9710

National Conference of Lieutenant Governors, Iron Works Pike, P.O. Box 11910, Lexington, Kentucky 40578. (606) 252-2291

National Conference of State Legislatures, 1125 17th Street, 15th Floor, Denver, Denver, Colorado 80202. (303) 623-6600

National Council on Governmental Accounting, 180 North Michigan Avenue, Suite 800, Chicago, Illinois 60601. (312) 977-9700

National Criminal Justice Association, 444 North Capitol Street, Suite 305, Washington, D.C. 20001. (202) 347-4900

National Governors' Association, 444 North Capitol Street, Washington, D.C. 20001. (202) 624-5300

National Intergovernmental Audit Forum, 441 G Street, NW, Washington, D.C. 20548. (202) 275-5200

National League of Cities, 1301 Pennsylvania Avenue, NW, Washington, D.C. 20006. (202) 293-7310

National Municipal League, 47 East 68th Street, New York, New York 10021. (212) 535-5700

State Auditor Coordinating Council, Iron Works Pike, P.O. Box 11910, Lexington, Kentucky 40578. (606) 252-2291

Urban Institute, 2100 M Street, NW, Washington, D.C. 20037. (202) 233-1950

U.S. Conference of Mayors, 1620 Eye Street, NW, Washington, D.C. 20006. (202) 293-7330

INTERSTATE COMPACTS AND AGREEMENTS: 1980-81

By Benjamin J. Jones

ONE MAJOR ADVANTAGE of the American Constitution is its flexibility in allowing government to use new structures and policies to meet changing needs and address new problems. A remarkably flexible provision of the Constitution, and one which is continuing to receive attention and see use, is that section relating to interstate compacts. Article I, Section 10 of the U.S. Constitution provides that "No state shall, without the consent of Congress . . . enter into agreement or compact with another state or with a foreign power." The words make possible an interesting, frequently used, and yet strangely obscure federal mechanism known as the interstate compact.

Interstate compacts are a level of government, between federal and state, created to deal with a specific problem. They are both contracts between the states and agreements with constitutional status, which create legitimate and important new government entities. They are typically set up by states, with only individual states constituting the compacts' membership. They may (and have on a few occasions) include the federal government or even Canadian Provinces as members along with the signatory states. Compacts are legislation in the sense that it is necessary that each compact be enacted into law by the legislatures of all states which wish to belong to it. Interstate compacts are typically the result of an effort among states facing a common problem to act jointly to deal with it in the common interest. Often states negotiate such compacts through their governors or other administrative officials before actual legislative consideration, and interstate organizations of state officials have identified the need and potential for compacts in particular problem areas.

The use of compacts was relatively infrequent until the 20th century. When used early in our history, such as settling boundary disputes, they effectively filled a need in the federal system. There was not a high demand for a mechanism other than the federal government to deal with interstate problems, however, during those less complex earlier decades of our history. From the first use of compacts (even before adoption of the Constitution) until 1920, only 36 interstate compacts were entered into by states. During the next 30 years, roughly the same number of new compacts were created. After 1950, however, the necessity to deal with ever more complex problems significantly increased the use of compacts by the states. At least 110 compacts have been negotiated since 1950, covering the gamut of subjects in which states have an interest. Some compacts now address national rather than strictly regional problems in areas where difficulties are nationwide but responsibility chiefly lies with the states. The last few decades have also seen vastly increased use of compacts to create interstate agencies, with continuing existence, their own source of funding and permanent staffs. These entities, because of their natures as agencies rather than just agreements, are able to perform functions and duties in areas such as regulation, public works and education, which cannot practically be handled by either states alone or by more traditional types of compacts and agreements.

Benjamin J. Jones is an attorney in private practice and serves as legal advisor for several Council of State Governments' projects.

Legally, interstate compacts are without analogy in our governmental system. As contracts between constitutionally recognized states, they are superior to, and have precedence over, conflicting statutes, either prior or subsequent, enacted by a signatory state. The U.S. Supreme Court has expressed a willingness to enforce such agreements where necessary and has indicated that withdrawal from them may only be accomplished in accord with the compacts' own withdrawal provisions. Although the compact clause of the Constitution would seem to require that all compacts receive the advance consent of Congress, this has not in fact been the requirement of that language. In *Virginia* v. *Tennessee* (148 U.S. 503 [1893]) and subsequent decisions, the U.S. Supreme Court has interpreted the compact clause to mean that consent can be validly given by implication as well as by express action. The U.S. Supreme Court has dealt with compacts and their characteristics in a number of decisions, covering such questions as the rules of judicial construction of compact texts, the binding nature of the agreements, and the extent to which governmental powers may be delegated to compact agencies. Since congressional consent is so important to compact creation and the federal government is involved in all major areas of interest to states, the policies and attitudes of federal executive branch agencies also constitute a significant part of the legal environment of compacts.

Recent Developments

From 1950 to 1970, the growth in the number of new compacts was dramatic. During the decade of the 1970s, however, that growth slowed to the smallest number for a 10-year period since World War II. Reasons for this decline probably included the growth in the responsibilities assumed by the federal government and the fact that the rapid growth already experienced in the number of compacts made new agreements less necessary. During 1980 and 1981, however, that trend away from new compacts may well have begun to reverse. During the last two years, at least five new compacts have reached various stages in the creation process, with major revisions in at least two others a distinct possibility. If, in fact, compact activity is again on the rise, it may be due to new policies in Washington intended to shift responsibility in many areas back to state and local governments. An additional factor may be the perception of compacts as an efficient solution to interstate problems in a time of fiscal difficulty. Several recent compact efforts illustrate both the creativity and the flexibility which compacts allow.

The Tahoe Regional Planning Compact was enacted by California and Nevada in 1968 and approved by Congress in 1969. It established an areawide planning agency with power to adopt and enforce a regional plan of resource conservation and development and to exercise various environmental controls over the Lake Tahoe area. In 1980, as the culmination of a five-year effort by both states, California and Nevada both adopted a major revision of the agreement to both limit some of the agencies' powers and grant expanded jurisdiction where experience had shown the need. The new compact changes the membership of the planning agency; sets up a new voting procedure for the approval of environmental standards, plans, ordinances and regulations; restricts certain types of construction in the Lake Tahoe basin area; and authorizes the drafting of a new regional plan using new environmental standards. Plans and regulations of the California Tahoe regional planning agency will be included in the bi-state agency's plans. Among these is a new transportation plan for the area covered by the agreement. A Tahoe transportation district will be created with limited taxing powers. The district will be prohibited from imposing property taxes or a user fee on vehicles in the lake area.

Many questions surrounding nuclear-powered generating plants are of vital interest to state governments. Perhaps no issue has been as troublesome as the question of how low-level radioactive waste disposal should be managed. With the passage in 1980 by Congress of the Low-Level Radioactive Waste Policy Act (96-573), states began considering the use of interstate compacts as a means of dealing with the problem of low-level waste disposal. In that legislation, Congress authorized and encouraged the states to enter into interstate compacts for the purpose of managing low-level radioactive waste. The act established a federal policy making each state responsible for the commercial low-level waste generated within its borders and encouraging compacts on the subject. As a result, by mid-1981 officials from the Western states had developed the Northwest Interstate Compact on Low-Level Radioactive Waste Management. That compact, which has now been adopted by Oregon, Idaho and Washington, is a first in the area of low-level waste management. Also eligible to join but not yet members are Alaska, Hawaii, Montana, Utah and Wyoming.

The compact provides that the party states cooperate in minimizing state handling and transportation required to dispose of wastes and cooperate in providing facilities for disposal that will conserve the entire region. The compact provides further that each member state will adopt practices that ensure low-level waste shipments originating within its borders and destined for another signatory state conform to the requirements of the destination state. These efforts are to include the maintenance of an inventory of each state's own low-level radioactive waste generators, unannounced inspections of such facilities and speedy action to halt violations. The compact further provides that disposal facilities located in any party state must accept low-level waste from any other party state. Such disposal facilities may not, however, accept wastes from non-party states without the approval of a body consisting of each party state's administrator for the compact. The agreement also provides that each party state shall cooperate with the other party states in identifying appropriate sites for common disposal facilities, and each party state pledges itself to act in good faith in such efforts.

In addition to the Northwest Interstate Compact on Low-Level Radioactive Waste Management, interested states in other regions may look to another recently developed model. The Low-Level Radioactive Waste Management Regional Compact was drafted by the State Planning Council on Radioactive Waste Management of the Southern States Energy Board in mid-1981 and is intended to offer to states options in forming a compact agreement similar to the Northwest. Alternative provisions are used liberally in the model compact draft, to enable states to use the language to achieve their own desired ends. Depending upon language chosen, states adopting this model could have in place a compact with strong regulatory authority or a more traditional advisory body.

Yet another new regional compact to be developed over the last two years is the Connecticut River Atlantic Salmon Compact. This agreement, which Connecticut, Vermont and New Hampshire have already joined, is a conservation-oriented agreement directed at re-establishing salmon as inhabitants of the Connecticut River. The compact requires member states to channel development along the river so as not to impede the movement of salmon up and downstream.

An indication of the wide range of subjects covered by interstate compacts may be gained from mention of yet another agreement which has been the subject of revision efforts during 1981. The Driver License Compact was created in 1960 to provide to states an arrangement to effectively ensure that each driver holds no more than one driver's license and that his driving offenses, no matter where committed, would be reflected on his driving record.

The compact requires signatory states (of which there are now 30) to send to a driver's home state the record of any infraction he may commit in other party states. The problem of multiple licenses from more than one state is addressed through requirements that a license applicant provide clearance from his former home state before obtaining a new license and that the former home state cancel his license when the new one is issued. Problems developed with the Driver License Compact over the period 1960-1980, principally due to the lack of a central coordinating mechanism to provide guidance on procedures and investigate specific problems. Accordingly, in 1981 The Council of State Governments prepared an initial draft of a revised Driver License Compact and a report recommending ways to implement a major revision. Currently CSG, the National Highway Traffic Safety Administration and the American Association of Motor Vehicle Administrators are working jointly to assist states in appropriate action to address these problems.

Future Role of Interstate Compacts

If no new interstate compacts were ever entered into, their current use would ensure their continued significance. Yet compacts are flexible and have been used in the complete range of subject areas addressed by state government. Accordingly, there is every reason to expect that in times of fiscal pressure states will maintain the compact option as visible and useful. In many ways the problem of low-level radioactive waste disposal demonstrates why we may continue to expect new compacts to be developed. The problem is relatively new, it is one in which states bear much of the responsibility for solution, it is one where solutions are complex and expensive, and it is a difficulty that inherently transcends the borders of a single state. In such situations, compacts can often provide a framework of interstate commitment in which the separate jurisdictions can rely upon one another to take joint action. Compacts can also delegate multi-state governmental power to a single agency—in effect merging jurisdictions for a particular, limited purpose. Often compacts can also provide economies of scale or otherwise offer financial advantages which would be difficult or impossible for individual states to achieve. It may, therefore, be expected that the usefulness of this 200-year-old mechanism will not soon expire, but will merely take new forms to meet new problems.

The Council of State Governments and Interstate Compacts

Since its inception in the 1930s, The Council of State Governments has been repeatedly involved in the creation and operation of interstate compacts. The Council's research materials and its history of compact involvement make it undoubtedly the nation's greatest source of information on the subject. Of the approximately 175 interstate compacts, the Council has to a greater or lesser degree been involved in the creation or operation of at least 100. As it has for several decades, the Council is ready to assist states in their interstate compact activities. In addition, the Council remains committed to maintenance of files on compacts and will continue to issue new publications on the subject and revise those of continuing interest.

As in the past, the Committee on Suggested State Legislation of the Council of State Governments continues to review proposed new compacts for publication in its annual *Suggested State Legislation* and also often uses that publication to disseminate information to states on proposed alterations in existing compacts and general background on the status of many of the more important agreements. Those individuals interested in additional information or assistance are welcome to contact the Council directly.

PARTICIPATION IN SELECTED INTERSTATE COMPACTS AND AGREEMENTS*

	Agreement on detainers	Agreement on qualification of educational personnel	Atlantic States Marine Fisheries Compact	Bus Taxation Proration & Reciprocity Agreement	Civil Defense & Disaster Compact	Colorado River Compact	Compact for Education	Compact on Mental Health	Compact on Motor Fuels Consumed by Interstate Buses	Delaware River & Bay Authority Compact	Delaware River Basin Compact	Delaware River Port Authority Compact	Driver License Compact	Great Lakes Basin Compact	Gulf States Marine Fisheries Compact	Interpleader Compact	Interstate Compact for Supervision of Parolees & Probationers	Interstate Compact on Juveniles
Alabama	★	★					★	★					★		★		★	★
Alaska		★					★	★					★				★	★
Arizona	★					★							★				★	★
Arkansas	★				★		★	★					★				★	★
California	★	★			★	★	★	★					★				★	★
Colorado	★				★	★	★	★					★				★	★
Connecticut	★	★	★	★			★	★									★	★
Delaware	★	★	★				★	★		★	★						★	★
Florida	★	★	★				★	★							★		★	★
Georgia	★		★		★		★	★									★	★
Hawaii	★	★					★	★					★				★	★
Idaho	★				★		★	★					★				★	★
Illinois	★				★		★	★									★	★
Indiana	★	★					★	★					★	★			★	★
Iowa	★						★	★									★	★
Kansas					★		★	★					★				★	★
Kentucky	★	★			★		★	★					★				★	★
Louisiana					★		★	★							★		★	★
Maine	★	★	★				★	★	★							★	★	★
Maryland	★	★	★		★		★	★								★	★	★
Massachusetts	★	★	★	★			★	★	★								★	★
Michigan	★	★			★		★	★						★			★	★
Minnesota	★	★					★	★						★			★	★
Mississippi	★						★						★		★		★	★
Missouri	★						★	★							★		★	★
Montana	★						★	★									★	★
Nebraska	★	★			★		★	★					★				★	★
Nevada	★					★							★				★	★
New Hampshire	★	★	★	★			★	★	★								★	★
New Jersey	★	★	★				★	★		★	★	★	★			★	★	★
New Mexico	★				★		★	★					★				★	★
New York	★	★	★	★			★	★			★		★	★		★	★	★
North Carolina	★	★	★		★		★	★					★		★		★	★
North Dakota	★			★	★		★	★									★	★
Ohio	★	★		★			★	★	★					★			★	★
Oklahoma	★	★					★	★					★				★	★
Oregon	★						★	★					★				★	★
Pennsylvania	★	★	★				★	★	★	★	★	★	★			★	★	★
Rhode Island	★	★	★	★			★	★								★	★	★
South Carolina	★		★		★		★	★									★	★
South Dakota	★						★	★									★	★
Tennessee	★						★	★									★	★
Texas	★				★		★	★								★	★	★
Utah	★	★				★	★										★	★
Vermont	★	★		★			★										★	★
Virginia	★	★	★		★		★						★				★	★
Washington	★	★					★	★					★				★	★
West Virginia	★	★		★			★	★					★				★	★
Wisconsin	★	★					★	★						★			★	★
Wyoming	★				★		★	★									★	★
Dist. of Col.	★	★		★			★	★									★	★
American Samoa							★											★
Guam																		★
Puerto Rico							★										★	
Virgin Islands							★										★	
U.S. govt.	★										★							

*This is only a partial listing of the 176 compacts and agreements listed in The Council of State Governments' *Interstate Compacts and Agencies* (1979 edition).

PARTICIPATION IN SELECTED INTERSTATE COMPACTS
AND AGREEMENTS—Continued

	Interstate Compact on Placement of Children	Interstate Corrections Compact	Interstate Library Compact	Interstate Mining Compact	Interstate Oil & Gas Compact	Kansas City Area Transportation Compact	Mentally Disordered Offender Compact	Middle Atlantic Forest Fire Protection Compact	Multistate Highway Transportation Agreement	Multistate Tax Compact	New England Corrections Compact	Non-resident Violator Compact of 1977	Northeastern Forest Fire Protection Compact	Pacific Marine Fisheries Compact	Potomac River Compact of 1958	Potomac Valley Compact	Red River Compact	Republican River Compact
Alabama	...	...	★	★	...	...	...	...	...	...	...	...	...	...	...	...	...	...
Alaska	★	...	...	...	★	...	...	...	...	★	...	...	...	★	...	...	...	...
Arizona	★	★	★	...	★	...	...	...	...	★	...	...	...	...	...	...	★	...
Arkansas	★	★	★	...	★	...	...	...	...	★	...	...	...	...	...	...	★	...
California	★	★	...	...	★	...	...	...	★	★	...	...	...	★	...	...	...	...
Colorado	★	★	★	...	★	...	...	...	...	★	...	...	...	...	...	...	...	★
Connecticut	★	★	★	...	...	...	...	...	...	...	★	★	...	...	...	...	...	...
Delaware	★	★	...	...	...	...	...	★	★	...	...	...	★	...	...	...	...	...
Florida	★	★	★	...	...	...	...	...	...	...	...	...	★	...	...	...	...	...
Georgia	★	★	★	...	...	...	...	...	...	...	...	...	...	...	...	...	...	...
Hawaii	...	...	...	...	...	...	...	...	...	★	...	...	...	...	...	...	...	...
Idaho	★	★	★	...	...	...	...	★	★	★	...	...	...	★	...	...	...	...
Illinois	★	★	★	★	★	...	★	...	...	...	...	...	...	...	...	...	...	...
Indiana	★	★	★	★	...	...	...	...	...	...	...	...	★	...	...	...	...	...
Iowa	★	★	★	...	...	...	...	...	...	...	...	...	...	...	...	...	...	...
Kansas	★	★	★	...	★	★	...	...	...	★	...	...	...	...	...	...	...	★
Kentucky	★	★	★	★	★	...	...	...	...	...	...	...	★	...	...	...	...	...
Louisiana	★	...	★	...	★	...	...	...	...	...	...	...	★	...	...	...	★	...
Maine	★	...	★	...	...	...	...	...	...	...	...	★	★	...	...	...	...	...
Maryland	★	★	★	★	★	...	...	★	...	...	...	...	★	...	...	★	★	...
Massachusetts	★	...	★	...	...	...	...	...	...	...	★	...	★	...	...	...	...	...
Michigan	...	...	...	...	★	...	...	...	...	★	...	...	...	...	...	...	...	...
Minnesota	★	★	★	...	...	...	...	...	...	...	...	...	★	...	...	...	...	...
Mississippi	★	★	★	...	★	...	...	...	...	...	...	...	★	...	...	...	...	...
Missouri	★	★	...	...	...	★	...	...	...	★	...	...	...	...	...	...	...	...
Montana	★	★	★	...	★	...	...	...	...	★	...	...	...	...	...	...	...	...
Nebraska	★	★	★	...	★	...	...	...	...	★	...	...	...	...	...	...	...	★
Nevada	...	★	★	...	...	...	...	...	★	★	...	...	...	...	...	...	...	...
New Hampshire	★	...	★	...	...	...	...	...	...	...	...	★	★	...	...	...	...	...
New Jersey	...	★	...	...	...	...	...	★	...	...	...	...	★	...	...	...	...	...
New Mexico	★	...	★	...	★	...	★	...	...	★	...	...	...	...	...	...	...	...
New York	★	...	★	...	★	...	...	...	...	★	...	★	★	...	...	...	...	...
North Carolina	★	★	★	★	...	...	...	...	...	...	...	...	★	...	...	...	...	...
North Dakota	★	...	★	★	★	...	★	...	...	★	...	...	★	...	...	...	...	...
Ohio	★	★	★	★	★	...	...	...	...	...	...	...	...	...	...	...	...	...
Oklahoma	★	...	★	★	★	...	...	...	...	...	...	...	...	...	...	...	...	...
Oregon	★	...	★	...	...	...	...	...	...	★	...	...	...	★	...	...	★	...
Pennsylvania	★	★	...	★	★	...	★	★	...	...	...	★	★	...	...	★	...	...
Rhode Island	★	...	★	...	...	...	★	...	...	...	★	★	★	...	...	...	...	...
South Carolina	...	★	...	★	...	...	...	...	...	...	...	...	★	...	...	...	...	...
South Dakota	★	★	★	...	★	...	...	...	...	★	...	...	...	...	...	...	...	...
Tennessee	★	★	★	★	★	...	...	...	...	★	...	...	...	...	...	...	...	...
Texas	★	...	...	★	★	...	...	...	...	★	...	...	...	...	...	...	★	...
Utah	★	★	★	...	★	...	...	...	...	★	...	...	...	...	...	...	...	...
Vermont	★	★	★	...	...	...	...	...	...	...	★	...	★	...	...	...	...	...
Virginia	★	★	★	★	...	...	★	...	...	...	...	★	...	...	★	★	...	...
Washington	★	...	★	...	...	...	...	...	...	★	...	...	...	★	...	...	...	...
West Virginia	★	...	★	★	★	...	★	★	...	★	...	...	★	...	...	★	...	...
Wisconsin	★	...	★	★	...	...	★	...	...	...	...	...	...	...	...	...	...	...
Wyoming	★	★	...	★	...	★	...	...	...	...	...	...	...	...	...	...	...	...
Dist. of Col.	★	...	...	...	...	...	...	...	...	★	...	★	...	...	...	★	...	...
American Samoa	...	...	...	...	...	...	...	...	...	...	...	...	...	...	...	...	...	...
Guam	★	...	...	...	...	...	...	...	...	...	...	...	...	...	...	...	...	...
Puerto Rico	...	...	...	...	...	...	...	...	...	...	...	...	...	...	...	...	...	...
Virgin Islands	...	...	...	...	...	...	...	...	...	...	...	...	...	...	...	...	...	...
U.S. govt.	...	...	...	...	...	...	...	...	...	...	...	...	...	...	...	...	...	...

PARTICIPATION IN SELECTED INTERSTATE COMPACTS AND AGREEMENTS—Concluded

	Rio Grande Interstate Compact	South Central Forest Fire Protection Compact	Southeastern Forest Fire Protection Compact	Southern Growth Policies Compact	Southern Interstate Energy Compact	Southern Regional Education Compact	Susquehanna River Basin Compact	Tahoe Regional Planning Compact	Thames River Flood Control Compact	Tri-State Regional Planning Compact	Tri-State Sanitation Compact	Unclaimed Property Compact	Uniform Vehicle Registration Proration & Reciprocity Agreement	Vehicle Equipment Safety Compact	Washington Metropolitan Area Transit Regulation Compact	Waterfront Compact	Western Corrections Compact	Yellowstone River Compact
Alabama			★	★	★	★												
Alaska													★					
Arizona													★				★	
Arkansas		★		★	★	★							★	★			★	
California								★					★	★			★	
Colorado	★												★	★			★	
Connecticut									★	★	★		★	★				
Delaware				★									★	★				
Florida			★	★	★	★							★	★				
Georgia			★	★	★	★							★	★				
Hawaii													★					
Idaho													★	★				
Illinois													★	★				
Indiana													★	★				
Iowa												★	★	★				
Kansas													★	★				
Kentucky			★	★	★	★							★	★				
Louisiana		★		★	★	★							★	★				
Maine													★	★				
Maryland				★	★		★						★		★			
Massachusetts									★				★	★				
Michigan													★	★				
Minnesota														★				
Mississippi		★	★	★	★	★							★	★				
Missouri					★								★	★				
Montana													★	★			★	★
Nebraska													★	★				
Nevada								★					★				★	
New Hampshire													★					
New Jersey										★	★	★	★	★		★		
New Mexico	★												★	★			★	
New York										★	★		★	★		★		
North Carolina			★	★	★	★							★	★				
North Dakota													★	★			★	★
Ohio													★	★				
Oklahoma		★		★	★								★	★				
Oregon													★	★			★	
Pennsylvania							★						★	★				
Rhode Island														★				
South Carolina			★	★	★	★												
South Dakota													★	★				
Tennessee			★	★	★	★							★	★				
Texas	★	★			★	★							★	★				
Utah													★	★			★	
Vermont														★				
Virginia			★	★	★	★							★	★	★			
Washington													★	★			★	
West Virginia			★	★	★	★							★	★			★	
Wisconsin												★		★				
Wyoming													★	★			★	★
Dist. of Col.													★		★			
American Samoa																		
Guam																		
Puerto Rico					★												★	
Virgin Islands																		
U.S. govt.						★												

2. Intergovernmental Relations

AMERICAN FEDERALISM—THEN AND NOW

By David B. Walker

IN THE ALMOST HALF CENTURY since the first *Book of the States*, there has been a revolution in federal-state-local relations. It began with the demise in the 1930s of dual federalism and its fundamental separation of basic governmental functions, powers and finances by governmental level. It proceeded with the gradual emergence during the next quarter century of a cooperative and commingled pattern of intergovernmental relations and continued to the spawning of various offshoots of cooperative federalism in the 1960s and 1970s under Presidents Johnson, Nixon and Carter.[1] At the moment, it is reflected in the new "New Federalism" of President Ronald Reagan with heavy emphasis on devolution and deregulation. This most recent development, to some, appears to be a reaction to the trends of the previous 50 years. But, as subsequent analysis will demonstrate, Reagan federalism, even if fully implemented, would not mean a return to the dual federalist principles and practice of the Hoover era.

The Initial Intergovernmental Pattern. The American system shifted dramatically toward greater centralization of governmental power and political influence and greater commingling of federal-state-local programs during the last 50 years. Some have argued that the seeds of this shift were sown in the federal regulatory and grant-in-aid efforts first launched in the 1880s. But, a careful examination of the intergovernmental impact of these earlier developments indicates that by 1930 only 15 grants were operating—all federal-state programs, and in total they represented less than 2 percent of all state revenues in 1927. While the states' regulatory, intrastate commerce and, in a few cases, taxing authorities were constrained by some of the federal government's regulations, none of these state powers was denied or in any real sense undermined. Most important, state and local governments enacted, performed and funded nearly all of the growing number of public services provided directly to the citizenry. In short, despite limited expansions of national authority during the 1865-1930 period, Madison's essentially compartmentalized system—dual federalism, if you will—was still essentially intact by the end of the third decade of this century.

From Dual to Cooperative Federalism (1933-1960). Between the elections of Franklin D. Roosevelt and John F. Kennedy, dual federalism declined precipitously. The earlier separation of services (and of funds) went first, followed by emergence of a full-blown theory of cooperative federalism during the late 1940s and early 1950s. Federal grant outlays rose to $2.9 billion by 1939, fell back to less than $1 billion by 1946, and then grew gradually to surpass the $7 billion mark by 1960. The federal government enacted 117 new permanent programs during this 30-year period. Despite the apparent proliferation, four programs—highways, old age assistance, aid to dependent children and employment security—accounted for almost three-quarters of all aid dollars in 1960. States were the dominant recipient partners—receiving 93 percent of the total in 1959. All but 1-2 percent

David B. Walker is Assistant Director of the Advisory Commission on Intergovernmental Relations.

(shared revenues from western lands) in any one year flowed through categorical conduits with project grants outnumbering formula grants by a two-to-one margin by the end of the Eisenhower years. Other than the normal programmatic, reporting and fiscal accountability provisions associated with categoricals, only the "single state agency" requirements and restrictions on political activity—chiefly in the Social Security Act programs—constituted what some state spokesmen deemed to be intrusive conditions.

In the realm of regulation, the national government carved out an even greater role than in the grant-in-aid field. The federal government began to dominate monetary, fiscal and banking policies. It moved into regulation of agriculture, stock exchanges, public utility holding companies and atomic energy uses, and a "federal presence" was established in labor-management relations in the private sector. In addition, the federal role that was initiated earlier in communications, shipping and airlines was expanded.

Not to be overlooked was the degree to which the federal government expanded its traditional functions as promoter of the economy and broker-subsidizer of major (usually economic or regional) interest groups in order to meet the exigencies of the Depression and post-war economic growth. Using both the regulatory and grant-in-aid approaches as well as many other forms of subsidies, 140 such programs were in place by 1960, about 90 percent of which had been enacted during the previous three decades.

At first glance, this dramatic growth in the grant-in-aid, regulatory and subsidy roles of the national government would appear to signify an extraordinary shift toward centralization, the collapse of the states' authority and influence in the system, and a nationally engineered cooperative federalism. Closer examination of the functional features of the system, however, reveals that most of the regulatory reforms were directed at interstate objects, that the states' police powers in intrastate commerce had not been undermined, that a majority of the states' executive departments and agencies were unaffected by federal grants, that only two (highway and welfare) were significantly but not exclusively involved with federal aid and another pair only minimally (natural resources and health), and that federal-local grant relationships were largely restricted to three aid programs (airports, urban renewal and public housing) and comparatively few local jurisdictions.

The collaborative and commingled pattern of intergovernmental functional and fiscal relations of this period, in fact, was far more descriptive of state-local relations than of the federal-state-local. Witness the emergence during these years of a strengthened state revenue raising role (with 154 new tax enactments), the ten-fold (four-fold in constant dollar terms) increase in state aid to localities between 1932 and 1958 (from $801 million to $8.1 billion), and the growing tendency of states to mandate.

From the vantage point of 1981, the system of 1961 was only moderately intergovernmentalized. The federal government directed the bulk of its regulatory and subsidy efforts toward the private sector, but the 117 new federal aid programs obviously constituted a major break with the network of intergovernmental relations that prevailed in 1931. Moreover, they heralded the decline of dual federalism, as did the growing interdependence of the states and their localities. Yet, it was a balanced, buoyant, functioning system, despite some complaints of duplication, uneven service delivery, and denied equity, due, in part, to the many residuals of dual federalism—e.g., the separation of services and funding—that still conditioned the operations of the system.

From Cooperative to Cooptive Federalism (1961-1980). Between the administrations of John Kennedy and Jimmy Carter, the residuals of dual federalism disappeared and cooptive federalism triumphed. This victory was costly, however, since the constraints that served to make cooperative federalism viable were demolished in the process, to be replaced, in effect, by a cooptive, overly crowded pattern of intergovernmental relations. Despite the apparent and real differences between Johnson's Creative Federalism, Nixon's New Federalism, Carter's Partnership Federalism and Congress' own eclectic but ascendant version, all four stressed governmental activism to lesser or greater degrees, a pivotal or primary role for the national government, and a federal-state-local sharing of various functional responsibilities. Hence, they all claim to be offspring of the cooperative federal concept that had risen to prominence in the 1950s and early 1960s. In practice, these various policy thrusts produced:

(1) About a 12-fold increase in total federal grant outlays, from $7.1 billion in 1961 to $91.5 billion by 1980, and a doubling of the funds (even in constant dollars) between 1968 and 1980.

(2) A dramatic hike in the number of grants from the 132 of 1960 to well over 500 authorized and funded programs two decades later (and this despite the mergers of some 46 categoricals).

(3) An expansion of the partnership concept to include all states, all counties, all cities, nearly all towns and townships, practically all school districts, at least half of all special districts and authorities, about 1,800 substate regional bodies and hundreds of non-profit organizations. At least 67,000 subnational governments directly received funds from at least one federal grant program by the late 1970s, and the proportion of federal-local "bypassing" aid rose to 14 percent by 1968, to 30 percent by 1977, and dropped to about 25 percent by 1980.

(4) A steady proliferation of wholly new programs (medical assistance for the needy, regional economic development, poverty), expansions of older ones (Aid to Families with Dependent Children, public health programs, natural resources conservation, programs for the aged), the continued reliance on grants as a means of furthering national purposes (income maintenance and employment security), a new reliance on the same device for advancing what formerly were purely local functions (libraries, fire control, police pensions, noise control, solid waste disposal) and a tendency to over-specify programs for narrowly defined areas (12 social service, 13 food and nutrition, 43 medical assistance, 36 primary and secondary education programs).

(5) A diversification of federal intergovernmental fiscal transfers through five block grants (Partnership for Health, 1966; Safe Streets, 1968; Social Services, 1972; Comprehensive Employment and Training, 1973; and Community Development, 1974) and general revenue sharing (GRS, 1972); however, the aggregate of these less conditional grants never exceeded 25 percent of total federal aid in any one year. New requirements or new categoricals became basic features of the subsequent history of four of the block grants, with procedural conditions being attached to GRS.

(6) The emergence of a new and unprecedented era of intergovernmental regulation; for example, the emergence by the late 1970s of some 60 cross-cutting national purpose conditions attached to most federal grants (civil rights, equal access, citizen participation, Davis-Bacon, etc.), the threat of cut-off of all funds for related grants for failure to comply with the requirements of one program (health planning, highway billboards, 55 mile speed limit), the resort to direct mandates (clear drinking water and education of the handicapped), and the expansion of partial preemption wherein a federal agency would assume regulation if a state's standards were not equal or superior to federal (water and air quality control, occupational safety) standards.

(7) The establishment of hundreds of quasi-governmental substate regional units, almost a score of multistate bodies and countless new agencies within state and local governments—resulting either directly or indirectly from federal grant conditions. The enactment of more than a score of federal grant programs (Safe Streets, economic development, health planning, coastal zone management, metropolitan transportation, air and water quality, etc.) prompted the creation of 1,300-1,500 single-purpose, multicounty planning bodies and the advent of nine multistate economic development and·eight river basin commissions. At the substate regional level, Congress and administration mandated a review and comment process

in metropolitan areas and encouraged it in non-metropolitan areas, thus causing a dramatic, 33-fold increase in regional councils; yet, these units have not been designated—at least half the time on the average—to carry out the functions of the other federal regional programs in their respective areas.

(8) A happenstantial handling of fiscal equalization in the allocation of federal grant funds. If per capita income is used as an indicator of state fiscal capacity, the low-income states received the highest average in 1960, but fell back to a second-rank position by the late 1970s. Conversely, the high-income states received the lowest average grants in 1960 but moved into the first rank in the next decade; moreover, at the metropolitan level, 32 central cities in the 66 largest Standard Metropolitan Statistical Areas enjoyed a greater marginal advantage over their suburbs in their per capita receipt of federal aid in 1970 compared to 1977, while for 34 the reverse was true.[2]

(9) The growing reliance by states and localities on federal aid funds. Consider here the hike in federal grants as a percentage of state-local expenditures, from 14.7 percent in 1960 to 19.4 percent by 1970, thence to 26.4 percent in 1978, and finally down slightly to 26.3 percent by 1980; note also the significant increases between 1957 and 1978 in direct federal aid as a percentage of local own source revenues (1.2 to 19.2 percent for counties, 1.4 to 25.0 percent for cities, 2.3 to 3.7 percent for school districts, and 8.9 to 34.0 percent for special districts).

(10) Finally, the expanding role of the federal judiciary as umpire of the system. The courts' grant-related decisions reaffirmed Congress' power to spend in furtherance of the general welfare and rarely checked Congress' power to attach conditions to grants, leaving protection of the 10th Amendment almost wholly to national political processes and to the capacity of recipient governments to refuse grants. At the same time, the National League of Cities and lower court EPA cases suggest that a latitudinarian exercise of the commerce power by Congress can lead to the gradual erosion of the states as quasi-sovereign political entities. Some sense of intergovernmental "comity" was reflected in certain Supreme Court decisions during the seventies relating to state judicial proceedings.

These ten dramatic developments suggest how drastic were the changes in American federalism between 1960 and 1980. They support the charge that the federal-state-local network is overloaded—due to the expansion of federal policy into nearly every program area, regulatory concern and subnational government and to the concomitant failure to use and expand federal manpower to implement directly the new policy responsibilities.

Were the states eclipsed by all this federal intergovernmental interventionism? The answer, of course, is an emphatic "no." Instead, the states significantly strengthened their own governmental institutions and processes and began to fashion a new state-local relationship.

Between 1960 and 1980, five state constitutions were completely overhauled and several others received major amendment. Eleven states gave their governors a four-year term (bringing the total to 45); six adopted a "short ballot" for state executive officers (making a total of nine); 23 major executive branch reorganizations were instituted between 1965 and 1979; the proportion of state employees covered by some form of merit system rose from 50 percent to 75 percent; the number of legislatures operating on a biennial basis was reduced from 31 to 14 (with the 14 usually meeting in special session in the second year); and the number of reformed and integrated state judiciaries rose from three in 1960 to about 37 by 1980. The reshaping of state government moved at a fast pace during these two decades—reflecting the states' new and expanded political, functional and intergovernmental roles.

Revenue systems were transformed, with the adoption of a personal income tax by 11 states, a corporate income levy by nine, and a general sales tax by nine. By 1980, 40 states had a broad-based income tax; 45 a corporate income tax; and a comparable number a general sales tax—with 36 generally using all three, compared to 19 only 20 years earlier.

Though many cuts and few increases in rates have been enacted since 1976 and though 18 states put lids on expenditures or revenues, state revenue systems are now more diversified and resilient overall than during the earlier period.

Yet, how did these state-level reforms affect directly or indirectly their localities? Drawing from the record of the 50 states, the following generalizations emerge:

• significantly more state aid (a 350 percent increase between 1960 and 1978) was provided but still largely in traditional areas, notably education.

• property tax relief was instituted (28 of the states financed a "circuit breaker" variety) in recognition that the local property tax angle had been too large.

• there was a propensity to assume directly some new responsibilities as well as to mandate a shift upward of some local functions.

• greater discretion was given cities and counties to adopt alternative forms of government, to enter interlocal service agreements and, to a much lesser degree, to transfer functions.

• a tendency grew to mandate local service levels, the conditions of local public employment, and sometimes new functions—more often than not without the "fiscal note" warning device.

• only modest expansions were made in allowing cities and counties all functional powers not denied by state constitutions or statutes, in permitting greater local revenue diversification, in liberalizing annexation statutes, and in curbing special district formation.

The above indicates that the states, like the federal government, no longer adhere to the compartmentalized (or layer-cake) theory of intergovernmental relations and with more reason! The states, after all, are the legal source of the structure, powers and finances as well as the overall jurisdictional pattern of the nation's localities, because the state-local relationship operates as a unitary system. Moreover, while some of the above findings can be viewed negatively from a local perspective, it also seems clear that the earlier state role of the "neglectful parent" has been scrapped. Finally, from both the state and local vantage points, there is a growing pattern of interdependency, reflected in 50 quite different systems—a fact frequently overlooked in Washington.

The Reagan Reaction (1981-). With the election of Ronald Reagan and a Republican Senate in 1980, the political and the pressure group dynamics that had nurtured the federal interventionism of the 1970s confronted a counterforce ready to do battle with them. In effect, the new administration accepted the diagnosis of the Advisory Commission on Intergovernmental Relations, Council of State Governments, National Governors' Association, National Conference of State Legislatures and others that the system was seriously overloaded.

In contrast with Nixonian New Federalism with its combined centralization (Family Assistance Plan) and devolution (GRS and six special revenue sharing proposals), the basic interrelated prescriptions of the Reagan "New Federalism" are: (1) to develop a dynamic, non-inflationary economy; (2) to launch a major effort to devolve power, programs and funding sources; and (3) to deregulate, or at least to curb overregulation. The Reagan budget and tax packages were geared primarily to the first goal. Yet, parts of the massive budget offensive were cuts in grants (usually at the 25 percent level for fiscal 1982), no appropriations for at least 90 categorical programs and seven proposed block grants adhering to the "special revenue sharing" format (very few conditions). The last involved the consolidation of some 85 aid programs into social services (12), health services (17), preventive health services (10), energy and emergency assistance (2), local special education needs (10), state programs for elementary and secondary education (33), and a new community development (1) block grant. In short, a major secondary effect of the 1981 battle of the budget was to further the devolution goal, with the block grants being described by the administration as transitional—to be followed by a turnback of revenue sources.

As of early June 1981, the fate of nearly all of the block grant proposals was in doubt, thanks to Senate modifications and House committee actions. With the advent of Gramm-Latta II and the House conservative coalition's drive to convert the budgetary reconciliation process into a vehicle for achieving program changes, the block grant initiatives took on new life. The president's social services and community development proposals re-emerged in roughly recognizable form, though political maneuvering required the adoption of a much more limited approach to the health services and preventive health block grants.

From the give and take of the marathon conference committee sessions, nine block grants emerged: community development (a mini-block to the states for non-entitlement local jurisdictions), education (combining 37 categoricals), community services (7), health prevention and health services (6), low-income home energy assistance (1), alcohol and drug abuse and mental health services (10), primary care (2), maternal and child health services (9) and social services (1). None of them was what the administration initially called for. Seventy-seven categorical aid programs were merged, but excluding 46 which the president wanted to consolidate. The latter remained as separate programs but with reduced funding. Moreover, none of the nine blocks adhered fully to the "special revenue" sharing features of the original Reagan proposals (quasi-automatic entitlement no plan approval, no matching or maintenance of effort requirements, etc.). A new state role, however, was established in the community service, primary care, energy assistance and community development areas, but with a match required in some cases.

In this struggle between categorical program interests and the consolidationists, the result was a draw with both sides scoring some points and losing others. Not to be overlooked in the story of the budget is the specific elimination of appropriations for at least 60 other categorical programs for fiscal 1982.

Turning to deregulation, the new administration soon established a cabinet-level task force on regulatory relief, chaired by Vice President Bush. Some 34 out of 104 actions taken during the spring of 1981 provided relief to state and local governments. Yet, these were administrative actions. A full-scale effort to reform federal regulations in their multiple manifestations also must involve the Congress, the real source of most of the regulatory proliferation and, of course, the courts.

To conclude, it is too soon to describe all of the features of Reagan federalism. Some new initiatives no doubt will emerge from the deliberations of the President's Federalism Advisory Committee. Moreover, the full effects of what already has been accomplished, as well as the outcome of promised new grant consolidations and revenue turnbacks, also are tough to forecast. Whether alternative approaches to decongesting the system will gain strength is also unknown. The Advisory Commission on Intergovernmental Relations, Council of State Governments, National Governors' Association, National Conference of State Legislatures and others have urged a sorting out of the major program responsibilities by governmental level—with some, like welfare and Medicaid, being federalized and others, like education and highways, turned over to the states.

It is predictable, however, that the cuts in federal aid will be felt; that the fiscal, political and management pressures on the states will mount; that many local jurisdictions, particularly in the Northeast and Great Lakes areas, will confront especially difficult challenges; that the success of much of the administration's new federalism depends heavily on the success of its economic program; and that the states and their respective localities will become even more intertwined.

In the final analysis, all that has been enacted or proposed is not a return to 1931 or even to 1961. Instead, the administration's intergovernmental goals and certainly Congress' response thus far add up to an attempt to cope with some of the more costly and intrusive manifestations of national governmental interventionism that emerged in the 1960s and 1970s.

So with The Council of State Governments preparing to celebrate its fiftieth anniversary, as with the first, American intergovernmental relations are entering a new but not yet clearly defined era.

Notes

1. David B. Walker, *Toward a Functioning Federalism* (Cambridge, Mass.: Winthrop Publishers, Inc., 1981), pp. 65-134.
2. Advisory Commission on Intergovernmental Relations (ACIR), *Central City-Suburban Fiscal Disparity and City Distress, 1977*, Report M-119 (Washington, D.C.: U.S. Government Printing Office, 1980), pp. 56-57.

SIGNIFICANT DEVELOPMENTS IN FEDERAL-STATE RELATIONS

By Jane F. Roberts

IN HIS INAUGURAL address, President Reagan declared that "it is my intention to curb the size and influence of the Federal establishment and to demand recognition of the distinction between the powers granted to the Federal Government and those reserved to the states or to the people. All of us need to be reminded that the Federal Government did not create the states; the states created the Federal Government." With this declaration, the president reiterated his campaign commitment to make federalism a major focus of his administration and to launch what some have termed a "quiet revolution" to change the American government system.

Federal budget cuts and economic recovery initiatives have dominated much of the news from Washington since inauguration day. However, there was considerable activity in a number of other areas which affect federal-state-local relationships.

The Congress initiated actions to bring federalism issues to the forefront in at least three important areas. First, legislation was introduced to create a "Commission on More Effective Government." This 18-member panel would have a two-part mandate: to examine the federal government and find ways to improve its organization and operations and to study the federal system and recommend ways to improve relationships among the three levels of government. The measures passed the Senate and await House action.

The second area addressed by the Congress is an omnibus approach to grant reform contained in the "Federal Assistance Improvement Act of 1981." The six-title measure encourages the consolidation of related federal grant programs; improves federal audit procedures of grants to states and localities; streamlines and simplifies generally applicable national policy requirements attached to most federal assistance programs; strengthens the joint funding process; enables recipients to shift grant funds between specific categories of functionally related programs; and implements several other improvements to grant administration procedures. The proposal is pending in both chambers.

A third Congressional measure called for federal "fiscal notes," estimating costs which proposed legislation would impose on state and local governments. The proposal has been a key federal legislative priority of state and local governments and ACIR for some time, and received broad support in both houses, as well as from the White House. The bill was signed into law at year's end.

The administration also moved quickly to implement its federalism reform agenda. Shortly after taking office, the president established a cabinet-level Task Force on Regulatory Relief chaired by Vice President Bush. Federal departments and agencies also were directed to review both administrative and legislative actions which would help reduce the regulatory burden on state and local governments as well as the private sector. Accord-

Jane F. Roberts is State-Local Relations Associate for the United States Advisory Commission on Intergovernmental Relations.

ing to a year-end tally, the task force completed a review of almost 2,500 regulations and over 3,700 paperwork clearance requests and estimated that its nearly 100 actions had saved the public and private sectors a total of $1.5 billion in annual costs and from $3.8 to $5.9 billion in one-time capital costs.

In April 1981, the president created a 40-member Advisory Committee on Federalism to advise him on the objectives and conduct of his overall federalism policy. The membership is drawn from the ranks of the cabinet, the Congress, state and local government and the public. Specifically, the committee has been charged with providing the president with information on the effects of federal policies on states and localities, developing long-term policies to reverse the centralization of program control by Washington and offering guidance to the administration in the implementation of its federalism proposals. A high-level task force, comprised of cabinet members and senior White House officials, also was formed to help coordinate the committee's work.

The president also proposed consolidating more than 90 categorical programs into seven block grants with a 25 percent reduction in funding. Although the proposal was modified significantly by the Congress, the Omnibus Reconciliation Act of 1981 did contain federal grant changes which will have a great impact upon state and local governments across the country.

Federal budget and appropriations actions are not yet complete, and the overall picture for the states is not totally clear. However, certain facts about the new federal grant arrangements have emerged. The Reconciliation Act created nine block grants by consolidating nearly 70 categorical programs with total authorizations of $7.596 billion for fiscal 1982. The functional areas involved are: maternal and child health care; preventive health and health services; alcohol, drug abuse and mental health; primary care (effective in 1983); social services; low-income energy assistance; community services; education; and community development non-entitlement programs. While the new block grants meet the prime requirement that they give more discretion to grant recipients, most still have an assortment of federal strings attached to them.

One of the most significant features of the grants is the designation of the state as the primary recipient and decision-maker. Many of the superseded categorical programs involved a direct federal-local relationship. Five of the grants carry no pass-through requirements, and the four which do still deal with the state as the lead actor. The number of categorical programs consolidated is relatively small and the amount of money involved relative to the total federal grants budget also is small, but the change in funding arrangements is of great significance.

Most intergovernmental analysts believe the block grants represent the beginning of an important trend. In the future, the states will be responsible for administering more programs and with fewer federal dollars. They will have to decide what the appropriate roles will be for governors, legislators and administrators. They will be making program decisions, allocating scarce resources among competing interests, pinpointing intergovernmental tension points and resolving conflicts. Mayors and county officials will look more frequently to state capitals for answers that used to come from Washington and will need to open new channels of communication with state officials in order to make their needs known.

The states now are involved in seeking solutions to the challenges and changes posed by the shift from categoricals to block grants. Some are establishing permanent, long-range processes and procedures. Others are concentrating on the short-run transition period, hoping to buy time before making final decisions. How quickly and how well individual states respond to the challenges and opportunities thrust upon them by the federal government will help to determine the viability of future block grant proposals.

Block grants, however, are only the first step in the administration's plans to reform federalism. As explained by the president at the annual conference of the National Association of Counties: "I have a dream of my own. I think block grants are only the intermediate steps. I dream of a day when the federal government can substitute for those, the turning back to local and state governments of the tax sources that we ourselves had preempted here at the federal level, so that you would have the resources."

In January 1982, President Reagan outlined his plan "to make our system of federalism work again" in his first State of the Union message. The initiative contained two major components: program tradeoffs and revenue turnbacks. Under the tradeoff proposal, the federal government would assume responsibility for the state portion of Medicaid, while states would take over the federal Food Stamp and Aid to Families with Dependent Children programs. The turnback component would return control of a number of federal categorical grant programs to the states and establish a trust fund to finance them. States could receive trust fund monies to continue operating these programs or, under certain conditions, receive a "super revenue sharing payment" from the fund to use at their discretion. The fund would be adjusted to equalize gains or losses resulting from the tradeoff portion of the plan and would be phased out over several years.

Numerous questions relating to important issues—such as which programs will be turned back, eligibility standards, benefit levels, pass-through requirements, state management and fiscal capacity, and the size and source of funding for the trust account, to name but a few—have yet to be resolved. The White House has expressed its willingness to "remain flexible" and has opened negotiations with state and local officials to reach a compromise plan. One of the major areas of disagreement centers around who will be responsible for welfare and income maintenance programs. As noted above, the administration has proposed a state takeover, while state officials strongly believe that this function should be maintained at the federal level.

Returning resources to states and localities could be accomplished by a variety of methods. Generally, however, there are four broad categories: *revenue sharing on a formula basis* that would distribute funds based on fiscal capacity and need, as well as on the magnitude of returned responsibilities; *tax sharing on an origin basis* that could provide a permanent state-local entitlement to a specific portion of federal tax receipts, with shares in the same proportion as the tax revenues; *conditional relinquishment of a federal tax* whereby Congress would give up part or all of a tax on the condition that a state or local government adopt that tax; and *unconditional relinquishment of a federal tax* whereby Congress would give up a portion of a tax or vacate an entire tax field *without* the requirement for state or local assumption.

To arrive at the best method of turning back resources, the president and Congress must weigh a variety of policy issues. First, the fiscal alignment or mismatch problem that plagued earlier turnback proposals is a problem today. Unless special safeguards are incorporated, some states would gain resources and others would lose under most packages of grant cuts and resource turnbacks. Secondly, since both the White House and the Congress will be attempting to balance the federal budget, it will be impossible to cut federal grants and yet provide enough of a resource turnback to hold states and localities "harmless" from an overall loss. And finally, a turnback package cannot be put together without agreement on what responsibilities should be turned back, which grants should be eliminated and what—if any—strings should be attached. Securing agreement will not be easy. Those served by grant programs have fought hard for the funding as well as for the complex network of federal controls and incentives attached to them.

Intergovernmental relationships will be tested, with key decisions expected in the states relating not only to how to spend federal dollars, but also with how to absorb federal aid cuts and turnbacks, and in many cases, with how to deal with reduced state revenues and how to modernize institutions. For example, a state's policy agenda quite reasonably could be expected to include: the authority exercised by state legislatures including appropriation and oversight of federal funds; the role of the courts; emergency or short-term actions required by state governments to mitigate transition problems; long-term executive and legislative institutional changes and reforms at the state level; the need for and role of intergovernmental consultation and coordination; the need for increasing the discretionary authority of local governments especially in the area of revenue raising capacity; new mechanisms for making grants and contracts with local governments and delegating more responsibility to those units; and the need for capacity building programs such as technical assistance and training activities.

It is the shift in decision-making authority that brings into sharpest focus the key intergovernmental issues. As additional federal programs and revenues are blocked or devolved and cuts are made at both the federal and state levels, these issues will take on an even greater importance.

In an address to the National Conference of State Legislatures in mid-1981, President Reagan observed: "This Nation has never fully debated the fact that over the past 40 years, federalism—one of the underlying principles of our Constitution—has nearly disappeared as a guiding force in American politics and government. My administration intends to initiate such a debate. . . ." The debate, indeed, has begun and may very well herald a new era for intergovernmental relationships.

TOTAL FEDERAL AID TO STATES: FISCAL 1976-1980
(In thousands of dollars)

State or other jurisdiction	1980	1979	1978	1977	T.Q(a)	1976
Total	$91,365,244	$82,853,473	$77,900,903	$68,436,840	$16,443,830	$59,107,874
Alabama	1,583,543	1,367,631	1,240,569	1,120,519	303,462	992,934
Alaska	451,170	388,580	408,211	382,004	89,305	318,553
Arizona	837,882	809,479	763,318	648,435	136,720	530,309
Arkansas	940,352	846,856	779,074	638,790	152,225	613,667
California	8,804,443	8,251,050	8,012,965	6,813,730	1,448,326	5,802,854
Colorado	995,230	942,865	825,855	714,543	206,957	672,597
Connecticut.........	1,156,824	1,074,780	1,052,697	894,981	192,889	723,950
Delaware	275,358	232,500	225,033	187,302	51,893	160,607
Florida	2,854,439	2,397,511	2,364,186	1,988,414	426,110	1,527,688
Georgia	2,373,419	2,181,048	2,036,993	1,861,105	342,370	1,421,097
Hawaii	463,258	407,881	413,391	400,144	82,267	306,796
Idaho	393,079	337,183	336,315	287,675	71,637	252,922
Illinois	4,476,964	3,782,934	3,467,151	3,202,188	777,293	2,808,813
Indiana.............	1,608,494	1,391,558	1,259,679	1,095,093	284,439	980,936
Iowa	994,733	877,823	796,893	714,420	183,964	675,156
Kansas	818,463	722,878	615,820	548,524	123,481	517,562
Kentucky	1,471,228	1,349,703	1,133,308	1,018,066	274,463	1,016,934
Louisiana	1,567,591	1,513,376	1,358,360	1,237,128	332,463	1,135,430
Maine	522,546	508,122	470,379	411,510	88,850	375,411
Maryland	1,843,192	1,577,979	1,318,423	1,244,922	319,042	1,113,997
Massachusetts	2,886,740	2,726,189	2,581,488	2,079,940	473,189	1,824,023
Michigan	3,928,527	3,568,596	3,280,231	2,915,254	680,219	2,600,513
Minnesota	1,667,347	1,515,431	1,350,915	1,224,464	325,347	1,106,679
Mississippi	1,190,010	1,045,969	915,855	800,688	205,146	781,581
Missouri............	1,702,897	1,514,482	1,278,467	1,142,323	316,406	1,040,933
Montana	486,363	434,433	397,300	347,632	79,763	283,675
Nebraska	546,513	474,570	458,783	367,820	125,173	401,112
Nevada.............	335,469	276,828	268,909	206,027	48,985	186,415
New Hampshire	345,912	292,753	289,298	233,703	57,986	218,844
New Jersey	2,833,075	2,716,267	2,552,215	2,199,862	522,298	1,863,012
New Mexico	668,500	617,016	608,411	449,345	102,655	424,224
New York	9,569,624	8,872,407	8,372,465	7,446,787	1,827,843	6,420,639
North Carolina	1,929,241	1,788,832	1,655,955	1,511,942	341,991	1,275,045
North Dakota	347,200	295,243	259,138	224,401	65,439	202,889
Ohio	3,433,736	3,071,195	2,904,685	2,510,305	616,141	2,136,835
Oklahoma	1,061,483	949,388	937,180	782,019	257,361	685,252
Oregon.............	1,237,294	1,070,598	1,075,400	836,132	241,514	795,966
Pennsylvania........	4,515,615	4,099,060	3,912,086	3,628,059	870,144	3,125,214
Rhode Island........	477,446	412,418	388,000	357,546	92,442	311,018
South Carolina	1,067,706	987,215	903,414	802,540	174,493	697,729
South Dakota	443,253	316,487	288,446	240,454	62,775	227,668
Tennessee	1,695,667	1,506,920	1,330,860	1,188,617	294,002	1,082,446
Texas	3,964,357	3,592,345	3,295,287	2,885,381	647,169	2,603,572
Utah	571,693	455,561	434,261	387,837	100,132	361,514
Vermont	355,597	241,813	240,659	222,501	61,836	176,110
Virginia	1,775,472	1,700,559	1,468,126	1,311,454	304,747	1,179,357
Washington..........	1,674,116	1,417,104	1,311,062	1,118,893	258,177	984,220
West Virginia	950,423	771,522	707,622	631,233	176,918	653,934
Wisconsin	2,024,519	1,725,467	1,607,427	1,493,308	326,427	1,204,165
Wyoming............	294,386	242,518	235,707	185,644	61,532	166,657
Dist. of Col.	1,336,361	1,138,639	1,105,199	942,136	265,795	749,043
Puerto Rico	1,430,471	1,308,739	1,156,550	939,008	182,662	812,955
Virgin Islands	295,798	228,784	237,699	235,033	12,458	218,680
Other(b)	215,163	281,269	269,315	179,576	63,323	163,389
Adjustments or undistributed to states....	-324,898	235,087	943,862	999,483	313,167	194,328

Source: U.S. Department of the Treasury, *Federal Aid to States, Fiscal Year 1980.*

(a) Transition quarter, July 1, through September 30, 1976.
(b) Includes American Samoa, Guam and Trust Territory.

GENERAL REVENUE SHARING

By Kent A. Peterson

THE REVENUE SHARING Program was first enacted with the passage of the State and Local Fiscal Assistance Act of 1972 (P.L. 92-512). The program was reauthorized under the State and Local Fiscal Assistance Amendments of 1976 (P.L. 94-488) and renewed again with the passage of the State and Local Fiscal Assistance Amendments of 1980 (P.L. 96-604). The revenue sharing legislation provides for the distribution of approximately $69 billion to more than 39,000 units of state and local government over a period of 11 years and nine months. According to the 1980 amendments, state governments are not eligible for fiscal 1981 funding but are authorized for fiscal 1982 and 1983 funding subject to annual appropriations. In addition, state government funding will depend upon the return or non-acceptance of federal categorical funds equal to the revenue sharing allocations. The current act, as amended, will expire in September 1983.

The Revenue Sharing Program is an "entitlement" program which means that no application is necessary to receive funds. Based upon data furnished by the Census Bureau and other federal agencies, funds are distributed to eligible general-purpose governments through formulas prescribed in the act. However, special purpose districts, such as school districts, special utility districts and library districts, are not eligible to receive funds. To receive funds, eligible governments must return a simple form which they automatically receive, assuring that funds will be spent in accordance with the law.

Payments to eligible governments are made quarterly, based on each unit's allocation for an entitlement period. Each of the first three entitlement periods was of six-month duration, followed by three 12-month periods beginning July 1973. Another six-month period began in 1976. Renewal in 1976 added a nine-month period starting January 1977 (to align the program with the new October-September federal fiscal year) and three 12-month entitlement periods. Renewal in 1980 authorized three more one-year entitlement periods. The amounts authorized for distribution for each entitlement period are shown in Table A.

Under the Revenue Sharing Program until September 30, 1980, one-third of the total appropriation was reserved for the state governments, with the remaining two-thirds distributed to local governments—counties, municipalities, townships, Indian tribes and Alaskan native villages. Payments made to the state and local governments since the beginning of the program are summarized in Tables 1 and 2 following this article.

Table 1 contains payments to state governments for Entitlement Periods 1 through 12, with payments and projected payments for Entitlement Period 13. Data on payments to local governments for Entitlement Periods 1 through 12 along with the payments and projected payments for Entitlement Period 13 are exhibited in Table 2. The payments reflected in these tables apply to the entitlement periods in which the funds are credited, not the entitlement periods in which they were paid. Payments for state and local governments for

---

Kent A. Peterson is Deputy Director, Office of Revenue Sharing, U.S. Department of the Treasury.

35

Table A
ENTITLEMENT PERIODS AND
AUTHORIZED DISTRIBUTION AMOUNTS

Entitlement period	Start	End	Amount (in millions)
1	January 1972	June 1972	$2,650.0
2	July 1972	December 1972	2,650.0
3	January 1973	June 1973	2,987.5
4	July 1973	June 1974	6,050.0
5	July 1974	June 1975	6,200.0
6	July 1975	June 1976	6,350.0
7	July 1976	December 1976	3,325.0
8	January 1977	September 1977	4,987.5
9	October 1977	September 1978	6,850.0
10	October 1978	September 1979	6,850.0
11	October 1979	September 1980	6,850.0
12	October 1980	September 1981	4,566.7*
13	October 1981	September 1982	4,566.7**
14	October 1982	September 1983	4,566.7**

*For local governments only.
**Additional funding for state governments is subject to appropriations for that purpose.

each entitlement period displayed in Tables 1 and 2 are different from those previously reported. This is because these payments include accounting and special adjustments for each entitlement period after initial payments were made. The previous payment data represented the sum of the unadjusted quarterly payments to state and local governments for each entitlement period.

The allocation amount for each government is determined by a mathematical formula using data as prescribed by the revenue sharing law. The data used to determine allocation amounts for local governments include per capita income, tax effort, population and intergovernmental transfers. Interstate data are population, urbanized population, income, state individual income tax, federal individual income tax, state and local taxes, aggregate personal income and general tax effort factor. The data are supplied by various governmental agencies, including the Bureau of the Census, the Bureau of Economic Analysis, the Internal Revenue Service and the Bureau of Indian Affairs.

According to the revenue sharing formula, each government competes against all other eligible governments for a portion of the total revenue sharing amount that is to be allocated. Because of the complexity of the formula and its relative nature, each government's share is computed simultaneously with all other governments. After allocations for local governments have been determined, the amount is then checked to assure that it does not exceed 50 percent of the total of the combined adjusted taxes and intergovernmental transfers of funds for the particular government. An allocation exceeding that amount is reduced to the 50 percent level, with the balance being transferred to the next higher level of government. The allocation amount for each government is also constrained by either the minimum or the maximum per capita entitlement permitted under the act. The minimum per capita allocation is 20 percent of the per capita amounts allocated to all governments in the state. The maximum amount allocated is 145 percent.

The Revenue Sharing Program was originally conceived as a way of sharing the relatively more progressive federal tax revenue, especially income tax revenue, with state and local governments which traditionally have had to rely on more regressive taxes and revenue sources. Its major goal is to disburse federal funds with minimum restrictions on use, permitting the local decision-making process to determine the programs and activities where the money is most needed.

Under the 1976 and 1980 amendments, revenue sharing funds may be used for any purpose which is a legal use of the government's own funds under state and local laws. The priority expenditure categories which restricted revenue sharing expenditures by governments were eliminated. Furthermore, the prohibition against recipients' use of funds for federal grant matching purposes was also repealed. However, recipients must spend, appropriate or obligate revenue sharing funds within 24 months from the end of the entitlement period for which the funds are received. Although there are no restrictions as to the uses of revenue sharing funds, recipient governments must comply with the public participation, audit and non-discrimination requirements specified by the revenue sharing law.

Table 1
GENERAL REVENUE SHARING PAYMENTS TO STATE GOVERNMENTS, BY STATE, BY ENTITLEMENT PERIOD
(In thousands of dollars)

State or other jurisdiction	Total 1/72-12/76	7/76-12/76	7/75-6/76	7/74-6/75	7/73-6/74	1/73-6/73	7/72-12/72	1/72-6/72
Total	$10,209,643.4	$1,137,196.7	$2,141,089.1	$2,085,768.3	$2,043,336.8	$1,013,029.8	$894,603.6	$894,619.1
Alabama	167,273.5	18,188.7	33,857.0	34,322.0	34,061.3	16,814.5	15,015.0	15,015.0
Alaska	14,010.2	2,084.7	3,089.1	2,735.7	2,609.2	1,291.9	1,100.9	1,098.7
Arizona	100,473.9	10,978.8	21,347.8	21,144.9	20,312.6	10,030.4	8,329.7	8,329.7
Arkansas	109,125.9	11,973.7	22,268.8	22,357.5	21,844.0	11,470.3	9,605.8	9,605.8
California	1,064,995.7	120,070.8	219,922.2	216,051.9	216,338.8	106,828.4	92,891.8	92,891.8
Colorado	106,935.6	12,422.2	23,010.9	21,939.0	21,076.5	10,407.6	9,039.7	9,039.7
Connecticut	129,129.9	14,326.0	28,486.8	26,577.6	25,061.6	12,379.3	11,150.0	11,148.6
Delaware	33,439.3	3,564.7	6,834.2	6,518.0	6,490.1	3,638.3	3,197.0	3,197.0
Florida	299,671.7	34,758.7	65,439.2	64,458.5	57,803.0	28,575.7	24,318.3	24,318.3
Georgia	210,386.6	23,980.1	43,940,1	44,040.0	41,565.5	20,528.7	18,166.1	18,166.1
Hawaii	44,384.6	5,078.6	9,274.8	8,932.6	8,859.9	4,379.1	3,929.8	3,929.8
Idaho	39,913.2	4,303.2	8,163.7	7,963.2	8,318.7	4,107.8	3,528.3	3,528.3
Illinois	512,538.9	57,579.7	107,742.7	103,580.1	102,270.5	50,501.3	45,432.3	45,432.3
Indiana	210,854.4	23,996.6	42,891.5	42,436.7	42,713.4	21,092.0	18,862.1	18,862.1
Iowa	137,568.6	13,758.9	28,138.0	28,221.2	28,397.4	14,022.7	12,515.2	12,515.2
Kansas	94,729.8	10,152.0	19,435.8	18,766.2	19,405.8	9,582.6	8,693.7	8,693.7
Kentucky	183,781.5	19,219.4	36,780.9	35,699.9	37,913.7	20,062.1	17,052.1	17,053.4
Louisiana	228,695.9	24,952.7	45,657.6	46,418.3	46,835.7	23,546.0	20,642.6	20,643.0
Maine	61,912.5	6,986.8	13,325.6	12,752.4	12,211.3	6,030.0	5,303.2	5,303.2
Maryland	199,270.5	22,500.1	42,099.8	40,116.6	39,521.7	19,515.9	17,758.2	17,758.2
Massachusetts	319,115.4	35,618.9	68,847.8	64,879.8	63,604.4	31,407.9	27,378.3	27,378.3
Michigan	424,061.4	46,128.5	89,145.2	87,213.1	85,115.7	42,030.3	37,214.3	37,214.3
Minnesota........	201,608.0	22,655.2	44,334.8	40,891.9	39,113.8	19,314.5	17,648.9	17,648.9
Mississippi	165,467.3	17,190.5	31,491.7	34,344.1	35,688.0	16,996.6	14,878.2	14,878.2
Missouri	189,597.6	21,185.8	40,778.4	39,254.5	37,293.9	18,462.0	16,311.5	16,311.5
Montana	38,971.2	4,129.4	7,835.7	8,526.5	7,822.2	3,862.6	3,397.4	3,397.4
Nebraska	69,851.0	7,100.8	14,128.2	13,761.6	14,710.1	7,263.9	6,443.2	6,443.2
Nevada	22,651.6	2,724.5	4,987.3	4,494.5	4,436.4	2,190.7	1,909.1	1,909.1
New Hampshire	32,188.2	3,617.2	6,807.4	6,716.3	6,391.3	3,156.0	2,750.0	2,750.0
New Jersey	315,025.1	35,266.6	66,450.4	64,410.1	62,683.4	30,953.2	27,630.7	27,630.7
New Mexico	65,051.8	7,519.2	13,402.5	13,085.6	13,104.6	6,616.7	5,661.6	5,661.6
New York	1,125,339.3	126,746.7	240,242.7	229,902.3	222,936.7	110,086.5	97,712.2	97,712.2
North Carolina	254,202.7	27,974.0	51,720.6	52,588.9	51,411.7	25,407.5	22,550.0	22,550.0
North Dakota	36,435.1	2,830.4	6,825.3	6,935.6	8,362.3	4,129.3	3,676.1	3,676.1
Ohio	403,265.2	45,373.3	86,486.3	82,198.6	79,165.8	39,092.2	35,474.5	35,474.5
Oklahoma........	111,930.3	12,548.2	23,151.7	23,300.8	22,354.2	11,038.6	9,768.4	9,768.4
Oregon	101,884.3	12,159.6	22,224.8	20,597.7	19,628.2	9,692.4	8,790.8	8,790.8
Pennsylvania	529,002.6	59,150.1	112,931.1	108,542.1	104,568.6	51,636.1	46,087.3	46,087.3
Rhode Island	44,579.2	4,834.7	9,175.5	9,047.4	9,043.5	4,465.7	4,006.2	4,006.2
South Carolina	140,659.0	15,850.5	29,592.3	28,639.7	27,756.6	14,264.5	12,269.0	12,286.4
South Dakota	42,086.0	3,661.8	8,384.6	8,507.7	9,061.0	4,474.3	3,998.3	3,998.3
Tennessee	188,776.8	20,827.5	39,622.2	39,670.4	37,411.2	18,473.7	16,385.9	16,385.9
Texas	481,591.9	56,673.4	101,911.5	98,365.4	95,175.0	47,178.2	41,144.2	41,144.2
Utah	58,889.2	6,292.9	12,537.4	12,005.1	11,983,1	5,929.3	5,070.7	5,070.7
Vermont	28,661.6	3,336.0	6,188.7	5,823.6	5,644.5	2,787.6	2,440.6	2,440.6
Virginia	200,291.1	22,774.3	42,661.0	40,798.2	39,357.6	19,434.8	17,632.6	17,632.6
Washington	146,153.7	16,757.0	31,277.1	28,935.3	29,002.7	14,321.6	12,930.0	12,930.0
West Virginia	121,940.3	12,008.7	22,427.0	25,810.3	25,683.3	13,453.8	11,278.6	11,278.6
Wisconsin	251,727.6	27,428.9	53,667.8	51,387.3	50,252.6	24,814.8	22,088.1	22,088.1
Wyoming	17,735.9	1,817.9	3,359.1	3,557.3	3,813.6	1,883.2	1,652.4	1,652.4
Dist. of Col.	131,810.8	14,137.8	26,786.5	26,544.3	27,150.1	13,406.7	11,892.7	11,892.7

Source: Office of Revenue Sharing, U.S. Department of the Treasury.

GENERAL REVENUE SHARING PAYMENTS TO STATE GOVERNMENTS, BY STATE, BY ENTITLEMENT PERIOD
(In thousands of dollars)

State or other jurisdiction	Total 1/72-9/80	10/79-9/80	10/78-9/79	10/77-9/78	1/77-9/77
Total..................	$18,760,823.4	$2,288,476.7	$2,301,240.8	$2,291,638.0	$1,669,754.9
Alabama..................	302,771.6	35,729.9	36,288.6	36,734.9	26,744.7
Alaska*	39,134.1	7,549.8	7,938.1	6,051.1	3,568.6
Arizona	194,645.5	26,671.3	26,466.8	24,890.2	16,143.3
Arkansas	193,875.2	22,716.2	22,666.5	21,768.6	17,598.0
California...............	2,020,345.0	266,231.2	259,045.5	253,520.0	176,552.6
Colorado	201,035.4	25,415.2	25,425.3	24,993.7	18,265.6
Connecticut*.............	235,864.0	28,567.2	28,658.8	28,395.2	21,066.6
Delaware	59,725.3	6,882.4	7,069.9	7,092.1	5,241.6
Florida	554,522.8	68,063.9	68,007.6	67,670.3	51,109.3
Georgia..................	395,222.9	50,158.1	50,450.6	48,967.2	35,260.4
Hawaii	85,715.3	10,695,9	11,129.7	11,334.5	8,170.6
Idaho	71,336.3	8,615.9	8,692.5	7,787.2	6,327.5
Illinois.................	939,580.3	112,900.0	113,629.2	115,846.8	84,665.4
Indiana	385,259.9	44,856.5	46,043.2	48,224.8	35,281.0
Iowa	241,101.9	28,354.0	28,485.1	26,463.1	20,231.1
Kansas	169,497.1	20,296.2	20,118.6	19,425.0	14,927.5
Kentucky	324,484.0	36,886.7	38,022.8	37,617.6	28,175.4
Louisiana	394,483.3	41,555.8	44,081.1	46,889.9	33,260.6
Maine	114,395.4	13,011.6	15,277.3	13,920.6	10,273.4
Maryland	367,500.1	44,193.4	45,435.1	45,516.8	33,084.3
Massachusetts	589.436.0	71,329.6	72,475.5	74,141.3	52,374.2
Michigan	779,885.3	98,147.7	95,734.1	94,114.6	67,827.5
Minnesota	371,418.4	45,396.2	45,660.4	45,441.4	33,312.4
Mississippi	289,038.2	31,666.5	33,310.8	33,333.8	25,259.8
Missouri	347,270.4	41,141.2	42,133.4	43,246.5	31,151.7
Montana	70,727.4	9,002.7	8,682.6	7,999.0	6,071.9
Nebraska	124,129.1	15,718.7	14,277.1	13,841.2	10,441.1
Nevada	43,797.1	5,765.4	5,675.9	5,698.1	4,006.1
New Hampshire	60,731.5	7,757.9	7,786.5	7,680.1	5,318.8
New Jersey...............	589,423.8	75,529.2	75,198.7	71,814.6	51,856.2
New Mexico...............	119,648.3	13,464.1	14,345.4	15,735.5	11,051.5
New York.................	2,072,715.6	248,555.8	255,048.4	257,403.1	186,369.0
North Carolina	464,015.0	56,407.5	56,334.5	55,937.2	41,133.1
North Dakota	58,394.5	6,480.5	6,324.3	4,992.8	4,161.8
Ohio	746,466.7	92,099.4	92,500.9	91,884.1	66,717.1
Oklahoma	205,885.8	25,554.7	24,798.4	25,151.5	18,450.9
Oregon	195,772.5	25,904.1	25,338.9	24,765.6	17,879.6
Pennsylvania	952,800.4	111,044.7	111,121.9	114,656.6	86,974.6
Rhode Island	81,193.9	9,844.5	9,798.2	9,863.0	7,109.0
South Carolina	255,186.1	30,532.4	30,705.9	29,985.1	23,303.7
South Dakota	69,793.5	7,767.3	7,665.3	6,890.6	5,384.3
Tennessee................	346,783.9	43,971.8	42,164.7	41,245.8	30,624.8
Texas	900,497.6	110,574.1	112,528.6	112,470.2	83,332.8
Utah	109,110.2	13,954.8	14,083.5	12,929.5	9,253.2
Vermont*.................	54,275.4	6,813.9	6,981.4	6,911.3	4,900.2
Virginia.................	374,683.6	46,856.4	47,478.9	46,569.8	33,487.4
Washington	267,152.6	31,727.0	30,766.0	33,866.4	24,639.5
West Virginia............	207,557.9	20,243.1	22,466.9	25,285.3	17,622.3
Wisconsin	451,398.3	52,960.1	53,634.7	52,744.4	40,331.5
Wyoming	33,432.8	4,692.1	4,428.9	3,902.8	2,673.1
Dist. of Col.............	237,706.2	28,222.1	28,857.8	28,027.2	20,788.3

*Total payments include prior period local funds waived to these states for entitlement period 12: Alaska—$16,300; Connecticut—$46,300; Vermont—$7,000.

Table 2
GENERAL REVENUE SHARING PAYMENTS TO LOCAL GOVERNMENTS, BY STATE, BY ENTITLEMENT PERIOD
(In thousands of dollars)

State or other jurisdiction	Total 1/72-12/76	7/76-12/76	7/75-6/76	7/74-6/75	7/73-6/74	1/73-6/73	7/72-12/72	1/72-6/72
Total	$19,988,650.1	$2,238,886.3	$4,209,071.7	$4,088,976.4	$3,987,804.0	$1,967,959.4	$1,747,994.6	$1,747,957.7
Alabama	334,855.6	36,385.4	67,716.9	68,645.3	68,007.1	33,754.6	30,173.1	30,173.2
Alaska	28,150.6	4,096.1	6,061.5	5,859.6	5,219.7	2,542.7	2,183.2	2,187.8
Arizona...........	202,202.1	21,983.4	42,723.3	42,289.8	41,184.1	20,273.5	16,874.0	16,874.0
Arkansas	204,231.3	23,550.4	43,885.6	42,409.7	40,187.0	19,160.8	17,518.9	17,518.9
California	2,130,070.6	240,148.3	439,848.7	432,177.7	432,671.3	213,657.0	185,783.8	185,783.8
Colorado	214,000.9	24,844.7	46,021.9	43,882.1	42,277.7	20,815.3	18,079.6	18,079.6
Connecticut	258,422.4	28,655.5	56,969.7	53,155.3	50,123.1	24,820.1	22,348.6	22,350.1
Delaware	57,702.0	7,129.8	12,400.8	12,079.2	11,336.7	5,165.5	4,795.0	4,795.0
Florida	599,885.7	69,517.5	130,880.9	128,917.1	115,862.4	57,194.8	48,756.5	48,756.5
Georgia	420,719.8	48,056.4	87,879.3	87,950.9	83,077.7	41,055.5	36,350.0	36,350.0
Hawaii	88,769.3	10,157.2	18,549.6	17,865.2	17,719.9	8,758.2	7,859.6	7,859.6
Idaho............	79,834.7	8,606.8	16,331.5	15,923.1	16,635.1	8,219.2	7,059.5	7,059.5
Illinois...........	1,025,056.1	115,212.0	215,487.2	207,074.0	204,537.0	101,007.7	90,869.1	90,869.1
Indiana	421,841.1	48,047.6	85,755.6	84,961.9	85,420.0	42,191.3	37,732.3	37,732.4
Iowa	275,209.6	27,517.5	56,276.9	56,444.2	56,794.2	28,071.2	25,052.8	25,052.8
Kansas...........	189,449.8	20,323.1	38,856.6	37,579.4	38,773.6	19,169.4	17,383.5	17,364.2
Kentucky	308,695.0	36,968.4	67,071.0	62,320.7	60,667.5	28,843.6	26,412.6	26,411.2
Louisiana	450,417.9	50,015.7	91,313.8	92,098.0	91,545.8	44,809.6	40,317.8	40,317.2
Maine	123,920.5	13,997.4	26,677.2	25,536.1	24,430.4	12,062.2	10,608.6	10,608.6
Maryland	398,463.9	44,922.8	84,199.6	80,233.5	79,043.2	39,031.8	35,516.5	35,516.5
Massachusetts	639,238.6	71,237.9	137,695.5	129,759.5	127,613.3	63,017.8	54,957.3	54,957.3
Michigan..........	848,596.9	92,523.9	178,289.2	174,434.5	170,203.2	84,076.5	74,532.9	74,536.7
Minnesota.........	403,952.0	45,289.8	88,695.0	81,781.8	78,236.6	39,105.6	35,424.8	35,418.4
Mississippi	315,191.4	33,744.4	62,195.3	64,560.5	64,148.2	32,315.2	29,113.9	29,113.9
Missouri	378,976.5	42,446.2	81,511.4	78,463.5	74,506.9	36,784.9	32,631.8	32,631.8
Montana..........	77,942.0	8,258.8	15,671.3	17,053.0	15,644.3	7,725.2	6,794.7	6,794.7
Nebraska	139,701.4	14,203.2	28,270.0	27,530.4	29,395.0	14,528.2	12,886.5	12,888.1
Nevada	45,333.6	5,452.6	9,969.0	9,021.2	8,872.8	4,381.4	3,818.3	3,818.3
New Hampshire	64,409.0	7,237.8	13,606.7	13,442.3	12,782.2	6,320.4	5,509.8	5,509.8
New Jersey	630,249.7	70,533.2	132,900.8	128,820.7	125,366.3	61,978.3	55,325.2	55,325.2
New Mexico	125,446.5	14,492.0	26,236.9	25,416.5	25,219.9	12,365.2	10,858.0	10,858.0
New York	2,250,650.5	253,497.4	480,494.3	459,753.4	445,873.4	220,176.8	195,427.6	195,427.6
North Carolina	509,118.8	55,951.2	103,450.7	105,177.3	102,826.9	51,038.3	45,337.2	45,337.2
North Dakota	72,875.5	5,657.2	13,649.0	13,872.1	16,723.1	8,262.5	7,355.7	7,355.9
Ohio	806,610.8	90,760.5	172,980.0	164,384.9	158,367.2	78,197.6	70,960.3	70,960.3
Oklahoma.........	223,851.6	25,091.2	46,301.9	46,599.1	44,707.7	22,077.5	19,537.1	19,537.1
Oregon	203,904.0	24,342.4	44,452.1	41,308.4	39,253.1	19,384.8	17,581.6	17,581.6
Pennsylvania	1,058,656.6	118,304.2	225,925.5	217,030.3	209,246.9	103,459.0	92,345.3	92,345.4
Rhode Island	89,158.4	9,669.5	18,350.9	18,094.8	18,087.0	8,931.4	8,012.4	8,012.4
South Carolina	275,232.8	31,625.8	59,182.1	56,752.6	54,269.2	26,241.7	23,590.7	23,570.7
South Dakota	84,492.9	7,324.4	16,772.2	17,011.8	18,255.5	9,016.4	8,056.3	8,056.3
Tennessee	380,069.8	41,653.1	79,376.1	79,342.3	74,822.3	37,824.2	33,526.6	33,525.2
Texas	961,875.4	113,450.3	203,826.6	196,545.9	190,056.2	93,676.1	82,159.9	82,160.4
Utah	117,794.6	12,586.8	25,071.5	24,010.2	23,990.1	11,834.8	10,150.8	10,150.4
Vermont	57,393.9	6,651.3	12,371.2	11,673.9	11,250.4	5,606.9	4,920.1	4,920.1
Virginia	417,160.1	45,766.8	85,181.3	86,538.8	83,473.2	41,299.1	37,450.4	37,450.5
Washington	292,334.1	33,508.3	62,578.8	57,887.3	57,993.6	28,644.3	25,860.9	25,860.9
West Virginia	167,154.1	18,986.1	35,096.2	35,428.7	32,973.6	15,528.7	14,570.4	14,570.4
Wisconsin	503,900.9	54,861.4	107,344.4	102,763.2	100,505.2	49,790.3	44,318.2	44,318.2
Wyoming	35,478.8	3,642.6	6,718.2	7,114.7	7,627.2	3,766.3	3,304.9	3,304.9
Dist. of Col.	0.0	0.0	0.0	0.0	0.0	0.0	0.0	0.0

Source: Office of Revenue Sharing, U.S. Department of the Treasury.

GENERAL REVENUE SHARING PAYMENTS TO LOCAL GOVERNMENTS, BY STATE, BY ENTITLEMENT PERIOD
(In thousands of dollars)

State or other jurisdiction	Total 1/72-9/82	Paid/proj. 10/81-9/82	Paid/proj. 10/80-9/81	10/79-9/80	10/78-9/79	10/77-9/78	1/77-9/77
Total....................	$46,039,669.4	$4,633,921.2	$4,500,256.7	$4,532,731.2	$4,556,284.1	$4,530,315.7	$3,297,510.4
Alabama....................	753,847.3	74,689.7	73,259.3	71,458.9	72,589.4	73,512.6	53,481.8
Alaska.....................	110,999.6	21,063.6	12,967.3	14,809.9	15,287.0	11,758.1	6,963.1
Arizona	513,047.0	65,450.8	56,991.0	53,339.1	52,948.5	49,772.3	32,343.2
Arkansas	465,721.4	48,592.5	43,313.9	45,420.2	45,460.5	43,833.4	34,869.6
California.................	5,055,551.8	523,694.6	490,705.7	532,530.9	518,288.1	507,045.8	353,216.1
Colorado	507,339.8	52,500.0	52,610.3	50,846.8	50,866.9	49,983.9	36,531.0
Connecticut................	583,403.2	55,654.9	56,018.9	57,074.4	57,317.6	56,786.0	42,129.0
Delaware	138,196.2	14,109.0	13,817.3	13,747.3	14,140.6	14,190.9	10,489.1
Florida	1,427,380.6	168,973.9	148,609.2	136,121.0	136,116.7	135,412.2	102,261.9
Georgia....................	1,008,884.8	114,596.2	103,910.6	100,365.8	100,884.5	97,909.4	70,498.5
Hawaii	215,014.0	22,341.0	21,242.4	21,391.7	22,259.5	22,668.9	16,341.2
Idaho	179,573.4	18,272.8	18,621.4	17,232.3	17,384.8	15,573.9	12,653.5
Illinois...................	2,325,322.2	223,463.5	222,512.9	225,836.0	227,329.1	231,692.5	169,432.1
Indiana....................	941,212.6	83,649.6	87,206.8	89,669.2	92,155.2	96,431.8	70,258.9
Iowa	594,633.3	56,181.4	56,173.3	56,707.9	56,976.8	52,926.0	40,458.3
Kansas	417,326.6	38,015.1	40,307.7	40,624.5	40,284.6	38,835.2	29,809.7
Kentucky	736,047.3	75,564.5	74,556.1	73,683.8	75,426.6	73,860.9	54,260.4
Louisiana	1,023,333.7	96,926.2	92,754.2	96,073.8	101,996.6	108,207.1	76,957.9
Maine	284,932.3	28,483.8	27,574.4	26,025.7	30,554.8	27,826.3	20,546.8
Maryland	911,168.3	87,382.5	88,684.1	88,389.9	90,870.7	91,032.7	66,344.5
Massachusetts	1,464,022.0	141,209.5	142,843.4	142,682.8	145,018.0	148,281.2	104,748.5
Michigan	1,934,284.8	184,383.7	188,795.7	196,281.9	191,866.6	188,275.9	136,084.1
Minnesota	922,158.0	87,047.2	91,528.0	90,783.4	91,234.1	90,886.9	66,636.4
Mississippi	685,642.3	63,217.6	60,849.0	63,533.2	66,612.8	66,483.6	49,754.7
Missouri...................	858,877.9	83,432.6	81,133.5	82,248.1	84,291.6	86,495.1	62,300.5
Montana....................	176,413.7	17,919.4	17,015.3	17,980.7	17,365.4	16,017.1	12,173.8
Nebraska	310,969.3	30,895.7	31,855.9	31,409.8	28,565.3	27,675.3	20,865.9
Nevada	113,516.0	13,430.2	12,456.8	11,530.1	11,353.1	11,398.6	8,013.6
New Hampshire	151,050.9	14,359.1	15,174.3	15,513.5	15,574.9	15,358.0	10,662.1
New Jersey.................	1,478,076.8	149,597.1	149.361.2	151,057.0	150,397.8	143,682.6	103,731.4
New Mexico.................	293,882.0	31,402.0	29,353.0	26,876.2	28,704.2	30,821.4	21,278.7
New York...................	5,103,660.8	482,575.9	475,303.7	497,265.9	510,245.8	514,789.7	372,829.3
North Carolina	1,164,877.6	122,139.8	113,952.1	112,847.1	112,673.7	111,880.9	82,265.2
North Dakota	141,938.5	13,039.6	12,112.7	12,944.5	12,648.5	9,988.5	8,329.2
Ohio	1,856,076.2	181,928.3	180,672.2	184,185.1	185,269.6	184,014.6	133,395.6
Oklahoma	520,860.2	55,954.7	53,101.2	51,120.7	49,601.2	50,303.1	36,907.7
Oregon	497,821.7	52,713.0	53,406.9	51,808.2	50,677.9	49,541.5	35,770.2
Pennsylvania	2,360,995.3	226,603.0	228,173.8	222,061.1	222,258.7	229,291.9	173,950.2
Rhode Island	202,110.1	19,558.6	20,191.8	19,689.1	19,568.2	19,726.0	14,218.0
South Carolina	637,242.2	69,999.5	63,045.1	61,074.7	61,410.6	59,986.0	46,493.5
South Dakota	170,505.6	15,317.8	15,298.0	15,534.4	15,328.8	13,767.3	10,766.4
Tennessee..................	866,157.0	84,698.8	85,327.1	87,954.5	84,339.2	82,502.7	61,264.9
Texas......................	2,256,813.1	238,486.3	218,417.9	221,198.3	225,142.6	224,985.9	166,706.7
Utah	284,637.5	34,624.7	31,087.6	27,950.6	28,798.1	25,877.2	18,504.7
Vermont....................	134,564.5	12,798.9	13,251.0	13,599.5	13,945.4	13,795.5	9,780.3
Virginia...................	957,057.6	96,942.6	94,162.8	93,714.9	94,959.4	93,156.2	66,961.6
Washington	671,495.6	69,148.6	67,993.7	63,454.2	61,530.8	67,731.8	49,302.4
West Virginia..............	402,592.3	43,704.7	41,496.2	39,774.6	41,536.3	40,957.5	27,968.9
Wisconsin..................	1,103,140.5	97,953.3	101,961.0	105,913.0	107,279.2	105,480.0	80,653.1
Wyoming....................	87,397.5	10,201.8	10,214.1	9,395.0	8,857.8	7,903.8	5,346.2
Dist. of Col...............	37,896.5	19,011.6	18,884.9	0.0	0.0	0.0	0.0

STATE-LOCAL RELATIONS

By Joseph A. Kayne

THE CHARACTER and direction of state-local relations in the coming years will depend largely on the answers to the following three questions:

- What will be the demand on all levels of government for public goods and services?
- How will the delivery of these goods and services be apportioned between levels of government?
- From what sources will the funds come to provide these goods and services?

Following his election in 1980, President Ronald Reagan focused attention on decreasing the role that government, particularly the federal government, assumes in our lives. Actions by the 97th Congress, especially passage of the Omnibus Budget Reconciliation Act (often referred to as the Gramm-Latta bill) in August 1981, set the tone of efforts to decrease and decentralize the existing system of federal domestic assistance. Through approximately $35 billion in budget reductions, the stage is set for a smaller federal presence in many areas of domestic assistance. In his 1982 State of the Union address, President Reagan proposed even more radical transfers of program responsibilities from the federal to the state governments, while concurrently returning to the states several traditional sources of federal revenues. The question that remains, however, is whether the general population—once these actions take effect—will accept the decreases in public goods and services. If not, will the states and localities be subjected to intense pressure to continue the level of services previously provided by the federal government?

A second element of the Reagan program for decreasing the size and power of the federal government in domestic assistance programs is the decentralization of decision-making authority. This objective is being achieved through the creation of several block grants (mandated in the 1981 Budget Reconciliation Act) which combine funding from previously categorical grants and turn it over to the states to decide the specific purposes for which the funds will be used and in what amounts. In most instances this has transferred to state governments the resources which can now be distributed according to state needs, policies and priorities. As states begin to design the process by which these funds will be distributed (either by formula or competition), a broad spectrum of solutions is emerging.

Finally, one is faced with the reality that even with the shift in authority for many programs to the state and local levels under the block grants, the lower spending authorizations in the fiscal 1982 federal budget mean that the activities under each of the block grants will have to be executed with fewer funds and resources. Additionally, tax initiatives such as Proposition 13 in California and Proposition 2½ in Massachusetts have further eroded the sources of revenues for state and local governments. For example, the mayor of one small California locality explained how the federal budget reductions and state tax initiatives have compounded the fiscal problems within her community: "In past years, we would

Joseph A. Kayne is Director of Program Development, Council of State Community Affairs Agencies, Washington, D.C.

total our share of federal and state transfers and the amount of assistance we might expect from various grant and loan programs. We would then compare these to our operating budget and adjust our property tax rate accordingly to balance our budget. Now federal and state transfers are declining. There are fewer grants and less funds to compete for. And now, the state tax law limits the amount of property tax we can raise. It is particularly hard on rural communities since property values, under Proposition 13, remain fixed until the time of sale and there just is not as much transfer of properties in rural areas as there is in the cities and suburbs.''

In some states, actions have been taken to shift the burden of taxation rather than limiting taxing authority. In April 1981, the Nevada State Legislature enacted a law which shifted the major source of revenue from property to sales, decreasing the property tax by 67 percent and raising the state sales tax proportionately. In addition to shifting the source of revenue, the act effectively gives control of local revenues to the state as the sales tax is collected by the state and redistributed to the localities. Several local officials felt uneasy about being beholden to the state legislature for their share of sales revenues. (A particular concern is that urban areas—the place of origin of an overwhelming majority of sales tax revenue—will want tax receipts to be returned to them.)

The future of state-local relations under these conditions is anything but clear. There must be concern that the competition for domestic assistance may force state and local governments into adversary positions. The same may be true among competing local governments. The domestic development agenda remains immense, including assistance to the needy and the growing demand for new basic expenditures to support the national and local economies.

There is evidence that states, in conjunction with their local governments, are seeking methods to resolve the issues surrounding the delivery of domestic assistance and the financing of these public goods and services. For example, the governor of Colorado has appointed a Commission on State and Local Government Finance, consisting of state and local officials, to examine how crucial government services can be continued during a period of reduced financial resources. In Florida, a task force is exploring the infrastructure needs of the states and means of financing required improvements. The remainder of this section will describe other instances in which state and local governments are addressing issues of government finance and administration, economic and community development and public infrastructure.

Community and Economic Development

Recently, states have actively pursued economic and community development objectives. Activities have included assistance to localities to apply for, and implement, Community Development Block Grant (CDBG) and Urban Development Action Grant (UDAG) programs, new business development financing instruments, enabling legislation to assist localities to establish their own economic and community development programs, and programs that increase local capacity to carry out these programs. Progress in this arena has proven to be most timely as now, more than ever, localities are looking to state governments to pick up the declining aid that is a result of federal administrative and legislative efforts to decrease the federal budget deficit.

The most visible anticipated change is the transfer of the non-entitlement portion of the CDBG program from the federal to state governments. While this represents the first time that states will have ultimate responsibility for the selection and administration of CDBG projects, two demonstration efforts over the past few years have provided some indication of the states' capacity to assume administration of the program. The first demonstration, co-sponsored by the U.S. Department of Housing and Community Development and the Farmers Home Administration (FmHA) of the U.S. Department of Agriculture, allowed four states—California, Colorado, Illinois and West Virginia—to increase the delivery of community development services and resources to previously underserved areas. Concentrating on remote, rural areas each of the states established outreach and implementation systems. In some instances, such as California, the system relied heavily on a state-staffed field office which provided direct technical assistance to the affected local governments. In Colorado, state officials encouraged the creation of new, multi-jurisdictional community development agencies that would remain in place after the demonstration. Where possible, all of the states relied on existing structures, either local government or regional agencies.

Program objectives for the four-state rural demonstration ranged from housing rehabilitation to better leveraging of CDBG resources with state and other federal development funds (particularly FmHA housing and community facilities programs). In both Colorado and West Virginia, state officials identified housing as the most urgent need in the target areas; therefore, these programs emphasized the rehabilitation of existing housing and the development of additional rental units for low- and moderate-income households. In contrast, leveraging of CDBG Title I funds was the major focus of the California demonstration with the state using the available resources as "seed" or "glue" money that ensured the feasibility of projects using other private and public resources. Finally, Illinois chose to run a project competition similar to the HUD-administered program. The state did, however, simplify the application process and lowered the grant maximum, the purpose being to demonstrate that smaller communities could use small grants effectively.

The second demonstration focused on the ability of states to design and then implement a CDBG selection process. The purpose of the effort, which involved Wisconsin and Kentucky, was to test several principles related to the effective use of community development resources. Among these were the contentions that states were more sensitive to the needs of smaller communities, that local government officials would have greater opportunities for input into the design of the selection process, that selection criteria tailored to state development priorities would result in greater project benefits and that states could devote more attention to potential applicants through site visits and concurrent technical assistance to local governments.

In both states, local officials felt that the state selection process had been more responsive to state and local needs. In Wisconsin, applicant communities were weighted according to degree of distress. This system was an extension of an existing state revenue sharing program in which a portion of the funds redistributed to local governments are allocated according to need. While the Kentucky program remained closer to the HUD model, state review and ranking procedures resulted in the funding of more small communities than the HUD-administered process. Although the final award of grants remained with the HUD area offices, in every instance HUD approved the state project recommendations.

Other state activities in the area of community development that affect local governments include the creation of a housing mortgage pool, use of monies from the state employees' and teachers' pension funds, provision of enabling legislation to create tax increment financing districts, and the targeted use of industrial development bonds for commercial businesses in distressed areas. Several Connecticut banks were able to pool available funds to provide mortgages at a 13.5 percent interest rate under an agreement by which the state purchased the mortgages with state public pension funds. Under the agreement, 40 percent of the pooled funds were initially made available to state employees and teachers.

Several states have implemented tax increment financing programs as a way to provide needed community development and encourage private investment in distressed areas. Under these programs, improvements are financed with tax revenues that result from new investment in the designated area. Enabling legislation in Iowa has resulted in the designation of a major portion of downtown Des Moines as a tax increment financing district. The program has substantially rehabilitated the commercial district of the city.

In the past few years, the use of industrial development bonds (IDBs) for financing commercial ventures has been under scrutiny by both the federal administration and Congress. Criticism has centered on providing bond financing to commercial enterprises that generally have not needed this incentive. To meet this concern, two states—Missouri and New Jersey—have amended the statutes that authorize IDB financing to preclude the use of IDBs for commercial firms except in instances where the location is part of a blighted area. In this manner the firm receives the benefits of the relatively low interest rates under IDB financing only as a result of assisting in state efforts to economically develop distressed areas.

During the past decade, the states' interest in economic development has been translated into efforts to improve their capacities to seize economic development opportunities and to assist their respective local governments. Several state technical assistance programs now include courses on development financing or the use of development incentives. Some states have encouraged localities to develop comprehensive community improvement programs to prepare the city or town for future economic development opportunities. The community is given some form of recognition such as ''Preferred Cities'' in Alabama or ''Communities of Excellence'' in North Carolina.

Most recently, state attention has turned to creating ''enterprise zones'' as a means of attracting new investment to distressed areas. Either in anticipation of some federal initiative (e.g., the Kemp-Garcia Urban Enterprise Act) or in response to severe local conditions (e.g., Liberty City in Florida), legislation has been introduced in several states. During 1980 and 1981, state legislatures in Florida, Connecticut and Louisiana enacted measures to attract private investment to blighted areas within the states. While not specifically labeled as enterprise zone proposals, the Florida legislature passed three bills providing tax incentives to encourage economic development in distressed areas. These include tax credits for contributions to eligible local, non-profit development corporations, for investments in distressed areas and for providing job opportunities for unemployed residents of designated blighted areas. In Connecticut, a series of tax incentives are further enhanced by the creation of a system of employment training vouchers for residents of the distressed areas and the establishment of a $1 million revolving loan fund to provide venture capital to businesses willing to locate in the designated needy areas. To assist in the development of rural areas, Louisiana provides a special tax credit against the state income and franchise tax liability as opposed to a 10-year moratorium on these taxes in urban enterprise zones in the state.

Taxation and Finance

That states are playing more active roles in local taxation and finance is evident from research provided by the Advisory Commission on Intergovernmental Relations, which shows that state revenue sharing increased tenfold between 1960 and 1980. These state-to-local transfers now represent 10 percent of all local aid. In some instances this increase is due to state efforts to minimize the negative impacts of local tax initiatives. In California, lost revenues at the local level have been offset for the past few years with state surplus funds. (These funds have been exhausted since the passage of Proposition 13, and only now do local officials expect to feel the real impact of the tax measure.) The Massachusetts legislature has appropriated $265 million in additional local aid, approximately half of the revenues foregone as a result of Proposition 2½.

In addition to these general local aid programs, states are responding to local financial stress in specific areas. Illinois, for example, provided an additional $13 million in state funds to support the Chicago public school system in 1981. Other states, such as Pennsylvania and Ohio, have opted for a system of uniform statewide property taxes to ensure full funding of local educational programs.

Highway construction and maintenance costs and subsidies for mass transit systems are two examples in which states have increased taxes to ensure adequate levels of public service. North Carolina has imposed a 3 percent increase in the state motor fuel tax to support the state's highway fund. New York has established a 2 percent gross receipts tax on oil products, the proceeds of which are used to maintain mass transportation systems across the state.

The lack of confidence in government bonds has hampered the ability of local governments to raise funds, and many localities have seen their bond ratings decline over concern about their fiscal health. Timidity on the part of buyers has meant higher interest rates. To relieve some of the concern in the bond market, Minnesota now guarantees local government bonds. In return, the localities place 2 percent of each bond issue into a guarantee fund.

Local Government Administration

With less funds available, it is imperative that local governments manage these resources effectively. A 1980 survey of state activities in the area of financial management assistance to local governments, prepared by the Council of State Community Affairs Agencies, found that some type of technical assistance—workshops, manuals, on-site aid or telephone inquiry services—is being provided by state agencies in 43 states. The survey also indicates that most of the assistance is directed to small- and medium-sized cities, towns and counties, partly due to large rates of turnover of local officials and professional staff. The type of assistance requested varies widely from accounting to budgeting to grantsmanship to cash management. The goals of state assistance in financial management include: fostering local fiscal control, ensuring financial solvency of the locality and promoting efficient resource utilization.

In addition to general training and technical assistance in administrative management, three specific methods by which states are working with local governments to ensure sound management practices are exhibited by the California program of supervising local property tax assessors, Pennsylvania's efforts to ensure sound employee pensions and Tennessee's monitoring of local budgets. Under the California program, local property tax assessors work under the supervision of the State Board of Equalization. Local assessors are monitored to ensure that property values across the state are assessed realistically.

One area in which local governments often face financial crises is the management of public pensions. In Pennsylvania, each municipality is required to submit to the state for review actuarial studies for any pension plans established. Additionally, larger jurisdictions with pensions covering 50 or more employees must prepare a biennial report of the status of their pension funds.

Tennessee's program of budget monitoring attempts to deal with potential local fiscal crises before they occur. State officials look for increasing rates of short-term debt as ". . . abuse of short term debt is an indication of more severe fiscal problems." The state is authorized to approve budgets of local governments that have outstanding short-term debt.

Conclusion

State and local governments can expect increasing pressure to provide a constant level of public goods and services in a number of program areas with decreasing financial assistance from the federal government. Additionally, the turnback of some domestic assistance programs to the states to administer portends increasing competition among local governments for state action to alleviate the specific needs in each of these communities. Early evidence suggests that states feel they are "under the gun" to perform effectively and equitably.

In the examples described above, states appear to recognize both the opportunities and liabilities associated with their increased responsibilities under the "New Federalism." The extent to which states can sustain and improve relationships with local governments and respond to local government needs with decreased resources may well determine the states' ability to assume a greater role in domestic assistance programs.

STATE AID TO LOCAL GOVERNMENTS IN 1980

INTERGOVERNMENTAL AID is one of today's most significant issues in government finance. As the federal government winds down or eliminates several intergovernmental aid programs and as local governments seek increased revenue in the wake of tax limitation measures, state governments become the middlemen in sorting out the proper roles of each level of government in our federal system. Recent events clearly signal a shift in the scope of state aid programs. Local governments (and particularly those in large urban areas) may now view their states as the primary source of all forms of financial aid, including grants for a variety of social programs, which were funded in the past directly by the federal government.

However, much remains uncertain as the Reagan administration and Congress continue to review and revise the federal budget and intergovernmental assistance programs. In the meantime, state governments most certainly will feel increased pressure from localities to finance or assume responsibility for additional services.

During fiscal 1980, state intergovernmental expenditures totaled $84.5 billion, or $374 per capita. Most state intergovernmental expenditure was for aid to local governments. Such state aid payments totaled $82.8 billion during fiscal 1980, with $1.7 billion in state funds paid to the federal government.

The rate of growth in state intergovernmental expenditure slowed during 1980, increasing by 11.2 percent. In comparison, state government direct expenditure for purchases of goods and services grew by 16.5 percent during the year.

There has been some variation in the percentage of state general spending going directly for state aid programs, as indicated in Table A. However, the overall variations have been modest, as state governments have maintained a consistently strong commitment to local assistance programs over the years.

Table A
DIRECT STATE AID TO LOCAL GOVERNMENTS AS A PERCENTAGE OF STATE GENERAL EXPENDITURE

Fiscal year	Percent	Fiscal year	Percent
1960	34.7	1972	37.2
1962	34.9	1974	38.0
1964	34.8	1976	36.9
1966	36.7	1978	36.6
1968	36.3	1979	37.1
1970	37.2	1980	36.3

Defining Intergovernmental Aid

Bureau of the Census data on state intergovernmental expenditure include two distinct features: state payments to the federal government (for services and Supplemental Security

Adapted by Maurice Criz and David Kellerman, Senior Advisor and Statistician, respectively, Governments Division, U.S. Bureau of the Census, from the Bureau's report, *State Payments to Local Governments* (vol. 6, no. 3 of the 1977 census of governments), and annual reports of *State Government Finances*.

Income aid) and payments to local governments. Total state intergovernmental expenditure also includes the amounts of federal funds which pass through the states to their local jurisdictions. Federal funds which states receive and then pass on to local governments are either distributed directly or in some combination with state funds. However, Bureau of the Census data cannot be used to identify state aid payments to local units by these two revenue sources.

In general, the Bureau of the Census defines state payments to local governments as consisting of grants-in-aid, payments in lieu of taxes, reimbursements for services performed, state-collected locally shared taxes, and the extension of contingent loans or advances (where repayment is on a conditional basis).

Excluded from the concept of state intergovernmental payments to local governments are the following:

1. Non-fiscal assistance to local governments in the form of advisory services or aid-in-kind.
2. Contributions by a state to trust funds it administers for the financing of retirement benefits to local government employees.
3. Shares of state-imposed taxes which are collected and retained by local governments.
4. Proceeds of state interest-bearing loans to local governments which, unlike contingent loans, are repayable over a specified time. Such loans are treated as debt and investment transactions.
5. Expenditure for the purchase of property, commodities and utility services to other governments.

State-to-federal payments for fiscal 1980 are shown in Table 5 on an individual state basis. These payments totaled only $341 million in fiscal 1974, but amounted to $1.7 billion by fiscal 1980. Not all states show payments to the federal government. State-to-federal payments consist almost entirely of state-supplemented shares of categorical welfare aid (Supplemental Security Income aid), a program administered by the federal government. Some states choose to supplement federal categorical welfare aid with their own direct payments to qualified recipients.

Administering Programs of State Aid

Programs of state aid payments to local governments involve the issues of the amounts of aid to be distributed, the methods of allocation and the methods of financing the programs.

The amount of aid to be distributed is generally predetermined, either by legislative action or participation in a federally funded program. In some cases, state aid payments are based upon the yield of a specific revenue source, such as a tax on gasoline. In education, state aid is quite often set at a particular amount per pupil or per teacher, with total amounts paid to any given unit varying accordingly.

The earmarking of gasoline taxes for local highway aid is a particular area of great concern to many state governments, at a time when gasoline tax revenues are on the decline. Gas tax receipts are not keeping pace with rising highway construction and maintenance costs, forcing many states to raise gas tax rates and to seek additional sources of funding for their highway programs.

The choice of how to finance and distribute state aid often depends upon the basic intent or purpose of particular aid programs. Most states now have some type of program for general local government support (revenue sharing type programs). Generally, broad-based revenue sources are used to finance these general local support programs. Payments can be made from a state's general fund or from a broad-based tax source such as the general sales tax or individual income tax. These taxes are levied on nearly all taxpayers and are logically used to finance programs considered beneficial to the general public.

For some specific types of state aid, there is a direct relation between the function being financed and the source and distribution of the aid payments. Aid for highways, as mentioned, is often financed from special trust funds comprised of gasoline tax revenue or highway user tax revenue. To some degree, the financing burden is borne by those who would use the highways most often, even though highways are a social commodity. The general approach is thus to finance the program through earmarked or designated revenue sources, with aid payments distributed according to origin or need.

Finally, some state aid programs might be designed so as to achieve specific goals. Financing is generally based upon appropriations, with distributions to localities which meet certain criteria, such as the establishment of a specific program. State aid of this type often involves the redistribution of federal funds and may involve some matching requirements.

Emergency Aid

Since the New York City fiscal crises in the mid-1970s, state governments have been called on to provide last-minute funding, or bail-outs, during local government financial emergencies. More and more states have found themselves facing such situations, as their local governments experienced varying degrees of cash shortages. These bail-outs initially were concerned with large city governments, but have subsequently spread to counties, school districts and even townships or special districts. Among the most notable emergency aid measures in recent years were those taken by New York State (to assist New York City and then later to aid upstate communities), Michigan (to assist Wayne County and Detroit) and Illinois (to assist Chicago schools and transit special district governments).

While state governments can respond in various ways to a local fiscal crisis, the most direct approaches remain state aid payments or advances of aid. Other less direct means of alleviating local fiscal or cash flow problems, which do not involve intergovernmental transfers, include the authorization of new taxing authority, the removal of debt or tax ceilings or the state guaranty of local borrowing.

However, the issue of emergency state assistance goes beyond such special aid measures. States constitutionally establish local governments and define their proper financial powers. They have certain responsibilities with respect to administration and oversight of local affairs, especially when unsound financial practices are among the primary causes of financial emergencies.

The extension of emergency aid by a state government has generally resulted in the creation of additional government agencies to deal with the needed financial and management oversight. New York created the Municipal Assistance Corporation, Michigan established a Michigan Municipal Finance Commission, and the Chicago School Finance Authority was created by the state of Illinois. Most often, such newly created agencies are directly associated with the state governments.

Statistical Findings

State intergovernmental expenditure increased in most major functional areas during fiscal 1980. State aid for education, the largest category for which states provide assistance, increased 14 percent to $52.7 billion. A number of states have made major changes in their education aid programs since fiscal 1978. In California, state aid for education increased nearly 22 percent in 1980, after a 57 percent increase in fiscal 1979 payments. These large increases were, of course, the result of Proposition 13 and the subsequent need to restructure local finance in California. The state government significantly increased its responsibilities for financing local schools while allowing the property tax to accrue principally to the local general purpose governments.

Other states that significantly revised their state education aid programs include Georgia, Idaho, Nevada and Washington. States have largely responded to tax and spending limitations (or the threat of them) by altering their programs for financing education aid, since education is perhaps the single most important function over which states (as opposed to local governments) have administrative control. State aid in the area of general local government support, on the other hand, showed only a very modest increase during fiscal 1980—up 5.1 percent. Such aid in California declined by over $500 million, for reasons cited above. State general purpose aid, or revenue sharing type grants, exists in every state except Delaware, but varies considerably. Per capita amounts range from $183 in Wyoming, $171 in Wisconsin and $108 in Alaska, to under $1 in Kentucky and Vermont.

State aid to localities in most other functional areas increased somewhat during the 1980 fiscal year, although not as significantly as did aid for education. Public welfare aid increased about 7 percent, aid for highways increased about 6 percent and aid for housing, libraries, airports and the like all showed some growth.

Table 5 presents state intergovernmental expenditure by type of receiving government. School districts received the largest share—over 50 percent of all aid. Counties received about 22 percent and municipalities about 15 percent. The remainder was spread out among the federal government, townships, and special districts, but with a large portion of the total being unidentifiable as to type of receiving government. However, most of the latter amount accrues to general purpose local governments, such as counties, cities and townships.

In total, the amount of state aid to local governments did not necessarily relate to the amount of federal aid received by the states, on a functional basis. Table B depicts state aid payments by function and corresponding intergovernmental revenue from the federal government by function for fiscal 1980.

Table B
STATE PAYMENTS TO LOCAL GOVERNMENTS
AND RECEIPTS FROM FEDERAL GOVERNMENT:
FISCAL 1980
(In millions)

Function	To local governments	From federal government
Total............................	$82,758	$61,892
Education	52,688	12,765
Public Welfare	9,242	24,680
General Support	8,644	2,278
Highways........................	4,383	8,860
Miscellaneous and Other	7,801	13,309

Unfortunately, Census Bureau statistics on intergovernmental transfers do not allow an analysis of federal pass-through aid to local governments, so the amount of state payments to local governments financed with federal funds cannot be determined.

Several of the tables present intergovernmental aid in terms of per capita amounts. This enables a clearer analysis of different levels of funding among the states. However, numerous factors help to determine funding levels in each state. Most important among these are the structure of responsibility for providing services and state constitutional and legislative restrictions on public spending and taxation.

Unreflected here are the significant changes in intergovernmental relations anticipated for 1981 and 1982. The state governments must respond to the decline in federal aid in general and federal categorical aid to localities in particular. The issue will not be whether state governments will assume more responsibility for financing local government programs, but will they be able to finance the programs? The large state budget surpluses of the late 1970s are expected to disappear, putting extreme pressure on state officials and forcing painful choices in program financing.

For example, the success of Proposition 13 in California can be, through 1980, attributable to the existence of surplus funds which were made available to localities. Overall state intergovernmental spending in California rose by 38 percent in 1979 and another 12 percent in 1980. What might happen as the state government surplus is depleted could be far different.

Table 1
SUMMARY OF STATE INTERGOVERNMENTAL PAYMENTS: 1942 to 1980
(In millions)

Fiscal year	Total	To federal government	For general local government support	To local governments — Total	Schools	Public welfare	Highways	All other	Per capita
1942	$ 1,780	...	$ 224	$ 1,556	$ 790	$ 390	$ 344	$ 32	$ 13.37
1944	1,842	...	274	1,568	861	368	298	41	13.95
1946	2,092	...	357	1,735	953	376	339	67	15.05
1948	3,283	...	428	2,855	1,554	648	507	146	22.64
1950	4,217	...	482	3,735	2,054	792	610	279	28.11
1951	4,678	...	513	4,165	2,248	974	667	276	30.78
1952	5,044	...	549	4,495	2,525	976	728	268	32.55
1953	5,384	...	592	4,971	2,740	981	803	267	34.19
1954	5,679	...	600	5,079	2,934	1,004	871	269	35.42
1955	5,986	...	591	5,395	3,154	1,046	911	284	36.62
1956	6,538	...	631	5,907	3,541	1,069	984	313	39.28
1957	7,439	...	668	6,771	4,212	1,136	1,083	340	43.86
1958	8,089	...	687	7,402	4,598	1,247	1,167	390	46.76
1959	8,689	...	725	7,964	4,957	1,409	1,207	391	49.37
1960	9,443	...	806	8,637	5,461	1,483	1,247	446	52.75
1961	10,114	...	821	9,293	5,963	1,602	1,266	462	55.51
1962	10,906	...	844	10,062	6,474	1,777	1,326	485	58.94
1963	11,885	...	1,012	10,873	6,993	1,919	1,416	545	63.31
1964	12,968	...	1,053	11,915	7,664	2,104	1,524	623	68.06
1965	14,174	...	1,102	13,072	8,351	2,436	1,630	655	73.43
1966	16,928	...	1,361	15,567	10,177	2,882	1,725	783	86.79
1967	19,056	...	1,585	17,471	11,845	2,897	1,861	868	96.70
1968	21,950	...	1,993	19,957	13,321	3,527	2,029	1,079	110.27
1969	24,779	...	2,135	22,644	14,858	4,402	2,109	1,275	123.20
1970	28,892	...	2,958	25,934	17,085	5,003	2,439	1,407	142.73
1971	32,640	...	3,258	29,382	19,292	5,760	2,507	1,823	158.82
1972	36,759	...	3,752	33,007	21,195	6,944	2,633	2,235	177.16
1973	40,822	...	4,280	36,542	23,316	7,532	2,953	2,741	195.22
1974	45,941	$ 341	4,804	40,796	27,107	7,028	3,211	3,450	218.07
1975	51,978	975	5,129	45,874	31,110	7,127	3,225	4,412	244.71
1976	57,858	1,180	5,674	51,004	34,084	8,296	3,241	5,383	270.42
1977	62,460	1,386	6,373	54,701	36,964	8,756	3,631	5,350	288.65
1978	67,287	1,472	6,819	58,995	40,125	8,586	3,821	6,463	309.52
1979	75,975	1,493	8,224	66,258	46,206	8,667	4,149	7,236	346.18
1980	84,504	1,746	8,644	74,114	52,688	9,242	4,383	7,801	374.13

Source: U.S. Bureau of the Census, *State Payments to Local Governments* (vol. 6, no. 3, of the 1977 census of governments) and annual reports of *State Government Finances*.

Table 2
STATE INTERGOVERNMENTAL EXPENDITURE, BY STATE:
1974 to 1980

State	Amount (in thousands)				Per capita amounts				Percentage change in per capita amounts		
	1980	1978	1976	1974	1980	1978	1976	1974	1978 to 1980	1976 to 1978	1974 to 1976
All states	$84,504,451	$67,287,260	$57,858,241	$45,941,111	$374.13	$309.52	$270.42	$218.07	20.9	14.5	24.0
Alabama	1,036,721	856,355	700,064	555,013	266.51	228.85	191.01	155.16	16.5	19.8	23.1
Alaska	340,319	265,975	207,088	146,623	850.80	659.99	542.12	435.08	28.9	21.7	24.6
Arizona	1,040,614	814,662	694,268	470,705	382.86	346.08	305.84	218.63	10.6	13.2	39.9
Arkansas	624,261	505,103	418,197	314,643	273.20	231.06	198.29	152.59	18.2	16.5	30.0
California	15,360,365	9,905,969	8,135,469	6,901,808	648.97	444.33	378.04	330.12	46.1	17.5	14.5
Colorado	947,692	746,746	675,431	482,735	328.03	279.68	261.49	193.40	17.3	7.0	35.2
Connecticut.........	671,287	593,857	525,225	429,011	215.99	191.63	168.50	138.93	12.7	13.7	21.3
Delaware	189,577	183,973	188,428	134,868	318.62	315.56	323.75	235.37	1.0	-2.5	37.6
Florida	2,925,889	2,235,987	1,834,215	1,560,305	300.40	260.18	217.81	192.87	15.5	19.5	12.9
Georgia	1,613,179	1,177,775	845,591	817,138	295.24	231.66	170.14	167.38	27.4	36.2	1.7
Hawaii	35,530	49,711	222,772	21,741	36.82	55.42	25.67	25.67	-33.6	115.9	0.0
Idaho	309,341	225,063	187,358	135,844	327.69	256.34	225.46	170.02	27.8	13.7	32.6
Illinois	3,817,128	2,869,480	2,652,553	2,043,053	334.31	255.22	236.22	183.55	31.0	8.0	28.7
Indiana.............	1,805,564	1,481,065	1,253,233	753,675	328.88	275.60	236.37	141.40	19.3	16.6	67.2
Iowa	1,148,360	969,801	797,891	584,348	394.22	334.88	278.01	204.68	17.7	20.5	35.8
Kansas	601,939	474,426	404,805	304,312	254.74	202.06	175.24	134.06	26.1	15.3	30.7
Kentucky	1,006,756	774,679	510,160	404,707	274.99	221.46	148.82	120.56	24.2	48.8	23.4
Louisiana...........	1,315,201	1,116,896	998,899	731,312	312.85	281.62	260.06	194.29	11.1	8.3	33.9
Maine	303,746	274,718	320,491	109,340	270.00	251.80	299.52	104.43	7.2	-15.9	186.8
Maryland	1,431,805	1,199,885	1,460,454	1,091,811	339.61	289.62	352.43	266.69	17.3	-17.8	32.2
Massachusetts........	2,116,477	1,577,703	1,429,110	916,244	368.92	273.24	246.02	157.97	35.0	11.1	55.7
Michigan	3,578,343	3,071,384	2,306,268	2,072,529	386.51	334.25	253.32	227.80	15.6	32.0	11.2
Minnesota	2,237,164	1,960,373	1,602,859	1,391,182	548.73	489.12	404.25	355.17	12.2	21.0	13.8
Mississippi	856,350	691,567	582,224	459,559	339.69	287.67	247.33	197.74	18.1	16.3	25.1
Missouri............	1,088,886	812,678	693,542	598,876	221.45	167.22	145.15	125.37	32.4	15.2	15.8
Montana	230,463	215,838	147,181	96,534	292.84	274.95	195.46	131.34	6.5	40.7	48.8
Nebraska	412,081	347,780	257,768	180,772	262.47	222.22	165.98	117.16	18.1	33.9	41.7
Nevada.............	265,956	197,202	143,910	119,059	332.86	298.79	235.92	207.78	11.4	26.7	13.5
New Hampshire	137,723	105,117	87,832	69,147	149.54	120.69	106.85	85.58	23.9	13.0	24.9
New Jersey	3,056,970	2,162,892	1,634,972	1,365,174	415.12	295.19	222.87	186.24	40.6	32.5	19.7
New Mexico	595,464	461,088	363,060	271,566	458.05	380.44	310.84	242.04	20.4	22.4	28.4
New York	10,252,802	10,075,469	9,977,102	7,914,358	583.97	567.70	551.71	436.99	2.9	2.9	26.3
North Carolina	2,028,170	1,960,984	1,652,666	1,179,995	345.28	351.62	302.19	220.03	-1.8	16.4	37.3
North Dakota	216,844	177,804	148,253	114,500	332.07	272.71	230.56	179.75	21.8	18.3	28.3
Ohio	3,249,696	2,610,757	2,095,547	1,828,135	300.98	242.88	196.03	170.26	23.9	23.9	15.1
Oklahoma	800,260	631,479	491,460	368,558	264.55	219.26	177.68	136.05	20.7	23.4	30.6
Oregon.............	879,899	608,505	421,079	353,141	334.18	248.98	180.80	155.84	34.2	37.7	16.0
Pennsylvania	3,541,232	3,054,225	2,762,409	2,352,901	298.41	259.93	232.88	198.81	14.8	11.6	17.1
Rhode Island	217,255	170,414	148,660	114,275	229.41	182.26	160.37	121.96	25.9	13.7	31.5
South Carolina	781,643	650,372	530,983	444,103	250.61	222.88	186.44	159.52	12.5	20.0	16.9
South Dakota	121,758	85,935	68,306	62,979	176.46	124.54	99.57	92.34	41.7	25.1	7.8
Tennessee	974,485	798,272	657,567	545,545	212.26	183.22	156.04	132.13	15.8	17.4	18.1
Texas	3,458,969	2,724,758	2,161,147	1,433,098	243.11	209.37	173.07	118.93	16.1	21.0	45.5
Utah	459,404	369,324	288,129	197,742	314.44	282.57	234.63	168.58	11.3	20.4	39.2
Vermont	110,786	97,068	81,941	69,620	216.80	199.32	172.14	148.13	8.8	15.8	16.2
Virginia	1,268,683	1,045,710	1,010,572	844,923	237.31	203.13	200.83	172.15	16.8	1.2	16.7
Washington..........	1,601,814	1,138,795	947,921	671,821	387.85	301.75	262.44	193.27	28.5	15.0	35.8
West Virginia	533,286	461,282	356,823	254,904	273.48	248.00	195.95	142.32	10.3	26.6	37.8
Wisconsin	2,643,133	2,149,735	1,868,145	1,587,473	561.77	459.44	405.33	347.67	22.3	13.4	16.6
Wyoming............	263,176	150,624	108,213	69,406	558.76	355.25	277.47	193.33	57.1	28.0	43.5

Source: U.S. Bureau of the Census, *State Government Finances in 1980,* and previous annual reports.

Table 3
PER CAPITA STATE INTERGOVERNMENTAL EXPENDITURE,
BY FUNCTION AND BY STATE: 1980

State	Total	General local government support	Specified functions			
			Education	Public welfare	Highways	Miscellaneous and unallocable
All states..................	$374.13	$ 38.27	$233.27	$ 48.60	$19.40	$ 34.59
Alabama.....................	266.51	9.98	208.77	0.84	20.20	26.72
Alaska......................	850.80	108.45	586.23	2.25	. . .	153.87
Arizona	382.86	90.12	248.79	0.97	24.27	18.71
Arkansas	273.20	16.15	192.56	0.52	31.87	32.10
California..................	648.97	51.24	361.19	167.88	16.44	52.22
Colorado	328.03	6.10	220.17	58.41	21.72	21.63
Connecticut.................	215.99	34.45	136.24	8.45	6.63	30.22
Delaware	318.62	. . .	264.35	0.85	3.36	50.06
Florida	300.40	29.71	240.93	. . .	13.26	16.50
Georgia.....................	295.24	2.95	229.96	1.35	18.83	42.15
Hawaii	36.82	18.88	. . .	4.25	4.26	9.43
Idaho	327.69	38.34	237.31	. . .	38.01	14.03
Illinois....................	334.31	40.77	231.23	8.36	22.41	31.54
Indiana.....................	328.88	69.91	178.17	26.23	38.46	16.11
Iowa	394.22	39.75	263.96	6.99	52.56	30.96
Kansas	254.74	15.41	207.74	0.05	18.11	13.43
Kentucky	274.99	0.35	239.67	. . .	6.05	28.92
Louisiana	312.85	40.77	232.02	0.10	13.42	26.54
Maine	270.00	20.95	212.32	6.74	4.23	25.76
Maryland	339.61	28.06	190.91	0.05	65.01	55.58
Massachusetts	368.92	30.65	198.81	23.16	12.97	103.33
Michigan	386.51	61.59	206.17	37.01	46.48	35.26
Minnesota	548.73	94.09	313.55	69.74	30.42	40.93
Mississippi	339.69	46.71	244.71	. . .	33.78	14.49
Missouri	221.45	1.50	172.76	2.48	17.49	27.22
Montana.....................	292.84	19.40	205.24	1.23	9.20	57.77
Nebraska	262.47	71.83	92.93	11.31	46.43	39.97
Nevada	332.86	20.32	284.15	6.76	8.72	12.93
New Hampshire	149.54	45.02	60.77	. . .	9.48	34.27
New Jersey	415.12	88.81	194.81	84.81	8.29	38.40
New Mexico..................	458.05	89.34	342.19	. . .	9.55	16.97
New York....................	583.97	72.17	243.29	209.99	7.22	51.30
North Carolina	345.28	17.23	269.34	16.48	6.96	35.27
North Dakota	332.07	44.94	221.51	12.50	41.29	11.83
Ohio	300.98	30.32	203.81	28.66	19.70	18.49
Oklahoma	264.55	3.24	211.80	2.84	36.11	10.56
Oregon	334.18	22.46	218.15	4.34	55.31	33.92
Pennsylvania	298.41	3.17	207.29	25.89	13.95	48.11
Rhode Island	229.41	14.90	171.11	21.82	0.41	21.17
South Carolina	250.61	24.01	182.08	. . .	13.36	31.16
South Dakota	176.46	36.09	111.63	0.27	7.51	20.96
Tennessee...................	212.26	19.49	148.91	0.31	32.69	10.86
Texas.......................	243.11	1.76	234.94	. . .	1.03	5.38
Utah	314.44	1.31	257.48	3.68	13.29	38.68
Vermont.....................	216.80	0.25	148.24	9.74	16.90	41.67
Virginia....................	237.31	7.36	171.42	26.17	8.60	23.76
Washington	387.85	12.55	300.99	5.33	28.10	40.88
West Virginia...............	273.48	5.25	255.63	. . .	. . .	12.60
Wisconsin...................	561.77	171.45	202.71	101.36	39.76	46.49
Wyoming	558.76	182.89	261.16	0.17	26.72	87.82

Source: U.S. Bureau of the Census, *State Government Finances in 1980.*

Table 4
STATE INTERGOVERNMENTAL EXPENDITURE, BY FUNCTION AND BY STATE: 1980
(In thousands)

State	Total	General local government support	Education	Public welfare	Highways	Miscellaneous and combined
All states.............	$84,504,451	$8,643,789	$52,688,101	$10,977,467	$4,382,716	$7,812,378
Alabama..................	1,036,721	38,815	812,117	3,280	78,595	103,914
Alaska....................	340,319	43,378	234,493	900	. . .	61,548
Arizona..................	1,040,614	244,944	676,221	2,650	65,977	50,822
Arkansas	624,261	36,903	439,999	1,180	72,816	73,363
California................	15,360,365	1,212,885	8,548,967	3,973,598	389,040	1,235,875 (a)
Colorado	947,692	16,919	636,083	168,758	62,758	63,174
Connecticut	671,287	107,058	423,437	26,250	20,618	93,924
Delaware	189,577	. . .	157,291	506	2,000	29,780
Florida	2,925,889	289,419	2,346,657	. . .	129,120	160,693
Georgia..................	1,613,179	16,117	1,256,498	7,373	102,888	230,303
Hawaii	35,530	18,223	. . .	4,100	4,111	9,096
Idaho	309,341	36,194	224,016	. . .	35,885	13,246
Illinois...................	3,817,128	465,456	2,640,206	95,504	255,907	360,055
Indiana..................	1,805,564	383,833	978,135	144,013	211,137	88,446
Iowa.....................	1,148,360	115,783	768,902	20,362	153,103	90,210
Kansas	601,939	36,409	490,894	125	42,790	31,721
Kentucky	1,006,756	1,285	877,446	. . .	22,138	105,887
Louisiana	1,315,201	171,415	975,406	430	56,437	111,513
Maine	303,746	23,574	238,857	7,586	4,759	28,970
Maryland	1,431,805	118,300	804,875	220	274,079	234,331
Massachusetts	2,116,477	175,861	1,140,549	132,857	74,412	592,798 (b)
Michigan	3,578,343	570,203	1,908,687	342,631	430,325	326,497
Minnesota	2,237,164	383,596	1,278,344	284,334	124,040	166,850
Mississippi	856,350	117,754	616,924	. . .	85,163	36,509
Missouri	1,088,886	7,374	849,470	12,216	85,977	133,849
Montana..................	230,463	15,269	161,526	971	7,238	45,459
Nebraska	412,081	112,767	145,896	17,758	72,900	62,760
Nevada	265,956	16,237	227,038	5,405	6,966	10,310
New Hampshire	137,723	41,464	55,969	. . .	8,728	31,562
New Jersey...............	3,056,970	653,993	1,434,564	624,540	61,036	282,837
New Mexico..............	595,464	116,143	444,847	. . .	12,414	22,060
New York................	10,252,802	1,267,133	4,271,473	3,686,773	126,759	900,664 (c)
North Carolina	2,028,170	101,208	1,582,103	96,832	40,857	207,170
North Dakota	216,844	29,344	144,647	8,163	26,961	7,729
Ohio	3,249,696	327,327	2,200,510	309,396	212,707	199,756
Oklahoma	800,260	9,803	640,682	8,599	109,219	31,957
Oregon	879,899	59,132	574,376	11,415	145,640	89,336
Pennsylvania	3,541,237	37,604	2,459,922	307,192	165,501	571,018 (d)
Rhode Island	217,255	14,114	162,045	20,665	390	20,041
South Carolina	781,643	74,883	567,896	. . .	41,674	97,190
South Dakota	121,758	24,901	77,026	185	5,183	14,463
Tennessee................	974,485	89,501	683,629	1,415	150,065	49,875
Texas....................	3,458,969	24,995	3,342,797	. . .	14,656	76,521
Utah	459,404	1,920	376,171	5,379	19,414	56,520
Vermont..................	110,786	130	75,752	4,979	8,634	21,291
Virginia..................	1,268,683	39,325	916,410	139,928	45,979	127,041
Washington	1,601,814	51,835	1,243,099	22,019	116,042	168,819
West Virginia.............	533,286	10,237	498,479	. . .	. . .	24,570
Wisconsin................	2,643,133	806,683	953,762	476,901	187,094	218,693
Wyoming	263,176	86,143	123,008	79	12,584	41,362

Source: U.S. Bureau of the Census, *State Government Finances in 1980.*

(a) Includes $499,649,000 health aid, $67,592,000 sewerage grants and $35,787,000 criminal justice grants.

(b) Includes $206,456,000 transit subsidies, $134,791,000 redistribution of federal CETA funds and $122,683,000 housing assistance.

(c) Includes $275,886,000 health aid, $81,557,000 lease payment to Albany County, $73,208,000 redistribution of federal CETA aid and $54,750,000 municipal overburden aid.

(d) Includes $219,956,000 health aid and $141,615,000 transportation grants.

Table 5
STATE INTERGOVERNMENTAL EXPENDITURE,
BY TYPE OF RECEIVING GOVERNMENT AND BY STATE: 1980
(In thousands of dollars)

State	Total intergovern- mental expenditure	Type of receiving government						
		Federal	School districts	Counties	Municipali- ties	Townships and New England "towns"	Special districts	Combined and un- allocable
All states	$84,504,451	$1,746,301(a)	$42,854,261	$18,334,151	$12,564,627	$1,041,160	$961,039	$7,002,912
Alabama	1,036,721	...	812,117	152,434	64,409	...	4	7,757
Alaska	340,319	1,938	...	163,022	125,261	...	...	50,098
Arizona	1,040,614	1,273	676,221	183,849	173,805	...	180	5,286
Arkansas	624,261	145	439,203	92,171	59,965	...	1,604	31,173
California	15,360,365	1,087,636	8,176,157	4,806,533	931,408	...	230,254	128,377
Colorado	947,692	196	636,083	194,257	101,312	...	15,596	248
Connecticut	671,287	1,173	22,854	...	256,135	323,214	4,898	63,013
Delaware	189,577	506	157,291	20,230	6,425	...	...	5,125
Florida	2,925,889	3,650	2,346,657	306,566	262,143	...	1,089	5,784
Georgia	1,613,179	59	1,256,498	215,350	39,558	...	6,268	95,446
Hawaii	35,5304,100	...	20,356	11,074	...	...	...	...
Idaho	309,341	917	224,016	38,570	13,487	...	4,836	27,515
Illinois	3,817,128	503	2,638,520	307,458	495,542	53,525	223,038	98,542
Indiana	1,805,564	2,808	978,135	249,374	172,259	...	11,438	391,550(b)
Iowa	1,148,360	9,447	768,902	169,406	128,514	...	6,718	65,373
Kansas	601,939	708	490,894	52,587	36,326	1,285	3,252	16,887
Kentucky	1,006,756	...	877,446	83,390	18,812	...	5,165	21,943
Louisiana	1,315,201	430	975,406	166,301	42,704	...	3,806	126,554
Maine	303,746	5,982	...	13,533	...	...	...	284,231
Maryland	1,431,805	220	...	843,275	479,971	...	1,541	106,798
Massachusetts	2,116,477	123,392	...	1,433	4,946	...	206,456	1,780,250(c)
Michigan	3,578,343	76,629	1,908,687	762,165	589,908	95,065	1,461	144,428
Minnesota	2,237,164	6	1,258,959	528,342	332,857	25,638	8,233	83,129
Mississippi	856,350	19	616,580	125,044	110,707	...	...	4,000
Missouri	1,088,886	...	849,470	49,099	82,054	...	2,073	106,190
Montana	230,463	801	160,661	42,714	14,320	...	406	11,561
Nebraska	412,081	767	145,896	62,637	57,968	...	11,009	133,804
Nevada	265,956	2,558	227,038	15,514	16,713	...	324	3,809
New Hampshire	137,723	...	15,374	1,999	30,473	25,047	364	64,466
New Jersey	3,056,970	21,550	...	709,136	127,483	346	1,421	2,197,034(d)
New Mexico	595,464	56	444,847	21,483	126,840	...	807	1,431
New York	10,252,802	289,636	2,508,331	2,207,021	5,116,414	127,096	4,304	...
North Carolina	2,028,170	...	...	1,874,396	139,305	...	11,204	3,265
North Dakota	216,844	...	144,647	34,857	22,128	...	91	15,121
Ohio	3,249,696	2,192	2,154,543	562,283	113,112	25,974	1,344	390,248(e)
Oklahoma	800,260	...	640,511	115,739	21,696	...	1,468	20,846
Oregon	879,899	...	574,376	207,300	72,170	...	2,785	23,268
Pennsylvania	3,541,237	52,884	2,459,922	529,833	215,821	75,710	137,295	69,772
Rhode Island	217,255	5,722	4,820	...	103,891	98,086	...	4,736
South Carolina	781,643	...	567,896	139,881	27,311	...	500	46,055
South Dakota	121,758	50	77,026	26,919	3,864	168	...	13,731
Tennessee	974,485	...	13,076	548,088	402,122	...	5,570	5,629
Texas	3,458,969	...	3,342,634	43,916	50,716	...	2,896	18,807
Utah	459,404	378	376,171	46,372	26,522	...	217	9,744
Vermont	110,786	4,979	75,752	...	3,147	10,088	332	16,488
Virginia	1,268,683	...	...	695,360	484,601	...	4,560	84,162
Washington	1,601,814	20,381	1,243,099	156,663	133,312	...	34,827	13,532
West Virginia	533,286	...	497,666	16,131	3,287	...	...	16,202
Wisconsin	2,643,133	22,465	946,871	694,789	622,125	179,918	672	176,293
Wyoming	263,176	145	123,008	36,375	89,704	...	733	13,211

Source: U.S. Bureau of the Census, *State Government Finances in 1980.*

(a) Includes $1,735,837,000 Supplemental Security Income payments (additional transfers not separately identified by other states may not be included).

(b) Includes $346,797,000 property tax relief and revenue distribution to local governments.

(c) Includes $1,283,549,000 education subsidies, $134,791,000 redistribution of CETA aid, $122,683,000 housing subsidies, $74,412,000 highway aid and $63,058,000 distribution of net lottery profits.

(d) Includes $1,246,329,000 education subsidies and $631,685,000 property tax relief and shared revenues.

(e) Includes $315,538,000 tax relief payments and $28,919,000 CETA payments to local governments.

Section II LEGISLATION, ELECTIONS AND CONSTITUTIONS
1. Legislation

TRENDS IN STATE LEGISLATION: 1980-81

By Elaine Stuart Knapp

THE NEW FEDERALISM and federal budget cuts in 1981 signaled a revolutionary change in state-federal relationships. Following the election of President Ronald Reagan, states welcomed the promise of increased authority and flexibility. By year's end, many state leaders complained that Congress was too generous with budget reductions and too stingy with flexibility.

The economy, high interest rates, the 1980 census, prison problems, high crime rates and deteriorating roads affected state legislative actions in the biennium. Hazardous waste remained a source of state concern.

The following is a summary of the major trends in state legislation in 1980 and 1981.

Taxes, Finance

The federal budget cuts came just as many states were in fiscal difficulties due to the economy. Hardest hit were Midwestern states dependent on the auto industry and Northwestern states reliant on timber sales. In addition, the taxpayers' revolt in the previous biennium and the resultant tax relief measures passed by states left little cushion for hard times. State general fund balances were projected to drop nationwide from $11.3 billion in fiscal 1980 to $4.7 billion in 1981 and to $2.3 billion in 1982, according to a spring 1981 survey by the National Governors' Association and National Association of State Budget Officers.

Many states imposed hiring freezes, laid-off workers, cut spending and raised taxes to deal with budget shortages. The taxpayers' revolt slowed considerably in 1980, when Proposition 13-style property tax rollbacks were rejected by voters in five states, and California voted down an initiative to halve income taxes. However, Massachusetts voted a 2.5 percent limit on property taxes.

Tax hikes were passed by 16 states in 1980, to raise a net $420 million, and by 30 states in 1981 for a net $2.5 billion a year, according to the Tax Foundation, a private non-profit organization. The 1981 tax hike total, released in September, climbed by year's end as Ohio and Washington raised sales taxes.

A survey by the Federation of Tax Administrators found that 1981 resulted in record excise tax hikes: the most motor fuel tax rate increases since the 1920s, the most cigarette tax hikes since 1971 and the most alcoholic beverage tax hikes in a decade.

Over the biennium, sales taxes were increased in six states (not including South Dakota which raised its sales tax for a one-year period), and a higher sales tax rate was not allowed to expire in Tennessee. Gasoline taxes were increased in 28 states and the District of Columbia. Cigarette taxes were raised in nine states. Severance taxes on coal, other minerals or

Elaine S. Knapp is editor of *State Government News*, the Council's monthly magazine.

timber were increased in 15 states. Alaska repealed the personal income tax. Indexing of income taxes to inflation passed in Montana, Oregon and South Carolina in 1980, but in 1981 Oregon postponed indexing until 1983.

The number of states with lids on spending increased by four in 1980; while Alaska scheduled a 1982 vote on a spending lid. Washington decided to set aside 5 percent of its revenues in a stabilization fund.

Government

The 1980 census launched the decennial reapportionment. Although the process was threatened with delay by court suits over the census in early 1981, by year's end 23 states had redrawn congressional districts and 30 had accomplished legislative redistricting. Six states with only one congressional seat required no congressional redistricting. Court suits were filed against a number of new plans, and review of the federal Voting Rights Act was required of certain state plans.

Party control of state legislatures remained heavily Democratic, and by the end of 1981 the composition was 28 Democratic, 15 Republican, six split and one non-partisan. Governorships were divided—27 Democratic to 23 Republican—over the biennium. In Illinois, voters in 1980 approved a one-third reduction in the size of the General Assembly. Two consecutive terms for governor were approved by South Carolina voters, but defeated by Kentucky voters. South Carolina designated the lieutenant governorship a part-time position.

Pennsylvania became the 35th state to provide for sunset (termination) of government agencies unless renewed by the legislature. Federal investigations of bid-rigging on highway contracts resulted in new laws in North Carolina and Tennessee. Oklahoma dealt with a kickback scandal among county commissioners. South Carolina consolidated its purchasing laws, and Colorado adopted a new purchasing code.

Law Enforcement

New or revised capital punishment laws were adopted in Alabama, Connecticut, Missouri, Ohio and Washington.

States continued to struggle with the problem of overcrowded prisons. Measures for early release or reduced sentences in times of prison overcrowding were adopted by several states. Others approved alternatives to prison, such as community service work or pre-trial intervention. Funds for new or expanded corrections facilities were appropriated by a number of states, but New York voted down a $500 million prison bond in 1981. A savage riot at the New Mexico penitentiary in 1980 was the worst of several prison incidents. The U.S. Supreme Court in 1981 upheld double-celling of Ohio inmates.

Compensation for crime victims is authorized in 33 states. However, budget cuts forced Washington to drop its program. At least five more states authorized restitution to victims by offenders.

Handguns cannot be carried without a permit in Connecticut and New York, which joined Massachusetts in imposing mandatory prison terms for violations. Additional penalties for use of a gun in certain crimes were prescribed in at least seven more states over the biennium. Some 10 states addressed the issue of insanity as a defense.

Drug paraphernalia (used for taking illegal drugs) was restricted by new laws in half the states, but court challenges were filed against many of the bans. Look-alike drugs (which mimic prescription stimulants) were outlawed by 11 states. Several states cracked down on drug dealers.

Drunk driving was penalized heavily by 11 states. Drinking ages were raised in three states: Florida to 19, and Nebraska and Rhode Island to 20.

Spousal rape was made a crime in three more states (Connecticut, Minnesota and New Hampshire). Strip searches by police were restricted in six states. Precious metals sales were regulated in at least five states due to thefts. Racial or religious harassment was banned in five states. Despite a U.S. Supreme Court ruling clearing the practice, cameras were banned in Maryland courts, but allowed on an experimental basis in Kentucky courts.

Bingo was authorized in four more states (for a total of 42) and the District of Columbia. Voters authorized government-operated lotteries in Arizona, Colorado and the District of Columbia—joining 14 states with lotteries. New York became the 12th state with a state-operated numbers game.

Education

A number of states revised school aid formulas. Kansas and Tennessee joined the many states which test student competency. Proficiency of teachers is to be tested in California, Oklahoma and Tennessee.

Moments of silent meditation were permitted in schools in Alabama, Florida and Maine. Voluntary prayer periods were allowed in Oklahoma, but struck down by a court in Massachusetts. Laws allowing posting of the Ten Commandments in schools in Kentucky and North Dakota were voided. Church schools were exempted from state rules in Alabama and South Dakota. Balanced treatment of scientific creation with evolution in the classroom was required in Arkansas and Louisiana; however, the Arkansas law lost its first test in federal court.

Texas mandated, but Colorado repealed, bilingual education for non-English speaking pupils.

The 50 states appropriated some $23 billion for annual operating expenses of higher education for fiscal 1982, for a 20 percent gain over the biennium, reported M. M. Chambers of Illinois State University.

Energy

Plentiful gasoline supplies took the edge off legislative interest in emergency energy measures. States continued to encourage alternative energy sources, as well as conservation, through tax and other incentives. Likewise, 27 states now tax gasohol, a blend of alcohol and unleaded fuel, at a lesser rate than gasoline. However, the market for gasohol eased in 1981 due to its higher price.

Nuclear power remained in the news as proposals were made to share the cost of cleaning up the reactor damaged by the 1979 accident at Three Mile Island, Pennsylvania. Voters in Maine, Missouri and South Dakota in 1980 defeated anti-nuclear measures, but Oregon rejected new nuclear plants pending acceptable methods to dispose of radioactive waste. Nuclear plants were assessed fees to pay for emergency planning in Arizona, Arkansas, Maine and New York.

State primacy in surface mine controls remained an issue as coal states vied for federal approval of new state plans.

Environment

Hazardous substances and waste were addressed by new laws in more than 30 states. Many laws were aimed at siting a hazardous waste facility or landfill. Love Canal, a residential area built on a former chemical dump in New York, was evacuated in 1980. Laws dealing with radioactive waste were passed in more than a dozen states. Regional compacts for disposal of low-level radioactive waste were advanced. Washington's 1980 voter-approved initiative to ban out-of-state nuclear waste was voided by a federal court, but the state was planning to appeal.

Bottle deposits were mandated in two more states (for a total of nine) and pull tabs on cans banned in three others. New Jersey adopted a statewide recycling plant funded by a landfill tax. Maine approved a $1 million bond for solid waste recovery efforts.

Water supply was the topic of new laws in a number of states, including a new groundwater law in Arizona. The Peripheral Canal was authorized in California to move water from north to south, but it faces a vote in 1982.

The sagebrush rebellion, begun with Nevada's call for state takeover of federal public lands, was joined by five other Western states in 1980 before fading in 1981 due to apparent satisfaction with Reagan administration policies. An Alaska lands bill, setting aside federal lands and distributing state lands, was signed by President Carter in 1980.

Legislation for auto emissions inspection was passed by 27 of 29 states under U.S. Environmental Protection Agency pressure in 1980. (California and Kentucky did not act.)

Income tax check-offs may be made to benefit programs for non-game species in four more states. Farmers were protected against nuisance suits in at least six states. Loans or tax breaks for agricultural endeavors, including loans for new farmers, were approved in a number of states. Pennsylvania passed a measure for farmland preservation. California spent some $100 million to combat a Medfly infestation.

Health, Social Legislation

Abortions for poor women need not be funded by federal or state governments, the U.S. Supreme Court ruled in 1980. Many states had already followed the federal law which severely restricted funds for abortions for the poor. Several states also banned public financing of abortion insurance coverage. At least nine states imposed notice or "informed consent" requirements on abortions. Tennessee requested a U.S. constitutional ban on abortions.

Another eight states permitted medical use of marijuana in certain cases, while two more approved use of laetrile for terminally ill cancer patients. The terminally ill in 11 states may now refuse further medical treatment under "right-to-die" laws. Four more states defined death by law. At least five states now permit use of DMSO (dimethyl sulfoxide) as a pain killer.

Some 30 states now regulate Medigap insurance, which covers costs not included in Medicare. Insurance availability for alcoholism treatment is required by 33 states, with at least four acting over the biennium. Abuse of elderly or disabled adults was addressed by new laws in at least 14 states.

Mental health facilities in Alabama were placed under the governor by court order. Various states revised their mental health laws.

Other trends included funding of programs for victims of domestic violence, protection for children from abuse, definition of patients' rights, higher standards for nursing homes, establishment of work fare programs for welfare recipients, passage of anti-discrimination laws for the handicapped, permission for joint custody of children in divorce cases and requirements for child passenger restraints in automobiles.

Commerce, Consumers

High interest rates were blamed for many of the nation's economic woes and contributed to the slumps in the housing and automobile industries. The interest rates allowed by Federal Reserve Board actions were higher than many state ceilings. Over the biennium, more than 30 states raised maximum rates allowed on various types of loans. At least eight states eliminated interest rate ceilings for specified loans. However, Arkansas voted down an amendment to lift the state's 10 percent interest rate lid. Graduated mortgages were allowed to replace fixed-rate mortgages by federal action and a number of states followed. State usury limits on home mortgages were preempted by federal law in 1980 and states were given three years to re-enact them.

Various actions were taken to make housing more affordable. Housing finance authorities were established in Louisiana and Mississippi, and their funding powers raised in at least seven other states. Many states issued single-family housing bonds. Conversion of rental units to condominiums was regulated in nine states.

Readable insurance policies were required in four more states. Bankruptcy laws were changed in several states in light of new federal law. Connecticut authorized enterprise zones to entice business to depressed areas, and financial incentives for business in blighted areas were offered in other states. A number of states revised jobless and workers' compensation benefits.

The ailing Chrysler Corporation was given loans by four states. New sources of state taxation were opened by a June 10, 1980, U.S. Supreme Court ruling that Wisconsin's taxation of a unitary business was legal and a March 19, 1980, decision that states may tax international earnings of companies doing business in their states.

Transportation

Highway financing was a major concern, and many states raised motor fuel taxes, truck or automobile fees or took other measures to keep up road funds. Heavier and/or longer trucks were allowed in 11 states over the biennium. Aid for railroads was provided in Iowa, South Dakota and Wisconsin. Mass transit received aid in Maryland, New York and Tennessee, but Illinois balked at rescuing the upstate mass transit system. Speed limits stayed at 55 mph despite proposals made in Western states. Nevada made exceeding 55 mph subject to a $5 energy violation fine.

Table 1
SELECTED LEGISLATIVE ACTIONS
(As of August 1981)

State or other jurisdiction	Ratified equal rights amendments to		Ratified U.S. Constitutional Amendment granting full representation to the District of Columbia	Call for U.S. Constitutional Convention to propose a balanced federal budget	Selected motorcycle regulations		
	U.S. Constitution	State constitution			Safety helmet required	Eye protection required	Operators license required
Alabama	...	...	...	★	★	...	...
Alaska	★	1972	...	...	★(a)	★(b)	★
Arizona	...	...	...	★	★(a)	★	★
Arkansas	...	...	...	★	★	★	★
California	★	...	...	...	...	...	★
Colorado	★	1972	...	★	...	★	★
Connecticut	★	1974	★	...	...	★(b)	★
Delaware	★	...	...	★	★(a,c)	★	★
Florida	...	...	...	★	★	★	...
Georgia	...	...	...	★	★	★(b)	★
Hawaii	★	1972	★	...	★(a,c)	★(b)	★
Idaho	★(d)	...	...	★	★(a)	...	★
Illinois	...	1971	...	★	...	★	★
Indiana	★	...	...	★	...	...	★
Iowa	★	...	...	★	...	...	★
Kansas	★	...	...	★	★(a)	★	★
Kentucky	★(d)	...	...	...	★	★	★
Louisiana	...	...	...	★	★	★(b)	★
Maine	★	...	...	...	★(a)	...	★
Maryland	★	1972	★	★	★(a,c)	★(b)	★
Massachusetts	★	1980	★	...	★	★(b)	★
Michigan	★	...	★	...	★	★(b)	★
Minnesota	★	...	★	...	★(a)	★	★
Mississippi	...	...	...	★	★	...	...
Missouri	...	...	...	...	★	...	★
Montana	★	1973	...	...	★(a)	...	★
Nebraska	★(d)	...	...	★	...	...	★
Nevada	...	...	...	★	★	★(b)	★
New Hampshire	★	1974	...	★	★(a)	★(b)	★
New Jersey	★	...	★	...	★(c)	★(b)	★
New Mexico	★	1973	...	★	★(a,c)	★(b)	★
New York	★	...	...	...	★(c)	★	★
North Carolina	...	...	...	★	★	...	★
North Dakota	★	...	...	★	★(a,c)	...	★
Ohio	★	...	★	...	★(a)	★	★
Oklahoma	...	...	...	★	★(a)	★(b)	...
Oregon	★	...	★	★	★(a)	...	★
Pennsylvania	★	1971	...	★	★	★	★
Rhode Island	★	...	...	...	...	★	★
South Carolina	...	...	...	★	★(a)	★(a)	★
South Dakota	★(d)	...	...	★	★(a)	★(b)	★
Tennessee	★(d)	...	...	★	★	★(b)	★
Texas	★	1972	...	★	★(a,c)	...	★
Utah	...	1896(e)	...	★	★(a)	...	★
Vermont	★	...	...	...	★(c)	★(b)	★
Virginia	...	1971	...	★	★	★(b)	★
Washington	★	1972	...	...	...	★(b)	★
West Virginia	★	...	...	...	★(c)	★	...
Wisconsin	★	...	★	...	★(a)	★(b)	★
Wyoming	★	1890(e)	...	★	★	...	★
Dist. of Col.	...	...	...	...	★	★(b)	★
Puerto Rico	...	...	...	...	★	★	★

Sources: Equal rights amendments—ERA America; D.C. amendment—Office of Delegate to U.S. House of Representatives for District of Columbia; Constitutional Convention—National Taxpayers Union; Motorcycle regulations—American Motorcyclist Association.

(a) Under specified age.

(b) Unless vehicle is equipped with windscreen or a windscreen of certain height.
(c) Reflectorization required.
(d) Voted to rescind. In Kentucky the vote to rescind was vetoed.
(e) Part of constitution when state admitted to Union.

Table 2
INITIATIVE PROVISIONS FOR STATE LEGISLATION

State or other jurisdiction	Type(a)	Established by constitutional provision	Petition requirement(b)
Alaska	D	★	10% of votes cast in last general election and resident in at least 2/3 of election districts
Arizona	D	★	10% of qualified electors
Arkansas	D	★	8% of those voting in the last general election for governor
California	D	★	5% of votes cast in the last general election for governor
Colorado	D	★	5% of votes cast in the last general election for secretary of state
Idaho	D	★	10% of votes cast in the last general election for governor
Maine	I	★	10% of votes cast in last general election for governor
Massachusetts	I	★	3% of votes cast in last general election for governor
Michigan	B	★	8% of votes cast in last general election for governor
Missouri	D	★	5% of voters in each of 2/3 of congressional districts
Montana	D	★	5% of qualified electors in each of at least 1/3 of legislative representative districts; total must equal 5% of total qualified electors
Nebraska	D	★	5% of votes cast in last general election for governor; the electors signing the petition shall be distributed so as to include 5% of the electors of each of 2/5 of the counties of the state
Nevada	B	★	10% of voters in last general election in 75% of the 17 counties
North Dakota	D	★	2% of the state's resident population from last federal decennial census
Ohio	B	★	3% of electors
Oklahoma	D	★	8% of total vote for state office receiving largest number of votes in last general election
Oregon	D	★	6% of total votes cast in last election for governor
South Dakota	B	★	5% of votes cast in last general election for governor
Utah	B	★	10% of total votes cast in last general election for governor with same percentage required from a majority of the counties (direct); 5% (indirect)(c)
Washington	B	★	8% of votes cast in last general election for governor
Wyoming	I	★	15% of voters in last general election and resident in at least 2/3 of counties in state
Guam	D	. . .	20% of persons voting for governor in last preceding general election at which governor was elected

(a) The initiative may be direct or indirect. The direct type, designated D in this table, places a proposed measure on the ballot for submission to the electorate, without legislative action. The indirect type, designated I, requires the legislature to act upon an initiated measure within a reasonable period before it is voted upon by the electorate. In some states both types, designated B, are used.

(b) In each state where the initiative may occur, a majority of the popular vote is required to enact a measure. Massachusetts: the measure must also be approved by at least 30 percent of the ballots cast.
(c) These requirements are established by law.

Table 3
PROVISIONS FOR REFERENDUM ON STATE LEGISLATION

State or other jurisdiction	Established by constitutional provision	Basis of referendum(a)	Petition requirement(b)
Alaska	★	Petition of people	10% of votes cast in last general election for governor and resident in at least 2/3 of election districts
Arizona	★	Petition of people Submitted by legislature	5% of qualified voters
Arkansas	★	Petition of people	6% of votes cast in last general election for governor
California	★	Petition of people(c) Constitutional requirement	5% of votes cast in last general election for governor
Colorado	★	Petition of people Submitted by legislature	5% of votes cast in last general election for secretary of state
Connecticut	...	Submitted by legislature	...
Florida	★	Constitutional requirement	...
Georgia	★ (d)	Submitted by legislature Constitutional requirement	...
Idaho	★	Petition of people	10% of votes cast in last general election for governor
Illinois	★	Submitted by legislature(e)	...
Iowa	★	Constitutional requirement(e)	...
Kansas	★	Constitutional requirement(e)	...
Kentucky	★	Petition of people(f) Constitutional requirement	5% of votes cast in last general election for governor
Maine	★	Petition of people Submitted by legislature Constitutional requirement	10% of votes cast in last general election for governor
Maryland	★ (d)	Petition of people Submitted by legislature	3% of votes cast in last general election for governor
Massachusetts	★	Petition of people	2% of votes cast in last general election for governor
Michigan	★	Petition of people(g) Submitted by legislature Constitutional requirement	5% of votes cast in last general election for governor
Missouri	★	Petition of people Submitted by legislature	5% of legal voters in each of 2/3 of congressional districts
Montana	★	Petition of people Submitted by legislature	5% of total qualified electors and 5% in at least 1/3 of legislative districts
Nebraska	★	Petition of people	5% of votes cast in last general election for governor
Nevada	★	Petition of people	10% of votes cast in last general election
New Jersey	★	Petition of people Constitutional requirement	...
New Mexico	★	Petition of people Constitutional requirement	10% of votes cast in last general election and 10% of electors in 3/4 of the counties
New York	★	Constitutional requirement	...
North Carolina	★	Submitted by legislature Constitutional requirement	...
North Dakota	★	Petition of people	2% of the state's resident population from last federal decennial census
Ohio	★	Petition of people Constitutional requirement	6% of electors
Oklahoma	★	Petition of people Submitted by legislature Constitutional requirement	5% of votes cast for state office receiving largest number of votes in last general election
Oregon	★	Petition of people Submitted by legislature	4% of votes cast in last election for governor

State or other jurisdiction	Established by constitutional provision	Basis of referendum(a)	Petition requirement(b)
Pennsylvania	★	Constitutional requirement	. . .
Rhode Island	★	Constitutional requirement	. . .
South Dakota	★	Petition of people	5% of votes cast in last general election for governor
Utah	★	Petition of people	10% of votes cast in last general election for governor and same percentage required from a majority of the counties
Virginia	★ (e)	Submitted by legislature Constitutional requirement	. . .
Washington	★	Petition of people Submitted by legislature Constitutional requirement	4% of votes cast in last general election for governor
Wisconsin	★ (d)	Submitted by legislature Constitutional requirement	. . .
Wyoming	★	Petition of people Constitutional requirement	15% of those voting in last general election and resident in at least 2/3 of counties of state
Guam	★	Petition of people Submitted by legislature	20% of persons voting for governor in last preceding general election at which governor was elected
Puerto Rico	. . .	Petition of people Submitted by legislature	20% of persons voting for governor in last preceding general election at which governor was elected

(a) Three forms of referendum exist: (1) Petition of people—the people may petition for a referendum, usually with the intention of repealing existing legislation; (2) Submitted by legislature—the legislature may voluntarily submit laws to the electorate for its approval; and (3) Constitutional requirement—the state constitution may require certain questions to be submitted to the people, often debt authorization.

(b) In each state where referendum may occur, a majority of the popular vote is required to enact a measure. Massachusetts: the measure must also be approved by at least 30 percent of the ballots cast.

(c) Amendments or repeals of initiative statutes by another statute must be submitted to the electorate for approval unless the initiative statute provides to the contrary.

(d) The type of referendum held at the request of the legislature is not established by a constitutional provision.

(e) Debt authorization and/or banking laws only.

(f) Applies only to referendum on legislation classifying property and providing for differential taxation on same.

(g) Does not extend to acts making appropriations for state institutions or to meet deficiencies in state funds.

Table 4
AGE OF MAJORITY FOR SPECIFIED ACTIVITIES

State or other jurisdiction	Serve on a jury	Make a contract	Own property	Make a will	Hold office(a)	Buy liquor(b)	Consent to medical care	Consent to sexual intercourse (c)	Stop attending school
Alabama	19	19	...	19	21	19	14	16(d)	16
Alaska	19	18	...	19	21	19	...	18	16
Arizona	18	18	...	18	25	19	18(e)	18	16
Arkansas	18	18	18	18	21	21	18	18	15
California	18	18(e)	...	18	18	21	18(e)	18, 14(f)	18(g)
Colorado	18	18	18	18	25	21(h)	18(i)	18	16
Connecticut	18	18	18	18	18	18	...	15	16(j)
Delaware	18	18	18	18	24	20	...	16	16
Florida(i)	18	18	18	18	21	19	18	18	16
Georgia	18	18	18	18	21	19	18(k)	14	16
Hawaii	18	18	18	18	18	18	14(l)	14	15
Idaho	18	18(i)	...	18(i)	18	19	18	18	16
Illinois	18	18	18	18	21	21	18	18	16
Indiana	18	18	18	18	21	21	18	18	16
Iowa	18	18	18	18	21	19	18	14	16(j)
Kansas	18	18	18	18	18	18	16	16	16
Kentucky	18	18	18	18	24	21	18	16	16
Louisiana	18	18(i)	...	16(i)	18	18	18(e)	17	16
Maine	18	18	18	18	21	20	18	14	17
Maryland	18	18	18	18	21	21(h)	18(e)	14	16
Massachusetts	18	18(m)	18	18	18	20	18	16	16
Michigan	18	18	18	18	21	21	18	16	16
Minnesota	18	18	18	18	21	19	18	13	17
Mississippi	21	18	...	18	21	21	21(n)	18	(o)
Missouri	21	18	18	18	24	21	18(e)	16(d)	16
Montana	18	18(m)	...	18	18	19	18(e)	16	16(p)
Nebraska	19	19	19	18	21	20	19	16	16
Nevada	18	18	18	18	21	21	18	18	17
New Hampshire	18	18	18	18	18	20	18	16	16
New Jersey	18	18	18	18	21	19	18	16	16
New Mexico	18	18	18	18	21	21	18	13	18(q)
New York	18	18	...	18	18	18	18(e)	17	17(q)
North Carolina	18	18(r)	...	18	18	21(h)	18(n)	13	16
North Dakota	18	18(m)	18	18	18	21	18(n)	15	16
Ohio	18	18	18	18	18	21(s)	18(n)	13	18
Oklahoma	18	18	...	18	21	21	18	16	16
Oregon	18	18	18	18	21	21	18	18	16(e)
Pennsylvania	18	18	...	18	21	21	18	14	16(e)
Rhode Island	21	18	18	18	18	20	16	16	16
South Carolina	18	18	18	18	21	21(h)	18	16	16
South Dakota	18	18	...	18	25	21(s)	18	15	16
Tennessee	18	18	18	18	21	19	18(t)	16	16
Texas	18	18	...	18(i)	21	19	16(i)	17	17
Utah	18	18	...	18	25	21	...	16	18
Vermont	18	18	18	18	18	18	18	18	18
Virginia	18	18	18	18	21	21(h)	18	13	17
Washington	18	18	...	18	18	21	18	16	18(e)
West Virginia	18	18	18	18	18	18	...	16	16
Wisconsin	18	18	18	18	18	18	18	18	16(e)
Wyoming	19	19	...	19	21	19	19(e)	19	19(e)
Dist. of Col.	18	18	...	18	18	18	18	16	16
American Samoa	...	...	...	...	25	21	...	14	18
Guam	18	18	18	18	25	18	18(n)	18	16
Puerto Rico	18	21(i)	21(i)	14	25	18	21(i)	14	...
Virgin Islands	21	18	18	18	21	18	18	16	16

(a) Some offices require higher ages, e.g., governor or lieutenant governor. The age indicated is that at which a person can serve in the lower house of the state legislature.

(b) The age indicated is that required to purchase "hard" liquor. The age required to purchase beer or wine is sometimes lower and when known is indicated by a footnote.

(c) Age of consent may be lower in certain circumstances, often depending on the age of the partner or the relationship between partners.

(d) Applies only to females.

(e) With certain exceptions.

(f) For males.

(g) Or, if graduate from high school, 16.

(h) Beer or wine at 18. In Virginia, 18 for on-premises consumption; 19 for off-premises consumption.

(i) Age may be lower for a minor living apart from parents or legal guardian and managing his or her own financial affairs, or who has contracted a lawful marriage.

(j) Unless getting education elsewhere; 14 if lawfully employed.

(k) Younger if pregnant.

(l) Restricted to treatment of venereal disease and pregnancy and family planning service.

(m) Minor can make a contract binding on an adult, but not on a minor. However, minor is bound on contracts for necessities.

(n) Younger for the prevention, diagnosis and treatment of venereal disease, pregnancy, abuse of alcohol and drugs, or emotional disturbances.

(o) 1982-83 school year—12 years old; 1983-84 school year—13 years old.

(p) Or completion of 8th grade, whichever is earlier.

(q) Or completion of high school, whichever is earlier. In New Mexico, age may be earlier with consent of parents and school officials.

(r) Minors over 15 may enter into insurance contracts; minors over 12 may enter into contracts with respect to shares in earnings and loan associations; all minors may enter into contracts for necessities.

(s) 18 for 3.2 percent beer.

(t) Younger for abortion or contraception; if emancipated.

68

Table 5
PRINCIPAL PROVISIONS OF STATE FIREARMS LAWS
(As of January 1982)

State	Permit to purchase		Registration of firearms		Licensing of owner		License or permit to carry		License or permit to possess		Constitutional provision†
	Rifles & shotguns	Hand-guns	Rifles & shotguns	Hand-guns	Rifles & shotguns	Hand-guns	Rifles & shotguns	Hand-guns	Rifles & shotguns	Hand-guns	
Alabama	...	...	...	...	...	...	...	★	...	...	★
Alaska	...	...	...	...	...	...	...	□	...	...	★
Arizona	...	...	...	...	...	...	□	□	...	...	★
Arkansas	...	...	...	...	...	...	...	(a)	...	...	★
California	...	(b)	...	(b)	...	...	...	■	...	...	...
Colorado	...	...	...	...	...	...	...	■	...	...	★
Connecticut	...	(b)	...	(b)	...	...	...	★	...	...	★
Delaware	...	...	...	...	...	...	...	■	...	...	★
Florida	...	...	...	...	...	...	...	★	...	...	★
Georgia	...	...	...	...	...	...	...	★	...	...	★
Hawaii	...	★	★	★	...	...	...	★	...	...	★
Idaho	...	...	...	...	...	...	■	■	...	...	★
Illinois	★(c)	★(c)	(d)	(d)	★(c)	★(c)	★(c)	□	★(c)	★(c)	★
Indiana	...	...	...	...	...	...	...	★	...	...	★
Iowa	...	★	(b)	(b)	...	...	...	■	...	...	...
Kansas	...	...	...	...	...	...	■	■	...	...	★
Kentucky	...	...	...	...	...	...	□	□	...	...	★
Louisiana	...	(e)	(f)	...	...	...	□	■	...	...	★
Maine	...	...	...	...	...	...	...	■	...	...	★
Maryland	...	(b)	...	(b)	...	...	...	★	...	...	...
Massachusetts	★(g)	★	...	...	★	★	★(g)	★	★(g)	★(g)	...
Michigan	...	★	...	★	...	...	...	★	...	(h)	★
Minnesota	...	...	...	...	...	...	...	★(i)	...	...	...
Mississippi	...	...	...	★	...	...	...	■	...	...	★
Missouri	...	★	...	(b)	...	...	...	□	...	...	★
Montana	...	...	...	...	...	...	...	■	...	...	★
Nebraska	...	...	...	...	...	...	□	□	...	...	★
Nevada	...	...	...	...	...	...	□(j)	□(j)	...	...	...
New Hampshire	...	(k)	...	...	...	...	...	★	...	...	...
New Jersey	★(g)	★	...	(b)	★	★	★(g)	★	★(g,j)	★(j)	...
New Mexico	...	...	...	...	...	...	...	□	...	...	★
New York	(l)	★	(l)	★	(l)	★	...	★	(l)	★	...
North Carolina	...	★	...	(b)	...	...	...	□	...	...	★
North Dakota	...	...	...	...	...	...	...	★	...	...	...
Ohio	(m)	(m)	...	...	...	...	□	...	...	...	★
Oklahoma	...	...	...	...	...	...	□	□	...	...	★
Oregon	...	...	...	(b)	...	...	...	■	...	...	★
Pennsylvania	...	...	...	(b)	...	...	...	★	...	...	★
Rhode Island	...	...	...	...	...	...	...	★	...	...	★
South Carolina	...	...	...	...	...	...	...	(n)	...	...	★
South Dakota	...	...	...	(b)	...	...	...	★	...	...	★
Tennessee	...	★	...	...	...	...	...	(n)	...	...	★
Texas	...	...	...	...	...	...	...	(n)	...	...	★
Utah	...	...	...	...	...	...	■	■	...	...	★
Vermont	...	...	...	...	...	...	(a)	(a)	...	...	★
Virginia	...	...	...	...	...	...	...	■	...	...	★
Washington	...	...	...	(b)	...	...	...	★	...	...	★
West Virginia	...	...	...	...	...	...	...	★	...	...	...
Wisconsin	...	...	...	...	...	...	□	□	...	...	...
Wyoming	...	...	...	...	...	...	...	■	...	...	★

Source: National Rifle Association. In addition to state law, the purchase, sale and, in certain circumstances, the possession and interstate transportation of firearms is regulated by the Federal Gun Control Act of 1968 and Title VII of the Omnibus Crime Control and Safe Streets Act. Also, cities and localities may have their own firearms ordinances in addition to federal and state laws. Details may be obtained by contacting local law enforcement authorities or by consulting the *Annual Guide to Firearms Regulation,* published by the Bureau of Alcohol, Tobacco and Firearms and available from the U.S. Government Printing Office, Washington, D.C. 20402. State firearm laws are subject to frequent change. *This summary is not to be considered as legal advice or a restatement of law.*

†State constitutional provisions on firearms vary considerably. The Connecticut constitution serves as an example of the basic features: "Every citizen has a right to bear arms in defense of himself and the state." (Article I, Section 15).

Key:
★—Provision applies.
■—If weapon concealed.
□—Carrying concealed weapon prohibited.
(a) Arkansas prohibits carrying a handgun "as a weapon" (that is, to fight with). Vermont prohibits carrying a firearm, concealed or openly, "with the intent or purpose of injuring another."

(b) Police record purchases from dealers.
(c) A Firearms Owner's Identification Card required.
(d) Only Chicago requires registration of all firearms.
(e) New Orleans requires a permit for purchase of any concealable firearm.
(f) If firearm is concealable.
(g) A Firearm Identification Card required.
(h) Handguns must be presented to the city chief of police or county sheriff to obtain a certificate of inspection.
(i) Exceptions to permit requirement are "keeping or carrying about one's place of business, dwelling house, premises or land."
(j) Permission to carry concealed may be granted by county sheriff upon written application.
(k) Permit required for purchase by a felon.
(l) Not required except in New York City.
(m) In Cleveland and Columbus, a police permit is required for the purchase of a handgun; in Toledo, a handgun owner's identification card is required for acquisition or purchase of a pistol or revolver; and in Cincinnati, an application is required for the purchase of a handgun.
(n) Carrying is restricted; no permit is required.

Table 6
LEGALIZED GAMING IN THE STATES
As of December 1981

State or other jurisdiction	Lotteries	Numbers	Sports betting	Off-track betting	Horse racing	Dog racing	Jai alai	Casinos	Card rooms	Bingo
Alabama	...	...	...	...	...	★	...	...	...	...
Alaska	...	...	...	...	...	...	...	...	...	★
Arizona	★	...	...	...	★	★	...	...	...	★
Arkansas	...	...	...	...	★	★	...	...	...	...
California	...	...	...	...	★	...	...	...	★	★
Colorado	(a)	...	...	...	★	★	...	...	...	★
Connecticut	★	★	...	★	•	★	★	...	...	★
Delaware	★	★	•	...	★	...	...	...	...	★
Florida	...	...	...	...	★	★	★	...	...	★
Georgia	...	...	...	...	...	...	...	...	...	★
Hawaii	...	...	...	...	...	...	...	...	...	...
Idaho	...	...	...	...	★	...	...	...	...	...
Illinois	★	★	...	...	★	...	...	...	...	★
Indiana	...	...	...	...	•	...	...	...	...	...
Iowa	...	...	...	...	...	...	...	...	★	★
Kansas	...	...	...	...	...	...	...	...	...	★
Kentucky	...	...	...	...	★	...	...	...	...	...
Louisiana	...	...	...	...	★	...	...	...	...	★
Maine	★	...	...	...	★	...	...	...	...	★
Maryland	★	★	...	...	★	...	...	...	...	...
Massachusetts	★	★	...	...	★	★	...	...	...	★
Michigan	★	★	...	...	★	...	...	...	...	★
Minnesota	...	...	...	...	...	...	...	...	...	★
Mississippi	...	...	...	...	...	...	...	...	...	...
Missouri	...	...	...	...	...	...	...	...	...	★
Montana	...	...	★(b)	...	★	...	...	...	★	★
Nebraska	...	...	...	...	★	...	...	...	...	★
Nevada	...	★(c)	★(d)	★(d)	★	★	★	★	★	★
New Hampshire	★	★	...	...	★	★	...	...	...	★
New Jersey	★	★	...	...	★	...	...	★	...	★
New Mexico	...	...	...	...	★	...	...	...	...	★
New York	★	★	...	★	★	...	...	...	...	★
North Carolina	...	...	...	...	...	...	...	...	...	★
North Dakota	...	...	...	...	...	...	...	...	...	★
Ohio	★	★	...	...	★	...	...	...	...	★
Oklahoma	...	...	...	...	...	...	...	...	...	★
Oregon	...	...	...	...	★	★	...	...	★	★
Pennsylvania	★	★	...	...	★	...	...	...	...	★
Rhode Island	★	★	...	...	★	★	★	...	...	★
South Carolina	...	...	...	...	...	...	...	...	...	★
South Dakota	...	...	...	...	★	★	...	...	...	★
Tennessee	...	...	...	...	...	...	...	...	...	★
Texas	...	...	...	...	...	...	...	...	...	★
Utah	...	...	...	...	...	...	...	...	...	...
Vermont	★	...	...	...	★	★	...	...	...	★
Virginia	...	...	...	...	...	...	...	...	...	★
Washington	...	...	★(b)	...	★	...	...	...	★	★
West Virginia	...	...	...	...	★	★	...	...	...	★
Wisconsin	...	...	...	...	...	...	...	...	...	★
Wyoming	...	...	...	...	★	...	...	...	...	★
Dist. of Col.	•	•	...	...	...	...	...	...	...	•

Source: Public Gaming Research Institute, Rockville, Md.
★—Legalized and operative.
•—Legalized but not now operative.

(a) Constitutional prohibition removed.
(b) Non-commercial.
(c) Keno.
(d) Operated by bookmakers licensed by state.

THE LEGAL STATUS OF WOMEN

By Ethel Mendelsohn and John H. Galvin

Introduction

THE COUNCIL OF STATE GOVERNMENTS' 50 years of service coincides with a period of progress for American women. The ratification of the 19th Amendment to the Constitution in 1920 granted women the right to vote and laid the groundwork for the resurgence of interest in women's issues during the sixties and the seventies.

During the thirties, women struggled alongside men to organize the labor force. Francis Perkins, the first woman to be a member of the president's cabinet, was the secretary of labor. During World War II, "Rosie the Riveter" became the symbol of the American woman's contribution to the war effort and the model for women in non-traditional jobs in the decade of the seventies.

In 1963, Congress passed the Equal Pay Act, which guaranteed equal pay for equal work, and a year later the Civil Rights Act of 1964 was enacted—outlawing, among other things, discrimination in employment based on sex and race. Over the past 18 years, numerous laws have passed at both the state and federal levels prohibiting sex discrimination in many phases of American life including credit, housing, education and public services. During the seventies, a major effort was mounted to amend the U.S. Constitution to guarantee equality of men and women under the law.

In 1981, Sandra Day O'Connor became the first woman justice appointed to the Supreme Court.

As the eighties begin to unfold, the legal status of women is at an all-time high. Most observers expect that the status of women will continue to improve over the next decade. In the immediate future, interest is expected to focus on employment-related issues such as part-time work, flextime, child care and retirement income.

The Fifty States Project

In the 1980s, many federal policy-makers shifted their attention to the states as crucial areas of decision-making. During 1981, the Reagan administration initiated the Fifty States Project to encourage the states to identify and to correct state laws that discriminate on the basis of sex. In May 1981, the president requested the governor of each state to appoint a representative to work with White House staff to accomplish this important task.

The immediate goals of the project are:
- to develop a state-by-state evaluation of what has been done, what is being done and what needs to be done in the future to ensure completion of the project.
- to develop a plan that is designed to meet each state's unique goals.
- to assist each state in meeting its goals.

The authors are in the Branch of Legislative Analysis, Women's Bureau, U.S. Department of Labor.

The Fifty States Project will be planned and implemented by the governors and the state legislatures with whatever encouragement, advice or assistance the White House can provide.

In recent years, a number of states have studied sex-based distinctions in the state codes and recommended changes on a range of issues. These studies vary widely in their scope and in the type of group that conducted the study. They include analyses of single issues, computer searches of the state code for gender-based terminology and comprehensive studies of discriminatory impact and the effects of stereotyped ideas about the roles and capabilities of women. The groups doing the studies range from law students or professors researching and writing papers or law review articles, to official government commissions appointed and funded by the legislature or governor.

On October 7, 1981, representatives of the states met at the White House to discuss the project. Panels described their experience with the legislative process and offered suggestions on strategy for implementing the project. At a luncheon for the group, the president said, "It's my hope that through the Fifty States Project we can alter or eliminate those State laws that continue to deny equality to women."

Women in Public Service

Although the number of women in the U.S. Congress has been fairly constant over the past 25 years, women have made gains consistently at state and local levels of government, particularly in state legislatures.

All 15 women incumbents who sought re-election to the U.S. House of Representatives in November 1980 were victorious, and at least four were added to their ranks. However, in February 1981, the 19 became 18 when the seat of Gladys Spellman (D-Md.) was declared vacant due to her extended illness.

There have never been more than two women U.S. senators at the same time. With the victory of Paula Hawkins (R-Fla.) in the 1980 general election, that number was equaled in the 97th Congress (1981-82). She joined Nancy Landon Kassebaum (R-Kans.) elected to the Senate in 1979 and the first woman to win a seat in that body without having been preceded in office by her husband.

Although women continue to be less likely than men to seek elective office, record numbers of women did stand for and win office in the November 1980 elections. There were 1,534 women who were major party candidates for state legislatures; of that number, 812 were elected. According to the National Information Bank on Women in Public Office, women held 12.1 percent of all seats in state legislatures nationwide in 1981. Since 1969, the number of women serving in state legislatures has nearly tripled.

In 1981, women were 7 percent of all state senators (138 out of 1,981) and 14 percent of state house or assembly members (770 out of 5,501). The average proportion of female state legislators is 11 percent. The 10 states with the highest proportions of female state legislators (including upper and lower houses) are as follows: New Hampshire, 29.2 percent; Washington, 23.8 percent; Connecticut, 23.5 percent; Colorado, 23 percent; Maine, 22.8 percent; Oregon, 22.2 percent; Vermont, 21.7 percent; Arizona, 18.9 percent; Wyoming, 18.5 percent; and Hawaii, 18.4 percent.

No state currently has a female governor at its helm. Seventy-two women now serve as mayors of cities with more than 30,000 population.

Unquestionably, the most newsworthy appointment of the Reagan administration to date has been that of Sandra Day O'Connor of Arizona to the Supreme Court. On September 25, 1981, she became the 102nd Supreme Court justice and the first woman to sit on the Court.

At the close of 1981, 46 of the 670 federal judges were women. According to the National Conference for State Courts, 617 women were serving at lower judicial levels in 1980, including 47 state appellate court judges, 520 trial and other court judges and 50 in such quasi-judicial posts as administrative law judges.

Forty-four women currently hold high-level positions in the federal government, according to White House sources. Jeane Kirkpatrick, U.S. Ambassador to the United Nations, is the first woman ever to serve in that post and the only woman in the cabinet. There are 43 women in subcabinet-level positions.

Although relatively few women are being elected or appointed to top positions, there is a trend for increasing proportions of office holders at local and state levels to be women. This should result, in the years ahead, in larger numbers of women joining the ranks of higher office holders.

Commissions on the Status of Women

Commissions on the status of women continue to serve as official advocates for women, advising governors, mayors, county executives and legislative bodies on the concerns of women in their jurisdictions. By the end of 1981, there were more than 175 state, local and regional commissions nationwide.

In a recent survey conducted by the Women's Bureau of the U.S. Department of Labor and the National Association of Commissions for Women (NACW), a confederation of all officially constituted state, county, municipal and regional commissions on the status of women, the issues found to be of most interest were employment and the economic status of women, including opportunities in non-traditional occupations and flextime jobs, apprenticeship programs, and the problems of minority and re-entry women in the job market. Violence against women, including programs to investigate and counter sexual assault and spouse abuse, made up the second largest area. The third major area was education, including the monitoring of projects to ensure implementation of laws such as Title IX, Vocational Education Amendments, etc.

Because child care is such a crucial factor in women's employability, the Women's Bureau has, over the years, consistently exchanged information on child day care with business, advocacy organizations, child care providers, state and local governments and individuals. In mid-1981, at the request of NACW, the Bureau agreed to serve as a national clearinghouse for the commissions on child care generally and employer-sponsored child care in particular. The clearinghouse will work to facilitate an exchange of information across state lines, give assistance where needed and provide feedback to commissions involved in promoting child care services and programs.

Credit

During the biennium there has been little change in state credit laws, perhaps because of the comprehensive legislation at the federal level.

By December 1981, at least 33 states,[1] the District of Columbia and numerous municipalities had legislation or regulations expressly prohibiting credit discrimination on the basis of sex or marital status. In some jurisdictions, credit discrimination is barred by omnibus human rights laws, ordinances or regulations.

The Federal Equal Credit Opportunity Act of 1974, as amended, prohibits discrimination against any credit worthy applicant in any credit transaction on the basis of sex, marital status, race, color, religion, national origin and age; because an applicant's income derives from assistance; or because an applicant has exercised any rights under the Federal Consumer Protection Act.

The law applies to mortgage financing as well as consumer and commercial credit and governs the practice of commercial banks, savings and loan associations, credit unions and other businesses that regularly grant credit, such as retail stores, travel and entertainment card companies, oil companies, common carriers and securities brokers.

In order to ensure that married women will have credit histories in their own names, information on joint credit accounts opened after November 1, 1976, must be reported to credit bureaus in the names of both spouses when both use or are liable for payment of the account. Creditors are also required to state in writing the reason for denial or revocation of credit privileges, upon request.

Enforcement of the law is delegated to the specific federal regulatory agency that has supervision over each class of credit. For example, the Comptroller of Currency handles complaints against national banks. The Federal Trade Commission has jurisdiction over retail credit and any other class of credit not supervised by a specified agency. The law authorizes private suits in federal district courts. Creditors may be liable for actual damages, attorney's fees and punitive damages up to $10,000. Class action suits and injunctive relief are also authorized. Complainants have the option of either filing a complaint with the federal agency which regulates the creditor, filing a suit under federal law, or pursuing remedies under state or local laws, whichever is most advantageous.

Abortion

During the nine years since the 1973 U.S. Supreme Court rulings in the cases of *Roe* v. *Wade*[2] and *Doe* v. *Bolton*[3] established national standards for abortion,[4] American society has become increasingly polarized on the issue. Well-organized groups on both sides of the issue have actively promoted their views through the news media, in mass demonstrations, in the courts and in legislative chambers. Several constitutional amendments outlawing abortion have been proposed in Congress, and at least 19 state legislatures have passed resolutions calling for a constitutional convention to consider the issue.[5]

In 1977, the Supreme Court ruled that the states have neither a constitutional nor a statutory obligation to provide non-therapeutic abortions for indigent women or access to public facilities for the performance of such abortions.[6] In June 1980, the Supreme Court held that neither the Medicaid legislation nor the Constitution requires the government to fund abortions, even if medically necessary.[7] In a companion case,[8] the Court held that a state does not have to pay for those medically necessary abortions for which federal reimbursement is not available and that restrictions in an Illinois statute similar to those of the Hyde Amendment[9] do not violate the Equal Protection Clause of the 14th Amendment.

The U.S. Supreme Court has also ruled on issues relating to the role of the family in abortion decisions. In *Planned Parenthood of Central Missouri* v. *Danforth*, 428 U.S. 52 (1976), the Court held that states do not have the constitutional authority to give a third party—a spouse or a parent—an absolute veto over the decision to terminate a pregancy.

In *Bellotti* v. *Baird*, 443 U.S. 622 (1979) (known as Bellotti II), the Court struck down a Massachusetts statute that required a minor seeking an abortion to obtain the consent of her parents or to obtain judicial approval following notification of her parents. "If the

State decides to require a pregnant minor to obtain one or both parents' consent to an abortion," the Court said, "it also must provide an alternative procedure whereby authorization for the abortion can be obtained. A pregnant minor is entitled in such a proceeding to show either: (1) that she is mature and well enough informed to make her abortion decision; or (2) that even if she is not able to make the decision independently, the desired abortion would be in her best interest."

In February 1981, a federal appeals court upheld a Massachusetts statute drawn in accord with the Bellotti II guidelines but also requiring all women seeking an abortion to sign a consent form. The court ruled unconstitutional the requirement that the consent form contain a description of the fetus and be signed at least 24 hours before the abortion. [10]

In *H.L.* v. *Matheson*, 450 U.S. 398 (1981), the Court upheld the constitutionality of a Utah statute requiring a physician, before performing an abortion on a minor, to notify her parents, if possible.

Equal Rights Amendment

In March 1972, Congress passed a resolution proposing the Equal Rights Amendment as the 27th Amendment to the Constitution of the United States and submitted it for ratification to the legislatures of the states. [11]

By 1977, 35 of the 38 required state legislatures had ratified the proposed amendment but a few states had voted to rescind their ratifications. In 1978, when supporters sought more time, Congress, by a simple majority vote, extended the time for ratification from the original March 22, 1979, deadline to June 30, 1982.

A federal District Court judge in Idaho ruled in late 1981 that Congress acted unconstitutionally when it extended the deadline for ratification and that states have the authority to rescind previous ratifications, an action that has never been recognized by Congress. [12] The Supreme Court, in January 1982, agreed to review the case and issued a stay of the District Court decision. The stay deprives the lower court ruling of any legal effect during the time it takes the Supreme Court to decide the appeal.

Women Offenders

By the end of 1981, state prisons housing women in 19 states[13] had developed apprenticeship programs for non-traditional job training for women inmates. The trades for which apprenticeship standards have been developed include millwright, maintenance mechanic, sewing machine mechanic, institutional cook, furniture refinisher, upholsterer, painter and auto mechanic.

The state apprenticeship programs are modeled after a pilot project developed in the Federal Prison System by a cooperative effort of the Women's Bureau of the U.S. Department of Labor, the Federal Prison System and the Bureau of Apprenticeship and Training of the U.S. Department of Labor.

The purpose of the training programs is to enable women inmates to use the time productively and to qualify for better-paying, non-traditional jobs upon release. The apprentices generally work under the supervision of a journeyperson at jobs within the prison. At a few prisons the women work at jobs in the community.

Pregnancy

As more American women remain in the work force after marriage and return to work within a short time after childbirth, legislation has been enacted to protect pregnant workers, and many employers have modified their personnel practices in order to retain the services of skilled women workers with young children.

At the federal level, Congress enacted the Pregnancy Discrimination Act in 1978. The new law amended Title VII of the Civil Rights Act of 1964 to prohibit discrimination in employment on the basis of pregnancy, childbirth and related medical conditions. The law requires employers to apply the same personnel policies to pregnancy as to any other type of temporary medical disability or inability to work for medical reasons. The period of medical disability is normally determined by the woman's doctor.

An increasing number of states and localities have similar provisions in their equal employment opportunity laws. In addition, two states—Massachusetts and Montana—have laws that obligate employers to grant maternity leave: at least eight weeks in Massachusetts and in Montana a "reasonable" leave. Both laws include job reinstatement rights. Five states (California, Hawaii, New Jersey, New York, Rhode Island) and Puerto Rico have temporary disability insurance (TDI) laws, which provide cash benefits for non-work related disabilities. Pregnancy is covered by these laws.

Although the new laws apply only to the period of medical inability to work, some employers have developed personnel policies to accommodate additional time away from work for "child rearing" purposes for both men and women.

Marriage

During the biennium, there were relatively few changes in state marriage laws. Colorado, Kansas and Ohio no longer require a medical examination for venereal disease. The reasons for this mini-trend are that almost no cases of venereal disease have been detected by the testing in recent years and the testing is not an effective method of preventing the spread of disease.

Forty-seven states and the District of Columbia have equalized age requirements for marriage without parental consent at 18 years for both sexes. In Nebraska and Wyoming both parties must be 19 years old, and in Mississippi and Puerto Rico both must be 21 years of age. In Delaware and Georgia parental consent is not required when the woman is pregnant or if the applicants are the parents of a living child.

By the end of 1981, 36 jurisdictions[14] had equalized the age at which men and women can marry with parental consent. In Kentucky and West Virginia, there is no minimum age for marriage with parental consent. In Michigan, there is no statutory provision for the marriage of men with parental consent, although women may do so at age 16.

Divorce

In April 1980, Pennsylvania added a "no fault" provision to its divorce laws. Under the provisions of the new law, divorce may be granted if both parties agree that the marriage is irretrievably broken or after the spouses have lived separate and apart for a period of at least three years. Divorce may also be granted on "traditional" grounds.

With the addition of Pennsylvania, 48 states, the District of Columbia and Puerto Rico now have some form of "no fault" provisions in their divorce laws. Only Illinois and South Dakota do not.

During the biennium, West Virginia reduced the time of separation required for divorce from two years to one year and the time period for divorce on the basis of desertion from one year to six months.

Marital Property

Although most American men and women view marriage as a partnership, the marital property laws in most jurisdictions are based upon feudal property concepts embedded in the common law during the early medieval period of English history. The major exceptions are found in the nine community property jurisdictions—Arizona, California, Idaho, Louisiana, Nevada, New Mexico, Texas, Washington and the commonwealth of Puerto Rico—where the laws provide that the wealth accumulated during marriage generally belongs equally to both spouses.

While many observers view the need to reform marital property laws along partnership lines as highly desirable, no jurisdiction has done so. Wisconsin has introduced such legislation, but it has not been enacted largely because of the difficulties of converting to a new system and the projected dislocation of state revenues under the proposed system. Nevertheless, a number of states have enacted legislation that provides the surviving spouse with a larger share of the estate of the deceased spouse than was customary under traditional common law rules. The trend is well established and clearly favors the surviving spouse over other family members in distribution of property at death.

In at least 35[15] jurisdictions the courts have authority to divide marital property between the spouses upon divorce. In most of these states the courts have broad discretion to decide how the property will be divided. The criteria included in the statutes or court rules to guide the court in arriving at an "equitable" or "equal" division of the property vary from state to state. The criteria frequently focus on the relative need and earning power of the separating spouse as well as the age, length of marriage and contributions of each spouse to the marriage including the value of homemaking services. The variable nature of the criteria injects a substantial element of uncertainty into the law of property, making the outcome of a particular proceeding difficult to predict. Observers generally agree that women are likely to benefit from the new procedures.

Joint Custody

During the biennium, several states[16] have passed legislation designed to highlight the possibility of awarding the custody of children of divorced parents to both parents jointly rather than one parent only—usually the mother. Although the courts generally have had authority to make joint custody awards under existing legislation, it has been rarely exercised until recently.

In the view of many observers joint custody is often not only "in the best interest of the child" but in the best interest of the parents as well. Both parents are more likely to remain interested in the child and the enormous demands of child rearing are more evenly shared under this arrangement.

Bills specifically authorizing joint custody have also been introduced in Massachusetts, Pennsylvania, New Jersey, New York and Ohio.

Child Support

The Census Bureau has developed figures, based on a 1975 population survey, that indicate that only about a quarter of the mothers who might be eligible for child support—or nearly 5 million—actually collect it. Deserting parents—mostly fathers—who abandon their families without financial support have become an increasingly serious and costly problem. When an absent parent evades child support obligations, families are often forced onto the welfare rolls—Aid to Families with Dependent Children (AFDC).

A major potential source of assistance has been the Child Support Enforcement (CSE) program. This combined federal-state program, authorized under a 1975 amendment to the Social Security Act, established a federal Office of Child Support Enforcement (OCSE) within the U.S. Department of Health and Human Services (DHHS) and a comparable agency in each of the 50 states, the District of Columbia, Guam, Puerto Rico and the Virgin Islands. Designed primarily to reduce welfare costs by collecting support on behalf of AFDC children, the services of the state are available free of charge to families receiving welfare payments and to non-welfare families for a nominal fee. Federal employees and armed services personnel, the latter previously free of garnishment of pay, are subject to its provisions.

The law mandates the efficient operation of an enforcement system by each state for obtaining child support orders and payments by use of its own collection mechanisms, any reciprocal arrangements adopted with other states and, as a last resort, referral to the federal courts or the Internal Revenue Service for collection. There is specific provision for the operation of a Federal-State Parent Locator Service to assist local welfare departments in obtaining information on the whereabouts of any absent parent when such information is to be used in the enforcement of child support obligations and in establishing paternity when necessary. The Locator Service has access to records of the Social Security Administration, the Department of Defense, the Internal Revenue Service and other federal government agencies.

Success in bringing delinquent parents to account has varied considerably from one state to another. The U.S. Treasury bears 75 percent of the costs incurred by state and local governments in finding them. However, states are assessed a 5 percent penalty against their welfare funds if they do not take the required actions to assist in locating and recovering funds from such parents. In fiscal 1980 (the latest reporting date) a dozen states recovered from $25 million to $290 million in child support collections.

On a national basis, the success of the program is evidenced by the more than doubling of child support collections over the five-year period since its initiation in 1975. Collections have grown from slightly over $500 million in fiscal 1976 to nearly $1.5 billion in fiscal 1980. Of this latter amount, slightly over $603 million was collected on behalf of families receiving AFDC.

Notes

1. Alaska, Arkansas, California, Colorado, Connecticut, Florida, Georgia, Hawaii, Illinois, Indiana, Iowa, Kansas, Kentucky, Louisiana, Maine, Maryland, Massachusetts, New York, North Carolina, Ohio, Oklahoma, Oregon, Pennsylvania, Rhode Island, South Dakota, Tennessee, Texas, Utah, Vermont, Virginia, Washington, West Virginia and Wisconsin.

2. 410 U.S. 113.

3. 410 U.S. 179.

4. *Wade* held that for the period of pregnancy prior to approximately the end of the first trimester, the attending physician, in consultation with the patient, is free to determine, without regulation by the state, that in his or her medical judgment the patient's pregnancy should be terminated. After this period, the state may, if it chooses, regulate the abortion procedure in ways that are reasonably related to maternal health. After the fetus has reached the point of viability, and "presumably has the capability of meaningful life outside the mother's womb," the Court ruled that a state may regulate and even prohibit abortion except where it is necessary to preserve the life or health of the mother. *Bolton* focused on state procedural requirements and prohibits procedures that are more burdensome for the abortion patient than for other patients.

5. Alabama, Arkansas, Delaware, Idaho, Indiana, Kentucky, Louisiana, Massachusetts, Mississippi, Missouri, Nebraska, Nevada, New Jersey, Oklahoma, Pennsylvania, Rhode Island, South Dakota, Tennessee and Utah.

6. *Beal* v. *Doe*, 432 U.S. 438; *Maker* v. *Roe*, 432 U.S. 464; and *Poellner* v. *Doe*, 432 U.S. 519.

7. *Harris* v. *McRae*, 448 U.S. 297.

8. *Williams* v. *Zbaras*, 448 U.S. 358.

9. Named after Congressman Henry J. Hyde of Illinois who proposed the amendments to the appropriation bills for the U.S. Departments of Labor and Health, Education and Welfare for fiscal years 1978, 1979 and 1980. The 1980 version which is still in effect permits federal funding of abortions only when the life of the mother would be endangered if the pregnancy continues, and for victims of rape or incest, providing the incidents have been properly reported to a law enforcement agency or to a public health service.

10. *Planned Parenthood of Massachusetts* v. *Bellotti*, 641 Fed. 2nd 1006.

11. The basic text of the proposed amendment reads as follows: "Equality of rights under the law shall not be denied or abridged by the United States or by any State on account of sex."

12. *Idaho* v. *Freeman* (Administrator of General Services Administration), (Civil No. 79-1097), U.S. District Court, District of Idaho.

13. California, Connecticut, Georgia, Illinois, Iowa, Louisiana, Maryland, Michigan, Missouri, Nebraska, New Jersey, New York, North Carolina, Oklahoma, Oregon, Pennsylvania, South Carolina, Tennessee and Virginia.

14. Alaska, Arizona, Colorado, Connecticut, Florida, Georgia, Hawaii, Idaho, Illinois, Indiana, Iowa, Kansas, Maine, Maryland, Massachusetts, Missouri, Montana, Nebraska, Nevada, New Jersey, New Mexico, North Carolina, North Dakota, Oklahoma, Oregon, Pennsylvania, South Dakota, Tennessee, Texas, Utah, Vermont, Virginia, Washington, Wisconsin, Wyoming and the District of Columbia.

15. Alaska, Arkansas, Colorado, Connecticut, Delaware, Florida, Hawaii, Illinois, Indiana, Iowa, Kansas, Kentucky, Maine, Massachusetts, Michigan, Minnesota, Missouri, Montana, Nebraska, New Hampshire, New Jersey, New York, North Dakota, Oklahoma, Oregon, Pennsylvania, Rhode Island, South Carolina, South Dakota, Tennessee, Utah, Vermont, Wisconsin, Wyoming and the District of Columbia.

16. Arkansas, California, Connecticut. States with similar provisions include: Alaska, Arizona (court guidelines), Arkansas, Kansas, Kentucky, Nevada, North Carolina, Texas and Wisconsin.

Table 1
MARRIAGE LAWS AS OF DECEMBER 31, 1981

State or other jurisdiction	Age at which marriage can be contracted without parental consent		Age at which marriage can be contracted with parental consent		Blood tests & other medical requirements		Waiting period		Common law marriage	
					Maximum period between examination & issuance of license (days)	Scope of medical inquiry	Before issuance of license	After issuance of license	May be contracted in state but not valid if attempted after date shown	Recognized if valid at time and place where contracted
	Male	Female	Male	Female						
Alabama	18	18	17(a)	14(a)	30	(b)	...	...	Yes	Yes
Alaska	18	18	16(c)	16(c)	30	(b)	3 da.	...	1917	(j)
Arizona	18	18	16(c)	16(c)	30	(b)	(d)	...	No	Yes(e)
Arkansas	18	18	17(c)	16(c)	30	(b)	3 da.	...	No	Yes
California	18	18	18(a,c)	16(a,c)	30	(b,f,g,h)	...	...	1895	Yes
Colorado	18	18	16(c)	16(c)	30	(g,i)	...	...	Yes	Yes
Connecticut	18	18	16(c)	16(c)	35	(b,g)	4 da.	...	No	No
Delaware	18	18	18(c,k)	16(c,k)	30	(b)	...	(l)	No	Yes(e)
Florida	18	18	16(a,c)	16(a,c)	60	(b)	3 da.	...	1/1/68	Yes
Georgia	18	18	16(c,k)	16(c,k)	30	(b,f,g)	3 da.(m)	...	Yes	Yes
Hawaii	18	18	16	16(c)	30	(b,g)	...	...	(n)	Yes
Idaho	18	18	16(c)	16(c)		(g)	(o)	...	Yes	Yes
Illinois	18	18	16(c)	16(c)	15	(b,f)	3 da.	...	6/30/05	(e,j)
Indiana	18	18	17(c)	17(c)	30	(b,f)	3 da.	...	1/1/58	(e,j)
Iowa	18	18	16	16	20	(b)	3 da.	...	Yes	Yes
Kansas	18	18	18(c)	18(c)	30	...	3 da.	...	Yes(p)	Yes
Kentucky	18	18	(a,q)	(a,q)	15	(b,f,r)	3 da.(r)	...	(n)	Yes
Louisiana	18	18	18(c)	16(c)	10	(b)	...	72 hrs.	(n)	(j)
Maine	18	18	16(c)	16(c)	60	(b)	5 da.	...	(j)	Yes
Maryland	18(s)	18(s)	16(c)	16(c)	...	...	48 hrs.	...	No	Yes
Massachusetts	18	18	18(c)	18(c)	30	(b,g)	3 da.	...	No	Yes(e)
Michigan	18	18	(t)	16	33	(b)	3 da.	...	1/1/57	Yes
Minnesota	18	18	18	16(u)	...	...	5 da.	...	4/26/41	(j)
Mississippi	21	21	17(c)	15(c)	30	(b)	3 da.	...	4/5/56	(j)
Missouri	18	18	15(c)	15(c)	15	(b)	3 da.	...	3/3/21	(j)
Montana	18	18	18(c)	18(c)	20	(b,g)	5 da.	3 da.	Yes	Yes
Nebraska	19	19	17	17	30	(b,g)	2 da.	...	1923	Yes
Nevada	18	18	16(a,c)	16(a,c)	...	...	...	...	3/24/43	Yes
New Hampshire	18	18	14(u)	13(u)	30(v)	...	3 da.	...	(n)	Yes(e)
New Jersey	18	18	16(c)	16(c)	30	(b)	72 hrs.	...	1/12/39	Yes
New Mexico	18	18	16(c)	16(c)	30	(b)	72 hrs.	...	No	Yes
New York	18	18	16	14(w)	30	(b,f)	...	24 hrs.(x)	4/29/33	Yes
North Carolina	18	18	16	16(c)	30	(b,g,y,z)	...	...	No	Yes
North Dakota	18	18	16	16	30	(b,aa)	...	...	No	Yes(e)
Ohio	18	18	18(c)	16(c)	30	...	5 da.	...	Yes	Yes
Oklahoma	18	18	16(c)	16(c)	30	(b)	(o)	...	Yes	Yes
Oregon	18	18	17	17	...	...	...	(ab)	(n)	Yes
Pennsylvania	18	18	16(c)	16(c)	30	(b,ac)	3 da.	...	Yes	Yes
Rhode Island	18	18	18(c)	16(c)	40	(b,g,z)	...	...	Yes	(j)
South Carolina	18	18	16(c)	14(c)	...	...	24 hrs.	...	Yes	Yes
South Dakota	18	18	16(c)	16(c)	20	(b)	...	...	7/1/59	Yes
Tennessee	18	18	16(c)	16(c)	30	(b)	3 da.(ad)	...	No	Yes
Texas	18	18	14(c)	14(c)	21	(b)	...	...	Yes	Yes
Utah	18	18	16(a)	16(a)	30	(b)	...	...	No	(j,e)
Vermont	18	18	16(c)	16(c)	30	(b)	...	3 da.	No	(j)
Virginia	18	18	16(a,c)	16(a,c)	30	(b)	...	...	1631	Yes
Washington	18	18	17(c)	17(c)	...	(b)	3 da.	...	No	Yes
West Virginia	18	18	(q)	(q)	30	(b)	3 da.	...	No	Yes
Wisconsin	18	18	16	16	20	(b)	5 da.	...	1913	(j)
Wyoming	19	19	16(c)	16(c)	30	(b)	...	...	No	Yes
Dist. of Col.	18	18	16(a)	16(a)	30	(b)	3 da.	...	Yes	Yes
Puerto Rico	21	21	18(c)	16(c)	10(ae)	(b,af)	...	...	No	(e,j)

LEGISLATION

Source: The Women's Bureau, U.S. Department of Labor, in cooperation with the attorneys general of the states.

(a) Parental consent not required if previously married.

(b) Venereal disease—usually syphilis.

(c) Legal procedure for younger persons to obtain license.

(d) Blood test must be on record at least 48 hours before issuance of license.

(e) If permanent residents attempt to contract a common law marriage in another state, such marriage is not valid in state where domiciled.

(f) Sickle cell anemia. Discretionary in Kentucky.

(g) Rubella immunity. If under age 45 in Colorado.

(h) Tay-Sachs disease.

(i) Rh factor. If under 45 in Colorado.

(j) Legal status uncertain; will probably recognize marriage if valid where contracted.

(k) Parental consent is not needed when the woman is pregnant, or the applicants are the parents of a living child.

(l) Residents, 24 hours; non-residents, 96 hours.

(m) Unless the parties are 18 years of age or older, or the woman is pregnant, or the applicants are the parents of a living child.

(n) Generally no, but may be recognized for limited purposes, e.g., legitimacy of children, workers' compensation benefits, etc. In New Hampshire for estate purposes, if the parties cohabited for three years before death.

(o) Three days if parties are under 18 years of age.

(p) However, contracting such a marriage is a misdemeanor.

(q) No minimum age.

(r) Not required if applicants are 60 years of age or older.

(s) Parental consent not needed if over 16 years of age and woman is pregnant or has given birth.

(t) No provision in the law for parental consent for males.

(u) Permission of judge also required.

(v) Maximum period between date of blood test and date of intended marriage.

(w) If under 16 years of age, consent of family court judge required too.

(x) However, marriage may not be solemnized within three days of date on which specimen for blood test was taken.

(y) Mental competence.

(z) Tuberculosis.

(aa) Some marriages prohibited if a party is severely retarded.

(ab) Licenses valid three days after application is signed and valid for 30 days thereafter.

(ac) Court order needed if party is weakminded, insane or of unsound mind.

(ad) May be waived if certain conditions are met.

(ae) Maximum time from blood test to expiration of license.

(af) Affidavit as to no epilepsy and mental competence required.

Table 2

DIVORCE LAWS AS OF DECEMBER 31, 1981

State or other jurisdiction	State residence required before filing suit(c)	"No fault" divorce(a)			"Traditional" grounds for absolute divorce(b)					
		Marriage break-down (d)	Separa-tion	Prior decree of limited divorce	Adultery	Mental and/or physical cruelty	Desertion	Alco-holism and/or drug addiction	Impo-tency	Non-support by hus-band
Alabama	6 mo.(g)	★	2 yrs.(h)	2 yrs.	★	...	1 yr.	★	★	★
Alaska	...	★	...	...	★	★	1 yr.	★	★	...
Arizona	90 days	★	...	...	...	...	...	...	...	...
Arkansas	60 days(k)	...	3 yrs.	...	★	...	1 yr.	★	★	★(l)
California	6 mo.(c)	★	...	...	...	...	...	...	...	...
Colorado	90 days	★	...	...	...	...	...	...	...	...
Connecticut	1 yr.(n)	★	18 mo.	...	★	★	1 yr.	★	...	...
Delaware	6 mo.	★(p)	6 mo.	...	(p)	(p)	(p)	(p)	...	...
Florida	6 mo.	★	...	...	...	...	...	...	...	...
Georgia	6 mo.	★	...	...	★	★	1 yr.	★	★	...
Hawaii	3 mo.	★	2 yrs.(h)	★(u)	...	...	...	...	...	...
Idaho	6 wk.	★	5 yrs.	...	★	★	★	★	...	★
Illinois	90 days.	...	...	...	★	★	1 yr.	2 yrs.	★	...
Indiana	6 mo.	★	...	...	...	...	...	...	...	...
Iowa	1 yr.	★	...	...	...	...	...	...	...	...
Kansas	60 days	★	...	...	★	★	1 yr.	★	...	★
Kentucky	180 days(x)	★	...	...	...	...	...	...	...	...
Louisiana	(y)	...	6 mo.(z)	...	★	★	★	★	...	★(l)
Maine	6 mo.(n)	★	...	...	★	★	3 yrs.	★	★	★(l)
Maryland	(ab)	...	(ac)	...	★	...	1 yr.	...	★	...
Massachusetts	(ae)	★	...	...	★	★	1 yr.	★	★	★(l)
Michigan	180 days(n)	★	...	...	...	...	...	...	...	...
Minnesota	180 days(n)	★	...	...	...	...	...	...	...	...
Mississippi	6 mo.	★	...	...	★	★	1 yr.	★	★	...
Missouri	90 days	★	...	...	...	...	...	...	...	...
Montana	90 days	★	180 days	...	...	...	...	...	...	...
Nebraska	1 yr.	★	...	...	...	...	...	...	...	...
Nevada	6 wks.(n)	★	1 yr.(t)	...	...	...	...	...	...	...
New Hampshire	1 yr.(n)	★	...	4 yrs.(t)	★	★	2 yrs.	★	★	★
New Jersey	1 yr.	...	18 mo.	...	★	★	1 yr.	★	...	...
New Mexico	6 mo.	★	...	...	★	★	★	...	...	...
New York	2 yrs.(n)	...	1 yr.(h)	...	★	★	1 yr.	...	(ak)	(al)
North Carolina	6 mo.	...	1 yr.	...	★	...	...	...	★	...
North Dakota	1 yr.	★	...	1 yr.	★	★	1yr.	★	★	★(l)
Ohio	6 mo.	★(am)	...	★	★	1 yr.	★	★	★	★(l)
Oklahoma	6 mo.(ao)	★	...	...	★	★	1 yr.	★	★	★(l)
Oregon	6 mo.	★	...	...	...	...	...	...	...	...
Pennsylvania	6 mo.	★(ap)	3 yrs.	...	★	★	1 yr.	...	(ak)	...
Rhode Island	1 yr.	★	3 yrs.	...	★	★	5 yrs.(as)	★	★	1 yr.
South Carolina	1 yr.(n)	...	1 yr.	...	★	★	1 yr.	★	...	...
South Dakota	...	...	...	...	★	★	1 yr.	1 yr.	...	1 yr.
Tennessee	6 mo.	★	...	2 yrs.(t)	★	★	1 yr.	★	★	★
Texas	6 mo.	★	3 yrs.	...	★	★	1 yr.	...	...	...
Utah	3 mo.	...	3 yrs.(h)	...	★	★	1 yr.	★	★	★(l)
Vermont	6 mo.(ax)	...	6 mo.	...	★	★	★	...	...	★(l)
Virginia	6 mo.	...	1 yr.	(ay)	★	★	1 yr.	...	...	...
Washington	...	★	...	...	...	...	...	...	...	...
West Virginia	1 yr.	...	1 yr.	...	★	★	6 mo.	★	...	...
Wisconsin	1 yr.	★	1 yr.	...	...	...	...	...	...	...
Wyoming	60 days(n)	★	...	...	...	...	...	...	(ak)	...
Dist. of Col.	6 mo.	...	6 mo.(az)	(ba)	...	...	...	...	...	...
Puerto Rico	1 yr.(n)	...	(bb)	2 yrs.	...	...	1 yr.	★	★	...

Source: The Women's Bureau, U.S. Department of Labor, in coopera-tion with the attorneys general of the states.

(a) "No fault" includes all proceedings where it is not necessary to prove one of the "traditional" grounds for divorce.

(b) "Traditional" grounds enacted into English and American law during mid-1800s. Before then, divorce was granted by state legislatures on an individual basis.

(c) Local residence also may be required.

(d) Expressed in statutes as irremediable or irretrievable breakdown of marriage relationship, irreconcilable differences, incompatibility, mar-riage unsupportable because of discord, etc.

(e) By another man; unknown to husband.

(f) Some lawyers advise no remarriage until time for appeal has passed—usually 30 days—particularly in contested divorce cases.

(g) Two years for wife filing on grounds of non-support.

(h) Under decree of separate maintenance and/or written separation agreement.

(i) Crime against nature.

(j) Except to each other. In Iowa, court can waive ban.

(k) Three-month residency required before final judgment.

(l) Grounds available to husband also.

(m) Incurable.

(n) In some cases a lesser period of time is allowed, i.e., parties mar-ried, or grounds arose in state or both parties residents of state.

(o) Fraud, force or duress.

(p) Grounds indicated, along with homosexuality, willful refusal to perform marriage obligations, and contracting venereal disease constitute basis for finding of marriage breakdown.

(q) Mental incompetence.

(r) Parties related by marriage or blood contrary to statute.

(s) Mental incapacity at time of marriage.

(t) At the discretion of the court.

(u) After expiration of term of separation decree.

(v) Loathsome disease.

(w) Attempt on life of spouse by poison or other means showing malice.

(x) No decree until the parties have lived apart for 60 days.

(y) Must be permanent residents (domiciliaries) of state and the grounds must have occurred in state.

(z) And parties sign affidavit of irreconcilable differences. Otherwise, one year.

(aa) Public defamation or fugitive from justice.

State or other jurisdiction	"Traditional" grounds for absolute divorce (b)						Period before parties may remarry after final decree(f)	
	Insanity	Pregnancy at marriage(e)	Bigamy	Unexplained absence	Felony conviction or imprisonment	Other	Plaintiff	Defendant
Alabama	5 yrs.	★	...	...	★	(i)	60 days(j)	60 days(j)
Alaska	18 mos.	...	...	...	★	...	...	...
Arizona	...	...	...	...	...	...	...	...
Arkansas	3 yrs.	...	★	...	★	...	...	...
California	(m)	...	...	...	...	...	...	...
Colorado	...	...	...	...	...	...	...	...
Connecticut	5 yrs.	...	...	7 yrs.	★	(o)	...	...
Delaware	(p)	...	(p)	...	(p)	(p)	30 days	30 days
Florida	3 yrs.(q)	...	...	...	...	(p)	...	...
Georgia	2 yrs.	★	...	...	★	(o,r,s)	(t)	(t)
Hawaii	...	...	...	...	...	...	...	...
Idaho	3 yrs.	...	...	...	...	...	...	...
Illinois	...	...	★	...	★	...	...	...
Indiana	2 yrs.	...	...	...	★	(v,w)	...	...
Iowa	...	...	...	...	...	...	1 yr.(j)	1 yr.(j)
Kansas	3 yrs.	...	...	...	★	...	30 days	30 days
Kentucky	...	...	...	...	★	...	...	...
Louisiana	...	...	...	...	...	...	...	...
Maine	7 yrs.	...	...	...	★	(aa)	...	...
Maryland	3 yrs.	...	...	...	★	(ad)	...	...
Massachusetts	...	...	...	...	★	...	...	...
Michigan	...	...	...	...	...	...	...	...
Minnesota	...	...	...	...	...	...	...	...
Mississippi	3 yrs.	★	★	...	★	(r,af)	...	...
Missouri	...	...	...	...	...	...	...	(ag)
Montana	...	...	...	...	...	...	...	...
Nebraska	...	...	...	...	...	...	...	...
Nevada	2 yrs.	...	...	...	...	...	...	...
New Hampshire	...	...	...	2 yrs.	★	(ah,ai)	...	...
New Jersey	2 yrs.	...	...	...	★	(aj)	...	...
New Mexico	...	...	...	...	...	...	...	...
New York	5 yrs.(ak)	...	...	...	★	...	...	...
North Carolina	3 yrs.	★	...	...	★	(i)	...	...
North Dakota	5 yrs.	...	...	...	★	...	(t)	(t)
Ohio	4 yrs.	...	★	...	★	(o,an)	...	...
Oklahoma	5 yrs.	★	...	...	★	(o,an)	6 mo.	6 mo.
Oregon	...	...	...	...	...	...	30 days	30 days
Pennsylvania	3 yrs.	...	★	...	★	(r,aq)	...	(ar)
Rhode Island	...	...	...	...	...	(at,au)	3 mo.	3 mo.
South Carolina	...	...	...	7 yrs.	...	...	...	...
South Dakota	5 yrs.	...	...	...	★	...	...	...
Tennessee	...	★	★	...	★	(w,av)	...	...
Texas	3 yrs.	...	...	...	★	...	30 days(j)	30 days(j)
Utah	(aw)	...	...	...	★	...	...	...
Vermont	5 yrs.	...	...	...	★	...	...	...
Virginia	...	...	...	...	★	...	...	...
Washington	...	...	...	...	...	...	...	...
West Virginia	3 yrs.	...	...	...	★	...	...	...
Wisconsin	...	...	...	...	...	...	...	...
Wyoming	2 yrs.	...	...	...	...	...	...	...
Dist. of Col.	...	...	...	...	...	...	...	...
Puerto Rico	7 yrs.	...	...	10 yrs.	★	(bc)	...	(bd)

(ab) One year if cause arose out of state; two years for insanity.
(ac) Voluntary living apart for one year or living separate and apart without interruption for three years.
(ad) Any cause which renders marriage null and void.
(ae) One year if grounds arose outside of commonwealth.
(af) Insanity or idiocy at time of marriage not known to other party.
(ag) When divorce is granted on grounds of adultery, court may prohibit remarriage. Disability may be removed after one year upon satisfactory evidence of reformation.
(ah) Membership in a religious sect not believing in marriage.
(ai) Wife out of state for 10 years without husband's consent.
(aj) Deviant sexual conduct without consent of spouse.
(ak) Grounds for annulment.
(al) Grounds for separation.
(am) On petition of both spouses, accompanied by separation agreement executed and confirmed by both spouses in court appearance not less than 90 days after filing of petition.
(an) Defendant obtained divorce from plaintiff in another state.
(ao) Five years for insanity if spouse in out-of-state facility.
(ap) Statute requires counseling.
(aq) Indignities.

(ar) If divorce is granted for adultery, the guilty party cannot marry the accomplice in adultery during lifetime of former spouse.
(as) Shorter period in court's discretion.
(at) Void or voidable marriage; in case party is deemed civilly dead from crime or other circumstances, party may be presumed dead.
(au) Gross misbehavior or wickedness.
(av) Refusal by wife to move to state with husband.
(aw) Adjudication of permanent and incurable insanity.
(ax) Two years if grounds are insanity.
(ay) Limited divorce granted on the grounds of cruelty, reasonable apprehension of bodily hurt, willful desertion or abandonment may be merged into an absolute divorce after one year.
(az) Voluntary separation; involuntary separation, one year.
(ba) Granted for six months voluntary separation, one year involuntary separation, adultery and cruelty.
(bb) By mutual consent.
(bc) Attempt by either parent to corrupt son or prostitute daughter, or by husband to prostitute wife.
(bd) If remarried before 301 days she must present certificate showing pregnancy or non-pregnancy. If pregnant, her former spouse is presumed to be the father. No certificate is required if she has given birth during the 301 days.

UNIFORM STATE LAWS

By John M. McCabe

IN 1980 and 1981, the National Conference of Commissioners on Uniform State Laws (NCCUSL) completed nine uniform and model acts:

1. Uniform Conservation Easement Act. This act authorizes the creation of permanent easements on real property for conservation and historic preservation purposes. Such easements may be held by non-profit associations organized for the purpose of holding such easements, or by governmental agencies. These easements persist with every transfer of the land and may be perpetually granted even to holders with no dominant estate in land to be served by the easement.

2. Uniform Extradition and Rendition Act (1980). This act contains an executive procedure for the extradition of accused persons from one state to another with an alternative procedure for the rendition of accused persons by a court. This combined act revises the Uniform Extradition Act, first offered in 1932 and amended in 1936, and the Uniform Rendition of Accused Persons Act, originally proposed in 1967. The new act combines, simplifies and modernizes the two older ones.

3. Uniform Information Practices Code. This code provides for the disclosure of governmental records and protection of the privacy of records concerning specific persons. It opens all governmental records to the public, with a few exceptions, such as current law enforcement files on criminal investigations. Each agency provides for access and copying. Individual records, however, cannot be disclosed, in general, except to the persons to whom they pertain. There are a few exceptions, carefully described. Violations of either aspect of this code subject agencies and employees to agency sanctions and civil and potential criminal liability.

4. Model Periodic Payment of Judgments Act. This act provides an alternative system for payment of future damages in personal injury cases. Rather than the traditional lump-sum award, this act allows parties to personal injury litigation to petition for payment as damages accrue. The act has particular application to large damage awards. No substantive damage rules are changed. Only the terms of payment are altered.

5. Uniform Planned Community Act. This act contains comprehensive legislation for real estate developments that combine private ownership of individual units with conditions, covenants and restrictions on title that bind unit owners into a community with other unit owners. The owners' association then owns all property, outside individual unit boundaries, which is common to the whole. The act covers all phases from creation to termination. It has comprehensive provisions for management, including transfer of developer control to the owners' association. It provides for disclosure to consumers and for warranties of sale. There is a final, optional article for regulation of condominium development.

6. Uniform Post-Conviction Procedure Act (1980). This act provides a procedure to

John M. McCabe is Legislative Director, National Conference of Commissioners on Uniform State Laws.

remedy defects in a criminal conviction. Grounds for seeking a remedy include violations of the federal constitution or the constitution of an enacting state, lack of jurisdiction, a sentence not authorized by law and the like. There are, also, sanctions to prevent frivolous use of the remedy and repetitive filings. The 1980 act is a revision of the original, first promulgated in 1955 and amended in 1966.

7. Model Real Estate Cooperative Act. This is a companion act to the Uniform Condominium Act and the Uniform Planned Community Act. Real estate cooperatives are created when an association assumes title to real property, which then is leased back to its members. Each member also owns a share of the association, itself. The model act provides comprehensive legislation governing the critical phases of cooperative development: creation, financing, management and termination. It deals also with buyer protection and tenants' rights in conversion buildings. An optional administrative agency is also provided for the registration, investigation and regulation of cooperative projects.

8. Model State Administrative Procedure Act (1981). This act is a substantial revision of earlier acts completed in 1954 and 1966. It establishes procedures for rule-making and for adjudication of cases and controversies. Rule-making requires notice and opportunity to comment by concerned citizens and, pursuant to a proper request, rule-making hearings. The act requires an administrative bulletin, for notice purposes, and an administrative code for final rules. It creates a comprehensive system of review for rules. Adjudication requires notice and hearing for serious cases and less rigorous procedures for less serious adjudications. A central office of administrative hearings provides administrative judges. Comprehensive provision for judicial review is provided.

9. Uniform Unclaimed Property Act. This act revises earlier acts completed in 1954 and 1966. It allows unclaimed intangible property, such as bank accounts and stock holdings, to be declared abandoned and transferred to the state as custodian for property owners in perpetuity. The new act solves jurisdictional difficulties with the earlier acts and provides for better cooperation between states claiming property.

In addition, the NCCUSL made minor amendments to the Uniform Condominium Act and to the Uniform Brain Death Act, which has now become the Uniform Determination of Death Act. NCCUSL work continues on a number of projects. More details on acts mentioned and on those in the accompanying table are available from NCCUSL, 645 North Michigan Avenue, Suite 510, Chicago, Illinois 60611.

RECORD OF PASSAGE OF UNIFORM ACTS
As of September 1, 1981

State	Acknowledgment (1939) (1960)	Adoption (1953) (1971)	Alcoholism and Intoxication Treatment (1971)	Anatomical Gift (1968)	Arbitration (1956)	Attendance of Out of State Witnesses (1931) (1936)	Audio-Visual Deposition (1978)	Certification of Questions of Law (1967)	Child Custody Jurisdiction (1968)	Civil Liability for Support (1954)	Class Actions (1976)	Commercial Code (1951) (1957) (1962) (1966)	Commercial Code—Article 8 (1977)	Commercial Code—Article 9 (1972)	Common Trust Fund (1938) (1952)	Comparative Fault (1977) (1979)	Condominium (1977) (1980)	Consumer Credit Code (1968) (1974)
Alabama	...	...	★	★	...	•	...	...	★	...	...	•	...	★	★	...	...	...
Alaska	...	...	★	★	★	•	...	...	★	...	...	•	...	...	★	★	...	...
Arizona	•	...	...	★	★	•	...	...	★	...	...	•	...	★	★	...	...	...
Arkansas	•	•	...	★	★	★	...	...	★	★	...	•	...	★	★	...	...	...
California	...	...	...	☆	...	...	...	...	★	...	...	•	...	★	★	...	...	...
Colorado	...	...	★	★	★	•	...	★	★	...	...	•	...	★	★	...	...	★
Connecticut	...	...	☆	★	☆	•	...	...	★	...	...	•	★	★	...	...	...	...
Delaware	•	...	★	★	★	•	...	...	★	...	...	•	...	★	★	...	...	...
Florida	★	...	☆	★	☆	•	...	☆	★	...	...	•	...	★	★	...	...	...
Georgia	...	...	★	★	☆	•	...	...	★	...	...	•	...	★	...	...	...	...
Hawaii	★	...	★	★	...	•	...	...	★	...	...	•	...	★	★	★	...	...
Idaho	★	...	★	★	★	★	...	...	★	...	...	•	...	★	★	★	...	★
Illinois	★	...	★	★	★	...	...	...	★	...	...	•	...	★	...	...	...	★
Indiana	...	...	...	★	☆	•	...	...	★	...	...	•	...	★	...	...	...	★
Iowa	★	•	★	★	★	☆	...	★	★	...	★	•	...	★	•	...	...	★
Kansas	•	...	★	★	★	•	...	★	★	...	...	•	...	★	★	...	...	★
Kentucky	...	...	...	★	...	•	...	...	★	...	...	•	...	★	...	...	...	...
Louisiana	...	...	☆	★	...	...	...	...	...	...	...	...	...	...	...	...	...	...
Maine	...	...	★	★	★	•	...	☆	★	★	...	•	...	★	★	...	...	★
Maryland	...	...	☆	★	★	•	...	...	★	...	...	•	...	★	...	...	...	...
Massachusetts	•	...	☆	★	★	•	...	...	★	...	...	•	...	★	★	★	...	...
Michigan	★	...	☆	★	★	☆	...	...	★	...	...	•	...	★	★	★	...	...
Minnesota	★	...	☆	★	★	•	...	★	★	...	...	•	★	★	...	...	★	...
Mississippi	...	...	...	★	...	•	...	...	...	...	...	•	...	★	...	...	...	...
Missouri	...	...	...	★	★	•	...	...	★	...	...	•	...	★	...	...	...	...
Montana	★	★	★	★	...	•	...	...	★	...	...	•	...	★	★	...	...	...
Nebraska	★	...	...	★	...	•	...	...	★	...	...	•	...	★	★	...	...	...
Nevada	★	...	...	★	★	•	...	...	★	★	...	•	...	★	★	...	...	...
New Hampshire	•	...	...	★	...	•	...	...	★	★	...	•	...	★	...	...	...	...
New Jersey	...	...	...	★	...	•	...	...	...	...	...	•	...	★	...	...	...	...
New Mexico	★	☆	★	★	★	•	...	...	★	...	...	•	...	★	★	...	...	...
New York	...	...	★	★	★	•	...	...	★	...	...	•	...	★	...	...	...	...
North Carolina	...	...	★	★	...	•	...	...	★	...	...	•	...	★	★	...	...	...
North Dakota	★	...	★	★	★	...	★	★	★	...	★	•	...	★	★	...	...	...
Ohio	...	...	...	★	☆	...	...	...	★	...	...	•	...	★	...	...	...	...
Oklahoma	...	★	★	★	★	•	...	...	★	...	...	•	...	★	★	...	...	★
Oregon	...	...	...	★	★	•	...	...	★	...	...	•	...	★	•	...	...	...
Pennsylvania	•	...	...	★	★	•	...	...	★	...	...	•	...	★	...	...	★	...
Rhode Island	...	...	☆	★	★	★	...	★	★	...	...	•	...	★	...	...	...	...
South Carolina	...	...	...	★	★	...	...	...	★	...	...	•	...	★	...	...	...	☆
South Dakota	★	...	★	★	★	...	...	...	★	...	...	•	...	★	...	...	...	...
Tennessee	...	...	...	★	...	•	...	...	★	...	...	•	...	★	...	...	...	...
Texas	...	...	...	★	★	•	...	...	...	...	...	•	...	★	...	...	...	...
Utah	★	...	...	★	☆	...	...	...	★	★	...	•	...	★	★	...	...	★
Vermont	...	...	...	★	...	•	...	...	★	...	...	•	...	★	...	...	...	...
Virginia	...	...	...	★	...	•	...	...	★	...	...	•	...	★	•	...	...	...
Washington	★	...	★	★	★	...	...	☆	★	...	...	•	...	★	★	★	☆	...
West Virginia	...	...	...	★	...	•	...	★	★	...	...	•	★	★	★	★	...	☆
Wisconsin	•	...	★	★	☆	•	...	...	★	...	...	•	...	★	...	...	...	☆
Wyoming	•	...	...	★	★	★	...	...	★	...	...	•	...	★	...	...	...	★
Dist. of Col.	...	...	☆	★	★	•	...	...	...	...	...	•	...	...	★	...	...	...
Puerto Rico	...	...	...	...	...	★	...	...	...	...	...	•	...	...	...	...	...	...
Virgin Islands	•	...	...	...	...	...	...	...	...	...	...	•	...	...	...	...	...	...

Source: Adapted from *Handbook of the National Conference of Commissioners on Uniform State Laws,* which lists all acts promulgated by the conference. The table records state adoptions of acts currently recommended by the conference for adoption by all jurisdictions, but does not include the following which have not been adopted by any jurisdictions: Conservation Easement (1981); Rules of Criminal Procedure (1974); Drug Dependence Treatment and Rehabilitation (1973); Eminent Domain Code (1974); Exemptions (1976, 1979); Extradition and Rendition (1980); Information Practices Code (1980); Land Transactions (1975, 1977); Metric System Procedure (1979); Motor Vehicle Accident Reparations (1972); Planned Community (1980); Simplification of Land Transfers (1976, 1977); Unclaimed Property (1981).

Key:
★—Enacted.
☆—Substantially similar.
•—As amended.

RECORD OF PASSAGE OF UNIFORM ACTS—Continued
As of September 1, 1981

State	Consumer Sales Practices (1970) (1971)	Controlled Substances (1970) (1973)	Crime Victims Reparations (1973)	Criminal Extradition (1926) (1936)	Deceptive Trade Practices (1964) (1966)	Declaratory Judgments (1922)	Determination of Death (1978) (1980)	Disclaimer of Property Interests ((1973) (1978)	Disclaimer of Transfers by Will, Intestacy or Appt. (1973) (1978)	Disclaimer of Transfers under Non-testamentary Instruments (1973) (1978)	Disposition of Community Property Rights at Death (1971)	Disposition of Unclaimed Property (1954) (1966)	Division of Income for Tax Purposes (1957)	Durable Power of Attorney (1979)	Duties to Disabled Persons (1972)	Enforcement of Foreign Judgments (1948) (1964)	Evidence, Rules of (1974)	Facsimile Signatures of Public Officials (1958)
Alabama	...	★	...	★	...	★	☆	•	...	...	...	★	...	★	★	...	...	...
Alaska	...	•	...	•	...	...	...	...	...	...	...	★	...	★	★	...	★	...
Arizona	...	★	...	★	...	★	☆	...	...	...	...	•	...	★	★	...	•	...
Arkansas	...	☆	...	★	...	★	...	•	...	...	...	★	•	★	★	...	•	★	★
California	...	☆	...	•	...	...	...	...	...	...	...	...	...	...	...	...	...	★
Colorado	...	...	...	•	•	★	...	...	...	...	★	...	★	★	★	...	...	★
Connecticut	...	★	...	•	...	★	...	...	...	...	...	☆	☆	★	★	...	★
Delaware	...	★	...	•	★	★	...	...	...	...	...	...	...	...	...	...	★
Florida	...	☆	...	•	•	★	...	•	...	...	...	...	...	...	...	...	★	★
Georgia	...	☆	...	•	•	★	...	...	...	...	☆	☆	...	...	☆	...	...
Hawaii	...	☆	...	•	•	★	★	...	...	...	★	•	★	★	...	...	...	★
Idaho	...	★	...	•	...	★	...	...	...	...	•	★	★	★	...	...	★
Illinois	...	☆	...	•	★	★	•	...	★	...	...	•	★	★	...	•	...	★
Indiana	...	•	...	★	...	★	•	•	...	...	...	•	★	★	...	•	★	★
Iowa	...	★	...	•	...	★	...	...	...	...	•	...	★	...	•	...
Kansas	★	★	☆	•	...	...	...	...	...	...	•	...	★	...	•	...	★
Kentucky	...	☆	★	•	...	...	...	•	...	★	...	...	•	☆	...	•	...	★
Louisiana	...	★	...	•	...	...	...	...	...	...	•	...	...	...	...	...
Maine	...	•	...	•	★	★	•	...	★	•	...	•	...	★	...	•	...	★
Maryland	...	★	...	•	...	★	...	•	...	...	★	...	★	...	•	...	★
Massachusetts	...	★	...	•	...	★	...	...	...	...	★	...	...	...	...	...
Michigan	...	★	...	•	•	★	...	•	...	★	...	•	...	...	•	...	★	...
Minnesota	...	☆	☆	•	•	★	...	...	...	...	☆	★	★	•	★	...
Mississippi	...	★	...	...	•	★	...	...	...	...	•	...	...	★	...
Missouri	...	★	...	•	...	★	...	...	...	...	★	...	...	★	...	★
Montana	...	☆	★	•	...	★	...	...	...	...	•	...	•	...	•	...	★
Nebraska	...	★	...	•	•	★	...	...	...	...	•	★	...	★	...	★	☆
Nevada	...	★	...	•	★	★	•	...	...	...	•	•	...	•	...	★
New Hampshire	...	★	...	•	...	★	...	...	...	...	•	☆	...	...	...	★
New Jersey	...	★	★	•	...	★	...	...	...	...	•	...	★	...	...	★
New Mexico	...	★	...	•	☆	★	...	...	...	...	•	★	★	...	...	★
New York	...	★	...	•	...	★	...	...	...	...	•	★	☆	...	•	...
North Carolina	...	☆	...	•	...	★	...	...	...	...	•	★	☆	...	•	...
North Dakota	...	★	★	•	...	★	•	★	...	...	★	★	★	•	★
Ohio	☆	...	...	•	•	★	...	...	...	...	☆	☆	★	...
Oklahoma	☆	★	...	•	★	★	...	...	...	...	•	★	...	★	•	★	...
Oregon	...	★	...	•	...	★	•	★	★	★	...	★	★	☆	...	★	•	★
Pennsylvania	...	★	...	•	...	★	...	...	...	...	★	★	☆	☆	•	...
Rhode Island	...	☆	...	•	...	★	...	☆	...	...	•	★	...	•	...	★
South Carolina	...	★	...	...	...	★	...	...	...	...	★	☆	...	...
South Dakota	...	★	...	•	...	★	...	...	...	...	•	★	...	•	...
Tennessee	...	★	☆	•	...	★	...	...	...	...	•	☆	...	•	...
Texas	...	★	...	•	•	★	...	...	...	...	•	★	☆	...	★
Utah	•	★	...	•	•	★	...	...	...	★	★	•	...	...
Vermont	...	★	...	★	•	★	★	...	...	...	•	★	...	...
Virginia	...	☆	★	•	...	★	...	...	...	...	★	☆	☆	...	...
Washington	...	★	...	•	•	★	...	...	...	...	★	★	★	...	★	★
West Virginia	...	★	...	•	•	★	☆	...	...	...	•	☆	...	...	...	★
Wisconsin	...	★	...	•	...	★	•	...	...	...	•	☆	...	•	...
Wyoming	...	★	...	★	...	★	☆	...	...	...	...	...	•	...	★
Dist. of Col.	...	☆	...	...	...	☆	...	...	...	...	☆	...	...	...
Puerto Rico	...	★	...	•	...	★	...	...	...	...	...	...	...	...
Virgin Islands	...	★	...	•	...	★	...	...	...	...	...	...	...	...

RECORD OF PASSAGE OF UNIFORM ACTS—Continued
As of September 1, 1981

State	Federal Lien Registration (1978)	Federal Tax Lien Registration (1926) (1966)	Fiduciaries (1922)	Foreign Money Judgments Recognition (1962)	Fraudulent Conveyance (1918)	Gifts to Minors (1956) (1965) (1966)	International Wills (1977)	Interstate Arbitration of Death Taxes (1943)	Interstate Compromise of Death Taxes (1943)	Jury Selection and Service (1970) (1971)	Juvenile Court (1968)	Limited Partnership (1916) (1976)	Management of Institutional Funds (1972)	Mandatory Disposition of Detainers (1958)	Marriage and Divorce (1970) (1973)	Parentage (1973)	Partnership (1914)	Photographic Copies as Evidence (1949)
Alabama			★			•						☆					☆	★
Alaska		★		★		•						★					★	★
Arizona		•	★		★	★						★		★	★		★	
Arkansas		★				•						•					★	★
California	★	•		★	★	•		★	★			★	☆			★	★	★
Colorado		•	★			•		★	★	★		•	★		★	★	★	★
Connecticut		•				•		★	★			★	★				★	★
Delaware		★			★	•						★	★				★	★
Florida						★						★	★				★	★
Georgia		•		★							☆	★			☆		★	★
Hawaii		☆	★			•						★				★	★	★
Idaho	★	•	★			•				★		★	★		★		★	★
Illinois		☆	★	★		•			☆			★	★	★			★	
Indiana		★	★			•			☆			★					★	★
Iowa		•			★	•						★					★	★
Kansas						•						★	☆	★			★	★
Kentucky		★				•						★	★		★		★	★
Louisiana		★	★			★											★	★
Maine		•				•		★	★	★		★	★				★	★
Maryland	★	•	★	★	★	•		★	★			•	★				★	★
Massachusetts		★		★	★	•		★	★			★	★	☆			★	★
Michigan		•		★	★	•		★	★			★	★				★	
Minnesota	★	•	★		★	•	★	☆	★	•		★	★	★	☆	★	★	★
Mississippi					★	•			☆			★		★			★	
Missouri		★	★			•						★	★	★			★	★
Montana		•			★	•						•	★		•	★	★	★
Nebraska		•			★	•		★	★			•	★				☆	
Nevada	★	•	★		★	•						★					★	★
New Hampshire		•			★	•			★			★	★				★	★
New Jersey			★		★	•			★			★	★				★	★
New Mexico		★			★	•						★					★	★
New York		★	☆	★		•			★			★	☆				★	★
North Carolina		•	★			•						★					★	★
North Dakota	★	•				•	★		★	★	★	★	★	★		★	★	★
Ohio		•		★		★	★					★	☆				★	★
Oklahoma		•		★	★	•						★					★	★
Oregon		•	★		★	•						☆	★				★	★
Pennsylvania		★	★		★	•		★	★			★					★	★
Rhode Island		★	☆			★						★	★	★			★	★
South Carolina		★				•						★					★	
South Dakota		•	★		★	•						★					★	★
Tennessee		★	★		★	•		☆	☆			★	★				★	★
Texas						•						★					★	★
Utah		★	★		★	•						★					★	★
Vermont						★		★	★			★					★	★
Virginia		•				★						★	★				★	★
Washington		•		★	★	•		★	★			•	★		☆	★	★	★
West Virginia						•		★	★			★	★				★	★
Wisconsin	★	★	★		★	•		★				★					★	★
Wyoming		★	★		★	•						•				★	★	★
Dist. of Col.			★			•						★	★				★	
Puerto Rico																		
Virgin Islands			★		★	★						★					★	☆

RECORD OF PASSAGE OF UNIFORM ACTS—Concluded
As of September 1, 1981

State	Post-Conviction Procedure (1955) (1966) (1980)	Principal and Income (1931) (1962)	Probate Code (1969) (1975) (1977) (1979)	Public Assembly (1972)	Reciprocal Enforcement of Support (1950) (1958) (1968)	Reciprocal Enforcement of Support (1950) (1958) (1968)	Recognition of Acknowledgments (1968)	Rendition of Accused Persons (1967)	Residential Landlord-Tenant (1972)	Securities (1956) (1958)	Simplification of Fiduciary Security Transfers (1958)	Simultaneous Death (1940) (1953)	State Antitrust (1973) (1979)	Status of Convicted Persons (1964)	Supervision of Trustees for Charitable Purposes (1954)	Testamentary Additions to Trusts (1960)	Trade Secrets (1979)	Trustees' Powers (1964)
Alabama	...	★	...	...	•	...	...	•	...	•	★	★	...	...	...	☆	...	...
Alaska	...	...	★	...	•	☆	...	★	...	•	★	★	...	...	...	★	...	...
Arizona	...	★	★	...	•	★	...	★	...	•	★	•	...	...	...	★	...	...
Arkansas	...	•	...	...	•	...	...	•	...	•	•	...	...	...	...	★	★	...
California	...	•	...	...	•	...	...	...	...	★	★	...	...	...	★	★	...	...
Colorado	...	★	•	...	•	★	★	...	...	•	•	•	...	...	...	☆	...	...
Connecticut	...	•	...	...	•	★	★	...	...	•	•	★	...	...	...	...	...	...
Delaware	...	...	...	...	•	...	...	...	...	★	★	...	...	...	...	...	...
Florida	...	★	...	...	•	...	...	★	...	•	★	★	...	...	...	☆	...	...
Georgia	...	...	...	...	•	...	...	...	...	•	★	...	...	...	...	★	...	...
Hawaii	•	•	★	...	•	...	★	★	•	★	★	...	...	★	...	★	...	...
Idaho	•	★	★	...	•	★	★	•	•	★	★	...	...	...	...	★	...	...
Illinois	•	★	...	...	•	★	★	...	...	★	★	...	...	...	★	☆	...	...
Indiana	...	•	...	...	•	...	...	...	☆	★	★	...	...	...	...	☆	...	...
Iowa	•	...	...	...	•	...	...	★	☆	★	★	★	...	...	...	★	...	...
Kansas	...	•	...	...	•	★	...	☆	•	★	•	...	...	...	...	★	★	★
Kentucky	...	★	...	...	•	★	...	★	☆	•	•	...	...	...	...	★	...	★
Louisiana	...	★	...	...	•	...	...	...	...	★	...	...	...	...	...	...	...	...
Maine	...	•	•	...	•	★	...	...	...	•	★	...	...	...	...	★	...	...
Maryland	★	•	...	...	•	...	...	...	•	★	★	...	...	...	...	☆	...	...
Massachusetts	...	...	...	...	•	...	...	...	•	•	...	...	...	...	...	...	...	...
Michigan	...	•	☆	...	•	★	★	★	•	★	★	...	...	★	★	★	...	...
Minnesota	•	•	★	...	•	★	...	•	•	★	★	...	...	...	★	★	★	☆
Mississippi	...	•	...	...	•	...	...	•	•	★	★	...	...	...	☆	...	★	...
Missouri	...	•	...	...	•	...	...	•	...	...	...	...	...	...	...	...	...	...
Montana	★	★	★	...	•	...	...	★	•	★	★	...	...	☆	...	☆	...	★
Nebraska	...	...	★	...	•	★	★	★	☆	•	★	...	...	...	...	...	...	...
Nevada	•	•	...	...	•	...	...	•	•	★	...	...	...	...	...	...	...	...
New Hampshire	...	...	...	...	•	★	...	•	★	★	...	...	★	...	★	...	★	...
New Jersey	...	...	☆	...	•	...	...	•	★	★	...	...	...	...	☆	...	...	...
New Mexico	...	•	★	...	•	...	★	...	•	...	...	...	...	...	★	...	...	...
New York	...	•	...	...	•	...	...	...	...	•	...	...	...	...	☆	...	...	...
North Carolina	...	•	...	...	•	...	...	★	★	...	...	...	...	...	☆	...	...	...
North Dakota	•	•	...	...	•	★	★	•	★	★	...	...	...	...	...	...	...	...
Ohio	...	•	...	...	•	...	...	...	...	...	...	...	...	...	1	...	...	...
Oklahoma	•	★	★	•	★	★	...	★	•	...	•	...	...	...	★	...	...	...
Oregon	★	•	☆	...	•	★	★	★	•	•	...	...	★	★	★	...	★	...
Pennsylvania	...	★	☆	...	•	...	...	...	☆	•	★	...	...	...	☆	...	...	...
Rhode Island	•	...	...	...	•	...	...	...	•	★	★	...	...	...	...	...	...	...
South Carolina	•	•	...	...	•	...	...	•	•	★	★	...	...	...	★	...	...	...
South Dakota	•	...	...	...	•	★	...	...	...	★	★	...	...	...	★	...	...	...
Tennessee	...	★	...	...	•	...	★	...	...	★	★	...	...	...	★	...	...	...
Texas	...	★	...	...	•	...	...	...	...	•	★	...	...	...	☆	...	...	...
Utah	...	★	★	...	•	...	...	...	•	★	★	...	...	...	☆	...	★	...
Vermont	★	•	☆	...	•	...	...	...	...	•	★	...	...	...	★	...	...	...
Virginia	...	★	...	...	•	★	...	★	...	★	★	...	...	...	...	...	...	...
Washington	...	•	...	...	•	★	☆	...	•	★	★	...	...	...	☆	★	...	...
West Virginia	...	★	...	...	•	★	★	...	•	★	★	...	...	...	★	...	...	...
Wisconsin	...	★	...	...	•	★	★	...	•	★	★	...	...	...	...	...	...	...
Wyoming	...	•	...	...	•	...	...	...	•	★	★	...	...	...	☆	...	...	★
Dist. of Col.	...	...	...	...	•	...	...	•	★	•	...	...	...	...	☆	...	...	...
Puerto Rico	...	...	...	...	•	...	...	...	...	...	...	...	...	...	...	...	...	...
Virgin Islands	...	...	...	...	•	...	...	...	...	...	...	...	...	...	...	...	...	...

RECORD OF PASSAGE OF MODEL ACTS
As of September 1, 1981

State	Act to Provide for the Appointment of Commissioners (1944)	Anti-Discrimination (1966)	Anti-Gambling (1952)	Court Administrator (1948) (1960)	Foreign Bank Loan (1959)	Land Sales Practices (1966)	Minor Student Capacity to Borrow (1969)	Post-Mortem Examinations (1954)	Public Defender (1970) (1974)	State Administrative Procedure (1946) (1961) (1981)	State Witness Immunity (1952)	Statutory Construction (1965)	Water Use (1958)
Alabama	★	...	...	...	...	...	...	...	...	...	...	...	...
Alaska	...	...	...	...	★	★	...	...	...	...	...	...	...
Arizona	★	...	...	...	...	...	★	...	...	...	...	...	...
Arkansas	★	...	...	...	...	...	...	...	...	•	...	...	...
California	...	...	...	...	...	...	...	...	...	...	...	...	...
Colorado	...	...	...	...	...	...	...	...	...	...	...	★	...
Connecticut	...	...	...	★	...	★	★	...	...	•	...	...	...
Delaware	...	...	...	...	...	...	...	...	...	•	...	...	...
Florida	...	...	...	...	...	★	...	...	...	...	...	...	...
Georgia	...	...	...	...	...	☆	...	...	...	•	...	...	...
Hawaii	...	★	...	...	...	★	...	...	...	★	...	...	☆
Idaho	...	...	...	...	...	...	...	...	...	...	...	...	...
Illinois	...	...	...	★	...	...	...	...	...	...	★	...	...
Indiana	...	...	★	...	...	...	...	...	...	•	...	...	...
Iowa	★	...	...	...	...	...	...	☆	...	•	...	★	...
Kansas	★	...	...	...	...	★	...	...	...	...	...	...	...
Kentucky	★	...	...	...	...	...	...	...	...	...	...	...	...
Louisiana	...	...	...	...	...	...	...	...	...	•	...	...	...
Maine	★	...	...	...	...	...	...	...	...	...	...	...	...
Maryland	...	...	...	...	...	...	...	☆	...	★	...	...	...
Massachusetts	...	...	...	...	...	...	...	...	...	...	...	...	...
Michigan	...	...	...	★	...	...	...	...	...	★	...	...	...
Minnesota	...	...	...	...	...	...	...	...	...	...	...	...	...
Mississippi	★	...	...	...	...	...	...	...	...	★	...	...	...
Missouri	...	...	...	...	...	...	...	...	...	★	...	...	...
Montana	★	...	...	☆	...	★	☆	...	...	•	...	...	...
Nebraska	★	...	...	...	...	...	...	...	...	...	...	...	...
Nevada	...	...	...	...	...	...	...	...	...	...	...	...	...
New Hampshire	★	...	...	...	...	...	...	...	...	...	...	...	...
New Jersey	...	...	...	...	...	...	...	...	...	...	...	...	...
New Mexico	...	...	...	...	...	...	...	...	...	...	...	...	...
New York	...	...	...	...	...	...	...	...	...	...	...	...	...
North Carolina	...	...	...	...	...	...	...	...	...	...	...	...	...
North Dakota	★	...	...	...	...	...	★	...	...	...	...	...	...
Ohio	...	...	...	...	...	...	...	...	...	...	...	...	...
Oklahoma	★	★	...	•	...	...	★	★	...	•	...	...	...
Oregon	★	...	...	...	...	...	★	...	...	★	...	...	...
Pennsylvania	...	...	...	...	...	...	...	...	...	•	...	...	...
Rhode Island	...	...	...	...	...	...	...	...	...	•	...	...	...
South Carolina	...	...	...	...	...	...	...	...	...	...	...	...	...
South Dakota	...	...	...	...	...	...	...	...	...	...	...	...	...
Tennessee	...	...	★	...	...	...	...	...	...	•	...	...	...
Texas	★	...	...	...	...	...	...	★	...	...	...	...	...
Utah	...	...	...	...	...	...	...	...	...	...	...	...	...
Vermont	...	...	...	...	...	...	...	...	...	...	...	...	...
Virginia	...	...	...	...	...	...	...	...	...	...	...	...	...
Washington	...	...	...	★	...	...	★	...	...	★	...	...	...
West Virginia	...	...	...	...	...	...	...	☆	...	☆	...	...	...
Wisconsin	★	...	...	...	...	...	...	...	...	★	...	★	...
Wyoming	...	...	...	...	...	...	...	...	...	•	...	...	...
Dist. of Col.	...	...	...	...	...	...	...	...	...	•	...	...	...
Puerto Rico	...	...	...	...	...	...	...	...	...	...	...	...	...
Virgin Islands	...	...	...	...	...	...	...	...	...	...	...	...	...

Source: Adapted from *Handbook of the National Conference of Commissioners of Uniform State Laws.*
Key:
★—Enacted.
☆—Substantially similar.
•—As amended.

2. Elections

ELECTION LEGISLATION

By Richard G. Smolka

STATE ELECTION LAWS passed during the 1980-81 biennium represented fine tuning of an election system that in most states has moved consistently during the last decade in the direction of expanding the franchise, easing ballot access and providing convenience for the voter. The campaign finance laws that emerged in a burst of legislative activity during the seventies have stabilized with only minor adjustments being made. Voter registration opportunities continued to expand, administratively as well as legislatively, and access to the polls or an absentee ballot became easier for all, including handicapped persons. As a result of court challenges by presidential candidate John Anderson during 1980, independent candidates have easier access to the ballot. If there was one new election procedure that gained significant attention during this period, it was an election conducted entirely by mail ballot.

Elections by All-Mail Ballot. Although there had been special district, all-mail ballot elections in California during the 1970s, none were conducted on as large a scale, nor prompted other jurisdictions to take as much note as the election conducted by San Diego in May 1981. The city mailed each of its 430,000 registered voters an official ballot and an explanation of the issue. More than 261,000 persons, 60 percent of the electorate, voted on this issue in contrast to the 25 to 35 percent who vote in such elections when they are conducted in the traditional manner. San Diego estimated that it saved about $175,000 by mailing all ballots.

Shortly thereafter, Oregon passed experimental legislation allowing communities to try an all-mail election based on the San Diego experience. In November 1981, Linn County, Oregon, conducted such an election for two school district levies and on a city charter revision. Voter turnout was much higher than in traditional elections on these types of issues. About 77 percent voted in the mail elections but only 21-23 percent voted in other elections conducted in the conventional manner in the same county on the same day.

Rochester, New York, used an all-mail ballot for a referendum on the creation of a municipal electric agency in February 1982, and a bill was introduced in the New York legislature to enable counties to use mail ballot elections.

Each jurisdiction that has experimented with all-mail elections reports greatly increased voter participation and expanded public awareness of the issue on the ballot. Two of the three report considerable cost savings as well. The disadvantage most frequently cited is fear of vote fraud, but there has been no allegation that any fraud has been attempted in the elections cited above. The San Diego election survived a court test when its procedure was challenged as violating the "secret ballot" requirement of the law. The court, after reviewing the processing procedures—basically identical to those for absentee ballots—found that the system met the "secret ballot" test.

Richard G. Smolka is Professor of Government, The American University, and Editor of *Election Administration Reports.*

Independent Candidate Access to the Ballot. John Anderson, as an independent candidate for president in 1980, became the most recent such candidate to mount a legal attack on state laws establishing early filing deadlines for presidential candidates and/or laws containing ''sore loser'' provisions. Anderson, who had begun the year as a Republican seeking his own party's nomination, switched his candidacy to that of an independent for the general election. Several states refused to place his name on the general election ballot, either because he failed to meet the filing deadline, or because he had been a candidate on a partisan primary ballot in the same state for the same office of president (the ''sore-loser'' provision). Some of the early filing deadlines challenged by Anderson came prior to the primary elections in the states involved.

Federal courts struck down or otherwise rendered inoperative such state laws in Ohio, New Mexico, Kentucky, Maine and Maryland in 1980.[1] In general, the courts held that the state had no ''compelling interest'' in establishing a filing deadline many months prior to the presidential election. They also held that the ''sore loser'' provision did not apply because the presidential primary was not a primary that nominated a candidate, pointing out that the presidential nominations of major parties are made at conventions.

Assistance to Handicapped Voters. 1981 was the Year of the Handicapped and several states responded by passing laws making it easier for physically disabled, elderly or illiterate voters to cast ballots. The laws broke no new ground but continued the trend toward making the ballot more accessible to all persons regardless of age or physical condition.

Recent legislation in Ohio allows handicapped voters to be aided by two election officials of opposite political parties. New Mexico permits such voters to be accompanied by a person of their own choosing, and Washington permits an option of two election judges or a person chosen by the voter. A new Vermont law deleted the requirement that a physician's certificate of illness or physical disability be filed before a ballot can be delivered to a voter, and a Tennessee law dropped the requirement that a physician's statement be a sworn statement on behalf of a voter who wishes to be included on a permanent absentee voting register. The statement is still made under penalty of perjury.

Voter Registration. The drive for easing voter registration continued although the procedures introduced were regarded as minor modifications and ''voter outreach'' rather than major new legislation. Registration in schools became more common. Georgia law made principals or their designated representatives registrars. Kentucky law called for the distribution of voter registration forms to every public high school and vocational school, and by law, Oklahoma permitted visits to schools by registrars. The mail registration procedure initiated in 19 states during the seventies found no new advocates, in part because there was no significant increase in voter registration and voting in those states collectively, compared to states without mail registration procedures. One 1980 California experiment, however, took advantage of that state's mail registration law to have elementary schoolchildren serve, in effect, as deputy registrars. Fifth and sixth graders in Riverside and San Bernardino Counties received voter registration cards with which to solicit registrations. Teachers monitored the dissemination and return of the forms. The students were credited with 2,606 new voter registrations.[2]

Voting Procedures

Ballots. As the trend toward punch card voting and computer vote counting continued, states made efforts to assure the integrity of the election by controlling various aspects of the process.

A California law on punch card ballots provides that the secretary of state adopt regulations governing the manufacture, distribution and inventory control of punch cards and requires the periodic inspection of the manufacturing and storage facilities involving punch cards. Punch card manufacturers must also be approved by the state. Kansas requires that local jurisdictions cease using any voting system if the secretary of state rescinds approval until changes required by the secretary have been made. Kansas also changed its definition of "election forgery" to include marking of another person's ballot without consent or contrary to the direction of the voter.

Punch card voting booths have also produced changes in laws relating to the size and shape of voting booths. Wisconsin redefined its size specifications, and Kansas deleted specifications regarding dimension and construction requirements for voting booths.

A foldover punch card ballot also became the subject of regulation, if not legislation in Illinois. The ballot card twice the size of a standard punch card is designed to be used without a secrecy envelope. To ensure privacy, the ballot card is folded over. The Illinois State Board of Elections, however, requires that there be additional security precautions to ensure that the holes in the ballot card cannot be seen from the back side. It suggested, but did not mandate, a third fold, the use of a secrecy envelope, or a ballot carrier to screen the card from view while the voter carries it to the judge and while the judge deposits it in the ballot box.

Training of Election Officials. Training of poll workers and others who are responsible for the conduct of elections in the polling place has traditionally been the responsibility of local election officials. Several states, however, have mandated poll worker training by law and the number doing so is increasing. Vermont has introduced a requirement that the secretary of state conduct regional workshops for election officials and that the presiding officer of each town attend at least one workshop every two years. Louisiana now requires an examination to be given after applicants complete the courses of instruction for certification for commissioners-at-large, commissioners or alternate commissioners for the election. Administratively, several states have developed training films, manuals of instruction or other teaching devices to aid in the training of local officials as well as poll workers.

Campaign Finance Regulation

There was little change in campaign finance laws during the past two years. For the most part, controversy in this area of election law tended to focus on administrative rulings and court decisions in the various states. The Supreme Court has agreed to look at disclosure requirements as they relate to unpopular political groups. The Socialist Workers Party received a state exemption in Wisconsin and in Ohio, and the Communist Party in New York was also exempted from reporting requirements by a federal court. The Court will hear the Ohio case during its fall 1982 term.

The Court issued a decision widely interpreted as effectively striking down any ban on expenditures or contributions by individuals or committees, including corporations, to issue committees or campaigns. The Court ruled unconstitutional, by an 8-1 vote, a City of Berkeley, California, ordinance that set a $250 limit on contributions to a referendum committee.[3] It ruled that the law violated the right of association and, in turn, the individual and collective rights of expression. The Court said the ordinance could not be justified as a safeguard against corruption because it referred to issues rather than to candidates.

LEGISLATION, ELECTIONS AND CONSTITUTIONS

Federal Legislation

The Voting Rights Act. The temporary provisions of the Voting Rights Act, renewed in 1970 and again in 1975, were due to expire in August 1982, but it appeared certain at press time that Congress would make these sections into permanent law, allowing the covered jurisdictions to "bail out" if they met certain tests for a 10-year period.

Under the temporary provisions of the act, states and localities, mostly in the South, are required to "pre-clear" any changes in election law or procedures before they can become effective. The law allows the jurisdictions to submit the proposed changes either to the Justice Department or the U.S. District Court for the District of Columbia. Any law or procedure to which the Justice Department or the court objects because it may be racially discriminatory may not be implemented. The temporary provisions of the act also require certain jurisdictions with minority language populations to print election materials in the minority language as well as English. These "bilingual" provisions are due to expire in 1985 but are expected to be made permanent under 1982 amendments to the Voting Rights Act.

The Department of Justice objected to original redistricting plans of congressional and/or state legislative districts in several states in 1981 and 1982 including those of North Carolina, Texas and Virginia, thereby preventing those states from implementing their preferred districts until they had been changed to meet objections that certain districts were discriminatory.

In a major voting rights development, the Supreme Court, in *City of Mobile* v. *Bolden*,[4] ruled that Section 2 of the act, a permanent provision applying nationally, requires proof of "intent to discriminate" before an election system can be found in violation of the act. Under at-large voting in effect since 1911, voters of Mobile, Alabama, had failed to elect one black to the city commission. After lower courts had found Mobile in violation of the Voting Rights Act, the Supreme Court reversed that decision. Subsequently, similar suits based on the "effect" of laws passed prior to 1965 in Southern states were dropped.

In 1981, the House of Representatives included in its Voting Rights Act amendments a provision to reverse this decision by making it explicit that Congress intended to outlaw discriminatory "effects" or "results" nationally. The bill, with this provision included, was expected to pass the Senate before August 1982. Although supporters of the change argued that the purpose was to remedy discriminatory effects of laws and procedures in effect prior to 1965, opponents charged that the "effects" or "results" could be measured only by proportional representation by race and language minority group and that proportional representation would thus become a national standard for election results. Whether or not the provision becomes law, substantial litigation challenging state and local election laws and procedures, including redistricting, is expected.

Presidential Primaries. In 1980, there were 33 Democratic and 32 Republican presidential preference primaries in the states, plus contests in the District of Columbia and Puerto Rico. In Arkansas and New York, only Democrats, and in South Carolina, only Republicans, conducted a presidential preference primary. In addition, Republicans in New York and Mississippi selected delegates without offering a direct presidential preference option to the voters.

Although there have been several bills introduced in Congress to provide for a direct national primary election, regional primaries or a commission to study the presidential primary situation, prospects for agreement on any legislation before the end of 1982 appeared dim. More likely was an impact on state law by revisions in the national political party rules, especially within the Democratic Party, that might reduce the significance of primaries by providing for greater numbers of uncommitted delegates.

Reporting Results Before the Close of the Polls. Congress also considered possible legislation designed to curb the potential or actual impact of reporting or projecting presidential election returns before the close of the polls across the nation. Among the solutions considered were requiring a simultaneous close of the polls at either 11 p.m. EST or 10 p.m. EST, simultaneous election hours on a national holiday or on a Sunday and prohibitions against tallying the votes and/or reporting any votes until all the polls have been closed.

Although representatives of West Coast states asked for action, there was little support for such legislation from other regions of the country. Further, although the states could change their voting hours to minimize the impact on federal elections, or change the date of state and local elections to eliminate any such effect, there was no legislation of this type seriously considered in the states. Even among those who believed that early reporting had made an impact on voter turnout, the differences over solutions made it unlikely that federal legislation would be passed.

Notes

1. See *Anderson* v. *Celebrezze*, No. C-2-80-400 (S.D. Ohio July 18, 1980); *Anderson* v. *Hooper*, No. 80-432-M (D. N.M. July 8, 1980); *Anderson* v. *Mills*, Civ. No. 80-18 (E.D. Ky. August 14, 1980); *Anderson* v. *Morris*, Y-80-1632 (D. Md. August 6, 1980) aff'd, No. 80-1534 (4th Cir. Sept. 17, 1980); and *Anderson* v. *Quinn*, No. 80-0176 P (D. Maine August 11, 1980).
2. *Election Administration Reports*, July 2, 1980.
3. *Citizens Against Rent Control* v. *City of Berkeley*, No. 80-737, decided Dec. 14, 1981.
4. *City of Mobile* v. *Bolden*, 455 U.S. 55, decided April 22, 1980.

Selected References

Alexander, Herbert E. and Haggerty, Brian A. *The Federal Election Campaign Act: After a Decade of Reform.* Los Angeles: Citizens' Research Foundation, University of Southern California, 1981.
_____. *Financing Politics: Money, Elections and Political Reform*, 2d. ed. Washington, D.C.: Congressional Quarterly Press, 1980.
Butler, David; Penniman, Howard; and Ranney, Austin, eds. *Democracy at the Polls.* Washington, D.C.: American Enterprise Institute, 1981.
Jones, Ruth S. "State Public Financing and the State Parties," in Michael Malbin, ed., *Parties Interest Groups and Campaign Finance Laws.* Washington, D.C.: American Enterprise Institute, 1980.
Library of Congress. *Federal-State Election Law Updates: An Analysis of State and Federal Legislation.* Prepared for the Federal Election Commission by the American Law Division of the Congressional Research Service, Library of Congress, quarterly.
_____. *Election Case Law '80.* Prepared for the Federal Election Commission, 1980.
Smolka, Richard G. *Election Administration Reports*, a biweekly newsletter for election officials. Washington, D.C.

Table 1

CAMPAIGN FINANCE LAWS: FILING REQUIREMENTS
(As of August 1981)

State or other jurisdiction	Statements required from	Statements filed with	Time for filing
Alabama	All political committees.	Secy. of state: statewide & judicial offices. Judge of probate in county of residence: legislative office.	15 days after primary & 30 days after any other election.
Alaska	State candidates, groups & individuals.	Alaska Public Offices Commission, central office.	30 days & 1 week before & 10 days after election; annually on Dec. 31.
Arizona	Candidates & committees.	Secy. of state. Legislative candidates in primaries also file with clerk of board of supervisors.	10-15 days before & 20 days after primary; 10-15 days before & 30 days after general or special election; supplemental reports annually by April 1.
Arkansas	Candidates & persons acting on their behalf.	Secy. of state and county clerk in county of residence.	Contributions: 25 & 7 days before & 30 days after election. Expenditures: 30 days after election. Supplemental post-election reports of contributions & expenditures.
California	Candidates, committees & elected officers(a).	Secy. of state, registrar of Los Angeles & San Francisco & clerk of county of residence; legislative candidates also file with clerk of county with largest number of registered voters in district.	Semiannual: July & Jan. 31; periodic: March & Sept. 22 & 12 days before 1st Tues. after 1st Mon. in June & Nov.; additional: 40 & 12 days before & 65 days after election.
Colorado	Candidates' campaign treasurers(b) & political committees.	Secy. of state or appropriate county clerk & recorder.	11 days before & 30 days after election.
Connecticut	Candidates' & committees' campaign treasurers spending over $500 in single election.	Secy. of state.	Generally, 2nd Thurs. of Jan., April, July, Oct.; 7 days before & 45 days after election, plus supplemental reports of contributions & expenditures(c).
Delaware	Candidates & committee treasurers.	State election commissioner.	20 days before election, Dec. 31 of election year, Dec. 31 of post-election year & annually by Dec. 31 until fund closes.
Florida	Candidates' or committees' campaign treasurers.	Candidates: qualifying officer & supervisor of elections in candidate's county of residence. Committees for statewide & district offices: division of elections & supervisor of elections in county where election is held.	Pre-election: Unopposed candidates—1st Fri. of each calendar quarter from time treasurer is appointed through last day of qualifying for office, then Mon. preceding election. Opposed candidates—Fri. of each week preceding election. 45 days after election.
Georgia	Candidates, chairmen or treasurers of campaign committees for specified offices, certain other individuals or organizations.	Generally, secy. of state & copy to probate judge in candidate's county of residence.	45 & 15 days before & 10 days after primary & 15 days before general or special election. Dec. 31 of election year & annually on Dec. 31.
Hawaii	Candidates, parties, campaign treasurers & committees.	Campaign Spending Commission.	10 working days before each election; 20 days after primary & 30 days after general or special election. Supplemental reports in event of surplus or deficit over $250.
Idaho	Treasurers for candidates & political committees.	Secy. of state.	14-7 days before & 30 days after elections. Supplemental reports on 10th day of Jan., April, July & Oct. annually(c).
Illinois	Treasurers of political committees.	State Board of Elections.	Contributions: 15 days before election & 90 days after each election, other than a primary. Annual reports of contribution & expenditures: July 31.
Indiana	Treasurers of political committees(b).	State Election Board; legislative candidate's committees file duplicate with elections board of candidate's county of residence.	10-8 days before election or convention; 20 days after convention, if no preconvention report filed; annually by Jan. 15
Iowa	Treasurers of candidates' & political committees(b).	Finance Disclosure Commission; statutory & political committees file with commissioner, copy to commission.	Jan. 25 & May 25 annually.
Kansas	Candidates' campaign treasurers & persons expending more than $100.	Secy. of state.	6 days before & 10 days after primary & 6 days before general election & Dec. 10 annually.
Kentucky	Campaign treasurers of candidates & committees. State & county executive committees.	Kentucky Registry of Election Finance with duplicates to clerk of county where candidate resides. Campaign committees file with appropriate central campaign committees.	32 & 12 days before election & 30 days after an election.
Louisiana	Candidates spending or receiving more than $5,000; political committees & others spending or receiving $500 or more.	Supervisory Committee.	Political committees: 180, 90, 30 & 10 days before primary; 10 & 40 days before general election; July 10 if deficit remains; Jan. 15 annually.

96

CAMPAIGN FINANCE LAWS: FILING REQUIREMENTS—Continued

State or other jurisdiction	Statements required from	Statements filed with	Time for filing
Maine	Candidates & treasurers of candidates and political committees.	Commission of Governmental Ethics and Election Practices.	7 days before & 42 days after election; supplemental reports every 90 days; gubernatorial candidates also file Jan. 15 & 42 days before election. Disposition of surplus or deficit in excess of $50 on 1st day of each quarter of fiscal year.
Maryland	Candidates & their treasurers; treasurers of political committees.	Board at which candidates filed certificate of candidacy. Central committees & continuing political committees file with State Administrative Board of Election Law.	2nd Fri. before election & 3rd Tues. after election or before taking office, whichever occurs first. Surplus or deficit: 7th Tues. after election & 6 months & then annually until eliminated.
Massachusetts	Candidates & treasurers of political committees.	Director of campaign & political finance.	8 days before election & Jan. 10 of year after general election.
Michigan	All political committees.	Secy. of state.	11 days before & 30 days after election; committees other than independent committees by Jan. 31.
Minnesota	Candidates, political committees, secretaries, treasurers & individuals expending over $100 (b).	State Ethics Commission. Legislative candidates file copies with auditor of each county in district.	10 days before election & Jan. 31 annually.
Mississippi	Candidates & their supporting political committees.	Secy. of state for statewide candidates; appropriate circuit clerk of legislative office.	Contributions: 5th day of each month of candidacy & Sat. before election. Expenditures: candidates report within 60 days after election; committees, within 30 days.
Missouri	Candidates, committees(b).	Secy. of state.	40 & 7 days before & 30 days after election.
Montana	Candidates & political committees.	Commissioner of campaign finance and practices & county clerk or recorder.	Statewide office: March 10 & Sept. 10 in election year. 5 & 15 days before & 20 days after election; supplemental reports March 10 & Sept. 10(c). Legislative office: 10 days before & 20 days after election(d).
Nebraska	Committees.	Nebraska Accountability and Disclosure Commission & election commissioner or clerk of candidate's county of residence.	30 & 10 days before & 40 days after election(e).
Nevada	Candidates.	Officer with whom candidate filed declaration of candidacy.	15 days after primary (30 if candidate loses) & 15 days before & 30 days after general election.
New Hampshire	Candidates, state committee & other political committees expending over $500.	Secy. of state.	Wed. 3 weeks before & immediately before election; 2nd Fri. after election.
New Jersey	Candidates, political information organizations, political committees(a).	Election Law Enforcement Commission.	25 & 7 days before & 15 days after election; March 1 annually. Supplemental reports filed every 60 days until no balance remains.
New Mexico	Candidates & treasurers of political committees spending more than $500.	Secy. of state.	10 days before & 30 days after election; 6 & 12 months after if balance remains.
New York	Candidates & treasurers of political committees expending or receiving more than $1,000 in a filing period.	State Board of Elections & other places required by the board.	Primary election reports filed Aug. 10 & 31 & Oct. 7; general election reports filed Oct. 2 & 23 & Nov. 30. Additional statements as required by State Board of Elections until fund balances(d).
North Carolina	Treasurers for candidates & political committees.	State Board of Elections for statewide & multicounty district offices. Others: county board of elections.	10 days before & after election (losing candidates in primary file 45 days after election). Supplemental reports due Jan.7 after general election & annually following years in which contributions are received or expenditures made.
North Dakota	Candidates & political parties receiving more than $100 in contributions.	Secy. of state. Legislative candidates file with county auditor.	30 days before & 15 days after election & 30 days after close of calendar year.
Ohio	Candidates, committees, political parties.	Secy. of state. Legislative offices file with Board of Elections for county with largest population.	12 days before(f) & 45 days after election & last business day of Nov. annually.
Oklahoma	Candidates & committees.	Office at which candidate declared candidacy.	10 days before election & 40 days after general election. Supplemental reports within 6 months & 10 days after general election(c).

CAMPAIGN FINANCE LAWS: FILING REQUIREMENTS—Concluded

State or other jurisdiction	Statements required from	Statements filed with	Time for filing
Oregon	Candidates & treasurers of political committees(g).	Secy. of state.	30-31 & 12-7 days before & 30 days after election. Supplemental reports 10 days after close of every other calendar quarter(c).
Pennsylvania	Treasurers & committees receiving or expending over $250.	Secy. of the commonwealth.	45 & 10 days before & 30 days after election.
Rhode Island	Candidates spending over $5,000 & political committees.	Secy. of state.	28 days before & after election. Party committees also file by March 1 annually.
South Carolina	Candidates & committees.	State Ethics Commission, except Senate or House Ethics Committee for legislative office.	30 days after election & 10 days after end of each calendar quarter in which funds are received or expended.
South Dakota	Candidates & committees.	Secy. of state. Legislative office: auditor of candidate's resident county.	7 days before election & 30 days after end of year(h).
Tennessee	Candidates & political campaign committees.	State librarian.	7 days before & 48 days after election.
Texas	Candidates & committees.	Secy. of state.	30-40 & 7 days before & 30 days after election; annually on Jan. 15(c).
Utah	Campaign committee for gov., secy. of state & atty. gen. & party committees	State auditor.	10th day of June, July, Aug., Sept., Oct. & Dec. of election year & 5th day preceding election.
Vermont	Candidates & political committees.	Secy. of state: state office & political committees. Legislative office: officers with whom nomination papers filed.	State office & political committees: 40 & 10 days after election. Legislative office: within 10 days after election.
Virginia	Treasurers of candidates, political party committees receiving or expending more than $100 in an election & others not reporting to candidate, treasurer or party committee.	State Board of Elections & election board where candidate resides.	8 days before & 30 days after election. Statewide candidates also report 30 days before election.
Washington	Candidates & political committees.	Public Disclosure Commission & county auditor in county of candidate's residence. Continuing political committees: commission & auditor in county of treasurer's residence.	Initial report at time of appointment of treasurer; 5 & 19 days before election; 10 days after primary & 20 days after general election; 10th day of each month in which no other report filed.
West Virginia	Candidates, their financial agents; persons & treasurers of associations supporting or opposing any candidate.	Secy. of state for multicounty office. Clerk of county commission: single-county office.	15 days after last Sat. in March before primary; 5-10 days before & 30 days after election.
Wisconsin	Candidates, committees, groups, others receiving or expending over $25.	State Elections Board. Legislative candidates also file duplicate with county clerk of counties in district.	8-14 days before election; continuing reports by committees & individuals, Jan. 1-31 & July 1-10 annually.
Wyoming	Candidates & their campaign committees & political action committees.	Secy. of state. Legislative candidates also file with county clerk.	10 days after election. Committees: 7 days after election. Committees formed after election report July 1 & Dec. 31 of odd-numbered years until all debts are paid.
Dist. of Col.	Candidates & political committee treasurers.	Director of campaign finance & appropriate "principal campaign committee."	Each year: Jan. 31. Election years: 10th day of March, June, Aug., Oct. & Dec. & 8 days before election. Nonelection years: July 31(i).

Source: Adapted from American Law Division, Congressional Research Service, Library of Congress, unpublished data.

Note: This table deals only with filing requirements for statewide and legislative offices in the most general terms. For detailed legal requirements or requirements for county and local offices, actual state statutes should be consulted.

(a) Candidates receiving or expending less than specified amount are not required to file certain statements.

(b) With certain exceptions.

(c) If necessary.

(d) Report within 24 hours $500 contribution received after pre-election report. New York: $1,000.

(e) Report late contributions within five days of receipt.

(f) Not required of candidate or committee spending or receiving less than $1,000 by 20 days before election or where person has become candidate less than 20 days before election.

(g) Special provisions for candidates who neither receive nor expend more than $500.

(h) Report contributions over $500 received within 9 days of election within 48 hours.

(i) Report contributions of $200 or more received after closing date within 24 hours.

Table 2

CAMPAIGN FINANCE LAWS: LIMITATIONS ON CONTRIBUTIONS
(As of August 1, 1981)

State or other jurisdiction	Corporate	Labor union	Individual	Government employee	Anonymous or in name of another
Alabama	Prohibited	...	...	Prohibited.	...
Alaska	Same as individual.	Same as individual.	"Persons" limited to $1,000 a year for each elective office.	Political assessment of, prohibited.	Prohibited.
Arizona	Prohibited.	Prohibited.	...	Prohibited.	...
Arkansas	Same as individuals.	Same as individuals.	Limited to $1,500 per candidate per election.	Political assessment of, prohibited. Employee may not solicit from other employees of his agency.	Anonymous: limited to $50 per year. In name of another: prohibited.
California	...	...	...	Solicitation by local agency employee or officer of another employee or officer, prohibited.	Must be in name of true contributor. Anonymous contributions under $100 permitted.
Colorado	...	...	...	Political assessments prohibited.	Prohibited. Anonymous contributions over $15 prohibited.
Connecticut	Prohibited to candidates & political parties. Permitted to corporation's political committee for administrative purposes or solicitation of contributions. Contributions for ballot question campaigns.	Must first organize a political committee. Limitations for such committees are the same as for individuals except no limits on org. pol. cmte. contributions to town, city & borough office candidates. Aggregate contributions to candidates (not including town, city & borough office candidates)—$50,000.	To candidates (P & G separately)—gov., $2,500; lt. gov., secy of state, treas., comptroller, atty. gen., $1,500; state senator or probate judge, $500; state rep., $250. Aggregate amounts to above may not exceed $15,000 in any single election. (a)		
Delaware	Same as individuals.	Same as individuals.	Per candidate: $1,000 in statewide elections; $500 in all other elections.	...	Prohibited.
Florida	Same as individuals.	Same as individuals.	Candidate for statewide office, $3,000; legislative office, $1,000; to political cmte., $1,000. (b)	Political assessment of, prohibited. No "contribution" of services during working hours.	In name of another, prohibited.
Georgia	Prohibited from agents of public utility corporations.	...	...	No state employee may coerce another into contributing.	Prohibited.
Hawaii	Same as individuals.	Same as individuals.	Limited to $2,000 aggregate in any primary, special primary, special or general election. (b)	Solicitation of, prohibited. Contributions to other employees prohibited.	Anonymous prohibited, with certain exceptions. Made in a false name, prohibited.
Idaho	Same as individuals.	Same as individuals.	Contributions over $50 must be accompanied by statement listing person's name and address.	Political assessments prohibited.	Prohibited.
Illinois	...	...	...	Receiving or making contributions during work hours prohibited.	Prohibited.
Indiana	Limited to $300 aggregate, statewide offices; plus $3,000 aggregate, state party central cmtes.; plus $1,000 aggregate, nonstatewide offices; plus $1,000 aggregate, all other party cmtes.	Same as corporations.	...	Employees may not solicit or receive contributions; political assessments prohibited.	Prohibited, in name of another.

99

CAMPAIGN FINANCE LAWS: LIMITATIONS ON CONTRIBUTIONS—Continued

State or other jurisdiction	Corporate	Labor union	Individual	Government employee	Anonymous or in name of another
Iowa	Generally prohibited, but may establish political action cmtes.	...	...	Receiving contributions during work hours prohibited.	Prohibited.
Kansas	Prohibited from certain corporations & their majority stockholders.	...	To candidates for gov. & lt. gov. or any statewide office: P-$2,500, G-$2,500; to any legislative or other specified candidate: P-$500, G-$500.	Political assessments prohibited.	Anonymous contributions of more than $10 prohibited. Contributions in the name of another prohibited.
Kentucky	Prohibited.	...	Limited to $3,000 per candidate per election.	Political assessments prohibited.	Anonymous: more than $50 prohibited. In name of another, prohibited.
Louisiana	Regulated—authorization by board of directors required.	Same as corporations.	...	Contributions may not be solicited.	Anonymous generally prohibited. Prohibited in name of another.
Maine	Limited to $5,000 per candidate in any election.	Limited to $5,000 per candidate in any election by associations.	Limited to $1,000 per candidate; $25,000 overall in any calendar year.	State classified service officers & employees may not coerce or advise other state officers or employees to make political contributions.	...
Maryland	Same as individuals.	Same as individuals.	Contributions limited to $1,000 per candidate, $2,500 overall, including ballot question expenditures, in any primary or general election.	Cannot be forced to contribute.	Prohibited.
Massachusetts	Prohibited.	...	Limited to $1,000 per candidate, committee, yearly. (b) Minors limited to $25 a year.	Prohibited.	Prohibited.
Michigan	Generally prohibited. Segregated funds may be established so long as contributions to fund are voluntary.	Same as individuals.	Limited to $1,700, state elective offices; $450, state sen.; $250, state rep. (b)	Political assessments prohibited.	Anonymous prohibited, except for certain transactions under $20. In name of another prohibited.
Minnesota	Prohibited. Specified activities permitted.	Regulated.	...	May not solicit or receive funds during office hours; no political assessments.	Anonymous limited to $20. In name of another, prohibited.
Mississippi	$1,000 limit.	...	...	No political assessments. Highway patrolmen: no contributions.	...
Missouri	Permitted if authorized by board of directors.	Permitted if authorized by majority of members present at meeting.	...	Solicitations of employees prohibited.	Up to $10.
Montana	Prohibited. Increases in salaries paid by corporations, with intention that increases be used by employees or officers as contributions to candidates, prohibited.	...	Aggregate individual limits: gov. & lt. gov. jointly: $1,500. State-wide offices: $750. Public service commission: $400. District court judge: $400. Senate: $400. Any other public office: $250.	Solicitation by public employees of contributions while on the job or at place of employment & coercion of contributions from public employees, prohibited.	...
Nebraska	Contributions made from separate segregated political funds established by corporations, labor organizations & industry, trade & professional associations must be limited to money and items of ascertainable value obtained from voluntary contributions.	Same as corporations.	...	...	Prohibited.

State				
Nevada	...	...	Employees may not solicit from other employees.	...
New Hampshire	Prohibited.	...	...	Prohibited.
New Jersey	Prohibited from certain corporations & their majority stockholders.	Limited to $800 for gubernatorial candidates in general election.	Prohibited.	Prohibited.
New Mexico	...	...	...	Acceptable, but if in excess of $50 must be reported as to date and amount.
New York	Non-political corporations limited to $5,000 in contributions per calendar year. No public utility may use revenues to make political contributions.	Limited: in statewide offices & party positions total number of voters in party or state x $0.0005. Other elections—total number of voters in party or in district x $0.05. For state senator: above amount or $4,000. For member of assembly: above amount or $2,500. Maximum permissible contribution shall not exceed $50,000 or be less than $1,000.	Voluntary specifically permitted, except police officers may not contribute to or solicit contributions for a "political fund." Political assessments prohibited.	...
North Carolina	Prohibited.	Limited to $4,000.	Political assessments prohibited.	Prohibited.
North Dakota	Prohibited.	Prohibitions regarding solicitations for separate segregated funds.	...	In name of another, prohibited.
Ohio	Prohibited. Employees may direct employers to deduct specified amounts from wages as political contributions.	...	Voluntary contributions specifically permitted. Employees may not solicit or receive contributions.	...
Oklahoma	Prohibited.	Limited to: $5,000 to political party of organization. $5,000 to candidate for state office.	Employees may not solicit or receive contributions.	In name of another, prohibited.
Oregon	Prohibited from certain corporations.	...	Political assessments prohibited; solicitations by employees during work hours prohibited.	In name of another, prohibited.
Pennsylvania	Prohibited from corporations, national or state banks.	Prohibited from "unincorporated associations."	Solicitations of, or by, employees prohibited. Political assessments of employees prohibited.	Prohibited.
Rhode Island	...	...	Solicitation of, or by, employees prohibited.	Prohibited.
South Carolina	...	...	...	...
South Dakota	Prohibited.	$1,000/yr. to statewide offices. $250/yr. to legislative or county office. $3,000/yr. to a political party.	No political assessments.	...

CAMPAIGN FINANCE LAWS: LIMITATIONS ON CONTRIBUTIONS—Concluded

State or other jurisdiction	Corporate	Labor union	Individual	Government employee	Anonymous or in name of another
Tennessee	Prohibited.	. . .	. . .	Political assessments prohibited.	. . .
Texas	Prohibited. Solicitation of contributions for separate segregated political funds permitted. Corporations and labor organizations may make contributions or expenditures for the purpose of aiding or defeating a measure.	Same as corporations.	. . .	Contributions to state office holders and members of the legislature are prohibited.	. . .
Utah	. . .	. . .	. . .	Political assessments prohibited; employees may not solicit during work hours.	. . .
Vermont	. . .	. . .	Candidates for state office & for rep. & sen. in general assembly may not accept contributions totaling more than $1,000 from a single source (except contributions from political cmtes). Political cmtes. may not accept contributions over $1,000 from a single source.	Employees may not solicit.	. . .
Virginia	. . .	. . .	. . .	. . .	. . .
Washington	. . .	. . .	. . .	Political assessments prohibited; no solicitations on state property.	Prohibited.
West Virginia	Prohibited	. . .	Limited to $1,000.	Solicitations of, prohibited. Voluntary contributions by, permitted.	. . .
Wisconsin	Corporations & cooperative associations may not contribute; however, they may establish & administer separate segregated funds made up of individual contributions so long as not more than $500 is spent on soliciting such contributions.	. . .	Aggregate yearly limit: $10,000. Limits to candidates for gov., lt. gov., secy. of state, treas., atty. gen., supreme ct. justice, supt. of public instruction: $10,000; state sen.: $1,000; state rep.: $500; other: greater of $250 or one cent x number of inhabitants of jurisdiction or district, but not more than $3,000.	Solicitation by or from employees on government time prohibited.	Prohibited.
Wyoming	Prohibited.	Prohibited.	Natural persons limited to $1,000 to any candidate ($25,000 in total political contributions) during general election year & preceding year(b).	. . .	. . .
Dist. of Col.	Same as individuals.	Same as individuals.	P & G combined: $2,000, mayor; $1,500, chairman of council; varies, other offices.	"Hatch Act" applicable.	Prohibited.

Source: American Law Division, Congressional Research Service, Library of Congress, unpublished data.
Key: P—Primary election; G—General election.
Note: For detailed legal requirements, actual state statutes should be consulted.

(a) Individual contribution to political committees also limited. Hawaii—limited to $50,000.
(b) Candidate's own contribution to campaign fund unlimited. Michigan—limited to $25,000.

Table 3
PUBLIC FUNDING OF STATE ELECTIONS
(As of August 1981)

| State | Source of funds | | | Funds distributed to | | For use in | | Acceptance of public funds limits total ex-penditures |
	Tax check-off	Tax add-on	Other	Candidates for	Parties	General election	Primary election	
Hawaii	★	...	(a)	Statewide offices and legislature.	...	★	★	★(b)
Idaho	★	...	...	...	★	★	...	...
Iowa	★	...	...	...	★	★	...	...
Kentucky	★	...	...	...	★	★	...	...
Maine	...	★	...	———————— No restrictions ————————				
Maryland	———————— Law enacted but never implemented ————————							
Massachusetts	...	★	...	Statewide offices.	...	★	★	...
Michigan	★	...	...	Governor.	...	★	★	★(c)
Minnesota	★	...	(d)	Statewide offices and legislature.	...	★	★	★(b)
Montana	...	★	...	Governor and supreme court justice.	...	★	...	...
New Jersey	★	...	(e)	Governor.	...	★	★	★(f)
North Carolina	★	...	...	...	★	★	...	...
Oklahoma(g)	★	...	...	...	★	★	...	...
Rhode Island	★	...	...	...	★	(h)	(h)	...
Utah	★	...	...	...	★	★	★	...
Wisconsin	★	...	...	Statewide offices, supreme court and legislature.	...	★	(i)	★(b)

(a) Tax deductions offered to contributors of $100 or less per candidate. Total deduction allowed: $500.
(b) Amount varies depending on office.
(c) $100,000 per election; additional $200,000 per election for fund raising.
(d) Tax credit.
(e) General appropriations.
(f) General election: $.70 per voter in last presidential election. Primary election: $.35 per voter in last presidential election.
(g) Statute is in litigation.
(h) To be used for administrative expenses only.
(i) Certain non-partisan candidates who run in the spring elections are also eligible for public funds.

Table 4
USE OF VOTING DEVICES

State or other jurisdiction	Statewide use required	Used in majority of voting areas	Used in some voting areas	Type of equipment used* Mechanical	Punch card	Optical scanning	Straight party vote†
Alabama	...	★	...	H	...	...	★
Alaska	...	...	★	...	H	...	...
Arizona	...	★	...	...	H	...	...
Arkansas	...	...	★	L	L	L	...
California	...	★	...	L	H	L	...
Colorado	...	★	...	H	H	H	...
Connecticut	★	...	...	H	...	...	★
Delaware	★	...	...	H	...	...	...
Florida	...	★	...	H	L	...	...
Georgia	...	...	★	L	L	...	★(a)
Hawaii	★	...	...	...	H	...	...
Idaho	...	...	★	L	H	...	...
Illinois	...	★	★	L	H	L	★
Indiana	...	★	...	H	L	...	★
Iowa	...	★	...	H	...	...	★
Kansas	...	...	★	L	...	...	...
Kentucky	★	...	...	H	...	...	★
Louisiana	★	...	...	H	...	...	(b)
Maine	...	...	★	L	L	...	...
Maryland	★	...	...	H	L	...	...
Massachusetts	...	...	★	H	L	L	...
Michigan	...	★	...	H	L	...	★
Minnesota	...	...	★	H	L	...	...
Mississippi	...	...	★	L	L	...	...
Missouri	...	...	★	L	L	L	★
Montana	...	...	★	L	L	...	...
Nebraska	...	...	★	L	L	H	...
Nevada	...	★	...	...	H	...	...
New Hampshire	...	...	★	H	L	...	★
New Jersey	...	★	...	H	L	L	...
New Mexico	★	...	...	H	...	...	★
New York	★(c)	★	...	H	...	...	...
North Carolina	...	...	★	H	L	L	★(d)
North Dakota	...	...	★	H	H	...	...
Ohio	...	...	★	H	H	...	...
Oklahoma	...	...	★	H	...	H	★(e)
Oregon	...	★	...	...	H	...	...
Pennsylvania	...	★	...	H	L	...	★
Rhode Island	★	...	...	H	...	...	★
South Carolina	...	...	★	L	L	...	★
South Dakota	...	...	★	L	L	...	★
Tennessee	...	★	...	H	L	...	...
Texas	...	★	...	H	H	L	★
Utah	...	...	★	...	L	L	★
Vermont	...	...	★	H	L	...	...
Virginia	...	★(f)	...	H	...	...	...
Washington	...	★	...	L	H	...	...
West Virginia	...	...	★	L	L	...	★
Wisconsin	...	★(g)	...	H	L	...	★
Wyoming	...	★	...	H	L	...	...
Dist. of Col.	★	...	...	...	H	...	...
Guam	★	...	...	...	...	H	...

*Mechanical, punch-card or optical scanning vote-counting devices are not used in American Samoa, Puerto Rico and the Virgin Islands.
H—indicates high frequency of use; L—indicates low frequency of use.
† The ballot allows the citizen to vote for all candidates of the same party by marking one box or lever.
(a) Except in presidential elections where candidates for the office of presidential electors are on a separate straight party ticket.
(b) Open elections preclude straight party voting.

(c) Mandatory in primaries, with certain exceptions.
(d) In primary only, crossover in general election.
(e) Straight party ticket can only be cast for each level of government.
(f) All precincts having 750 or more registered voters must have voting machines.
(g) Mandatory for municipalities of 10,000 or more population; optional for smaller communities.

Table 5

QUALIFICATIONS FOR VOTING

State or other jurisdiction	Minimum residence requirement before election (days)*	Closing date for registration before general election (days)	Cancellation of registration for failure to vote (years)	Registration covers all elections	Mail registration
Alabama	Close of registration	10	. . .	★	. . .
Alaska	30	30	2	★	★
Arizona	50	50	Last general election	★	. . .
Arkansas	None	20	4	★	. . .
California	None	29	. . .	★	★
Colorado	32	32	Last general election	★	. . .
Connecticut.........	Resident	21	. . .	★	. . .
Delaware	Resident	3rd Sat. in Oct.	2 consecutive elections	★	★
Florida	None	30	2	★	. . .
Georgia	Resident	30	3	(a)	. . .
Hawaii	Resident	30	2	★	. . .
Idaho	Resident	17/10(b)	4	(a)	. . .
Illinois	30	28	4	★	. . .
Indiana..............	30 (in precinct)	29	2	★	. . .
Iowa	None	10	4	★	★
Kansas	Close of registration	20	2 consec. state gen. elections	★	★
Kentucky	30	30	4	★	★
Louisiana...........	Resident	30	4	★	. . .
Maine	Resident	Election day	. . .	★	. . .
Maryland	Resident	29	5	(a)	★
Massachusetts.......	Close of registration	28	. . .	★	. . .
Michigan	30	30	6	★	★
Minnesota	20	20(c)	4	(d)	★
Mississippi	30	30	. . .	★	. . .
Missouri............	None	4th Wed. before election	. . .	★	★
Montana	30	30	(e)	★	★
Nebraska	None	2nd Fri. before election	. . .	★	. . .
Nevada.............	30	5th Sat. before election	General election	★	. . .
New Hampshire	10	10	. . .	★	. . .
New Jersey	30	29	4	★	★
New Mexico	Resident	42	2	★	. . .
New York	30	(f)	4	★	★
North Carolina	30	21	8	★	. . .
North Dakota	30	No registration	. . .	. . .	. . .
Ohio	30	30	4	★	★
Oklahoma	Resident	10	8	★	. . .
Oregon	20	8 p.m. election day	. . .	★	★
Pennsylvania........	30	30	2	★	★
Rhode Island........	30	30	5	★	. . .
South Carolina	Resident	30	2	★	. . .
South Dakota	None	15	4	★	. . .
Tennessee	20	29	4, excluding yr. of registration	★	★
Texas	30	30	. . .	★	★
Utah	30	10	. . .	★	★
Vermont	None	17	. . .	★	. . .
Virginia	Resident	31	4	★	. . .
Washington	30	30	2	★	. . .
West Virginia	29	30	2 elections	★(g)	. . .
Wisconsin	10	2nd Wed. before elec. (c)	. . .	★	★
Wyoming............	Resident	30	General election	★	. . .
Dist. of Col.	None	30	4	★	★
American Samoa	(h)	30	2 consec. general elections	★	N.A.
Guam	None	30	Last general election	★	N.A.
Puerto Rico	50	50	Last general election	★	. . .

*When law specifies no residence requirement, "None" is listed; when law states only that the voter must be a bona fide resident, "Resident" is listed.

N.A.—Not available.

(a) Registration covers national and state elections; municipal registration is separate.
(b) With precinct registrar 17 days before; with county clerk 10 days.
(c) Registration at polls with identification.

(d) All except school elections.
(e) Challenge of qualifications; failure to vote in presidential elections.
(f) Varies according to date set for local registration day.
(g) In order for permanent registration to be applicable for municipal registration, municipality must pass an ordinance implementing the state law and integrating the city registration with the state law.
(h) Two years in territory; 12 months in election district next preceding the election.

Table 6
POLLING HOURS: GENERAL ELECTIONS

State or other jurisdiction	Polls open	Polls close	Notes on hours
Alabama	8 a.m.	6 p.m.	Opening and closing times not mandatory: polls must be open at least 10 consecutive hours.
Alaska	8 a.m.	8 p.m.	....
Arizona	6 a.m.	7 p.m.	....
Arkansas	8 a.m.	7:30 p.m.	Polls may open at 7 a.m.
California	7 a.m.	8 p.m.	Charter cities may set different hours for municipal elections.
Colorado	7 a.m.	7 p.m.	....
Connecticut	6 a.m.	8 p.m.	....
Delaware	7 a.m.	8 p.m.	....
Florida	7 a.m.	7 p.m.	....
Georgia	7 a.m.	7 p.m.	In cities of 300,000 or more, polls remain open until 8 p.m.
Hawaii	7 a.m.	6 p.m.	Voters standing in line at 6 p.m. may vote. No one may join line after 6 p.m.
Idaho	8 a.m.	8 p.m.	Polls close 8 p.m. or earlier when all registered electors of the precinct have appeared and voted. County clerk has option of opening polls at 7 a.m.
Illinois	6 a.m.	7 p.m.	....
Indiana	6 a.m.	6 p.m.	....
Iowa	7 a.m.	9 p.m.	....
Kansas	7 a.m.	7 p.m.	Hours may be changed by election authorities, but polls must be kept open at least 12 consecutive hours between 6 a.m. and 8 p.m.
Kentucky	6 a.m.	6 p.m.	Persons in line may vote until 7 p.m.
Louisiana	6 a.m.	8 p.m.	Persons in line at 8 p.m. are entitled to vote.
Maine	Between 6 a.m. & 10 a.m.	Between 8 p.m. & 9 p.m.	Only municipalities using voting machines have the option of staying open until 9 p.m.
Maryland	7 a.m.	8 p.m.	....
Massachusetts	May open as early as 5:45 a.m.; must be opened by 10 a.m.	8 p.m.	In cities and towns, the polls shall be kept open at least 10 hours.
Michigan	7 a.m.	8 p.m.	....
Minnesota	7 a.m.	8 p.m.	Municipalities of less than 1,000 may establish hours of 9 a.m. to 8 p.m.
Mississippi	7 a.m.	6 p.m.	....
Missouri	6 a.m.	7 p.m.	....
Montana	8 a.m. 12 p.m.	8 p.m. 8 p.m. or earlier when all registered in any precinct have voted.	In precincts of less than 100 registered voters.
Nebraska	7 a.m. 8 a.m.	7 p.m. 8 p.m.	Mountain Time Zone. Central Time Zone.
Nevada	7 a.m.	7 p.m.	....
New Hampshire	Varies	Varies	Cities: Polls open not less than 4 hours and may be opened not earlier than 6 a.m. nor later than 8 p.m. Small towns: In towns of less than 700 population the polls shall be open not less than 5 consecutive hours. On written request of 7 registered voters the polls shall be kept open until 6 p.m. In towns of less than 100 population, the polls shall close if all on the checklist have voted. Other towns: Polls shall open not later than 10 a.m. and close not earlier than 6 p.m. On written request of 10 registered voters the polls shall be kept open until 7 p.m.
New Jersey	7 a.m.	8 p.m.	....
New Mexico	8 a.m.	7 p.m.	....
New York	6 a.m.	9 p.m.	....
North Carolina	6:30 a.m.	7:30 p.m.	In voting precincts where voting machines are used, county board of elections may permit closing at 8:30 p.m.
North Dakota	Between 7 a.m. & 9 a.m.	Between 7 p.m. & 9 p.m.	....
Ohio	6:30 a.m.	7:30 p.m.	....
Oklahoma	7 a.m.	7 p.m.	....
Oregon	8 a.m.	8 p.m.	....
Pennsylvania	7 a.m.	8 p.m.	....
Rhode Island	Between 7 a.m. & 12 noon	9 p.m.	....

State or other jurisdiction	Polls open	Polls close	Notes on hours
South Carolina	8 a.m.	7 p.m.	Lancaster County is allowed to keep polls open until 8 p.m.
South Dakota	7 a.m. 8 a.m.	7 p.m. 8 p.m.	Mountain Time Zone. Central Time Zone.
Tennessee	Varies.	8 p.m. EST 7 p.m. CST	Polls must be open minimum of 10 and maximum of 13 continuous hours.
Texas	7 a.m.	7 p.m.	In counties of more than one million population the polls may be opened at 6 a.m.
Utah	7 a.m.	8 p.m.	....
Vermont	Between 6 a.m. & 10 a.m.	Not later than 7 p.m.	Polls must be open at least 9 consecutive hours during the day.
Virginia	6 a.m.	7 p.m.	....
Washington	7 a.m.	8 p.m.	....
West Virginia	6:30 a.m.	7:30 p.m.	....
Wisconsin	7 a.m. 9 a.m.	8 p.m. 8 p.m.	1st, 2nd and 3rd class cities. 4th class cities, villages and towns. Opening hours extendable by governing body to not earlier than 7 a.m.
Wyoming	8 a.m.	7 p.m.	....
Dist. of Col.	7 a.m.	8 p.m.	....
American Samoa	6 a.m.	6 p.m.	....
Guam	8 a.m.	8 p.m.	....
Puerto Rico	9 a.m.	3 p.m.	....

Table 7
OFFICERS WITH STATEWIDE JURISDICTION TO BE ELECTED: 1982 AND 1983*

State or other jurisdiction	Date of general elections in 1982 (a)	Governor	Lt. governor	Secretary of state	Attorney general	Treasurer	Auditor	Supreme court Judge or justice	Court of appeals Judge	Board of education members	Public utilities commissioners	Superintendent of public instruction	Other	State legis. Senate	State legis. House	U.S. Cong. Senate	U.S. Cong. House
Alabama	Nov. 2	★	★	★	★	★	★	2	3(b)	4	2		Commr. of ag. & industries	all	all	0	7
Alaska	Nov. 2	★	★											9/10	all	0	1
Arizona	Nov. 2	★		★	★	★		2	6			★	State mine inspec., 1 corporation commr.	all	all	1	5
Arkansas	Nov. 2	★	★	★	★	★	★	1					Commr. of state lands	all	all	0	4
California	Nov. 2	★	★	★	★	★		3				★	Controller, board of equalization	½	all	1	45
Colorado	Nov. 2	★	★	★	★	★				4			3 Univ. of Colorado regents	½(c)	all	0	6
Connecticut	Nov. 2	★	★	★	★	★							Comptroller	all	all	1	6
Delaware	Nov. 2				★	★								½	all	1	1
Florida	Nov. 2	★	★	★	★	★		4			2	★	Comptroller, commr. of agriculture	½	all	0	19
Georgia	Nov. 2	★	★	★	★	★		3		2	2	★	Comptroller gen., commrs. of ag. & labor	all	all	0	10
Hawaii	Nov. 2	★	★										4 Office of Hawaii affairs trustees	½(c)	all	1	2
Idaho	Nov. 2	★	★	★	★	★	★	1(d)				★	Comptroller	all	all	0	2
Illinois	Nov. 2	★	★	★	★	★								all	all	1	22
Indiana	Nov. 2			★	★	★	★			4				½	all	0	10
Iowa	Nov. 2	★	★	★	★	★	★						Secretary of ag.	½	all	0	6
Kansas	Nov. 2	★	★	★	★	★		1	3				Insurance commr.	0	all	0	5
Kentucky ...... (1983)	Nov. 8	★	★	★	★	★	★	1		4	1		Commr. of ag., 3 railroad commrs.			0	7
Louisiana ..... (1983)	Dec. 10	★	★	★	★	★	★	1		4			Commrs. of ag., insurance & elections			0	8
Maine	Nov. 2	★			★									all	all	1	2
Maryland	Nov. 2	★	★		★	★			1(e)				Comptroller	all	all	1	8
Massachusetts	Nov. 2	★	★	★	★	★	★			2			6 trustees of state universities	all	all	1	11
Michigan	Nov. 2	★	★	★	★		★	2		2				all	all	1	18
Minnesota	Nov. 2	★	★	★	★	★	★	2						all	all	1	8
Mississippi ... (1983)	Nov. 1	★	★	★	★	★	★	2			3		Commrs. of land, ag., insurance; 3 highway commrs.; supreme court clerk		all		5
Missouri	Nov. 2			★	★		★						Clerk of supreme court	½	all	1	9
Montana	Nov. 2			★	★	★		2			2		2 board of regents	½	all	1	2
Nebraska	Nov. 2	★	★	★	★	★	★	4		4	1		Controller, 2 university board of regents	½(c)	(f)	1	3
Nevada	Nov. 2	★	★	★	★	★	★	1		3				½	all	0	2
New Hampshire	Nov. 2	★											5 executive councilors	all	all	1	2
New Jersey .... (1983)	Nov. 8													all	all	1	14

108

Table (rotated 90° on page) — Elections to be held, by state:

State	Election date	Supreme court judges	Appellate court judges	Other state officials to be elected	State Senate	State House	U.S. Senate	U.S. House
New Mexico	Nov. 2	2	1	Commr. of public lands, 2 corporation commrs.	1/6	all	1	3
New York	Nov. 2		1	Comptroller	all	all	1	34
North Carolina	Nov. 2			...	all	all	0	11
North Dakota	Nov. 2		1	Commr. of labor	1/2(c)	all	1	1
Ohio	Nov. 2			...	1/2(c)	all	1	21
Oklahoma	Nov. 2	4(g)	2	2 corporation commrs., commr. of insurance, auditor & inspector	1/2	all	0	6
Oregon	Nov. 2	3	4	Commr. of labor	1/2	all	0	5
Pennsylvania	Nov. 2			...	1/2	all	1	23
Rhode Island	Nov. 2			...	all	all	1	2
South Carolina	Nov. 2			Comptroller, commr. of ag., adjutant general	0	all	0	6
South Dakota	Nov. 2		1	Commr. of schools and public lands	all	all	0	1
Tennessee	Nov. 2	6(h)	(i)	...	1/2(c)	all	1	9
Texas	Nov. 2	(i)	8	Commr. of ag., comptroller, commr. of general land office, 1 railroad commr.	all	all	1	27
Utah	Nov. 2	1		...	1/2	all	1	3
Vermont	Nov. 2		5	...	all	all	1	1
Virginia	(1983)			...	all	all	1	10
Washington	Nov. 2	3		...	1/2(c)	all	0	8
West Virginia	Nov. 2			...	1/2	all	1	4
Wisconsin	Apr. 6(i) / Nov. 2		4	...	1/2(c)	all		9
Wyoming	(1983) Apr. 5(j) / Nov. 2	1	1	...	1/2	all	1	1
Dist. of Col.	Nov. 2 (1983)	(k)		Advry. neighborhood comm.—single-district commrs.		(l)		1(m)
American Samoa	Nov. 2 / Nov. 8			...	0			1(m)
Guam	Nov. 2			...	all	(f)		1(m)
Puerto Rico	Nov. 2			...	(f)			0(m)

*In several states, some or all elected officials with statewide jurisdiction do not appear on the table, because due to their terms, no elections for their office occur in 1982 or 1983. Also, election dates and number of state legislators to be elected are subject to change because of reapportionment decisions.

(a) Elections in 1983 are indicated by 1983 before the date.
(b) One court of civil appeals and two courts of criminal appeals; all circuit judges.
(c) Approximately.
(d) The vote for supreme court justice is usually decided at the primary election.
(e) And one court of special appeals judge.
(f) Unicameral legislature.
(g) Three justices of supreme court, one court of criminal appeals judge.
(h) Presiding judge of court of criminal appeals, three justices of supreme court, and two judges of court of criminal appeals.
(i) Approximately one-third of the judges of court of civil appeals.
(j) Nonpartisan election.
(k) Mayor.
(l) Eight members of the Council of the District of Columbia, including chairman.
(m) Non-voting delegate to U.S. House of Representatives; Puerto Rico's delegate is called the Resident Commissioner.

Table 8
PRIMARY ELECTIONS FOR STATE OFFICERS*

State or other jurisdiction	Dates for 1982 primaries for officers with statewide jurisdiction(a)		Method of nominating candidates	Party affiliation for primary voting		Voters receive ballot of	
	1982 primary	Runoff primary		Recorded on registration form	Declare for party ballot	One party	All parties participating
Alabama	Sept. 7	Sept. 28	C,P(b)	...	★(c)	★	...
Alaska	Aug. 24	...	P	...	...	...	★(d)
Arizona	Sept. 7	...	P	★	...	★	...
Arkansas	May 25	June 8	C,P(b)	...	★(c)	★	...
California	June 8	...	P	★	...	★	...
Colorado	Sept. 14	...	X(e)	★	...	★	...
Connecticut	Sept. 7(f)	...	X	★	...	★	...
Delaware	Sept. 11	...	P	★	...	★	...
Florida	Sept. 7	Oct. 5	P	★	...	★	...
Georgia	Aug. 10	Aug. 31	C,P	...	★(g)	★	...
Hawaii	Sept. 18	...	P	...	...	...	★(h)
Idaho	May 25	...	P	...	...	...	★(h)
Illinois	March 16	...	C,P(i)	...	★(j)	★	...
Indiana	May 4	...	C,P(k)	...	★(j)	★	...
Iowa	June 8	...	X(l)	★(m)	...	★	...
Kansas	Aug. 3	...	C,P	...	★(n)	★	...
Kentucky	May 25	...	P	★	...	★	...
(1983)	May 24	...	P	★	...	★	...
Louisiana	Sept. 11	...	P	★	...	...	★(d)
(1983)	Oct. 29	...	P	★	...	...	★(d)
Maine	June 8	...	P	★	...	★	...
Maryland	Sept. 14	...	P	★	...	★	...
Massachusetts	Sept. 14	...	P	★(o)	...	★	...
Michigan	Aug. 3	...	P(p)	...	...	...	★(h)
Minnesota	Sept. 14	...	P	...	...	...	★(h)
Mississippi	June 1	June 22	P	...	★(c)	★	...
(1983)	June 7	June 28	P	...	★(c)	★	...
Missouri	Aug. 3	...	P	...	★(j)	★	...
Montana	June 8	...	P	...	...	...	★(h)
Nebraska	May 11	...	P	★	...	★	...
Nevada	Sept. 14	...	P	★	...	★	...
New Hampshire	Sept. 14	...	P	★(o)	...	★	...
New Jersey............	June 8	...	P	...	★(n)	★	...
(1983)	June 7	...	P	...	★(n)	★	...
New Mexico	June 1	...	C,P	★	...	★	...
New York	Sept. 14	...	CC,P	★	...	★	...
North Carolina	May 4	June 1	P	★	...	★	...
North Dakota	June 8	...	P	...	...	...	★(h)
Ohio	June 8	...	P	...	★(g)	★	...
Oklahoma	Aug. 24	Sept. 21	P	★	...	★	...
Oregon	May 18	...	P	★	...	★	...
Pennsylvania	May 18	...	P	★	...	★	...
Rhode Island	Sept. 14	...	P	...	★(j)	★	...
South Carolina	June 8	(q)	C,P(b)	...	★	★	...
South Dakota	June 1	...	C,P(l)	★	...	★	...
Tennessee	Aug. 5	...	P	...	★(j)	★	...
Texas	May 1	June 5	P	...	★(c)	★	...
Utah	Sept. 14	...	X(e)	...	...	...	★(h)
Vermont..............	Sept. 14	...	P	...	...	...	★(h)
Virginia	June 8	...	C,P(b)	...	★(c)	★	...
(1983)	June 14	...	C,P(b)	...	★(c)	★	...
Washington...........	Sept. 14	...	P	...	...	...	★(d)
West Virginia	June 1	...	P	★	...	★	...
Wisconsin	Sept. 14(r)	...	P	...	...	...	★(h)
Wyoming..............	Sept. 14	...	P	★(s)	...	★	...
Dist. of Col.	Sept. 14	...	P	★	...	★	...
American Samoa	(t)	...	...	...	...	...	...
Guam	Sept. 4	...	P	...	...	...	★(h)
Puerto Rico	(u)	(u)	C	...	★	...	...

*Subject to change depending on difficulties encountered with re-apportionment.

Key: C—Convention; P—Direct primary; C,P—Some candidates in convention, some in direct primary; CC,P—State central committees or direct primary; X—Combination of convention and direct primary.

(a) Primaries for statewide offices in 1983 have (1983) before the date. For a listing of candidates to be voted upon, see Table 6.

(b) The party officials may choose whether they wish to nominate candidates in convention or by primary elections. Usually major party candidates are elected by primary.

(c) Political party law prescribes individual party membership.

(d) Blanket primary—voting is permitted for candidates of more than one party.

(e) Pre-primary designation assemblies are held in Colorado, and pre-primary convention assemblies are held in Utah. If one candidate in Utah receives 70 percent of the delegate vote, he is certified the candidate and is not required to run in the primary.

(f) If candidate endorsed by party convention is challenged by one receiving at least 20 percent of delegate vote at convention.

(g) By written declaration. Ohio: party selection in primary is noted on registration slip at each election.

(h) Voter is restricted to candidates of one party only. Ballots of all parties are received by voter, and his party registration is private.

(i) Trustees of the University of Illinois are the only state officers nominated in convention.

(j) Declaration or request for ballot.

(k) Republican and Democratic parties must nominate candidates by primary in all cases except towns under 3,000 population. In those towns, candidates are nominated by convention.

(l) If for any office no candidate receives 35 percent of votes cast at the primary, a convention is held to select a candidate.

(m) Party affiliation may be changed at the primary, but if challenged, a voter must take an oath that the change is made in good faith. The new party designation is entered on the registration form.

(n) Party designation is made the first time a voter participates in a primary election by his selection of a "party ballot." This becomes permanent until changed at the election officer's office prior to another primary. Kansas: 20 days prior; New Jersey: 50 days prior.

(o) A voter who is a member of no party may declare to vote in a party's primary up to and including election day. By filling out a card after he votes, an elector may return to being a member of no party after the election.

(p) The governor is the only state officer nominated by primary election.

(q) First runoff held two weeks after primary; second runoff held two weeks after that, if necessary.

(r) For partisan election only. Non-partisan primary held February 16, election April 6.

(s) Party affiliation can be declared if uncommitted, or changed at the polls on primary election day.

(t) There are no primary elections or political parties in the election process. Candidates are nominated by petition of qualified voters.

(u) Primaries are not mandatory unless party regulations require them.

Table 9
VOTER TURNOUT FOR PRESIDENTIAL ELECTIONS: 1972, 1976 AND 1980
(In thousands)

State or or other jurisdiction	1980 Voting age population (a)	1980 Number registered (b)	1980 Number voting (b)	1976 Voting age population (a)	1976 Number registered	1976 Number voting	1972 Voting age population (a)	1972 Number registered	1972 Number voting
United States	160,491	103,615	93,067	150,041	105,837	81,556	140,068	92,702	77,899
Alabama	2,702	1,849	1,485	2,501	1,865	1,183	2,314	1,764	1,006
Alaska	257	167	143	231	207	124	197	149	95
Arizona	1,779	1,028	937	1,555	980	743	1,295	862	654
Arkansas	1,562	1,032	888	1,503	1,021	768	1,354	1,010	648
California	16,956	9,877	8,854	15,294	9,982	7,867	13,969	10,466	8,368
Colorado	2,050	1,376	1,257	1,773	1,349	1,082	1,586	1,220	954
Connecticut	2,321	1,658	1,539	2,211	1,669	1,382	2,089	1,648	1,384
Delaware	420	274	251	403	301	236	378	293	236
Florida	6,876	4,245	3,732	6,326	4,094	3,151	5,242	3,487	2,583
Georgia	3,629	2,321	1,896	3,375	2,302	1,467	3,098	2,043	1,173
Hawaii	657	373	337	600	363	291	536	338	270
Idaho	634	460	439	567	520	344	491	397	310
Illinois	8,046	5,783	5,270	7,718	6,252	4,719	7,532	6,215	4,723
Indiana	3,849	2,649	2,355	3,640	3,010	2,220	3,496	3,019	2,126
Iowa	2,093	1,576	1,410	2,010	1,407	1,279	1,936	(c)	1,226
Kansas	1,756	1,189	1,087	1,610	1,113	958	1,553	(c)	916
Kentucky	2,532	634	1,402	2,374	1,713	1,167	2,204	1,455	1,067
Louisiana	2,780	1,974	1,735	2,532	1,866	1,278	2,373	1,785	1,051
Maine	790	628	527	741	696	483	683	616	417
Maryland	3,039	1,994	1,759	2,863	1,950	1,440	2,690	1,816	1,354
Massachusetts	4,298	3,068	2,777	4,173	2,912	2,548	3,968	3,096	2,459
Michigan	6,557	4,735	4,163	6,268	5,202	3,654	5,868	4,763	3,490
Minnesota	2,957	2,444 (d)	2,140	2,721	2,566	1,950	2,546	(c)	1,742
Mississippi	1,650	1,325	1,100	1,544	(c)	769	1,435	N.A.	646
Missouri	3,569	2,662	2,375	3,348	2,553	1,954	3,228	(c)	1,853
Montana	560	410	374	518	455	329	469	387	318
Nebraska	1,138	796	703	1,080	841	608	1,030	712	577
Nevada..........	533	277	254	424	251	202	357	231	182
New Hampshire	657	475	437	574	478	340	520	450	334
New Jersey	5,398	3,557	3,173	5,154	3,770	3,014	4,997	3,673	2,997
New Mexico	869	571	501	771	527	418	671	505	386
New York	12,900	7,524	6,931	12,910	8,199	6,534	12,663	9,207	7,323
North Carolina	4,055	2,368	2,040	3,847	2,554	1,679	3,496	2,358	1,519
North Dakota	469	(c)	329	432	(c)	297	413	(c)	281
Ohio	7,701	5,070	4,631	7,459	4,693	4,112	7,123	4,628	4,095
Oklahoma	2,131	1,374	1,234	1,937	1,401	1,092	1,809	1,247	1,030
Oregon	1,909	1,344	1,223	1,653	1,420	1,030	1,503	1,198	928
Pennsylvania......	8,652	5,327	4,717	8,441	5,750	4,621	8,193	5,872	4,592
Rhode Island.....	687	494	438	648	545	411	671	532	416
South Carolina	2,069	1,157	1,021	1,933	1,113	803	1,748	1,034	674
South Dakota	485	383	353	469	426	301	447	392	307
Tennessee	3,205	2,123	1,789	2,958	1,912	1,476	2,758	1,990	1,201
Texas	9,648	5,630	4,763	8,503	6,319	4,072	7,655	5,500 (e)	3,471
Utah	901	681	641	783	705	541	699	621	478
Vermont	359	261	217	329	284	188	306	273	187
Virginia..........	3,817	2,261	2,006	3,528	2,124	1,697	3,202	2,107	1,457
Washington.......	2,978	1,885	1,728	2,536	2,065	1,556	2,306	1,975	1,471
West Virginia	1,357	921	776	1,281	1,084	751	1,221	1,063	762
Wisconsin	3,446	2,936 (d)	2,512	3,211	2,566	2,104	2,991	(c)	1,853
Wyoming.........	335	205	191	266	195	156	229	N.A.	146
Dist. of Col.	475	264	227	514	268	169	530	305	163

Sources: Compiled from U.S. Department of Commerce, Bureau of the Census, *Statistical Abstract of the United States*; unpublished data from Voting and Registration Division, Bureau of the Census, U.S. Department of Commerce; and National Republican Congressional Committee.

N.A.—Not available.

(a) Estimated as of November 1 of the year indicated. Includes armed forces in each state, aliens and institutional population.
(b) Estimated as of November 1980 from sample of 68,000 households. Unpublished data covers civilian non-institutional population only.
(c) No statewide registration required.
(d) Registration at polls with identification.
(e) Estimated by secretary of state.

Table 10
VOTER TURNOUT IN NON-PRESIDENTIAL ELECTION YEARS:
1970, 1974 AND 1978
(In thousands)

State or other jurisdiction	1978 Voting age population (a,b)	1978 Number registered	1978 Number voting (c)	1974 Voting age population (a,b)	1974 Number registered	1974 Number voting (c)	1970 Voting age population (a,d)	1970 Number registered	1970 Number voting (c)
United States	155,492	104,829	61,038	145,035	97,303	57,357	124,498	76,373	58,983
Alabama	2,604	1,938	730 (e)	2,404	1,793	598 (f)	2,042	1,626	855 (f)
Alaska	272	238	130	213	169	99	178 (g)	107	82
Arizona	1,642	969	551	1,444	891	564	1,056	618	421
Arkansas	1,535	1,047	524 (f)	1,420	997	546 (f)	1,180	881	609 (f)
California	16,052	10,130	7,132	14,595	9,928	6,635	12,376	8,706	6,633
Colorado	1,900	1,345	848	1,710	1,227	829 (f)	1,328	969	668 (f)
Connecticut	2,279	1,626	1,061	2,149	1,562	1,125	1,886	1,393	1,121
Delaware	418	278	166	390	279	160 (h)	326	246	161 (i)
Florida	6,502	4,217	2,530	5,856	3,621	1,828 (f)	4,451	2,797	1,731 (f)
Georgia	3,543	2,183	663 (f)	3,251	2,090	936 (f)	2,985 (b)	1,961	1,045 (f)
Hawaii	637	395	293	574	343	273	473 (j)	292	248
Idaho	597	526	297	528	440	264	418	365	245 (f)
Illinois	7,975	5,809	3,343	7,612	5,906	3,085	6,795	5,338	3,731
Indiana	3,752	2,851	1,405	3,577	2,937	1,753 (i)	3,104	2,716	1,738 (i)
Iowa	2,057	1,588	843 (f)	1,958	1,013	920 (f)	1,712	(k)	791 (f)
Kansas	1,694	1,182	749 (i)	1,581	1,143	794 (i)	1,380	(k)	745 (f)
Kentucky	2,457	1,666	477 (i)	2,284	1,473	746 (i)	2,136 (b)	1,506	474 (h)
Louisiana	2,674	1,821	840 (l)	2,443	1,727	546 (h)	2,058	1,439	363 (h)
Maine	776	692	375 (i)	714	632	364 (f)	601	522	325 (f)
Maryland	2,991	1,888	1,012 (f)	2,783	1,738	949 (f)	2,372	1,597	973 (f)
Massachusetts	4,230	2,920	2,044	4,052	2,928	1,896	3,538	2,629	2,043
Michigan	6,405	5,230	2,985	6,077	4,786	2,657 (f)	5,200	4,060	2,656 (f)
Minnesota	2,828	2,511	1,625	2,631	1,922	1,296	2,248	(k)	1,389
Mississippi	1,612	1,150	584 (i)	1,505	1,152	306 (h)	1,253	1,006	324 (i)
Missouri	3,471	2,579	1,546 (m)	3,306	2,165	1,224 (i)	2,913	(k)	1,283 (i)
Montana	538	410	297	494	374	260	410	325	255
Nebraska	1,117	833	511	1,056	788	467	906	708	471
Nevada	461	268	195	390	237	172	303	193	150
New Hampshire	614	489	279	551	421	236	452	387	229
New Jersey	5,305	3,602	2,060	5,070	3,502	2,184	4,507	3,168	2,209
New Mexico	815	598	357	717	504	229	561	406	301
New York	12,967	7,801	4,929	12,701	8,341	5,544	11,543	7,931	6,150
North Carolina	3,964	2,430	1,136 (i)	3,677	2,280	1,020 (i)	3,043	1,899	930 (h)
North Dakota	461	(k)	235	425	(k)	242	360	(k)	226
Ohio	7,589	5,222	3018	7,296	4,442	3,151	6,419	(k)	3,276
Oklahoma	2,043	1,366	801	1,872	1,341	822	1,605	1,202	712
Oregon	1,750	1,473	911 (f)	1,581	1,143	793	1,308	955	681
Pennsylvania	8,611	5,590	3,742 (f)	8,312	5,529	3,500 (f)	7,412	5,420	3,700 (f)
Rhode Island	678	534	332	654	514	322 (f)	596	462	345 (f)
South Carolina	2,011	1,098	633 (i)	1,842	998	523 (f)	1,487	889	485 (f)
South Dakota	484	421	260 (f)	459	402	279 (i)	389	351	240 (f)
Tennessee	3,107	2,138	1,190 (f)	2,859	1,960	1,064	2,410	1,709	1,108 (f)
Texas	9,063	5,682	2,370 (f)	8,075	5,348	1,655 (f)	6,658	4,149	2,236 (f)
Utah	827	667	385	741	620	423	583	561	374 (i)
Vermont	344	286	125	316	267	145	265	230	156
Virginia	3,736	2,027	1,251	3,375	2,051	924 (h)	2,823	1,765	946 (i)
Washington	2,651	1,961	1,029	2,419	1,896	1,044	2,078	1,563	1,121
West Virginia	1,341	1,021	493	1,240	1,025	416 (h)	1,077	931	446 (i)
Wisconsin	3,319	1,682	1,501 (f)	3,090	(k)	1,199 (i)	2,615	(k)	1,343 (f)
Wyoming	290	201	142	245	185	132	198	135	122
Dist. of Col.	499	250	103	515	273	108 (n)	483	260 (o)	117 (o)

Sources: Compiled from U.S. Department of Commerce, Bureau of the Census, *Statistical Abstract of the United States,* and unpublished data from the National Republican Congressional Committee.

(a) Estimated as of November 1 of the year indicated. Includes armed forces stationed in each state, aliens and institutional population.

(b) Population age 18 and over.

(c) Number represents total voting in general election for all races for the year indicated, except where noted. Total persons voting restricted to number of ballots recorded by secretaries of state as having been cast.

(d) Population age 21 and over, except where noted.

(e) Senate unexpired term.

(f) Total vote for largest race—governor.

(g) Population age 19 and over.

(h) Total vote for largest race—congressperson.

(i) Total vote for largest race—senator.

(j) Population age 20 and over.

(k) No statewide registration required.

(l) Open senatorial primary, September 16, 1978.

(m) Total vote for largest race—auditor.

(n) Total vote for largest race—mayor.

(o) For election which took place March 23, 1971.

Table 11
VOTING STATISTICS FOR GUBERNATORIAL ELECTIONS

State	Primary			General election						
	Republican	Democrat	Total	Republican	Per-cent	Democrat	Per-cent	Other	Per-cent	Total
Alabama	18,832	834,686	853,518	196,963	25.9	551,886	72.6	11,625	1.6	760,474
Alaska	81,422	20,845	102,267	49,580	39.1	25,656	20.2	51,674	40.6	126,910
Arizona	112,637	139,667	252,304	241,093	44.8	282,605	52.5	14,858	2.7	538,556
Arkansas‡	8,131	144,111	452,442	435,684	51.9	403,241	48.1	...	...	838,925
California	2,299,017	3,122,614	5,421,631	2,526,534	36.5	3,878,812	56.0	515,927	7.5	6,921,273
Colorado	134,871	unopposed	134,871	317,292	38.5	483,985	58.7	22,530	2.8	823,807
Connecticut	unopposed	203,504	203,504	422,316	40.7	613,109	59.1	...	...	1,035,425
Delaware‡	unopposed	unopposed	...	159,004	70.7	64,217	28.5	1,815	0.8	225,036
Florida	369,413	1,015,156	1,384,569	1,123,888	44.4	1,406,580	55.6	...	...	2,530,568
Georgia	23,769	640,104	663,873	128,139	19.3	534,572	80.7	...	...	662,711
Hawaii	22,330	259,458	281,788	124,610	44.3	153,394	54.5	3,583	1.3	281,587
Idaho	116,628	unopposed	116,628	114,149	39.6	169,540	58.8	4,877	1.7	288,566
Illinois	unopposed	684,578	684,578	1,859,684	59.0	1,263,134	40.1	27,283	1.0	3,150,001
Indiana‡	unopposed	536,594	536,594	1,257,383	57.7	913,116	41.9	7,904	0.4	2,178,403
Iowa	155,562	106,667	262,229	491,713	58.3	345,519	41.0	5,882	0.7	843,114
Kansas	204,051	124,948	328,999	348,015	47.3	363,835	49.4	24,396	3.3	736,246
Kentucky†	565,814	132,642	698,456	379,932	41.0	553,077	59.0	...	...	933,009
Louisiana†	...	...	1,385,852(a)	690,691	50.3	681,134	49.7	...	...	1,371,825
Maine	73,440	70,671	144,111	126,862	34.3	176,493	47.7	65,889	17.8	369,244
Maryland	129,388	563,748	693,136	293,635	29.0	718,328	71.0	...	...	1,011,963
Massachusetts	247,197	845,905	1,093,102	926,072	47.2	1,030,297	52.5	...	...	1,956,366
Michigan	unopposed	605,199	605,199	1,628,485	56.8	1,237,256	43.2	...	...	2,865,741
Minnesota	207,708	481,719	689,427	830,019	52.3	718,244	45.3	37,331	2.3	1,585,594
Mississippi†	688,274	30,399	718,673	247,162	39.0	382,512	61.0	...	...	629,674
Missouri‡	342,692	639,392	982,084	1,098,950	52.6	981,884	47.0	7,193	0.4	2,088,027
Montana‡	69,959	131,793	201,752	160,892	44.6	199,574	55.4	...	...	360,466
Nebraska	194,757	128,617	323,374	275,473	56.0	216,754	44.0	...	...	492,227
Nevada	43,392	81,020	124,412	108,097	56.2	76,361	39.7	7,987	4.2	192,445
New Hampshire‡	98,076	46,257	144,333	156,178	40.7	226,436	59.0	1,318	0.3	383,932
New Jersey§	385,146	612,562	997,708	1,145,999	49.5	1,144,202	49.4	27,038	1.1	2,317,239
New Mexico	46,105	145,253	191,358	170,848	49.5	174,631	50.5	...	...	345,479
New York	...	717,779	717,779	2,156,404	45.2	2,429,272	50.9	182,643	3.8	4,768,319
North Carolina‡	149,294	750,601	899,895	691,449	37.4	1,143,145	61.9	12,838	0.7	1,847,432
North Dakota‡	67,027	unopposed	67,027	160,230	53.6	140,391	46.4	...	...	300,621
Ohio	579,693	581,709	1,161,402	1,402,167	49.3	1,354,631	47.6	86,528	3.0	2,843,326
Oklahoma	96,314	552,416	648,730	367,055	47.2	402,240	51.7	8,119	1.0	777,414
Oregon	244,214	276,804	521,018	498,452	54.7	409,411	44.9	...	...	907,863
Pennsylvania	972,693	1,242,289	1,214,982	1,966,042	52.5	1,737,888	46.4	37,655	1.0	3,741,585
Rhode Island‡	unopposed	unopposed	...	106,729	26.3	299,174	73.7	...	...	405,903
South Carolina	23,683	331,835	355,518	236,949	37.8	385,016	61.4	5,338	0.9	627,300
South Dakota	90,934	69,481	160,415	147,116	56.6	112,679	43.4	...	...	259,795
Tennessee	230,300	704,872	935,172	661,959	55.6	523,495	44.0	4,139	0.4	1,189,593
Texas	126,980	1,780,564	1,907,544	1,183,839	50.0	1,166,979	49.2	18,834	0.8	2,369,652
Utah‡	...	...	...	566,578	44.4	330,974	55.2	2,467	0.4	600,019
Vermont‡	43,660	31,006	74,666	123,229	58.6	77,363	36.8	9,538	4.5	210,130
Virginia§	...	...	...	659,398	46.4	760,357	53.5	856	0.1	1,420,611
Washington‡	363,589	220,660	584,249	981,083	56.7	749,813	43.3	...	...	1,730,896
West Virginia‡	unopposed	312,747	312,747	337,240	45.4	401,863	54.2	3,047	0.4	742,150
Wisconsin	314,673	338,631	653,304	816,056	54.4	673,813	44.9	10,935	0.7	1,500,804
Wyoming	66,049	42,210	108,259	67,595	49.1	69,972	50.9	...	...	137,567

Source: Congressional Quarterly Weekly Reports and state election administration offices. Figures are for 1978 except where indicated: †1979; ‡1980; §1981.

(a) Louisiana has an open primary which requires all candidates, regardless of party affiliation, to appear on a single ballot. Persons receiving over 50 percent of the vote are elected. If no majority on first ballot, a single election is held between the two candidates receiving the most votes.

3. Constitutions

STATE CONSTITUTIONS AND CONSTITUTIONAL REVISION: 1980-81 AND THE PAST 50 YEARS

By Albert L. Sturm and Janice C. May

SINCE THE FIRST analysis of constitutional developments in *The Book of the States* was published in the 1930s, more than four-fifths of the states have attempted to modernize their constitutions. Although no state adopted a new constitution between 1921 and 1945, during the ensuing 36 years 15 new organic laws have been approved by the voters and become effective in 14 states.[1] This reflects efforts in many states to adapt basic charters to the changing needs of government in the aftermath of the Great Depression and World War II. State constitutional modernization reached its peak during the late 1960s and early 1970s, mainly as a result of the "reapportionment revolution" in the mid- and late-1960s. In the wake of *Baker* v. *Carr*[2], mandates of the U.S. Supreme Court resulted in more equitable representation in state lawmaking bodies, which, for many years, had been hostile to modernization by general constitutional revision. With representation aligned on the "one person, one vote" principle, many legislatures, no longer malapportioned under rural domination, proved more responsive to reform. Following the exceptional record of revision in the 1960s, constitutional revision continued into the 1970s, but slackened substantially in later years of the decade. In retrospect, a significant legacy of constitutional revision has been its contribution to the remarkable resurgence and modernization of state governments during the past 20 years.[3]

Preceding volumes of *The Book of the States* have reported the major state constitutional developments during the past half century. This summary analysis provides a general overview in addition to more specific data on alterations proposed and adopted during the 1980-81 biennium.

General Features of State Constitutions

In the 1930s, only seven state constitutions were products of the 20th century. Table 1 indicates that by 1982 the number had increased to 18, or more than one-third of all state charters. Twenty-nine organic laws, now in effect, date from the 19th century, and three New England constitutions—Massachusetts (1780), New Hampshire (1784) and Vermont (1793)—were drafted in the 18th century. The Massachusetts document is the oldest constitution now in operation in the world. Of the present state organic laws that have been extensively revised since 1930, perhaps the most typical are those that were adopted orginally

Albert L. Sturm is Professor Emeritus, Center for Public Administration and Policy, Virginia Polytechnic Institute and State University, and Janice C. May is Associate Professor in the Department of Government, The University of Texas at Austin. Data for this summary analysis were provided by correspondents in the 50 states. Principal sources were elections divisions in the offices of secretaries of state, state legislative service agencies, state libraries, and university institutes and bureaus of governmental research and public affairs.

during the last quarter of the 19th century; approximately a third of current state constitutions date from this period. The average age of state constitutions operative in 1982 was approximately 82 years.

As shown in Table 1, since the first state constitutions became effective in 1776, American states have operated under at least 145 constitutions. Nineteen states in 1982 were functioning with their first state constitutions. Louisiana leads all the states with 11 constitutions, and the South leads all sections of the nation in constitution-making. With the single exception of Pennsylvania, all states that have adopted five or more constitutions are southern. Much of the constitution-making in these states occurred during the Civil War and Reconstruction era.[4]

The average estimated length of state constitutions effective in 1982 was approximately 26,150 words, excluding the local amendments to the Georgia constitution which comprise the largest part of the document's verbiage. The Georgia constitution is by far the longest document if the local amendments are included; they have never been counted, but certainly exceed 500,000 words. Estimated length of the published part of the constitution of Georgia, which includes only those provisions of statewide applicability, is approximately 48,000 words. Second in length to the Georgia constitution is Alabama's organic law with an estimated 129,000 words. Shortest and also one of the oldest is the constitution of Vermont with an estimated 6,600 words. The median estimated length of the 50 documents falls between that of South Carolina with 22,500 words and the Pennsylvania constitution with 21,675.

Table A shows the number of constitutional changes proposed and adopted in the 50 states through 1981 by all authorized methods of initiating change. Excepting Delaware, where legislative action only is required to change the constitution, a total of 7,953 proposed constitutional changes have been submitted to the voters in 49 states, and 4,988 have been adopted. As Table A indicates, the number of constitutional alterations varies greatly, ranging from 735 proposals with 438 adoptions in California and 626 proposals with 443 adoptions in South Carolina (both 19th-century documents) down to the five proposals with two adoptions in Illinois, where the new constitution (effective since 1971) was unamended until 1980.

The Georgia constitution provides a special case in any consideration of amendments to state charters now operative. The present Georgia document, adopted in 1976, was an editorial revision of the 1945 Georgia constitution proposed by the Georgia General Assembly to facilitate later substantive revision on an article-by-article basis. The General Assembly, however, made little change in the substance of the 1945 Georgia constitution, which has resulted in submission to the voters of more than a thousand proposed amendments, most of which were of local effect only. Georgia voters will have an opportunity in November 1982 to approve a new constitution that eliminates provisions for local amendments.

Use of Authorized Methods of Change

Since the Florida constitution became effective in 1969, the states have authorized four methods of initiating proposals for constitutional amendment and revision. These are: proposal by the state legislature, available in all states; the constitutional initiative, authorized in 17 state constitutions; the constitutional convention, which is expressly authorized in 41 organic laws but may be used in all states; and the constitutional commission, which is

Table A
AMENDMENTS TO STATE CONSTITUTIONS: PROPOSED AND ADOPTED
BY METHOD OF INITIATION
(As of December 31, 1981)

State	Total amendments: all methods		Proposals by the legislature		Proposals by constitutional initiative		Proposals by constitutional convention or commission	
	Proposed	Adopted	Proposed	Adopted	Proposed	Adopted	Proposed	Adopted
Total..........	7,953 (49 states)	4,988 (50 states)	7,021	4,430	539	184	393(a)	267(b)
Alabama	583(c)	393(c)	583(c)	393(c)	...	...	...	...
Alaska	23	16	23	16	...	...	...	...
Arizona	171	102	124	83	47	19	...	...
Arkansas	148	67	83	40	62	27	3	0
California........	735(c)	438(c)	641(c)	412(c)	94	26	...	...
Colorado	218	101	139	77	79	24	...	...
Connecticut......	17	16	17	16	...	...	...	...
Delaware	N/A	107	N/A	107	...	...	...	...
Florida	53	32	43	31	2	1	8(d)	0
Georgia	260(c)	193(c)	260(c)	193(c)	...	...	...	...
Hawaii	79(e)	74(e)	18	14	...	...	57	56
Idaho	173	94	173	94	...	...	...	...
Illinois...........	5	2	4	1	1	1	...	...
Indiana	63	34	63	34	...	...	...	...
Iowa	46	43	46	43	...	...	...	...
Kansas	107	80	107	80	...	...	...	...
Kentucky	53	25	53	25	...	...	...	...
Louisiana	8	8	8	8	...	...	...	...
Maine	170	146	170	146	...	...	...	...
Maryland	221(c)	189(c)	221(c)	189(c)	...	...	...	...
Massachusetts	139	115	92	81	2	2	45	32
Michigan	34	13	21	8	13	5	...	...
Minnesota	192	102	192	102	...	...	...	...
Mississippi	117	48	117	48	...	...	...	...
Missouri	81	52	74	50	7	2	...	...
Montana	12	7	9	6	3	1	...	...
Nebraska	265	176	211	129	13	6	41	41
Nevada..........	149	94	143	92	6	2	...	...
New Hampshire ...	173	75	20	8	...	...	153(f)	67(f)
New Jersey........	38	28	37	27	...	...	1	1
New Mexico.......	205	99	205	99	...	...	...	...
New York	256	191	244	185	...	...	12	6
North Carolina	21	19	21	19	...	...	...	...
North Dakota	193	110	163	92	30	18	...	...
Ohio	234	140	151	97	42	10	41	33
Oklahoma	233	107	188	95	45	12	...	...
Oregon	335	169	244	141	91	28	...	...
Pennsylvania	20	15	20	15	...	...	...	...
Rhode Island	81	43	81	43	...	...	...	...
South Carolina	626(c)	443(c)	626(c)	443(c)	...	...	...	...
South Dakota	173	89	171	89	2	0	...	...
Tennessee.........	54	31	22	0	...	...	32	31
Texas	391	247	391	247	...	...	...	...
Utah	112	64	112	64	...	...	...	...
Vermont..........	205	48	205	48	...	...	...	...
Virginia..........	14	13	14	13	...	...	...	...
Washington	131	73	131	73	...	...	...	...
West Virginia......	88	53	88	53	...	...	...	...
Wisconsin	159	116	159	116	...	...	...	...
Wyoming	84	47	84	47	...	...	...	...

(a) Eight by the Florida Constitution Revision Commission; 385 by conventions.
(b) All were proposed by constitutional conventions.
(c) Includes local amendments.
(d) Proposals by the Florida Constitution Revision Commission. All other proposals in this column were by constitutional conventions.
(e) Includes four amendments by the U.S. Congress.
(f) Until 1964 all proposed amendments in New Hampshire were initiated by constitutional conventions.

specifically authorized only in the Florida constitution. Only the Florida document provides expressly for the use of all four methods. In all states except Delaware, where action by the General Assembly only is required for proposal and adoption,[5] all proposed changes in the constitution must be submitted to the electorate for approval or rejection. Tables 2, 3 and 4 summarize the salient procedural requirements in state constitutions for use of the first three methods listed above.

During the past half century the states have used all methods of initiating constitutional change. Except for the constitutional initiative, which is designed only for limited changes, the various methods have been employed for all degrees of constitutional alteration up to revision or rewriting of an entire constitution.

Table B summarizes state constitutional changes by each of the four authorized methods of formal initiation during 1980-81 and the two preceding bienniums. In addition to the number of states involved, the table provides the totals of proposals, adoptions, percentages of adoptions and the aggregates for all methods.

Table B
STATE CONSTITUTIONAL CHANGES BY METHOD OF INITIATION
(1976-77, 1978-79 and 1980-81)

Method of initiation	Number of states involved			Total proposals			Total adopted			Percentage adopted		
	1980 -81	1978 -79	1976 -77	1980 -81	1978 -79	1976 -77	1980 -81	1978 -79	1976 -77	1980 -81	1978 -79	1976 -77
All methods	46	43	42	388	395	399	272	277	280	70.1	70.1	70.2
Legislative proposal	46	40	42	362	319	369	265	223	273	73.2	69.0	74.0
Constitutional initiative	11	10	8	18	17	18	5	6	3	27.8	35.3	16.7
Constitutional convention	2	3	1	8	51	12	2	48	4	25.0	94.1	33.3
Constitutional commission	...	1	...	...	8	...	...	0	...	...	0	...

Forty-six states were involved in formal constitutional change during 1980-81. All 46 used the legislative proposal technique, 11 states had initiative proposals, and two (Arkansas and New Hampshire) acted on proposals by constitutional conventions. Of the total of 388 proposed, 272 (70.1 percent) were adopted, which was the same percentage as during 1978-79. In contrast, the voters approved only a fourth of the proposals by constitutional initiative and conventions. No proposals by constitutional commissions were submitted directly to state electorates during the past biennium.

Legislative Proposals

Proposal of constitutional change by the state lawmaking body is by far the most commonly used method of originating proposed alterations in state constitutions. Table A shows that through 1981 this method accounted for 7,021, or 88.3 percent, of the 7,953 proposals by all methods that have been submitted to the voters in 49 states. The adoption rate for legislative proposals in all states is even higher—4,430 of 4,881 by all methods, or 90.8 percent. During the operation of present state constitutions, all states have used the legislative proposal method, and at least one proposal has been adopted in every state except Tennessee. In a few states, especially in the South, legislative proposals have included large numbers of local amendments that place a heavy burden on the voters. At the November 1980 general election in Georgia, for example, the electorate voted on a total of 137 proposed amendments, including 16 of statewide effect and 121 of local applicability only.

These figures are indicative of the key role that legislatures play in the process of constitutional reform. At least three state constitutions (Florida, Georgia and Oregon) expressly authorize the legislature to propose an entire constitution. In 1970, new constitutions were proposed by the Idaho, Oregon and Virginia legislatures, and similar extensive proposals have occurred both before and since. Less extensive legislative proposals involving proposed revisions of entire articles of state constitutions have been made during each biennium of the past decade.[6] Phased constitutional revision proposed by state lawmaking bodies is another modern trend that became increasingly popular in the past two decades. During the 1970s, constitutional revision by stages achieved at least partial success in California, Minnesota, Nebraska, Ohio, South Carolina, South Dakota and Utah.

Since the late 1960s, legislatures have given increased attention to "editorial" revision of state charters, often called "codification," "rearrangement," or "simplification" in earlier years. In 1950, for example, the voters of Maine approved an amendment permitting codification without substantive change of existing provisions. In 1953, the Connecticut document was revised editorially, and in November 1962, the New York electorate approved two amendments that shortened the organic law by 4,000 words. There were more extensive editorial revisions of state charters during the 1960s and 1970s in North Carolina (1970), Georgia (1976) and South Carolina (1968-1980s). One purpose of recent editorial revision is to remove gender bias from constitutional language.

Proposed New Constitution in Georgia. The most far-reaching proposal for constitutional reform by a legislative body during the past biennium was the proposed new constitution approved by the Georgia General Assembly on September 18, 1981. Drafted initially under the coordinative supervision of the Georgia Select Committee on Constitutional Revision, the proposed document was reviewed by a 62-member Legislative Overview Committee representing both houses of the General Assembly before it was debated and approved during a special legislative session for submission to the voters at the November 1982 general election. By a vote of 148 to 25 in the House and 39 to 27 in the Senate, the Georgia General Assembly capped years of sustained effort to modernize the state's organic law.

The proposed new constitution is more than 50 percent shorter than the published general statewide provisions of the 1976 document. Other major features include greater clarity, deletion of archaic language, more flexibility and use of gender-neutral language throughout its contents. Probably the most significant change is the elimination of local amendments, which have been the principal reason for the "bedsheet" ballot that has confronted Georgia voters at recent general elections. Deletion of much legislative minutiae would extend additional power to the General Assembly. Other salient alterations in the proposed document provide for open sessions of the General Assembly and all standing committees; more extensive legislative power over constitutional boards and commissions; a streamlined, unified judiciary; non-partisan election of most judges; reduction of tax assessments on farmland from 100 to 75 percent of fair market value; and authorization for consolidation of local governments, subject to approval in a local referendum. Retained in the proposed constitution are provisions for two successive terms for the governor and strong home rule for local governments. Also left untouched is the board of the higher education system, although approval by the General Assembly is required to establish higher educational institutions. Substantive contents of the proposed document are subject to change during the 1982 regular session.

The Constitutional Initiative

Unlike legislative proposal, which is available for all forms of constitutional revision, the constitutional initiative is appropriate only for limited alterations in the organic law. First adopted in Oregon in 1902, the constitutional initiative was available in 13 states by the 1930s,[7] and in 17 states by the early 1980s. Despite the objections of its critics that it encourages proposals by special interest groups, that many initiatives are poorly drafted and that initiatives may add undesirable matter to state constitutions,[8] since 1968 four states (Florida, Illinois, Montana and South Dakota) have added this method of proposing amendments to their organic laws. In Illinois, where the initiative is authorized only to change provisions in the legislative article, the voters approved a constitutional initiative proposal in 1980 that reduced the Illinois House of Representatives from 177 to 118 members, with one member elected from each of 118 districts. Table 3 summarizes the salient requirements for use of the constitutional initiative.

As shown in Table A, a total of 539 constitutional initiatives have been submitted to the voters in the 17 states authorizing this technique under their present constitutions; 184, or 34.1 percent, have been adopted, including at least one in each of the 17 states providing for its use except South Dakota. States that have employed this method most frequently are California (94 proposals, 26 adoptions), Oregon (91 proposals, 28 adoptions), Colorado (79 proposals, 24 adoptions) and Arkansas (62 proposals, 27 adoptions). Four other states (Arizona, North Dakota, Ohio and Oklahoma) each have had at least 30 initiative proposals, and each of the remaining nine states has voted on 13 or fewer.

Although this method has been used sparingly and the percentage of adoptions has been low, it has been the instrument for several historic changes, including the overwhelming approval of Proposition 13 by California voters in June 1978. This popularly initiated measure substantially reduced increases in local property taxes and gave impetus to a taxpayers' revolt that spawned 16 taxing and spending limitations in 1978 elections alone and many more since. Other significant changes resulting from use of the constitutional initiative include the Gateway Amendment that paved the way for the Michigan constitutional convention of 1961-62 and the Missouri plan for selection of judges adopted in 1940.

Table B indicates that 18 initiative proposals were voted on in 11 states during 1980-81; of these only five were adopted, or 27.8 percent. The numbers proposed and adopted in each state were: Arizona (1-0), Arkansas (1-0), California (2-0), Colorado (2-1), Illinois (1-1), Michigan (2-0), Missouri (1-1), Nevada (3-2), Ohio (2-0), Oregon (1-0), South Dakota (2-0). Thus, the voters of only four of 11 states approved constitutional initiatives during the biennium. The results of referendums on these measures during 1980-81 and preceding bienniums reflect the ephemeral nature of popular support for initiative proposals to alter the states' basic laws.

Constitutional Conventions

Probably no governmental institution is more uniquely American than the constitutional convention, which is the oldest, best-known and the traditional method for extensive revision of an old constitution or writing a new one. Through 1981, at least 230 such bodies had been convened in American states.[9] Table C shows the number of state constitutional conventions operative during each quarter-century through 1950, and in the 31 years since mid-century. Sixty conventions, or more than one-fourth the total number, are 20th-century bodies, and more than half of these have been called since mid-century. If the conventions assembled in preparation for statehood and the exceptional number convened during the Civil War and Reconstruction era are excluded, the scope and significance of state constitutional modernization activity during the past three decades becomes more apparent. Table D provides additional data on the number of unlimited and limited constituent assemblies convened during the past half-century. Significantly, 12 unlimited conventions or more than half the total of 23 and eight of the 17 limited conventions were assembled during the period 1965-81. In the mid- and late-1960s the reapportionment revolution reached its high point.

Table C
STATE CONSTITUTIONAL CONVENTIONS
Grouped Periodically: 1776-1981

Period	Number of conventions
Before 1801	26
1801-1825	14
1826-1850	38
1851-1875	67
1876-1900	25
1901-1925	20
1926-1950	9
1951-1981	31
Total	230

Table D
STATE CONSTITUTIONAL CONVENTIONS
Grouped Periodically by Date of Assembly: 1930-1981

Period	Unlimited conventions	Limited conventions	Total conventions
1930-49	5	3	8
1950-59	3	6	9
1960-64	3	0	3
1965-69	7	3	10
1970-74	3	4	7
1975-81	2	1	3
Totals	23	17	40

It should be noted that the voters have rejected the proposed documents of a number of these bodies, all of which were unlimited in their authority to propose changes. During the past 20 years, new or revised constitutions proposed by seven unlimited constitutional conventions failed to win acceptance by the electorates in six states: New York (1967), Rhode Island (1968), Maryland (1968), New Mexico (1969), North Dakota (1972) and Arkansas (1970 and 1980). Also, the 1974 Texas constitutional convention failed to agree on a proposed constitution for submission to the voters.[10]

Several constitutional conventions during the past 50 years are especially noteworthy. The Missouri convention of 1943 was the first in 35 years to rewrite completely an existing state constitution. The New Jersey convention of 1947, after a decade of preparation and abortive effort, succeeded in drafting one of the best constitutions, which has served as a model for executive and judicial reform ever since. Similarly, the Alaska constitution, drafted during 1955-56 in anticipation of statehood, is often cited for its brevity, flexibility, modern provisions and general excellence. The Texas constitutional convention of 1974 was one of the most procedurally unusual bodies. A hybrid, legally it was a convention whose membership was comprised entirely of the members of the Texas Legislature, who met in a unicameral assembly at a different time from the regular legislative session. Financed by separate appropriations, the Texas convention followed convention rules and procedures and considered only convention business. Membership of the Louisiana convention of 1973-74 was unusual in that 27 delegates, representing a variety of interests, were appointed by the governor, and 105 delegates were elected.[11] In Arkansas, a limited convention consisting only of appointed delegates and called without popular referendum was declared unconstitutional by the Arkansas Supreme Court in 1975.[12]

Major characteristics and features of state constitutional conventions have been reported in *The Book of the States* since the 1930s. During the past half-century, there has been considerable procedural experimentation with aspects of convention activity. Use of new ballot forms to present convention proposals, the conduct of public hearings in the various sections of the state, pre-session briefings for members of the press and increased distribution of voter information pamphlets explaining convention proposals are illustrative.

Since 1930, the question of whether a convention shall be called has been submitted to the electorates of at least 27 states. Table E shows the results of voter action on convention calls during the past half-century. Of the total of 62 referendums on the convention question, the voters approved 35, including 22 unlimited and 13 limited conventions. They rejected 27, including 25 unlimited and 2 limited bodies. The tabulation indicates the increased constitutional revision activity by the convention method during the late 1960s and early 1970s, and also the greater reluctance of state electorates to approve calls for unlimited conventions as compared with constituent bodies whose power to propose changes was limited to specified subjects or areas.

Table E
VOTER ACTION ON CONVENTION CALLS
By Periods: 1930-1981

Period	Unlimited conventions		Limited conventions		Totals	
	Approved	Rejected	Approved	Rejected	Approved	Rejected
1930-49...............	4	6	1	0	5	6
1950-54...............	2	4	2	0	4	4
1955-59...............	0	3	4	0	4	3
1960-64...............	3	3	1	1	4	4
1965-69...............	6	1	2	1	8	2
1970-74...............	4	5	2	0	6	5
1975-81...............	3	3	1	0	4	3
Totals...............	22	25	13	2	35	27

An increasing number of state constitutions require periodic submission to the voters of the question of calling a convention to consider constitutional revision. The number of such submissions required in state constitutions has grown from eight in 1939 to 14 in 1982. As shown in Table 4, eight states provide for automatic submission of the question every 20 years (Connecticut, Illinois, Maryland, Missouri, Montana, New York, Ohio and Oklahoma), four states every 10 years (Alaska, Iowa, New Hampshire and Rhode Island), one every 16 years (Michigan) and one every nine years (Hawaii).

During the past biennium, Iowa was the only state to hold a referendum on the convention question, and this occurred under the constitutional mandate for periodic submission each 10 years. On November 4, 1980, Iowa voters rejected by a three-to-two margin a call for an unlimited convention (640,130 to 404,249).

Only one constitutional convention was convened during 1980-81, the eighth Arkansas constitutional convention which assembled initially for organizational purposes in late 1978. The results of its work are discussed later in this article. In addition, however, proposals of one other convention were submitted to the voters during the past biennium, namely, six proposals of the New Hampshire convention held in 1974. Legally, the sixteenth New Hampshire convention that met for 12 days in 1974 (during the period May 8-June 26) is a continuing body for 10 years or until its successor is authorized and selected. Of the six New Hampshire convention proposals submitted to the electorate in 1980, the voters adopted two. In the aggregate, of the 27 amendments proposed by the 1974 New Hampshire body to be voted on during 1974-80, the electorate approved 10.

Arkansas' Eighth Constitutional Convention. Action leading to the eighth Arkansas constitutional convention, its membership, organization, work and initial proposals have been summarized in the two preceding volumes of *The Book of the States.*[13] Approved by the voters in 1976, this body convened initially in organizational session December 11-12, 1978, reconvened in plenary session on May 14, 1979, and remained in session until July 16, drafting a proposed new constitution. A 1979 amendment to the enabling act of 1977 provided for the convention to reconvene on June 16, 1980, for a maximum period of two weeks, to provide the convention an opportunity to alter the draft document after the electorate reacted to it.[14] The convention reconvened on June 16, 1980, made some modifications in the original draft document, approved a separate proposition for submission to the voters offering a choice between merit selection and election by the voters of appellate court judges, and adjourned sine die on June 30, 1980.

At the 1979 plenary session, the most controversial issue was the usury provision, and the delegates decided tentatively to submit to the electorate alternative proposals on this issue separate from the proposed new constitution. In 1980, however, the convention reversed this decision, provided for legislative determination of the interest rate by a two-thirds vote, and substituted alternative proposals concerning selection of appellate court judges for separate submission to the voters. As changed during the 1980 reconvened session, the proposed constitution included provisions for: right of privacy, establishment of a statewide public defender system, mandate for open meetings and records of public bodies, recall of local officers, mandate for voting machines, single-member legislative districts, four-year term for the governor, a system of county trial courts, extensive local home rule, increased flexibility in property tax provisions and overhaul of property evaluation and assessment.

Controversial issues, to which major opposition developed, included the potential costs of implementation, the usury provision, and local home-rule provisions that would enlarge the taxing power of local governments. The proposed document was endorsed by the governor, the congressional delegation, the Democratic Party, the Arkansas Bar Association, city and county organizations and other private groups. The AFL-CIO and the Arkansas Education Association led the opposition. At the referendum on November 4, 1980, Arkansas voters overwhelmingly rejected the new constitution by a vote of 276,257 (37.3 percent) in favor to 464,210 (62.7 percent) against. The failure rendered moot the separate issue offering a choice between alternative methods of selecting appellate court judges.[15]

Constitutional Commissions

Constitutional commissions serve two principal purposes: to study the state constitution and recommend appropriate changes, and to make preparations for a constitutional convention. By far the larger number are study commissions, usually serving as auxiliary staff arms of legislative assemblies, which normally have full discretion to accept, modify or reject their recommendations. Constitutional commissions are established by statute, executive order, legislative resolution or, in the unique case of Florida, by the state constitution. General characteristics of constitutional commissions have been summarized in preceding volumes of *The Book of the States.*

Table F shows the numbers of constitutional commissions established since 1930, grouped periodically according to date of creation and classified by purpose. The 88 commissions, including 76 with primarily "study and recommend" responsibilities and 12 preparatory bodies, were established in 43 states.[16] Two states, Florida and New York, each had five commissions, four states had four commissions each (Georgia, Kentucky, Michigan and Oklahoma), seven states had three, 11 states had two, and 19 states each had one commission.

Table F
CONSTITUTIONAL COMMISSIONS:
1930-1981

Period	Study commissions	Preparatory commissions	Total
1930-49	9	0	9
1950-59	12	2	14
1960-64	17	2	19
1965-69	26*	6	32
1970-74	4	1	5
1975-81	8	1	9
Totals	76	12	88

*Three of these bodies had both study and preparatory responsibilities.

Peak use of constitutional commissions occurred in the late 1960s when state lawmaking bodies relied increasingly on these special organs to prepare proposals for state constitutional revision. Many commissions have prepared draft constitutions. During the 1970s, constitutional commissions wrote the initial drafts of all revised constitutions proposed to state electorates by legislatures.[17]

Most unusual of the constitutional commissions was the Florida Constitution Revision Commission of 1977-78, established under the 1969 Florida constitution, which is the only state organic law to accord constitutional status to such an organ. Following extensive hearings and study, the Florida commission submitted eight proposed revisions to the voters at the November 1978 general election. All were defeated. In 1980, a proposed amendment initiated by the Florida legislature would have deleted from the constitution the unique provision for periodic establishment of a constitution revision commission. The voters rejected this proposal, which was the only one of 12 legislative proposals to be rejected at the three elections held during the year.[18]

Increased use of constitutional commissions has been one of the significant developments in the procedure of state constitutional revision during the past 30 years. In large measure this may be attributed to the lack of time, energy and resources of state lawmaking bodies for thorough study of the complex issues involved in constitutional reform. Burdened with the growing pressures of the modern legislative process, state legislatures will necessarily rely on the expertise potentially available through auxiliary commissions in discharging their responsibilities for initiating proposals for constitutional change.

During 1980-81, fewer state constitutional commissions or committees operated than in any biennium of the 1970s. Table 6 lists four such bodies active during the period. Oldest of these is the Utah Constitutional Revision Study Commission, which was created in 1969 and was made permanent in 1977. Through 1980, Utah voters' action on commission recommendations, which were submitted initially to the legislature, has included approval of revised articles on the legislative and executive branches, elections, amending procedure and labor. Voters rejected articles on the executive (1979), taxation and legislative compensation. The Utah commission will submit revisions of the judicial and tax articles to the legislature in 1982.

In Alaska, where a referendum on the question of calling a convention is scheduled to be held in 1982, the legislature in 1980 renewed its mandate to the interim committee created in 1979 to evaluate the need for calling a convention. The committee, which was reconstituted as a seven-member joint legislative committee, was asked to study the organization and procedures of the 1955-56 constitutional convention, matters relating to a convention call and issues that could arise at such a constituent assembly, for the purpose of preparing guidelines and recommendations for conducting a constitutional convention. Although not renewed by the legislature in 1981, the committee had assembled materials for a "Citizens Guide to the Alaska Constitution" and may be reauthorized and funded in 1982.

Potentially the most significant development in state constitutional reform in 1981 grew out of the staff work of the Georgia Select Committee on Constitutional Revision. This 11-member body, chaired by the governor, was established in 1977 to provide overall policy direction and coordination for a continuing study and revision of the constitution. This action followed the voters' approval in 1976 of an "editorial" revision of the 1945 Georgia constitution to facilitate substantive modernization on an article-by-article basis. This method failed, however, in 1978 when the voters rejected proposed revisions of the articles on the "Elective Franchise" (Article II) and "Retirement Systems and Educational Scholarships" (Article X), which had been approved by the Georgia General Assembly. Following defeat of proposed revisions of additional articles during the 1980 legislative session, the General Assembly in 1981 established a 62-member Legislative Overview Committee to review constitutional revision proposals. Under the auspices of the Select Committee on Constitutional Revision, nine individual article revision committees prepared proposed revisions which were reviewed by the Legislative Overview Committee and submitted to the General Assembly. At the end of a special legislative session, on September 18, 1981, the Georgia lawmaking body approved a proposed new constitution for submission to the voters in November 1982.[19]

Substantive Changes

The procedure of change selected for constitutional modernization is important, but the primary concerns of constitution-makers are the substantive contents of the organic law. The following paragraphs summarize principal substantive developments both during the 1980-81 biennium and the past 50 years. Table G is a composite of state constitutional changes classified under appropriate substantive headings during each biennium of the 1970s and 1980-81. The tabulation includes proposals of statewide applicability classified by subject-matter areas and local amendments that apply to only one or a few political subdivisions. As indicated in Table A, only a few states, located mainly in the South, account for most local amendments. There is no breakdown of local amendments, which apply to constitutions currently operative in only five states (Alabama, California, Georgia, Maryland and South Carolina).

In 1980-81, of the 388 proposed changes by all methods, 254 were statewide proposals in 46 states, of which 160 or approximately 63 percent were adopted. The 134 local amendments were proposed in three states, with 112 or 83.6 percent adopted (Alabama, 10 proposed, 7 adopted; Georgia, 121 proposed, 103 adopted; and Maryland, 3 proposed, 2 adopted). Comparison of adoptions indicates that the adoption rate for local amendments exceeded that for statewide proposals during the past four bienniums.

By far the largest number of proposed changes during the entire period covered in Table G was in the general area of state and local finance, including taxation, debt and financial administration. Particularly since California voters approved the popularly initiated Prop-

Table G
SUBSTANTIVE CHANGES IN STATE CONSTITUTIONS:
PROPOSED AND ADOPTED: 1970-71 to 1980-81

Subject matter	Total proposed						Total adopted						Percentage adopted					
	1980 -81	1978 -79	1976 -77	1974 -75	1972 -73	1970 -71	1980 -81	1978 -79	1976 -77	1974 -75	1972 -73	1970 -71	1980 -81	1978 -79	1976 -77	1974 -75	1972 -73	1970 -71
Proposals of statewide applicability	254	295	283	253	389	300	160	200	189	171	275	176	63.0	67.8	66.8	67.6	70.7	58.2
Bill of rights.........	13	17	10	9	26	13	10	15	6	6	22	11	76.9	88.2	60.0	66.7	84.6	84.6
Suffrage & elections..	5	12	17	23	34	39	5	9	14	20	24	23	100.0	75.0	82.4	86.9	70.6	59.0
Legislative branch ...	43	37	40	40	46	42	21	25	18	27	25	19	48.8	67.6	45.0	67.5	54.3	45.2
Executive branch	21	16	32	34	36	27	10	12	23	20	25	22	47.6	75.0	71.9	58.8	69.4	81.5
Judicial branch	23	25	34	20	35	17	17	19	32	18	26	11	73.9	76.0	94.1	90.0	74.3	64.7
Local government ...	11	27	7	13	30	21	4	13	3	12	23	15	36.4	48.1	42.9	92.3	76.7	71.4
Taxation & finance...	77	68	56	49	85	50	52	39	41	33	56	29	67.5	57.4	73.2	67.3	65.9	58.0
State & local debt	20	19	36	18	24	25	13 ·	9	20	6	15	10	65.0	47.4	55.6	33.3	62.5	40.0
State functions	23	31	42	23	40	46	16	24	25	16	36	26	69.6	77.4	59.5	69.6	90.0	56.5
Amendment & revision	9	11	2	8	19	13	7	10	1	7	12	7	77.8	90.9	50.0	87.5	63.1	53.8
General revision proposals.........	1	1	1	12	2	7	0	1	1	3	1	3	0	100.0	100.0	25.0	50.0	42.9
Misc. proposals......	8	31	6	4	12	*	5	25	5	3	10	*	62.5	80.6	83.3	75.0	83.3	*
Local amendments....	134	100	116	99	141	103	112	77	91	85	93	48	83.6	77.0	78.4	85.9	65.9	46.6

*Not compiled for 1970-71.

osition 13 in June 1978, electorates in many states have voted on numerous proposals to limit taxing and spending by the states and their political subdivisions. Other major subjects of constitutional proposals relating to finance include extension and modification of tax exemptions, property classification and assessment, and requirement of state funding support for new or expanded local programs mandated by state legislatures. Further reference to changes shown in Table G is made in the following discussion of the subject areas.

The Bill of Rights, Suffrage and Elections. Although state bills of rights have undergone relatively little basic change in recent state constitutional revision, some newly recognized rights have emerged and have been incorporated into state constitutions. One such addition has been new "legal equality" and "antidiscrimination" guarantees, especially prohibitions against gender discrimination, in several states. Currently 16 states have such provisions although all are not recent adoptions, Utah (1896) and Wyoming (1890) having entered the union with them. Other recent substantive additions include the rights of privacy, of handicapped persons, to a clean and healthy environment, to work or to bargain collectively and to strike, and to an education or equal educational opportunity. Changes in procedural rights have usually related to bail, juries, indictment procedures and counsel. A significant recent development is the increased emphasis on state bills of rights to protect persons in the wake of diminished leadership in the protection of civil rights by the U.S. Supreme Court.[20]

In 1980-81, there were at least 13 proposals related to bills of rights, with 10 adopted. Significant adoptions included limitation on the right to bail (Nevada, New Mexico, Wisconsin), guarantee of the right to privacy (Florida), prohibition of discrimination against handicapped persons (Massachusetts) and authorization for juries of less than 12 persons in specified cases (California, Wyoming).

National directives during the past 25 years have overshadowed state-originated efforts to liberalize the suffrage. Most states have adopted constitutional amendments conforming their constitutions to federal requirements, relating especially to voting age and residency requirements.[21] During the 1980-81 biennium, five proposals relating to suffrage and elections were adopted, three of which liberalized requirements for voting.

The Three Branches. A major concern of state constitution-makers in recent modernization of state charters has been to strengthen the basic framework of government. This applies especially to the legislative branch, where apportionment provisions have had top priority. Many state organic laws have been modified to conform to the "one man, one vote" standard laid down by the U.S. Supreme Court.[22] These and other changes include new or revised provisions for independent or bipartisan apportionment commissions, changes in sessions usually to annual meetings and extending legislators' control over special sessions, organization or orientation and veto sessions, requirements for open sessions and committee meetings, compensation of legislators, qualifications, legislative terms, method of filling vacancies, eligibility for other offices and conflict of interest.

As shown in Table G, in 1980-81 proposals affecting the legislative branch almost equaled the aggregate for the executive and judicial branches. Of the 43 proposed alterations in legislative articles, 21 (48.8 percent) were adopted, as compared with 21 proposals and 10 adoptions (47.6 percent) involving changes in executive provisions, and 23 proposed alterations in judicial articles of which 17 (73.9 percent) were approved—by far the highest adoption rate of the three branches. North Dakota voters rejected a proposed editorial revision of the legislative article and a revision of the executive department. In Utah, the electorate approved a general revision of the executive article, including provisions for a lieutenant governor, elimination of the office of secretary of state, and joint election of the governor and lieutenant governor.

Since the 1930s basic principles of executive and administrative reform long advocated have continued to dominate efforts to modernize state executive departments. Major trends in proposals to revise state executives include longer terms for the governor and other state officers, strengthening the governor's authority (both legislative and administrative), shortening the ballot, limiting the number of executive departments, joint election of the governor and lieutenant governor, procedure for determining the inability of the governor to perform his functions, and others. Currently, 46 states grant their governors four-year terms as compared with 35 in 1960, but two-fifths of state constitutions limit the governor to two successive terms. By 1980, tandem election of the governor and lieutenant governor had been adopted in 21 states. In 1976, Maine abolished its 155-year-old executive council.

The past few decades also have witnessed numerous reforms in state judicial systems. Principal alterations involve judicial structure and unification, selection and tenure of judges, jurisdiction, and judicial performance and discipline. New Jersey provided an outstanding example of judicial reform when the state court system was thoroughly overhauled under the leadership of Judge Arthur T. Vanderbilt after adoption of the 1947 constitution. Approximately a third of the states have adopted the Missouri plan for merit selection of judges. With California leading the way in 1960, all except a few states now provide some method for monitoring judicial performance. Usually this function is vested in a judicial qualifications commission with duties relating to the retirement, removal, disqualification and censure of judges. Most revised state judiciaries feature administrative leadership under the chief justice of the supreme court. In effecting these reforms, approximately a third of the states have adopted new or revised judicial articles; others have made adjustments by amendments of lesser scope.

Local Government and Finance. Constitutional modernization of local government structure has lagged behind reform in other areas in many states. Yet, a rapidly urbanizing population in recent decades has imposed growing strain on local resources, especially in metropolitan areas. Increased financial stress, demands for new and increased services, and growing interdependence are major contributors to extensive changes in federal-state-local governmental relationships since the 1930s. The principal lines of attack by state constitution-makers in meeting the problems growing out of the "New Federalism," aside from financial adjustments, have been constitutional home rule for municipalities and counties, provisions for merger, consolidation and boundary changes of local units, and permissive authority for various kinds of intergovernmental cooperative arrangements.

In 1980-81, four of 11 proposed amendments to local government articles were approved or only 36.4 percent. This was the lowest percentage of adoptions of all constitutional areas, and substantially lower than the adoption rate of local government proposals in any biennium of the 1970s shown in Table G. Few, if any, areas of state constitutional systems encounter greater resistance to change than local government.

As noted previously and indicated in Table G, by far the largest number of proposed constitutional changes during the 1970s and 1980-81 concerned state and local finance. In 1980-81, of the total of 97 proposals dealing with taxation, finance and debt, 65 or approximately two-thirds were adopted. Approximately half of the popularly initiated proposals during the biennium dealt with financial matters, mainly tax and spending limitations.

A distinct trend in the past 50 years has been toward greater flexibility for state and local governments, including the general area of finance. This was a reaction against crippling restraint of earlier decades, particularly those of 19th-century origin. But Proposition 13 signaled a change in course toward limitation of both taxing and spending. Although the tide of popular support has ebbed since 1978, an era of greater fiscal restraint and retrenchment has emerged. The U.S. Advisory Commission on Intergovernmental Relations, however, declares that one of the major trends of the past 20 years has been the development of "more powerful state revenue systems."[23] It remains to be seen what effect "Reaganomics" and diminution or withdrawal of federal support from intergovernmental programs will have on financial provisions in state constitutions.

State Functions. State constitutions include a variety of provisions on policy areas of special concern to the states. Most important of these by far is education. Other traditional functional areas include health, welfare, highways, institutions, corporations and business regulation. Since the Great Depression of the 1930s, various provisions reflecting the emerging, as well as existing, needs and problems of our times have been added to state constitutions. Illustrative of these are promotion of economic development, promotion of tourism, conservation of natural resources, environmental protection, energy conservation and restrictions on nuclear energy, and similar provisions. These new functional governmental concerns, as well as modification of the more traditional policy areas, have contributed substantially to the verbiage of state constitutions.

Table G indicates a total of 23 proposals related to state policy or functional areas during the past biennium, somewhat fewer than similar proposals during most of the bienniums of the 1970s. Of these, 16 or 69.6 percent were adopted. The largest number of proposals were in education. The most extensive change in constitutional provisions for state functions during the biennium occurred in Kansas where the voters adopted a revision of the article on banks and currency.

Constitutional Amendment and Revision. Procedural provisions for altering state constitutions are among the most important parts of these documents. Compared with other areas, however, they were reformed relatively little during the past few decades. As has been noted above, the number of state charters that expressly authorize the calling of a constitutional convention has increased to 41, and the new constitutions of Florida, Illinois and Montana, plus an amendment in South Dakota, increased authorizations for use of the constitutional initiative to 17. Also, express authorization in the 1969 Florida document for use of a constitutional commission to propose changes was a significant procedural development. In 1964, New Hampshire became the 50th state to authorize legislative proposal of amendments; previously the state had relied solely on conventions to initiate constitutional alterations. Other recent changes, most of a liberalizing nature, include provisions for: revision of an entire article by a single amendment, increasing the number of amendments that may be submitted to the voters at any one election, reducing the number of voters that must approve an amendment, periodic submission of the convention question to the voters, repeal of obsolete provisions and various other detailed changes.

During 1980-81, as Table G indicates, seven of nine proposed changes concerning amendment and revision procedures were adopted. These proposals were submitted to the voters of four states (Florida, Hawaii, Kansas and New Hampshire) and dealt mainly with procedural requirements for proposing and adopting amendments. In Florida, the voters in 1980 rejected a legislative proposal to eliminate authorization for periodic establishment of a constitution revision commission. Rejection of the only general revision proposal to be submitted to the voters during the biennium occurred at the November 1980 general election when Arkansas voters turned down the new constitution proposed by the state's eighth constitutional convention.

Constitutional Materials

Over the past 50 years, a large body of material on state constitutions and constitutional revision has been written, much of it of high quality and readily accessible to interested persons. In addition, a vast quantity of ephemeral materials is stored in state archives and libraries in individual states where major constitutional reform efforts have occurred. Principal producers of constitutional materials have been the staffs of constitutional conventions and commissions, legislative research and service agencies, university institutes of governmental research, and contributors to law reviews. Particularly valuable are the records of proceedings and debates of constitutional conventions and special studies prepared for constitution-making.

Illustrative of the materials prepared in the 1970s are the published proceedings of the Illinois, North Dakota and Texas conventions, the reports of the Arkansas and Texas constitutional commissions, and the special studies prepared for the Montana and Hawaii conventions. Of continuing significance and value are the publications and work of the National Municipal League, The Council of State Governments, the Advisory Commission on Intergovernmental Relations and the League of Women Voters. The *Model State Constitution*, first published by the National Municipal League in 1921 and since revised six times, most recently in 1968, has been widely recognized and used as a valuable resource for constitutional revision. The Legislative Drafting Fund of Columbia University has provided drafting assistance, and in 1956 and most recently in 1969, published new, up-to-date editions of the *Index-Digest of State Constitutions*, which was first prepared for the New York State Constitutional Convention of 1915. In 1980, the Fund introduced the first of a series of subject-matter indices that will replace the *Index-Digest*. An innovation of particular merit during the 1970s was the preparation of complete, annotated and comparative analyses of the Illinois and Texas constitutions for the delegates to constitutional conventions in these states.

Major publications of state constitutional conventions and commissions active between 1776 and 1959 are available on microfiche from the Congressional Information Service (CIS). A bibliographic guide compiled for this collection by Cynthia E. Browne is available separately from Greenwood Press. CIS also offers a microfiche file of constitutional revision documents from all 50 states covering the period 1959-1978. This file contains official publications of revision bodies, as well as state publications relating to amendment by legislative proposal and constitutional initiative; also included is a selection of unofficial items concerning special revision efforts. The two-volume bibliographic guide issued by CIS to accompany the 1959-1978 file is a helpful reference work in its own right.

Secondary materials of special value to students, planners and participants in state constitution-making include most of the items listed in the selected references at the end of this summary analysis. The National Municipal League's two series of *State Constitution Studies* (10 volumes) and *State Constitutional Convention Studies* (10 volumes) were heavily used by constitution-makers during the 1970s. Of special reference value is the 10-volume collection, *Sources and Documents of United States Constitutions*, edited and annotated by William F. Swindler. Included in this collection are annotations of significant sections, historical background notes, analytical tables tracing the development of specific provisions in successive constitutions, a selected bibliography and a separate index for each state. Excepting the holdings of the Library of Congress, probably the most extensive collections of fugitive and published materials on state constitutions and constitutional reform are those of the National Municipal League and The Council of State Governments.

The biennial summary analysis of state constitutional developments published in *The Book of the States* provides a concise overview of official action in this general area. Since 1970, the January (or February) issues of the *National Civic Review* have carried annual reviews of state constitutional revision activity by one of the authors, including a state-by-state summary of the substantive contents of all state constitutional changes of statewide effect during the preceding year.

District of Columbia Statehood Constitutional Convention

Although not related to an existing state constitution, a potentially significant event in American state constitutional development is the District of Columbia Statehood Constitutional Convention. This constituent assembly was called to prepare a constitution for submission to Congress as a basis for statehood. Authorization for convening it was the District of Columbia Statehood Constitutional Convention Initiative of 1979 (1 D.C. *Code*, secs. 111 et seq.), which was approved by the City Council on June 9, 1979. At the referendum on the question of calling the convention on November 4, 1980, District of Columbia voters approved the call by a vote of 104,899 (63.2 percent) to 60,972 (36.8 percent), with 12,563 not voting on the issue. Election of the convention's 45 delegates occurred a year later on November 3, 1981, when five delegates were elected from each of eight wards, with an additional five delegates elected at large, all on a non-partisan basis.

Supported by an appropriation of $150,000 the convention held its opening session on January 30, 1982, and is authorized to be in session 90 days. Officers of the convention include a president (Charles I. Cassell), three vice-presidents, a secretary, assistant secretary, treasurer and historian. Ten substantive committees covering the principal areas of state constitutional systems have been designated to prepare the initial draft of a constitution. If the voters reject the constitution to be proposed by the convention, the delegates are authorized to reconvene to revise the proposed document for resubmission to the District electorate. The mayor is mandated to take all steps necessary for resubmission of the revised constitution within 60 days after the convention completes its revision.

Notes

1. Alaska (1956), Connecticut (1965), Florida (1968), Georgia (1945 and 1976), Hawaii (1950), Illinois (1970), Louisiana (1974), Michigan (1963), Missouri (1945), Montana (1972), New Jersey (1947), North Carolina (1970), Pennsylvania (1968) and Virginia (1970).

2. Especially *Reynolds* v. *Sims*, 377 U.S. 533 (1964). *Baker* v. *Carr*, 369 U.S. 186 (1962).

3. The U.S. Advisory Commission on Intergovernmental Relations has cited "strengthened states" as one of the major intergovernmental trends of the past 20 years. Carl W. Stenberg, "Federalism in Transition: 1959-79," *Intergovernmental Perspective* 6, 1 (Winter 1980): 8. David B. Walker of the Advisory Commission on Intergovernmental Relations has written: "No other 20-year period in American history [1959-1979] produced as many changes in the architecture and activities of state government as the last two decades." "The States and the System: Changes and Choices," *Intergovernmental Perspective* 6, 4 (Fall 1980): 6.

4. Nine states have operated with two constitutions; four states with three constitutions; nine states with four constitutions; three states with five; three states with six; one state with seven; and one state with nine constitutions. See Table 1.

5. In Delaware, amendment or revision of the constitution is accomplished by a two-thirds favorable vote in each of two successive General Assemblies between which an election has intervened.

6. Alabama, California, Indiana, Minnesota, Nebraska, North Carolina, South Carolina, South Dakota and Utah are major examples.

7. Arizona, Arkansas, California, Colorado, Massachusetts, Michigan, Missouri, Nebraska, Nevada, North Dakota, Ohio, Oklahoma and Oregon.

8. For more detailed discussion, see Sturm, *Thirty Years of State Constitution Making: 1938-1968* (N.Y., N.Y.: National Municipal League, 1970), ch. 2, and Sturm, *Methods of State Constitutional Reform* (Ann Arbor: University of Michigan Press, 1954), ch. IV.

9. See Sturm, *Thirty Years of State Constitution Making*, pp. 52-53; this section of the last five volumes of *The Book of the States*; and Sturm, "State Constitutional Conventions during the 1970s," *State Government* 52, 1 (Winter 1979): 24-30.

10. The Texas convention, whose members were the state's 31 senators and 150 representatives, failed by three votes to muster the required two-thirds majority required for submission of convention proposals to the voters. See Janice C. May, *The Texas Constitutional Revision Experience in the Seventies* (Austin, Texas: Sterling Swift Publishing Company, 1975), and "Texas Constitutional Revision: Lessons and Laments," *National Civic Review* 66, 2 (February 1977): 64-69.

11. In *Bates et al.* v. *Edwards, Governor*, 294 So. 2d 532 (1974), the Louisiana Supreme Court rejected plaintiff's contention that the "one man, one vote" requirement applies to a constitutional convention, and declared that there is no requirement that the call for a constitutional convention must be submitted to and approved by the voters.

12. *David Pryor et al.* v. *Lynne Lowe et al.*, 258 Ark. 188 (1975).

13. See *The Book of the States*, vol. 22, p. 202 and vol. 23, pp. 11-12.

14. Act 622 of 1979, amending Act 3, Extraordinary Session, 1977.

15. The vote on the alternate proposals was as follows: merit selection by appointment—264,849 (44.2 percent); non-partisan election—334,092 (55.8 percent).

16. States that did not establish constitutional commissions during this period were Arizona, Colorado, Hawaii, Iowa, Mississippi, Nevada and Wyoming.

17. Constitutional commissions drafted proposed new documents or extensive revisions for legislatures in Alabama, California, Delaware, Georgia, Idaho, Minnesota, Nebraska, Ohio and South Dakota.

18. The vote was 1,164,824 for abolition of the commission, and 1,512,682 against it.

19. In the preparation of a proposed revised document for submission to the Georgia General Assembly, over a four-year period 1977-81, committees on the individual articles of the constitution included 231 appointed citizens and elected officials.

20. For an overview, see Robert Welsh and Ronald L. K. Collins, "Taking State Constitutions Seriously," *The Center Magazine* 14, 5 (September/October 1981): 16-35, 38-43. See also William J. Brennan Jr., "State Constitutions and the Protection of Individual Rights," *Harvard Law Review* 90 (January 1977): 489-504, and A. E. Dick Howard, "State Courts and Constitutional Rights in the Day of the Burger Court," *Virginia Law Review* 62 (June 1976): 874-944. The U.S. Advisory Commission on Intergovernmental Relations has cited the landmark California Supreme Court case of *Serrano* v. *Priest*, 487 P.2d 1241, 557 P.2d 929 (Cal. 1971 and 1976) as one of the major intergovernmental events of the past 20 years, Stenberg, "Federalism in Transition," p. 5. The case,

which promoted greater equity in the financing of public schools, protected the right to equality in the state constitution.

21. The 26th Amendment to the U.S. Constitution in 1971, the Voting Rights Act and various U.S. Supreme Court decisions, including *Dunn* v. *Blumstein*, 405 U.S. 330 (1972), which struck down durational residence requirements, exemplify these federal requirements.

22. See the cases cited in footnote 2.

23. See the articles by Stenberg, "Federalism in Transition" and Walker, "The States and the System."

Selected References

Bard, Dean F., ed. *Debates of the North Dakota Constitutional Convention of 1972.* 2 vols. Bismarck, N.D.: Quality Printing Service, 1972.

Braden, George D. *Citizens' Guide to the Texas Constitution.* Prepared by the Institute for Urban Studies, University of Houston for the Texas Advisory Commission on Intergovernmental Relations, Austin, 1972.

_____ et al. *The Constitution of the State of Texas: An Annotation and Comparative Analysis.* 2 vols. Austin, Texas: Texas Advisory Commission on Intergovernmental Relations, 1978.

Browne, Cynthia E., comp. *State Constitutional Conventions: From Independence to the Completion of the Present Union. A Bibliography.* Westport, Conn.: Greenwood Press, 1973.

Clem, Alan L., ed. *Contemporary Approaches to State Constitutional Revision.* Vermillion, S.D.: Governmental Research Bureau, University of South Dakota, 1970.

Constitutions of the United States: National and State. 2 vols. Dobbs Ferry, N.Y.: Oceana Publications, 1962. Loose leaf.

Cornwell, Elmer E., Jr., et al. *Constitutional Conventions: The Politics of Revision.* New York, N.Y.: National Municipal League, 1974.

Dishman, Robert B. *State Constitutions: The Shape of the Document.* Rev. ed. New York, N.Y.: National Municipal League, 1968.

Edwards, William A., ed. *Index-Digest of State Constitutions.* Dobbs Ferry, N.Y.: Oceana Publications, 1959. Prepared by the Legislative Research Fund, Columbia University.

Elazar, Daniel J., ed. Series of articles on American state constitutions and the constitutions of selected foreign states. *Publius: The Journal of Federalism* 11, 4 (Fall 1982): entire issue. [Forthcoming].

Grad, Frank P. *The State Constitution: Its Function and Form for Our Time.* New York, N.Y.: National Municipal League, 1968. Reprinted from *Virginia Law Review* 54, 5 (June 1968).

Graves, W. Brooke. "State Constitutional Law: A Twenty-five Year Summary." *William and Mary Law Review* 8, 1 (Fall 1966): 1-48.

_____, ed. *Major Problems in State Constitutional Revision.* Chicago: Public Administration Service, 1960.

Howard, A. E. Dick. *Commentaries on the Constitution of Virginia.* 2 vols. Charlottesville, Va.: The University Press of Virginia, 1974.

Leach, Richard H., ed. *Compacts of Antiquity: State Constitutions.* Atlanta, Ga.: Southern Newspaper Publishers Association Foundation, 1969.

Lutz, Donald S. "The Theory of Consent in the Early State Constitutions." *Publius* 9, 21 (Spring 1979): 11-42.

May, Janice C. *Amending the Texas Constitution: 1951-1972.* Austin, Texas: Texas Advisory Commission on Intergovernmental Relations, 1972.

_____. "Texas Constitutional Revision: Lessons and Laments." *National Civic Review* 66, 2 (February 1977): 64-69.

_____. *The Texas Constitutional Revision Experience in the Seventies.* Austin, Texas: Sterling Swift Publishing Company, 1975.

Model State Constitution. 6th ed. New York, N.Y.: National Municipal League, 1963. Revised 1968.

Nunn, Walter H., and Collett, Kay G. *Political Paradox: Constitutional Revision in Arkansas.* New York, N.Y.: National Municipal League, 1973. Mimeographed.

Ohio Constitutional Revision Commission. *Recommendation for Amendments to the Ohio Constitution. Final Report, Index to Proceedings and Research.* Columbus, Ohio: June 30, 1977.

Record of Proceedings: Sixth Illinois Constitutional Convention, December 8, 1968-September 3, 1970. 7 vols. Springfield, Ill.: July 1972. Published by the secretary of state in cooperation with the Sixth Illinois Constitutional Convention.

Sachs, Barbara Faith, ed. *Fundamental Liberties and Rights: A Fifty-State Index.* London, Rome and New York: Oceana Publications, 1980. Prepared by the Legislative Research Fund, Columbia University.

Stafman, Ed., spec. projects ed. [Florida]. "Constitutional Revision Symposium." *Florida State University Law Review* 5, 4 (Fall 1977).

State Constitutional Convention Studies. New York, N.Y.: National Municipal League, 1969-75.

Number One—Elmer E. Cornwell Jr., and Jay S. Goodman. *The Politics of the Rhode Island Constitutional Convention*. 1969.

Number Two—George D. Wolf. *Constitutional Revision in Pennsylvania: The Dual Tactic of Amendment and Limited Convention*. 1969.

Number Three—John P. Wheeler Jr., and Melissa Kinsey. *Magnificent Failure: The Maryland Constitutional Convention of 1967-1968*. 1970.

Number Four—Richard J. Connors. *The Process of Constitutional Revision in New Jersey: 1940-1947*. 1970.

Number Five—Norman Meller. *With an Understanding Heart: Constitution Making in Hawaii*. 1971.

Number Six—Martin L. Faust. *Constitution Making in Missouri: The Convention of 1943-1944*. 1971.

Number Seven—Donna E. Shalala. *The City and the Constitution: The 1967 New York Convention's Response to the Urban Crisis*. 1972.

Number Eight—Samuel K. Gove and Thomas R. Kitsos. *Revision Success: The Sixth Illinois Constitutional Convention*. 1974.

Number Nine—Victor Fischer. *Alaska's Constitutional Convention*. Published by the University of Alaska Press, Fairbanks, 1975.

Number Ten—Thomas Schick. *The New York State Constitutional Convention of 1915 and the Modern State Governor*. Lebanon, Pa.: Sowers Printing Company, 1978.

State Constitution Studies. 10 vols. in two series. New York, N.Y.: National Municipal League, 1960-65.

State Constitutional Conventions, Commissions, and Amendments, 1959-1978: An Annotated Bibliography. 2 vols. Washington, D.C.: Congressional Information Service, 1981.

State Constitutional Conventions, Commissions, and Amendments on Microfiche. 4 pts. [Microform]. Westport, Conn.: Greenwood Press, 1972-1976; Washington D.C.: Congressional Information Service, 1977-1981.

Stewart, William H. Jr. *The Alabama Constitutional Commission: A Pragmatic Approach to Constitutional Revision*. University, Ala.: Bureau of Public Administration, University of Alabama, 1975.

Studies in Illinois Constitution Making. Urbana, Ill.: University of Illinois Press, 1972-75.

Elmer Gertz. *For the First Hours of Tomorrow: The New Illinois Bill of Rights*. 1972.

Janet Cornelius. Constitution Making in Illinois, 1818-1970. 1972.

Rubin G. Cohn. *To Judge with Justice: The History and Politics of Judicial Reform*. 1973.

Ian D. Burman. *Lobbying at the Illinois Constitutional Convention*. 1973.

Alan G. Gratch and Virginia H. Ubik. *Ballots for Change: New Suffrage and Amending Articles for Illinois*. 1973.

Joyce H. Fishbane and Glenn W. Fisher. *Politics of the Purse: Revenue and Finance in the Sixth Illinois Constitutional Convention*. 1974.

Jane Gallaway Buresh. *A Fundamental Goal: Education for the People of Illinois*. 1975.

David Kenny, Jack R. VanDerSlik, and Samuel J. Pernacciaro. *Roll Call! Patterns of Voting in the Sixth Illinois Constitutional Convention*. 1975.

Sturm, Albert L. *A Bibliography on State Constitutions and Constitutional Revision, 1945-1975*. Englewood, Colo.: The Citizens Conference on State Legislatures [now Legis/50], August 1975.

_____. "State Constitutional Conventions during the 1970s." *State Government* 52, 1 (Winter 1979): 24-30.

_____. Annual summary analyses of state constitutional developments. Published in the January (or February) issues of the *National Civic Review* since 1970.

_____. "The Procedure of State Constitutional Change with Special Emphasis on the South and Florida." *Florida State University Law Review* 5, 4 (Fall 1977).

_____. *Thirty Years of State Constitution Making, 1938-1968*. New York, N.Y.: National Municipal League, 1970.

_____. *Trends in State Constitution Making: 1966-1972*. Lexington, Ky.: The Council of State Governments, 1973.

Swindler, William F., ed. *Sources and Documents of United States Constitutions*. 10 vols. Dobbs Ferry, N.Y.: Oceana Publications, Inc., 1973-1979.

Wheeler, John P., Jr. *The Constitutional Convention: A Manual on Its Planning, Organization and Operation*. New York, N.Y.: National Municipal League, 1961.

_____, ed. *Salient Issues of Constitutional Revision*. New York, N.Y.: National Municipal League, 1961.

Table 1
GENERAL INFORMATION ON STATE CONSTITUTIONS
(As of December 31, 1981)

State or other jurisdiction	Number of constitutions*	Dates of adoption	Effective date of present constitution	Estimated length (number of words)	Number of amendments Submitted to voters	Number of amendments Adopted
Alabama	6	1819, 1861, 1865, 1868, 1875, 1901	Nov. 28, 1901	129,000	582	383
Alaska	1	1956	Jan. 3, 1959	12,880	23	16
Arizona	1	1911	Feb. 14, 1912	28,779(a)	171	102
Arkansas	5	1836, 1861, 1864, 1868, 1874	Oct. 30, 1874	40,469(a)	148	67(b)
California	2	1849, 1879	July 4, 1879	33,000	735	438
Colorado	1	1876	Aug. 1, 1876	39,800	218	101
Connecticut	4	1818(c), 1965	Dec. 30, 1965	7,900	17	16
Delaware	4	1776, 1792, 1831, 1897	June 10, 1897	18,700	(d)	107
Florida	6	1839, 1861, 1865, 1868, 1886, 1968	Jan. 7, 1969	25,000	53	32
Georgia	9	1777, 1789, 1798, 1861, 1865, 1868, 1877, 1945, 1976	Jan. 1, 1977	48,000(e)	260	193
Hawaii	1(f)	1950	Aug. 21, 1959	17,450(a)	79	74
Idaho	1	1889	July 3, 1890	21,323(a)	173	94
Illinois	4	1818, 1848, 1870, 1970	July 1, 1971	13,200	5	2
Indiana	2	1816, 1851	Nov. 1, 1851	10,225(a)	63	34
Iowa	2	1846, 1857	Sept. 3, 1857	12,500	46	43(g)
Kansas	1	1859	Jan. 29, 1861	11,865	107	80(g)
Kentucky	4	1792, 1799, 1850, 1891	Sept. 28, 1891	23,500	53	25
Louisiana	11	1812, 1845, 1852, 1861, 1864, 1868, 1879, 1898, 1913, 1921, 1974	Jan. 1, 1975	35,387(a)	8	8
Maine	1	1819	March 15, 1820	13,500	170	146(h)
Maryland	4	1776, 1851, 1864, 1867	Oct. 5, 1867	40,775	221	189
Massachusetts	1	1780	Oct. 25, 1780	36,612(a,i)	139	115
Michigan	4	1835, 1850, 1908, 1963	Jan. 1, 1964	20,000	34	13
Minnesota	1	1857	May 11, 1858	9,491(a)	197	103
Mississippi	4	1817, 1832, 1869, 1890	Nov. 1, 1890	23,500	117	48
Missouri	4	1820, 1865, 1875, 1945	March 30, 1945	40,134(a)	81	52
Montana	2	1889, 1972	July 1, 1973	11,812(a)	12	7
Nebraska	2	1866, 1875	Oct. 12, 1875	18,802(a)	265	176
Nevada	1	1864	Oct. 31, 1864	19,735	149	94(g)
New Hampshire	2	1776, 1784(k)	June 2, 1784	9,175	173(j)	75(j)
New Jersey	3	1776, 1844, 1947	Jan. 1, 1948	17,086	38	28
New Mexico	1	1911	Jan. 6, 1912	27,066	205	99
New York	4	1777, 1822, 1846, 1894	Jan. 1, 1895	47,000	256	191
North Carolina	3	1776, 1868, 1970	July 1, 1971	10,500	21	19
North Dakota	1	1889	Nov. 2, 1889	30,000	193(k)	110(k)
Ohio	2	1802, 1851	Sept. 1, 1851	36,300	234	140
Oklahoma	1	1907	Nov. 16, 1907	68,500	233(l)	107(l)
Oregon	1	1857	Feb. 14, 1859	25,000	335	169
Pennsylvania	5	1776, 1790, 1838, 1873, 1968(m)	1968	21,675	20(m)	15(m)
Rhode Island	2	1842(c)	May 2, 1843	19,026(a,i)	81	43
South Carolina	7	1776, 1778, 1790, 1861, 1865, 1868, 1895	Jan. 1, 1896	22,500(n)	626(o)	443(o)
South Dakota	1	1889	Nov. 2, 1889	23,250	173	89
Tennessee	3	1796, 1835, 1870	Feb. 23, 1870	15,300	54	31
Texas	5	1845, 1861, 1866, 1869, 1876	Feb. 15, 1876	61,000	391	247
Utah	1	1895	Jan. 4, 1896	17,300	112	64
Vermont	3	1777, 1786, 1793	July 9, 1793	6,600	205	48
Virginia	6	1776, 1830, 1851, 1869, 1902, 1970	July 1, 1971	18,500	14	13
Washington	1	1889	Nov. 11, 1889	29,350	131	73
West Virginia	2	1863, 1872	April 9, 1872	25,550(a)	88	53
Wisconsin	1	1848	May 29, 1848	13,435	159	116(g)
Wyoming	1	1889	July 10, 1890	27,600	84	47
American Samoa	2	1960, 1967	July 1, 1967	6,000	13	7
No. Mariana Islands	1	1977	Oct. 24, 1977	. . .	. . .	. . .
Puerto Rico	1	1952	July 25, 1952	9,281(a)	6	6

CONSTITUTIONS

*The constitutions referred to in this table include those Civil War documents customarily listed by the individual states.

(a) Actual word count.

(b) Eight of the approved amendments have been superseded and are not printed in the current edition of the constitution. The total adopted does not include five amendments that were invalidated.

(c) Colonial charters with some alterations served as the first constitutions in Connecticut (1638, 1662) and in Rhode Island (1663).

(d) Proposed amendments are not submitted to the voters in Delaware.

(e) Estimated length of the printed constitution, which includes only provisions of statewide applicability. Local amendments comprise most of the total constitution.

(f) As a kingdom and a republic, Hawaii had five constitutions.

(g) The figure given includes amendments approved by the voters and later nullified by the state supreme court in Iowa (three), Kansas (one), Nevada (six) and Wisconsin (two).

(h) The figure does not include one amendment approved by the voters in 1967 that is inoperative until implemented by legislation.

(i) The printed constitution includes many provisions that have been annulled. The length of effective provisions is an estimated 24,122 words (12,490 annulled) in Massachusetts and 11,399 words (7,627 annulled) in Rhode Island.

(j) The constitution of 1784 was extensively revised in 1792. Figures show proposals and adoptions since 1793, when the revised constitution became effective.

(k) The figures do not include submission and approval of the constitution of 1889 itself and of Article XX; these are constitutional questions included in some counts of constitutional amendments and would add two to the figure in each column.

(l) The figures include one amendment submitted to and approved by the voters and subsequently ruled by the supreme court to have been illegally submitted.

(m) Certain sections of the constitution were revised by the limited constitutional convention of 1967-68. Amendments proposed and adopted are since 1968.

(n) Of the estimated length, approximately two-thirds is of general statewide effect; the remainder is local amendments.

(o) Of the 626 proposed amendments submitted to the voters, 130 were of general statewide effect and 496 were local; the voters rejected 83 (12 statewide, 71 local). Of the remaining 543, the General Assembly refused to approve 100 (22 statewide, 78 local), and 443 (96 statewide, 347 local) were finally added to the constitution.

Table 2
CONSTITUTIONAL AMENDMENT PROCEDURE: BY THE LEGISLATURE
Constitutional Provisions

State or other jurisdiction	Legislative vote required for proposal(a)	Consideration by two sessions required	Vote required for ratification	Limitation on the number of amendments submitted at one election
Alabama	3/5	No	Majority vote on amendment	None
Alaska	2/3	No	Majority vote on amendment	None
Arizona	Majority	No	Majority vote on amendment	None
Arkansas	Majority	No	Majority vote on amendment	3
California	2/3	No	Majority vote on amendment	None
Colorado	2/3	No	Majority vote on amendment	None(b)
Connecticut	(c)	(c)	Majority vote on amendment	None
Delaware	2/3	Yes	Not required	No referendum
Florida	3/5	No	Majority vote on amendment	None
Georgia	2/3	No	Majority vote on amendment	None
Hawaii	(d)	(d)	Majority vote on amendment(e)	None
Idaho	2/3	No	Majority vote on amendment	None
Illinois	3/5	No	(f)	3 articles
Indiana	Majority	Yes	Majority vote on amendment	None
Iowa	Majority	Yes	Majority vote on amendment	None
Kansas	2/3	No	Majority vote on amendment	5
Kentucky	3/5	No	Majority vote on amendment	4
Louisiana	2/3	No	Majority vote on amendment(g)	None
Maine	2/3(h)	No	Majority vote on amendment	None
Maryland	3/5	No	Majority vote on amendment	None
Massachusetts	Majority(i)	Yes	Majority vote on amendment	None
Michigan	2/3	No	Majority vote on amendment	None
Minnesota	Majority	No	Majority vote in election	None
Mississippi	2/3(j)	No	Majority vote on amendment	None
Missouri	Majority	No	Majority vote on amendment	None
Montana	2/3(h)	No	Majority vote on amendment	None
Nebraska	3/5	No	Majority vote on amendment(e)	None
Nevada	Majority	Yes	Majority vote on amendment	None
New Hampshire	3/5	No	2/3 vote on amendment	None
New Jersey	(k)	(k)	Majority vote on amendment	None(l)
New Mexico	Majority(m)	No	Majority vote on amendment(m)	None
New York	Majority	Yes	Majority vote on amendment	None
North Carolina	3/5	No	Majority vote on amendment	None
North Dakota	Majority	No	Majority vote on amendment	None
Ohio	3/5	No	Majority vote on amendment	None
Oklahoma	Majority	No	Majority vote on amendment	None
Oregon	(n)	No	Majority vote on amendment	None
Pennsylvania	Majority(o)	Yes(o)	Majority vote on amendment	None
Rhode Island	Majority	No	Majority vote on amendment	None
South Carolina	2/3(p)	Yes(p)	Majority vote on amendment	None
South Dakota	Majority	No	Majority vote on amendment	None
Tennessee	(q)	Yes(q)	Majority vote in election(r)	None
Texas	2/3	No	Majority vote on amendment	None
Utah	2/3	No	Majority vote on amendment	None
Vermont	(s)	Yes	Majority vote on amendment	None
Virginia	Majority	Yes	Majority vote on amendment	None
Washington	2/3	No	Majority vote on amendment	None
West Virginia	2/3	No	Majority vote on amendment	None
Wisconsin	Majority	Yes	Majority vote on amendment	None
Wyoming	2/3	No	Majority vote in election	None
American Samoa	3/5	No	Majority vote on amendment(t)	None
Puerto Rico	2/3(u)	No	Majority vote on amendment	3

(a) In all states not otherwise noted, the figure shown in the column refers to the proportion of elected members in each house required for approval of proposed constitutional amendments.

(b) Legislature may not propose amendments at the same session to more than six articles in Colorado.

(c) Three-fourths vote in each house at one session, or majority vote in each house in two sessions between which an election has intervened.

(d) Two-thirds vote in each house at one session, or majority vote in each house in two sessions.

(e) Majority on amendment must be at least 50 percent of the total votes cast at the election; or, at a special election, a majority of the votes tallied which must be at least 30 percent of the total number of registered voters.

(f) Majority voting in election or three-fifths voting on amendment.

(g) If five or fewer political subdivisions of state affected, majority in state as a whole and also in affected subdivision(s) is required.

(h) Two-thirds of both houses.

(i) Majority of members elected sitting in joint session.

(j) The two-thirds must include not less than a majority elected to each house.

(k) Three-fifths of all members of each house at one session, or majority of all members of each house for two successive sessions.

(l) If a proposed amendment is not approved at the election when submitted, neither the same amendment nor one which would make substantially the same change for the constitution may be again submitted to the people before the third general election thereafter.

(m) Amendments concerning certain elective franchise and education matters require three-fourths vote of members elected and approval by three-fourths of electors voting in state and two-thirds of those voting in each county.

(n) Majority to amend constitution, two-thirds to revise (revise includes all or a part of the constitution).

(o) Emergency amendments may be passed by two-thirds vote of each house, followed by ratification by majority vote of electors in election held at least one month after legislative approval.

(p) Two-thirds of members of each house, first passage; majority of members of each house after popular ratification.

(q) Majority of members elected to both houses, first passage; two-thirds of members elected to both houses, second passage.

(r) Majority of all citizens voting for governor.

(s) Two-thirds vote senate, majority vote house, first passage; majority both houses, second passage. As of 1974, amendments may be submitted only every four years.

(t) Within 30 days after voter approval, governor must submit amendment(s) to Secretary of the Interior for approval.

(u) If approved by two-thirds of members of each house, amendment(s) submitted to voters at special referendum; if approved by not less than three-fourths of total members of each house, referendum may be held at next general election.

136

Table 3
CONSTITUTIONAL AMENDMENT PROCEDURE: BY INITIATIVE
Constitutional Provisions

State	Number of signatures required on initiative petition	Distribution of signatures	Referendum vote
Arizona	15% of total votes cast for all candidates for governor at last election.	None specified.	Majority vote on amendment.
Arkansas	10% of voters for governor at last election.	Must include 5% of voters for governor in each of 15 counties.	Majority vote on amendment.
California	8% of total voters for all candidates for governor at last election.	None specified.	Majority vote on amendment.
Colorado	5% of legal voters for secretary of state at last election.	None specified.	Majority vote on amendment.
Florida	8% of total votes cast in the state in the last election for presidential electors.	8% of total votes cast in each of 1/2 of the congressional districts.	Majority vote on amendment.
Illinois(a)	8% of total votes cast for candidates for governor at last election.	None specified.	Majority voting in election or 3/5 voting on amendment.
Massachusetts(b)	3% of total votes cast for governor at preceding biennial state election (not less than 25,000 qualified voters).	No more than 1/4 from any one county.	Majority vote on amendment which must be 30% of total ballots cast at election.
Michigan	10% of total voters for governor at last election.	None specified.	Majority vote on amendment.
Missouri.............	8% of legal voters for all candidates for governor at last election.	The 8% must be in each of 2/3 of the congressional districts in the state.	Majority vote on amendment.
Montana	10% of qualified electors, the number of qualified electors to be determined by number of votes cast for governor in preceding general election.	The 10% to include at least 10% of qualified electors in each of 2/5 of the legislative districts.	Majority vote on amendment.
Nebraska	10% of total votes for governor at last election.	The 10% must include 5% in each of 2/5 of the counties.	Majority vote on amendment which must be at least 35% of total vote at the election.
Nevada..............	10% of voters who voted in entire state in last general election.	10% of total voters who voted in each of 75% of the counties.	Majority vote on amendment in two consecutive general elections.
North Dakota	4% of population of the state.	None specified.	Majority vote on amendment.
Ohio	10% of total number of electors who voted for governor in last election.	At least 5% of qualified electors in each of 1/2 of counties in the state.	Majority vote on amendment.
Oklahoma	15% of legal voters for state office receiving highest number of voters at last general state election.	None specified.	Majority vote on amendment.
Oregon	8% of total votes for all candidates for governor elected for 4-year term at last election.	None specified.	Majority vote on amendment.
South Dakota	10% of total votes for governor in last election.	None specified.	Majority vote on amendment.

(a) Only Article IV, The Legislature, may be amended by initiative petition.
(b) Before being submitted to the electorate for ratification, initiative measures must be approved at two sessions of a successively elected legislature by not less than one-fourth of all members elected, sitting in joint session.

Table 4
PROCEDURES FOR CALLING CONSTITUTIONAL CONVENTIONS
Constitutional Provisions

State or other jurisdiction	Provision for convention	Legislative vote for submission of convention question(a)	Popular vote to authorize convention	Periodic submission of convention question required(b)	Popular vote required for ratification of convention proposals
Alabama	Yes	Majority	ME	No	Not specified
Alaska	Yes	No provision(c,d)	(c)	10 yrs. (c)	Not specified(c)
Arizona	Yes	Majority	(e)	No	MP
Arkansas	No	...	...	No	...
California	Yes	2/3	MP	No	MP
Colorado	Yes	2/3	MP	No	ME
Connecticut	Yes	2/3	MP	20 yrs. (f)	MP
Delaware	Yes	2/3	MP	No	No provision
Florida	Yes	(g)	MP	No	Not specified
Georgia	Yes	(d)	None	No	MP
Hawaii	Yes	Not specified	MP	9 years	MP(h)
Idaho	Yes	2/3	MP	No	Not specified
Illinois	Yes	3/5	(i)	20 years	MP
Indiana	No	...	...	No	...
Iowa	Yes	Majority	MP	10 yrs.; 1970	MP
Kansas	Yes	2/3	MP	No	MP
Kentucky	Yes	Majority(j)	MP(k)	No	No provision
Louisiana	Yes	(d)	None	No	MP
Maine	Yes	(d)	None	No	No provision
Maryland	Yes	Majority	ME	20 yrs.; 1970	MP
Massachusetts	No	...	...	No	...
Michigan	Yes	Majority	MP	16 yrs.; 1978	MP
Minnesota	Yes	2/3	ME	No	3/5 on P
Mississippi	No	...	...	No	...
Missouri	Yes	Majority	MP	20 yrs.; 1962	Not specified(l)
Montana	Yes(m)	2/3(n)	MP	20 years	MP
Nebraska	Yes	3/5	MP(o)	No	MP
Nevada	Yes	2/3	ME	No	No provision
New Hampshire	Yes	Majority	MP	10 years	2/3 on P
New Jersey	No	...	...	No	...
New Mexico	Yes	2/3	MP	No	Not specified
New York	Yes	Majority	MP	20 yrs.; 1957	MP
North Carolina	Yes	2/3	MP	No	MP
North Dakota	No	...	...	No	...
Ohio	Yes	2/3	MP	20 yrs.; 1932	MP
Oklahoma	Yes	Majority	(e)	20 years	MP
Oregon	Yes	Majority	(e)	No	No provision
Pennsylvania	No	...	...	No	...
Rhode Island	Yes	Majority	MP	10 years	MP
South Carolina	Yes	(d)	ME	No	No provision
South Dakota	Yes	(d)	(d)	No	MP(p)
Tennessee	Yes(q)	Majority	MP	No	MP
Texas	No	...	...	No	ME
Utah	Yes	2/3	ME	No	...
Vermont	No	...	...	No	...
Virginia	Yes	(d)	None	No	MP
Washington	Yes	2/3	ME	No	Not specified
West Virginia	Yes	Majority	MP	No	Not specified
Wisconsin	Yes	Majority	MP	No	No provision
Wyoming	Yes	2/3	ME	No	Not specified
American Samoa	Yes	(r)	None	No	ME(s)
Puerto Rico	Yes	2/3	MP	No	MP

Key:
MP—Majority voting on the proposal.
ME—Majority voting in the election.

(a) In all states not otherwise noted, the entries in this column refer to the proportion of members elected to each house required to submit to the electorate the question of calling a constitutional convention.

(b) The number listed is the interval between required submissions on the question of calling a constitutional convention; where given, the date is that of the first required submission of the convention question.

(c) Unless provided otherwise by law, convention calls are to conform as nearly as possible to the act calling the 1955 convention, which provided for a legislative vote of a majority of members elected to each house and ratification by a majority vote on the proposals. The legislature may call a constitutional convention at any time.

(d) In these states, the legislature may call a convention without submitting the question to the people. The legislative vote required is two-thirds of the members elected to each house in Georgia, Louisiana, South Carolina and Virginia; two-thirds concurrent vote of both branches in Maine; three-fourths of all members of each house in South Dakota; and not specified in Alaska, but bills require majority vote of membership of each house. In South Dakota, the question of calling a convention may be initiated by the people in the same manner as an amendment to the constitution (see Table 3) and requires a majority vote on the question for approval.

(e) The law calling a convention must be approved by the people.

(f) The legislature shall submit the question 20 years after the last con-

vention, or 20 years after the last vote on the question of calling a convention, whichever date is last.

(g) The power to call a convention is reserved to the people by petition.

(h) The majority must be 35 percent of the total votes cast at a general election or 30 percent of the number of registered voters if at a special election.

(i) Majority voting in the election, or three-fifths voting on the question.

(j) Must be approved during two legislative sessions.

(k) Majority must equal one-fourth of qualified voters at last general election.

(l) Majority of those voting on the proposal is assumed.

(m) The question of calling a constitutional convention may be submitted either by the legislature or by initiative petition to the secretary of state in the same manner as provided for initiated amendments (see Table 3).

(n) Two-thirds of all members of the legislature.

(o) Majority must be 35 percent of total votes cast at the election.

(p) Convention proposals are submitted to the electorate at a special election in a manner to be determined by the convention.

(q) Conventions may not be held more often than once in six years.

(r) Five years after effective date of constitutions, governor shall call a constitutional convention to consider changes proposed by a constitutional committee appointed by the governor. Delegates to the convention are to be elected by their county councils.

(s) If proposed amendments are approved by the voters, they must be submitted to the Secretary of the Interior for approval.

Table 5
STATE CONSTITUTIONAL COMMISSIONS
(Operative during January 1, 1980-December 31, 1981)

State	Name of commission	Method and date of creation and period of operation	Membership: number and type	Funding	Purpose of commission	Proposals and action
Alaska	Constitutional Convention Committee	Legislative; created by Legislative Council; June 26, 1979-Jan. 9, 1980	2 members: one senator and one representative	$87,000	Study organization and procedures of 1955-56 constitutional convention, matters relating to a convention call, and issues likely to arise in convention in order to prepare guidelines and recommendations for conducting a convention	Prepared work papers; background work for committee established in 1980.
	Interim Committee on the Constitutional Convention	Legislative; SCR 43; January 1980-January 12, 1981	7: appointed from the two houses, 4 senators and 3 representatives	$143,000	Study (see above)	Continued work of previous committee. Prepared material for "A Citizen's Guide to the Alaska Constitution."
Georgia	Select Committee on Constitutional Revision	Statutory; HR 135-588, Res. Act No. 26, March 30, 1977; May 9, 1977-June 30, 1982	11 (most ex officio): gov., lt. gov., speaker of house, chf. justice of sup. ct., chf. judge of ct. of appeals, atty. gen., chrnn. of sen. jud. cmte., chrnn. of house jud. cmte., trial judge apptd. by jud. council, pres. pro tem of sen., pres. pro tem of house	No specified amount; funded from General Assembly appropriation	Provide overall policy direction and coordination for a continuing study and revision of the constitution	Under the auspices of the select committee, nine article revision committees prepared proposed revisions which were reviewed in 1981 by a 62-member Legislative Overview Committee and submitted to the General Assembly. On Sept. 18, 1981, the General Assembly approved a proposed new constitution for submission to the voters in Nov. 1982.
Utah	Utah Constitutional Revision Study Commission	Statutory; Ch. 89, *Laws of Utah*, 1969; amended by Ch. 107, *Laws*, 1975; amended by Ch. 159, *Laws*, 1977, which made the commission permanent as of July 1, 1977	16; 1 ex officio, 9 apptd. by speaker of house (3), pres. of sen. (3) and gov. (3)—no more than 2 of each group to be from same party; and 6 additional members apptd. by the 9 previously apptd. members	Appropriations through 1981 totaled $265,000. (The 1981 appropriation was $54,000.)	Study constitution and recommend desirable changes, including proposed drafts	Mandated to report recommendations at least 60 days before legislature convenes. Voter action through 1980 on commission recommendations included approval of revised articles on the legislative and executive branches, elections, amending procedure and labor; rejection of articles on the executive (1979), taxation and legislative compensation. Proposed revisions of the judicial and tax articles will be submitted to the legislature in 1982.

Table 6
CONSTITUTIONAL CONVENTIONS
1980-81

State	Convention dates	Type of convention	Referendum on convention question	Preparatory bodies	Appropriations	Convention delegates	Convention proposals	Referendum on convention proposals
Arkansas	Dec. 11-12, 1978; May 14-July 16, 1979; and June 16-30, 1980	Unlimited	Nov. 2, 1976 Vote: 314,385 239,491	Constitutional Convention Preparatory Commitee	$800,000	100 (elected Nov. 7, 1978 and at run-off election Nov. 21, 1978, from representative districts; non-partisan)	Proposed a new constitution plus 2 alternative proposals on the method of selecting judges submitted separately	Nov. 4, 1980: constitution rejected; vote: 276,257 (37%) 464,210 (63%). Alternative proposals (selection of judges): For merit selection by appointment—264,849; For non-partisan election—334,092. (Rejection of the proposed constitution nullified votes on the alternatives.)
New Hampshire ...	May 8-June 26, 1974 (met 12 days). The 16th constitutional convention is a continuing body for 10 years or until successor is authorized and selected.	Unlimited	Nov. 7, 1972 Vote: 96,793 73,365	Commisssion to Study the State Constitution	$180,000	400 (elected March 5, 1974 from house districts; non-partisan)	27 proposed amendments to be voted on during the period 1974-80	Nov. 5, 1974: 5 proposed amendments, 2 adopted; Feb. 24, 1976: 5 proposed, 5 rejected; Nov. 2, 1976: 7 proposed, 4 adopted; Nov. 7, 1978: 4 proposed, 2 adopted; Feb. 26, 1980: 3 proposals, 3 rejected; Nov. 4, 1980: 3 proposals, 2 adopted. (Total convention proposals: 27; 10 adopted).

Section III
THE GOVERNORS AND THE EXECUTIVE BRANCH

THE GOVERNORS AND THE EXECUTIVE BRANCH, 1980-81

By Thad L. Beyle

TRENDS in state administrative organizations begun in the late 1970s continued during the first two years of the 1980s. The concerns of governors, legislators and administrators have turned from the structure and power of state government toward budget and management processes, additional revenue requirements and critical policy decisions.

In part this can be attributed to the rather extensive efforts since the mid-1960s to modernize most state governments. While some reforms remain to be carried out, as Larry Sabato was able to report "within the last fifteen years, there has been a virtual reform in state government. In most of the states as a result, the governor is now truly the master of his own house, not just the father figure."[1]

In part this shift is due to a changing federal system in which the demands on state governments and their leaders from above and below are increasing. The federalism revolution being wrought under the Reagan administration is a most visible part of these changes. But the demands for more adequate education, safer and more productive corrections policies and structures, preventive measures tied to hazardous waste disposal and health care cost containment, as well as the concern over decreasing highway revenues and increasing costs of maintaining transportation facilities, etc., all have high positions on the states' agendas.[2] With a general slow-down in additional revenues, the state tax reduction and reform efforts of the mid- to late-1970s have shifted to the state tax increases and expansions of the 1980s.

Governors

Fifteen governorships were up for election during the two-year period; in 12 of these the incumbent stood for an additional term with seven of these being re-elected. Of the five defeated governors, two were unseated in their own party's primary (Montana, Washington), and three were beaten in the general election (Arkansas, Missouri and North Dakota).

The cost of becoming governor is high, as measured by those elections. In 1980, the 13 campaigns cost the various candidates over $35 million, paced by the $12.7 million West Virginia and $6 million Missouri campaigns. This is an average of $2.7 million per gubernatorial chair, with the winners spending the greater amount (63.8 percent) as would be expected. Deleting those two largest campaigns, the average was $1.5 million per chair with the winners spending 53.4 percent.

Thad L. Beyle is Professor of Political Science at the University of North Carolina at Chapel Hill.

The two parties nearly split gubernatorial elections with eight Republican and seven Democratic winners. Previously, these seats had been held by 11 Democrats and four Republicans, which meant a net gain of four for the Republicans. As of January 1982, the political lineup was 27 Democrats and 23 Republicans. The eight new governors inaugurated in 1981-82 included three former lieutenant governors (Indiana, Montana, Virginia), a former governor (Missouri), a former attorney general (North Dakota), a former speaker of the house (New Jersey), a former county executive (Washington) and a banker who had held an appointive position in an earlier administration (Arkansas).

The Governor's Office. The size, ability and structure of governors' immediate offices have changed considerably in recent years. The average number of staff has grown from 11 persons in 1956 to 34 in 1979. The range from high to low in 1956 was from 3 to 43; in 1979 it was from 6 to 262.[3]

Much of this growth has been in the traditional staff functions such as political liaison, press relations and working with the public, but a sizable portion is tied to policy. There is increasing use of agency liaisons or aides concerned with the programs and activities that cut across several agencies or departments. In the 1979 survey, 41 states reported an average of nearly four people in each governor's office involved in federal-state relations, and at least one gubernatorial aide involved in policy development activities.

At the same time there has been a distinct trend toward more formal hierarchical structures with increasing specialization of functions. This is seen in the shift from the typical offices of the 1950s, which operated with several gubernatorial aides of relatively equal stature[4] to the adoption of a "chief of staff" model in most states by 1976, when only five states lacked an executive assistant or chief of staff to run the office.[5] The executive assistant performs many roles: advising the governor; easing communication within the office and among key administration people; working to see that decisions are made and made at the appropriate level of authority; ensuring the governor's decisions are carried out; providing the governor with a manageable span of control; and running the governor's office.[6]

Governors have also adopted new approaches to greater contact with the public. In 1981, West Virginia opened a regional governor's office in Welch, West Virginia. The governor of Idaho announced in 1980 a "Capital for a Day" meeting in each of that state's 44 counties, with two such meetings a month. These meetings include the governor, key state agency representatives, local officials and citizens in question and answer sessions with provision for follow-up action and reports. Eight other states had developed similar programs over the past few years in order to supplement the more conventional means of public communication through media, ceremonial duties, public appearances and such personal contacts as the mail and telephone provide.[7]

The Governor and the Lieutenant Governor. During the biennium at least five governors came into conflict with lieutenant governors. The governor of Montana was defeated by his lieutenant governor in the primary fight for the Democratic nomination for governor in 1980. In New Mexico, the conflict was over personnel matters, pardons and control over the National Guard when the governor was out of state.[8] In Missouri, the conflict concerned the state's constitutional provision giving all the powers and salary of the governor to the lieutenant governor when the governor is out of state unless he is accompanied by the lieutenant governor.[9] Even then the power and salary devolve to the next in line: the president pro tem of the senate. In effect, the governor became a captive in his own state. In Nebraska, the two actors were caught in a constitutional question over the lieutenant governor's right to break a tie vote in the unicameral legislature on a banking bill and then signing the bill into law as acting governor when the governor was out of state.[10]

The most well-known situation was in California where the governor had to go to court to determine the limits of the lieutenant governor's gubernatorial power while the governor was out of state. The specific issue was an appointment of a judge by the lieutenant governor, which the governor later withdrew upon return to the state. The California Supreme Court ruled in December 1979 the lieutenant governor could exercise this power under the circumstances but that the governor could withdraw the appointment until it was confirmed by the legislature.

Separate elections had much to do with these problems. In California and Missouri, both officers were separately elected and from opposite parties. In Nebraska and New Mexico, while they were jointly elected in the general election, they won the party's nomination separately. Only in Montana were governor and lieutenant governor jointly elected in both the primary and general elections.

Another area of conflict between these two offices is based on the extent of legislative powers and duties assigned some lieutenant governors by their constitutions. The greater the lieutenant governor's legislative powers, the greater the potential for a power base separate from the governor. While 28 states call on the lieutenant governor to preside over the senate, 10 provide some committee appointment power and 16 give bill assignment power.[11] Michigan voters in 1980 rejected a constitutional amendment to remove the presiding powers from their lieutenant governor or to allow the governor to fill a vacancy in the office subject to approval of both houses of the legislature.

Separation of Powers: Governors and Legislatures

There were several developments in the relationship between these two major actors in state government, including restriction of gubernatorial power of veto in several states. The Delaware Supreme Court in 1980 limited the governor's pocket veto power, stipulating it can be used after formal dissolution of the legislature or when the legislature ceases to exist on election day. Both Utah and Virginia amended their constitutions in 1980 to allow their legislatures to either reconvene or be called into special session to act on vetoes.

In 1981, New Jersey voters, through constitutional amendment, eliminated the long-held custom of gubernatorial courtesy whereby the legislature waited for the governor to call for passed bills for signature or veto, which had given the governor a most effective pocket veto. Following a New Jersey Supreme Court decision upholding the custom and the pocket veto, the constitution was amended to require all bills passed by the legislature to be presented to the governor on that or the next day, and for the governor to have 45 days to sign or veto a bill. Special sessions at the close of each term were also provided to enable the legislature to reconsider bills the governor vetoes—thereby eliminating the pocket veto.

The use of the item veto was revived in New York when the state's Court of Appeals declared the governor's impoundment of appropriated funds unconstitutional. Thus, the gubernatorial power to control appropriations by the legislature shifted from budget administration to item veto.[12]

The entire area of budget control is a major source of conflict between governors and legislatures. State legislatures have become more aggressive in budget-making, especially in doling out federal grants-in-aid and in reviewing executive branch administrative activities. According to a 1980 National Conference on State Legislatures' report, 38 states appropriate federal funds in some manner, and by late 1981, at least 11 state legislatures had created formal roles for themselves in the state response to the new federal block grants.[13] This has become an especially volatile issue with the federal aid cutbacks under the Reagan administration and the general shift to the less-structured block grant approach.

In Pennsylvania, the legislature was given the authority to appropriate federal grant dollars on a line item basis in executive and judicial budgets in 1980. The Massachusetts General Court in 1981 overrode a gubernatorial veto in order to gain some authority in the administration of federal block grants. In 1981 the governor of North Carolina, already sharing his budgetary power with a joint legislative-executive Advisory Budget Commission, found the legislature not only adding review of federal block grants to its own authority but gaining a review and approval power over any transfer by the governor of more than 10 percent of the money from one budget line to another.[14] This was challenged as an unconstitutional violation of the separation-of-powers clause of the state constitution as well as the clause giving reponsibility for administering the budget to the governor. The seed for such a challenge was sown by a state Supreme Court decision in early 1982 striking down a 1980 legislative act which mandated legislative representation on the Environmental Management Commission, an executive branch agency. The landmark decision was based on the constitutional separation of powers doctrine. A month later, the Court, in an advisory opinion, also ruled that the legislature had acted unconstitutionally in assuming review power over federal block grants and gubernatorial executive branch transfers.

Related to budget control is the issue of legislative review of executive branch activities. Over three-quarters of the state legislatures have established such a process, and while general legislative oversight of the executive branch is not questioned, the notion of a "legislative veto" of administrative rules is. Nearly one third of the states provide their legislatures with veto power, but two state court cases within the past two years may significantly affect further expansion of this power in the states. A law providing the Alaska legislature with a legislative veto over administrative regulations was declared unconstitutional by the Alaska Supreme Court in 1980 on the narrow grounds that the legislature could not exercise its legislative veto power without following the constitutionally stipulated enactment procedures. In other words, such a procedure must be similar to enacting legislation—including the governor's signature. A lower court in Connecticut in 1980 held on broader grounds that a legislative veto was an "unpermitted incursion" or violation of the separation of powers doctrine and therefore unconstitutional. The legislature is appealing to the state Supreme Court.[15] In New Jersey in 1980, the governor vetoed a legislative veto bill as inconsistent with the separation of powers principle. He argued such a legislative power would deny him his own veto power.

The third branch of government—the state courts—plays a crucial role in sharpening the issues and determining boundary lines in these questions of separation of powers between the executive branch and the legislature. The trend seems clear, however, with the legislatures becoming more assertive and intruding on previously executive turf.

Elective Officials

There were a few changes in the states' elective offices in the two-year period. Voters approved a constitutional amendment allowing the governor of South Carolina to succeed himself (1980), while the voters of New Mexico (1980) and Kentucky (1981) rejected similar amendments. In addition to these latter two states, only Mississippi and Virginia still restrict their governors to a single term. Utah voters determined gubernatorial disability and established gubernatorial succession in a revision of the executive article of the Utah constitution in 1980.

In 1980, voters in Nebraska agreed to authorize the governor to fill a vacancy in the office of lieutenant governor, and in Utah they eliminated the title of secretary of state and added a lieutenant governor who would run jointly with the governor for election. The South Carolina legislature in 1981 designated the office of lieutenant governor as a half-time position beginning in 1983.

In actions affecting other offices, the Arizona constitution was amended in 1980 to allow the treasurer to hold consecutive terms and in Delaware the auditor and treasurer had their terms extended from 2 to 4 years by legislation. In 1981, Oregon voters refused to make their superintendent of public instruction appointive rather than elective, and Maine voters refused an elected state energy commission.

State Government Organization

Many states have made changes over the past decades to make state government more manageable as well as more responsive and accountable. And, some argue it is the governor who must be the manager.[16] Several structural and procedural changes and trends support this argument.

Reorganization. Between 1965 and 1977, 21 states underwent a major executive branch reorganization.[17] Since then, no additional states have done so, but several have taken some

Table A
GOVERNORS' REORGANIZATION POWER: 1981

	Legislative veto of reorganization requires:		Legislature considers re-organization as normal bill	Reorganization power revoked
	Both houses	Either house		
Alaska(a)	C			
California		S		
Georgia				★
Illinois(a)		C		
Kansas(b)		C		
Kentucky			S	
Maryland		C		
Massachusetts(b)		C		
Michigan(a)		C		
Minnesota			S	
Missouri		S		
New Jersey	S			
North Carolina(b)		C		
Oklahoma(a)				★
Pennsylvania		S		
Rhode Island(b)				★
South Dakota		C		
Utah(a)			I	
Vermont		S		

Key:
C—Constitutional authority
S—Statutory authority
I—Informal power

(a) Executive order by governor.
(b) Plan proposed by governor.

steps to address organizational problems. In 1980, the Kentucky governor established by executive order an Executive Management Commission to review 20 agencies of the executive branch. A joint effort of private-sector "loaned executives" and state employees, the commission sought "to introduce business practices into the operation of State Government."[18] In 1981, Louisiana's governor set up a Cost Control Commission "to examine State Government operations," using private-sector executives as consultants. Since 1973 when 15 governors called for reoganization in their "State of the State" addresses, gubernatorial concern about overall reorganization has generally declined. No governors called for it in their 1981 messages.[19]

In a closely related issue, North Dakota voters in 1980 defeated a revision of the executive article of their constitution which would have authorized the governor to initiate reorganization proposals subject to vote of the legislature. This left at 15 the number of states authorizing their governors to initiate reorganization subject to legislative veto or concurrence. Other states may allow their governor to do so informally, as in Utah. In fact no state has successfully provided this power to a governor since 1972.

Functional Reorganization. As in the past, some states undertook specific functional reorganization but with no overall discernible patterns. The efforts of recent years had accomplished most that needed to be done across the states. Some of the functional area shifts were:

- *Education:* Kentucky (1980) consolidated its formerly separate secondary, elementary and occupational school boards into a single board; Massachusetts (1980) consolidated its separate boards for colleges, universities and community colleges into one Board of Regents to enhance central administration and budgetary control; Rhode Island (1981) abolished its overall Board of Regents and replaced it with three new and separate boards for higher education, elementary and secondary education and educational television; North Dakota (1981) established a higher education study commission.
- *Energy:* Mississippi (1980) consolidated its energy and transportation planning; Kentucky (1980) abolished separate energy and transportation regulation commissions, merging them into a full-time Public Service Commission; Minnesota (1980) created a more independent Public Utilities Commission out from its Public Service Department; Arkansas (1981) reduced its Energy Department to an office in the Department of Economic Development; Utah and Illinois (1981) established new Departments of Energy and Natural Resources.
- *Human Resources:* Mississippi (1980) established a Health Care Commission; Utah (1981) established a Division of Youth Corrections and authorized an ombudsman for the institutional elderly; North Dakota (1981) consolidated various human service agencies into an umbrella Department of Human Services; Washington (1981) established a separate Department of Corrections and instituted several correctional reforms; Mississippi (1981) renewed its Department of Corrections.
- *Local/Community Affairs:* Montana (1981) created a Department of Commerce by merging the Departments of Community Affairs, Professional and Occupational Licensing and Business Regulation; Wisconsin (1981) merged its Department of Local Affairs and Development into a new Department of Development; Louisiana (1980) established a Housing Finance Agency in the Department of Urban and Community Affairs to provide funds for low- and moderate-income residential housing mortgage loans; Mississippi (1980) established a Housing Finance Authority to provide tax-exempt bonds for moderate- and low-income housing.

- *Transportation:* Indiana (1980) reorganized some of its transportation agencies, creating a new Department of Highways; Mississippi (1980) abolished the Office of Motor Vehicle Comptroller and transferred its responsibilities to the State Tax Commission; Tennessee (1981) reorganized its Department of Transportation in an economy effort.

Sunset. Another reason for the lack of formal reorganization activity is the involvement of many states in sunset activities over the past six years. Beginning in 1976 with Colorado, 35 states have adopted some form of sunset legislation, the most recent being Delaware in 1980. This legislation is generally action forcing, in that it calls for the automatic termination of an agency, board or commission unless the legislature reauthorizes or re-establishes it. A legislative or executive agency usually reviews the activities and programs of the agencies under consideration before legislative action. The tendency has been for most states to focus their sunset activities on licensing and regulatory agencies. Kansas in 1980 and Montana in 1981 reported several agency and board terminations, and several other states conducted sunset reviews over the 1980-81 biennium.

However, there appears to be a lessening of interest in the states in the sunset concept. The legislation in Michigan was vetoed in 1980 by the governor as being too broad in scope, and the legislature of North Carolina abolished that state's Sunset Commission in 1981, replacing it with a legislative commission on agency review. A six-state study of sunset activities found some unanticipated results: few agencies or boards being terminated, but changes occurring in management and operations. Further, legislators were provided the opportunity to examine the issues involved in the regulatory area of state government.[20]

Cabinet Systems. There has been an increase in the states which use a cabinet system from 10 in 1969 to 35 in 1981. They vary in their composition, responsibility and frequency of meeting. While they may not wield policy-making and implementing authority, they can serve as a problem-solving group, a vehicle by which the governor can interact with key administrators.[21] Some states have turned to sub-cabinets to achieve coordination within policy areas.

Policy Management. Traditionally, the budget has been the policy management device for state government. While this still is the most significant tool available, governors have been bringing the budget office closer to their own office and blending it with planning. The most recent trend is to develop an aggressive office of policy management, following the federal Office of Management and Budget model. While such offices perform many functions, the most important is "to provide the governor with an adequate source of advice on a broad range of state policy issues."[22]

Kansas abolished its Division of Planning and Research and transferred its duties to the Division of the Budget in 1980, and North Dakota in 1981 changed the name of the Department of Accounts and Purchases to the Office of Management and Budget. However, Texas voters rejected a constitutional amendment in 1980, which would have given the governor the authority to oversee and manage the state budget.

In the budgetary process itself more attention is being paid by states to indicators and measurements other than the dollar. The increasing number of formula-based programs in which the focus of attention is on the factors that generate the allocation formulas has caused budget offices to pay considerable attention to a variety of socio-economic factors. In addition, a recent survey of 38 states indicated 25 states using some form of effectiveness measures for some or most agencies in their budget documents and 29 using productivity measures in a similar manner. The same survey also indicated that in 22 responding states the governor issues written policy guides for preparation of agency budget requests, and in 25 states the governor required the agencies to rank programs according to priorities. This is a considerable increase in the number of states doing so since surveys in 1970 and 1975.[23] These findings were consistent with another survey of the financial management systems of the states which reported over half the states working to coordinate and enhance the availability and use of data through various projects. And there was a trend toward integrating budgeting, accounting, electronic data processing, personnel, performance reporting and auditing systems more closely.[24]

The policy management process in the states has been tested by the very rapid changes in grant-in-aid programs instituted by the Reagan administration. Some states have established permanent and long-range processes and procedures. Others concentrate mainly on the short-run transition period, putting off longer-range questions. The usual process in the states is to develop information gathering and dissemination to aid in setting priorities. As of mid-December 1981, 23 states had created a new agency, committee or task force; 17 had designated a lead or coordinating agency; 18 had conducted public hearings; and four had convened convocations or retreats.[25]

Appointments. A significant tool in the management process is the governor's ability to appoint department and agency heads. This power has been enhanced over the past decade and a half, in good part due to the extensive reorganization activity in the states.[26] Louisiana in 1980 made the terms of the members of 40 appointed boards and commissions concurrent with the appointing governor, and Texas voters in 1980 approved a constitutional amendment giving the governor the power to remove his own appointments with concurrence of two-thirds of the senate.

In conflicting court cases, the Georgia Supreme Court in 1980 ruled unconstitutional the delegation of executive authority in making appointments to the State Board of Medical Examiners from a list submitted by the state medical association, while the Mississippi Supreme Court upheld the procedure, as have the federal courts.

Personnel. Management of the state government work force is another important aspect of overall management of state government. There were several states which took steps to strengthen their personnel management capacity. In 1980, Minnesota established a new Department of Employee Relations and outlined the collective bargaining and strike rights of state public employees. The governor of California, under his executive reorganization power, reorganized the state civil service system by establishing a central office of Personnel Administration which will take over the functions previously scattered among six separate agencies. Alaska split its personnel agency into a personnel management and administrative management branches and established separate divisions of labor relations and personnel.

Most significant activities in this area have been tied to the necessity for cutbacks in state budgets and personnel, due to declining revenues in the states. In a 50-state survey of the salary increases for state government employees in 1981, the median increase was in the 8-9 percent range. Increases varied considerably from a low of zero percent in Alabama to a high of 17 percent in Oklahoma.[27] However, several states operated under hiring freezes over the biennium in attempts to cut back the size of the state government work force and thereby cut back budget expenditures, and other governors instituted percentage spending cuts or holdbacks which served a similar purpose. Michigan led the states in having to undertake major budget cutbacks and reduced employee paychecks which had severe implications for that state's workers.[28]

The specter of state employee strikes over these serious actions was real. Sixty percent of Minnesota state employees walked out in 1981 over their grievances, and a 22-day strike ensued. Massachusetts employees held a 4-day strike over the serious budget cuts necessitated by the impact of Proposition 2½ on that state's budget. With the full impact of the federal aid cutbacks still to be felt, the states will undoubtedly face more problems in personnel management.

Administration. Several states took steps to better their own housekeeping functions that provide support for state government agencies. Utah in 1981 established a Department of Administrative Services, joining a growing number of states that have separated policy and service administrative activities. In 1980, Massachusetts created a Division of Capital Planning and Operations to control and supervise all state agency and building authority construction, and Arizona established a State Board of Deposit to manage public dollars. Utah in 1981 created a Risk Management Fund; however, Texas voters rejected authorization for the legislature to empower a state finance management committee, chaired by the governor with six other ex-officio members to manage the expenditure of certain appropriated funds. Alabama, North Carolina and Vermont adjusted their administrative rule-making procedures by new legislation in 1981.

Other Activities

Open Government. At least two states furthered the definition of open meetings. In the Wisconsin attorney general's 1980 opinion, state government bodies are required to hold meetings where those with functional disabilities have access without assistance. In a later opinion the attorney general also ruled telephone conference calls between members of a public body constitute a meeting under Wisconsin's open meetings law and must meet the requirements as to notice and public accessibility. Illinois' Open Meetings Act was revised in 1981 to define a meeting as "any gathering of a majority of a quorum of a public body to discuss public business."

Ethics. Ethical questions continued to be a problem in the states. Former Tennessee Governor Ray Blanton was convicted in 1981 of crimes committed while in office, along with 14 other relatives and aides. Former Maryland Governor Marvin Mandel was pardoned from his sentence in federal prison for misdeeds while in office only to be sued by the state for removing property from the official mansion. He counter-sued on the value of property he left behind.

Several states took action to correct ethical problems. The use of the state-funded computer for political campaign purposes in California led in 1981 to a written code of conduct to be communicated and enforced by the governor's office—the source of the problem. Massachusetts established an Office of Inspector General in 1980 to prevent corruption in the purchase of goods and services by both state and local governments and set new penalties for fraud and bribery in obtaining a public contract. The Massachusetts Ethics Commission in 1980 allowed media coverage of its hearings, creating trial-like proceedings for officials accused of misconduct.

Responding to a growing scandal outside of government but an integral part of the contract process, two states took action to control bid-rigging activities by contractors. North Carolina made it a felony offense with increased penalties, and Tennessee permitted its attorney general to look into contracts on request of a state district attorney.

THE GOVERNORS

Notes

1. Larry Sabato, *Goodbye to Good-Time Charlie: The American Governor Transformed, 1950-1975* (Lexington, Mass.: Lexington Books, 1978), p. 63.

2. Eric Herzik, "Governors and Issues: A Typology of Concerns," paper presented at the Annual Meeting of the Southern Political Science Association, Memphis, Tenn., November 1981.

3. Coleman B. Ransone Jr., *The Office of Governor in the United States* (University, Ala.: University of Alabama Press, 1956), p. 44, and Office of State Services Survey, National Governors' Association, 1979.

4. Ransone, *Office of the Governor*, pp. 302-62.

5. Center for Policy Research, *Governor's Office Series: 2, The Governor's Executive Assistant* (Washington, D.C.: National Governors' Association, 1976), p. 6.

6. Office of State Services reports, National Governors' Association, 1979-1981.

7. Frank H. Olander Jr. and Sydney Duncombe, "Capital-for-a-Day Program: A New Approach to Public Contact," *State Government* 54, 1 (1981): 21-27.

8. Janet Clark, "Conflict between Governor and Lieutenant Governor in New Mexico," *Comparative State Politics Newsletter* 1, 2 (January 1980): 11.

9. Phill Brooks, "Missouri's Captive Governor," *Comparative State Politics Newsletter* 1, 6 (October 1980): 12-13.

10. "Nebraska: Bankers and State Officials Battle over New Regulations," *Congressional Quarterly Weekly Report*, August 29, 1981, p. 1622.

11. For discussion of this relationship see: Thad L. Beyle and Nelson C. Dometrius, "Governors and Lieutenant Governors," *State Government* 52, 4 (Autumn 1979): 187-95.

12. Joseph F. Zimmerman, "Rebirth of the Item in the Empire State," *State Government* 54, 2 (1981): 51-52.

13. National Conference of State Legislatures, and Jean Lawson and Carl Stenberg, "Reagan Federalism: The State's Role and Response," *Intergovernmental Perspective* 8, 1 (Winter 1982): 30-41.

14. Thad L. Beyle, "How Powerful is the North Carolina Governor?" and Ran Coble, "Legislators and Governor Clash over Budget Provisions—The Legal Issues at Stake," *NC Insight* 4, 4 (Winter 1981): 3-11, 28-29.

15. Jane F. Roberts, "Fiscal Issues Dominate As States Meet the Eighties," *Intergovernmental Perspective* 7, 1 (Winter 1981): 26-27.

16. See symposium on "The Governor as Manager," *State Government* 54, 3 (1981).

17. Arkansas (1968), California (1968), Colorado (1968), Connecticut (1977), Delaware (1969), Florida (1969), Georgia (1972), Idaho (1974), Kentucky (1972), Louisiana (1975), Maine (1971), Maryland (1969), Massachusetts (1969), Michigan (1965), Missouri 1974), Montana (1971), New Mexico (1977), North Carolina (1971), South Dakota (1973), Virginia (1972) and Wisconsin (1967).

18. For discussion of this effort see: David H. Bland and Pat Ray Reese, "Kentucky's Executive Management Commission: What the Executives Thought," *State Government* 54, 2 (1981): 39-44.

19. Herzik, "Governors and Issues."

20. Doug Roederer, *Sunset: Expectation and Experience* (Lexington, Ky.: The Council of State Governments, 1981).

21. Judith Nicholson, "State Administrative Organization Activities, 1976-1977," *The Book of the States, 1978-1979* (Lexington, Ky.: The Council of State Governments, 1978), p. 107.

22. H. Edward Flentje, "Knowledge and Gubernatorial Policy Making" (Wichita: Center for Urban Studies, Wichita State University, 1980), p. 26.

23. Robert D. Lee Jr., "Developments in State Budgeting: Preliminary Results from 38 States," presentation to the Annual Meeting of the American Society for Public Administration, April 1981.

24. Stanley B. Botner, "The Quiet Revolution in State Financial Management," *State and Local Government Review* (in press).

25. Lawson and Stenberg, "Reagan Federalism."

26. Thad L. Beyle and Robert Dalton, "Appointment Power: Does It Belong to the Governor?," *State Government* 54, 1 (1981): 2-12.

27. Office of State Services Report, National Governors' Association, January 5, 1982.

28. For a state perspective on cutback management see: Harold A. Hovey, "Cutback Management in State Government," *State Government* 54, 3 (1981), 82-86.

Table 1
THE GOVERNORS
January 1982

State or other jurisdiction	Name and party	Length of regular term in years	Present term ends	Number of previous terms	Maximum consecutive terms allowed by constitution	Joint election of governor and lieutenant governor	Official who succeeds governor
Alabama	Forrest James (D)	4	Jan. 1983	...	2	No	LG
Alaska	Jay S. Hammond (R)	4	Dec. 1982	1	2	Yes	LG
Arizona	Bruce Babbitt (D)	4	Jan. 1983	(a)	...	(b)	SS
Arkansas	Frank White (R)	2	Jan. 1983	...	...	No	LG
California	Edmund G. Brown Jr. (D)	4	Jan. 1983	1	...	No	LG
Colorado	Richard D. Lamm (D)	4	Jan. 1983	1	...	Yes	LG
Connecticut	William A. O'Neill (D)	4	Jan. 1983	(c)	...	Yes	LG
Delaware	Pierre S. du Pont IV (R)	4	Jan. 1985	1	2(d)	No	LG
Florida	Bob Graham (D)	4	Jan. 1983	...	2	Yes	LG
Georgia	George D. Busbee (D)	4	Jan. 1983	1	2	No	LG
Hawaii	George R. Ariyoshi (D)	4	Dec. 1982	1	2(e)	Yes	LG
Idaho	John V. Evans (D)	4	Jan. 1983	(f)	...	No	LG
Illinois	James R. Thompson (R)	4	Jan. 1983	1(g)	...	Yes	LG
Indiana	Robert D. Orr (R)	4	Jan. 1985	...	2	Yes	LG
Iowa	Robert D. Ray (R)	4	Jan. 1983	4(h)	...	No	LG
Kansas	John Carlin (D)	4	Jan. 1983	...	2	Yes	LG
Kentucky	John Y. Brown Jr. (D)	4	Dec. 1983	...	(i)	No	LG
Louisiana	David C. Treen (R)	4	Mar. 1984	...	2	No	LG
Maine	Joseph E. Brennan (D)	4	Jan. 1983	...	2	(b)	PS
Maryland	Harry R. Hughes (D)	4	Jan. 1983	...	2	Yes	LG
Massachusetts	Edward J. King (D)	4	Jan. 1983	...	...	Yes	LG
Michigan	William G. Milliken (R)	4	Jan. 1983	1(j)	...	Yes	LG
Minnesota	Albert H. Quie (R)	4	Jan. 1983	...	...	Yes	LG
Mississippi	William Winter (D)	4	Jan. 1984	...	(i)	No	LG
Missouri	Christopher S. Bond (R)	4	Jan. 1985	1(k)	2(d)	No	LG
Montana	Ted Schwinden (D)	4	Jan. 1985	...	...	Yes	LG
Nebraska	Charles Thone (R)	4	Jan. 1983	...	2	Yes	LG
Nevada	Robert List (R)	4	Jan. 1983	...	2	No	LG
New Hampshire	Hugh J. Gallen (D)	2	Jan. 1983	1	...	(b)	PS
New Jersey	Thomas H. Kean (R)	4	Jan. 1986	...	2	(b)	PS
New Mexico	Bruce King (D)	4	Jan. 1983	1(l)	(i)	Yes	LG
New York	Hugh L. Carey (D)	4	Jan. 1983	1	...	Yes	LG
North Carolina	James B. Hunt Jr. (D)	4	Jan. 1985	1	2(d)	No	LG
North Dakota	Allen I. Olson (R)	4	Jan. 1985	...	...	Yes	LG
Ohio	James. A. Rhodes (R)	4	Jan. 1983	3(m)	2	Yes	LG
Oklahoma	George Nigh (D)	4	Jan. 1983	...	2	No	LG
Oregon	Victor Atiyeh (R)	4	Jan. 1983	...	2	(b)	SS
Pennsylvania	Richard L. Thornburgh (R)	4	Jan. 1983	...	2	Yes	LG
Rhode Island	J. Joseph Garrahy (D)	2	Jan. 1983	2	...	No	LG
South Carolina	Richard W. Riley (D)	4	Jan. 1983	...	2	No	LG
South Dakota	William J. Janklow (R)	4	Jan. 1983	...	2	Yes	LG
Tennessee	Lamar Alexander (R)	4	Jan. 1983	...	2	No	SpS(n)
Texas	William P. Clements (R)	4	Jan. 1983	...	...	No	LG
Utah	Scott M. Matheson (D)	4	Jan. 1985	1	...	Yes(o)	LG
Vermont	Richard A. Snelling (R)	2	Jan. 1983	2	...	No	LG
Virginia	Charles S. Robb (D)	4	Jan. 1986	...	(i)	No	LG
Washington	John Spellman (R)	4	Jan. 1985	...	...	No	LG
West Virginia	John D. Rockefeller IV (D)	4	Jan. 1985	1	2	(b)	PS
Wisconsin	Lee Sherman Dreyfus (R)	4	Jan. 1983	...	...	Yes	LG
Wyoming	Ed Herschler (D)	4	Jan. 1983	1	...	(b)	SS
American Samoa	Peter T. Coleman(p)	4	Jan. 1985	1(q)	2(r)	Yes	LG
Guam	Paul M. Calvo (R)	4	Jan. 1983	...	2	Yes	LG
No. Mariana Is.	Pedro P. Tenorio (R)	4	Jan. 1986	...	3(s)	Yes	LG
Puerto Rico	Carlos Romero-Barcelo (NP)	4	Jan. 1985	1	...	(b)	SS
Virgin Islands	Juan Luis (I)	4	Jan. 1983	(t)	2	Yes	LG

Key:
D—Democrat; R—Republican; I—Independent Citizens Movement; NP—New Progressive; LG—Lieutenant Governor; SS—Secretary of State; PS—President of the Senate; SpS—Speaker of the Senate.
(a) Succeeded to governor's office March 1978. Was elected to a full term November 1978.
(b) No lieutenant governor. In Puerto Rico, resident commissioner runs jointly with governor.
(c) Succeeded to governor's office December 1980.
(d) Absolute two-term limitation, but not necessarily consecutive.
(e) Governor Ariyoshi may serve three consecutive terms.
(f) Succeeded to governor's office January 1977. Was elected to a full term November 1978.
(g) Two-year term.
(h) Has served three two-year terms. Is now serving his second four-year term.
(i) Successive terms forbidden.

(j) Succeeded to governor's office January 1969. Was elected to full terms in 1970, 1974 and 1978.
(k) Served 1973-1976. Was elected again in 1980.
(l) Served 1971-1974. Was elected again in 1978.
(m) Served two terms from 1963-1966 and 1967-1970. Was elected again in 1974 and 1978.
(n) This official bears the additional statutory title of "lieutenant governor."
(o) Effective with 1984 election.
(p) American Samoa has no political party system. However, Governor Coleman is personally a member of the National Republican Party.
(q) Three-year term.
(r) Limitation is statutory.
(s) Absolute three-term limitation, but not necessarily consecutive.
(t) Succeeded to governor's office in January 1978. Was elected to a full term in November 1978.

Table 2
GOVERNOR'S COMPENSATION

State or other jurisdiction	Salary	Governor's office		Transportation provided			Travel allowance	Official residence
		Staff	Budget	Automobile	Airplane	Helicopter		
Alabama	$50,000	42	$1,629,600	★	★	★	(a)	★(b)
Alaska	74,196	41	N.A.	★	...	...	(c)	★
Arizona	50,000	26	1,405,100	★	★	(d)	$ 31,000	...
Arkansas	35,000	48	1,714,498	★	...	...	61,055	★
California	49,100	87.6	5,029,000	★	...	...	(e)	★(b)
Colorado	50,000	30.5	882,102	★	(f)	...	(c)	★
Connecticut	42,000	30	804,000	★	...	...	(a)	★
Delaware	35,000	25	748,200	★	...	★	17,000	★
Florida	65,000	46	2,048,238	★	★	...	(a)	★
Georgia	65,934	28	1,587,999	★	(f)	(d)	(a)	★
Hawaii	50,000	33	984,481	★	...	...	(c)	★
Idaho	40,000	21	637,900	★	★	...	(a)	★
Illinois	58,000	6	2,528,000	★	★	★	164,864(e)	★
Indiana	48,000(g)	24	755,904	★	★	...	(c)	★
Iowa	60,000	17	607,032	★	★	...	N.A.	★
Kansas	45,000	29	1,065,559	★	★	...	(c)	★
Kentucky	50,000	32	1,625,000	★	★	★	70,000	★(b)
Louisiana	73,400	28	1,460,159	★	★	★	7,000	★
Maine	35,000	11	436,110	★	★	...	(a)	★
Maryland	60,000	77	2,292,897	★	★(f)	★	(a)	★
Massachusetts	40,000	53	1,207,440	★	(f)	★	(a)	...
Michigan	70,000	53.5	2,781,100	★	(f)	...	10,000	★
Minnesota	66,500	38	1,256,794	★	★	★	(c)	★
Mississippi	53,000	23	993,405	★	★	★	19,200	★
Missouri	55,000	42	896,853	★	(f)	(d)	(a)	★
Montana	43,360	19.5	863,071	★	★	...	64,283(e)	★
Nebraska	40,000	6	194,477	★	★	...	(a)	★
Nevada	50,000	16	666,986	★	(f)	...	31,400(e)	★
New Hampshire	51,830(g)	19	806,206	...	...	(d)	10,000(e)	★
New Jersey	85,000(g)	64	1,709,764	★	...	(d)	36,000(h)	★
New Mexico	60,000	29	910,000	★	★	★	43,000	★
New York	85,000	N.A.	6,800,000	★	★	★	(c)	★
North Carolina	57,864	36.5	1,194,894	★	★	★	59,973	★
North Dakota	47,000(g)	14	493,146	★	(f)	...	(a)	★
Ohio	50,000(i)	20	791,000	★	★	...	...	★(b)
Oklahoma	48,000	43	1,225,520	★	★	...	(c)	★
Oregon	55,423	29	(j)	...	(f)	...	(a)	★
Pennsylvania	66,000	64	2,361,000(k)	★	★	...	(l)	★
Rhode Island	49,500	7	1,725,000	★	★	★	19,000(e)	...
South Carolina	60,000	15	680,593	★	★	★	...	★
South Dakota	46,750	10	525,000	★	(f)	...	(a)	★
Tennessee	68,226	44	1,671,600	★	★	★	161,900(e)	★
Texas	78,700	4	3,187,550	...	★	...	(c)	★
Utah	48,000	11	370,000	★	(f)	...	15,000	★(b)
Vermont	44,850	12	509,350	★	...	...	(a)	...
Virginia	75,000	25	728,660	★	★	★	52,600	★
Washington	63,000	34	(m)	★	★	...	45,000	★
West Virginia	60,000	55	1,294,791	★	(f)	(d)	N.A.	★
Wisconsin	65,801	29.9	1,076,500	★(n)	★	...	(a)	★
Wyoming	55,000	6	399,238	★	★	...	43,030(e)	★
American Samoa	40,000	18	680,500	★	...	...	45,000(e)	★
Guam	50,000	25	862,000	★	...	...	40,000	★
No. Mariana Is.	20,000	5	158,000(j)	★	...	...	...	★
Puerto Rico	35,000	N.A.	5,493,600	★	...	★	60,000	★
Virgin Islands	51,000	7	811,689	★	...	...	100,000(h)	★

N.A.—Not available.

(a) Travel allowance is included in office budget.

(b) Governor does not occupy residence.

(c) Travel allowance is flexible: in Alaska, governor is reimbursed per diem; in Minnesota, governor's travel allowance is $18,300 for in-state and $16,800 for out-of-state travel; in New York, governor is reimbursed for out-of-state travel expenses and up to $15,000 for actual in-state expenses.

(d) In Arizona, governor is provided with a helicopter for emergency use; in Georgia, governor has access to state helicopter; in Missouri, governor has access to State Highway Patrol helicopter; in New Hampshire, governor has access to National Guard helicopter; in New Jersey and West Virginia, governor has use of State Police helicopter.

(e) Travel allowance includes travel expenses for all staff.

(f) Governor has access to state plane: in Maryland, governor has a yacht; in Massachusetts, governor has access to Massachusetts Aeronautics Commission rental; in Oregon, governor pays state agency an hourly rate for plane; in Utah and West Virginia, governor's office is billed for each use of state plane.

(g) In Indiana, governor receives an additional $12,000 for expenses; in New Hampshire, governor accepted a salary of $44,520; in New Jersey, governor receives an additional $55,000 for expenses; in North Dakota, governor receives an $11,608 supplement.

(h) Contingency fund includes travel allowance.

(i) In Ohio, governor turned down salary increase of $5,000.

(j) In Oregon, the 1981-83 biennial budget is $2,284,846; in Northern Mariana Islands, budget is for nine employees.

(k) Included are Washington office ($381,000), governor's home ($147,000) and dues to interstate organizations ($118,000).

(l) A separate amount is not appropriated. An estimated amount of $120,000 for 1981-82 includes all officials in governor's office.

(m) $1,775,000 appropriated; 10.1 percent budget cut by executive order—$1,597,500.

(n) Governor is provided with a van for a mobile office.

Table 3
THE GOVERNORS: PROVISIONS AND PROCEDURES FOR TRANSITION

State or other jurisdiction	Legislation pertaining to gubernatorial transition	Appropriations available to gov.-elect	Gov.-elect participation in preparing state budget for coming fiscal year	Gov.-elect hires staff to assist during transition	State personnel made available to assist gov.-elect	Office space in buildings available to gov.-elect	Provisions for acquainting gov.-elect staff with office procedures and routine office functions	Provisions for transfer of information (records, files, etc.)
Alabama	...	...	...	...	...	...	...	...
Alaska	...	...	...	...	...	☆	...	☆
Arizona	...	...	☆	...	☆	☆	☆	☆
Arkansas	★	$ 60,000	★	★	...	☆	...	...
California	★	348,000	★	★	★	★	☆	☆
Colorado	★	10,000	★	★	...	★	★	★
Connecticut	★	10,000	☆	★	☆	★	...	★
Delaware	★	10,000 (a)	...	...	☆	★	☆	☆
Florida	★	75,000	...	★	☆	★	☆	☆
Georgia	★	★	☆	☆	☆	★	☆	☆
Hawaii	★	50,000	★	...	★	★	★	★
Idaho	★	15,000	★	★	★	★	★	★
Illinois	★	...	★	★(b)	★(c)	★	★	★
Indiana	★	40,000	★	★	★	★	★	★
Iowa	★(d)	10,000	★	★	☆(e)	...	★	★(f)
Kansas	★	100,000	★	★	★	★	★	★
Kentucky	★	Unspecified	★	★	★	★	★	★
Louisiana	...	10,000	★	★	...	★	☆	☆
Maine	★	5,000	★	★	★(g)	...	★	☆
Maryland	...	50,000	★	★	★	★	★	★
Massachusetts	...	★	☆	★	★	★	☆	☆
Michigan	...	...	...	...	...	...	☆	☆
Minnesota	★	29,600	★	★	★	★	☆	☆
Mississippi	★	25,000	★	★	★	★	★	★
Missouri	★	100,000	★	★	☆	★	...	...
Montana	★	30,000	★(h)	★	★	★	★	★
Nebraska	★	30,000 (i)	☆	★	☆	☆	☆	☆
Nevada	...	...	★	★	☆	★	☆	☆
New Hampshire	★	5,000	★	★	★	★	★	...
New Jersey	★	150,000	★	★	★	★	☆	★
New Mexico	★	25,000	★	★	☆	★	☆	☆
New York	...	...	☆	☆	☆	☆	☆	☆
North Carolina	★	3,500 (j)	★	★	★	★	★	★
North Dakota	...	★	...	...	☆	...	☆	★
Ohio	★	30,000	...	★	★	★	...	☆
Oklahoma	★	10,000	★	★	...	☆	...	...
Oregon	★	20,000	★	★	★	★	★	★
Pennsylvania	★	100,000	...	★	☆	★	★	...
Rhode Island	...	...	★	...	...	★	...	...
South Carolina	★	50,000	★	★	...	★	...	☆
South Dakota	★	10,000	...	★	☆	★	☆	★
Tennessee	★	(k)	☆	★	★	★	☆	★
Texas	...	...	★(l)	★	☆	...	...	☆
Utah	...	5,000 (m)	★	★	...	★	...	...
Vermont	...	18,000	★(n)	★	★	★	...	(o)
Virginia	...	40,000	★	★	★	★	★	★
Washington	★	80,000	☆	☆	☆	☆	☆	☆
West Virginia	...	...	...	...	...	☆	☆	...
Wisconsin	★	Unspecified	★	★	★	★	★	★
Wyoming	...	10,000 (i)	★	★	...	...	...	...
American Samoa	...	Unspecified	★(p)	☆	☆	☆	☆	☆
Guam	...	...	...	...	...	...	...	...
No. Mariana Is.	...	...	...	...	...	...	...	...
Puerto Rico	...	56,000 (a)	...	☆	☆	☆	☆	☆
Virgin Islands	...	...	...	...	...	...	...	...

Key:
... —No provisions or procedures.
★ —Formal provisions or procedures.
☆ —No formal provisions; occurs informally.
(a) Inaugural expenses are paid from this amount.
(b) On a contractual basis.
(c) Voluntary assistance.
(d) Pertains only to funds.
(e) Provided on irregular basis.
(f) Arrangement for transfer of criminal files.
(g) Budget personnel.
(h) Can submit supplemental budget.
(i) Made available in 1979.
(j) In addition, $1,500 is made available for the lieutenant governor-elect.
(k) Money made available from emergency and contingency funds.
(l) Outgoing governor and incoming governor present separate budgets to the legislature.
(m) Allocated from the governor's emergency fund.
(n) Responsible for the preparation of the budget; staff made available.
(o) Not transferred but use may be authorized.
(p) Can submit reprogramming or supplemental appropriation measures for current fiscal year.

Table 4
LIEUTENANT GOVERNORS: QUALIFICATIONS AND TERMS*
(In years)

State or other jurisdiction	Minimum age	State citizen	U.S. citizen	State resident	Qualified voter	Length of term	Maximum consecutive terms allowed
Alabama	30	7	10	7	...	4	2
Alaska	30	...	7	7	(a)	4	...
Arizona				(b)			
Arkansas	30	...	(a)	7	...	2	...
California	18	5	5	5	(a)	4	...
Colorado	30	...	(a)	2	...	4	...
Connecticut	30	...	...	...	(a)	4	...
Delaware	30	...	12	6	...	4	...
Florida	30	...	...	7	(a)	4	...
Georgia	30	6	15	...	...	4	...
Hawaii	30	...	...	5	(a)	4	2
Idaho	30	...	(a)	2	...	4	...
Illinois	25	...	(a)	3	...	4	...
Indiana	30	...	5	5	...	4	...
Iowa	30	...	(a)	2	...	4	...
Kansas	...	...	...	...	...	4	2
Kentucky	30	6	...	6	...	4	(c)
Louisiana	25	5	5	5	(a)	4	...
Maine				(b)			
Maryland	30	5	5	5	5	4	...
Massachusetts	...	...	...	7	...	4	...
Michigan	30	...	...	...	4	4	...
Minnesota	25	...	(a)	1	...	4	...
Mississippi	30	...	20	5	...	4	...
Missouri	30	...	15	10	...	4	...
Montana	25	...	(a)	2	(a)	4	...
Nebraska	30	5	5	5	...	4	...
Nevada	25	...	...	2	(a)	4	2
New Hampshire				(b)			
New Jersey				(b)			
New Mexico	30	...	(a)	5	...	4	(c)
New York	30	...	(a)	5	...	4	...
North Carolina	30	...	5	2	...	4	2
North Dakota	30	...	(a)	5	(a)	4	...
Ohio	...	...	...	...	(a)	4	...
Oklahoma	31	...	(a)	...	10	4	...
Oregon				(b)			
Pennsylvania	30	...	(a)	7	...	4	2
Rhode Island	18	...	(a)	...	(a)	2	...
South Carolina	30	5	5	5	...	4	...
South Dakota	...	...	(a)	2	...	4	2
Tennessee				(b)			
Texas	30	...	(a)	5	...	4	...
Utah	30	...	...	5	(a)	4	...
Vermont	...	...	...	4	...	2	...
Virginia	30	...	(a)	5	5	4	...
Washington	...	...	(a)	...	(a)	4	...
West Virginia				(b)			
Wisconsin	18	...	(a)	...	(a)	4	...
Wyoming				(b)			
American Samoa	35	...	(d)	5	...	4	2
Guam	30	...	5	...	(a)	4	2
Puerto Rico				(b)			
Virgin Islands	30	...	5	...	(a)	4	2

*This table includes constitutional and some statutory qualifications.
(a) Required by constitution but number of years not specified.
(b) No lieutenant governor. In Tennessee, the senate president, who bears the statutory title of lieutenant governor, is elected from the senate membership by the senate rather than by statewide election.
(c) Successive terms forbidden.
(d) U.S. citizen or National.

Table 5
LIEUTENANT GOVERNORS: POWERS AND DUTIES

State or other jurisdiction	Presides over senate	Appoints committees	Breaks roll-call ties	Assigns bills	Authority for governor to assign duties	Head of executive department	Serves when governor out of state
Alabama	★	★	★	★	...	...	★(a)
Alaska	...	★	...	...	★	★(b)	★
Arizona					(c)		
Arkansas	★	...	★	...	...	...	★
California	★	...	★	...	★	...	★
Colorado	...	...	...	...	★	...	★
Connecticut	★	...	★	...	★	...	★
Delaware	★	...	★	★	...	...	...
Florida	...	...	...	...	★	...	(d)
Georgia	★	(e)	...	★	...	...	...
Hawaii	...	...	...	...	★	★(b)	★
Idaho	★	...	★	...	★	...	★
Illinois	...	...	...	...	★	...	...
Indiana	★	...	★	...	★	Dept. of Commerce	...
Iowa	★	★(f)	★(g)	★(f)	...	...	...
Kansas	...	...	...	...	★	...	★(h)
Kentucky	★	...	★	★	★	...	★
Louisiana	...	...	...	...	★	...	★
Maine					(c)		
Maryland	...	...			★	...	...
Massachusetts	...	...	...	...	★	...	★
Michigan	★	...	★	...	★(i)	...	★
Minnesota	...	...	...	...	★(i)	...	★
Mississippi	★	★(j)	★	★	...	...	★
Missouri	★	...	★(g)	...	...	...	★
Montana	...	...	...	...	★(i)	...	★(a)
Nebraska	★	...	★	...	★	...	★
Nevada	★	...	...	...	...	...	★
New Hampshire					(c)		
New Jersey					(c)		
New Mexico	★	...	★	★(k)	★		★
New York	★	...	★	...	★	...	★
North Carolina	★	★	★	★	★	...	★
North Dakota	★	★(l)	★	★	★	...	★
Ohio	...	★	...	...	★	...	...
Oklahoma	★	...	★	...	...	Tourism & Recreation	★
Oregon					(c)		
Pennsylvania	★	...	★(g)	★	★	...	...
Rhode Island	★	...	★	★	...	...	★
South Carolina	★	★(m)	★	★	★	...	★(h)
South Dakota	★	...	★	★	★	...	★(n)
Tennessee					(c)		
Texas	★	★	★	★	...	...	★
Utah	...	...	...	...	★	...	...
Vermont	★	(e)	★	★	...	...	★
Virginia	★	...	★	...	★	...	...
Washington	★	★(o)	★(g)	★	★	...	★
West Virginia					(c)		
Wisconsin	...	...	...	...	★	...	★
Wyoming					(c)		
American Samoa	...	...	...	...	★	...	★
Guam	...	...	...	...	...	Federal Liaison Office	★
Puerto Rico					(c)		
Virgin Islands	...	...	...	...	...	...	★

(a) After 20 days absence, except for Montana which is after 45 days.

(b) Performs the function generally granted to a secretary of state.

(c) No lieutenant governor, except in Tennessee the speaker of the senate bears the additional statutory title "Lieutenant Governor."

(d) Lieutenant governor does not serve as governor in his absence, but the governor leaves lieutenant governor in charge of operations of governor's office.

(e) The lieutenant governor is a member of the Committee on Committees which appoints the committees. In Georgia he is chairman.

(f) When the lieutenant governor is a member of the senate majority party.

(g) Except for final passage.

(h) Has authority to act in an emergency when the governor is absent from the state.

(i) May perform duties requested by the governor, but no power vested in the governor may be delegated.

(j) Except rules and legislative service committees.

(k) Only with sponsor's request.

(l) By tradition, the lieutenant governor appoints those persons suggested by the party leaders.

(m) Appoints study committees but not standing committees.

(n) Only when governor is continuously absent or suffers a temporary disability. The state supreme court must determine when such a situation exists.

(o) Subject to senate confirmation.

Table 6
ATTORNEYS GENERAL AND SECRETARIES OF STATE:
QUALIFICATIONS FOR OFFICE

State or other jurisdiction	Attorneys General						Secretaries of State			
	Minimum age	U.S. citizen (years)	State resident (years)	Qualified voter	Licensed attorney (years)	Membership in the state bar (years)	Minimum age	U.S. citizen (years)	State resident (years)	Qualified voter
Alabama	25	7	5	...	...	...	25	7	5	★
Alaska	...	★	...	...	...	...	(a)	(a)	(a)	(a)
Arizona	25	10	5	...	...	...	25	10	5	★
Arkansas	...	★	★	★(b)	...	...	...	...	★	★(b)
California	18	...	★	...	★(c)	★(c)	...	...	...	★(b)
Colorado	25	★	2	...	★	...	25	★	2	★
Connecticut	21	★	6 mos.	★	10	10	21	★	★	★
Delaware	...	...	...	...	...	...	...	...	...	...
Florida	30	★	7	★	5	5	30	★	7	★
Georgia	25	10	6	★	7	6	25	10	6	...
Hawaii	...	★	1	...	...	...	(a)	(a)	(a)	(a)
Idaho	30	★	2	★	★	★	25	★	2	...
Illinois	25	★	3	...	...	...	25	★	3	...
Indiana	...	★	★	★(b)	★	...	...	...	...	★(b)
Iowa	...	...	...	...	...	...	...	...	★	...
Kansas	...	★	...	...	★	★	...	...	...	★(b)
Kentucky	30	2	2	...	8	2	30	...	2	...
Louisiana	25	5	5	★	5	5	25	5	5	★
Maine	...	...	...	...	...	...	...	...	...	...
Maryland	...	...	10	★(b)	10	10(d)	...	...	...	...
Massachusetts	...	★	5	★	★	★	18	★	5	★
Michigan	18	★	30 days	★	★	★	...	★	30 days	★(b)
Minnesota	21	3 mos.	30 days	★	...	...	21	★	★	★
Mississippi	26	★	5	★	5	5	25	5	5	★
Missouri	...	...	...	...	...	...	...	...	...	...
Montana	25	★	2	...	5	5(d)	25	2	2	...
Nebraska	21(e)	...	★(d)	...	★(d)	...	18	★	★	...
Nevada	25	2	2	★	...	...	18	2	2	★
New Hampshire	...	...	...	...	★	★	...	...	...	...
New Jersey	18(f)	...	★	...	★	★	...	...	...	...
New Mexico	30	★	5	...	★	★	30	★	5	★
New York	30	★	5	...	★(d)	...	21	★	1	...
North Carolina	21	★	30 days	★	...	...	21	★	1	...
North Dakota	25	★	★	★	...	...	25	...	30 days	★
Ohio	18	30 days	30 days	★	...	...	...	...	...	★(b)
Oklahoma	31	★	10	★	...	...	31	★	10	★
Oregon	...	...	...	★(b)	...	...	18	★	★	★
Pennsylvania(g)	30	★	7	★(d)	★(d)	★	...	...	...	...
Rhode Island	18	30 days	30 days	★	...	...	18	30 days	30 days	★
South Carolina	...	...	★	★(b)	...	...	21	★	1	★
South Dakota	...	★	★	★(b)	★	★	...	...	...	...
Tennessee	...	...	...	...	...	...	...	★	★	...
Texas	...	★	...	...	★	★	...	★	★	...
Utah	25	★	5	★	★	★	(a)	(a)	(a)	(a)
Vermont	...	...	...	...	...	...	...	...	...	★(b)
Virginia	...	...	★	★(b)	★	...	...	...	...	...
Washington	...	★	★	★(b)	★	★	...	★	★	★(b)
West Virginia	25	5	5	★	...	...	18	5	5	★
Wisconsin	...	...	...	...	...	...	...	...	...	...
Wyoming	...	...	★	...	4	4	25	★	★	★
American Samoa	...	...	...	...	...	...	(a)	(a)	(a)	(a)
Guam	N.A.	N.A.	N.A.	N.A.	N.A.	N.A.	(a)	(a)	(a)	(a)
Northern Mariana Is.	...	...	...	...	5(d)	...	(a)	(a)	(a)	(a)
Puerto Rico	21(e)	...	...	...	★(d)	★(d)	...	...	...	...
Virgin Islands	...	★	...	...	★(h)	...	(a)	(a)	(a)	(a)

N.A.—Not available.

(a) No secretary of state.

(b) Although there may be no specific requirement for minimum age of U.S. citizen, it can be inferred that the individual must be 18 years old and a U.S. citizen since he or she must be a qualified voter. In addition, some states have residency requirements to be a qualified voter and these can be found in the table "Qualifications for Voting."

(c) No statute specifically requires this, but the State Bar Act can be construed as making this a qualification.

(d) Implied.

(e) Implied, since the attorney general must represent the state in all legal matters and, therefore, must be an attorney. To be an attorney in Nebraska and Puerto Rico, one must be at least 21 years old.

(f) Implied, since the attorney general must be a practicing attorney and to be an attorney in New Jersey, one must be at least 18 years old.

(g) These qualifications took effect for the first time with the attorney general entering office in 1981.

(h) Must be admitted to practice before highest court of a state or territory.

Table 7
SECRETARIES OF STATE: LEGISLATIVE LICENSING, REGISTRATION AND CUSTODIAL DUTIES

State or other jurisdiction	Legislative				Licensing and registration				Custodial duties				
	Opens legislative sessions(a)	Custodian or recorder of documents	Registers lobbyists	Engrosses & enrolls bills	Prepares extradition papers or warrants of arrest	Licenses professions	Registers charitable organizations	Commissions notaries public	Keeps records of lands of state	Files agency reports, rules & regulations	Administers uniform commercial code provisions	Files articles of incorporation for corporations	Collects taxes from corporations(b)
Alabama	...	...	...	...	★	...	...	...	★	★	★	★	...
Alaska(c)	★	...	...	★	...	...	...	★	...	★(d)	...	...	...
Arizona	...	★	★	...	...	...	...	★	...	★	★	...	...
Arkansas	H	...	★	...	...	★	★	★	...	★	★	★	...
California	...	★	★	...	★	...	...	★	...	★	★	★	...
Colorado	...	...	★	...	...	...	★	★	...	★	★	★	D,F
Connecticut	★	...	...	...	...	...	...	★	...	★	★	★	D,F
Delaware	...	...	...	...	...	...	★	★	★	★	★	★	D,F
Florida	...	...	...	...	★	...	...	★	...	...	★	★	D,F
Georgia	...	★	★	...	...	...	★	★	★	★	★	★	...
Hawaii(c)	★	...	...	...	...	...	...	...	★	...	...	...	...
Idaho	...	★	★	...	...	...	★(e)	...	...	★	★	★	...
Illinois	H	★	★	...	...	...	★	★	★	★	★	★	D,F
Indiana	H	...	★	...	★	...	...	★	...	★	★	★	...
Iowa	...	★	...	...	...	...	★(e)	★	★	...	★	★	...
Kansas	★	★	★	...	...	...	★	★	★	...	★	★	D,F
Kentucky	...	★	...	★	★(f)	★	★	★	...	★	★	★	...
Louisiana	...	★	...	...	★(g)	...	★(e)	★(f)	...	...	...	★	D,F(h)
Maine	...	...	★	★	★	...	...	★	...	★	★	★	...
Maryland	...	★	...	★	★	...	★	★	...	★	★	...	...
Massachusetts	...	★	★	...	★	...	★	★	...	★	★	★	...
Michigan	...	★	★	...	...	...	...	★	...	★	★	★	...
Minnesota	★	★	★	...	...	...	...	...	...	★	★	★	...
Mississippi	...	★	★	★	★	...	...	★	★	★	★	★	...
Missouri	★	★	...	...	...	...	★(e)	★	★	★	★	★	...
Montana	H	★	★	...	...	...	★(e)	...	...	★(i)	★	★	...
Nebraska	...	★	...	★	★	★	★	★	★	★	★	★	D,F
Nevada	H	...	...	...	...	...	★	★	★	★	★	★	D,F
New Hampshire	...	★	★	★	...	...	...	★	...	★	★	★	...
New Jersey	...	...	...	...	★	...	...	★	...	★	★	★	...
New Mexico	H	★	★	...	★	...	...	★	...	★	...	★	...
New York	...	★	...	...	...	★	★	★	★	★	★	★	...
North Carolina	H	★	★	...	...	...	★	★	...	...	★	★	...
North Dakota	...	★	★	...	★	...	★	★	...	★	★	★	D,F(h)
Ohio	...	★	...	...	...	...	...	...	...	★	★	★	F(j)
Oklahoma	...	★	...	...	★	★	★	★	...	★	...	★	F
Oregon	...	★	...	...	...	...	...	★	...	★	★	★	...
Pennsylvania	...	★	...	★	★	★	★	★	...	★	★	★	...
Rhode Island	...	★	...	...	...	...	★	★	...	★	★	★	...
South Carolina	...	★	★	...	...	...	...	★	...	...	★	★	...
South Dakota	H	★	★	...	★	...	★(e)	★	...	★	★	★	...
Tennessee	...	★	...	...	...	★	★	★	...	★	★	★	...
Texas	H	★	★	...	★	...	...	★	...	★	★	★	...
Utah(c)	S	★	★	★	★	...	★	★	★	★	★	★	...
Vermont	★	★	★	★	...	★	...	...	★	★	★	★	...
Virginia	...	...	★	...	★	...	...	★	...	...	...	...	...
Washington	...	★	...	...	...	...	...	★	...	...	...	★	D,F
West Virginia	★	★	★	★	★	...	★	★	...	★	★	★	...
Wisconsin	...	★	★	...	...	...	...	★	★	★	★	★	...
Wyoming	H	★	...	...	...	...	...	★	...	★	★	★	D,F
American Samoa(c)	...	...	...	★	...	...	...	...	...	...	...	...	...
Puerto Rico	...	★	...	...	...	★	★	★	...	★	...	★	★

(a) In this column only: ★—Both houses; H—House; S—Senate.
(b) D—Domestic; F—Foreign.
(c) No secretary of state. Duties indicated are performed by lieutenant governor.
(d) Administrative regulations only.
(e) Only as corporations.
(f) On instructions from governor.
(g) Extradition only.
(h) Collects fees for filing certain corporate reports and papers.
(i) Rules only.
(j) Annual fee only.

Table 8
SECRETARIES OF STATE: ELECTION AND PUBLICATION DUTIES

State or other jurisdiction	Election								Publication				
	Chief election officer	Registers political parties & determines ballot eligibility	Files nomination papers	Receives initiative or referendum petition	Submits constitutional amendments to voters	Issues certificates of nomination & election	Supplies election ballots or material to local officials	Files candidates' expense papers	State manual or directory	Session laws	State constitution	Statutes	Administrative rules & regulations
Alabama	★	★	★	...	★	★	...	★	...	★	...	...	...
Alaska(a)	...	...	...	★	...	...	...	...	...	★	...	...	★
Arizona	★	★(b)	★	★	★	★	...	★	...	★	★	★	★
Arkansas	★	★	★	★	★	★	★	★	...	★	★	...	★
California	★	★	★(b)	★(b)	★	★(b)	★	★(b)	★	...	...	...	...
Colorado	★	★	★	★	★	★	...	★	...	★	...	★	
Connecticut	★	★	★	...	★	★	★	★	★	★(c)	★	★(c)	★
Delaware	...	...	...	...	...	...	...	★	...	...	...	...	★
Florida	★	★	★	★	...	★	...	★	★	...	★	★	★
Georgia	★	★	★	...	★	★	★	★	★	★	★	★	★
Hawaii(a)	★	★	★	...	★	★	★	★(d)	...	(e)	...	(e)	(f)
Idaho	★	★	★(g)	★	★	★(g)	★	★(g)	★	★	★	★	...
Illinois	...	...	...	...	★	...	...	...	★	★	★	...	★
Indiana	...	...	★	...	...	★	...	★(h)	...	...	...	...	★
Iowa	★	★(b)	★	...	★	★(i)	...	★(h)	...	...	...	...	...
Kansas	★	★	★	...	★	★	...	★	★	★	★(c)	★(c)	★(c)
Kentucky	★	★	★	★	★	★	★	★	...	...	...	...	...
Louisiana	★	...	★(g)	★	★	...	...	★(h)	★	★	...	...	...
Maine	★	★	★	★	★	★	★	★(j)	★	...	★	...	★
Maryland	...	...	...	★	★	...	...	★	★	...	★	★	★
Massachusetts	★	★	★	★	★	★	...	...	★	★	★	★	★
Michigan	★	★	★	★	★	★(k)	★	...	★	★	★	...	...
Minnesota	★	★	★	...	★	★	★	★	★	★	★	...	...
Mississippi	★(l)	...	...	...	...	★(k)	...	★	★	★	★	★	...
Missouri	★	★	★	★	★	★	★	★	★	★	★	...	★
Montana	★	...	...	★	★	...	...	★(h)	...	★	★	...	★
Nebraska	★	★	★	★	★	★	★	...	...	★	★	...	★
Nevada	★	★	★	★	★	★	★	★	...	★	★	...	★
New Hampshire	★	★	★	★	★	★	★	★	★	★	★	...	★
New Jersey	★	...	★	...	...	★	★	★	★	★	★	★	★
New Mexico	★	★	★	★	...	★	★	★	...	★	★	...	★
New York	...	...	...	...	...	...	...	...	★	★	★	★	★
North Carolina	...	...	★	...	...	★(k)	...	...	★	★	★	★	★
North Dakota	★	...	★	★	★	★	...	★(b)	...	★	★	★	...
Ohio	★	★	★	★	★	★	...	★	...	★	★	...	...
Oklahoma	...	...	...	★	★	...	...	★	...	★	★	★	★
Oregon	★	★	★	★	★	★	★	★	...	★	★	★	★
Pennsylvania	★	★	★	...	★	★(k)	★	★	...	...	...	...	★
Rhode Island	...	...	★	...	★	...	...	...	★	★	★	★	★
South Carolina	...	...	...	...	...	...	...	...	...	...	...	...	...
South Dakota	★	★	★(g)	★	★	★	...	★	...	★	★	...	★
Tennessee	...	★	★	★	...	★	★	★	★	★	★	★	★
Texas	★	★	...	...	★	★	...	★	★	★	★	★	★
Utah(a)	★	★	★	★	★	★	...	★	★	★	★	...	★
Vermont	★	★	★	...	★	★(k)	★	★	★	★	★	...	★
Virginia	...	...	...	...	...	...	...	...	★	...	...	...	...
Washington	★	★	★	★	★	★	★	...	...	★	★	...	★
West Virginia	★	★	★	★	★	★	...	★	...	★	...	...	...
Wisconsin	...	...	...	...	...	...	...	...	...	★	★	...	...
Wyoming	★	★(g)	★	★	★	★(m)	★	★	★	...	★	...	...
American Samoa(a)	...	...	...	...	...	...	...	...	...	...	...	...	★
Puerto Rico	...	...	...	...	...	...	...	...	...	...	★	★	★

(a) No secretary of state. Duties indicated are performed by lieutenant governor.
(b) On state level only.
(c) Distribution only.
(d) By Campaign Spending Commission attached to lieutenant governor's office for administrative purposes.
(e) Sales of session laws and statutes to public.
(f) Maintains central file of administrative rules for public inspection.
(g) On state and federal level.

(h) On federal level only.
(i) Certifies candidates' names to counties for ballots.
(j) Commission on Governmental Ethics and Election Practices attached to secretary of state's office.
(k) Files certificates of election only.
(l) State Election Commission composed of governor, secretary of state and attorney general.
(m) Nomination only; governor issues certificates of election.

Table 9

ATTORNEYS GENERAL: PROSECUTORIAL AND ADVISORY DUTIES

State or other jurisdiction	Authority to initiate local prosecutions	May intervene in local prosecutions	May assist local prosecutor	May supersede local prosecutor	Issues advisory opinions					Reviews legislation	
					To state executive officials	To legislators	To local prosecutors	On the interpretation of statutes	On the constitutionality of bills or ordinances	Prior to passage	Before signing
Alabama	A	A,D	A,D	A	★	★	★	★	★	★	...
Alaska	A(a)	A(a)	A(a)	A(a)	★	★	...	★	★	★	★
Arizona	A,B,C,D,F	B,D	B,D	B	★	★	★	★	★	★	★
Arkansas	...	D	D	...	★	★	★	★	★	★	★
California	A, E	A,D,E	A,B,D	A	★	★	★	★	★	★	★
Colorado	B,F	B	D,F(b)	B	★	★	★	★	★	★	★
Connecticut	...	...	...	...	★	...	★	★	★	★	★
Delaware	(c)	(c)	(c)	(c)	★	★	(c)	★	★	★	★
Florida	F	D	D	...	★	★	★	★	...	★	★
Georgia	A,B,F	A,B,D,G	A,B,D,F	B	★	★	★	★	...	★	★
Hawaii	E	A,D,G	A,D	A,G	★	★	★	★	★	★	★
Idaho	A,D,F	A	A,D	A	★	★	★	★	...	★	★
Illinois	A,D,E,F,G	A,D,E	A,D	F	★	★	★	★	★	(d)	(d)
Indiana	F(b)	...	A,D,E,F	G	★	★	★	★	...	★	★
Iowa	D,F	D	D	...	★	★	★	★	★	★	★
Kansas	B,C,D,F	D	D	A,F	★	★	★	★	★	★	★
Kentucky	A,B	B,D	B,D,F	G	★	★	★	★	★	★	...
Louisiana	G	G	D	G	★	★	★	★	★	★	★
Maine	A	A	A	A	★	★	★	...	★	★	★
Maryland	B,C,F	B,C,D	B,C,D	B,C	★	★	★	★	★	★	★
Massachusetts	A,B,C,D,E,F,G	A,B,C,D,E,G	A,B,C,D,E	A,B,C,E	★	★	...	★	★	★	★
Michigan	A	A	D	A	★	★	★	★	★	★	★
Minnesota	B	B,D,G	A,B,D	B	★	★	★	★	★	...	(d)
Mississippi	B,E,F	...	B,F	...	★	★	★	★	★	(d)	(d)
Missouri	F	...	B	...	★	★	★	★	...	★	★
Montana	C,F	A,B,C,D	A,B,C,D,F	A,C	★	★(e)	★	★	★	...	...
Nebraska	A	A	A,D	A	★	★	★	★	★	...	...
Nevada	D,F,G(f)	D(f)	(f,g)	G,F	★	...	★	★	★	...	...
New Hampshire	A	A	A	A	★	★	★	★	★	★	★
New Jersey	A	A,B,D,G	A,D	A,B,D,G	★	★	★	★	★	★	★
New Mexico	A,B,E,F,G	B,D,G	D	B	★	★	★	★	★	★	★
New York	B,F,	B	D	B	★	★	★	★	★	★	★
North Carolina	...	D	D	...	★	★	...	★	★	★	...
North Dakota	A,G	A,D	A,D	A	★	★	★	...	...	...	(d)
Ohio	B,C,F	B,F	F	B,C	★	★(e)	★	...		...	...
Oklahoma	B,C	B,C	B,C	B,C	★	★	★	★	★	★	★
Oregon	B,F	B,D	B,D	B	★	★	★	★	★	(d)	(d)
Pennsylvania	A,D,G	D,G	D	G	★	★	★	...	...	★	★
Rhode Island	A	D	D	...	★	★	...	★	★	★	...
South Carolina	A	A,D	A,D	A	★	★	★	★	★	★	★
South Dakota	A(h)	A	A	A	★	★	★	★	★	★	★
Tennessee	D,F,G(b)	D,G(b)	D	F	★	★	★	★	★	(d)	(d)
Texas	F	...	D	...	★	★	★	★	★	★	★
Utah	A,B,D,E,F,G	E,G	D,E	E	★	...	★	★	★	(d)	(d)
Vermont	A	A	A	A	★	★	★	★	★	★	★
Virginia	B,F	A,B,D,F	B,D,F	B	★	★	★	★	★	★	★
Washington	B,D,G	B,D,G	D	B	★	★	★	★	★	★	★
West Virginia	...	...	...	...	★	★	★	★	★	(i)	(i)
Wisconsin	B,C,F	B,C,D	D	B,C(j)	★	★	★	★	★	(i)	(i)
Wyoming	B,D(b)	B,D	B,D	...	★	★	★	★	...	★	★
American Samoa	A,E	A,E	A,E	A,E	★	★	...	★	★	★	★
No. Mariana Is.	A	...	...	...	★	★	...	★	★	★	★
Puerto Rico	A,B,E	A,B,E	A,E	A,B,E	★	★	...	★	★	★	★
Virgin Islands	A	...	...	...	★	★	...	★	★	★	★

Key:
A—On own initiative.
B—On request of governor.
C—On request of legislature.
D—On request of local prosecutor.
E—When in state's interest.
F—Under certain statutes for specific crimes.
G—On authorization of court or other body.
(a) Local prosecutors serve at pleasure of attorney general.
(b) Certain statutes provide for concurrent jurisdiction with local prosecutors.

(c) No local prosecutions or prosecutors.
(d) Only when requested by governor or legislature.
(e) To legislative leadership only or to legislature as a whole.
(f) In connection with grand jury cases.
(g) Will prosecute as a matter of practice when requested.
(h) Has concurrent jurisdiction with states' attorneys.
(i) No legal authority, but sometimes informally reviews laws at request of legislature.
(j) If the governor removes the district attorney for cause.

Table 10

ATTORNEYS GENERAL: CONSUMER PROTECTION ACTIVITIES AND SUBPOENA AND ANTITRUST POWERS

State or other jurisdiction	May commence civil proceedings	May commence criminal proceedings	Represents the state before regulatory agencies	Administers consumer protection programs	Handles consumer complaints	Subpoena powers (a)	Antitrust duties
Alabama	★	★	. . .	★	★	•	A, B
Alaska	★	★	★	★	★	★	B, C
Arizona	★	. . .	. . .	★	★	★	A, B, D
Arkansas	★	. . .	★	★	★	★	B, C, D
California	★	. . .	. . .	. . .	★	★	B, C, D
Colorado	★	★	★	★	★	•	B, C, D(b)
Connecticut	★	. . .	★	★	. . .	•	A, B, D
Delaware	★	★	★	★	. . .	★	A, B, C
Florida	★	★	. . .	★	★	★	A, B, C, D
Georgia	★	★	★	. . .	. . .	★	B, C, D
Hawaii	★	★	★	. . .	. . .	★	A, B, C, D
Idaho	★	. . .	★	★	★	•	D
Illinois	★	★	★	★	★	•	A, B, D
Indiana	★	. . .	. . .	★	★	. . .	B, C, D
Iowa	★	★	★	★	★	•	A, B, C, D
Kansas	★	★	★	★	★	★	B, C, D
Kentucky	★	★	★	★	★	★(c)	A, B, D
Louisiana	★	. . .	★	. . .	★	★	B, C
Maine	★	★	★	★	★	★	B, C
Maryland	★	★	★	★	★	★	B, C, D
Massachusetts	★	★	★	★	★	•	A, B, C, D
Michigan	★	★	★	★	★	•	A, B, C, D
Minnesota	★	. . .	★	★	★	•	B, D
Mississippi	★	. . .	★	★	★	•	B, C
Missouri	★	. . .	. . .	. . .	★	•	A, B, C, D
Montana	★	★	★	. . .	. . .	★	B, C, D
Nebraska	★	. . .	★	★	★	•	A, B, C(d), D
Nevada	★	★	. . .	. . .	★	•	A, B, C, D
New Hampshire	★	★	★	. . .	★	•	B, C, D
New Jersey	★	★	★	★	★	•	A, B, C, D
New Mexico	★	★	★	★	. . .	•	A, C
New York	★	★	. . .	. . .	★	•	A, B, C, D
North Carolina	★	. . .	★	★	★	•	A, B, C, D
North Dakota	★	★	. . .	★	★	★	C, D
Ohio	★	★	★	★	★	★	B, C, D
Oklahoma	★	. . .	★(e)	★	★	•	B, D
Oregon	★	★	★(c)	★	★	•	A, B, C, D
Pennsylvania	★	. . .	★	★	★	•	D
Rhode Island	★	★	★	★	★	•	A, B, C, D
South Carolina	★	★	★	. . .	★	•	A, B, C, D
South Dakota	★	★	. . .	★	★	•	A, B, C, D
Tennessee	★	★	★(c)	★	★	•	A, B, C, D
Texas	★	. . .	★	★	★	•	B, D
Utah	★	★(d)	★(d)	. . .	★(f)	★	A(g), B, C, D(g)
Vermont	★	★	★	★	★	•	A, B, C, D
Virginia	★	★(e)	★	★(f)	★(f)	•	A, B, C, D
Washington	★	. . .	★	★	★	★	A, B, D
West Virginia	★	. . .	★	★	★	★	A, B, D
Wisconsin	★	. . .	★	★	★	•	A, B, C, D
Wyoming	★	. . .	. . .	★	★	. . .	. . .
American Samoa	★	★	★	. . .	. . .	★	. . .
Northern Mariana Is.	★	★	★	★	★	★	B, C, D
Puerto Rico	★	★	★	★(e)	★(e)	★	A, B, C
Virgin Islands	★	★(h)	★	. . .	. . .	★	A, B(i), C, D

Key:
A—Has parens patriae authority to commence suits on behalf of consumers in state antitrust damage actions in state courts.
B—May initiate damage actions on behalf of state in state courts.
C—May commence criminal proceedings.
D—May represent cities, counties and other governmental entities in recovering civil damages under federal or state law.
(a) In this column only: ★ indicates broad powers and • indicates limited powers.
(b) Only under Rule 23 of the Rules of Civil Procedure.

(c) When permitted to intervene.
(d) Attorney general has exclusive authority.
(e) Limited.
(f) Attorney general handles legal matters only with no administrative handling of complaints.
(g) Opinion only, since there are no controlling precedents.
(h) May always prosecute in inferior courts. May prosecute in District Court by request or consent of U.S. Attorney General.
(i) May initiate damage actions on behalf of territory in District Court.

Table 11

ATTORNEYS GENERAL: DUTIES TO ADMINISTRATIVE AGENCIES AND MISCELLANEOUS DUTIES

State or other jurisdiction	Serves as counsel for state	Appears for state in criminal appeals	Issues official advice	Interprets statutes or regulations	Conducts litigation — In behalf of agency	Against agency	Prepares or reviews legal documents	Represents the public before the agency	Involved in rule-making	Reviews rules for legality
Alabama	A, B, C	★(a)	★	★	★	★	★	★(b)	...	★
Alaska	A, B, C	★	★	★	★	★	★	...	★	★
Arizona	A, B, C	★(c,d)	★	★	★	★	★	...	★	★
Arkansas	A, B, C	★(a)	★	★	★	...	★	★	★	★
California	A, B, C	★(a)	★	★	★	★	★	...	...	...
Colorado	A, B, C	★(a)	★	★	★	★	★	...	★	★
Connecticut	A, B, C	...	★	★	★	...	★	...	★	★
Delaware	A, B, C	★(a)	★	★	★	★	★	★	★	★
Florida	A, B, C	★(a)	★	★	★	...	★	★	★	★
Georgia	A, B, C	★(b,c)	★	★	★	★	★	...	★	★
Hawaii	A, B	★(b,c)	★	★	★	★	★	★	★	★
Idaho	A, B, C	★(a)	★	★	★	★	★	...	★	★
Illinois	A, B*, C	★(b,c,e)	★	★	★	★	★	...	...	...
Indiana	A, B, C	★(a)	★	★	★	...	★	...	★	★
Iowa	A, B, C	★(a)	★	★	★	...	★	...	...	★
Kansas	A, B, C	★(a)	★	★	★	★	★	...	...	★
Kentucky	A, B*, C	★	★	★	★	★	★	...	★	★
Louisiana	A, B, C	★(c)	★	★	★	★	★	...	★	★
Maine	A, B, C	★(b,d)	★	★	★	...	★	...	★	★
Maryland	A, B, C	★	★	★	★	★(b)	★	★	★	★
Massachusetts	A, B, C	★(b,c,d)	★	★	★	★	★	★	★	★
Michigan	A, B, C	★(b,c,d)	★	★	★	...	★	★	...	★
Minnesota	A, B, C	★(c)	★	★	★	★	★	...	★	...
Mississippi	A, B, C	★	★	★	★	...	★	...	★	★
Missouri	A, B, C	★	★	★	★	...	★	...	★	★
Montana	A, B, C	★	★	★	★	...	★	...	★	★
Nebraska	A, B, C	★	★	★	★	★	★	...	★	★
Nevada	A, B, C	★(d)	★	★	★	★	★	★	★	★
New Hampshire	A, B, C	★(a)	★	★	★	★	★	...	★	★
New Jersey	A, B, C	★(d)	★	★	★	★	★	...	★	★
New Mexico	A, B, C	★(a)	★	★	★	★	★	★	★	★
New York	A, B, C	★(b)	★	★	★	...	★	...	...	★
North Carolina	A, B, C	★	★	★	★	★	★	★(b)	★	★
North Dakota	A, B, C	★(b)	★	★	★	...	★	...	★	★
Ohio	A, B, C	...	★	★	★	★	★	...	★	...
Oklahoma	A, B, C	★(b)	★	★	★	★	★	...	★	★
Oregon	A, B, C	★	★	★	★	...	★	...	★	★
Pennsylvania	A, B, C	★(c)	★	★	★	★	★	...	★	★
Rhode Island	A, B, C	★(a)	★	★	★	...	★	★	★	★
South Carolina	A, B, C	★(d)	★	★	★	...	★	...	★	★
South Dakota	A, B, C	★(a)	★	★	★	...	★	...	★	★
Tennessee	A, B, C	★(a)	★	★	★	...	★	★(b)	★	★
Texas	A, B, C	★(c)	★	★	★	★	★	...	★	★
Utah	A, B, C	★(a)	★	★	★	★	★	★	★	★
Vermont	A, B, C	★(b)	★	★	★	★	★	★(b)	...	★
Virginia	A, B, C	★(a)	★	★	★	★	★	★	★	★
Washington	A, B, C	★(c,f)	★	★	★	★	★	★	★	★
West Virginia	A, B, C	★(a)	★	★	★	★(f)	★	★	★	...
Wisconsin	A, B, C	★(b)	★	★	★	★	★	★(b)	★	...
Wyoming	A, B, C	★(a)	★	★	★	...	★	...	★	★
American Samoa	A, B, C	★(a)	★	★	★	...	★	...	★	★
Northern Mariana Is.	A, B, C	★(g)	★	★	★	...	★	...	★	★
Puerto Rico	A, B, C	★	★	★	★	...	★	...	★	★
Virgin Islands	A, B, C(h)	★	★	★	★	...	★	...	★	★

Key: A—Defend state law when challenged on federal constitutional grounds.
B—Conduct litigation on behalf of state in federal and other states' courts.
C—Prosecute actions against another state in U.S. Supreme Court.
*Only in federal courts.
(a) Attorney general has exclusive jurisdiction.

(b) In certain cases only.
(c) When assisting the local prosecutor in the appeal.
(d) Can appear on own discretion.
(e) In certain courts only.
(f) If authorized by the governor.
(g) Because there are no local prosecutors.
(h) Except in cases in which the U.S. Attorney is representing the Government of the Virgin Islands.

Table 12

STATE CABINET SYSTEMS

State or other jurisdiction	Authorization for cabinet system				Criteria for membership			Number of members in cabinet (including governor)	Frequency of cabinet meetings	Open cabinet meetings
	Statute	Constitution	Governor	Tradition	Appointed to specified office	Election to specified office	Gubernatorial appointment regardless of office			
Alabama	...	...	...	★	...	...	★	25	Gov.'s discretion	Yes
Alaska	...	...	★	...	★	...	...	16		No
Arizona	...	...	...	...	...	...	...			
Arkansas	★	...	...	...	★	...	...	15	Gov.'s discretion	No
California	...	...	★	...	★	...	★	9	Gov.'s discretion	No
Colorado	...	★	...	...	★	...	...	19	Once a month	No
Connecticut	★	...	...	...	★	...	...	15	Gov.'s discretion	Yes(a)
Delaware	★	...	...	...	...	...	★(b)	16	Gov.'s discretion	Yes
Florida	...	★	...	...	...	★	...	6	Every other week	Yes
Georgia	...	...	...	...	...	...	...			
Hawaii	★	...	...	...	★	...	...	18	Gov.'s discretion	No
Idaho	...	...	★	...	...	...	★	29	Gov.'s discretion	Yes
Illinois	...	...	...	★	★	...	...	21	Gov.'s discretion	Yes
Indiana	...	...	...	...	...	...	...			
Iowa	★	...	...	...	...	★	...	5	Weekly	Yes(c)
Kansas	...	...	★	...	...	...	★	15(d)	Monthly(e)	(f)
Kentucky	★	...	...	...	★	...	...	11	At least every other month	Yes(g)
Louisiana	...	...	...	...	...	...	...			
Maine	...	...	...	★	...	...	★(b)	22	Monthly	(f)
Maryland	★	...	...	...	★(b)	...	...	22	Gov.'s discretion	No
Massachusetts	★	...	...	...	★	...	★	11	Gov.'s discretion	No
Michigan	...	...	★	...	...	...	...	(h)	Gov.'s discretion	...
Minnesota	...	...	...	...	...	...	...			
Mississippi	...	...	★	...	...	...	★	6	Gov.'s discretion	No
Missouri	...	...	...	...	...	...	...			
Montana	...	...	★	...	★	...	...	17	3-4 times a year	Yes
Nebraska	...	...	...	...	...	...	...			
Nevada	...	...	...	...	...	...	...			
New Hampshire	...	...	...	...	...	...	...			
New Jersey	...	★	...	...	★	...	...	19	Gov.'s discretion(i)	No
New Mexico	★	...	...	...	★	...	...	12	Gov.'s discretion	Yes
New York	...	...	...	★	★	...	...	22	Gov.'s discretion	Yes(a)
North Carolina(j)	...	...	★	...	...	...	★	10	Weekly	No
North Dakota	...	...	...	...	...	...	...			
Ohio	★	...	...	...	★	...	★	23	Gov.'s discretion	(f)
Oklahoma	...	...	★	...	...	...	★	9	Monthly	Yes
Oregon	...	...	★	...	★	...	...	(k)	Weekly	No
Pennsylvania	★	...	...	...	★	...	...	19	Gov.'s discretion	Yes(l)
Rhode Island	...	...	★	...	★	...	...	17	Every 4-6 weeks	No
South Carolina	...	...	...	...	...	...	...			
South Dakota	...	...	...	...	★	...	★	23	Gov.'s discretion	No
Tennessee	...	...	...	★	★	...	...	21	Gov.'s discretion	Yes
Texas	...	...	...	...	...	...	...			
Utah	...	...	...	(m)	(m)	...	...	(m)	(m)	Yes
Vermont	...	...	★	...	...	...	★	17	Gov.'s discretion	No
Virginia	★	...	...	...	...	...	★	7	Usually monthly	No
Washington	...	...	★	...	...	...	★	(h)	Gov.'s discretion	No
West Virginia	...	...	...	...	...	...	...			
Wisconsin	...	...	...	...	...	...	...			
Wyoming	...	...	...	...	...	...	...			
Virgin Islands	...	...	★	...	...	...	...		Gov.'s discretion	

(a) Except when in executive session.
(b) With the consent of senate.
(c) Except when closed meeting is called for in law.
(d) Typically about 15.
(e) Weekly during the legislative session.
(f) In practice, the media and others do not attend, but cabinet meetings have not been formally designated closed.
(g) With some restrictions.
(h) No formal cabinet system, but the governor meets periodically with various cabinet heads or other advisors.
(i) Usually every other week.

(j) North Carolina constitution provides for a Council of State made up of the state elective administrative officials, which makes policy decisions for the state while the cabinet acts more in an advisory capacity.
(k) Governor meets with all department heads once a week. Three separate meetings are set up each week for this purpose. All statewide elected officials are also invited to the meetings.
(l) Except when in policy-making session.
(m) State Planning Advisory Committee, composed of all department heads, serves as an informal cabinet. Committee meets at discretion of state planning coordinator.

Table 13

STATE ADMINISTRATIVE OFFICIALS: ANNUAL SALARIES*

State or other jurisdiction	Governor	Lieutenant governor	Secretary of state	Attorney general	Treasurer	Adjutant general	Administration	Agriculture	Banking	Budget
Alabama	$50,000	(b)	25,800	49,000	25,800	43,277	. . .	35,471	43,277	39,702
Alaska	74,196	58,500	(a-4)	57,500	(a-5)	57,500	57,500	64,452	64,452	64,452
Arizona	50,000	. . .	28,000	45,000	30,000	44,629	58,766	48,901	44,629	48,901
Arkansas	35,000	14,000	22,500	26,500	22,500	34,240	(a-10)	(a-11)	33,500	35,360
California	49,100	42,500	42,500	47,500	42,500	53,119	(c)	54,556	54,556	63,628
Colorado	50,000	32,500	32,500	40,000	32,500	45,400	50,000	50,000	45,816	52,000
Connecticut	42,000	25,000	25,000	38,500	25,000	49,561	67,624	51,467	54,356	67,624
Delaware	35,000	15,500	41,900	37,000	24,000	32,300	35,300	27,800	39,300	41,900
Florida	65,000	56,500	55,500	55,500	55,500	50,112	48,651	55,500	32,956	46,879
Georgia	65,934	28,846	38,400	46,000	35,742	60,456	38,400	38,400	38,400	50,000
Hawaii	50,000	45,000	(a-4)	42,500	. . .	42,500	. . .	42,500	(a-25)	42,500
Idaho	40,000	12,000	28,000	35,000	28,000	43,221	43,075	43,075	39,150	41,029
Illinois	58,000	45,500	50,500	50,500	48,000	32,500	45,000	43,000	39,000	54,600
Indiana	48,000	43,600	34,000	39,000	34,000	44,460	48,880	(a-4)	48,880	50,128
Iowa	60,000	18,000	35,600	46,980	35,600	40,248	. . .	35,600	37,400	(a-5)
Kansas	45,000	13,500	27,500	40,000	27,500	36,636	50,724	45,972	24,348	47,340
Kentucky	50,000	43,229	43,229	43,229	43,229	44,000	47,500	43,229	41,500	45,000
Louisiana	73,400	63,367	55,712	60,169	55,712	60,169	60,311	60,168	43,079	52,908
Maine	35,000	. . .	25,000	36,637	25,000	25,230	39,749	39,811	34,050	31,928
Maryland	60,000	52,500	36,000	50,000	50,000	41,773	. . .	52,200	40,800	55,200
Massachusetts	40,000	30,000	30,000	37,500	30,000	40,644	55,000	22,671	35,053	36,796
Michigan	70,000	50,000	60,000	60,000	58,400	50,305	58,400	49,100	45,200	(a-8)
Minnesota	66,500	40,000	36,000	56,000	36,000	60,456	47,000	40,000	36,500	46,291
Mississippi	53,000	34,000	34,000	41,000	34,000	33,000	. . .	34,000	30,000	40,934
Missouri	55,000	30,000	42,500	45,000	42,500	34,000	40,000	40,000	34,000	34,000
Montana	43,360	31,077	28,685	39,555	26,175	43,000	43,000	43,000	(a-11)	42,500
Nebraska	40,000	32,000	32,000	39,500	32,000	39,231	41,500	34,430	37,788	39,800
Nevada	50,000	8,000	32,500	40,500	31,500	32,500	46,827	35,382	33,103	(a-8)
New Hampshire	51,830	. . .	36,406	45,039	36,406	29,615	(a-5)	34,553	36,406	36,406
New Jersey	85,000	. . .	56,000	56,000	56,000	53,500	. . .	56,000	56,000	55,500
New Mexico	60,000	38,500	38,500	44,000	38,500	40,128	45,000	(c)	42,432	43,824
New York	85,000	60,000	69,000	60,000	49,029	59,800	. . .	65,700	65,700	67,000
North Carolina	57,864	47,918	47,918	53,966	47,918	39,010	51,307	47,918	46,091	51,337
North Dakota	47,000	46,500	33,500	38,000	33,500	54,600	49,800	33,000	38,000	53,500
Ohio	50,000	30,000	50,000	50,000	50,000	51,000	55,000	43,000	43,000	45,000
Oklahoma	48,000	27,500	24,000	35,000	30,000	45,990	. . .	40,000	51,000	41,772
Oregon	55,423	. . .	45,629	53,308	45,619	43,440	52,800	47,844	43,440	47,844
Pennsylvania	66,000	57,500	48,000	55,000	48,000	48,000	49,000	48,000	48,000	49,000
Rhode Island	49,500	35,500	35,500	41,875	35,500	34,620	58,141	(a-12)	30,002	47,284
South Carolina	60,000	30,000	45,000	45,000	45,000	45,000	(a-22)	45,000	37,222	50,234
South Dakota	46,750	8,500	31,749	39,749	31,749	33,850	36,652	33,850	28,036	37,750
Tennessee	68,226	(f)	51,504	73,015	51,504	46,526	(a-10)	46,526	46,526	42,636
Texas	78,700	7,200	52,800	56,200	56,200	56,200	. . .	56,200	59,496	55,200
Utah	48,000	33,500	. . .	36,500	33,500	50,363	60,281	42,533	42,533	53,286
Vermont	44,850	19,200	24,380	31,400	24,380	28,579	47,278	32,032	32,115	34,507
Virginia	75,000	16,000	29,200	45,000	53,000	35,500	59,000	44,400	48,723	47,900
Washington	63,000	28,600	31,000	47,100	37,200	50,112	(a-6)	54,000	41,928	66,800
West Virginia	60,000	. . .	36,000	42,000	39,000	31,500	(a-6)	39,000	33,750	38,316
Wisconsin	65,801	36,151	32,608	50,780	32,608	40,068	65,313	56,000	46,782	(a-8)
Wyoming	55,000	. . .	37,500	55,500	37,500	40,400	69,216	52,764	52,764	59,712
Dist. of Col.	67,410(i)	. . .	. . .	. . .	50,112	52,618	58,500	. . .	. . .	52,618
American Samoa	40,000	35,000	(a-4)	35,000	35,000	. . .	(c)	25,000	. . .	30,000
Guam	50,000	45,000	. . .	29,000	24,460	. . .	27,300	N.A.	(a-38)	29,900
Puerto Rico	35,000	. . .	32,500	30,000	32,000	28,000	. . .	32,000	(a-21)	32,000
No. Mariana Is.	20,000	18,000	. . .	36,000	14,664	. . .	24,000	(a-12)	. . .	N.A.
Virgin Islands	51,000	47,000	. . .	36,000	. . .	. . .	(c)	34,776	(a-4)	38,640

*Salary figures are presented as submitted by the states except when ranges were given. In those instances, the maximum figure was chosen. When necessary, figures have been rounded. Methods of selection for the officials listed on this table may be found in Table 20.

N.A.—Not available.

(a) Chief administrative official or agency in charge of function:
(a-1) Attorney General
(a-2) Secretary of State
(a-3) Social Services
(a-4) Lieutenant Governor
(a-5) Comptroller
(a-6) General Services
(a-7) Planning
(a-8) Administration
(a-9) Transportation
(a-10) Finance
(a-11) Commerce
(a-12) Natural Resources
(a-13) Parks & Recreation
(a-14) Labor & Industrial Relations
(a-15) Consumer Affairs
(a-16) Adjutant General
(a-17) Health
(a-18) Community Affairs
(a-19) Highways
(a-20) Environmental Conservation
(a-21) Treasurer
(a-22) Budget
(a-23) Education (chief state school officer)
(a-24) Mental Health
(a-25) Licensing
(a-26) Personnel
(a-27) Industrial Development
(a-28) Highway Patrol
(a-29) Agriculture
(a-30) Post Audit
(a-31) Welfare
(a-32) Education—higher
(a-33) Fish & Game
(a-34) Tourism
(a-35) Energy Resources
(a-36) Banking
(a-37) Disaster Preparedness
(a-38) Taxation

STATE ADMINISTRATIVE OFFICIALS: ANNUAL SALARIES

State or other jurisdiction	Civil rights	Commerce	Community affairs	Comp- troller	Consumer affairs	Correc- tions	Data processing	Disaster prepar- edness	Education (chief school officer)	Education —higher
Alabama	...	$43,277	$43,277	$39,702	(a-1)	$50,622	$39,702	$36,000	$49,461	...
Alaska	$64,452	57,500	57,500	64,452	50,640	64,452	64,452	64,452	57,500	$64,452
Arizona	58,766	48,901	...	48,901	(a-1)	53,624	53,624	40,716	36,000	63,000
Arkansas	...	(a-12)	39,096	(a-10)	(a-1)	41,119	44,101	26,500	48,150	49,000
California	49,978	44,011	54,556	42,500	49,990	54,556	52,980	45,452	42,500	56,757
Colorado	51,556	39,576	35,892	50,508	(a-1)	54,000	(a-8)	(a-16)	62,519	64,140
Connecticut	54,356	58,101	34,817	25,000	58,101	62,488	51,467	34,817	62,488	50,000
Delaware	29,600	48,600	48,600	45,700	27,600	46,100	43,200	22,800	64,500	(c)
Florida	30,900	50,699	48,150	55,500	37,606	49,460	40,068	29,089	48,981	55,500
Georgia	...	52,750	43,475	38,400	43,308	38,400	42,870	(a-16)	43,200	81,700
Hawaii	...	(a-7)	...	42,500	(a-25)	(a-3)	(a-22)	(a-16)	42,500	45,000
Idaho	22,174	35,454	(a-11)	28,000	(a-1)	37,897	(a-5)	29,754	28,000	43,326
Illinois	44,000	39,000	46,000	48,000	(a-1)	46,000	47,544	32,500	58,000	69,550
Indiana	33,592	(a-4)	36,816	...	35,802	47,632	33,592	26,520	34,000	70,000
Iowa	28,944	39,312	28,080	37,565	(a-1)	(a-3)	41,392	27,800	48,200	44,496
Kansas	32,064	47,184	35,304	48,624	35,928	50,724	52,548	36,204	58,045	46,000
Kentucky	39,000	41,500	41,500	(a-10)	42,000	47,500	34,500	45,000	43,229	62,652
Louisiana	...	50,812	34,042	(a-8)	30,928	47,386	50,496	38,661	60,169	69,109
Maine	24,482	(a-27)	32,968	33,530	32,469	32,802	31,512	25,688	39,479	(a-23)
Maryland	42,400	39,400	36,200	50,000	41,400	44,000	(a-5)	30,000	56,800	51,200
Massachusetts	25,000	30,741	45,000	35,053	45,000	47,500	63,180	26,025	41,584	41,584
Michigan	49,000	53,500	...	...	(a-1)	58,400	(a-8)	(a-28)	58,400	56,400
Minnesota	33,000	37,521	(a-11)	46,291	30,000	45,000	46,291	38,962	45,000	42,000
Mississippi	...	(a-29)	32,000	(a-30)	35,000	38,000	39,915	22,000	34,000	54,000
Missouri	34,000	34,000	(a-11)	34,000	30,600	40,000	34,000	34,000	51,780	40,000
Montana	26,713	43,000	(a-11)	26,713	25,409	43,000	30,368	27,668	34,120	50,800
Nebraska	35,748	38,063	(a-11)	35,200	(a-1)	43,600	38,500	(a-16)	48,000	41,366
Nevada	28,000	40,000	29,000	31,500	25,982	44,000	38,500	25,127	34,812	40,509
New Hampshire	20,885	34,553	23,985	45,039	(a-1)	34,553	36,406	24,750	41,333	30,654
New Jersey	53,461	56,000	56,000	54,052	55,500	56,000	55,500	39,892	56,000	56,000
New Mexico	30,516	45,000	43,128	43,128	(a-1)	50,000	43,824	(a-16)	50,000	44,520
New York	59,800	65,700	69,000	60,000	55,300	69,200	(a-6)	53,330	76,100	(a-23)
North Carolina	(a-8)	49,178	39,753	(a-22)	48,145	49,178	43,160	43,760	53,966	78,750
North Dakota	...	42,000	...	36,000	30,000	35,300	44,500	33,100	34,000	60,700
Ohio	35,000	47,000	(a-11)	(a-21)	(a-1)	47,000	36,000	(a-16)	53,500	85,000
Oklahoma	24,000	40,000	40,000	32,000	35,000	49,500	...	29,864	35,000	78,000
Oregon	34,020	47,844	44,532	43,440	43,440	47,844	43,440	32,400	45,619	69,516
Pennsylvania	42,152	48,000	48,000	43,000	42,152	47,511	42,152	42,152	49,000	49,000
Rhode Island	26,680	50,902	38,238	40,046	24,613	47,956	38,238	27,269	53,140	(a-23)
South Carolina	38,475	(a-27)	28,355	45,000	41,000	49,269	(a-22)	(a-16)	45,000	54,249
South Dakota	25,013	34,347	(a-27)	26,499	(a-1)	37,749	48,000	23,594	36,005	46,057
Tennessee	32,220	51,510	(a-11)	51,510	32,220	46,526	42,636	32,220	51,510	59,900
Texas	...	(a-27)	41,000	56,200	38,800	55,000	35,000	27,500	55,000	55,000
Utah	...	53,286	53,286	47,606	36,498	50,363	53,286	38,419	60,281	64,519
Vermont	(a-1)	41,308	31,220	(a-10)	(a-1)	34,985	29,370	24,024	37,876	...
Virginia	...	36,700	44,400	47,900	(a-29)	50,100	43,200	42,000	59,500	56,200
Washington	45,500	47,200	(a-11)	(a-22)	(a-1)	56,388	51,180	36,100	42,800	52,680
West Virginia	30,942	50,628	34,860	(a-10)	(a-1)	33,750	36,312	28,125	56,200	64,692
Wisconsin	42,462	51,482	(a-11)	(a-8)	(a-1)	52,866	(a-8)	35,588	58,139	42,500
Wyoming	...	(a-27)	(a-27)	37,900	(a-1)	52,764	59,712	41,232	37,500	32,300
Dist. of Col.	52,618	...	...	52,618	52,618	52,618	52,618	52,618	55,400	62,475
American Samoa	(a-26)	30,000	(a-11)	(a-21)	(c)	(a-37)	31,500	30,000	31,000	30,000
Guam	...	27,300	N.A.	(a-8)	31,345	27,300	35,000	27,300	36,000	N.A.
Puerto Rico	27,960	32,000	25,800	34,000	32,000	27,000	...	26,000	32,000	(j)
No. Mariana Is.	...	14,644	20,064	...	...	11,494	...	15,517	25,000	17,821
Virgin Islands	N.A.	43,500	(c)	...	34,776	34,779	(c)	26,368	38,640	N.A.

(b) Receives $400 per month, plus $67 per day during legislative session.

(c) No single agency or official.

(d) Responsibilities handled by three positions: Director of Pre-Construction & Design, $47,500; Director of Construction, $47,500; Director of Maintenance, $47,500.

(e) State Library, Board of Education, $34,640.

(f) The speaker of the senate is elected by the senate from among its membership and, by statute, is lieutenant governor. For that part of the job the salary is $9,053.

(g) Salary: $61,000 plus house, utilities and $9,000 supplement.

(h) Departments of Fisheries and Game: $54,000 each.

(i) Mayor.

(j) $25 per meeting.

STATE ADMINISTRATIVE OFFICIALS: ANNUAL SALARIES

State or other jurisdiction	Elections adminis- tration	Employ- ment services	Energy resources	Environ- mental conser- vation	Finance	Fish & game	General services	Health	Highway patrol	Highways	Historic preser- vation
Alabama	(a-2)	$39,702	35,000	(c)	$43,277	$34,463	$25,337	$68,003	$43,277	$43,277	$31,629
Alaska	$64,452	64,452	64,452	57,500	64,452	57,500	64,452	57,500	64,452	64,452	64,452
Arizona	(a-2)	40,716	(a-7)	58,766	53,624	53,624	(a-8)	77,349	51,224	(a-9)	40,716
Arkansas	. . .	46,061	32,464	33,254	48,853	40,000	. . .	49,552	35,360	(a-9)	26,624
California	(a-2	54,556	49,888	49,990	63,628	49,990	54,556	59,079	54,556	(a-9)	(a-13)
Colorado	(a-2)	41,556	39,576	(a-17)	50,000	45,816	(a-8)	65,000	48,108	53,028	35,520
Connecticut	36,211	54,356	51,467	62,488	67,624	32,188	(a-8)	67,088	51,467	54,356	32,188
Delaware	26,000	(a-14)	34,500	42,600	46,200	30,500	(a-8)	44,500	38,000	(a-9)	34,300
Florida	40,250	42,200	41,166	49,731	(a-5)	48,150	49,500	59,400	40,660	(d)	36,150
Georgia	(a-2)	(a-14)	39,500	(a-12)	(c)	41,200	(a-8)	61,626	42,315	(a-9)	(a-12)
Hawaii	(a-4)	(a-26)	(a-7)	(a-17)	(a-22)	(a-12)	(a-5)	42,500	. . .	(a-9)	(a-12)
Idaho	(a-2)	45,247	34,389	41,217	41,029	44,140	(a-8)	46,353	34,765	(a-9)	34,034
Illinois	25,000	55,296	43,000	43,000	(c)	43,000	(a-8)	52,000	37,000	(a-9)	41,256
Indiana	24,388	40,404	30,524	57,148	(c)	29,562	25,272	63,128	48,800	52,910	29,692
Iowa	26,770	36,900	34,668	35,856	(a-5)	34,050	36,936	39,312	35,714	(a-9)	26,244
Kansas	28,104	40,776	41,196	40,860	(c)	33,864	(a-8)	50,724	39,384	47,340	37,776
Kentucky	38,568	45,000	43,500	47,500	47,500	55,000	(a-10)	61,464	47,500	(a-9)	28,788
Louisiana	60,168	50,812	(a-12)	48,602	(a-8)	53,020	(a-8)	35,000	47,497	(a-9)	25,860
Maine	(a-2)	34,528	36,982	32,802	(a-8)	28,434	. . .	49,670	36,920	29,869	23,338
Maryland	34,100	34,736	38,800	(a-12)	(a-5)	37,516	52,200	52,174	44,000	48,200	32,800
Massachusetts	31,610	34,991	43,000	30,071	55,000	28,021	36,796	48,394	30,705	34,876	(a-2)
Michigan	(a-2)	50,800	45,200	. . .	(a-8)	49,485	(a-8)	69,300	53,500	58,400	41,488
Minnesota	(a-2)	46,291	46,291	40,000	50,000	(a-12)	47,000	49,000	43,347	(a-9)	. . .
Mississippi	(a-2)	34,000	37,600	39,600	(a-22)	38,750	. . .	46,000	31,000	38,580	27,000
Missouri	23,700	34,000	34,000	34,000	(a-8)	39,100	. . .	45,000	32,500	47,500	25,000
Montana	(a-2)	42,074	31,108	(a-17)	(c)	43,000	25,131	48,000	31,436	43,000	29,349
Nebraska	(a-2)	(a-14)	32,330	34,288	(a-8)	(a-13)	(a-8)	53,600	38,121	41,113	32,883
Nevada	(a-2)	38,231	38,800	36,236	(a-5)	33,103	40,240	34,812	40,509	(a-9)	38,231
New Hampshire	(a-2)	25,506	32,000	(c)	(a-5)	34,553	. . .	45,039	34,553	41,333	20,027
New Jersey	(a-2)	50,914	56,000	56,000	(a-21)	50,914	(a-21)	56,000	55,500	(a-9)	28,353
New Mexico	29,064	45,000	45,000	42,432	(a-8)	43,128	(a-8)	42,432	44,520	50,000	43,824
New York	56,500	57,910	65,700	65,700	. . .	(a-20)	65,700	69,200	65,700	(a-9)	(a-13)
North Carolina	48,145	46,091	43,760	44,777	(c)	36,750	(a-8)	82,139	45,877	46,229	32,848
North Dakota	(a-2)	45,600	35,000	51,500	(a-22)	36,000	41,900	52,000	34,000	52,500	31,800
Ohio	(a-2)	35,000	43,000	35,000	(a-22)	35,000	(a-8)	51,000	(a-19)	52,000	. . .
Oklahoma	44,000	40,000	28,590	(a-17)	(a-21)	42,500	32,648	71,500	41,888	(a-9)	29,240
Oregon	45,619	47,844	47,844	47,844	(a-8)	45,576	47,844	43,440	47,844	47,844	(a-9)
Pennsylvania	34,856	42,152	44,538	55,000	(a-8)	42,152	51,500	51,500	51,500	47,600	34,856
Rhode Island	22,859	43,665	32,295	(a-12)	(a-8)	24,613	34,620	49,093	48,363	31,151	27,788
South Carolina	38,640	52,360	38,101	(a-17)	(a-22)	49,972	(a-22)	63,412	41,606	54,587	30,168
South Dakota	(a-2)	31,154	33,250	39,000	37,750	26,956	(a-8)	34,346	32,749	36,450	23,737
Tennessee	26,784	46,526	39,264	42,636	51,510	45,924	46,526	56,339	46,526	(a-9)	29,376
Texas	(a-2)	46,300	39,600	(c)	(c)	(a-13)	47,400	55,000	55,000	55,700	39,200
Utah	(a-4)	56,376	42,533	50,363	53,286	47,606	(a-8)	42,533	38,419	(a-9)	42,533
Vermont	(a-2)	34,507	29,993	42,411	34,507	33,758	(a-8)	48,484	38,147	(a-9)	28,849
Virginia	37,900	43,200	(a-37)	(c)	(a-8)	39,200	47,900	59,500	43,200	54,100	31,300
Washington	31,176	54,000	40,300	(a-33)	(a-22)	(h)	54,000	68,700	54,000	(a-9)	36,100
West Virginia	(a-2)	31,500	29,520	41,112	42,192	33,252	21,804	50,675	39,375	43,875	33,750
Wisconsin	40,165	(a-14)	(a-8)	(a-12)	. . .	(a-12)	(a-8)	47,521	44,472	(a-9)	31,729
Wyoming	(a-2)	61,188	37,344	58,236	(c)	67,500	(a-8)	69,216	52,764	70,956	34,692
Dist. of Col.	52,618	52,618	. . .	52,618	52,618	. . .	52,618	52,618	. . .	52,618	. . .
American Samoa	(a-1)	. . .	21,000	(c)	(c)	25,000	(c)	35,000	(a-37)	35,000	. . .
Guam	N.A.	27,680	29,000	N.A.	(a-8)	(a-29)	(a-8)	(a-8)	32,510	25,240	21,340
Puerto Rico	28,000	28,000	23,340	29,000	(a-21)	(a-12)	30,000	32,000	20,520	30,000	19,500
No. Mariana Is.	17,821	18,000	36,000	20,000	25,000	. . .	. . .	36,000	8,174	. . .	13,967
Virgin Islands	29,998	(a-14)	36,000	30,390	38,640	23,990	(c)	43,058	. . .	. . .	20,965

STATE ADMINISTRATIVE OFFICIALS: ANNUAL SALARIES

State or other jurisdiction	Industrial development	Insurance	Labor & Industrial relations	Licensing	Mental health	Natural resources	Parks & recreation	Personnel	Planning	Post Audit
Alabama	$43,277	$43,277	$43,277	...	$45,292	$43,277	$36,101	$43,277	$43,277	$40,000
Alaska	64,452	64,452	64,452	64,452	64,452	57,500	64,452	64,452	54,000	50,640
Arizona	48,901	44,629	53,624	...	93,078	...	44,629	53,624	44,629	53,597
Arkansas	41,176	37,450	40,018	...	60,060	42,592	36,989	35,360	...	...
California	(a-14)	54,556	54,556	(a-15)	59,079	63,628	49,990	54,556	50,778	(a-10)
Colorado	(a-11)	45,816	50,000	50,000	48,108	58,000	45,816	52,000	41,556	48,000
Connecticut	(a-11)	54,356	58,101	...	67,088	(a-20)	34,817	54,356	44,726	51,546
Delaware	29,600	24,000	37,300	23,700	44,400	41,900	31,000	31,400	44,900	24,000
Florida	46,999	(a-21)	47,250	41,250	43,000	49,500	36,500	44,075	(a-22)	58,000
Georgia	(a-11)	(a-5)	53,460	(a-2)	65,000	50,572	42,027	44,820	(a-22)	38,400
Hawaii	(a-7)	(a-25)	42,500	42,500	(a-17)	42,500	(a-12)	42,500	42,500	(a-5)
Idaho	(a-11)	36,331	38,126	36,331	33,742	...	42,031	44,140	(a-22)	38,126
Illinois	(a-11)	43,000	43,000	44,000	52,000	40,000	47,544	43,000	...	48,000
Indiana	35,074	44,460	32,084	...	48,880	46,566	33,384	46,566	30,524	34,000
Iowa	34,050	32,000	34,128	...	(a-3)	37,800	34,050	36,000	35,640	35,600
Kansas	36,000	35,000	36,420	...	47,340	...	38,016	45,684	(a-22)	35,334
Kentucky	(a-11)	45,000	41,500	(a-10)	(a-17)	45,000	41,500	45,000	...	43,229
Louisiana	50,812	55,712	50,812	(c)	39,766	53,020	47,497	50,760	38,159	48,600
Maine	34,445	30,930	25,230	...	28,933	44,445	28,475	39,479	38,750	23,067
Maryland	36,200	47,800	44,600	34,736	(a-17)	52,200	38,800	52,200	52,200	46,500
Massachusetts	30,741	35,000	29,086	16,095	48,394	30,071	27,882	36,796	(a-18)	30,000
Michigan	56,710	45,200	53,500	49,000	69,300	53,500	48,734	60,552	...	64,800
Minnesota	46,000	36,500	40,000	...	46,291	47,000	43,347	47,000	46,291	46,000
Mississippi	45,000	34,000	...	...	53,000	39,520	36,500	36,500	31,500	34,000
Missouri	(a-11)	34,000	40,000	29,000	63,768	40,000	34,000	34,000	...	42,500
Montana	(a-11)	28,685	43,000	(a-11)	43,000	43,000	(a-33)	27,435	(a-11)	31,824
Nebraska	(a-11)	35,967	33,983	(a-17)	(a-31)	38,000	48,143	35,292	32,659	32,000
Nevada	38,800	36,236	31,445	...	40,240	38,944	30,824	38,231	33,103	...
New Hampshire	30,654	41,333	34,553	...	45,039	34,553	34.553	41,333	29,755	45,039
New Jersey	48,493	56,000	56,000	43,979	55,500	56,000	53,461	56,000	55,500	...
New Mexico	38,580	41,736	35,328	...	(a-17)	45,000	40,128	43,824	40,128	38,500
New York	(a-11)	65,700	65,700	48,351	69,200	(a-20)	65,700	65,700	...	(a-5)
North Carolina	43,760	47,918	47,918	(c)	86,247	49,178	39,753	47,489	...	47,918
North Dakota	(a-11)	33,500	33,500	...	(a-3)	...	36,000	43,500	...	33,500
Ohio	33,000	43,000	43,000	...	55,000	47,000	36,000	39,000	35,000	17,000
Oklahoma	32,700	32,000	24,000	...	71,510	...	(a-34)	42,000	...	(a-21)
Oregon	44,532	43,440	45,619	(a-11)	64,152	(c)	43,440	(a-8)	47,844	(a-2)
Pennsylvania	34,856	48,000	33,389	37,907	47,600	40,700	42,152	42,152	44,538	48,000
Rhode Island	(a-11)	26,680	36,947	24,613	56,332	43,665	26,680	38,238	34,620	(c)
South Carolina	55,730	49,059	40,247	...	61,591	...	43,064	46,326	42,941	50,234
South Dakota	34,347	27,706	27,750	28,000	29,215	39,000	26,952	33,750	34,999	32,318
Tennessee	38,808	46,526	46,526	(c)	56,339	46,526	35,340	46,526	38,808	(a-5)
Texas	39,200	49,600	38,600	...	(g)	(a-35)	49,300	...	(a-22)	55,200
Utah	40,465	42,533	44,955	38,419	50,363	53,286	47,606	53,286	38,419	33,500
Vermont	33,779	(a-36)	32,115	(a-2)	45,822	(a-20)	34,403	36,067	37,190	24,380
Virginia	48,900	48,723	40,200	(c)	60,000	44,400	(a-12)	47,900	(a-22)	51,230
Washington	(a-11)	37,200	54,000	37,056	68,700	42,800	51,000	54,000	41,928	37,200
West Virginia	34,860	31,500	31,500	...	(a-17)	42,192	33,252	33,750	(a-11)	44,874
Wisconsin	(a-11)	42,000	55,000	35,866	(a-3)	61,026	(a-12)	52,458	(a-22)	(c)
Wyoming	52,764	48,996	46,644	...	50,244	...	47,832	59,712	50,244	46,644
Dist. of Col.	...	52,618	...	52,618	52,618	...	...	52,618	52,618	...
American Samoa	(a-11)	...	...	(c)	(a-17)	...	30,000	30,000	(a-11)	27,000
Guam	N.A.	(a-38)	27,300	N.A.	27,000	...	27,300	28,360	26,000	N.A.
Puerto Rico	32,000	30,000	32,000	15,300	25,800	32,000	32,000	30,000	32,000	(a-5)
No. Mariana Is.	...	...	13,304	(a-11)	17,821	23,000	12,068	30,000	N.A.	30,000
Virgin Islands	34,779	(a-4)	34,776	(a-15)	(a-17)	34,500	25,000	34,776	32,200	(c)

STATE ADMINISTRATIVE OFFICIALS: ANNUAL SALARIES

State or other jurisdiction	Pre audit	Public library	Public utility regulation	Purchasing	Social services	Solid waste	Taxation	Tourism	Transportation	Welfare
Alabama	$39,702	$38,506	$29,315	$32,877	43,277	. . .	$43,227	$43,227	. . .	(a-3)
Alaska	34,140	64,452	49,000	(a-6)	64,452	$64,452	57,500	64,452	$57,500	(a-3)
Arizona	48,901	40,716	36,000	44,629	44,629	. . .	58,766	40,716	70,603	53,624
Arkansas	28,288	27,916	34,240	35,360	39,202	28,288	38,026	33,254	57,270	(a-3)
California	32,976	50,537	54,709	48,387	54,556	49,888	49,990	44,016	54,556	(a-3)
Colorado	(a-5)	48,433	40,000	45,816	55,000	(a-17)	54,000	(a-18)	(a-19)	(a-3)
Connecticut	(a-5)	49,561	57,983	44,726	58,101	37,660	54,356	33,477	67,624	58,101
Delaware	(a-10)	27,000	29,600	31,000	36,700	50,200	43,700	27,900	45,700	(a-3)
Florida	(a-5)	36,150	53,000	36,504	(a-17)	29,422	49,500	42,000	55,361	41,808
Georgia	(a-5)	(a-23)	44,520	35,742	(a-24)	46,734	38,400	40,764	59,160	42,666
Hawaii	(a-5)	(a-23)	(a-22)	(a-5)	42,500	(a-17)	42,500	(a-7)	42,500	(a-3)
Idaho	(a-5)	(e)	32,340	31,361	38,210	35,746	30,150	(a-11)	53,682	(a-17)
Illinois	48,000	(a-2)	47,500	44,400	46,000	38,556	46,000	(a-11)	52,000	52,000
Indiana	42,400	37,934	51,376	29,120	40,404	24,388	41,418	24,388	42,420	(a-3)
Iowa	30,867	30,024	39,312	34,050	48,467	34,050	43,600	30,867	48,467	(a-3)
Kansas	33,336	30,708	45,492	36,420	36,552	43,776	47,184	23,772	47,184	37,872
Kentucky	45,000	37,500	45,000	43,500	41,500	45,000	44,500	41,500	47,500	41,500
Louisiana	(a-22)	44,184	50,796	37,744	49,707	41,700	47,497	47,497	53,020	57,439
Maine	33,030	27,123	36,166	29,869	23,110	(a-12)	32,448	(a-27)	37,939	30,160
Maryland	(a-21)	40,518	45,400	34,736	41,500	(a-12)	50,000	34,000	56,800	(a-3)
Massachusetts	30,000	30,700	33,146	35,053	36,770	30,317	45,000	28,045	47,500	37,826
Michigan	(a-8)	48,734	48,900	48,734	54,100	(a-12)	41,900	48,734	(a-19)	(a-3)
Minnesota	46,291	. . .	36,000	40,424	46,291	45,000	47,000	37,521	48,000	48,000
Mississippi	34,000	27,000	31,000	(a-22)	(a-31)	24,357	33,000	28,590	(a-19)	40,000
Missouri	(c)	(a-32)	40,000	34,000	40,000	30,000	40,000	34,000	(a-19)	34,000
Montana	. . .	26,713	31,077	26,175	43,000	(a-17)	43,000	24,126	. . .	(a-3)
Nebraska	(a-5)	35,250	25,000	30,300	(a-31)	23,100	37,855	24,300	. . .	71,298
Nevada	(a-8)	34,335	42,522	35,942	41,074	(a-12)	38,231	27,500	47,500	(a-3)
New Hampshire	34,553	34,553	46,270	34,553	(a-31)	24,648	41,333	21,972	. . .	36,406
New Jersey	(a-22)	46,177	56,000	(a-21)	56,000	34,461	55,500	43,979	56,000	55,500
New Mexico	(a-8)	37,092	42,432	43,824	43,128	(a-17)	45,000	35,328	45,000	(a-3)
New York	(a-5)	43,463	69,200	57,910	69,200	(a-20)	65,700	(a-11)	72,400	69,200
North Carolina	(a-8)	43,760	48,968	43,760	50,564	34,461	49,178	41,744	49,178	(a-3)
North Dakota	(a-22)	29,000	30,000	33,300	52,500	38,500	33,500	(a-11)	. . .	(a-3)
Ohio	17,000	36,000	43,000	34,000	29,000	32,000	47,000	29,000	50,000	47,000
Oklahoma	(a-22)	31,763	40,000	(a-6)	87,450	(a-17)	47,600	40,000	50,000	(a-3)
Oregon	. . .	39,372	52,800	34,020	52,800	39,372	47,844	39,372	52,800	47,844
Pennsylvania	(a-5)	36,342	42,500	36,342	40,700	41,272	51,500	34,856	55,000	47,600
Rhode Island	23,653	34,620	42,450	43,665	47,284	(a-12)	45,475	28,898	44,285	(a-3)
South Carolina	42,941	34,677	43,058	33,936	55,229	41,606	45,743	36,705	(a-19)	(a-3)
South Dakota	31,750	25,680	31,749	24,810	32,231	31,720	35,498	27,180	36,924	36,924
Tennessee	(a-5)	35,340	46,526	35,340	38,808	38,808	46,526	46,526	51,510	46,526
Texas	(a-5)	39,200	43,800	(a-6)	(a-31)	30,200	(a-5)	38,100	(a-19)	55,000
Utah	(a-5)	42,533	44,955	44,955	56,376	(a-17)	50,363	40,465	64,519	50,363
Vermont	(a-10)	25,854	41,000	27,206	36,316	30,035	33,176	33,633	44,200	38,084
Virginia	(a-5)	43,200	48,723	(a-6)	(a-31)	(c)	49,600	(a-12)	59,000	44,900
Washington	44,052	47,200	51,100	40,908	53,664	39,900	54,000	34,416	66,800	53,664
West Virginia	39,000	49,750	35,000	31,716	33,252	32,433	43,875	29,520	(a-19)	42,192
Wisconsin	(a-8)	47,792	46,747	49,718	(a-17)	39,530	51,941	41,791	54,083	47,682
Wyoming	42,264	45,528	61,188	46,644	47,832	43,308	52,764	45,528	. . .	(a-3)
Dist. of Col.	. . .	52,618	52,618	52,618	52,618	52,618	52,618	. . .	52,618	52,618
American Samoa	(a-21)	(a-23)	. . .	25,000	(c)	(a-19)	(a-21)	(a-11)	(c)	. . .
Guam	. . .	27,580	27,300	27,580	30,222	21,340	26,800	N.A.	(c)	(a-3)
Puerto Rico	(a-21)	(a-23)	29,000	21,360	32,000	27,720	(a-21)	28,000	32,000	(a-3)
No. Mariana Is.	. . .	13,304	. . .	17,881	12,068	8,174	12,671	. . .	. . .	22,000
Virgin Islands	(c)	31,911	25,000	36,000	22,933	. . .	38,640	34,776	. . .	36,000

Table 14
CONSTITUTIONAL AND STATUTORY ELECTIVE ADMINISTRATIVE OFFICIALS*

State or other jurisdiction	Governor	Lt. governor	Secretary of state	Attorney general	Treasurer	Auditor	Controller	Education	Agriculture	Labor	Insurance	Mines	Land	University regents	Board of education	Public utilities commission	Executive council	Miscellaneous	Total agencies	Total officials
Alabama	C	C	C	C	C	C			C(a)						C8	S3			9	18
Alaska	C	C																	1(b)	2
Arizona	C		C	C	C			C				C				C3			7	9
Arkansas	C	C	C	C	C	C							C						7	7
California	C	C	C	C	C		C	C										Board of Equalization—C4(c)	8	11
Colorado	C	C	C	C	C									C9	C5				7	19
Connecticut	C	C	C	C	C		C												6	6
Delaware	C	C		C	C	C					C								6	6
Florida	C	C	C	C	C(d)		C	C	C		(d)				(e)				8	8
Georgia	C	C	C	C				C	C	C	(f)					C5			9	13
Hawaii	C	C													C13				3	15
Idaho	C	C	C	C	C	C		S											7	7
Illinois	C	C	C	C	C		C											Bd. of Trustees, Univ. of Ill.—S9(g)	7	15
Indiana	C	C	C	S	C	C		C											7	7
Iowa	C	C	C	C	C	C			S										7	7
Kansas	C	C	C	C	S						S		(h)		C10				7	16
Kentucky	C	C	C	C	C	C		C	C									Railroad Commission—C3	9	11
Louisiana	C	C	C	C	C			C	C		C				C8(i)	C5		Elections commissioner	11	22
Maine	C																		1	1
Maryland	C	C		C			C												4	4
Massachusetts	C	C	C	C	C	C											C8		7	14
Michigan	C	C	C	C										C24(j)	C8(k)				8	36
Minnesota	C	C	C	C	C	C													6	6
Mississippi	C	C	C	C	C	C			S(l)		S					S3		Highway Commission—S3	11	13
Missouri	C	C	C	C	C	C													6	6

168

Key: C—Constitutional; S—Statutory; numbers indicate number of officials.

State													Other			No. Const.	Total
Montana	C	C	C	C	C											7	11
Nebraska	C	C	C	C	C		C	C	C							9	27
Nevada	C	C	C													8	24
New Hampshire	C		C													2	6
New Jersey	C															1	1
New Mexico	C	C	C	C	C	C					C8	S5		Corporation Commission—C3		9	20
New York	C	C		C					C8	C						4	4
North Carolina	C	C	C	C	C	C		C9	S9	C5	C10		C			10	10
North Dakota	C	C	C	C	C	S(n)							C			12	14
Ohio	C	C	C	C	C				C23	C3		Tax commissioner—C				7	29
Oklahoma	S	C	C	C	C	C				C3			C			8	10
Oregon	C	S	C		S								C			6	6
Pennsylvania	C	C			C								C			5	5
Rhode Island	C	C	C													5	5
South Carolina	C	C	C	C	C					C3		Adjutant & inspector general—C				9	9
South Dakota	C	C	C	C	C				S3				C			8	10
Tennessee	C								S3							2	4
Texas	C	C	C	C			S		S24			Railroad Commission—C3	C			9	34
Utah	C	C	C	C	S				C11				C			5	15
Vermont	C	C	C	C	C											6	6
Virginia	C		C	C			S						C			3	3
Washington	C	C	C	C	C											9	9
West Virginia	C	C	C	C	C											6	6
Wisconsin	C	C	C	C	S								C			6	6
Wyoming	C		C		C											5	5
American Samoa	C	C														2	2
Guam	C															4	37
Puerto Rico	C															1	1
Virgin Islands									S11(o)			Village Commissioners—S24				2	2

*Includes only officials who are popularly elected.
Key: C—Constitutional; S—Statutory; numbers indicate number of officials.
(a) Commissioner of agriculture and industries.
(b) Lieutenant governor's office is part of governor's office.
(c) Plus controller, ex officio.
(d) The state treasurer also serves as insurance commissioner.
(e) Governor and cabinet, ex officio.
(f) Comptroller general is ex officio insurance commissioner.
(g) Plus governor, ex officio.
(h) Secretary of state holds this office.

(i) Eight elective members, three appointive.
(j) Three universities with eight regents each.
(k) Plus governor and superintendent of public instruction, ex officio, non-voting.
(l) Commissioner of agriculture and commerce.
(m) State auditor is also insurance commissioner.
(n) The constitution provides for a secretary of agriculture and labor. If the legislature provides for a secretary of labor, which it has, then it must be a separate and distinct office. The secretary of agriculture and labor then becomes just the secretary of agriculture. Therefore the constitution does not provide for a secretary of labor, as do the statutes.
(o) Elected school board, by districts.

Table 15
CONSTITUTIONAL AND STATUTORY PROVISIONS FOR LENGTH AND NUMBER OF TERMS OF ELECTED STATE OFFICIALS*

State or other jurisdiction	Governor	Lt. governor	Secretary of state	Attorney general	Treasurer	Auditor	Controller	Education	Agriculture	Labor	Insurance	Mines	Land	Univ. regents	Bd. of education	Public util. comm.	Exec. council	Miscellaneous
Alabama	4/2	4/2	4/2	4/2	4/2	4/2	…	…	4/2	…	…	…	…	…	4/1	4/U	…	…
Alaska	4/2(a)	4/1	…	…	…	…	…	…	…	…	…	…	…	…	…	…	…	…
Arizona	4/U	…	4/U	4/U	4/O(b)	…	…	4/U	…	…	…	2/U	…	…	…	6/U	…	…
Arkansas	2/U	2/U	2/U	2/U	2/U	2/U	…	…	…	…	…	…	2/U	…	…	…	…	…
California	4/U	4/U	4/U	4/U	4/U	…	4/U	4/U	…	…	…	…	…	…	…	…	…	Bd. of Equalization—4/U
Colorado	4/U	4/U	4/U	4/U	4/U	…	…	…	…	…	…	…	…	6/U	…	…	…	…
Connecticut	4/U	4/U	4/U	4/U	4/U	…	4/U	…	…	…	…	…	…	…	6/U	…	…	…
Delaware	4/2(c)	4/U	…	4/U	4/U	4/U	…	…	…	…	4/U	…	…	…	…	…	…	…
Florida	4/2	4/U	4/U	4/U	…	4/U	4/U	4/U	4/U	…	(d)	…	…	…	(e)	…	…	…
Georgia	4/2	4/U	4/U	4/U	…	4/U	4/U	4/U	4/U	4/U	(f)	…	…	…	…	6/U	…	…
Hawaii	4/2(a)	4/2(a)	…	…	…	…	…	…	…	…	…	…	…	…	…	…	…	…
Idaho	4/U	4/U	4/U	4/U	4/U	4/U	4/U	4/U	…	…	…	…	…	…	…	…	…	…
Illinois	4/U	4/U	4/U	4/U	4/U	…	4/U	4/U	…	…	…	…	…	…	4/1	…	…	Bd. of Trustees, Univ. of Illinois—6/U
Indiana	4/2	4/U	4/2(g)	4/U	4/2(g)	4/2(g)	…	4/U	…	…	…	…	…	…	…	…	…	…
Iowa	4/1	4/1	4/1	4/1	4/1	4/1	…	4/U	4/1	…	…	…	…	…	…	…	…	…
Kansas	4/2	4/2	4/U	4/U	4/U	4/U	…	4/O	…	…	4/U	…	…	…	4/U	…	…	…
Kentucky	4/O	4/O	4/O	4/O	4/O	4/O	…	4/O	4/O	…	…	…	…	…	6/U	6/U	…	…
Louisiana	4/2	4/U	4/U	4/U	4/U	…	…	4/U	4/U	…	4/U	…	…	…	…	…	…	Railroad Comm.—4/U
Maine	4/2(a)	…	…	4/1	…	…	4/U	…	…	…	…	…	(h)	…	…	…	…	Election commr.—4/U
Maryland	4/2(a)	4/U	…	…	…	4/U	4/U	…	…	…	…	…	…	…	…	…	…	…
Massachusetts	4/U	4/U	4/U	4/U	4/U	4/U	…	…	…	…	…	…	…	…	4/U	4/U	2/U	…
Michigan	4/U	4/U	4/U	4/U	…	4/U	…	…	…	…	…	…	…	8/U	6/U	…	…	…
Minnesota	4/U	4/U	4/U	4/U	4/O	4/U	…	…	…	…	…	…	…	…	…	…	…	…
Mississippi	4/O	4/U	4/U	4/U	4/O	4/U	…	4/U	4/U	…	4/U	…	…	8/U	8/U	…	…	…
Missouri	4/2(c)	4/U	4/U	4/U	4/2(c)	4/1	4/U	4/U	4/U	…	4/U	…	…	…	…	4/U	…	Highway Comm.—4/U

170

State												Other
Montana	4/U	4/U	4/U	4/U	4/U						4/U	
Nebraska	4/2	4/U	4/U	4/U	4/U	6/U		4/U	6/U			
Nevada	4/2	4/I	4/U	4/U	4/U	6/U		4/U	6/U			
New Hampshire	2/U	2/U	2/U	2/U						2/I		
New Jersey	4/2	4/2			4/U							
New Mexico	4/O(k)	4/O(k)	4/O(k)	4/O(k)	4/O(k)		4/O(k)	6/U				Corporation Commission—6/U
New York	4/U	4/U	4/U	4/U	4/U							
North Carolina	4/2(c)	4/2(c)	4/U	4/U	4/U	4/U	4/U					
North Dakota	4/U	4/U	4/U	4/2	4/U	4/U	4/U	6/U				Tax commissioner—4/U
Ohio	4/2(a)	4/U	4/U	4/U			6/I		6/I			
Oklahoma	4/2	4/U	4/I	4/I	4/1	4/1	4/U		6/U			
Oregon	4/2(g)	4/2(g)	4/2	4/2	4/U	4/U						
Pennsylvania	4/2	4/2	4/2	4/2(g)	4/2(l)							
Rhode Island	2/U	2/U	2/U	2/U	2/U							
South Carolina	4/2	4/U	4/U	4/U	4/U	4/U						Adjutant & inspector general—4/U
South Dakota	4/2	4/2	4/U	4/U	4/U	4/U						
Tennessee	4/U	4/U					6/U		6/U			
Texas	4/U	4/U	4/U	4/U	4/U	4/U	6/I		6/U			Railroad Commission—6/U
Utah	4/U	4/U	4/U	4/U	4/U		4/U					
Vermont	2/U	2/U	2/U	2/U								
Virginia	4/O	4/1	4/U	4/U	4/U	4/U						
Washington	4/U	4/U	4/U	4/U	4/U	4/U						
West Virginia	4/2	4/U	4/U	4/U	4/U		4/1					
Wisconsin	4/U	4/U	4/U	4/U	4/U							
Wyoming	4/U											
American Samoa	4/2	4/2										
Guam	4/2	4/2					4/U	4/U				
Puerto Rico	4/U											
Virgin Islands	4/2(a)	4/2(a)									4/1	

*First entry refers to number of years per term. Second entry refers to number of terms. This table reflects the literal state constitutions and statutes.

Key:

U—No provision for number of terms allowed.
O—Cannot succeed himself.
I—May hold office for unlimited number of terms.
(a) Must wait two years before being eligible again.
(b) Governor and cabinet ex officio.
(c) Absolute two-term limit, not necessarily consecutive.
(d) Comptroller general is ex officio insurance commissioner.

(e) Eligible for eight out of 12 years.
(f) Secretary of state holds this office.
(g) After two consecutive terms, must wait two years before being eligible again.
(h) Must wait one full term before being eligible for any office, with the exception of lieutenant governor who is eligible immediately for the office of governor.
(i) After two consecutive terms, must wait four years before being eligible again.
(j) State treasurer also serves as insurance commissioner.
(k) State auditor is also insurance commissioner.
(l) State treasurer is not eligible for Office of Auditor General until four years after leaving office.

Table 16
QUALIFICATIONS FOR ELECTION TO STATE OFFICE*

State or other jurisdiction	Governor Age	Governor U.S. citizen (years)	Governor State citizen/resident (years)	Governor Other	Legislature Age House	Legislature Age Senate	Legislature State resident (years) House	Legislature State resident (years) Senate	District resident, house & senate (years)	Legislature Other
Alabama	30	10	7(a)	...	21	25	3	3	1	(b)
Alaska	30	7	7	...	21	25	3	3	1	(c)
Arizona	25	10	5(a)	...	25	25	3	3	1	(c)
Arkansas	30	(d)	7	...	21	25	2	2	1	(c)
California	18	5	5	(b)	18	18	3	3	...	(b,c)
Colorado	30	(d)	2	...	25	25	...	...	(e)	(c)
Connecticut	30	...	...	(b)	18	18	...	...	1	(b)
Delaware	30	12	6	...	24	27	3	3	(e)	(c)
Florida	30	...	7	(b)	21	21	2	2	1	(c)
Georgia	30	15	6(a)	...	21	25	2	4	...	(b,c)
Hawaii	30	...	5	(b)	18	18	3	3	1	(b,c)
Idaho	30	(d)	2	...	18	18	...	...	2(f)	(c)
Illinois	25	(d)	3	...	21	21	...	...	1	(c)
Indiana	30	5	5	...	21	25	2	2	60 da.	(c)
Iowa	30	(d)	2	...	21	25	1	1	...	
Kansas(g)	...	...	6(h)	...	18	18	...	...	(e)	(b)
Kentucky	30	...	6	(b)	24	30	2	6	1	(a)
Louisiana	25	5	5	(i)	18	18	2	2	1	(a,b)
Maine	30	15	5	(b)	21	18	1	1	3 mo.	(a,c)
Maryland	30	...	5	...	21	25	1	1	(i)	(c)
Massachusetts	...	...	7	(b)	18	18	1	5	(e)	(b,c,k)
Michigan	30	(d)	1	...	21	21	...	...	(e)	(b)
Minnesota	25	...	1	...	21	21	1	1	6 mo.	(b)
Mississippi	30	20	5	...	21	25	4	4	2	(b)
Missouri	30	15	10	...	24	30	2	3	1	
Montana	25	(d)	2	(b,l,m)	18	18	1	1	6 mo.(n)	(b,l,m)
Nebraska	30	5	5(h)	(b)	U	21	U	1	1	(b)
Nevada	25	...	2	...	(o)	(o)	(o)	(o)	(o)	...
New Hampshire	30	...	7	...	18	30	2	7	(e)	(b)
New Jersey	30	20	7	...	21	30	2(a)	4(a)	1	(b)
New Mexico	30	(d)	5	...	21	25	...	...	(e)	(c)
New York	30	(d)	5	...	18	18	5	5	1	(c)
North Carolina	30	5	2	...	21(p)	25	1	2	(e)	(b)
North Dakota	30	(d)	5	(b,q)	18	18	...	...	1	(b)
Ohio(g)	18	(d)	...	(b,q)	18	18	...	...	...	(b,q)
Oklahoma	31	(d)	(b)	(b)	21	25	...	...	(e)	(b)
Oregon	30	(d)	3	...	21	21	...	...	1	(c)
Pennsylvania	30	(d)	7	...	21	25	4(a)	4(a)	1	...
Rhode Island	18	1 mo.	1 mo.	(b,r)	18	18	1 mo.	1 mo.	1 mo.	(b,r)
South Carolina	30	5	5(h)	...	21	25	...	...	...	(b)

172

State								
South Dakota	. . .	(d)	. . .	. . .	25	25	2	(b,c,r)
Tennessee	30	(d)	7(a)	. . .	30	21	1	(c)
Texas	30	. . .	5	. . .	26	25	. . .	(b,c)
Utah	30	. . .	5(i)	. . .	25	25	6 mo.	(b,c)
Vermont	4	. . .	. . .	. . .	30	18	(e)	. . .
Virginia	30	(d)	5	. . .	21	21	(e)	(b,c)
Washington	18	(d)	. . .	. . .	18	18	. . .	(b,p,r)
West Virginia	30	(d)	5(a)	(a,b)	25	18(a)	1	(b)
Wisconsin	18	(d)	(b)	(b)	18	18	. . .	(b)
Wyoming	30	(d)	5	(b)	25	21	. . .	(a,c)
American Samoa	35	(s)	5	(t)	30	25	(u)	(u,v,w)
Guam	35	(d)	5	(b)	25	U	5	. . .
Puerto Rico	30	5	5	. . .	30	25	2	1	(w)
Virgin Islands	30	. . .	. . .	(b)	21	U	3	3	(b,c)

*This table includes constitutional and some statutory qualifications.

U—Unicameral legislature.

(a) Citizen of the state.

(b) Must be a qualified voter. Maryland: five years; Michigan: governor four years; Oklahoma: 10 years prior to election for governor, 6 months prior to filing for legislature; Virginia: five years.

(c) U.S. citizen. California: three years; Maine: five years.

(d) Number of years not specified.

(e) Reside in district, no time limit. Massachusetts: House one year; Oklahoma: six months prior to filing and must be registered in party six months prior to filing; Vermont: House one year.

(f) Following redistricting, a candidate may be elected from any district which contains a part of the district in which he resided at the time of redistricting, and re-elected if a resident of the new district he represents for 18 months prior to re-election.

(g) Kansas and Ohio have no constitutional qualifications for the office of governor. Ohio provides that no member of Congress or other person holding a state or federal office shall be governor.

(h) Resident and citizen.

(i) Governor must be resident of the state during the term for which he is elected.

(j) If the district has been established for at least six months, residency is six months. If the district was established for less than six months, residency is length of establishment of district.

(k) No person convicted of a felony for breach of public trust within preceding 20 years or convicted for subversion shall be eligible.

(l) No person convicted of a felony shall be eligible to hold office until his final discharge from state supervision.

(m) No person of unsound mind, as determined by a court, is qualified and hence eligible to hold office.

(n) Shall be a resident of the county if it contains one or more districts or of the district if it contains all or parts of more than one county.

(o) By statute an age of 21 minimum and a one-year state residency have been established for membership in the legislature.

(p) A conflict exists between two articles of the constitution specifying age for house members. Depending on interpretation, minimum age is 21 or age of qualified voter (18).

(q) No person convicted of embezzlement of public funds shall hold any office.

(r) No bribery convictions. South Dakota, West Virginia: No bribery, perjury or infamous crimes.

(s) Must be a U.S. citizen or U.S. national.

(t) No dishonorable discharge.

(u) Live in American Samoa for five years and bona fide resident one year.

(v) Senator must be a registered Matai.

(w) Write and speak English and Spanish.

Table 17

COMPENSATION COMMISSION FOR STATE OFFICIALS

State or other jurisdiction	Name of commission	Number of members	Salaries — Elected officials	Salaries — Administrative officials	Salaries — Legislators	Salaries — Judges	Benefits and/or expenses — Elected officials	Benefits and/or expenses — Administrative officials	Benefits and/or expenses — Legislators	Benefits and/or expenses — Judges	Recommendation submitted to — Legislature	Recommendation submitted to — Governor	Recommendation submitted to — Other	Authority — Advisory only	Authority — Other
Alabama	...														
Alaska	Salary Commission	5	★	★	★	★	★	★	★	★	★	★	(a)		May be accepted or rejected only; no action constitutes rejection.
Arizona	Commission on Salaries for Elective State Offices	5	★		★	★							(b)		
Arkansas	...														
California	...														
Colorado	State Officials' Compensation Commission	9	★	★	★	★	★	★	★	★	★	★	(a)		
Connecticut	Compensation Commission for Elected State Officials & Judges	11	★	★		★	★	★		★	★			★	
Delaware	...														
Florida	State Officers Compensation Commission	9	★	★	★	★	★	★	★	★	★	★	(c)	★	
Georgia	State Commission on Compensation	12	★	★			★	★			★	★		★	
Hawaii	Commission on Legislative Salary	10			★						★	★			May be accepted or rejected only; no action constitutes acceptance. May be reduced; no action constitutes acceptance
Idaho	Citizens' Committee on Legislative Compensation	6	★	★			★	★			★	★		★	
Illinois	Commission on Compensation of State and Local Government Officials	5	★	★	★	★	★	★	★	★		★			
Indiana	Advisory Committee on Compensation of General Assembly Members	7									(d)			★	
Iowa	Commission on Compensation Expenses & Salaries for Elected State Officials	15	★	★		★	★	★		★	★			★	
Kansas	Public Officials Compensation Commission	5			★	★		★		★	★			★	
Kentucky	Legislative Compensation Commission	7			★	★		★			★			★	
Louisiana	Compensation Review Commission	19	★	★	★	★	★	★			★			★	
Maine	General Assembly Compensation Commission	9									★				May be reduced; no action constitutes acceptance.
Maryland	Governor's Salary Commission	7	(e)			(f)	★		★		★				May decrease but not lower than the salary of incumbent.
Massachusetts	Advisory Board on Legislative & Constitutional Officers' Compensation	7	★		★		★		★		★			★	
Michigan	State Officers Compensation Commission	7	(e)		★	(f)	(e)		(g)	(f)	★				May be rejected by 2/3 votes of members in each house.
Minnesota	...														
Mississippi	...														
Missouri	...														

174

State	Commission											Notes
Montana	Montana Salary Commission	8	★			★		★		(h)	★	
Nevada	...											
New Hampshire	...											
New Jersey	...											
New Mexico	Temporary State Commission on Judicial Compensation	7		★		★		★				
New York	Advisory Budget Commission	12			★	★		★		★	★	
North Carolina				★		★					★	May be amended by legislative action.
North Dakota	...											
Ohio	...											
Oklahoma	Board on Legislative Compensation	11			★		★			★		Final and binding.
Oregon	...	★										
Pennsylvania	Commission on Compensation of Executive & Judicial State Officers	7	★									
Rhode Island	...			★			★					
South Carolina	Legislative & Constitutional Officers Pay Committee	10	★				★				★	Any increase which is passed by legislature cannot take effect until January 1, 1983.
South Dakota	Commission on Salaries for Elective State Officials	5	★			★				★		
Tennessee	...		★									
Texas	...		★			★						
Utah	Executive Compensation Commission	5	★(i)			★						
Vermont	...			★		★						
Virginia	...	7	★			★		★				
Washington	State Committee on Salaries	7	★		★		★				★	
West Virginia	Citizens Legislative Compensation Commission									(j)		May be reduced. May be accepted, rejected or reduced.
Wisconsin	...										★	
Wyoming	...											
American Samoa	Executive, Judicial & Legislative Compensation	9	★		★		★			★		
Guam	...										★	
Puerto Rico	...											
Virgin Islands	...											

(a) And chief justice.
(b) For legislature, referendum; for elected officials and judiciary, to governor.
(c) And lieutenant governor, house speaker, house clerk, senate clerk, legislative counsel, chief justice, and court of appeals justices.
(d) First session.
(e) Governor and lieutenant governor only.
(f) Judges of supreme court only.
(g) Expenses only.
(h) Commissioner of Campaign Finances and Practices and members of the State Tax Appeal Board.
(i) Makes recommendations on grade levels; therefore, indirectly affects salaries.
(j) And other salary authority.

175

Table 18

PROVISIONS FOR RECALL OF STATE OFFICIALS

State or other jurisdiction	Officers to whom applicable	Established by constitutional provision	Petition requirement*
Alabama	All elective officials except judicial officers	★	25% of voters in last general election in district in which election occurred
Arizona	All elective officials	★	25% of votes cast in last election for office of official sought to be recalled
California	All elective officials	★	State officer: 12% of votes cast in last election for officer sought to be recalled; state legislators, members of Board of Equalization, and judges: 20%
Colorado	All elective officials	★	25% of votes cast in last election for office of official sought to be recalled
Georgia	All elective officials	(a)	15% of number of electors who were registered and qualified to vote at the last preceding general election. To recall district or local officials: 30% of the number of electors registered and qualified to vote at the last preceding general election for any candidate offering for the office held by the officer.
Idaho	All elective officials except judicial officers	★	20% of the number of electors registered to vote in the last general election held in the jurisdiction from which the officer was elected
Kansas	All elected public officials in the state except judicial officers	★	40% of votes cast at the last general election for office of official sought to be recalled
Louisiana	All elective officials except judges of courts of record	★	33-1/3% of voters voting; 40% of voters in districts of less than 1,000 voters
Michigan	All elective officials except judges of courts of record	★	25% of voters in last election for governor in electoral district of officer sought to be recalled
Montana	All public officials elected or appointed	(a)	10% of registered voters at preceding general election is required, except for officials chosen from a district, in which case 15% of the number registered to vote in the preceding election in that district is required
Nevada	All elective officials	★	25% of voters voting in the jurisdiction electing official sought to be recalled
North Dakota	All elective officials	★	25% of electors voting in last general election for governor
Oregon	All elective officials	★	25% of votes cast in last election for supreme court justice
Washington	All elective officials except judges of courts of record	★	25%-35% of qualified electors depending on unit of government
Wisconsin	All elective officials	★	25% of votes cast in last general election for governor within the district of officeholder recalled
Guam	Governor	★	Petition for referendum: 2/3 vote of legislature or petition of legislature by 50% of voters voting in last gubernatorial election. Referendum election: "yes" votes must total 2/3 of votes cast in last gubernatorial election, and majority vote on issue must be "yes"
Virgin Islands	Governor	★	50% of votes cast for governor in last election or by 2/3 vote of legislature in favor of referendum

*In each state where a recall election may occur, a majority of the popular vote is required to recall an official.

(a) Allowable under the constitution; provision is statutory.

Table 19
STATE ADMINISTRATIVE OFFICIALS: METHODS OF SELECTION

State or other jurisdiction	Governor	Lt. governor	Secretary of state	Attorney general	Treasurer	Adjutant general	Administration	Agriculture	Banking	Budget	Civil rights	Commerce	Community affairs	Comptroller	Consumer affairs	Corrections	Data processing
Alabama	CE	CE	CE	CE	CE	G	...	CE	G	CS	...	G	G	AG	(a-1)	G	CS
Alaska	CE	CE	(a-4)	GB	(a-5)	GB	A	A	A	A	G	GB	GB	GB	A	A	A
Arizona	CE	...	CE	CE	CE	G	GS	B	GS	L	A	G	...	AG	(a-1)	GS	AG
Arkansas	CE	CE	CE	CE	CE	G	(a-10)	(a-11)	AG	AG	...	(a-12)	G	(a-10)	(a-1)	GS	GS
California	CE	CE	CE	CE	CE	GS	(b)	GS	GS	GS	G	GS	GS	CE	GS	GS	G
Colorado	CE	CE	CE	CE	CE	G	GS	GS	A	GS	A	A	A	A	(a-1)	GS	(a-8)
Connecticut	CE	CE	CE	CE	CE	G	GE	GE	GE	A	B	GE	A	CE	GE	GE	A
Delaware	CE	CE	GS	CE	CE	GS	GS	GS	GS	GS	GS	AG	AG	A	AG	GS	AG
Florida	CE	CE	CE	CE	CE	GS	GS	CE	CE	A	A	GS	GS	CE	A	GS	A
Georgia	CE	CE	CE	CE	A	G	GS	CE	GS	G	...	B	G	CE	G	B	A
Hawaii	CE	CE	(a-4)	GS	...	GS	GS	GS	(a-25)	GS	...	(a-7)	...	GS	(a-25)	(a-3)	(a-22)
Idaho	CE	CE	CE	CE	CE	GS	GS	GS	GS	G	BGS	G	(a-11)	CE	(a-1)	BGS	(a-5)
Illinois	CE	CE	CE	CE	CE	G	GS	GS	GS	G	GS	GS	CE	(a-1)	AT	G	A
Indiana	CE	CE	CE	SE	CE	G	G	(a-4)	G	G	G	(a-4)	A	...	AT	G	A
Iowa	CE	CE	CE	CE	CE	GS	...	SE	GS	(a-5)	GS	GS	A	GS	(a-1)	(a-3)	CS
Kansas	CE	CE	CE	CE	SE	GS	GS	B	GS	CS	B	GS	A	A	A	GS	A
Kentucky	CE	CE	CE	CE	CE	G	G	CE	G	AG	B	G	G	(a-10)	A	AG	AG
Louisiana	CE	CE	CE	CE	CE	G	GS	G	CE	GS	...	GS	GS	(a-8)	GS	GS	A
Maine	CE	...	CL	CL	CL	G	GLS	GLS	GLS	AG	B	(a-27)	G	AG	GLS	AG	CS
Maryland	CE	CE	GS	CE	CL	GS	...	GS	AGS	GS	GS	A	AG	CE	A	AGS	(a-5)
Massachusetts	CE	CE	CE	CE	CE	G	G	G	G	AG	AT	G	G	G	G	G	A
Michigan	CE	CE	CE	CE	GS	GS	GS	B	GS	(a-8)	B	GS	...	(a-11)	(a-1)	B	(a-8)
Minnesota	CE	CE	CE	CE	CE	G	GS	GS	BS	GS	GS	(g)	(a-11)	A	GS	GS	A
Mississippi	CE	CE	CE	CE	CE	GS	GS	...	SE	GS	B	...	(a-29)	B	(a-30)	B	B
Missouri	CE	CE	CE	CE	CE	GS	GS	GS	AS	A	B	A	(a-11)	A	GS	GS	A
Montana	CE	CE	CE	CE	A	G	GS	GS	(a-11)	G	G	G	(a-11)	A	G	A	A
Nebraska	CE	CE	CE	CE	CE	G	GS	GS	GS	A	B	GS	(a-11)	A	(a-1)	GS	A
Nevada	CE	CE	CE	CE	CE	G	G	BG	A	(a-8)	G	G	G	CE	A	G	A
New Hampshire	CE	...	CL	GC	CL	GC	(a-5)	GC	GC	A	B	GOC	GOC	GOC	(a-1)	GOC	B
New Jersey	CE	...	GS	GS	GS	GS	...	BG	GS	GS	A	GS	GS	GS	GS	GS	A
New Mexico	CE	CE	CE	CE	CE	GS	(b)	GS	G	G	G	GS	AG	G	(a-1)	A	A
New York	CE	CE	GS	CE	A	GS	...	G	G	G	G	GS	GS	CE	GS	GS	(a-6)
North Carolina	CE	CE	CE	CE	CE	G	G	CE	GS	AG	(a-8)	G	A	(a-22)	A	G	AG
North Dakota	CE	CE	CE	CE	CE	G	A	CE	GS	A	...	A	...	A	A	GS	A
Ohio	CE	CE	CE	CE	CE	G	GS	GS	A	GS	A	GS	(a-11)	(a-21)	(a-1)	A	A
Oklahoma	CE	CE	CE	SE	CE	GS	...	GS	GS	GS	B	G	G	AG	B	B	...
Oregon	CE	...	CE	SE	CE	G	GS	GS	AG	A	CS	GS	A	A	A	AG	A
Pennsylvania	CE	CE	GS	GS	CE	GS	GS	GS	GS	GS	GS	GS	GS	A	A	AG	AG
Rhode Island	CE	CE	CE	CE	CE	G	GS	(a-12)	G	CS	B	GS	GS	A	BS	A	A
South Carolina	CE	CE	CE	CE	CE	CE	(a-22)	SE	B	B	B	(a-27)	A	CE	B	B	(a-22)
South Dakota	CE	CE	CE	CE	CE	GS	G	GS	A	G	GS	GS	(a-27)	CE	(a-1)	AG	A
Tennessee	CE	(i)	CL	SC	CL	GS	(a-10)	G	A	B	G	(a-11)	A	A	A	A	A
Texas	CE	CE	GS	CE	CE	GS	...	SE	BS	G	...	(a-27)	GS	CE	A	B	B
Utah	CE	CE	...	CE	CE	GS	GS	GS	G	GS	...	GS	GS	CE	AG	BA	AG
Vermont	CE	CE	CE	SE	CE	SL	GS	GS	GS	GS	(a-1)	A	GS	(a-10)	(a-1)	GS	CS
Virginia	CE	CE	GB	CE	GB	GB	GB	GB	B	GB	...	GB	A	GB	(a-29)	GB	GB
Washington	CE	CE	CE	CE	CE	GS	(a-6)	GS	A	GS	B	GS	(a-11)	(a-22)	(a-1)	GS	B
West Virginia	CE	...	CE	CE	CE	GS	(a-10)	CE	GS	A	GS	GS	A	(a-10)	(a-1)	GS	A
Wisconsin	CE	CE	CE	CE	CE	G	GS	B	GS	(a-8)	A	GS	(a-11)	(a-8)	(a-1)	A	(a-8)
Wyoming	CE	...	CE	GS	CE	G	G	B	G	G	...	(a-27)	(a-27)	G	(a-1)	BG	A
Guam	CE	...	...	CE	A	...	GS	GS	(a-38)	GS	...	GS	G	(a-8)	A	GS	A
Puerto Rico	CE	...	GB	GS	GS	GS	...	GS	(a-21)	G	G	A	G	GS	GS	GS	...
Virgin Islands	CE	CE	...	GS	...	...	(b)	GS	(a-4)	G	GS	GS	(b)	...	GS	GS	(b)

Note: Salary figures for these officials may be found in Table 18.

Key:
CE —Constitutional, elected
CL —Constitutional, elected by legislature
SE —Statutory, elected
SL —Statutory, elected by legislature
L —Selected by legislature or one of its organs
SC —Statutory, elected by state supreme court

Appointed by:
G —Governor / ...
GS —Governor / Senate
GB —Governor / Both houses
GE —Governor / Either house
GC —Governor / Council
GD —Governor / Departmental board
GLS —Governor / Appropriate legislative committee & senate
GLG —Governor & Lt. governor / ...
GOC —Governor & council or cabinet / ...
LG —Lieutenant governor / ...

Appointed by:
AT —Attorney general / ...
A —Agency head / ...
AB —Agency head / Board
AG —Agency head / Governor
AGC —Agency head / Governor & council
AS —Agency head / Senate
ALS —Agency head / Appropriate legislative committee & senate
AGS —Agency head / Governor & senate
ASH —Agency head / Senate president & house speaker

B —Board or commission / ...
BG —Board / Governor
BGC —Board / Governor & council
BGS —Board / Governor & senate
BS —Board or commission / Senate
BA —Board or commission / Agency head
CS —Civil Service / ...
ACB —Nominated by audit committee / Both houses

STATE ADMINISTRATIVE OFFICIALS: METHODS OF SELECTION

State or other jurisdiction	Disaster preparedness	Education (chief state school officer)	Education—higher	Elections administration	Employment services	Energy resources	Environmental conservation	Finance	Fish & game	General services	Health	Highway patrol	Highways	Historic preservation	Industrial development	Insurance	Labor & industrial relations
Alabama	CS	B	...	(a-2)	A	CS	(b)	G	G	CS	B	G	G	B	G	G	G
Alaska	A	BG	BG	LG	A	A	GB	GB	GB	A	A	A	A	A	A	A	GB
Arizona	G	CE	B	(a-2)	GS	(a-7)	GS	AG	B	(a-8)	GS	A	(a-9)	B	G	GS	B
Arkansas	AG	BG	BG	...	G	GS	G	G	B	...	GS	AG	(a-9)	GS	GS	AG	GS
California	GS	CE	B	(a-2)	GS	B	GS	GS	GS	GS	GS	GS	(a-9)	(a-13)	(a-14)	GS	GS
Colorado	(a-16)	B	B	(a-2)	A	G	(a-17)	GS	BA	(a-8)	GS	A	GS	GD	(a-11)	A	A
Connecticut	GE	GE	B	GE	AG	A	GE	GE	GE	(a-8)	GE	GE	A	G	(a-11)	GE	GE
Delaware	AG	B	(b)	GS	(a-14)	G	A	GS	A	(a-8)	AG	A	(a-9)	AG	AG	CE	GS
Florida	A	CE	B	A	A	GS	(a-5)	GS	GOC	A	G	A	A	A	A	(a-21)	A
Georgia	(a-16)	CE	B	(a-2)	(a-14)	G	(a-12)	(b)	A	(a-8)	BG	BG	(a-9)	(a-12)	(a-11)	(a-5)	CE
Hawaii	(a-16)	B	B	(a-4)	(a-26)	(a-7)	(a-17)	(a-22)	(a-12)	(a-5)	GS	...	(a-9)	(a-12)	(a-7)	(a-25)	GS
Idaho	A	CE	BGS	(a-2)	GS	G	GS	G	GS	(a-8)	A	A	(a-9)	B	(a-11)	GS	GS
Illinois	GS	B	B	(e)	GS	GS	GS	(b)	A	(a-8)	GS	GS	(a-9)	A	(a-11)	GS	GS
Indiana	GC	SE	B	B	G	G	A	(b)	A	G	G	G	G	B	LG	G	G
Iowa	A	GS	GS	A	GS	GS	A	(a-5)	GD	GS	GS	GS	(a-9)	B	GS	G	GS
Kansas	A	B	B	A	GS	GS	A	(b)	A	(a-8)	GS	GS	A	B	A	SE	GS
Kentucky	G	CE	B	B	AG	G	G	G	B	(a-10)	AG	AG	(a-9)	BG	(a-11)	G	G
Louisiana	GS	CE	B	CE	GS	(a-12)	GS	(a-8)	GS	(a-8)	GS	GS	(a-9)	GS	GS	CE	GS
Maine	AG	GLS	(a-23)	(a-2)	GLS	G	GLS	(a-8)	GLS	...	A	AG	A	B	G	GLS	A
Maryland	G	B	B	G	AG	A	(a-12)	(a-5)	G	GS	GS	GS	AG	A	AG	GS	GS
Massachusetts	G	B	B	A	G	G	G	G	G	G	G	G	G	(a-2)	G	G	A
Michigan	(a-28)	B	CS	(a-2)	B	G	...	(a-8)	B	(a-8)	GS	GS	A	CS	CS	GS	GS
Minnesota	G	BG	GS	(a-2)	GS	GS	GS	GS	(a-12)	GS	GS	G	(a-9)	...	A	BS	GS
Mississippi	G	CE	B	(a-2)	G	G	B	(a-22)	B	...	B	GS	SE	B	G	SE	...
Missouri	GS	B	B	A	A	A	A	(a-8)	B	...	A	GS	B	A	(a-11)	AS	GS
Montana	A	CE	GS	(a-2)	A	G	(a-17)	(b)	GS	A	GS	AT	GS	B	(a-11)	(h)	GS
Nebraska	(a-16)	B	B	(a-2)	(a-14)	GS	GS	(a-8)	(a-13)	(a-8)	GS	G	GS	B	(a-11)	GS	GS
Nevada	G	B	B	(a-2)	G	G	A	(a-5)	G	A	A	A	(a-9)	A	A	A	G
New Hampshire	G	B	A	(a-2)	GC	G	(b)	(a-5)	B	...	GC	GC	GC	A	GC	GC	GC
New Jersey	A	GS	BG	(a-2)	A	GS	GS	(a-21)	AGC	(a-21)	GS	GS	(a-9)	A	GS	GS	GS
New Mexico	(a-16)	B	B	A	GS	GS	A	(a-8)	A	(a-8)	GS	GD	GS	A	A	B	GS
New York	G	B	(a-23)	G	A	GS	G	...	(a-20)	GS	GS	GS	(a-9)	(a-13)	(a-11)	GS	GS
North Carolina	G	CE	BG	G	G	AG	A	(b)	A	(a-8)	G	G	AG	G	A	CE	CE
North Dakota	A	CE	B	(a-2)	G	G	A	(a-22)	G	GS	G	G	G	B	(a-11)	CE	SE
Ohio	(a-16)	B	BG	(a-2)	GS	GS	GS	(a-22)	A	(a-8)	GS	(a-19)	GS	...	A	GS	GS
Oklahoma	GS	CE	B	L	B	B	(a-17)	(a-21)	AB	A	B	GS	(a-9)	B	G	CE	GS
Oregon	CS	CE	B	A	AG	GS	B	(a-8)	B	GS	AG	GS	AB	(a-9)	A	AG	SE
Pennsylvania	B	B	AG	G	CS	GS	AG	(a-8)	B	GS	GS	GS	A	BG	GS	GS	GS
Rhode Island	G	B	(a-23)	B	G	G	(a-12)	(a-8)	B	A	GB	G	A	B	(a-11)	G	G
South Carolina	(a-16)	CE	B	B	B	B	(a-17)	(a-22)	B	(a-22)	B	B	B	B	B	GS	GS
South Dakota	A	GS	B	(a-2)	A	A	A	G	G	(a-8)	GS	AG	A	GS	GS	A	GS
Tennessee	A	G	B	A	G	BG	A	G	B	G	G	A	(a-9)	AB	A	G	G
Texas	G	BS	B	(a-2)	B	GLG	(b)	(b)	(a-13)	B	B	B	B	B	B	B	G
Utah	BG	B	B	(a-4)	AG	A	B	AG	BA	(a-8)	GS	AG	(a-9)	AB	A	GS	GS
Vermont	G	BG	...	(a-2)	GS	G	GS	AGS	AS	(a-8)	GS	A	(a-9)	A	A	(a-36)	GS
Virginia	GB	GB	GB	GB	GB	(a-37)	(b)	(a-8)	B	GB	GB	GB	GB	GB	GB	B	GB
Washington	GS	CE	B	A	GS	GS	(a-33)	(a-22)	(j)	GS	A	GS	(a-9)	GS	A	SE	GS
West Virginia	G	B	B	(a-2)	GS	B	B	GS	A	A	CS	GS	GS	A	A	GS	GS
Wisconsin	GS	CE	BG	BA	(a-14)	(a-8)	(a-12)	...	(a-12)	(a-8)	GS	GS	(a-9)	G	(a-11)	GS	GS
Wyoming	G	CE	G	(a-2)	G	G	G	(b)	A	(a-8)	G	AB	B	B	AG	B	G
Guam	G	BGS	B	B	GS	G	BGS	(a-8)	GS	(a-8)	GS	A	B	GS	A	B	(a-38)
Puerto Rico	G	GS	GS	G	A	G	G	(a-21)	(a-12)	GS	GS	A	GS	G	G	GS	GS
Virgin Islands	G	GS	B	L	(a-14)	G	GS	GS	GS	(b)	GS	...	...	A	GS	(a-4)	GS

(a) Chief administrative official or agency in charge of function:

(a-1) Attorney General	(a-15) Consumer Affairs
(a-2) Secretary of State	(a-16) Adjutant General
(a-3) Social Services	(a-17) Health
(a-4) Lieutenant Governor	(a-18) Community Affairs
(a-5) Comptroller	(a-19) Highways
(a-6) General Services	(a-20) Environmental Conservation
(a-7) Planning	(a-21) Treasurer
(a-8) Administration	(a-22) Budget
(a-9) Transportation	(a-23) Education (chief state school officer)
(a-10) Finance	(a-24) Mental Health
(a-11) Commerce	(a-25) Licensing
(a-12) Natural Resources	(a-26) Personnel
(a-13) Parks & Recreation	(a-27) Industrial Development
(a-14) Labor & Industrial Relations	

- (a-28) Highway Patrol
- (a-29) Agriculture
- (a-30) Post Audit
- (a-31) Welfare
- (a-32) Education—higher
- (a-33) Fish & Game
- (a-34) Tourism
- (a-35) Energy Resources
- (a-36) Banking
- (a-37) Disaster Preparedness
- (a-38) Taxation
- (b) No single agency or official.

STATE ADMINISTRATIVE OFFICIALS: METHODS OF SELECTION

State or other jurisdiction	Licensing	Mental health	Natural resources	Parks & recreation	Personnel	Planning	Post audit	Pre audit	Public library	Public utility regulation	Purchasing	Social services	Solid waste	Taxation	Tourism	Transportation	Welfare
Alabama	...	B	G	G	B	G	CE	CS	B	SE	CS	G	...	G	G	...	(a-3)
Alaska	A	A	GB	A	A	G	CL	A	A	GB	(a-6)	A	GB	GB	A	GB	(a-3)
Arizona	...	A	...	B	AG	G	GB	AG	B	CE	AG	GS	...	GS	GS	GS	GS
Arkansas	...	AG	GS	GS	AG	...	...	CE	B	AG	AG	AG	AG	AG	AG	B	(a-3)
California	(a-15)	GS	GS	GS	G	A	(a-10)	CE	GS	GS	GS	GS	(c)	BS	G	GS	(a-3)
Colorado	GS	A	GS	BA	GS	A	ACB	(a-5)	A	GS	A	GS	(a-17)	GS	(a-18)	(a-19)	(a-3)
Connecticut	...	GE	(a-20)	CS	A	A	L	(a-5)	B	GB	A	GE	CS	GE	CS	GE	GE
Delaware	AG	AG	AG	AG	GS	GS	CE	(a-10)	AG	GS	AG	AG	GS	AG	AG	GS	(a-3)
Florida	GS	A	GOC	A	A	(a-22)	L	(a-5)	A	GC	A	(a-17)	GS	GOC	A	GS	A
Georgia	(a-2)	BG	BG	A	GD	(a-22)	SL	(a-5)	(a-23)	CE	A	(a-24)	A	GS	A	B	G
Hawaii	GS	(a-17)	GS	(a-12)	GS	GS	(a-5)	(a-5)	(a-23)	(a-22)	(a-5)	GS	(a-17)	GS	(a-7)	GS	(a-3)
Idaho	G	A	...	GS	BGS	(a-22)	L	(a-5)	(d)	GS	A	GS	A	GS	(a-11)	BGS	(a-17)
Illinois	GS	GS	GS	A	GS	...	L	CE	(a-2)	(f)	A	A	A	GS	(a-11)	GS	GS
Indiana	...	G	G	A	G	LG	G	CE	B	G	A	G	A	G	A	G	(a-3)
Iowa	...	(a-3)	GB	GD	BG	G	CE	GS	BS	GS	CS	GB	GS	GS	GS	GD	(a-3)
Kansas	...	AS	...	BG	A	(a-22)	L	CS	GS	GS	A	GS	A	GS	A	GS	GS
Kentucky	(a-10)	(a-17)	AG	G	G	...	CE	AG	G	B	A	AG	AG	G	G	A	AG
Louisiana	(b)	GS	GS	GS	B	GS	SL	(a-22)	B	CE	A	GS	GS	GS	GS	GS	GS
Maine	...	AG	GLS	B	GLS	G	SL	AG	BG	GLS	AGS	(a-12)	AG	(a-27)	GLS	A	
Maryland	GS	(a-17)	GS	A	GS	GS	ASH	(a-21)	A	GS	CS	AG	(a-12)	CE	GS	(a-3)	
Massachusetts	G	G	G	A	A	(a-18)	CE	G	A	G	G	G	A	G	A	G	G
Michigan	GS	GS	B	CS	CS	...	CL	(a-8)	CS	GS	CS	GS	(a-12)	A	CS	(a-19)	(a-3)
Minnesota	...	GS	GS	A	GS	G	L	GS	...	GS	A	GS	A	GS	A	GS	GS
Mississippi	...	GS	B	AB	G	G	CE	G	B	SE	(a-22)	(a-31)	A	GS	A	(a-19)	B
Missouri	A	B	GS	A	A	...	CE	(b)	(a-32)	GS	A	GS	A	GS	B	(a-19)	A
Montana	(a-11)	GS	AG	(a-33)	AG	(a-11)	L	...	B	SE	A	GS	(a-17)	GS	A	...	(a-3)
Nebraska	(a-17)	(a-31)	B	B	GS	G	CE	(a-5)	B	CE	A	(a-31)	A	GS	A	...	GS
Nevada	...	A	G	A	GS	A	...	(a-8)	G	A	GS	(a-12)	G	GS	G	B	(a-3)
New Hampshire	...	GC	GC	GC	BGC	G	G	L	AG	B	GC	AGC	(a-31)	A	GC	A	...	GC
New Jersey	A	A	GS	A	A	GS	...	(a-22)	A	GS	(a-21)	GS	A	GS	A	GS	AB
New Mexico	...	(a-17)	GS	A	G	G	CE	(a-8)	A	GS	GS	G	(a-17)	G	A	GS	GS
New York	A	GS	(a-20)	G	GS	...	(a-5)	(a-5)	CS	GS	GS	GS	(a-20)	GS	(a-11)	GS	GS
North Carolina	(b)	G	G	G	AG	...	CE	(a-8)	G	GS	AG	G	G	A	G	A	(a-3)
North Dakota	...	(a-3)	...	G	AB	...	CE	(a-22)	A	CE	A	G	A	CE	(a-11)	...	(a-3)
Ohio	...	GS	GS	A	A	A	CE	CE	B	GS	GS	GS	GS	A	GS	GS	
Oklahoma	...	B	...	(a-34)	B	...	(a-21)	(a-22)	B	CE	(a-6)	GS	(a-17)	GS	B	B	(a-3)
Oregon	(a-11)	AG	(b)	AB	(a-8)	B	(a-2)	...	B	GS	A	GS	A	GS	A	BS	AG
Pennsylvania	G	AG	GS	CS	AG	G	CE	(a-5)	A	GS	AG	GS	CS	GS	A	GS	A
Rhode Island	G	GS	GS	A	GS	CS	(b)	A	GS	GS	CS	GS	(a-12)	GS	A	GS	(a-3)
South Carolina	...	B	...	B	B	B	B	CE	B	L	B	B	B	GS	A	(a-19)	(a-3)
South Dakota	A	A	GS	GS	GS	G	SL	CE	B	SE	A	GS	GS	A	GS	AG	
Tennessee	(b)	G	G	A	G	G	(a-5)	(a-5)	A	SE	A	A	A	G	G	G	
Texas	...	B	(a-35)	B	...	(a-22)	L	(a-5)	B	B	(a-6)	(a-31)	A	(a-5)	B	(a-19)	BS
Utah	AG	AB	GS	BA	AG	G	CE	(a-5)	AB	GS	AG	GS	(a-17)	GS	AB	GS	GS
Vermont	(a-2)	GS	(a-20)	A	GS	G	CE	(a-10)	G	GS	G	GS	A	GS	A	GS	
Virginia	(b)	GB	GB	(a-12)	GB	(a-22)	GB	(a-5)	GB	L	(a-6)	(a-31)	(b)	GB	(a-12)	GB	GB
Washington	GS	A	CE	B	G	G	AG	A	B	GS	A	A	A	GS	A	B	A
West Virginia	...	(a-17)	GS	A	A	(a-11)	A	A	B	GS	A	A	B	GS	A	(a-19)	GS
Wisconsin	GS	(a-3)	B	(a-12)	GS	(a-22)	(b)	(a-8)	A	GS	A	(a-17)	A	GS	A	GS	A
Wyoming	...	A	G	G	G	L	CE	B	G	A	G	G	G	G	...	(a-3)	
Guam	A	A	...	GS	A	GS	L	(a-5)	(a-21)	(a-23)	GS	A	GS	A	GS	B	(b)	(a-3)
Puerto Rico	B	GS	GS	G	GS	GS	(a-5)	(a-21)	(a-23)	GS	A	GS	A	(a-21)	G	GS	(a-3)
Virgin Islands	(a-15)	(a-17)	A	A	G	G	(b)	(b)	A	GS	GS	GS	...	GS	A	...	GS

(c) Solid Waste Management Board is composed of nine voting members: seven appointed by the governor subject to senate confirmation; one each appointed by the speaker of the assembly and the senate Committee on Rules.

(d) State Library, Board of Education, B.

(e) Function performed by eight-member board (GS). Four members are nominated by governor and four are nominated by the highest ranking constitutional officer of the political party opposite that of the governor. Executive director of the board is chosen by the board.

(f) Members appointed by the governor with consent of senate; chairman is chosen by the governor from among the members.

(g) Commerce Commission, composed of commissioners of banking, securities and insurance, all GS.

(h) State auditor is ex officio commissioner of insurance, CE.

(i) The speaker of the senate is elected by the senate from among its membership and, by statute, is lieutenant governor.

(j) Function performed by two agencies: Fisheries, GS; Game, B.

Section IV   THE LEGISLATURES

THE STATE LEGISLATURES

By William Pound

THE MAJOR THEME in state legislatures during the 1980s promises to be consolidation and integration of the reforms and changes of the preceding two decades. Reform and revitalization of state legislatures were clearly the predominant characteristics in the period from 1965 to 1977. In the last five years, however, there has been a noticeable slowing in the pace of legislative reform. Emphasis has turned from change and expansion to management of legislative resources. Several of the organizations most active in the reform movement have either ceased to exist or turned their attention to other issues. This is not to imply that legislative change has occurred at the same pace or with similar impact in each state. Perhaps the most important fact to note about state legislatures is that while they have many common features, each is unique. A review of the tables in *The Book of the States* will illustrate the diversity of American state legislatures.

The legislative reform movement received much of its stimulus from the U.S. Supreme Court decisions on legislative reapportionment, particularly *Baker* v. *Carr* (1963) and *Reynolds* v. *Sims* (1965). As the composition of state legislatures changed and the growth of state government accelerated, legislative institutions underwent rapid change in areas such as constitutional restrictions on authority, length of sessions, legislator compensation, professional staff, and rules and procedures. Restrictions on the length of sessions were eliminated or relaxed to allow more time for legislative deliberation. Forty-three states now meet annually through formal or informal arrangements leaving only Arkansas, Kentucky, Montana, Nevada, North Dakota, Oregon and Texas on biennial schedules. Limitations on matters which legislatures can consider during their second session have been eased, although seven states (Colorado, Connecticut, Indiana, Maine, New Mexico, Utah and Wyoming) still restrict their second year primarily to budget and fiscal matters.

Legislative staff expanded dramatically during this period. The National Conference of State Legislatures estimated that there were more than 16,000 full-time legislative employees in 1980 and the employment of temporary staff during sessions increased this number to over 25,000. Staff specialization increased with the development of strong fiscal, audit and evaluation units and the expansion of administrative, research and bill drafting staffs. Committee and caucus staffs developed in several states, notably California and Florida. Legislative rules and procedures were reviewed in most states, committee numbers were reduced and committees were given more time to work and more authority. Legislatures also modernized their facilities and began more frequently to provide office space and individual staff assistance to their members. Yet even with this expansion of legislative capability, state legislatures still spend less than half of 1 percent of state general fund expenditures on their own operations.

Significant issues currently confronting state legislatures include the erosion of leadership power, the amount and use of time by legislators, accommodating legislative structure to

William Pound is Director of State Services for the National Conference of State Legislatures.

the increased responsibilities of state government, improving the effectiveness of legislative oversight, and the management of information and accommodation of legislatures to technological change. Of particular concern to many observers has been a decline in the powers of legislative leadership and a sense that many legislators are more concerned with their individual roles and status than they are with the functioning of the legislature as an institution.[1]

The Legislative Institution

There are several elements involved in the decline perceived in leadership power and institutional patriotism. To some extent, the reform and democratization of legislative rules and procedures with their corollary "opening" of the legislative process have weakened the powers of leadership and diffused those powers over more members of the legislature. The committee process has been made more effective and more powerful in a number of states. The growth of legislative staff has likewise increased the knowledge and capability of the individual legislator. In particular, in recent years, the personal staff of legislators in many states has grown much faster than have central staff services. Legislators in many states find themselves increasingly involved with providing constituent services and dealing with specific constituent problems. The decline in power of political parties and the growth in influence of interest group and political action committee contributions to campaigns have also been factors in emphasizing the "legislator" as opposed to the "legislature."

There are several facets to the concern about time spent in the legislative process. The pressures increase yearly to make the legislature a full-time, as opposed to a part-time, occupation. The "New Federalism" proposals of the Reagan administration promise to accelerate this tendency. In at least seven states (California, Illinois, Massachusetts, Michigan, New York, Ohio and Pennsylvania), the majority of members consider themselves to be full-time legislators. These legislatures, as well as those in New Jersey and Wisconsin, can be found in session throughout the year and are appropriately classified as full-time. In other states, such as Alaska, Arizona, Colorado, Iowa, Oklahoma and South Carolina, there has been a gradual increase in the number of days spent in session, but this trend is meeting resistance, and the legislatures themselves are attempting by rule and procedure to manage their time more efficiently. Examples of such efforts include committee hearing and floor action deadlines, increasing committee time early in the session to facilitate workflow and establishing adjournment dates or limits on the number of days for which legislators may receive per diem expenses. In 1980, the states which had the most formal session days were California, Michigan, South Carolina, Alaska, Arizona, Colorado, Massachusetts and Oklahoma, ranging from 120 to 90.

Two other facets to the problem of time management are legislative salaries and time spent during the interim on legislative activities. The increase in legislator salaries, a trend for more than a decade, continued during the past biennium. As legislators are required to spend more time on legislative business, there appears both more demand and more justification for increased salaries. An effect of the reform movement in many states was to remove fiscal limits on legislator compensation from state constitutions and allow salaries to be determined by compensation commissions or by statute. The full-time status of legislators in the states listed above is reflected in the rates of compensation.

The interim work of the legislature has been re-emphasized as an important part of the legislative process. Some complex issues are better studied and managed when the legislature is not under the pressures of committee and floor activity and bill passage. Interim activity dates from the beginning of the legislative council movement in the 1930s. Today, interim activity is conducted through legislative councils or by a continuation of the work of the standing committees of the legislature. Legislatures in 29 states now use the regular standing committees during the interim. The importance of adequate time and analysis to deal with complex issues cannot be overstated. Thus, the time pressures on state legislators both in and out of session continue to grow. Several states, notably Florida, Minnesota, Utah and Washington, have developed committee weeks or weekends during the interim when virtually the entire legislature is in the capitol at the same time. Both houses of 11 state legislatures, and one house in two others, have established scheduling procedures to control interim activities. Florida, which meets in 60-day annual sessions, has sought to manage its workload through extensive and effective use of interim time.

Legislative Oversight

Program oversight by legislatures has become an important aspect of legislative activity. The traditional and most essential tool of legislative oversight is the appropriations process. But in recent years, oversight activity has become more specialized in such areas as program evaluation, review of administrative rules, review and control of federal funds, and sunset reviews. During the past two years, oversight of federal block grants has received special attention from a growing number of legislatures.

The integration of oversight activity in the legislative process is of concern to many legislators and staff. When a specialized oversight agency finds programs or policies that are not in compliance with statute or legislative intent or operating ineffectively, the most efficient way to deal with them is through the budget process. Instances of effective oversight are most often found where appropriations committees assume a strong oversight role or where other oversight activity is closely related to the budget process and has strong leadership support. Colorado, Florida, Mississippi, Texas and Virginia provide examples of effective oversight integration.

The growth of new oversight activities has slowed in the last biennium, being primarily confined to federal funds and block grant review. There have been no new independent legislative program evaluation agencies established since the 1970s. Program or performance evaluation activity continues to be an area of growth, but its spread is within existing audit, fiscal or research agencies. Sunset activity has been similarly characterized by retrenchment as legislatures find that the sunset concept may have been oversold and that many sunset review schedules were over-ambitious.

An assessment of the experience of the 35 states which have sunset laws indicates mixed results. On the positive side, the action-forcing mechanism of sunset compels the legislature to evaluate programs or agencies and exercise its oversight responsibilities, forces affirmative legislative action to re-create or maintain agencies facing termination, institutionalizes the evaluation process and creates an incentive for agencies to implement corrective administrative changes on their own. On the negative side, sunset has required a significant amount of legislative time to conduct sunset reviews, detracting from time spent on other legislative responsibilities, and the costs of thorough sunset reviews have been considerable while there have been relatively small financial savings in the programs reviewed. Sunset seems to have been most effective when reviews have focused on the lesser regulatory agencies and probably cannot be expected to have significant impact on the broader areas of government or major regulatory agencies. However, the sunset experience may be judged positive if it has caused legislators to be more aware of their oversight responsibilities and results in more effective program evaluation.

Legislative review of the administrative rule-making process now takes place in some form in 41 states. In 29 states, the legislature has the power to veto, temporarily suspend or require modifications in proposed administrative rules. Constitutional challenges to the legislative rule review authority, largely on the grounds of violation of the separation of powers concept, have been mounted in several states with mixed results. Important variables are the structure and procedures of the review process. Legislative rule review may be vested in a special oversight committee or placed in the regular standing committees, or a combination. Also, all proposed rules may be reviewed or the process may be applied selectively. Most importantly, the states vary as to whether rules may be suspended by resolution or only through a bill and as to whether the suspension or veto power may be exercised by a legislative committee or only by the legislature.

The review and control of federal funds by state legislatures was stimulated by the growth of federal grant-in-aid programs to more than 25 percent of state budgets during the past 20 years. During the 1970s, legislatures became increasingly concerned about federal dictation of state priorities and situations where legislatures were expected to contribute ever-greater state funds to programs begun with federal monies. State administration of federal aid programs also often increased the independence of state executive branch personnel from legislative direction. Thus, even as the overall amount of federal aid began to decline in the last biennium and federal aid programs assumed new forms, legislatures continued to develop new mechanisms to increase their involvement in the oversight of federal funds.

In 1981, almost half the state legislatures enacted statutes increasing their oversight of federal funds and placing controls on the administration and expenditure of federal block grants. Thirty-six state legislatures are actively involved in the appropriation of federal funds other than open-ended appropriations, and 23 states have recently developed new or specialized procedures to deal with block grants. Again, as in other areas of oversight, there is a wide variation in the procedures and strength of legislative control mechanisms. However, it is clear that state legislatures intend to play an active role in the review and control of federal aid programs. This is, in part, a result of the development of highly qualified professional fiscal and research staffs in legislatures in recent years. Four legislatures (Iowa, Massachusetts, New York and Oklahoma) greatly strengthened their roles regarding federal funds in 1981. The legislatures in Alaska, Florida, Louisiana, Maine, Michigan, Montana and Oregon are examples of states which have long and effective traditions of federal funds oversight.

Legislatures continue to search for means to improve the effectiveness of oversight and to expand its scope. Oversight has the potential to bring legislatures into frequent conflict with the other branches of government. It is clear that significant questions exist about the procedures and limits of legislative oversight. Of these, the powers which may be exercised by a legislature during an interim period and the extent to which authority may be delegated to a committee are among the most important.

The state legislative appropriations process, whose effective functioning is the strongest element of oversight, will be enhanced in the 1980s by several factors. The proposed return of authority and financial responsibility for some federal programs to the states and the continued expansion of staff expertise will be contributing factors. As in other areas of legislative operations, the tendency will be to consolidate the improvements of the past two decades. All 50 state legislatures have asserted their role in state budgeting, but the legislative role in budget development and consideration still varies widely, ranging from Maryland, where the legislature may only review and reduce executive expenditure proposals, to Arkansas, Colorado, New Mexico and Texas, where the budget process is dominated by the legislature. The recent movement to expand the number of legislators directly involved in the appropriations process seems to have slowed. Hawaii, Wisconsin and the Tennessee Senate involve the relevant substantive standing committees in review of the budget, and Iowa, North Carolina and Utah use an elaborate subcommittee system with every member of the legislature serving on at least one subcommittee. Likewise, the movements to zero-base budgeting and to require economic impact statements have lost momentum. Only Florida has had extensive experience with economic impact statements, with very mixed results. Like sunset, many observers doubt that the costs in time and staff resources justify the results. There has been renewed examination of the budget cycle in several states. Florida returned to biennial budgeting in 1981. On the other hand, the difficult economic situation facing many states during the biennium has created a situation of perpetual budget consideration in states such as Michigan, Ohio, Oregon and Washington.

Technological change has affected legislatures both in terms of their need for more technical policy analysis and in their internal information management. Specialized science and technology advisory units were created in many state legislatures in the 1970s, notably in Arkansas, Illinois, Massachusetts, New York, Pennsylvania and Wisconsin. Many legislatures use computer systems in some way to perform tasks such as bill drafting and tracking. Computers and word processing equipment promise to have a significant impact on the administration of the legislative process. Information can be rapidly and widely shared among legislators, and the processing of bills and reports can be speeded and simplified. Sophisticated legislative information systems exist in states such as Alaska, Colorado, Florida, Illinois, Louisiana, Michigan, North Dakota, Oregon, South Dakota and Washington. The effective management and use of information management systems will continue to present a challenge to legislatures.

Recent Developments

Party Affiliation and Leadership. The legislative elections of 1980-81 continued the trend toward increased Republican Party strength in state legislatures. Republican strength and control of legislative houses during the 1981-82 biennium closely approximate the level of 10 years earlier, prior to the Democratic Party dominance of the mid-1970s. Republicans control 35 legislative chambers and Democrats control 62 with the Alaska Senate in a tie and the Nebraska Unicameral organized on a non-partisan basis. Approximately 60 percent of state legislative seats are held by members elected as Democrats.

However, party affiliation as the determining factor in the organization of state legislatures appears to be under stress. Coalition control of legislative houses is becoming more frequent. When this occurs, committee chairmen are usually drawn from both parties. The Alaska Senate and House, the California Assembly, the Hawaii Senate and the New Mexico House have recently experienced coalition organization. Control of two legislative chambers, the House in Alaska and the Senate in Washington, changed during 1981 sessions as a result of party switches and coalition formation. Minority parties are represented in very small number in state legislatures but may be influential in a close situation such as the recent Alaska experience.

Caucuses. Another element of state legislative practice which has come under recent scrutiny is the use of caucuses. Party caucuses have traditionally played a key role in legislative organization in most states, and in policy decisions in a somewhat lesser number. Only five one-party states (Alabama, Arkansas, Louisiana, Mississippi and Texas) have not used party caucuses. Recently, other types of caucuses have arisen in a few states, organized along geographic, racial or issue lines. Nebraska, with its non-partisan organization, has caucused by congressional districts for certain purposes. The "bush caucus" has become influential in Alaska, and in Florida and Maryland, county delegations regularly meet on matters of common interest.

Where party caucuses meet regularly, their formation may be either informational or extend to the development of party positions and strategy. In some states, party caucuses are an almost daily occurrence and exert heavy control over party policy and action on the floor of the legislative body. Caucus votes which are binding on their members are sometimes employed in Alaska, Colorado, Florida and Utah. In Colorado and Wisconsin the budget bill may be discussed extensively in caucus, with numerous amendments agreed to, before it receives floor action.

Size and Apportionment. For the second time in four years, there will be a major reduction in the size of a legislative house in 1983. Illinois voters in 1980 approved an initiated measure which reduced the size of the Illinois House by one-third, from 177 to 118 members, and eliminated Illinois' unique electoral system of cumulative voting. The Massachusetts House was reduced from 240 to 160 members effective in 1979. The number of state legislators will thus be less in 1983 than the 7,482 holding office in 1981-82, although the exact number will not be determined until legislative reapportionment is completed in all 50 states. Several states, including Nevada, North Dakota and Wyoming, will adjust the size of one or both of their houses to facilitate reapportionment.

Staffing. As previously noted, the growth of new legislative staff units has slowed. However, major reorganization of the staff structure took place during 1981 in Louisiana and Oklahoma, where both eliminated their long-time legislative council structure and organized separate House and Senate staff services. The primary areas of recent staff increase have been in specialized oversight units and in public information and media offices. The increasing professionalization of legislative staff is reflected in several ways. There is growing recruitment and transfer of staff between states, and there is heightened interest and concern about legislative personnel systems and training and professional development.

Special Sessions. Special legislative sessions took place in 28 states in 1981, the greatest number in recent years. Several states did not adjourn sine die and met periodically during the year. At least four states (Alaska, Colorado, Oregon and South Carolina) set records for time spent in session. The primary causes of this activity were state budget problems and reapportionment.

Note

1. See, for example, "Separate Roads: The Legislator as an Individual and the Legislature as an Institution," *State Legislatures* 5, 3 (March 1979): 21-25.

Table 1
NAMES OF STATE LEGISLATIVE BODIES AND CONVENING PLACE

State or other jurisdiction	Both bodies	Upper house	Lower house	Convening place
Alabama	Legislature	Senate	House of Representatives	State Capitol
Alaska	Legislature	Senate	House of Representatives	State Capitol
Arizona	Legislature	Senate	House of Representatives	State Capitol(a)
Arkansas	General Assembly	Senate	House of Representatives	State Capitol
California	Legislature	Senate	Assembly	State Capitol
Colorado	General Assembly	Senate	House of Representatives	State Capitol
Connecticut	General Assembly	Senate	House of Representatives	State Capitol
Delaware	General Assembly	Senate	House of Representatives	Legislative Hall
Florida	Legislature	Senate	House of Representatives	State Capitol(b)
Georgia	General Assembly	Senate	House of Representatives	State Capitol
Hawaii	Legislature	Senate	House of Representatives	State Capitol
Idaho	Legislature	Senate	House of Representatives	State Capitol
Arizona	General Assembly	Senate	House of Representatives	State House
Indiana	General Assembly	Senate	House of Representatives	State House/State Capitol
Iowa	General Assembly	Senate	House of Representatives	State Capitol
Kansas	Legislature	Senate	House of Representatives	State House
Kentucky	General Assembly	Senate	House of Representatives	State Capitol
Louisiana	Legislature	Senate	House of Representatives	State Capitol
Maine	Legislature	Senate	House of Representatives	State House
Maryland	General Assembly	Senate	House of Delegates	State House
Massachusetts	General Court	Senate	House of Representatives	State House
Michigan	Legislature	Senate	House of Representatives	State Capitol
Minnesota	Legislature	Senate	House of Representatives	State Capitol
Mississippi	Legislature	Senate	House of Representatives	New Capitol(c)
Missouri	General Assembly	Senate	House of Representatives	State Capitol
Montana	Legislature	Senate	House of Representatives	State Capitol
Nebraska	Legislature	(d)	. . .	State Capitol
Nevada	Legislature	Senate	Assembly	Legislative Building
New Hampshire	General Court	Senate	House of Representatives	State House
New Jersey	Legislature	Senate	General Assembly	State House
New Mexico	Legislature	Senate	House of Representatives	State Capitol
New York	Legislature	Senate	Assembly	State Capitol
North Carolina	General Assembly	Senate	House of Representatives	State Legislative Building
North Dakota	Legislative Assembly	Senate	House of Representatives	State Capitol
Ohio	General Assembly	Senate	House of Representatives	State House
Oklahoma	Legislature	Senate	House of Representatives	State Capitol
Oregon	Legislative Assembly	Senate	House of Representatives	State Capitol
Pennsylvania	General Assembly	Senate	House of Representatives	Main Capitol
Rhode Island	General Assembly	Senate	House of Representatives	State House
South Carolina	General Assembly	Senate	House of Representatives	State House
South Dakota	Legislature	Senate	House of Representatives	State Capitol
Tennessee	General Assembly	Senate	House of Representatives	State Capitol
Texas	Legislature	Senate	House of Representatives	State Capitol
Utah	Legislature	Senate	House of Representatives	State Capitol
Vermont	General Assembly	Senate	House of Representatives	State House
Virginia	General Assembly	Senate	House of Delegates	State Capitol(e)
Washington	Legislature	Senate	House of Representatives	Legislative Building
West Virginia	Legislature	Senate	House of Delegates	State Capitol
Wisconsin	Legislature	Senate	Assembly(f)	State Capitol
Wyoming	Legislature	Senate	House of Representatives	State Capitol
American Samoa	Legislature	Senate	House of Representatives	Maota Fono
Guam	Legislature	(d)	. . .	Congress Building
Northern Mariana Is.	Legislature	Senate	House of Representatives	Civic Center
Puerto Rico	Legislative Assembly	Senate	House of Representatives	Capitol
Federated States of Micronesia	Congress	(d)	. . .	Congress Office Building
Virgin Islands	Legislature	(d)	. . .	Government House

(a) Senate Wing, House Wing.
(b) Senate: Capitol South Wing. House: Capitol North Wing.
(c) New Capitol Senate Chamber; New Capitol House Chamber.

(d) Unicameral legislature. Members go by the title Senator.
(e) Senate addition; House addition.
(f) Members of the lower house go by the title Representative.

Table 2
THE LEGISLATORS
Numbers, Terms, and Party Affiliations

State or other jurisdiction	Senate						House						House and senate totals
	Demo-crats	Repub-licans	Other	Vacan-cies	Total	Term	Demo-crats	Repub-licans	Other	Vacan-cies	Total	Term	
United States	1,221	774	2	6	2,070	...	3,323	2,218	9	13	5,588	...	7,653
Alabama	35	0	...	...	35	4	100	4	...	1	105	4	140
Alaska	11	9	...	...	20	4	22	16	2(a)	...	40	2	60
Arizona	14	16	...	...	30	2	17	43	...	...	60	2	90
Arkansas	34	1	...	...	35	4	93	7	...	...	100	2	135
California	23	17	...	...	40	4	48	32	...	...	80	2	120
Colorado	13	22	...	...	35	4	26	39	...	..	65	2	100
Connecticut.........	22	13	...	1	36	2	83	68	...	...	151	2	187
Delaware	12	9	...	...	21	4	16	25	...	...	41	2	62
Florida	27	13	...	...	40	4	81	39	...	...	120	2	160
Georgia	51	5	...	...	56	2	156	23	...	1	180	2	236
Hawaii	17	8	...	...	25	4	39	12	...	...	51	2	76
Idaho	12	23	...	...	35	2	14	56	...	...	70	2	105
Illinois	30	29	...	...	59	4(b)	86	91	...	...	177	2	236
Indiana	15	35	...	...	50	4	35	63	...	2	100	2	150
Iowa	22	28	...	...	50	4	42	58	...	...	100	2	150
Kansas	16	24	...	...	40	4	53	72	...	...	125	2	165
Kentucky (1981)	29	9	...	...	38	4	75	24	...	1	100	2	138
Louisiana (1979)	39	...	...	...	39	4	95	10	...	...	105	4	144
Maine	16	17	...	...	33	2	84	67	...	...	151	2	184
Maryland	40	7	...	...	47	4	125	15	1(c)	...	141	4	188
Massachusetts	32	7	1(c)	...	40	2	128	31	1(c)	...	160	2	200
Michigan	24	14	...	...	38	4	64	46	...	...	110	2	148
Minnesota	45(d)	22(e)	...	...	67	4	70(d)	64(e)	...	...	134	2	201
Mississippi (1979)	48	4	...	...	52	4	115	4	2(c)	1	122	4	174
Missouri	23	10	...	1	34	4	111	52	...	...	163	2	197
Montana	21	29	...	...	50	4(f)	43	57	...	...	100	2	150
Nebraska	—— Nonpartisan election ——				49	4	————Unicameral————						49
Nevada	15	5	...	...	20	4	26	14	...	...	40	2	60
New Hampshire	10	13	...	1	24	2	160	238	...	2	400	2	424
New Jersey (1981).....	22	18	...	...	40	4(g)	43	37	...	...	80	2	120
New Mexico	22	20	...	...	42	4	41	29	...	...	70	2	112
New York	25	35	...	...	60	2	86	63	...	1	150	2	210
North Carolina	40	10	...	...	50	2	95	24	...	1	120	2	170
North Dakota	10	40	...	...	50	4	27	73	...	...	100	2	150
Ohio	15	18	...	...	33	4	54	45	...	...	99	2	132
Oklahoma	37	11	...	...	48	4	73	28	...	...	101	2	149
Oregon	22	8	...	...	30	4	33	27	...	...	60	2	90
Pennsylvania	23	25	...	2	50	4	100	103	...	...	203	2	253
Rhode Island	43	7	...	...	50	2	82	18	...	...	100	2	150
South Carolina	41	5	...	...	46	4	107	17	...	...	124	2	170
South Dakota	10	25	...	...	35	2	21	49	...	...	70	2	105
Tennessee	20	12	1(c)	...	33	4	57	39	2(c)	1	99	2	132
Texas	23	7	...	1	31	4	114	35	...	1	150	2	181
Utah	7	22	...	...	29	4	17	58	...	...	75	2	104
Vermont	14	16	...	...	30	2	64	86	...	...	150	2	180
Virginia (1981)........	31	9	...	...	40	4	66	33	1(c)	...	100	2	140
Washington..........	24	25	...	...	49	4	42	56	...	...	98	2	147
West Virginia	27	7	...	...	34	4	78	22	...	...	100	2	134
Wisconsin	19	14	...	...	33	4	59	39	...	1	99	2	132
Wyoming............	11	19	...	...	30	4	23	39	...	...	62	2	92
American Samoa	—— Nonpartisan election ——				18	4	———— Nonpartisan election————				20	2	38
Guam	10	11	...	...	21	2	————————Unicameral————————						21
N. Mariana Is. (1981)..	3(h)	6(h)	...	...	9	4	10(h)	4(h)	...	...	14	2	23
Puerto Rico..........	15(i)	11(j)	...	...	26	4	24(i)	24(j)	...	...	48	4	74
Virgin Islands	11	4(k)	...	...	15	4	————————Unicameral————————						15

*Table reflects the legislatures as of January 1, 1981, except for Kentucky, New Jersey, Virginia, the Northern Mariana Islands, Puerto Rico and the Virgin Islands; information for those jurisdictions is as of January 1, 1982.

(a) Libertarian.

(b) All senators ran for election in 1972 and all will run every 10 years thereafter. Senate districts are divided into thirds. One group elects senators for terms of four years, four years and two years; the second group for terms of four years, two years and four years; the third group for terms of two years, four years and four years.

(c) Independent.

(d) Democratic-Farmer-Labor.

(e) Independent-Republican.

(f) After each decennial reapportionment, lots will be drawn for 1/2 the senators to serve an initial two-year term. Subsequent elections will be for four-year terms.

(g) Senate terms beginning in January of second year following the U.S. decennial census are for two years only.

(h) The Democratic and Republican parties are not affiliated with the national parties.

(i) Popular Democratic Party.

(j) New Progressive Party.

(k) Independent Citizens Movement.

Table 3
SELECTED LEGISLATIVE LEADERSHIP POSITIONS—SENATE

State or other jurisdiction	President	President pro tem	Majority leader	Assistant majority leader	Majority floor leader	Assistant majority floor leader	Majority whip	Majority caucus chairman	Minority leader	Assistant minority leader	Minority floor leader	Assistant minority floor leader	Minority whip	Minority caucus chairman
Alabama	□	■	★						★					
Alaska	■		★						★					
Arizona	■	●	★				★		★	★			★	
Arkansas	□	■	★											
California	□			★			★			★			★	★
Colorado	■	■	★	★			★		★					★
Connecticut	□	■	●	●8(a)					★	●3(b)			●	
Delaware	□	■	★				★		★				★	
Florida	■	■	★	★					★(c)	★				
Georgia	□	■	★				★		★				★	
Hawaii	■	■(d)	★		*		(e)		★	★	★	★		
Idaho	□	■	★				★	★	★				★	★
Illinois	■		(f)	●4				●	★	●3				●
Indiana	□	■			●	☆	☆	★	★		★	★		★
Iowa	□	■	★	★3				★	★	★2				
Kansas	■	■(d)	★	★			★	★	★				★	★
Kentucky	□	■			★		★	★			★		★	★
Louisiana	■													
Maine	■				★		★				★		★	
Maryland	■		★				●		★					
Massachusetts	■	●	●		★		●	●	★	●	●		●	●
Michigan	■	★	★	★	★		★	★	★	★	★		★	★
Minnesota	■	★	★						★					
Mississippi	□	■												
Missouri	□				★		★				★			
Montana	■	■(g)					★		■				★	
Nebraska	□	■(g)												
Nevada	■		★	★					★	★				
New Hampshire	■	●	●	●				★(h)	★	★2			★	
New Jersey	■	■	★	★3					★	★				(e)
New Mexico	□	■			★		★				★			
New York	□	■(i)	★						★	●(j)				
North Carolina	□	■(i)	★											
North Dakota	□		★		★		★		★	★		★		★
Ohio	■	■		■(k)					■	■			■	
Oklahoma	□			■	■	■	★		★	★	★		★	★
Oregon	■		★	★2			★		★				★	
Pennsylvania	□	■	★				★	★	★				★	★
Rhode Island	□	■	★				★		★	●(j)				
South Carolina	□	■												
South Dakota	□	■	★	★			★		★	★				
Tennessee	□(l)		★	★2			★	★	★					★
Texas	□	■												
Utah	■		★				★		★				★	
Vermont	□	■(i)												
Virginia	□	■					★							★
Washington	■	■	★				★	★	★				★	★
West Virginia	■	●	★				★		★				★	
Wisconsin	■		★	★			★		★				★	
Wyoming	■	■(d)												
American Samoa	■	■												
Guam	■(l)	■(m)	★											
Puerto Rico	■	★(d)	★	★	★	★	★	★	★	★	★	★	★	★
Virgin Islands	■	■	★						★					

Key:

■—Formally elected or confirmed by all members of their respective chambers.
★—Formally elected by the respective caucuses.
●—Appointed by presiding officer or party leader.
☆—Appointed by president pro tem.
□—Lieutenant governor.

(a) Connecticut has a deputy majority leader, an assistant majority leader at large for fiscal policy, and six assistant majority leaders.
(b) Connecticut has a deputy minority leader and two assistant minority leaders.

(c) Minority leader pro tem.
(d) Vice president.
(e) Majority policy leader.
(f) The president of the senate is the majority leader.
(g) Speaker of the senate.
(h) Senate whip.
(i) President pro tem/majority leader.
(j) Deputy minority leader.
(k) Assistant president pro tem.
(l) Speaker.
(m) Vice speaker.

Table 4
SELECTED LEGISLATIVE LEADERSHIP POSITIONS—HOUSE

State or other jurisdiction	Speaker	Speaker pro tem	Majority leader	Assistant majority leader	Majority floor leader	Assistant majority floor leader	Majority whip	Majority caucus chairman	Minority leader	Assistant minority leader	Minority floor leader	Assistant minority floor leader	Minority whip	Minority caucus chairman
Alabama	■	■	..	★	...	...	...	...	★	...	...	...	...	...
Alaska	■	...	..	★	...	...	...	...	★	...	...	...	...	...
Arizona	■	●	★	...	...	...	★	...	●	★	...	...	★	...
Arkansas	■	■	★	...	...	...	...	...	★	...	...	...	...	...
California	■	...	..	...	●(a)	★	...	★	...	...	★	...	★	★
Colorado	■	...	★	★	...	...	...	★	...	★	...	...	...	★
Connecticut	★	●(b)	★	(c)	...	...	...	★	...	●6	...	...	●	...
Delaware	■	...	..	...	...	...	★	...	★	...	...	...	★	...
Florida	■	■	●	...	...	...	●	...	★	...	★	...	●	★
Georgia	■	■	★	...	...	...	...	★	...	★	...	...	★	★
Hawaii	■	■(d)	★	★2	★	★6	...	★	...	★	...	★	★3	...
Idaho	■	...	★	★	...	...	...	★	...	★	...	...	...	...
Illinois	■	...	●	●4	...	...	●2	★	★	●4	...	...	●2	●
Indiana	■	●	..	●	★	★	★	●	★	...	...	●	●	★
Iowa	■	■	★	★4	...	...	...	★	...	★4	...	...	★	★
Kansas	■	■	..	...	●	★	...	★	...	★	...	...	★	★
Kentucky	■	■	..	...	★	★	★	★	...	★	...	...	★	★
Louisiana	■	...	..	...	...	...	...	...	...	...	...	...	...	...
Maine	■	...	..	...	★	★	...	...	★	...	★	...	...	...
Maryland	■	...	★	...	...	...	...	...	★	...	...	...	...	...
Massachusetts	■	■	●	...	...	...	●	...	★	...	●	...	...	...
Michigan	■	■	■	...	★	★3	★14	★	■	★	★	★	★	★
Minnesota	■	●	★	★	...	...	...	★	...	★	...	...	...	...
Mississippi	■	●	..	...	...	...	...	...	...	...	...	...	...	...
Missouri	■	■	..	...	★	★	★	★	...	...	★	★	★	★
Montana	■	■	..	...	■	...	★	...	...	...	■	...	★	...
Nebraska(e)	...	...	...	...	...	...	...	...	...	...	...	...	...	...
Nevada	■	■	..	...	★	...	★	★	...	★	...	...	★	★
New Hampshire	■	●	●	●4	...	...	●4(f)	★	★	★7(g)	★	...	●	...
New Jersey	■	■	★3	★(h)	...	...	★2	★	★	★	★	...	★2	(i)
New Mexico	■	...	..	...	★	...	●	★	...	★	...	...	●	★
New York	■	●	●	★(c)	...	...	●	★	●	★	...	...	●	...
North Carolina	■	■(j)	..	...	...	...	★	★	★	...	...	...	...	★
North Dakota	■	■	..	...	★	★	●	★	★	...	★	★	●	...
Ohio	■	■	■	...	■	★	●	★	■	★	★	★	●	★
Oklahoma	■	■	..	...	...	●3	●	★	...	★	...	★2	★	★
Oregon	■	■	★	...	4(k)	...	★	...	★	...	★2	●3(l)	...	...
Pennsylvania	■	●	★	...	...	...	★	★	★	...	...	...	★	★
Rhode Island	■	●	★	★10	...	...	★	...	★	★4(m).	...	...	★	...
South Carolina	■	...	★(n)	★(o)	...	...	...	...	★	...	...	...	...	...
South Dakota	■	■	★	★	...	...	...	★	...	★	★	...	...	...
Tennessee	■	■	★	★	...	...	★	★	...	★	★	...	...	...
Texas	■	●	..	...	...	...	...	...	...	...	...	...	...	...
Utah	■	...	★	...	...	...	★	★	...	★	...	...	★	★
Vermont	■	...	..	...	...	...	★	★	...	★	...	...	...	...
Virginia	■	...	★(o)	...	...	...	...	★	★	...	...	...	★	★
Washington	■	■	★	★2	...	...	★	★	★	...	★	...	★	★
West Virginia	■	●	●	...	...	...	●	■	●	...	...	...	...	★
Wisconsin	■	■	●	...	...	...	★	★	★	...	...	...	★	...
Wyoming	■	...	★	...	...	...	...	★	...	★	...	...	★	...
American Samoa	■	...	...	...	...	...	...	...	...	...	...	...	...	...
Guam(e)	...	...	...	...	...	...	...	...	...	...	...	...	...	...
Puerto Rico	■	★(p)	..	...	...	...	...	...	...	...	...	...	...	...
Virgin Islands(e)	...	...	...	...	...	...	...	...	...	...	...	...	...	...

Key:
■—Formally elected or confirmed by all members of their respective chambers.
★—Formally elected by the respective caucuses.
●—Appointed by presiding officer or party leader.
(a) Appointed by speaker after consultation with members of supporting majority.
(b) Deputy speaker.
(c) Connecticut has a deputy majority leader, a majority leader at large, and eight assistant majority leaders: two selected by speaker, two selected by majority leader, and four elected by caucus; New York has a deputy majority leader and an assistant majority leader.
(d) Vice speaker.
(e) The legislatures of Nebraska, Guam and the Virgin Islands are unicameral. Members go by the title senator. The leadership positions are listed in the senate table.
(f) Assistant majority whip.
(g) New Hampshire has six assistant minority leaders and a deputy minority leader.
(h) Deputy assistant minority leader.
(i) Assistant minority whip.
(j) Speaker pro tem/majority leader.
(k) Appointed by majority whip.
(l) With approval of caucus.
(m) Deputy minority leader.
(n) Majority leader/majority caucus chairman.
(o) Majority leader/majority floor leader.
(p) Vice president.

Table 5
LEGISLATIVE COMPENSATION: REGULAR AND SPECIAL SESSIONS

State or other jurisdiction	Regular sessions Amount per day	Limit on days	Annual salaries	Special sessions Amount per day	Limit on days	Travel allowance Per mile	Round trips home to capital	Living expenses per day
Alabama	$10	105C	...	$10	30C	10	One	$65 up to 105C (U)
Alaska	...	...	$18,768	...	...	25	One	Depending on residence $50 to $67 (U)
Arizona	...	...	$15,000	...	...	22.5	Unlimited	$40 ($20 for legislators from Maricopa County) for first 120 days of regular session; after that, legislators receive $20 and $10 respectively (V)
Arkansas	$20	None	$7,500	$20	None	23	Weekly	$308/wk. (V)
California	...	...	$28,110	...	...	15(a)	One	$50/7-day week except when in recess four or more days (U)
Colorado	...	...	$14,000	...	...	20 (24/4-wheel drive)	Weekly	$40 ($20 for legislators from Denver metro area) (U)
Connecticut	...	...	$9,500(b)/$7,500(c)	...	...	15	Unlimited	...
Delaware	...	...	$11,400	...	...	15	Unlimited	...
Florida	...	...	$12,000	...	...	20	Weekly	$50/7-day week (U)
Georgia	...	...	$7,200	...	...	18	Weekly	$44/7-day week (U)
Hawaii	...	...	$13,650	...	...	20	Unlimited	$20 for legislators from outside Oahu (U)
Idaho	...	...	$4,200	...	...	18	Five	$44 each calendar day of session if residence in capital ($25 if lives at home) (U)
Illinois	...	...	$28,000	...	...	20	Weekly	$36/L (U)
Indiana	...	...	$9,600	...	30L	22	Weekly	$50/7-day week (U)
Iowa	...	...	$13,700	$40	None	20	Weekly	$30/7-day week for 120 days in odd years and 100 days in even years (U)
Kansas	$42	...	...	$42	None	22	Weekly	$50/7-day week (U)
Kentucky	$50 / $100(e)	None (odd) 90C (even)	...	$50	None	22.5	Eleven	$75/7-day week (U)
Louisiana	$75	60L(d)	$16,800	$75	30C	21(g)	Weekly	$35/day before and each day of session, or $17/day meals; mileage up to $20/day (V)
Maine	...	60L(f)	$4,500(b)/$2,500(c)	$25	...	20	Weekly	$50 max. meals & lodging ($20 max. for meals); out of state: $75/diem max. meals & lodging actual & necessary for travel (V)
Maryland	...	...	$18,500/$21,000(b)	...	...	18	Daily if not lodging; weekly if lodging	...
Massachusetts	...	...	$19,125	...	...	Varies	Unlimited	Each member depending on residence receives a per diem allowance for mileage, meals and lodging from $5 to $45/L (U)
Michigan	...	...	$31,000	...	...	26.5	Weekly	$6,200 max. (V)
Minnesota	...	...	$18,500	...	...	24	Weekly	Up to $23 metro; up to $36 out of state (U)
Mississippi	...	...	$8,100	$50	...	20	Weekly	$44 actual daily attendance (U)
Missouri	...	...	$15,000	...	...	17	Weekly	$35 actual daily attendance (U)
Montana	$43.74(b)	90L	...	$43.74(b)	None	20(b)	Two (U) / Two (V)	$45/7-day week (U)
Nebraska	...	...	$4,800	...	...	21	One	...
Nevada	$104	60C	...	$104	20C	20	Unlimited(h)	$44/C (U)

New Hampshire	...	...	$100	$3	15L	38/1st 45 mi. $19/in excess of 45 miles $50 max.	Unlimited	...
New Jersey	...	...	$18,000	...	...	Intrastate railroad pass	...	...
New Mexico	$40	60C (odd) 30C (even)	...	$40	30C	10	One	...
New York	...	...	$30,804	...	...	23	Weekly	$55/day for actual & necessary expenses (V)
North Carolina	...	...	$6,936	...	...	25	Weekly	$50/7-day week (U); plus addtl. expense allowance of $172/mo.
North Dakota	$5	80L	...	$5	None	10	Weekly	$85/7-calendar days (U)
Ohio	...	...	$22,500	...	...	20	Weekly	...
Oklahoma	...	...	$18,000	...	...	22	Weekly	$35/4-day week paid only to legislators spending the night (U)
Oregon	...	...	$8,400	...	...	...	...	$44/7-day week (U)
Pennsylvania	...	...	$25,000	...	...	17	Weekly	$10,000 max. (V)
Rhode Island	$5	60L	...	...	...	8	Each day of attendance	...
South Carolina	$250	40L	$10,000	$250	None	23	Weekly	$50 (V)
South Dakota	...	...	$3,200(b) $2,800(c)	$90	None	21	Weekly	$50/5-day week (U)
Tennessee	...	...	$8,308	...	...	$19.96(i)	Weekly	$66.47/90L plus up to 15 org. days (U)
Texas	...	...	$7,200	...	...	23/car; 30/single-engine aircraft; 40/twin-engine aircraft	Weekly	$30/7-day week (U)
Utah	$25	60C (odd) 20C (even)	...	$25	30C	23	Unlimited	$15/7-day week (U)
Vermont	...	...	$7,500(j) $2,000(j)	...	...	22	Daily for commuters, weekly for boarders	$17.50 for food if commuting; $25 for room and $20 for meals if boarding in capital (U)
Virginia	...	...	$8,000	...	...	20	Weekly	Up to $50 but no more than is allowed as a non-vouchered expense by the federal Internal Revenue Service (U)
Washington	...	...	$11,200 $9,800(k)	...	...	10	One	$44/L (U)
West Virginia	...	...	$5,136	$35	None	17	Weekly	$30/7-day week lodging, or up to $30 travel expenses if commuting (V); legislators living in Charleston, $20 meals but may not receive travel & lodging expenses (U)
Wisconsin	...	...	$22,638 $19,767(k)	...	...	20.5	Weekly	$30 outside Madison, $15 inside Madison (U)
Wyoming	$30(d)	40L (odd) 20L (even)	...	$30	None	12	One	$44/7-day week (U)
American Samoa	...	...	$12,000	...	...	(l)	...	(l)
Puerto Rico	...	...	$20,000	...	...	30/km. & no less than $20	Weekly	$35 if in residence within 50 km. of capitol; $45 if over 50 km. (U)

Key:
C—Calendar day
L—Legislative day
U—Unvouchered
V—Vouchered

(a) Members are furnished a leased car up to $265/month including gasoline and maintenance. Actual and necessary for commercial air fare.
(b) 1983. Maryland: unless reduced or rejected by General Assembly.
(c) 1982.
(d) Paid on calendar day basis.
(e) 1984.
(f) Within an 85C period; paid for 85C.
(g) For travel exceeding 100 miles air travel may be paid in lieu of 21 cents per mile.
(h) Allowance up to $3,500 maximum per regular session and $1,000 per special session.
(i) Actual commercial travel expenses on out-of-state travel; however, not to exceed amount which would have been allowed for travel in a personal vehicle.
(j) Up to this amount during the biennium, to be paid at a rate of $250 weekly during regular sessions and $50 for each day of special session.
(k) For holdover senators only.
(l) Same as all other government employees.

Table 6
ADDITIONAL COMPENSATION FOR SENATE LEADERS

State or other jurisdiction	President	President pro tem	Majority leader	Minority leader	Other
Alabama	$2/d(a)	...	...	...	...
Alaska	$500/y	...	...	...	...
Arizona	...	...	...	...	...
Arkansas	...	$2,500/y	...	...	...
California	...	...	...	...	...
Colorado	$50/d(b)	...	$50/d(b)	$50/d(b)	...
Connecticut	...	$4,000/b	$3,000/b	$3,000/b	Dep. Maj. Ldr., Dep. Min. Ldr.: $2,000/b; Asst. Maj. Ldrs. (5), Asst. Min. Ldrs. (2): $1,000/b
Delaware	...	$180.80/m	$150.70/m	$150.70/m	Chmn., V-Chmn., Finance Cmte.: $150.70/m Maj. Whip, Min. Whip: $120.50/m; Mbrs. Joint Finance Cmte: $60.30/m
Florida	$25,000/y	...	...	...	...
Georgia	...	$2,800/y	$2,400/y(c)	$2,400/y(c)	Admin. Flr. Ldr.: $2,400/y(c) Asst. Admin. Flr. Ldr.: $1,200/y(c)
Hawaii	...	...	...	...	...
Idaho	...	...	...	...	...
Illinois	$10,000/y	...	...	$10,000/y	Asst. Maj. Ldrs. (4), Asst. Min. Ldrs. (3): $6,000/y
Indiana	...	$3,000/y	$1,500/y	$2,000/y	Asst. Min. Flr. Ldr., Maj. Caucus Chmn., Min. Caucus Chmn., Finance Cmte. Chmn.: $1,500/y
Iowa	$6,800/y(a,d)	...	$2,300/y	$2,300/y	...
Kansas	$4,200/y	$1,800/y	$3,240/y	$3,240/y	Ways & Means Cmte. Chmn.: $3,240/y
Kentucky	...	$25/d	$20/d	$20/d	Asst. Pres. Pro Tem., Caucus Chmn., Whips: $15/d
Louisiana	$32,000/y(e)	...	...	...	...
Maine	$3,500/b(f)	...	$1,750/b	$1,750/b	Asst. Maj. Ldr., Asst. Min. Ldr.: $875/b
Maryland	$5,000/y	...	...	...	...
Massachusetts	$38,000/y	...	$32,000/y	$32,000/y	Chmn., Ways & Means Cmte.: $34,000/y; Asst. Maj. Flr. Ldrs. (2), Asst. Min. Flr. Ldrs. (3), Chmn., Post Audit & Oversight Cmte.: $28,000/y; Chmn., Jt. Standing Cmtes., Chmn., Bills in Third Reading Cmte., V-Chmn., Post Audit & Oversight Cmte., Asst. V-Chmn., Ways & Means Cmte.: $24,000/y
Michigan	...	...	$14,000/y	$8,000/y	Chmn., Appropriations Cmte.: $1,000/y
Minnesota	$7,400/y(f)	...	$7,400/y(f)	$7,400/y(f)	Sen. Rules Cmte. designates up to 3 leadership positions to receive up to 140% of compensation of other members
Mississippi	$34,000(a,g)	...	...	...	...
Missouri	...	$2,500/y	$1,500/y	$1,500/y	...
Montana	$5(h)	...	...	...	...
Nebraska	...	...	...	...	...
Nevada	$2/d(a,f)	(f)	(f)	(f)	Cmte. Chmn.: (f)
New Hampshire	$50/b	...	...	...	...
New Jersey	$6,000/y	...	...	...	...

State or other jurisdiction	President	President pro tem	Majority leader	Minority leader	Other
New Mexico	...				
New York	...	$30,000/y	...	$25,000/y	Dep. Maj. Ldr.: $24,500/y; Maj. Conf. Chmn.: $18,000/y; Min. Conf. Chmn.: $10,500/y; Maj. Conf. Secy.: $7,000/y; Min. Conf. Secy.: $3,000/y; Cmte. Chmn. & Ranking Min. Mbrs.: Education, Finance: $13,000/y & 24,500/y; Judiciary, Codes: $13,000/y; Banks, Health, Cities, Corp.: $11,000/y; All other cmtes.: $9,000 & 6,500/y
North Carolina	...	$8,664/y(f)	...	$8,664/y(f)	...
North Dakota	...	...	$5/d(i)	$5/d(i)	Maj. Flr. Ldr., Min. Flr. Ldr.: $5/d(i); All Standing Cmte. Chmn: $3/d(i)
Ohio	$12,500/y	$9,500/y	...	$8,500/y	Asst. Pres. Pro Tem.: $7,500/y; Asst. Min. Ldr.: $6,500/y; Min. Whip: $4,500/y; Chmn. Standing Cmtes.: $1,500/y; Chmn. Standing Sub-Cmtes.: $750/y
Oklahoma	...	$8,400/y	$5,800/y	$5,800/y	...
Oregon	$700/m				
Pennsylvania	...	$14,000/y(d) $20,000/y(f)	$11,200/y(d) $6,000/y(f)	$11,200/y(d) $6,000/y(f)	Maj. Whip, Min. Whip: $5,300/y(d) & 3,000/y(f) Maj. Caucus Chmn., Min. Caucus Chmn.: $4,600/y(d), $3,000/y(f) Maj. Caucus Secy., Min. Caucus Secy.: $2,700/y(d), $3,000/y(f); Maj. Caucus Admin., Min. Caucus Admin., Maj. Policy Chmn., Min. Policy Chmn.: $2,700/y(d), $2,000/y(f); Maj. & Min. Appropriations Chmn.: $6,000/y(f)
Rhode Island	...	...	...	...	...
South Carolina	$30,000(a,g)	$3,600/y	...	...	...
South Dakota	...	...			
Tennessee	$4,154/y(j)	...	...	...	...
Texas	...	...	...	...	...
Utah	...	...	...	...	...
Vermont	...	...	...	...	...
Virginia	...	...	...	...	...
Washington	...	...	...	...	...
West Virginia	$35/d(h,k)	...	$15/d(h)	$15/d(h)	...
Wisconsin	...	...	...	...	...
Wyoming	$3/d	...	...	...	...
American Samoa	$3,000/y	...	...	...	...
Puerto Rico	$16,600/y	$4,500/y	$4,500/y	$4,500/y	Cmte. on Finance Chmn., Cmte. on Government Chmn.: $4,500/y

Note: This table reflects the amount paid the leadership in addition to their regular legislative compensation.

Key: d—day; y—year; b—biennium; m—month.
(a) Lieutenant governor.
(b) During the interim up to $5,000/year.
(c) Up to $2,800/year provided by resolution.
(d) Additional salary. Iowa: $20/diem salary for special sessions and interim business.
(e) Reimbursement for actual expenses not to exceed $10,000/year.
(f) Plus additional expenses. Maine: paid at discretion of president as lump sum at end of session; Nevada: $300/regular session, $40/special session for postage, phone, and other communications; North Carolina: $230/month.
(g) In lieu of all per diem salary and monthly expense allowances.
(h) While in session. West Virginia: paid each day of actual floor sessions.
(i) Expenses only.
(j) Upon request, the Speaker may also receive $750 ex officio payment, $2,400 annual office allowance, $3,000 county office allowance, $300 supplies.
(k) During interim when committees are not meeting, up to maximum of 80 days in capitol offices.

Table 7
ADDITIONAL COMPENSATION FOR HOUSE LEADERS

State or other jurisdiction	Speaker	Speaker pro tem	Majority leader	Minority leader	Other
Alabama	$2/d	...	...	...	...
Alaska	$500/y	...	...	...	...
Arizona	...	...	...	...	...
Arkansas	$2,500/y	...	...	...	...
California	...	...	...	...	...
Colorado	$50/d(a)	...	$50/d(a)	$50/d(a)	...
Connecticut	$4,000/b	...	$3,000/b	$3,000/b	Dep. Spkr.: $3,000/b; Dep. Maj. Ldr., Dep. Min. Ldr.: $2,000/b; Asst. Maj. Ldr., Asst. Min. Ldr.: $1,000/b
Delaware	$180.80/m	...	$150.70/m	$150.70/m	Chmn., V-Chmn. Finance Cmte.: $150.70/m Maj. Whip, Min. Whip: $120.50/m; Mbrs. Joint Finance Cmte: $60.30/m
Florida	$25,000/y	...	...	...	...
Georgia	$17,800/y	$2,800/y	$2,400/y(b)	$2,400/y(b)	Admin. Flr. Ldr.: $2,400/y(b)
Hawaii	...	...	...	...	...
Idaho	...	...	...	...	...
Illinois	$10,000/y	...	$7,500/y	$10,000/y	Asst. Maj. Ldrs. (4), Asst. Min. Ldrs. (4): $6,000/y; Maj. Whips (2), Min. Whips (2): $5,000/y
Indiana	$3,000/y	$1,500/y	$1,500/y	$2,000/y	Maj. Whip, Asst. Min. Flr. Ldr., Maj. Caucus Chmn., Min. Caucus Chmn., Ways & Means Cmte. Chmn.: $1,500/y
Iowa	$6,800/y(c)	...	$2,300/y	$2,300/y	...
Kansas	$4,200/y	$1,800/y	$3,240/y	$3,240/y	Ways & Means Cmte. Chmn.: $3,240/y
Kentucky	$25/d	$15/d	$20/d	$20/d	Maj. & Min. Caucus Chmn., Maj. & Min. Whips: $15/d
Louisiana	$32,000/y(d)	...	...	...	...
Maine	$3,500/b(e)	...	$1,750/b	$1,750/b	Asst. Maj. Ldr., Asst. Min. Ldr.: $875/b
Maryland	$5,000/y	...	...	...	...
Massachusetts	$38,000/y	...	$32,000/y	$32,000/y	Chmn., Ways & Means Cmte.: $34,000/y; Asst. Maj. Flr. Ldrs. (2), Asst. Min. Flr. Ldrs. (3), Chmn., Post Audit & Oversight Cmte.: $28,000/y; Chmn., Jt. Standing Cmtes., Chmn., Bills in Third Reading Cmte., V-Chmn., Post Audit & Oversight Cmte., Asst. V-Chmn., Ways & Means Cmte.: $24,000/y
Michigan	$16,000/y	...	...	$8,000/y	Chmn. Appropriations Cmte.: $1,000/y
Minnesota	$7,400/y(e)	...	$7,400/y(e)	$7,400/y(e)	House Rules Cmte. designates up to 3 leadership positions to receive up to 140% of compensation of other members
Mississippi	$34,000(f)	...	...	...	...
Missouri	$2,500/y	$1,500/y	$1,500/y	$1,500/y	...
Montana	$5/d(g)	...	...	...	...
Nebraska	———————————————————————— Unicameral ———————————————————————————				
Nevada	$2/d(e)	(e)	(e)	(e)	Cmte. Chmn.(e)
New Hampshire	$50/b	...	...	...	...
New Jersey	$6,000/y	...	...	...	...

State or other jurisdiction	Speaker	Speaker pro tem	Majority leader	Minority leader	Other
New Mexico	...	...	...	...	...
New York	$30,000/y	$18,000/y	$25,000/y	$25,000/y	Chmn., Cmte. on Cmtes.: $18,000/y; Dep. Maj. Ldr., Asst. Maj. Ldr.: $14,000/y; Asst. Min. Ldr., Dep. Min. Ldr., Ranking Min. Member, Cmte. on Cmtes.: $13,000/y; Maj. Whip: $13,000/y; Min. Whip: $12,000/y; Maj. Conf. Chmn.: $12,000/y; Min. Conf. Chmn.: $11,000/y; Maj. Conf. V-Chmn.: $9,000/y; Min. Conf. V-Chmn.: $8,000/y; Cmte. Chmn. & Ranking Min. Mbrs.: Ways & Means: $24,500/y & $15,000/y; Education, Judiciary, Codes: $13,000/y & 8,000/y; Banks, Cities, Health, Local Gov.: $11,000/y & $7,000/y; All other cmtes.: $9,000/y & 6,500/y
North Carolina	$13,960/y(e)	$8,664/y(e)	...	$8,664/y(e)	...
North Dakota	$5/d(h)	...	$5/d(h)	$5/d(h)	All Standing Cmte. Chmn: $3/d(h)
Ohio	$12,500/y	$9,500/y	$9,500/y	$8,500/y	Asst. Min. Fl. Ldr.: $6,500/y;Asst. Maj. Fl. Ldr.: $4,500/y; Maj. Whip, Min. Whip: $2,500/y; Chmn. Standing Cmtes.: $1,500/y; Chmn. Standing Sub-Cmtes.: $750/y
Oklahoma	$8,400/y	...	$5,800/y	$5,800/y	...
Oregon............	$700/m	...	...	...	...
Pennsylvania.......	$14,000/y(c) $20,000/y(e)	...	$11,200/y(c) $6,000/y(e)	$11,200/y(c) $6,000/y(e)	Maj. Whip, Min. Whip: $5,300/y(c) & 3,000/y(e) Maj. Caucus Chmn., Min. Caucus Chmn.: $4,600/y(c), $3,000/y(e) Maj. Caucus Secy., Min. Caucus Secy.: $2,700/y(c), $3,000/y(e); Maj. Caucus Admin., Min. Caucus Admin., Maj. Policy Chmn., Min. Policy Chmn.: $2,700/y(c), $2,000/y(e); Maj. & Min. Appropriations Cmte. Chmn.: $6,000/y(e)
Rhode Island.......	$5/d	...	...	...	...
South Carolina	$11,000/y	$3,600/y	...	...	Spkr. Emeritus: $1,500/y
South Dakota	...	...	...	...	...
Tennessee	$4,154/y(i)	...	...	...	...
Texas	...	...	...	...	...
Utah...............	...	...	...	...	...
Vermont	$200/bw(e)	...	...	...	...
Virginia	$12,000/y	...	...	...	...
Washington........	...	...	...	...	...
West Virginia	$35/d(j)	...	$15/d(g)	$15/d(g)	...
Wisconsin	$25/m	...	...	...	...
Wyoming..........	$3/d	...	...	...	...
American Samoa ...	$3,000/y	...	...	...	...
Puerto Rico........	$16,000/y	$4,500/y	$4,500/y	$4,500/y	Cmte. on Finance Chmn., Cmte. on Government Chmn.: $4,500/y

Note: This table reflects the amount paid the leadership in addition to their regular legislative compensation.

Key: d—day; y—year; b—biennium; m—month; bw—biweekly.
(a) Per day during the interim up to $5,000/year.
(b) Up to $2,800/year provided by resolution.
(c) Additional salary. Iowa: $20/diem salary for special sessions and interim business.
(d) Reimbursement for actual expenses not to exceed $10,000/year.
(e) Plus additional expenses. Maine: paid at discretion of speaker as lump sum at end of session; Nevada: $300/regular session, $40/special session for postage, phone, and other communications; North Carolina: speaker—$345/month, speaker pro tem and minority leader—$230 month; Vermont: $275/week plus expenses when general assembly in session.
(f) In lieu of all per diem salary and monthly expense allowances.
(g) While in session. West Virginia: paid each day of actual floor sessions.
(h) Expenses only.
(i) Upon request, the speaker may also receive $750 ex officio payment, $2,400 annual office allowance, $3,000 county office allowance, $300 supplies.
(j) While in session: paid each day of actual floor session. During interim: up to a maximum of 80 days in capitol when committees are not meeting.

Table 8
LEGISLATIVE COMPENSATION: INTERIM PAYMENTS AND OTHER DIRECT PAYMENTS

State or other jurisdiction	Compensation for committee or official business (amount per day)	Travel allowance (cents per mile)	Living expenses (per day)	Other direct payments or services to legislators
Alabama	$65	10	...	$400/mo., 12 mo. (U)
Alaska	...	25	Legislators are compensated by residence and away from residence based on regional per diem rates. Out of state: varies(V)	$4,000/yr. for secretarial services, stationery & postage (U)
Arizona	...	22.5	$20 max. inside county of residence & $40 outside (V); up to $75 with documentation	...
Arkansas	$45	23	...	Members are entitled to reimbursement not to exceed $385/mo. 1981-82, $420/mo. 1982-83 for expenses incurred in the interim (V).
California	$50 up to $2,500(b)	15(a)	$50 (U)	...
Colorado	...	20 24/4-wheel drive	Actual and necessary (V)	$2,000/yr. expenses (U)
Connecticut	...	15	...	$30 postage/yr. and $2,500/yr.
Delaware	...	15	...	$1,000 max./mo. for intradistrict expenses; office rental equip., supplies & travel (U)
Florida	...	20	$40 (V)	$3,600/yr. for intradistrict expenses, e.g., rent, district office, supplies, materials, equipment, secretarial assistance (V)
Georgia	...	18	$44 (V)	$2,500 total allowance for incidental expenses connected with legislative duties.
Hawaii	...	20	$10 inside island of residence; $45 inter-island travel; $60 out of state (U)	...
Idaho	$35	18	Actual and necessary (V)	Not more than $17,000/yr. for legislative staff (secretarial, clerical, research, technical); telephone & other utility services, stationery, postage, office equip. rental and office rental costs (V)
Illinois	...	20	Varies. $36 to $49 depending upon party and position (V)	$12.50/day, 6 days/wk., paid monthly during interim only for supplies, etc. (U)
Indiana	...	22	$50 (V)	...
Iowa	$40	20	Actual and necessary (V)	$400/mo. April through Dec. to defray expenses, travel, postage, telephone, office (U)
Kansas	$42	22	$50 (U)	$50 supplies per regular & special session, $750 monthly expense allowance between sessions
Kentucky	$50	22.5	Actual and necessary (V)	$325/mo. for rent, utilities and expenses of district office (V); $1,047 base, not to exceed $1,652/mo. for assistants in home districts (V); $1,000 one-time allowance plus $250 for each additional four-year term for office and equipment and furniture which reverts to state when legislator leaves office; $16,800 annual salary and expense allowance for secretarial assistance, travel, telephone, other, paid monthly (U)
Louisiana	$75	21(c)	...	...
Maine	$25	20 plus turnpike tolls	$35 meals and housing; or $17/day meals, mileage up to $20/day (V)	Telephone & telegraph service, postage, newspapers; $200/yr. allowance for constituent services (U)
Maryland	...	18	$50 max. meals and lodging ($20 max. meals) (V); $75/diem max. out-of-state travel (V)	Senate $6,300 plus full-time secretary and House $9,660 annual for district office rent, staff, equipment, telephone (V)
Massachusetts	...	...	...	$2,400 annual expense allowance (U)
Michigan	...	26.5	$6,200 max. (V)	...
Minnesota	...	24	$36 (U); $45 lodging in state, actual and necessary out of state (V)	Postage allotment: House 3,000 1st class stamps-odd years, 1,400 1st class stamps—even years. Senate: chairmen 3,000 1st class stamps/yr., other senators 2,000 1st class stamps/yr. Telephone allotment: House $600/yr.; Senate $55/mo. during interim

State				
Mississippi	$40	20	Actual and necessary (V)	$210/mo. during interim (U)
Missouri	...	17	Actual and necessary (V)	Senate: actual, necessary and reasonable office expenses paid directly by Senate Accounts Cmte.; House: up to $450/mo. for office expenses (V)
Montana	$43.74	20(d)	In state: $24 lodging, $13.50 meals; out of state: $50 lodging, $22.50 meals, max. (V)	$7/day allowed for other than commercial lodging
Nebraska	...	21	Actual and necessary for authorized interim activity only (V)	$200 postage/yr.
Nevada	$104	20	In state: $26.50 food, $21 room; out of state: $21 food, actual and necessary lodging (V)	Travel out of state at reasonable rate; $60 postage & stationery; $60 printing allowance; $1,000 regular session, $200 special session telephone allowance (U); additional travel allowance $3,500 regular, $1,000 special session (V)
New Hampshire	...	38/1st 45 miles; 19/in excess of 45 miles to $50 max.	Actual and necessary (V)	...
New Jersey	...	...	...	Free stationery, postage, district office expenses, Western Union telegraph, telephone; $22,000 annually for salaries (V)
New Mexico	$40	10	...	Stationery, postage, telephone and telegraph
New York	...	23	$55/day (V)	$5,000 district office expenses (V); $20,000 staff allowance for Albany (V)
North Carolina	...	25	$50 (U)	$172/mo., annually, for office expenses and other miscellaneous expenses in home district office (U)
North Dakota	$62.50	25	$25 lodging in state, actual out of state (V); $17 food in state, up to $23 out of state (U)	$180/mo., annually for expenses (U)
Ohio	...	20	...	...
Oklahoma	$25 for 20 days	22	...	Telephone credit card up to $600/yr.; 3,000 1st class stamps
Oregon	...	18 cmte. business only	$44 (U)	$300/mo. interim expenses (U); where technically possible, may have state centrex line whose rental does not exceed $58/mo.; also $10/mo. for toll charge calls up to $180 (V). Where centrex would cost more than $58/mo., receives a phone credit card and may charge up to $75/mo. (V)
Pennsylvania	...	20	$58 non-legislative days, in or outside capital (V) or actual expenses (documented)	...
Rhode Island	...	...	...	...
South Carolina	$50	23	$50 (V)	$300/session for postage
South Dakota	$50	21	In state: $14.50 meals, $18 lodging; out of state: $19 meals, $70 lodging (V)	...
Tennessee	...	19.96(e)	$66.47 (U)	$166.15/mo. for telephone, secretary and other assistance, home office (U)
Texas	...	23/car; 30/single engine aircraft; 40/ twin engine aircraft	Actual and necessary (V)	Senate: all necessary office expenses except $10,000/mo. in session, $19,000/mo. interim limit on staff salaries (V); House: $5,500/mo. in session, $4,500/mo. interim office expenses (V)
Utah	$25	23	In state: max. $35 lodging, $16 meals; out of state: actual and necessary for travel and lodging, $20 max. meals (V)	...
Vermont	$50	22	Overnight: $25 lodging, $20 meals; commuting: $17.50 meals only (U); out of state: actual and necessary (V)	...
Virginia	$50	20	$50 (V)	$6,760 annually for secy. or admin. asst. (V)
Washington	...	18.5	$44 (U)	$5,000 annually (U)

LEGISLATIVE COMPENSATION: INTERIM PAYMENTS AND OTHER DIRECT PAYMENTS

State or other jurisdiction	Compensation for committee or official business (amount per day)	Travel allowance (cents per mile)	Living expenses (per day)	Other direct payments or services to legislators
West Virginia	$35 up to $1,050 for mbrs. of cmtes. authorized to meet during interim	17	$30 lodging (V), $20 meals and misc. (U); out of state: actual and necessary for travel and lodging (V), $25 max. meals and misc. (U)	Individual telephone credit cards, stationery, desk supplies
Wisconsin	...	...	Actual and necessary (V)	$75 senators, $25 representatives monthly interim expense allowance (U)
Wyoming	$30	12	$44 max. in state only (U); actual expenses for out of state travel (V)	Stationery, postage, telephone credit cards, misc. supplies
American Samoa	...	...	...	...
Puerto Rico	...	30/km.	$35 if residence within 50 km. of capitol; $45 if over 50 km. (U)	$800 in postage stamps per fiscal year; $2,000 annually for communications with constituents (V)

Key:
U—Unvouchered
V—Vouchered
(a) Members are furnished a leased car up to $265 per month, including gasoline and maintenance.
(b) Leadership and Joint Budget and Legislative Audit Committee members have added $5,000 maximum.
(c) For travel exceeding 100 miles; air travel may be paid in lieu of 21 cents per mile.
(d) 1983.
(e) Actual commercial travel expenses on out-of-state travel; however, not to exceed amount which would have been allowed for travel in a personal vehicle.

Table 9
CONSTITUTIONAL PROVISIONS ON LEGISLATIVE COMPENSATION

State or other jurisdiction	Set by constitution	Set by compensation commissions and legislatures, or referendum	Set by law			No restrictions
			Not effective during legislature adopting law(a)	Not effective during session adopted	Not effective during member's term(b)	
Alabama	★	...	...	...	...	...
Alaska	...	...	...	...	...	★
Arizona	...	★	...	..	...	...
Arkansas	★	...	...	...	...	...
California	...	...	★(c)	...	...	...
Colorado	...	...	...	...	★	...
Connecticut	...	...	...	...	...	★
Delaware	...	...	...	...	...	★
Florida	...	...	...	...	...	★
Georgia	...	...	★	...	...	...
Hawaii	...	★	...	..	...	...
Idaho	...	★	...	..	..	...
Illinois	...	...	...	..	★	...
Indiana	...	...	..	★	...	...
Iowa	...	...	★	...	...	...
Kansas	...	...	...	...	...	★
Kentucky	...	...	★	...	...	...
Louisiana	...	...	..	...	...	★
Maine	...	..	★	...	...	...
Maryland	...	★	...	..	...	...
Massachusetts	...	...	...	...	...	★
Michigan	...	★	...	...	...	...
Minnesota	...	...	★	...	...	...
Mississippi	...	...	..	★	...	...
Missouri	...	...	★	...	...	...
Montana	...	...	★	...	...	...
Nebraska	★	...	...	...	...	...
Nevada	...	...	...	...	★	...
New Hampshire	★	...	..	...	...	...
New Jersey	...	...	★	...	...	...
New Mexico	★	...	...	...	..	...
New York	...	...	...	...	★	...
North Carolina	..	...	★	...	...	...
North Dakota	★	...	...	...	...	...
Ohio	...	...	...	...	★	...
Oklahoma	...	★	...	...	...	...
Oregon	...	...	...	..	...	★
Pennsylvania	..	...	...	...	★	...
Rhode Island	★	...	...	...	...	...
South Carolina	...	...	★	...	...	...
South Dakota	...	...	..	...	...	★
Tennessee	..	...	★	...	...	...
Texas	★	...	...	...	...	...
Utah	★	...	...	...	...	..
Vermont	...	...	...	...	...	★
Virginia	...	...	...	...	★	...
Washington	...	...	...	...	★	...
West Virginia	...	★	...	...	..	...
Wisconsin	...	...	...	...	★	...
Wyoming	...	...	...	...	★	...
American Samoa	...	...	★	...	...	...
Guam	...	...	...	...	...	★
Puerto Rico	...	...	...	...	...	...
Virgin Islands	...	★	...	..	...	...

(a) Effective after intervening election.
(b) Senators serving the second half of a four-year term cannot receive the increase until they are re-elected.
(c) Amount of increase limited by constitution.

Table 10
INSURANCE PROGRAMS FOR STATE LEGISLATORS

State or other jurisdiction	Health insurance		Life insurance			Same programs as other state employees
	Legislative membership	State contribution	Legislative membership	Maximum coverage	State contribution	
Alabama	—— No program ——		———— No program ————			...
Alaska	Yes	100%	Yes	Annual salary	0	Yes
Arizona	Yes	90% I; 62% F	Yes	Annual salary	1st $5,000—100%; above $5,000—0	Yes
Arkansas	Yes	(a)	Yes	$20,000	(b)	Yes
California	Yes	0	———— No program ————			...
Colorado	Yes	$42.12	Yes	$3,800; Addtl. optional $25,000	$0.88/mo.; addtl. 0	Yes
Connecticut	Yes	100% I; 70% F	———— No program ————			...
Delaware	Yes(c)	100%	Yes(d)	Annual salary	0	Yes
Florida	Yes	75%	Yes	$18,000	66.6%	Yes
Georgia	Yes	70%	Yes	18 x monthly reported salary	75%	Yes
Hawaii	Yes	$14.88 I; $47.34 F	Yes	$15,000	100%	Yes
Idaho	Yes	100%	Yes	$10,000	100%	...
Illinois	Yes	100%	Yes	50% annual salary(e); addtl. optional	100%; addtl. 0	Yes
Indiana	Yes	97% I; 73% F	Yes	$13,000; $10,000-$20,000 addtl. optional	71%; addtl. 0	Yes
Iowa	—— No program ——		———— No program ————			...
Kansas	Yes	100%	Yes	$15,624	100%	Yes
Kentucky	Yes	100% I; 40% F(f)	Yes	$5,000; over $5,000 up to $36,000	100%; addtl. 0	Yes
Louisiana	Yes	50%	Yes	$40,000	50%	Yes
Maine	Yes	100%	Yes	Annual salary	0	...
Maryland	Yes	90% average	———— No program ————			...
Massachusetts	Yes	90%	Yes	$2,000 basic; addtl. optional to annual salary	90%; addtl. 0	Yes
Michigan	Yes	100%	Yes	1½ x annual salary	(g)	...
Minnesota	Yes	Up to $56.06/mo. I; up to $76.94/mo. F	Yes	$20,000; up to $100,000 addtl. optional	100%; addtl. 0	Yes
Mississippi	Yes	100%	Yes	$15,000 max.	50%	Yes
Missouri	Yes	(h)	Yes	$5,000	100%	Yes
Montana	Yes	(i)	Yes	$10,000; addtl. optional	(b)	Yes
Nebraska	Yes	0	Yes	$10,000	0	...
Nevada	—— No program ——		(j)	(j)	(j)	...
New Hampshire	—— No program ——		———— No program ————			...
New Jersey	Yes	100%	Yes	3 x annual salary	50%	Yes
New Mexico	—— No program ——		———— No program ————			...
New York	Yes	(a)	Yes	3 x annual salary, salary up to $150,000	0	...
North Carolina	Yes	0	———— No program ————			Yes
North Dakota	Yes	100% I & F for $300 deduct.; $27.87/mo. for $50 deduct.	Yes	Nearest $1,000 above annual salary to max. $3,000	1st $1,000—100%	Yes
Ohio	Yes	70%	Yes	(c,k)	100%	...
Oklahoma	Yes	100%	Yes	$18,000; addtl. $18,000	100%; addtl. 0	Yes
Oregon	Yes	100%	Yes	Annual salary(k)	100%	Yes
Pennsylvania	Yes	100%	Yes	$20,000	100%	Yes
Rhode Island	Yes	0	Yes	$1,000	0	...
South Carolina	Yes	$36.22/mo.	Yes	$3,000	$0.67/mo.	Yes
South Dakota	—— No program ——		———— No program ————			...
Tennessee	Yes	60%	Yes	$12,000	60%	Yes
Texas	Yes	(i)	Yes(i)	2 x annual salary	(i)	Yes
Utah	Yes	80% I & F	Yes	$18,000; addtl. $30,000	56%	Yes
Vermont	—— No program ——		———— No program ————			...

| State or other jurisdiction | Health insurance | | Life insurance | | | Same programs as other state employees |
	Legislative membership	State contribution	Legislative membership	Maximum coverage	State contribution	
Virginia	——— No program ———		Yes	Up to $1,000 above annual compensation x 2(l)	27%	Yes
Washington	Yes	100%	Yes	$100,000	1st $5,000—100%; above—0	Yes
West Virginia	Yes	0	Yes	$10,000; optional to $20,000	0	Yes(m)
Wisconsin	Yes	90%	Yes	Nearest $1,000 above annual salary; addtl. optional up to 2 x annual salary	75%; addtl. 0	Yes
Wyoming	——— No program ———		———————— No program ————————			...
American Samoa	Yes	100%	———————— No program ————————			...
Puerto Rico	Yes	$25/mo.	Yes	Annual salary	100%	...

Key: I—Individual coverage; F—Family coverage.
(a) Varies; 100 percent on some individual plans depending on plan and coverage.
(b) Included with health coverage.
(c) After one year.
(d) After three months.
(e) Reduces by 5 percent a year from age 56 on.
(f) HMO offered as optional health coverage.
(g) State contributes balance after actuarial evaluation.
(h) Members pay $10.70/mo.; remainder of cost paid by state.

(i) Per month: Montana—$70.00 fiscal 1982; Texas—combined for health and life, not more than $48.00 fiscal 1982.
(j) Covered with survivors benefits under retirement plan.
(k) Salary rounded to next higher thousand. Ohio—leaders and committee chairmen receive additional coverage equal to their compensation for the leadership and/or chair positions held.
(l) Creditable compensation (which includes salary, travel expense per diem, office allowance) is used in computing benefits for legislators.
(m) Legislators pay full premium.

Table 11
RETIREMENT PROGRAMS FOR STATE LEGISLATORS

State or other jurisdiction	Retirement system type	Membership type	Legislator's contribution as percentage of compensation	State government contribution	Minimum years legislative service for retirement	Age normally required for retirement
Alabama	— No program —					
Alaska	Public employee	Optional(a)	4.25(b)	Yes	5	55
Arizona	Public employee	Compulsory	5.0	Yes	5	60
Arkansas	Public employee(c)	Compulsory	6.0	Yes	10	60
California	Special legislative	Optional	8.0	Yes	4	60
Colorado	Public employee	Optional	8.0	Yes	5	65
Connecticut	Special legislative	Optional	10.0	No	10	55
Delaware	Public employee	Compulsory	0.0(d)	Yes	5	60
Florida	Public employee/ Special legislative(e)	Compulsory/ Optional(e)	8.0	Yes	8	62
Georgia	Public employee/ Special legislative	(f) (f)	5.5 8.0	Yes Yes	10 8	60 62
Hawaii	Public employee	Optional	6.0	Yes	10	55
Idaho	Public employee	Compulsory	4.84	Yes	0	65
Illinois	Special legislative	Optional	10.0	Yes	4	62
Indiana	Public employee	Optional	3.0	Yes	10	65
Iowa	Public employee	Optional	3.75	Yes	4	65
Kansas	Public employee	Optional	4.0	Yes	10	65
Kentucky	Public employee/ Special legislative	Compulsory/ Optional	4.0 5.0	Yes Yes	8 5	65 65
Louisiana	Public employee	Optional	11.0	Yes	10(g)	60(g)
Maine	Public employee	Optional	6.5	Yes	10	60
Maryland	Special legislative	Optional	5.0	Yes	8	60
Massachusetts	Public employee	Optional	7.0	Yes	6	55
Michigan	Special legislative	Optional	7.0	Yes	8(h)	55
Minnesota	Special legislative	Compulsory	9.0	Yes	6	62
Mississippi	Public employee	Compulsory(i)	6.0	Yes	10	65
Missouri	Special legislative	Compulsory	0.0	Yes	6	60
Montana	Public employee	Optional	6.0	Yes	5(j)	60(j)
Nebraska	— No program —					
Nevada	Special legislative	Compulsory	15.0	Yes	8	60
New Hampshire	— No program —					
New Jersey	Public employee(c)	Compulsory	5.0	Yes	8	60
New Mexico	Public employee(c)	Optional	$125/yr.	Yes	5	65
New York	Public employee	Optional/ Compulsory(k)	5.0 3.0	Yes Yes	0 10	55 62
North Carolina	— No program —					
North Dakota	Public employee(l)	. . .	. . .	. . .	. . .	. . .
Ohio	Public employee	Optional(e)	8.5	Yes	5	55
Oklahoma	Public employee	Optional	10.0	Yes	6	60(m)
Oregon	Public employee	Optional	0.0	Yes	6 mo.	70
Pennsylvania	Public employee	Optional	5.0	Yes	10(n)	50(o)
Rhode Island	Public employee(c)	Optional	30.0	Yes	8	55
South Carolina	Special legislative	Compulsory	10.0	Yes	8	60
South Dakota	— No program —					
Tennessee	Public employee	Optional	0.0(p)	Yes	4	55
Texas	Public employee	Optional	8.0	Yes	12 8	55 60
Utah	Special legislative	Optional	3.95	Yes	8	65
Vermont	— No program —					
Virginia	Public employee	Compulsory	5.0	Yes	5	65
Washington	Public employee(c)	Optional	7.5/5.51	Yes	5	60
West Virginia	Public employee	Optional	3.5/4.5	Yes	5	62
Wisconsin	Public employee	Compulsory	5.5	Yes	0	62
Wyoming	— No program —					
American Samoa	Public employee	Optional	2.85	Yes	0	. . .
Puerto Rico	Public employee	Optional	7.0	Yes	10	58

(a) If the legislator was serving in 1975-76 he is covered under a special elected public officers retirement system.

(b) If the legislator had qualified under the separate Teachers Retirement Act before election, he may elect coverage under that act. Legislator contribution is 8 percent.

(c) Special provisions for legislators.

(d) Up to $6,000. 5 percent on all above.

(e) Legislators may choose to join the compulsory statewide public employee pension system or the optional (elected officers class) special legislative retirement system. Florida: If assumed office after July 1, 1972, participation is compulsory.

(f) Legislator must join one or the other.

(g) Twelve years legislative service, age 55; 16 years legislative service, any age; 20 years public service, at least 12 of which is legislative, age 50.

(h) Not less than six years service if elected to at least four full or partial house terms, or two full or partial senate terms.

(i) Unless over age 64.

(j) Eligible for full retirement at age 65 regardless of years of service as a legislator, or after 30 years of service as a legislator regardless of age.

(k) Compulsory for members elected after July 1, 1976.

(l) Legislative authority for a retirement program exists. Implementation has never taken place.

(m) Age 55 with reduced benefits.

(n) Number of years of total state service if under superannuation age.

(o) With three years of legislative service.

(p) Litigation is pending which could adjust legislators' contributions to 5 percent of earnings until November 1982 when the non-contributory plan would go into effect.

Table 12
MEMBERSHIP TURNOVER IN THE LEGISLATURES*
(1980 and 1981)

State	Senate			House		
	Total number of members	*Number of membership changes*	*Percentage change of total*	*Total number of members*	*Number of membership changes*	*Percentage change of total*
All states	1,981	388	20	5,501	1,272	23
Alabama	35 (a)	...	...	105 (a)	...	...
Alaska	20 (b)	4	20	40	12	30
Arizona	30	5	17	60	9	15
Arkansas	35 (b)	4	11	100	16	16
California	40 (b)	6	15	80	18	23
Colorado	35 (b)	5	14	65	21	32
Connecticut...........	36	10	28	151	55	36
Delaware	21 (b)	7	33	41	13	32
Florida	40 (b)	10	25	120	23	19
Georgia	56	8	14	180	30	17
Hawaii	25	5	20	51	16	31
Idaho	35	13	37	70	15	21
Illinois	59 (b)	10	17	177	43	24
Indiana...............	50 (b)	11	22	100	17	17
Iowa	50 (b)	8	16	100	19	19
Kansas	40	10	25	125	31	25
Kentucky(c)	38 (b)	5	13	100	19	19
Louisiana	39 (a)	...	...	105 (a)	...	...
Maine	33	8	24	151	58	38
Maryland	47 (a)	...	...	141 (a)	...	...
Massachusetts	40	7	18	160	26	16
Michigan	38 (a)	...	...	110	20	18
Minnesota	67	25	37	134	28	21
Mississippi	52 (a)	...	...	122 (a)	...	...
Missouri..............	34 (b)	4	12	163	30	18
Montana	50 (b)	12	24	100	33	33
Nebraska	49 (b)	13	27	———Unicameral———		
Nevada................	20 (b)	5	25	40	12	30
New Hampshire	24	9	38	400	140	35
New Jersey(c)	40	17	43	80	27	34
New Mexico	42 (b)	16	38	70	12	17
New York	60	3	5	150	23	15
North Carolina	50	15	30	120	37	31
North Dakota	50 (b)	13	26	100	27	27
Ohio	33 (b)	6	18	99	15	15
Oklahoma	48 (b)	8	17	101	26	26
Oregon	30 (b)	4	13	60	20	33
Pennsylvania..........	50 (b)	8	16	203	50	25
Rhode Island	50	11	22	100	26	26
South Carolina	46	15	33	124	30	24
South Dakota	35	11	31	70	20	29
Tennessee	33 (b)	2	6	99	14	14
Texas	31 (b)	8	26	150	37	25
Utah	29	5	17	75	29	39
Vermont...............	30	7	23	150	56	37
Virginia(c)..........	40 (a)	...	...	100	23	23
Washington...........	49 (b)	14	29	98	25	26
West Virginia	34 (b)	11	32	100	39	39
Wisconsin	33 (b)	7	21	99	19	19
Wyoming	30 (b)	3	10	62	13	21

*Data was obtained by comparing the 1979 and 1981-82 editions of *State Elective Officials and the Legislatures*, published by The Council of State Governments.

(a) No election in 1980 or in 1981.
(b) Entire senate membership not up for election.
(c) State held statewide elections in 1981.

Table 13
1979 AND 1980 SESSIONS, INTRODUCTIONS AND ENACTMENTS:
REGULAR SESSIONS

State or other jurisdiction	Duration of session*	Introductions Bills	Introductions Resolutions	Enactments Bills	Enactments Resolutions	Measures vetoed by governor	Length of session
Alabama	April 17-July 30, 1979	1,717	510	582	198	2	30L
	Feb. 5-May 19, 1980	1,772	250	562	249	0	30L
Alaska	Jan. 15-May 6, 1979			263	110	20	112C
	Jan. 14-June 6, 1980	1,625	366				145C
Arizona	Jan. 8-April 21, 1979	800	66	221	27	8	103C
	Jan. 14-May 1, 1980	817	45	253	18	7	109C
Arkansas	Jan. 8-April 20, 1979	1,964	359	1,118	221	47	87C
	Jan. 7-Jan. 17, 1980(a)	3	48	3	4	1	11C
California	Dec. 4, 1978-Nov. 30, 1980	5,556	509	2,588	298	122	(b)
Colorado	Jan. 3-July 6, 1979	1,148	183	433	126	23	116L
	Jan. 2-May 7, 1980	419	113	174	66	3	80L
Connecticut	Jan. 3-June 4, 1979	4,672	1,332	734	N.A.	19(e)	(b)
	July 30-July 30, 1979(f)	. . .	. . .	. . .		. . .	1L
	Feb. 6-May 5, 1980	1,822	159	564	N.A.	21(e)	(b)
	June 16-June 16, 1980(f)	. . .	. . .	. . .		. . .	1L
Delaware	Jan. 9-June 30, 1979						54L
	Jan. 8-June 30, 1980	1,858	676	425	0	45	55L
Florida	April 3-June 6, 1979	2,996	177	599	54	20	60C
	April 8-June 7, 1980	3,040	224	617	82	13	60C
Georgia	Jan. 8-March 27, 1979	1,393	646	677	484	5	40L
	Jan. 14-March 8, 1980	1,199	683	766	333	15	40L
Hawaii	Jan. 17-April 20, 1979	3,584	1,533	230	749	14	94C(c)
	Jan. 16-April 28, 1980	2,616	1,236	309	822	6	104C(c)
Idaho	Jan. 8-March 26, 1979	599	71	338	39	13	78C
	Jan. 7-March 31, 1980	714	68	410	53	10	85C
Illinois	Jan. 10-July 10, 1979	4,381	1,091	1,220	1,085	256	89L
	Oct. 3-Nov. 9, 1979						
	Jan. 9-July 2, 1980	1,109	652	114	655	245	71L
	Nov. 6-Dec. 5, 1980						
Indiana	Jan. 8-April 6, 1979	1,706	261	337	94	14	60L
	Jan. 7-Feb. 26, 1980	949	197	224	101	1	29L
Iowa	Jan. 8-May 11, 1979	1,269	32	169	3	2	124C
	Jan. 14-April 26, 1980	983	22	206	0	2	84C
Kansas	Jan. 8-May 14, 1979	1,204	109(d)	335	22(d)	9	(b)
	Jan. 14-May 21, 1980	996	109(d)	333	22(d)	17	(b)
Kentucky†	Jan. 8-April 15, 1980	1,366	245	392	30(d)	17(e)	60L
Louisiana†	March 18-March 18, 1980(g)	. . .	. . .	. . .	. . .	. . .	1L
	April 21-July 14, 1980	2,937	533	881	399	37	(b)
	April 20-July 13, 1981	3,049	634	1,027	457	83	(b)
Maine	Jan. 3-June 15, 1979	1,602	22	664	1	5	101C
	Jan. 2-April 3, 1980	317	5	231	3	0	53C
Maryland	Jan. 10-April 9, 1979	2,945	170	748	170	110(e)	(b)
	Jan. 9-April 7, 1980	3,139	195	879	195	94	(b)
Massachusetts	Jan. 3-Nov. 4, 1979	8,951	256	791	24	25	306C
	Jan. 2-July 5, 1980	9,103	225	575	10	21	186C
Michigan	Jan. 10-Jan. 11, 1979						(b)
	Jan. 23-April 11, 1979						
	April 24-July 13, 1979	2,272	1,808	220	N.A.	15	
	Sept. 18-Nov. 15, 1979						
	Nov. 27-Dec. 15, 1979						
	Dec. 29-Dec. 29, 1979						
	Jan. 9-July 30, 1980						(b)
	Sept. 3-Sept. 30, 1980	1,220	1,777	524	N.A.	5	
	Oct. 8-Oct. 9, 1980						
	Nov. 12-Dec. 17, 1980						
	Dec. 30-Dec. 30, 1980						
Minnesota	Jan. 3-May 21, 1979	1,643	3	314	3	5	59L
	Jan. 22-April 12, 1980	859	0	578	0	5	40L
Mississippi†	Jan. 8-May 11, 1980	2,472	312	679	152	0	120C
	Jan. 6-April 1, 1981	2,637	306	636	186	7	90C
Missouri	Jan. 3-June 29, 1979	1,463	64	207	4	11	(b)
	Jan. 9-May 15, 1980	1,339	50	120	0	2	(b)
	Sept. 3-Sept. 3, 1980(f)	. . .	. . .	. . .	. . .	. . .	1C
Montana	Jan. 3-April 20, 1979	1,448	110(d)	743	67(d)	10	90L
Nebraska	Jan. 3-May 23, 1979	635	178	310	0	7(e)	89C
	Jan. 9-April 18, 1980	458	348	251	56	20(e)	60C
Nevada	Jan. 15-May 29, 1979	1,441	254	697	153	2	(b)
New Hampshire	Jan. 3-June 28, 1979						90L
	March 27-March 27, 1980	1,181	103	501	75	6	1L
	May 29-May 29, 1980(a)						1L
New Jersey†	Jan. 9, 1979-Jan. 8, 1980	1,185	169	501	7	19(h)	(b)
	Jan. 8, 1980-Jan. 13, 1981	4,047	494	187	9	12(h)	(b)
New Mexico	Jan. 16-March 17, 1979	1,086	37	440	7	36	60C
	Jan. 15-Feb. 14, 1980	458	33	157	1	2	30C

206

State or other jurisdiction	Duration of session*	Introductions		Enactments		Measures vetoed by governor	Length of session
		Bills	Resolutions	Bills	Resolutions		
New York	Jan. 3-Nov. 27, 1979	(i)	1,503	734	1,408	98(e)	(b)
	Jan.9-Nov. 22, 1980	(i)	1,865	881	1,795	132(e)	(b)
North Carolina	Jan. 10-June 8, 1979	2,328	152	1,077	90	(j)	108L
	June 5-June 25, 1980	399	52	255	20	(j)	15L
North Dakota	Jan. 3-March 29, 1979	1,183	189	681	143	31	61L
Ohio	Jan. 2-Nov. 30, 1979	1,258	90	204	15	5	(b)
	Jan. 2-Dec.19, 1980	465	43	234	7	12	(b)
Oklahoma	Jan. 2-July 2, 1979	906	248	292	142	2	89L
	Jan. 8-June 16, 1980	683	191	365	23	2(e)	80L
Oregon	Jan. 8-July 4, 1979	2,288	146	903	62	19	176C
Pennsylvania	Jan. 2, 1979-Jan. 1, 1980	3,294	260	211	78	2	(b)
	Jan. 1-Nov. 19, 1980	1,322	157	385	70	12	(b)
Rhode Island	Jan. 2-May 4, 1979	2,692	N.A.	499	440	13	62C
	Jan. 1-May 9, 1980	2,079	N.A.	525	384	26	(b)
South Carolina	Jan. 9-Aug. 16, 1979	1,337	N.A.	307	N.A.	...	(b)
	Jan. 8-Aug. 28, 1980	853	N.A.	348	N.A.	23(e)	(b)
South Dakota	Jan. 16-March 30, 1979	614	57	346	43	18	45L
	Jan. 8-March 12, 1980	631	52	385	42	30	30L
Tennessee	Jan. 9-Jan. 20, 1979(g)	...	...	...	...	...	12C
	Jan. 20-May 17, 1979	2,919	775	616	N.A.	3	47L
	Jan. 8-April 18, 1980	2,269	711	646	N.A.	7	(b)
Texas	Jan. 9-May 28, 1979	3,598	1,477	890	1,135	48	140C
Utah	Jan. 8-March 8, 1979	773	89	260	25	12	60C
	Jan. 14-Feb. 2, 1980	184	64	90	22	2	20C
Vermont	Jan. 3-April 21, 1979	611	85	85	65	0	67L
	Jan. 8-April 22, 1980	392	93	120	71	1	66L
Virginia †	Jan. 9-March 8, 1980	1,566	381	760	151	35	60C
	Jan. 14-Feb. 21, 1981 April 1-April 2, 1981	1,117	248	638	179	29	41C
Washington	Jan. 8-March 8, 1979	2,642	85	159	6	7	60C
	Jan. 14-March 13, 1980	1,096	36	191	5	16(e)	59C
West Virginia	Jan. 10-March 12, 1979	1,308	195	124	49	2	62C
	Jan. 9-March 11, 1980	1,611	203	136	60	2(e)	63C
Wisconsin	Jan. 3-Jan. 3, 1979 Jan. 9-Jan. 9, 1979 Jan. 23-March 1, 1979 April 17-June 29, 1979 Oct. 2-Nov. 1, 1979 Jan. 29-April 2, 1980 May 28-May 29, 1980	1,920	243	350	105	19(e)	(b)
Wyoming	Jan. 9-Feb. 23, 1979	702	27	171	1	8	40L
	Feb. 12-March 5, 1980	147	13	80	3	5	20L
American Samoa	Feb. 16, 1979	133	48	28	26	9	30C
	Sept. 21, 1979	122	13	35	8	13	45C
	March 24, 1980	128	77	31	29	12	45C
	Sept. 20, 1980	168	167	24	36	12	45C

*Actual adjournment dates are listed regardless of constitutional limitations. Legal provisions governing legislative sessions, regular and special, are reflected in the table "Legislative Sessions: Legal Provisions."

†—Legislatures in these states begin new legislatures in even-numbered years. These figures reflect this calendar. Alabama, Louisiana, Maryland and Mississippi have four-year legislatures.

Key: C—Calendar days; L-Legislative days; N.A.—Not available.
(a) Extended session.
(b) California: A-251L, S-262L; Connecticut: 1979 H-83L, S-64L; 1980 H-49L, S-51L; Kansas: 1979 H-70L, S-68L; 1980 H-67L, S-65L; Louisiana: 1980 H-54L, S-45L; 1981 H-57L, S-45L; Maryland: 1979 H-64L, S-65L; 1980 H-67L, S-66L; Michigan: 1979 H-136L, S-128L; 1980 H-133L, S-134L; Missouri: 1979 H-93L, S-96L; 1980 H-68L, S-69L; Nevada: A-93L, S-98L; New Jersey: 1979 H-35L, S-38L; 1980 H-32L, S-35L; New York: 1979 A-216L, S-147L; 1980 A-212L, S-144L; Ohio:

1979 H-119L, S-129L; 1980 H-97L, S-102L; Pennsylvania: 1979 H-89L, S-71L; 1980 H-70L, S-65L; Rhode Island: H-66C, S-68C; South Carolina: 1979 H-123C, S-125C; 1980 H-96C, S-94C; Tennessee: H-90L, S-86L; Wisconsin: A-98L, S-82L.
(c) Includes mandatory five-day recess required by constitution.
(d) Concurrent resolutions only.
(e) Passed over governor's veto. Connecticut: 1979-1, 1980-3; Kentucky: 1; Maryland: 7; Nebraska: 1979-1, 1980-4; New York: 1979-2, 1980-1; Oklahoma: 1; South Carolina: 13; Washington: 1; West Virginia: 1; Wisconsin: 4.
(f) Veto session.
(g) Organizational session.
(h) Plus 44 conditional vetoes, 83 pocket vetoes and 9 conditional vetoes in 1979; 17 conditional vetoes and 5 line-item vetoes in 1980.
(i) 1979 and 1980 sessions, 21,682.
(j) Governor has no veto power.

Table 14
1979 AND 1980 SESSIONS, INTRODUCTIONS AND ENACTMENTS: SPECIAL SESSIONS

State or other jurisdiction	Duration of session*	Introductions		Enactments		Measures vetoed by governor	Length of session
		Bills	Resolutions	Bills	Resolutions		
Alabama	Jan. 18-Jan. 24, 1979	20	34	10	16	0	5L
Alaska	Aug. 6-Aug. 8, 1979	5	0	4	0	0	3C
	Sept. 22-Sept. 24, 1980	19	0	3	0	0	3C
Arizona	July 2-July 2, 1979	6	0	2	0	0	1C
	Nov. 12, 1979-April 3, 1980	58	17	11	6	0	144C
	June 10-June 10, 1980	3	0	3	0	0	1C
	June 11-June 11, 1980	1	0	1	0	0	1C
Arkansas	Jan. 17-Jan. 24, 1980	93	20	71	18	2	8C
	April 15-April 18, 1980	27	25	11	23	9	4C
California	None	...	...	...	...	...	...
Colorado	None	...	...	...	...	...	...
Connecticut	July 30-Aug. 13, 1979	0	31	0	0	0	2C
	Oct. 31-Nov. 20, 1979	158	33	15	0	0	12C
Delaware	July 1-July 1, 1980	(a)	(a)	(a)	(a)	(a)	1C
Florida	Dec. 6-Dec. 6, 1978	13	2	6	1	0	1C
	June 6-June 6, 1979	4	1	3	1	0	1C
	Nov. 27-Dec. 4, 1979	35	26	12	7	0	8C
	June 9-June 11, 1980	21	4	9	1	3	3C
	June 30-June 30, 1980	15	21	8	11	0	1C
Georgia	None	...	...	...	...	...	...
Hawaii	None	...	...	...	...	...	...
Idaho	May 12-May 14, 1980	15	8	1	5	0	3C
Illinois	Aug. 6-Aug. 6, 1979	0	0	1	0	0	1L
	Sept. 5-Sept. 6, 1979	0	0	3	0	0	2L
	Oct. 17-Nov. 8, 1979	27	0	1	3	0	7L
	Jan. 12-Jan. 23, 1980	0	0	0	0	0	3L
Indiana	None	...	...	...	...	...	...
Iowa	None	...	...	...	...	...	...
Kansas	None	...	...	...	...	...	...
Kentucky	Jan. 8-Feb. 10, 1979	132	96	21	6	0	28L
Louisiana	Sept. 2-Sept. 11, 1980	29	54	18	37	1	7L
Maine	Oct. 4-Oct. 5, 1979	3	0	2	0	0	2C
	Oct. 10-Oct. 11, 1979	1	0	1	0	0	2C
	May 22-May 22, 1980	5	0	5	0	0	1C
Maryland	None	...	...	...	...	...	...
Massachusetts	Sept. 18-Nov. 12, 1980	N.A.	N.A.	N.A.	N.A.	N.A.	N.A.
	Nov. 17-Nov. 20, 1980						
	Dec. 1-Dec. 7, 1980						
Michigan	None	...	...	...	...	...	...
Minnesota	May 24-May 24, 1979	4	3	3	3	0	1C
Mississippi	May 1-May 3, 1979	18	18	8	5	0	3C
Missouri	Dec. 3-Dec. 13, 1979	1	0	1	0	0	11C
	Sept. 3-Nov. 2, 1980	9	0	3	0	0	17L
Montana	None	...	...	...	...	...	...
Nebraska	None	...	...	...	...	...	...
Nevada	Sept. 13-Sept. 13, 1980	2	2	2	2	2	1L
New Hampshire	None	...	...	...	...	...	...
New Jersey	None	...	...	...	...	...	...
New Mexico	None	...	...	...	...	...	...
New York	July 18-July 18, 1979						1L
	Nov. 27-Nov. 27, 1979	(a)	(a)	(a)	(a)	(a)	1L
	Nov. 1-Nov. 2, 1980						2L
	Nov. 20-Nov. 22, 1980						3L
North Carolina	None	...	...	...	...	...	...
North Dakota	None	...	...	...	...	...	...
Ohio	None	...	...	...	...	...	...
Oklahoma	July 7-July 11, 1980	3	5	2	3	0	5C
Oregon	Aug. 4-Aug. 8, 1980	24	2	17	2	0	5C
Pennsylvania	None	...	...	...	...	...	...
Rhode Island	June 8-June 8, 1979	10	1	3	1	0	1C
	Sept. 20-Sept. 20-1979	0	0	0	0	0	1C
	Nov. 13-Nov. 13, 1979	0	0	0	0	0	1C
South Carolina	None	...	...	...	...	...	...
South Dakota	None	...	...	...	...	...	...
Tennessee	None	...	...	...	...	...	...
Texas	None	...	...	...	...	...	...

THE LEGISLATURES

State or other jurisdiction	Duration of session*	Introductions Bills	Introductions Resolutions	Enactments Bills	Enactments Resolutions	Measures vetoed by governor	Length of session†
Utah	Dec. 15-Dec. 16, 1980	6	3	4	3	0	2C
Vermont	None	...	...	...	...	...	...
Virginia..................	None	...	...	...	...	...	...
Washington	March 22-June 2, 1979	0	...	276 (b)	...	18	74C
West Virginia.............	April 9-April 11, 1979	2	17	1	1	0	2C
Wisconsin	Sept. 5-Sept. 5, 1979	10	5	5	5	0	1L
	Jan. 22-Jan. 25, 1980	8	5	0	2	0	(c)
	June 3-Aug. 3, 1980	20	16	7	12	0	(c)
Wyoming	None	...	...	...	...	...	...
American Samoa	May 11, 1979	2	8	2	8	0	10C
	Dec. 18, 1979	4	9	2	3	0	15C
	May 2, 1980	8	10	6	4	0	10C

*Actual adjournment dates are listed regardless of constitutional limitations. Legal provisions governing legislative sessions, regular and special, are reflected in the table "Legislative Sessions: Legal Provisions."

Key: C—Calendar days; L—Legislative days; N.A.—Not available.
(a) Data included in regular sessions.
(b) Carried over from regular session.
(c) Second Special A-4L, S-2L; Third Special A-12L, S-13L.

Table 15
LEGISLATIVE SESSIONS: LEGAL PROVISIONS

State or other jurisdiction	Regular sessions — Legislature convenes* — Year	Month	Day	Regular sessions — Limitation on length of session	Special sessions — Legislature may call†	Special sessions — Legislature may determine subject	Special sessions — Limitation on length of session
Alabama	Annual	Apr. Feb.	3rd Tues. (a,b) 1st Tues. 2nd Tues. (c)	30 L in 105 C	No	2/3 vote, each house	12 L in 30 C
Alaska	Annual	Jan.	3rd Mon. (a) 2nd Mon.	None	Vote 2/3 members	Yes(d)	30 C
Arizona	Annual	Jan.	2nd Mon.	None(e)	Petition 2/3 members, each house	Yes(d)	None
Arkansas	Odd(f)	Jan.	2nd Mon.	60 C(f)	No	(g)	None(g)
California	Even(h)	Dec.	1st Mon.	None	No	No	None
Colorado	Annual(i)	Jan.	Weds. after 1st Tues.	None	Vote 2/3 members, each house	Yes(d)	None
Connecticut	Annual(i)	Odd: Jan. Even: Feb.	Wed. after 1st Mon. Wed. after 1st Mon.	(j) (j)	No	No	None
Delaware	Annual(k)	Jan.	2nd Tues.	June 30	Joint call, presiding officers, both houses	Yes	None
Florida	Annual	Apr.	Tues. after 1st Mon. (b)	60 C(f)	Joint call, presiding officers, both houses.	Yes	20 C(f)
Georgia	Annual(k)	Jan.	2nd Mon.	40 L	Petition 3/5 members, each house	Yes(d)	(l)
Hawaii	Annual(k)	Jan.	3rd Wed.	60 L(f)	Petition 2/3 members, each house	Yes	30 L(f)
Idaho	Annual	Jan.	Mon. on or nearest 9th day	None	No	No	20 C
Illinois	Annual(k)	Jan.	2nd. Wed.	None	Joint call, presiding officers, both houses	Yes	None
Indiana	Annual	Jan.	2nd Mon. (b)	Odd: 61 L or Apr. 30 Even: 30 L or March 15	No	Yes	30 L in 40 C
Iowa	Annual(k)	Jan.	2nd Mon.	None(m)	Petition 2/3 members, each house	Yes	None
Kansas	Annual(k)	Jan.	2nd Mon.	Odd: None; Even: 90 C(f)	Petition to governor or 2/3 members, each house	Yes	None
Kentucky	Even	Jan.	Tues. after 1st Mon.	60 L	No	No	None
Louisiana	Annual	Apr.	3rd Mon.	60 L in 85 C	Petition majority, each house	Yes(d)	30 C
Maine	Even(h) Even(i)	Dec. Jan.	1st Wed. 1st Wed. after 1st Tues. (b)	100 L 50 L	Vote of majority of each party, each house	Yes(d)	None
Maryland	Annual	Jan.	2nd Wed.	90 C(f,n)	Petition majority, each house	Yes	30 C
Massachusetts	Annual	Jan.	1st Wed	None	Yes	Yes	None
Michigan	Annual(k)	Jan.	1st Wed	None	No	No	None
Minnesota	Odd(o)	Jan.	Tues. after 1st Mon.	120 L or 1st Mon. after 3rd Sat. in May	No	Yes	None
Mississippi	Annual	Jan.	Tues. after 1st. Mon.	(f,p)	No	No	None
Missouri	Annual	Jan.	Wed. after 1st Mon.	Odd: June 30. Even: May 15.	No	No	60 C
Montana	Odd	Jan.	1st Mon. (q)	90 L	Petition majority, each house	Yes	None
Nebraska	Annual(k)	Jan.	1st Wed. after 1st Mon.	Odd: 90 L(f). Even: 60 L(f)	Petition 2/3 members	Yes	None
Nevada	Odd	Jan.	3rd Mon.	60 C(m)	No	No	20 C(m)
New Hampshire	Odd	Jan.	1st Wed. after 1st Tues. (b)	(m)	Yes	Yes	None(m)
New Jersey	Annual	Jan.	2nd Tues.	None	Petition majority, each house	Yes	None
New Mexico	Annual(i)	Jan.	3rd Tues.	Odd: 60 C; Even: 30 C	Petition 3/5 members, each house	Yes(d)	30 C
New York	Annual(k)	Jan.	Wed. after 1st Mon.	None	Petition 2/3 members, each house	Yes(d)	None
North Carolina	Odd(o)	Jan.	Wed. after 2nd Mon.	None	Petition 3/5 members, each house	Yes	None
North Dakota	Odd	Jan.	1st Tues. after 3rd day (b,q)	80 L	No	Yes	None
Ohio	Annual	Jan.	1st Mon. (q)	None	Joint call, presiding officers, both houses	Yes	None

Oklahoma	Annual(k)	Jan.	Tues. after 1st Mon.	90 L	Vote 2/3 members, each house	Yes	None
Oregon	Odd	Jan.	2nd Mon.	None	Petition majority, each house	Yes	None
Pennsylvania	Annual(k)	Jan.	1st Tues.	None	Petition majority, each house	No	None
Rhode Island	Annual(k)	Jan.	1st Tues.	60 L(m)	No	No	None
South Carolina	Annual(k)	Jan.	2nd Tues. (b)	1st Thurs. in June(f)	No	Yes	None
South Dakota	Annual	Jan.	Tues. after 1st Mon.	40 L	No	No	None
Tennessee	Odd(o)	Jan.	1st Tues.(b)	35 L	Petition 2/3 members, each house	Yes	30(m)
Texas	Odd	Jan.	2nd Tues.	90 L(m)	No	No	30 C
Utah	Annual(i)	Jan.	2nd Mon.	140 C	No	No	30 C
Vermont	Odd(o)	Jan.	Wed. after 1st Mon.	None(m)	No	Yes	None
Virginia	Annual(k)	Jan.	2nd Wed.	Even: 60 C(f) Odd: 30 C(f)	Petition 2/3 members, each house	Yes	None
Washington	Annual	Jan.	2nd Mon.	Odd: 105 C; Even: 60 C	Petition, 2/3 members each house	Yes	30 C
West Virginia	Annual	Jan.	2nd Wed. (r)	60 C(f,n)	Petition 3/5 members, each house	Yes(s)	None
Wisconsin	Annual	Jan.	1st Tues. after Jan. 8(t)	None	No	No	None
Wyoming	Annual(i)	Feb.	Odd: 2nd Tues. Even: 2nd Tues.	40 L / 20 L	No	Yes	None
American Samoa	Annual	Jan.; July	2nd Mon.	45 L / 45 L	No	No	None
Guam	Annual(k)	Jan.	2nd Mon.(u)	None	No	No	None
Puerto Rico	Annual(k)	Jan.	2nd Mon.	Apr. 30(f)	No	No	20 C
Virgin Islands	Annual(k)	Jan.	2nd Mon.	75 L	No	No	15 C

*All states elect new legislatures in November of even-numbered years except Kentucky, Louisiana, Mississippi, New Jersey and Virginia. Alabama, Louisiana, Maryland and Mississippi elect all legislators at the same time to four-year terms.

†The following states provide for a special session only to consider bills vetoed after adjournment sine die: Connecticut, Hawaii, Louisiana, Missouri (even years only), Utah, Virginia and Washington.

Key: L—Legislative day
C—Calendar day
N—Natural day

(a) In the year immediately following the quadrennial general election.

(b) Legislature meets in organizational session. Alabama: second Tuesday in January after quadrennial election. Florida: fourteenth day following each general election. Indiana: third Tuesday after first Monday in November for one day only. New Hampshire: first Wednesday in December, even-numbered years. North Dakota: first Tuesday after first Monday in December in even years. South Carolina: first Tuesday after certification of the election of its members for no more than three days. Tennessee: first Tuesday in January for no more than 15 C days to organize and introduce bills; reconvenes on first Tuesday next following the conclusion of the organizational session, unless the General Assembly by joint resolution sets another date.

(c) During the election year.

(d) Only if legislature convenes itself. Special sessions called by the legislature are unlimited in scope in Arizona, Georgia, Maine and New Mexico.

(e) House and Senate rules require that regular sessions be adjourned sine die no later than the third Friday in April of each year.

(f) Session may be extended for an indefinite period of time by vote of members in both houses. Hawaii: petition of 2/3 membership for not more than 15 days. Maryland: 3/5 vote for 30 additional days. Mississippi: 2/3 vote of those present may extend for 30 C days, no limit on extensions. Nebraska: 4/5 vote. South Carolina: concurrent resolution, 2/3 vote, both houses. Puerto Rico: joint resolution.
Arkansas: 2/3 vote. Florida: 3/5 vote. Hawaii: petition of 2/3 membership for not more than 15 days. Kansas: 2/3 vote elected members. Maryland: 3/5 vote for 30 additional days. Mississippi: 2/3 vote of those present may extend for 30 C days, no limit on extensions. Nebraska: 4/5 vote. South Carolina: 4/5 vote, both houses. West Virginia: 2/3 vote. Puerto Rico: 2/3 vote.

(g) After the legislature has disposed of the subject(s) in the governor's call, it may by a 2/3 vote of members of both houses take up subject(s) of its own choosing in a session of up to 15 days.

(h) Regular sessions commence in December of each even-numbered year following the general election. California: the legislature continues in session until November 30 of the next even-numbered year. It may recess from time to time and may be recalled into regular session.

(i) Second session of legislature is basically limited to budget and fiscal matters. Exceptions: Colorado—items on governor's call; Maine—legislation; in the governor's call, study committee legislation and initiated measures; New Mexico—legislature may consider bills vetoed by the governor at the preceding session; Utah—legislature may consider non-budget matters after 2/3 vote of each house.

(j) Odd years: not later than first Wednesday after first Monday in June; even years: not later than first Wednesday after first Monday in May.

(k) The legislature meets in two annual sessions, each adjourning sine die. Bills carry over from first to second session. Delaware, Illinois, Virgin Islands: legislature adjourns sine die at end of second year only; Puerto Rico: four annual sessions.

(l) Limited to 70 days if called by governor and 30 days if called at petition of legislature, except for impeachment proceedings.

(m) Indirect restrictions only since legislator's pay, per diem, or daily allowance stops, but session may continue. Iowa: limit on per diem expenses, 120 days first session, 100 days second session. Nevada: limit on pay only. New Hampshire: constitutional limit on expenses of 90 days or July 1, whichever occurs first, 15 days salary and expenses for special sessions. Tennessee: constitutional limit on per diem and travel allowance only, excluding organizational session.

(n) Governor must extend until the general appropriation is passed.

(o) The legislature may divide and in practice has divided the session to meet in even years also.

(p) The first session of a new legislature. Every other even year of the gubernatorial term is limited to 125 C days; odd years 90 C days.

(q) If the first day falls on a legal holiday: Montana—following Wednesday; North Dakota—or falls on January 2, a date to be selected by the Legislative Council between Jan. 2 and Jan. 11; Ohio—the day after.

(r) Following each gubernatorial election, the legislature convenes on the second Wednesday of January to organize but recesses until the second Wednesday in February for the start of the 60-day session.

(s) According to a 1955 attorney general's opinion, when the legislature has petitioned to the governor to be called into session, it may then act on any matter.

(t) The legislature by joint resolution establishes the session schedule of activity for the remainder of the biennium at the beginning of the odd-numbered year. These dates may be subject to change.

(u) The legislature meets on the first Monday of each month following its initial session in January.

Table 16
ENACTING LEGISLATION: VETO, VETO OVERRIDE AND EFFECTIVE DATE

State or other jurisdiction	Legislature may recall bill before governor acts	Governor may return bill before action	Item veto on appropriation bills: Amount	Item veto on appropriation bills: Other	Days allowed governor to consider bill(a) — During session: Bill becomes law unless vetoed	After session: Bill becomes law unless vetoed	After session: Bill dies unless signed	Votes required in each house to pass bills or items over veto(b)	Effective date of enacted legislation(c)
Alabama	★	★	★	★	6	20 P	10 A	Majority elected	Immediately(d)
Alaska			★(e)		15	10 A		Two-thirds elected(f)	90 days after enactment
Arizona	★		★		5	10 A		Two-thirds elected	90 days after adjournment
Arkansas	★		★		5	20 A(g)		Majority elected	90 days after adjournment
California		★	★(e)		12(g)	P(h)		Two-thirds elected	(i)
Colorado	★		★	★	10(g)	30 A(g)		Two-thirds elected	Immediately
Connecticut	★(j)		★		5	15 P(g)		Two-thirds elected	Oct. 1
Delaware			★	★	10		30 A(g)	Three-fifths elected	Immediately
Florida		★	★	★	7(g)	15 P(g)		Two-thirds elected	60 days after adjournment
Georgia(k)			★		5	30 A(l)		Two-thirds elected	July 1(m)
Hawaii(k)	★		★(n)		10(o,p)	45 A(o,p)	(p)	Two-thirds elected	Immediately
Idaho		★(q)	★(e)		5	10 A		Two-thirds present	July 1(m)
Illinois			★(e)		60(g)	60 P(g)		Three-fifths elected(f)	Jan. 1(m,r)
Indiana					7	7A		Majority elected	Set by law
Iowa		★	★	★	3	30 A(s)	30 A(s)	Two-thirds elected	July 1(m)
Kansas	★		★		10	10 P		Two-thirds elected	Upon publication
Kentucky			★		10	10 A		Majority elected	90 days after adjournment
Louisiana(k)			★	★	10(g)	20 P(g)		Two-thirds elected	60 days after adjournment
Maine					10	(l)		Two-thirds present	June 1(u)
Maryland(k)			★(t)	★	6	30 P(l)		Three-fifths elected	
Massachusetts	★(v)	★	★(e)	★	10(o)		10 P	Two-thirds present	90 days
Michigan			★	★	14(g)		14 P(g)	Two-thirds elected and serving	90 days after adjournment
Minnesota	★		★		3		14 P	Two-thirds elected	Aug. 1(w)
Mississippi			★(e)		5	15 P(l)		Two-thirds elected	60 days
Missouri			★	★	15(s)	45 P(l,s)		Two-thirds elected	90 days after adjournment(w,x)
Montana		★(q)	★(y)	★	5(g)	25 A(g)		Two-thirds present	July 1
Nebraska	★	★	★		5	5 A		Three-fifths elected	3 mos. after adjournment
Nevada	★	★			5	10 A		Two-thirds elected	July 1
New Hampshire		★(q)	★(e)		5		5 P	Two-thirds elected	60 days
New Jersey		★(q)	★(e)		45(z)		(aa)	Two-thirds elected	July 4
New Mexico	★	★	★		3		20 A	Two-thirds present	90 days after adjournment(w)
New York			★		10		30 A(f)	Two-thirds elected	20 days
North Carolina			(ab)		(ab)	(ab)	(ab)	Two-thirds elected	30 days after adjournment
North Dakota			★(e)	★	3	15 A		Two-thirds elected	July 1
Ohio	★		★	★	10	10 A		Three-fifths elected	91 days after filed with secretary of state(ac)
Oklahoma	★		★		5		15 A	Two-thirds elected(f)	90 days after adjournment
Oregon	★		★(e)	★	5	30 A(g)		Two-thirds present	90 days after adjournment
Pennsylvania			★		10(g)	30 A(g)		Two-thirds elected	60 days
Rhode Island					6	10 A(g)		Three-fifths present	10 days after adjournment
South Carolina	★		★		5			Two-thirds present	20 days

State or other jurisdiction				Days	Days (P/A)	Vote required to pass over veto	Effective date
South Dakota	★		★		5	15 A	Two-thirds elected	July 1(m)
Tennessee	★	★(e)			10	10 A	Majority elected	40 days
Utah	★(ad)	★	★(ad)		10(g)	20 A	Two-thirds present	90 days after adjournment
Vermont	★				5	3 A	Two-thirds present	60 days after adjournment July 1
Virginia		★	★		7(g)	30 A(g)	Two-thirds present(ae)	Julyl 1(af)
Washington	★	★	★(e)		5	20 A	Two-thirds present	90 days after adjournment
West Virginia	★		★(e)		5	15 A(ag)	Majority elected(f)	90 days after final passage by legislature
Wisconsin	★		★		6	6 P	Two-thirds present	Day after publication
Wyoming		★			3	15(g)	Two-thirds elected	Immediately
American Samoa	★		★(e)		10	30 P	Two-thirds elected	Immediately(ai)
Guam					10	30 P	14 members	(ah)
No. Mariana Islands	★		★(e)		10	30	Three-fourths elected	(ah)
Puerto Rico		★	★(e)		10	30 P(g)	Two-thirds elected	Specified in act
Virgin Islands	★				10(a)	30 P(g)		Immediately
U.S. Congress					10	10 P	Two-thirds present	Immediately

Key: P—days after presentation to governor

A—days after adjournment of legislature

(a) Sundays excluded.

(b) Bill is returned to house of origin with objections.

(c) The effective date may be established by the law itself. Special or emergency acts are usually effective immediately.

(d) Penal acts, 60 days.

(e) The governor can also reduce items in appropriations measures.

(f) Revenue and appropriations bills. Illinois: appropriations reductions, majority elected. Oklahoma: emergency bills, three-fourths. West Virginia: budget and supplementary appropriations, two-thirds elected.

(g) Sundays included.

(h) Regular sessions: the last day which either house may pass a bill, except statutes calling elections, majority elected. Special sessions: statutes providing for tax levies or appropriations for usual current expenses of the state and urgency statutes. All bills given to the governor during the 12 days prior to August 31 of that year become law unless vetoed by September 30. Special sessions: 12 days.

(i) Regular sessions: January 1 next following 90-day period from date of enactment. Special sessions: 91st day after adjournment; except statutes calling elections, statutes providing for tax levies or appropriations for the usual current expenses of the state and urgency statutes, all of which take immediate effect.

(j) Only by originating house.

(k) Constitution withholds right to veto constitutional amendments.

(l) Bills vetoed after adjournment shall be returned to the legislature for reconsideration. Georgia: bills returned within 35 days from the date of adjournment for reconsideration within the first 10 days of the next session. Maine: returned within three days after the next meeting of the same legislature which enacted the bill or resolution. Maryland: reconsidered at the next meeting of the same General Assembly. Mississippi: returned within three days after the beginning of the next session. Missouri: bills returned within four days of adjournment or later in first session are considered at beginning of second session. Bills returned in second session are considered in automatic veto session held for no more than 10 days beginning on the first Wednesday following the first Monday in September. South Carolina: within two days after the next meeting.

(m) Effective date for acts which become law on or after July 1. Georgia: January 1. Idaho: special sessions, 60 days after adjournment. Illinois: July 1 of next calendar year. Iowa: if governor signs bill after July 1, bill becomes law on August 15; special sessions: 90 days after adjournment. South Dakota: 91st day after adjournment.

(n) The governor can only reduce items in the executive appropriations measures. The governor can neither reduce nor item veto items in the legislative or judicial budgets, but he may veto the budget as a whole.

(o) Except Sundays and legal holidays. Hawaii: except Saturdays, Sundays, holidays and any days in which the legislature is in recess prior to adjournment.

(p) The governor must notify the legislature 10 days before the 45th day of his intent to veto a measure on that day. The legislature may convene on 45th day after adjournment to consider vetoed measures. If the legislature fails to reconvene, it may pass the measure over the governor's veto or it may amend the law to meet the governor's objections. If the law is amended, the governor must sign the bill within 10 days after it is presented to him for it to become law.

(q) Amendatory veto.

(r) Any law may have another effective date specified. Bills passed after June 30 which specify an earlier effective date must receive the approval of three-fifths of the members elected to each house. Iowa: during the last three days of the session. Missouri: if the governor fails in his constitutional duty to return the approved or vetoed bill, the legislature by joint resolution may direct the enrollment of the bill and it becomes law.

(s) The governor must sign or veto all bills presented to him.

(t) Item veto on supplementary appropriation bills and capital construction bill only. The general appropriation bill may not be vetoed.

(u) Bills passed over the governor's veto are effective in 30 days or on date specified in bill, whichever is later.

(v) Senate only.

(w) Appropriations acts. Minnesota: July 1. Missouri: immediately. New Mexico: immediately.

(x) In event of a recess of 30 days or more, legislature may prescribe by joint resolution that laws previously passed and not effective shall take effect 90 days from beginning of recess.

(y) No appropriation can be made in excess of the recommendations contained in the governor's budget unless by a two-thirds vote. The excess is not subject to veto by the governor.

(z) If house of origin is in temporary adjournment on the 45th day, Sundays excepted, after presentation to governor, bill becomes law on day house of origin reconvenes unless returned by governor on that day. If bill is passed between 45th day and 10th day before end of second legislative year of two-year legislature, bill becomes law on day of expiration of legislative year unless returned by governor on day preceding that day. If bill is passed during last 10 days of second legislative year, bill does not become law unless governor signs it by expiration of legislative year.

(aa) A special session of the legislature convenes for the purpose of acting on bills returned by the governor on the 45th day after a sine die adjournment of the legislature in the first year of a two-year legislature. A special session of the legislature convenes for the purpose of acting on bills returned by the governor on the day before the expiration of the second year of a two-year legislature.

(ab) Governor has no approval or veto power.

(ac) Ninety days are required to permit filing of any referendum petition.

(ad) To correct a technical error only.

(ae) Special sessions: first day of the fourth month of adjournment.

(af) Special sessions: first day of the fourth month of adjournment.

(ag) Five days for appropriations bills.

(ah) All laws require approval by secretary of interior.

(ai) Congress may annul.

Table 17
LEGISLATIVE PROCEDURE: TIME LIMITATIONS ON
BILL INTRODUCTION

State or other jurisdiction	Time limit on introduction of legislation	Exceptions granted to time limits on bill introduction
Alabama	24th L day.	House: 4/5 vote of quorum present and voting. Senate: must suspend rules.
Alaska	2nd session only: 35th C day.	2/3 vote of membership. Standing committees. Governor's legislation introduced through the Rules Committee.
Arizona	Regular session: 29th day. Special session: 10th day.	Permission of Rules Committee.
Arkansas	Appropriation bills: 50th day; other bills: 55th day.	2/3 vote of membership.
California	None, except legislative schedule established for committee action.	Legislative schedule may be waived by approval of Rules Committee and a vote of 2/3 of the House.
Colorado	1st session: 60th L day. 2nd session: 30th L day.	Committee on Delayed Bills. Appropriations bills.
Connecticut	Fixed by legislature when adopting rulres for the biennium.	Bills at request of governor for emergency or necessity. Emergency legislation designated by presiding officers. Legislative revision and omnibus validation acts.
Delaware	Discretion of each house.	. . . .
Florida	House: noon 1st day of regular session, except for bills and joint resolutions sponsored by a standing committee. Senate: 11th day, except for general appropriations bills, local bill and joint resolutions.	2/3 vote. Recommendation of Rules Committee.
Georgia	House: 30th L day. Senate: 33rd L day.	House: 3/5 vote. Senate: 2/3 vote.
Hawaii	Constitutional limit: after 19th day and before the mandatory recess held between the 20th and 40th days. Actual deadlines established during the session.	2/3 vote.
Idaho	20th day for individual house members and 12th day for individual senators. 35th day for committees except—House: Appropriations, State Affairs, Revenue and Taxation, and Ways and Means; Senate: Finance, State Affairs, Judiciary, and Rules.	Speaker may designate any committee to serve as a privileged committee either temporarily or for the remainder of the session.
Illinois	House: odd year, April 6 except Senate bills in House, June 1; even year, all bills except committee bills and appropriation bills referred to Rules Committee. Senate: odd year, April 11; even year, bills allowed by the Rules Committee and bills implementing state budget or introduced by standing committees.	House rules governing limitations on the introduction of bills may not be suspended. Senate rules may be suspended by affirmative vote of a majority of senators elected, or if suspension is approved by a majority of Rules Committee, or by a majority of senators present.
Indiana	House: odd year, 16th session day; even year, 4th session day. Senate: odd year, 12th session day; even year, 4th session day.	House: 2/3 vote. Senate: consent of Rules and Legislative Procedure Committee.
Iowa	Individual legislators. House: odd year, Friday of 7th week; even year, Friday of 3rd week; Senate: odd year, Friday of 7th week; even year, Friday of 2nd week. Committee bills: odd year, 11th week; even year, 9th week.	Committee-sponsored bills. Majority vote of membership, unless written request for drafting the bill was submitted before deadline. Senate and House bills co-sponsored by the majority and minority floor leaders.
Kansas	Individuals: 31st C day. Committees: 45th C day. Either house, by resolution, may set an earlier date.	By resolution, either house may make specific exceptions to the deadline for committee bills. Ways and Means and Federal-State Affairs Committees not subject to deadline.
Kentucky	No introductions during final 10 days.	Majority vote of elected members.
Louisiana	15th C day.	2/3 vote of elected members of each house.
Maine	2nd Friday after convening in 1st regular session for drafting requests to Legislative Research: final form to be introduced no later than the 7th Friday following. Second regular session deadlines established by Legislative Council.	Approval of a majority of the members of the Legislative Council. Committee bills. Bills to facilitate legislative business.
Maryland	No introductions during last 35 days. Appropriations bills, 3rd Wednesday of January. New governors, 10 days after convening of legislature.	2/3 vote.
Massachusetts	1st Wednesday of December.	4/5 vote. Request of governor, secretary of administration and finance, special commission or committee with specific reporting dates and home rule petitions.
Michigan	None.	. . . .
Minnesota	None.	. . . .
Mississippi	90-day session: 16th day. 125-day session: 51st day.	2/3 present and voting. Revenue, local and private, and appropriation bills.
Missouri	Odd year: 60th L day. Even year: 30th L day.	Majority of elected members. Request of governor. Appropriation bills.
Montana	Bill drafting requests: individuals, 10th day; committees, 38th day. Introductions: individuals, 18th day; appropriation and revenue bills, 21st day; committees, 40th day.	2/3 vote. Appropriations bills.
Nebraska	10 L days.	Request of governor. With approval of majority of members of a committee and 3/5 elected members of legislature.
Nevada	Bill drafting request only: 30th day.	House: 2/3 present. Committee bills.
New Hampshire	House: all drafting requests must be filed by 5 p.m. Jan. 31; all bills must be approved by signature by April 5 for introduction as House bills. Senate: April 12.	2/3 vote of membership or approval of Joint Rules Committee.
New Jersey	None.	. . . .

State or other jurisdiction	Time limit on introduction of legislation	Exceptions granted to time limits on bill introduction
New Mexico	Odd year only: 30th L day. Appropriations bill. Odd year: final passage in house of origin by 40th C day, second house by 50th C day; even year: final passage 16th and 21st C day.	At request of governor.
New York	Assembly: 1st Tuesday in March for unlimited introduction; each member may introduce up to 10 bills until the last Tuesday in March. Senate: temporary president may designate a final date but not prior to first Tuesday of March; bills recommended by a state department or agency must be submitted to the temporary president by the 1st day of March.	Assembly: unanimous vote except for Fridays; Committee on Rules; by message from Senate; bills from governor, Senate; members elected at special elections after 1st Tuesday in March; Friday introductions only. Senate: bills by governor, attorney general, comptroller, Dept. of Education or the Office of Court Administration must be to the temporary president by the 1st Tuesday of April.
North Carolina	House: local bills and state agency bills by April 1. Senate: local bills and state agency bills, by April 1; all resolutions except those honoring deceased persons, by April 1.	2/3 vote.
North Dakota	Bills: 15th L day. State agency bills: none introduced after Dec. 15 prior to a session except upon approval of a majority of Committee on Delayed Bills. Resolutions: 18th L day. Resolutions proposing constitutional amendments or Legislative Council studies: 33rd L day.	2/3 vote or approval of majority of Committee on Delayed Bills.
Ohio	House: after March 15 of the second regular session, a resolution to end introduction of bills may be passed by a majority vote. Senate: no bills can be introduced after April 30 of first regular session or after last day in February of second regular session.	Majority vote on recommendation of bill by Reference Committee.
Oklahoma	1st session: none. 2nd session: 19th L day.	2/3 vote. Revenue and appropriation bills.
Oregon	House: 29th C day. Senate: 36th C day following the election of a Senate President.	Approval of House Committee on Legislative Rules and Operations, Senate Rules Committee, Speaker of House, Joint Committee on Ways and Means, substitute measures sponsored by a committee, priority bills and measures requested to be drafted by counsel no later than 36th C day and received by the senator no later than the 50th C day.
Pennsylvania	None.	. . . .
Rhode Island	Senate: 40th L day; House: 38th L day. Except for private and local bills and certain resolutions.	Senate: Majority members present. House: 2/3 members present.
South Carolina	House: April 15, or if received from Senate prior to May 1. After April 15, introduction and committee reference only. Senate: received from House prior to May 1.	House: 2/3 vote. General or deficiency appropriations act or joint resolution approving or disapproving state agency regulations. Senate: 2/3 vote.
South Dakota	40-day session: 14th day. 35-day session: 10th day. All committee bills one day later.	2/3 vote. General appropriations act.
Tennessee	House: general bills, 20th L day. Senate: general bills, 10th L day. Resolutions, 30th L day.	House: 2/3 vote. Senate: unanimous consent of Committee on Delayed Bills or 2/3 vote.
Texas	60 C days.	4/5 vote. Local bills. Emergency appropriations. Emergency matters by governor.
Utah	30th C day.	Majority vote.
Vermont	House: odd year, 5 weeks except proposals delivered to the Legislative Drafting Division by that time, then 12 weeks; even year, by agreement of Rules Committee may be prefiled by Sept. 1 of odd year for next year. Senate: odd year, 53rd C day; even year must be filed with the Legislative Drafting Division 25 days before session begins.(a)	2/3 vote. Consent of Rules Committee. Appropriations and revenue bills. House only: committee bills introduced within 10 days after 1st Tuesday in March.
Virginia	Deadlines are set during the session. Municipal charter bills must be introduced on the 1st day of session.	Unanimous vote. At request of governor.
Washington	Constitution: by 50th day. Stricter limits usually established by concurrent resolution at beginning of each session. 1981 limit: code revisor's list, 30th day, introduced by 36th day. Senate: 46th day.	2/3 vote of elected members.
West Virginia	House: 50th C day. Senate: 41st C day.	House: 2/3 vote of all members of appropriate house present and voting.
Wisconsin	None.	. . . .
Wyoming	Odd year: 18th L day. Even year: 5th L day.	Senate: unanimous vote of elected members. House: 2/3 vote.
American Samoa	House: 15th L day. Senate: 15th L day.	2/3 vote of elected members.
Guam	None.	. . . .
Puerto Rico	60th day.	Majority vote.
Virgin Islands	None.	. . . .

Key: L—Legislative day
  C—Calendar day.
  (a) For 1982 session only, and for House bills only; the deadline for introductions will depend on date of submission of draft requests. If received prior to second Monday in December 1981, it will be drafted in long form (normal); if after, will be drafted only in short form (narrative). Dates for introduction have changed to 10 days following town meetings, which is first Tuesday in March.

Table 18
LEGISLATIVE PROCEDURE: BILL INTRODUCTION AND REFERENCE

State or other jurisdiction	Pre-season bill filing		Bills referred to committee by		Bill referral restricted by rule		Bill carryover†
	First session	Second session	House	Senate	House	Senate	
Alabama	B	B(a,b)	Spkr.	Pres.	...	...	No
Alaska	B	B	Spkr.	Pres.	★	★	Yes
Arizona	B	B	Spkr.	Pres.	...	...	No
Arkansas	B	...	Spkr.	Rules Cmte.	★	★	...
California	(c)	(c)	Rules Cmte.	Rules Cmte.	...	★	Yes(d)
Colorado	B	B	Spkr.	Pres.	...	...	No
Connecticut	B	B	Spkr.	Pres. Pro Tem.	★	★	No
Delaware	B	B	Spkr.	Pres.	★	...	Yes
Florida	B	B	Spkr.	Pres.	★	★	No
Georgia	No	No	Spkr.	Pres.	...	...	Yes
Hawaii	No	No	Spkr.	Pres.	★	★	Yes
Idaho	No	No	Spkr.	Pres.	...	...	No
Illinois	B	B	Cmte. on Assignment	Cmte. on Assignment	...	...	Yes(e)
Indiana	B	B	Spkr.	Pres. Pro Tem.	...	...	No
Iowa	B	B	Spkr.	Pres.	...	★	Yes
Kansas	B	B	Spkr.	Pres.	★	★	Yes
Kentucky	B	...	Cmte. on Cmtes.	Cmte. on Cmtes.	★	★	...
Louisiana	B	B(a)	Spkr.(f)	Pres.(f)	★	★	No
Maine	B	No	—Secy. of Senate & Clerk of House(f,g)—		...	...	No
Maryland	B	B(a,b)	Spkr.	Pres.	(h)	(h)	No
Massachusetts	B	B	Clerk(f)	Clerk(f)	★	★	No
Michigan	No	No	Spkr.	Maj. Ldr.	...	...	Yes
Minnesota	No	B	Spkr.	Pres.	(h)	(h)	Yes
Mississippi	B	B(a)	Spkr.	Pres.	...	...	No
Missouri	B	B	Spkr.	Pres. Pro Tem.	★	★	Yes(i)
Montana	B	...	Spkr.	Pres.	...	...	...
Nebraska	S	S	U	Ref. Cmte.	U	★	Yes
Nevada	B	...	Spkr.	Maj. Ldr.	...	★	...
New Hampshire	B	...	Spkr.	Pres.	★	★	...
New Jersey	B	No	Spkr.	Pres.	...	...	Yes
New Mexico	No	No	Spkr.	Presid. Offr.(j)	(h)	(h)	No
New York	B	B	Spkr.	Pres. Pro Tem.	...	...	Yes
North Carolina	No	No	Spkr.	Pres.	(h)	(h)	Yes
North Dakota	B	...	Spkr.	Pres.	★	★	...
Ohio	B	B	Ref. Cmte.	Ref. Cmte.	...	...	Yes
Oklahoma	B	B	Spkr.	Pres. Pro Tem.	...	...	Yes
Oregon	B	...	Spkr.	Pres.	★	...	...
Pennsylvania	B	B	Spkr.	Pres.	...	...	Yes
Rhode Island	B	B	Spkr.	Pres.	...	...	Yes
South Carolina	B	B	Spkr.	Presid. Offr.	...	...	Yes
South Dakota	B	B	Spkr.	Pres.	...	...	No
Tennessee	B	B	Spkr.	Spkr.	...	★	Yes
Texas	B	...	Spkr.	Pres.	★	...	...
Utah	B	B	Spkr.	Pres.	...	...	No
Vermont	B	B	Spkr.	Pres.	★	★	Yes
Virginia	B	B	Spkr.	Clerk	★	★	Yes
Washington	B	B	Spkr.	Pres.	...	...	Yes
West Virginia	B	B	Spkr.	Pres.	...	...	No
Wisconsin	B	B	Presid. Offr.	Presid. Offr.	...	...	Yes
Wyoming	B	No	Spkr.	Pres.	...	...	No
American Samoa	B	B	Spkr.	Pres.	★	★	Yes
Guam	S	S	U	Rules Cmte.	U	★	Yes
Puerto Rico	B	B	Pres.	Pres.	★	★	Yes
Virgin Islands	S	S	U	Pres.	U	...	Yes

† Bills carry over from the first year of a legislature to the second. Bills generally do not carry over after an intervening legislative election.

Key: B—Both chambers.
S—Senate
H—House
U—Unicameral

(a) Four-year legislature. Louisiana: pre-season filing allowed before every session.

(b) Bills cannot be pre-filed after last session of the term.

(c) California has a continuous legislature. Bills may be introduced at any time during the biennium. However, legislative schedule is established for committee action.

(d) Only bills which have passed the house of origin by Jan. 30 of the second year of the biennium may carry over.

(e) Some limitation by legislative rule.

(f) Subject to approval or disapproval. Louisiana: majority of those present and voting. Maine: by membership of either house. Massachusetts: by presiding officer.

(g) Should there be no agreement between the clerk and secretary, the speaker and president make the assignment. If they cannot agree, the Legislative Council resolves the issue.

(h) No, except: Maryland—local bills in house, and local bills and bills creating judgeships in senate; Minnesota—bills on government structure which go to governmental operations committees and bills appropriating funds which go to Finance Committee; New Mexico—House Appropriation and Finance Committee, Senate Finance Committee; North Carolina—Appropriations, Finance and Ways and Means Committees.

(i) The constitution authorizes bill carryover; however, the House and Senate refuse to hear any bill carried over by the other house.

(j) At request of sponsoring senator.

Table 19
LEGISLATIVE PROCEDURE: STANDING COMMITTEES*

State or other jurisdiction	Committee members appointed by		Committee chairmen appointed by		Number of standing committees during regular 1981 session			Average number of committee assignments per legislator	
	Senate	House	Senate	House	Senate	House	Joint	Senate	House
Alabama	P(a)	S	P(a)	S	12	21	...	5	3
Alaska	CC,E	CC,E	CC,E	CC,E	9	9	...	3	2
Arizona	P	S	P	S	11	17	...	3.5	4
Arkansas	CC	S	CC	S	10	10	3	2	2
California	CR	S	CR	S	19	25	...	4	4
Colorado	MjL, MnL	S, Mnl	MjL	S	10	13	...	2	3
Connecticut	PT	S	PT	S	...	...	17	2.5	2
Delaware	PT	S	PT	S	16	18	1	4	3
Florida	P	S	P	S	18	28	...	3	3
Georgia	CC	S	CC	S	21	28	...	3	3
Hawaii	(b)	(b)	(c)	(c)	16	21	...	6	6
Idaho	P	S	P	S	9	13	...	2.3	2.5
Illinois	CC	S, MnL	P	S	19	23	...	3.66	2.29
Indiana	PT	S	PT	S	16	22	...	4	3
Iowa	P(a)	S	P(a)	S	15	16	...	3.5	4
Kansas	CC	S	CC	S	18	20	2	4.8	2.8
Kentucky	CC	CC	CC	CC	15	15	...	3	3
Louisiana	P	S	P	S	15	15	...	2.9	2.3
Maine	P	S	P	S	...	...	19	2	1.5
Maryland	P	S	P	S	5	6	...	1	1
Massachusetts	P	S	P	S	5	5	21	(d)	(d)
Michigan	MjL	S	MjL	S	15	33	...	2.3	3.4
Minnesota	(e)	S	(e)	S	17	18	...	3	3
Mississippi	P(a)	S	P(a)	S	32	28	4	7	4
Missouri	PT(f)	S	PT	S	24	50	...	7	3
Montana	CC	S	CC	S	16	15	...	2.9	2.5
Nebraska	CC	U	(g)	U	14	U	...	2.2	U
Nevada	MjL, MnL	S, MnL	MjL	S	9	13	...	3	3
New Hampshire	P	S	P	S	16	23	...	3.25	1
New Jersey	P	S	P	S	14	16	7	3.1	1.8
New Mexico	CC	S	CC	S	7	12	...	2	2
New York	PT	S	PT	S	28	31	...	6.5	4
North Carolina	P	S	P	S	38	59	...	8	9
North Dakota	CC	S	CC	S	11	11	1	2	2
Ohio	CC	S	CC	S	11	22	...	3	3
Oklahoma	PT	S	CR	S	9	28	1	4	4
Oregon	P	S	P	S	18	17	...	3	2
Pennsylvania	PT	CC,E	PT	S	20	24	...	4.8	2.6
Rhode Island	MjL	S	MjL	S	6	4	7	2	1
South Carolina	Sr	S	E	E	15	11	3	5	1
South Dakota	MjL	S	MjL	S	10	10	...	2.5	2
Tennessee	S	S	S	S	9	11	...	2	2
Texas	P(a)	S(h)	P(a)	S	9	31	...	3	3
Utah	P	S	P	S	11	11	2	3	3.2
Vermont	CC	S	CC	S	12	15	3	3	1
Virginia	E	S	(i)	S	11	20	...	4	3
Washington	P,CC	S,CC	CC	S,CC	16	19	...	3	3
West Virginia	P	S	P	S	16	13	...	6	3
Wisconsin	(j)	S, MnL	(j)	S	12	32	9	2	3
Wyoming	P(b)	S(b)	P(b)	S(b)	12	12	1	2	2
American Samoa	P,E	S,E	P	S	16	15	1	4	4
Guam	(k)	U	E	U	10	U	...	4	U
Puerto Rico	P	S	P	S	15	18	...	N.A.	N.A.
Virgin Islands	P	U	P	U	15	U	...	5.25	U

*Committees which regularly consider legislation during a legislative session.

Key: S—Speaker
P—President
CC—Committee on Committees
E—Election
CR—Committee on Rules
MjL-Majority leader
MnL—Minority leader
PT—President pro tempore
Sr—Seniority
U—Unicameral
N.A.—Not available.

(a) Lieutenant governor.
(b) Party caucus.
(c) Majority caucus.
(d) Senate: Democrats 3.7, Republicans 4.5; House: Democrats 1.8, Republicans 1.8
(e) Subcommittee of Rules Committee.
(f) Minority caucus.
(g) Secret ballot by legislature as a whole.
(h) Modified seniority system.
(i) Senior member of the committee is automatically chairman.
(j) Committee on Senate Organization.
(k) Chairman of each committee.

Table 20
LEGISLATIVE PROCEDURE: STANDING COMMITTEE ACTION

State or other jurisdiction	Uniform rules of committee procedure			Public access to committee meetings required				Recorded roll call on vote to report bill to floor	
				Open to public		Advance notice (in days)			
	House	Senate	Joint	House	Senate	House	Senate	House	Senate
Alabama	No	Yes	...	Yes	Yes	...	...	Al	Nv
Alaska	No	No	...	Yes	Yes	...	...	Sm	Sm
Arizona	No	Yes	...	Yes	Yes	5	(a)	Nv	Nv
Arkansas	Yes	Yes	Yes	Yes	Yes	2	2	Sm	Sm
California	Yes	Yes	Yes	Yes	Yes	4	4	Al	Al
Colorado	Yes	Yes	...	Yes	Yes	...	...	Al	Al
Connecticut	No	No	Yes	Yes(b)	Yes(b)	1	1	Al	Al
Delaware	Yes	Yes	No	Yes	Yes	(c)	(c)	Al	Al
Florida	Yes	Yes	...	Yes	Yes	7	2(d)	Al	Al
Georgia	No	No	...	Yes	Yes	...	...	Nv	Nv
Hawaii	Yes	Yes	...	Yes	Yes	2	2	Al	Al
Idaho	Yes	Yes	...	Yes	Yes	...	...	Us	Us
Illinois	Yes	Yes	No	Yes	Yes	6	6.5	Al	Al
Indiana	No	No	...	Yes	Yes	3	1	Al	Al
Iowa	Yes	Yes	...	Yes	Yes	...	...	Al	Al
Kansas	Yes	Yes	...	Yes	Yes	...	(c)	Sm	Sm
Kentucky	No	No	...	Yes	Yes	...	3	Al	Al
Louisiana	Yes	Yes	...	Yes	Yes	1(e)	1(e)	Sm	Al
Maine	No	No	Yes	Yes	Yes	(c)	(c)	Sm	Sm
Maryland	Yes	Yes	...	Yes	Yes	(c)	(c)	Al	Al
Massachusetts	No	No	No	Yes	Yes	...	...	Nv	Nv
Michigan	Yes	Yes	...	Yes	Yes	(f)	(f)	Al	Al
Minnesota	Yes	Yes	Yes	Yes	Yes	3	3	Sm	Sm
Mississippi	No	No	No	Yes	Yes	...	...	Sm	Sm
Missouri	Yes	Yes	Yes	Yes	Yes	1	1	Al	Al
Montana	No	No	...	Yes	Yes	(g)	(g)	Al	Al
Nebraska	Yes	U	U	Yes	U	5-7	U	Al	U
Nevada	Yes	Yes	...	Yes	Yes	(c)	5(h)	Al	Al
New Hampshire	No	Yes	...	Yes	Yes	3	3	Al	Al
New Jersey	Yes	Yes	...	Yes	Yes	5	5	Al	Al
New Mexico	No	No	...	Yes	Yes	...	...	Sm	Al
New York	Yes	Yes	...	Yes	Yes	7	7	Al	Al
North Carolina	No	No	No	Yes(b)	Yes(b)	(c)	(c)	Sm	Sm
North Dakota	No	No	...	Yes	Yes	(i)	(i)	Al	Al
Ohio	Yes	Yes	...	Yes	Yes	5	(c)	Al	Al
Oklahoma	Yes	Yes	...	Yes	Yes	(c)	(c)	Sm	Sm
Oregon	Yes	Yes	...	Yes	Yes	1(j)	1(k)	Al	Al
Pennsylvania	No	No	...	Yes	Yes	3	3	Al	Al
Rhode Island	Yes	Yes	Yes	Yes	Yes	...	...	Sm	Sm
South Carolina	Yes	Yes	Yes	Yes	Yes	1	1	Sm	Sm
South Dakota	Yes	Yes	...	Yes	Yes	2	2	Al	Al
Tennessee	Yes	Yes	...	Yes	Yes	(l)	(l)	Sm	Sm
Texas	No	Yes	...	Yes	Yes	1	5	Sm	Al
Utah	Yes	Yes	Yes	Yes	Yes	1	1	Al	Al
Vermont	Yes	Yes	Yes	Yes	Yes	...	...	Sm	Sm
Virginia	Yes	Yes	...	Yes	Yes(m)	(c)	(c)	Al	Al
Washington	Yes	Yes	...	Yes	Yes	5	5	Sm	Sm
West Virginia	No	No	...	Yes	Yes	...	...	Sm	Sm
Wisconsin	Yes	Yes	Yes	Yes	Yes	7	7	Al	Al
Wyoming	No	No	No	Yes	Yes	...	...	Sm	Sm
American Samoa	No	No	No	Yes	Yes	(d)	1.5	Nv	Nv
Guam	Yes	U	U	Yes(b)	U	7	U	Al	U
Puerto Rico	Yes	Yes	...	Yes	Yes	...	...	Nv	Nv
Virgin Islands	Yes	U	U	Yes	U	7(n)	U	Us	U

Key: U—Unicameral
Al—Always
Us—Usually
Sm—Sometimes
Nv—Never

(a) Rules: Thursday of previous week. Statute: 24 hours.
(b) Certain matters specified by statute can be discussed in executive session. Connecticut: upon a 2/3 vote of committee members present and voting and stating the reason for such executive session. North Carolina: appropriations committees are required to sit jointly in open session. Guam: hearings are open to the public but meetings may be closed.
(c) No specified time. Kansas: "due notice" is required by house rules. Maine: usually seven days notice given. Maryland: "from time to time," usually seven days. Nevada: "adequate notice." North Carolina: notice must be given in the House or Senate; two methods to waive notice in the Senate. Ohio: "due notice," usually seven days. Virginia: notice is published in the daily calendar.
(d) During session: two days notice for first 45 days, two hours thereafter.
(e) One day during session, five days during interim.
(f) Committees meet on regular schedule during sessions. Eighteen-hour notice for rescheduled or special meetings unless legislature is adjourned or recessed for less than 18 hours.

(g) There is an informal agreement to give three days notice.
(h) Public hearings on bills or resolutions of "high public importance" must receive five calendar days notice. All other committee meetings must have 24 hours notice.
(i) Rules require posting of bills and resolutions to be considered at each meeting and provide deadlines for such posting depending upon the schedules for particular committees.
(j) Except in case of meeting to resolve conflicts or inconsistencies among two or more measures, in which case posting and notice to the public shall be given immediately upon call of the meeting, and notice of the meeting shall be announced on the floor if the Senate is in session.
(k) In case of actual emergency, a meeting may be held upon such notice as is appropriate to the circumstances.
(l) Committees meet on a fixed schedule during sessions. Five days notice required during interim.
(m) Committee meetings are required to be open for final vote on bill.
(n) Advanced notice may be waived if the "committee determines there is good cause to conduct a meeting sooner." In that case, notice must be given at least 48 hours in advance. Items on the agenda may be considered by unanimous consent.

218

Table 21
STAFF FOR LEGISLATIVE STANDING COMMITTEES

State or other jurisdiction	Committees receiving staff assistance				Organizational source of staff services†							
	Professional		Secretarial/ clerical		Joint central agency(a)		Chamber agency(b)		Caucus or leadership		Committee or committee chairman	
	Senate	House	Senate	House	Prof.	Clerk	Prof.	Clerk	Prof.	Clerk	Prof.	Clerk
Alabama	(c)	(c)	★	★	B	...	...	...	...	...	B	B
Alaska	★	★	★	★	B	...	...	B	B	B	B(d)	B
Arizona	★	★	★	★	B(e)	...	B	B	B	...	B	...
Arkansas	★	★	★	★	B	B	...	B	...	...	...	...
California	★	★	★	★	...	...	B	B	...	...	...	...
Colorado	★	★	...	...	B	...	...	...	...	...	...	...
Connecticut	★(f)	★(f)	★(f)	★(f)	★(f)	★(f)	...	...	...	...	...	...
Delaware	★(c)	★(c)	★(g)	★(g)	B	B	...	B	B	...	...	...
Florida	★	★	★	★	...	...	...	...	...	...	B	B
Georgia	★	★	★(g)	★(g)	B	...	S	...	...	B	H	...
Hawaii	(h)	(h)	★	★	L	L	B	B	B	B	B	B
Idaho	(c)	(c)	★	★	B	...	...	...	...	...	...	B
Illinois	★	★	★	★	...	...	...	...	B	B	...	...
Indiana	★	★	★	...	B	...	...	...	...	S	...	...
Iowa	★	★	★	★	B	...	...	B(i)	B	...	...	B(i)
Kansas	★	★	★	★	B	B	...	B	...	B	...	B
Kentucky	★	★	★	★	B	B	...	...	...	...	...	...
Louisiana	★	★	★	★	...	...	...	B	...	...	B	B
Maine	★(f)	★(f)	★(f)	★(f)	L	...	...	...	...	...	...	(g)
Maryland	★	★	★	★	B	...	...	...	...	...	...	B
Massachusetts	★	★	★	★	B	...	B	...	B	B	B	...
Michigan	★	★	★	★	...	...	...	H	B	...	B	B
Minnesota	★	★	★	★	...	...	...	...	...	...	B	B
Mississippi	•	•	★	★	B	B	...	...	...	...	...	...
Missouri	★(c,g)	★(c,g,j)	★	★	...	...	...	...	B	B	B	B
Montana	★	★	★	★	B	B	...	...	...	...	...	B
Nebraska	★	U	★	U	...	...	L	L	...	...	L	L
Nevada	(c)	(c)	★	★	B	...	...	B	...	...	...	...
New Hampshire	•	•	★(g)	★(g)	B	B	...	...	H	...	...	...
New Jersey	★	★	★	★	B	B	...	...	...	...	...	...
New Mexico	•	•	★	★	B	...	...	B	...	...	...	...
New York	★	★	★	★	B	B	B	B	B	B	B	B
North Carolina	•	•	★	★	B	...	B	B	B	...	...	...
North Dakota	(c)	(c)	★	★	B	...	...	B	...	...	...	...
Ohio	★	★	★	★	B	...	...	...	B	B	...	...
Oklahoma	•	•	★	★	...	...	B	B	...	...	...	...
Oregon	★	★	★	★	...	...	...	...	...	...	B	B
Pennsylvania	★	★	★	★	...	...	B	B	...	...	B	B
Rhode Island	★	★	★	★	...	...	...	...	...	...	B	B
South Carolina	•	•	★	★	B	B	...	...	...	B	B	B
South Dakota	★	★	★	★	B	...	...	...	...	B	...	...
Tennessee	★	★	★	★	B	...	...	...	B	B	S	B
Texas	★	★	★	★	B	B	B(g)	...	...	...	B	B
Utah	★	★	★	★	B	...	...	...	...	B	...	...
Vermont	★	★	★	★	B	...	...	...	...	...	...	...
Virginia	★	★	★	★	B	...	B	B	...	...	...	B(i)
Washington	★	★	★	★	...	...	B	B	B	B	B	...
West Virginia	★	★	★	★	B	B	B	B	...	...	...	B
Wisconsin	★	★	★	★	B	...	B	B	...	...	B	B
Wyoming	★(g)	★(g)	★	★	B	...	...	B	...	...	...	...
American Samoa	★(g)	★(g)	...	...	B	...	...	...	...	...	...	...
Guam	★	U	★	U	L	L	...	...	L	L	L	L
Puerto Rico	★	★	★	★	B	...	...	...	...	...	B	L
Virgin Islands	★	U	★	U	L	L	...	...	...	...	...	L

†Multiple entries reflect a combination of organizational location of services.

Key:
H—House
S—Senate
B—Both chambers
L—Legislature
U—Unicameral
★—All committees
•—Some committees
...—None

(a) Includes legislative council or service agency, central management agency.
(b) Includes chamber management agency, office of clerk or secretary and house or senate research office.

(c) Financial Committee(s) only.
(d) Some committees are provided additional funding for special studies for the purpose of hiring expanded staff.
(e) The Joint Budget Committee provides staff assistance to both appropriations committees.
(f) Standing committees are joint house and senate committees.
(g) Provided on a pool basis.
(h) All professional committee staff (except finance committees) during session only. During interim, assistance provided by year-round majority and minority research offices.
(i) The senate secretary and house clerk maintain supervision of committee clerks. Iowa: during the session each committee selects its own clerk.
(j) Judicial committee only.

Table 22
LEGISLATIVE APPROPRIATIONS PROCESS:
BUDGET DOCUMENTS AND BILLS

State or other jurisdiction	Legal source of deadline: Constitutional	Statutory	Submission date relative to convening: Prior to session	Within one week	Within two weeks	Within one month	Over one month	Budget bill introduction: Same time as budget document	Another time	None until cmte. review	Usual member of budget bills
Alabama	...	★	...	2nd da.	...	...	...	★	...	...	2
Alaska	...	★	...	★	...	...	...	★	...	...	1
Arizona	...	★	...	★	...	...	...	...	...	★(a)	3-4
Arkansas	...	...	...	...	★(b)	...	...	...	...	★	450
California	★	...	...	...	...	...	★(c)	★	...	...	1
Colorado	...	★	...	...	★(d)	...	...	...	...	★	1
Connecticut	...	★	...	...	...	★(e)	...	★	...	...	1
Delaware	...	★	...	...	...	Feb. 1	...	★(f)	...	...	1
Florida	...	★	30 da.	...	...	...	...	...	...	★(g)	1
Georgia	★	...	...	★	...	...	...	★	...	...	2(h)
Hawaii	...	★	20 da.	...	...	...	...	...	★	...	1
Idaho	...	★	...	★	...	...	...	...	★	★	100
Illinois	...	★	...	...	...	...	★	...	★	...	100
Indiana	...	★	7 da.(i)	...	...	...	...	★	...	...	3(j)
Iowa	...	★	...	...	...	★	...	...	...	★(g)	20
Kansas	...	★	...	...	...	★(e)	...	...	★(k)	...	15-25
Kentucky	...	...	...	...	...	...	★(l)	★	...	...	1
Louisiana	...	★	...	1st da.	...	...	...	...	(m)	...	2
Maine	...	★	...	...	★(n)	...	...	★	...	...	2
Maryland	★	...	★(n)	...	...	...	...	★(o)	...	...	1
Massachusetts	★	...	...	...	...	★(n)	...	★(p)	...	...	5
Michigan	...	★	...	...	★(q)	...	...	★	...	...	15-16
Minnesota	...	★	...	...	...	★	...	...	...	★	7
Mississippi	...	★	Dec. 15	...	...	...	...	...	...	★	240
Missouri	★	...	...	...	...	★	...	★	...	...	13-16
Montana	...	★	...	1st da.	...	...	...	...	★	...	6
Nebraska	...	★	...	...	★	...	...	...	...	★(f)	5-8
Nevada	...	★	...	...	★	...	...	...	...	★	5
New Hampshire	...	★	...	...	...	...	★	...	...	★	2
New Jersey	...	★	...	...	...	★(n)	...	...	...	★	1
New Mexico	...	★	★(r)	...	...	...	...	★	...	...	1
New York	★	...	...	...	★(n)	...	...	★(s)	...	...	30-40
North Carolina	...	...	★(b)	...	...	...	...	★	...	...	2
North Dakota	...	★	3rd da.(t)	...	...	...	...	★	...	...	80
Ohio	...	★	...	...	...	★(n)	...	★	...	...	3-4
Oklahoma	...	★	...	★	...	...	...	★	...	...	90
Oregon	...	★	Dec. 1(n)	...	...	...	...	★	...	...	150
Pennsylvania	...	★	...	...	...	...	★(n,u)	...	...	★	141
Rhode Island	...	★	...	...	...	...	★(v)	★	...	...	1
South Carolina	...	★	1st Tues. in Jan.	...	...	...	...	...	...	★	2
South Dakota	...	★	Dec. 1	...	...	...	...	...	...	★	1
Tennessee	...	★	...	...	★(n)	...	...	★	...	...	1
Texas	...	★	...	★	...	...	...	★	...	...	1
Utah	...	★	...	...	★(e)	...	...	...	...	★	1
Vermont	...	★	...	...	...	★	...	...	...	★	1
Virginia	...	★	...	★	...	...	...	★	...	...	1
Washington	...	★	Dec. 20	...	...	...	...	...	★	...	3(j)
West Virginia	★	...	...	1st da.(n)	...	...	...	★	...	...	1
Wisconsin	...	★	...	...	...	★(x)	...	★	...	...	1
Wyoming	...	★	Jan. 1	...	...	...	...	...	...	★	4
American Samoa	...	...	★(b)	...	...	...	...	★	★(y)	...	1
Guam	...	★	...	...	...	...	...	★	...	...	1
Puerto Rico	★	...	...	...	...	★	...	...	...	★	2
Virgin Islands	...	★	...	...	...	★(z)	...	★	...	...	8-10

(a) General appropriations bill only.

(b) By custom only.

(c) Session begins in December. Within the first 10 days of each calendar year.

(d) Copies of agency budgets to be presented to the legislature by November 1. Governor's budget usually is presented in January.

(e) Even year. Connecticut—first day; Kansas—second day; Utah—first day.

(f) Executive budget bill is introduced and used as working tool for committee. Delaware: after hearings on executive bill, a new bill is then introduced. The committee bill is considered by the legislature.

(g) Executive submits bill, but it is not introduced; used as a working tool by committee.

(h) One appropriations bill amends the current appropriation, the other appropriates funds for the coming fiscal year.

(i) Budget document submitted prior to session does not necessarily reflect budget message which is given sometime during the first three weeks of session.

(j) There are three basic budget bills: one for conduct of state government, one for construction of state properties, one for highways.

(k) Within one month for most bills; however, some are introduced later.

(l) No set time.

(m) Subject to same 15-day constitutional limit as other bills.

(n) Later for first session of a new governor. Maine—six weeks; Maryland—10 days; Massachusetts—two months; New Jersey—February 15; New York—February 1; Ohio—March 16; Oregon—February 1;

Pennsylvania—first full week in March; Tennessee—March 1; West Virginia—one month.

(o) Appropriations bills other than the budget bill (supplementary) may be introduced at any time. They must provide their own tax source and may not be enacted until the budget bill is enacted.

(p) General Appropriations Act only.

(q) Long-range capital budget: 30 days.

(r) Statutes provide for submission by 25th legislative day; however, the executive budget is usually presented by the first day of the session. The legislative budget is usually presented on the first day or at the prelegislative session conference of the standing finance committees.

(s) Governor has 30 days to amend or complete submission bills which enact the recommendations contained in this executive budget, computed from the designated submission date for the budget.

(t) For whole legislature. The Legislative Council only receives budget on December 1.

(u) Submitted by governor as soon as possible after General Assembly organizes, but not later than the first full week in February.

(v) Twenty-fourth legislative day. Legislature normally meets for four legislative days per week.

(w) Must submit confidential copy to fiscal analyst 30 days prior to session.

(x) Last Tuesday in January. A later submission date may be requested by the governor.

(y) Budget presented prior to session.

(z) Organic Act specifies at opening of each regular session; statute specifies on or before May 30.

Table 23
STAFF FOR INDIVIDUAL LEGISLATORS

State or other jurisdiction	Senate — Capitol — Personal	Senate — Capitol — Shared — Number(a)	Senate — Capitol — Shared — Pool	Senate — District	House — Capitol — Personal	House — Capitol — Shared — Number(a)	House — Capitol — Shared — Pool	House — District
Alabama	...	...	SO	...	...	...	YR	...
Alaska	YR(b)	...	...	YR(b)	YR(b)	...	...	YR(b)
Arizona	...	YR 2	...	...	...	YR 5	...	...
Arkansas	...	...	SO	IO(c)	...	...	SO	IO(c)
California	YR	...	...	YR	YR	...	...	YR
Colorado	...	...	YR	...	...	...	YR	...
Connecticut	SO(d)	...	YR	...	SO(d)	...	YR	...
Delaware	YR(e)	...	SO	...	YR(e)	...	SO	...
Florida	YR	...	...	YR(c)	YR	...	...	YR(c)
Georgia	...	...	YR	...	...	...	YR	...
Hawaii	SO(f)	YR(f)	...	...	SO(f)	YR(f)	...	...
Idaho	...	...	...	...	...	...	...	...
Illinois	YR	...	...	YR(c)	...	YR 2-3	...	YR
Indiana	...	YR 5-6	...	...	...	YR 8-9	...	...
Iowa	YR(e)	YR 1.25	...	...	YR(e)	YR 2.2	...	...
Kansas	SO	...	SO	...	...	SO 1-3	SO	...
Kentucky	...	...	YR	...	...	...	YR	...
Louisiana	SO	...	...	YR(g)	...	...	...	YR(g)
Maine	...	...	SO	...	...	...	SO	...
Maryland	SO(c)	...	...	YR(c)	...	...	...	SO(c)
Massachusetts	YR	...	...	...	YR	...	...	...
Michigan	YR	...	...	...	YR	...	...	...
Minnesota	YR	YR 2	SO	...	YR	YR 3	SO	...
Mississippi	...	...	SO	...	...	...	SO	...
Missouri	YR	...	...	YR	SO	...	IO	...
Montana	...	...	SO	...	...	...	SO	...
Nebraska	YR	...	...	...	Unicameral			
Nevada	...	...	YR	...	...	...	YR	...
New Hampshire	...	...	SO	...	...	...	YR	...
New Jersey	YR(g)	...	...	YR(g)	YR(g)	...	...	YR(g)
New Mexico	...	SO 2-10	...	...	...	SO 2-10	...	...
New York	YR,SO(c)	...	...	YR(c)	YR(c)	...	...	YR(c)
North Carolina	SO	...	...	...	SO	...	...	...
North Dakota	...	...	SO	...	...	...	SO	...
Ohio	YR	...	...	...	YR(e)	...	YR	...
Oklahoma	SO	...	...	...	SO	...	...	...
Oregon	SO	...	...	...	YR(c)	...	...	...
Pennsylvania	YR	...	...	YR	YR	...	...	(b)
Rhode Island	...	...	SO	...	...	...	SO	...
South Carolina	...	YR 2	...	YR(h)	...	...	YR	YR(h)
South Dakota	...	...	...	...	...	...	...	...
Tennessee	...	SO 2-3	SO	...	...	SO 2-4	SO	...
Texas	YR(c)	...	SO	YR(c)	YR(c)	...	SO	YR(c)
Utah	...	SO 4-5(d)	YR	...	...	SO 7(d)	YR	...
Vermont	...	...	YR	...	...	...	YR	...
Virginia	YR(c)	SO 2	...	YR(c)	YR(c)	SO 3	...	YR(c)
Washington	YR	...	...	...	SO	...	...	...
West Virginia	...	...	SO	...	...	...	SO	...
Wisconsin	YR	...	...	YR(c)	...	YR 2	...	...
Wyoming	...	...	SO	...	...	...	SO	...
American Samoa	...	...	SO	...	...	...	SO	...
Guam	YR	...	...	...	Unicameral			
Puerto Rico	YR	...	...	...	YR	...	...	...
Virgin Islands	YR(c)	...	...	...	Unicameral			

Key:
YR—Year-round
SO—Session only
IO—Interim only

(a) Number of legislators per staff assistant.

(b) District office staff is available year-round, part of the year, full time or part time as authorized.

(c) Staff is provided by the legislator through an expense allotment given for this purpose. All other staff is hired directly by the legislature.

(d) There is an intern program which provides session staff to some legislators.

(e) Leaders only. Delaware: some legislative leaders also have part-time clerical assistance during interim. Ohio: includes committee chairmen.

(f) Varies. Hawaii: during interim, each legislator is allowed staff assistance for not more than 20 hours a week.

(g) District legislative assistants are often used at the capitol during the session, and in the district the rest of the year. Louisiana: in some cases this is not the same person.

(h) Most county legislative delegations have an office in their county with a secretary. Some large counties have additional staff.

Table 24
FISCAL NOTES: CONTENT AND DISTRIBUTION

State or other jurisdiction	Content						Distribution						
							Legislators			Appropriations committee			
	Intent or purpose of bill	Cost involved	Projected future cost	Proposed source of revenue	Fiscal impact on local government	Other	All	Available on request	Bill sponsor	Members	Chairman only	Fiscal staff	Executive budget staff
Alabama	...	★	...	★	★(a)	...	★(b)	...	...	...	...	...	...
Alaska	...	★	★	★(c)	...	...	★(d)	...	...	...	...	...	...
Arizona	...	★	★	★	★	...	★	...	...	...	...	★	★
Arkansas	★(e)	★(e)	★(e)	...	★	...	★	...	...	...	...	...	...
California	★	★	★	★	★	...	★	...	...	...	...	★	★
Colorado	★	★	★	★	★	...	★	...	...	...	...	★	...
Connecticut	...	★	★	...	★	...	...	★	...	...	...	★	...
Delaware	...	★	★	...	...	★(f)	...	★	...	★	...	★	★
Florida	★	★	★	★	★	★(g)	★	...	...	...	...	★	★
Georgia	...	★	★	★	★	...	...	★	...	...	...	...	...
Hawaii	...	...	...	...	...	...	...	...	...	...	...	...	...
Idaho	★	★	★	★(h)	★	...	★	...	...	...	...	...	...
Illinois	...	★	★	★	★	(i)	...	★(j)	★(j)	...	...	...	...
Indiana	★	★	★	★	★	...	★	...	...	...	...	★	★
Iowa	...	★	★	★	★	...	...	...	...	...	...	...	...
Kansas	★	★	★	★	★	...	...	★	...	...	★(k)	★	★
Kentucky	★	★	★	★	...	...	...	★	★	★	...	★	...
Louisiana	...	★	★	...	★	...	...	★	★	...	...	★(l)	★
Maine	...	★	★	...	...	...	★	...	...	...	...	★	...
Maryland	★	★	★	★	...	...	...	★	★	★(k)	...	...	★
Massachusetts	...	★(m)	...	...	...	...	★	...	...	...	...	★	...
Michigan	★	★	★	★	★	★(n)	★(o)	...	...	...	...	★	...
Minnesota	★	★	★	★	...	...	...	★	★	...	...	★	...
Mississippi	★	★	★	★	...	...	...	★	...	...	★	...	...
Missouri	...	★	★	★	...	...	...	★	...	...	...	...	...
Montana	★(p)	★	★	★	★	★(g)	★	...	...	...	...	...	...
Nebraska	...	★	★	★	★	...	★	...	...	...	...	...	★
Nevada	★	★	★	★	★	...	★	...	...	...	...	...	★
New Hampshire	★	★	★	★	★	...	★	...	...	...	...	★	★
New Jersey	★	★	★	...	★	★	★(q)	...	...	...	...	★	...
New Mexico	★	★	★	...	(h)	★(r)	...	(s)	...	...	★(s)	...	...
New York	★	★(t)	...	...	★	...	...	★	★	★	...	★	...
North Carolina	★	★	★	...	...	★(u)	...	★	★	...	★	...	...
North Dakota	★	★	★(v)	★	...	...	...	★	...	...	...	★	★
Ohio	★	★	★	★	...	...	★(w)	★	...	★	...	★	...
Oklahoma	...	...	...	...	...	...	...	...	...	...	...	...	...
Oregon	...	★	★	★	★	...	...	...	...	...	...	...	...
Pennsylvania	...	★	★	★	★	★(i)	★	...	...	...	...	★	★
Rhode Island	...	★	★	...	★	★(x)	...	★	...	...	★	★	★
South Carolina	...	★	★	...	...	...	...	★	...	...	...	...	...
South Dakota	...	★	★	★	★	...	...	★	...	...	...	...	...
Tennessee	★	★	★	★	★	★(y)	★	...	...	...	...	★	★
Texas	...	★	★	★	★	...	...	★	★	★(k)	...	...	★
Utah	...	★	★	★	★	...	★	...	...	...	...	...	...
Vermont	★	★	★	★	...	...	...	...	...	...	★	...	...
Virginia	★	★	★	★(z)	...	★	...	★	★	★	...	...	...
Washington	★	★	★	★	★	...	...	★	...	...	...	★	★
West Virginia	★	★	★	★	★(aa)	...	★	...	...	...	...	...	...
Wisconsin	★	★	★	★	★	...	★	...	...	...	...	...	...
Wyoming	...	★	★	★	...	...	★	...	...	...	...	...	...
American Samoa	...	...	...	...	...	...	...	...	...	...	...	...	...
Guam	★	★	★	★	★	...	★	...	...	...	...	★	★
Puerto Rico	...	★	...	...	★	...	★	...	...	...	...	...	...
Virgin Islands	★	★	...	★	...	...	★	...	...	...	...	...	...

(a) Senate only.
(b) Fiscal notes are included in bills for final passage calendar. A computerized fiscal note status, tally and reporting system is currently being implemented. Printout information will be distributed to fiscal committees and will be available on request.
(c) Contained in the bill, not in the fiscal note.
(d) Fiscal notes are required only on bills which would require increased appropriations by the state. Fiscal notes are to be attached to the bill before it is reported to the rules committee. Governor's bills must have fiscal note before introduction.
(e) Required on retirement and local government bills.
(f) Relevant data and prior fiscal year cost information.
(g) Mechanical defects in bill and effective date.
(h) Occasionally.

(i) Bill proposing changes in retirement system of state or local government must have an actuarial note.
(j) A summary of the fiscal note is attached to the summary of the relevant bill in the Legislative Synopsis and Digest. Fiscal notes are prepared for the sponsor of the bill and are attached to the bill on file in either the office of the clerk of the house or the secretary of the senate.
(k) Or to committee to which referred.
(l) Prepared by Central Legislative Fiscal Office; copies sent to house and senate staff offices respectively.
(m) Fiscal notes are prepared only if cost exceeds $100,000 or matter has not been acted upon by the Joint Commission on Ways and Means.
(n) Other relevant data.
(o) Analyses prepared by Senate Fiscal Agency, distributed to senate

FISCAL NOTES: CONTENT AND DISTRIBUTION
Footnotes

members only; analyses prepared by House Fiscal Agency, distributed to house members only.

(p) Comment or opinion on the merits of the bill is prohibited.

(q) Sponsor may disapprove fiscal note; if disapproved, fiscal note is not printed or distributed.

(r) Impact of revenue bills reviewed by Legislative Council Service and executive agencies.

(s) Legislative Finance Committee staff prepares fiscal notes for Appropriations Committee chairman; other fiscal impact statements prepared by Legislative Council Service and executive agencies are available to anyone upon request.

(t) Rules of the Assembly require sponsors' memoranda to include estimate of cost to state and/or local government. Fiscal note required by law to be included on all pension bills.

(u) Fiscal note required in Senate. In House, staff prepares a summary.

(v) A two-year projection.

(w) If a bill comes up for floor consideration.

(x) Technical or mechanical defects may be noted.

(y) Effects of revenue bills.

(z) The Department of Taxation prepares revenue impact notes including the intent and revenue impact.

(aa) House of Delegates only.

Table 25
LEGISLATIVE REVIEW OF ADMINISTRATIVE REGULATIONS—POWERS

State or other jurisdiction	No objection constitutes approval of proposed rule	Advisory power only	Committee may initiate rule	Committee may suspend rule	Legislature must sustain committee action	Time limit for legislative action	Legislature can amend or modify rule	Legislature can repeal rule
	Committee powers					*Legislative powers*		
Alabama	★	...	...	★	★	End of regular session	★	★
Alaska	★	...	...	★	★	30 days after convening of a reg. sess.	...	★
Arizona	...	★	...	...	...	1 year	...	★
Arkansas	...	★	...	...	...	...	...	...
California						No program		
Colorado	...	...	...	...	★	Next regular session	★	★
Connecticut	★	...	...	★	★(a,b)	65 days after date of submission	★(c)	...
Delaware						No program		
Florida	★	★	...	...	...	...	...	...
Georgia	★	...	★	...	★	30 days after convening next reg. ses.	...	★
Hawaii	...	★	...	...	...			
Idaho	★	★	★	...	★	End of regular session	★	★
Illinois	★	...	...	...		None	★	★
Indiana						No program		
Iowa	★	(d)	...	★	★	45 session days	...	...
Kansas	★	...	★	...	★	End of regular session	★	★
Kentucky	★	...	...	(e)		...	...	...
Louisiana	★	★	...	...		...	...	...
Maine	...	★	...	...				
Maryland	★	...	...	...				
Massachusetts						No program		
Michigan	...	...	...	★(f)		(g)	...	...
Minnesota	...	...	...	★	★	End of regular session	...	...
Mississippi						No program		
Missouri	...	★	...	...		...	...	...
Montana	...	...	★	...	★(h)	None	★	★
Nebraska	...	...	...	★	★	Next regular session	...	★
Nevada	★	...	...	...	★(i)	30 session days	...	...
New Hampshire						No program		
New Jersey	...	★	...	...	★	60 days after submission(j)	(k)	★
	...	★	...	...	★	None	...	(l)
New Mexico						No program		
New York	★	★	...	...	★	None	...	...
North Carolina	...	★	...	...		...	...	...
North Dakota	...	★	...	...		...	...	...
Ohio	★	...	...	★	★	59 days	★	★(m)
Oklahoma	...	★	...	...	★	30 days(n)	...	(o)
Oregon	★	★	...	...		...	...	...
Pennsylvania	★	(p)	...	...		30 or 60 days	...	...
Rhode Island						No program		
South Carolina	★	...	...	...	★	90 days after rule filed with legis.	★(q)	...
South Dakota	★	...	...	★	★	30 days after convening of reg. ses.	★(r)	...
Tennessee	★	...	...	★		...	...	...
Texas	★	★	...	...		...	...	...
Utah						No program		
Vermont	★	(d)	★	...	★	End of next regular session	★	★
Virginia	★	...	...	...	★	End of regular session	...	★
Washington	...	(s)	...	...		...	...	...
West Virginia	★	...	...	...		...	...	...
Wisconsin	...	...	...	★	★	End of next regular session	★	★
Wyoming	★(t)	...	...	...		...	...	
American Samoa						No program		
Guam	...	★	...	...	...	45 days after rule filed with legis.	★	★
Puerto Rico						No program		

(a) Committee disapproval of state agency rules can only be reversed by the legislature. Connecticut—it is not mandatory for legislature to approve or disapprove committee action.

(b) Disapproval of a rule implementing a federally subsidized program must be sustained by the legislature before the end of the regular session, or the committee's action is reversed.

(c) Committee may disapprove a part of a rule.

(d) If the committee objects to a rule on the grounds it is "unreasonable, arbitrary, capricious or otherwise beyond the authority delegated to the agency," the agency must then prove this to the contrary in any judicial review.

(e) Until an interim committee or the next legislature may review.

(f) Committee may suspend rules, during interim only, if granted authorization to do so by concurrent resolution of legislature.

(g) If joint committee neither approves nor disapproves, legislature may approve rules, by concurrent resolution, within 60 calendar days.

(h) During the interim, the committee may poll the members of the legislature by mail to determine if a rule is consistent with legislative intent.

(i) Committee action to disapprove a regulation must be sustained by concurrent resolution of next regular session of the legislature.

(j) Legislature may extend deadline up to an additional 60 days by concurrent resolution.

(k) Legislature may veto part of the rule.

(l) Existing rules may be suspended for 60 days.

(m) In addition to outright repeal of a rule, the legislature may modify an agency's statutory rule-making authority—which may have the implicit effect of modifying or "repealing" a rule.

(n) If the rule or regulation is filed while the legislature is not in session, it may be disapproved within the first 30 days of the next session.

(o) Either house may disapprove by simple resolution.

(p) Some rules and regulations may be submitted to standing committees of each house for "review and comment."

(q) Committee cannot initiate rule; legislature cannot repeal an existing rule.

(r) Legislature's authority to amend has never been used.

(s) Committee may publish notice of objection in register and administrative code.

(t) The Legislative Management Council submits its report to the governor. If the governor objects to the report, he must file his objections with the council within 15 days.

Table 26
LEGISLATIVE REVIEW OF ADMINISTRATIVE REGULATIONS—
STRUCTURES AND PROCEDURES

State or other jurisdiction	Type of reviewing committee	All rules reviewed	Review of proposed rules	Review of existing rules	Time limits for submission of rules for review
Alabama	Joint	★	★	★	60 days
Alaska	Joint	★	★	★	45 days
Arizona	(a)	(b)	. . .	★	Immediately after adoption
Arkansas	Joint	★	★	★	10 days before agency hearing
California	————————————————— No program —————————————————				
Colorado	Joint	★	. . .	★	20 days after approval by attorney general
Connecticut	Joint bipartisan	. . .	★	. . .	After approval of attorney general
Delaware	————————————————— No program —————————————————				
Florida	Joint	★	★	★	21 days
Georgia	Standing cmte.	★	★	. . .	30 days
Hawaii	(c)	(d)	(d)	. . .	
Idaho	Standing cmtes. & germane sub-cmtes. for proposed rules	★	★	★	Beginning of each session for existing rules. Proposed rules to be submitted to germane subcmte. through Legislative Council to allow for a minimum 30-day review period.
Illinois	Joint bipartisan	★	★	★	45 days
Indiana	————————————————— No program —————————————————				
Iowa	Joint	★	★	★	35(e)
Kansas	Joint	★	★	★	By Dec. 31 of each year
Kentucky	Joint	★	★	★	None, but cannot go into effect unless filed with LRC and reviewed by subcmte.
Louisiana	Standing cmtes.	★	★	. . .	15 days prior to adoption of rule(f)
Maine	Joint standing cmtes.	(g)	. . .	(g)	None
Maryland	Joint	★	★	★	At least 45 days and not more than one year before adoption
Massachusetts	————————————————— No program —————————————————				
Michigan	Joint	★(h)	★	★	None
Minnesota	Joint	★	★(i)	★	None
Mississippi	————————————————— No program —————————————————				
Missouri	Joint	★	. . .	★	None
Montana	Joint bipartisan	★	. . .	★	None
Nebraska	Standing cmte.	★	. . .	★	By Jan. 1 of each year
Nevada	Joint	★	★(j)	★	After adoption
New Hampshire	————————————————— No program —————————————————				
New Jersey	Standing cmte.	★	★	. . .	Prior to adoption
	Joint	★	. . .	★	No submission
New Mexico	————————————————— No program —————————————————				
New York	Joint(k)	★	★	★	21 days prior to effective date
North Carolina	Joint	★	★	★	Prior to filing with attorney general, usually 30 days prior to effective date
North Dakota	Joint interim	(l)	★	★	None
Ohio	Joint	★(m)	★(n)	★(n)	60 days before adoption by agency
Oklahoma	Standing cmtes.	★	. . .	★	10 days after adoption
Oregon	Joint	★(o)	★	★	Within 10 days after filing with the secretary of state
Pennsylvania	Standing cmtes. or entire membership of each house	(p)	★	. . .	None
Rhode Island	————————————————— No program —————————————————				
South Carolina	Standing cmtes.	★	★	. . .	None, but cannot go into effect until 90 days after submission(q)
South Dakota	Joint	★	★	★	20 days before agency hearing
Tennessee	House & Senate Government Operations Cmtes.	(l)	. . .	★	45 days prior to effective date
Texas	Standing cmtes.	★	★	. . .	30 days prior to adoption
Utah	————————————————— No program —————————————————				
Vermont	Joint	★	★	★	30 days prior to adoption
Virginia	Standing cmtes.	★	★	★	Emergency regulations with immediate effective dates can be issued with approval from the governor
Washington	Joint	★(l)	★	★	Immediately upon filing with code revisor
West Virginia	Joint	. . .	★	. . .	None
Wisconsin	Joint	★	★	★	None
Wyoming	Joint	★	. . .	★	20 days prior to adoption
American Samoa	————————————————— No program —————————————————				
Guam	(a)	(d)	. . .	. . .	After adoption
Puerto Rico	————————————————— No program —————————————————				

(a) Not specified; presumably review done by appropriate committee.

(b) Provides for legislative review of only those rules promulgated by State Parks Board.

(c) Review is by the Office of the Legislative Auditor which submits reports to the legislature for appropriate action.

(d) Reviews rules when adopted, amended or repealed.

(e) Published in Iowa Administrative Code 35 days prior to adoption.

(f) Agencies also must submit an annual report to the legislature on all rules adopted over the past year, 30 days prior to the regular session.

(g) All rules expire in five years unless legislation is enacted to terminate them in less than five years.

(h) Except emergency rules.

(i) If the chief hearing examiner determines that an agency has not demonstrated the need and reasonableness of a proposed rule, and the agency does not make the corrections suggested by the the chief hearing examiner, the agency must submit the proposed rule to the Legislative Commission to Review Administrative Rules (LCRAR) for advice and comment. The agency must wait at least 30 days for a response from the LCRAR, but the commission's advice is not binding on the agency.

(j) Optional with legislative commission.

(k) The committee was established by joint resolution and has no statutory authority.

(l) Rules reviewed selectively. North Dakota: rules to be reviewed are selected by the chairman of the Legislative Council.

(m) Certain rules are exempt from review.

(n) During interim, agencies may adopt rules before the time limit for review has expired. Those rules are subject to review when the legislature reconvenes.

(o) Committee may review or may direct the legislative counsel to review a rule. Review is not automatic.

(p) Review includes only fraud and abuse control (public welfare), emergency medical services, health care facilities, professional engineers licensing, licensing and fees of Bureau of Professional and Occupational Affairs, mass transit inspection, real estate broker licensing, solid waste management, coal refuse disposal control.

(q) During interim, emergency regulations can be issued with an immediate effective date.

Table 27
SUMMARY OF SUNSET LEGISLATION

State or other jurisdiction	Scope	Termination schedule	Preliminary evaluation conducted by	Other legislative review	Other oversight mechanisms in bill	Phase-out period	Life of each agency (in years)	Other provisions
Alabama	C	28 in 1980 15 in 1981 24 in 1982	Select Joint Committee	…	Zero-base budg.	180/d	4	1-hour time limit on floor debate on each bill.
Alaska	R	13 in 1980 1 in 1981	Standing committees	…	Perf. audit	1/y	4	In addition to regulatory agencies, programs in other broad areas terminate in 1980-83; specific programs authorized for termination by Legislative Budget & Audit Cmte.
Arizona	C	3 in 1980 1 in 1981 15 in 1982 18 in 1984 3 in 1985 28 in 1986 14 in 1988 19 in 1990 9 in 1992 5 in 1994 9 in 1996	Committees of reference	Jt. Legislative Oversight Committee	Perf. audit	(a)	6	…
Arkansas	C	113 in 1981 60 in 1983	Joint interim committees	…	Perf. audit	1/y	(b)	…
California	(c)	…	…	…	…	…	…	…
Colorado	R	1 in 1980 14 in 1981 6 in 1983 2 in 1984 15 in 1985 15 in 1986	Until July 1, 1984, by the Dept. of Regulatory Agencies; after, by the Dept. of Admin. Reports to Legis. Council by July 1, preceding year of termination	Standing committees	Perf. audit	1/y	6	There is also legislation requiring a study of 20 principal depts. of state government on a schedule concluding in 1994.
Connecticut	R(d)	19 in 1980 17 in 1981 19 in 1982 26 in 1983 23 in 1984 19 in 1985 11 in 1986	Legis. Prog. Review & Investigations Cmte.	Govt. Adminis. & Elections Cmte.	Perf. audit	1/y	5	…
Delaware	C	9 in 1981 9 in 1982 9 in 1983 9 in 1984	Agencies under review submit report to Del. Sunset Comm. based on criteria for review and set forth in statute. Comm. staff conducts separate review	…	Perf. audit	Dec. 31 of next succeeding calendar year	4	Yearly Sunset Review schedules must include at least nine agencies. If the number automatically scheduled for review or added by the General Assembly is less than a full schedule, additional agencies shall be added in order of their appearance in the Del. Code to complete the review schedul.
Florida	R	24 in 1980 18 in 1982 23 in 1983 15 in 1984 10 in 1985 15 in 1986 9 in 1988 7 in 1989 9 in 1990 7 in 1991	Appropriate substantive cmte. shall begin review 15 months prior to repeal date	…	…	1/y	10	Provides for periodic review of limitations on the initial entry in to a profession, occupation, business, industry or other endeavor.

State		Termination dates	Agency	Review body	Program/method	Frequency	No.	Comments
Georgia	R	19 in 1980 4 in 1981 20 in 1982 4 in 1983 5 in 1984	Standing committees	...	Perf. audit	1/y	6	The termination dates of the 10 agencies reviewed & scheduled for termination in 1978 were extended.
Hawaii	R	3 in 1980 8 in 1981 8 in 1982 7 in 1983 4 in 1984 2 in 1985 3 in 1986	Legislative Auditor	...	...	None	...	...
Idaho				— No program —				
Illinois	R	7 in 1981 6 in 1983 9 in 1985 6 in 1987 7 in 1989	Bur. of the Budget & gov.; Select Jt. Cmte.	Standing cmtes. of each house	Performance evaluation; agency demonstrates need for continued existence	1/y	10	Upon receipt of report from Bur. of the Budget, the gov. may recommend continuation or abolition of agency. Gov. may also submit Select Jt. Cmte.'s recommendations as a reorganization plan.
Indiana	C	25 in 1980 35 in 1981 52 in 1982 75 in 1983 45 in 1984 29 in 1985 47 in 1986 84 in 1987	Legis. Serv. Agency, Off. of Fiscal & Mgt. Analysis	Jt. Interim Sunset Evaluation Cmte.	Gov. submits recommendations	None(e)	...	Each newly established agency subject to termination with 10-year life span. Agencies established by exec. order. terminate when a gov. leaves office. Agencies established by concurrent resolution by a General Assembly terminate after adjournment of the 2nd session.
Iowa	(c)							
Kansas	R(d)	12 in 1980 8 in 1981 5 in 1982 4 in 1983 3 in 1984 4 in 1985 2 in 1986 2 in 1987	Legis. Post Audit nine months prior to termination	Standing committees	Perf. audit	1/y	8	Act terminates in July 1984 unless re-enacted.
Kentucky				— No program —				
Louisiana	C	2 in 1982 1 in 1983 3 in 1984 2 in 1985 1 in 1986 3 in 1987 1 in 1988 3 in 1989 4 in 1990	Standing cmtes. of the two houses which have usual jurisdiction over the affairs of the entity. Process begins 2 years prior to the termination date	Bill authorizing re-creation referred to committee performing initial review	Zero-base budgeting	July 1 of year before end of legislative authority	9	Standing cmtes. may conduct a more extensive evaluation of selected statutory entities under their jurisdiction or of particular programs of such entities.
Maine	R	7 in 1980 23 in 1982 11 in 1984 14 in 1986 11 in 1988	State Auditor	...	Perf. eval.	1/y	10	Performance reviews also scheduled for executive departments (no terminations).
Maryland	R	13 in 1980 16 in 1981 18 in 1982 15 in 1983	Dept. of Fiscal Serv.	Standing committees	...	None	6	...
Massachusetts				— No program —				

SUMMARY OF SUNSET LEGISLATION—Continued

State or other jurisdiction	Scope	Termination schedule	Preliminary evaluation conducted by	Other legislative review	Other oversight mechanisms in bill	Phase-out period	Life of each agency (in years)	Other provisions
Michigan	(c)	...	...	...	...	...	...	...
Minnesota	(c)	...	...	...	...	...	...	...
Mississippi	C	20 in 1980, 16 in 1981, 14 in 1982, 20 in 1983	Standing committees	...	Perf. audit; agency demonstrates need for continued existence	By Dec. 31 of year terminated	8	Act terminates in 1984 unless re-enacted. Newly created agencies subject to termination with 8-year life span. Governmental units established by exec. order shall terminate unless enacted into statutory law. (Those established after effective date of sunset legislation.)
Missouri				No program				...
Montana	R(f)	22 in 1981, 10 in 1983, 11 in 1985	Legis. Audit Cmte.	Standing committees	...	1/y	6	...
Nebraska	D/C	7 in 1980, 5 in 1981, 5 in 1982, 8 in 1983	Perf. Review & Audit Cmte.	Standing committees	Perf. review	1/y	6	Act terminates in 1983.
Nevada	S	None	Legis. Commission with assistance from the Legis. Council Bureau & cmtes. or sub-cmtes. appropriated to carry out review	Legislature	...	1/y	...	...
New Hampshire	D/C	All by 1985	Jt. Legis. Cmte. on Review of Agencies & Programs	Standing committees	...	9/m	6	...
New Jersey	(c)	...	...	...	...	...	...	...
New Mexico	R	16 in 1980	Legis. Finance Cmte.	...	...	1/y	6	...
New York				No program				...
North Carolina	R	62 by 1982	Cmte. on Agency Review	Standing committees	Perf. eval.	...	...	...
North Dakota				No program				...
Ohio	(c)	...	...	...	...	...	...	...
Oklahoma	C	18 in 1980, 16 in 1981, 20 in 1982, 21 in 1983	Standing or interim cmte.	...	Zero-base budgeting	1/y	6	Rules & regulations of terminated agencies continue in effect unless terminated by law; includes agencies established by exec. order.
Oregon	R	9 in 1980, 13 in 1982, 8 in 1984, 16 in 1986	Interim cmte.	Standing committees	...	None	8	...
Pennsylvania	S	3 in 1980, 1 in 1982, 1 in 1984	Standing committee	...	Perf. eval.	...	2 to 6	...
Rhode Island	C	25 in 1980, 20 in 1981	Oversight Commission	...	Zero-base budgeting	1/y	5	Oversight Commission established to conduct sunset reviews.
South Carolina	R	7 in 1980, 6 in 1981, 7 in 1982, 7 in 1983, 7 in 1984, 7 in 1985	Legis. Audit Council	Reorganization Commission, standing committees	Perf. audit	1/y	6	...

State		Scheduled	Review body	Other reviewers	Type of review	Freq.	No.	Comments
South Dakota	S	0 in 1980 1 in 1981	Special interim cmte.	...	Perf. audit	180/d	...	The legislature, through a special committee, may also review for sunset an agency's authorization to promulgate rules & the rules currently in existence.
Tennessee	C	35 in 1980 12 in 1981 20 in 1982 66 in 1983 43 in 1984 46 in 1985	Special eval. cmte. in each house	Standing cmtes. review (only in tie vote in evaluation cmte.)	Limited prog.	1/y	6	Establishment of new agencies subject to review by evaluation committee.
Texas	C	33 in 1983 33 in 1985 25 in 1987 29 in 1989 19 in 1991 32 in 1993	Sunset Advisory Commission	...	Perf. eval.	1/y	12	Initial review conducted by agencies themselves.
Utah	R	30 in 1981	Interim study cmte.	...	Interim cmte.'s discretion	1/y	6	...
Vermont	R	All by 1988	Legis. Council staff	Standing committees	...	1/y	6	Act terminates.
Virginia	(g)	...	...	...	...	...	...	...
Washington	C	22 in 1981 20 in 1983	Legis. Budget Cmte.	Standing committees	Prog. review	1/y	6	Select Jt. cmte. prepares termination legislation. Act terminates in 1984.
West Virginia	S	11 in 1982 4 in 1983 12 in 1984 5 in 1985 4 in 1986 6 in 1987 6 in 1988 7 in 1989 3 in 1990	Jt. Cmte. on Govt. Operations	Legislature when in session	Perf. audit	1/y	6	Jt. Cmte. on Govt. Operations composed of 5 house members, 5 senate members & 5 citizens appointed by governor.
Wisconsin	(c)	...	...	...	...	...	...	...
Wyoming	S	11 in 1981 8 in 1983	Legis. Serv. Office	11-mbr. cmte. apptd. by Mgt. Council	...	1/y	6	...
American Samoa	...	...	No program					
Guam	...	...	No program					A sunset bill is pending.
Puerto Rico	...	...	No program					
Virgin Islands	...	...	No program					

Key:
C—Comprehensive
R—Regulatory
S—Selective
D—Discretionary
d—day
y—year
m—month

(a) Agency termination is scheduled on July 1 of the year prior to the scheduled termination of statutory authority for that agency.
(b) Permanent.
(c) While they have not enacted sunset legislation in the same sense as the other 33 states with detailed information in this table, the legislatures in California, Delaware, Iowa, Michigan, Minnesota, New Jersey, Ohio and Wisconsin have included sunset clauses in selected programs.
(d) Primarily.
(e) Through an executive order, the governor may provide a terminated agency with one year to wind up its affairs.
(f) Plus certain agencies within Departments of Social and Rehabilitative Services, Community Affairs and Institutions.
(g) By joint resolution, Senate and House of Delegates establish a schedule for review of "functional areas" of state government. Program evaluation is carried out by Joint Legislative Audit and Review Commission. Agencies are not scheduled for automatic termination. Commission reports are made to standing committees which conduct public hearings.

Table 28
LEGISLATIVE APPLICATIONS OF ELECTRONIC DATA PROCESSING

State or other jurisdiction	Statutory retrieval	Bill drafting	Bill typing	Bill status report	Statutory revision	Case law retrieval	Redistricting	Other	Revenue forecasting	Revenue analysis	Budget comparison	Budget effects of legislation	Fiscal notes	Local fiscal notes	Economic impact note	Impact of salary and fringe changes	State aid formulas	Tracking federal dollars	Other	Computer printing	Legislative accounting	Mailing lists	Other
Alabama	★	★	★	★					★		★	★	★					★	(a,b)		★★		
Alaska			★	★					★		★	★	★					★		★	★	★	
Arizona			☆								☆		☆			☆							
Arkansas						☆		(c)											(d)				(d)
California	★	★	★	★	★	★	★		(e)	(e)	★	★	★					★		★	(e)	★	(f)
Colorado	★	★	★	★	★		★				★	★					★			★	★	★	
Connecticut	★	(g)	(g)	★	★		★				★	★					★			★	★	★	
Delaware	★	★	★	★	★																		
Florida	★	★	★	★	★		★	(h)			★	★	★			★	★				★	★	
Georgia	★	★	★	★	★						★	★											
Hawaii	★	★	★	★	★			(a)											(d)				
Idaho							★				☆	☆							(i)	☆	★	★	(i)
Illinois	★	★	★	★	★		★			☆	★	★	★	★			★	★			★	★	
Indiana	★	★	★	★	★		★		★	★	★	★	★	★	★	★	★	★		☆	★	★	
Iowa	★			★	★		★		★	★	★	★	★	★		★	★			★	★		
Kansas	★	★	★	★	★		★				★	★					★			★	★	★	
Kentucky						(k)					★											★	
Louisiana	★	★	★	★	★		★	(a)		★	★	★	★				★			★	★	★	
Maine	☆			★						★	★						★	★				★	
Maryland	★	★	★	★	★			(a)			★	★	★				★			(j)	★		(j)
Massachusetts	★	☆	★	★	★		★	(j,l,m)			★								(j,l,m)	★		★	(j,l,m)
Michigan	☆	☆	★	★	★ ☆		★		★	★	★	★	★		★		★	★		★	★		
Minnesota	★	★	★	★			★				★	★					★	★	(m)	★	★		
Mississippi	★	★	★	★							★					★	★	★	(o)	★	★ (p)		
Missouri				★							★	★				★					★	★	

Montana													(q)							
Nebraska													(a)							
Nevada																				
New Hampshire																				
New Jersey																				
New Mexico																	(p)				(s)
New York							(l)														(t)
North Carolina																				
North Dakota								(m)												
Ohio																				
Oklahoma													(a)							
Oregon													(v)				(w)				(f,x,y)
Pennsylvania																				
Rhode Island																				
South Carolina																				
South Dakota																				
Tennessee													(z)							
Texas																				
Utah																				
Vermont																				
Virginia													(a)				(j)				(g)
Washington													(aa)								(ab)
West Virginia																				
Wisconsin																				
Wyoming																				
American Samoa																				
Guam									(ac)								(d)				
Puerto Rico																				
Virgin Islands																				

Key:
★—Actual application
☆—Planned application
(a) Bill index. Nebraska—daily journal; Virginia—attorney general opinions.
(b) Act index.
(c) House engrossing and journal typing. Arkansas: planned only.
(d) Budget preparation.
(e) Tracking system only.
(f) Selected personnel record-keeping.
(g) Delaware: Word processing system only; West Virginia: for interim committee agencies.
(h) Lobbyist registration, law book distribution, appropriations, calendar preparation, audit reports.
(i) Expenditure analysis and tracking, expense forecasting and comparison to appropriations.
(j) Photo composition.
(k) In use for attorney general.
(l) Status of bill in committee.
(m) Bill registry—tracking method for bills being drafted.
(n) Higher education/community college budget requests.
(o) Appropriations (experimental).
(p) Payroll only.

(q) Data files include bill index, photo composition, bill registry, act name file, statute chronology, session history publication, session laws, house and senate journals, legislative rules, publications of the Montana Code Annotated.
(r) For education only.
(s) Inventory control.
(t) Calendar.
(u) House only.
(v) Act name file (word searching), statute chronology and session history publications, senate congratulatory resolutions.
(w) Computer typeset products are: session slip laws and pamphlet law volume, all senate and house calendars, senate congratulatory resolutions, verbatim senate and house journals.
(x) Present election results and survey tabulations.
(y) Administration of the senate and house, including personnel listings, payroll and expense accounting, fringe and retirement benefits, inventory control and registered lobbyists and represented organizations.
(z) Statutes affected by pending and passed bills.
(aa) Data files include federal and state constitutions, attorney general opinions, supreme court reports and administrative rules.
(ab) Public opinion questionnaire analysis.
(ac) Available for the Law Revision Commission and Compiler, not other legal services.

Table 29
REGISTRATION OF LOBBYISTS

State or other jurisdiction	Lobbyist registers with	Filed with	Activity reports — Frequency	Activity reports — Expenditures reported	Penalties for non-compliance
Alabama	Ethics Commission	Ethics Commission	Monthly(a,b)	★	Fine of not more than $10,000 or more than 10 years imprisonment, or both.
Alaska	Public Offices Commission	Public Offices Commission	Monthly(c)	★	Fine of not more than $1,000 or more than 1 year imprisonment, or both; civil penalty of $1 per day (after 30 days, $10 per day).
Arizona	Secretary of State	Secretary of State	Annually(d,e)	★	Prosecuted as a misdemeanor.
Arkansas	Clerk of House, Secy. of Sen.	…	…	…	None specified.
California	Secretary of State	Secretary of State	Quarterly	… ★	Prosecuted as misdemeanor, subject to civil fines and 4-year prohibition from public office following conviction.
Colorado	Secretary of State	Secretary of State	Monthly(f)	★	Fine of not more than $5,000 or 1 year imprisonment, or both; registration may be revoked.
Connecticut	Ethics Commission	Ethics Commission	Quarterly(g)	★	Fine of not more than $1,000 or more than 1 year imprisonment, or both.
Delaware	Legislative Council	Legislative Council	Quarterly	★	(h)
Florida	Clerk of House, Secy. of Sen.	Clerk of House, Secy. of Sen.	Monthly(i); Semi-annually	★	Reprimand, censure or prohibit from lobbying(j)
Georgia	Secretary of State	…	…	…	Prosecuted as a misdemeanor.
Hawaii	Ethics Commission	Ethics Commission	Biannually	★	Prosecuted as a misdemeanor.
Idaho	Secretary of State	Secretary of State	Quarterly(c)	★	Prosecuted as a misdemeanor subject to civil fines and possible per diem penalty.
Illinois	Secretary of State	Secretary of State	Jan., April & July (during ses.)(k)	…	Prosecuted as a Class 3 felony (fine of not more than $10,000 or more than 5 years imprisonment, or both).
Indiana	Secretary of State	Secretary of State	Following session	★	Prosecuted as a felony.
Iowa	Clerk of House, Secy. of Sen.	Clerk of House, Secy. of Sen.	Monthly	★	House: suspension from lobbying; Senate: cancellation of registration.
Kansas	Secretary of State	Secretary of State	Jan-April(l)	★	Prosecuted as a Class B misdemeanor.
Kentucky	Attorney General	Attorney General	Following session	★	Fine up to $5,000 or up to 5 years imprisonment, or both.
Louisiana	Clerk of House, Secy. of Sen.	…	…	…	Fine of not more than $500 or more than 6 months imprisonment, or both.
Maine	Secretary of State	Secretary of State	Monthly following ses. & annually	★	Fine of not more than $1,000 or more than 11 months imprisonment, or both.
Maryland	Ethics Commission	Ethics Commission	Semiannually	★	Prosecuted as a misdemeanor.
Massachusetts	Secretary of State	Secretary of State	Semiannually	★	Fine of not less than $100 or more than $5,000.
Michigan	Secretary of State	Secretary of State(m)	Four times yearly	…	Prosecuted as a felony.
Minnesota	Ethical Practices Board	Ethical Practices Board		★	Fine of $5 per business day to maximum of $100 and prosecuted as a misdemeanor.
Mississippi	Secretary of State	Secretary of State	Following session	★	Fine of not more than $1,000 or 6 months in county jail for first offense, or both.
Missouri	Clerk of House, Secy. of Sen.	Clerk of House, Secy. of Sen.	Three times/session	★	Prosecuted as a misdemeanor.
Montana(n)	Secy. of State	Secy. of State	Monthly	… ★	Prosecuted as a misdemeanor.
Nebraska	Clerk of Legislature	Clerk of Legislature	(o)	★	Prosecuted as a misdemeanor.
Nevada	Legis. Counsel Bureau	Legis. Counsel Bureau	Following session	★	Prosecuted as a misdemeanor; perjury is a felony.
New Hampshire	Secretary of State	Secretary of State	Quarterly	★	Prosecuted as a misdemeanor.
New Jersey	Attorney General	Attorney General	Quarterly	★	Prosecuted as a crime of the fourth degree.

State	Registration authority	Reports filed with	Frequency		Penalties
New Mexico	Secretary of State	Secretary of State	(p)	*	Prosecuted as a misdemeanor; revocation of registration and prohibited from lobbying.
New York	N.Y. Temporary State Commission on Regulation of Lobbying	N.Y. Temporary State Commission on Regulation of Lobbying	Following session	*	Prosecuted as a misdemeanor.
North Carolina	Secretary of State	Secretary of State	Annually	*	Prosecuted as a misdemeanor.
North Dakota	Secretary of State	Secretary of State	Annually	*	Prosecuted as a Class B misdemeanor.
Ohio	Senate Clerk	Senate Clerk	Jan. & July(q)	*	Prosecuted as a first or fourth degree misdemeanor.
Oklahoma	Joint Legis. Ethics Cmte.	Joint Legis. Ethics Cmte.	Annually	*	Prosecuted as a misdemeanor.
Oregon	Ethics Commission	Ethics Commission	Quarterly	*	Civil penalty for individuals not to exceed $250; for other than individual, not to exceed $1,000 for each violation.
Pennsylvania	Clerk of House, Secy. of Sen.	Clerk of House, Secy. of Sen.	Biannually	*	Prosecuted as a third degree misdemeanor.
Rhode Island	Secretary of State	Secretary of State	Three times/session	*	Fine of not less than $100 or more than $1,000 for agent; fine of not less than $200 or more than $5,000 for corporation; disbarment from agent capacity for 3 years from date of conviction.
South Carolina	Secretary of State	Secretary of State	Annually	*	Prosecuted as a misdemeanor.
South Dakota	Secretary of State	Secretary of State	Annually(r)	*	Fine of not more than $1,000 or 1 year imprisonment, or both.
Tennessee	State Library & Archives	State Library & Archives	Following session	*	Prosecuted as a misdemeanor.
Texas	Secretary of State	Secretary of State	Monthly(d)	*	Prosecuted as a Class A misdemeanor and subject to additional fine; prosecuted as third degree felony if compensation contingent upon passage, defeat, approval or veto of a bill.
Utah	Lieutenant Governor	…	…	…	Prosecuted as a Class C misdemeanor.
Vermont	Secretary of State	Secretary of State	Annually(s)	*	Fine of not less than $100 or more than $500.
Virginia	Secy. of Commonwealth	Secy. of Commonwealth	Following session	*	Penalty of $50/day for late filing for lobbyist and employer individually plus $50 for each day after tenth day late.
Washington	Pub. Disclosure Commission	Pub. Disclosure Commission	Monthly	*	Prosecuted as a civil offense. Fine of not more than $10,000. Registration can be revoked.
West Virginia	Clerk of House, Clerk of Sen.	Clerk of House, Clerk of Sen.	Following session	*	None specified.
Wisconsin	Secretary of State	Secretary of State	Semiannually	…	Fine of not more than $5,000 depending on offense.
Wyoming	Dir., Legis. Service Office	…			Prosecuted as a misdemeanor. Subject to fine of not more than $200.
Guam	Legislative Secretary	Legislative Secretary	Quarterly	*	Misdemeanor fine not more than $5,000 or imprisonment of not more than 12 months, or both; prohibited from lobbying for three years.

(a) Established by secretary of state.
(b) During session.
(c) In months when lobbying occurs.
(d) During session; quarterly during interim.
(e) Supplemental reports shall be filed monthly, on or before the 10th day of the following month, to list any expenditures in excess of $25 occurring during the month and which must be reported pursuant to this section.
(f) Plus cumulative statement yearly.
(g) Monthly during session, if lobbyist attempts to influence legislative action.
(h) Criminal penalty for a false financial report. Failure to report cancels the registration.
(i) For senate only.
(j) For house only.
(k) And within 20 days after special session.

(l) Quarterly basis thereafter; only when required expenses are made.
(m) Name and address of person retaining records (lobbyist, his employer, or agent).
(n) Information presented reflects current laws. The constitutionality of an initiative that would change the lobbying laws is presently being considered by the Supreme Court.
(o) Final report must be filed within 30 days after the close of the legislative session. In addition, each registrant who attempts to influence legislative action must file, between the first and the 10th day of the month subsequent to each month that the legislature is in session, a report concerning his lobbying activities during the previous month.
(p) Upon filing of registration statement and prior to the 60th day after the end of any regular or special session.
(q) Report of certain financial transactions must be filed within 30 days after the transaction.
(r) Following year of registration.
(s) And after two months of session.

Table 30
LOBBYISTS AS DEFINED IN STATE STATUTES

State or other jurisdiction	Anyone receiving compensation to influence legislative action	Anyone spending money to influence legislation	Anyone representing someone else's interest	Anyone attempting to influence legislation	Any executive branch employee attempting to influence legislation	Public officials acting in an official capacity	Persons who speak only before committees or boards	Any person with professional knowledge acting as a professional witness	Religious organizations	Members of the media	Attorneys representing clients on legal matters	Professional bill drafters	Others†
Alabama	★					•	•	•	•			•	
Alaska	★					•	•	•			•		
Arizona	★	★			★						•	•	
Arkansas	★		★			•						•	
California	★				★	•				•	•		
Colorado	★					•	•	•			•		A•,B•
Connecticut	★(d)	★(d)				•	•(e)				•		C•
Delaware	★	★	★(f)			•	•(f)	•	★		•		
Florida				★		•	•						
Georgia	★			★(c)		•	•	•			★		
Hawaii	★	★(g)	★(g)	★(g)	•	•				•		•	
Idaho	★					•	•			•	•	•	
Illinois	★		★			•	•	•		•	•	•	
Indiana	★	★	★		•	•	•(h)			•	•		E•
Iowa	★	★	★	★(a)		•		•(a)		•			E•
Kansas	★	★	★			•							F•
Kentucky			★(c)			•							C•
Louisiana	★(i)					•	•	•					
Maine	★					•	•	•					
Maryland	★	★				•	•		★	•	★	•	G★,C•,I•
Massachusetts	★					•	•	•					
Michigan						•							
Minnesota	★	★(b)				•				•		•	H•
Mississippi	★					•		•			•		
Missouri	★					•							
Montana	★					•	•						
Nebraska			★		•	•	•	•					
Nevada			★	★		•	•	•					N•,O•,P•
New Hampshire	★					•	•	•			•		
New Jersey	★					•				•			E•
New Mexico	★					•					•		
New York	★					•					•		
North Carolina	★					•	•			•			
North Dakota				★		•		•			•	•	
Ohio	★	★	★		★	★(m)	•	•	★	•	★	•	E★,G★, J★,M•
Oklahoma	★(a)		★			•							B•,K•
Oregon	★	★	★		★		•						B•,K•
Pennsylvania	★	★	★	★		•							(j)
Rhode Island	★	★	★	★		•							L•,M•
South Carolina			★			•	•	•	•		•		
South Dakota			★	★(c)	★	•				•			
Tennessee		★			★	•			•	•	•		
Texas	★(k)	★(k)				•	•		•	•	•		E•
Utah	★				★	•	•			•	•		
Vermont	★					•	•						
Virginia	★	★				•	•				•		D•
Washington				★(l)			•						C•,Q★(l)
West Virginia													
Wisconsin	★					•	•						
Wyoming	★					•							
American Samoa													
Guam						•	•						
Puerto Rico													
Virgin Islands													

Key:

★—Definitions of who is a lobbyist.

•—Exceptions to who is a lobbyist.

†—Abbreviations used in last column:

A—Communications made by a person in response to a statute, rule, regulation or order requiring such communication.

B—In Colorado, any legislative department employee performing department duties; in Oregon, any legislative official acting in an official capacity.

C—Any lobbyist not compensated and not making expenditures.

D—Any uncompensated individual who expends or directs expenditure of less than $100 in a given session.

E—Political parties.

F—Non-profit interstate organization.

G—Anyone spending money to influence executive action.

H—Any paid expert witness whose testimony is requested.

I—Members of associations engaged exclusively in lobbying for counties and local governments.

J—Charitable organizations.

K—Persons who do not spend more than 16 hours and $50 on lobbying in any calendar quarter.

L—Anyone employed, appointed or retained, with or without compensation, to influence an act or vote concerning any bill, resolution, amendment, report, claim, act or veto pending or to be introduced.

M—Anyone expressing a personal opinion to members of the legislature.

N—Employees of departments, divisions or agencies of the state government who appear before legislative committees only to explain the effect of legislation related to their departments, divisions or agencies.

O—Employees of the legislature, legislators, legislative agencies or legislative commissions.

P—Persons who contact the members of the legislature who are elected from the district in which they reside.

Q—State and local officials and employees if they spend pubic funds to influence legislation.

(a) For senate only.

(b) More than $250 or five hours in any month.

(c) Affecting private pecuniary interests.

(d) Compensation, reimbursement, expenditures or combination totaling at least $500 per calendar year.

(e) Under certain conditions.

(f) Must register if "committee" is of the General Assembly.

(g) More than $275 of own or any person's money in a six-month period or five hours in any month.

(h) At request of legislator.

(i) Or for any consideration.

(j) Anyone who accepts reimbursement of $100 or more within one year for the purpose of influencing legislation.

(k) Expenditure or compensation in excess of $200/quarter.

(l) Lobbyists are exempt from reporting if they lobby no more than four days in a three-month period during which time they spend less than $15.

(m) Except governor, lieutenant governor, attorney general, secretary of state, treasurer, auditor.

REAPPORTIONMENT IN THE 1980s

By Andrea J. Wollock

OVER THE PAST 20 YEARS, state legislatures have become more concerned with their reapportionment responsibility. Case law on the subject has grown dramatically since the U.S. Supreme Court decided the case of *Baker* v. *Carr* in 1962, ruling that districting cases are subject to the courts. Since then, the courts have played an increasing role in the re-apportionment process, setting ever-stricter standards for redistricting. The changes in reapportionment criteria because of the Court's decisions have been many, and the federal courts are currently showing little hesitation about becoming involved in the process.

The 1980 census and ensuing reapportionment have already shown a great deal more sophistication than the data and procedures used in the 1970s. This is the result not only of the larger body of case law but also a more detailed and accurate census. In addition, a number of innovative methods have been used for redrawing district lines, including the formation of reapportionment commissions and the employment of private consultants and computer technology. Some of the more significant changes follow.

Case Law

The all-important "one-person, one-vote" dictum was first enunciated by the Court in 1963 in the case of *Gray* v. *Sanders* and was reiterated in *Wesberry* v. *Sanders* in 1964. The Court stated, "As nearly as is practicable, one man's vote is to be worth as much as another's." Though the Court set no specific standards, it did begin the trend of subjecting congressional redistricting plans to a higher standard of population equality than legislative reapportionment maps. *Reynolds* v. *Sims*, decided shortly after *Wesberry*, reaffirmed the Court's distinction between the two by granting broader latitude to the states in legislative reapportionment standards.

While the Supreme Court has decided only a handful of congressional redistricting cases, all on the issue of population variance, it has ruled on a great many more legislative re-apportionment issues. The Court has never set an upper limit over which the "as nearly as practicable" standard is violated in congressional redistricting. It has, however, in the case of *Chapman* v. *Meier*, indicated that legislative reapportionment plans with less than 10 percent overall population range, where there is no showing of invidious discrimination, are permissible.[1]

Census Data

Public Law 94-171, acknowledged as the most important census legislation in recent history, was enacted December 23, 1975. The law required some specific improvements in timing and data tabulation for the 1980 census.

Andrea J. Wollock is Senior Staff Associate, Legislative Management, National Conference of State Legislatures.

Nearly every state uses census data to redraw congressional and legislative districts. Exceptions are: Hawaii, which redistricts using a registered voter population base; Massachusetts, which uses a state-conducted census to reapportion its legislative seats; and Kansas, which conducted its last state census and reapportioned its legislative seats in 1979 but will use federal census data beginning in 1990.

As a result of P.L. 94-171, the U.S. Bureau of the Census was mandated to release all census block statistics to the states by April 1, 1981, and the bureau was required to develop block data for all cities of 10,000 or more people. After the 1970 census, block data had been available for urbanized areas only and had not been delivered to the states until the fall of 1971, too late for their use in conducting a timely redistricting. For the 1980 census, 22 states chose to participate in a new, optional census program providing information by election precinct for all or a portion of their states.

Despite the efforts of the federal government to provide the most accurate population counts possible, a wide range of cases challenging the census were filed following release of 1980 census data. The most important of these were two cases charging undercounts in the populations of the city of Detroit and the state and city of New York. In late February and early March 1982, the U.S. Supreme Court refused to hear either of the cases, thus effectively ending the undercount dispute which had threatened to delay redistricting efforts. Though the New York case was remanded back to a U.S. District Court, there is little likelihood that any future decision could influence the current reapportionment.

Two other significant census cases were decided by the Court in late February as well. The disputes, brought by Essex County, New Jersey (Newark) and Denver, Colorado, officials, involved the confidentiality of the census address records, needed by the plaintiffs to prove the inaccuracy of the census. The Court unanimously ruled that the records are indeed confidential, laying to rest another major census issue.

The accompanying table lists census population statistics and the gains and losses in congressional districts, by state, as used for reapportionment.

Voting Rights Act

The Voting Rights Act of 1965, along with the 14th and 15th Amendments to the U.S. Constitution, provides the grounds on which racial discrimination cases have been brought against reapportionment plans. Section 5 of the act, commonly referred to as the "preclearance provision," requires that states and political subdivisions covered under Section 5 "preclear" any changes in district boundaries (or other voting-related standards, practices or procedures) with the U.S. Department of Justice before putting them into effect. Nine states in whole and 13 in part are subject to the "preclearance provision." The entire states of Alabama, Alaska, Arizona, Georgia, Louisana, Mississippi, South Carolina, Texas and Virginia are covered. Portions of California, Colorado, Connecticut, Florida, Hawaii, Idaho, Massachusetts, Michigan, New Hampshire,. New York, North Carolina, South Dakota and Wyoming are also subject to the scrutiny of the Justice Department.

Section 5 requires the specially covered jurisdictions to affirmatively seek approval for their district changes by proving that such changes are not discriminatory. Section 2 of the act, however, applies nationwide and, in lawsuits where plaintiffs charge racial discrimination, requires the plaintiffs to prove that such districts are discriminatory.

In April 1980, the U.S. Supreme Court potentially weakened the Section 2 provision by ruling, in the case of *City of Mobile* v. *Bolden*, that a government's *intent* to discriminate must be proved in order for a racial vote dilution case to be successful. Thus, if a redistricting plan has a discriminatory *effect*, that alone does not prove a violation of the Constitution's Equal Protection Clause. The Court's decision was divided, producing no majority opinion and creating a great deal of confusion about the state of the law.

The act's special provisions (including Section 5) are up for renewal in August 1982. If they are not extended by Congress by that time, the jurisdictions covered under Section 5 can easily terminate their coverage. In 1981, the U.S. House of Representatives voted to extend the special provisions and, with regard to Section 2, specifically outlawed any voting rule or reapportionment plan that is discriminatory in effect, eliminating some of the confusion arising from the *Mobile* decision. As this book goes to press, the extension is pending in the U.S. Senate.

The upshot is that the U.S. Department of Justice still has the ability to object to legislative and congressional districting plans for those jurisdictions currently covered under the act. The department had already objected to plans in six states, as of March 26, 1982: Arizona (House and Senate), Georgia (House, Senate and congressional), South Carolina (House), Texas (House, Senate and congressional) and Virginia (House twice and Senate).

What's Different in the 1980s

Within the past 10 years, state legislatures have considered various means by which to improve the reapportionment process. Three innovations were instituted in time for the 1980 round of redistricting: the use of private consultants, computer technology and reapportionment commissions.

The use of private consultants to perform the redistricting chore increased tremendously in the 1980 reapportionment. The consultants, most of whom had not been actively involved in drawing district lines in the 1970s, are largely partisan and most often sell their computer software as part of their overall packages. Current computerization of reapportionment activity is highly sophisticated, using a variety of mapping and digitizing techniques developed within the last decade. Digitizing involves using a small electronic pad to enter map lines and coordinates into the computer. While most states used computers to some degree in drawing their new maps, they did not widely use the more complex technology. Some states, most notably New York, developed their own sophisticated computer systems that were the envy of the private consultants.

The concept of reapportionment commissions began to catch on in the 1970s, with encouragement from such organizations as Common Cause, as a means of reducing the politics involved in drawing districts. The commissions have not, however, had a significantly better track record than the legislatures in drawing reapportionment plans acceptable to the courts. Only two states, Hawaii and Montana, redistrict congressional seats by commission. Hawaii's plan was held unconstitutional late in March 1982 while Montana is not due to complete redistricting until 1983. Seven additional states reapportion legislative seats through the use of commissions: Arkansas, Colorado, Michigan, Missouri (separate House and Senate commissions), New Jersey, Ohio and Pennsylvania. Again, at the end of March, only three of those states (Arkansas, Missouri and New Jersey) were not the subject of court challenge.

This book goes to press at the height of reapportionment activity in the states. Some trends have already developed, however, in the types of law suits filed against reapportionment plans. Most common have been those cases brought because of the legislature's failure to complete its legislative or congressional remaps. At the end of March, five states' congressional redistricting plans had either been drawn or selected by federal courts: Colorado, Illinois, Minnesota, Missouri and South Carolina.

Furthermore, suits charging racial discrimination and denial of one-person, one-vote equal population standards have been successful in overturning two congressional redistricting plans. Three-judge federal panels in Arkansas and New Jersey ruled those states' congressional maps unconstitutional because the legislature had considered other plans with lower population variances. The plans had overall population ranges (the sum of the greatest deviations above and below the ideal district population) of 1.87 and 0.7 percent respectively. The Arkansas court drew a new plan; however, at the end of March, the U.S. Supreme Court, having issued a stay on the New Jersey order and denied a request for an expedited appeal, permitted the state's 1982 congressional elections to be held under the districts enacted by the legislature. The Court was expected to hear the case but had not definitely decided to do so. At question is the strictness of the "as nearly as practicable" standard of population equality.

The New Jersey case could potentially signal the beginning of the Supreme Court's involvement in 1980s reapportionment. To what extent the Court becomes further embroiled in the "political thicket" is yet to be seen as future and possibly more stringent reapportionment criteria emerge.

Note

1. For a more detailed review of the 1970s case law, see *Reapportionment: Law and Technology* (National Conference of State Legislatures, June 1980).

1980 POPULATION AND NUMBER OF U.S. REPRESENTATIVES BY STATE

State	Resident population used as the basis for apportionment	Number of representatives based on 1980 census	Change from 1970 apportionment	State	Resident population used as the basis for apportionment	Number of representatives based on 1980 census	Change from 1970 apportionment
United States(a) ..	226,504,825	435	...	Montana	786,690	2	...
				Nebraska	1,570,006	3	...
Alabama	3,890,061	7	...	Nevada...........	799,184	2	+1
Alaska	400,481	1	...	New Hampshire	920,610	2	...
Arizona	2,717,866	5	+1	New Jersey	7,364,158	14	-1
Arkansas	2,285,513	4	...				
California	23,668,562	45	+2	New Mexico	1,299,968	3	+1
				New York	17,557,288	34	-5
Colorado	2,888,834	6	+1	North Carolina	5,874,429	11	...
Connecticut	3,107,576	6	...	North Dakota	652,695	1	...
Delaware	595,225	1	...	Ohio.............	10,797,419	21	-2
Florida	9,739,992	19	+4				
Georgia	5,464,265	10	...	Oklahoma	3,025,266	6	...
				Oregon...........	2,632,663	5	+1
Hawaii	965,000	2	...	Pennsylvania......	11,866,728	23	-2
Idaho	943,935	2	...	Rhode Island......	947,154	2	...
Illinois	11,418,461	22	-2	South Carolina	3,119,208	6	...
Indiana	5,490,179	10	-1				
Iowa.............	2,913,387	6	...	South Dakota	690,178	1	-1
				Tennessee	4,590,750	9	+1
Kansas	2,363,208	5	...	Texas	14,228,383	27	+3
Kentucky	3,661,433	7	...	Utah.............	1,461,037	3	+1
Louisiana.........	4,203,972	8	...	Vermont	511,456	1	...
Maine............	1,124,660	2	...				
Maryland	4,216,446	8	...	Virginia	5,346,279	10	...
				Washington........	4,130,163	8	+1
Massachusetts.....	5,737,037	11	-1	West Virginia	1,949,644	4	...
Michigan	9,258,344	18	-1	Wisconsin	4,705,335	9	...
Minnesota	4,077,148	8	...	Wyoming.........	470,816	1	...
Mississippi........	2,520,638	5	...				
Missouri...........	4,917,444	9	-1	Dist. of Col.(b).....	637,651	...	...

Source: U.S. Bureau of the Census.
(a) Includes the District of Columbia. The total excluding the District of Columbia is 225,867,174.
(b) Excluded in determination of apportionment.

Section V   THE JUDICIARY

STATE OF THE JUDICIARY

By Charlotte A. Carter

Introduction

THE INCREASING COMPLEXITY of the society in which we live has had a tremendous impact upon state judicial systems as more and more citizens turn to the courts for resolution of disputes. The sharp rise in the number of cases filed in the courts has resulted in severe court congestion and increasing difficulty in allocating judicial resources within a jurisdiction. Predictably, the increase in judicial workload has created corresponding problems in the administration of the court system and the processing of cases.

In the face of increasing constraints, the courts have been criticized for their inefficient administration, their cumbersome procedures, the lengthy delay in processing cases, and the high cost of litigation. Considering the operation of the courts 25 years ago, however, it is obvious that tremendous strides have been made. Most of the significant criminal law decisions of the Warren Court were yet to come. Concern was focused on civil calendars while criminal, juvenile and appellate caseloads were thought to present little or no problem. Judicial education was non-existent, and rule-making powers were still thought to reside solely in the province of the legislature. The idea of managing the courts was a novelty, and a professional support staff was unheard of.

Today, however, as the concept of court management has gained widespread acceptance, many structural and management improvements have been achieved. Speedy trial in criminal cases is the accepted rule, although not one universally attained, and judicial education is considered essential to maintain the quality of justice. Courts routinely rely upon express constitutional or statutory authority or a claim of inherent power to promulgate rules of practice, procedure, administration or evidence. Trained court managers and support staff have introduced modern business management practices and the latest technology into the courts to speed case processing and to reduce costs.

Although the courts are rising to the challenges presented by an ever-changing society, time and research are required to find effective solutions to the yet unsolved problems facing the state courts. The remainder of this article will examine some of these problems and concerns as they are perceived and expressed by the state chief justices either individually in their state of the judiciary messages or collectively as the Conference of Chief Justices.

Fiscal Concerns

Sufficient Funding. Funding for state court systems is a crucial issue, frequently addressed by chief justices in their state of the judiciary reports. The combination of the increasing volume of litigation, rising inflation and a growing trend in government toward fiscal conservatism has resulted in mounting pressure to reduce state court budgets, creating a serious threat to the ability of courts to operate. The situation has reached crisis proportion in some jurisdictions with courts threatening to close down operations, either partially

---

Charlotte A. Carter is a staff attorney with the National Center for State Courts.

or completely, due to lack of funds.[1] Moreover, expanded jurisdiction, redistricting and the creation of additional judgeships have exacerbated the need for capital improvements in state court systems. Many trial courts lack sufficient courtrooms and support facilities to try cases promptly and to conduct clerical business efficiently.

A majority of state supreme courts have rule-making authority and general administrative and supervisory control over all courts within their state, in addition to their primary responsibility of appellate review. Accordingly, the chief justices in these states are all too cognizant of the critical impact that the availability of financial resources has on all aspects of court operations. In order to ensure a solid financial base for the state courts, these chief justices have supported legislation to provide full or partial state funding of general or limited jurisdiction courts. State funding is urged based on the rationale that, because local resources are limited and because state laws dictate the structure and operation of the court system, the state should bear ultimate responsibility for managing the courts.

The court systems in 22 states are completely or substantially state-funded, and several other jurisdictions are considering state court funding.[2] These states have achieved a more equitable fiscal operation because state funding has permitted them to: take a unified approach to budgeting; implement a merit-based, statewide personnel plan; and provide uniform services to the public. Furthermore, state funding of local courts has freed funds for important services that are best provided on a local basis.

Adequate Compensation. Additionally, judicial budget constraints significantly affect the quality of those who administer justice. Highly skilled, qualified judges are essential for an effective judicial system. Adequate salaries and fringe benefits are necessary to retain qualified judges currently on the bench and to attract to the judiciary the best members of the legal profession who would otherwise stay in private practice. The judicial salaries of state judges have failed to keep pace with either inflation or the overall rise in income for lawyers in the private sector. Recognizing the threat inadequate compensation presents to the caliber of the judiciary, several chief justices have strongly advocated passage of legislation that would provide appropriate judicial compensation by ensuring adequate cost-of-living increases for judicial personnel and by adjusting the benefits of retired judges to keep pace with inflation.[3]

Assistance for Court Improvements. In view of dwindling resources, the state judiciaries have placed increased emphasis on improved efficiency in court operations, especially through the use of research and technology. With reduced levels of federal funding generally and the loss of Law Enforcement Assistance Administration (LEAA) funds specifically, however, it is feared that court improvement efforts, which have resulted in effective structural and organizational changes in a number of state court systems and in essential educational, technical assistance, and research programs at the state and national levels, will cease to be maintained. The Conference of Chief Justices as well as individual chief justices have called upon state legislatures and local governing bodies to make funding available to continue and expand research and development programs for court improvement.[4]

The Conference also has advocated the establishment of a State Justice Institute to provide federal financial assistance to state courts to promote more efficient court operations.[5] The Conference maintains that a legitimate basis exists for federal aid to the state judiciaries as long as the use of federal funds is consistent with the doctrine of separation of powers and federalism. The basis is founded on the following assertions: the quality of justice at the national level is largely determined by the quality of justice in the state courts which handle over 98 percent of the cases filed in a given year;[6] the state courts share with the federal courts the obligation of enforcing the requirements of the U.S. Constitution and the laws of the United States; efforts to maintain high-quality justice in the federal courts and the implementation of the Speedy Trial Act of 1974 have resulted in the diversion of numerous federal cases to the state courts; and decisions of the U.S. Supreme Court have placed increased responsibility on state courts to guarantee procedural due process in criminal, civil, juvenile and mental health proceedings.

The federal courts' greater reliance upon the state judiciaries and the increasing procedural complexity of state court litigation necessitate the development of new and more efficient court operations and the provision of high-quality continuing education programs for members of the state judiciary. The proposed State Justice Institute would meet these needs through its authority to fund judicial education and training programs, information clearinghouses, and research, demonstration and evaluation projects. Moreover, it is contemplated that the institute would assist the state courts through the allocation of federal funds to nationwide organizations that support state judicial systems through education, research and technical assistance programs. Illustrative of national organizations working in the judicial system and deserving of continuing support are the National Judicial College, the Institute for Court Management, the National Center for State Courts, the Institute for Judicial Administration and the American Judicature Society.

Increasing Litigation and Delay

The volume of litigation in the state courts has been rising out of all proportion to increases in both population and court resources. According to the most recent national statistics available, state courts process annually some 90 million cases; 25 million of these are non-traffic and include approximately 130,000 appeals, 12 million civil cases, 11 million criminal cases and 1.2 million juvenile proceedings.[7] In 1981, several chief justices reported an annual increase of 10 to 25 percent in case filings in state trial and appellate courts.[8] Legislation enacted over the past decade that created new legal rights or new opportunities for legal controversy, such as environmental and consumer protection laws and revisions in small claims and domestic violence statutes, may account for much of this increase. A related problem of equal importance to the state judiciaries is the delay in processing and adjudicating cases filed in state courts. The substantial backlog of pending cases traditionally has been attributed to an imbalance in caseloads and workloads among judicial districts, a shortage of judges, inefficient case processing and an overabundance of procedural options and safeguards.

Finding efficient, prompt measures for coping with the problems of increasing caseloads and delay is of paramount concern to the state judiciaries. They have responded in a variety of ways. Some jurisdictions have attempted to reduce caseloads by requiring prehearing settlement conferences or by diverting certain kinds of cases to arbitration boards or mediation or dispute settlement centers. Other jurisdictions have adopted measures that permit more flexibility and efficiency in handling increasing workloads with current judicial resources. Others have instituted procedural reforms, including rules that provide for tighter control and accounting of case flow, expedite the criminal appeals process, reduce time limits for filing briefs, require prompt preparation of transcripts on appeal, and restrict formal written opinions to cases that involve new or significant legal issues.

Despite such measures, considerable research remains to be conducted concerning the causes of and cures for delay in the processing of cases. The findings of two major studies of delay contradict many of the commonly held assumptions. The Appellate Justice improvement Project, conducted by the National Center for State Courts, was aimed at reducing appellate courts' case-processing time, increasing their efficiency and determining the effectiveness of appellate case-processing techniques. Two important findings of the study were that the relationship between increasing case volume and appellate court delay has been over-emphasized and that the amount of backlog in a given court is a function of the "complex interplay of volume, decision-making efficiency and managerial style."[9] The study also found that appellate court structures and procedures have a greater effect on case processing times than do volume and case type. The study concludes that structure, or organization, and procedures can be modified or altered to deal with larger caseload demands and reduce case-processing time.[10]

The second major study of delay was conducted by the National Center for State Courts in cooperation with the National Conference of Metropolitan Courts. The Reducing Trial Court Delay Project studied major metropolitan courts throughout the country and found that: court size as determined by the number of sitting judges is not related to case processing speed; increase in workload does not result in a corresponding increase in delay; an inverse relationship exists between time spent on settlement activity and case processing time; courts with a relatively high proportion of jury trials are no less productive than courts with few jury trials; and courts with individual calendars have a faster mean disposition time than do courts using master calendars.[11] The most significant finding of this study, however, is that the pace of litigation is determined primarily by the local legal culture, defined as a stable set of expectations and informal rules of behavior on the part of judges and lawyers. The study concluded that local legal cultures can be changed to improve the pace of litigation if judicial personnel accept responsibility for reducing delay.[12] Suggested techniques for partial or total court management of the pace of litigation include total case management from commencement to disposition, imposition of firm trial dates, limitations on continuances and special emphasis on the movement of older cases. Testing in pilot courts has demonstrated that these techniques do, in fact, work.[13]

Quality of Court Personnel

The state judicial leadership has recognized that the quality of performance from the primary actors in the judicial system has a decisive impact upon the overall improvement of the administration of justice. Judicial qualifications commissions and disciplinary boards have been established in most states to evaluate the performance of judges, disseminate information to the public prior to retention elections, investigate complaints of judicial misconduct and remove judges from office.

The need for professional administrators and trained support staff to apply principles and techniques of modern business management to the courts has gained increasing support over the years. Professional organizations for managers at all court levels, such as the Conference of State Court Administrators, the National Association of Trial Court Administrators and the National Association for Court Administration, have contributed to the growth and education of the profession. The First National Symposium on Court Management, held in September 1981, testified to the significant progress that has been made. The symposium was the result of cooperative efforts between five court management associations to undertake a comprehensive and constructively critical view of court management and the role of court administration. Heightened professionalism in court management has increased efficiency, reduced costs and improved financial, record and case flow management.

State judiciaries also are becoming increasingly aware of the need to maintain high-quality professional performance through continuing education for judicial and non-judicial personnel. In many jurisdictions administrative offices of the courts, state judicial colleges or special committees under the auspices of the supreme courts or state judicial councils have undertaken responsibility for in-state training sessions and educational seminars for employees of all levels of the court systems. Valuable training programs are offered on the national level by such organizations as the National Judicial College, the National Center for State Courts and the Institute for Court Management to keep judges abreast of recent developments in law and procedures and to sharpen the management skills of administrators and clerks. Faced with the withdrawal of federal funds, chief justices have encouraged state and local funding of continuing education programs for judges and court personnel.[14]

Lawyer Training and Competence

The chief justices have expressed concern over the quality of lawyers practicing in state courts. There has been a growing awareness that the current processes of legal education, bar admission exams, continuing legal education and attorney discipline are insufficient to ensure that lawyers in general, and those entering the courtroom in particular, are competent practitioners. The highest court in each state promulgates and enforces state rules governing the legal profession. Accordingly, it has a special responsibility to assure the public that members of the bar are qualified to render professional legal service.

To that end, the Conference of Chief Justices has maintained a Task Force on Lawyer Competence since 1979 and has taken an active role in efforts to improve performance levels in the legal profession. The states have adopted various measures to ensure lawyer competency including increased emphasis on clinical programs in law school curriculums, higher standards for bar admissions, continuing legal education and certification programs, and peer review or mentorship programs. Based on its findings that no one program will ensure lawyer competency, the task force has advocated a comprehensive approach to the problem, which encompasses a variety of different programs focusing on all levels and all aspects of law practice, and has called for a strong commitment to lawyer competence by the states' highest courts. Furthermore, the task force has recommended the creation of a Coordinating Council on Lawyer Competence to: provide a forum for discussion of lawyer competency issues; coordinate the many programs being developed and tested; maintain information on this topic; provide continuing review of programs, processes and rule changes; and recommend those most conducive to improvements in lawyer competence.[15]

Public Image of the Judicial System

In 1978, a nationwide survey was sponsored by the National Center for State Courts and conducted by one of the leading polling firms to ascertain the public's opinion of the courts. The two major conclusions that emerged from the study were: the general public's confidence in their state and local courts is extremely low in sharp contrast to the confidence judges and lawyers have in the courts, and the general public has little knowledge of or contact with the courts.[16] It has been suggested that the widespread public dissatisfaction with the administration of justice is created in part by the public's lack of knowledge and understanding about how the court system actually works. In response, leaders of the state judiciary have adocated measures to increase the public's understanding of and confidence in the judicial system. These measures include: public education programs aimed at school and civic organizations; experimentation, under controlled conditions, with extended media coverage of courtroom proceedings; establishment of bench, bar and media committees; and improvement of public relations by inviting citizen participation on court improvement committees and by adding lay members to such policy-making bodies as judicial nominating commissions and judicial councils.[17] Furthermore, courts are giving greater attention to their relationship with and treatment of those who come in direct contact with the courts—jurors, witnesses and litigants. For example, numerous courts have undertaken measures to minimize the inconvenience of jury duty and to improve citizens' attitudes about the judicial systems. These include shortened terms of service, increases in juror compensation and use of telephone call-in procedures to notify jurors whether they need to report to the courthouse on a particular day.

Jurisdictional Issues

Of long-standing concern to the Conference of Chief Justices are issues dealing with state-federal sovereignty and with lower federal court review of state court decisions. The conference has voiced support for legislative proposals that would allocate jurisdiction between federal and state courts in such a manner as to eliminate wasteful duplication of federal and state court efforts.

Limitations on Federal Collateral Review of State Court Convictions. The conference has strongly criticized the continued duplication, overlapping and redundancy of collateral review of state criminal convictions in the federal courts which unduly delays and calls into question the legitimacy of state criminal proceedings. Accordingly, the conference has endorsed proposed amendments to the federal criminal code that would bar federal habeas corpus review of issues not properly raised in state courts unless cause and prejudice is shown for failure to do so, establish reasonable time limits within which a federal habeas corpus action must be commenced and bar federal habeas corpus review when the state court record provides a factual basis for the state court findings and such record was made under circumstances affording the petitioner a full and fair hearing on the factual issue.[18] Enactment of this legislation would permit orderly and timely presentation of state prisoners' claims while promoting the finality of state criminal processes and ensuring proper respect for state court factual determinations.

Diversity Jurisdiction. The Conference of Chief Justices has expressed support for proposed legislation that would eliminate federal diversity jurisdiction.[19] It is urged that diversity cases are the proper responsibility of state courts because of the state interests involved. Diversity cases generally involve the type of litigation that is routinely handled by state courts, such as claims arising out of contracts or suits for damages for personal injuries, and is not considered within the federal courts' expertise. Because these cases involve interpretations of state law, errors and inconsistencies are bound to occur when federal trial judges attempt to interpret state laws and precedents. Furthermore, state assumption of diversity cases would help relieve the critical case overload facing federal courts as a result of an increasing number of criminal and federal question cases filed in federal courts. Moreover, the original rationale behind diversity jurisdiction—that a non-resident party suffers from local prejudice—is no longer seriously contended. Finally, the implication of diversity jurisdiction that state courts will not provide a "hospitable forum" demeans state court systems and ignores improvements that have been made in the administration of justice in state courts.

Limitations on Federal Court Jurisdiction. The conference also has questioned the wisdom of proposed congressional legislation to limit the jurisdiction of federal courts, including the U.S. Supreme Court, in cases involving school desegregation and busing, prayer in public schools and abortion. The conference warns that eliminating the "unifying function of Supreme Court review" could produce different constitutional interpretation in the several states and maintains that the "resulting inconsistencies in legal precedent and the more frequent jurisdictional disputes would further overload state courts."[20] Furthermore, the conference views such proposals as an attempt to bypass the amendment process and obtain changes in constitutional law by circumscribing the powers of federal courts.

Conclusion

The foregoing discussion reveals that the state judicial leaders are sensitive to the problems facing the courts and are working to meet the challenges presented. As caseload demand increases and budgeting levels decrease, courts are responding positively with administrative, structural and procedural changes to improve the efficiency of court operations and reduce costs. Courts have relied increasingly upon court resource organizations that have contributed significantly to court improvement efforts through research, technical assistance and educational programs. Accordingly, the state judiciaries are pledged to the continuation and expansion of such research and development programs and have urged continued federal and state financial support for these organizations. Major studies of appellate and trial delay suggest delay is not inevitable, and pilot testing has shown that case processing time can be reduced if courts will accept responsibility for implementing case management techniques. The impact of the performance of judges, lawyers and court support staff on the quality of justice has been acknowledged, and measures are being undertaken to ensure the competency of these individuals. Recognizing the need to restore and maintain the public's confidence in and respect for the judicial system, courts have assumed an active role in informing and educating the public about the judicial process. The Conference of Chief Justices as the collective voice of state judicial leadership has expressed concern over issues involving state and federal court jurisdiction and their possible effect on the independence and operations of state courts.

Although problems remain to be resolved and worsening economic conditions will undoubtedly intensify existing problems and create new ones, the state judiciaries are committed to finding effective solutions to these problems in order to increase the efficiency of the judicial process and enhance the quality of justice.

Notes

1. Gilmore, "The Day the Detroit Courts Ran Out of Money," *Judges Journal* 19 (1980): 36; Burke, "Court Closing Threatened," *National Law Journal*, May 19, 1980; Eisen, "Judges Warn Fund Lack Could Close City Courts for Summer," *Washington Post*, May 30, 1980, and "Lack of Funds May Halt Superior Court Jury Trial," *Washington Post*, April 3, 1980.

2. Institute for Advanced Studies in Justice, Criminal Courts Technical Assistance Project, *State Funding of Court Systems: An Initial Examination* Washington, D.C.: American University Law School, 1979).

3. Rausch, "The State of the Judiciary: An Agenda for Change, *State Court Journal* 5 (1981): 23, 41.

4. See Conference of Chief Justices Resolutions on Loss of LEAA Funds for Courts, Thirty-second Annual Meeting, July 28, 1980.

5. Conference of Chief Justices Resolution on State Judicial Institute, Thirty-first Annual Meeting, August 8, 1979.

6. Joint Committee of the Conference of Chief Justices and Conference of State Court Administrators, Report of the Task Force on a State Court Improvement Act 5 (May 1979); Memorandum from Nora Blair of the

National Center for State Courts to Francis J. Taillefer, Project Director, National Court Statistics Project (April 16, 1979) indicates that 98.8 percent of current cases are handled in state courts.

7. These figures were obtained from data contained in National Court Statistics Project, *State Court Caseload Statistics: Annual Report, 1976* (National Center for State Courts, 1980).

8. See Rausch, "State of the Judiciary," Note 3, pp. 23-24.

9. Martin and Prescott, *Appellate Court Delay: Structural Responses to the Problems of Volume and Delay* (National Center for State Courts, 1981), p. xviii.

10. Ibid, p. xxi.

11. Church, et al., *Justice Delayed: The Pace of Litigation in Urban Trial Courts* (National Center for State Courts, 1978), pp. 3-13.

12. Ibid., p. 14.

13. Sipes, et al., *Managing to Reduce Delay* (National Center for State Courts, 1980).

14. Rausch, "State of the Judiciary," Note 3, p. 41.

15. Conference of Chief Justices Task Force on Lawyer Competence, Report with Findings and Recommendations (Draft, January 7, 1981).

16. National Center for State Courts, *State Courts: A Blueprint for the Future* (1978), p. 5.

17. Rausch, "State of the Judiciary," Note 3, p. 42.

18. Conference of Chief Justices Resolution on Amendments to the Federal Criminal Code Concerning Federal Court Collateral Review of State Court Criminal Convictions, "Thirty-third Annual Meeting, August 5, 1981.

19. Sheran, "State Courts and Federalism in the 1980's," *William and Mary Law Review* 22 (1981): 789, 793; Diversity of Citizenship Jurisdiction/Magistrates Reform: Hearings on H.R. 1046 and H.R. 2202 Before the Subcommittee on Courts, Civil Liberties and the Administration of Justice of the House Committee on the Judiciary, 96th Cong., 1st Sess. 109-14 (Statement of Robert J. Sheran).

20. Conference of Chief Justices Resolution Relating to Proposed Legislation to Restrict the Jurisdiction of the Federal Courts, Fifth Midyear Meeting, January 30, 1982.

Table 1
STATE COURTS OF LAST RESORT

State or other jurisdiction	Name of court	Justices chosen* At large	Justices chosen* By district	Chief justice† Method of selection	Chief justice† Term
Alabama	S.C.	★	...	Popular election	6 years
Alaska	S.C.	★(a)	...	By court	3 years(b)
Arizona	S.C.	★	...	By court	5 years
Arkansas	S.C.	★	...	Popular election	8 years
California	S.C.	★(a)	...	First apptd. by gov., then subject to approval by popular election	12 years
Colorado	S.C.	★(a)	...	By court	Pleasure of court
Connecticut	S.C.	★(c)	...	Nominated by gov., apptd. by legislature	8 years
Delaware	S.C.	★(d)	...	Apptd. by gov., confirmed by senate	12 years
Florida	S.C.	...	★	By court	2 years
Georgia	S.C.	★	...	Appointed by court	6 years
Hawaii	S.C.	★(e)	...	Apptd. by gov., with consent of senate	10 years
Idaho	S.C.	★	...	By court	4 years
Illinois	S.C.	...	★	By court	3 years
Indiana	S.C.	★	...	Judicial Nominating Commission	5 years
Iowa	S.C.	★(a)	...	By court	Remainder of term as justice
Kansas	S.C.	★(a)	...	Seniority of service	Remainder of term as justice
Kentucky	S.C.	...	★	By court	4 years
Louisiana	S.C.	...	★	Seniority of service	Remainder of term as justice
Maine	S.J.C.	★(d)	...	Apptd. by gov., with consent of senate	7 years
Maryland	C.A.	...	★(a)	By governor	Remainder of term as judge
Massachusetts	S.J.C.	★(d)	★	Apptd. by gov., with consent of exec. council	To age 70
Michigan	S.C.	★	...	By court	2 years
Minnesota	S.C.	★	...	Popular election	6 years
Mississippi	S.C.	...	★	Seniority of service	Remainder of term as justice
Missouri	S.C.	★(f)	...	By court rotation	2 years
Montana	S.C.	★	...	Popular election	8 years
Nebraska	S.C.	...	★(a)	By governor	6 years
Nevada	S.C.	★	...	Justice whose commission is oldest—rotation	2 years
New Hampshire	S.C.	★(d)	...	Apptd. by gov. and council	To age 70
New Jersey	S.C.	★(d)	...	Apptd. by gov., with consent of senate	7 years, reapptd. to age 70
New Mexico	S.C.	★	...	By court	2 years
New York	C.A.	★(d)	...	Apptd. by gov., with consent of senate	14 years(g)
North Carolina	S.C.	★	...	Popular election	8 years
North Dakota	S.C.	★	...	By supreme & district court judges sitting together	5 years or until expiration of term as justice, whichever is first
Ohio	S.C.	★	...	Popular election	6 years
Oklahoma	S.C.	...	★(a)	By court	2 years
	C.C.A.	...	★(a)	By court	2 years
Oregon	S.C.	★	...	By court	6 years
Pennsylvania	S.C.	★	...	Seniority of service	Remainder of term as justice
Rhode Island	S.C.	★(h)	...	By legislature	Life
South Carolina	S.C.	★(h)	...	By legislature	10 years
South Dakota	S.C.	...	★	By court	4 years
Tennessee	S.C.	★(i)	...	By court rotation	Approximately 19 months
Texas	S.C.	★	...	Popular election	6 years
	C.C.A	★	...	Popular election	6 years
Utah	S.C.	★(a)	...	Justice with shortest time to serve on a regularly elected term	Remainder of term as justice
Vermont	S.C.	★(d)	...	By governor, with consent of senate	6 years
Virginia	S.C.	★(h)	...	Seniority of service	Remainder of term as justice
Washington	S.C.	★	...	Judge with shortest time to serve(j)	2 years
West Virginia	S.C.A.	★	...	By court	Pleasure of court
Wisconsin	S.C.	★	...	Seniority of service	Remainder of term as justice
Wyoming	S.C.	★(f)	...	By court	2 years
Dist. of Col.	C.A.	★	...	By Judicial Nomination Commission	4 years
American Samoa	H.C.	★(k)	...	By U.S. Secretary of the Interior	Life
Puerto Rico	S.C.	★(d)	...	Apptd. by gov., with consent of senate	To age 70

Key:
S.C.—Supreme Court
S.J.C.—Supreme Judicial Court
C.A.—Court of Appeals
C.C.A.—Court of Criminal Appeals
S.C.A.—Supreme Court of Appeals
H.C.—High Court
*See table on Final Selection of Judges for details.
† Title is Chief Justice, except Chief Judge in Maryland, New York and D.C. and Presiding Judge in Oklahoma, Texas (Court of Criminal Appeals) and South Dakota.
(a) Justice originally appointed by governor (in Maryland and Utah, with consent of the senate), subsequently stand for retention on their records.
(b) A justice may serve more than one term as chief justice but may not serve consecutive terms in that office.

(c) Justices nominated by governor, appointed by legislature.
(d) Justices appointed by governor, with consent of senate. In Massachusetts and New Hampshire, with consent of council.
(e) Appointed by governor with consent of senate after nomination on a list of at least six names by Judicial Selection Committee.
(f) Justices apppointed by governor from a list of three submitted by Nominating Committee.
(g) Or until age 70, whichever occurs first.
(h) Justices elected by legislature.
(i) Justices chosen at large (each voter may vote for five), but not more than two may reside in any one of the three geographical regions of the state.
(j) Senior judge next up for election who has not yet served as chief justice. Must have served a full term to be eligible for chief justice.
(k) Appointed by U.S. Secretary of the Interior.

Table 2
NUMBER OF JUDGES AND TERMS FOR APPELLATE COURTS AND MAJOR TRIAL COURTS

State or other jurisdiction	Appellate courts						Major trial courts		
	Court of last resort	No. of judges	Term (in years)	Intermediate appellate court	No. of judges	Term (in years)	Major trial courts	No. of judges	Term (in years)
Alabama	Supreme Court	9	6	Court of Criminal Appeals	5	6	Circuit courts	113	6
				Court of Civil Appeals	3	6			
Alaska	Supreme Court	5	10				Superior courts	21	6
Arizona	Supreme Court	5	6	Court of Appeals	15	6	Superior courts	81	4
Arkansas	Supreme Court	7	8	Court of Appeals	6	8	Chancery & probate courts	33	6
							Circuit courts	30	4
California	Supreme Court	7	12	Courts of Appeal	59	12	Superior Courts	628	6
Colorado	Supreme Court	7	10	Court of Appeals	10	8	District Court	107	6
Connecticut	Supreme Court	6(a)	8	. . .			Superior Court	121(a)	8
Delaware	Supreme Court	5	12				Court of Chancery	3	12
							Superior Court	11	12
Florida	Supreme Court	7	6	District courts of appeal	45	6	Circuit courts	326	6
Georgia	Supreme Court	7	6	Court of Appeals	9	6	Superior courts	116	4-8
Hawaii	Supreme Court	5	10	Intermediate Appellate Court	3	10	Circuit courts	21	10
Idaho	Supreme Court	5	6	Court of Appeals	3	6	District courts	31	4
Illinois	Supreme Court	7	10	Appellate Court	34(b)	10	Circuit courts	650(c)	6(c)
Indiana	Supreme Court	5	10	Court of Appeals	12	10	Superior courts	92	6
							County courts	64	4
Iowa	Supreme Court	9	8	Court of Appeals	5	6	District Court	307(d)	6(d)
Kansas	Supreme Court	7	6	Court of Appeals	7	4	District courts	211(e)	4
Kentucky	Supreme Court	7	8	Court of Appeals	14	8	Circuit courts	91	8
Louisiana	Supreme Court	7	10	Courts of appeals	48	10	District courts	167	6
Maine	Supreme Judicial Court	7	7				Superior Court	14	7
Maryland	Court of Appeals	7	10	Court of Special Appeals	13	10	Circuit courts of counties	80	15
							Courts of Supreme Bench of Baltimore City	23	15
Massachusetts	Supreme Judicial Court	7	To age 70	Appeals Court	10	To age 70	Trial Court	264	To age 70
Michigan	Supreme Court	7	8	Court of Appeals	18	6(f)	Circuit courts	165	6(f)
							Recorder's Court (Detroit)	29	6(f)
Minnesota	Supreme Court	9	6	. . .			District courts	72	6
Mississippi	Supreme Court	9	8	. . .			Chancery courts	38	4
							Circuit courts	35	4
Missouri	Supreme Court	7	12	Court of Appeals	31	12	Circuit courts	131	6
Montana	Supreme Court	7	8	. . .			District courts	31	6
Nebraska	Supreme Court	7	6	. . .			District courts	47	6
Nevada	Supreme Court	5	6	. . .			District courts	35	6
New Hampshire	Supreme Court	5	To age 70	. . .			Superior court	15	To age 70
New Jersey	Supreme Court	7	7(g)	Appellate division of Superior Court	21	7(g)	Superior Court	236	7(g)

State	Court of last resort	No.	Term	Intermediate appellate court	No.	Term	General trial court	No.	Term
New Mexico	Supreme Court	5	8	Court of Appeals	7	8	District courts	49	6
New York	Court of Appeals	7	14(h)	Appellate divisions of Supreme Court(i)	24(j)	5(k)	Supreme Court	263	14(h)
North Carolina	Supreme Court	7	8	Court of Appeals	12	8	Superior Court	66	8
North Dakota	Supreme Court	5	10	…	…	…	District courts	26	6
Ohio	Supreme Court	7	6	Courts of appeals	52	6	Courts of common pleas	321	6
Oklahoma	Supreme Court	9	6	Court of Appeals	6	6	District courts	202	4(l)
	Court of Criminal Appeals	3	6						
Oregon	Supreme Court	7	6	Court of Appeals	10	6	Circuit courts	85	6
Pennsylvania	Supreme Court	7	10	Superior Court	15	10	Courts of common pleas	309	10
				Commonwealth Court	9	10			
Rhode Island	Supreme Court	5	Life	…	…	…	Superior Court	19	Life
South Carolina	Supreme Court	5	10	…	…	…	Circuit Court	31	6
South Dakota	Supreme Court	5	8	…	…	…	Circuit courts	36	8
Tennessee	Supreme Court	5	8	Court of Appeals	12	8	Circuit courts	27	8
				Court of Criminal Appeals	9	8	Chancery courts	58	8
							Criminal courts	26	8
							Law-equity courts	5	8
Texas	Supreme Court	9	6	Court of Civil Appeals	79(m)	6	District courts	347(m)	4
	Court of Criminal Appeals	9	6						
Utah	Supreme Court	5	10	…	…	…	District courts	25	6
Vermont	Supreme Court	5	6	…	…	…	Superior courts	10	6(n)
							District courts	14	6
Virginia	Supreme Court	7	12	…	…	…	Circuit courts	113	8
Washington	Supreme Court	9	6	Court of Appeals	16	6	Superior courts	127	4
West Virginia	Supreme Court of Appeals	5	12	…	…	…	Circuit courts	60	8
Wisconsin	Supreme Court	7	10	Court of Appeals	12	6	Circuit courts	190	6
Wyoming	Supreme Court	5	8	…	…	…	District courts	17	6
Dist. of Col.	Court of Appeals	9	15	…	…	…	Superior Court	44	15
American Samoa	High Court: Appellate	8(o)	(p)	…	…	…	High Court: Trial	8(o)	8(o)
Guam	…	…	…	…	…	…	Superior Court	5	7
Northern Mariana Is.	…	…	…	…	…	…	Commonwealth Court	3	6
Puerto Rico	Supreme Court	8	To age 70	…	…	…	Superior Court	92	12

(a) Does not include senior judges, i.e., judges between the ages of 65 and 70 who are eligible for assignment to judicial duties but who have retired from full-time service as a judge.

(b) Elective judgeships. Retired and sitting circuit judges are assigned full time to appellate court as needed.

(c) Composed of circuit and associate judges who have full jurisdiction of circuit court. Associate judges serve four-year terms.

(d) A unified system with 95 district court judges who possess full jurisdiction of the court. An additional 39 district associate judges, nine senior judges and 166 part-time judicial magistrates have limited jurisdiction. District associate judges serve four years; part-time magistrates, two years.

(e) 71 district judges, 67 associate district judges and 73 district magistrate judges.

(f) Terms for new judgeships are for 10, eight or six years; elected thereafter for six-year term.

(g) With reappointment to age 70.

(h) To age 70; judges may be certificated thereafter as supreme court justices for two-year terms up to age 76.

(i) The appellate divisions may establish appellate terms to hear appeals from local courts. County courts, although basically trial courts, may hear appeals from certain local courts.

(j) 24 justices permanently authorized; in addition, 21 justices and certificated retired justices have been temporarily assigned.

(k) Or until term as supreme court justice expires. Presiding justices of four appellate divisions are appointed for remainder of their terms as supreme court justices.

(l) Special judges serve at pleasure of district judges by whom they are appointed.

(m) Effective January 1, 1983.

(n) Six years for superior judges; four years for assistant judges.

(o) Chief justice and associate justice sit in all divisions as well as court of last resort except in Matai cases; trial court judges sit in all divisions of the High Court by designation of the chief justice.

(p) Appointed. See table on Final Selection of Judges for details.

Table 3
COMPENSATION OF JUDGES OF APPELLATE COURTS AND MAJOR TRIAL COURTS*

| State or other jurisdiction | Appellate courts | | | | Major trial courts | Salary |
	Court of last resort	Salary	Intermediate appellate court	Salary		
Alabama	Supreme Court	$49,000(a)	Court of Criminal Appeals	$48,000(b)	Circuit courts	$36,550(c)
			Court of Civil Appeals	48,000(b)		
Alaska	Supreme Court	52,992(d)	. . .	. . .	Superior courts	48,576(d)
Arizona	Supreme Court	47,500	Court of Appeals	45,500	Superior courts	43,500(e)
Arkansas	Supreme Court	46,214(a)	Court of Appeals	44,603	Chancery & probate courts	42,991
					Circuit courts	42,991
California	Supreme Court	76,498(a,f)	Courts of Appeal	71,718(f)	Superior courts	62,670(f,g)
Colorado	Supreme Court	55,600(a)	Court of Appeals	51,152	District Court	47,260
Connecticut	Supreme Court	46,600(a,b)	. . .	. . .	Superior Court	36,806-43,873
Delaware	Supreme Court	52,920(a)	. . .	. . .	Court of Chancery	49,680(b)
					Superior Court	49,680(b)
Florida	Supreme Court	61,500	District courts of appeal	55,500	Circuit courts	53,000
Georgia	Supreme Court	52,412	Court of Appeals	51,840	Superior courts	43,867(h)
Hawaii	Supreme Court	45,000(a)	Intermediate Appellate Court	43,750(b)	Circuit courts	42,500
Idaho	Supreme Court	43,000	Court of Appeals	42,000	District courts	41,000
Illinois	Supreme Court	58,000	Appellate Court	53,000	Circuit courts	50,500(i)
Indiana	Supreme Court	42,000(j)	Court of Appeals	42,000(j)	Circuit courts	35,500-37,500(k)
					Superior courts	35,500-37,500(k)
					County courts	30,500(k)
Iowa	Supreme Court	52,900(a)	Court of Appeals	50,200(b)	District courts	47,000(b,l)
Kansas	Supreme Court	47,500(a)	Court of Appeals	45,500(b)	District courts	44,000(m)
Kentucky	Supreme Court	51,940(a)	Court of Appeals	49,820(b)	Circuit courts	47,700
Louisiana.........	Supreme Court	66,566	Court of Appeals	63,367	District courts	60,169
Maine	Supreme Judicial Court	40,392(a)	. . .	. . .	Superior Court	39,760
Maryland	Court of Appeals	56,200(a)	Court of Special Appeals	53,500(b)	Circuit courts of counties	52,500
					Courts of Supreme Bench of Baltimore City	52,500
Massachusetts......	Supreme Judicial Court	50,000(a)	Appeals Court	45,000(b)	Trial Court	42,500(b)
Michigan	Supreme Court	69,000	Court of Appeals	66,240	Circuit courts	48,160-63,480(k)
					Recorder's Court (Detroit)	63,480
					District courts	34,155-60,720(k)
Minnesota	Supreme Court	56,000(a)	. . .	. . .	District courts	48,000
Mississippi	Supreme Court	46,000(a)	. . .	. . .	Chancery courts	41,000
					Circuit courts	41,000
Missouri..........	Supreme Court	50,000(a)	Court of Appeals	47,500	Circuit courts	45,000
Montana	Supreme Court	43,360(a)	. . .	. . .	District courts	42,273
Nebraska	Supreme Court	48,314	. . .	. . .	District courts	44,382
Nevada...........	Supreme Court	61,500	. . .	. . .	District courts	57,000
New Hampshire	Supreme Court	47,513(a)	. . .	. . .	Superior Court	46,270(b)
New Jersey	Supreme Court	63,000(a)	Appellate division of Superior Court	60,000	Superior Court	55,000(n)
New Mexico	Supreme Court	49,500(a)	Court of Appeals	47,000(b)	District courts	45,000
New York	Court of Appeals	75,600(a)	Appellate divisions of Supreme Court	65,100(b)	Supreme Court	60,900
North Carolina	Supreme Court	54,288(a)	Court of Appeals	51,396(b)	Superior Court	45,636(j)
North Dakota	Supreme Court	49,900(a)	. . .	. . .	District courts	46,900(b)
Ohio	Supreme Court	51,000(a)	Court of Appeals	47,000	Courts of common pleas	33,000-43,500(o)
Oklahoma	Supreme Court	53,760(a)	Court of Appeals	50,400	District Court	33,000-44,800(p)
	Court of Criminal Appeals	53,760(a)				
Oregon...........	Supreme Court	53,308	Court of Appeals	52,039	Circuit courts	48,356
Pennsylvania.......	Supreme Court	64,500(a)	Superior Court	62,500(b)	Courts of Common pleas	55,000(q)
			Commonwealth Court	62,500(b)		
Rhode Island......	Supreme Court	46,622(a,r)	. . .	. . .	Superior Court	44,139(b,r)
South Carolina	Supreme Court	55,088(a)	. . .	. . .	Circuit Court	55,088
South Dakota	Supreme Court	44,750(a)	. . .	. . .	Circuit courts	41,750(b)
Tennessee	Supreme Court	73,015(a,s)	Court of Appeals	66,931(b,s)	Chancery courts	60,846(s)
			Court of Criminal Appeals	66,931(b,s)	Circuit courts	60,846(s)
					Criminal courts	60,846(s)
					Law equity courts	60,846(s)
Texas	Supreme Court	71,400(a)	Court of Civil Appeals	60,100(b,t)	District courts	50,400(u)
	Court of Criminal Appeals	71,400(a)				
Utah	Supreme Court	47,500	. . .	. . .	District courts	43,500(b)
Vermont	Supreme Court	41,000(a)	. . .	. . .	Superior courts	39,000(b)
					District courts	39,000(b)
Virginia	Supreme Court	59,000(a,j)	. . .	. . .	Circuit courts	54,820
Washington........	Supreme Court	51,000	Court of Appeals	48,100	Superior courts	44,700
West Virginia	Supreme Court of Appeals	49,000	. . .	. . .	Circuit courts	45,000
Wisconsin	Supreme Court	56,016(a)	Court of Appeals	51,372	Circuit courts	49,180
Wyoming..........	Supreme Court	63,500	. . .	. . .	District courts	61,000
Dist. of Col.	Court of Appeals	63,810(a)	. . .	. . .	Superior Court	60,390
American Samoa ...	High Court: Appellate	44,547-50,112(v)	. . .	. . .	High Court Trial	9,000(w)
Guam	. . .	. . .	. . .	. . .	Superior Court	43,500(b)
No. Mariana Is.	. . .	. . .	. . .	. . .	Commonwealth Court	38,000(b)
Puerto Rico........	Supreme Court	36,000(a)	. . .	. . .	Superior Court	30,000

THE JUDICIARY

*Compensation is shown according to most recent legislation even though laws may not yet have taken effect.

(a) These jurisdictions pay additional amounts to chief justices or presiding judges of court of last resort:
Alabama, Delaware, Texas, District of Columbia—$500.
Arkansas—$4,201.
California—$4,781.
Colorado—$3,336.
Connecticut—$4,493.
Hawaii, Missouri, New Jersey, Pennsylvania—$2,500.
Iowa—$5,000.
Kansas, Kentucky, New Mexico, Virginia—$1,000.
Maine—$1,894.
Maryland—$1,600.
Massachusetts, South Dakota, Vermont—$2,000.
Minnesota—$3,000.
Mississippi—chief justice, $1,000; presiding judges, $500.
Montana—$1,087.
New Hampshire—$1,842.
New York—$3,150.
North Carolina—$1,152.
North Dakota—$1,500.
Ohio—$3,500.
Oklahoma—$2,400.
Rhode Island—$1,241.
South Carolina—$7,089.
Tennessee—$6,084.
Wisconsin—$7,308.
Puerto Rico—$600.

(b) Additional amounts paid to various judges:
Alabama—presiding judges, $500.
Connecticut—chief court administrator, if he is a judge of supreme or superior court, $2,246.
Delaware—presiding judge of chancery and superior courts, $500.
Hawaii—chief judge of intermediate appellate court, $1,250.
Iowa—chief judge of district court, $2,100; chief judge of court of appeals, $1,100.
Kansas, New Mexico—chief judge of court of appeals, $1,000.
Kentucky—chief judge of court of appeals, $500.
Maryland—presiding judge of intermediate appellate court, $1,700.
Massachusetts—chief justice of appeals court, $2,000; trial court chief administrative justice, $4,500; trial court department administrative justice, $2,000.
New Hampshire—presiding judge of superior court, $1,243.
New York—presiding justice of intermediate appellate court, $4,200.
North Carolina—presiding judge of intermediate appellate court, $1,164.
North Dakota—presiding judge of district court, $1,200.

Pennsylvania—presiding judge of intermediate appellate court and commonwealth court, $1,500.
Rhode Island—presiding judge of superior court, $1,241.
South Dakota—presiding judge, $1,000.
Tennessee—presiding judge, $2,434.
Texas—chief justice, $500.
Utah—chief justice, $500; chairman of judicial council, $1,000.
Vermont—administrative judge, $2,000.
Guam—presiding judge, $1,500.
Northern Mariana Islands—chief judge, $6,000.

(c) Local supplements up to 40 percent of state salary.
(d) Base figures may be adjusted for geographical cost-of-living supplements.
(e) One-half paid by state, one-half by county.
(f) Cost-of-living annual increase based on average percentage salary increase granted state employees.
(g) Partially paid by state, partially by county, based on statutory formula.
(h) Plus county supplements, if any.
(i) Associate judges of circuit court, $45,000.
(j) These jurisdictions pay an expense allowance: Indiana—$3,000; North Carolina—$5,500; Virginia—$4,000 in lieu of per diem.
(k) Range based on varying optional county supplements. Indiana—range depends on population of circuit.
(l) District associate judges and full-time judicial magistrates, $38,900; part-time judicial magistrates, $10,800.
(m) Associate district judges may have a state-paid salary of $42,000. District magistrate judges' salaries are paid entirely by state; amounts average $19,000.
(n) Assignment judges receive $58,000 salary.
(o) Variation in salary based on population.
(p) Unified court system. District judges, $44,800; associate district judges paid on basis of population ranges.
(q) Additional amounts up to $2,500 paid president judges and administrative and president judges of divisions. Variations based on number of judges and population.
(r) Salary supplemented by state service longevity at 7, 11, 15, 20 and 25 years up to 20 percent.
(s) Cost-of-living increase limited to 5 percent yearly until July 1982 for new judges coming on the bench. Salaries as follows: supreme court justices, $61,251; appellate judges, $56,147; trial judges, $51,043.
(t) Counties may supplement to a total salary of $70,400-$70,900 for chief judges of intermediate appellate courts.
(u) Counties may supplement up to a total of $1,000 less than that received by justices of intermediate appellate courts.
(v) Salary plus 25 percent post differential.
(w) Associate judges, $12,000; chief associate judge receives $14,000.

Table 4
QUALIFICATIONS OF JUDGES OF STATE APPELLATE COURTS AND TRIAL COURTS OF GENERAL JURISDICTION

Years of minimum residence spans the *In state* and *In district* column groups.

State or other jurisdiction	U.S. citizenship		In state		In district		Minimum age		Learned in law		Years of legal experience		Other	
	A	T	A	T	A	T	A	T	A	T	A	T	A	T
Alabama	★	★	5	5	...	1	25	25	★(a)	★(a)	...	...	...	...
Alaska	★	★	3	3	...	...	...	...	★(a)	★(a)	8	5	...	...
Arizona	★	★	10(b)	5	3(c)	...	30(c)	30	★(a)	★(a)	10(b)	5	(d)	(d)
Arkansas	★	★	2	2	...	...	30	28	★	★	8	6	(d)	(d)
California	★	★	...	...	...	...	28	28	★(a)	★(a)	10	10	...	...
Colorado	★	★	1	1	...	★	...	...			5	5	...	...
Connecticut	...	...	...	...	...	...	...	...	★(a)	★(a)	...	...	...	...
Delaware	...	...	(e)	(e)	...	(f)	...	...	★	★	...	...	(g)	(h)
Florida	★	★	(e)	(e)	...	...	...	...	★(a)	★(a)	10(a)	5(a)	...	...
Georgia	★	★	3	3	...	...	30	30	★	★	7	7	...	...
Hawaii	★	★	...	...	...	...	...	...	★(a)	★(a)	10(i)	10(i)	(j)	(j)
Idaho	★	★	1	1	...	1	...	30	★(a)	★(a)	...	5	(k,l)	(k,l)
Illinois	★	★	...	...	★	★	...	...	★(a)	★(a)	...	...	...	...
Indiana	★	★	5	★	★	★	21	21	★(a)	★	10(m)	★	...	...
Iowa	★	★	...	...	...	...	...	...	★	★(n)	...	...	(o)	(o)
Kansas	★	★	...	★	...	★	30	30	★	★(p)	10	5	...	...
Kentucky	★	★	2	2	2	2	...	...	★	★	8	8	...	...
Louisiana	...	...	2	2	2	2	...	...	★(a)	★(a)	5	5	...	...
Maine	★	★	...	...	...	...	...	...	★	★	...	...	(q)	(q)
Maryland	★	★	5	5	★	★	30	30	★(a)	★(a)	...	...	(d)	(d)
Massachusetts	— No legal qualifications in state constitution —								★(a)	★(a)	...	...	(l)	(l)
Michigan	...	...	...	...	...	★	...	21	★	★	...	...	...	...
Minnesota	...	...	5	5	...	...	...	...	★	★	★	5	...	(k)
Mississippi	...	...	5	5	...	...	30	26	★	★	...	...	(k)	(k)
Missouri	★	★	9(r)	3(r)	★	1	30	30	★	★	...	...	(k)	(k)
Montana	★	★	2	2	...	...	...	...	★(a)	★(a)	5	5	...	...
Nebraska	★	★	5	5	★	★	30	30	★(a)	★(a)	5(s)	5(s)	(k)	(k)
Nevada	★	★	2	2	...	...	25	25	★(a)	★(a)	...	...	(k)	(k)
New Hampshire	— No legal qualifications —													
New Jersey	— Residence or principal law office in state —						...	...	★(a)	★(a)	10	10	...	...
New Mexico	★	★	3	3	...	...	30	30	...	...	3	3	...	...
New York	★	★	★	★	...	★	...	...	★(a)	★(a)	10	10	...	...
North Carolina	★	★	1 mo.	1 mo.	...	★	21	21	★(a,t)	★(a,t)	...	...	(k)	(k)
North Dakota	★	★	★(e)	★(e)	...	...	...	...	★	★	...	...	...	...
Ohio	★	★	1	...	...	1	...	...	★(a)	★(a)	6	6	...	...
Oklahoma	★	★	...	1	1	6 mo.	30	18(u)	★	★	5	4(u)	(v)	(v)
Oregon	★	★	...	...	...	★	21	21	★(a)	★(a)	...	...	(k)	...
Pennsylvania	★	★	1(e)	1(e)	...	1	...	...	★(a)	★(a)	...	...	...	...
Rhode Island	★	★	...	...	...	...	...	...	★	★	...	...	...	...
South Carolina	★	★	5	5	...	★	26	26	★(a)	★	5	5	(w)	...
South Dakota	★	★	★	★	★	★	19	19	★(a)	★(a)	...	...	...	...
Tennessee	...	...	5	5	...	1	35(x)	30	★	★	...	...	...	...
Texas	★	★	(e)	(e)	...	2	35	25	★	★	10	4	...	...
Utah	★	...	5	3	...	★	30	25	★	★	★	★	...	...
Vermont	★	★	★	★	...	...	...	...	★	★	5(y)	5(y)	...	...
Virginia	★	★	...	...	...	...	21	21	★(a)	★(a)	5	5	(z)	(z)
Washington	★	★	1	1	...	...	21	21	★(a)	★(a)	...	...	...	...
West Virginia	★	★	5	5	...	...	30	30	...	...	10	5	(k)	(k)
Wisconsin	★	★	10 da.(k)	10 da.(k)	...	...	18	18	★(a)	★(a)	5	5	...	...
Wyoming	★	★	3	2	...	...	30	28	★	★	9	5	(aa)	(aa)
Dist. of Col.	★	★	90 da.	90 da.	...	...	...	...	★	★	5	5	...	...
American Samoa	★	★	...	...	...	...	...	...	★(a)	★(a)	...	...	...	...
Guam	...	★	...	...	...	...	...	...	...	★	...	...	...	...
No. Mariana Is.	...	★	...	...	...	...	...	30	...	★	...	5	...	...
Puerto Rico	★	★	5	...	...	...	...	25	★(a)	★(a)	10	5	...	...

Key:

A—Judges of courts of last resort and intermediate appellate courts.

T—Judges of trial courts of general jurisdiction.

★—Indicates requirement exists; length of time for requirement not specified.

(a) Member of or admitted to bar. Alabama—licensed to practice law in the state. Connecticut, Illinois, Nebraska, New Jersey, New York, Virginia, Washington—shall not engage in private practice. Montana, Virginia, Washington (for appellate courts), Wisconsin—member of bar at least five years.

(b) For court of appeals, five years.

(c) For court of appeals.

(d) Good character. Maryland—integrity and wisdom.

(e) State citizenship.

(f) There must be one judge residing in each of state's three counties.

(g) No more than three justices can be of same major political party; at least two justices must be of other major political party.

(h) No more than bare majority of judges can be of same major political party; remainder of judges must be of other major political party.

(i) Supreme Court, intermediate appellate court and circuit court judges must be licensed to practice law for at least 10 years preceding nomination for office.

(j) Shall not engage in practice of law or run for or hold any other office or position of profit under the United States, the state or its political subdivisions during judicial term.

(k) Qualified voter. Nevada—qualified elector in state for supreme court justices; in state and district for trial court judges. Oregon—qualified elector in county of residence for court of appeals judges. Wisconsin—qualified elector for 10 days in the jurisdiction of the office for which the judge is running.

(l) Judges must be under 70 at time of election or appointment.

(m) Member of state bar 10 years, or five years a trial judge.

(n) Part-time judicial magistrates not required to be learned in law, but must be an elector of the county of appointment, less than 72 years of age, and retire upon attaining that age.

(o) Justices of supreme court, judges of court of appeals, district court judges, and district associate judges, at time of appointment, must be of an age which will permit them to serve an initial and one regular term before reaching age 72. Magistrates must be of an age which will permit them to serve a full term of office before reaching age 72.

(p) District and associate district judges must be regularly admitted to the bar; district magistrate judges need not be admitted to the bar, but if not they must be certified by the supreme court as qualified to serve.

(q) Sobriety of manner.

(r) Required number of years as qualified voter.

(s) In Nebraska.

(t) Does not apply to persons elected to or serving in such capacity before January 1, 1981.

(u) Associate district judges required to be licensed to practice in the state; two years of practice required; age not specified.

(v) Shall continue to be licensed attorney while holding office.

(w) Must be pronounced qualified by the Legislative Screening Committee.

(x) Thirty years for judges of court of appeals and court of criminal appeals.

(y) Five out of 10 years preceding appointment.

(z) Shall not seek or accept non-judicial elective office, or hold any other office of public trust, or engage in any other incompatible activity.

(aa) Shall have practiced law in state at least one year immediately preceding election or appointment.

Table 5
FINAL SELECTION OF JUDGES

Alabama	Appellate, circuit, district and probate judges elected on partisan ballots. Judges of municipal courts are appointed by the governing body of the municipality.
Alaska	Supreme court justices and superior court judges appointed by governor from nominations by Judicial Council. Supreme court justices and superior court judges approved or rejected at first general election held more than 3 years after appointment. Reconfirmation every 10 and 6 years, respectively. Magistrates appointed by and serve at pleasure of the presiding judges of each judicial district.
Arizona	Supreme court justices and court of appeals judges appointed by governor from a list of not less than 3 for each vacancy submitted by a 9-member Commission on Appellate Court Appointments. Maricopa and Pima County superior court judges appointed by governor from a list of not less than 3 for each vacancy submitted by a 9-member commission on trial court appointments for each county. Superior court judges of other 12 counties elected on non-partisan ballot (partisan primary); justices of the peace elected on partisan ballot; city and town magistrates selected as provided by charter or ordinance, usually appointed by mayor and council.
Arkansas	All elected on partisan ballot.
California	Supreme court and courts of appeal judges appointed by governor with approval of Commission on Judicial Appointments. Run for re-election on record. All judges elected on non-partisan ballot.
Colorado	Judges of all courts, except Denver County and municipal, appointed initially by governor from lists submitted by non-partisan nominating commissions; run on record for retention. Municipal judges appointed by city councils or town boards. Denver County judges appointed by mayor from list submitted by nominating commission; judges run on record for retention.
Connecticut	All appointed by legislature from nominations submitted by governor, except that probate judges are elected on partisan ballot.
Delaware	All appointed by governor with consent of senate.
Florida	All trial judges are elected on a non-partisan ballot. All appellate judges are appointed by the governor with recommendations by a Judicial Nominating Commission. The latter are retained by running on their records.
Georgia	All elected on partisan ballot except that county and some city court judges are appointed.
Hawaii	Supreme court and intermediate appellate court justices and circuit court judges appointed by the governor with consent of the senate. District judges appointed by chief justice of the state. Candidates are to be nominated (on a list of at least 6 names) to governor or chief justice by Judicial Selection Committee.
Idaho	Supreme court, court of appeals and district court judges initially are nominated by Idaho Judicial Council and appointed by governor; thereafter, they are elected on non-partisan ballot. Magistrates appointed by District Magistrate's Commission for initial 2-year term; thereafter, run on record for retention for 4-year term on non-partisan ballot.
Illinois	All elected on partisan ballot and run on record for retention. Associate judges are appointed by circuit judges and serve 4-year terms.
Indiana	Judges of appellate courts appointed by governor from a list of 3 for each vacancy submitted by a 7-member Judicial Nomination Commission. Governor appoints members of municipal courts and several counties have judicial nominating commissions which submit a list of nominees to the governor for appointment. All other judges are elected.
Iowa	Judges of supreme, appeals and district courts appointed initially by governor from lists submitted by non-partisan nominating commissions. Appointee serves initial 1-year term and then runs on record for retention. District associate judges are initially appointed by district judges in the judicial election district from nominees submitted by county judicial magistrate appointing commission; thereafter, run on record for retention. Part-time judicial magistrates appointed by county judicial magistrate appointing commission.
Kansas	Judges of appellate courts appointed by governor from list submitted by nominating commission. Run on record for retention. Non-partisan selection method adopted for judges of courts of general jurisdiction in 20 of 29 districts.
Kentucky	All judges elected on non-partisan ballot.
Louisiana	All elected on open (bipartisan) ballot.
Maine	All appointed by governor with confirmation of the senate, except that probate judges are elected on partisan ballot.
Maryland	Judges of circuit courts and Supreme Bench of Baltimore City appointed by governor, elected on non-partisan ballot after at least one year's service. District court judges appointed by governor subject to confirmation by senate. Judges of appellate courts appointed by governor with the consent of the senate. Run on record after at least one year of service for retention.
Massachusetts	All appointed by governor with consent of Executive Council. Judicial Nominating Commission, established by executive order, advises governor on appointment of judges.
Michigan	All elected on non-partisan ballot, except municipal judges in accordance with local charters by local city councils.
Minnesota	All elected on non-partisan ballot. Vacancy filled by gubernatorial appointment.
Mississippi	All elected on partisan ballot, except that city police court justices are appointed by governing authority of each municipality.
Missouri	Judges of supreme court, court of appeals and circuit courts in St. Louis City and County, Jackson County, Platte County and Clay County appointed initially by governor from nominations submitted by special commissions. Run on record for re-election. All other judges elected on partisan ballot.
Montana	All elected on non-partisan ballot. Vacancies on supreme or district courts and Worker's Compensation Court filled by governor according to established appointment procedure (from 3 nominees submitted by Judicial Nominations Commission). Vacancies at end of term may be filled by election, except Worker's Compensation Court. Gubernatorial appointments face senate confirmation.
Nebraska	Judges of all courts appointed initially by governor from lists submitted by bipartisan nominating commissions. Run on record for retention in office in general election following initial term of 3 years; subsequent terms are 6 years.
Nevada	All elected on non-partisan ballot.
New Hampshire	All appointed by governor with confirmation of Executive Council.
New Jersey	All appointed by governor with consent of senate except that judges of municipal courts serving only one municipality are appointed by the governing body.
New Mexico	All elected on partisan ballot.

New York	All elected on partisan ballot except that governor appoints chief judge and associate judges of court of appeals, with advice and consent of senate, from a list of persons found to be well qualified and recommended by the bipartisan Judicial Nominating Commission, and also appoints judges of court of claims and designates members of appellate division of supreme court. Mayor of New York City appoints judges of the criminal and family courts in the city.
North Carolina	All elected on partisan ballot. By executive order, present governor uses a nominating commission for merit selection of superior court judges when he is authorized to make such an appointment.
North Dakota	All elected on non-partisan ballot.
Ohio	All elected on non-partisan ballot except court of claims judges who may be appointed by chief justice of supreme court from ranks of supreme court, court of appeals, court of common pleas or retired judges.
Oklahoma	Supreme court justices and court of criminal appeals judges appointed by governor from lists of 3 submitted by Judicial Nominating Commission. If governor fails to make appointment within 60 days after occurrence of vacancy, appointment is made by chief justice from the same list. Run for retention on their records at first general election following completion of 12 months' service for unexpired term. Judges of court of appeals, and district and associate district judges elected on non-partisan ballot in adversary popular election. Special judges appointed by district judges. Municipal judges appointed by governing body of municipality.
Oregon	All judges except municipal judges are elected on non-partisan ballot for 6-year terms. Municipal judges are mostly appointed by city councils except 2 Oregon cities elect their judges.
Pennsylvania	All originally elected on partisan ballot; thereafter, on non-partisan retention ballot, except police magistrates, city of Pittsburgh—appointed by mayor of Pittsburgh.
Rhode Island	Supreme court justices elected by legislature. Superior, family and district court justices and justices of the peace appointed by governor, with consent of senate (except for justices of the peace); probate and municipal court judges appointed by city or town councils.
South Carolina	Supreme court, circuit court and family court judges elected by legislature. Magistrates appointed by governor with advice and consent of the senate. Municipal judges appointed by municipal governing body. Probate judges elected on partisan ballot.
South Dakota	Supreme court justices and circuit court judges appointed by governor from nominees submitted by the Judicial Qualifications Commission; thereafter, run for retention. Magistrates (law trained and others) are appointed by the presiding judge of the judicial circuit.
Tennessee	Judges of intermediate appellate courts appointed initially by governors from nominations submitted by special commission. Run on record for re-election. The supreme court judges and all other judges elected on partisan ballot, except for some municipal judges who are appointed by the governing body of the city.
Texas	All elected on partisan ballot except municipal judges, most of whom are appointed by municipal governing body.
Utah	Supreme court, district court and circuit court judges appointed by governor from lists of 3 nominees submitted by nominating commissions with advice and consent of senate. If governor fails to make appointments within 30 days, chief justice appoints. Judges run for retention in office at next succeeding election; they may be opposed by others on non-partisan judicial ballots. Juvenile court judges are initially appointed by the governor from a list of not less than 2 nominated by the Juvenile Court Commission, and retained in office by gubernatorial appointment. Town justices of the peace are appointed for 4-year terms by town trustees. County justices of the peace are elected for 4 years on non-partisan ballot.
Vermont	Supreme court justices, superior court judges (presiding judges of superior courts) and district court judges appointed by governor, with consent of senate from list of persons designated as qualified by the Judicial Nominating Board. Supreme, superior and district court judges retained in office by vote of legislature. Assistant judges of superior courts and probate judges elected on partisan ballot in the territorial area of their jurisdiction.
Virginia	Supreme court justices and all judges of circuit courts, general district, and juvenile and domestic relations district courts elected by legislature.
Washington	All elected on non-partisan ballot except that municipal judges in second-, third- and fourth-class cities are appointed by mayor.
West Virginia	Judges of all courts of record and magistrate courts elected on partisan ballot.
Wisconsin	All elected on non-partisan ballot.
Wyoming	Supreme court justices, district court judges and county judges appointed by governor from a list of 3 submitted by nominating committee and stand for retention at next election after 1 year in office. Justices of the peace elected on non-partisan ballot. Municipal judges appointed by mayor.
Dist. of Col.	Nominated by the president of the United States from a list of persons recommended by the District of Columbia Judicial Nomination Commission; appointed upon the advice and consent of the U.S. Senate.
American Samoa ...	Chief justice and associate justice(s) appointed by the U.S. Secretary of the Interior pursuant to presidential delegation of authority. Associate judges appointed by governor of American Samoa on recommendation of the chief justice, and subsequently confirmed by the senate of American Samoa.
Guam	All appointed by governor with consent of legislature from list of 3 nominees submitted by Judicial Council for term of 7 years; thereafter, run on record for retention every 7 years.
No. Mariana Is.	All appointed by governor with consent of senate.
Puerto Rico	All appointed by governor with consent of senate.

Table 6

METHODS FOR REMOVAL OF JUDGES AND FILLING OF VACANCIES

State or other jurisdiction	How removed	Vacanies: how filled
Alabama	A Judicial Inquiry Commission and Court of the Judiciary were created in new constitution for purpose of investigating and acting upon complaints. Court of the Judiciary is empowered to remove, suspend, censure or otherwise discipline a judge.	By governor, until the next general election, when judge is elected to fill unexpired term. All interim appointees customarily elected for a full term.
Alaska	All justices and superior court judges subject to impeachment for malfeasance or misfeasance. Impeachment by 2/3 vote of senate; trial in house, with a supreme court justice, designated by the court, presiding. Concurrence of 2/3 vote of house required for removal. On recommendation of Judicial Qualifications Commission or on own motion, supreme court may suspend judge from office without salary when in U.S. he pleads guilty or no contest or is found guilty of a crime punishable as a felony under Alaska or federal law or of any other crime, involving moral turpitude under that law. If conviction is reversed, suspension terminates, and he shall be paid salary for period of suspension. If conviction becomes final, removal from office by supreme court. On recommendation of Judicial Qualifications Commission, supreme court may (1) retire judge for disability that seriously interferes with performance of duties and is or is likely to become permanent, and (2) censure or remove judge for action occurring not more than 6 years before commencement of current term which constitutes willful misconduct in office, willful and persistent failure to perform duties, habitual intemperance, or conduct prejudicial to the administration of justice that brings the judicial office into disrepute.	Filled by governor from nominations by Judicial Council.
Arizona	Every public officer subject to recall. Electors, equal to 25% of votes cast at last preceding general election, may petition for recall. All judges, except justices of courts not of record, subject to impeachment by 2/3 of vote of senate. Upon recommendation of Comission on Judicial Qualifications, supreme court may remove judges from all courts (except city magistrate) for willful misconduct in office, willful and persistent failure to perform duties, habitual intemperance or conduct prejudicial to the administration of justice that brings the judicial office into disrepute, or may retire them for disability that seriously interferes with performance of duties and is, or is likely to become, permanent.	Supreme court justices, court of appeals judges and Maricopa and Pima County superior court judges selected in manner provided for in original appointment. Superior court judges of the other 12 counties by governor, until the next general election when judge is elected to fill unexpired term. Justices of the peace by county board of supervisors for balance of term. City magistrates by the mayor and council.
Arkansas	Judges of the supreme, appellate, and circuit courts and chancellors are subject to removal by impeachment or by the governor upon the joint address of 2/3 of the members elected to each house of the legislature.	By governor until next general election. Ad interim appointees ineligible for election.
California	Judges of all state courts subject to impeachment. All judges subject to recall by voters. Suspension without salary by supreme court when they plead guilty or no contest or are found guilty of a crime punishable as a felony under California or federal law or of any other crime that involves moral turpitude, and removal by the supreme court upon final conviction of such crimes. Upon recommendation of Commission on Judicial Performance, supreme court may remove judges from all courts for willful misconduct in office, persistent failure or inability to perform duties, habitual intemperance, or conduct prejudicial to the administration of justice that brings the judicial office in disrepute, or may retire them for disability that seriously interferes with performance of duties and is, or is likely to become, permanent.	Supreme court and courts of appeal judges, by governor with approval of Commission on Judicial Appointments, until next gubernatorial election. If elected, fills unexpired term of predecessor. Superior court judges, by governor, until next election. Judge then elected serves full term. Municipal court judges, by governor, for unexpired term of predecessor. Justice court judges, by board of supervisors of county or by special election, until next election, when judge is elected to serve unexpired term.
Colorado	Judges of supreme, appeals, district and county courts, by impeachment or (except judges of the Denver County court) on recommendation of the Commission on Judicial Qualifications, by the supreme court, for willful misconduct in office, willful or persistent failure to perform duties, or habitual intemperance, as well as for disability seriously interfering with performance of duties and likely to become of a permanent character. Denver County court and municipal judges may be removed according to charter and ordinance provisions.	By the governor, from lists submitted by judicial nominating commissions.
Connecticut	Judges of the supreme and superior courts may be removed by impeachment, with trial by the senate and 2/3 vote. Governor may also remove them on the address of 2/3 of each house of the legislature. The supreme court, acting on its own motion or upon a recommendation of the Judicial Review Council, may remove or suspend a judge of the supreme court or superior court. An investigation and hearing are required. If the alleged conduct involves a member of the supreme court, such judge is disqualified from participating in the proceedings. If a judge becomes permanently incapacitated from fulfilling adequately the duties of his office, he may be retired for disability by the Judicial Review Council on its own motion or on application of the judge.	By governor until the next legislature or until a successor shall be elected or appointed.
Delaware	Court on the Judiciary has power to retire judge for permanent mental or physical disability, or to censure or remove judge from office for misconduct. All civil officers may be impeached.	As in case of original appointment.

State or other jurisdiction	How removed	Vacancies: how filled
Florida	Justices of the supreme court, and judges of the district courts of appeal and circuit courts may be impeached for misdemeanor in office. Any such justice or judge may be disciplined or removed by the supreme court on recommendation of a Judicial Qualifications Commission for willful or persistent failure to perform his duties or for conduct unbecoming a member of the judiciary, or may be retired for disability seriously interfering with the performance of his duties, which is, or is likely to become, of a permanent nature.	By the governor, until the next general election, from recommendations provided by an appropriate Judicial Nominating Commission.
Georgia	Judges are subject to impeachment for cause, and removal from office. Trial by senate. 2/3 vote. A Judicial Qualification Commission investigates charges of alleged misconduct or incapacity and certifies its findings to the supreme court. Any justice or judge may then be retired, removed or censured by the supreme court upon recommendation of the Judicial Qualification Commission.	By the governor, until the next general election.
Hawaii	A Commission on Judicial Discipline appointed by the supreme court investigates charges and makes recommendation to the supreme court.	Supreme court, intermediate and circuit court vacancies by governor, by and with advice and consent of senate after nomination on a list of at least 6 names by the Judicial Selection Committee. Pending official appointment, chief justice may assign circuit judge to serve temporarily on supreme court or on any vacant circuit court bench. District court vacancies filled by chief justice.
Idaho	Judges are subject to impeachment for cause, and removed from office. Impeachment trial by senate, 2/3 vote. Supreme court, court of appeals and district court judges subject to removal by supreme court after investigation and recommendation by Judicial Council. Magistrates may be removed for cause by district court judges or judicial district sitting en banc, upon majority vote, in accordance with supreme court rules; may be removed without cause during first 18 months of service by District Magistrate's Commission.	Supreme court, court of appeals and district court vacancies filled by governor, from names recommended by Judicial Council, for unexpired term; magistrates by District Magistrate's Commission for unexpired term.
Illinois	A judge or associate judge can be removed for willful misconduct in office, persistent failure to perform duties, or other conduct prejudicial to the administration of justice or that which brings the judicial office into disrepute. He can be suspended with or without pay or retired if physically or mentally unable to perform his duties. The Judicial Inquiry Board investigates complaints and may initiate investigations of judges, and file complaints with the Court Commission on a "reasonable basis" to charge misconduct or disability. The Courts Commission's function is to hear complaints initiated by the Judicial Inquiry Board and make rulings on the disposition of such complaints. It has authority after notice and public hearing to remove, suspend without pay, censure or reprimand a judge for misconduct; and to suspend with or without pay or retire a judge for disability. The commission is composed of one judge of the supreme court selected by that court, two judges of the appellate court selected by that court, and two circuit judges selected by the supreme court. Judicial officers may be impeached by the legislature.	Vacancies in supreme, appellate, and circuit courts may be filled by appointment by the supreme court until general election when vacancy is filled by election. Associate judge vacancies in circuit court filled by appointment by circuit judges (same as original appointment).
Indiana	Appellate judges may be removed by vote of the supreme court on own motion or that of Judicial Qualifications Commission. Non-appellate judges are also subject to disciplinary power of supreme court, which includes the power to suspend a judge without pay. For pleading guilty or no contest to felony or crime involving moral turpitude, the supreme court may, on its own motion or upon the commission's recommendation, suspend and remove. For other matters, the supreme court may, upon commission's recommendation, retire, censure or remove judge.	Appellate vacancies are filled in the same manner as initial selection. If a trial judge is suspended, supreme court appoints a pro tem to serve. If a trial judge is removed, governor appoints a person to serve until next general election.
Iowa	Supreme and district court judges subject to impeachment. Upon recommendation of Commission on Judicial Qualifications, such judges and district associate judges also may be retired for permanent disability or removed for failure to perform duties, habitual intemperance, willful misconduct, or substantial violations of the canons of judicial ethics, by order of the supreme court. Judicial magistrates may be removed by a tribunal consisting of 3 district court judges in the judicial election district of the magistrate's residence.	All vacancies created by removal are filled in the same manner as original final selection.
Kansas	All officers under constitution subject to impeachment. In addition to impeachment, all judges below supreme court level are subject to retirement for incapacity, and to discipline, suspension and removal, for cause by the supreme court after appropriate hearing before the Judicial Qualifications Committee.	For supreme court, by governor from list submitted by Nominating Commission, until next general election, when appointee runs for retention on his record. For court of appeals, appointment is for unexpired term; by governor from list submitted by Nominating Commission. For district court in 20 districts by governor from list submitted by district judicial nominating commission until next general election when appointee runs for retention on record; in 9 districts the governor appoints until next general election.

State or other jurisdiction	How removed	Vacancies: how filled
Kentucky	Removal by impeachment; removal by the Retirement and Removal Commission, subject to rules of procedure established by the supreme court. Actions of the Retirement and Removal Commission are subject to review by the supreme court.	By the governor, from a list of three names submitted by the appropriate Judicial Nominating Commission, or by the chief justice should the governor fail to act within 60 days. Appointees serve until next general election after their appointment, at which time election is held to fill the vacancy.
Louisiana	Upon investigation and recommendation by Judiciary Commission, supreme court can censure, suspend with or without salary, remove from office, or retire involuntarily a judge for misconduct relating to his official duties or willful and persistent failure to perform his duties, persistent and public conduct prejudicial to the administration of justice that brings the judicial office into disrepute, conduct while in office which would constitute a felony, or conviction of a felony, as well as retire a judge for disability which is, or is likely to become, of a permanent character. All state and district officers may be impeached.	By special election called by the governor and held within 6 months after the vacancy occurs. Until the vacancy is filled, the supreme court appoints a qualified person, who is ineligible as a candidate at the election.
Maine	Judges may be impeached by the house; removal upon 2/3 vote at trial by senate. Judges also may be removed by the governor on the address of both branches of the legislature. Judges of supreme judicial, superior and district courts may be retired for disability.	Vacancies filled as in case of original appointment, except that vacancies in office of judges of probate are filled by the governor, with the advice and consent of the council, until January 1 after the next November election.
Maryland	Judges of court of appeals, court of special appeals, trial courts of general jurisdiction, and district court by the governor, on conviction in a court of law or on impeachment; or for physical or mental disability; or on the address of the legislature, 2/3 of each house concurring in such address. Impeachment trial by senate, conviction on 2/3 vote. Removal or retirement by court of appeals after hearing and recommendation by Commission on Judicial Disabilities, for misconduct in office, persistent failure to perform duties, conduct prejudicial to the proper administration of justice, or disability seriously interfering with the performance of duties, which is, or is likely to become, of a permanent character. Elected judge convicted of felony or misdemeanor relating to his public duties and involving moral turpitude is removed from office by operation of law when conviction becomes final.	By the governor, from Nominating Commission list, until first biennial election for congressional representative after the expiration of the term or the first general election 1 year after the occurrence of the vacancy. Appointees customarily elected to full term. District court judges appointed and confirmed by senate (no election). Appellate judges run on record.
Massachusetts	The governor, with the consent of the Executive Council, may remove judges upon the address of both houses of the legislature. Also, after hearing, he may, with the consent of the council, retire a judge because of advanced age or mental or physical disability. All officers may be removed by impeachment.	As in the case of an original appointment.
Michigan	House of representatives directs impeachment by a majority vote. Impeachment trial by senate, 2/3 vote for conviction. Governor may remove judge for reasonable cause insufficient for impeachment with concurrence of 2/3 of the members of each house of the legislature. On recommendation of Judicial Tenure Commission, supreme court may censure, suspend with or without salary, retire or remove a judge for conviction of a felony, physical or mental disability, or persistent failure to perform duties, misconduct in office, or habitual intemperance or conduct clearly prejudicial to the administration of justice.	For all courts of record, by governor, until January 1, next succeeding first general election held after vacancy occurs, at which successor is elected for unexpired term of predecessor. Vacancies on municipal courts filled by local city councils. Supreme court may authorize persons who have been elected and served as judges to perform judicial duties for limited periods or specific assignments.
Minnesota	Supreme and district court judges may be impeached. On recommendation of Board of Judicial Standards, supreme court may censure, suspend with or without salary, retire or remove a judge for conviction of a felony, physical or mental disability, or persistent failure to perform duties, misconduct in office, or habitual intemperance or conduct prejudicial to the administration of justice.	Filled by governor until next general election occurring more than 1 year after appointment.
Mississippi	Presentment, indictment by a grand jury, and conviction of a high crime or misdemeanor in office. All civil officers may be impeached by 2/3 of members present of the house, and removed after trial by senate. Also, for reasonable cause which shall not be sufficient ground for impeachment, the governor shall, on the joint address of 2/3 of each branch of the legislature, remove from office the judges of the supreme and inferior courts.	By governor during recess of senate. Filled at next congressional election if there is one prior to the expiration of the term.
Missouri	All judges are subject to retirement, removal or discipline by the supreme court on recommendation of a majority of members of a committee composed of two citizens (not members of the bar) appointed by the governor, two lawyers appointed by the governing body of the Missouri bar, one judge of the court of appeals elected by a majority of that court, and one circuit judge selected by a majority of circuit judges in the state.	By governor until next general election, except that vacancies in the supreme court, court of appeals, circuit courts of City of St. Louis, St. Louis, Clay, Platte and Jackson Counties are filled by governor from nominations by a nonpartisan commission until the next general election after the judge has been in office at least a year.

State or other jurisdiction	How removed	Vacancies: how filled
Montana	All judicial officers subject to impeachment. Impeachment by 2/3 vote of house. Upon recommendation of Judicial Standards Commission, supreme court may suspend a judicial officer and remove same upon conviction where a felony or other crime involves moral turpitude; also, can order censure, suspension, removal or retirement for cause.	Justices of supreme court, district court judges and worker's compensation judge by governor; justices of peace by boards of county commissioners. Judge so appointed holds until next general election or senate confirmation, whichever comes sooner.
Nebraska	Impeachment by majority of legislature; in case of impeachment of supreme court justice, all judges of district courts sit as court of impeachment—2/3 concurrence required; in case of other judicial impeachments, heard by supreme court as court of impeachment. Also, provisions similar to those in California for removal of judges by supreme court on recommendation of a Judicial Qualifications Commission.	By governor, from lists submitted by bipartisan judicial nominating commissions.
Nevada	All judicial officers except justices of peace subject to impeachment. Impeachment by 2/3 vote of each branch of legislature, provided that no member of either branch shall be eligible to fill the vacancy so created. Trial by senate, 2/3 vote. Also subject to removal by legislative resolution and by recall. A justice of the supreme court or district judge may be censured, retired or removed by the Commission on Judicial Discipline. The commission is composed of 2 justices or judges appointed by the supreme court; 2 members of the State Bar of Nevada, a public corporation created by statute, appointed by its board of governors; and 3 persons, not members of the legal profession, appointed by the governor. A justice or judge may appeal action of commission to supreme court, which may reverse the action or take alternative actions. No justice or judge may be removed except for willful misconduct, willful or persistent failure to perform duties of office, or habitual intemperance, or be retired except for advanced age which interferes with proper performance of judicial duties or for mental or physical disability which prevents the proper performance of judicial duties and which is likely to be permanent in nature.	By governor, from list of 3 nominees submitted by Commission on Judicial Selection.
New Hampshire	Governor with consent of council may remove judges upon the address of both houses of the legislature. Any officer of the state may be impeached.	Vacancies filled by governor with consent of council.
New Jersey	Except for justices of the supreme court, all judges are subject to a statutory removal proceeding that is initiated only by the filing of a complaint by the supreme court on its own motion, the governor, or either house of the legislature acting by a majority of its total membership. However, prior to institution of such formal statutory removal proceedings, complaints are almost without exception referred to the supreme court's Advisory Committee on Judicial Conduct, which conducts a preliminary investigation, makes findings of fact, and may dismiss the charges or, after providing the accused judge with a hearing, recommend to the supreme court that formal proceedings be instituted. This committee is composed of nine members: (1) at least 2 retired justices of the supreme court or judges of the superior court or county court, (2) at least 3 other members of the state bar, and (3) not more than 4 laymen who do not hold public office of any nature. Although the supreme court is supplied with the record created by this committee, the supreme court's determination is based on a plenary hearing procedure. The formal statutory removal hearing may be either before the supreme court sitting en banc or before 3 justices or judges, or a combination thereof, specially designated by the chief justice. Justices of the supreme court and judges of the superior court are also subject to impeachment by the legislature. If the supreme court certifies to the governor that it appears that any justice of the supreme court or judge of the superior court is so incapacitated as to substantially prevent him from performing his judicial duties, the governor appoints a commission of 3 persons to inquire into the circumstances. On their recommendation, the governor may retire the justice or judge from office, on pension, as may be provided by law.	By governor, with advice and consent of senate, except municipal courts serving only one municipality, for which judges are appointed by the governing body of the municipality.
New Mexico	All state officers and judges of the district court may be impeached. Through the Judicial Standards Commission, any justice, judge or magistrate may be disciplined or removed for willful misconduct in office or willful and persistent failure to perform his duties or habitual intemperance, or may be retired for disability seriously interfering with the performance of his duties, which is, or is likely to become, of a permanent character.	Governor appoints to fill vacancy until next general election.
New York	Any judge may be removed by impeachment. Judges of the court of appeals and justices of the supreme court may be removed by 2/3 concurrence of both houses of the legislature. Judges of the court of claims, county courts, surrogate's court, family court, the civil and criminal courts of the city of New York, and district courts may be removed by 2/3 vote of the senate, on recommendation of the governor. Commission on Judicial Conduct has the power to determine that a judge or justice be admonished, censured or removed from office for cause or retired for disability, subject to an appeal to the court of appeals.	Vacancies in elective judgeships filled at the next general election for full term; until the election, governor makes the appointment (with the concurrence of the senate if it is in session). This does not apply in the following cases: civil court of the city of New York appointed by the mayor; district courts appointed by the appropriate district governing body or official; city courts (outside the city of New York), town courts and village courts appointed by appropriate governing body as prescribed by the legislature.

State or other jurisdiction	How removed	Vacancies: how filled
North Carolina	Upon recommendation of the Judicial Standards Commission, the supreme court may censure or remove any trial court judge or any judge of the court of appeals for willful misconduct in office, willful and persistent failure to perform duties, habitual intemperance, conviction of a crime involving moral turpitude, conduct prejudicial to the administration of justice that brings the judicial office into disrepute, or for mental or physical incapacity interfering with the performance of duties which is or is likely to become permanent. Any member of the supreme court may be censured or removed for the reasons just enumerated, by a 7-member panel of the court of appeals upon recommendation of the Judicial Standards Commission.	By governor until next general election. Ad interim appointees customarily elected for remainder of unexpired term.
North Dakota	Supreme and district court judges by impeachment for habitual drunkenness, crimes, corrupt conduct, malfeasance or misdemeanor in office. County judges by governor after hearing. Impeachment trial by senate, conviction 2/3 vote. All judges may be recalled. Upon recommendation of Commission on Judicial Qualifications, supreme court may remove judges from all courts for willful misconduct in office, willful and persistent failure to perform duties, habitual intemperance or conduct prejudicial to the administration of justice that brings the judicial office into disrepute, or may retire them for disability that seriously interferes with performance of duties and is, or is likely to become, permanent.	Supreme and district court judges by governor from candidates nominated by Judicial Nominating Committee until next general election, unless governor calls for a special election to fill vacancy for the remainder of the term.
Ohio	By concurrent resolution of 2/3 members of both houses of the legislature. All judges may be removed by impeachment. Trial by senate, conviction on 2/3 vote. By disqualification as a result of disciplinary action as provided in Rule V, supreme court. Removal for cause upon filing of a petition signed by at least 15% of the electors in the preceding gubernatorial election; trial by court or jury. Removal, retirement or suspension without pay for cause following complaint filed in the supreme court; hearing before a commission of judges named by the supreme court. Appeal from commission to supreme court.	By governor until next election, when judge is elected to fill unexpired term.
Oklahoma	By impeachment for willful neglect of duty, corruption in office, habitual drunkenness, incompetency or any offense involving moral turpitude. Upon recommendation of the Council on Judicial Complaints, the chief justice of the supreme court may bring charges against any justice or judge in the Court on the Judiciary. Court on the Judiciary may order removal for gross neglect of duty, corruption in office, habitual drunkenness, commission while in office of any offense involving moral turpitude, gross partiality in office, oppression in office or any other grounds hereinafter specified by the legislature. Compulsory retirement, with or without compensation, for mental or physical disability preventing proper performance of office duties, or incompetence to perform duties of the office.	Vacancies on supreme court and court of criminal appeals by governor, as in case of original appointment. Appointee to vacancy occurring during unexpired term serves for remainder of that term if retained by election after completing 12 months' service. Vacancies on court of appeals and district court filled by governor for unexpired term; in making appointment, he must use Judicial Nominating Committee.
Oregon	Any judge may be involuntarily retired for mental or physical disability after certification by a special commission; he may appeal to supreme court. On recommendation of Commission on Judicial Fitness, supreme court may remove a judge of any court for conviction of a felony or a crime involving moral turpitude, willful misconduct in a judicial office involving moral turpitude, willful or persistent failure to perform judicial duties, habitual drunkenness, illegal use of narcotic drugs, willful violation of rules of conduct prescribed by supreme court or general incompetence.	By governor until next general election, at which time a judge is elected to fill the unexpired term.
Pennsylvania	All judges, as all civil officers, may be impeached by house for any misdemeanor in office. Trial by senate, 2/3 vote for conviction. Upon recommendation of the Judicial Inquiry and Review Board, any justice or judge may be suspended, removed or otherwise disciplined by the supreme court for specified forms of misconduct, neglect of duty or disability.	By governor, until the first Monday of January following next judicial election which shall occur more than 10 months after vacancy occurs or for the remainder of the unexpired term, whichever is less. Appointment is with the advice and consent of 2/3 of the senate, except majority for justices of the peace.
Rhode Island	Supreme court judges, by a resolution of the legislature voted by a majority in each house at the annual session for the election of public officers. All judicial officers may be impeached. Trial by senate, 2/3 vote of all members elected thereto for conviction.	In case of vacancy on supreme court, the office may be filled by the Grand Committee of the Legislature until the next annual election. In case of impeachment, inability or temporary absence, governor appoints a person to fill vacancy. Vacancies on superior, family and district courts may be filled by governor with advice and consent of senate.
South Carolina	By impeachment or by governor on address of 2/3 of each house of the legislature. Also by supreme court for mental and/or physical disability. Judicial Standards Commission enforces code of judicial conduct.	By governor if unexpired term does not exceed 1 year; otherwise, by General Assembly to fill unexpired term.
South Dakota	Supreme court justices and circuit court judges may be removed by impeachment. Trial by senate, 2/3 vote for conviction. Recommendation by Judicial Qualifications Commission to supreme court for removal.	Supreme court justices and circuit court judges by the governor from 1 of 2 or more persons nominated by the Judicial Qualifications Commission for balance of term.

State or other jurisdiction	How removed	Vacancies: how filled
Tennessee	By impeachment for misfeasance or malfeasance in office; by concurrent resolution of 2/3 of each house of the legislature when the judge is physically or mentally unable to perform his duties; upon recommendation of the Court of the Judiciary, legislature can remove a judge by concurrent resolution of 2/3 of each house for physical or mental disability or willful misconduct in office.	By governor until next general election.
Texas	Supreme court, and appeals and district court judges may be removed by impeachment, senate, 2/3 vote, or by joint address, 2/3 vote of both houses. District judges may be removed also by the supreme court. County judges and justices of the peace may be removed by district judges. Upon charges filed by the Commission on Judicial Conduct, any judge in the state may be involuntarily retired for disability or removed for misconduct by the supreme court.	Appellate, district court judges by governor, until next general election. County courts by county commissioner's court. Municipal judges by governing body of municipality. Judge elected fills unexpired term.
Utah	By concurrent vote of 2/3 of the members of each house of the legislature. All judicial officers except justices of the peace may be impeached. Trial by senate, conviction on 2/3 vote. Removal from office by supreme court upon recommendation of Commission on Judicial Qualifications for willful misconduct in office, final conviction of a crime punishable as a felony, persistent failure to perform duties, habitual use of alcohol or drugs which interferes with performance of judicial duties; retirement for disability seriously interfering with performance of duties which is, or is likely to become, of a permanent character. Lay justices of the peace may be removed for willful failure to participate in judicial education program.	By governor, upon recommendation of Judicial Selection Commission, until next general election. Judge elected fills unexpired term.
Vermont	All judicial officers impeachable. Trial by senate, conviction on 2/3 vote. Supreme court has disciplinary control over all judicial officers not inconsistent with constitutional powers of the legislature; it has power to impose sanctions, including suspension from judicial duties for the balance of the term of the judicial officer charged.	Supreme, superior and district court vacancy filled by governor, from list of persons selected by Judicial Nominating Board.
Virginia	All judges may be impeached by house. Trial by senate. Conviction on 2/3 vote of members present. By supreme court after charges against judge have been certified by Judicial Inquiry and Review Commission.	A successor shall be elected for the full term by the legislature. If legislature not in session, governor makes appointment to expire 30 days after commencement of next session.
Washington	Any judge of any court of record may be impeached. Trial by senate. Conviction on 2/3 vote. Any judge may be censured, suspended or removed for violating a rule of judicial conduct or retired for disability, which is permanent or likely to become permanent and which seriously interferes with the performance of judicial duties, following notice, hearing and recommendation of the Judicial Qualifications Commission.	Vacancies on appellate and general trial courts filled by governor until next general election when an election is held to fill the unexpired term.
West Virginia	Removal by concurrent vote of both houses of the legislature in which 2/3 of the members of each house must concur, when a judge is incapable of discharging the duties of his office because of age, disease, mental or bodily infirmity, or intemperance. By impeachment by a 2/3 vote of the legislature for maladministration, corruption, incompetency, gross immorality, neglect of duty, or any crime or misdemeanor.	By governor if unexpired term is less than 2 years; if more than 2 years, governor may appoint judge until next general election when a judge is elected to fill the unexpired term.
Wisconsin	All judges subject to impeachment. Supreme, circuit and court of appeals judges by the address of both houses of the legislature, 2/3 of all members of each house concurring and hearing, and by recall. Since all judges of courts of record must be licensed to practice law in Wisconsin, removal also can be by disbarment. The office of a justice of the supreme court, court of appeals or circuit court judge may be declared temporarily vacant by the supreme court for disability or misconduct upon petition of the Judicial Commission or upon its own motion. The disabled justice or judge continues to receive the salary and other benefits of the office for the balance of his or her term or until the temporary vacancy terminates, whichever occurs first.	By governor until next regular judicial election is held, when judge is elected for a full term. At any election only one supreme court justice and one court of appeals judge from each district may be elected, so that appointee holds until next available election. Disabled supreme court justice replaced by governor. Disabled circuit court or court of appeals judge may be replaced through appointment by chief justice from list of reserve judges (retired judges on assignment); if not available, governor may fill the temporary vacancy which continues during disability of judge or until he dies or his term expires. If temporary disability of a judge is determined by supreme court, a temporary vacancy exists which is filled by appointment of chief justice of supreme court of a reserve judge. If temporary disability of a supreme court justice, governor makes the appointment.

THE JUDICIARY

State or other jurisdiction	How removed	Vacancies: how filled
Wyoming	All judicial officers, except justices of peace, by impeachment. Trial by senate, 2/3 vote for conviction. May be retired or removed by supreme court on recommendation of Judicial Supervisory Commission. Justices of the peace by supreme court after hearing before panel of 3 district judges.	By governor from a list of 3 submitted by Judicial Nominating Commission, for approximately 1 year, then stand for election for retention in office. Justices of the peace by appointment by county commissioners.
Dist. of Col.	All judges shall be removed from office by the Commission on Judicial Disabilities and Tenure, upon conviction of a felony (including a federal crime), for willful misconduct in office, for willful and persistent failure to perform judicial duties, or for other conduct prejudicial to the administration of justice or which brings the office into disrepute.	Nominated by the president of the United States from a list of persons recommended by the D.C. Judicial Nomination Commission; appointed upon the advice and consent of the U.S. Senate.
American Samoa	Chief and associate justices shall hold office during good behavior, but may be removed by the U.S. Secretary of Interior for cause. Associate judges shall hold office during good behavior, but may be removed by the chief justice for cause, upon the recommendation of the governor.	Appointed by the U.S. Secretary of Interior. Appointed by the governor upon the recommendation of the chief justice.
Guam	Any justice or judge may be removed by a special court of 3 judges on recommendation of a Judicial Qualification Commission for misconduct or incapacity.	By governor for term of 7 years.
No. Mariana Is.	Any judge is subject to impeachment for treason, commission of a felony, corruption or neglect of duty. House of representatives initiates proceedings, and senate may convict by 2/3 vote after hearing.	By governor.
Puerto Rico	Supreme court justices by impeachment for treason, bribery, other felonies and misdemeanors involving moral turpitude. Indictment by 2/3 of total number of house members and trial by senate. Conviction by 3/4 of total number of senators. All other judges may be removed by supreme court for cause as provided by judiciary act, after hearing upon complaint on charges brought by order of the chief justice, who shall disqualify himself in the final proceedings.	By governor, as in case of original appointment.

Table 7
SELECTED DATA ON COURT ADMINISTRATIVE OFFICES

State or other jurisdiction	Title	Estab-lished	Appointed by(a)	Salary	Number on staff	Appropriation for office Amount(b)	Fiscal
Alabama	Administrative Director of Courts(c)	1971	CJ	$42,250	80	$ 3,352,711	1982
Alaska	Administrative Director	1959	CJ(d)	72,196	57	2,918,000	1981
Arizona	Administrative Director of the Courts	1960	SC	40,280	27	(e)	(e)
Arkansas	Executive Secretary, Judicial Dept.	1965	CJ(f)	36,457	17	549,420	1982
California	Administrative Director of the Courts	1960	JC	66,665	66	5,490,422(g)	1982
Colorado	State Court Administrator	1959	SC	51,152	49	5,343,515	1982
Connecticut	Chief Court Administrator	1965	CJ	46,846(h)	100(i)	2,853,000	1982
Delaware	Director, Administrative Office of the Courts	1971	CJ	40,716	17(i)	2,263,000(j)	1982
Florida	State Court Administrator	1972	SC	44,144	37	2,494,646	1981
Georgia	Director, Administrative Office of the Courts	1973	JC	39,500	17	546,200	1980
Hawaii	Administrative Director of the Courts	1959	CJ(d)	40,000	57	2,050,287	1981
Idaho	Administrative Director of the Courts	1967	SC	44,500	13(i)	320,000	1982
Illinois	Administrative Director of the Courts	1959	SC	53,000	41(i)	1,971,000	1981
Indiana	Supreme Court Administrator—Commissioner	1968	SC	37,550	5	(e)	(e)
	Executive Director, Div. of State Court Administration	1975	...	43,000	4	(e)	(e)
Iowa	Court Administrator	1971	SC	37,800	20.5	589,956(k)	1982
Kansas	Judicial Administrator	1965	CJ	42,000	22	(e)	(e)
Kentucky	Director, Administrative Office of the Courts	1976	CJ	40,810	83.5(i)	1,673,246	1982
Louisiana	Judicial Administrator	1954	SC	60,169	11	362,215	1982
Maine	State Court Administrator	1975	CJ	34,347	9	185,196	1982
Maryland	State Court Administrator(c)	1955	CJ	48,700	104(i)	4,022,490(i)	1982
Massachusetts	Administrative Assistant, Supreme Judicial Court(c)	1978	SC	42,500	8	1,818,900(e)	1981
Michigan	Court Administrator	1952	SC	60,385	102	7,205,500	1982
Minnesota	Court Administrator	1963	SC	47,000	40	1,576,400	1982
Mississippi	Executive Assistant	1974	SC	41,000	2	(e)	(e)
Missouri	State Courts Administrator	1970	SC	40,000	50	1,270,059	1982
Montana	State Court Administrator	1975	SC	27,821	6(i)	(e)	(e)
Nebraska	State Court Administrator	1972	CJ	36,500	6(i)	203,500(e)	1981
Nevada	Director, Administrative Office of the Courts	1971	SC	30,250	7(i)	221,000	1982
New Hampshire	Director of Administrative Servics	1980	SC	35,000	5	152,429	1982
New Jersey	Administrative Director of the Courts	1948	CJ	60,000	210(i)	3,821,738(l)	1979
New Mexico	Director, Administrative Office of the Courts	1959	SC	40,000	37(i)	1,676,000	1982
New York	Chief Administrator of the Courts(m)	1978	CJ(n)	71,300	315	12,792,645	1982
North Carolina	Director, Administrative Office of the Courts	1965	CJ	48,504	79	2,217,805	1981
North Dakota	State Court Administrator, Judicial Council(o)	1971	CJ	42,792	11	500,000	1982&1983
Ohio	Administrative Director of the Courts	1955	SC	50,107	13(i)	(e)	(e)
Oklahoma	Administrative Director of the Courts	1967	SC	50,400	5	(e)	(e)
Oregon	State Court Administrator	1971	CJ	41,376	25	1,430,097	1982&1983
Pennsylvania	State Court Administrator	1968	SC	60,000	52	3,969,000	1980&1981
Rhode Island	Court Administrator	1969	CJ	37,958-43,104(p)	17	372,000(e)	1981
South Carolina	Court Administrator	1973	CJ	40,831	25	499,726(q)	1981
South Dakota	State Court Administrator	1974	SC	40,750	18	1,616,822(r)	1982
Tennessee	Executive Secretary to the Supreme Court	1963	SC	66,931	17	486,700	1981
Texas	Administrative Director of the Courts(s)	1977	SC	47,600	19	1,198,161	1982&1983
Utah	State Court Administrator	1973	SC	43,500	8	271,600	1982
Vermont	Court Administrator(t)	1967	SC	39,000	14	(e)	(e)
Virginia	Executive Secretary to the Supreme Court	1952	SC	54,820	62	2,894,400	1981
Washington	Administrator for the Courts	1957	SC(u)	40,200	82(i)	11,554,000	1982&1983
West Virginia	Director, Administrative Office of the Supreme Court of Appeals	1975	SC	46,000	14	430,000	1982
Wisconsin	Director of State Courts	1978	SC	51,372	47	2,348,400(v)	1980&1981
Wyoming	Court Coordinator	1974	SC	30,000	3(i)	(e)	(e)
Dist. of Col.	Executive Officer of D.C. Courts	1971	(w)	60,390	64	5,787,100	1981
American Samoa	Court Administrator	1977	CJ	16,617	3	(e)	(e)
No. Mariana Is.	Court Administration Officer	1978	CJ	13,000	6	140,000	1981
Puerto Rico	Administrative Director, Office of Court Administration	1952	CJ	34,896	366	5,199,979	1981

Key:
SC—State court of last resort.
CJ—Chief justice or chief judge of court of last resort.
JC—Judicial council.

(a) Term of office for all court administrators is at pleasure of appointing authority.
(b) Appropriations for the various offices are not necessarily comparable because of variations in the time periods covered and the pur-

poses of the appropriations. In some states amounts shown include appropriations for travel and expenses of trial court judges.

(c) In addition, there is a court administrator to administer state trial courts.

(d) With approval of Supreme Court.

(e) Appropriation not segregated from general appropriation of court of last resort. Where figure given, it is an estimate. In Massachusetts, appropriation includes Supreme Judicial Court expenses except for judges' salaries and expenses.

(f) With approval of Judicial Council.

(g) Total appropriation for Judicial Council, including administrative office of the courts, but not including salaries of assigned judges, including 12 positions with assignment judges with duties not directly related to administrative office. Includes $158,746 for reimbursement to trial courts for expenses made necessary by the coordination of civil actions.

(h) Salary conditioned on administrator being a judge of the supreme or superior court.

(i) Breakdown of staff from information supplied:
Connecticut—61 are professional.
Delaware—6 professional, 7 technical, 4 clerical.
Idaho—3 professional, 2 computer and 8 clerical.
Illinois—12 professional, 29 semi-professional.
Kentucky—In addition, 121.5 pretrial service officers and 24.5 mediation/diversion officers of Kentucky Pretrial Services Agency.
Maryland—Including 49 judicial data processing employees and judicial processing budget of $2,847,923.
Montana—4 professional, 2 secretarial.

Nebraska—3 professional, 3 clerical.
Nevada—4 professional, 3 clerical.
New Jersey—96 professional (33 federally funded), 114 clerical (14 federally funded).
New Mexico—14 professional, 23 clerical.
Ohio—6 professional, 7 clerical.
Washington—85.5 in 1983.
Wyoming—1 professional, 2 clerical.

(j) Includes such items as pension costs for entire judiciary, all court rentals, all juror and witness fees and data processing costs for all courts.

(k) For administrative and budgetary purposes, supreme court clerk's office has been incorporated into the office of the court administrator.

(l) Salaries only including both state-funded and federally funded positions.

(m) If incumbent is a judge, the title is Chief Administrative Judge of the Courts.

(n) With advice and consent of Administrative Board of the Courts.

(o) Serves as secretary to Judicial Council.

(p) Longevity payments at 7, 11, 15, 20 and 25 years of state service.

(q) Does not include cost-of-living raises or fringe benefits.

(r) Includes $161,333 in federal funds for training and studies and $1,031,905 in purchase-of-service monies for out-of-home placement of juveniles.

(s) Serves as executive director of Judicial Council.

(t) Also clerk of the supreme court.

(u) Appointed from list of five submitted by governor.

(v) Includes $271,600 in federal funds.

(w) Joint Committee on Judicial Administration.

Section VI ADMINISTRATION
1.   Administrative Activities

STATE BUDGETING

By Robert P. Kerker

A FIFTIETH anniversary offers a unique opportunity for institutions to take stock, to look once again at their roots, to examine the assumptions under which they were created and to compare current performance with other eras. It also offers an opportunity for institutions to look ahead, to ask themselves if the structures and relationships designed for one set of problems will prove adequate for new challenges.

For state budgeting these are relevant questions, and the answers are apt to be considerably different than those we might have given just a decade ago. State budget officers, even those who administer executive budget systems securely lodged in state constitutions, are subject virtually everywhere to unprecedented pressure to change: to share power with a once docile body of legislators and legislative staff; to adjust accounting systems from cash to accrual and to make other changes which will, in sum, reduce executive discretion in the classification and timing of transactions; to recognize the increasing tendency of the courts to intervene in ways which have enormous consequences for policy-making, resource allocation and administration; to react to the federal government's efforts to shift part of its burden of financing social programs to states and localities at the very time that economic stagnation and tax revolts have limited the ability of government at all levels to absorb new responsibilities.

The early 1930s, which saw the birth of The Council of State Governments, also marked in many ways the culmination of an intense and on the whole productive movement for structural reform in state administration which had flowered in the preceding quarter century. The campaign for structural reform—which followed and was in some ways modeled on federal and municipal prototypes—had produced uneven and in some cases uncertain results. But, in essence, by 1930 there had emerged a consensus that chief executives in state government should have longer terms, should share power with fewer elected officials, should have the power of appointment and the authority to restructure, manage and administer the executive branch, and should be responsible for developing, presenting, defending and executing the state's financial plan.

The 1920s had been a heady period for the proponents of structural reform. The scholars and administrators who dominated the New York Bureau of Municipal Research had succeeded in making these principles an article of faith at virtually every level of government. Students of budgeting committed to reform dominated the professional, and even the popular, literature, and "tested" the budgetary systems of the states for their degree of conformity to the principles of executive budget norms. Active governors, such as Republican Frank O. Lowden in Illinois and Democrat Alfred E. Smith in New York, gave the issue of reform a bipartisan hue and owed at least part of their national prominence to

Robert P. Kerker is Chief of Administrative Management, New York State Division of the Budget.

their vigorous efforts to overhaul their respective state governments and financial management systems. In the eyes of both, the budget system was clearly the keystone of the new governmental structure. "The reorganization of the government is absolutely necessary," Governor Smith told his cabinet in 1927 as he filled in the last pieces of his restructuring program, but "no more so . . . than the Executive Budget." The latter, he observed, is "probably . . . the biggest reform in the manner and method of the State doing business of all that has been so far suggested."

The executive budget movement emerged in a period of almost constant increase in the scope and cost of governmental functions. Its diverse constituency included not only those concerned with more orderly administration, but those who saw the budget system as a way to enforce economy and those who saw the government as a vehicle of social improvement or physical growth and looked to the governor to sponsor, organize and finance new public undertakings. Popular conceptions of government during the 1920s have too often emphasized a relaxed and even negative federal establishment, presided over by a dour Calvin Coolidge. But in the states and many municipalities, progressive reform lingered long after its demise in Washington.[1] Expenditures for education rose sharply, financed in many areas by state grants to municipalities or school districts. Responsibility for dependent populations was centralized in many states, and government responded by constructing new institutions to house their expanding numbers of clients. Water and power development and park land acquisition demanded and often got increasing attention. Most important, the emergence of the automobile and the truck brought an unquenchable demand for intercity highways, parkways, farm-to-market roads, and associated policing, maintenance, repair and upgrading.

The Great Depression of the early 1930s was devastating in its impact, and provided a far sterner test of the working of the new budget systems—as well as the capacity of governors to govern—than the growth of the 1920s. As Lester Thurow has noted, society faces its principal challenge in apportioning losses, not in distributing gains.[2] And losses there were—appalling losses—which bear discussion if only to help the public officials of a later era put their troubles in perspective. In New York State, for example, receipts from the personal income tax fell from $40.2 million in 1930 to $19.7 million in 1931, a drop of 51 percent. Although comparisons over a half-century are hazardous—the personal income tax of 1930, for example, provided only 15 percent of New York State's revenues—such a reduction in personal income tax receipts today would cut the state's revenues by nearly $4 billion, or almost 25 percent of the state budget, if one excludes federal funds.

On the whole, the Depression enhanced the standing of state executive budget systems in the eyes of public officials and scholars alike. But it also exposed the weaknesses of many of the budget systems that had been developed, including many which on examination revealed little "system" at all. Changing the "manner and method of . . . doing . . . business" was in some states in its infancy. In other cases, reorganizations which, in theory, had given the governor responsibility for preparing a financial plan, often had provided no staff for this purpose or had required him to rely upon officials who either were not appointed by him or were already charged by law with other duties. Many states (the South had numerous examples) earmarked such a large proportion of their revenues—especially those related to the ownership or operation of motor vehicles—that they had little discretion in adjusting their expenditures to economic crisis. Debt, which had pyramided from 1920 on, now exerted a heavy claim on the state revenues. Those functions which depended upon general revenues bore the brunt of the cutbacks, with education, perhaps, hit hardest of all. Competition between roads and schools, the two great objects of the growth of public expenditure in most of the nation in the 1920s, became the focus of political debate in state after state.

The Depression taught many lessons. And one of the lessons public administrators thought the crisis had taught or confirmed was the "benefit of a responsible budget system." In the final analysis, summed up one observer of the efforts of nine Southern states to cope with the crisis, "There can be no way out of financial chaos except by leadership. . . . The stage seems to be set for the exercise of responsible executive power."[3] It was high time to complete the reforms begun three decades before.

Today, executive budget systems once again find themselves challenged, and the challengers are by no means uniform in exalting the need to increase the power or responsibility of the executive budget role. There has been a curious and qualitative shift in the nature of the debate over budgetary "reform." Where the debates of the 1950s, 1960s and 1970s over performance budgeting, program budgeting, PPBS, zero-base budgeting and a variety of their combinations and derivatives were essentially debates over the process of "resource allocation," the current ferment in state budgeting reflects an effort to control the resources themselves. Thus, the federal judiciary has intervened in several states to define standards of care for institutional populations and to establish both precise program and spending targets and a lien on the necessary revenues.

Legislative bodies, increasingly well staffed, are less and less ready to accept the executive's budgetary agenda or definition of priorities. As fiscal problems multiply, however, a greater share of the budgetary authority may not be an unmixed blessing. It will often bring with it a greater share of the unpleasant task of telling people "No." Almost on the eve of this year's heavy cuts in federal aid, New York State's highest court ruled that a provision resident in the state constitution since 1846 required the legislature to appropriate federal funds received by the state. "Now that we've got it," observed Arthur J. Kremer, chairman of the State Assembly's Ways and Means Committee, somewhat ruefully, "I'm not sure that it's the greatest idea. Maybe it's an idea whose time has passed."[4]

Still a third challenge is ironically descended from the same progressive era that produced the executive budget system. Propositions 2½, 13 and other efforts in Massachusetts, California and other states to establish constitutional restrictions on government spending and taxing are nothing if not a rediscovery of the virtues of the initiative and referendum. Again, they are concerned less with the system and the completeness of the supporting evidence for decisions on resource allocation than with the distribution of the resource burden within the community.

To some degree, it can be argued that such challenges to institutional prerogatives are a manifestation of a deeper social issue: the weakening of the legitimacy that once protected both private and public bodies from outside intervention. Businesses, labor unions and universities have been pushed to demonstrate both their social and economic value and their right to hire, fire and manage their employees. In a society struggling with economic stagnation and apportioning loss, not dividends, the erosion of the legitimacy of its institutions seems inevitable. Full financial disclosure, expanded public access to governmental records, and even the accelerated demand to extend "generally accepted accounting principles" to all governmental operations are in some ways reflections of a challenge to once unquestioned authority. We are only now beginning to explore the implications of these issues for state government; our energies have been devoted to coping with the demands of full disclosure, not placing it in a larger social and historical context. But, as The Council of State Governments faces its next half century, it seems apparent that in financial management as in its other functions its members will be dealing with a vastly different set of assumptions.

The outcome of this debate and pressure to change both our methods and our way of looking at the problems of government cannot be forecast with any degree of confidence. The federal model, for example, seems less and less serviceable as a guide to state budgeting and management practice.[5] Nevertheless, the key actors in the struggles for control over state budgetary processes—the three branches of government, the taxpaying public and the various interest groups—will in the long run find it difficult to discard the fundamental assumptions which guided the reformers early in this century:

- A budgetary process which cannot assume deficit financing will continue to demand accountability, particularly in its execution. The fragmentation of responsibility for state financial management characteristic of much of our history cannot be tolerated— not least of all by an increasingly sophisticated financial community.
- State budgeting will increasingly require a balancing of competing demands against a relatively fixed pool of resources. Gains by one interest group mean a "loss" for another; limits on the pool eventually limit services.

In short, while executive prerogatives may emerge somewhat diminished, the essential goals of the reformers who plumped for the adoption of the executive budget—coherence, responsibility, accountability—will remain intact as the bedrock of budgetary systems.

Notes

1. Arthur S. Link, "What Happened to the Progressive Movement in the 1920's?" *American Historical Review* 64 (July 1959).

2. Lester C. Thurow, *The Zero-Sum Society: Distribution and the Possibilities for Economic Change* (New York: Penguin Books, 1981).

3. James E. Pate, "Balancing State Budgets in Southern Commonwealths during the Economic Crisis," *Social Forces* 13 (December 1934): 282.

4. New York *Times*, October 6, 1981.

5. For a succinct discussion of the "retreat" of the presidency from the budgeting system established by the Budgeting and Accounting Act of 1921, see Louis Fisher, "Developing Fiscal Responsibility," in "The Power to Govern: Assessing Reform in the United States," *Proceedings of the Academy of Political Science* 34 (1981): 62-75.

Table 1
STATE BUDGETARY PRACTICES

State or other jurisdiction	Budget-making authority	Official or agency preparing budget	Date estimates must be submitted by dept. or agencies	Date submitted to legislature	Power of legislature to change budget*	Power of item veto by governor	Fiscal year begins	Frequency of budget
Alabama	Governor	Div. of the Budget, Dept. of Finance	Oct. 15 for Jan. session; Nov. 15 for Feb. session	By the 5th day regular business session	Unlimited	Yes	Oct. 1	Annual
Alaska	Governor	Div. of Budget & Management, Office of the Governor	Oct. 1	3rd legislative day of session	Unlimited	Yes	July 1	Annual
Arizona	Governor	Finance Div., Dept. of Administration	Sept. 1 each year	By the 5th day of regular session	Unlimited	Yes	July 1	Annual
Arkansas	Governor	Office of Budget, Dept. of Finance & Administration	Sept. 1 in even years	Date of convening session	Unlimited	Yes	July 1	Biennial, odd yr.(a)
California	Governor	Dept. of Finance	Specific date for each agency set by Dept. of Finance	Jan 10	Unlimited	Yes	July 1	Annual
Colorado	Governor	Executive Director, Office of State Planning & Budgeting	Aug. 1-15	Dept. budgets submitted Nov. 1; governor's full recommendation submitted within first 10 days of legislative session	Unlimited	Yes	July 1	Annual
Connecticut	Governor	Div. of Budget & Financial Management, Office of Policy & Management	Sept. 1	1st session day after third of Feb. in odd years, except if change in governor; then 1st session day after Feb. 14. In even years, on the Wed. following the 1st Mon. in Feb.	Unlimited	Yes	July 1	Annual
Delaware	Governor	Office of Budget Director, Office of the Governor	Sept. 15; schools, Oct. 15	By Feb. 1	Unlimited	Yes	July 1	Annual
Florida	Governor	Office of Planning & Budget, Office of the Governor	Nov. 1 each year	45 days prior to regular	Unlimited	Yes	July1	Biennial
Georgia	Governor	Office of Planning & Budget	Sept. 1	By 5th day of session or sooner	Unlimited	Yes	July 1	Annual
Hawaii	Governor(b)	Budget, Planning & Management Div., Dept. of Budget & Finance	Aug. 31	20 days prior to convening of session on 3rd Wed. in Jan.	Unlimited	Yes	July 1	Biennial, odd yr.(a,c)
Idaho	Governor	Office of the Governor	Sept. 1 before Jan. session	Not later than 5th day of session	Unlimited	Yes	July 1	Annual
Illinois	Governor	Bureau of the Budget, Office of the Governor	Specific date for each agency set by Bureau of the Budget	First Wed. in March	Unlimited	Yes	July 1	Annual
Indiana	Governor	Budget Agency(d)	Sept. 1 in even years, flexible policy	Within the 1st two weeks after the session convenes(e)	Unlimited	No	July 1	Biennial, odd yr.(a)
Iowa	Governor	Comptroller	Sept. 1	Feb. 1 or before	Unlimited	Yes	July 1	Biennial, odd yr.(a)
Kansas	Governor	Div. of the Budget, Dept. of Administration	Not later than Oct. 1	Within 3 weeks after convening of session in odd years and within 2 days after convening of session in even years	Unlimited	Yes	July 1	Annual
Kentucky	Governor	Office for Policy & Management, Dept. of Finance	Specific date set by administrative action but may not be later than Nov. 15 of each odd year	As governor desires	Unlimited	Yes	July 1	Biennial, even yr.(a)

State	Budget-making authority	Budget agency	Date budget submitted to legislature	Deadline for submission	Legislature's power over budget	Item veto	Fiscal year begins	Budget period
Louisiana	Governor	State Executive Budget Director, Div. of Administration	Dec. 15	Not later than 1st day of each regular session	Unlimited	Yes	July 1	Annual
Maine	Governor	Bureau of the Budget, Dept. of Finance & Administration	Sept. 1 in even years	Not later than the Fri. following the first Mon. in Jan. of the 1st regular legislative session. Governor-elect to 1st term, not later than Fri. following 1st Mon. in Feb. of 1st regular legislative session	Unlimited	No	July 1	Biennial, odd yr. (a)
Maryland	Governor	Secretary, Dept. of Budget & Fiscal Planning	Sept. 1	3rd Wed. of Jan. annually	Limited: legislature may decrease but not increase, except appropriations for legislature and judiciary	No	July 1	Annual
Massachusetts	Governor	Budget Director, Div. of Fiscal Affairs, Executive Office for Administration & Finance	Set by administrative action	Within 3 weeks after convening of the legislature	Unlimited	Yes	July 1	Annual
Michigan	Governor	Office of the Budget, Dept. of Management & Budget	Set by administrative action	10th day of session	Unlimited	Yes	Oct. 1	Annual
Minnesota	Governor	Budget Div., Dept. of Finance	Oct. 1 preceding convening of legislature	Within 3 weeks after the 1st Mon. in Jan. in each odd year	Unlimited	Yes	July 1	Biennial, odd yr. (a)
Mississippi	Commission of Budget & Accounting(f)	Commission of Budget & Accounting	Aug. 1 preceding convening of legislature	Dec. 15	Unlimited	Yes	July 1	Annual
Missouri	Governor	Div. of Budget & Planning, Office of Administration	Oct. 1	By the 30th day	Unlimited	Yes	July 1	Annual
Montana	Governor	Director, Office of Budget & Program Planning, Governor's Office	Sept. 1 of year before each session	1st day of session	Unlimited	Yes	July 1	Biennial, odd yr.
Nebraska	Governor	Budget Div., Dept. of Administrative Services	Not later than Sept. 15	Jan. 15	Limited: three-fifths vote required to increase governor's recommendations; majority vote required to reject or decrease such items	Yes	July 1	Annual
Nevada	Governor	Budget Director, Budget Div., Dept. of Administration	Sept. 1	10th day of session or before	Unlimited	No	July 1	Biennial, odd yr. (a)
New Hampshire	Governor	Comptroller, Dept. of Administration & Control	Oct. 1 in even years	Feb. 15 in odd years	Unlimited	No	July 1	Biennial, odd yr. (a)
New Jersey	Governor	Director, Div. of Budget & Accounting, Dept. of the Treasury	Oct. 1	Third Tues. after opening of session	Unlimited	Yes	July 1	Annual
New Mexico	Governor	Budget Div. Dept. of Finance & Administration	Sept. 1	On or before 25th day of regular session	Unlimited	Yes	July 1	Annual
New York	Governor	Div. of Budget, Executive Dept.	Early in Sept.	Second Tuesday following the first day of the annual session, except on or before Feb. 1 in years following gubernatorial election	Limited: may strike out items, reduce items, or add separate items of expenditure	Yes	April 1	Annual

State or other jurisdiction	Budget-making authority	Official or agency preparing budget	Date estimates must be submitted by dept. or agencies	Date submitted to legislature	Power of legislature to change budget*	Power of item veto by governor	Fiscal year begins	Frequency of budget
North Carolina	Governor	Office of State Budget	Sept. 1 preceding session	1st week of session	Unlimited	No	July 1	Biennial, odd yr. (a)
North Dakota	Governor	Office of Management & Budget	July 15 in even years; may extend 45 days	Dec. 1, prior to biennial session	Unlimited	Yes	July 1	Biennial, odd yr.
Ohio	Governor	Office of Budget & Management	Nov. 1; Dec. 1 when new governor is elected	Within four weeks of convening in odd years unless change in governor; then March 15	Unlimited	Yes	July 1	Biennial, odd yr. (a)
Oklahoma	Governor	Director of State Finance, Div. of Budget	Sept. 1	Immediately after convening of regular legislative session; an incoming governor, following inaugural	Unlimited	Yes	July 1	Annual
Oregon	Governor	Budget & Management Div., Executive Dept.	Sept. 1 in even year preceding legislative year	Dec. 1 in even year preceding legislative year	Unlimited	Yes	July 1	Biennial, odd yr.
Pennsylvania	Governor	Secretary of Budget & Administration, Governor's Office of Budget & Administration	Nov. 1 each year	As soon as possible after organization of legislature, but no later than 1st full week in Feb. Governor-elect to 1st term, no later than 1st week in March	Unlimited	Yes	July 1	Annual
Rhode Island	Governor	Div. of Budget, Dept. of Administration	Oct. 1	24th day of session	Unlimited	No	July 1	Annual
South Carolina	State Budget & Control Board(g)	Finance Div., State Budget & Control Board	Sept. 15 or discretion of board	2nd Tues. in Jan.	Unlimited	Yes	July 1	Annual
South Dakota	Governor	Commissioner, Bureau of Finance & Management, Dept. of Executive Management	Sept. 1	1st Tues. after 1st Mon. in Dec.	Unlimited	Yes	July 1	Annual
Tennessee	Governor	Budget Div., Dept. of Finance & Administration	Oct. 1	Prior to Feb. 1, except prior to March 1 in first year of governor's term	Unlimited	Yes	July 1	Annual
Texas	Governor, Legislative Budget Board	Budget & Planning Office, Office of Governor; Legislative Budget Board	Date set by budget director and legislative board	7th day of sesion or before	Unlimited	Yes	Sept. 1	Biennial, odd yr. (a)
Utah	Governor	State Budget Office	Sept. 1-30(h)	After convening of legislature, 3 days regular session; 1 day budget session	Unlimited	Yes	July 1	Annual
Vermont	Governor	Commissioner, Dept. of Budget & Management; Agency for Administration	Sept. 1	3rd Tues. in Jan.	Unlimited	No	July 1	(i)
Virginia	Governor	Director, Dept. of Planning & Budget, Office of Administration & Finance	Feb.-Sept. in odd years	Within 5 days after convening of regular session on 2nd Wed. in Jan. in even years	Unlimited	Yes	July 1	Biennial, even yr. (a)
Washington	Governor	Director, Office of Financial Management	Date set by governor	20th day of Dec. prior to session	Unlimited	Yes	July 1	Biennial, odd yr. (a)

State	Prepared by	Budget agency	Date submitted to governor	Date submitted to legislature	Legislature's power*	Public hearings	Fiscal year begins	Annual/Biennial
West Virginia	Governor	Planning Div. & Div. of Budget, Dept. of Finance & Administration	Aug. 15	1st day of session except for 1st year of new gov. when it may be submitted 1 month after convening of session	Limited: may not increase items of budget bill except appropriations for legislature and judiciary	Yes	July 1	Annual
Wisconsin	Governor	Div. of State Executive Budget & Planning, Dept. of Administration	Dates as set by secretary, Department of Administration	On or before the last Tues. in Jan. in odd-numbered years	Unlimited	Yes	July 1	Biennial, odd yr.(a)
Wyoming	Governor	Budget Div., Dept. of Administration & Fiscal Control	Sept. 15 preceding session in Feb.	Jan. 1	Unlimited	Yes	July 1	Biennial, even yr.(a)
Dist. of Col.	Mayor	Office of Budget & Management Systems	Date set by mayor	(j)	Unlimited	Yes	Oct. 1	Annual
American Samoa(k)	Governor	Planning & Budget Office	July 1	August	Unlimited (local funds)	Yes	Oct. 1	Annual
Guam	Governor	Bureau of Budget & Management Research	Date set by director, Bureau of Budget & Management Research. Usually not later than Feb. 15	By April 30	Unlimited	Yes	Oct. 1	Annual
Puerto Rico	Governor	Bureau of the Budget, Office of the Governor	Oct. 15	2nd Mon. in Jan.; opening day of regular session	Unlimited	Yes	July 1	Annual
Virgin Islands	Governor	Director of the Budget, Office of the Governor	Dec. 30	Upon convening	Unlimited	Yes	Oct. 1	Annual

*Limitations listed in this column relate to legislative power to increase or decrease budget items generally. Specific limitations, such as constitutionally earmarked funds or requirement to enact revenue measures to cover new expenditure items, are not included.

(a) Budget is adopted biennially, but appropriations are made for each year of the biennium separately. Maine—budget is reviewed annually. Minnesota and Wisconsin—a few appropriations are made for the biennium. Virginia—amendments to current budget can be made in any year, but there is no formal provision for annual review of the entire biennial appropriation. North Carolina, Washington and Wyoming—biennial appropriations with annual review. Wisconsin—statutes authorize an annual budget review, and the governor may in even years recommend changes.

(b) Governor has budget-making authority for executive branch only. Judiciary and legislative branch budgets are the responsibility of the respective branches, and the governor may only veto the budget bills as a whole, not by item.

(c) Increases or decreases may be made in even-year sessions.

(d) Budget Committee serves in advisory capacity.

(e) Convenes on first Thursday after first Monday in January in odd years.

(f) Composition of commission: governor as ex officio chairman, lieutenant governor, chairman House Ways and Means Committee, chairman House Appropriations Committee, chairman Senate Finance Committee, president pro tem of senate, chairman Senate Appropriations Committee, one member of senate appointed by lieutenant governor, speaker of house, two house members appointed by the speaker.

(g) Composition of board: governor as chairman, treasurer, comptroller general, chairman Senate Finance committee, chairman House Ways and Means Committee.

(h) Thirty days prior to each department or agency hearing before the governor.

(i) 1981 legislature authorized annual or biennial budget at governor's discretion. Submission of annual budget began with fiscal 1982.

(j) Budget submitted to both council and Congress. Council sets date of submission for its review; the Office of Management and Budget, Executive Office of the President, sets the date for submission to Congress.

(k) Information from 1980-81 *Book of the States.*

Table 2
BUDGET AGENCY FUNCTIONS

State or other jurisdiction	Revenue estimating primary	Revenue estimating secondary	Fiscal research	Fiscal notes	Organization and management analysis	Accounting primary	Accounting secondary	Data processing primary	Data processing secondary	Legislative review	Planning†	Program policy issue analysis	Program evaluation	Federal/state relations†	Debt management	Economic analysis
Alabama	★		★		★★		★			★★		★★★	★★	X,Y,Z	★	
Alaska			★	★	★					★		★				
Arizona	★		★	★	★					★		★				★
Arkansas	★★		★	★	★		★		★	★	C	★	★	X,Y,Z		★
California	★★		★★		★★★					★★		★★	★	V		★
Colorado			★	(e)	(a)					★	C,P	★	★	(a)		★
Connecticut	★★	(b)	★		★★★		(c)			★	C,P	★	★	W,X,Y,Z		★
Delaware	★ (d)		★	(f)	★		★	★		★	C,P	★	★	V,W,X,Y,Z		★
Florida	★★		★	★★	★					★	P	★	★	V,W,X		★
Georgia			★		★					★		★	★			
Hawaii	★ (g)		★		★			★		★	P	★	★	Y	★	★
Idaho	★		★	★	★					★		★	★	Y,W		★
Illinois	★		★	★	★★					★	C,F,P	★	★	W,X,Y,Z	★	★
Indiana	★		★	★	★					★	P	★	★	V,X		★
Iowa	★		★		★	★	★			★		★		V,W,Y		
Kansas			★		★★					★	P	★	★	V(h)		★
Kentucky		(i)	★	★	★					★	P	★	★	Y(i)	★	★
Louisiana			★		★					★		★	★	V,X		
Maine	★	★ (k)	★	★	★				★	★		★		V,Y		★
Maryland	★	★ (l)	★		★					★	P	★			★	★
Massachusetts	★ (m)		★		★★★					★	C,P	★	★★	V	★	(n)
Michigan	★ (n)	★ (i)	★★ (n)		★ (o)	(n)		★ (o)		★★	P	★	★★	V,W(n)	(n)	★★
Minnesota	★ (n)	★ (s)	★	★	★					★		★	★		(n)	★
Mississippi	★ (q)		★		★				★	★	C,L,P	★★	★★	X,Y,Z		★
Missouri			★		★					★		★	★			★
Montana	★ (r)	★ (i)	★	★	★★					★★	F,P	★	★	V,X	★	★
Nebraska	★	★ (s)	★		★★					★★	P	★	★	(j)		★
Nevada	★		★		★			★		★	P	★	★			★
New Hampshire	★	★ (t)	★		★★					★	P	★	★	X,Y		★
New Jersey	★		★	★	★★	★★★			★	★★★	P	★★	★	V,W,X,Y,Z	★	★★★
New Mexico	★★		★★		★★★	★★★				★★★	P	★	★	V,W,X,Y,Z	★	★
New York			★★		★★★	★	★★			★★	P	★★	★			
North Carolina		(u)	★★	★	★★	★		★	★	★		★	★	V,X,Y,Z		★
North Dakota	★★		★★		★		★★			★		★				★
Ohio			★	★	★	★ (w)		(w)	★	★		★★				★
Oklahoma	★ (v)		★★		★							★				★
Oregon	★		★★	★	★						C,P	★	★	V,X	★	★
Pennsylvania			★★	★						★		★		V	★ (x)	★
Rhode Island	★		★★	★	★				★	★		★				★
South Carolina	★	★	★★	★	★		★		★	★	C,P	★	★		★	★

State											
South Dakota	★	…	★★	…	★	★	(z) ★	★★	…	…	★
Tennessee	★	(y)	★★	…	…	…	★★★	★★★	…	v	★
Texas	★★	(aa) ★	★★★	…	…	★	★★★	C,L,P ★★★	…	v,w,x	★
Utah	★★	…	★★	★	…	…	★★	★★	…	…	★
Vermont	★★	★	★	★	…	★	★	…	…	…	★
Virginia	…	(ab)	★★	…	…	…	★★	C,P ★★	…	w,X,Z	★
Washington	(ac)	…	★★	★★	…	★	★★	C,P ★★	…	v	★
West Virginia	(ad)	★★	★★	…	(ad)	★	…	L	…	v,w,X,Z	★
Wisconsin	(ae)	(af) ★	★★	…	(ad) ★	…	★	C,F,P ★	…	X	★
Wyoming	(af) ★	…	★★	★	★	…	…	…	…	…	★
Guam	(ag) ★	…	★★	…	…	…	★★	P ★★	…	w	★★
Puerto Rico	…	★	★★	…	…	…	★★	P ★★	…	…	★★
Virgin Islands	★	(ah)	★	★	…	★	★	C,P …	★	X	★

Source: National Association of State Budget Officers; updated by The Council of State Governments. In addition to the functions listed, the following states indicated additional duties: Alabama—keep all allotment records; Colorado—approval of fund transfers; Delaware—coordinate state policies and federal programs and resources by providing staff support to State Clearinghouse Committee and operating Washington, D.C. office; New Hampshire—management supervision of all state agencies; New Jersey—monitor programs and their objectives to determine progress in reaching objectives; New Mexico—review contracts for professional services and out-of-state travel requests, propose and administer salary plans for exempt employees (political appointments), serve as revenue sharing liaison, draft general appropriations act, prepare capital budgets and plans, budget adjustments; New York—participates in management assistance and coordination, state-local relations, employee relations and compensation; Rhode Island—negotiations of hospital rates; Virginia—development, storage, retrieval and dissemination of data on social, economic, physical and governmental aspects of the state to provide information for use by state and other governmental bodies; Guam—local auditing of territorial programs within the executive branch; Virgin Islands—coordination of state energy policy.

†:
C—Comprehensive state
F—Functional
L—Local
P—Policy

‡:
V—Approval of agency grant applications.
W—Planning assistance for and monitoring of grant applications.
X—A-95
Y—Information on grant awards; 1082 reports, etc.
Z—Assistance to agencies and local governments on obtaining grants or information on grant.

(a) Performed in Office of Policy and Management by other than the Division of the Budget and Financial Management.
(b) Delaware Economic Financial Advisory Council (advisory); governor (budget); legislature (resolution).
(c) Executed through Revenue Estimating Committee comprised of representatives from Division of Budget, legislature, comptroller, Departments of Revenue, Business Regulation, and Motor Vehicles and Highway Safety.
(d) Budget director establishes and maintains accounting system and procedures; secretary, Department of Finance, processes documents, conducts preaudits and maintains central accounting records.

(e) Upon request of governor, legislature or other.
(f) Joint responsibility with state auditor's office and Office of Planning and Budget.
(g) Council on Revenues (constitutional requirement).
(h) Recommendations on agency grant applications.
(i) Department of Revenue.
(j) Review only.
(k) Agency collecting revenue.
(l) Board of Revenue Estimates.
(m) Responsibility of Budget Bureau with aid and counsel of Department of Corporation and Taxation.
(n) Performed in Department of Finance by a unit other than the Budget Division.
(o) Department of Administration.
(p) Legislative auditor.
(q) Approval of estimates made by tax commission.
(r) General Fund only.
(s) Revenue Department makes projections with only review function served by Budget Division.
(t) Division of Taxation.
(u) Governor, Advisory Budget Commission; legislature.
(v) Provides input and data to the State Board of Equalization which makes the official estimate.
(w) Performed in Office of Budget and Administration in unit other than the Budget Bureau.
(x) Recommend bond sale, including amount by project and term.
(y) Only at request of presiding officer or committee hearing bill.
(z) All departments review bills introduced which apply to them.
(aa) Controller of Public Accounts.
(ab) Department of Revenue is responsible for primary revenue estimating for most major taxes; however, budget agency has responsibility for all the estimates used for the budget.
(ac) Tax Department and Department of Finance and Administration.
(ad) Department of Finance and Administration.
(ae) By statute, budget agency responsible for revenue estimating; however, Department of Revenue provides assistance.
(af) Research and Statistics Division, Department of Administration and Fiscal Control.
(ag) Department of Revenue and Taxation and Department of Commerce.
(ah) Approval of personnel action and fund transfers.

Table 3

BUDGET: OFFICIALS OR AGENCIES RESPONSIBLE FOR PREPARATION, REVIEW AND CONTROLS

State or other jurisdiction	Preparation of budget	Special budget review agency in legislative branch	Budgetary and related accounting controls
Alabama	Governor; Finance Director (G)	Legislative Fiscal Officer (L); Senate Finance and Taxation Committee (L); House Ways and Means Committee (L)	Finance Director (G)
Alaska	Governor; Div. of Budget & Management(a)	Legislative Budget & Audit Committee (L)	Dept. of Admin.(a)
Arizona	Governor; Finance Div., Dept. of Admin. (G)	Joint Legislative Budget Committee (L)	Finance Div., Dept. of Admin. (G)
Arkansas	Governor; Director, Dept. of Finance & Admin. and its Office of Budget (G)	Legislative Council, Bureau of Legislative Research (L)	Dept. of Finance & Admin.(a)
California	Governor; Finance Director (G)	Joint Legislative Budget Committee (L)	Finance Director (G)
Colorado	Governor; Office of State Planning & Budgeting (G)	Joint Budget Committee (L)	Controller (CS); Office of State Planning & Budgeting (G)
Connecticut	Governor; Div. of Budget & Financial Mgt., Office of Policy & Mgt. (G)	Office of Fiscal Analysis (L)	Secretary of Office of Policy & Mgt. (G); Comptroller (E)
Delaware	Governor; Budget Director (G)	Joint Legislative Finance Committee (L); Controller General (L)	Budget Director (G); Secretary, Dept. of Finance (G)
Florida	Governor; Office of Planning & Budget, Office of the Governor (G)	House & Senate Appropriation Committees (L)	Director, Office of Planning & Budget (G); Comptroller (E)
Georgia	Governor; Office of Planning & Budget (G)	Office of Legislative Budget Analyst (L)	Auditor (L); Budget Director (G)
Hawaii	Governor; Director of Finance (G)	Legislative Auditor (L)	Comptroller (G)
Idaho	Governor; Administrator, Div. of Financial Mgt.(a)	Legislative Fiscal Office, Joint Finance-Appropriations Committee (L)	State Board of Examiners(b)
Illinois	Governor; Budget Bureau (G)	Fiscal & Economic Commission (L); Senate & House Appropriations Committees (L)	Dept. of Administrative Services (G); Bureau of the Budget (G); Comptroller (E)
Indiana	State Budget Agency (G); Budget Committee(c)	Senate Finance Committee (L); House Ways & Means Committee (L); Legislative Council (L)	State Budget Agency (G)(d); Auditor (E)
Iowa	Governor; Budget Dept., Office of Comptroller (G)	Legislative Fiscal Bureau (L)	Comptroller (G)
Kansas	Governor; Div. of the Budget, Dept. of Admin.(e)	Legislative Research Dept. (L)	Div. of Accounts & Reports, Dept. of Admin.(f)
Kentucky	Governor; Secretary, Dept. of Finance (G); Executive Director, Office for Policy & Mgt. (g)	Appropriations & Revenue Committees (L)	Secretary, Dept. of Finance (G); Executive Director, Office for Policy & Mgt. (g)
Louisiana	Governor; Commissioner of Admin. (G); Budget Office(e)	Legislative Fiscal Office (L)	Commissioner of Admin. (G); Budget Office(e)
Maine	Governor; Budget Officer(h)	Joint Committee on Appropriations & Financial Affairs (L); Legislative Finance Officer (L)	Controller, Dept. of Finance & Admin.(h)
Maryland	Governor; Secretary, Dept. of Budget & Fiscal Planning (G)	Div. of Budget Review, Dept. of Fiscal Services (L)	Secretary, Dept. of Budget & Fiscal Planning (G)
Massachusetts	Governor; Budget Director, Executive Office for Admin. & Finance(h)	House & Senate Ways & Means Committees (L)	Executive Office for Admin. & Finance (G)
Michigan	Governor; Director, Dept. of Mgt. & Budget (G)	House Fiscal Agency (L); House Appropriations Committee, Senate Appropriations Committee & Senate Fiscal Agency (L)	Director, Dept. of Mgt. & Budget (G)
Minnesota	Governor; Commissioner of Finance (G)	House Appropriations Committee (L); Senate Finance Committee (L)	Commissioner of Finance (G)
Mississippi	Commission of Budget & Accounting(i)	(i)	Commission of Budget & Accounting(i)
Missouri	Governor; Commissioner of Admin. (G)	House & Senate Appropriations Committees (L); Legislative Committee on State Fiscal Affairs (L)	Commissioner of Admin. (G)

State			
Montana	Governor; Office of Budget & Program Planning (G)	Legislative Fiscal Analyst & Finance Committee (L)	Director, Dept. of Admin. (G)
Nebraska	Governor; Budget Administrator; Dept. of Administrative Services(j)	Legislative Fiscal Analyst, Legislative Council (L); Legislative Budget Committee (L)	Budget Administrator, Dept. of Administrative Services(j)
Nevada	Governor; Budget Director (G)	Div. of Fiscal Analysis, Legislative Counsel Bureau (L)	Budget Administrator (G)
New Hampshire	Governor; Comptroller (G)	Legislative Budget Assistant (L)	Comptroller (G); head of Dept. of Admin. & Control (G)
New Jersey	Governor; Director of Budget & Accounting, Treasury Dept. (G)	Legislative Budget Officer, Office of Legislative Services (L)	Director, Div. of Budget & Accounting, Treasury Dept. (G)
New Mexico	Governor; Director, Budget Div., Dept. of Finance & Admin. (a)	Legislative Finance Committee (L)	Budget & Financial Control Divisions, Dept. of Finance & Admin.(a)
New York	Governor; Budget Director (G)	Legislative Finance Committees (L)	Budget Director (G); Comptroller (E)
North Carolina	Governor; Office of State Budget(k,l)	Advisory Budget Commission (L & G)	Office of State Budget(k)
North Dakota	Budget Director, Office of Mgt. & Budget (G)	Budget Committee, Legislative Council (L)	Office of Mgt. & Budget(m)
Ohio	Governor; Director, Budget & Mgt. (G)	Legislative Budget Office (L)	Director, Administrative Services (G); Director, Office of Budget & Mgt. (G)
Oklahoma	Director of State Finance (G)	Legislative Fiscal Office (L)	Director of State Finance (G)
Oregon	Governor; Director, Executive Dept. (G)	Legislative Fiscal Office (L)	Director, Executive Dept. (G)
Pennsylvania	Governor; Secretary of Budget & Admin. (G)	House & Senate Appropriations Committees (L); Legislative Budget & Finance Committee (L)	Secretary of Budget & Admin. (G)
Rhode Island	Governor; Budget Div., Dept. of Admin.(a)	House Finance Committee staff (L)	Div. of Budget & Div. of Accounts & Control, Dept. of Admin.(a)
South Carolina	State Budget & Control Board(n)	None	Comptroller General (E)
South Dakota	Governor; Commissioner, Bur. of Finance & Mgt. (G)	Legislative Research Council (L)	Commissioner, Bureau of Finance & Mgt. (G)
Tennessee	Governor; Budget Director (G); Legislative Budget Board (L)	House & Senate Finance, Ways & Means Committees (L); Fiscal Review Committee (L)	Budget Director (G)
Texas		Legislative Budget Board (L)	Auditor (L)
Utah	Governor; Budget Director (G)	Office of Legislative Fiscal Analyst (L)	Director of Finance (G)
Vermont	Governor; Secretary of Admin. (G); Commissioner, Budget & Mgt. Dept. (G)	Joint Legislative Fiscal Review Committee (L)	Secretary of Admin.; Budget & Mgt., & Finance Departments (G)
Virginia	Governor; Secretary of Admin. & Finance (G); Director, Dept. of Planning & Budget (G)	House Appropriations Committee & Senate Finance Committee (L); House & Senate Ways & Means Committees (L)	Secretary of Admin. & Finance (G); Comptroller (G); Director, Dept. of Planning & Budget (G)
Washington	Governor; Director, Office of Financial Mgt. (G)	Legislative Auditor, Joint Committee on Government & Finance (L)	Director, Office of Financial Mgt. (G)
West Virginia	Governor; Commissioner and Budget Div., Dept. of Finance & Admin. (G)(a)	Joint Committee on Finance (L); Legislative Fiscal Bureau (L)	Governor; Dept. of Finance & Admin. (a)
Wisconsin	Governor; Secretary, Dept. of Admin. (G)	Legislative Services Office (L)	Finance Bureau, Div. of State Finance & Program Mgt., Dept. of Admin. (CS)
Wyoming	Governor; Director, Budget Div., Dept. of Admin. & Fiscal Control (G)		Budget Div. & Centralized Accounting-Data Processing(o)
Dist. of Col.	Mayor (E); Off. of Budget & Resource Develop. (CS)	Committee on Budget & City Council (E)(p)	Office of Budget & Resource Develop. (CS)
American Samoa	Governor; Director, Office of Program Planning & Budget Develop. (G)	Legislative Financial Officer (L)	Director, Administrative Services (G)
Guam	Governor; Budget Director, Bureau of Budget & Mgt. Research (G)	Legislative Committee on Ways & Means (L)	Budget Director (G); Director, Dept. of Admin. (G)
Puerto Rico	Governor; Budget Director (G)	Legislative Finance Committees (L)	Budget Bureau(a); Treasury Dept.(a)
Virgin Islands	Governor; Budget Director (G)	Legislative Finance Committee (L)	Budget Director; Commissioner, Finance Dept. (G)

BUDGET: OFFICIALS OR AGENCIES RESPONSIBLE FOR PREPARATION, REVIEW AND CONTROLS
(Footnotes)

Key:
E—Elected
G—Appointed by governor, in some states with one or both houses approving.
L—Chosen by legislature or, in some cases, by an officer or group thereof.
CS—Civil Service.

(a) Director, appointed by governor, selects section or division chiefs.

(b) Comprised of: governor, secretary of state and attorney general.

(c) Budget committee: two senators of opposite parties, two representatives of opposite parties, and budget director who is the head of the state budget agency. The legislative members of the budget committee are appointed by their party leaders in the legislature.

(d) The legislative division of the budget committee acts in an advisory capacity.

(e) Department director appointed by governor; budget director chosen by department head in accordance with civil service act.

(f) Department secretary appointed by governor; director of accounts and reports heads division and is chosen by department head in accordance with civil service act.

(g) Appointed by secretary of the Executive Department for Finance and Administration with governor's approval.

(h) Appointed by commissioner of finance and administration with approval of governor.

(i) The Commission of Budget and Accounting is primarily a legislative agency. Its membership is as follows: governor as ex officio chairman; lieutenant governor; president pro tempore of senate; chairman of senate finance committee; chairman of senate appropriations committee; one senate member appointed by lieutenant governor; speaker of the house; chairman of house ways and means committee; chairman of house appropriations committee; and two house members appointed by speaker.

(j) Appointed by director of administrative services.

(k) State budget officer, appointed by governor, selects division chiefs, subject to approval of the governor.

(l) Division of state budget prepares budget subject to review of the governor and advisory budget commission.

(m) Director appointed by governor.

(n) Governor as chairman, treasurer, comptroller general, chairman of senate finance committee, chairman of house ways and means committee.

(o) Appointed by the director of administration and fiscal control with governor's approval.

(p) Also, U.S. Senate and House of Representatives subcommittees on appropriations for District of Columbia.

(q) Information from 1980-81 Book of the States.

STATE PURCHASING ISSUES FOR THE 1980s

By John Short

PUBLIC PURCHASING is an evolutionary process, and the dynamics of state government purchasing have changed over the years.

Some issues, important in their time, have proved transitory. Some, like the question of centralization/decentralization of purchasing authority, ebb and flow but are not likely to be wholly resolved. Procurement of high technology gear, an issue of the 1960s and 1970s, is handled more comfortably in the 1980s as state purchasing offices apply more sophisticated strategies to the procurement of data processing hardware, word processing systems and related products.

The issues of the 1980s are many—some inherited from the past, some peculiar to the present. This chapter cannot address every issue but will examine six that will come to the fore in this decade. All of these issues involve the relationship and influence of the federal government on state procurement and call for policy decisions to solve the problems brought on by this symbiosis. The first of these issues addresses directly federal-state relationships, and in one way or another, the others are influenced by these relationships:

1. The New Federal Procurement System proposed to the Congress by the Office of Federal Procurement Policy concerns procurement under grants and will modify Attachment O, Procurement Standards of OMB Circular A-102, Revised, *Uniform Administration Requirements for Grants-in-Aid to State and Local Governments*, the present rules of the game.

2. The issue of adoption or adaptation of the American Bar Association Model Procurement Code by state—and local—government purchasing operations will continue to be debated over the coming years.

3. Closely allied to the Model Procurement Code are questions of drafting or redrafting administrative law, the rules and regulations necessary to implement statute purchasing law. The oversight role of the legislative branch creates a subset of policy issues.

4. The growth of federal and state legislation intended to redress socioeconomic inequities through public purchasing presents a dilemma to the traditionally conservative craft of public purchasing.

5. Like the federal government, states are beginning to raise questions about government consultants. More state central purchasing offices are assuming authority and responsibility for contracting professional services.

6. As state buying becomes increasingly diverse and technically complex, purchasing officers have to look beyond competitive sealed bidding to other methods of selection. This is a challenge for this decade, not without risk.

John Short is Assistant to the Administrator, Division of State Agency Services, for Wisconsin.

Attachment "O"

The Office of Management and Budget issued an amended Attachment "O"—*Standards Governing State and Local Grantee Procurement*—to OMB Circular A-102, Revised, *Uniform Administrative Requirements for Grants-in-Aid to State and Local Governments*, effective October 1, 1979. Changes in this document have had an impact on the relationship of public purchasers to federal grantor agencies and further proposed changes may alter the whole environment of purchasing under grants.

It is the position of the National Association of State Purchasing Officials (NASPO) that the attachment responds to the concepts of the New Federal Procurement System proposal and is reasonably responsive to the real world of state procurement under grants. The amended procurement standards have hardly had time to be tested and should be fine tuned only after major problems are identified. Nothing should be done to alter the policy of maximum reliance on state and local government grantee management of their own procurement and prohibiting grantor agency's unwarranted intervention in that process.

NASPO has conveyed to the Administrator of Federal Procurement Policy reservations about the concept of federal certification of state and local purchasing programs. Certification appears to run counter to the concept of reducing bureaucratic interference and placing more reliance on local monitoring and remedies. There is the concern that a review and certification program would tend toward standardization and could be an impediment to creativity, initiative and innovation.

The Model Procurement Code

The first edition of *State and Local Government Purchasing* (1975) served as the overture to the American Bar Association's Model Procurement Code (MPC). The second edition (1982) contains a reprise of the code and an update on its status.

Both the National Association of State Purchasing Officials and the National Institute of Governmental Purchasing have endorsed the *concept* of the Model Procurement Code and remain among those advocating clear-headed discretion in adaptation of those portions of the code meeting the need for revision of existing purchasing laws.

Several states have adapted versions of the code; more are giving serious consideration to changes in their purchasing laws influenced by comparison to the MPC and the essential elements identified in *State and Local Government Purchasing*. A modified draft of the ` code more appropriate to smaller jurisdictions has been proposed by the American Bar Association and would have an impact on county, municipal and other local purchasing programs.

For many states and political subdivisions, a major decision point in consideration of the MPC is raised in Article II—*Procurement Organizations*. The conceptual basis of the code, the separation of policy-making and operational functions, is proposed through the establishment of an independent policy body. The code provides for placement of the policy office either as an independent entity within the executive branch of the government or within an existing department of government such as general services, finance or administration. The first is recommended as it is seen to ensure the professional integrity of the policy-making body and elevate the entire procurement process in the state organizational structure.

The concept differs with the current development of administrative organization in state government, and the organizational distinction between policy-making and operations is seen as federally oriented. The Office of Federal Procurement Policy was an early implementation of the recommendations of the Federal Commission on Government Procurement.

Rules and Regulations

Any change in purchasing statute law requires drafting or redrafting of the implementing rules or regulations. For a state contemplating adoption or adaptation of the MPC, this is a massive undertaking. Public purchasing must respond not only to specific statutory purchasing law, but also the Uniform Commercial Code and other statute contract laws, to appropriate case law, common law and precedents, and to diverse trade and industry practice with the force of custom, if not law.

In several instances of state adaptation of the code, the period from passage of the legislation to effective date of the new law was so brief that the drafting of implementing rules or regulations became a race against time. The American Bar Association Model Procurement Code Project has prepared model rules and regulations to support the code, but these have not been widely circulated.

Most purchasing rules and regulations are promulgated under administrative practices acts and have the force of administrative law. State legislatures are taking an increasing role in overseeing the adoption of administrative law, and state purchasing officials find that stressful relationships between the executive and legislative branches make drafting and modification of rules and regulations a lengthy and arduous task. Overly detailed rules and regulations are seen to diminish the administrative discretion accorded public purchasing by case law.

Socioeconomic Issues

The procurement process has become more complex because of attempts to effect social change through the leverage of government purchasing. The public purchasing officer should not—and probably could not—pass judgment on questions of industrial safety, environmental protection, the redress of inequity or other social objectives being integrated into the procurement process at both the federal or state level. But questions must be raised about diffused legislative intent in the implementation of these objectives.

For example, Attachment "O" directs that procurement under grants be aggregated for the savings inherent in volume purchasing, a time-honored precept. A few paragraphs later the grantee purchasing offices are instructed to subdivide solicitations for bids so as to attract offerings by small business!

Almost without exception, the thrust of socioeconomic provisions is to increase the cost of acquisition without supplemental funding to cushion the impact on government operations. The law simply avoids putting a cash value on the desired effect, leaving purchasing and program managers to wrestle with a balance between worthy goals and practical reality.

Contracting for Services

In contracting for professional services, evaluation and award must on occasion call for the exercise of subjective judgment, as well as absolutes of criteria. It is an area where many central purchasing offices have not had responsibility but where recent trends indicate that these responsibilities will become common.

Competitive Negotiation

Many professional services contracts can be competitively bid—sometimes only through the innovation and ingenuity of the purchasing office and in the face of opposition from both program managers and those with whom they would contract. When there are demonstrable impediments to competitive bidding, purchase of service contracts as well as high technology procurements may be awarded by competitive negotiation. Where clear specifications are not possible, the principal impediment to competitive bidding is prohibition against changes in technical aspects and prices after bids are submitted, whereas such changes are permissible under competitive negotiation. Where competitive negotiation is used, however, price or overall cost continues to be a major competitive element.

Competitive negotiation must seek the widest possible range of prospective proposers. The competitive negotiation procedure should include all elements of the competitive bid procedure if possible: legal notice where required for sealed bidding; specified data and time of receipt of proposals; inclusion of all procedural specifications; and standard contract clauses.

The Request for Proposals must specify the factors to be considered with their relative weight. Wherever possible, these should be objective, measurable criteria. Equal written or oral discussions must be conducted with all responsible offerers who submit proposals and should not disclose any information from competing offerers. Non-competitive negotiation is the least desirable method of award. Sole source procurement must be documented with demonstrable, objective findings that will stand the test of judicial review.

Competitive bidding is a clean, comfortable and historically sound approach to source selection. However, there are transactions in which it cannot and should not be used. Competitive negotiation is not without risk, particularly in those states where the statutes are vague or mute on the subject. Competitive negotiation is encouraged in Attachment "O" and well defined in the Model Procurement Code. This may be the issue of the 1980s most easily resolved.

SELECTED STATE PURCHASING PROCEDURES

State	Purchasing rules and regulations prescribed by: Name of agency or official	Authority	Authority under which written conditions for waiving competitive bidding are established	Two-step/multi-step bidding used Yes	No	Authority under which documentation required to waive competitive bidding
Alabama	Dir. of Fin.	S	O	O	...	S
Alaska	Dir. of Gen. Ser.	R	S	O	...	R
Arizona	Dir., Dept. of Admin.		S(a)	O	...	O
Arkansas	Dir. of Off. of St. Purch.		S	S	...	S
California	Dir. of Gen. Ser.	S,R	S,R	R(b)	...	S,R
Colorado	Dir., Dept. of Admin.	S	S,R	S,R	...	S
Connecticut	Commr., Bur. of Purchases		S	O	...	O
Delaware	Secy. of Adm. Ser.	S	S	...	★	S
Florida	Bd. of Dept. of Gen. Ser.		S,R	R	...	R
Georgia	Dir. of State Purch.		R	★	...	...
Hawaii	Gov.	S	(c)	...	★	...
Idaho	Dir., Dept. of Admin.		S	S	...	O
Illinois	Dir., Dept. of Admin. Ser.	S	S,R	O	...	O
Indiana	Commr., Dept. of Admin.	S	S	S	....	S,R
Iowa	Dir. of Gen. Ser.		S,R	O	...	R
Kansas	Secy., Dept. of Admin.		S	...	★	O
Kentucky	Secy., Dept. of Fin.		(d)	S	...	S,R,O
Louisiana	Commr. of Admin.	S	S,R	R,O	...	S,R
Maine	St. Purch. Agent	S	S	(e)	...	...
Maryland	Bd. of Pub. Works		S,R	S,R	...	S,R
Massachusetts	St. Purch. Agt.	O	O	O	...	O
Michigan	Dir., Dept. of Mgt. & Budg.		O(f)	O	...	...
Minnesota	Commr., Dept. of Admin.		R	NA	...	R
Mississippi	Supr., Div. of Purch.		S	...	★	...
Missouri	Commr. of Admin.	S	O	...	★	O
Montana	Dir., Dept. of Admin.	S	S	...	★	R
Nebraska	Dir., Dept. of Admin. Ser.	S	S	...	★	...
Nevada	Dir., Dept. of Gen. Ser.		S	...	★	(g)
New Hampshire	Dir., Div. of Purch. & Property or St. Treas.	S	S	...	★	R
New Jersey	Dir., Div. of Purch. & Prop.		S	...	R	S,R
New Mexico	Dir., Purch. Div.		S	...	S	O
New York	Commr. of Gen. Ser.		S(h)	(i)	...	S,O
North Carolina	Advry. Budg. Comm.	S	S	O	...	R
North Dakota	Dir., Off. of Mgt. & Budg.	S	S	(i)	...	S
Ohio	Admin. Purch. Off.	R	R	(j)	...	S
Oklahoma	Bd. of Pub. Aff.	S	S	O	...	S,R
Oregon	Pub. Contract Review Bd.	S,R	,R	★	...	S
Pennsylvania	Secy., Dept. of Gen. Ser.	S	S	...	S	O
Rhode Island	St. Purch. Agt.		O	...	★	...
South Carolina	Budg. & Control Bd.		S	S	...	S
South Dakota	Dir., Purch. & Printing		S	O	...	S
Tennessee	Bd. of Standards		R	(k)	...	(c)
Texas	St. Purch. & Gen. Ser. Comm. Ser. Comm.	S	S	O	...	S
Utah	Policy Bd.		R	R	...	R
Vermont	Purch. Dir.		(l)	...	★	(g)
Virginia	Dir., Div. of Purch. & Supply		O	...	★	O
Washington	Dir., Purch. & Material Cont.	S	S	S	...	R
West Virginia	Commr., Fin. & Admin.	S,R	R	O	...	R
Wisconsin	Dir., St. Bur. of Procurement	S	S	O	...	S
Wyoming	Administr., Div. of Purch. & Property Control	S	S	O	...	O

Source: National Association of State Purchasing Officials, *State and Local Government Purchasing* (2nd ed., 1982).

Key: S— Authority in statute.
R— Authority in rules and regulations.
O— Authority in operating procedures.
★— Yes.
(a) No authority for waiver except professional services.
(b) Primarily EDP acquisitions.
(c) Sole source only.
(d) No authority cited.
(e) Contracts only.
(f) Partially.
(g) No documentation required.
(h) Also opinions of Atty. Gen.
(i) Occasionally.
(j) Ohio does unilateral contracting only.
(k) Infrequent.
(l) No written conditions.

STATE INFORMATION SYSTEMS

By Carl W. Vorlander

A SIGNIFICANT CHANGE faces the states as they plan for the management of their information resources. A major part of this change centers on technology, which has accelerated at an exponential rate in recent years and has far outstripped the user's capacity to realize its potential.

A second part of the change is only now making itself known, and knowledge is still hazy. This change is being wrought by the Omnibus Budget Reconciliation Act. To quote Jule Sugarman, managing director of the Human Services Information Center, "Never have so many programs changed at the same time; never has so much authority been shifted virtually simultaneously to the states; never has there been a reduction in federal funding of this magnitude; and never have the states been allowed such flexibility to decide what federal law means without benefit of federal regulations."

Perhaps this part of the change will be a greater challenge than incorporating new technologies into on-going procedures. The program changes which will face government policy-makers and administrators will require new kinds of information not now available and the presentation of currently available information in new formats. These needs will have to be met in the face of diminishing financial backing and an inability to recruit qualified personnel in a period of scarcity of such skills generally and non-competitive salaries. The following table taken from the 1980-81 National Association for State Information Systems' annual report, "Information Systems Technology in State Government," points up the concerns of state information systems administrators.

EXTERNAL PROBLEMS RELATED TO INFORMATION SYSTEMS, 1976-1980

Problem category	Aggregate rank					Number of states identifying the category					Number of states reporting problems 1980	
	1976	1977	1978	1979	1980	1976	1977	1978	1979	1980	More serious	Less serious
Management understanding	1	1	2	2	2	43	43	41	42	39	12	14
Lack of definitive plan	2	3	3	3	4	41	40	36	43	39	18	11
Management commitment	3	2	4	4	3	42	43	40	43	38	13	17
Management interest	4	6	6	8	7	43	43	40	40	39	5	24
Resistance to consolidation	5	4	5	7	8	42	40	37	39	37	8	17
User unfamiliarity with information system	6	8	7	5	6	43	41	40	42	41	3	23
User agency cooperation	7	7	8	9	8	43	42	38	41	38	6	21
Recruitment of qualified personnel	8	5	1	1	1	45	45	42	45	41	26	10
Inadequate financing	9	10	10	10	5	42	38	39	40	38	19	9
Lack of standards	10	9	9	6	10	41	39	38	42	39	8	17
Need for documentation	11	11	10	11	12	40	40	38	44	38	11	16
Need for common data base	12	12	12	12	11	42	41	39	40	37	11	16

Carl W. Vorlander is Executive Director of the National Association for State Information Systems.

Over the past five years, the impact of inadequate financing has moved from tenth to fifth place in the rank order of seriousness as an external problem over which the administrator has no control. Even more dramatic has been the movement from eighth to first place in the seriousness of problems in recruiting qualified staff. One further finding that adds gravity to the table is that both of these problems are considered to be getting more serious by a ratio of more than two to one.

The National Association for State Information Systems has recognized these challenges and altered its committee structure to encompass the area of management policies and procedures. A committee has been appointed which will devote time and effort to the questions raised in the foregoing paragraphs. The entire question of the management of change is of serious concern to the people who represent the NASIS member states.

The challenge of technological change is not a new one in the areas of information resource management; however, it is one that is being heightened by the accelerated rate of such change. The chart below has been used to indicate but one aspect of this remarkable situation. In only five years the use of "mini" computers has grown from 8 percent of the total inventory of state computers to 34 percent. In terms of growth ratios the use of minis has grown by 600 percent, while the aggregate of other so-called mainframe computers has only grown by 7 percent. While the minis may have taken some of the workload off of the larger mainframes, it is much more likely that their growth in numbers represents new work or new methods of handling data so as to make it more useful and readily accessible.

COMPUTERS BY SIZE*
1973-1980

Year	Large	Medium	Small	Mini	Total
1973 (36 states)					
Number	100	102	118	6	326
Percentage of total	31	31	36	2	100
1974 (49 states)					
Number	101	176	175	44	496
Percentage of total	20	36	35	9	100
1975 (50 states)					
Number	159	189	212	39	599
Percentage of total	27	31	35	7	100
1976 (49 states)					
Number	161	169	222	51	603
Percentage of total	27	28	37	8	100
1977 (50 states)					
Number	183	167	224	70	644
Percentage of total	28	26	35	11	100
1978 (50 states)					
Number	200	152	168	161	681
Percentage of total	29	22	25	24	100
1979 (50 states)					
Number	210	145	189	221	768
Percentage of total	28	19	24	29	100
1980 (50 states)					
Number	249	130	215	310	904
Percentage of total	28	14	24	34	100

*Size comparisons between 1973 and 1974 cannot be made due to reclassification.

A second area of technological change which must be given very serious consideration is communication between systems. This is having almost as great an impact on the decade of the eighties as did the stored program computer on the decade of the sixties. When combined with the mini or microcomputer, it creates a network capable of providing computational capabilities directly to the desk of the user and distributing the information so developed to any part of the organization where it is needed. Communications is at the very heart of the successful development of the automated office, with the written word transmitted through electronic pulses capable of being stored, forwarded on a selective basis or reformatted for further processing. Techniques such as "piggy backing" of messages or data on state-owned television networks, the leasing of resources from private carriers and even using satellite transmission will have to be considered in view of the ever-rising cost of using common carrier facilities. A recent report by a NASIS ad hoc committee concluded:

1. Telecommunication facilities are becoming the central nervous system for the information communications, processing and overall business operations of state government.

2. There appears to be a trend toward central organization, design, management, operation and planning of multimodal telecommunication within the states.

3. Telecommunication technology is in a period of major transition and will probably remain so for the next two to five years. (For instance, the trend and transition to digital from analog transmission appears more a matter of "when" or "how long" rather than "if.")

4. It appears prudent that each state develop "in-house" multimodal telecommunication expertise since there are a variety of management options, including multiple architectures, vendors and technologies/methodologies to help solve both generic and special telecommunication needs of the states.

These changes, both programmatic and technological, demand that this article conclude by calling attention to the increasingly serious vulnerabilities which face the states in terms of safeguarding the larger amount of information which they will find necessary to collect and protecting more widespread information resources from wrongful use. This concern is best stated by quoting the most recent NASIS annual report, "It can happen here! What more can be said. The accompanying table indicates only too well the extent to which we are leaving ourselves open to future woes. Although NASIS found it worthwhile to have one of its standing committees develop guidelines for drafting computer crime legislation and prepare a sample draft bill which has been included in The Council of State Governments' 1981 publication, *Suggested State Legislation* (Volume 40), many of its members cannot find the backing and the resources to develop a comprehensive security program. We must again cite the 1973 annual report which said 'we are courting potential catastophies of great dimension.'"

SECURITY
(38 states reporting)

States reporting	Physical security					
	Total physical security plan				I.D. badges required	Entrance guards required
	Issued	Implemented	Enforced	Audited		
Yes	22	26	24	22	30	20
No.........................	13	10	11	12	7	18

States reporting	Data security					
	Total data security plan				Off-site back-up storage used	S & P documentation included
	Issued	Implemented	Enforced	Audited		
Yes	14	14	12	14	32	23
No.........................	19	15	16	14	4	12

Table 1
COORDINATION AND CONTROL OF INFORMATION SYSTEMS
IN STATE AGENCIES

State or other jurisdiction	Authority	Functions*				
		Planning	Systems design	Programming	Hardware acquisition	Operations
Alabama	Statute	C/O	C	C	A	C
Alaska(a)	Statute	C/O	C/O	C/O	A	A
Arizona	Statute	C/O	C	C	C	C
Arkansas(b)	Statute	C/O	C/O	O	A	O
California(h)	Statute	C	C	C	C	C
Colorado(g)	Statute/Admin. Code	C/O	C	C	C/O	C
Connecticut	Statute	C	C	C	C/O	C
Delaware	State Code	A	A	A	A	A
Florida	Statute	C	C	C	A	C/O
Georgia(a,f)	Statute/Exec. Order	C	A	A	A	A
Hawaii	Exec. Order	A	C	C	A	A
Idaho	Statute	C	...	...	C	...
Illinois(b,f,g,k)	Statute	A	C	C	A	A
Indiana(a,c,i,j)	Statute	A	C	C	A	C
Iowa(c)	Statute/Admin. Code	O	O	O	C	O
Kansas(f)	Statute	C	...	...	C	C/O
Kentucky(b,f)	Statute	C	...	...	C	C/O
Louisiana	Statute	C	C	C	A	...
Maine	Statute	A	C	C	A	A(d)
Maryland	Statute/Exec. Order	C	...	...	C	...
	Admin. Reg.	...	C	C	C	C
Massachusetts	Statute/Exec. Order	C	C		C	...
Michigan	Statute/Exec. Order	C	...	...	C	...
Minnesota(d)	Statute	C	C/O	A	A	A
Mississippi(a)	Statute	C	C	C	A	C
Missouri	Statute	C	C	C	C	C
Montana	Statute	C	C	C	A	A
Nebraska	Statute	A	A	A	A	A
Nevada	Statute	...	A	A	C	...
	Admin. Reg.	C	...	...	...	C
New Hampshire	Statute	A(a,c,f)	A(a,c,f)	A(a,c,f)	A	A(a,c,f)
New Jersey	Statute	C	C/O	C/O	C	C/O
New Mexico	Statute	C	C	C	A	C
New York	Statute	...	...	...	C	...
	Exec.Order/Admin. Reg.	C	...	...	C	...
North Carolina	Statute	C	...	...	...	C
	Exec. Order	C	...	...	C	...
North Dakota(a,e)	Statute	A	A	A	A	A
Ohio	Statute	C	X	X	C	C
Oklahoma	Statute	C	C	C	C	C
Oregon	Statute/Exec. Order	C/O	C/O	C/O	C/O	C/O
Pennsylvania	Exec. Order	C	C	C	C	C
Rhode Island	Statute	A	A	A	A	A
South Carolina	Statute	C	C	C	C	...
South Dakota(f)	Statute	A	A	A	A	A
Tennessee(a)	Exec. Order	C/O	C/O	A	A	A
Texas	Statute	C	C	X	C	C
Utah	Statute	A	A	A	A	A
Vermont(a,f)	Exec. Order	C/O	C/O	C/O	C/O	C/O
Virginia(f)	Statute	C/O	C	C	A	O
Washington	Statute	C	C	C	C	C
West Virginia	Statute/Exec. Order	A	C	C	A	A
Wisconsin	Statute	A	C/O	C/O	A	C
Wyoming(f)	Statute	A	A	A	A	A
Guam	Statute	A	A	A	A	A

*Key:
C—Controlling or coordinating authority.
O—Execution of the function.
A—Authority is all-inclusive.
X—Scope of authority not stated.
  (a) Excludes employment security.
  (b) Excludes constitional officers.
  (c) Excludes highway.
  (d) Should be "C" for employment services.

  (e) Excludes adjutant general.
  (f) Operation control excludes higher education.
  (g) Excludes Judicial Department.
  (h) Excludes legislature, Univ. of Calif. Community College District, and Industrial Insurance Comp. Fund.
  (i) Excludes auditor of state.
  (j) Excludes institutions of higher education.
  (k) Excludes legislature.

Table 2
TREND OF COMPUTER INVENTORIES: 1969-1980

State or other jurisdiction	Years										
	1980	7/1/79	7/1/78	7/1/77	7/1/76	7/1/75	7/1/74	7/1/73	7/1/72	7/1/71	1969-70
Total	909	773	686	644	603	599	496	474	421	373	478
Alabama	10	10	10	11	12	12	11	...	9	11	...
Alaska	23	23	20	9	3	3	3	3	3	3	3
Arizona	11	11	11	13	12	7	8	12	15	11	15
Arkansas	21	13	13	17	17	18	16	15	...	...	...
California	58	63	49	46	34	37	29	28	...	...	49
Colorado	10	10	10	10	10	10	9	...	7	...	8
Connecticut	17	16	11	11	12	11	11	11	...	...	...
Delaware	6	2	3	3	3	4	3	3	3	3	...
Florida	23	23	29	26	...	20	13	...	14	14	11
Georgia	5	17	18	18	19	20	11	...	14	...	21
Hawaii	3	3	3	3	3	4	4	4	5	3	3
Idaho	13	11	11	10	6	3	3	4	4	...	3
Illinois	20	21	14	12	12	15	12	20	28	28	33
Indiana	8	13	9	9	9	8	6	6	6	10	...
Iowa	14	9	13	7	8	8	6	9	6	4	5
Kansas	21	21	19	4	4	3	3	3	5	5	6
Kentucky	5	5	6	6	4	5	1	14	14	...	...
Louisiana	20	21	21	19	19	19	10	17	17	22	21
Maine	13	9	4	5	5	5	4	4	5	5	4
Maryland	21	18	18	18	17	17	17	17	12	16	5
Massachusetts	12	15	15	15	15	14	15	14	20	..	16
Michigan	45	34	30	24	30	29	28	26	21	17	14
Minnesota	3	4	4	4	5	4	4	5	6	7	6
Mississippi	2	2	2	2	2	2	1	4	8	10	10
Missouri	13	14	12	20	20	16	...	14	...	...	9
Montana	3	3	3	4	4	5	4	4	4	4	3
Nebraska	15	6	6	6	6	6	6	6	4	3	...
Nevada	28	20	15	9	9	8	4	5	2	1	2
New Hampshire	16	12	7	8	6	5	3	4	4	3	3
New Jersey	27	24	25	36	37	19	20	15	17	13	23
New Mexico	6	6	6	5	5	5	9	7	6	7	2
New York	77	53	43	40	40	37	33	33	...	31	49
North Carolina	24	19	13	18	13	11	8	9	9	8	6
North Dakota	5	5	5	3	3	3	3	3	3	2	2
Ohio	37	36	29	27	29	47	34	16	16	...	16
Oklahoma	12	12	11	12	9	10	10	9	9	11	12
Oregon	8	8	10	10	19	10	8	12	12	9	9
Pennsylvania	38	35	28	27	27	27	18	22	22	22	20
Rhode Island	10	4	3	3	3	3	3	4	4	...	6
South Carolina	14	14	14	22	22	24	20	14	14	14	12
South Dakota	2	2	3	3	3	3	3	3	2	3	2
Tennessee	4	4	5	5	5	5	4	6	8	16	9
Texas	58	45	35	38	36	32	29	27	21	22	24
Utah	5	5	7	7	7	7	3	4	3	6	4
Vermont	3	3	3	3	3	2	3	1	1	...	3
Virginia	11	7	8	8	9	10	10	6	11	...	11
Washington	46	38	26	9	11	10	11	10	11	12	10
West Virginia	17	4	5	4	4	4	6	4	4	8	...
Wisconsin	32	11	13	13	11	11	13	13	9	9	8
Wyoming	9	4	3	2	1	1	3	4	3	...	...
Guam	5	5	5	...	...	...	...	...	...	...	...

Figure 1
STATE EDP BUDGETS

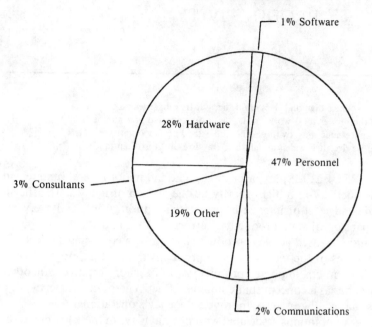

PRODUCTIVITY

By James E. Jarrett

Productivity is like a diamond. It is multi-faceted. Its value is enhanced when those with the proper tools work on it. It can be measured in a number of ways. It is appreciated most by those who understand its many subtleties. It is obtained at a price. It is widely sought after; as a result, it is often faked.[1]

STATE BUDGETARY PROBLEMS, taxpayer discontent and major federal funding cutbacks have elevated productivity to a high priority on the agenda of many state officials. There was an unprecedented level of interest in productivity during 1981, and every sign points to continued expansion of state productivity efforts in 1982 and 1983.

Despite the interest and increased activity, productivity can be a confusing subject. For instance, there are many uses of the term. To some productivity directors, productivity is viewed as a process while to others, improved productivity is a goal or objective. Still others categorize productivity either as a concept that combines effectiveness and efficiency, or as a bundle of techniques that can be used to improve an agency's operations.

There are also negative connotations associated with productivity. In these less charitable interpretations, it is a buzzword, another faddish technique, a term denoting work speedups and increased workloads and responsibilities without commensurate pay increases, and a facade for budget and personnel retrenchment. In this way, productivity becomes synonymous with cost *and* service reduction. True productivity improvement, however, does not necessarily require cost-cutting and certainly does not require reduction of services.

Another source of confusion is that productivity is used in both broad and narrow ways and has both non-technical and technical definitions.[2] In this article, productivity is broadly interpreted as being those programs, procedures, techniques and processes which improve governmental performance and operations. More specifically, this includes new programs and approaches which: (1) increase service levels while holding costs constant, or (2) decrease costs for current service levels, or ideally, (3) increase performance and service levels while simultaneously reducing costs.

Even by taking such a broad view of productivity improvement, one must realize that most productivity initiatives never are labeled as such. Most improvements in state governments' operations are evolutionary and achieved without fanfare. Therefore, any inventory of state productivity initiatives necessarily will omit much of what is going on.

Diverse Organizational Approaches

State government officials are following diverse paths to improve their operations. This can be attributed to differences in state needs, leadership styles and levels of commitment, resources and staff expertise, and to the fact that no single approach has emerged as the

James E. Jarrett directs The Council of State Governments' work in productivity and government employment.

best. Just like productivity improvement in the private sector, there is no universally accepted sequence and approach for success. As a result, there is considerable diversity in how state efforts are organized, where they are located and what they have as their key objectives and activities.

Because of the diversity, there are only a few detectable trends. First, most states still do not have a comprehensive, formal productivity improvement program. Second, except for legislative sunset review mechanisms and several other isolated cases, productivity projects have been a distinctly executive branch activity. Most efforts have been initiated and implemented without extensive legislative support and involvement, and legislation has been rare. Third, a common and highly visible approach, the establishment of temporary task forces of private-sector managers who conduct operational audits and reviews over a three-to-six-month period, has continued. Fourth, most efforts have emphasized cost control or cost reduction rather than improvement in services and outputs. Fifth, these productivity efforts are generally planned, implemented and supported in a political context. While better government operations would seem to be a goal which would stand outside of politics, most efforts depend greatly on support and leadership by key elected officials. Sixth, there are few guides and rules available to state officials on how to start, support and maintain a new productivity improvement program. Consequently, there are numerous methods being used to improve performance. And seventh, the interest in productivity activities is growing rapidly. This surge of interest has been in comprehensive, coordinated productivity programs as well as more narrow issues like monetary incentives and contracting out for services, subjects which in better economic times rarely generated interest.

Because there is no typical state government productivity program, there can be no easy listing or description of current efforts. The variety of approaches, however, is stimulating and instructive as well as disconcerting. Organizationally, there are formal executive branch programs, informal executive branch programs and legislative programs for executive branch productivity.

Some states, notably North Carolina and Arizona, have formal programs involving a gubernatorially appointed Productivity Commission, a central coordinating staff unit and productivity designees in line agencies. States such as South Carolina and New Jersey have adopted only some of the components. And in other cases, like Pennsylvania, a formal and integrated improvement effort has been concentrated in a single line agency.

Informal executive branch efforts have been the most frequent. Included under this category are two major types of structures. First, the temporary task force of private-sector managers, and secondly, the use of existing staff units, which are not designated as productivity units as such but perform work designed to improve operations. In some states these units are known as internal consulting groups; in other states they are called management analysis, management service, program review or administrative analysis units. These units, sometimes located within the budget operation but usually not, are important to the productivity efforts in states such as Georgia, Washington, Oregon, Virginia, Michigan, Colorado, Iowa, Pennsylvania and New Jersey.

Legislative initiatives focused on executive branch programs and activities have been of three types. In a handful of states such as Mississippi, a legislative staff group has been the key force for new productivity improvement activities. In several other states, there have been temporary, interim or select committees. This has occurred in Texas and Indiana as well as in Arizona and Washington on a specific productivity topic. And in one case there has been a permanent legislative body established: New York's Legislative Commission on

Economy and Efficiency in Government. Besides being more permanent than some other states' legislative efforts, this commission is unique in that staff conduct productivity studies and research rather than perform post audits or sunset reviews.

Diverse Methods

Just as there is diversity in the structure and organization of state productivity projects, so too is there diversity in the methods and activities used to achieve better performance. The enormous range of methods in use is striking. Under the category of human or people-oriented approaches, state officials have concentrated on six primary topics and areas: (1) employee suggestion systems—additional states are now starting them, other states are attempting to keep them alive, and several states have taken steps to rejuvenate existing procedures; (2) training—the emphasis clearly has been on improving the skills and overall management capabilities of both executive administrators and middle managers; (3) sick leave—a host of state officials have conducted studies on possible methods of reducing absenteeism through new alternatives like personal leave, paid time off, and well-pay annual bonuses; (4) quality circles—this employee participation method has grown rapidly in government on a pilot basis as it has in the private sector; (5) quality of work life projects—this collection of techniques, to foster job enrichment, job enlargement and higher job satisfaction, is more and more viewed positively in its own right and as a motivational approach; and (6) monetary incentives—these range from new pay-for-performance plans for the individual state employee to less commonly used approaches such as monetary bonuses and bonuses for groups of employees.

Under the category of technical approaches, state officials also are using a variety of techniques and methods. Office automation and investment in new technologies have increased, and there has been an emphasis on all types of measurement: program evaluations for effectiveness and efficiency, work measurement and new work standards for groups and individual employees, and integration of program performance measures into the budgetary review cycle. Work simplification, planning and scheduling techniques and even value engineering and analysis have been used. Operational audits are widespread and the use of organizational diagnostic tools and employee attitude surveys is increasing. Other projects have centered on administrative consolidations, alternative service delivery forms such as provision of services by for-profit firms instead of by state employees, and the use of volunteer, retired private executives on productivity projects.

What are the most useful ways to improve state operations? Based on a national survey of state officials in 1980 by The Council of State Governments' Productivity Center, there are several key approaches which are favored. State officials believe improving the capability of managers would be the most useful avenue, while the next best means would be to provide more incentives and rewards for outstanding state employees. Improved productivity measurement techniques and improved operating procedures were also seen as high priorities. And elimination of unnecessary state programs was viewed as important by state legislators and key legislative staff.

Selected State Efforts

During 1980-81, many state governments started or expanded programs or began serious study of a major productivity-oriented program or project. While the activities highlighted below deserve special mention, this is by no means a complete inventory.

New productivity programs were started in five states. In Arizona, a Governor's Commission on Productivity was formed in 1980 and a staff group was created in the Department of Administration. Initial activities were devoted to a resource management measurement system and a statewide conference. In Ohio, a productivity center was started in mid-1981 within the Office of Management and Budget. In Texas, a multi-faceted Government Effectiveness Program was started in the governor's office. The key elements of the program are: (1) a major briefing package for members of the governing boards of state agencies and institutions; (2) reduction of the state work force; (3) more management-by-objective and zero-base budgeting; (4) increased management training; and (5) a large number of operational audits using state employees and retired senior executives. In Minnesota, a productivity improvement program was started in 1980. Minnesota's program was unique for at least two reasons. First, much more effort has been spent on strategic planning and multi-agency planning than in other states, and the program was organized to have an Operating Advisory Board (consisting of the several sponsoring agencies) and a larger Advisory Council that included staff agencies and major line agencies. Another state that started a formal effort was South Carolina. As a result of a gubernatorial task force recommendation, a Council on Productivity was created to look at both state management issues and the impact of state government actions on private firms' operations.

Special studies and projects occurred in many other states. New Hampshire, Louisiana, Nebraska and Kentucky had state efficiency task forces at some point during the two years. In Colorado, a major personnel bill was enacted which has a pay-for-performance component along with several other productivity-oriented features. Significant improvements in the Pennsylvania Department of Transportation were achieved with a departmental productivity improvement effort. According to Pennsylvania officials, over an 18-month period, staff was reduced while production, quantity and quality increased in virtually every unit. Kentucky's Department of Transportation also implemented a large number of management initiatives and reduced staff significantly while generating more output, according to transportation administrators. And Tennessee held a governor's conference on productivity and started an innovative sick leave incentive program to reduce absenteeism. As of January 1982, the results of the sick leave program were impressive.

Several states continued or expanded their programs. New Jersey and New York, for the most part, carried on with previous lines of effort.[3] North Carolina's formal program was expanded even further, and in September 1980, a retired senior executives project was started to take advantage of the management expertise of retired high executives living in the state. A talent bank of these individuals who are willing to provide advice and counsel was created, and more than a dozen individuals are already working directly with senior government managers on projects. Other new moves have included: designation of a person at the assistant or deputy secretary level in each agency to be responsible for an agency's management improvement activities; creation of a Management Council comprised of all agencies' assistant secretaries for productivity; and a process to identify and communicate productivity priorities through the use of governor's management directives and information sharing among the assistant secretaries. These new components and others are in addition to the numerous continuing productivity activities in North Carolina.

The number of state productivity programs is likely to increase, and perhaps rather quickly. In early 1982, Michigan officials announced creation of an Executive Council on Productivity, and Missouri officials had begun planning for a program. Serious consideration was being given to productivity program options in Utah, Connecticut, Virginia and Kansas and to a proposed Council on State Government Productivity in California. Also, legislation, which stood a realistic chance of passage, had been introduced in Delaware to create a Management Advisory Committee, and in Washington, to begin a Council on Management Advisers. Because of the very favorable outlook for an increase in the number of state programs, there will be more emphasis in the future on implementation and an assessment of accomplishments rather than on mobilizing support for creation of new programs.

Problems

In spite of the overall outlook for new productivity programs, not all of the trends are positive. One major problem has been the limited scope of most programs. Rarely have they covered the higher educational system, the judicial branch and legislative operations, and grant programs to local governments. In most states, if these major categories of expenditures are left untouched, any productivity program will be limited. A second major problem has been in the low level and degree of support for the productivity improvement effort. Many employees and managers perceive that they have nothing to gain and much to lose. State legislators often seem more apt to suggest elimination of a service than its improvement. Resources have proven unstable both for the productivity analysts and staff *and* for investments in people and equipment that may be necessary for long-term improvements. Moreover, the level of funds for state productivity programs has been insignificant, and the withdrawal of federal funding for productivity initiatives will only make the situation much worse. A third major problem has been with some productivity efforts themselves. Few devote adequate time to strategic planning or to in-depth diagnosis. Most of the efforts do not seem to have the luxury of a slow start, as there is a demand for quick results. Perhaps even more important, many of the productivity projects have been designed to cut costs without regard for services—outputs are being cut along with inputs. Retrenchment is not the same as productivity improvement, however.

Although there are some major problems, it seems clear that steady gains in productivity can be made, once the period of major service cutbacks is over. This conclusion is based on the growing recognition that the problem is long-term and the increasing understanding that nearly everyone benefits in the long-run from productivity increases in *both* the public and private sectors.

A Look Ahead

Many state officials will begin new productivity programs and projects during the next two years. Some of the programs will be labeled as productivity projects, while others will improve performance without falling under the category of productivity. In both cases, the important point will be the achievements, not the label. State officials do not need to have a coordinated productivity plan and program to increase productivity and performance. Often it helps; sometimes it is a detriment.

Fortunately, state officials will not adopt a consistent or uniform approach to productivity improvement. Diversity, based on local needs and problems, will predominate. However, there are likely to be a number of topics and issues that will receive more attention. These include the aforementioned monetary and non-monetary incentives, contracting out, technology and office automation, and more sophisticated measurement and control techniques. And, there is likely to be more cooperation between private firms and state government agencies toward the objective of increasing both organizations' performances.

State government productivity activities must be viewed primarily as long-term ventures.

Given the size of most productivity programs, the difficult problems encountered, and the nature of the bureaucratic and political environments, short-term major successes will be very infrequent. Nor will productivity efforts be a panacea for the shock of major federal funding cutbacks.

The goal of improving state governmental performance by better serving the public is an on-going process because improvements will always be possible. There are many, many ways to improve productivity. Most will be undramatic, but they will be significant, for even small improvements in state government operations will produce benefits for years to come.

Notes

1. Judy B. Rosener, "Improving Productivity in the Public Sector: An Analysis of Two Tools—Marketing and Citizen Involvement," *Public Productivity Review* 2, 3 (Spring-Summer 1977): 3.

2. Because most introductory works on productivity deal with these issues, they will not be covered here. Readers interested in pursuing this should read Walter L. Balk, *Improving Government Productivity: Some Policy Perspectives* (Beverly Hills, Calif.: Sage Publications, 1975), and Brian J. Usilaner, "Productivity Measurement," in *Productivity Improvement Handbook for State and Local Government* (New York, N.Y.: John Wiley and Sons, 1979).

3. When this article was being prepared, the Florida productivity program was being altered. Rather than being a separate effort within the office of the governor, it appeared as if the program would be merged with another. For more information, contact the author at The Council of State Governments.

STATE LIBRARY AGENCIES

By Lester L. Stoffel and Kathryn J. Gesterfield

AS PUBLIC LIBRARIES entered the modern age, it became evident that no single library could satisfy the wide information needs of an increasingly sophisticated public. In response to this problem, New York State, in 1958, formed the first state-supported public library system, bringing together the public libraries in a region to share materials and provide central services more economically than on a local basis. The responsibility for public library support and control remained at the local level, while the state recognized its obligation to move toward equalizing local library service through its support of the regional systems. Within a decade, most states had followed New York's lead in fostering public library systems in some form.

State library agencies, realizing that the library user does not care where his information comes from as long as he gets it, have developed ways to share resources of all types of libraries in the state for the benefit of the user. Although some states have legislation enabling library systems to serve all types of libraries, others are studying their laws to determine the best ways to establish library systems. In the meantime, state library agencies continue to promote resource sharing by means of cooperative projects and programs which make it possible for libraries of every type to call upon other libraries in order to satisfy their users' needs.

The federal Library Services and Construction Act (LSCA), which had supplied funds to states to strengthen public library services throughout the nation, was broadened in 1966 by the addition of Title III. Under the new title, funds were appropriated to "establish and maintain local, regional, state or interstate networks for the systematic and effective coordination of the resources of school, public, academic and special libraries or special information centers." Eligibility for funding depended on all types of libraries collaborating in the development of comprehensive statewide plans for access to all of the state's resources. This legislation furthered the evolution to multitype library systems.

The National Commission on Libraries and Information Science (NCLIS) has declared that "information is a vital national resource and essential to well-being in a democratic society. . . ." NCLIS envisions "the development of a full-service national library and information service network"[1] with the state library agencies stimulating, initiating and coordinating the development of statewide networks which would become the nodes of the envisioned national network.

Meanwhile, the library profession has adopted networking as a useful means of sharing materials to satisfy the needs of library clientele. The 1980 *American Library Directory* lists 330 "Networks, Consortia and Other Cooperative Organizations,"[2] of which 161 include public libraries. Also listed are 445 library systems, six of which include other than public libraries. Only seven states have no library systems. A number of the networks cross state

Lester L. Stoffel is Executive Director of Suburban Library System in Burr Ridge, Illinois. Kathryn J. Gesterfield is Director of Illinois State Library, Springfield, Illinois.

boundaries, such as the New England Library Network (NELINET), while others are computer-based and are open to libraries anywhere in the nation, for example, the not-for-profit On Line Computer Library Center (OCLC), which in 1981 was a network with over 4,000 terminals in over 2,500 libraries in 50 states and seven foreign countries.

Automation has also proved extremely useful in library systems and facilitates resource sharing among systems statewide. Through a grant program using LSCA funds, the Illinois State Library has stimulated the development of data bases which are accessible to several systems in the state. Illinois systems also are able to gain access to the University of Illinois data base. A statewide service delivers the materials needed by the requester.

Movements toward cooperation among all types of libraries have reinforced the planning role of state agencies. In order to carry out resource sharing in an efficient and effective manner, joint planning with all the libraries is required. The state agency then is able to see the whole picture of library service and development in the state and can design projects to reinforce strengths and shore up weaknesses.

State library agencies traditionally have provided continuing education for librarians and trustees, and with the development of new, multitype library systems, continuing education has been extended to include librarians from all types of libraries. While many traditional kinds of continuing education, such as improving reference skills, administration of libraries and budgeting, continue to be popular, increased use of automated library methods has called for many specialized presentations. Searching on automated reference data bases, for example, requires special training. Use of the various sub-systems of OCLC and the changes in the second edition of the *Anglo-American Cataloging Rules* required extensive re-education.

The influx to all states of people whose second language is English (or will be when learned) requires specialized library service. State libraries have been alert to this need, and projects have provided materials for the new residents, in their own language, as well as learning aids to help them in their study of English. While the Spanish-speaking population has been growing, the sudden addition of populations from Southeast Asia has made demands on libraries that few were able to meet without aid from state agencies.

Although service for the blind and physically handicapped has been in place in state library agencies (or in other libraries with fiscal support from the state agencies), partly as a result of need expressed during the White House Conference on Library and Information Services (WHCLIS), a new realization of a great unserved population has become apparent—that of the hearing-impaired. More and more state library agencies are looking for ways to serve this part of the population.

Services to state-supported institutions—especially correctional institutions—have been the responsibility of state library agencies, either directly or through assignment to libraries for some time. Currently, more and more state agencies are becoming concerned about state institutions for mental health, and the development of these services increases each year.

A constant concern of state agencies is the number of people within each state who do not live in an area in which tax-supported public library service is available. State libraries have used a variety of methods to serve these people, from bookmobiles, to books by mail, to efforts to establish service libraries in areas where there is sufficient population and sufficient tax base to provide library service. Since usually even the most remote areas have schools with libraries, multitype library development is expected to make the resources of the state available.

Notes

1. Alphonse F. Trezza, "The Role of State Library Agencies in National Plans for Library and Information Services," *Library Trends*, 27 (Fall 1978): 213-16.

2. *American Library Directory*, 33rd edition (New York: R. R. Bowker Co., 1980), pp. 1649-1664.

Table 1
STATE LIBRARY AGENCIES
Structure and Appropriations
Fiscal 1981

State	Organi-zation struc-ture*	Agency reports to:†	Appropriations				Other sources of income	Total
			State(a)		Federal			
			Agency appro-priation	Direct assistance to public libraries & networks	Library Services and Con-struction Act	Other		
All states			$112,601,622	$174,220,361	$68,746,580	$7,978,144	$2,439,657	$365,986,364
Alabama	I	B	1,262,273	1,703,379	1,278,313	89,659	7,800	4,341,424
Alaska	U	E	2,767,400	400,000	330,600	...	...	3,498,000
Arizona	U	B	...	300,000	...	...	...	300,000
Arkansas	U	E	1,200,272	1,353,000	843,000	...	...	3,396,272
California	U	E	6,037,253	5,229,256	5,690,460	...	...	16,956,969
Colorado	U	E	668,761	1,477,427	823,446	...	55,277	3,024,911
Connecticut.........	I	B	4,798,035	428,000	1,029,620	...	34,077	6,289,732
Delaware	U	D	360,000	75,000	384,221	...	...	819,221
Florida	U	S	928,353	3,751,692	2,414,136	19,700	...	7,113,881
Georgia	U	E	440,602	8,371,162	1,387,622	...	...	10,199,386
Hawaii	U	E	9,871,991	(b)	430,493	...	...	10,302,484
Idaho	U	B,E	897,400	362,500	444,500	41,200	107,700	1,853,300
Illinois	U	S	2,706,200	20,289,796	3,389,656	...	...	26,385,652
Indiana	I	G	1,516,572	1,778,095	1,725,984	...	...	5,020,651
Iowa	I	B	715,938	983,390	1,049,372	...	...	2,748,700
Kansas	I	G	560,898	854,375	824,814	...	13,932	2,254,019
Kentucky	I	G	6,841,826	2,400,000	1,212,026	44,262	87,000	10,585,114
Louisiana...........	U	R	667,623	1,597,119	1,505,836	105,827	7,883	3,884,288
Maine	U	E	2,086,753	363,188	465,586	159,853	...	3,075,380
Maryland	U	E	240,000	13,061,603	3,754,000	4,371,000	...	21,426,603
Massachusetts	I	A	8,700,000	7,200,000	1,500,000	...	...	17,400,000
Michigan	U	E	3,986,700	7,933,007	1,052,700	2,100,000	...	15,072,407
Minnesota	U	E	737,560	4,044,864	1,360,754	...	...	6,143,178
Mississippi..........	I	C	2,550,674	1,334,700	910,948	...	...	4,796,322
Missouri............	U	E	840,617	1,667,603	1,239,737	75,000	267,778	4,090,735
Montana	U	C	647,902	...	457,244	...	...	1,105,146
Nebraska	I	C	1,320,048	579,100	575,915	9,478	12,559	2,497,100
Nevada.............	I	G	841,933	49,770	425,492	...	24,585	1,341,780
New Hampshire	I	G	1,200,000	750,000	428,000	...	...	2,378,000
New Jersey	U	E	2,908,840	8,742,426	2,277,634	162,858	409,486	14,501,244
New Mexico	U	R	1,954,002	208,000	537,837	...	...	2,699,839
New York	U	E	5,160,347	33,649,880	5,182,571	435,307	...	44,428,105
North Carolina	U	R	2,110,045	4,354,056	1,613,388	...	...	8,077,489
North Dakota	U	I	422,928	500,000	401,000	60,000	...	1,383,928
Ohio	I	B	2,370,685	969,073	3,229,050	...	415,430	6,984,238
Oklahoma	I	B	1,559,698	1,075,000	1,031,825	100,000	81,000	3,847,523
Oregon.............	I	B	1,300,278	471,455	702,181	...	18,074	2,491,988
Pennsylvania.........	U	E	2,092,000	12,968,000	3,516,000	124,000	5,000	18,705,000
Rhode Island........	I	G	2,274,686	1,979,088	502,589	...	...	4,756,363
South Carolina	I	B	1,014,339	1,942,887	1,048,258	...	...	4,005,484
South Dakota	U	G	1,700,000	...	410,000	...	35,000	2,145,000
Tennessee	U	E	1,243,200	2,789,700	1,159,050	...	97,000	5,288,950
Texas	I	C	3,278,772	2,025,079	3,873,817	...	...	9,177,668
Utah	U	C	1,626,700	...	588,300	...	640,000	2,855,000
Vermont	I	G	780,200	252,659	341,199	...	6,000	1,380,058
Virginia	I	G	2,750,000	4,700,000	1,440,000	...	...	8,890,000
Washington..........	I	C	3,577,592	...	1,296,417	...	73,376	4,947,385
West Virginia	I	G	6,264,885	4,679,147	758,321	...	...	11,702,353
Wisconsin	U	E	1,938,738	4,575,885	1,544,298	80,000	40,700	8,179,621
Wyoming............	I	B	880,103	...	358,370	...	...	1,238,473

Source: Kathryn J. Gesterfield, Illinois State Library.

* Abbreviations: I—Independent; U—Unit within larger unit.

† Abbreviations: A—Department of Administration; B—Board; C—Commission; D—Department of Community Affairs and Economic Development; E—Department of Education; G—Governor or Governor's Board; I—Director of Institutions; R—Department of Cultural Resources; S—Secretary of State.

(a) State appropriations in some states may vary from data reported here due to administrative decisions.

(b) Hawaii has a totally integrated system; all public and state library support included in previous column.

Table 2
FUNCTIONS AND RESPONSIBILITIES
OF STATE LIBRARY AGENCIES

State	Library services to state governments							Statewide library services development															
	Documents	Information and reference service	Legislative reference	Law library	Genealogy and state history	Archives	Liaison with institutional libraries	Coordination of academic libraries	Coordination of public libraries	Coordination of school libraries	Coordination of institutional libraries	Research	Coordination of library systems	Consulting services	Interlibrary loan, reference and bibliographic service	Statistical gathering and analysis	Library legislation review	Interstate library compacts and other cooperative efforts	Specialized resource centers	Direct service to the public	Annual reports	Public relations	Continuing education
Alabama	..	★	†	†	★	..	★	†	★	..	★	★	★	★	★	★	★	★	★	★	†	★	★	★
Alaska	★	★	†	†	★	★	★	★	★	†	★	★	★	★	★	★	★	★	★	★	†	★	★	★
Arizona	★	★	★	★	★	★	★	★	★	†	†	★	★	★	★	★	★	★	★	★	★	★	†	★
Arkansas	★	★	..	..	..	..	★	†	†	†	†	★	★	★	★	★	★	★	★	★	..	..	★	★
California	★	★	★	★	★	..	★	†	★	..	†	†	★	★	★	★	★	†	★	†	..	★	†	†
Colorado	†						★	†	★	†	★	★	★	★	★	★	★	†	★		★	†	★
Connecticut	★	★	†	†	★	†	★	..	★	..	†	†	★	★	★	★	★	★	★	★	★	★	★	★
Delaware	†	★	†	..	†	..	★	..	..	..	†	★	★	★	★	★	★	★	★	★	★	★	★	★
Florida	★	★	†	..	★	..	★	†	..	★	†	★	★	★	★	★	★	★	★	..	★	★	†	†
Georgia	†	★					★	..	★	†	†	★	★	★	★	★	★	★	★	★	★	★	★	†
Hawaii	†	★	†	..	†	†	★	..	..	..	★	†	†	★	★	★	..	..	★	★	†	†	★
Idaho	†	★	†	..	†	†	★	..	★	★	†	★	★	★	★	★	†	★	..	..	★	..	★	★
Illinois	★	★	†	..	..	..	†	†	†	†	★	†	★	★	★	★	†	†	†	†	..	★	†	†
Indiana	★	★	†	..	..	..	★	†	†	★	†	★	★	★	★	★	★	★	★	★	..	★	★	†
Iowa	★	★	†	★	†	..	★	..	..	..	†	†	★	★	★	★	★	★	★	..	★	★	★	†
Kansas	★	★	★	..	†	..	★	†	★	†	★	★	★	★	★	★	★	★	★	†	★	†	†	†
Kentucky	†	★	†	..	†	★	★	†	..	†	†	†	★	★	★	★	★	★	★	†	..	★	★	★
Louisiana	†	★	†	..	★	..	★	†	★	..	†	★	★	★	★	★	★	★	†	†	★	★	★	★
Maine	★	★	†	..	..	..	★	★	★	★	†	★	★	★	★	★	†	★	★	†	★	†	★	★
Maryland	†	†	..	..	..	..	★	★	★	..	★	★	★	★	★	★	..	★	★	†	★	★	†
Massachusetts	..	†	..	..	..	..	★	..	★	..	★	★	★	★	†	★	†	★	★	..	..	★	†	†
Michigan	★	★	★	★	★	..	★	★	★	..	★	†	†	★	★	†	★	†	★	†	★	★	★	★
Minnesota	..	†	..	..	..	..	†	†	★	†	†	†	★	★	★	★	†	★	†	†	..	★	†	★
Mississippi	★	†	†	..	..	..	★	†	★	†	★	†	★	★	★	★	†	★	★	†	★	†	★	★
Missouri	†	†	..	..	..	..	★	†	★	†	★	..	★	★	★	★	†	★	★	★	★	★	★	★
Montana	†	★	..	..	†	..	★	†	★	†	†	†	★	★	★	★	†	★	★	★	★	★	★	★
Nebraska	★	★	..	..	..	..	★	†	★	†	†	†	†	★	★	★	†	★	★	★	★	★	★	★
Nevada	★	★	†	..	†	★	★	..	★	..	†	★	★	★	★	★	†	★	★	★	★	★	★	★
New Hampshire	★	★	★	★	★	..	★	★	★	..	†	★	★	★	★	†	★	★	★	★	★	★	★	★
New Jersey	★	★	†	★	★	★	†	†	★	★	†	†	★	★	†	★	†	★	★	..	..	★	†	★
New Mexico	★	★	†	..	†	..	★	†	★	†	★	★	★	★	★	†	★	★	★	★	★	★	★	★
New York	★	★	†	†	..	†	★	†	★	†	†	★	★	★	★	★	★	★	★	★	★	★	†	†
North Carolina	★	★	†	..	†	..	★	†	†	†	†	★	★	★	★	★	†	★	★	★	★	★	★	★
North Dakota	★	★	†	..	..	..	★	★	★	★	★	★	★	★	★	★	†	★	★	★	†	★	★	★
Ohio	★	★	†	..	†	..	★	†	★	†	★	★	★	★	★	★	†	★	★	★	†	†	†	†
Oklahoma	★	★	★	★	†	★	★	†	★	†	★	★	★	★	★	★	★	★	★	★	..	★	†	★
Oregon	★	★	★	..	†	..	★	..	★	†	★	†	★	★	★	★	★	★	†	..	★	★	★	★
Pennsylvania	★	★	†	★	†	..	★	★	★	..	..	★	★	★	★	★	†	★	..	★	†	★	†	†
Rhode Island	..	†	..	..	..	..	★	★	★	..	†	★	★	★	★	★	†	†	★	..	★	†	★	†
South Carolina	†	★	★	..	..	†	..	..	†	..	†	★	★	★	★	★	★	★	..	★	★	★	†
South Dakota	★	★	★	..	†	..	★	†	†	†	†	★	★	★	★	★	★	★	★	★	★	★	★	★
Tennessee	★	†	†	†	★	★	†	..	..	★	†	★	★	★	★	†	★	†	†	★	★	★	★	†
Texas	★	★	..	..	★	★	★	..	★	†	..	★	★	★	★	★	†	†	★	†	★	★	★	★
Utah	★	★	†	..	..	..	★	..	†	★	..	★	★	★	★	†	†	★	★	†	★	★	★	†
Vermont	★	★	†	★	†	..	★	..	★	..	†	★	★	★	★	★	†	..	★	★	★	★	★	★
Virginia	★	†	†	..	★	★	★	..	†	..	★	★	★	★	★	†	★	★	†	†	†	†	★	†
Washington	★	★	★	..	†	†	★	†	..	..	★	★	★	★	★	★	★	★	†	★	★	★	★	★
West Virginia	..	†	†	..	..	..	★	†	★	†	★	★	★	★	★	★	†	★	★	★	†	★	★	★
Wisconsin	†	★	†	..	..	..	★	†	★	★	★	★	★	★	★	†	★	★	★	★	★	★	★	★
Wyoming	★	★	..	†	†	..	★	★	★	†	★	†	..	★	★	★	..	★	..	†	★	★	†

Source: Modified by Kathryn J. Gesterfield, Illinois State Library,
from the Association for State Library Agencies.
Key: ★—Primary. †—Shared. ..—None.

State	Long-range planning	Determination of size and scope of collections in the state	Mobilization of resources	Subject and reference centers	Resources—books	Resources—other printed materials	Resources—multimedia	Resources—materials for the blind and handicapped	Coordination of resources	Little-used materials	Planning of information networks	Provision of centralized facilities	Exchange of information and materials	Interstate cooperation	Administration of federal aid	Administration of state aid	Financing of library systems and networks
Alabama	★	★	★	★	★	★	★	★	★	..	★	†	★	★	★	★	★
Alaska	★	†	†	†	†	†	★	★	★	†	★	★	†	★	★	★	†
Arizona	★	★	★	★	★	★	★	★	★	..	★	★	★	★	★	★	★
Arkansas	★	★	★	★	★	★	★	★	★	★	★	★	★	★	★	★	★
California	★	†	†	†	†	†	†	†	★	†	†	†	†	★	★	★	★
Colorado	★	†	†	†	†	†	†	★	†	†	†	†	†	★	★	★	★
Connecticut	★	★	★	★	★	★	★	★	★	★	★	★	★	★	★	★	★
Delaware	★	†	★	†	★	★	†	★	★	†	★	★	★	★	★	★	★
Florida	★	†	†	★	†	†	†	†	†	★	★	★	★	★	★	★	★
Georgia	★	★	★	★	★	★	★	★	★	★	★	★	★	★	★	★	★
Hawaii	†	†	†	†	†	†	†	★	†	★	†	†	†	†	†	†	†
Idaho	★	†	★	†	★	★	★	★	★	†	★	†	★	★	★	★	★
Illinois	†	†	†	†	†	†	†	†	†	..	†	†	†	†	★	★	★
Indiana	★	..	†	†	†	†	†	†	★	†	★	†	†	†	★	★	★
Iowa	★	★	★	★	★	★	★	†	★	★	★	†	★	★	★	★	★
Kansas	★	★	†	†	†	†	†	†	†	†	★	†	†	★	★	★	★
Kentucky	★	†	†	†	†	†	†	★	†	†	★	†	★	★	★	★	★
Louisiana	†	†	†	†	†	†	†	†	★	†	..	★	†	★	★	..	★
Maine	★	★	★	★	★	★	★	★	★	†	★	★	†	★	★	★	★
Maryland	★	..	..	★	..	..	..	★	..	★	★	★	★	★	★	★	★
Massachusetts	†	..	†	..	†	†	†	†	†	†	†	†	†	★	★	★	★
Michigan	★	★	★	★	★	★	★	★	★	★	★	★	★	★	★	★	★
Minnesota	★	†	★	★	†	†	†	†	★	★	★	†	★	★	★	★	†
Mississippi	★	★	★	★	★	★	★	★	★	★	★	†	★	★	★	★	†
Missouri	★	†	★	★	★	★	†	†	★	★	★	†	†	†	★	★	†
Montana	★	★	★	★	★	★	★	★	†	†	★	★	★	★	★	★	★
Nebraska	★	..	★	★	★	★	★	★	★	..	★	..	†	★	★	★	★
Nevada	★	†	†	†	†	†	†	★	★	†	★	★	★	★	★	★	★
New Hampshire	★	★	★	★	★	★	★	★	★	†	★	★	★	★	★	★	★
New Jersey	★	..	★	†	†	†	†	†	★	†	†	★	★	★	★	★	★
New Mexico	★	†	†	..	†	†	†	★	★	..	★	★	★	★	†	★	★
New York	★	†	†	★	†	★	★	★	†	†	★	★	★	†	★	★	★
North Carolina	★	†	†	†	★	★	★	†	★	†	★	★	★	★	★	★	★
North Dakota	★	..	★	★	★	★	★	★	★	†	★	★	..	★	★	★	★
Ohio	★	†	†	†	†	†	†	†	★	†	★	..	★	★	★	★	★
Oklahoma	★	†	★	★	★	★	★	★	★	†	★	★	★	★	★	★	★
Oregon	★	★	★	..	..	★	..	★	★	..	★	..	†	★	★	★	★
Pennsylvania	★	†	†	†	†	†	†	★	★	†	★	†	★	..	★	★	★
Rhode Island	★	†	★	†	†	†	†	★	★	★	★	†	★	★	★	★	★
South Carolina	★	†	..	★	†	†	†	★	★	..	★	★	★	★	★	★	..
South Dakota	★	†	★	★	†	†	★	★	★	★	★	★	★	★	★	★	★
Tennessee	★	..	★	†	†	†	†	★	★	†	★	†	★	★	★	★	★
Texas	★	†	†	†	★	★	..	★	★	†	★	†	★	★	★	★	★
Utah	..	†	†	†	..	†	★	†	..	★	†	★	★	★	★	†	..
Vermont	★	†	†	†	†	†	†	★	★	†	†	†	★	★	†	★	..
Virginia	★	†	†	†	†	†	†	†	†	†	★	★	★	★	★	★	†
Washington	★	..	★	†	..	..	..	†	..	★	★	★	★	★	★	..	★
West Virginia	†	..	†	†	★	..	★	★	..	★	†	★	★	★	★	†	..
Wisconsin	★	†	†	†	†	†	†	★	†	†	†	★	†	★	★	★	★
Wyoming	★	†	†	†	†	†	†	★	..	★	†	†	★	★	★	..	..

2. Employment

DEVELOPMENTS IN STATE PERSONNEL SYSTEMS

By David R. Cooke

RARELY CAN TWO YEARS be called an era, yet the changes in the focus and scope of governmental human resource services between 1980 and 1982 could be termed just that. These changes have affected and will continue to affect the core of human services within government for decades ahead.

Funding cuts, the deletion of federal support, cutback management, comparative pay, productivity and unionization, sexual harassment, abolishment of the merit system and the demand for increased professionalism have left some human service personnel spinning, while others have met these challenges by being on the cutting edge of innovation and change in the personnel and human resources services area.

The issue has been to find ways to increase or maintain the current level of services in the face of overall budget and personnel cuts.

Budget Cuts

During the period from July 1981 to July 1982, 17 of the 42 states reporting either cut or anticipated cutting their budgets up to 12 percent, the average cut being 6.36 percent. In addition, at least one other state cut personnel service by 2 percent. Of the states reporting, 20 states increased their budgets. Of the 20, nine (45 percent) increased their budgets to cover inflation and rising costs only. Eleven states (26 percent of the 42 reporting) increased their budgets to cover inflation and to fund some new programs. Two states reported no change in overall budget appropriations, and two states did not respond.

The most pertinent question is: how have these budget cuts, both at the federal and state levels, affected the states' personnel and human service systems?

Reductions in Force. The most dramatic effect can be illustrated by the need to reduce the numbers of state employees while maintaining an existing service level. Between July 1980 and July 1981, 17 (40.4 percent of the 42 states reporting) indicated an employee reduction of between .0009 and 12 percent, with an average reduction of 3.72 percent. Four additional states experienced some reduction but did not provide percentages. Between July 1981 and July 1982, the projected reductions are to be more dramatic. Nineteen states (45.2 percent of the 42 states reporting) indicated a definite employee reduction between 1 and 15 percent, with an average reduction of 4.8 percent. Not only were the anticipated reductions in force at this writing greater for the period July 1981-July 1982, but a larger number of states indicated such reductions appeared inevitable.

In addition to those states with definite employee reductions in 1981 and 1982, 14 other

David R. Cooke is Director, Management Development and Research Programs, The Council of State Governments. The author expresses appreciation to state personnel directors and staff and the executive committee of the National Association of State Personnel Executives for their cooperation in gathering much of the information for this overview.

states anticipate an employee reduction at some level in the near future. By way of comparison, 21 states had no employee reduction between July 1980 and July 1981, while between July 1981 and July 1982, only nine states anticipate no reduction.

Salary Increases. Basically, four general methods were used to reduce the number of state employees:

1. Attrition, including retirement with no replacements.
2. Elimination of non-essential services.
3. Consolidation of essential program areas.
4. Elimination of needed but unaffordable service with the least perceived impact.

With some reduction in the number of state employees, states were able to more easily fund both cost-of-living or across-the-board increases and merit increases, while at the same time holding the line on new taxes. Between July 1980 and July 1981, 39 (92.8 percent) of the 42 states reporting granted some type of across-the-board increase. At the same time, 28 (66.6 percent) of these 42 states provided for some type of merit increase. The across-the-board increases ranged from a low of approximately 2.5 percent to a high of 16.5 percent, with an average of approximately 7.3 percent. The merit increase for July 1980-July 1981 ranged from 1 to 10 percent with an average of 3.58 percent of payroll being allocated for this purpose. The projected figures for merit increase for July 1981-July 1982 are lower, with 17 (40.4 percent) of the 42 states anticipating a merit increase of from 1 to 8 percent, with an average of 3.38 percent of anticipated payroll being allocated for merit purposes.

Productivity

From the data, two definite trends appear—one, that state governments are experiencing both budget and employee reductions on a significant scale, and two, that their reductions appear to be much more than a one-time event, requiring many states to seek and implement long-term innovations and improvements that can provide adequate services while absorbing budget and personnel reductions.

Increasingly, the question is asked: how can governments help employees to become more effective and efficient? In seeking answers to this question, a number of states have established productivity centers, charged with the responsibility to focus efforts in improving the effectiveness and efficiency of state employees. Eleven of the 42 states reporting (26 percent) have already established such centers. One reported setting up a governor's council and another eight (19 percent) of the 42 states reported moving toward the establishment of such a center in the near future.

Literally hundreds of ideas are being considered to increase and maintain the productiveness and morale of employees remaining on state payrolls. The 10 most significant areas are:

- *Incentive*—cash payments for both individual and employee groups who initiate and implement cost-saving measures.
- *Bonuses*—bonus payments for not using sick leave.
- *Lump-Sum Sick Pay*—payment of accrued sick leave to the estate of any deceased employee.
- *Salary Continuity*—continuation of an employee's salary even when an employee is demoted (i.e., lead worker and supervisor) due to a reduction in force.
- *Discipline*—expunging of disciplinary record after satisfactory performance for a certain time period.

- *Quality Circles and Employee Involvement*—the establishment of quality circles and inclusion of employees in the development of effectiveness and efficiency schemes.
- *Performance Pay*—the granting of merit performance pay from funds accumulated due to increased productivity.
- *Work Sharing and Pairing*—the creation of pools of part-time employees with varied skills who can be called in on short notice to handle emergencies and extremely heavy work loads.
- *Performance Measure*—the establishment of performance systems that combine universal characteristics and management by objective scales which can be altered by employees and supervisors based on a work planning and progress review scheme.
- *Management Involvement*—the establishment of management advisory task forces and training institutes to encourage the blending of human resource systems (personnel systems) into total management at the various organizational levels. The seeking and reaching out to the private sector, universities and the community for ideas and assistance in meeting the productivity challenge.

More than in any other decade, it appears that in the eighties, the traditional personnel function will become more of a management tool for increasing the effectiveness and efficiency of state government. The search for solutions to the problem of increased service with the same or fewer human resources will bring a blending of ideas from all levels of management and from the individual worker, as well as the community at large.

Sources: Much of the data for this chapter is extracted from a survey of developments in state personnel systems by The Council of State Governments (November 1981) and from *Report of the States* for 1980 and 1981. These reports are a collection of papers containing information on the changes, current trends, innovations, etc., within the states, as presented by each state personnel director attending the National Association of State Personnel Executives annual conference in July of each year. Note: Elaboration on specific civil service reform efforts can be obtained by contacting the author.

Table 1
STATE PERSONNEL AGENCIES
Coverage, Organization and Selected Policies*
(As of October-November 1981)

State or other jurisdiction	General coverage(a)	Number of employees covered	Board members No.	Board members How appld.	Board members Term (years)	Work week for office workers(b) (hours)	No. paid vacation days	Sick leave After 1 yr.	Sick leave Cumulative	Group insurance Hospitalization	Group insurance Medical or surgical	Group insurance Life
Alabama Personnel Dept.	*	25,151	3	G(c)	6	40	13(d)	13	150	100	100 %	...
Alaska Div. of Personnel	*	11,128	3	G(c)	6	37.5	15(d)	15	No limit	100 %		(e)
Arizona Personnel Div.	(g)	18,000	5	G(c)	5	40(f)	12(d)	12	No limit	$45.46/mo.		100%
Arkansas Merit System Council	(g)	6,000	...	G(c)	...	40	12(d)	12	90		66%	
Off. of Personnel Mgt.		16,000	...	...	...	40	12(d)	12	90		66%	
California Personnel Board	*	135,465	5	G(c)	10	40	10(d)	12	No limit	(h)		100%
Colorado Dept. of Personnel	*	26,561	5	(i)	5	40(f)	12(d)	15	No limit	$42.12/mo.		$.88/mo.
Connecticut Personnel Div.	*	32,000	...		...	35	12(j)	15	No limit	(h)		40%
Delaware Off. of Personnel	*	9,800	5	G	3	37.5	15(d)	15	No limit	$11.46/mo.		(e)
Florida Career Service System	*	94,195	7	G(k)	4	40	13(d)	13	No limit	(h)		75%
Georgia Merit System	*	48,382	5	G(c)	5	40	15(d)	15	90	4.5%	(e)	.5%
Hawaii Dept. of Personnel Services	*	18,221	7	G(c)	4	40	21	21	No limit	67%		100%
Idaho Personnel Commission	*	8,400	5	G(c)	6	40	12(d)	12	No limit	$63.22/mo.		100%
Illinois Dept. of Personnel(l)		61,000	...		...	37.5	10(d)	12	No limit		100%	
Indiana State Personnel Dept.	*	29,329	4	G	4	37.5	12(d)	12	No limit	(h)		93%
Iowa Merit Employment Dept.	*	22,000	5	G(c)	6	40	10(d)	18	No limit	100%	100%	100%(m)
Kansas Div. of Personnel Services	*	28,000	5	G(c)	4	40	12(d)	12	No limit		100%(n)	
Kentucky Dept. of Personnel	(o)	32,881	5	G	4	37.5	12(d)	12(d)	No limit	$39.84/mo.		100%
Merit System Council		1,900	5	A	3	37.5	12(d)	12(d)	No limit	(p)		100%
Louisiana Dept. of Civil Service	*	68,000	7	G(q)	6	40	12(d)	12	No limit		50%	
Maine Dept. of Personnel	*	13,014	5	G(c)	4	40	12(d)	12	120	100%		(e)
Maryland Dept. of Personnel	*	53,391	...		...	35.5	10(d)	15	No limit	92%		
Massachusetts Div. of Pers. Admin.	*	72,701	5	G	5	37.5	10(d)	15	No limit		90%	
Michigan Dept. of Civil Service	*	70,000	4	G	8	40	15(d)	13	No limit	90%		100%
Minnesota Dept. of Employee Rels.	*	29,607	3	G(c)	3	40	13(d)	13	112.5	$56.06/mo.		100%
Merit System	(r)	3,050	3		...	35-40	12	12	100		(s)	
Mississippi State Personnel Board	*	29,509	8	(t)	4	40	6(d)	15	120	100%		50%
Missouri Personnel Div.	*	27,000	3	G(c)	6	40	15(d)	15	No limit		$12/mo.	
Montana Joint Merit System	(g)	2,230	3	G	6	40	15(d)	12	No limit	$70/mo.	$70/mo.	...
Personnel Div.	*	14,000	...		...	40	15(d)	12	No limit			...
Nebraska Joint Merit System	(g)	1,800	3	A	3	40	12(d)	12	180	(h)		100%
Personnel Dept.	*	11,000	5	G	5	40	12(d)	12	180	(h)		100%
Nevada Personnel Div.	*	9,000	5	G	4	40	15(d)	15	No limit		100%	100%
New Hampshire Dept. of Personnel	*	9,562	3	GC	3	37.5	15	15	90(d)	100%	100%	41%

Agency										
New Jersey Dept. of Civil Service	★	211,000	5	G(c)	35	12(d)	15	No limit	100%	100%
New Mexico Personnel Office	★	14,846	5	G	40	15	12	No limit	60%	
New York Dept. of Civil Service	★	173,100	3	G(c)	37.5	13(d)	13	180-200	(h)	(e)
North Carolina Off. of State Pers.	★	64,000	7	G(c)	40	10(d)	10	No limit	(h)	...
North Dakota Central Personnel Div.	★	10,500	5	(u)	40	12(d)	12	No limit	(v)	(e)
Ohio Div. of Personnel	★	70,000	6	...	40	10(d)	15	No limit	70%	100%
Oklahoma Personnel Board	★	26,757	7	G	40	15	15	45	100%	...
Oregon Personnel Div.	★	36,500	...	G	40	12(d)	12	No limit	$85/mo.	(e)
Pennsylvania Civil Service System	(w)	73,560	3	G(c)	37.5(x)	10(d)	15	200	100%	100%
Gov's. Off., Bur. of Pers.	★	109,853	★		37.5(x)	10(d)	15	200	100%	100%
Rhode Island Div. of Personnel	★	20,772	...		35	15(d)	15	120	100%	partial
South Carolina Personnel Div.	★	54,800	4	(y)	37.5-40	15(d)	15(d)	90	100%	(e)
South Dakota Bureau of Personnel	★	8,000	5	G(c)	40	15(d)	14	No limit	100%	...
Tennessee Dept. of Personnel	★	38,000	5	G	37.5	12(d)	12	No limit	60%	...
Texas Merit System Council	(g)	23,513	6	G	40	10.5(d)	12	No limit	$48/mo.	56%
Utah Personnel Office	★	12,000	5	G	40	12(d)	12	No limit	80%	75%
Vermont Dept. of Pers. & Trng.	★	6,500	3	G(c)	40	12(d)	12	No limit	100%	
Virginia Dept. of Personnel	★	69,066	3		40	12(d)	15	No limit	100%	
Washington Dept. of Personnel	(g)	34,707	3	G(c)	40	12(d)	12	No limit	100%	(z)
West Virginia Civil Service System	★	15,000	3	G(c)	37.5	15(d)	12	No limit	$96.95/mo.	(aa)
Wisconsin Div. of Personnel	★	35,854	5	G(c)	40	10(d)	13	No limit	90%	43%
Wyoming Personnel Div.	(g)	5,000	3	G	40	12(d)	12	No limit	$45/mo.	$5/mo.
Career Service	(g)	1,191	3		40	12(d)	12	No limit	$45/mo.	$5/mo.
Dist. of Col. Personnel Office	(ab)	25,000	...	...	40	13(d)	13	No limit	(h)	33-1/3%
Amer. Samoa Off. of Manpower Res.	★	3,800	7	G	40	13(d,ac)	11	No limit	...	...
Guam Dept. of Admin.	★	3,397	7	G(c)	40	13(d)	13	No limit	$46.70/mo.	...
Puerto Rico Off. for Pers. Admin.	★	206,901	8	G(c)	37.5	30	18	90	$1.52/mo.	(ad)
Virgin Islands Personnel Office	★	11,000	5	G	40	15(d)	13	No limit	75%	...

*Excluding school employees, fire fighters and police.

Key: G—governor; A—agencies; GC—governor and cabinet.

(a) The pattern of personnel agency coverage varies widely from state to state. Where coverage is shown as "General" (★), most employees in state agencies are covered by the program. Seldom, however, is coverage complete.

(b) All jurisdictions listed have a five-day workweek.

(c) With confirmation of legislature.

(d) Additional days after a specified number of years. In Kentucky, one-time bonus of 10 days sick leave after 10 years.

(e) The state has group insurance, but employee pays the premium.

(f) Some agencies work four 10-hour days.

(g) The program covers employees engaged in activities aided by the U.S. Department of Health and Human Services.

(h) California: 100% for employee, 90% for dependents; Connecticut: 100% for employees, 70% for dependents; Florida: $18.72/mo. for individual, $20.70/mo. for family; Indiana: $23/mo. for individual, $41.22/mo. for family; Nebraska: $23/mo. for individual, $85/mo. for family; New York: 100% for employees, 75% for dependents; North Carolina: 100% for employees, 37% for dependents; Vermont: 75% for employees, 50% plus $1.38 for one dependent and 50% plus $1.75 for

two or more dependents; District of Columbia: $32.16/mo. for individual, $66.13/mo. for family.

(i) Governor appoints three members with legislative confirmation; employees elect two.

(j) Those hired after July 1977 get additional days after a specified number of years. Those hired before July 1977 get 15 days.

(k) With the approval of three members of cabinet and confirmation by the senate.

(l) The offices of secretary of state (3,802 employees) and comptroller (370 employees) are covered by their own merit codes.

(m) For $10,000 policy. Employee may purchase an additional $10,000.

(n) Life insurance benefit is 100% of employee's annual salary. Employee may purchase additional $50,000.

(o) Program covers only local government employees administering grant-in-aid programs dealing with health.

(p) Under negotiation at time of compilation.

(q) Six appointed by governor, one elected by employees.

(r) Program covers only local government employees administering grant-in-aid programs dealing with health, welfare and civil defense.

(s) Varies from county to county according to collective bargaining agreement.

(t) Governor appoints four, legislature appoints four.

(u) Governor, Board of Higher Education, and elected officials each appoint one; employees elect two.

(v) Full family medical with $300 deductible paid by state; $27.87/mo. for $50 deductible is paid by employee.

(w) Program covers employees under the merit system and those engaged in activities aided by the grant-in-aid programs administered by the U.S. Department of Health and Human Services.

(x) Approximately 25% of all employees have a 40-hour work schedule.

(y) Three constitutionally elected, two legislative appointees.

(z) 40% of employee contribution.

(aa) State pays 70% the first year, 100% thereafter.

(ab) Personnel system centralized; covers all employees including school and college employees, police and fire fighters.

(ac) No annual leave for teachers and other school personnel who work 10 out of 12 months/year.

(ad) Territory pays flat rate of $25 on the premium, and employee pays the difference according to his personal needs.

Table 2
STATE GOVERNMENT EMPLOYEES: FRINGE BENEFITS
(Excluding school employees, fire fighters and police)

| State or other jurisdiction | Retirement plans | | | | | | | Education | | |
| | No. of years before eligible | | No. of years after which interest is vested in employee | Percent of state contribution | Percent of employee contribution | Longevity pay plans* | | Paid leave during working hours | Maximum hours | Percent of maximum tuition paid by state |
	Full-time employees	Part-time employees				Full-time employees	Part-time employees			
Alabama	0	0	15	10.13	5	...	...	★	Varies	Varies
Alaska	0	0	5	12.69	4.25	★1	...	...	...	100
Arizona	0(a)	0(a)	5	7	7	...	...	Varies	40	Varies
Arkansas	0	...	10	12	0	...	...	Varies	Varies	Varies
California	0	0(b)	5	Varies	Varies	...	...	★	Varies	0
Colorado	0(a)	0(a)	...	12.2	8	(c)	(c)	Varies	Varies	(c)
Connecticut	0(a)	0(a)	10	Varies	Varies	★2	★2	★	Varies	(d)
Delaware	1	1	10	14.2	2	...	...	...	(e)	(f)
Florida	0	0	10	100	0	...	...	...	...	(g)
Georgia	0	...	10	99.5	Varies	★3	★3	...	...	...
Hawaii	0	0(b)	5	10.97	7.8	★4	★4	...	Varies	Varies
Idaho	0	0(b)	5	9.5	4.84	★5	★5	★	(h)	(h)
Illinois(i)	0	0	8	7.76	Varies	...	...	★	(j)	80
Indiana	0	...	15	97	3	...	...	★	...	...
Iowa	0	0	4	5.75	3.7	...	...	...	Varies	Varies
Kansas	1	1(b)	10	5.2	4	★6	★6	...	...	...
Kentucky	0	0(b)	5	7.25	4	★7	★7	(k)	(k)	(l)
Louisiana	0	0	...	9	7	...	...	...	(m)	Varies
Maine	0(a)	0(a)	10	15.47	6.5	...	...	★	Varies	Varies
Maryland	0	0(b)	5	(n)	(n)	...	...	★	7.1	100(o)
Massachusetts	1/2	1/2	10	(p)	(p)	...	...	★	Varies	100(q)
Michigan	0	0	10	19.1	...	★8	★8	★	Varies	Varies
Minnesota	0	0	10	6	4	...	...	★	100	75
Mississippi	0	0	10	8	6	★9	...	...	...	Varies
Missouri	0	...	10	100	0	...	...	...	...	...
Montana	0	0	...	6.2	6	★10	★10	★	Varies	Varies
Nebraska	2(r)	2(r)	10	(r)	(r)	...	...	...	6	50-75
Nevada	0	0	10	8	8	★11	★11	★	Varies	Varies
New Hampshire	1/2	(b)	10	3	(s)	★12	★12	★	Varies	Varies
New Jersey	0	0	10	7.4	Varies	...	...	★	Varies	Varies
New Mexico	0	...	5	6.115	6.115	...	...	★	8	0
New York	0	0	10	Varies	Varies	...	...	★	Varies	Varies
North Carolina	1/12	...	5	9.92	6	★13	...	★	(t)	(t)
North Dakota	0	0	10	5.12	4	...	...	★	Varies	100
Ohio	5	5	5	13.7	8.5	★14	★14	★	Varies	Varies
Oklahoma	0	0	10	100	1(u)	★15	★15	★	(v)	(v)
Oregon	1/2	1/2	5	16.9	0	...	...	Varies	Varies	Varies
Pennsylvania	0	(w)	10	14.41	5	...	...	★	(x)	100
Rhode Island	0	0	10	62.5	37.5	★16	★16	...	...	...
South Carolina	0	0	5	7.1	(y)	★17	...	...	Varies	Varies
South Dakota	0	0	5	5	5	...	...	...	24 months	Varies
Tennessee	0	0	10	12.21	0	★18	...	★	8	100
Texas	0	0	10	8	6	★19	...	Varies	Varies	Varies
Utah	0	...	0	13.95	3.95	...	...	...	...	(z)
Vermont	0	0	10	9.2	0	...	...	★	Varies	Varies
Virginia	0	...	5	4.67	5	...	...	★	Varies	100
Washington	0	...	5	(aa)	(aa)	...	...	★	4	Varies
West Virginia	0	0(b)	10	9.5	4.5	...	...	...	...	...
Wisconsin	0	0	0	11.1	1	...	...	...	Varies	50
Wyoming	0(ab)	0(ab)	4	7.43	3.71	★20	★20	★	Varies	Varies
Dist. of Col.	0	Varies	...	7	7	...	...	★	120	100
American Samoa	0	0	0	16.78	3	★21	★21	...	Varies	Varies
Guam	0	0	3	10.104	6.5	★22	...	★	8	Varies
Puerto Rico	0	0	...	Varies	Varies	...	...	★	8	Varies
Virgin Islands	1	...	10	11	6	★23	...	★	8	80

*Longevity pay plan notes:

(1) Paid after employee has remained in final step within given salary range for two years, provided that the employee has worked continuously for the state for seven years, and provided that his current annual performance rating is "good" or higher; the amount awarded is approximately 3.75 percent for each of four additional increments.

(2) Permanent full-time employees are eligible after 10 years of service. Permanent part-time employees are eligible after the equivalent of 10 years of full-time service. Semi-annual lump sum payments based on a schedule related to salary level.

(3) Permanent full- and part-time employees are eligible after 8½ years of continuous service and two years at step 7.

(4) The white-collar salary schedule consists of five annual increments and four triennial longevity steps which are provided to employees for satisfactory performance ratings. The blue-collar wage board schedule consists of four annual increment steps which are provided to employees for satisfactory performance ratings. However, increment/longevity steps of both schedules are not implemented during the years in which a negotiated pay increase is granted to employees.

5. Permanent full-time and permanent part-time (half-time or more)

employees are eligible after five years of service: 2½ percent of base pay after five years; 5 percent after 10 years; 7½ percent after 15 years; 10 percent after 20 years.

6. Permanent full- and part-time employees are eligible after five, 10, 15 and 20 continuous years. The employee must have been at the top step of the salary range for a year or more, have a good or better evaluation rating, and be recommended for a longevity increase by the appointing authority of the agency.

7. An employee is given a continuous service award of 5 percent of his current annual salary rate after each completion of 12 months service in the last step of the salary range for his class. The 5 percent continuous service award is in a lump sum payment.

8. Permanent full- and part-time employees are eligible after six years continuous service.

9. 5 percent after end of maximum pay step.

10. Permanent full- and part-time employees are eligible after one year of service. Each year, employee automatically receives 2 percent of salary or one additional step. Each five years employee automatically receives 1 percent of salary.

11. Permanent full-time employees are eligible after eight years; permanent part-time employees are eligible after the equivalent of eight years full-time service, standard or better performance ratings: $150 per year for eight years increasing by $50 increments yearly to maximum of $750 for 20 years service.

12. Permanent full-time employees are eligible after 10 years; permanent part-time employees are eligible after the equivalent of 10 years full-time service; after 10 years, $200 flat rate and $200 added each five-year anniversary.

13. Permanent full-time employees are eligible after 10 years: 10-14 years—1.5 percent of base salary; 15-19 years—2.25 percent of base salary; 20-24 years—3.25 percent of base salary; 25 or more years—4.5 percent of base salary.

14. Awarded 1/2 percent of base salary for each year of service, beginning with 2½ percent after five total years of service, up to a maximum of 10 percent of base salary after 20 years of service.

15. Longevity pay plan available for certain groups only, such as the Oklahoma Highway Patrol.

16. Permanent full- and part-time employees are eligible after seven years service; pay awarded is: seven years—5 percent, 11 years—10 percent, 15 years—15 percent, 20 years—17.5 percent, 25 years—20 percent.

17. Permanent full-time employees are eligible; length of service varies. If employee has received no increases in 24 months and is at maximum of grade and has received only the across-the-board general increases, then pay awarded is 5 percent of salary.

18. Permanent full-time employees are eligible after three years of service; pay awarded is $75 times the number of years of service, up to 15 years.

19. Permanent full-time employees are eligible after five years of service.

20. Permanent full- and part-time employees are eligible after five years of continuous service; pay awarded is $30 per month for each five years of service; years of credit given for non-continuous state employment when employee has completed 24 months of continuous service since most recent entry.

21. $500 for 20 years of service; $750 for 30 years of service; $1,000 for 40 years of service; part-time employees prorated.

22. Permanent full-time employees are eligible after one year of service; upon annual certification of satisfactory service, pay awarded is one step of pay range.

23. Permanent full-time employees are eligible after one year of service; pay awarded is approximately 5 percent of salary.

(a) Required to participate.

(b) To be eligible, employee must be half-time or more; in Hawaii, employee must work 20 hours or more per week; in Idaho, employee must be employed at least five months per year and be half-time or more; in Kansas, employee must work more than 1,000 hours per year; in Kentucky, employee must work 100 hours or more per month; in Maryland, employee must work 700 hours per year.

(c) Rules providing for longevity pay and statute providing for tuition assistance have not been funded by the legislature.

(d) Varies depending on negotiated contract.

(e) Leave of absence without pay.

(f) $180 per semester reimbursable after satisfactory completion; must sign agreement of six months service after completion.

(g) Six hours free course work per term at any state university on a space-available basis.

(h) Appropriate travel time and duration of course; 100 percent paid tuition if attendance during working hours is approved.

(i) The offices of secretary of state (3,802 employees) and comptroller (370 employees) are covered by their own merit codes.

(j) Based on course credit hours.

(k) Educational leave with pay may be granted for a period not to exceed 24 months. Agency in-service training may be granted without requesting leave for a period not to exceed 30 days.

(l) 100 percent for six semester hours of graduate study per semester and three hours per summer semester; nine semester hours for undergraduate study per semester and six hours per summer semester; nine classroom hours per week for non-college training.

(m) Up to 240 hours per year.

(n) State contribution to retirement system 14.72 percent, employee contribution 5 percent; state contribution to pension system 5.16 percent, employee contributes 0 to Social Security base and 5 percent thereafter. Approximately 60 percent of employees are in retirement system and 40 percent are in the pension system.

(o) Up to $600 per calendar year, except $300 maximum for clerical and paraprofessional training.

(p) State contribution funded via annual appropriation; employee contribution 5 percent if hired before and 7 percent if hired after January 1, 1975.

(q) For job-related courses, based on availability of funds.

(r) Employees eligible after two years of service and 30 years of age. State contribution is 5.62 percent of the first $24,000/year earned and 7.49 percent of anything above $24,000. Employee contribution is 3.6 percent of salary up to $24,000/year and 4.8 percent thereafter.

(s) Employee contributes 4.6 percent and 9.2 after maximum of Social Security has been reached.

(t) Employee is allowed up to five semester hours during working hours. $80 per course or maximum of $320 per year per employee tuition paid by state.

(u) Increase 1 percent each succeeding July until employee is contributing 5 percent.

(v) Education benefits are offered only by the Department of Institutions, Social, and Rehabilitative Services.

(w) Part-time salaried employees are eligible immediately; part-time wage employees are eligible if they work a minimum of 100 days per calendar year.

(x) 20 days a calendar year.

(y) Employee contributes 4 percent of the first $4,800; then 6 percent of the excess salary.

(z) Up to $500.

(aa) State contribution: Plans 1 and 2—6.5 percent. Employee contribution: Plan 1—6 percent and Plan 2—5.11 percent.

(ab) Eligible for benefits at age 50 and after four years continuous service.

Table 3
STATE EMPLOYEES: HOLIDAYS

State or other jurisdiction	Five major holidays(a)	Martin Luther King's Birthday	Lincoln's Birthday	Washington's Birthday	Presidents Day	Good Friday	Memorial Day	Columbus Day	Veterans Day	Day after Thanksgiving	Day before or after Christmas	Day before or after New Year's	Election day(b)	Personal leave days(c)	Other(d)	Total
Alabama	★		★	★			★	·	★	★(e)					4	13
Alaska	★		·	★			★	·	★						2	11
Arizona	★		★	★			★	·	★		Both(e)					10
Arkansas	★		·	·		★	★		★	★(e)				1	2	10-13
California	★						★	·	★					1	1	12
Colorado	★						★	★	★				★		1	11
Connecticut	★	★	★	★		★	★	★	★	★				3		15
Delaware	★			★		★	★	★	★	★			★			11
Florida	★						★	·	★						3	8
Georgia	★		★	★			★		★							12
Hawaii	★			★			★		★		Before(e)		★		4	13
Idaho	★						★	·	★							9
Illinois	★		★	★			★	★	★				★	3		15
Indiana	★						★	·	★	★			★			11
Iowa	★						★		★				★	2		11
Kansas	★						★		★	★(f)	Before(e)	★(f)		1		9-10
Kentucky	★					1/2	★		★	★	★(f)		★		1(g)	10½
Louisiana	★					★	★	★	★	★(e)	Both(e)				1	8-13
Maine	★	★		★	★		★	★	★		Both(e)		★			11
Maryland	★			★			★	★	★				★	3	2	17
Massachusetts	★	★		★			★	★	★		Before(e)	Before(e)		3	3	16
Michigan	★				★		★	★	★	★			★	1		10-12
Minnesota	★				★		★	★	★	★					3	10
Mississippi	★						★	·	★					1	1	10
Missouri	★			★			★	★	★							10
Montana	★				★		★	★	★				★			10
Nebraska	★			★			★	★	★	★					1	11
Nevada	★						★		★	★			★		1	9
New Hampshire	★		★	★			★	★	★				★		1	11
New Jersey	★		★	★		★	★	★	★				★	3		15
New Mexico	★						★	★	★					1		11
New York	★		★	★			★	★	★		★(i)		★(h)	5	1	15
North Carolina	★						★		★	★	★(i)					10-11
North Dakota	★						★	★	★							9
Ohio	★						★	★	★							10
Oklahoma	★		★	★	★		★		★	★	Before		★	3		14
Oregon	★						★		★				★	3	1	10
Pennsylvania	★	★	★	★			★	★	★				★	3	1	14
Rhode Island	★						★	·	★				★			12
South Carolina	★						★	·	★	★	After		★		3(j)	11

316

		Total days
South Dakota	★	9-11½
Tennessee	★	10
Texas	★ ... (e) ... 1½(e)	16
Utah	★	12
Vermont	★	13
Virginia	★ ... Both	—
Washington	★	10
West Virginia	★ ... Before, 1/2	11
Wisconsin	★ ... Before, 1/2	11½
Wyoming	★ ... Before, 1/2	10½
		9
Dist. of Col.	★	10
American Samoa	★ ... Before	11
Guam	★ ... Before	15
No. Mariana Is.	★	12
Puerto Rico	★ ... Before, 1/2 & after	17
Virgin Islands	★	23½

Note: This table may not pertain to school employees, fire fighters and police.

(a) New Year's Day, Independence Day, Labor Day, Thanksgiving Day and Christmas Day.

(b) May be *any* election day. Not included in total.

(c) Days of the employee's choosing. Generally, not cumulative from one year to another.

(d) Date holiday is celebrated is in parentheses:

Alabama—Robert E. Lee's Birthday (Jan. 19), Mardi Gras Day (varies), Thomas Jefferson's Birthday (April 3), and Jefferson Davis' Birthday (June 1).

Alaska—Seward's Day (last Mon. in March) and Alaska Day (Monday nearest Oct. 18).

Arkansas—Robert E. Lee's Birthday (Jan. 19) and employee's birthday.

California—California Admission Day (Sept. 9).

Colorado—Colorado Day (Aug. 3).

Georgia—Robert E. Lee's Birthday (Jan. 19); Confederate Memorial Day (April 26) and Jefferson Davis' Birthday (June 3).

Hawaii—Prince Kuhio Day (March 26), King Kamehameha Day (June 11), Admission Day (3rd Fri. in Aug.) and Discoverer's Day (2nd Mon. in Oct.).

Louisiana—Mardi Gras Day (varies).

Maine—Patriots' Day (3rd Mon. in April).

Maryland—Maryland Day (March 25) and Defender's Day (Sept. 11).

Massachusetts—Evacuation Day (March 17), Patriots' Day (3rd Mon. in April) and Bunker Hill Day (June 17).

Mississippi—Robert E. Lee's Birthday (3rd Mon. in Jan.), Confederate Memorial Day (last Mon. in April) and Jefferson Davis' Birthday (1st Mon. in June).

Missouri—Harry S. Truman's Birthday (May 18).

Nebraska—Arbor Day (April 22).

Nevada—Nevada Day (Oct. 31).

New Hampshire—Fast Day (last Mon. in April).

North Carolina—Easter Monday.

Pennsylvania—Flag Day (June 14).

Rhode Island—Victory Day (3rd Mon. in Aug.).

Texas—Confederate Heroes Day (Jan. 19), San Jacinto Day (April 21), Emancipation Day (June 19) and Lyndon B. Johnson's Birthday (Aug. 27).

Utah—Pioneer Day (June 24).

Vermont—Town Meeting Day (1st Tues. in March) and Battle of Bennington Day (Aug. 16).

Virginia—Lee-Jackson Day (3rd Mon. in Jan.).

West Virginia—West Virginia Day (June 20).

American Samoa—Flag Day (April 17).

Guam—Guam Discovery Day (1st Mon. in March), Liberation Day (July 21) and Lady of Camarin Day (Dec. 8).

Northern Mariana Islands—Commonwealth Day (Jan. 9), Covenant Day (March 24) and Constitution Day (Dec. 8).

Puerto Rico—Three Kings Day (Jan. 6), De Hostos' Birthday (Jan. 11), Jose de Diego's Birthday (April 16), Luis Munoz Rivera's Birthday (July 17), Commonwealth Constitution Day (July 25), Jose C. Barbosa's Birthday (July 27) and Discovery of Puerto Rico Day (Nov. 19).

Virgin Islands—Three Kings Day (Jan. 6), Transfer Day (March 31), Holy Thursday (April-day varies), Easter Monday, Traditional Market Fair (3rd Tues. after Easter), Carnival Children's Parade (3rd Fri. after Easter), Organic Act Day (3rd Mon. in June), Virgin Islands Emancipation Day (July 3), Hurricane Supplication Day (4th Mon. in July), and Local Thanksgiving (3rd Mon. in Oct.).

(e) Depends on governor's proclamation.

(f) One extra day granted per holiday. Governor designates day before or day after.

(g) Mardi Gras is a statutory holiday. In addition, governor may proclaim two of the following as holidays: Martin Luther King's Birthday, Robert E. Lee's Birthday, Washington's Birthday, Confederate Memorial Day, Memorial Day, and Huey P. Long's Birthday (Aug. 30).

(h) For certain employees, Martin Luther King's Birthday is an alternative to election day.

(i) If Christmas Day falls on Tuesday, Wednesday or Thursday, two extra holidays are granted; otherwise only one day extra.

(j) Employee chooses three of following four holidays to observe each year: Martin Luther King's Birthday, Robert E. Lee's Birthday, Confederate Memorial Day and Jefferson Davis' Birthday.

Table 4

STATE EMPLOYEE LABOR RELATIONS: CHARACTERISTICS AND SCOPE
(Excluding school employees, fire fighters and police)

State or other jurisdiction	Legislation enacted (a)	Coverage (a)	Administrative body	Bargaining rights conferred	Impasse resolution provisions (mandatory or permissive) — Mediation	Fact-finding	Arbitration	Scope of bargaining (b)	Strike policy (c)
Alabama	...	...	...	...	...	...	...	...	Prohibited(c)
Alaska	★	★	State Personnel Board	★	★	...	★	★	Prohibition varies by class of employee
Arizona	...	...	...	...	...	...	...	...	...
Arkansas	★†	...	...	(d)	...	...	...	★	Prohibited(e)
California	★†	★	Public Employment Relations Board	★	★	...	...	★	Prohibited(f)
Colorado	...	...	...	...	...	...	...	...	...
Connecticut	★	★	State Board of Labor Relations	★	★	★	...	★	Prohibited
Delaware	★	★	State Department of Labor	★	★	★	★(g)	★	Prohibited
Florida	★	★	Public Employees Relations Commission	★	★	★	(h)	★	Prohibited; penalties
Georgia	...	...	...	...	...	...	...	...	Prohibited(f); penalties
Hawaii	★	★	Public Employment Relations Board	★	★	★	★	★(i)	Limited right to strike for all employees; unlawful public health and safety endangered; enjoinable
Idaho	...	...	...	...	...	...	...	...	...
Illinois	★(j)	★(j)	Office of Collective Bargaining	★(j)	(k)	...	...	★(j)	Prohibited
Indiana	★	...	...	★	★	...	...	...	Prohibited; enjoinable; penalties
Iowa	★	★	Public Employment Relations Board	★	★	★	★	★	...
Kansas	★†	...	Public Employees Relations Board	★	★	★	...	★	Prohibited
Kentucky	...	...	...	★	★	...	...	★	Prohibited(l); penalties
Louisiana	...	...	...	...	...	...	...	...	...
Maine	★	★	Maine Labor Relations Board	★	★	★	★(m)	★	Prohibited; enjoinable
Maryland	...	...	...	★	...	...	...	★	...
Massachusetts	★	★	Labor Relations Commission	★	★	★	★	★	Prohibited; employees subject to discipline and discharge
Michigan	★	★	Civil Service Commission	★	★	★	★	★	Prohibited
Minnesota	★	★	Public Employment Relations Board	★	★	...	★	★(n)	Permitted for non-essential employees after exhaustion of mediation
Mississippi	★†	★	State Personnel Board	...	...	...	...	...	Prohibited
Missouri	★†	★	State Board of Mediation	★	...	...	...	★	...
Montana	★	★(p)	Board of Personnel Appeals	★	★	★	★	★	Most contracts bar strikes as long as contract runs. Otherwise, strikes permitted, except nurses may not strike if there is another health care facility on strike within 150-mile radius.
Nebraska	★	★	Commission on Industrial Relations	★	★	★	★	★	Prohibited; penalties
Nevada	★	...	...	★	★	★	...	★	Prohibited; enjoinable; penalties
New Hampshire	★	★	Public Employee Labor Relations Board	★	★	★	...	★	Prohibited; enjoinable
New Jersey	★	★	Public Employment Rels. Commission	★	★	★	★	★	Prohibited(e)

Sources: Public Personnel Administration: Labor-Management Relations, vols. 1 and 2 (Englewood Cliffs, N.J.: Prentice-Hall, Inc., loose-leaf updated biweekly) in addition to Council of State Governments' survey.

★—Yes.
†—Meet and confer law.
(a) In this column only: ★—All state employees; normal exemptions usually include elected and appointed officials, agency heads and designated managerial or confidential employees. •—Limited state employee coverage.
(b) Wages, hours and terms and conditions of employment.
(c) Opinion of attorney general.
(d) Public employees may join unions and bargain collectively (attorney general's opinion); however, employers not required to bargain (state supreme court decision).
(e) State supreme court decision.
(f) By case law. In Georgia, strikes prohibited by statute; bargaining prohibited by case law.
(g) Except for issues of wages and salaries.
(h) Legislature may make final determination if issue remains unresolved.
(i) Health insurance and retirement benefits are excluded from negotiations. For Hawaii, classification is also excluded.
(j) Executive order.
(k) Impasse provisions are provided by the rules and regulations of the director of personnel.
(l) Memorandum, Department of Personnel.
(m) Binding on all issues except salaries, pensions and insurance.
(n) Except retirement benefits.
(o) The State Personnel Board has issued regulations for the conduct of employee-management relations with classified state employees. Management determines the degree of collective bargaining or consultation, if any.
(p) Personnel matters over which employer may lawfully exercise discretion.
(q) Rules and regulations of State Personnel Board.

State	Administering agency	Strikes
New Mexico	State Personnel Board	Prohibited(o)
New York	Public Employment Relations Board	Prohibited; penalties
North Carolina	...	...
North Dakota	...	Prohibited(e)
Ohio	...	Prohibited(f); penalties
Oklahoma	...	Prohibited(c)
Oregon	Employment Relations Board	Permitted for some employees after exhaustion of fact-finding; enjoinable if public health, safety or welfare is threatened
Pennsylvania	Governor's Office, Bureau of Labor Relations	Limited right after impasse procedures exhausted unless public health, safety or welfare threatened
Rhode Island	Division of Labor Relations.	Prohibited
South Carolina	...	Prohibited(c)
South Dakota	Department of Labor	Prohibited; enjoinable; penalties
Tennessee	...	Prohibited(e)
Texas	...	Prohibited(f)
Utah	...	Prohibited(c); terminates employment
Vermont	State Labor Relations Board	Prohibited
Virginia	...	Prohibited; terminates employment
Washington	Department of Personnel	Prohibited(q)
West Virginia	...	Prohibited(e)
Wisconsin	Employment Relations Commission	Prohibited; enjoinable; penalties
Wyoming	...	...
Dist. of Col.	Office of Labor Relations and Collective Bargaining	Prohibited
American Samoa	...	...
Guam	...	...
Puerto Rico	...	...
Virgin Islands	Office of Collective Bargaining	Limited for all employees; unlawful for essential workers

Table 5
STATE EMPLOYEE LABOR RELATIONS: PUBLIC UNIONS
(Excluding school employees, fire fighters and police)

State or other jurisdiction	Number of unions representing state employees	Union affiliation		Number of bargaining units	Number of full-time equivalent employees in unions	Union security: at least one of the unions has the following(c):
		Affiliated with AFSCME (a)	Other(b)			
Alabama	...	...	...	...	...	...
Alaska	7	...	★	8	11,846	Closed shop
Arizona	...	...	...	...	...	...
Arkansas	2	★	★	0	Unknown	...
California	(d)	★	★	20	130,000(e)	(d)
Colorado	...	...	...	...	...	...
Connecticut	7	★	★	15	38,000	Agency shop
Delaware	7	★	★	28	4,473	Union shop
Florida	3	★	★	6	65,000(e)	...
Georgia	...	...	...	...	...	...
Hawaii	2	★	...	7	17,000(e)	Agency shop
Idaho	...	...	...	...	...	...
Illinois	7	★	★	17	47,000	...
Indiana	...	...	...	...	...	...
Iowa	2	★	★	10	15,000(e)	...
Kansas	13	★	★	30	9,500(e)	...
Kentucky	...	...	...	...	...	...
Louisiana	4(f)	★	★	45	8,200	...
Maine	4	★	★	9	11,900	...
Maryland	4	★	★	0	32,200(e)	...
Massachusetts	6	★	...	9	48,690	Agency shop
Michigan	6	★	★	9	52,850	Agency shop
Minnesota	11	★	★	16	29,607	...
Mississippi	...	...	...	...	...	...
Missouri	3	★	★	8	7,000(e)	...
Montana	19	★	★	74	6,100(e)	Agency shop
Nebraska	4	★	★	11	2,300(e)	...
Nevada	1	...	★	0	4,300(e)	...
New Hampshire	1	...	★	29	6,252	...
New Jersey	4	★	★	7	52,000	...
New Mexico	3	★	★	7	3,000(e)	...
New York	4	★	★	7	161,700	Agency shop
North Carolina	...	...	...	...	...	...
North Dakota	...	...	...	...	...	...
Ohio	14	★	★	0	17,260	...
Oklahoma	...	...	...	...	...	...
Oregon	9	...	★	70(e)	32,164(e)	...
Pennsylvania	14	★	★	45	85,788(e)	...
Rhode Island	17	★	★	20	14,000	...
South Carolina	...	...	...	...	...	...
South Dakota	1	★	...	1	690	...
Tennessee	...	...	...	...	...	...
Texas	...	...	...	...	...	...
Utah	...	...	...	...	...	...
Vermont	1	...	★	3	3,800	...
Virginia	...	...	...	...	...	...
Washington	8	★	★	62	24,780	Union shop
West Virginia	...	...	...	...	...	...
Wisconsin	7	★	★	12	26,904	Agency shop
Wyoming	...	...	...	...	...	...
Dist. of Col.	12	★	★	75	31,150	...
American Samoa	...	...	...	...	...	...
Guam	3	...	★	18	2,544	...
Puerto Rico	64	...	★	153	33,835	Union shop/closed shop(g)
Virgin Islands	8	...	★	29	80%(e)	...

★—Indicates yes.

(a) American Federation of State, County, and Municipal Employees (AFSCME) is an affiliate of the American Federation of Labor-Congress of Industrial Organizations (AFL-CIO).

(b) A star in this column indicates the state has one or more unions which are not affiliated with AFSCME. These may or may not be affiliated with the AFL-CIO.

(c) In a closed shop, the union supplies all candidates for employment. In a union shop, all employees hired must, after a period of time, join the union. In an agency shop, all employees must allow the check-off from their salaries for union dues whether they join the union or not.

(d) Still in process of selection.

(e) Approximately.

(f) Louisiana does not have public employee collective bargaining legislation, but it is lawful for public employees to engage in collective bargaining with their employers by an attorney general's opinion.

(g) Most of the unions are union shops; three are closed shops.

FINANCES OF STATE-ADMINISTERED PUBLIC EMPLOYEE RETIREMENT SYSTEMS

By Maurice Criz and David Kellerman

THE 1977 CENSUS OF GOVERNMENTS indicated there were 3,075 public employee retirement systems administered by state and local governments. While only 197 (6 percent) of these were state-administered, they provided pension coverage for 86 percent of all public employees enrolled under government-administered retirement programs.

The 196 state-administered systems currently in existence are an important part of total state government financial activity. These state systems accounted for over 7 percent of all state revenue in fiscal year 1980, 4 percent of all state government expenditure, and over 52 percent of all state government cash and security holdings. Retirement systems also have a long-term impact on state government operations, as they constitute significant future liabilities and play key roles in the maintenance of sound state government personnel systems.

The Census Bureau defines retirement systems for public employees as only those systems sponsored by a recognized unit of government and whose members are public employees compensated with public funds. There must be an identifiable employee retirement fund, financed in whole or in part with public contributions. Excluded from this census count are public employee pension plans in which direct payments to retired or disabled individuals are made by appropriation of general funds or payments are made to a private trustee or insurance carrier who administers the investments and benefit payments. Selected information on such retirement plans, as well as on state and locally administered retirement systems, has been gathered in two special studies undertaken at the request of the U.S. Congress.[1]

Unfortunately, there is a shortage of detailed information concerning the operations of state (as well as local) systems. This impedes the ability of analysts and policy-makers to assess the current and future conditions of these systems, upon which 2.2 million public employees or survivors rely for retirement income.

The lack of data is particularly evident in determining actuarial soundness—the extent to which public employee retirement systems have set aside adequate funds to provide for future pension benefits.

Efforts at the federal level to establish guidelines for public employee retirement systems have met with little success. Calls for universal coverage under the Social Security program, mandatory reporting requirements in conjunction with the Employee Retirement Income Security Act of 1974 and the establishment of a similar public employee act[2] have generally not been well received by state (and local) retirement officials and employees.

Coverage

The 196 state-administered public employee retirement systems provided coverage to over

Maurice Criz and David Kellerman are Senior Advisor and Statistician, respectively, Governments Division, U.S. Bureau of the Census. Data are from the Bureau of the Census report, *Finances of Employee Retirement Systems of State and Local Governments in 1979-80*, and reports from prior years.

10 million members in 1980. These systems tend to be very broad in scope, frequently covering local employees, or some combination of state and local employees, in addition to state employees only (see Table 1).

The 62 general coverage systems are open to all employees with little or no exception. All states except Nebraska have general, state-administered systems which provide coverage for the bulk of state employees, either uniquely or in some combination with local employees. Nebraska maintains a privately administered pension plan for its state employees, which is not included here in the count of government-operated retirement systems.

Limited coverage systems are restricted by occupational area and therefore tend to be smaller in size. There were 134 limited coverage state systems in 1980.

One controversial aspect of public employee retirement system operations is the question of integration with the Social Security program. Figures in Table 1 indicate that 4.9 million active members of state-administered systems were also covered by Social Security in 1980. Table A depicts the trend, since 1957, of integration with Social Security. It should also be noted that 5 percent of all state and local government employees were under Social Security as their sole retirement coverage in 1977, and were not members of any state or local government retirement system.

Table A
COVERAGE OF MEMBERS OF STATE-ADMINISTERED
PUBLIC EMPLOYEE RETIREMENT SYSTEMS BY FEDERAL SOCIAL SECURITY

Type of system	Percentage of systems					Percentage of membership				
	1977	1972	1967	1962	1957	1977	1972	1967	1962	1957
All members also covered by Social Security	33.0	39.8	40.4	41.8	27.9	29.8	40.7	28.8	33.5	27.3
Some members covered by Social Security	17.3	14.2	20.2	24.1	21.1	32.6	22.2	40.7	46.9	29.9
No members covered by Social Security	49.8	46.0	39.3	34.1	51.0	37.6	37.3	30.5	19.6	42.9

Integration with (or coverage under) the Social Security program has the distinct advantage of portability—the ability to transfer membership and vested interests among different employers. Yet many state-administered systems have not made coverage under Social Security available to their membership, as benefits under the state systems tend to exceed those under Social Security, and length of service or age provisions for retirement tend to be more liberal under state systems. The average monthly benefit payment under the state-administered systems was $355 in fiscal 1980, compared with the average benefit payment under Social Security of approximately $300 in June 1980.[3]

These factors, combined with the financial difficulties of the Social Security program, are dampening any move toward integration or universal coverage, at least as far as the state and local government employees are concerned. Indeed, public employee systems have continued to drop out from Social Security coverage (principally at the local government level). During 1979 and 1980, about 175 governments, with 58,000 employees, withdrew from coverage under Social Security.

Benefit Operations

The ratio of beneficiaries receiving periodic benefit payments to total membership of state-administered systems continued to increase, reaching 19.4 percent as of the last month of fiscal 1980. In comparison, this figure was 19.3 percent in fiscal 1978, 13.9 percent in fiscal 1972 and 11.7 percent in fiscal 1967. To a large extent, this measure reflects changing demographic characteristics nationwide, as well as greater maturity of the systems themselves. In view of the current national efforts to reduce or limit the scope of government, it is unlikely that government employment will grow very much in the near future. Thus the ratio of beneficiaries to total membership can be expected to continue to increase.

Average benefit payments vary considerably by state (Table 5) and class (Table 1). By state, the average monthly payments for all persons receiving periodic benefits varied from less than $150 in five states to over $500 in four states. By coverage class, average benefit payments ranged from $161 for fire fighters to $1,331 for judges.

Numerous factors affect the computation of average benefit payments. Differences in salary levels among professions, varying length-of-service requirements, regional economic differences, and the degree of employee unionization all contribute to the variation. Also affecting the computations are particular nuances in the survey data. For example, the low average benefit in Nebraska reflects the absence of any general coverage, statewide system, as noted previously. The low average benefit for fire fighters reflects the inclusion of many supplemental systems for volunteer firemen.

While much is made of the comparison of benefits between public employee retirement systems and private employee plans and systems, direct comparison is not always meaningful. Public employee retirement systems play a different role in many circumstances, serving to attract employees into professions that might otherwise be less desirable. The traditionally earlier retirement offered by many police systems is an example.

Assets

State-administered employee retirement systems are an important source of funds for the nation's credit markets, with cash and security holdings that amounted to $144.7 billion at the close of fiscal 1980. Table 5 provides the percent distribution of cash and security holdings, by type, on a state-by-state basis while Table 2 provides a more detailed breakdown of holdings at the national summary level.

Since the early 1970s, there has been a significant change in the composition of cash and security holdings for state retirement systems. Holdings of federal government securities have increased from approximately 9 percent to 18.1 percent of the total since 1972.[4] Correspondingly, the level of corporate bond holdings has dropped from 57.8 percent of total assets to 42.1 percent over the same time period. The percentage of holdings invested in corporate stocks has remained fairly steady since 1977, while investments in mortgages has decreased slightly over the past decade.

Investment behavior has generally changed in response to economic conditions. The high rate of inflation during the 1970s, combined with the unpredictable nature of the corporate stock and bond market, resulted in the increase in federal security holdings, which provide a high rate of return with minimal risk. The high rate of inflation has also resulted in increased returns on certain types of investments. Investment earnings rose 25.7 percent between fiscal years 1979 and 1980 and were the fastest growing source of funds for state-administered systems.

Most states followed the national pattern of overall investment holdings, but with some variation evident. Restrictions do exist on the type of investments that can be made by state retirement systems and represent another element in determining the composition of security holdings, especially on a state-by-state basis.

Finances

The overall financial condition of state government retirement systems was greatly affected by the high rate of inflation and generally unstable economic conditions which prevailed during 1979-80. Inflation particularly has had a severe impact upon systems, eroding the value of fixed-income assets, increasing member salary levels and frequently triggering increased benefit payments in instances where cost-of-living or indexing provisions exist. Unstable economic conditions, particularly in the bond and stock markets, have proven difficult for many retirement systems. Depending upon their particular investment portfolio, systems with extensive bond or stock holdings did not perform as well during 1979-80, in terms of investment earnings, as did systems with other types of investments.

Perhaps most important of all, inflation and unstable economic conditions have tended to render unrealistic the assumptions upon which the retirement systems' operations are based. Projected rates of return on investment, future salary and benefit levels and the value of investment holdings themselves have generally been unpredictable in recent years.

The extent to which retirement systems rely upon different financial resources is important in analyzing fiscal soundness. Contributory systems would be less affected by budgetary restrictions imposed upon governments than would non-contributory systems, wherein no employee share is paid into the system. The impact of the many budget and spending limitations is difficult to measure, but with government contributions the largest source of retirement system revenue (see Table B), it is likely that the impact is strong.

During recent years, state government retirement systems' receipts have grown at a slightly faster pace than payments. Most of the growth in receipts has been the result of rapidly rising earnings on investments, which increased by 25 percent and 19 percent in fiscal years 1980 and 1979, respectively. Government contributions have also risen, although not as sharply, while employee contributions have increased only minimally in recent years. Table B depicts the resulting change in the composition of retirement system receipts since 1962.

Table B
PERCENTAGE DISTRIBUTION OF TOTAL RECEIPTS, SELECTED YEARS: 1962 TO 1980

Item	1979-80	1978-79	1976-77	1971-72	1966-67	1962
Employee contributions	18.5	20.1	21.9	28.4	32.1	35.0
Government contributions	45.5	46.6	46.1	43.3	44.1	44.3
Earnings on investments	36.0	33.3	32.0	28.2	23.8	20.7

The importance of specific sources of revenue varies considerably among the states (Table 5). The state-by-state differences are a consequence of many of the factors cited above, including the existence of non-contributory systems and restrictions on the type of investments that can be made.

State government contributions to the retirement systems they administer totaled $7.4 billion in fiscal 1980, or 26 percent of total system receipts nationwide. (It should be noted that government contributions in Table B include local government contributions.) These contributions are significant because they represent a use of funds that would have been available for spending during the current fiscal year by state governments, but which instead had to be set aside into retirement funds. Over the past decade, such contributions have represented between 2.4 percent and 3.1 percent of state general revenue and an even larger share of state general revenue from own sources. For particular states, the retirement system contribution of the state government can be even larger, exceeding 4 percent in several states.

There is an important distinction in Census Bureau reporting on state government finances between employee retirement system revenue and expenditure, and the receipts and payments of employee retirement systems as discussed in this article.[5] For example, a government's contribution to a retirement system that it administers is not counted as state "revenue," since this constitutes a transfer of funds from one state agency to another, but is treated as a "receipt" in the presentation of data on state retirement systems. Hence, the employee retirement system receipts presented here do not correspond to census data shown elsewhere for employee retirement revenue. The same holds true for employee retirement systems' benefits and payments as compared to employee retirement system expenditure shown elsewhere.

The relationship between benefit payments and total receipts of retirement systems has changed somewhat in recent years. From 1957 to 1978, the ratio of payments to receipts increased steadily from 23.7 percent to 31.7 percent. In fiscal 1979 and 1980, the ratio declined to 31.2 percent and 30.8 percent, respectively. Again, however, there is great variation among the states in this ratio. Arizona, Utah and Wyoming all had ratios of less than 15 percent, while in Maine, Massachusetts and West Virginia, the ratios exceed 50 percent. To some extent, a higher ratio of benefit payments to total receipts is undesirable, reflecting an inadequate funding level and operations on a pay-as-you-go basis. This is especially true if the ratio remained high over a time span of a number of years.

Similarly, the ratio of benefit payments to total cash and security holdings could be indicative of financial difficulties, particularly if a high ratio of benefit payments to assets is sustained over a long period of time. Nationally, this ratio was 6.1 percent in fiscal 1980, with state ratios ranging from 2.5 percent to 24.9 percent.

Any examination of the relationship between benefit payments and revenues, or benefit payments and assets, should be undertaken with other factors in mind before reaching conclusions regarding the financial condition of a retirement system. The maturity of the system, the long-term trend of benefit payments in relation to receipts or assets, the existence of recent actuarial studies and a host of other factors need also be evaluated.

Data Presentation

Data presented in Tables 1 through 5 reflect national and statewide totals only, with no individual state-administered systems shown.[6] In some cases, as indicated in the tables, data for certain systems were not available. For other systems, data were available in total, but with no breakdown into detailed categories. Because of these omissions, a certain degree of caution should be used in interpreting the data presented herein, especially when using data which reflect a high degree of detail.

For individual states (Tables 3-5), data include diverse coverage of groups of employees represented by between one and 11 state-administered systems. Generalized comparisons are especially difficult to make, as employee coverage, the existence or absence of locally administered employee retirement systems, and extensive variations in the size of the governments themselves all contribute to differences in the size and nature of state-administered employee retirement systems.

Notes

1. Approximately 2,800 of the privately administered pension plans for public employees were identified by the Pension Task Force of the House Committee on Education and Labor, in "Pension Task Force Report on Public Employee Retirement Systems" (1978). See also "Funding of State and Local Government Pension Plans: A National Problem" (U.S. General Accounting Office, 1979).

2. The President's Commission on Pension Policy has made such a recommendation in its final report, submitted to the president and the Congress in February 1981.

3. Compiled from statistics in the "Social Security Bulletin" (monthly, U.S. Department of Health and Human Services, Social Security Administration).

4. In Census Bureau reporting prior to 1974, federal securities were defined to include only U.S. Treasury obligations, with securities of federal agencies (such as the TVA) classified as non-governmental. In fiscal 1972, holdings of U.S. Treasury securities were 5.7 percent of the total; holdings of federal agency securities were estimated at 3.3 percent.

5. The operation of state-administered employee retirement systems is treated as part of the insurance trust sector of state government financial activity in Bureau of the Census reporting. The insurance trust sector is comprised, in addition to employee retirement activity, of unemployment compensation, workmen's compensation, and selected miscellaneous state insurance programs. For further information on the various "sectors" of state government financial activity, see the section on "State Finances in 1980."

6. Data on major individual state systems (at least 500 members) can be found in the Bureau of the Census' annual report, *Finances of Employee Retirement Systems of State and Local Governments.*

EMPLOYMENT

Table 1
NUMBER, MEMBERSHIP AND BENEFITS OF STATE-ADMINISTERED EMPLOYEE RETIREMENT SYSTEMS, BY SYSTEM CHARACTERISTICS: 1979-80

Systems	Number of systems	Membership, last month of fiscal year Number(a)	Covered by Social Security(b,c)	Recurrent benefit operations, last month of fiscal year Number of beneficiaries	Amount (in thousands)(c)	Average per beneficiary (c)	Lump-sum survivors benefit payments during the month (in thousands)
All systems	196	10,326,512	4,914,040	2,008,155	$713,037	$355	$15,124
General coverage	62	6,356,683	3,547,249	1,229,377	361,128	294	9,006
State employees only	12	847,401	450,124	191,121	67,249	352	1,713
State employees and all local employees	16	2,214,750	1,457,446	356,839	94,082	264	3,450
State employees and local nonschool employees	18	2,531,652	1,079,199	559,536	168,778	302	2,888
State employees and local school employees	2	264,862	262,731	42,815	15,122	353	333
State employees and teachers	1	29,984	N.A.	7,417	3,180	429	88
Local employees other than teachers	13	468,034	297,749	71,649	12,717	177	534
Limited coverage	134	3,969,829	1,366,791	778,778	351,909	458	6,118
Teachers only	24	1,990,622	511,549	425,424	215,772	507	3,314
All school employees	15	1,503,603	806,459	261,782	102,645	392	2,552
School employees, nonteaching	3	263,147	6,447	36,888	6,215	168	22
Peace officers	31	70,534	19,761	14,351	5,986	417	97
Fire fighters	8	46,160	56	4,692	758	161	3
Peace officers and fire fighters	6	67,650	9,265	28,220	15,658	555	125
Judicial	26	5,945	2,351	2,530	3,375	1,334	0
State legislators	7	1,484	292	736	408	554	1
Other	14	20,684	10,611	4,155	1,092	263	4

Source: Compiled from unpublished data received in the U.S. Bureau of the Census annual survey on finances of public employee retirement systems.
N.A.—Not available.

(a) Includes both active and inactive membership.
(b) Includes only active members also covered under Social Security.
(c) Data not available for all systems.

327

Table 2
NATIONAL SUMMARY OF FINANCES OF STATE-ADMINISTERED
EMPLOYEE RETIREMENT SYSTEMS, SELECTED YEARS: 1967-1980

Item	Amount (in millions of dollars)							Percentage distribution			
	1979-80	1978-79	1977-78	1976-77	1975-76	1971-72	1966-67	1979-80	1976-77	1971-72	1966-67
Receipts..........................	$28,603	$24,659	$21,488	$19,287	$16,415	$9,285	$4,656	100.0	100.0	100.0	100.0
Employee contributions..............	5,285	4,968	4,619	4,223	3,854	2,637	1,494	18.5	21.9	28.4	32.1
Government contributions............	13,010	11,490	10,000	8,898	7,641	4,026	2,052	45.5	46.1	43.3	44.1
From states........................	7,399	6,318	5,736	4,847	4,672	2,428	1,305	25.9	25.1	26.1	28.0
From local governments.............	5,611	5,173	4,264	4,051	2,969	1,598	747	19.6	21.0	17.2	16.0
Earnings on investments..............	10,308	8,200	6,868	6,167	4,920	2,621	1,110	36.0	32.0	28.2	23.8
Benefits and withdrawal payments	10,257	8,937	7,811	6,930	6,045	3,187	1,606	100.0	100.0	100.0	100.0
Benefits...........................	8,809	7,704	6,821	6,048	5,327	2,694	1,280	85.9	87.3	84.5	79.7
Withdrawals........................	1,448	1,233	990	882	718	493	326	14.1	12.7	15.5	20.3
Cash and security holdings at											
end of fiscal year, total	144,682	125,803	110,357	94,913	85,979	51,158	27,266	100.0	100.0	100.0	100.0
Cash and deposits	2,647	1,883	1,304	818	728	419	236	1.8	0.9	0.8	0.9
Governmental securities	26,724	20,872	14,743	10,096	8,457	2,925	5,296	18.5	10.6	5.7	19.1
Federal	26,213	20,510	14,425	9,500	7,234	2,241	4,594	18.1	10.0	4.4	16.6
U.S. Treasury....................	13,814	10,375	6,680	4,729	2,426	N.A.	N.A.	9.5	5.0	N.A.	N.A.
Federal agency	12,399	10,136	7,745	4,770	4,808	N.A.	N.A.	8.6	5.0	N.A.	N.A.
State and local	511	362	318	596	1,223	684	1,720	0.4	0.6	1.3	2.5
Nongovernmental securities...........	115,311	103,048	94,309	83,998	76,794	47,814	9,525	79.7	88.5	93.5	80.0
Corporate bonds	60,871	55,108	51,266	45,364	45,123	29,570	6,700	42.1	47.8	57.8	51.8
Corporate stocks	31,146	26,987	24,404	21,733	19,002	9,209	512	21.5	22.9	18.0	6.9
Mortgages.......................	11,966	10,711	9,794	10,228	7,225	6,138	1,893	8.3	10.8	12.0	15.4
Other securities	10,677	8,944	7,637	6,361	4,496⟩ 2,897		420	7.4	6.7⟩	5.7	6.0
Other investments	651	1,298	1,208	312	948			0.4	0.3		

Source: U.S. Bureau of the Census, *Finances of Employee Retirement Systems of State and Local Governments in 1979-80,* and prior annual reports.

N.A.—Not available.

Table 3
MEMBERSHIP AND BENEFIT OPERATIONS OF STATE-ADMINISTERED EMPLOYEE RETIREMENT SYSTEMS: LAST MONTH OF FISCAL 1980

State	Membership, last month of the fiscal year	Members covered by Social Security	Benefit Operations, last month of fiscal year								Lump-sum survivors benefit payments during the month (dollars)
			Beneficiaries receiving periodic benefit payments				Periodic benefit payment for the month (dollars)				
			Total(a)	Persons retired on account of age or length of service	Persons retired on account of disability	Survivors of deceased former members (no. of payees)	Total(a)	Persons retired on account of age or length of service	Persons retired on account of disability	To survivors of deceased former members	
All states	10,326,512	4,914,040	2,008,155	1,559,432	141,535	124,805	$713,037,437	$572,330,539	$51,491,412	$32,815,367	$15,123,792
Alabama	154,770	131,395	25,464	22,713	1,429	1,322	8,592,448	8,070,940	352,931	168,577	87,712
Alaska	33,830(b)	19,313(b)	3,690(b)	3,370(b)	184(b)	136(b)	2,853,185(b)	2,610,117(b)	142,659(b)	100,409(b)	N.A.
Arizona	142,834	117,750	17,690(a)	658	169	244	4,197,002(a)	431,548	84,331	71,952	240,369
Arkansas	97,052	68,369	15,299	12,759	1,578	962	3,837,051	3,332,598	336,800	167,653	12,326
California	956,312	428,676	236,658	203,378	26,807	6,473	108,950,898	94,622,636	11,555,287	2,772,975	2,604,742
Colorado	96,939	20	18,268	16,468(b)	1,300(b)	500(b)	5,808,625	5,088,625(b)	470,000(b)	250,000(b)	102,118
Connecticut	99,528(b)	45,436(b)	26,276(b)	23,187(b)	2,036(b)	1,053(b)	13,845,345(b)	12,640,840(b)	912,323(b)	292,182(b)	N.A.
Delaware	25,217	25,100	5,670	4,342	512	816	1,794,571	1,549,427	116,624	128,520	...
Florida	382,968	382,968	58,893	48,218	4,460	6,215	18,619,903	16,129,677	1,071,824	1,418,402	N.A.
Georgia	266,712	154,065(c)	32,081	26,380	2,561	3,140	12,035,627	10,309,242	986,016	740,369	12,500
Hawaii	51,300(b)	45,000(b)	14,215(b)	13,000(b)	990(b)	225(b)	5,285,000(b)	5,000,000(b)	260,000(b)	25,000(b)	N.A.
Idaho	50,465	39,910	10,927	9,752	477	698	2,682,320	2,367,868	135,958	178,494	18,600
Illinois	431,486	169,374	97,139	77,662	5,142	14,355	32,550,761	28,004,956	2,190,261	2,355,544	758,784
Indiana	213,184(b)	189,389	42,524(b)	40,206(b)	2,240(b)	78(b)	11,565,572(b)	11,120,272(b)	406,886(b)	38,414(b)	19,145
Iowa	158,472	142,964(c)	32,002(a)	106	18	67	5,121,437(a)	80,955	13,022	21,601	288,856(c)
Kansas	111,511	107,588	27,478	26,247	87	1,144	3,941,378	3,786,299	22,364	132,715	1,189,523
Kentucky	150,535	40,650	27,407(a,b)	12,335	484	1,253	8,494,805(a,b)	5,660,175	321,429	316,540	8,462(c)
Louisiana	224,004(b)	20,315(b)	37,328(a,b)	17,214(b)	1,845(b)	3,069(b)	18,887,914(a,b)	7,553,999	633,370	1,033,545(b)	63,851(c)
Maine	65,528	N.A.	16,286	13,336	531	2,419	6,569,317	5,671,266	319,621	578,430	34,976
Maryland	167,126	N.A.	27,044	22,892(b)	2,333(b)	1,819(b)	13,383,985	11,393,719(b)	1,190,526(b)	799,740(b)	675,805
Massachusetts	159,166		44,206	40,266(b)	1,072(b)	2,868(b)	23,579,215	20,804,667(b)	844,664(b)	1,929,884(b)	151,804
Michigan	404,889(b)	399,540(b)	69,108(a,b)	56,090(b)	3,356(b)	1,162(b)	22,171,404(a,b)	17,113,195	804,995	428,214	N.A.(c)
Minnesota	232,321(b)	187,359(b,c)	35,525(a,b)	29,479(b)	1,461(b)	4,463(b)	8,426,855(a,b)	7,447,623(b)	388,656(b)	585,485(b)	56,416(b)
Mississippi	195,897	123,913	20,329	17,452	1,254	1,623	4,677,690	4,154,084	237,655	285,951	1,424,510
Missouri	129,043(b)	71,797(b)	26,646(b)	23,123(b)	1,818(b)	1,705(b)	7,497,345(b)	6,820,679(b)	363,649(b)	313,017(b)	109,584(b)
Montana	58,984	N.A.	10,880	9,702	529	649	3,278,592	2,967,880	158,763	151,949	21,310
Nebraska	32,602	25,192	5,430	5,178	63	189	650,677	621,114	7,902	21,661	383
Nevada	51,197		5,590	4,595	396	599	2,490,872	2,232,837	160,857	97,178	23,195
New Hampshire	32,504	29,254	5,925	5,447	291	187	821,550	669,560	101,238	50,752(c)	35,797(c)
New Jersey	343,607	274,646	72,191(a)	35,690(b)	26,277(b)	9,865(b)	30,904,779(a)	15,275,397(b)	11,117,904(b)	4,319,124(b)	652,276

MEMBERSHIP AND BENEFIT OPERATIONS OF STATE-ADMINISTERED EMPLOYEE RETIREMENT SYSTEMS: LAST MONTH OF FISCAL 1980—Concluded

State	Membership, last month of the fiscal year	Members covered by Social Security	Benefit Operations, last month of fiscal year								Lump-sum survivors benefit payments during the month (dollars)
			Beneficiaries receiving periodic benefit payments				Periodic benefit payment for the month (dollars)				
			Total(a)	Persons retired on account of age or length of service	Persons retired on account of disability	Survivors of deceased former members (no. of payees)	Total(a)	Persons retired on account of age or length of service	Persons retired on account of disability	To survivors of deceased former members	
New Mexico	88,426	41,049	11,078	10,407	644	27	3,347,285	3,226,336	105,135	15,814	825,407
New York	817,563	N.A.	202,728	182,468	8,522	11,738	74,531,508	68,812,482	2,500,389	3,218,637	467,504
North Carolina	324,259	310,201	47,277 (a)	35,672	5,809	3,769	15,081,147 (a)	12,333,490 (b)	1,858,628 (b)	787,678 (b)	6,942
North Dakota	22,993	11,543	5,049	4,684	78	287	711,209	663,916	13,824	33,469	285,331
Ohio	764,711	....	160,387	129,572	11,329	19,486	55,677,236	46,322,194	4,913,368	4,441,674	
Oklahoma	95,455	35,531	22,286	20,752	884	650	6,997,276 (b)	6,636,801 (b)	203,852 (b)	156,623 (b)	9,135 (c)
Oregon	115,892	102,056 (c)	31,067	28,455	2,588	24	6,295,080	5,690,348	592,117	12,615	85,948
Pennsylvania	420,761	235,778	113,344	100,985	5,619	6,740	53,556,765	49,795,260	2,123,229	1,638,276	2,942,878
Rhode Island	34,817	N.A.	8,635 (a)	7,310	N.A.	107	3,459,093 (a)	3,144,590	N.A.	35,216	104,400
South Carolina	264,970 (b)	195 (c)	25,799 (b)	21,505 (b)	2,862 (b)	1,432 (b)	8,169,043 (b)	7,040,791 (b)	812,535 (b)	315,717 (b)	N.A.
South Dakota	27,186	27,181	5,592	4,955	95	542	824,306	736,532	15,136	72,638	104,533
Tennessee	182,851	135,900	35,639	32,564	2,050	1,025	9,737,454	9,144,394	313,347	279,713	879,453
Texas	608,482	93,426	83,397 (a)	70,074	4,529	4,645	28,213,281 (a)	25,110,491	1,077,931	1,280,291	89,255
Utah	69,925	...	11,374 (a)	9,885	633	N.A.	2,127,692 (a)	1,700,928	100,294	N.A.	N.A.
Vermont	16,157	14,602	3,863 (a)	3,301	177	306	1,128,371 (a)	1,000,298	52,185	67,225	6,123
Virginia	300,000 (b)	230,000 (b)	36,500 (a,b)	N.A.	N.A.	N.A.	10,871,093 (a,b)	N.A.	N.A.	N.A.	N.A.
Washington	246,680	169,047 (b)	52,366 (a)	732	6	20	19,567,552 (a)	N.A.	N.A.	N.A.	N.A.
West Virginia	116,620	82,615	27,138	23,870	1,244	2,024	7,553,124	6,883,580	306,883	362,661	94,766
Wisconsin	248,817	181,019 (b)	51,528	46,557	2,691	2,280	10,889,343	9,855,264	774,365	259,714	589,251
Wyoming	39,964	3,914	4,939	4,439	75	425	783,456 (b)	700,649 (b)	19,679 (b)	63,128 (b)	39,825

Source: Compiled from unpublished data received in the U.S. Bureau of the Census' annual survey on finances of public employee retirement systems.

N.A.—Not available.

... Represents zero.

(a) Detail does not add to totals because, for those states indicated, detail was not always available. Total of such nonsegregable amounts was 182,383 for beneficiaries receiving periodic benefit payments and $56,400,119 for periodic benefit payments.

(b) State totals include some estimated figures.

(c) Data not available for all systems.

Table 4
FINANCES OF STATE-ADMINISTERED EMPLOYEE RETIREMENT SYSTEMS, BY STATE: 1979-80
(In thousands of dollars)

	Receipts					Benefits and withdrawal payments		
			Government contributions					
State	Total	Employee contributions	From state	From local governments	Earnings on investments	Total	Benefits	Withdrawals
All states...............	$28,603,259	$5,285,218	$7,399,276	$5,611,093	$10,307,672	$10,256,545	$8,808,549	$1,447,996
Alabama...................	429,561	81,768	188,316	20,782	138,695	126,139	111,421	14,718
Alaska....................	194,999	37,549	51,076	36,404	69,970	43,086	34,238	8,847
Arizona	407,365	113,464	34,938	87,565	171,398	87,675	50,813	36,862
Arkansas	199,145	34,923	77,131	12,908	74,183	58,609	45,581	13,029
California................	4,288,463	683,734	965,718	1,061,369	1,577,642	1,510,865	1,294,192	216,673
Colorado	440,123	106,909	63,170	92,119	177,926	104,290	74,836	29,454
Connecticut	374,686	70,049	181,637	6,335	116,664	177,433	162,340	15,093
Delaware	76,405	9,529	47,480	. . .	19,397	21,955	20,729	1,225
Florida	783,709	10,536	129,094	308,926	335,153	215,988	201,916	14,072
Georgia	530,797	142,773	163,233	48,911	175,881	168,517	140,082	28,435
Hawaii(a)	241,500	63,000	57,500	23,000	98,000	84,300	76,000	8,300
Idaho	95,492	24,178	17,127	27,392	26,794	38,967	31,108	7,859
Illinois..................	1,217,050	317,332	377,079	108,986	413,654	461,925	392,733	69,191
Indiana	320,397	63,609	129,915	29,337	97,536	153,925	138,981	14,945
Iowa	262,333	58,621	37,781	65,505	100,427	84,767	58,924	25,843
Kansas	206,572	48,343	60,315	22,525	75,389	64,078	47,199	16,879
Kentucky	345,418	89,875	119,518	25,065	110,960	116,562	101,929	14,634
Louisiana	478,946	137,049	108,631	54,173	179,094	238,324	220,455	17,869
Maine	140,969	33,706	56,971		34,544	85,223	77,972	7,251
Maryland	481,550	116,907	207,076	6,565	151,002	249,640	179,790	69,850
Massachusetts	516,454	141,577	260,602	. . .	114,276	323,083	288,343	34,740
Michigan	1,093,090	14,651	499,865	216,428	362,145	286,352	271,843	14,508
Minnesota	488,411	124,540	124,934	70,299	168,639	128,982	103,258	25,723
Mississippi	244,256	66,090	43,778	56,054	78,335	77,478	59,412	18,066
Missouri	379,416	83,615	60,920	89,070	145,812	156,956	88,869	68,088
Montana...................	106,045	34,856	14,351	22,688	34,151	50,712	39,914	10,799
Nebraska	43,278	11,146	7,087	6,387	18,659	11,422	8,358	3,064
Nevada	153,339	15,376	16,302	53,227	68,434	36,924	29,429	7,495
New Hampshire	62,979	21,653	12,243	11,107	17,975	24,442	18,329	6,113
New Jersey................	1,067,651	204,768	302,051	171,237	389,596	367,791	345,351	22,440
New Mexico	169,266	51,901	20,500	36,972	59,893	52,181	38,677	13,505
New York	3,175,046	65,186	556,701	1,298,909	1,254,250	1,023,027	974,789	48,238
North Carolina	730,918	178,423	184,756	71,353	296,386	228,418	191,495	36,923
North Dakota	40,259	13,989	4,636	10,327	11,308	12,533	8,036	4,497
Ohio	2,226,078	538,173	208,629	659,709	819,567	883,693	763,005	120,688
Oklahoma	246,104	39,492	142,978	6,265	57,369	96,185	87,956	8,230
Oregon	318,095	93,701	53,581	91,147	79,666	98,799	75,764	23,035
Pennsylvania	1,481,133	270,978	477,945	198,681	533,529	780,044	709,821	70,223
Rhode Island	107,207	28,852	31,328	10,038	36,989	49,011	45,451	3,559
South Carolina	336,677	83,478	55,564	63,480	134,155	108,303	89,218	19,085
South Dakota	53,309	17,473	7,532	10,704	17,599	14,730	8,922	5,807
Tennessee.................	422,940	81,676	189,707	26,849	124,708	136,406	114,730	21,677
Texas.....................	1,199,220	361,311	382,722	26,959	428,229	440,663	337,889	102,775
Utah	191,048	69,443	20,511	55,772	45,322	44,962	27,820	17,142
Vermont...................	47,753	10,105	15,827	427	21,394	15,942	13,246	2,696
Virginia..................	435,654	126,357	111,983	40,835	156,479	162,413	130,453	31,960
Washington	752,648	166,252	347,078	10,300	229,019	278,275	244,125	34,151
West Virginia	170,894	50,461	59,933	11,044	49,456	101,154	90,796	10,357
Wisconsin.................	766,806	62,442	104,384	211,389	388,591	160,410	133,256	27,154
Wyoming	61,802	13,400	7,145	19,823	21,434	12,987	8,755	4,232

Source: U.S. Bureau of the Census, *Finances of Employee Retirement Systems of State and Local Governments in 1979-80*.

Note: Because of rounding, detail may not add to totals.
(a) Data estimated.

FINANCES OF STATE-ADMINISTERED EMPLOYEE RETIREMENT SYSTEMS, BY STATE: 1979-80
(In thousands of dollars)

State	Total	Cash and deposits	Total	U.S. Treasury	Federal agency	State and local	Non-governmental securities
All states	$144,681,650	$2,647,356	$26,213,095	$13,813,955	$12,399,140	$510,577	$115,310,623
Alabama	1,784,433	10,084	91,504	...	91,504	...	1,682,845
Alaska	719,558	93,810	192,175	149,394	42,781	...	443,573
Arizona	2,062,413	559	380,671	380,211	460	...	1,681,183
Arkansas	932,095	25,277	257,102	170,296	86,806	...	649,715
California	22,789,620	196,106	3,310,459	884,487	2,425,972	19,955	19,263,100
Colorado	2,297,758	1,877	190,086	129,950	60,136	...	2,105,795
Connecticut	1,576,398	8,594	117,669	117,669	...	...	1,450,135
Delaware	253,428	385	16,691	15,091	1,600	...	236,351
Florida	3,790,885	212,393	1,103,070	436,955	666,115	15	2,475,407
Georgia	2,489,568	45,539	527,801	469,075	58,726	...	1,916,227
Hawaii(a)	1,214,850	206,500	269,000	27,000	242,000	350	739,000
Idaho	335,942	19,678	31,404	15,501	15,903	...	284,860
Illinois	5,481,894	9,581	792,838	291,320	501,518	...	4,679,475
Indiana	1,253,121	29,092	529,718	163,401	366,317	...	694,311
Iowa	1,297,038	1,699	430,662	287,529	143,133	...	864,677
Kansas	879,107	1,940	109,183	12,114	97,070	16,986	750,998
Kentucky	1,585,812	62,969	331,894	80,181	251,713	940	1,190,010
Louisiana	2,440,465	237,690	654,819	261,625	393,195	18,696	1,529,259
Maine	313,271	44,748	51,914	37,939	13,975	...	216,609
Maryland	2,415,039	29,157	...	...	...	...	2,385,881
Massachusetts	1,541,985	677	400,052	69,167	330,885	...	1,141,256
Michigan	4,907,546	638,556	590,537	552,741	37,795	425	3,678,028
Minnesota	2,719,074	1,187	389,129	103,070	286,059	2,917	2,325,842
Mississippi	1,037,977	97,673	474,795	67,900	406,895	...	465,509
Missouri	1,932,778	6,752	319,321	99,105	220,216	...	1,606,705
Montana	467,858	4,341	28,835	27,856	979	1,548	433,134
Nebraska	218,650	3	55,079	13,542	41,537	...	163,568
Nevada	722,742	73	95,462	21,850	73,612	...	627,207
New Hampshire	315,326	36,069	50,104	18,171	31,933	...	229,153
New Jersey	6,233,685	166	727,868	45,938	681,930	877	5,504,773
New Mexico	797,072	24,402	284,424	109,927	174,498	...	488,246
New York	19,585,218	9,506	6,073,742	4,749,206	1,324,536	439,046	13,062,924
North Carolina	4,587,427	9,205	1,900	1,900	...	...	4,576,322
North Dakota	143,858	1,069	70,728	32,165	38,563	...	72,061
Ohio	11,735,379	7,030	1,181,171	630,425	550,745	2,607	10,544,571
Oklahoma	795,620	39,531	148,505	71,528	76,977	...	607,584
Oregon	1,574,202	14,864	102,917	1	102,916	...	1,456,422
Pennsylvania	7,638,010	148	586,128	341,985	244,144	101	7,051,633
Rhode Island	463,279	19,956	125,851	109,049	16,802	...	317,473
South Carolina	1,839,171	7,435	699,512	312,361	387,151	5,000	1,127,224
South Dakota	245,829	46,233	91,206	72,836	18,371	...	108,390
Tennessee	1,752,701	122,346	560,729	513,133	47,596	...	1,069,626
Texas	6,227,738	15,614	1,973,679	781,673	1,192,005	...	4,238,445
Utah	823,946	43,280	140,337	74,323	66,014	...	640,329
Vermont	232,640	1,532	43,116	37,441	5,675	...	187,992
Virginia	1,713,073	264,912	463,000	259,280	203,720	189	984,973
Washington	3,160,357	5,693	734,976	498,797	236,179	555	2,419,134
West Virginia	608,283	864	244,226	110,935	133,291	371	362,822
Wisconsin	4,476,495	3	40,288	40,288	...	...	4,436,204
Wyoming	271,036	557	126,816	117,623	9,193	...	143,663

332

Table 5
COMPARATIVE STATISTICS FOR STATE-ADMINISTERED PUBLIC EMPLOYEE RETIREMENT SYSTEMS: 1979-80

State	Percent of receipts paid by			Annual benefit payments as a percentage of		Average benefit payments(a)	Investment earnings as a percentage of cash and asset holdings	Percentage distribution of cash and security holdings				
										Governmental securities		Nongovernmental securities
	Employee contribution	State government	Local government	Annual receipts	Cash and security holdings			Total	Cash and deposits	Federal	State and local	
All states	18.5	25.9	19.6	30.8	6.1	$355	7.1	100.0	1.8	18.1	0.4	79.7
Alabama	19.0	43.8	4.8	25.9	6.2	337	7.8	100.0	0.6	5.1	...	94.3
Alaska(b)	19.3	26.2	18.7	17.6	4.7	773	9.7	100.0	11.6	26.7	...	61.6
Arizona	27.9	8.6	21.5	12.5	2.5	237	8.3	100.0	...	18.4	...	81.5
Arkansas	17.5	38.7	6.5	22.9	4.9	251	8.0	100.0	2.7	27.6	...	69.7
California	15.9	22.5	24.7	30.2	5.7	460	6.9	100.0	0.9	14.5	...	84.5
Colorado	24.3	14.4	20.9	17.0	3.3	318	7.7	100.0	0.1	8.3	...	91.6
Connecticut	18.7	48.5	1.7	43.3	10.3	527	7.4	100.0	0.5	7.5	...	92.0
Delaware	12.5	62.1	...	27.1	8.2	317	7.7	100.0	0.2	6.6	...	93.2
Florida	1.3	16.5	39.4	25.8	5.3	316	8.8	100.0	5.6	29.1	...	65.3
Georgia	26.9	30.8	9.2	26.4	5.6	375	7.4	100.0	1.8	21.2	...	77.0
Hawaii(b)	26.1	23.8	9.5	31.5	6.3	372	8.1	100.0	17.0	22.1	...	60.8
Idaho	25.3	17.9	28.7	32.6	9.2	245	8.0	100.0	5.9	9.4	...	84.8
Illinois	26.1	31.0	9.0	32.3	7.2	335	7.5	100.0	0.2	14.5	...	85.4
Indiana	19.9	40.5	9.2	43.4	11.1	272	7.8	100.0	2.3	42.3	...	55.4
Iowa	22.3	14.4	25.0	22.5	4.5	160	7.7	100.0	0.1	33.2	...	66.7
Kansas	23.4	29.2	10.9	22.8	5.4	143	8.6	100.0	0.2	12.4	1.9	85.4
Kentucky	26.0	34.6	7.3	29.5	6.4	310	7.0	100.0	4.0	20.9	0.1	75.0
Louisiana	28.6	22.7	11.3	46.0	9.0	506	7.3	100.0	9.7	26.8	0.8	62.7
Maine	23.9	40.4	11.2	55.3	24.9	403	11.0	100.0	14.3	16.6	...	69.1
Maryland	24.3	43.0	1.4	37.3	7.4	495	6.3	100.0	1.2	...	...	98.8
Massachusetts	27.4	50.5	...	55.8	18.7	533	7.4	100.0	...	25.9	...	74.0
Michigan(b)	1.3	45.7	19.8	24.9	5.5	321	7.4	100.0	13.0	12.0	...	74.9
Minnesota	25.5	25.6	14.4	21.1	3.8	237	6.2	100.0	...	14.3	0.1	85.5
Mississippi	27.1	17.9	22.9	24.3	5.7	230	7.5	100.0	9.4	45.7	...	44.8
Missouri(b)	22.0	16.1	23.5	23.4	4.6	256	7.5	100.0	0.3	16.5	...	83.2
Montana	32.9	13.5	21.4	37.6	8.5	301	7.3	100.0	0.9	6.2	0.3	92.6
Nebraska	25.8	16.4	14.8	19.3	3.8	120	8.5	100.0	...	25.2	...	74.8
Nevada	10.0	10.6	10.5	19.2	4.1	446	9.5	100.0	...	13.2	...	86.8
New Hampshire	34.4	19.4	17.6	29.1	5.8	139	5.7	100.0	11.4	15.9	...	72.7
New Jersey	19.2	28.3	16.0	32.3	5.5	428	6.2	100.0	...	11.7	...	88.3

COMPARATIVE STATISTICS FOR STATE-ADMINISTERED PUBLIC EMPLOYEE RETIREMENT SYSTEMS: 1979-80
—Concluded

State	Percent of receipts paid by			Annual benefit payments as a percentage of		Average benefit payments(a)	Investment earnings as a percentage of cash and asset holdings	Total	Cash and deposits	Governmental securities		Nongovernmental securities
	Employee contribution	State government	Local government	Annual receipts	Cash and security holdings					Federal	State and local	
New Mexico	30.2	12.1	21.8	22.8	4.9	302	7.5	100.0	3.1	35.7	...	61.3
New York	2.1	17.5	40.9	30.7	5.0	368	6.4	100.0	...	31.0	2.2	66.7
North Carolina	24.4	25.3	9.8	26.2	4.2	319	6.5	100.0	0.2	...	...	99.8
North Dakota	34.7	11.5	25.6	20.0	5.6	141	7.9	100.0	0.7	49.2	...	50.0
Ohio	24.2	9.4	29.6	34.3	6.5	347	7.0	100.0	0.1	10.1	...	89.9
Oklahoma	16.0	58.1	2.5	35.7	11.1	314	7.2	100.0	5.0	18.7	...	76.4
Oregon	29.5	16.8	28.7	23.8	4.8	203	5.1	100.0	0.9	6.5	...	92.5
Pennsylvania	18.3	32.3	13.4	47.9	9.3	439	7.0	100.0	...	7.7	...	92.3
Rhode Island	26.9	29.2	9.4	42.3	9.8	401	8.0	100.0	4.3	0.8	...	68.5
South Carolina(b)	24.8	16.5	18.9	26.5	4.9	317	7.3	100.0	0.4	38.0	0.3	61.3
South Dakota	32.8	14.1	20.1	16.7	3.6	147	7.2	100.0	18.8	37.1	...	44.1
Tennessee	19.3	44.8	6.3	27.1	6.5	273	7.1	100.0	7.0	32.0	...	61.0
Texas	30.1	31.9	2.2	28.2	5.4	338	6.9	100.0	0.3	31.7	...	68.1
Utah	36.3	10.7	29.2	14.6	3.4	187	5.5	100.0	5.3	17.0	...	77.7
Vermont	21.2	33.1	0.9	27.7	5.7	292	9.2	100.0	0.7	18.5	...	80.8
Virginia(b)	29.0	25.7	9.4	29.9	7.6	298	9.1	100.0	15.5	27.0	...	57.5
Washington	22.1	46.1	1.4	32.4	7.8	374	7.2	100.0	0.2	23.3	...	76.5
West Virginia	29.5	35.1	6.5	53.1	14.9	278	8.1	100.0	0.1	40.2	0.1	59.6
Wisconsin	8.1	13.6	27.6	17.4	3.0	211	8.7	100.0	...	0.9	...	99.1
Wyoming	21.7	11.6	32.1	14.2	3.2	159	7.9	100.0	0.2	46.8	...	53.0

Source: U.S. Bureau of the Census, *Finances of Employee Retirement Systems of State and Local Governments, 1979-80*, Table 5.

... Represents zero or rounds to zero.

(a) Average benefit payment for last month of fiscal year.
(b) Includes estimated data.

STATE GOVERNMENT EMPLOYMENT IN 1980

MORE THAN 3.7 MILLION persons were employed by state governments in October 1980, an increase of 1.5 percent from October 1979. This increase was considerably less than the average annual rate of increase during the decade of the 1970s, 3.5 percent, when state government employment increased by over 1 million workers. The ratio of state government workers to state population, using full-time equivalent employment, was 13.7 per 1,000 population in October 1980; in October 1970 the ratio was 11.3 per 1,000 population.[1]

October 1980 payrolls for state government workers were nearly $4.3 billion, up 10.7 percent from the same month in 1979. The average annual increase in payrolls during the 1970s, using October payroll amounts, was 10.5 percent.

The average earnings of full-time state workers for the month of October 1980 was $1,373, an increase of 9.2 percent from the average for the same period in 1979.

Change in Government Employment, 1970-1980

Civilian employment for all levels of government totaled more than 16.2 million in October 1980, and civilian government payrolls for that month exceeded $19.9 billion. The federal government accounted for 17.9 percent of the civilian government work force and 26.1 percent of civilian government payrolls; local governments accounted for 58.9 percent of this work force and 52.4 percent of the payrolls; the states' shares were 23.1 percent and 21.5 percent, respectively. The following table summarizes and compares government employment and payrolls, by level of government, in 1980 and 1970.

Table A

Employment and payrolls	All governments	Federal government	State governments	Local governments
Employment (thousands):				
October 1980	16,222	2,907	3,753	9,562
October 1970	13,028	2,881	2,755	7,392
Payrolls (millions of dollars):				
October 1980	19,945.8	5,215.7	4,284.7	10,445.4
October 1970	8,334.2	2,427.9	1,612.2	4,294.2
Average annual rate of change, Oct. 1970-Oct. 1980 (percent):				
Employment	2.2	0.1	3.1	2.6
Payrolls...................	9.1	7.9	10.3	9.3

Although federal civilian employment increased only slightly during the past 10 years, there were significant changes in individual functional areas. Civilian employment in na-

Adapted by Alan V. Stevens, Chief, Employment Branch, Governments Division, U.S. Bureau of the Census, from *Public Employment in 1980* and *Labor-Management Relations in State and Local Governments: 1980.*

tional defense and international relations activities had a decline from 1970 to 1980 of 224,000 employees, or 18.7 percent, and similarly, postal service employment declined by 67,000 or 9.2 percent. Federal employment increased considerably, however, in several functional categories—health and hospital employment increased by 73,000 (37.8 percent) and employment in natural resources activities grew by 70,000 (31.7 percent).

State governments recorded a decrease in only one functional area, highways, during the past 10 years. State highway employment dropped by 44,000 (14.6 percent) to 258,000 employees, its lowest level since 1961. Increases were recorded in nearly all other functional categories; some of the more significant increases over the past 10 years were in higher education (up 380,000 employees, 34.7 percent), hospitals (up 128,000 employees, 28.4 percent), public welfare (up 75,000 employees, 75.6 percent), general control[2] (up 65,000 employees, 127.5 percent), health (up 62,000 employees, 121.6 percent) and correctional activities (up 61,000 employees, 66.3 percent).

Local governments had minor decreases in employment for two functional activities from 1970 to 1980: highways (down 1.4 percent) and sanitation other than sewerage (down 3.8 percent). Nearly all other functional categories of local government employment reflected increases during this 10-year period. The most significant categories of increase were elementary and secondary education (up 937,000 employees, 24.0 percent), higher education (up 189,000 employees, 92.6 percent), hospitals (up 147,000 employees, 34.3 percent), police protection (up 135,000 employees, 29.9 percent), general control (up 120,000 employees, 37.6 percent), public transit (up 67,000 employees, 72.8 percent), health (up 63,000 employees, 79.7 percent) and public welfare (up 61,000 employees, 38.4 percent).

States' Portion of Government Employment

Six state governments employed over 150,000 workers as of October 1980 and nine employed less than 20,000 workers. These state governments and their October 1980 employment and population rankings are as follows:

Table B

Largest state government employers			Smallest state government employers		
State	Number of employees	Population ranking		Number of employees	Population ranking
California	309,872	1	Wyoming	11,146	49
New York	230,938	2	Vermont	12,289	48
Texas	200,496	3	Nevada	14,571	43
Michigan	161,323	8	South Dakota	16,435	45
Illinois	154,954	5	North Dakota	17,089	46
Ohio	152,573	6	Delaware	17,396	47
			Alaska	17,759	50
			New Hampshire	18,537	42
			Idaho	19,172	41

While the level of a state government's employment generally depends on the size of the state's population, several other factors also influence the employment level: provision of public services by local governments (e.g., public welfare activities) based on state law or local option; provision of certain services by the private sector (most notably hospitals); and the proportion of urban population.

As can be seen from Table 3 at the end of this chapter, the ratio of local government to state government full-time equivalent employment per 10,000 population is generally in the range of 2:1 to 3:1. Some notable exceptions to this generality include Hawaii, where the state operates all elementary and secondary schools, and Alaska, where the state operates elementary and secondary schools in the unorganized areas of the state.

State Employment by Function

More than one-third of state government full-time equivalent employment is in education, and over 17 percent is in hospitals. Highways rank third and account for another 8.2 percent. All remaining functions account for less than 6 percent each.

The ratio of full-time equivalent employment to population varies significantly from state to state because of the several factors mentioned above. While the most populous states often have the highest numbers of employees in many functions, the ratio of their employment to population is frequently lower than the less populous states. The following table lists the state governments with the highest and lowest ratios of full-time equivalent employment to population in the four functions with the largest number of employees.

Table C
(Amounts equal number of full-time equivalent employment per 1,000 population)

Education		Hospitals		Highways		Public welfare	
Hawaii	22.3	Rhode Island	4.7	Alaska	6.0	Oklahoma	2.8
Alaska	12.6	Louisiana	4.7	West Virginia	4.2	Michigan	1.7
New Mexico	9.9	New York	3.9	Wyoming	3.5	Rhode Island	1.6
All states average	4.7	All states average	2.4	All states average	1.1	All states average	0.8
Florida	2.7	Idaho	1.2	Illinois	0.7	Virginia	0.2
Pennsylvania	2.0	Alaska	1.0	Michigan	0.5	North Carolina	0.1
New York	1.8	Nevada	0.9	Wisconsin	0.4	Ohio	0.1

Average Earnings for State Workers

Full-time employees of state governments earned an average gross wage of $1,373 for the month of October 1980, a 9.2 percent increase over the corresponding amount for October 1979. The average for full-time instructional staff in educational institutions was $2,162, and for all other full-time employees it was $1,282.

The average annual increase from October 1970 to October 1980 in full-time state worker's average pay was 7 percent. The annual rate of increase during this 10-year period was in excess of 8 percent in seven states and less than 6 percent in three states as shown in Table D.

Table D

State	Annual rate of change, full-time average pay Oct. 1970-Oct. 1980	Average full-time employee pay, Oct. 1980
Alabama	8.4	$1,280
Colorado	8.4	1,588
Delaware	8.1	1,265
Idaho	8.2	1,353
Maine	8.7	1,266
South Carolina	8.0	1,234
Wyoming	8.6	1,470
All states average	7.0	1,373
Connecticut	5.3	1,264
Hawaii	5.8	1,403
Massachusetts	5.2	1,214

Full-time state employee average pay for October 1980 was highest in Alaska ($2,065) and California ($1,867), and lowest in Mississippi ($1,052) and West Virginia ($1,066).

Labor-Management Relations in State Government

Forty state governments had a labor-management relations policy covering part or all of their work force in 1980. Of these 40 states, 33 had provisions allowing for collective negotiations with employee groups.

There were nearly 1,163,000 full-time state employees who belonged to employee organizations in October 1980, or more than 40 percent of all full-time state workers. The functions with the highest proportion of full-time employees belonging to employee organizations were highways (52.9 percent), police protection (51.8 percent) and hospitals (49.8 percent). In eight states, more than two-thirds of all full-time workers belonged to employee organizations (Alaska, Connecticut, Florida, Hawaii, Maine, Massachusetts, New York and Rhode Island), and in three states less than 10 percent belonged to employee organizations (Kentucky, Oklahoma and West Virginia).

Labor-management contracts between the state government and employee organizations existed in 29 of the 33 states having provisions for collective negotiations in October 1980. These states had a total of 728 contractual agreements covering 837,628 employees, or slightly more than 22 percent of all state employees. Thirty-four of these contractual agreements were new agreements reached during the October 1979-October 1980 period, 240 were renegotiated during this period, and the remainder were multi-year agreements negotiated before October 1979.

Twenty-two work stoppages by state employees occurred during the 12-month period which ended in October 1980. New Jersey, New York and Pennsylvania each experienced three work stoppages, and Massachusetts had two stoppages during this period. These 22 stoppages involved over 16,000 workers and accounted for nearly 90,000 days of idleness.[3]

A summary of state government labor-management relations activities is provided in Table 7.

Notes

1. Full-time equivalent employment is a computed statistic representing the number of full-time workers that could be employed with no increase in total salary and wage costs if all personnel were engaged on a full-time basis at the average October pay prevailing for full-time employees.

2. The general control function includes judicial and legislative activities, the chief executive's office and government-wide administrative agencies.

3. Days of idleness are computed by multiplying the number of employees idled in a work stoppage by the number of work days or work shifts scheduled for the period of the stoppage.

Table 1

SUMMARY OF STATE GOVERNMENT EMPLOYMENT: 1950-1980

	Employment (in thousands)						Monthly payrolls (in millions of dollars)			Average monthly earnings of full-time employees		
	Total, full-time and part-time			Full-time equivalent								
Year	All	Educa-tion	Other	All	Educa-tion	Other	All	Educa-tion	Other	All	Educa-tion	Other
October:												
1980	3,753	1,599	2,154	3,106	1,063	2,044	$4,284.7	$1,608.0	$2,676.6	$1,373	$1,523	$1,305
1979	3,699	1,577	2,122	3,072	1,046	2,026	3,869.3	1,451.4	2,419.9	1,257	1,399	1,193
1978	3,539	1,508	2,032	2,966	1,016	1,950	3,483.0	1,332.9	2,150.2	1,167	1,311	1,102
1977	3,491	1,484	2,007	2,903	1,005	1,898	3,194.6	1,234.4	1,960.1	1,096	1,237	1,031
1976	3,343	1,434	1,910	2,799	973	1,827	2,893.7	1,112.5	1,782.1	1,031	1,163	975
1975	3,271	1,400	1,870	2,744	952	1,792	2,652.7	1,022.7	1,631.1	964	1,080	909
1974	3,155	1,357	1,798	2,653	929	1,725	2,409.5	932.7	1,476.9	906	1,023	856
1973	3,013	1,280	1,733	2,547	887	1,660	2,158.2	822.2	1,336.0	843	952	805
1972	2,957	1,267	1,690	2,487	867	1,619	1,936.6	746.9	1,189.7	778	871	734
1971	2,832	1,223	1,609	2,384	841	1,544	1,741.7	681.4	1,060.2	731	826	686
1970	2,755	1,182	1,573	2,302	803	1,499	1,612.2	630.2	981.8	701	797	655
1969	2,614	1,112	1,501	2,179	746	1,433	1,430.5	554.4	876.0	655	743	597
1968	2,495	1,037	1,458	2,085	694	1,391	1,256.6	477.0	779.6	602	687	544
1967	2,335	940	1,395	1,946	620	1,326	1,105.5	406.3	699.3	567	666	526
1966	2,211	866	1,344	1,864	575	1,289	975.2	353.0	622.2	523	614	483
1965	2,028	739	1,289	1,751	508	1,243	849.2	290.1	559.1	485	571	450
1964	1,873	656	1,217	1,639	460	1,179	761.1	257.5	503.6	464	560	427
1963	1,775	602	1,173	1,558	422	1,136	696.4	230.1	466.3	447	545	410
1962	1,680	555	1,126	1,478	389	1,088	634.6	201.8	432.8	429	518	397
1961	1,625	518	1,107	1,435	367	1,068	586.2	192.4	393.8	409	482	383
1960	1,527	474	1,053	1,353	332	1,021	524.1	167.7	356.4	384	439	365
1959	1,454	443	1,011	1,302	318	984	485.4	136.0	349.4	372	427	352
1958	1,408	406	1,002	1,259	284	975	446.5	123.4	323.1	355	416	333
April 1957	1,300	375	925	1,153	257	896	372.5	106.1	266.4	320	355	309
October:												
1956	1,268	353	915	1,136	250	886	366.5	108.8	257.7	321	358	309
1955	1,199	333	866	1,081	244	837	325.9	88.5	237.4	302	334	290
1954	1,149	310	839	1,024	222	802	300.7	78.9	221.8	294	325	283
1953	1,082	294	788	966	211	755	278.6	73.5	205.1	289	320	278
1952	1,060	293	767	958	213	745	260.3	65.1	195.2	271	298	262
1951	1,070	316	754	973	240	733	245.8	68.1	177.7	253	284	242
1950	1,057	312	745	N.A.	N.A.	N.A.	218.4	61.0	157.4	N.A.	N.A.	N.A.

Source: U.S. Bureau of the Census, annual *Public Employment* reports.

Note: Because of rounding, detail may not add to totals. N.A.—Not available.

Table 2
EMPLOYMENT AND PAYROLLS OF STATE AND LOCAL GOVERNMENTS, BY FUNCTION: OCTOBER 1980

Function	All employees, full-time and part-time (in thousands)			October payrolls (in millions of dollars)			Average October earnings of full-time employees
	Total	State governments	Local governments	Total	State governments	Local governments	
All functions	13,315	3,753	9,562	$14,730	$4,285	$10,445	$1,337
Education	6,841	1,599	5,242	7,451	1,608	5,843	1,402
Local schools	4,868	20	4,848	5,522	26	5,496	1,364
Instructional personnel only	3,164	14	3,149	4,324	21	4,303	1,513
Institutions of higher education	1,868	1,474	393	1,797	1,450	347	1,560
Instructional personnel only	655	452	202	937	721	216	2,167
Other education	105	105	...	132	132	...	1,347
Functions other than education	6,474	2,154	4,320	7,279	2,677	4,603	1,279
Highways	559	258	301	660	346	314	1,238
Public welfare	394	174	220	413	205	208	1,112
Hospitals	1,154	578	576	1,175	616	558	1,096
Health	254	113	142	301	145	156	1,289
Police protection	659	73	586	869	119	750	1,483
Police officers only	492	50	441	734	91	643	1,574
Local fire protection	308	...	308	355	...	355	1,579
Fire fighters only	281	...	281	336	...	336	1,596
Natural resources	228	192	36	254	220	34	1,294
Correction	249	153	96	319	201	119	1,329
Social insurance administration	124	124	...	155	155	...	1,351
Financial administration	316	121	195	344	153	191	1,211
General control	555	116	439	543	172	370	1,347
Local utilities	386	17	369	578	34	545	1,584
Other	1,287	235	1,053	1,321	319	1,002	1,225

Source: U.S. Bureau of the Census, *Public Employment in 1980.*

Note: Statistics for local governments are subject to sampling variation.
Because of rounding, detail may not add to totals.

Table 3
STATE AND LOCAL GOVERNMENT EMPLOYMENT, BY STATE:
OCTOBER 1980

| State or other jurisdiction | All employees (full-time and part-time) | | Full-time equivalent employment | | | | | |
| | | | Number | | | Number per 10,000 population | | |
	State	Local	Total	State	Local	Total	State	Local
United States	3,753,106	9,561,944	11,046,909	3,106,291	7,940,618	488	137	351
Alabama	74,578	150,064	196,225	62,530	133,695	504	161	344
Alaska	17,759	17,975	32,118	16,642	15,476	803	416	387
Arizona	41,760	119,779	137,439	37,310	100,129	506	137	368
Arkansas	45,145	80,157	106,323	37,577	68,746	465	164	301
California	309,872	1,107,109	1,108,151	248,833	859,318	468	105	363
Colorado	58,394	128,486	148,726	42,537	106,189	515	147	368
Connecticut	57,083	109,234	138,382	46,390	91,992	445	149	296
Delaware	17,396	18,071	31,318	15,563	15,755	526	262	265
Florida	119,223	399,345	458,804	104,664	354,140	471	107	364
Georgia	94,572	253,611	307,514	83,300	224,214	563	152	410
Hawaii	43,310	12,926	48,538	36,454	12,084	503	378	125
Idaho	19,172	38,532	45,391	14,881	30,510	481	158	323
Illinois	154,954	483,140	509,288	123,816	385,472	446	108	338
Indiana	91,097	214,821	247,573	66,564	181,009	451	121	330
Iowa	55,004	129,983	147,850	45,110	102,740	508	155	353
Kansas	49,763	112,527	126,727	37,815	88,912	536	160	376
Kentucky	70,359	113,680	154,813	57,719	97,094	423	158	265
Louisiana	93,704	154,910	223,723	81,292	142,431	532	193	339
Maine	22,736	43,824	51,492	18,131	33,361	458	161	297
Maryland	87,513	176,611	230,625	81,754	148,871	547	194	353
Massachusetts	88,509	249,954	286,900	78,226	208,674	500	136	364
Michigan	161,323	396,723	435,054	125,630	309,424	470	136	334
Minnesota	73,291	198,812	203,118	54,868	148,250	498	135	364
Mississippi	46,008	104,260	129,551	39,973	89,578	514	159	355
Missouri	76,523	193,531	228,706	65,268	163,438	465	133	332
Montana	22,273	35,126	43,732	15,639	28,093	556	199	357
Nebraska	33,486	81,712	92,582	28,211	64,371	590	180	410
Nevada	14,571	31,990	40,004	12,125	27,879	501	152	349
New Hampshire	18,537	34,108	41,437	14,413	27,024	450	156	293
New Jersey	102,351	331,488	369,902	87,350	282,552	502	119	384
New Mexico	41,787	47,695	76,599	33,730	42,869	589	259	330
New York	230,938	864,951	945,949	215,271	730,678	539	123	416
North Carolina	101,917	247,299	298,127	86,603	211,524	508	147	360
North Dakota	17,089	34,198	32,810	12,624	20,186	502	193	309
Ohio	152,573	444,583	472,790	114,997	357,793	438	107	331
Oklahoma	67,806	118,174	158,458	56,220	102,238	524	186	338
Oregon	54,891	116,610	135,224	43,076	92,148	514	164	350
Pennsylvania	148,992	420,120	475,386	127,145	348,241	401	107	293
Rhode Island	25,143	27,254	44,634	20,004	24,630	471	211	260
South Carolina	67,505	114,273	160,784	61,138	99,646	515	196	319
South Dakota	16,435	31,368	34,468	12,416	22,052	500	180	320
Tennessee	74,401	180,363	224,783	62,814	161,969	490	137	353
Texas	200,496	591,734	694,992	168,995	525,997	488	119	370
Utah	32,244	55,305	67,673	25,793	41,880	463	177	287
Vermont	12,289	17,987	24,603	10,984	13,619	481	215	267
Virginia	113,667	200,565	268,850	94,165	174,685	503	176	327
Washington	94,222	156,361	204,354	71,419	132,935	495	173	322
West Virginia	46,794	65,432	99,624	39,693	59,931	511	204	307
Wisconsin	82,505	224,664	225,913	59,531	166,382	480	127	354
Wyoming	11,146	27,729	30,265	9,088	21,177	643	193	450
Dist. of Col.	. . .	52,790	48,617	. . .	48,617	762	. . .	762

Source: U.S. Bureau of the Census, Public Employment in 1980.
Note: Statistics for local governments are estimates subject to sampling variation. Because of rounding, detail may not add to totals.

Table 4

STATE AND LOCAL GOVERNMENT PAYROLLS AND AVERAGE EARNINGS OF FULL-TIME EMPLOYEES, BY STATE: OCTOBER 1980

State or other jurisdiction	Amount of payroll (in thousands of dollars)			Percentage of October payroll		Average earnings of full-time state and local government employees		
	Total	State government	Local governments	State government	Local governments	All	Education employees	Other
United States	$14,730,088	$4,284,687	$10,445,402	29.1	70.9	$1,337	$1,403	$1,280
Alabama	214,405	80,235	134,170	37.4	62.6	1,098	1,181	1,032
Alaska	69,439	34,225	35,214	49.3	50.7	2,178	2,136	2,208
Arizona	198,047	52,602	145,445	26.6	73.4	1,446	1,455	1,436
Arkansas	104,933	41,662	63,272	39.7	60.3	986	1,050	919
California	1,863,702	458,958	1,404,744	24.6	75.4	1,691	1,724	1,667
Colorado	205,880	67,144	138,736	32.6	67.4	1,392	1,407	1,378
Connecticut.........	192,950	61,156	131,794	31.7	68.3	1,367	1,545	1,197
Delaware	38,788	19,911	18,878	51.3	48.7	1,231	1,287	1,180
Florida	546,606	130,319	416,287	23.8	76.2	1,191	1,256	1,144
Georgia	321,270	99,483	221,787	31.0	69.0	1,049	1,083	1,021
Hawaii	68,360	51,522	16,838	75.4	24.6	1,401	1,507	1,323
Idaho	53,616	19,983	33,634	37.3	62.7	1,187	1,177	1,197
Illinois	745,017	179,239	565,778	24.1	75.9	1,477	1,546	1,413
Indiana............	295,018	94,073	200,945	31.9	68.1	1,193	1,314	1,063
Iowa	187,596	61,746	125,850	32.9	67.1	1,265	1,346	1,167
Kansas	146,027	49,364	96,662	33.8	66.2	1,156	1,206	1,101
Kentucky	177,384	71,740	105,644	40.4	59.6	1,136	1,205	1,061
Louisiana..........	239,571	94,735	144,836	39.5	60.5	1,073	1,165	991
Maine	58,674	22,893	35,781	39.0	61.0	1,147	1,155	1,138
Maryland	318,724	106,024	212,700	33.3	66.7	1,386	1,486	1,299
Massachusetts.......	394,623	94,859	299,765	24.0	76.0	1,387	1,523	1,280
Michigan	695,019	202,521	492,498	29.1	70.9	1,605	1,671	1,533
Minnesota	291,917	86,628	205,289	29.7	70.3	1,448	1,483	1,411
Mississippi	121,742	41,656	80,085	34.2	65.8	949	1,009	890
Missouri	260,813	81,099	179,715	31.1	68.9	1,145	1,156	1,134
Montana	53,825	20,591	33,234	38.3	61.7	1,241	1,285	1,196
Nebraska	109,078	32,281	76,796	29.6	70.4	1,191	1,186	1,195
Nevada	57,131	18,244	38,886	31.9	68.1	1,429	1,427	1,431
New Hampshire	46,923	17,843	29,080	38.0	62.0	1,133	1,129	1,137
New Jersey	517,540	123,803	393,737	23.9	76.1	1,408	1,591	1,246
New Mexico	90,842	42,350	48,492	46.6	53.4	1,190	1,235	1,143
New York	1,393,310	308,274	1,085,037	22.1	77.9	1,479	1,696	1,362
North Carolina	342,068	112,329	229,739	32.8	67.2	1,151	1,194	1,104
North Dakota	42,802	16,759	26,043	39.2	60.8	1,314	1,434	1,175
Ohio	614,271	153,527	460,743	25.0	75.0	1,304	1,410	1,205
Oklahoma	171,324	66,985	104,339	39.1	60.9	1,084	1,141	1,028
Oregon	189,163	60,859	128,303	32.2	67.8	1,401	1,404	1,398
Pennsylvania	635,029	175,314	459,714	27.6	72.4	1,345	1,432	1,270
Rhode Island	61,872	26,576	35,297	43.0	57.0	1,391	1,529	1,280
South Carolina	172,367	75,765	96,603	44.0	56.0	1,075	1,115	1,033
South Dakota	37,286	15,292	21,994	41.0	59.0	1,083	1,100	1,064
Tennessee	247,932	73,816	174,116	29.8	70.2	1,109	1,206	1,031
Texas	825,963	215,519	610,444	26.1	73.9	1,193	1,218	1,164
Utah	88,424	36,181	52,243	40.9	59.1	1,321	1,285	1,368
Vermont	28,071	13,713	14,358	48.9	51.1	1,148	1,119	1,186
Virginia	321,382	116,644	204,738	36.3	63.7	1,207	1,266	1,143
Washington	314,233	109,679	204,554	34.9	65.1	1,545	1,599	1,498
West Virginia	107,848	42,469	65,379	39.4	60.6	1,081	1,174	977
Wisconsin	325,165	92,794	232,371	28.5	71.5	1,447	1,540	1,350
Wyoming...........	40,429	13,302	27,126	32.9	67.1	1,342	1,398	1,282
Dist. of Col.	85,689	...	85,689	...	100.0	1,775	1,870	1,741

Source: U.S. Bureau of the Census, Public Employment in 1980.
Note: Statistics for local governments are estimates subject to sampling variation. Because of rounding, detail may not add to totals.

Table 5

STATE GOVERNMENT EMPLOYMENT (FULL-TIME EQUIVALENT), TOTAL AND FOR SELECTED FUNCTIONS, BY STATE: OCTOBER 1980

State	All functions	Education		Selected functions other than education							
		Institutions of higher education	Other education	Highways	Public welfare	Hospitals	Correction	Police protection	Natural resources	Financial administration	General control
All states	3,106,291	947,661	115,090	255,335	171,512	540,975	150,571	72,466	167,634	118,057	108,345
Alabama	62,530	20,531	5,692	3,948	4,170	10,820	1,821	1,177	3,113	1,957	2,293
Alaska	16,642	2,870	2,161	2,405	533	402	562	375	2,127	907	1,228
Arizona	37,310	14,071	2,994	3,309	1,833	3,833	1,840	1,425	1,896	1,662	748
Arkansas	37,577	10,974	3,519	3,960	2,173	5,120	1,105	820	2,747	1,309	799
California	248,833	82,676	4,685	15,828	2,238	28,930	9,386	8,488	18,293	11,012	5,447
Colorado	42,537	20.198	560	3,146	1,045	6,297	1,601	827	1,892	1,751	1,574
Connecticut	46,390	10,203	2,311	4,567	2,046	10,336	3,347	1,418	765	1,436	3,780
Delaware	15,563	4,309	243	1,335	629	2,660	1,003	600	493	687	906
Florida	104,664	24,208	2,293	7,351	5,968	14,641	10,651	2,395	7,839	3,770	5,522
Georgia	83,300	24,653	2,414	6,564	5,204	13,319	5,488	1,928	4,852	1,558	2,369
Hawaii	36,454	5,578	15,921	896	863	2,873	670	. . .	1,391	957	1,324
Idaho	14,881	4,901	477	1,447	1,190	1.098	472	217	1,564	665	376
Illinois	123,816	40,597	3,894	7,551	11,379	20,258	7,564	3,274	4,216	6,076	3,505
Indiana	66,564	30,933	3,080	5,285	1,191	10,546	3,136	1,771	2,508	2,027	971
Iowa	45,110	16,615	1,772	3,447	3,276	8,525	1,595	720	2,738	1,595	797
Kansas	37,815	14,892	659	3,825	915	5,829	1,478	573	2,344	1,631	1,877
Kentucky	57,719	17,434	4,154	6,933	4,873	4,782	2,347	1,578	4,873	1,587	3,112
Louisiana	81,292	19,870	3,903	7,528	4,145	19,752	4,405	1,336	4,429	2,359	1,557
Maine	18,131	4,605	1,095	2,729	1,150	1,841	681	338	1,691	762	571
Maryland	81,754	22,840	2,260	4,919	6,196	13,964	5,383	2,140	3,407	3,576	2,703
Massachusetts	78,226	14,619	1,666	5,302	8,460	20,238	3,475	1,582	2,427	3,701	7,150
Michigan	125,630	48,159	2,474	4,457	15,633	20,604	6,112	2,995	5,072	3,742	2,834
Minnesota	54,868	22,729	1,485	4,717	1,232	9,141	1,568	872	3,448	2,067	1,573
Mississippi	39,973	12,988	1,339	2,954	2,797	6,070	1,248	833	3,427	927	630
Missouri	65,268	16,773	1,912	6,212	5,499	15,056	2,850	1,771	4,016	1,928	1,941
Montana	15,639	4,735	441	2,009	1,011	1,266	576	292	1,801	1,106	381
Nebraska	28,211	12,059	965	2,271	1,097	3,570	1,253	525	2,093	697	1,030
Nevada	12,125	3,706	260	1,307	672	684	921	291	771	1,257	407
New Hampshire	14,413	4,516	355	1,892	1,092	2,086	486	275	703	391	441
New Jersey	87,350	21,170	2,477	8,301	4,978	17,217	4,139	4,162	2,463	3,964	4,034
New Mexico	33,730	12,041	886	2,453	1,709	3,594	1,068	611	1,605	1,610	1,766
New York	215,271	27,180	4,672	14,925	3,223	68,947	9,010	4,797	8,681	11,689	17,648
North Carolina	86,603	25,037	3,225	11,744	844	16,417	7,401	2,948	5,040	2,058	4,383
North Dakota	12,624	4,827	389	1,107	408	1,843	254	174	1,161	345	227
Ohio	114,997	45,074	2,294	7,566	1,510	23,129	6,586	1,966	5,429	4,580	2,290
Oklahoma	56,220	19,956	2,033	3,578	8,551	6,380	3,378	892	2,306	1,352	1,485
Oregon	43,076	11,654	1,123	3,350	3,967	6,203	1,921	1,120	3,462	1,886	1,218
Pennsylvania	127,145	21,458	2,610	15,846	11,225	29,703	4,260	4,660	7,060	6,197	3,251
Rhode Island	20,004	4,260	1,077	924	1,466	4,487	731	237	677	914	1,042
South Carolina	61,138	19,199	3,206	4,671	4,680	10,234	3,214	1,292	2,503	1,924	1,052
South Dakota	12,416	3,933	410	1,269	708	1,446	302	323	949	344	684
Tennessee	62,814	19,061	2,799	5,454	4,981	10,192	3,858	995	4,019	2,257	1,604
Texas	168,995	63,595	3,878	14,392	12,464	34,076	5,745	1,705	8,539	4,962	1,848
Utah	25,793	12,057	749	1,791	851	3,001	785	516	1,224	953	682
Vermont	10,984	3,553	340	1,071	744	1,121	389	432	709	503	489
Virginia	94,165	31,575	2,826	11,652	840	17,113	6,713	1,825	3,946	2,112	2,137
Washington	71,419	27,507	1,617	5,610	4,945	8,153	3,683	1,270	5,379	2,830	1,282
West Virginia	39,693	9,983	1,813	8,112	3,347	5,155	764	846	2,108	1,239	1,178
Wisconsin	59,531	28,790	1,497	1,776	1,083	7,044	3,103	690	2,614	2,552	1,926
Wyoming	9,088	2,509	185	1,649	478	979	243	169	824	686	273

Source: U.S. Bureau of the Census, *Public Employment in 1980*.

Table 6
STATE GOVERNMENT PAYROLLS,
TOTAL AND FOR SELECTED FUNCTIONS, BY STATE: OCTOBER 1980
(In thousands of dollars)

State	All functions	Education — Institution of higher education	Education — Other education	Highways	Public welfare	Hospitals	Correction	Police protection	Natural resources	Financial administration	General control
All states	4,284,687	1,450,130	157,913	345,865	204,876	616,445	20,507	119,077	220,075	153,022	172,436
Alabama	80,235	29,235	7,019	4,876	5,019	11,469	2,349	1,749	4,172	2,401	3,383
Alaska	34,225	5,645	4,457	4,675	875	708	1,249	1,067	4,546	1,839	2,811
Arizona	52,602	22,418	3,570	4,272	2,484	3,943	2,738	2,354	2,675	1,987	1,291
Arkansas	41,662	14,118	3,871	4,452	2,051	4,490	1,078	929	2,947	1,313	862
California	458,958	157,146	8,417	32,965	3,992	44,581	17,195	21,753	29,130	17,453	9,009
Colorado	67,144	33,142	852	5,345	1,490	8,774	2,557	1,257	3,051	2,404	2,684
Connecticut	61,156	15,141	3,387	5,979	2,429	11,171	4,544	1,931	1,133	1,764	5,774
Delaware	19,911	6,493	430	1,693	700	2,558	1,413	930	596	762	1,215
Florida	130,319	38,871	2,910	7,314	5,920	13,982	12,211	2,569	9,994	4,317	8,057
Georgia	99,483	33,839	3,252	7,458	5,707	13,151	5,925	2,578	5,771	1,950	2,835
Hawaii	51,522	9,793	22,798	1,283	980	3,326	777	. . .	2,072	1,347	1,825
Idaho	19,983	6,281	583	2,107	2,002	1,204	565	315	2,064	841	691
Illinois	179,239	66,987	5,369	11,780	14,266	25,907	10,520	5,602	5,601	7,486	4,523
Indiana	94,073	48,811	4,704	6,402	1,339	12,348	4,225	3,029	2,838	2,456	1,625
Iowa	61,746	27,229	1,646	5,026	3,619	9,678	2,129	570	3,431	1,964	1,474
Kansas	49,364	20,863	894	4,909	1,186	6,582	1,788	871	3,098	1,935	2,400
Kentucky	71,740	23,141	5,400	8,750	4,086	6,752	2,539	2,248	4,866	2,038	4,173
Louisiana	94,735	27,070	5,189	9,951	2,660	18,321	5,618	1,939	5,208	3,168	2,039
Maine...........	22,893	6,135	1,393	3,346	1,352	2,018	958	562	2,115	868	882
Maryland	106,024	28,521	3,440	6,186	7,572	15,152	7,607	3,524	3,863	4,856	5,451
Massachusetts....	94,859	19,946	2,104	7,525	9,823	19,834	4,438	2,308	2,297	4,479	10,112
Michigan	202,521	77,166	4,372	8,193	24,054	30,321	10,489	6,000	8,426	6,223	5,368
Minnesota	86,628	40,393	2,385	7,714	1,696	11,378	2,455	1,551	5,094	2,717	2,623
Mississippi.......	41,656	14,878	1,414	2,961	2,332	4,888	1,355	1,113	3,666	1,017	964
Missouri.........	81,099	25,507	1,948	7,866	5,770	15,820	3,018	2,485	5,311	1,944	2,864
Montana	20,591	6,377	579	2,919	1,187	1,459	710	430	2,338	1,285	599
Nebraska........	32,281	13,455	1,241	2,668	1,082	3,864	1,447	870	2,393	847	1,359
Nevada	18,244	5,806	400	2,039	970	990	1,261	383	1,189	1,724	657
New Hampshire ..	17,843	5,430	529	3,495	1,065	1,884	568	288	933	434	593
New Jersey	123,803	34,786	3,855	12,218	6,255	19,790	5,829	5,855	3,227	5,005	7,114
New Mexico	42,350	16,096	999	3,297	1,953	3,417	1,403	629	2,326	1,915	2,441
New York	308,274	41,262	6,180	19,695	4,368	85,504	13,027	7,709	10,087	13,980	33,222
North Carolina...	112,329	36,302	4,370	13,346	1,203	18,563	8,909	3,734	7,036	2,970	5,995
North Dakota....	16,759	7,023	495	1,416	402	1,810	289	263	1,805	420	374
Ohio	153,527	68,700	3,098	10,103	1,104	24,934	8,430	2,907	6,817	5,699	3,434
Oklahoma	66,985	26,942	2,567	4,073	9,374	6,085	3,513	1,336	2,383	1,518	1,982
Oregon	60,859	19,430	1,442	4,923	4,923	7,258	2,635	1,955	4,574	2,443	2,153
Pennsylvania.....	175,314	35,707	3,945	20,088	15,343	35,940	6,272	7,976	8,884	7,859	4,741
Rhode Island	26,576	5,649	1,586	1,152	1,927	5,864	1,064	517	839	1,204	1,541
South Carolina ...	75,765	27,363	4,119	4,740	4,970	10,322	3,701	1,777	2,893	2,272	1,785
South Dakota ...	15,292	5,206	551	1,679	773	1,382	364	416	1,266	444	947
Tennessee	73,816	26,220	3,298	5,612	5,166	9,766	4,032	1,249	4,504	2,602	2,629
Texas	215,519	91,723	4,593	19,423	14,316	33,167	6,742	2,524	10,607	6,344	3,523
Utah............	36,181	16,091	1,225	2,972	1,259	3,115	1,294	918	1,865	1,251	1,126
Vermont	13,713	4,544	425	1,525	838	1,023	476	721	943	569	662
Virginia	116,644	46,314	3,352	12,434	913	16,608	7,691	2,568	4,683	2,442	2,994
Washington	109,679	47,089	2,527	9,631	6,563	10,371	5,388	2,320	7,202	4,182	2,217
West Virginia	42,469	12,826	1,966	7,954	3,196	4,355	696	1,083	2,452	1,308	1,508
Wisconsin	92,794	46,938	2,469	3,294	1,672	9,492	4,717	1,103	3,579	3,844	3,436
Wyoming........	13,302	4,080	298	2,192	652	1,128	312	310	1,284	932	469

Source: U.S. Bureau of the Census, *Public Employment in 1980*. Note: Because of rounding, detail may not add to totals.

Table 7
STATE GOVERNMENT LABOR-MANAGEMENT RELATIONS: OCTOBER 1980

State	Labor-management relations policy		Full-time employees who belong to an employee organization		Labor-management agreements Contractual agreements		Memoranda of understanding	Bargaining units		Work stoppages Oct. 1979-Oct. 1980
	Collective negotiations	Meet and confer	Number	Percentage of total full-time	Number	Number of employees covered		Number	Employees represented	
All states	...	...	1,162,878	40.5	728	837,628	231	978	1,001,842	22
Alabama	Yes	Yes	14,405	24.4	9	2,735	1	16	4,484	...
Alaska	Yes	Yes	10,837	67.9	28	11,269	1	29	11,314	...
Arizona	No	Yes	6,323	18.1	...	...	...	...	...	...
Arkansas	No	No	4,892	14.0	...	...	...	...	...	...
California	Yes	Yes	105,146	48.1	...	...	...	...	...	...
Colorado	Yes	Yes	13,742	37.8	...	...	...	...	...	1
Connecticut.........	Yes	Yes	37,961	78.5	21	40,228	1	28	40,228	...
Delaware	Yes	Yes	5,978	40.0	25	5,888	8	31	6,290	...
Florida	Yes	Yes	82,969	84.5	3	50,443	...	8	94,950	1
Georgia	No	No	13,409	17.0	...	...	...	...	...	...
Hawaii	Yes	Yes	30,226	88.5	12	30,418	1	12	30,418	...
Idaho	No	No	3,512	25.4	...	...	...	...	...	...
Illinois	Yes	Yes	50,529	44.5	104	56,420	6	105	56,998	1
Indiana.............	Yes	Yes	10,881	18.7	2	574	1	8	3,730	...
Iowa................	Yes	No	6,999	18.2	4	18,200	...	7	18,200	...
Kansas	No	Yes	5,949	17.3	...	...	27	29	9,295	...
Kentucky	No	No	1,680	2.9	...	...	...	...	...	...
Louisiana...........	Yes	Yes	12,336	15.7	39	10,002	5	50	11,039	...
Maine	Yes	Yes	11,794	69.4	8	11,937	...	8	11,937	...
Maryland	Yes	Yes	31,942	41.3	3	1,992	...	5	2,053	...
Massachusetts........	Yes	Yes	50,212	67.4	35	70,496	3	35	70,496	2
Michigan	Yes	Yes	56,155	54.0	49	28,714	35	70	55,534	1
Minnesota	Yes	Yes	26,281	54.3	35	32,400	3	16	32,442	...
Mississippi	Yes	Yes	4,440	12.1	...	...	...	...	...	...
Missouri............	No	Yes	16,181	27.3	...	...	8	16	17,550	...
Montana	Yes	No	7,583	53.7	55	7,392	...	107	7,773	1
Nebraska	Yes	Yes	4,415	17.9	15	5,501	1	17	6,012	...
Nevada.............	No	Yes	4,012	36.4	...	...	...	...	...	...
New Hampshire	Yes	Yes	5,334	41.5	1	8,884	4	2	8,884	1
New Jersey	Yes	Yes	36,986	45.2	27	64,711	24	28	64,711	3
New Mexico	Yes	Yes	4,590	14.7	9	4,865	3	10	5,650	...
New York	Yes	Yes	173,271	82.6	10	183,378	9	10	183,378	3
North Carolina	No	No	31,164	38.1	...	...	...	...	...	...
North Dakota	Yes	Yes	3,540	30.9	1	76	2	2	293	...
Ohio	Yes	Yes	29,060	27.5	...	...	15	45	32,624	1
Oklahoma	No	No	2,101	4.2	...	...	...	...	...	...
Oregon	Yes	Yes	18,976	48.3	69	28,291	8	70	28,357	1
Pennsylvania........	Yes	Yes	73,208	60.3	26	80,323	19	40	100,511	3
Rhode Island........	Yes	Yes	16,817	88.3	20	15,135	19	20	15,135	1
South Carolina	No	No	7,669	13.2	...	...	...	...	...	...
South Dakota	Yes	Yes	1,554	13.7	6	1,028	...	9	1,242	...
Tennessee	No	Yes	13,995	23.7	...	...	1	1	311	...
Texas	No	No	21,658	14.0	...	...	...	...	...	...
Utah	No	No	8,578	35.8	...	...	...	...	...	...
Vermont	Yes	No	6,824	65.5	4	5,036	...	4	5,036	...
Virginia	No	No	18,908	21.8	...	...	...	...	...	...
Washington..........	Yes	Yes	23,293	36.2	100	32,822	26	128	36,497	1
West Virginia	No	Yes	3,301	8.8	...	...	...	...	...	...
Wisconsin	Yes	No	28,223	53.9	8	28,470	...	12	28,470	1
Wyoming............	No	No	3,039	36.5	...	...	...	...	...	...

Source: U.S. Bureau of the Census, *Labor-Management Relations in State and Local Governments: 1980.*

Section VII   FINANCES

1. Revenue, Expenditure and Debt

AN EVENTFUL HALF-CENTURY
OF STATE GOVERNMENT FINANCES

By Maurice Criz and David Kellerman

OURS IS A NATION of great diversity. We are a variety of peoples, we maintain a broad and varied economic base, and we adapt constantly to change. Such diversity is reflected in our system of government, with three levels working in relative harmony to balance resources against the changing needs of the citizens.

Among the three levels of government, the states have been most effective at meeting changing public needs while maintaining a constant position. In contrast, the federal government has undergone change in its position in society, having become a more dominant social and economic force. Local governments—the cities, counties and special purpose governments—have likewise undergone a transformation in their ability to respond to public needs, largely due to their lack of the economic and statutory wherewithal to provide new services and develop new sources of revenue.

The past 50 years have been interesting for state governments. They have managed through depression and prosperity, war and peace, and rapid change, always finding ways to raise the funds necessary to provide services called for by the public. A review of the period from 1932 to 1980, in terms of dollar volume of state government fiscal activity, gives the impression that we are comparing different solar systems. Revenues went from $2.5 billion in 1932 to $277.0 billion in 1980; expenditures, from $2.8 billion to $257.8 billion; and debt outstanding, from $2.8 billion to $122.0 billion. Little would be gained by reciting how many billions this tax or that tax furnishes now compared to then, or similarly for this functional expenditure or that one. Rather, we believe it will be more useful to analyze the composition of state revenue sources, how some tax groups have grown in relative importance while others have decreased, and the larger role played by federal grants-in-aid. As to expenditures, we will see a changing pattern among the various functions and the growth in support of local governments.

Providing the Funds

In 1932, state governments raised 78 percent of their general revenue (i.e., excluding insurance trust, liquor stores and utility revenue) from taxes, 11 percent from charges and miscellaneous sources, and 11 percent from intergovernmental revenue from the federal and local governments. General sales taxes were practically non-existent in that year, while selective sales taxes furnished 30 percent of general revenue—motor fuel taxes alone provided

The authors are Senior Advisor and Statistician, respectively, Governments Division, U.S. Bureau of the Census. Sources are U.S. Bureau of the Census, *Historical Statistics on Governmental Finances and Employment* (vol. 6, no. 4, of the 1977 Census of Governments) and annual reports of *State Government Finances, Governmental Finances*, and *Public Employment*.

21.7 percent. Motor vehicle and operators licenses produced an additional 13.8 percent. Property taxes were still effective revenue producers for the states, yielding 13.5 percent of general revenue. Individual income taxes were in force in 19 states, but produced only 3.1 percent, while corporate income taxes in 20 states provided 3.3 percent.[1]

Clearly, state governments then were not in the habit of taxing economic activity generally, but rather targeted, specific activities (such as the sale of motor fuel or the privilege of driving a motor vehicle) as their primary revenue sources. This was very much in keeping with the spirit of the times, characterized by a strong sense of laissez-faire.

The Great Depression changed things, however. During the 1930s, the many pressures for funds established a new star producer for the states—general sales and gross receipts taxes. These were frequently enacted as "emergency" taxes for a single year, but as the public grew accustomed to paying the slight add-on to price, and as state tax collectors and budget directors came to rely on sales tax productivity, the taxes were transformed to permanent status. Twenty-three states and Hawaii enacted general sales taxes in that decade, and in 1940, they produced 11.4 percent of general revenue. Other excise taxes were also adopted by states from coast to coast—liquor taxes by 29 states and cigarette taxes by 19 states. Individual income taxes were adopted by 16 states and corporate income taxes by 15—both of these were at much lower rates and lacked the progressive rate structures used today.

At the same time, withdrawal of states from the property tax field continued, so that in 1940 only 5.9 percent of general revenue came from this source, as against 13.5 percent in 1932.

A strongly expanding national economy resulting from war production before and during World War II, postwar conversion to production of civilian goods and manufacturing facilities worldwide, and more states adopting general sales and cigarette taxes continued the shifting trend in revenue sources during the 1940s. General sales taxes were enacted by five states, and the percentage of general revenue from this source increased to 14.8 in 1950. Cigarette taxes were passed by 15 states, so that taxes on tobacco products rose to 3.7 percent. Individual income taxes increased to 6.4 percent, and corporate income taxes produced 5.2 percent. Property taxes fell further to 2.7 percent of general revenue.

The period from 1950 to 1980 continued the trends described above. More states broadened their tax bases and increased tax rates, so that currently all 50 states have gasoline, alcoholic beverage and tobacco taxes, 45 have general sales and gross receipts taxes, 44 have individual income taxes and 45 have corporation income taxes. During this period, growth in population and the labor force, an expanding national economy, and increasing income and price levels all worked in favor of taxes based on incomes or prices. Thus, in 1980 state individual income taxes accounted for 15.9 percent of general revenue, corporate income taxes were 5.7 percent, and general sales and gross receipts taxes were 18.5 percent. At the same time, taxes based on volume of commodities purchased or taxes with flat rates diminished in relative importance. Motor fuel taxes fell to 4.2 percent of general revenue (a contributing factor being reduction in consumption), and motor vehicle and operators licenses dropped to 2.3 percent. Property taxes declined further to 1.2 percent, with taxation of property in general now having largely disappeared as a state revenue source. Charges and miscellaneous revenue, which are looked to as alternative revenue sources, increased to a high of 13.8 percent of general revenue.

An outstanding feature of this half-century has been the growth in intergovernmental revenue from the federal government. Federal grants-in-aid have ranged over practically the entire spectrum of state activities, from public welfare, education and highways to health, hospitals, natural resources, airports and many others. In 1932, these provided 9.2 percent of state government general revenue and increased sharply to 15.2 percent in 1940. They rose steadily through the years, with general revenue sharing being added in 1972, and reached a high point of 26.5 percent in 1980. This compared with 72.4 percent state governments raised from their own revenue sources. An additional 1 percent came from local intergovernmental revenue.

Funds for capital outlay (construction, purchase of land and existing structures, and equipment) come primarily from the sale of bonds and notes. Short-term debt was used generally to meet temporary needs for operating funds. It is interesting that during the deep depression year of 1932 total debt outstanding was 10 percent more than total state revenue.

During the balance of the half-century, total debt outstanding ranged narrowly between 27 and 57 percent of total revenue. The relationship is significant because the amount of funds required to meet principal and interest obligations is a prime factor in determining the tax revenue that has to be produced and the service charges to be collected from toll roads, bridges and other revenue bond projects.

The amount of state debt outstanding began a 30-year period of sharp expansion in the 1950s, due primarily to construction of classrooms and dormitories for institutions of higher education and improvement or replacement of road systems. Much of this construction was necessary at the outset to catch up with projects postponed during World War II. Also, states entered into an era of extensive construction of administrative office buildings.

The composition of the type of debt issued has altered significantly over the years. In 1942, the earliest year for which these data are available, 85 percent of long-term debt (payable more than one year after date of issue) was full-faith and credit debt, for which the credit of the government is unconditionally pledged. In contrast, 15 percent was non-guaranteed debt, payable solely from pledged specific sources such as earnings of revenue producing activities, or from specific non-property taxes. In 1950, the distribution was about the same, but by 1960 the percentage for non-guaranteed debt increased to one-half, by 1970 to slightly more than one-half (54 percent), and then to 59 percent in 1980.

This radical change in the character of debt issued was the result of large demands for funds by the states and favorable reception by the bond market of issues backed by revenues from toll roads and bridges, university dormitories, sports centers, etc., or by revenues from specific taxes. This relieved states of the need to convince taxpayers to support issuance of full-faith and credit debt in such large amounts.

Providing the Services

The period from 1932 to the present was characterized by significant changes in the level of state government expenditure and the scope of state government activities. Statistically, this was reflected by the changing distribution of state spending among different functions, and between capital outlay and current operation.

It is interesting to note, however, that the distribution of total state spending between direct expenditure and indirect expenditure (intergovernmental payments to local governments) remained relatively stable over the years, hovering around a split of two-thirds and one-third. This reflects little change in the overall intent of the states to provide services or to provide financial assistance to their localities and let them meet public needs directly.

The composition of state spending, in terms of function and object (such as for capital outlay), has undergone considerable change over the years in response to economic conditions and social needs. Capital outlay—that is, construction of buildings or roads and the purchase of equipment, land and structures—has lost much of its place. Amounting to 25 percent of total expenditure in 1932, capital outlay fell off to half this ratio in 1940 and 1950, then increased to 21 percent in 1960, but diminished again to 16 percent in 1970 and 9 percent in 1980.

This is quite indicative of one evolving emphasis of state governments—their emergence as providers of specific services for people rather than as forces which shape the economic or social environment. State governments now operate more universities and hospitals, take active roles in equitable financing of local education, provide direct assistance to the needy and aged and so forth. In contrast, the role of state governments at the outset of the period under study was more one of a business and economic regulator, or a builder of transportation systems (e.g., the infrastructure necessary for business and society to function smoothly). States have not abandoned this latter role, and it still is an important aspect of state government activity. In terms of the level of financial activity, however, such functions have become less significant.

Table A depicts the change in the relative importance of selected services provided by state governments, as measured by the percentage distribution of state spending for selected categories. The split between direct and indirect spending shows the consistency of the states. Also, quite evident is the rapid decline in capital outlay relative to current operating expenditure. For 1980, this clearly reflected the states' response to the condition of the economy and the high rates of interest which prevailed, holding down borrowing for capital projects.

Table A
PERCENTAGE DISTRIBUTION, SELECTED ITEMS OF
STATE GOVERNMENT EXPENDITURE, 1932 TO 1980

Item	1980	1970	1960	1950	1940	1932
Total expenditure	100	100	100	100	100	100
Intergovernmental	33	34	30	28	32	28
Direct	67	66	70	72	68	72
Current operation	42	36	30	30	30	35
Capital outlay	9	16	21	15	14	28
Interest on debt	3	2	2	1	3	4
Assistance and subsidies	4	5	6	13	10	3
Insurance benefits	10	7	11	14	12	2
General expenditure, by function	100	100	100	100	100	100
Highways	11	17	27	22	26	39
Education	39	40	33	28	25	24
Health and hospitals	8	7	7	8	7	8
Public welfare	19	17	14	19	22	4
Interest on general debt	3	2	2	1	3	4
All other	20	17	17	22	17	21

Note: Detail may not add to totals due to rounding.

Assistance and subsidies to citizens or private institutions went up sharply in relative terms from 1932 to 1950, and then reversed direction. This category includes cash assistance payments to public welfare recipients, veterans' bonuses, direct cash grants for tuition and scholarships, and aid to non-public educational institutions.

Insurance benefits and repayments expanded sharply in the 1930s. This category includes cash payments to beneficiaries of employee retirement, unemployment compensation, workers' compensation and disability benefit social insurance programs. Regardless of peaks and recessions in the economy, higher or lower rates of unemployment, inflation or deflation, insurance trust benefits grew during the 1930s to become a major sector of state government activity and continue to maintain that role. From 2 percent of total expenditure in 1932, insurance benefits have stayed at between 7 and 14 percent of total spending since 1940.

State expenditure for general government functions (i.e., excluding insurance trust, liquor stores and utilities) increased strongly in percentages spent for education and public welfare, while the proportion for highways fell off sharply.

Expenditure for education increased steadily from about one-fourth of state expenditure in 1932 and 1940 to about 40 percent in 1970 and 1980. Public welfare expenditure during the 1930s jumped from 4 percent to 22 percent, fell back to 14 percent by 1960, then increased again to 19 percent in 1980. Health and hospitals expenditure remained at 7 to 8 percent for the entire half-century. Expenditure for highways, in contrast to the other major functions, experienced a steep drop from 39 percent in 1932 to 22 percent in 1950, then increased to 27 percent in 1960, but declined sharply to 11 percent in 1980. Highway expenditure has been outpaced by growth in the other major functions mentioned above, but in the latter part of the period was also subject to construction and maintenance cutbacks due to revenue shortages that resulted from the OPEC crisis and much higher gasoline prices, fuel conservation of various types including more efficient automobiles, the flattening out of motor fuel tax collections, effects of price inflation on construction costs, and all-time highs in interest rates for bond issues.

State intergovernmental expenditure to local governments, including federal funds passed through states, has exhibited some interesting features since 1932. Overall, intergovernmental expenditure ranged from 29 to 41 percent of state general expenditure, and was 37 percent in 1980. Education, throughout the half-century, was always the leading function, growing steadily from one-half of state intergovernmental expenditure to slightly less than two-thirds today. State aid programs for education were reorganized substantially following the California Supreme Court decision in *Serrano* v. *Priest* in 1971, which led to a broader role for states in ensuring equality of spending on education.

Public welfare is second in importance of state aid, comprising 13 percent of state intergovernmental expenditure in 1980. It has grown steadily through the years from 3.5 percent in 1932, although it was as high as 25 percent of the total in 1940.

General local government support ranks third, with 10 percent of the total. It has generally maintained a narrow range between 8 and 11 percent. These general support funds may be applied at the discretion of the local governments to any of their functions. This has been an especially significant category in recent years since passage of Proposition 13 in California restricting local property tax assessments, similar legislation in other states and restrictions on taxation and/or spending in still more states. State surplus funds were initially used to relieve fiscal stress of local governments, but these surpluses are reported to be no longer available so that local governments will be forced to devise additional revenue sources or cut expenditures.

Grants for highways, roads and streets accounted for 5 percent of state intergovernmental expenditure in 1980, a low point from the 29 percent they represented in 1932.

What we have seen, then, with respect to states and the services they provide, has been a solid historical record of responding to the changing needs of society. State governments have served well in this sense, as clearly indicated by the changing distribution of state government expenditure.

The states have also been successful in their role as intermediaries, financially assisting their local governments. From this viewpoint, total state payments to local governments were a substantial 36 percent of total local government general revenue in 1980, considerably higher than the 14 percent of funds which local governments received from their states in 1932. For individual functions, state intergovernmental expenditure in 1980 was 54 percent of local general expenditure for education, 35 percent for highways and 89 percent for public welfare. In 1932, the comparable percentages were education, 20 percent; highways, 26 percent; and public welfare, 8 percent.

In conclusion, state governments have emerged from a half-century in which they experienced major changes, both in how funds were raised and in how funds were spent. Current events give every indication that states will continue to be challenged to adapt to changes as the decade of the 1980s progresses. Recently, states lost the $2.25 billion that they have been receiving annually from the federal government under general revenue sharing, and they are facing reductions in other grants-in-aid. Their tax collections are being threatened by a depressed national economy and increasing unemployment. At the same time, costs of operation and capital outlay continue at high levels because of high prices and interest rates, growing requirements for retirement systems and financial needs of local governments. Maintaining fiscal solvency will be a difficult, though not insurmountable, challenge.

Note

1. For dates of adoption of major state taxes, see Advisory Commission on Intergovernmental Relations, *Significant Features of Fiscal Federalism* (1979-80 edition), Table 74.

STATE AND LOCAL GOVERNMENT FINANCES
IN 1979-80

STATE AND LOCAL government finances performed well during the 1979-80 biennium, even though the fiscal screw tightened late in the period. Gross National Product (GNP) in current dollars increased at rates of 12 to 16 percent during the last two quarters of calendar year 1978 and the first quarter of 1979, but went up by only 6 percent in the second quarter of 1979. It then picked up in the next three quarters to increases ranging from 9 to 13 percent, but fell sharply during the second quarter of 1980 to a recessionary decrease of 1 percent.

The unemployment rate was nearly level in calendar 1979, starting the year at 5.8 percent, and increasing to 6 percent at the close of the year.[1] By mid-1980, it had increased to 7.7 percent. Automobile and construction employment were hit especially hard due to imports of cars, high interest rates and inflation.

Inflation during 1979 was seriously aggravated by sharp increases in oil prices, due to cutbacks in Iranian production and three increases in the Saudi benchmark price. By January 1980, the world price of oil reached $28 per barrel, more than double the level of a year earlier. The Consumer Price Index (CPI) rose by 13 percent, largely due to sharp advances in energy prices and the costs of home purchase and finance.

The rise in real income flattened out in the last three quarters of 1979, but personal consumption expenditure increased about 1.5 percent during the year, as the personal saving rate fell. This, of course, benefited state and local government collections of sales and income taxes.

Fiscal and monetary policies of the federal government were somewhat restrictive during the year and, combined with oil-induced inflation, resulted in sharply higher interest rates in the second half of 1979. During that period, interest on the 91-day treasury bill went from 9.3 to 12.1 percent, and the prime rate rose from 11.5 to 15.5 percent. Early in March 1980, inflation of the CPI rose to an annual rate of 18 percent, and the prime rate reached 17.75 percent. However, in the second quarter real GNP dropped at an annual rate of 9.9 percent. Interest rates dropped sharply due to weakening loan demand and a declining economy. By July 1980 the prime rate had fallen to 11 percent from a peak of 20 percent.

Through all of these events, state and local general revenue increased by 11 percent in each of the fiscal years 1979 and 1980, and general expenditure increased at the same rate. General revenue exceeded expenditure by $15.8 billion in 1979 and by $13.2 billion in 1980.

Adapted by Maurice Criz, Senior Advisor, and David Kellerman, Statistician, Governments Division, U.S. Bureau of the Census, from the Bureau's report, *Government Finances in 1979-80* and prior annual reports. The financial statistics for 1979-80 relate to governmental fiscal years which ended June 30, 1980, or at some date within the previous 12 months, with the following exceptions: the state government and the school districts of Alabama, having fiscal years which ended September 30, 1980; the state government and the school districts of Texas, having fiscal years which ended August 31, 1980; and the state government of Michigan having a fiscal year which ended September 30, 1980.

The demand for capital outlay funds continued at a high level. Long-term debt issued increased $42 billion in both 1979 and 1980, to a total of $335.6 billion long-term debt outstanding at the end of 1980. Short-term debt outstanding amounted to $13.1 billion.

Government Revenue

Tax collections of state and local governments rose constantly, but at a somewhat slower rate of increase than previously. Taxes increased by 6.1 percent in fiscal 1979 and by 8.7 percent in 1980, compared to 10 to 12 percent in the preceding three years. State and local taxes totaled $223.5 billion in 1980, or $987 per capita.

Overall, tax collections of all three levels of government (federal, state and local) reached $574.2 billion in 1980, an increase of 9.5 percent over fiscal 1979 collections. On a per capita basis, this amounted to $2,535. It should be noted that the Social Security taxes collected by the federal government from employees and employers are treated as federal insurance trust revenue in Census Bureau data, and thus are not reflected in the federal total of tax collections. These collections for Social Security amounted to $136.4 billion in fiscal 1980.

State and local government income taxes continued as the fastest growing major tax source. Total income tax collections rose 12.9 percent during fiscal 1980 and accounted for 14.5 percent of all state and local government general revenue. With personal income increasing at annual rates of 12.0 percent in calendar 1978 and 12.9 percent in 1979, individual income tax collections of state and local governments rose sharply, by 13.9 percent during fiscal 1980. Corporate net income taxes grew at a slower rate, by 9.8 percent.

Sales and gross receipts taxes remained the largest source of tax revenue for states and localities in total. Such taxes, including both those on general sales and those on the sale of selective items, totaled $79.9 billion in 1980 or 20.9 percent of all state and local government general revenue.

Property tax collections continued to decline in relative importance as a government revenue source. Ten years ago, property tax collections accounted for 26 percent of all state and local government general revenue and 41 percent of all local government general revenue. By fiscal 1980, such taxes were 18 percent of all state and local government general revenue and 28 percent of all local government general revenue.

As property taxes have declined as a revenue source, governments have relied increasingly on intergovernmental revenue, especially from the federal government. As indicated in Table 2, intergovernmental aid accounted for 44 percent of total local government general revenue in fiscal 1980, substantially exceeding tax collections in importance as a revenue source. Revenue from the federal government accounted for 22 percent of all state and local general revenue. Ten years ago, such federal aid accounted for about 17 percent of all state and local general revenue. Included in the total of federal aid is the receipt of federal general revenue sharing monies, which have accounted for between 2 and 3 percent of all state and local general revenue annually since the program's inception.

The complexity of financing state and local government programs can be seen from Table 6, which shows the significance of intergovernmental aid among the levels of government. The importance of federal aid varied among the state areas, ranging from between 12.1 to 31.1 percent of total state and local general revenue, and contributing 51.1 percent of the general revenue of the District of Columbia.

Non-tax revenue from own sources has become more significant to state and local governments, as tax limitation measures have taken effect in numerous states. Revenue from user charges has increased slightly in relative importance since 1978, particularly at the local government level. Interest earnings of state and local governments also have increased in relative importance, from 2.6 percent of general revenue in fiscal 1978 to 4.5 percent in fiscal 1980. Overall, these charges and miscellaneous revenues now account for nearly 20 percent of state and local general revenue, up from 16.7 percent in fiscal 1978.

Government Expenditure

State and local government expenditure increased at the same rate as revenue through fiscal 1980. General expenditure increased 11.3 percent to $369 billion, utility expenditure rose 18.2 percent to $34 billion, and government-operated liquor stores expenditure increased 7.2 percent to $2.6 billion. The insurance trust financial sector showed an increase of 22.5 percent in total expenditure during the year, the largest portion being an increase of $3.2 billion in payments from unemployment compensation funds.

As indicated in Table 8, per capita direct general expenditure of state and local governments amounted to $1,622. There was a great deal of variation, however, among the states, both in terms of total general expenditure and for the many functional categories of expenditure. Total per capita direct general expenditure of all levels of government amounted to $3,192 with the federal government accounting for $1,571 of this total.

There was little functional change in the distribution of state and local government direct general expenditure. Education ($133.2 billion), public welfare ($45.6 billion), highways ($33.3 billion), hospitals ($23.8 billion) and police ($13.5 billion) continued to account for most state and local outlays during fiscal 1980.

Interest payments on general debt for state and local governments amounted to $14.7 billion. If interest payments on utility debt of state and local governments are combined with payments on general government debt, the total would amount to $17.6 billion, or $78 per capita. When combined with the interest payments on federal debt, total interest expenditure for fiscal 1980 was $78.9 billion, or $348 per capita.

Government Debt

Indebtedness of all levels of government amounted to $5,518 per capita at the close of fiscal 1980. The federal share of this figure was $4,037, the state government share $538 and the local government share $943.

Table 1 gives an indication of the extent to which variation in per capita indebtedness exists among the states. Alaska had the largest per capita state and local debt burden ($10,098), with the District of Columbia ($4,166) and Nebraska ($2,933) ranked next. Idaho had the lowest per capita debt ($712), along with Indiana ($715) and North Carolina ($752). Of the state and local long-term debt of $322 billion, 46 percent was full faith and credit (guaranteed) debt.

Data Presentation

Tables presented here contain data covering state and local governments only, except for Table 2, which presents summary data for all three levels of government—federal, state and local. National summaries are presented in Tables 2 and 3, with all other tables presenting data on a state-by-state basis.

Per capita amounts were computed on the basis of estimated resident population of the United States as of July 1 of the specified year, except for the fiscal 1980 amounts, which were computed on the basis of the April 1, 1980 population from the decennial census.

Table 9 shows selected items of state and local government finance in relation to personal income. Estimates of personal income can be used as one of the measures of the relative fiscal capacity of states.

Use of the terms "general" revenue, "general" expenditure and "general" debt refers to the general government sector, i.e., all government activity excluding liquor stores operation, insurance trust systems and utilities. The latter sector is comprised of electric, gas and water supply, as well as transit systems operated by government units. Effective with fiscal 1977, the coverage of the utility sector was expanded to include state-operated utilities. For years prior to 1977, utility coverage was applicable only to local governments. This classification change should be kept in mind if current data are being compared with pre-1977 data.

Note

1. Reflects seasonally adjusted data.

Table 1
INDEBTEDNESS OF STATE AND LOCAL GOVERNMENTS
AT END OF FISCAL 1980, BY STATE
(In millions of dollars, except per capita amounts)

State or other jurisdiction	Total	Long-term debt		Short-term debt	Per capita debt	
		Total	Full faith and credit		Total	Long-term only
United States............	$335,603.1	$322,455.8	$149,802.2	$13,147.3	$1,481.66	$1,423.62
Alabama..................	4,081.2	3,890.2	1,209.6	191.0	1,049.14	1,000.05
Alaska...................	4,039.2	4,038.6	144.1	0.7	10,098.03	10,096.41
Arizona	4,752.2	4,606.0	1,617.2	146.2	1,748.42	1,694.64
Arkansas	2,017.2	1,984.1	472.8	33.0	882.79	868.34
California................	24,209.4	23,928.5	13,779.5	280.9	1,022.83	1,010.97
Colorado	3,801.2	3,756.2	1,567.6	45.0	1,315.76	1,300.17
Connecticut..............	5,787.3	5,358.5	3,427.8	428.8	1,862.07	1,724.09
Delaware	1,621.8	1,583.8	634.0	38.0	2,725.79	2,661.87
Florida..................	10,473.8	10,315.0	3,323.5	158.8	1,075.34	1,059.04
Georgia..................	6,204.8	6,080.3	1,644.4	124.6	1,135.58	1,112.78
Hawaii	2,181.1	2,146.3	1,696.8	34.8	2,260.25	2,224.16
Idaho	672.4	647.0	203.8	25.5	712.33	685.36
Illinois..................	15,282.9	14,165.3	6,814.4	1,117.6	1,338.49	1,240.61
Indiana	3,924.8	3,769.5	917.7	155.3	714.90	686.61
Iowa	2,294.9	2,278.0	810.9	16.9	787.82	782.01
Kansas	3,276.6	3,158.2	1,000.0	118.4	1,386.64	1,336.51
Kentucky	7,421.8	7,391.7	1,139.7	30.2	2,027.27	2,019.03
Louisiana	7,088.9	7,026.7	3,733.3	62.1	1,686.22	1,671.44
Maine	1,339.2	1,285.0	724.5	54.3	1,190.43	1,142.19
Maryland	7,500.6	7,288.3	5,186.2	212.3	1,779.07	1,728.71
Massachusetts	10,237.1	9,117.4	6,107.5	1,119.7	1,784.41	1,589.24
Michigan	11,117.7	10,832.2	6,639.2	285.5	1,200.87	1,170.04
Minnesota	8,680.4	8,563.5	5,601.6	117.0	2,129.13	2,100.43
Mississippi	2,130.8	2,095.5	1,513.4	35.3	845.24	831.22
Missouri	4,229.5	4,128.2	1,514.6	101.3	860.17	839.58
Montana	852.7	845.7	186.0	7.0	1,083.49	1,074.63
Nebraska	4,604.3	4,417.4	638.3	186.9	2,932.67	2,813.62
Nevada..................	1,314.7	1,311.4	653.4	3.3	1,645.41	1,641.31
New Hampshire	1,294.7	1,220.8	564.2	74.0	1,405.80	1,325.50
New Jersey...............	12,617.4	11,484.0	5,059.7	1,133.4	1,713.39	1,559.48
New Mexico..............	1,892.5	1,888.8	319.3	3.8	1,455.80	1,452.89
New York................	46,496.3	43,733.8	18,767.0	2,762.5	2,648.31	2,490.96
North Carolina	4,416.9	4,188.9	2,364.1	228.0	751.94	713.12
North Dakota	825.8	822.4	210.3	3.4	1,264.62	1,259.45
Ohio	10,481.4	9,249.0	5,114.3	1,232.4	970.77	856.63
Oklahoma	3,374.1	3,324.1	1,168.7	50.0	1,115.42	1,098.88
Oregon	7,026.0	6,906.4	5,730.4	119.6	2,668.45	2,623.01
Pennsylvania	20,392.6	19,641.0	7,756.4	751.6	1,718.43	1,655.09
Rhode Island	2,028.9	1,866.2	584.9	162.8	2,142.49	1,970.60
South Carolina	3,347.7	3,221.4	1,232.8	126.3	1,073.32	1,032.83
South Dakota	1,133.6	1,131.5	99.0	2.1	1,642.95	1,639.86
Tennessee................	6,039.9	5,679.9	2,864.2	360.0	1,315.59	1,237.18
Texas	20,660.1	20,411.4	9,681.3	248.7	1,452.07	1,434.59
Utah	1,414.4	1,413.4	627.2	1.0	968.12	967.42
Vermont.................	788.9	754.0	333.6	34.9	1,543.84	1,475.53
Virginia..................	5,863.4	5,517.8	2,509.3	345.6	1,096.77	1,032.13
Washington	11,624.7	11,506.6	3,854.8	118.1	2,814.70	2,786.10
West Virginia.............	324.71	3,223.3	1,131.5	23.9	1,665.18	1,652.92
Wisconsin	5,673.2	5,494.0	4,027.8	179.3	1,205.79	1,167.68
Wyoming	1,166.6	1,166.0	297.9	0.5	2,476.76	2,475.68
Dist. of Col...............	2,657.9	2,602.8	1,305.6	55.1	4,165.98	4,079.64

Source: U.S. Bureau of the Census, *Governmental Finances in 1979-80.*

Note: Because of rounding, detail may not add to total.

Table 2
SUMMARY OF GOVERNMENTAL FINANCES, BY LEVEL OF GOVERNMENT: 1979-80
(In millions of dollars, except per capita amounts)

Sources	All governments	Federal government	State and local governments			Per capita		
			Total	State	Local	Total	Federal government	State and local governments
Total revenue	$932,199 (a)	$565,477	$451,537 (a)	$276,962	$258,298 (a)	$4,115.58 (a)	$2,496.53	$1,993.50 (a)
Total general revenue	716,629 (a)	419,123	382,322 (a)	233,592	232,453 (a)	3,163.86 (a)	1,850.39	1,687.92 (a)
Intergovernmental revenue	(a)	1,787	83,029	64,326	102,425	(a)	7.89	366.56
From federal government	(a)		83,029	61,892	21,136	(a)		366.56
From state governments	(a)	1,787	(a)		81,289	(a)	7.89	(a)
From local governments	(a)		(a)	2,434	(a)	(a)		(a)
Revenue from own sources	932,199	563,690	368,509	212,636	155,873	4,115.58	2,488.64	1,626.93
General revenue from own sources	716,629	417,336	299,293	169,266	130,027	3,163.86	1,842.50	1,321.35
Taxes	574,244	350,781	223,463	137,075	86,387	2,535.24	1,548.67	986.57
Property	68,499		68,499	2,892	65,607	302.42		302.42
Individual income	286,149	244,069	42,080	37,089	4,990	1,263.32	1,077.54	185.78
Corporation income	77,921	64,600	13,321	13,321		344.02	285.20	58.81
Sales and gross receipts	111,961	32,034	79,927	67,855	12,072	494.30	141.43	352.87
Customs duties	7,436	7,436				32.83	32.83	
General sales and gross receipts	51,328		51,328	43,168	8,160	226.61		226.61
Selective sales and gross receipts	53,197	24,598	28,599	24,687	3,912	234.86	108.60	126.26
Motor fuel	14,709	4,887	9,822	9,722	100	64.94	21.58	43.36
Alcoholic beverages	8,327	5,685	2,642	2,478	164	36.76	25.10	11.66
Tobacco products	6,320	2,446	3,874	3,738	136	27.90	10.80	17.10
Public utilities	8,755	2,867	5,888	3,359	2,529	38.65	12.66	25.99
Other	15,087	8,713	6,374	5,392	982	66.61	38.47	28.14
Motor vehicle and operators licenses	5,713		5,713	5,325	388	25.22		25.22
Death and gift tax	8,424	6,389	2,035	2,035		37.19	28.21	8.99
All other	15,577	3,689	11,888	8,557	3,330	68.77	16.29	52.48
Charges and miscellaneous general revenue	142,385	66,555	75,830	32,190	43,640	628.62	293.83	334.78
Current charges	80,132	35,759	44,373	16,545	27,828	353.78	157.87	195.90
Miscellaneous general revenue	62,253	30,796	31,457	15,646	15,812	274.84	135.96	138.88
Utility revenue	22,359		22,359	1,304	21,055	98.71		98.71
Liquor stores revenue	3,201		3,201	2,765	435	14.13		14.13
Insurance trust revenue	190,010	146,354	43,656	39,301	4,355	838.88	646.14	192.74
Total expenditure	958,657 (a)	617,166	434,073 (a)	257,812	260,777 (a)	4,232.39 (a)	2,724.73	1,916.39 (a)
Intergovernmental expenditure	(a)	90,836	1,746 (a)	84,504	1,757 (a)	(a)	401.03	7.71 (a)
To federal government	(a)		1,746	1,746		(a)		7.71
To state governments	(a)	64,249	(a)		1,757	(a)	283.65	(a)
To local governments	(a)	26,587	(a)	82,758	(a)	(a)	117.38	(a)
Direct expenditure	958,657	526,330	432,327	173,307	259,019	4,232.39	2,323.70	1,908.69
By type:								
General expenditure	723,094	355,754	367,340	143,718	223,621	3,192.40	1,570.62	1,621.77
Utility expenditure	33,599		33,599	2,401	31,198	148.34		148.34
Liquor stores expenditure	2,591		2,591	2,207	385	11.44		11.44
Insurance trust expenditure	199,373	170,576	28,797	24,981	3,815	880.21	753.08	127.14
By character and object:								
Current operation	517,011	209,200	307,811	108,131	199,680	2,282.56	923.60	1,358.96
Capital outlay	99,386	36,492	62,894	23,325	39,568	438.78	161.11	277.67
Construction	58,410	6,918	51,492	19,736	31,755	257.88	30.54	227.33
Equipment, land and existing structures	40,976	29,574	11,402	3,589	7,313	180.91	130.57	50.34

Assistance and subsidies	63,998	48,776	15,222	9,818	5,404	282.55	215.34	67.20
Interest on debt	78,890	61,286	17,604	7,053	10,552	348.29	270.57	77.72
Insurance benefits and repayments	199,373	170,576	28,797	24,981	3,815	880.21	753.08	127.14
Exhibit: expenditure for salaries and wages	250,886	86,990(b)	163,896	48,793	115,103	1,107.64	384.05	723.59
Direct general expenditure, by function	723,094	355,754	367,340	143,718	223,621	3,192.40	1,570.62	1,621.77
Selected federal programs:								
National defense and international relations	149,459	149,459	...	...	...	659.85	659.85	...
Postal service	18,177	18,177	...	...	...	80.25	80.25	...
Space research and technology	4,892	4,892	...	...	...	21.60	21.60	...
Education services:								
Education	143,830	10,619	133,211	35,251	97,960	635.00	46.88	588.11
Local schools	92,930	...	92,930	964	91,966	410.28	...	410.28
Institutions of higher education	33,919	...	33,919	27,927	5,993	149.75	...	149.75
Other	16,981	10,619	6,362	6,360	2	74.97	46.88	28.09
Libraries	2,026	332	1,694	127	1,566	8.94	1.47	7.48
Social services and income maintenance:								
Public welfare	64,764	19,212	45,552	33,242	12,310	285.93	84.82	201.11
Categorical cash assistance	19,583	7,998	11,585	6,831	4,754	86.46	35.31	51.15
Other cash assistance	1,336	...	1,336	687	650	5.90	...	5.90
Other public welfare	43,845	11,214	32,631	25,725	6,906	193.57	49.51	144.06
Hospitals	29,208	5,421	23,787	11,277	12,510	128.95	23.93	105.02
Health	14,102	5,715	8,387	4,389	3,997	62.26	25.23	37.03
Social insurance administration	4,537	2,528	2,009	2,001	7	20.03	11.16	8.87
Veterans' services	12,504	12,443	61	61	...	55.20	54.93	.27
Transportation:								
Highways	33,745	434	33,311	20,661	12,650	148.98	1.92	147.07
Air transportation	5,071	2,570	2,501	360	2,141	22.39	11.35	11.04
Water transport and terminals	3,278	2,110	1,168	360	808	14.47	9.32	5.16
Parking facilities	343	...	343	...	343	1.51	...	1.51
Public safety:								
Police protection	15,233	1,739	13,494	2,060	11,433	67.25	7.68	59.57
Fire protection	5,718	...	5,718	...	5,718	25.25	...	25.25
Correction	6,835	387	6,448	4,212	2,235	30.17	1.71	28.47
Protective inspection and regulation	2,318	...	2,318	1,564	754	10.23	...	10.23
Environment and housing:								
Natural resources	35,243	29,734	5,509	4,124	1,385	155.60	131.27	24.32
Sewerage	9,892	...	9,892	334	9,558	43.67	...	43.67
Housing and urban renewal	12,142	6,080	6,062	331	5,731	53.60	26.84	26.76
Parks and recreation	8,184	1,664	6,520	1,274	5,247	36.13	7.35	28.79
Sanitation other than sewerage	3,322	...	3,322	...	3,322	14.67	...	14.67
Governmental administration:								
Financial administration	10,228	3,509	6,719	2,994	3,725	45.15	15.49	29.66
General control	10,518	1,821	8,697	3,120	5,578	46.44	8.04	38.40
General public buildings (state-local)	3,018	...	3,018	726	2,292	13.32	...	13.32
Interest on general debt	76,033	61,286	14,747	6,763	7,984	335.68	270.57	65.11
Other and unallocable	38,475	15,622	22,853	8,487	14,366	169.86	68.97	100.89
Indebtedness								
Gross debt outstanding at end of fiscal year	1,249,919	914,316	335,603	121,958	213,645	5,518.28	4,036.63	1,481.66

Source: U.S. Bureau of the Census, *Governmental Finances in 1979-80.*
Note: Because of rounding, detail may not add to totals. Local government amounts are estimates subject to sampling variations.

... Represents zero.
(a) Duplicative transactions between levels of government are excluded.
(b) Includes pay and allowance for military personnel, amounting to $45,704 million.

Table 3
SUMMARY OF STATE AND LOCAL GOVERNMENT FINANCES: 1975-76 TO 1979-80
(In millions of dollars, except per capita amounts)

Sources	1979-80 Total	1979-80 State	1979-80 Local	1978-79	1977-78	1976-77	1975-76	Per capita 1979-80	Per capita 1978-79	Per capita 1977-78	Per capita 1976-77	Per capita 1975-76
Revenue, total	$451,537	$274,528	$177,009	$404,934	$371,607	$337,747	$303,287	$1,993.50	$1,839.78	$1,704.11	$1,561.24	$1,412.88
From federal government	83,029	61,892	21,136	75,164	69,592	62,575	55,589	366.56	341.50	319.14	289.25	258.96
Revenue from own sources	368,509	212,636	155,873	329,770	302,014	275,172	247,697	1,626.93	1,498.28	1,384.97	1,271.99	1,153.91
General revenue from own sources	299,293	169,266	130,027	268,115	246,368	223,221	200,586	1,321.35	1,218.15	1,129.75	1,031.85	934.44
Taxes	223,463	137,075	86,387	205,514	193,642	175,879	156,813	986.57	933.74	888.00	813.01	730.52
Property	68,499	2,892	65,607	64,944	66,422	62,535	57,001	302.42	295.07	304.60	289.07	265.54
Sales and gross receipts	79,927	67,855	12,072	74,247	67,596	60,595	54,547	352.87	337.34	309.98	280.10	254.11
General	51,328	43,168	8,160	46,559	41,473	36,313	32,044	226.61	211.53	190.19	167.86	149.28
Selective	28,599	24,687	3,912	27,689	26,123	24,282	22,502	126.26	125.80	119.80	112.24	104.83
Individual income	42,080	37,089	4,990	36,932	33,176	29,245	24,575	185.78	167.80	152.14	135.19	114.48
Corporation net income	13,321	13,321	(a)	12,128	10,738	9,174	7,273	58.81	55.10	49.24	42.41	33.88
Other taxes	19,636	15,918	3,718	17,264	15,710	14,330	13,417	86.69	78.44	72.04	66.24	62.50
Charges and miscellaneous	75,830	32,190	43,640	62,600	52,726	47,343	43,774	334.78	284.42	241.79	218.84	203.92
Insurance trust revenue	43,656	39,301	4,355	39,027	35,635	35,148	31,985	192.74	177.31	163.42	162.47	149.00
Utility revenue	22,359	1,304	21,055	19,730	17,252	14,191	12,573	98.71	89.64	79.12	65.60	58.57
Liquor stores revenue	3,201	2,765	435	2,898	2,759	2,612	2,553	14.13	13.17	12.65	12.07	11.89
Expenditure, total	434,073	175,054	259,020	381,867	346,786	322,780	304,228	1,916.39	1,734.98	1,590.29	1,492.06	1,417.26
To federal government	1,746	1,746		1,493	1,472	1,387	1,181	7.71	6.78	6.75	6.41	5.48
Direct expenditure by character and object	432,327	173,307	259,019	380,374	345,313	321,393	303,047	1,908.69	1,729.86	1,583.54	1,485.65	1,411.78
Current operation	307,811	108,131	199,680	274,167	249,222	224,241	204,387	1,358.96	1,245.65	1,142.88	1,036.56	952.15
Capital outlay	62,894	23,325	39,568	53,196	44,769	44,896	46,531	277.67	241.69	205.30	207.53	216.77
Construction	51,492	19,736	31,755	43,326	36,199	36,068	38,299	227.33	196.85	166.00	166.72	178.42
Equipment(b)	11,402	3,589	7,813	9,870	8,570	8,829	5,375	50.34	44.84	39.30	40.47	25.04
Land and existing structures(b)							2,857					13.31
Assistance and subsidies	15,222	9,818	5,404	14,044	13,753	13,103	12,494	67.20	63.81	63.07	60.57	58.21
Interest on debt	28,797	24,981	3,815	23,504	23,525	26,141	27,954	127.14	106.79	107.89	120.84	130.23
Insurance benefits and repayments	17,604	7,053	10,552	15,463	14,044	13,012	11,681	77.72	70.25	64.40	60.15	54.42
Exhibit: Expenditure for salaries and wages	163,896	48,793	115,103	149,104	137,703	125,525	116,466	723.59	677.44	631.48	580.24	542.56
Direct expenditure, by function	432,327	173,307	259,019	380,374	345,313	321,393	303,047	1,908.69	1,729.86	1,583.54	1,485.65	1,411.78
Direct general expenditure	367,340	143,718	223,621	326,024	295,510	273,001	255,550	1,621.77	1,481.26	1,355.15	1,261.96	1,190.51
Education	133,211	35,251	97,960	119,448	110,758	102,805	97,216	588.11	542.70	507.91	475.22	452.89
Local schools	92,930	964	91,966	83,385	76,703	71,343	67,674	410.28	378.85	351.74	329.78	315.26
Institutions of higher education	33,919	27,927	5,993	30,059	28,391	26,205	24,304	149.75	136.57	130.19	121.13	113.22
Other education	6,362	6,360	2	6,004	5,664	5,257	5,239	28.09	27.28	25.98	24.30	24.41
Public welfare	45,552	33,242	12,310	40,418	37,679	34,564	31,435	201.11	190.36	172.79	159.73	146.44
Highways	33,311	20,661	12,650	28,440	24,609	23,105	23,907	147.07	129.22	112.85	106.80	111.37
Hospitals	23,787	11,277	12,510	21,039	18,648	17,201	15,726	105.02	95.59	85.51	79.51	73.26
Police protection	13,494	2,060	11,433	12,207	11,306	10,380	9,531	59.57	55.46	51.85	47.98	44.40
Sewerage	9,892	334	9,558	8,795	7,142	6,537	5,937	43.67	39.96	32.75	30.22	27.66
General control	8,697	3,120	5,578	7,742	7,001	6,264	5,711	38.40	35.17	32.11	28.96	26.61
Health	8,387	4,389	3,997	7,179	6,303	5,342	4,960	37.03	32.62	28.90	24.69	23.11
Natural resources	5,509	4,124	1,385	4,706	4,225	5,004	4,662	24.32	21.38	19.38	23.13	21.72
Financial administration	6,719	2,994	3,725	6,071	5,292	4,433	3,960	29.66	27.58	24.27	20.49	18.45
Fire protection	5,718		5,718	5,147	4,802	4,293	3,898	25.25	23.38	22.02	19.84	18.16
Parks and recreation	6,520	1,274	5,247	5,896	5,270	3,871	3,864	28.79	26.79	24.17	17.89	18.00

Correction	6,448	4,212	2,235	5,534	4,981	4,347	3,784	28.47	25.15	22.84	20.09	17.63
Housing and urban renewal	6,062	331	5,731	4,724	3,699	3,410	3,151	26.76	21.46	16.96	15.76	14.68
General public buildings	3,018	726	2,292	2,829	2,561	2,409	2,557	13.32	12.85	11.74	11.14	11.91
Sanitation other than sewerage	3,322		3,322	2,992	2,727	2,336	2,302	14.67	13.59	12.51	10.80	10.73
Employment security administration	2,009	2,001	7	1,806	1,764	1,706	1,576	8.87	8.21	8.09	7.89	7.34
Airports	2,501	360	2,141	1,906	1,617	1,327	1,501	11.04	8.66	7.42	6.13	6.99
Interest on general debt	14,747	6,763	7,984	12,987	11,983	11,394	10,269	65.11	59.01	54.95	52.67	47.84
Other and unallocable	28,436	10,599	17,838	26,157	23,143	22,273	19,605	125.54	118.84	106.13	103.02	91.38
Insurance trust expenditure	28,797	24,981	3,815	23,504	23,525	26,140	27,954	127.14	106.79	107.89	120.83	130.23
Utility expenditure	33,599	2,401	31,198	28,429	23,960	20,108	17,451	148.34	129.17	109.88	92.95	81.30
Liquor stores expenditure	2,591	2,207	385	2,416	2,317	2,143	2,091	11.44	10.98	10.63	9.91	9.74
Debt outstanding at end of fiscal year	335,603	121,958	213,645	304,103	280,433	257,532	240,532	1,481.66	1,381.66	1,286.01	1,190.46	1,120.53
Long-term	322,456	119,821	202,635	292,302	269,003	244,147	221,754	1,423.62	1,328.05	1,233.59	1,128.59	1,033.05
Full faith and credit	149,802	49,364	100,439	145,385	142,523	137,749	131,064	661.36	660.54	653.58	636.75	610.57
Nonguaranteed	172,654	70,457	102,196	146,917	126,481	106,398	90,690	762.25	667.50	580.01	491.83	422.48
Short-term	13,147	2,137	11,011	11,801	11,430	13,385	18,777	58.04	53.62	52.41	61.87	87.47
Long-term debt issued	42,364	16,424	25,940	42,085	39,980	32,342	31,671	187.03	191.21	183.34	149.50	147.54
Long-term debt retired	17,404	5,688	11,717	27,056	16,715	13,219	11,348	76.84	122.93	76.65	61.11	52.87
Cash and security holdings, by type	407,815	272,396	135,418	362,359	318,676	270,621	243,304	1,800.47	1,646.35	1,461.38	1,250.66	1,133.44
Unemp. Comp. Fund balance in U.S. Treasury	11,994	11,969	25	11,341	7,431	4,931	4,435	52.95	51.53	34.08	22.79	20.66
Other deposits and cash	89,743	30,854	58,889	85,138	73,296	65,744	59,463	396.20	386.82	336.12	303.83	277.01
Securities	306,077	229,573	76,504	265,881	237,950	199,946	179,405	1,351.30	1,208.01	1,091.19	924.04	835.77
Federal	81,669	51,904	29,765	72,284	63,449	48,467	38,746	360.56	328.41	290.96	223.99	180.50
State and local government	11,379	6,168	5,211	10,248	12,078	10,551	10,150	50.24	46.56	55.38	48.76	47.28
Other	213,031	171,502	41,529	183,350	162,422	140,929	130,505	940.51	833.03	744.83	651.29	607.96

Source: U.S. Bureau of the Census, *Governmental Finances in 1979–80*, and prior annual reports.

(a) Minor amount included in individual income tax figure.

(b) Equipment and land and existing structures are combined into a single category effective with fiscal 1976–77 data.

Table 4
GENERAL REVENUE OF STATE AND LOCAL GOVERNMENTS
BY SOURCE AND BY STATE: 1979-80
(In millions of dollars)

State or other jurisdiction	Total general revenue	From federal government	All general revenue from own sources	Taxes Total	Taxes Property	Taxes Other	Charges and miscellaneous general revenue
United States..........	$382.321.6	$83,028.5	$299,293.0	$223,462.6	$68,498.7	$154,963.9	$75,830.4
Alabama	5,306.1	1,472.2	3,833.8	2,528.4	306.0	2,222.4	1,305.4
Alaska	3,567.2	430.9	3,136.3	1,675.5	360.0	1,315.5	1,460.8
Arizona	4,365.9	806.9	3,558.9	2,738.2	956.0	1,782.2	820.8
Arkansas	2,897.5	835.8	2,061.7	1,495.3	305.2	1,190.1	566.5
California..............	46,012.3	9,435.7	36,576.6	27,745.5	6,477.5	21,268.0	8,831.0
Colorado	5,066.1	1,000.6	4,065.5	2,859.2	951.6	1,907.6	1,206.3
Connecticut............	5,044.7	976.1	4,068.6	3,326.4	1,470.5	1,855.9	742.2
Delaware	1,167.6	279.1	888.4	629.9	99.6	530.3	258.5
Florida	13,240.9	2,746.7	10,494.3	7,381.6	2,184.4	5,197.2	3,112.7
Georgia	8,028.0	1,927.1	6,100.9	4,207.0	1,087.0	3,120.0	1,894.0
Hawaii	2,049.1	476.8	1,572.3	1,232.8	186.2	1,046.6	339.5
Idaho	1,351.6	336.0	1,015.7	712.0	213.8	498.2	303.6
Illinois	19,347.3	4,034.9	15,312.4	12,375.2	4,191.5	8,183.7	2,937.2
Indiana................	6,875.5	1,213.7	5,661.8	4,083.1	1,348.9	2,734.2	1,578.7
Iowa	4,746.7	915.5	3,831.1	2,817.6	1,048.3	1,769.3	1,013.6
Kansas	3,735.9	735.4	3,000.5	2,188.4	863.8	1,324.6	812.1
Kentucky	5,032.2	1,349.8	3,682.4	2,709.3	495.9	2,213.4	973.1
Louisiana..............	7,054.8	1,692.7	5,362.1	3,534.0	466.3	3,067.7	1,828.2
Maine	1,680.1	485.9	1,194.2	965.5	359.4	606.1	228.7
Maryland	7,929.0	1,672.4	6,256.7	4,655.5	1,215.7	3,439.8	1,601.2
Massachusetts..........	11,201.4	2,720.8	8,480.5	7,133.2	3,183.5	3,749.7	1,347.3
Michigan	17,483.6	3,897.3	13,586.3	9,956.4	3,832.5	6,123.9	3,629.8
Minnesota	8,035.6	1,584.9	6,450.6	4,585.5	1,321.7	3,263.8	1,865.1
Mississippi	3,462.9	1,073.5	2,389.5	1,629.6	354.3	1,275.3	759.9
Missouri...............	6,588.1	1,655.6	4,932.5	3,734.3	1,058.1	2,676.2	1,198.2
Montana	1,500.8	433.9	1,066.9	786.8	358.3	428.5	280.2
Nebraska..............	2,626.7	472.0	2,154.7	1,512.3	629.0	883.3	642.4
Nevada................	1,449.2	302.1	1,147.1	776.8	204.5	572.3	370.4
New Hampshire	1,220.9	311.6	909.3	681.5	415.0	266.5	227.8
New Jersey............	12,686.5	2,279.0	10,407.5	8,376.5	3,672.6	4,703.9	2,031.1
New Mexico............	2,514.3	554.3	1,960.1	1,143.0	184.8	958.2	817.1
New York	40,820.3	8,469.9	32,350.3	26,245.5	8,791.1	17,454.4	6,104.8
North Carolina	7,732.2	1,958.7	5,773.5	4,395.2	1,002.7	3,392.5	1,378.3
North Dakota	1,249.4	279.5	970.0	553.0	175.6	377.4	417.0
Ohio	14,959.3	3,081.3	11,878.1	8,747.7	3,034.3	5,713.4	3,130.4
Oklahoma	4,552.2	997.8	3,554.4	2,500.7	458.0	2,042.7	1,053.8
Oregon	5,113.1	1,267.7	3,845.4	2,576.5	1,006.1	1,570.4	1,268.8
Pennsylvania...........	18,296.1	3,680.5	14,615.6	11,605.9	2,957.9	8,648.0	3,009.7
Rhode Island	1,696.4	431.3	1,265.1	939.9	391.5	548.4	325.3
South Carolina	4,020.6	968.5	3,052.1	2,209.1	497.6	1,711.5	843.0
South Dakota	1,106.7	315.8	790.9	544.1	242.0	302.1	246.8
Tennessee.............	5,888.9	1,586.9	4,301.9	3,012.3	723.3	2,289.0	1,289.7
Texas	20,275.8	3,763.1	16,512.7	11,466.3	3,979.6	7,486.7	5,046.4
Utah	2,284.5	581.1	1,703.5	1,226.8	342.8	884.0	476.6
Vermont...............	885.0	275.4	609.6	459.9	192.5	267.4	149.7
Virginia	7,807.7	1,725.6	6,082.0	4,574.1	1,260.1	3,314.0	1,507.9
Washington	7,426.6	1,522.8	5,903.8	4,083.9	1,199.5	2,884.4	1,819.8
West Virginia..........	2,901.9	806.4	2,095.5	1,551.7	266.8	1,284.9	543.8
Wisconsin	8,510.5	1,783.0	6,727.5	4,993.9	1,696.3	3,297.6	1,733.7
Wyoming...............	1,277.5	275.7	1,001.7	659.1	259.8	399.3	342.6
Dist. of Col.	2,248.4	1,148.2	1,100.2	940.9	219.4	721.5	159.4

Source: U.S. Bureau of the Census, *Governmental Finances in 1979-80.*

Note: Because of rounding, detail may not add to total.

Table 5
PER CAPITA GENERAL REVENUE OF STATE AND LOCAL GOVERNMENTS
BY SOURCE AND BY STATE: 1979-80

State or other jurisdiction	Total	From federal government	All general revenue from own sources	Taxes Total	Property	Other	Charges and miscellaneous general revenue
U.S. Average...........	$1,687.92	$ 366.56	$1,321.35	$ 986.57	$ 302.42	$ 684.15	$ 334.78
Alabama	1,364.03	378.47	985.56	649.96	78.65	571.31	335.59
Alaska	8,917.91	1,077.23	7,840.68	4,188.68	900.01	3,288.67	3,652.00
Arizona	1,606.28	296.89	1,309.39	1,007.42	351.72	655.70	301.97
Arkansas	1,268.04	365.76	902.28	654.38	133.56	520.82	247.90
California.............	1,943.99	398.65	1,545.34	1,172.23	273.67	898.56	373.10
Colorado	1,753.57	346.34	1,407.23	989.70	329.38	660.32	417.53
Connecticut	1,623.15	314.07	1,309.07	1,070.27	473.14	597.13	238.80
Delaware	1,962.28	469.14	1,493.14	1,058.67	167.36	891.31	434.47
Florida	1,359.44	282.00	1,077.44	757.86	224.27	533.59	319.58
Georgia	1,469.26	352.68	1,116.57	769.94	198.94	571.00	346.63
Hawaii	2,123.43	494.08	1,629.35	1,277.52	192.96	1,084.55	351.83
Idaho	1,431.83	355.90	1,075.92	754.28	226.51	527.76	321.65
Illinois	1,694.46	353.38	1,341.08	1,083.83	367.10	716.73	257.24
Indiana	1,252.37	221.08	1,031.29	743.73	245.69	498.04	287.56
Iowa	1,629.47	314.29	1,315.18	967.24	359.87	607.37	347.94
Kansas	1,581.00	311.21	1,269.79	926.12	365.53	560.59	343.67
Kentucky	1,374.54	368.70	1,005.84	740.06	135.46	604.59	265.78
Louisiana	1,678.12	402.65	1,275.47	840.62	110.92	729.69	434.86
Maine	1,493.46	431.93	1,061.53	858.26	319.47	538.79	203.27
Maryland	1,880.70	396.67	1,484.03	1,104.23	288.36	815.88	379.79
Massachusetts	1,952.48	474.26	1,478.22	1,243.37	554.91	688.46	234.85
Michigan	1,888.49	420.97	1,467.51	1,075.44	413.97	661.47	392.07
Minnesota	1,970.95	388.75	1,582.20	1,124.73	324.19	800.54	457.48
Mississippi	1,373.64	425.81	947.83	646.42	140.54	505.88	301.41
Missouri	1,339.86	336.70	1,003.16	759.46	215.19	544.28	243.69
Montana	1,906.98	551.34	1,355.65	999.69	455.27	544.42	355.96
Nebraska	1,673.07	300.64	1,372.43	963.25	400.66	562.59	409.18
Nevada	1,813.81	378.13	1,435.68	972.17	255.89	716.28	463.51
New Hampshire	1,325.61	338.37	987.24	739.98	450.63	289.34	247.26
New Jersey.............	1,722.78	309.48	1,413.30	1,137.49	498.73	638.77	275.81
New Mexico.............	1,934.11	426.36	1,507.75	879.24	142.16	737.07	628.52
New York	2,325.01	482.43	1,842.59	1,494.87	500.72	994.16	347.72
North Carolina	1,316.35	333.45	982.90	748.25	170.69	577.56	234.65
North Dakota	1,913.38	427.96	1,485.42	846.81	268.93	577.87	638.61
Ohio	1,385.51	285.38	1,100.13	810.20	281.03	527.17	289.93
Oklahoma	1,504.86	329.84	1,175.02	826.66	151.41	675.26	348.36
Oregon	1,941.92	481.47	1,460.45	978.54	382.11	596.44	481.90
Pennsylvania	1,541.76	310.15	1,231.61	978.00	249.25	728.75	253.61
Rhode Island	1,791.30	455.40	1,335.90	992.46	413.42	579.04	343.44
South Carolina	1,289.07	310.52	978.55	708.27	159.55	548.72	270.28
South Dakota	1,603.93	457.70	1,146.23	788.55	350.74	437.81	357.68
Tennessee..............	1,282.69	345.66	937.03	656.12	157.55	498.57	280.91
Texas	1,425.06	264.49	1,160.58	805.90	279.70	526.20	354.68
Utah	1,563.69	397.72	1,165.97	839.71	234.63	605.08	326.26
Vermont................	1,731.84	538.85	1,192.99	900.02	376.71	523.30	292.97
Virginia	1,460.47	322.79	1,137.68	855.61	235.71	619.91	282.07
Washington.............	1,798.20	368.72	1,429.48	988.85	290.43	698.42	440.63
West Virginia..........	1,488.14	413.53	1,074.61	795.75	136.80	658.95	278.85
Wisconsin	1,808.83	378.96	1,429.87	1,061.40	360.53	700.88	368.47
Wyoming	2,712.26	585.41	2,126.85	1,399.36	551.70	847.66	727.49
Dist. of Col.	3,524.18	1,799.67	1,724.50	1,474.71	343.88	1,130.84	249.79

Source: U.S. Bureau of the Census, *Governmental Finances in 1979-80.*

Table 6
ORIGIN AND ALLOCATION, BY LEVEL OF GOVERNMENT,
OF GENERAL REVENUE OF STATE AND LOCAL GOVERNMENTS: 1979-80
(In millions)

State or other jurisdiction	Total general revenue	By originating level of government (before transfers among governments)						By final recipient level of government (after intergovernmental transfers)			
		Amount			Percent			Amount		Percent	
		Federal	State	Local	Federal	State	Local	State(a)	Local	State	Local
United States	$382,321.6	$83,028.5	$169,265.6	$130,027.4	21.7	44.3	34.0	$152,302.8	$230,018.7	39.8	60.2
Alabama	5,306.1	1,472.2	2,381.1	1,452.7	27.7	44.9	27.4	2,640.4	2,665.6	49.8	50.2
Alaska	3,567.2	430.9	2,630.8	505.5	12.1	73.7	14.2	2,714.7	852.5	76.1	23.9
Arizona	4,365.9	806.9	2,008.5	1,550.4	18.5	46.0	35.5	1,620.1	2,745.7	37.1	62.9
Arkansas	2,897.5	835.8	1,379.1	682.6	28.8	47.6	23.6	1,511.9	1,385.6	52.2	47.8
California	46,012.3	9,435.7	22,346.0	14,230.5	20.5	48.6	30.9	14,729.3	31,282.9	32.0	68.0
Colorado	5,066.1	1,000.6	2,010.4	2,055.1	19.8	39.7	40.6	1,922.4	3,143.6	37.9	62.1
Connecticut	5,044.7	976.1	2,294.8	1,773.8	19.3	45.5	35.2	2,583.5	2,461.3	51.2	48.8
Delaware	1,167.6	279.1	685.9	202.5	23.9	58.7	17.3	709.1	458.5	60.7	39.3
Florida	13,240.9	2,746.7	5,513.0	4,981.2	20.7	41.6	37.6	4,362.2	8,878.8	32.9	67.1
Georgia	8,028.0	1,927.1	3,155.5	2,945.4	24.0	39.3	36.7	3,142.7	4,885.3	39.1	60.9
Hawaii	2,049.1	476.8	1,263.2	309.1	23.3	61.6	15.1	1,604.6	444.5	78.3	21.7
Idaho	1,351.6	336.0	632.8	382.9	24.9	46.8	28.3	632.0	719.6	46.8	53.2
Illinois	19,347.3	4,034.9	8,175.3	7,137.1	20.9	42.3	36.9	7,895.3	11,452.0	40.8	59.2
Indiana	6,875.5	1,213.7	3,424.5	2,237.3	17.7	49.8	32.5	2,592.5	4,283.0	37.7	62.3
Iowa	4,746.7	915.5	2,176.1	1,655.0	19.3	45.8	34.9	1,875.0	2,871.7	39.5	60.5
Kansas	3,735.9	735.4	1,574.1	1,426.4	19.7	42.1	38.2	1,600.2	2,135.7	42.8	57.2
Kentucky	5,032.2	1,349.8	2,643.4	1,039.0	26.8	52.5	20.6	2,740.4	2,291.8	54.5	45.5
Louisiana	7,054.8	1,692.7	3,488.0	1,874.0	24.0	49.4	26.6	3,524.6	3,530.2	50.0	50.0
Maine	1,680.1	485.9	767.0	427.2	28.9	45.7	25.4	935.0	745.1	55.7	44.3
Maryland	7,929.0	1,672.4	3,668.4	2,588.3	21.1	46.3	32.6	3,498.3	4,430.8	44.1	55.9
Massachusetts......	11,201.4	2,720.8	4,651.2	3,829.3	24.3	41.5	34.2	4,958.8	6,242.6	44.3	55.7
Michigan	17,483.6	3,897.3	7,460.4	6,125.9	22.3	42.7	35.0	6,977.9	10,505.7	39.9	60.1
Minnesota	8,035.6	1,584.9	3,978.6	2,472.1	19.7	49.5	30.8	3,136.8	4,898.7	39.0	61.0
Mississippi	3,462.9	1,073.5	1,553.2	836.3	31.0	44.9	24.2	1,634.4	1,828.5	47.2	52.8
Missouri	6,588.1	1,655.6	2,514.1	2,418.4	25.1	38.2	36.7	2,690.4	3,897.7	40.8	59.2
Montana	1,500.8	433.9	575.1	491.8	28.9	38.3	32.8	743.0	757.8	49.5	50.5
Nebraska	2,626.7	472.0	1,030.1	1,124.6	18.0	39.2	42.8	1,108.5	1,518.2	42.2	57.8
Nevada...........	1,449.2	302.1	587.9	559.2	20.8	40.6	38.6	546.1	903.1	37.7	62.3
New Hampshire	1,220.9	311.6	416.3	493.0	25.5	34.1	40.4	555.3	665.6	45.5	54.5
New Jersey	12,686.5	2,279.0	5,291.1	5,116.4	18.0	41.7	40.3	4,725.2	7,961.4	37.2	62.8
New Mexico	2,514.3	554.3	1,545.9	414.2	22.0	61.5	16.5	1,404.5	1,109.8	55.9	44.1
New York	40,820.3	8,469.9	14,677.6	17,672.7	20.7	36.0	43.3	10,868.3	29,952.0	26.6	73.4
North Carolina	7,732.2	1,958.7	3,808.5	1,965.1	25.3	49.3	25.4	3,556.7	4,175.5	46.0	54.0
North Dakota	1,249.4	279.5	660.5	309.5	22.4	52.9	24.8	703.2	546.2	56.3	43.7
Ohio..............	14,959.3	3,081.3	5,994.9	5,883.1	20.6	40.1	39.3	4,780.0	10,179.3	32.0	68.0
Oklahoma	4,552.2	997.8	2,337.5	1,217.0	21.9	51.3	26.7	2,336.2	2,216.0	51.3	48.7
Oregon...........	5,113.1	1,267.7	2,126.5	1,718.9	24.8	41.6	33.6	2,204.0	2,909.1	43.1	56.9
Pennsylvania.......	18,296.1	3,680.5	8,422.9	6,192.7	20.1	46.0	33.8	7,624.3	10,671.8	41.7	58.3
Rhode Island......	1,696.4	431.3	827.8	437.3	25.4	48.8	25.8	1,006.2	690.1	59.3	40.7
South Carolina	4,020.6	968.5	2,056.0	996.0	24.1	51.1	24.8	2,188.5	1,832.1	54.4	45.6
South Dakota	1,106.7	315.8	433.7	357.2	28.5	39.2	32.3	596.0	510.7	53.9	46.1
Tennessee	5,888.9	1,586.9	2,330.5	1,971.4	26.9	39.6	33.5	2,605.7	3,283.2	44.2	55.8
Texas	20,275.8	3,763.1	9,009.8	7,502.9	18.6	44.4	37.0	8,541.2	11,734.6	42.1	57.9
Utah	2,284.5	581.1	1,051.8	651.7	25.4	46.0	28.5	1,126.3	1,158.2	49.3	50.7
Vermont	885.0	275.4	385.0	224.6	31.1	43.5	25.4	555.6	329.4	62.8	37.2
Virginia	7,807.1	1,725.6	3,642.9	2,439.1	22.1	46.7	31.2	3,821.4	3,986.3	48.9	51.1
Washington	7,426.6	1,522.8	3,593.8	2,310.0	20.5	48.4	31.1	3,054.5	4,372.1	41.1	58.9
West Virginia	2,901.9	806.4	1,465.0	630.5	27.8	50.5	21.7	1,645.0	1,256.9	56.7	43.3
Wisconsin	8,510.5	1,783.0	4,063.1	2,664.4	21.0	47.7	31.3	3,170.7	5,339.9	37.3	62.7
Wyoming..........	1,277.5	275.7	555.8	445.9	21.6	43.5	34.9	604.1	673.4	47.3	52.7
Dist. of Col.	2,248.4	1,148.2	. . .	1,100.2	51.1	. . .	48.9	. . .	2,248.4	. . .	100.0

Source: U.S. Bureau of the Census, *Governmental Finances in 1979-80.*
Note: Because of rounding, detail may not add to totals. Local government data are estimates subject to sampling variation.

(a) Data not adjusted for federal receipts of $1,787 million from state governments (mainly for Supplemental Security Income program).

Table 7
DIRECT GENERAL EXPENDITURE OF STATE AND LOCAL GOVERNMENTS, FOR SELECTED ITEMS, BY STATE: 1979-80
(In millions of dollars)

State or other jurisdiction	Total	Other than capital outlay	Education		Public welfare	Health and hospitals	Highways		Interest on general debt
			Total	Local schools only			Total	Other than capital outlay	
United States	$367,339.9	$314,389.6	$133,210.8	$92,930.0	$45,552.2	$32,173.5	$33,311.3	$14,177.8	$14,746.8
Alabama	5,159.8	4,428.9	1,992.9	1,175.1	549.8	697.4	518.1	251.7	168.9
Alaska	2,502.7	2,001.4	725.0	539.0	115.2	60.1	223.6	88.2	216.4
Arizona	4,204.7	3,351.7	1,828.6	1,176.7	185.3	299.3	427.0	135.4	121.8
Arkansas	2,742.3	2,264.5	1,084.5	748.3	322.3	266.1	406.4	173.4	65.0
California	43,412.7	39,177.7	15,062.8	9,967.9	6,761.5	3,641.2	2,311.9	1,264.9	902.0
Colorado	4,558.4	3,877.5	1,924.3	1,295.7	402.1	383.5	474.2	222.2	124.2
Connecticut	4,918.8	4,362.6	1,715.5	1,311.4	658.9	306.2	356.7	189.2	289.1
Delaware	1,076.5	932.3	435.3	249.6	98.3	49.2	99.3	47.6	63.2
Florida	12,753.7	10,545.9	4,486.0	3,309.1	760.8	1,512.0	1,201.6	369.6	436.6
Georgia	7,462.6	6,067.4	2,602.2	1,887.3	707.1	1,179.5	820.5	256.1	206.9
Hawaii	1,876.8	1,524.4	559.7	337.6	231.9	136.7	130.3	38.8	112.2
Idaho	1,289.1	1,074.2	483.6	317.8	116.4	117.6	170.6	63.3	28.8
Illinois	18,122.1	15,394.0	6,407.0	4,630.2	2,543.1	1,152.2	1,838.9	720.5	738.7
Indiana	6,826.7	5,784.6	2,920.0	1,955.8	662.6	732.9	692.7	281.5	203.4
Iowa	4,910.6	4,192.6	2,032.6	1,355.3	550.3	506.1	697.8	338.1	81.8
Kansas	3,748.2	2,955.6	1,376.8	920.0	373.6	303.1	570.0	230.9	114.8
Kentucky	5,406.3	4,191.7	1,853.5	1,149.8	648.3	334.1	981.7	240.0	358.4
Louisiana.........	6,558.2	5,495.4	2,242.9	1,550.9	645.6	749.1	793.6	324.6	306.2
Maine	1,581.0	1,399.5	544.0	396.9	264.4	71.9	211.0	116.7	63.8
Maryland	7,626.1	6,251.0	2,691.0	1,854.5	756.0	607.7	679.4	234.8	323.3
Massachusetts......	10,301.3	9,419.5	3,230.4	2,653.6	1,800.6	848.1	616.8	347.3	493.0
Michigan	17,401.8	15,234.9	6,442.8	4,404.4	2,705.5	1,620.1	1,263.4	536.8	569.7
Minnesota	7,723.6	6,384.1	2,658.8	1,877.0	1,035.6	640.5	892.3	385.0	318.3
Mississippi........	3,412.2	2,866.1	1,264.7	776.9	393.0	433.8	492.8	192.1	99.9
Missouri..........	6,294.6	5,275.9	2,324.9	1,689.5	659.3	669.8	701.4	280.3	164.9
Montana	1,392.0	1,121.9	544.2	422.0	107.8	75.8	244.5	100.0	43.9
Nebraska	2,424.6	1,965.1	972.9	651.6	191.0	224.6	359.7	127.2	52.1
Nevada	1,491.9	1,153.3	459.5	332.8	77.0	142.0	188.3	64.9	57.3
New Hampshire	1,233.9	1,058.2	432.7	298.6	167.9	59.4	176.7	93.6	70.6
New Jersey	12,427.1	11,058.2	4,452.4	3,403.6	1,532.1	796.0	780.3	430.3	591.9
New Mexico	2,156.0	1,758.4	924.2	631.7	166.4	177.2	252.7	92.4	83.6
New York	38,689.9	35,009.1	11,774.0	8,748.8	6,286.7	3,459.1	2,159.9	1,097.3	2,692.7
North Carolina	7,639.3	6,561.1	3,186.4	2,060.6	769.3	727.7	702.4	289.2	185.4
North Dakota	1,201.2	952.7	426.5	259.5	91.6	52.7	197.8	72.0	35.9
Ohio	15,447.0	13,022.3	5,929.2	4,334.4	1,827.7	1,624.5	1,180.6	535.4	509.0
Oklahoma	4,254.6	3,505.2	1,683.2	1,087.6	548.2	353.7	454.4	210.8	120.7
Oregon...........	5,000.9	4,170.9	1,925.4	1,318.9	476.3	286.7	473.2	188.2	314.2
Pennsylvania	17,429.8	15,328.4	6,123.3	4,761.5	2,803.4	1,112.6	1,128.8	740.7	1,067.9
Rhode Island......	1,661.0	1,509.2	549.2	349.0	298.7	139.9	83.9	44.8	109.0
South Carolina	3,958.4	3,405.5	1,698.5	1,061.1	363.1	564.7	286.6	141.6	95.7
South Dakota	1,094.6	906.6	399.3	270.4	104.7	49.7	205.7	108.3	39.2
Tennessee	5,928.6	4,922.0	2,113.4	1,380.9	596.0	762.1	688.5	278.4	229.2
Texas	19,376.0	15,204.6	8,238.6	5,643.9	1,500.9	1,779.8	2,285.3	613.8	696.2
Utah	2,359.0	1,827.4	1,073.6	699.3	188.0	148.4	279.3	83.9	61.6
Vermont	817.5	719.8	321.1	190.8	95.5	44.4	100.3	60.9	41.3
Virginia	7,700.0	6,420.7	2,909.9	1,960.1	768.2	682.5	935.0	371.0	282.7
Washington........	7,358.9	5,992.8	3,009.1	2,031.1	788.0	459.5	802.0	297.0	230.3
West Virginia	2,966.1	2,372.1	1,068.1	753.9	253.7	210.5	601.5	210.4	151.3
Wisconsin	8,464.2	7,423.9	3,292.8	2,145.1	1,227.5	656.6	917.4	494.0	261.1
Wyoming	1,100.0	804.9	430.3	297.0	42.8	96.2	179.6	49.7	57.0
Dist. of Col.	1,896.6	1,761.9	383.4	305.6	332.3	178.1	75.2	53.2	95.8

Source: U.S. Bureau of the Census, *Governmental Finances in 1979-80.*

Note: Because of rounding, detail may not add to totals.

Table 8
PER CAPITA DIRECT GENERAL EXPENDITURE OF STATE AND
LOCAL GOVERNMENTS, FOR SELECTED ITEMS, BY STATE: 1979-80

State or other jurisdiction	Total	Other than capital outlay	Education Total	Local schools only	Public welfare	Health and hospitals	Highways Total	Other than capital outlay	Interest on general debt
United States	$1,621.77	$1,388.00	$ 588.11	$ 410.28	$201.11	$142.04	$147.07	$ 84.47	$ 65.11
Alabama	1,326.42	1,138.52	512.32	302.08	141.33	179.28	133.19	68.48	43.41
Alaska	6,256.70	5,003.53	1,812.41	1,347.39	288.06	150.16	558.94	338.60	541.02
Arizona	1,547.00	1,233.17	672.77	432.92	68.16	110.12	157.10	107.28	44.83
Arkansas	1,200.13	991.04	474.62	327.50	141.06	116.46	177.84	101.98	28.43
California	1,834.16	1,655.23	636.39	421.14	285.67	153.84	97.67	44.23	38.11
Colorado	1,577.85	1,342.16	666.09	448.50	139.18	132.73	164.12	87.24	42.99
Connecticut	1,582.63	1,403.67	551.96	421.93	211.99	98.51	114.78	53.90	93.02
Delaware	1,809.18	1,566.82	731.58	419.42	165.16	82.76	166.85	86.91	106.29
Florida	1,309.42	1,082.74	460.58	339.74	78.11	155.24	123.36	85.42	44.82
Georgia	1,365.77	1,110.43	476.24	345.41	129.41	215.87	150.17	103.30	37.86
Hawaii	1,944.88	1,579.69	580.05	349.81	240.29	141.70	135.01	94.81	116.31
Idaho	1,365.57	1,137.97	512.25	336.69	123.29	124.54	180.73	113.67	30.55
Illinois	1,587.15	1,348.23	561.13	405.52	222.72	100.91	161.05	97.95	64.70
Indiana	1,243.47	1,053.65	531.88	356.25	120.70	133.49	126.17	74.91	37.06
Iowa	1,685.76	1,439.29	697.78	465.25	188.91	173.75	239.54	123.49	28.09
Kansas	1,586.20	1,250.76	582.65	389.34	158.10	128.26	241.23	143.49	48.58
Kentucky	1,476.72	1,144.96	506.27	314.06	177.09	91.26	268.14	202.59	97.91
Louisiana..........	1,560.00	1,307.18	533.52	368.92	153.57	178.19	188.77	111.55	72.84
Maine.............	1,405.33	1,244.04	483.52	352.82	234.99	63.87	187.57	83.82	56.70
Maryland	1,808.85	1,482.70	638.27	439.87	179.32	144.15	161.15	105.45	76.69
Massachusetts.....	1,795.59	1,641.88	563.08	462.55	313.85	147.83	107.52	46.97	85.93
Michigan	1,879.65	1,645.60	695.92	475.74	292.24	174.99	136.46	78.48	61.53
Minnesota	1,894.42	1,565.87	652.16	460.40	254.00	157.09	218.87	124.43	78.07
Mississippi	1,353.51	1,136.89	501.66	308.16	155.91	172.09	195.48	119.29	39.61
Missouri..........	1,280.18	1,072.99	472.83	343.60	134.09	136.22	142.65	85.64	33.54
Montana	1,768.80	1,425.57	691.48	536.24	136.94	96.27	310.62	183.64	55.77
Nebraska	1,544.35	1,251.71	619.70	415.02	121.67	143.05	229.12	148.11	33.18
Nevada...........	1,867.19	1,443.35	575.07	416.48	96.31	177.78	235.68	154.46	71.72
New Hampshire ...	1,339.74	1,148.92	469.79	324.24	182.31	64.45	191.89	90.27	76.70
New Jersey	1,687.55	1,501.66	604.61	462.19	208.06	108.09	105.96	47.54	80.37
New Mexico	1,658.44	1,352.59	710.94	485.92	128.03	136.31	194.36	123.29	64.29
New York	2,203.67	1,994.02	670.62	498.31	358.07	197.02	123.02	60.52	153.37
North Carolina	1,300.53	1,116.98	542.45	350.80	130.97	123.89	119.57	70.34	31.56
North Dakota	1,839.55	1,458.96	653.09	397.37	140.33	80.69	302.88	192.61	54.94
Ohio	1,430.67	1,206.10	549.15	401.44	169.28	150.46	109.35	59.75	47.14
Oklahoma	1,406.47	1,158.73	556.44	359.53	181.22	116.94	150.20	80.52	39.91
Oregon...........	1,899.31	1,584.09	731.26	500.91	180.90	108.87	179.72	108.24	119.33
Pennsylvania......	1,468.76	1,291.68	515.99	401.24	236.24	93.76	95.12	32.70	89.99
Rhode Island	1,753.96	1,593.62	579.96	368.57	315.39	147.73	88.61	41.25	115.13
South Carolina	1,269.13	1,091.87	544.55	340.20	116.42	181.05	91.89	46.50	30.67
South Dakota	1,586.37	1,313.89	578.72	391.92	151.74	71.96	298.08	141.22	56.86
Tennessee	1,291.35	1,072.08	460.33	300.79	129.82	165.99	149.98	89.33	49.92
Texas	1,361.82	1,068.64	579.04	396.68	105.49	125.09	160.62	117.48	48.93
Utah.............	1,614.64	1,250.80	734.81	478.64	128.66	101.59	191.15	133.71	42.16
Vermont	1,599.83	1,408.64	628.32	373.35	186.97	86.81	196.18	77.04	80.73
Virginia	1,440.33	1,201.03	544.31	366.65	143.69	127.67	174.89	105.50	52.88
Washington........	1,781.81	1,451.04	728.60	491.80	190.79	109.08	194.19	122.28	55.77
West Virginia	1,521.09	1,216.47	547.72	386.61	130.11	107.92	308.48	200.54	77.58
Wisconsin	1,798.99	1,577.89	699.84	455.92	260.90	139.55	194.99	89.99	55.50
Wyoming..........	2,335.46	1,708.91	913.63	630.58	90.85	204.25	381.42	275.73	120.96
Dist. of Col.	2,972.71	2,761.66	600.92	479.02	520.90	279.19	117.82	34.50	150.21

Source: U.S. Bureau of the Census, *Governmental Finances in 1979-80.*

Table 9
RELATION OF SELECTED ITEMS OF STATE AND LOCAL GOVERNMENT FINANCES TO PERSONAL INCOME: 1979-80

State or other jurisdiction	General revenue per $1,000 of personal income					Direct general expenditure per $1,000 of personal income				
	Total	From federal government	All state and local general revenue sources	Taxes	Charges and miscellaneous general revenue	All general expenditures	Education	Highways	Public welfare	Health and hospitals
U.S. Average...........	$198.02	$ 43.00	$155.01	$115.74	$ 39.28	$190.26	$ 68.99	$17.25	$23.59	$16.66
Alabama	202.21	56.11	146.11	96.36	49.75	196.64	75.95	19.75	20.95	26.58
Alaska	783.13	94.60	688.53	367.83	320.70	549.44	159.16	49.08	25.30	13.19
Arizona	211.56	39.10	172.45	132.68	39.77	203.75	88.61	20.69	8.98	14.50
Arkansas	191.33	55.19	136.14	98.74	37.41	181.08	71.61	26.83	21.28	17.57
California..............	201.79	41.38	160.41	121.68	38.73	190.39	66.06	10.14	29.65	15.97
Colorado	200.36	39.57	160.79	113.08	47.71	180.28	76.11	18.75	15.90	15.17
Connecticut............	159.98	30.96	129.03	105.49	23.54	155.99	54.40	11.31	20.89	9.71
Delaware	215.10	51.43	163.67	116.05	47.63	198.32	80.19	18.29	18.10	9.07
Florida	174.88	36.28	138.61	97.49	41.11	168.45	59.25	15.87	10.05	19.97
Georgia	205.61	49.36	156.26	107.75	48.51	191.13	66.65	21.02	18.11	30.21
Hawaii	245.23	57.06	188.17	147.54	40.63	224.61	66.99	27.75	27.75	16.36
Idaho	197.26	49.03	148.23	103.92	44.31	188.13	70.57	24.90	16.99	17.16
Illinois	175.83	36.67	139.16	112.47	26.69	164.70	58.23	16.71	23.11	10.47
Indiana	148.57	26.23	122.34	88.23	34.11	147.51	63.10	14.97	14.32	15.84
Iowa	186.47	35.97	150.51	110.69	39.82	192.91	79.85	27.41	21.62	19.88
Kansas	170.80	33.62	137.18	100.05	37.13	171.36	62.95	26.06	17.08	13.86
Kentucky	193.06	51.79	141.27	103.94	37.33	207.41	71.11	37.66	24.87	12.82
Louisiana	231.56	55.56	176.00	115.99	60.00	215.26	73.62	26.05	21.19	24.59
Maine	217.58	62.93	154.65	125.04	29.61	204.74	70.44	27.33	34.24	9.31
Maryland	204.85	43.21	161.65	120.28	41.37	197.97	69.52	17.55	19.53	15.70
Massachusetts	218.34	53.04	165.30	139.04	26.26	200.79	62.97	12.02	35.10	16.53
Michigan	201.95	45.02	156.94	115.01	41.93	201.01	74.42	14.59	31.25	18.71
Minnesota	223.27	44.04	179.23	127.41	51.82	214.60	73.88	24.79	28.77	17.80
Mississippi	230.76	71.53	159.22	108.59	50.63	227.37	84.27	32.84	26.19	28.91
Missouri	164.07	41.23	122.84	93.00	29.84	156.76	57.90	17.47	16.42	16.68
Montana	248.48	71.84	176.64	130.26	46.38	230.46	90.10	40.47	17.84	12.54
Nebraska	192.18	34.53	157.65	110.65	47.00	177.39	71.18	26.32	13.98	16.43
Nevada	196.21	40.91	155.31	105.17	50.14	201.99	62.21	25.50	10.42	19.23
New Hampshire	164.83	42.07	122.76	92.01	30.75	166.59	58.42	23.86	22.67	8.01
New Jersey.............	177.53	31.89	145.64	117.22	28.42	173.90	62.31	10.92	21.44	11.14
New Mexico............	267.97	59.07	208.90	121.82	87.08	229.78	98.50	26.93	17.74	18.89
New York	254.08	52.72	201.36	163.36	38.00	240.82	73.29	13.44	39.13	21.53
North Carolina	186.77	47.31	139.46	106.17	33.29	184.53	76.97	16.97	18.58	17.58
North Dakota	231.04	51.68	179.36	102.25	77.11	222.11	78.86	36.57	16.94	9.74
Ohio	159.96	32.95	127.02	93.54	33.47	165.18	63.40	12.63	19.54	17.37
Oklahoma	185.00	40.55	144.45	101.62	42.83	172.90	68.41	18.46	22.28	14.38
Oregon	226.37	56.13	170.25	114.07	56.18	221.41	85.24	20.95	21.09	12.69
Pennsylvania	182.24	36.66	145.58	115.60	29.98	173.61	60.99	11.24	27.92	11.08
Rhode Island	214.57	54.55	160.02	118.88	41.14	210.09	69.47	10.61	37.78	17.70
South Carolina	194.33	46.81	147.52	106.77	40.75	191.32	82.09	13.85	17.55	27.29
South Dakota	215.44	61.48	153.96	105.92	48.04	213.08	77.73	40.04	20.38	9.67
Tennessee..............	183.10	49.34	133.76	93.66	40.10	184.34	65.71	21.41	18.53	23.70
Texas	172.44	32.00	140.43	97.52	42.92	164.78	70.07	19.44	12.76	15.14
Utah	232.22	59.06	173.15	124.70	48.45	239.78	109.12	28.39	19.11	15.09
Vermont................	244.94	76.21	168.73	127.29	41.44	226.27	88.87	27.75	26.45	12.28
Virginia	174.95	38.67	136.28	102.49	33.79	172.54	65.20	20.95	17.21	15.29
Washington	197.77	40.55	157.22	108.75	48.46	195.97	80.13	21.36	20.98	12.00
West Virginia...........	209.61	58.25	151.36	112.09	39.28	214.25	77.15	43.45	18.33	15.20
Wisconsin	212.54	44.53	168.01	124.71	43.30	211.38	82.23	22.91	30.66	16.40
Wyoming...............	286.11	61.75	224.36	147.61	76.74	246.36	96.38	40.24	9.58	21.55
Dist. of Col.	324.26	165.59	158.67	135.69	22.98	273.52	55.29	10.84	47.93	25.69

Source: U.S. Bureau of the Census, Governmental Finances in 1979-80.

Table 10
LIMITATIONS ON STATE DEFICITS:
CONSTITUTIONAL AND STATUTORY

State or other jurisdiction	Constitutional debt restrictions		Balanced budget appropriations		Execution		Prohibitory provisions: at least one is
	Debt limit	Exceed limit by popular vote	Budget must balance expenditure with revenue	Legis. approp. must balance expenditure with revenue	Reduce expenditure if revenue short fall	Must tax to cover deficit	
Alabama	$300,000		C(a)				C
Alaska	V						C
Arizona	$350,000				S(b)		S
Arkansas	V						C
California	$300,000	(c)	C				C
Colorado	$100,000			C	C		C
Connecticut			S(d)	S	S(e)		S
Delaware	1.5 x state general fund revenue			C	S		C
Florida				C			C
Georgia	(f)			C			C
Hawaii	(g)		S	S	S		S
Idaho	$2,000,000	★		C			C
Illinois	(h)	(h)	C	C			C
Indiana	(i)						C
Iowa	$250,000						C
Kansas	$1,000,000	★			S		S
Kentucky	$500,000	★	S		S(j)		C
Louisiana				C	S(j)		C
Maine	$2,000,000	★	S				C
Maryland			C	C			C
Massachusetts			C	C			C
Michigan			C		S		C
Minnesota	P				S		C
Mississippi	1.5 x revenue of any one of 4 preceding years		S	S			
Missouri	$1,000,000	★			C(j)		C
Montana				C			C
Nebraska	$100,000		S	C,S(k)		C	C
Nevada	1% of assessed valuation of the state		S				C
New Hampshire			S		S(j)		C
New Jersey	1% of approp.	★		C			C
New Mexico	$200,000	★(l)					C
New York			C		C		C
North Carolina			C		S		C
North Dakota	(m)		S		S		C
Ohio	$750,000	(n)					
Oklahoma				C(o)	C		C
Oregon	$50,000 + AV[P]			C	C		C
Pennsylvania	(p)	★	C	C	S		C
Rhode Island	$50,000	★		C,R	S	C	C
South Carolina	(q)						C
South Dakota	$100,000		S	C	S		C
Tennessee			C		C		C
Texas	$200,000		S	C	S	C	C
Utah	AV						
Vermont							
Virginia	T(r),T[P,V]		S		S		C
Washington	(s)	★	S(d)		S		S
West Virginia	No debt allowed			C	S		C
Wisconsin	AV,P(t)		C				
Wyoming	AV,T						
Dist. of Col.				C(u)	S		C
Guam	AV		S				
Puerto Rico				C			

Key:
AV—Percentage of property value
C—Constitution
P—Specified purposes only
R—Rule of house
S—Statute
T—Percentage of taxes
V—Popular vote required for any debt
(a) Implicit—governor shall submit bills for budget and revenue recommendations.
(b) Responsibility of each agency.
(c) Specified circumstances.

(d) Recommendation can include increased debt.
(e) Permissive if projected deficit is under 3 percent; mandatory if over 3 percent of original budget.
(f) Total not to exceed 15 percent of the total revenue receipts in the preceding fiscal year.
(g) Not to exceed 18.5 percent of general fund revenue average of state in the three preceding fiscal years.
(h) Three-fifths vote of total membership of each house, or vote of majority of voters at general election required to issue new debt.
(i) No debt except to meet casual deficits in the revenue payment of interest and defense. A deficit budget or appropriation is not considered a casual deficit.

(j) Permissive, not mandatory.

(k) Statute covers supplemental appropriations only.

(l) In no case over 1 % of assessed valuation.

(m) Limit on basis of value of state property.

(n) General debt limit has been exceeded by constitutional amendments authorizing debt for capital improvements.

(o) Constitution limits appropriation ceiling to five-year average revenue increase.

(p) Debt may be incurred without electoral approval for capital budget if debt will not cause all net debt to exceed one and three-fourths times the average of annual tax revenues in previous five fiscal years.

(q) In any fiscal year the maximum annual debt service on general obligation bonds may not exceed 7 percent of the general revenues for the fiscal year next preceding.

(r) Limit for casual deficits is 30 percent of 1.15 x previous year's income and sales tax collections and must be paid off in 12 months.

(s) Percentage of revenues.

(t) $100,000 limit on casual deficits.

(u) District charter.

STATE FINANCES IN 1980

REVENUE OF ALL STATE governments exceeded expenditure by $19.2 billion in fiscal 1980, reflecting a slight decline from fiscal 1979, when the excess was $22.4 billion. Only 46 states had an excess of revenue over expenditure, compared to 48 in 1979 and 50 in 1978.

In Census Bureau reporting, state government financial statistics include four sectors of activity: general government, state-operated utilities, state alcoholic beverage monopolies and insurance trust operations. Total revenue exceeded expenditure in all but the utility sector during fiscal 1980.

Census Bureau statistics on state government finances do not allow direct comparison of revenue and expenditure as a way to determine overall surplus or deficit. Total revenue and expenditure include such transactions as the operations of trust funds for employee retirement or other insurance trust activities, and exclude transactions that might be crucial to determining total spending requirements, such as liabilities or debt redemption. The Census statistics can be used to approximate the revenue excess or deficiency of state governments, however, with some adjustment to the standard data presentation. Table A depicts this for the last 10 years.

Current revenue is defined to include general, utility and liquor stores revenue. Insurance trust revenue is excluded.

Current expenditure includes current operation, assistance and subsidies, interest on debt and intergovernmental expenditure. Expressed another way, total expenditure includes general, utility and liquor stores expenditure for all purposes other than capital outlay financed by long-term debt. The insurance trust sector is covered by including state government contributions to their own employee retirement and workers' compensation systems as part of current expenditures. Also included as current expenditure are long-term debt redeemed and any net decrease in short-term debt. These debt service payments replace capital outlay funded from bond issues. Finally, capital outlay funded from current revenues is also included as current expenditures.

Table A

CURRENT REVENUE, CURRENT EXPENDITURE AND EXCESS (DEFICIENCY) OF STATE GOVERNMENTS

(In billions of dollars)

Fiscal year	Current revenue	Current expenditure	Calculated excess (deficiency)
1980	$237.7	$228.2	$9.5
1979	211.7	203.3	8.4
1978	192.4	183.1	9.3
1977	172.1	169.0	3.1
1976	154.3	148.8	5.5
1975	136.7	138.9	(2.2)
1974	124.4	120.8	3.6
1973	115.1	108.4	6.7
1972	100.5	98.6	1.9
1971	86.9	88.6	(1.7)

Adapted by Maurice Criz and David Kellerman, Senior Advisor and Statistician, respectively, Governments Division, U.S. Bureau of the Census, from the Bureau's report, *State Government Finances in 1980*. Fiscal 1980 data is for fiscal years which ended on June 30, 1980, except for four states with other closing dates: Alabama, September 30; Michigan, September 30; New York, March 31; and Texas, August 31.

As indicated in Table A, the state government sector of the economy was in good fiscal shape through 1980.

Among the major factors affecting state government finances during 1980 were the economic recession, continued high rates of inflation and an emerging review of the role of state governments in the federal system (a continuation of the public's call for tax or budget restrictions begun a few years earlier). These all contributed to rising costs for states in pro-. viding services, while at the same time revenue and expenditure limitations (or the threat of them) continued to be imposed. Eleven states had some form of broad-based tax or spending limit in effect by fiscal 1980. Limitation measures in three more states are scheduled to take effect for fiscal 1981, and two more are scheduled for fiscal 1982.

The General Government Sector

For the second consecutive year, general expenditure of all state governments increased at a slightly faster pace than general revenue. Expenditure levels were pushed upward by rising costs, while revenues (particularly taxes) were affected by public pressure for restraint. State governments responded accordingly with changes in state taxes, including indexing the individual income tax or reducing its rates and exempting food or medicine from sales tax.

During the 1980 fiscal year, state government general expenditure exceeded $1,000 per capita for the first time. Excluding Alaska (where state general spending per capita amounted to $4,827), per capita general expenditure ranged from over $1,500 in Hawaii and Wyoming to under $750 in Florida and Missouri.

State general expenditure increases were led by growth in capital outlays (up 21.8 percent during 1980). Capital outlay had been restrained in the late 1970s as long-term capital projects became susceptible to state efforts at holding down spending. Growth in the level of capital outlay during 1980 reflected, to some extent, state catch-up spending. A number of states increased general capital outlay during the year more than 50 percent.

The increased level of capital spending accounted for much of the growth in specific state programs, especially highways, natural resources, and housing and urban renewal. Expenditures for state highways were up 21 percent to $20.7 billion, with capital outlay for state highway facilities increasing by almost 25 percent.

Other programs for which state spending increased considerably included health, corrections, natural resources and interest expenditure on general debt. Interest payments increased to $6.8 billion, making interest the fifth largest general purpose for which state governments spent public funds during 1980.

State aid payments for education increased 14 percent to $52.7 billion. This increase reflected major shifts in the method of financing public education that took place in a handful of states during 1980. In some cases, these were the direct result of limitations imposed upon local property taxation. Most notable among the states in which education aid programs were revised were those in California, Georgia, Idaho, Nevada and Washington. Aid for education also increased considerably in Illinois, New Hampshire and Wyoming.

Public welfare spending increased by 13.7 percent, to $44.2 billion. Most of the growth was in vendor payments for medical care, up 17.5 percent to $19 billion.

State government general revenue patterns showed little change from prior years. Of the $233.6 billion total, over 58 percent was attributable to tax revenue. Severance taxes were the fastest growing tax source, up 44 percent. While a relatively small source of state general revenue in terms of national totals (1.8 percent), severance taxes account for significant portions of total general revenue in the energy producing states of Alaska, Kentucky, Louisiana, Montana, New Mexico, Oklahoma, Texas and Wyoming.[1]

State individual income taxes increased 13.7 percent nationally, as inflation pushed salary and wage earners into higher brackets. However, there was wide variation with respect to growth among those states that impose individual income taxes. A number of states established large tax credits or indexing provisions, or reduced tax rates and thereby showed a decline or little growth in individual income tax revenue. Percentage change in individual income tax collections ranged from -13.4 percent in Alaska and -31.7 percent in New Mexico, to increases of over 35 percent in Arkansas and California. As for other major state tax sources, general sales tax revenue increased 9.1 percent nationally, corporation net income taxes were up 9.8 percent, and motor fuel sales tax collections dropped by 2.6 percent. This drop was particularly significant in view of the dedication of large parts of motor fuel tax revenue to highway construction and maintenance programs in most states.

After tax revenue, the largest source of state funds continued to be intergovernmental aid. State revenue from the federal government increased by 13.5 percent to $61.9 billion during 1980, accounting for 26.5 percent of state general revenue nationally. Federal aid for highways increased by 26.3 percent, with aid for education up 19.2 percent, and aid for health and hospitals up 16.1 percent. The increased highway aid was a significant factor in the growth of highway capital outlays mentioned above.

Intergovernmental aid may take on a new significance in forthcoming years, as states have to contend with cutbacks in federal aid and more important roles as conduits for aid to local governments. With federal aid accounting for over 26 percent of state general revenue, any major shifts in federal-state and state-local intergovernmental relationships will have a considerable impact upon state government financial activity.

Included in state government general revenue were net proceeds from 14 state-operated lotteries. Vermont became the latest state to establish a lottery when it began operations during fiscal 1980. Net lottery revenue of all 14 states amounted to about $1 billion, less than 1 percent of state general revenue nationwide.

Table B
STATE LOTTERY PROCEEDS: FISCAL 1980
(In thousands of dollars)

| | | | Disposition of funds | |
| | | | Administration and other | Proceeds available for other purposes |
States	Gross revenue	Prizes		
Connecticut	$122,776	$ 67,275	$ 9,342	$ 46,159
Delaware	15,142	8,103	1,507	5,532
Illinois	90,012	45,813	9,461	34,738
Maine	5,365	2,797	1,690	878
Maryland	353,653	174,339	12,611	166,703
Massachusetts	152,130	89,761	13,758	48,611
Michigan	444,240	237,414	11,737	195,089
New Hampshire	11,455	5,668	2,258	3,529
New Jersey	320,433	173,766	6,057	140,610
New York	165,788	72,811	12,856	80,121
Ohio	118,399	61,363	11,924	45,112
Pennsylvania	357,059	189,811	16,292	150,956
Rhode Island	28,950	14,965	2,077	11,908
Vermont	2,695	1,337	534	824

Insurance Trust Finances

Every state operates a system of unemployment insurance and one or more public employee retirement systems. Most of the states also administer workers' compensation systems, and a few have other insurance systems involving the payment of cash benefits from accumulated fund reserves. Transactions of these various systems, exclusive of administrative costs (treated as general expenditure) and of state contributions (classified as intergovernmental transactions), are reported as insurance trust revenue and insurance trust expenditure in Tables 1 and 2.

The increased level of unemployment as a result of the 1980 recession led to a 36 percent jump in state expenditures for unemployment compensation benefits. Unemployment compensation payments had declined annually since fiscal 1976, when state governments paid out a record $17.8 billion in benefits. Fiscal 1980 benefit payments totaled $12.0 billion.

Benefit payments of state-administered employee retirement systems also increased considerably during 1980, up nearly 15 percent to $10.3 billion.[2]

In total, insurance trust operations accounted for 14.2 percent of all state revenue and 9.7 percent of all state expenditures during the fiscal year.

Utility and Liquor Store Operations

Thirteen states had some form of utility operation during fiscal 1980. There were three water supply systems, six electric power systems and six transit systems operated by state governments or their agencies during the year. Nationally, state government utility expenditure of $2.4 billion exceeded revenue of $1.3 billion.

New York state utility operations accounted for about 75 percent of utility revenue and 60 percent of utility expenditure nationally. The Power Authority of the State of New York, the Metropolitan Transportation Authority and a number of other transportation authorities are all treated as agencies of the state government, thus accounting for the large dollar volume of utility transactions for New York in Census Bureau statistical reports.

Seventeen state governments maintained alcoholic beverage monopolies during 1980. In total, liquor stores revenue ($2.8 billion) exceeded expenditure ($2.2 billion), as all 17 states recorded a profit on their liquor store operations during 1980.

Indebtedness and Debt Transactions

Total indebtedness of all state governments reached $122 billion at the end of fiscal 1980, or $540 per capita. Long-term debt increased by 9.5 percent to $119.8 billion, while short-term debt declined 6.7 percent to $2.1 billion.

Full faith and credit debt (backed by state government powers of taxation) continued to decline relative to total state borrowing. Such debt increased by only 2.2 percent during 1980, while revenue bonds and other forms of non-guaranteed borrowing increased by 15.2 percent. The increased use of non-guaranteed debt reflects greater state involvement in financing enterprise-type operations (sewage facilities, hospitals, utilities, public housing, etc.) as well as an increased level of state financing of facilities for private enterprise. These include activities for pollution control, industrial development and housing construction for private ownership.

High interest rates prevailing in the credit markets made for a significant drop in the issuance of refunding bonds. During 1978 and 1979, $4.1 and $1.6 billion in refunding bonds were issued. For 1980, only a negligible amount ($30 million) of refunding bonds were issued.

States varied greatly in the extent to which they have relied upon debt financing. Per capita indebtedness ranged from lows of $35 in Arizona and $111 in Indiana to highs of $3,861 in Alaska, $1,932 in Hawaii, and $1,856 in Oregon.

Notes

1. More information on severance tax collections can be found in the section on "State Tax Collections in 1981."

2. More detailed information on insurance trust finances can be found in the section on "Finances of State-Administered Public Employee Retirement Systems."

Table 1
SUMMARY FINANCIAL AGGREGATES, BY STATE: 1980
(In millions of dollars)*

State	Revenue						Expenditure					Debt redemption
	Total	General	Insurance trust	Liquor stores	Utilities	Borrowing	Total	General	Insurance trust	Liquor stores	Utilities	
All states	$276,962	$233,592	$39,301	$2,765	$1,304	$16,734	$257,812	$228,223	$24,981	$2,207	$2,401	$6,022
Alabama	4,154	3,634	393	127	...	31	4,002	3,579	304	118	...	52
Alaska	3,230	3,011	218	...	...	258	2,033	1,931	102	...	...	76
Arizona	3,187	2,566	614	...	7	...	2,637	2,447	184	...	7	2
Arkansas	2,295	2,103	192	...	...	125	2,148	1,993	155	...	...	7
California	36,087	29,603	6,459	...	25	1,098	32,812	29,427	3,381	...	4	408
Colorado	3,366	2,792	574	...	...	57	2,805	2,581	224	...	...	26
Connecticut.........	3,472	3,111	350	...	12	506	3,341	2,957	319	...	65	217
Delaware	970	893	74	...	3	251	886	820	59	...	7	56
Florida	8,223	7,304	914	...	6	52	7,387	7,005	364	...	17	96
Georgia	5,194	4,583	611	...	...	114	4,901	4,574	327	...	...	80
Hawaii	1,895	1,637	258	...	...	254	1,660	1,539	121	...	...	87
Idaho	1,108	917	153	37	...	111	1,041	917	97	27	...	8
Illinois	12,730	11,045	1,685	...	...	874	12,429	11,045	1,383	...	...	310
Indiana.............	4,794	4,323	471	...	...	53	4,867	4,448	418	...	...	26
Iowa	3,479	2,958	394	127	...	16	3,412	3,107	213	91	...	8
Kansas	2,419	2,162	257	...	...	...	2,254	2,104	150	...	...	21
Kentucky	4,168	3,744	425	...	...	316	4,569	4,213	356	...	...	91
Louisiana...........	5,412	4,792	620	...	...	480	4,887	4,463	424	...	...	108
Maine	1,369	1,179	150	41	...	84	1,326	1,143	141	41	...	49
Maryland	5,564	4,833	697	...	34	475	5,435	4,740	461	...	234	204
Massachusetts........	7,457	6,749	706	...	2	734	7,336	6,715	603	...	18	364
Michigan	12,357	10,277	1,674	406	...	614	12,634	10,513	1,779	342	...	207
Minnesota	5,700	5,253	447	...	...	349	5,418	5,066	351	...	...	162
Mississippi	2,885	2,482	304	98	...	13	2,691	2,460	142	89	...	40
Missouri............	4,258	3,670	587	...	...	303	3,996	3,617	379	...	...	43
Montana	1,153	946	169	39	...	169	1,005	864	109	32	...	7
Nebraska...........	1,506	1,420	86	...	...	150	1,392	1,341	52	...	...	3
Nevada	1,221	829	366	...	25	163	1,098	817	190	...	90	6
New Hampshire	894	672	88	133	...	192	889	735	48	106	...	31
New Jersey	8,822	7,148	1,675	...	...	1,025	8,537	7,288	1,249	...	...	167
New Mexico	2,183	1,984	199	...	...	237	1,744	1,663	81	...	...	33
New York	27,199	22,051	4,172	...	976	2,476	24,978	21,345	2,205	...	1,428	1,498
North Carolina	6,202	5,370	832	...	...	219	5,733	5,340	392	...	...	61
North Dakota	1,013	907	106	...	...	97	910	854	56	...	...	8
Ohio	12,180	8,231	3,589	361	...	657	11,397	8,808	2,314	275	...	388
Oklahoma	3,433	3,135	241	...	57	70	3,249	2,868	192	...	189	51
Oregon.............	4,041	3,079	815	147	...	1,213	3,456	2,987	382	87	...	110
Pennsylvania	14,004	11,277	2,119	608	...	208	12,644	10,316	1,849	480	...	262
Rhode Island........	1,393	1,187	200	...	6	349	1,361	1,184	162	...	15	63
South Carolina	3,484	2,906	427	...	151	331	3,325	2,799	200	...	326	68
South Dakota	762	703	59	...	...	154	740	712	27	...	...	16
Tennessee	4,028	3,572	456	...	...	108	3,874	3,543	330	...	...	91
Texas	12,924	11,927	997	...	...	212	11,487	10,815	672	...	...	84
Utah	1,889	1,558	278	53	...	162	1,755	1,597	120	38	...	18
Vermont	711	630	52	29	...	177	676	608	40	28	...	34
Virginia	5,656	5,034	394	227	...	323	5,393	4,919	289	186	...	60
Washington..........	6,324	4,831	1,275	218	...	137	5,715	4,856	689	170	...	59
West Virginia	2,640	2,178	376	87	...	243	2,679	2,263	346	69	...	64
Wisconsin	6,588	5,596	991	...	...	342	6,074	5,574	500	...	...	88
Wyoming	937	802	106	30	...	150	797	720	51	27	...	3

Source: U.S. Bureau of the Census, *State Government Finances in 1980.*

*Details do not add up to totals due to rounding.
... Represents zero.

Table 2

NATIONAL TOTALS OF STATE GOVERNMENT FINANCES: 1960-80

Item	1980	1979	1978	1976	1974	1972	1970	1968	1966	1964	1962	1960	Percentage change 1979 to 1980	Per capita 1980
Revenue and borrowing	$293,696	$262,648	$238,475	$199,626	$148,775	$120,931	$93,463	$73,237	$58,970	$47,885	$40,589	$35,149	11.8	$1,300
Borrowing	16,734	15,644	13,464	15,805	7,959	8,622	4,523	4,777	3,724	2,717	2,994	2,312	7.0	74
Revenue total	276,962	247,004	225,011	183,821	140,816	112,309	88,939	68,460	55,246	45,167	37,595	32,838	12.1	1,226
General revenue	233,592	207,993	189,099	152,118	122,327	98,632	77,755	59,132	46,757	37,648	31,157	27,363	12.3	1,034
Taxes total	137,075	124,903	113,261	89,256	74,207	59,870	47,961	36,400	29,380	24,243	20,561	18,036	9.8	607
Intergovernmental revenue	64,326	57,087	53,461	44,717	33,170	27,981	20,248	15,935	12,246	9,464	7,480	6,745	12.7	285
From federal government	61,892	54,548	50,200	42,013	31,632	26,791	19,252	15,228	11,743	9,046	7,108	6,382	13.5	274
Public welfare	24,680	22,313	20,007	16,867	13,320	12,289	7,818	5,240	3,573	2,977	2,449	2,048	10.5	109
Education	12,765	10,710	9,819	8,661	6,720	5,984	4,554	3,891	2,654	1,152	985	727	19.2	57
Highways	8,860	7,015	6,301	6,262	4,503	4,871	4,431	4,198	3,972	3,652	2,746	2,883	26.3	39
General revenue sharing	2,278	2,261	2,255	2,102	2,045								0.7	10
Employment security administration	2,050	1,928	1,887	1,658	1,295	1,148	769	619	506	437	423	319	6.4	9
Other	11,258	10,322	9,931	6,463	3,749	2,499	1,681	1,280	1,037	828	504	406	9.1	49
From local governments	2,434	2,539	3,261	2,704	1,538	1,191	995	707	503	417	373	363	-4.1	11
Charges and miscellaneous revenue	32,190	25,998	22,377	18,145	14,950	10,780	9,545	6,797	5,131	3,942	3,116	2,583	23.8	143
Utility revenue(a)	1,304	1,137	962										14.7	6
Liquor stores revenue	2,765	2,504	2,388	2,196	2,049	1,904	1,748	1,557	1,361	1,195	1,134	1,128	10.4	12
Insurance trust revenue	39,301	35,370	32,562	29,508	16,439	11,773	9,437	7,771	7,128	6,324	5,304	4,347	11.1	174
Unemployment compensation	13,468	12,866	13,083	15,068	5,711	3,588	3,090	2,963	3,326	3,250	2,812	2,316	4.7	60
Employee retirement	21,146	18,341	16,026	12,171	8,919	6,827	5,205	3,831	2,918	2,369	1,942	1,558	15.3	94
Other	4,686	4,162	3,452	2,269	1,809	1,359	1,143	977	884	706	550	472	12.6	20
Debt outstanding at end of fiscal year, total	121,958	111,740	102,569	84,825	65,296	53,833	42,008	35,666	29,564	25,041	22,023	18,543	9.1	540
Long-term	119,821	109,449	99,671	78,814	61,697	50,379	38,903	33,622	28,504	24,401	21,612	18,128	9.5	530
Non-guaranteed	70,457	61,163	53,356	39,972	30,842	25,314	21,167	18,923	15,795	13,254	11,300	9,216	15.2	312
Full faith and credit	49,364	48,286	46,316	38,842	30,855	25,065	17,736	14,698	12,709	11,147	10,313	8,912	2.2	219
Short-term	2,137	2,291	2,897	6,011	3,599	3,454	3,104	2,045	1,060	641	411	415	-6.7	9
Net long-term	79,810	81,338	72,089	62,488	53,847	45,082	34,479	29,366	24,488	20,922	18,645	15,595	-1.9	353
Full faith and credit only	39,357	40,401	39,147	33,708	26,967	21,932	14,832	11,886	9,925	8,434	7,780	6,711	-2.6	174
Expenditure and debt redemption	263,834	230,154	208,533	184,511	134,948	111,933	87,152	67,754	52,385	43,620	37,392	32,496	14.6	1,168
Debt redemption	6,022	5,497	4,701	3,585	2,814	2,690	2,096	1,500	1,262	1,036	990	900	9.6	27
Expenditure total	257,812	224,666	203,832	180,926	132,134	109,243	85,055	66,254	51,123	42,583	36,402	31,596	14.7	1,141
General expenditure	228,223	200,534	179,802	153,690	119,891	98,810	77,642	60,395	46,090	37,242	31,281	27,228	13.8	1,010
Education	87,939	77,722	69,702	59,630	46,860	38,348	30,865	24,279	17,749	13,129	10,744	8,857	13.1	389
Intergovernmental expenditure	52,688	46,206	40,125	34,084	27,107	21,195	17,085	13,321	10,177	7,664	6,474	5,461	14.0	233
State institutions of higher education	27,927	24,680	23,259	19,707	15,395	13,381	11,011	8,982	6,353	4,649	3,634	2,856	13.2	124
Other	7,324	6,837	6,318	5,839	4,358	3,773	2,769	1,976	1,220	816	636	540	7.1	32
Public welfare	44,219	38,893	35,776	29,633	22,538	19,191	13,206	8,649	6,020	4,904	4,285	3,704	13.7	196
Intergovernmental expenditure	10,977	10,146	10,047	9,476	7,369	6,944	5,003	3,527	2,882	2,108	1,777	1,483	8.2	49
Cash assistance, categorical programs	6,831	6,151	5,712	5,203	4,984	5,089	3,534	2,421	1,986	1,935	1,863	1,728	11.0	30
Cash assistance, other	687	602	623	353	212	192	145	57	57	59	61	76	14.1	3
Other public welfare	25,725	21,994	19,393	14,601	9,974	6,967	4,523	2,644	1,096	801	585	417	17.0	114
Highways	25,044	21,228	18,479	18,100	15,847	15,380	13,483	11,848	10,349	9,374	7,961	7,317	18.0	111
Regular state highway facilities	19,652	16,275	13,970	14,223	11,887	12,089	10,482	9,286	8,297	7,437	6,374	5,812	20.7	87
State toll highway facilities	1,009	804	687	636	749	658	562	533	327	413	260	259	25.5	4
Intergovernmental expenditure	4,383	4,149	3,821	3,241	3,211	2,633	2,439	2,029	1,725	1,524	1,327	1,247	5.6	19

Health and hospitals	17,855	15,529	13,883	11,110	8,443	6,963	5,355	4,202	3,241	2,699	2,351	2,072	15.0	79
State hospitals and institutions for handicapped	11,015	9,922	8,979	7,572	5,957	4,825	3,941	3,198	2,483	2,073	1,824	1,618	11.0	49
Other	6,840	5,608	4,905	3,538	2,486	2,138	1,414	1,044	758	626	527	454	22.0	30
Natural resources	4,346	3,808	3,411	3,863	3,053	2,595	2,223	2,005	1,567	1,208	992	862	14.1	19
Corrections	4,449	3,770	3,275	2,480	1,812	1,389	1,104	874	691	605	524	433	18.0	20
Financial administration	3,031	2,723	2,482	1,955	1,594	1,235	1,032	819	660	582	512	447	11.3	13
General control	3,232	2,812	2,331	1,688	1,273	944	717	510	388	301	259	216	14.9	14
Employment security administration	2,001	1,799	1,757	1,570	1,304	1,133	767	606	500	426	399	313	11.2	9
Police	2,263	2,034	1,826	1,569	1,262	983	741	539	390	319	281	251	11.3	10
Miscellaneous and unallocable	33,843	30,214	26,879	22,091	15,906	10,647	8,149	6,066	4,546	3,696	2,972	2,755	12.0	147
State aid for unspecified purposes	8,501	8,224	6,819	5,674	4,804	3,752	2,958	1,993	1,361	1,053	839	806	3.4	37
Interest	6,763	5,790	5,268	4,140	2,863	2,135	1,499	1,128	894	765	635	536	16.8	30
Veterans' services	61	53	54	64	156	51	67	33	21	19	95	112	14.3	. . .
Other (includes intergovernmental aid for specified purposes not elsewhere classified)	18,518	16,146	14,738	12,213	8,083	4,709	3,626	2,912	2,270	1,859	1,402	1,300	14.7	81
Utility expenditure(a)	2,401	1,957	1,544	. . .	. . .	. . .	. . .	. . .	. . .	. . .	. . .	. . .	22.7	11
Liquor store expenditure	2,206	2,068	1,991	1,781	1,653	1,495	1,404	1,233	1,081	977	882	907	6.7	10
Insurance trust expenditure	24,981	20,107	20,495	25,455	10,590	8,938	6,010	4,626	3,952	4,364	4,238	3,461	24.2	111
Unemployment compensation	12,006	8,828	10,672	17,780	4,673	4,722	2,713	2,042	1,884	2,627	2,802	2,359	36.0	53
Employee retirement	10,257	8,937	7,811	6,045	4,591	3,175	2,376	1,810	1,398	1,125	933	700	14.8	45
Other	2,718	2,342	2,011	1,629	1,326	1,041	921	774	671	612	502	402	16.1	12
Total expenditure by character and object	257,812	224,666	203,832	180,926	132,134	109,243	85,055	66,254	51,123	42,583	36,402	31,596	14.7	1,141
Direct expenditure	173,307	148,691	136,545	123,069	86,193	72,483	56,163	44,304	34,195	29,616	25,495	22,152	16.5	767
Current operation	108,131	94,533	86,153	68,175	50,803	39,790	30,971	23,379	16,855	13,492	11,290	9,534	14.4	479
Capital outlay	23,325	19,124	16,064	18,009	15,417	15,283	13,295	12,210	10,193	8,820	7,214	6,607	22.0	103
Construction	19,736	15,930	13,260	15,285	12,655	13,022	11,185	10,053	8,287	7,263	5,960	5,509	23.9	87
Purchase of land and existing structures	1,345	1,229	1,171	1,274	1,540	1,369	1,240	1,389	1,360	1,134	903	802	9.5	6
Equipment	2,243	1,965	1,633	1,450	1,222	892	870	769	546	424	351	296	14.2	10
Assistance and subsidies	9,818	8,878	8,341	7,290	6,521	6,337	4,387	2,960	2,301	2,175	2,118	2,015	10.6	43
Interest on debt	7,052	6,048	5,493	4,140	2,863	2,135	1,499	1,128	894	765	635	536	16.6	31
Insurance benefits and repayments	24,981	20,107	20,495	25,455	10,590	8,938	6,010	4,626	3,952	4,364	4,238	3,461	24.2	111
Intergovernmental expenditure	84,504	75,975	67,287	57,858	45,941	36,759	28,892	21,950	16,928	12,968	10,906	9,443	11.2	374
Cash and security holdings at end of fiscal year	273,047	241,217	212,107	157,210	134,493	99,791	84,810	69,412	58,201	45,862	38,543	33,940	13.2	1,209
Unemployment fund balance in U.S. Treasury	11,945	11,359	7,450	4,425	10,773	8,964	12,236	10,849	8,835	6,580	5,603	6,597	5.2	53
Cash and deposits	30,782	30,251	25,345	18,477	18,387	12,372	8,463	8,226	7,469	5,572	4,650	4,175	1.8	136
Securities	230,320	199,607	179,312	134,308	105,332	78,456	64,110	50,337	41,898	33,710	28,290	23,168	15.4	1,020
Total by purpose:														
Insurance trust	166,656	144,422	124,371	94,679	80,840	62,991	54,995	44,333	35,515	28,058	22,789	20,264	15.4	738
Debt offsets	40,011	28,111	27,582	15,880	7,849	5,309	4,424	4,256	4,016	3,479	2,968	2,533	42.3	177
Other	66,381	68,564	60,154	46,651	45,804	31,514	25,404	20,824	18,671	14,325	12,786	11,144	-3.2	294

Source: U.S. Bureau of the Census, annual reports on *State Government Finances* and *Historical Statistics on Governmental Finances and Employment* (vol. 6, no. 4, of the 1977 Census of Governments).
. . . Represents or rounds to zero.

(a) Reported separately only since 1977; previously included with general revenue or general expenditure.

Table 3
STATE GENERAL REVENUE, BY SOURCE AND BY STATE: 1980
(In thousands of dollars)

State	Total general revenue(a)	Taxes Total	Sales and gross receipts Total	General	Motor fuels	Licenses Total	Motor vehicle	Individual income	Corporation net income	Intergovernmental revenue	Charges and miscellaneous general revenue
All states	$233,592,124	$137,075,178	$67,854,790	$43,167,534	$9,721,569	$8,690,435	$4,935,633	$37,089,481	$13,321,331	$64,326,479	$32,190,467
Alabama	3,633,716	1,856,789	1,146,256	577,089	172,922	116,586	38,344	396,570	109,238	1,252,576	524,351
Alaska	3,011,436	1,437,601	54,422		26,175	39,136	10,960	100,481	565,329	380,637	1,193,192
Arizona	2,566,150	1,684,399	1,056,991	814,588	118,158	88,039	58,180	287,498	117,764	557,616	324,135
Arkansas	2,102,719	1,160,767	625,315	371,825	136,166	105,565	72,964	316,644	83,714	723,598	218,354
California	29,603,059	19,366,696	8,599,792	6,695,242	854,185	629,387	414,881	6,463,736	2,507,183	7,257,017	2,979,346
Colorado	2,791,974	1,490,898	757,961	537,379	113,442	93,434	49,153	461,325	110,607	781,549	519,527
Connecticut	3,110,767	1,839,678	1,326,202	802,950	153,155	111,142	69,951	100,953	246,129	815,919	455,170
Delaware	892,558	515,715	74,169		29,319	144,468	23,007	235,763	40,553	206,657	170,186
Florida	7,303,596	4,804,298	3,544,031	2,252,113	417,133	379,845	244,009		371,405	1,790,579	708,719
Georgia	4,583,376	2,728,961	1,506,923	931,976	330,485	85,896	46,797	872,073	239,713	1,427,845	426,570
Hawaii	1,636,835	998,383	614,237	498,293	34,778	15,892	8,398	311,404	50,259	373,608	264,844
Idaho	917,331	490,346	223,490	137,114	52,793	58,510	35,163	159,138	42,604	284,566	142,419
Illinois	11,045,235	7,073,077	3,681,186	2,379,123	388,097	459,805	349,804	1,900,676	797,927	2,869,941	1,102,217
Indiana	4,322,869	2,695,759	1,761,331	1,331,594	256,149	127,788	98,411	556,709	179,191	898,400	728,710
Iowa	2,957,634	1,746,828	778,242	502,055	167,463	176,985	132,742	602,385	138,564	781,538	429,268
Kansas	2,161,779	1,269,671	634,819	418,389	118,937	103,096	70,063	336,061	149,517	587,664	304,444
Kentucky	3,743,692	2,144,941	1,007,078	607,604	187,446	94,969	51,133	505,832	158,846	1,100,282	498,469
Louisiana	4,792,318	2,397,215	1,190,267	739,347	188,281	162,152	41,560	247,438	249,338	1,304,273	1,090,830
Maine	1,178,755	619,160	347,675	214,113	51,652	56,179	33,782	142,689	45,086	411,739	147,850
Maryland	4,833,162	2,760,818	1,247,724	712,815	186,658	112,453	81,390	1,097,009	165,857	1,164,803	907,541
Massachusetts	6,748,678	3,927,303	1,349,502	745,996	212,035	93,375	55,556	1,860,033	532,383	2,097,467	723,908
Michigan	10,277,168	5,947,650	2,556,716	1,706,728	473,593	340,358	248,587	1,916,626	910,732	2,816,792	1,512,726
Minnesota	5,253,033	3,202,581	1,216,226	650,138	204,955	194,485	134,506	1,262,697	381,217	1,274,458	775,994
Mississippi	2,482,408	1,257,932	899,777	671,086	127,647	80,247	26,612	150,296	64,369	929,212	295,264
Missouri	3,670,190	2,094,540	1,146,337	792,290	203,177	178,442	108,107	603,319	135,103	1,156,044	419,606
Montana	945,678	435,751	95,191		51,089	38,026	21,188	135,012	45,623	370,572	139,355
Nebraska	1,419,516	816,767	446,856	277,014	104,331	67,038	42,489	235,821	57,579	389,420	213,329
Nevada	829,112	476,604	391,327	182,925	34,625	64,193	23,467			241,219	111,289
New Hampshire	672,172	267,495	133,372		48,046	40,768	21,917	10,474	62,786	255,892	148,785
New Jersey	7,147,524	4,265,830	2,091,599	1,180,267	288,264	469,863	256,307	1,004,781	497,205	1,856,391	1,025,303

New Mexico	1,984,036	926,048	537,085	402,909	69,999	55,534	34,423	46,846	46,272	438,166	619,822
New York	22,051,223	12,716,772	4,607,665	2,844,869	474,798	496,160	312,044	5,780,045	1,235,340	7,373,613	1,960,838
North Carolina	5,369,967	3,215,348	1,413,025	693,564	295,143	240,715	128,089	1,180,507	291,752	1,561,501	593,118
North Dakota	907,133	371,861	191,814	124,012	33,488	41,424	25,631	53,346	36,348	246,633	288,639
Ohio	8,230,517	4,766,665	2,658,567	1,445,788	397,133	367,242	209,315	1,039,728	517,344	2,235,588	1,228,264
Oklahoma	3,135,059	1,776,044	678,807	317,578	129,545	173,470	118,998	361,895	89,869	797,599	561,416
Oregon	3,079,327	1,455,352	172,186	...	92,880	159,261	102,189	867,976	177,425	952,828	671,147
Pennsylvania	11,277,432	7,240,808	3,518,743	1,995,829	575,891	748,786	278,116	1,671,842	861,682	2,854,579	1,182,045
Rhode Island	1,186,593	550,787	297,993	169,061	39,260	23,270	18,466	153,912	53,620	358,799	277,007
South Carolina	2,905,665	1,678,049	939,284	576,489	173,412	65,557	31,905	494,789	153,475	849,619	377,997
South Dakota	703,253	270,518	232,851	147,171	41,809	24,690	15,770	30,800	3,292	269,558	163,177
Tennessee	3,571,842	1,886,992	1,415,967	982,251	226,785	181,522	93,089	...	198,222	1,241,306	443,544
Texas	11,926,955	6,758,706	4,368,968	2,536,805	480,946	741,680	302,348	265,327	40,377	2,917,195	2,251,054
Utah	1,557,722	785,755	433,964	324,744	74,074	33,661	18,364	83,182	22,425	505,902	266,065
Vermont	630,156	266,317	128,010	40,836	21,745	27,467	20,174	...	...	245,133	118,706
Virginia	5,034,342	2,743,325	1,212,363	595,060	275,141	149,138	99,121	1,103,006	193,847	1,391,394	899,623
Washington	4,830,772	2,917,445	2,176,618	1,625,006	254,637	158,134	78,162	252,362	32,889	1,236,987	676,340
West Virginia	2,177,916	1,219,492	845,791	598,512	101,467	71,480	49,987	1,430,475	311,321	712,959	245,465
Wisconsin	5,596,130	3,366,310	1,305,000	853,863	194,684	161,745	99,035	...	...	1,533,017	696,803
Wyoming	801,644	388,125	215,075	163,134	37,576	41,377	30,979	...	...	245,829	167,690

Source: U.S. Bureau of the Census, *State Government Finances in 1980.*

... —Represents zero.

(a) Total general revenue equals total taxes plus intergovernmental revenue plus charges and miscellaneous revenue. Columns do not add to totals due to rounding.

Table 4
SUMMARY OF EXPENDITURE, BY CHARACTER AND OBJECT AND BY STATE: 1980
(In thousands of dollars)

| State | Intergovernmental expenditure | Direct expenditure | | Capital outlay | | | | Assistance and subsidies | Interest on debt | Insurance benefits and repayments | Exhibit: Total salary and wages |
		Total	Current operation	Total	Construction	Land and existing structures	Equipment				
All states	$84,504,451	$173,307,530	$108,130,998	$23,325,066	$19,736,347	$1,345,482	$2,243,237	$9,817,816	$7,052,537	$24,981,113	$48,792,921
Alabama	1,036,721	2,965,135	2,046,616	384,046	321,139	16,513	46,394	175,686	54,571	304,216	900,550
Alaska	340,319	1,692,399	1,178,760	290,342	262,280	15,949	12,113	33,944	87,403	101,950	487,038
Arizona	1,040,614	1,596,673	1,047,370	296,164	246,429	11,105	38,630	65,091	4,366	183,682	560,152
Arkansas	624,261	1,523,281	1,005,555	276,253	244,261	6,493	25,499	67,925	18,765	154,783	449,673
California	15,360,365	17,451,834	12,260,454	1,226,545	895,621	177,079	153,845	173,727	410,072	3,381,036	5,519,251
Colorado	947,692	1,857,078	1,353,448	223,503	187,352	6,257	29,894	30,621	25,266	224,240	731,269
Connecticut	671,287	2,669,979	1,675,257	259,173	188,664	20,555	49,954	211,485	205,415	318,649	719,279
Delaware	189,577	696,574	448,232	107,123	85,144	6,164	15,815	38,964	42,973	59,282	216,278
Florida	2,925,889	4,460,865	2,837,944	898,467	745,101	85,330	68,036	216,454	143,819	364,181	1,596,566
Georgia	1,613,179	3,287,555	2,059,597	686,989	631,819	3,156	52,014	147,736	66,120	327,113	1,032,358
Hawaii	35,530	1,624,498	1,013,006	284,158	250,097	10,872	23,189	110,118	96,540	120,676	604,735
Idaho	309,341	731,946	473,387	112,725	92,016	6,400	14,309	32,046	16,618	97,170	225,266
Illinois	3,817,128	8,611,630	4,671,241	1,169,989	1,034,273	53,420	82,296	1,035,428	351,587	1,383,385	1,908,596
Indiana	1,805,564	3,061,239	2,053,949	503,829	426,476	12,029	65,324	55,141	29,924	418,396	909,323
Iowa	1,148,360	2,263,452	1,546,852	311,948	233,265	36,197	42,486	170,489	20,856	213,307	691,732
Kansas	601,939	1,652,092	1,088,829	280,482	245,992	10,992	23,498	110,378	22,073	150,330	551,574
Kentucky	1,006,756	3,562,379	1,955,619	904,646	810,647	26,119	67,880	179,541	166,835	355,738	994,941
Louisiana	1,315,201	3,571,507	2,292,574	568,066	465,040	48,009	55,017	142,137	145,145	423,585	1,112,154
Maine	303,746	1,022,133	673,415	98,448	88,820	3,266	6,362	72,324	36,505	141,441	248,563
Maryland	1,431,805	4,003,010	2,339,971	753,921	663,172	55,486	35,263	276,574	171,991	460,553	948,613
Massachusetts	2,116,477	5,219,624	3,377,550	344,360	302,129	14,648	27,583	564,330	330,437	602,947	1,284,370
Michigan	3,578,343	9,055,263	5,352,988	720,420	606,070	32,734	81,616	1,010,937	192,149	1,778,769	2,160,607
Minnesota	2,237,164	3,180,712	2,228,028	445,935	368,413	46,128	31,394	40,835	114,428	351,486	948,157
Mississippi	856,350	1,834,467	1,257,368	288,927	260,083	6,949	21,895	102,084	44,444	141,644	441,517
Missouri	1,088,886	2,907,186	1,804,329	474,459	384,579	48,839	41,041	197,529	51,908	378,961	863,214
Montana	230,463	774,508	480,737	146,143	126,970	8,236	10,937	23,185	15,023	109,420	220,507
Nebraska	412,081	980,139	656,013	217,437	174,613	15,938	26,886	52,641	2,368	51,680	355,515
Nevada	265,956	831,602	405,032	202,920	181,723	9,310	11,926	11,926	21,928	189,796	198,894
New Hampshire	137,723	751,725	527,562	96,112	84,231	3,613	8,268	32,446	47,442	48,163	190,362
New Jersey	3,056,970	5,479,878	3,266,778	558,175	460,400	64,242	33,533	108,013	298,045	1,248,867	1,278,270

State											
New Mexico	595,464	1,148,708	773,263	211,305	189,801	3,982	17,522	47,684	35,356	81,100	415,777
New York	10,252,802	14,725,137	8,630,006	1,526,689	1,365,609	69,294	91,786	539,358	1,824,137	2,204,947	4,203,343
North Carolina	2,028,170	3,704,372	2,469,199	540,970	440,866	35,510	64,594	208,014	93,905	392,284	1,254,667
North Dakota	216,844	693,071	483,284	126,990	108,918	4,793	13,279	17,886	8,622	56,289	189,633
Ohio	3,249,696	8,147,675	3,905,179	1,142,766	1,017,222	28,055	97,489	567,353	218,721	2,313,656	1,812,086
Oklahoma	800,260	2,448,736	1,608,983	431,926	366,376	16,251	49,299	131,785	84,134	191,908	680,239
Oregon	879,899	2,576,057	1,430,149	341,948	280,731	13,370	47,847	178,662	243,791	381,507	685,704
Pennsylvania	3,541,237	9,102,767	5,011,095	457,311	361,410	25,643	70,258	1,359,968	425,687	1,848,706	2,031,383
Rhode Island	217,255	1,143,748	745,553	70,038	58,604	4,220	7,214	84,170	81,825	162,162	318,945
South Carolina	781,643	2,543,668	1,742,805	425,117	331,326	12,038	81,753	82,238	93,336	200,172	838,938
South Dakota	121,758	617,745	422,297	96,835	76,726	2,524	17,585	38,548	32,884	27,181	167,595
Tennessee	974,485	2,899,251	1,897,272	489,408	412,802	36,652	39,954	108,740	73,473	330,358	849,647
Texas	3,458,969	8,027,882	5,176,160	1,775,329	1,541,791	71,637	161,901	285,066	119,587	671,740	2,400,040
Utah	459,404	1,295,400	832,260	264,849	224,992	7,715	32,142	54,607	24,034	119,650	378,923
Vermont	110,786	565,081	387,889	61,255	47,798	4,980	8,477	41,325	35,018	39,594	146,259
Virginia	1,268,683	4,124,537	2,861,043	665,470	560,635	51,847	52,988	181,655	127,596	288,773	1,332,865
Washington	1,601,814	4,112,798	2,483,568	599,494	483,844	36,124	79,526	262,521	78,445	688,770	1,132,918
West Virginia	533,286	2,145,277	1,225,282	433,191	371,503	31,292	30,396	61,799	78,717	346,288	497,345
Wisconsin	2,643,133	3,430,984	2,378,312	371,203	293,248	18,845	59,110	61,811	119,883	499,775	949,889
Wyoming	263,176	534,273	288,938	161,267	135,326	8,682	17,259	14,891	18,370	50,807	157,401

Source: U.S. Bureau of the Census, *State Government Finances in 1980*.

Table 5
STATE GENERAL EXPENDITURE IN TOTAL AND FOR SELECTED FUNCTIONS, BY STATE: 1980
(In thousands of dollars)

	Total general expenditure(b)	Education	Public welfare	Highways	Hospitals	Natural resources	Health	Corrections	Financial administration	General control	Employment security administration	Police
All states(a)	$228,222,861	$87,938,702	$44,219,541	$25,043,948	$11,369,866	$4,345,758	$6,485,136	$4,449,188	$3,031,211	$3,232,143	$2,001,385	$2,263,352
Alabama	3,579,438	1,665,103	544,039	408,280	236,329	74,625	104,068	55,972	35,881	47,717	21,007	29,378
Alaska	1,930,768	598,629	115,348	173,526	14,034	104,983	34,631	30,501	34,259	65,105	16,631	17,775
Arizona	2,446,907	1,181,970	150,445	337,104	80,446	34,874	75,593	64,469	44,420	23,586	24,319	45,347
Arkansas	1,992,759	780,569	319,091	376,460	82,764	57,184	57,252	28,254	32,265	15,217	19,882	17,958
California	29,427,390	12,086,100	7,572,428	1,550,739	851,670	602,904	854,170	490,507	390,465	203,081	166,549	268,392
Colorado	2,580,530	1,242,988	378,808	335,573	139,952	59,154	66,094	53,671	32,212	48,683	16,557	33,206
Connecticut	2,957,260	827,564	629,706	246,590	212,312	27,461	64,664	74,627	39,564	72,323	35,257	32,558
Delaware	820,076	343,025	98,502	87,535	28,669	12,852	20,050	26,211	17,809	21,533	6,109	13,336
Florida	7,005,078	3,147,477	704,884	947,295	307,574	217,918	327,079	204,641	70,816	161,537	54,478	85,503
Georgia	4,573,621	1,964,825	702,241	701,878	234,024	118,712	165,600	119,152	42,386	43,415	41,304	49,393
Hawaii	1,539,352	559,207	233,492	101,595	80,496	52,179	51,318	17,170	17,927	42,598	12,782	1,144
Idaho	917,042	376,193	112,706	145,251	17,108	43,200	33,347	13,136	13,134	10,029	14,045	8,052
Illinois	11,045,373	4,043,667	2,553,056	1,351,701	431,968	125,100	214,956	222,315	132,252	123,253	96,239	89,529
Indiana	4,448,407	1,942,354	574,462	645,229	197,412	90,448	119,411	82,411	50,159	33,530	39,577	47,803
Iowa	3,107,350	1,319,403	512,058	491,435	192,970	71,774	32,926	51,787	40,918	24,612	27,690	22,455
Kansas	2,103,701	871,304	366,001	378,526	120,974	59,840	30,837	33,775	32,192	39,035	19,904	11,984
Kentucky	4,213,397	1,587,883	637,301	904,110	150,147	87,970	105,793	73,493	48,413	80,832	12,405	65,529
Louisiana	4,463,123	1,684,364	639,455	621,619	337,794	114,202	107,252	87,967	53,407	55,164	16,950	59,553
Maine	1,143,068	389,019	265,686	151,212	29,766	46,218	31,303	16,351	20,973	16,426	12,860	11,513
Maryland	4,739,936	1,475,980	749,280	722,651	358,555	52,274	143,174	153,678	99,876	68,815	25,082	126,394
Massachusetts	6,714,912	1,714,205	1,887,682	423,051	294,127	41,370	319,055	118,165	71,111	156,831	52,977	35,010
Michigan	10,512,780	3,642,925	2,842,865	986,504	524,498	129,953	369,212	188,084	106,361	109,887	134,019	110,547
Minnesota	5,066,390	2,060,152	842,576	542,691	249,655	135,491	78,767	75,401	51,944	55,541	33,817	42,353
Mississippi	2,460,057	1,009,957	384,680	370,853	114,601	71,176	61,444	35,291	16,311	17,664	38,886	23,769
Missouri	3,617,111	1,410,083	660,584	530,313	240,922	102,232	95,664	67,130	44,709	43,661	45,105	43,265
Montana	863,516	279,333	94,928	186,695	25,690	48,464	24,581	18,303	28,185	12,177	7,708	10,989
Nebraska	1,340,540	416,260	191,036	264,553	80,907	54,027	37,018	33,281	15,864	17,042	14,435	14,487
Nevada	817,272	353,749	75,189	150,480	17,528	17,629	24,575	29,257	26,171	10,294	24,405	7,380
New Hampshire	735,310	190,021	132,551	129,145	33,983	13,657	20,666	11,070	9,969	9,326	7,547	9,005
New Jersey	7,287,981	2,305,071	1,489,671	435,287	455,868	122,773	114,597	145,545	82,751	108,220	49,938	77,574

State											
New Mexico	1,663,072	753,375	161,577	205,654	75,611	41,124	60,122	34,973	30,204	31,443	15,372	16,338
New York	21,344,548	6,440,798	5,283,597	1,115,054	1,414,682	104,524	520,775	462,952	307,623	728,592	192,899	133,334
North Carolina	5,340,258	2,500,036	729,418	630,611	285,217	123,885	162,407	171,800	58,494	78,919	29,400	65,572
North Dakota	853,626	311,633	88,045	138,316	32,574	31,502	16,506	6,270	11,119	6,406	4,528	3,715
Ohio	8,808,482	3,688,166	1,651,591	829,547	528,361	123,021	442,700	140,178	132,054	49,563	92,702	53,652
Oklahoma	2,867,812	1,243,058	552,963	375,192	160,390	49,574	42,618	53,240	35,143	30,163	27,493	33,176
Oregon	2,987,314	1,037,427	463,784	431,512	135,813	120,159	76,615	58,102	86,034	41,508	17,217	36,448
Pennsylvania	10,315,687	3,695,387	2,729,367	867,897	610,729	158,065	304,206	131,044	161,170	129,489	142,093	137,857
Rhode Island	1,184,157	362,215	303,627	52,367	96,385	9,249	41,770	19,510	19,029	27,419	14,953	11,080
South Carolina	2,799,322	1,264,205	354,749	269,959	187,079	65,475	112,191	60,969	36,157	32,080	29,600	32,907
South Dakota	712,322	205,913	101,423	144,276	21,342	28,210	18,684	7,247	16,517	15,014	10,014	6,551
Tennessee	3,543,378	1,416,092	570,382	609,508	164,931	71,906	124,162	98,408	37,805	42,482	42,241	23,629
Texas	10,815,111	5,518,003	1,455,431	1,687,625	620,025	174,030	203,269	161,825	116,788	63,495	104,915	96,359
Utah	1,597,377	750,430	186,645	228,888	77,852	48,618	38,474	22,400	21,721	16,838	19,284	15,890
Vermont	607,883	206,038	100,396	72,660	21,121	19,421	22,161	12,102	11,957	12,221	9,046	9,601
Virginia	4,918,756	1,866,198	696,804	833,538	389,728	66,183	171,665	160,226	72,356	59,050	39,486	84,464
Washington	4,855,948	2,296,485	804,147	617,959	144,330	152,640	112,536	97,287	60,260	36,373	42,596	40,720
West Virginia	2,263,143	812,642	249,257	576,526	76,159	46,235	48,299	14,391	31,587	27,213	20,835	19,371
Wisconsin	5,574,342	1,877,861	1,232,948	509,766	168,216	96,927	164,295	92,536	69,887	59,938	49,787	23,707
Wyoming	719,878	223,360	42,639	149,212	16,308	24,366	16,584	22,113	12,602	7,403	8,730	7,800

Source: U.S. Bureau of the Census, *State Government Finances in 1980.*

(a) Totals do not add, due to rounding.

(b) Does not represent sum of state figures because total includes miscellaneous expenditure not shown separately.

383

Table 6
STATE DEBT OUTSTANDING AT END OF FISCAL YEAR, BY STATE: 1980
(In thousands of dollars, except per capita amounts)

State	Total	Per capita	Long-term Total	Long-term Full faith and credit	Long-term Non-guaranteed	Short-term	Net long-term(a) Total	Net long-term(a) Full faith and credit
All states	$121,957,862	$ 539.95	$119,821,093	$49,363,682	$70,457,411	$2,136,769	$79,810,494	$39,356,578
Alabama	1,032,338	265.38	1,032,338	129,410	902,928	...	1,001,505	124,924
Alaska	1,544,554	3,861.38	1,544,554	631,723	912,831	...	976,090	630,343
Arizona	94,007	34.59	94,007	...	94,007	...	79,016	...
Arkansas	362,579	158.68	362,579	...	362,579	...	132,719	...
California	8,361,705	353.28	8,259,704	6,317,952	1,941,752	102,001	5,329,440	4,000,095
Colorado	460,497	159.40	455,944	...	455,944	4,553	178,281	...
Connecticut.........	3,879,197	1,248.13	3,873,366	2,187,299	1,686,067	5,831	2,432,403	1,998,923
Delaware	1,044,499	1,755.46	1,037,535	402,383	635,152	6,964	927,564	388,862
Florida	2,626,926	269.70	2,626,926	618,585	2,008,341	...	1,846,285	163,602
Georgia	1,404,635	257.07	1,404,635	547,206	857,429	...	1,059,104	540,178
Hawaii	1,864,213	1,931.83	1,838,854	1,418,764	420,090	25,359	1,835,378	1,415,978
Idaho	327,334	346.75	327,334	795	326,539	...	46,164	795
Illinois	6,277,201	549.76	6,229,741	2,611,510	3,618,231	47,460	3,688,767	2,416,665
Indiana............	607,581	110.67	540,379	...	540,379	67,202	427,744	...
Iowa	380,999	130.79	380,999	...	380,999	...	144,348	...
Kansas	438,137	185.42	438,137	27,800	410,337	...	386,585	27,800
Kentucky...........	3,035,267	829.08	3,035,267	281,715	2,753,552	...	1,867,389	281,715
Louisiana..........	2,977,031	708.14	2,476,972	1,908,419	1,068,553	59	2,775,056	1,770,930
Maine	730,266	649.13	718,677	254,835	463,842	11,589	496,927	254,835
Maryland	3,502,248	830.70	3,502,248	2,120,398	1,381,850	...	2,877,248	2,067,000
Massachusetts........	5,784,878	1,008.35	5,337,717	3,252,853	2,084,864	447,161	3,636,202	3,238,922
Michigan	2,916,082	314.98	2,914,869	676,410	2,238,459	1,213	1,623,381	657,587
Minnesota	2,069,902	507.70	2,067,640	896,805	1,170,835	2,262	1,033,372	895,525
Mississippi	815,045	323.30	812,692	752,346	60,346	2,353	780,532	730,188
Missouri............	1,017,862	207.01	1,017,862	63,745	954,117	...	481,089	57,272
Montana	309,533	393.31	309,533	6,500	303,033	...	146,063	5,900
Nebraska..........	199,341	126.97	199,341	...	199,341	...	25,416	...
Nevada............	527,969	660.79	527,969	106,844	421,125	...	330,952	85,345
New Hampshire	899,050	976.17	863,295	252,490	610,805	35,755	504,004	244,184
New Jersey	6,526,797	886.31	6,517,097	1,853,466	4,663,631	9,700	4,509,245	1,834,811
New Mexico	707,783	544.45	704,521	23,071	681,450	3,262	239,368	18,635
New York	23,640,088	1,346.48	22,965,711	3,781,179	19,184,532	674,377	14,687,874	3,030,199
North Carolina	1,265,720	215.48	1,262,773	730,504	532,269	2,947	1,039,564	692,562
North Dakota........	219,276	335.80	219,276	11,350	207,926	...	44,236	...
Ohio	4,014,977	371.86	4,009,151	2,291,560	1,717,591	5,826	3,687,646	2,286,590
Oklahoma	1,525,740	504.38	1,525,740	197,740	1,328,000	...	1,341,428	131,613
Oregon	4,886,286	1,855.79	4,866,186	4,521,716	344,470	20,100	166,261	166,261
Pennsylvania.........	6,347,873	534.92	6,197,617	3,872,315	2,325,302	150,256	5,689,281	3,770,244
Rhode Island........	1,463,092	1,544.98	1,448,092	250,315	1,197,777	15,000	1,404,133	248,880
South Carolina	1,937,234	621.11	1,866,934	501,307	1,365,627	70,300	1,253,824	315,793
South Dakota........	714,274	1,035.18	713,764	...	713,764	510	101,881	...
Tennessee	1,405,948	306.24	1,359,277	651,350	707,927	46,671	746,083	585,560
Texas	2,468,627	173.50	2,468,627	908,545	1,560,082	...	1,788,110	374,553
Utah	537,074	367.61	536,919	88,490	448,429	155	251,838	65,785
Vermont	654,159	1,280.15	634,851	238,280	396,571	19,308	330,920	238,280
Virginia	1,926,291	360.32	1,681,786	23,572	1,658,214	244,505	758,040	5,717
Washington	1,600,407	387.51	1,600,407	1,322,620	277,787	...	1,407,058	1,322,620
West Virginia	1,816,478	931.53	1,816,478	925,120	891,358	...	1,291,509	594,155
Wisconsin	2,445,967	519.87	2,331,877	1,704,395	627,482	114,090	1,944,437	1,676,752
Wyoming...........	362,895	770.48	362,895	...	362,895	...	58,734	...

Source: U.S Bureau of the Census, *State Government Finances in 1980.*

(a) Long-term debt outstanding minus long-term debt offsets.

Note: Debt figures include revenue bonds and other special obligations of state agencies as well as state general obligations.

... Represents zero.

2. Taxation

RECENT TRENDS IN STATE TAXATION

By John Gambill

STATE TAX LEGISLATION enacted in 1980 and 1981 emphasized sales and excise tax rate increases and personal income tax reductions. A majority of the states increased their motor fuel tax rates, and variable rate motor fuel tax laws were adopted in seven states and the District of Columbia. Seven states and the District of Columbia increased their sales tax rates, while eight states increased cigarette taxes. Twenty states increased taxes on one or more kinds of alcoholic beverages.

Reductions in the personal income tax took various forms: repeal in Alaska, restructuring in Louisiana and North Dakota, reduced rates, higher personal exemptions and standard deductions, and more rebates and credits.

ACTION IN 1980

General Sales Taxes

Tax Rates. Connecticut increased its sales tax rate from 7 to 7.5 percent on July 1, 1980. The District of Columbia increased its rate from 5 to 6 percent on August 1. Ohio increased its sales tax rate from 4 to 5 percent for the period January 1, 1981, through June 30, 1981. South Dakota increased its rate from 4 to 5 percent for the period April 1, 1980, to July 1, 1981, but the increase did not take effect until May 1 because of litigation. Tennessee again extended its 4.5 percent rate, to July 1, 1981.

Local Sales Taxes. Alabama authorized four more counties to impose sales taxes. Alaska raised the maximum sales tax rate of boroughs (counties) from 3 to 6 percent. Georgia permanently extended its local option sales and use tax. Illinois authorized the East St. Louis metropolitan area transit district to impose a 0.25 percent tax in three counties. Washington State authorized King County to raise the rate of the sales tax levied for transit purposes from 0.3 to 0.6 percent.

Exemptions. Arizona exempted food from the sales tax. Illinois reduced the tax on food and drugs from 3 to 2 percent, effective January 1, 1981; the general rate of the Illinois sales tax is 4 percent. South Dakota kept the rate on food at 4 percent when it increased the general rate to 5 percent.

Individual Income Taxes

Repeal. Alaska repealed its individual income tax retroactively to the beginning of 1979.

Indexing. South Carolina indexed its rate brackets, personal exemptions and standard deduction, beginning with 1982 tax years. The adjustment may not exceed 6 percent per year. The Montana electorate approved indexing the tax brackets, personal exemptions and standard deduction beginning in 1981.

John Gambill is Senior Research Associate and Director of Publications, Federation of Tax Administrators.

Three states that adopted indexing in earlier years enacted related legislation in 1980. Arizona permanently extended its indexing law. Colorado provided that the inflation adjustment for 1980 would be 9 percent. Iowa extended indexing to the 1981 tax year, but no indexing adjustment was made for 1980 and 1981 because the balance in the state treasury was below the legal limit to initiate the adjustment.

Restructuring. Louisiana restructured and reduced its personal income tax. The previous system of directly relating state income tax to federal income tax was replaced by a system that uses federal adjusted gross income as a starting point. The new law provides for a combined personal exemption and standard deduction of $6,000 for single taxpayers and $12,000 for joint returns and heads of households. An additional deduction of $1,000 is allowed for each exemption.

Rates. Nebraska reduced its tax from 17 to 15 percent of federal tax liability. Vermont reduced its tax from 25 to 23 percent of federal tax liability. (In 1979, Vermont had reduced the tax from 25 to 23 percent for 1979 only.)

Personal Exemptions. Hawaii increased its personal exemption from $750 to $1,000.

Standard Deductions. Colorado increased the standard deduction from 10 percent of adjusted gross income or $1,000, whichever was less, to a flat $1,000. Maryland made the 13 percent standard deduction permanent; it was scheduled to revert to 10 percent on July 1, 1981.

Sales Tax Credit. Hawaii increased the amounts of its excise tax credit, which is graduated according to income. The amounts now range from $48 down to $8; previously the range was $40 to $6. Nebraska increased the amount of its food sales tax credit from $20 to $28.

Rebates and General Credits. Colorado provided a credit of 20 percent of normal tax liability for the 1980 tax year. Rhode Island provided a rebate of $10 for each personal exemption claimed on the 1979 income tax return.

Corporation Income Taxes

Tax Rates. Alaska increased the surtax exemption from $25,000 to $50,000. Kentucky revised its tax rates. The new rates, effective January 1, 1980, ranged from 3 to 6 percent, with four brackets. The previous rates were 4 and 5.8 percent. New Jersey increased its rate from 7.5 to 9 percent, effective January 1, 1980. Ohio imposed a one-time surtax of 15 percent on its corporation tax. It also imposed a litter tax of 0.11 percent on the first $25,000 of taxable income and 0.22 percent on additional amounts.

Taxes on Specific Industries. Iowa revised the rate and base of its tax on financial institutions. Utah imposed a gross receipts tax on corporations that are not otherwise required to pay income or franchise taxes to the state or to declare dividends. Connecticut and New York imposed taxes on the gross receipts of oil companies.

New and Expanding Business. Florida enacted a jobs creation credit and a credit for new and expanding businesses. Louisiana enacted a credit for new or expanding businesses, equal to $100 for each new employee (with larger amounts for employees who are economically disadvantaged or who are residents of neighborhoods with an unemployment rate above 10 percent). Missouri enacted a 10-year income tax credit for new business facilities, based on the number of new employees and the value of the new business facility investment. Tennessee enacted a credit for purchases of industrial machinery, ranging from 0.2 to 1.0 percent of the purchase price, depending on the year of purchase.

TAXATION

Motor Fuel Taxes

Variable Rate Taxes. Indiana, Kentucky, Massachusetts and Nebraska adopted legislation that periodically resets the per gallon tax rates on the basis of the wholesale or retail price of motor fuel. As a result of this legislation, the Indiana tax rose from 8 to 8.5 cents per gallon, the Massachusetts tax rose from 8.5 to 10 cents and then dropped to 9.8 cents, and the Nebraska tax rose from 10.5 cents to 13.3 and then to 13.6 cents. As the result of a variable rate tax enacted in 1979, New Mexico's rate increased from 7 to 8 cents per gallon.

Other Rate Increases. Excluding states with variable rate laws, motor fuel tax rate increases were enacted in seven states: Alabama, from 7 to 11 cents per gallon on gasoline and from 8 to 12 cents on diesel fuel; District of Columbia, from 10 to 11 cents; Minnesota, from 9 to 11 cents; South Carolina, from 10 to 11 cents; South Dakota, from 9 to 12 cents for gasoline and diesel fuel, from 7 to 10 cents for liquid propane, and from 5 to 8 cents for gasohol; Virginia, from 9 to 11 cents; and Wisconsin, from 7 to 9 cents. Michigan raised the diesel fuel tax rate to 11 cents, which is the rate on gasoline.

Gasohol. The tax on gasohol was reduced or eliminated in nine states: Alabama, Alaska, Florida, Maryland, Michigan, Minnesota, New Mexico, North Carolina and Utah. Iowa, which had exempted gasohol in 1978, raised the tax to 5 cents per gallon.

Local Taxes. South Dakota authorized second and third class municipalities to levy a 1 cent per gallon tax on motor fuel. Virginia imposed a 2 percent tax on the retail sale of motor fuel in the five Virginia cities and counties that are members of the Washington Metropolitan Area Transit Authority; the rate will rise to 4 percent on July 1, 1982.

Cigarette, Tobacco and Alcoholic Beverage Taxes

Two states increased their cigarette tax rates: Alabama, from 12 to 16 cents per pack, and Maryland, from 10 to 13 cents. Alabama imposed an additional 10 percent tax on distilled spirits and wines sold by the alcoholic beverage control board and a 35 percent tax on table wine (not over 14 percent alcohol). Minnesota permanently extended a two-year reduction of the tax on sparkling wines. New Jersey imposed a tax of 6.5 percent of the receipts of wholesalers from sales of alcoholic beverages (except draught beer sold by the barrel). Ohio increased the taxes on beer and wine for a six-month period. Virginia increased its tax on wine.

Property Tax Relief

Tax Limits. Arkansas amended its constitution to require an automatic rollback of property tax rates whenever a reassessment raises the value of all the property in a taxing unit by 10 percent or more. Louisiana amended the constitution to provide for millage adjustments to keep taxes constant in the event of a reappraisal. Massachusetts amended its constitution to limit state and local property taxes to 2.5 percent of the full and fair cash value of the property. In addition, a city or town may increase its revenues by no more than 2.5 percent a year. By constitutional amendment, Ohio classified all real property into two classes (residential or agricultural and other) and provided that the taxes on each class of property in each jurisdiction would remain constant.

Residential Relief. Arizona amended its constitution to limit taxes on residential real estate to 1 percent of full value and limited increases in value to 10 percent per year. Florida, Illinois, Iowa and Louisiana increased their homestead exemptions. Oregon voters approved the continuation of homestead tax payments of 30 percent of the property tax, up to

$800 on each homestead and increased the amount of the property tax refund, which is graduated according to household income. Utah repealed its property tax refund for homeowners and renters and enacted an income tax credit for property tax and rent.

Senior Citizen Relief. Property tax relief for senior citizens, including homestead exemptions and circuit breakers, was revised and increased in Alaska, Colorado, Connecticut, Georgia, Idaho, Illinois, Indiana, Nebraska, New Jersey, New York, Ohio, Rhode Island, South Carolina, Utah, Washington and West Virginia.

Classification and Use Value Assessment. Arizona reduced the assessment ratios for all classes of property. Arkansas amended its constitution to provide that agricultural, pasture, timber, residential and commercial land must be valued according to its productivity or use. Illinois provided that the equalized assessed value of farmland in each county in 1980 may not increase by more than 8 percent over 1979. Minnesota lowered the assessment ratios for various classes of property.

Limits on State Taxes and Spending

Delaware amended its constitution to require a three-fifths vote of each house of the legislature to increase taxes or fees. Missouri amended its constitution to limit the increase in state revenues to the increase in Missouri personal income and to prohibit an increase of local taxes without voter approval.

ACTION IN 1981

General Sales Taxes

Tax Rates. Five states increased their sales tax rates and one state reduced its rate. Minnesota increased its sales tax rate from 4 to 5 percent for the period July 1, 1981, to June 30, 1983. The rate on farm machinery was kept at 4 percent. Nevada increased its tax rate to 5.75 percent, including uniform school and county taxes, from May 1, 1981, through June 30, 1983. The previous rate was 3 percent plus an optional county tax of 0.5 percent, levied in all but two counties. New Mexico reduced its rate from 3.75 to 3.5 percent on July 1, 1981. Ohio raised its rate from 4 to 5 percent, effective November 15, 1981. Washington raised its rate from 4.5 to 5.5 percent, effective December 4, 1981. West Virginia increased its rate from 3 to 5 percent on June 1, 1981. The rate on mobile homes was kept at 3 percent. Tennessee again extended its 4.5 percent rate, to July 1, 1982.

Local Sales Taxes. Arkansas authorized counties and first class cities to impose 1 percent sales taxes, if approved by the voters. Louisiana increased the maximum rate of the municipal sales tax from 1.5 to 2.5 percent, except for municipalities located in six designated parishes (counties). Missouri extended its authorization for cities to impose sales tax for transportation purposes through December 31, 1983. Nebraska permanently extended its authorization for Omaha to impose a sales tax of 1.5 percent, rather than the 1 percent allowed other municipalities. Nevada authorized counties to impose a 0.25 percent tax for public mass transportation, if approved by the voters. New York imposed a 0.25 percent tax within the Metropolitan Transportation District (New York City and seven nearby counties). Ohio raised the limit on county sales tax rates from 0.5 to 1 percent. Utah authorized municipalities to impose a 0.25 percent tax to fund a public transportation system, if approved by the voters.

Exemptions. Alabama and Oklahoma exempted prescription medicines and drugs from the sales tax.

TAXATION

Individual Income Taxes

Tax Rates. Montana repealed its 10 percent surtax. New Mexico reduced its income tax rates. Pennsylvania extended its temporary 2.2 percent tax rate through 1983. Utah increased the tax rates on single taxpayers and estates and trusts to make them equal to the tax rates on married couples.

Restructuring. North Dakota gave individuals, estates and trusts the option of computing their state income tax at 7.5 percent of their adjusted federal income tax liability before credits.

Rebates and General Credits. Hawaii granted taxpayers a refundable credit of $100 per personal exemption, to be applied against their tax liability for 1981. New York increased the amount of its household credit. North Dakota provided that, if the revenue credited to the general fund during the 1981-82 fiscal year exceeded $460 million, individuals, estates and trusts would receive a credit equal to 10 percent of the tax liability for the 1982 tax year.

Personal Exemptions. New Hampshire increased the personal exemption under its interest and dividends tax from $600 to $1,200. New York increased the personal exemption from $750 to $800, beginning in 1982. North Dakota increased the personal exemption from $750 to $1,000.

Standard Deduction. Georgia, Montana, New York, North Dakota and South Carolina increased their standard deductions (minimum amount, maximum amount or percentage).

Indexing. Minnesota revised its formula for indexing its personal income tax. Oregon postponed the indexing of its personal exemption (which was to begin with 1981 tax years) until 1983.

Unincorporated Business Tax. Connecticut enacted a 5 percent tax on the net income of unincorporated businesses.

Sales Tax Credit. New Mexico increased the amount of its sales tax rebate from $40 to $45 per exemption and the amount of its graduated rebate for state and local taxes.

Local Income Tax. Michigan increased the maximum rate of tax that Detroit may impose on its residents from 2 to 3 percent and the maximum rate on non-residents from 0.5 to 1.5 percent. Ohio authorized school districts to levy income taxes. Oregon authorized mass transit districts to impose a tax of 0.6 percent on net earnings from self-employment.

Corporation Income Taxes

Tax Rates. Alaska revised its tax rates, replacing a set of two rates with 12 brackets in 1981 and 10 brackets in later years. New Hampshire imposed a 13.5 percent surtax on its business profits tax from July 1, 1981 through June 30, 1983. New Mexico replaced its flat 5 percent tax rate with a graduated set of rates ranging from 4 percent on the first $1 million of taxable income to 6 percent on income over $2 million. North Dakota reduced its corporate tax rates. Ohio increased its rates from 4 to 4.6 percent on the first $25,000 of taxable income and from 8 to 8.7 percent on additional amounts. Pennsylvania extended its temporary 10.5 percent rate through 1983. Wisconsin replaced its set of graduated rates (ranging from 2.3 to 7.9 percent) with a flat 7.9 percent rate. Connecticut increased its minimum and alternate corporation taxes and exacted a second alternate tax. Colorado enacted a tax reduction that varies with taxable income and increases each year through 1985. North Dakota provided that, if revenue credited to the general fund during the 1981-82 fiscal year exceeds $460 million, corporations would receive a credit equal to 10 percent of the tax liability for the 1982 tax year.

Depreciation. Hawaii and Wisconsin adopted the federal Accelerated Cost Recovery System, effective with 1981. Maine adopted ACRS for 1981 only. Oregon provided that ACRS would not apply in 1981 and 1982. Ohio and Pennsylvania provided for phasing in ACRS.

Investment Tax Credit. Illinois enacted an investment tax credit and New York increased the amount of its investment tax credit.

Financial Depositories. Delaware provided an inverse graduated rate structure for banks and trust companies: 8.7 percent of the first $20 million of taxable income, 6.7 percent of the next $5 million, 4.7 percent of the next $5 million, and 2.7 percent over $30 million. Previously, the rate was a flat 8.7 percent. New Mexico, North Carolina and Ohio made financial depositories subject to the corporation income tax and repealed the separate taxes that had applied to them.

Motor Fuel Taxes

Variable Rate Taxes. Three states and the District of Columbia enacted variable rate laws and increased their tax rates. Arizona increased its tax rate from 8 to 9.6 cents per gallon, effective January 1, 1982. The rate increase was suspended by a referendum petition to be voted on at the 1982 election. Beginning January 1, 1983, the tax is to be redetermined every six months, based on the average retail price of motor fuel. The District of Columbia increased its rate from 11 to 13 cents and provided that, beginning June 1, 1982, the rate will be indexed annually according to changes in the consumer price index for Washington, D.C. Ohio enacted an additional 3.3 cents per gallon tax, making the total tax 10.3 cents per gallon. The rate will be changed each March 1, according to a formula that takes into account highway maintenance cost and fuel consumption. Rhode Island provided for changing its rate each January 1 and July 1 based on the average wholesale selling price of fuel; this raised the tax from 10 to 12 cents per gallon.

In all six states that already had variable rate taxes, the tax increased during 1981 by legislative or administrative action. Indiana amended the formula for setting the rate and raised the rate from 8.5 to 10.5 cents. In Kentucky, where the rate changes quarterly, the rate went from 9 to 9.5 to to 10.4 to 10.1 cents per gallon. In Massachusetts, the rate went from 9.8 to 11.6 to 11.4 to 11.2 cents per gallon. The Nebraska rate, which could change monthly, went from 13.6 to 13.7 to 13.9 cents; in future years, changes will be made quarterly. The New Mexico rate increased from 8 to 9 cents. Washington set the rate at 13.5 cents by legislative action and revised the formula, minimum, and maximum for future rate changes.

Other Rate Changes. Excluding states with variable rate laws, motor fuel taxes were increased in 16 states: California, from 7 to 9 cents per gallon, effective January 1, 1983; Colorado, from 7 to 9 cents; Delaware, from 9 to 11 cents; Idaho, from 9.5 to 11.5 cents; Iowa, from 10 to 13 cents (11.5 to 13.5 cents for diesel fuel, rising to 15.5 cents on July 1, 1982); Minnesota, from 11 to 13 cents; Nevada, from 6 to 10.5 cents, rising to 12 cents on July 1, 1982; New Hampshire, from 11 to 14 cents, through June 30, 1983; North Carolina, from 9 to 12 cents; Oregon, from 7 to 8 cents on January 1, 1982, and rising one cent each year on July 1, 1982, 1983 and 1984 (subject to approval at the May 1982 election); South Carolina, from 11 to 13 cents; South Dakota, from 12 to 13 cents, through March 30, 1984; Tennessee, from 7 to 9 cents (8 to 12 cents for diesel fuel); Utah, from 9 to 11 cents; Vermont, from 9 to 11 cents; and Wisconsin, from 9 to 13 cents.

Gasohol. Idaho, Nevada and Virginia provided special rates for gasohol. Iowa and

Maryland terminated their special provisions for gasohol. The preferential rate in Virginia also applies to synthetic fuel made from coal.

Cigarette and Tobacco Taxes

Six states increased their cigarette tax rates: Iowa, from 13 to 18 cents per pack, through June 30, 1983; Nebraska, from 13 to 14 cents; Oregon, from 9 to 16 cents, through June 30, 1983; South Dakota, from 14 to 15 cents; and Washington and Wisconsin, from 16 to 20 cents per pack. Wisconsin also imposed a 20 percent tax on all other tobacco products. Ohio reduced its rate from 15 to 14 cents per pack, when it made cigarettes subject to the sales tax.

Alcoholic Beverage Taxes

Taxes on beer, wine and distilled spirits were increased in Colorado, Indiana, Maine, Nebraska, New Mexico, South Dakota, Vermont, West Virginia and Wisconsin. Utah and Washington increased their taxes on beer. Michigan and Ohio increased their taxes on wine. Nevada increased its tax on distilled spirits. New Hampshire increased the gallonage tax imposed on manufacturers and wholesalers of beverages containing not more than 6 percent alcohol. Tennessee increased the tax on beverages having an alcoholic content of not more than 5 percent. Mississippi extended its 3 percent markup on alcoholic beverages through June 30, 1985, and imposed a 1 percent surcharge on the gross proceeds of sales of alcoholic beverages.

Virginia repealed the additional tax on alcoholic beverages bought for resale by the drink. Georgia and New Mexico converted their tax rates on wine and distilled spirits into metric units. Michigan and Washington converted their wine tax to metric units.

Property Tax Relief

Tax Limits. North Dakota provided that tax districts may not increase property taxes by more than 7 percent over the previous year in 1981 and 1982.

Residential Relief. New York and Wisconsin increased the amount of property tax relief provided under their circuit breaker programs. Utah repealed its income tax credit for property tax and rent.

Senior Citizen Relief. Montana enacted an income tax credit for senior citizen homeowners and renters. Property tax relief for senior citizens, including homestead exemptions and circuit breakers, was revised and increased in Illinois, Maine, Michigan, Nevada, New Hampshire, New Jersey, North Carolina, North Dakota, South Dakota, Virginia, West Virginia and Wisconsin.

Classification and Use Value Assessment. North Dakota established a classified property tax system with different assessment ratios for residential property, commercial and railroad property, agricultural property and centrally assessed (utility) property. Illinois and North Dakota provided that farmland would be valued on the basis of its income.

Table 1
FOOD AND DRUG SALES TAX EXEMPTIONS
(As of January 1, 1982)

State or other jurisdiction	Tax rate	Exemptions Food	Exemptions Pre-scription drugs	Related income tax credit	State or other jurisdiction	Tax rate	Exemptions Food	Exemptions Pre-scription drugs	Related income tax credit
Alabama	4	...	★	...	New Jersey	5	★	★	...
Arizona	4	★	★	...	New Mexico	3.5	...	...	★
Arkansas	3	...	★	...	New York	4	★	★	...
California	4.75	★	★	...	North Carolina	3	...	★	...
Colorado	3	★	★	...	North Dakota	3	★	★	...
Connecticut	7.5	★	★	...	Ohio	5	★	★	...
Florida	4	★	★	...	Oklahoma	2	...	★	...
Georgia	3	...	...	...	Pennsylvania	6	★	★	...
Hawaii	4	...	...	★	Rhode Island	6	★	★	...
Idaho	3	...	★	★	South Carolina	4	...	★	...
Illinois	4	(a)	(a)	...	South Dakota	4	...	★	...
Indiana	4	★	★	...	Tennessee	4.5	...	★	...
Iowa	3	★	★	...	Texas	4	★	★	...
Kansas	3	...	★	...	Utah	4	...	★	...
Kentucky	5	★	★	...	Vermont	3	★	★	★
Louisiana	3	★	★	...	Virginia	3	...	★	...
Maine	5	★	★	...	Washington	5.5	★	★	...
Maryland	5	★	★	...	West Virginia	5	★	★	...
Massachusetts	5	★	★	★	Wisconsin	4	★	★	...
Michigan	4	★	★	...	Wyoming	3	...	★	...
Minnesota	5	★	★	...	Dist. of Col.	6	★	★	...
Mississippi	5	...	★	...					
Missouri	3.125	...	★	...					
Nebraska	3	...	★	★					
Nevada	5.75	★	★	...					

Source: The Federation of Tax Administrators (based on legislation enacted at 1981 session).

(a) Food and drugs are taxed at 2 percent.

Table 2
AGENCIES ADMINISTERING MAJOR STATE TAXES
(As of January 1, 1982)

State or other jurisdiction	Income	Sales	Gasoline	Motor vehicle
Alabama	Dept. of Rev.	Dept. of Rev.	Dept. of Rev.	Dept. of Rev.
Alaska	Dept. of Rev.	. . .	Dept. of Rev.	Dept. of Pub. Sfty.
Arizona	Dept. of Rev.	Dept. of Rev.	Dept. of Trans.	Dept. of Trans.
Arkansas	Dept. of Fin. & Admin.	Dept. of Fin. & Admin.	Dept. of Fin. & Admin.	Dept. of Fin. & Admin.
California	Fran. Tax Bd.	Bd. of Equal.	Bd. of Equal.	Dept. of Mot. Veh.
Colorado	Dept. of Rev.	Dept. of Rev.	Dept. of Rev.	Dept. of Rev.
Connecticut	Dept. of Rev. Serv.	Dept. of Rev. Serv.	Dept. of Rev. Serv.	Commr. of Mot. Veh.
Delaware	Div. of Rev.	. . .	Dept. of Pub. Sfty.	Dept. of Pub. Sfty.
Florida	Dept. of Rev.	Dept. of Rev.	Dept. of Rev.	Div. of Mot. Veh.
Georgia	Dept. of Rev.	Dept. of Rev.	Dept. of Rev.	Dept. of Rev.
Hawaii	Dept. of Tax.	Dept. of Tax.	Dept. of Tax.	County Treasr.
Idaho	Dept. of Rev./Tax.	Dept. of Rev./Tax.	Dept. of Rev./Tax.	Dept. of Law Enf.
Illinois	Dept. of Rev.	Dept. of Rev.	Dept. of Rev.	Secy. of State
Indiana	Dept. of Rev.	Dept. of Rev.	Dept. of Rev.	Bur. of Mot. Veh.
Iowa	Dept. of Rev.	Dept. of Rev.	Dept. of Rev.	Dept. of Trans.
Kansas	Dept. of Rev.	Dept. of Rev.	Dept. of Rev.	Dept. of Rev.
Kentucky	Dept. of Rev.	Dept. of Rev.	Dept. of Rev.	Dept. of Trans.
Louisiana	Dept. of Rev./Tax.	Dept. of Rev./Tax.	Dept. of Rev./Tax.	Dept. of Pub. Sfty.
Maine	Bur. of Tax.	Bur. of Tax.	Bur. of Tax.	Secy. of State
Maryland	Comptroller	Comptroller	Comptroller	Dept. of Trans.
Massachusetts	Dept. of Rev.	Dept. of Rev.	Dept. of Rev.	Reg. of Mot. Veh.
Michigan	Dept. of Treas.	Dept. of Treas.	Dept. of Treas.	Secy. of State
Minnesota	Dept. of Rev.	Dept. of Rev.	Dept. of Rev.	Dept. of Pub. Sfty.
Mississippi	Tax Com.	Tax Com.	Tax Com.	Tax Com.
Missouri	Dept. of Rev.	Dept. of Rev.	Dept. of Rev.	Dept. of Rev.
Montana	Dept. of Rev.	. . .	Dept. of Rev.	Reg. of Mot. Veh.
Nebraska	Dept. of Rev.	Dept. of Rev.	Dept. of Rev.	Dept. of Mot. Veh.
Nevada	. . .	Dept. of Tax.	Dept. of Tax.	Dept. of Mot. Veh.
New Hampshire	Dept. of Rev. Admin.	. . .	Dept. of Sfty.	Dept. of Sfty.
New Jersey	Dept. of Treas.	Dept. of Treas.	Dept. of Treas.	Dept. of Law & Pub. Sfty.
New Mexico	Dept. of Tax. & Rev.	Dept. of Tax. & Rev.	Dept. of Tax. & Rev.	Dept. of Trans.
New York	Dept. of Tax. & Fin.	Dept. of Tax. & Fin.	Dept. of Tax. & Fin.	Dept. of Mot. Veh.
North Carolina	Dept. of Rev.	Dept. of Rev.	Dept. of Rev.	Dept. of Trans.
North Dakota	Tax Commr.	Tax Commr.	Tax Commr.	Dept. of Mot. Veh.
Ohio	Dept. of Tax.	Dept. of Tax.	Dept. of Tax.	Reg. of Mot. Veh.
Oklahoma	Tax Com.	Tax Com.	Tax Com.	Tax Com.
Oregon	Dept. of Rev.	. . .	Dept. of Trans.	Dept. of Trans.
Pennsylvania	Dept. of Rev.	Dept. of Rev.	Dept. of Rev.	Dept. of Trans.
Rhode Island	Dept. of Admin.	Dept. of Admin.	Dept. of Admin.	Dept. of Trans.
South Carolina	Tax Com.	Tax Com.	Tax Com.	Dept. of Hwy./Pub. Trans.
South Dakota	. . .	Dept. of Rev.	Dept. of Rev.	Dept. of Mot. Veh.
Tennessee	Dept. of Rev.	Dept. of Rev.	Dept. of Rev.	Dept. of Rev.
Texas	. . .	Comptroller	Comptroller	Highway Dept.
Utah	Tax. Com.	Tax Com.	Tax Com.	Tax Com.
Vermont	Commr. of Taxes	Commr. of Taxes	Commr. of Taxes	Mot. Veh. Dept.
Virginia	Dept. of Tax.	Dept. of Tax.	Div. of Mot. Veh.	Div. of Mot. Veh.
Washington	. . .	Dept. of Rev.	Dept. of Licensing	Dept. of Licensing
West Virginia	Tax Dept.	Tax Dept.	Tax Dept.	Dept. of Mot. Veh.
Wisconsin	Dept. of Rev.	Dept. of Rev.	Dept. of Rev.	Dept. of Trans.
Wyoming	. . .	Dept. of Rev. & Tax.	Dept. of Rev. & Tax.	Dept. of Rev. & Tax.
Dist. of Col.	Dept. of Fin. & Rev.	Dept. of Fin. & Rev.	Dept. of Fin. & Rev.	Dept. of Fin. & Rev.

Source: The Federation of Tax Administrators

FINANCES

AGENCIES ADMINISTERING MAJOR STATE TAXES
(As of January 1, 1982)

State or other jurisdiction	Tobacco	Death	Alcoholic beverage	Number of agencies
Alabama	Dept. of Rev.	Dept. of Rev.	Al. Bev. Cont. Bd.	2
Alaska	Dept. of Rev.	Dept. of Rev.	Dept. of Rev.	2
Arizona	Dept. of Rev.	Dept. of Rev.	Dept. of Rev.	2
Arkansas	Dept. of Fin. & Admin.	Dept. of Fin. & Admin.	Dept. of Fin. & Admin.	1
California	Bd. of Equal.	Controller	Bd. of Equal.	4
Colorado	Dept. of Rev.	Dept. of Rev.	Dept. of Rev.	1
Connecticut	Dept. of Rev. Serv.	Dept. of Rev. Serv.	Dept. of Rev. Serv.	2
Delaware	Div. of Rev.	Div. of Rev.	Div. of Rev.	2
Florida	Dept. of Bus. Regln.	Dept. of Rev.	Dept. of Bus. Regln.	3
Georgia	Dept. of Rev.	Dept. of Rev.	Dept. of Rev.	1
Hawaii	Dept. of Tax.	Dept. of Tax.	Dept. of Tax.	2
Idaho	Dept. of Rev./Tax.	Dept. of Rev./Tax.	Dept. of Rev./Tax.	2
Illinois	Dept. of Rev.	Atty. Gen.	Dept. of Rev.	3
Indiana	Dept. of Rev.	Dept. of Rev.	Dept. of Rev.	2
Iowa	Dept. of Rev.	Dept. of Rev.	Dept. of Rev.	2
Kansas	Dept. of Rev.	Dept. of Rev.	Dept. of Rev.	1
Kentucky	Dept. of Rev.	Dept. of Rev.	Dept. of Rev.	2
Louisiana	Dept. of Rev./Tax.	Dept. of Rev./Tax.	Dept. of Rev./Tax.	2
Maine	Bur. of Tax.	Bur. of Tax.	Liquor Com.	3
Maryland	Comptroller	Local	Comptroller	3
Massachusetts	Dept. of Rev.	Dept. of Rev.	Dept. of Rev.	2
Michigan	Dept. of Treas.	Dept. of Treas.	Liquor Contr. Com.	3
Minnesota	Dept. of Rev.	Dept. of Rev.	Dept. of Rev.	2
Mississippi	Tax Com.	Tax Com.	Tax Com.	1
Missouri	Dept. of Rev.	Dept. of Rev.	Dept. of Rev.	1
Montana	Dept. of Rev.	Dept. of Rev.	Dept. of Rev.	2
Nebraska	Dept. of Rev.	Dept. of Rev.	Liquor Cont. Com.	3
Nevada	Dept. of Tax.	. . .	Dept. of Tax	2
New Hampshire	Dept. of Rev. Admin.	Dept. of Rev. Admin.	Liquor Com.	3
New Jersey	Dept. of Treas.	Dept. of Treas.	Dept. of Treas.	2
New Mexico	Dept. of Tax. & Rev.	Dept. of Tax. & Rev.	Dept. of Tax. & Rev.	2
New York	Dept. of Tax. & Fin.	Dept. of Tax. & Fin.	Dept. of Tax. & Fin.	2
North Carolina	Dept. of Rev.	Dept. of Rev.	Dept. of Rev.	2
North Dakota	Tax Commr.	Tax Commr.	Treasurer	3
Ohio	Dept. of Tax.	Dept. of Tax.	Dept. of Tax.	2
Oklahoma	Tax Com.	Tax Com.	Tax Com.	1
Oregon	Dept. of Rev.	Dept. of Rev.	Liquor Cont. Com.	3
Pennsylvania	Dept. of Rev.	Dept. of Rev.	Dept. of Rev.	2
Rhode Island	Dept. of Admin.	Dept. of Admin.	Dept. of Admin.	2
South Carolina	Tax Com.	Tax Com.	Tax Com.	2
South Dakota	Dept. of Rev.	Dept. of Rev.	Dept. of Rev.	2
Tennessee	Dept. of Rev.	Dept. of Rev.	Dept. of Rev.	1
Texas	Comptroller	Comptroller	Al. Bev. Com.	3
Utah	Tax. Com.	Tax Com.	Tax Com.	1
Vermont	Commr. of Taxes	Commr. of Taxes	Commr. of Taxes	2
Virginia	Dept. of Tax.	Dept. of Tax.	Dept. of Tax.	2
Washington	Dept. of Rev.	Dept. of Rev.	Liquor Cont. Bd.	3
West Virginia	Tax Dept.	Tax Dept.	Al. Bev. Cont. Commr.	3
Wisconsin	Dept. of Rev.	Dept. of Rev.	Dept. of Rev.	2
Wyoming	Dept. of Rev. & Tax.	Dept. of Rev. & Tax.	Liquor Com.	2
Dist. of Col.	Dept. of Fin. & Rev.	Dept. of Fin. & Rev.	Dept. of Fin. & Rev.	1

394

Table 3
STATE EXCISE RATES
(As of January 1, 1982)

State or other jurisdiction	Sales and gross receipts (percent)	Cigarettes (cents per pack)	Distilled spirits(b) (dollars per gallon)	Gasoline	Motor fuel(a) (cents per gallon) Diesel	Liquefied petroleum gas	Gasohol
Alabama	4	16	...	11	12	No tax	8
Alaska	...	8	4.00	8	...	No tax	No tax
Arizona	4(c)	13	2.50	8	...	...	...
Arkansas	3	17.75	2.50	9.5	10.5	7.5	No tax
California	4.75	10	2.00(d)	7	...	6	...
Colorado	3	10	2.28(e)	9	...	...	4
Connecticut	7.5(f)	21	2.50	11	...	...	10
Delaware	...	14	2.25	11	...	...	...
Florida	4(g)	21	4.75(h)	8	...	...	3
Georgia	3	12	3.77(e)	7.5	...	...	...
Hawaii	4(i)	40% of wholesale price	20% of wholesale price	8.5	...	6	...
Idaho	3	9.1	...	11.5	...	...	7.5
Illinois	4	12	2.00	7.5	...	...	...
Indiana	4(j)	10.5	2.68	11.1	...	...	...
Iowa	3	18	...	13	13.5	...	6
Kansas	3	11	2.50	8	10	7	5
Kentucky	5	3	1.92	10(k)	...	...	...
Louisiana	3	11	2.50(e)	8	...	...	No tax
Maine	5	16	...	9	...	...	...
Maryland	5	13	1.50(e)	9	...	...	...
Massachusetts	5	21	4.05	11.1	...	...	...
Michigan	4	11	...	11	...	...	6
Minnesota	5(l)	18	4.39(e)	13	...	...	9
Mississippi	5(m)	11	...	9	10	8	...
Missouri	3.125	9	2.00	7	...	...	...
Montana	...	12	...	9	11	No tax	2
Nebraska	3(n)	14	2.75	13.9	...	...	8.9
Nevada	5.75(o)	10	2.05	10.5	...	...	9.5
New Hampshire	...	12	...	14	...	...	9
New Jersey	5	19	2.80	8	...	4	...
New Mexico	3.5	12	1.63(e,p)	9	...	...	No tax
New York	4	15	3.25(e)	8	10	...	...
North Carolina	3(q)	2	...	12	...	...	9
North Dakota	3(r)	12	2.50	8	...	...	4
Ohio	5	14	...	10.3	...	...	...
Oklahoma	2	18	4.00	6.58	6.5	6.5	.08
Oregon	...	16	...	8	...	...	...
Pennsylvania	6	18	...	11	...	...	...
Rhode Island	6	18	2.50	12	...	...	...
South Carolina	4	7	2.96(e,s)	13	...	...	6
South Dakota	4	15	3.80	13	...	11	9
Tennessee	4.5(t)	13	4.00	9(u)	12	...	...
Texas	4	18.5	2.00	5	6.5	...	...
Utah	4	10	...	11	...	...	6
Vermont	3	12	...	11	No tax	No tax	...
Virginia	3	2.5	...	11(v)	...	...	3
Washington	5.5(w)	20	...	12	...	No tax	...
West Virginia	5(x)	17	...	10.5	...	...	...
Wisconsin	4	20	3.25(e)	13	...	...	...
Wyoming	3	8	...	8	...	...	4
Dist. of Col.	6(y)	13	1.50	13	No tax	No tax	...

STATE EXCISE RATES
Footnotes

Source: The Federation of Tax Administrators (based on legislation enacted at the 1981 sessions).

(a) Nine states and the District of Columbia have variable rate motor fuel taxes, under which the motor fuel tax rate is periodically changed by administrative action according to a statutory formula. The states that have thse provisions, the variable on which the formula is based, and the dates that the rate changes become effective are: Arizona, retail price of motor fuel, every January 1 and July 1, beginning January 1, 1983. Indiana, retail price of motor fuel, every January 1 and July 1. Kentucky, wholesale price of motor fuel, January 1, April 1, July 1 and October 1. Massachusetts, wholesale price of motor fuel, January 1, April 1, July 1 and October 1. Nebrska, price of fuel purchased by state government, January 1, April 1, July 1 and October 1. New Mexico, wholesale price of motor fuel, July 1. Ohio, highway maintenance costs and fuel consumption, every March 1, beginning in 1982. Rhode Island, wholesale price of motor fuel, every January 1 and July 1. Washington, retail price of motor fuel, every January 1 and July 1. District of Columbia, consumer price index for Washington, D.C., every June 1, beginning in 1982.

(b) Seventeen states have liquor monopoly systems (Alabama, Idaho, Iowa, Maine, Michigan, Mississippi, Montana, New Hampshire, Ohio, Oregon, Pennsylvania, Utah, Vermont, Virginia, Washington, West Virginia and Wyoming). (North Carolina has county-operated stores on a local option basis.) Some of the monopoly states impose taxes, generally expressed in terms of percentage of retail price. Only gallonage taxes imposed by states with license systems are reported in the table. Excise tax rates shown are general rates; some states tax distilled spirits manufactured in the state from state-grown products at lower rates.

(c) Arizona: This rate is for retailers. Selected businesses are taxed at rates ranging from 0.375 to 4 percent.

(d) California: If not over 50 percent alcohol by weight. If over 50 percent, $4.00 per gallon.

(e) In several states, the tax rate is expressed in metric units: Colorado—$0.6026 per liter; Georgia—$1.00 per liter; Louisiana—$0.66 per liter; Maryland—$0.3963 per liter; Minnesota—$1.16 per liter; New Mexico—$0.43 per liter; New York—$0.859 per liter; South Carolina—$0.7828925 per liter (includes 9 percent surcharge); and Wisconsin—$0.8586 per liter.

(f) Connecticut: Certain business services are taxed at 3.5 percent.

(g) Florida: Self-propelled or power-driven farm equipment is taxed at 3 percent.

(h) Florida: On beverages containing 14 to 48 percent alcohol. The tax rate on beverages containing more than 48 percent alcohol is $9.53 per gallon.

(i) Hawaii: Wholesalers and manufacturers, 0.5 percent; retailers, 4 percent.

(j) Indiana: In addition to the 4 percent sales tax, a gross income tax is imposed, under which wholesale and retail sales are taxed at 0.325 percent in 1982. Thereafter, the gross income tax will be reduced annually until 2008, when it goes out of existence.

(k) Kentucky: Heavy equipment motor carriers pay a 12.2 cents per gallon tax on a use basis.

(l) Minnesota: Farm machinery is taxed at 4 percent. General rate reverts to 4 percent on July 1, 1983.

(m) Mississippi: Among other rates imposed under the tax: wholesale sales, 0.125 percent; aircraft, automobiles, trucks and truck tractors, 3 percent; manufacturing or processing machinery and farm tractors, 1.0 percent; contractors (on compensation exceeding $10,000), 2.5 percent.

(n) Nebraska: State board of equalization and assessment determines rate annually.

(o) Nevada: Includes mandatory, statewide, state-collected 3.75 percent county and school sales tax, which drops to 1.5 percent on July 1, 1983.

(p) New Mexico: If not over 100 proof. If over 100 proof, $0.69 per liter ($2.61 per gallon).

(q) North Carolina: Motor vehicles, boats, railway cars and locomotives, and airplanes, 2 percent with a maximum tax of $120. A tax of 1 percent is imposed on various items used in agriculture and industry. On some items subject to the 1 percent rate, the maximum tax is $80 per article.

(r) North Dakota: The tax on farm machinery, agricultural irrigation equipment and mobile homes is 2 percent.

(s) South Carolina: Includes 9 percent surtax. In addition, there is a tax of $4.88 ($4.48 plus 9 percent surtax) per case on wholesale sales.

(t) Tennessee: Rate scheduled to revert to 3 percent on June 30, 1982.

(u) Tennessee: Also subject to special privilege tax of 1.0 cents per gallon.

(v) Virginia: A 13 cents per gallon tax is imposed on motor carriers of property on a use basis. Synthetic fuel taxed at 3 cents per gallon.

(w) Washington: Also has a gross income tax with rates varying from 0.01 percent to 1 percent according to type of business. Retailers are subject to a 0.44 percent tax under the business and occupation tax.

(x) West Virginia: Sales of mobile homes to be used by purchasers as their principal year-round residence and dwelling are taxed at 3 percent. West Virginia also has a gross income tax at rates ranging from 0.27 to 8.63 percent, according to type of business. Retailers are subject to a 0.55 percent rate under this tax.

(y) District of Columbia: Parking charges are taxed at 12 percent; hotel lodging and accommodations at 10 percent; food or drink for immediate consumption at 8 percent; rental vehicles at 8 percent; and food or drink sold from vending machines at 2 percent.

Table 4
STATE INDIVIDUAL INCOME TAXES

State	Rate range(a) (percent)	Income brackets — Lowest (ends)	Income brackets — Highest (over)	Personal exemptions — Single	Personal exemptions — Married	Personal exemptions — Dependents	Federal income tax deductible
Alabama	1.5-5.0(4)	$1,000	$5,000	$1,500	$3,000	$300	★
Arizona(b)	2.0-8.0(7)	1,000(c)	6,000(c)	1,589	3,178	954	★
Arkansas	1.0-7.0(6)(d)	3,000	25,000	17.50(e)	35(e)	6(e)	. . .
California(b)	1.0-11.0(11)	2,850(f)	22,140(f)	35(e)	70(e)	11(e)	. . .
Colorado(b)	3.0-8.0(11)(g)	1,335	13,352	1,135	2,270	1,135	★
Delaware	1.4-13.5(15)	1,000	50,000	600	1,200	600	★(h)
Georgia	1.0-6.0(6)	750(i)	7,000(i)	1,500(j)	3,000(j)	700	. . .
Hawaii	2.25-11.0(11)(k)	500	30,000	1,000	2,000	1,000	. . .
Idaho	2.0-7.5(6)(l)	1,000	5,000	1,000(l,m)	2,000(l,m)	1,000(l,m)	. . .
Illinois	2.5	——— Flat rate ———		1,000	2,000	1,000	. . .
Indiana	1.9	——— Flat rate ———		1,000	2,000(n)	500	. . .
Iowa(b)	0.5-13.0(13)(o)	1,023	76,725	19(e)	38(e)	14(e)	★
Kansas	2.0-9.0(8)	2,000(c)	25,000(c)	1,000	2,000	1,000	★
Kentucky	2.0-6.0(5)	3,000	8,000	20(e)	40(e)	20(e)	★
Louisiana	2.0-6.0(3)(p)	10,000	50,000	6,000(q)	12,000(q)	1,000	★
Maine	1.0-10.0(8)	2,000(c)	25,000(c)	1,000	2,000	1,000	. . .
Maryland	2.0-5.0(4)	1,000	3,000	800	1,600	800	. . .
Massachusetts	5.375(r)	——— Flat rate ———		2,000	2,800(s)	700	. . .
Michigan	4.6	——— Flat rate ———		1,500	3,000	1,500	. . .
Minnesota(b)	1.6-16.0(13)(d)	654	35,915	66(e)	132(e)	66(e)	★
Mississippi	3.0-4.0(2)	5,000	5,000	6,000	9,500	1,500	. . .
Missouri	1.5-6.0(10)	1,000	9,000	1,200	2,400	400	★
Montana(b)	2.0-11.0(10)	1,100	38,400	880	1,760	880	★
Nebraska	15% U.S. tax(t)	. . .	. . .	. . .	. . .	. . .	. . .
New Jersey	2.0-2.5(2)(u)	20,000	20,000	1,000	2,000	1,000	. . .
New Mexico	0.5-6.0(18)(v)	2,000	100,000	1,000(m)	2,000(m)	1,000(m)	. . .
New York	2.0-14.0(13)	1,000	23,000	800	1,600	800	. . .
North Carolina	3.0-7.0(5)	2,000	10,000	1,100	3,300	800	. . .
North Dakota	1.0-7.5(6)(w)	3,000	30,000	1,000(m)	2,000(m)	1,000(m)	★
Ohio	0.5-3.5(6)	5,000	40,000	650	1,300	650	. . .
Oklahoma	0.5-6.0(7)(x)	1,000	7,500	750	1,500	750	(x)
Oregon(b)	4.0-10.0(7)	500	5,000	1,000	2,000	1,000	★(h)
Pennsylvania	2.2	——— Flat rate ———		0	0	0	. . .
Rhode Island	19% of U.S. tax	. . .	. . .	. . .	. . .	. . .	. . .
South Carolina(b)	2.0-7.0(6)	2,000	10,000	800	1,600	800	★(h)
Utah	2.75-7.75(6)	750(c)	3,750(c)	750(m)	1,500(m)	750(m)	★
Vermont	23% of U.S. tax(y)	. . .	. . .	. . .	. . .	. . .	. . .
Virginia	2.0-5.75(4)	3,000	12,000	600	1,200	600	. . .
West Virginia	2.1-9.6(24)	2,000(z)	200,000(z)	600	1,200	600	. . .
Wisconsin(b)	3.4-10.0(8)	3,600	48,200	20(e)	40(e)	20(e)	. . .
Dist. of Col.	2.0-11.0(10)	1,000	25,000	750	1,500	750	. . .

Source: The Federation of Tax Administrators (based on legislation enacted at 1981 sessions).

Note: The table excludes the following state taxes: Connecticut taxes dividends at 1 to 9 percent, capital gains at 7 percent and unincorporated businesses at 5 percent. New Hampshire taxes interest and dividends at 5 percent. Tennessee taxes dividends and interest at 6 percent; it imposes a 4 percent tax on dividends from corporations with property at least 75 percent of which is assessable for property tax in Tennessee.

(a) Figure in parentheses is the number of steps in range.

(b) Nine states have statutory provisions for automatic adjustment of tax brackets or personal exemptions, as well as other features, to reflect changes in the price level. Adjustments to be made for 1982 tax years will generally not be made until the latter part of 1982. The 1981 adjustment is shown when available.

(c) For joint returns, the tax is twice the tax imposed on half the income.

(d) Provides for the exemption of or the imposition of lower rates on taxpayers with incomes below certain levels.

(e) Tax credits.

(f) The range reported is for single persons. For married persons, the tax is twice the tax imposed on half the income. For heads of households, brackets range from $5,720 to $25,710.

(g) Imposes a surtax of 2 percent on gross income from intangibles which exceed $15,000. A credit is allowed on taxable income up to $9,000, computed by dividing taxable income by 200.

(h) The federal tax deduction is limited: in Delaware to $300 for single persons and $600 for joint returns; in Oregon to $7,000; and in South Carolina to $500.

(i) The range reported is for single persons. For joint returns and heads of households the same rates are applied to income brackets ranging from $1,000 to $10,000. For married persons filing separately, the income brackets range from $500 to $5,000.

(j) In addition, low-income taxpayers are allowed a tax credit up to $15 for single persons and $30 for heads of households or married persons filing jointly.

(k) The range reported is for single persons. For joint returns, the tax is twice the tax imposed on half the income. Different rates and brackets apply to heads of households.

(l) In the case of joint returns, the tax is twice the tax imposed on half the income. A filing fee of $10 is imposed on each return. A credit of $15 is allowed for each personal exemption.

(m) These states by definition allow personal exemptions provided in the Internal Revenue Code. Under existing law, Idaho follows the federal

code as of January 1, 1981; North Dakota as of December 31, 1980; and Utah (for purposes of personal exemptions) as of December 31, 1974. New Mexico automatically accepts amendments to the federal code.

(n) Allows $1,000 for individual taxpayers and $500 for dependents. On joint returns, each spouse may subtract the lesser of $1,000 or adjusted gross income; the minimum exemption is $500 for each spouse.

(o) No tax is imposed on persons whose net income does not exceed $5,000.

(p) The tax due for any year shall not exceed 70 percent of the tax that would have been due if the tax were determined under Louisiana income tax provisions in effect on December 31, 1979, using federal tax liability determined under the Internal Revenue Code in effect on December 31, 1979.

(q) Combined personal exemption and standard deduction.

(r) A 10.75 percent rate is applied to interest and dividends (other than from savings deposits) and on net capital gains. The 5.375 percent rate applies to all other income, including earned income and interest and dividends from savings deposits. These rates include a 7.5 percent surtax.

(s) Minimum allowance; permits exemption on a spouse's earnings up to $2,000.

(t) The rate is determined annually by the State Board of Equalization and Assessment.

(u) A separate tax is levied on New York-New Jersey commuters; taxpayers are liable only for the larger of the applicable taxes.

(v) The rate range reported is for single persons. For joint returns and heads of households, tax rates range from 0.5 percent on income not over $2,000 to 6 percent on income over $200,000. For married persons filing separately, tax rates range from 0.5 percent on the first $1,000 to 6 percent on income over $100,000.

(w) Taxpayers have the option of paying 7.5 percent of adjusted federal income tax liability.

(x) The rate range is for single persons not deducting federal income tax. Married persons filing jointly, surviving spouses, and heads of households have the same rates and brackets that are twice as wide. Separate schedules, with rates ranging from 0.5 percent to 17 percent apply to taxpayers deducting federal income taxes.

(y) If Vermont tax liability for any taxable year exceeds Vermont tax liability determinable under federal law in effect January 1, 1980, the taxpayer will be entitled to a credit equal to the excess plus 6 percent of that amount.

(z) The range reported is for single persons and heads of households. For joint returns, the same rates are applied to brackets ranging from $4,000 to $400,000.

397

Table 5
STATE SEVERANCE TAXES: 1981

State	Title and application of tax(a)	Rate
Alabama	Iron Ore Mining Tax	3¢/ton
	Forest Products Severance Tax	Varies by species and ultimate use
	Oil and Gas Severance Tax	6% of gross value at point of production; 4% for wells producing less than 40 bbls./day
	Oil and Gas Production Tax	2% of gross value at point of production
	Coal Severance Tax(b)	13.5¢/ton
	Coal and Lignite Severance Tax	20¢/ton in addition to Coal Severance Tax
Alaska	Fisheries Business Tax	3% to 5% of fish value based on type of fish
	Oil and Gas Production Tax	Percentage of gross value determined annually
Arkansas	Natural Resources Severance Tax	Separate rate for each substance
	Oil and Gas Conservation Tax	Not more than 25 mills/bbl. of oil nor more than 5 mills/1,000 cu. ft. of gas
California	Oil and Gas Production Tax	Rate determined annually by Department of Conservation
Colorado	Severance Tax(c)	Separate rate for each substance
	Oil and Gas Conservation Tax	9/10 mill/$1 of market value at wellhead
Florida	Oil and Gas Production Tax	8% (oil) and 5% (gas) of gross value at point of production. Wells producing less than 100 bbls./day or producing oil by tertiary methods are taxed 5% of gross value at point of production
	Solid Minerals Tax(d)	5% of market value at point of production
Georgia	Oil and Gas Production Tax	5 mills/bbl. of oil and 1/2 mill/1,000 cu. ft. of gas
Idaho	Ore Severance Tax	2% of net value
	Oil and Gas Production Tax	Maximum of 5 mills/bbl. of oil and 5 mills/1,000 cu. ft. of gas(e)
	Additional Oil and Gas Production Tax	2% of market value at site of production
Indiana	Petroleum Production Tax(f)	1% of value
Kansas	Oil and Gas Production Tax	$.001/bbl. of petroleum and $.00005/1,000 cu. ft. of gas, in addition to $.003/bbl. of oil or petroleum and $.0008/1,000 cu. ft. of gas produced, sold, marketed or used(g)
Kentucky	Oil Production Tax	4½% of market value
	Coal Severance Tax	4½% of gross value
	Natural Resource Severance Tax(h)	4½% of gross value
Louisiana	Natural Resources Severance Tax	Rate varies according to substance
Maryland	Coal and Gas Severance Tax(i)	40¢/ton; 7% of wholesale market value of gas
Michigan	Gas and Oil Severance Tax	5%, 6.6%, and 4% of gross cash market value of gas, oil, and oil from stripper wells and marginal properties(j)
Minnesota	Iron Severance Tax(k)	15% to 15.5% of value (depending on ore) minus credits
	Ore Royalty Tax	15% to 15.5% of royalty (depending on ore) minus credits
	Taconite, Iron Sulphides and Agglomerate Taxes	(l)
	Semi-Taconite Tax	(l)
	Copper-Nickel Taxes	1% of value of ores mined or produced(m)
Mississippi	Oil and Gas Severance Tax	The greater of 6% of value or 6¢/bbl. of oil or 6% of value or 3 mills/1,000 cu. ft. of gas
	Timber Severance Tax	Varies depending on type of wood and ultimate use
	Salt Severance Tax	3% of value of amount produced
Montana	Coal Severance Tax	Varies by quality of coal and type of mine
	Metalliferous Mines License Tax(n)	Progressive gross value tax from 0.15% to 1.438% of value
	Oil or Gas Producers' Severance Tax	License Tax: 5% of gross value until March 31, 1983 (6% thereafter) on oil; 2.65% of gross value of gas. Maximum conservation tax: 2/10 of 1% of market value/bbl. of oil and of each 10,000 cu. ft. of gas(e)
	Micaceous Minerals License Tax	5¢/ton
	Cement License Tax(o)	22¢/ton of cement, 5¢/ton of gypsum or plaster
	Mineral Mining Tax	$25 plus 1/2% of gross value over $5,000
Nebraska	Oil and Gas Severance Tax	3% of the value (wells averaging 10 bbls./day or less, 2%)
	Oil and Gas Conservation Tax	Not to exceed 4 mills/$1 of value at the wellhead(e)
Nevada	Net Proceeds of Mine Tax	Property tax rate of place where mine is located
	Oil and Gas Conservation Tax	5 mills/bbl. of oil and 5 mills/50,000 cu. ft. of gas
New Hampshire	Refined Petroleum Products Tax	1/10 of 1% of market value
New Mexico	Resources Excise Tax(p)	3/4 of 1% for most substances
	Severance Tax(p)	Varies according to substance
	Oil and Gas Severance Tax	3-3/4% of value (less credits) of oil or liquid hydrocarbon; 12.6¢/1,000 cu. ft. of gas based on volume of gas severed
	Oil and Gas Privilege Tax	2.55% of value
	Natural Gas Processor's Tax	0.45% of value
	Oil and Gas Ad Valorem Production Tax	Varies
	Oil and Gas Conservation Tax(q)	Variable percentage

State	Title and application of tax(a)	Rate
North Carolina.....	Oil and Gas Conservation Act	Not to exceed 5 mills/bbl. of oil nor 1/2 mill/1,000 cu. ft. of gas(e)
	Primary Forest Product Assessment Tax	40¢ to 50¢/1,000 board ft. and 12¢ to 20¢/cord depending on type of wood and use
North Dakota......	Oil and Gas Production Tax	5% of gross value at well
	Coal Severance Tax	85¢/ton and 1¢/ton for every four-point increase in wholesale price index
	Oil Extraction Tax	6½% of gross value at well
Ohio..............	Resource Severance Tax(r)	Separate rate for each substance
Oklahoma.........	Oil, Gas, and Mineral Gross Production Tax(s)	Separate rate for each substance
	Natural Gas and Casinghead Gas Conservation Excise Tax	7¢/1,000 cu. ft. less 7% of the gross value of each 1,000 cu. ft. of gas
Oregon...........	Forest Products Severance Tax	20¢/1,000 board ft.
	Oil and Gas Gross Production Tax	6% of gross value at well
	Severance Tax on Eastern Oregon Timber	5% of value
	Severance Tax on Western Oregon Timber	6½% of value
South Dakota......	Precious Metals Severance Tax(t)	6% of gross yield
	Energy Minerals Severance Tax	4½% of taxable value of any energy mineral
Tennessee	Oil and Gas Severance Tax	1½% of the sales price
	Coal Severance Tax	20¢/ton(u)
Texas	Natural Gas Production Tax	7½% of market value
	Oil Production Tax	4.6% of market value if it exceeds $1/bbl., otherwise 4.6¢/bbl.
	Sulphur Production Tax	$1.03/long ton
	Cement Distributor's Tax	2-3/4¢/100 lbs.
Utah..............	Mining Occupation Tax(v)	1% of value for metals, 2% of value for oil and gas
	Oil and Gas Conservation Tax	Up to 2 mills/$1 of wellhead value
Virginia	Forest Products Severance Tax	Varies by species and ultimate use
Washington........	Uranium and Thorium Milling Tax	5¢/lb.
	Food Fish and Shellfish Tax	0.07% to 5% of the selling price depending on species
Wisconsin	Metalliferous Minerals Occupation Tax	Progressive net proceeds tax from 6% to 20%
Wyoming..........	Oil and Gas Production Tax	Not to exceed 4/5 mill/$1 of value at the well(e)
	Mining Excise and Severance Taxes	Varies by substance from 1.5% to 3% of value

Source: Commerce Clearing House, *State Tax Guide.*

(a) Application of tax is same as that of title unless otherwise indicated by a footnote.

(b) Tax scheduled to terminate upon the redemption of all bonds issued by the Alabama State Docks Department.

(c) Metallic minerals, coal, oil shale, and oil and gas.

(d) Clay, gravel, phosphate rock, lime, shells, stone, sand, heavy minerals and rare earths.

(e) Actual rate set by administrative actions.

(f) Petroleum, oil, gas and other hydrocarbons.

(g) Figures are the total parts of the tax designed for conservation and pollution prevention.

(h) Coal and oil excepted.

(i) Limited to certain counties. Coal tax expires June 30, 1983.

(j) Plus a fee (not to exceed 1 percent of gross value) on oil and gas produced the previous year.

(k) All ores.

(l) $1.25/ton plus a surcharge up to 1.6 percent based on the percentage iron content of the ore, except for semi-taconites which are taxed at 10¢/ton plus the surcharge.

(m) Plus miscellaneous taxes on royalties and additional tax based on the percentage copper-nickel content of the ore.

(n) Metals, gems and precious stones.

(o) Cement and gypsum or allied products.

(p) Natural resources except oil and gas.

(q) Oil, gas, geothermal energy, coal and uranium.

(r) Coal, salt, limestone, dolomite, sand, gravel and natural gas.

(s) Asphalt, oil, gas, uranium and metals.

(t) Does not apply if less than 1,000 ozs. of gold or silver severed annually.

(u) Subject to change following federal approval of Tennessee's surface coal mining program.

(v) Metals, oil, gas and uranium.

Table 6
PROPERTY TAX RELIEF: STATE-FINANCED CIRCUIT-BREAKER PROGRAMS

State	Description of beneficiaries					Income ceiling	Form of relief				Notes:
	Homeowners with qualifying age	Renters with qualifying age	Disabled	Widows	Other		Income tax credit	Rebate	Reduction in tax bill	Other	
Alabama	...	...	★	...	Retired persons over 65; blind	...	...	...	...	Exempt from state property tax	...
Arizona	65	65	...	...	...	...	★	...	★	...	Renters receive a property tax credit on their income tax returns. Homeowners qualify for a general property tax reduction keyed to school district spending levels.
Arkansas	65	...	...	62	...	...	★	★	...	...	Relief based on amount by which property taxes exceed a specified percentage of household income.
California	62	All	...	...	...	$12,000	...	★	...	...	...
Colorado	65	65	★	...	...	$5,000 if single $8,700 if married	★	★	...	...	...
Connecticut	65	65	...	...	...	$6,000	...	...	...	Housing subsidy or property tax freeze	...
Delaware	65	...	...	...	...	$3,000	...	...	...	Partly exempt	Exempt from paying a property tax on the first $5,000 of assessed valuation of property.
Idaho	65	...	...	★	Blind; disabled veterans; fatherless children under 18	$7,500	...	...	★	...	Reduction based on income.
Illinois	65	65	★	...	...	...	...	★	...	...	Relief based on amount by which property tax (or rent equivalent) exceeds 4 percent of household income; relief also provided for first $3,000 of increased assessed value over the 1977 value.
Indiana	65	65	...	...	...	$5,000	★	★	...	...	...
Iowa	65	65	★	...	...	$9,000	...	★	...	...	Relief is given for taxes in excess of various percentages of income.
Kansas	58	58	★	52	Families with children under 18	$13,000	...	★	...	...	Relief is equal to the amount of tax up to $400.
Maine	62	62	...	...	...	$5,000 if single $6,000 if married	...	★	...	...	Relief is equal to the amount of tax up to $400.
Maryland	All	All	...	...	...	...	★	...	...	...	Relief based on extent to which tax exceeds various percentages of income.
Massachusetts	...	...	...	...	...	...	...	...	...	...	Small program for certain elderly, certain retired citizens, and certain veterans.

400

State	Age	Age		Category	Amount				Provisions
Michigan	All	All	...	Veterans	...	...	...	★	Eligibility requires payment in excess of 3.5% of income for property tax.
Minnesota	All	All	★	Senior citizens	...	...	★	★	Relief based on extent of the property tax over various percentages of income.
Missouri	65	...	...	...	$7,500	...	★	★	...
Nevada	62	...	...	...	$12,000	...	★	★	Relief ranges from 90% of property tax for incomes of less than $1,999 to 10% for incomes between $10,000 and $11,000. Maximum relief is $300 (17 percent of rent equals tax equivalent).
New Mexico	65	...	...	...	$16,000	...	★	★	Relief based on various property tax liability and gross income classes.
New York	All	...	...	...	$16,000	...	★	★	Relief applies to households with gross incomes up to $16,000 for whom 50% of real property tax exceeds scaled threshold amounts of gross income. Credits range from $10 to a maximum of $250.
North Dakota	65	...	★	...	...	★	...	...	Relief applies to persons with incomes under $3,500 and assessed value of the property is reduced 100% (maximum reduction).
Ohio	65	...	★	...	...	★	★	...	Relief ranges from a 70% reduction or $5,000, whichever is less.
Oklahoma	65	...	★	...	...	...	★	...	Relief is equal to property taxes due in excess of 1% of household income.
Oregon	All	All	...	(a)	$17,500	...	★	★	Relief depends on level of income.
Pennsylvania	65	65	★	...	$7,500	★	★	...	...
Rhode Island	65	65	...	...	$5,000	...	★	★	Relief equals amount by which property taxes paid exceed various percentages of household income.
South Dakota	65	...	★	...	...	...	★	...	Relief based on a percentage of real estate tax according to income.
Utah	65	...	...	...	...	...	★	...	Relief ranges from 95% of property taxes for incomes under $1,000 to 20% for incomes between $6,000 and $7,000.
Vermont	All	All	...	...	...	...	★	...	Relief based on amount of taxes paid exceeding 4% of income for incomes less than $4,000 up to 6% for incomes over $16,000.
Washington	62	...	★	Retired	...	...	...	...	...
West Virginia	65	65	...	...	...	★	★	...	$10,000 homestead exemption. State reimburses local levying bodies for amount of property tax lost on $5,000 of exemption.
Wisconsin	All	All	...	...	$14,000	★	...	★	Maximum rebate or credit is 80% of rent paid or property tax paid up to $1,000.
Wyoming	65	...	★	...	...	...	...	...	...

(a) Widows and widowers age 50 and over.

Sources: Education Commission of the States and Advisory Commission on Intergovernmental Relations. Updated by Education Commission of the States.

Table 7
RANGE OF STATE CORPORATE INCOME TAX RATES
(As of January 1, 1982)

State or other jurisdiction	Tax rate* (percent)	Federal income tax deductible	State or other jurisdiction	Tax rate* (percent)	Federal income tax deductible
Alabama		★	**Minnesota**		...
Business corporations	5		Business corporations	12	
Banks & financial corps.	6		Banks	12	
Alaska		...	**Mississippi**		...
Business corporations:			$0 to $5,000	3	
$0 to $10,000	1		Over $5,000	4(2)	
Over $90,000	9.4(10)		**Missouri**		★
Banks & finan. institutions	7(a)		Business corporations	5	
Arizona		★	Banks & trust companies	7	
$0 to $1,000	2.5		**Montana**	6.75(m)	
Over $6,000	10.5(7)		**Nebraska**		...
Arkansas		...	$0 to $25,000	3.75	
$0 to $3,000	1		Over $25,000	4.125(2)(n)	
Over $25,000	6(5)		**New Hampshire**	9.08(o)	...
California		...	**New Jersey**	9(p)	...
Business corporations	9.6(b)		**New Mexico**		...
Banks & financial corps.	11.6(b)		$0 to $1 million	4	
Colorado	5(c)	...	Over $2 million	6(3)	
Connecticut	10(d)	...	**New York**		...
Delaware	8.7	...	Business corporations	10(q)	
Florida	5(e)	...	Banks & financial corps.	12(r)	
Georgia	6	...	**North Carolina**	6	...
Hawaii		...	**North Dakota**		★
Business corporations			Business corporations		
$0 to $25,000	5.85(f)		$0 to $3,000	2	
Over $25,000	6.435(2)		Over $50,000	7(6)	
Banks & financial corps.	11.7		Banks & financial corps.	5(s)	
Idaho	6.5(g)	...	**Ohio**		...
Illinois	6.5(h)	...	$0 to $25,000	4.6(t)	
Indiana	6(i)	...	Over $25,000	8.7(2)(t)	
Iowa		(j)	**Oklahoma**	4	...
Business corporations			**Oregon**	7.5(u)	...
$0 to $25,000	6		**Pennsylvania**	10.5	...
Over $100,000	10(3)		**Rhode Island**	8(v)	...
Financial institutions	5		**South Carolina**		...
Kansas		...	Business corporations	6	
Business corporations	4.5(k)		Banks	4.5	
Banks	4.25(k)		Financial associations	8	
Trust companies & savings			**South Dakota**		★
& loan associations	4.5(k)		Banks & financial corps.	6(w)	
Kentucky		...	**Tennessee**	6	...
$0 to $25,000	3		**Utah**	4(x)	...
Over $100,000	6(4)		**Vermont**		...
Louisiana		★	$0 to $10,000	5	
$0 to $25,000	4		Over $250,000	7.5(4)(y)	
Over $200,000	8(5)		**Virginia**	6	...
Maine		...	**West Virginia**	6	...
$0 to $25,000	4.95		**Wisconsin**	7.9	...
Over $25,000	6.93(2)				
Maryland	7	...			
Massachusetts		...			
Business corporations	9.4962(l)				
Banks & trust companies	12.54				
Utility corporations	6.5				

Source: The Federation of Tax Administrators (based on legislation enacted at 1981 sessions.)

*Figure in parentheses is number of steps in range.

(a) Banks and other financial institutions are subject to a license tax.

(b) Minimum tax is $200.

(c) For tax years beginning in 1982, the tax is reduced by 1 percent of the first $25,000 of net income and 0.5 percent of the next $50,000 of net income; the maximum reduction is $500.

(d) Or 3.1 mills per dollar of capital stock and surplus (maximum tax $100,000), or $250, or 5 percent of 50 percent of net income of corporation plus salaries and other compensation paid to officers and certain shareholders, whichever is greater.

(e) An exemption of $5,000 is allowed.

(f) Taxes capital gains at 3.08 percent.

(g) An additional tax of $10 is imposed on each return.

(h) Includes 2.5 percent personal property tax replacement tax.

(i) Consists of 3 percent basic rate plus a 3 percent supplemental tax.

(j) 50 percent of federal income tax deductible.

(k) Plus a surtax of 2.25 percent of taxable income in excess of $25,000 (2.125 percent for banks).

(l) Rate includes a 14 percent surtax, as does the following: Plus a tax of $2.60 per $1,000 on taxable tangible property (or net worth allocable to state, for intangible property corporations). Minimum tax of $228 including surtax. Corporations engaged exclusively in interstate or foreign commerce are taxed at 5 percent of net income, and are not subject to surtax.

(m) Minimum tax is $50; for small business corporations, $10.

(n) 25 and 27.5 percent of individual income tax rate, determined annually by State Board of Equalization and Assessment, imposed on net taxable income. Rate shown is for 1981.

(o) Business profits tax imposed on both corporations and unincorporated business. Includes a 13.5 percent surtax. Minimum tax is $250 for businesses with more than $12,000 in gross business income.

(p) This is the corporation business franchise tax rate, plus a net worth tax at millage rates ranging from 2 mills to 0.2 mill; minimum tax is $250.

Corporations not subject to the franchise tax are subject to a 7.25 percent income tax. Savings institutions are subject to a 3 percent tax.

(q) Or $250; 1.78 mills per dollar of capital; or 10 percent of 30 percent of net income plus salaries and other compensation to officers and stockholders owning more than 5 percent of the issued capital stock less $15,000 and any net loss, if any of these is greater than the tax computed on net income.

(r) Minimum tax is $250 or 1.6 mills per dollar of capital stock; for savings institutions, the minimum tax is $250 or 2 percent of interest credited to depositors in preceding year.

(s) Minimum tax is $50; plus an additional 2 percent tax.

(t) Or 5.5 mills times the value of the taxpayer's issued and outstanding shares of stock as determined according to the total value of capital surplus, undivided profits, and reserves; minimum tax $50. An additional litter tax is imposed equal to 0.11 percent on the first $25,000 of income, 0.22 percent on income over $25,000, or 0.14 mills on net worth. Corporations manufacturing or selling litter stream products are subject to an additional 0.22 percent tax on income over $25,000 or 0.14 mills on net worth.

(u) Minimum tax is $10.

(v) Or, for business corporations, the tax is 40 cents per $100 of net worth, if greater than the tax computed on net income. For banks, if a greater tax results, the alternative tax is $2.50 per $10,000 of capital stock; minimum tax is $100.

(w) Minimum tax is $200 per authorized location.

(x) Minimum tax is $25. There is a graduated gross receipts tax on corporations not otherwise required to pay income or franchise taxes, ranging up to 6 percent on receipts in excess of $5 billion.

(y) Minimum tax is $50.

(z) Includes 10 percent surtax. Minimum tax is $25.

Note: Michigan imposes a single business tax (sometimes described as a business activities or value added tax) of 2.35 percent on the sum of federal taxable income of the business, compensation paid to employees, dividends, interest and royalties paid, and other items.

STATE TAX COLLECTIONS IN 1981

STATE GOVERNMENT TAX collections totaled nearly $150 billion at the close of fiscal 1981, an increase of almost $13 billion from 1980 and $25 billion from the 1979 collections. The 1981 total amounted to $663 per capita nationally.

There was a wide variation in the behavior of particular types of taxes during the period, as inflation, a struggling domestic economy, and the political environment all affected specific taxes in a slightly different manner. Generally speaking, the broad group of sales and gross receipts taxes (with the exception of such taxes on public utilities) grew at a slower pace than did other taxes during fiscal 1981. Sales and gross receipts tax collections increased 7.2 percent during the year, while the broad category of license tax revenue increased by 9.2 percent.

Individual income tax collections showed a 10.2 percent increase, despite indexing provisions and taxpayer rebate programs in effect in a number of states. While inflation and rising personal income levels were helping to increase the individual income tax yields, corporate net income tax collections were up by a more modest 6.2 percent in 1981, as the pressures of recession were an overriding factor on business performance.

Even within the broad tax groups, specific tax yields seemed at odds with the overall trend of the group. Thus, while sales taxes showed only a slow rate of growth, sales and gross receipts taxes imposed upon public utilities were up 27.9 percent. This resulted from generally increasing price levels for gas and electricity, as well as the inclusion of a previously local utility tax in New Jersey being taken over by the state.

The 1981 period was also characterized by an exceptionally large number of tax rate changes, particularly for motor fuel taxes. Fourteen states increased the motor fuel tax rate during their 1981 fiscal year (which generally ended June 30), and another 13 states increased the rate through January 1, 1982. In addition, nine states have imposed a variable rate, which will result in periodic fuel tax rate changes.

Tax amounts presented here are net of refunds paid, but include any state-imposed taxes collected or received by the state and subsequently distributed to local governments as grants-in-aid or shared revenues. Taxes collected and retained locally are not included. The fiscal 1981 figures are preliminary.

Major Tax Sources

While sales taxes have traditionally been the most significant source of state government tax revenue, they have declined steadily since 1967 in terms of their relative importance. By the 1981 fiscal period, sales taxes accounted for less than half (48.6 percent) of all state tax revenue, having dipped below the 50 percent figure for the first time in a half-century.

Adapted by Maurice Criz and David Kellerman, Senior Advisor and Statistician, respectively, Governments Division, U.S. Bureau of the Census, from the annual report *State Government Tax Collections in 1981*.

Table A depicts the percentage distribution of state tax revenue among the major tax categories since 1957.

Table A
PERCENTAGE DISTRIBUTION OF STATE TAX COLLECTIONS,
BY MAJOR TAX CATEGORY

Year	Sales taxes	Income taxes	License taxes	Other
1957	58.1	17.6	15.1	9.2
1962	58.6	19.6	13.0	8.8
1967	58.2	22.4	11.4	8.0
1972	55.5	29.1	9.0	6.4
1977	51.8	34.3	7.1	6.8
1981	48.6	36.7	6.3	8.4

Sales taxes include both general sales and gross receipts taxes, currently in use in 45 states, and the many types of selective sales taxes on specific goods or services. General sales tax collections totaled $46.4 billion during fiscal 1981, amounting to $205 per capita nationwide (see Table 1). General sales tax collections grew by a modest 7.5 percent during fiscal 1981, somewhat less than the rate of growth in the consumer price index for all urban consumers, which grew by about 10 percent between 1980 and 1981.

Income taxes continued to increase as a percentage of total state tax revenue, amounting to 36.7 percent of all collections during fiscal 1981. Income taxes on individuals were up 10.2 percent to $40.9 billion, despite indexing, new or increased tax credits and the repeal of the tax in Alaska during the year. In part, this reflected the rise in personal income nationwide, which increased between 10 and 11 percent during the 1980-81 period. Income taxes on corporate net earnings increased a more modest 6.2 percent during the 1981 fiscal year.

Motor fuel tax collections of state governments were virtually unchanged from the fiscal 1980 total. These taxes accounted for only 6.5 percent of all state government tax revenue in fiscal 1981. As recently as fiscal 1973, immediately before the oil embargo, motor fuel taxes had accounted for 11.8 percent of all state tax collections. The lack of growth in this tax category was evident despite increased tax rates in many states, reflecting increases in the fuel efficiency of automobiles and other conservation efforts. The lack of growth in motor fuel tax collections poses a particularly acute problem for state governments, most of which finance their highway construction and maintenance operations from this revenue.

Severance tax collections showed the most significant increase during fiscal 1981, up 51.6 percent, after a 47.6 percent rise during 1980. These collections totaled $6.4 billion, or 4.3 percent of state taxes nationwide. Severance taxes are concentrated in a handful of energy-producing states and as such have become a source of dispute among the states themselves and in Congress. Issues such as tax exportation, ceilings on energy-related taxes, and royalties and lease-bonus payments have grown in controversy as severance tax revenues have grown.

License taxes, imposed either to regulate or to produce revenue, totaled $9.5 billion, accounting for 6.3 percent of all state tax revenue. All states impose license taxes on motor vehicles, hunting and fishing, and various occupations and businesses. Other types of license taxes include corporation franchise and filing, public utility regulation, alcoholic beverage production and distribution, and amusement regulation.

The dominance of one tax source over another varies considerably from state to state. The state's major tax source is often determined by whether or not the state has historically resorted to a particular tax, such as an individual income or general sales tax. More recently, the issue of principal tax sources has depended on the existence of energy-related mineral resources in a state.

For fiscal 1981, the general sales tax was the single largest source of tax revenue in 31 states. The individual income tax was the largest source in 16 states. Severance taxes were dominant in Oklahoma and Alaska, while in New Hampshire the corporate net income tax yielded the most revenue.

Individual State Comparisons

All but two states increased tax collections from 1980 to 1981. Taxes went up from 0.5 to 4.9 percent in 11 states, from 5.1 to 9.9 percent in 17 states, from 10.1 to 17.9 percent in 14 states, and from 20.9 to 61.2 percent in six states. Thus, in over half of the states, tax collections failed to keep pace with inflation.

Alaska's tax collections continued to increase rapidly, rising 61.2 percent during 1981, after a record 76 percent increase during 1980. Alaska's favorable position in taxing oil and gas production was a key factor. Alaska's severance tax collections alone accounted for 50.5 percent of that state's total tax revenue in fiscal 1981. Corporate net income taxes and state property taxes, consisting to a large degree of payments from oil and gas companies, accounted for another 44.8 percent of the state's total tax collections.

Alaska actually repealed the income tax on individuals in 1980, retroactive to January 1, 1979. Alaska also has no general sales or gross receipts tax, making it now the only state without either of the two largest revenue-producing taxes nationally.[1] Nevertheless, Alaska's per capita tax collections stood at $5,792 during fiscal 1981, far outpacing the next highest per capita collections of $1,128 found in Hawaii.

Other states with large increases in tax revenue during 1981 were New Mexico (27.3 percent), Oklahoma (25.7 percent), North Dakota (21.2 percent), and Texas and Wyoming (20.9 percent each). It is interesting to note that in every one of these states, growth in tax revenue can be largely attributed to their taxation of energy-related activities, such as oil and gas exploration and mining.

The two states that declined in their total tax collections between the 1980 and 1981 fiscal years were Colorado and Nebraska (down 3 percent and 1.6 percent, respectively). In Colorado, food products were exempted from the general sales tax base effective with fiscal 1981, an individual income tax credit program was established, and corporate net income tax rates were reduced for 1981, all of which led to declining tax revenues. In Nebraska, individual income tax collections dropped by about 15 percent as a result of a rate reduction in calendar year 1980 and a temporary moratorium on the withholding of individual income taxes.

As with most other items of government finances, a few states account for a large fraction of the national totals. Thus for tax collections, the following eight states accounted for almost half of the taxes collected by all state governments (amounts in millions): California, $20,505; New York, $13,918; Texas, $8,174; Pennsylvania, $7,597; Illinois, $7,323; Michigan, $6,177; Florida, $5,314; Ohio, $5,241. Despite their large volume of tax collections, none of these states were among the five highest in per capita taxation nationally.

As an indication of relative tax burden in each state, per capita amounts are presented in Table 2. As mentioned, Alaska had the highest level of per capita taxes, followed by Hawaii. Other states with high levels of per capita tax collections were Wyoming ($996), Delaware ($926), New Mexico ($907) and California ($866). The lowest per capita tax collections for fiscal 1981 were in New Hampshire ($292), Tennessee ($427), South Dakota ($432) and Missouri ($436).

Interstate differences in per capita state tax collections should not be viewed as necessarily indicative of differing state personal tax burdens, however. Responsibility for the provision and financing of services varies considerably among the states. In many cases, local governments are authorized to impose taxes that are elsewhere imposed by state governments. Regional economic differences and service levels also play important roles in determining the per capita tax distribution among the states.

The Importance of State Taxation

State tax collections in fiscal 1981, as in past years, continued to exceed local government collections in a comparable time period:

State tax collections, fiscal 1981 (millions) $149,739

Local government tax collections, July 1980 to
    June 1981[2] (millions) . . . .$ 92,191

Local tax collections as a percentage of
    state tax collections 61.6

With the exception of property taxation, states have largely opted to retain authority for imposing the major types of taxes (sales, income, licensing, etc.) rather than permit their local jurisdictions to impose such taxes.

After a period (1976 to 1979) in which tax revenues increased at a faster pace than expenditures, the trend shifted in 1980. Taxes increased by 9.7 percent during 1980, while state government expenditure rose 14.7 percent. The fiscal 1981 trend is expected to be similar.

The growth of tax revenue, especially in relation to other areas of state government finances, should be viewed with respect to political actions as well as economic actions. While inflation has a clear impact upon taxation, the creation of new taxes, increased tax rates or expanded tax bases also are important in determining the role of tax collections in the state revenue system.

The Advisory Commission on Intergovernmental Relations (ACIR) annually assesses the sources of changes in state tax revenue.[3] The analysis applies to the income and sales tax categories only and assesses tax revenue changes as attributable to economic factors (real growth or inflation) and to political factors. For 1980, inflation accounted for the entire growth in the level of tax collections. According to ACIR, inflation actually contributed to 106 percent of the growth in tax revenue, which was offset by a 6 percent decline in the level of taxes as a result of political actions. None of the increased tax collection during 1980 was attributable to real economic growth.

In contrast, during the 1976 to 1979 period, real economic growth contributed between 31 percent and 40 percent of the increased level of tax collections. Through the 1970s, inflation was the major source of increase in the level of taxation. Political actions had a dampening effect on tax revenues in 1979 (as well as 1980).

Notes

1. New Hampshire has no general sales tax, and a limited income tax, on interest and dividend earnings.
2. U.S. Bureau of the Census, *Quarterly Summary of State and Local Tax Revenue*, April-June 1981.
3. Advisory Commission on Intergovernmental Relations, *Significant Features of Fiscal Federalism, 1980-81 Edition*, Report M-132 (Washington, D.C., December 1981), p. 29.

Table 1
NATIONAL SUMMARY OF STATE GOVERNMENT TAX REVENUE, BY TYPE OF TAX: 1979 TO 1981

Tax source	Amount (in thousands)			Percent change year-to-year		Percent distribu- tion, 1981	Per capita, 1981
	1981 (prelim.)	1980	1979	1980 to 1981	1979 to 1980		
Total collections	$149,739,329	$137,056,630	$124,892,913	9.3	9.7	100.0	$662.95
Sales and gross receipts	72,751,238	67,854,790	63,724,112	7.2	6.5	48.6	322.10
General......................	46,412,126	43,167,534	39,562,064	7.5	9.1	31.0	205.48
Selective	26,339,112	24,687,256	24,162,048	6.7	2.2	17.6	116.61
Motor fuels	9,733,528	9,721,569	9,980,104	0.1	-2.6	6.5	43.09
Tobacco products..........	3,893,171	3,737,798	3,640,466	4.2	2.7	2.6	17.24
Public utilities	4,295,626	3,358,768	2,933,584	27.9	14.5	2.9	19.02
Insurance	3,321,350	3,113,231	2,937,657	6.7	6.0	2.2	14.70
Alcoholic beverages	2,613,426	2,477,569	2,400,322	5.5	3.2	1.7	11.57
Other	2,482,011	2,278,321	2,269,915	8.9	0.4	1.7	10.99
Licenses	9,493,603	8,690,435	8,223,860	9.2	5.7	6.3	42.03
Motor vehicles..............	5,266,082	4,935,633	4,781,488	6.7	3.2	3.5	23.31
Corporations in general	1,611,720	1,387,780	1,261,522	16.1	10.0	1.1	7.14
Hunting and fishing	464,003	417,479	382,337	11.1	9.2	0.3	2.05
Motor vehicle operators.......	428,988	389,408	376,379	10.2	3.5	0.3	1.90
Alcholic beverages	212,407	179,026	186,244	18.6	-3.9	0.1	0.94
Other	1,510,403	1,381,109	1,235,890	9.4	11.8	1.0	6.69
Individual income	40,895,235	37,121,319	32,583,405	10.2	13.9	27.3	181.06
Corporation net income..........	14,143,497	13,321,331	12,127,524	6.2	9.8	9.4	62.62
Severance	6,379,191	4,207,758	2,850,518	51.6	47.6	4.3	28.24
Property......................	2,948,883	2,892,105	2,491,507	2.0	16.1	2.0	13.06
Death and gift	2,228,968	2,035,269	1,973,230	9.5	3.1	1.5	9.87
Other........................	898,714	933,623	918,757	-3.7	1.6	0.6	3.98

Source: U.S. Bureau of the Census, *State Government Tax Collections in 1981.*

Note: Because of rounding, detail may not add to totals. Per capita and percent figures are computed on the basis of amounts rounded to the nearest thousand. Population figures as of April 1, 1980 were used to calculate per capita amounts.

Table 2
SUMMARY OF STATE GOVERNMENT TAX REVENUE, BY STATE:
1979 TO 1981

	Amount (in thousands)			Percent change year-to-year		
	1981 (prelim.)	1980	1979	1980 to 1981	1979 to 1980	Per capita, 1981
United States............	$149,739,329	$137,056,630	$124,892,913	9.3	9.7	$ 662.95
Alabama..................	2,148,415	1,856,789	1,747,350	15.7	6.3	552.29
Alaska	2,316,823	1,437,607	816,710	61.2	76.0	5,792.06
Arizona	1,785,775	1,716,237	1,515,826	4.1	13.2	657.02
Arkansas	1,188,851	1,160,767	995,955	2.4	16.5	520.28
California................	20,504,787	19,366,696	16,351,959	5.9	18.4	866.31
Colorado	1,445,777	1,490,898	1,440,844	-3.0	3.5	500.44
Connecticut..............	2,071,885	1,839,678	1,718,112	12.6	7.1	666.63
Delaware	550,943	515,715	491,906	6.8	4.8	925.95
Florida	5,314,376	4,804,298	4,290,975	10.6	12.0	545.62
Georgia..................	3,019,847	2,728,961	2,448,148	10.7	11.5	552.68
Hawaii	1,088,330	998,383	875,953	9.0	14.0	1,127.80
Idaho	536,757	490,346	466,371	9.5	5.1	568.60
Illinois..................	7,322,572	7,073,077	6,322,766	3.5	11.9	641.32
Indiana..................	2,808,811	2,695,759	2,668,124	4.2	1.0	511.62
Iowa	1,835,807	1,746,828	1,644,621	5.1	6.2	630.21
Kansas	1,392,277	1,269,671	1,187,670	9.7	6.9	589.20
Kentucky	2,276,170	2,144,941	2,075,732	6.1	3.3	621.73
Louisiana	2,804,570	2,397,215	2,197,623	17.0	9.1	667.12
Maine	674,316	619,160	554,375	8.9	11.7	599.39
Maryland	2,956,088	2,760,818	2,647,157	7.1	4.3	701.16
Massachusetts	4,335,648	3,927,303	3,618,785	10.4	8.5	755.73
Michigan	6,176,957	5,947,650	6,024,565	3.9	-1.3	667.20
Minnesota	3,373,726	3,242,940	3,133,761	4.0	3.5	827.50
Mississippi	1,396,745	1,257,932	1,157,436	11.0	8.7	554.04
Missouri.................	2,142,965	2,094,540	2,013,027	2.3	4.0	435.83
Montana	466,575	435,751	399,438	7.1	9.1	592.85
Nebraska	803,960	816,767	742,560	-1.6	10.0	512.08
Nevada	515,303	476,604	462,703	8.1	3.0	644.93
New Hampshire	268,752	267,495	264,107	0.5	1.3	291.80
New Jersey	5,029,336	4,265,830	3,729,258	17.9	14.4	682.96
New Mexico..............	1,179,280	926,048	827,035	27.3	12.0	907.14
New York................	13,918,245	12,626,027	11,633,728	10.2	8.5	792.75
North Carolina	3,430,723	3,215,348	2,915,053	6.7	10.3	584.05
North Dakota	450,755	371,861	324,791	21.2	14.5	690.28
Ohio	5,240,844	4,766,665	4,619,880	9.9	3.2	485.40
Oklahoma	2,232,278	1,776,044	1,515,918	25.7	17.2	737.94
Oregon	1,608,423	1,455,352	1,384,493	10.5	5.1	610.87
Pennsylvania	7,597,010	7,240,808	6,781,837	4.9	6.8	640.18
Rhode Island	607,951	550,787	537,827	10.4	2.4	641.98
South Carolina	1,825,935	1,678,049	1,522,968	8.8	10.2	585.42
South Dakota	297,813	270,518	245,535	10.1	10.2	431.61
Tennessee................	1,958,427	1,886,992	1,843,906	3.8	2.3	426.58
Texas	8,173,759	6,758,706	5,738,430	20.9	17.8	574.48
Utah	849,148	785,755	694,907	8.1	13.1	581.21
Vermont.................	294,243	266,317	267,473	10.5	-0.4	575.82
Virginia.................	3,027,348	2,743,325	2,563,713	10.4	7.0	566.28
Washington	3,125,815	2,917,445	2,718,277	7.1	7.3	756.86
West Virginia.............	1,269,671	1,219,492	1,150,055	4.1	6.0	651.11
Wisconsin	3,629,459	3,366,310	3,260,448	7.8	3.2	771.40
Wyoming	469,058	388,125	342,822	20.9	13.2	995.88

Source: U.S. Bureau of the Census, *State Government Tax Collections in 1981.*

Note: Because of rounding, detail may not add to totals. Population figures as of April 1, 1980 were used to calculate per capita amounts; see Table 6.

Table 3
STATE GOVERNMENT TAX REVENUE, BY TYPE OF TAX: 1981
(In thousands of dollars)

State	Total	Sales and gross receipts	Licenses	Individual income	Corporation net income	Property	Death and gift	Severance	Documentary and stock transfer	Other
Number of states using tax	50	50	50	44	46	42	49	33	28	15
United States	$149,739,329	$72,751,238	$9,493,603	$40,895,235	$14,143,497	$2,948,883	$2,228,968	$6,379,191	$862,202	$36,512
Alabama	2,148,415	1,284,001	128,250	515,870	99,095	46,192	8,071	60,669	6,267	...
Alaska	2,316,823	53,310	46,709	7,172	894,843	143,179	460	1,170,180	...	970
Arizona	1,785,775	1,063,563	97,580	364,131	126,510	124,099	9,892	...	...	...
Arkansas	1,188,851	655,502	101,772	311,929	80,683	4,500	4,730	26,745	2,623	367
California	20,504,787	9,206,628	705,574	6,589,203	2,731,111	727,867	522,502	21,902	...	...
Colorado	1,445,777	750,944	100,869	437,649	103,465	4,525	8,963	35,879	...	3,483
Connecticut	2,071,885	1,511,012	126,555	117,786	248,720	12	67,350	...	...	450
Delaware	550,943	79,424	155,880	261,916	32,914	...	8,460	...	12,349	...
Florida	5,314,376	3,908,552	395,998	...	402,471	101,756	70,619	169,213	265,767	...
Georgia	3,019,847	1,609,766	90,059	1,035,899	252,235	13,201	11,667	...	6,312	708
Hawaii	1,088,330	678,253	15,990	334,750	52,745	...	4,589	...	2,003	...
Idaho	536,757	229,316	63,962	185,507	50,875	274	4,602	2,221	...	...
Illinois	7,322,572	3,690,010	458,546	2,037,453	835,017	154,119	142,223	...	5,204	...
Indiana	2,808,811	1,797,195	142,225	642,911	154,873	29,862	39,934	1,811	...	...
Iowa	1,835,807	785,600	183,494	673,470	135,868	...	54,970	...	2,405	...
Kansas	1,392,277	668,426	107,863	415,015	150,421	20,642	28,903	1,007	...	...
Kentucky	2,276,170	1,045,782	98,682	573,091	154,786	180,111	28,322	194,441	955	...
Louisiana	2,804,570	1,327,943	184,606	185,663	266,611	...	24,517	815,230	...	...
Maine	674,316	372,170	56,438	176,600	39,193	14,581	14,236	...	1,098	...
Maryland	2,956,088	1,329,779	116,662	1,205,507	156,338	90,134	22,266	...	29,008	6,394
Massachusetts	4,335,648	1,508,216	137,963	2,057,945	536,069	468	82,020	...	12,967	...
Michigan	6,176,957	2,601,050	327,140	2,028,437	943,909	142,849	50,715	82,857	...	...
Minnesota	3,373,726	1,286,364	210,082	1,396,432	331,718	4,431	28,776	98,858	17,065	...
Mississippi	1,396,745	950,020	92,940	191,138	63,832	4,877	6,052	87,886	...	...
Missouri	2,142,965	1,126,939	186,031	669,728	128,282	5,136	26,777	19	...	53

Montana	466,575	95,273	42,691	146,036	52,901	23,500	6,195	99,248	…	731
Nebraska	803,960	465,580	69,824	201,161	54,128	3,110	4,346	4,196	1,615	…
Nevada	515,303	425,489	66,636	…	…	23,167	…	11	…	…
New Hampshire	268,752	134,193	43,079	12,618	57,339	8,068	10,372	52	3,031	…
New Jersey	5,029,336	2,563,504	535,339	1,147,834	574,920	67,566	123,280	…	16,893	…
New Mexico	1,179,280	664,996	54,518	70,937	53,523	10,013	2,701	322,592	…	…
New York	13,918,245	4,813,869	507,753	6,612,289	1,524,968	…	143,210	…	316,156	…
North Carolina	3,430,723	1,496,382	252,883	1,303,517	279,937	51,016	45,603	1,385	…	…
North Dakota	450,755	196,548	42,293	62,419	41,051	2,495	2,559	103,390	…	…
Ohio	5,240,844	2,939,811	483,430	1,134,381	490,637	147,787	40,631	4,167	…	…
Oklahoma	2,232,278	773,561	188,173	494,023	128,697	107	38,917	601,486	4,771	2,650
Oregon	1,608,423	186,944	167,703	1,005,104	155,503	…	35,427	56,937	698	…
Pennsylvania	7,597,010	3,673,505	843,761	1,884,756	821,962	98,934	196,298	…	77,794	…
Rhode Island	607,951	314,322	24,430	192,976	50,340	6,260	16,300	…	1,271	2,052
South Carolina	1,825,935	999,569	73,357	571,001	152,674	6,759	12,148	…	10,427	…
South Dakota	297,813	254,019	26,786	3,680	…	…	7,249	6,079	…	…
Tennessee	1,958,427	1,484,207	184,116	35,678	195,065	…	27,218	2,552	19,555	…
Texas	8,173,759	5,027,519	839,606	…	…	12,592	96,360	2,197,682	…	10,036
Utah	849,148	459,613	35,736	294,947	40,667	98	2,046	16,041	…	…
Vermont	294,243	137,487	29,191	98,574	22,918	339	1,981	…	3,253	500
Virginia	3,027,348	1,311,141	161,170	1,288,796	182,301	28,256	19,780	1,087	31,432	3,385
Washington	3,125,815	2,314,879	169,255	…	…	526,646	54,274	54,489	6,272	…
West Virginia	1,269,671	869,613	81,997	268,124	32,039	1,152	13,057	…	2,767	922
Wisconsin	3,629,459	1,379,343	186,290	1,654,862	255,663	92,177	54,515	554	2,244	3,811
Wyoming	469,058	250,106	51,716	…	…	26,026	2,885	138,325	…	…

Source: U.S. Bureau of the Census, *State Government Tax Collections in 1981.*
Note: Because of rounding, detail may not add to totals.

Table 4

STATE GOVERNMENT SALES AND GROSS RECEIPTS TAX REVENUE: 1981

(In thousands of dollars)

State	Total	General sales or gross receipts	Selective sales and gross receipts								
			Total	Motor fuels	Alcoholic beverages	Tobacco products	Insurance	Public utilities	Parimutuels	Amusements	Other
Number of states using tax	50	45	50	50	50	50	50	40	30	28	31
United States	$72,751,238	$46,412,126	$26,339,112	$9,733,528	$2,613,426	$3,893,171	$3,321,350	$4,295,626	$751,844	$259,577	$1,470,590
Alabama	1,284,001	595,173	688,828	241,735	91,642	69,851	70,605	179,499	...	81	35,415
Alaska	53,310	...	53,310	23,227	8,326	4,539	10,619	1,136	...	...	5,463
Arizona	1,063,563	805,745	257,818	120,432	22,801	39,744	41,722	22,256	10,863	...	...
Arkansas	655,502	398,950	256,552	133,004	22,859	51,892	32,303	...	16,494	...	...
California	9,206,628	7,262,497	1,944,131	839,317	141,752	283,898	460,447	23,805	133,288	233	61,391
Colorado	750,944	529,881	221,063	108,382	24,075	37,112	40,861	1,279	9,060	294	40,066
Connecticut	1,511,012	916,668	594,344	151,309	25,685	74,830	67,013	170,465	53,271	11,705	...
Delaware	79,424	...	79,424	29,112	5,334	12,441	13,250	15,936	1,517	...	1,834
Florida	3,908,552	2,542,895	1,365,657	420,972	300,845	266,172	103,269	137,372	105,246	2,300	29,481
Georgia	1,609,766	1,009,237	600,529	348,792	97,336	84,196	70,205	...	...	...	...
Hawaii	678,253	548,914	129,339	33,660	6,964	13,799	24,766	50,150	...	...	...
Idaho	229,316	144,993	84,323	50,694	7,539	8,313	15,875	1,602	300	...	...
Illinois	3,690,010	2,333,028	1,356,982	367,513	76,733	181,762	84,684	537,026	70,726	7,213	31,325
Indiana	1,797,195	1,361,250	435,945	258,687	35,380	84,337	57,426	...	...	115	...
Iowa	785,600	514,727	270,873	156,864	17,019	49,853	45,721	1,157	...	...	259
Kansas	668,426	449,213	219,213	114,632	32,479	33,952	36,756	701	...	693	...
Kentucky	1,045,782	630,472	415,310	180,915	16,231	21,726	90,497	...	14,361	251	91,329
Louisiana	1,327,943	858,604	469,339	187,792	54,422	63,807	89,670	31,272	21,973	196	20,207
Maine	372,170	235,678	136,492	49,154	28,637	24,376	13,989	18,612	1,724	...	...
Maryland	1,329,779	753,674	576,105	187,175	29,787	73,485	59,896	70,571	16,465	842	137,884
Massachusetts	1,508,216	859,716	648,500	237,526	84,747	148,555	114,083	...	32,268	9,227	22,094
Michigan	2,601,050	1,792,675	808,375	438,035	92,793	140,564	113,002	...	23,853	128	...
Minnesota	1,286,364	686,668	599,696	231,225	55,501	88,168	64,298	73,317	...	104	87,083
Mississippi	950,020	723,568	226,452	118,923	33,611	34,510	39,169	...	...	239	...
Missouri	1,126,939	787,185	339,754	186,323	25,302	60,974	66,451	704	...	...	...
Montana	95,273	...	95,273	48,903	14,683	11,627	14,264	5,015	...	...	781
Nebraska	465,580	281,212	184,368	115,410	12,939	22,592	21,649	...	7,591	621	3,566
Nevada	425,489	203,109	222,380	35,333	11,369	13,119	13,742	1,493	382	146,660	282
New Hampshire	134,193	...	134,193	47,028	4,701	26,623	14,130	1,674	9,405	...	30,632
New Jersey	2,563,504	1,263,650	1,299,854	285,364	58,919	176,203	96,607	581,503	16,074	72,314	12,870

State											
New Mexico	664,996	515,692	149,304	79,014	8,224	15,410	21,303	4,017	3,146	79	18,111
New York	4,813,869	2,965,313	1,848,556	449,896	148,159	336,153	206,267	590,931	116,180	970	22,279
North Carolina	1,496,382	738,879	757,503	282,742	110,846	18,247	86,531	236,858			
North Dakota	196,548	129,509	67,039	31,756	6,578	9,725	9,247	3,343			6,390
Ohio	2,939,811	1,636,100	1,303,711	374,187	93,368	209,796	136,653	464,886	24,821		
Oklahoma	773,561	382,649	390,912	128,875	41,233	77,649	75,919	8,374			58,862
Oregon	186,944		186,944	88,844	10,450	33,055	47,950	1,913	4,732	99	93
Pennsylvania	3,673,505	2,086,165	1,587,340	579,262	124,829	254,661	170,852	432,324	25,220	101	
Rhode Island	314,322	177,542	136,780	38,885	7,530	25,067	13,790	44,463	6,944		
South Carolina	999,569	616,081	383,488	184,822	88,652	29,543	42,773	20,129		4,197	13,372
South Dakota	254,019	158,022	95,997	51,958	7,915	10,554	11,238	273	2,418		11,641
Tennessee	1,484,207	1,044,155	440,052	220,433	52,865	77,582	66,630	16,372		439	5,731
Texas	5,027,519	2,994,496	2,033,023	480,845	236,521	339,583	189,167	223,443		278	563,186
Utah	459,613	349,502	110,111	69,911	7,810	11,257	19,128	2,005			
Vermont	137,487	44,761	92,726	21,361	13,571	10,099	6,653	11,961	1,086		27,995
Virginia	1,311,141	645,203	665,938	312,716	78,294	17,952	80,157	101,989		88	74,742
Washington	2,314,879	1,716,251	598,628	246,828	88,286	81,654	60,888	112,286	8,639	47	
West Virginia	869,613	623,793	245,820	96,082	5,124	38,130	36,905		13,782		55,797
Wisconsin	1,379,343	901,496	477,847	209,606	41,555	88,296	44,384	93,514		63	
Wyoming	250,106	197,135	52,971	38,067	1,205	5,738	7,946		15		429

Source: U.S. Bureau of the Census, *State Government Tax Collections in 1981.*

Note: Because of rounding, detail may not add to totals.

Table 5

STATE GOVERNMENT LICENSE TAX REVENUE: 1981

(In thousands of dollars)

State	Total	Motor vehicles	Motor vehicle operators	Corporations in general	Public utilities	Alcoholic beverages	Amusements	Occupations and businesses, n.e.c.	Hunting and fishing	Other
Number of states using tax		50	49	49	31	49	33	50	50	47
United States	$9,493,603	$5,266,082	$428,988	$1,611,720	$147,534	$212,407	$90,535	$1,193,051	$464,003	$79,283
Alabama	128,250	40,175	8,309	50,731	997	2,157	117	17,575	8,306	...
Alaska	46,709	10,881	520	857	...	1,494	157	24,011	8,759	70
Arizona	97,580	65,784	4,374	2,836	...	3,532	...	7,240	6,527	7,130
Arkansas	101,772	71,640	3,912	3,058	3,732	838	305	8,494	9,649	144
California	705,574	446,902	16,283	6,225	17,673	35,507	692	142,715	35,495	4,082
Colorado	100,869	52,538	5,436	2,831	...	1,946	80	13,053	22,414	2,571
Connecticut	126,555	82,237	12,896	4,412	...	6,001	43	18,564	1,398	1,004
Delaware	155,880	23,336	1,062	70,942	3,632	478	62	56,429	426	513
Florida	395,998	240,495	27,892	9,841	9,248	14,319	635	79,190	8,883	5,495
Georgia	90,059	47,423	7,990	9,819	...	1,119	...	15,226	8,267	215
Hawaii	15,990	8,386	...	809	1,593	...	...	4,995	139	68
Idaho	63,962	36,342	1,881	1,334	224	710	...	14,902	8,493	76
Illinois	458,546	348,447	32,319	40,705	...	1,782	768	21,880	11,293	1,352
Indiana	142,225	107,692	(a)	3,762	182	8,782	37	13,958	7,324	488
Iowa	183,494	144,095	5,971	11,373	46	4,817	...	9,662	5,593	1,937
Kansas	107,863	69,851	3,800	7,087	1,900	1,060	19	17,271	6,344	531
Kentucky	98,682	50,012	5,940	13,322	1,830	1,769	482	18,083	6,434	810
Louisiana	184,606	53,231	10,305	72,287	855	2,143	107	40,384	4,934	360
Maine	56,438	31,662	3,360	652	...	1,401	143	11,607	6,624	989
Maryland	116,662	83,908	6,404	3,118	...	244	365	18,240	3,849	534
Massachusetts	137,963	81,403	23,725	5,757	...	1,643	476	20,991	3,460	508
Michigan	327,140	224,581	11,789	5,435	5,190	19,329	31	31,115	23,408	6,262
Minnesota	210,082	141,713	8,002	1,547	...	392	...	38,496	16,111	3,821
Mississippi	92,940	29,724	5,099	32,985	1,702	1,184	...	15,762	6,484	...
Missouri	186,031	109,594	5,730	31,995	4,313	1,987	559	19,834	11,324	695

414

Montana	42,691	22,199	1,270	458	785	1,448	...	6,445	10,020	66
Nebraska	69,824	44,327	1,823	2,746	...	163	28,522	10,571	5,278	4,916
Nevada	66,636	25,150	1,148	2,527	...	23	...	6,121	2,085	1,060
New Hampshire	43,079	22,714	2,325	2,966	868	1,008	46	9,034	2,602	1,516
New Jersey	535,339	255,415	20,090	201,249	50	3,000	30,686	17,252	5,966	1,631
New Mexico	54,518	35,108	2,032	4,228	44	458	90	6,204	6,354	...
New York	507,753	309,117	15,326	8,165	39,714	34,293	19,973	67,061	12,561	1,543
North Carolina	252,883	132,245	9,425	56,127	...	1,475	2,012	42,589	8,267	743
North Dakota	42,293	25,179	1,006	406	356	221	553	12,712	1,700	160
Ohio	483,430	326,854	11,115	75,209	11,389	15,064	...	27,048	13,482	3,269
Oklahoma	188,173	132,027	6,617	19,228	3	1,004	664	12,527	8,627	7,476
Oregon	167,703	104,787	6,866	2,561	3,889	1,301	544	31,350	15,226	1,179
Pennsylvania	843,761	317,089	58,728	337,529	18,574	9,102	17	74,368	25,837	2,517
Rhode Island	24,430	18,698	(a)	1,953	...	136	43	3,042	360	198
South Carolina	73,357	36,492	3,251	6,033	...	2,997	2,090	15,118	4,654	2,722
South Dakota	26,786	16,278	1,244	363	1,181	150	...	3,569	4,729	453
Tennessee	184,116	91,517	10,582	47,383	3,489	1,249	...	23,035	8,268	901
Texas	839,606	314,047	25,543	431,383	...	11,255	39	36,686	14,560	2,604
Utah	35,736	19,580	1,892	...	...	148	...	5,989	7,900	227
Vermont	29,191	21,311	1,528	188	...	433	162	2,254	2,983	332
Virginia	161,170	104,214	11,394	6,947	5,831	1,982	16	26,517	9,318	782
Washington	169,255	83,508	11,567	3,523	8,039	4,058	...	43,867	16,811	90
West Virginia	81,997	51,932	(a)	3,622	33	6,715	...	5,821	5,753	115
Wisconsin	186,290	120,671	10,861	2,278	83	...	...	23,130	24,230	5,004
Wyoming	51,716	33,571	356	928	1,172	7	...	1,064	14,494	124

Source: U.S. Bureau of the Census, *State Government Tax Collections in 1981.*
Note: Because of rounding, detail may not add to total.

(a) Included with motor vehicle license taxes.

Table 6
FISCAL YEAR, POPULATION AND PERSONAL INCOME, BY STATE

State	Date of close of fiscal year in 1981	Total population (excluding armed forces overseas) (in thousands)(a)		Personal income, calendar year 1980(b)		State government portion of state-local tax revenue in fiscal 1979-80(c) (percent)
		April 1, 1980	July 1, 1979	Amount (in millions)	Per capita	
United States		225,867	219,443	$2,155,237	$ 9,514	61.3
Alabama....................	September 30	3,890	3,769	29,199	7,488	73.4
Alaska.....................	June 30	400	406	5,136	12,790	85.8
Arizona....................	June 30	2,718	2,450	23,951	8,791	61.5
Arkansas	June 30	2,285	2,180	16,651	7,268	77.6
California..................	June 30	23,669	22,694	259,551	10,938	69.8
Colorado	June 30	2,889	2,772	29,029	10,025	52.1
Connecticut	June 30	3,108	3,115	36,510	11,720	55.3
Delaware	June 30	595	582	6,172	10,339	81.9
Florida	June 30	9,740	8,860	88,675	8,996	65.1
Georgia....................	June 30	5,464	5,117	44,217	8,073	64.9
Hawaii	June 30	965	915	9,775	10,101	81.0
Idaho	June 30	944	905	7,626	8,056	68.9
Illinois....................	June 30	11,418	11,229	120,434	10,521	57.2
Indiana	June 30	5,490	5,400	49,177	8,936	66.0
Iowa	June 30	2,913	2,902	27,328	9,358	62.0
Kansas	June 30	2,363	2,369	23,648	9,983	58.0
Kentucky	June 30	3,661	3,527	27,939	7,613	79.2
Louisiana	June 30	4,204	4,018	35,645	8,458	67.8
Maine	June 30	1,125	1,097	8,940	7,925	64.1
Maryland	June 30	4,216	4,148	44,210	10,460	59.3
Massachusetts	June 30	5,737	5,769	58,232	10,125	55.1
Michigan	September 30	9,258	9,207	92,339	9,950	59.7
Minnesota	June 30	4,077	4,060	39,744	9,724	69.8
Mississippi	June 30	2,521	2,429	16,626	6,580	77.2
Missouri	June 30	4,917	4,867	44,273	8,982	56.1
Montana...................	June 30	787	786	6,732	8,536	55.4
Nebraska	June 30	1,570	1,574	14,738	9,365	54.0
Nevada	June 30	799	702	8,597	10,727	61.4
New Hampshire	June 30	921	887	8,429	9,131	39.3
New Jersey.................	June 30	7,364	7,332	80,724	10,924	50.9
New Mexico.................	June 30	1,300	1,241	10,219	7,841	81.0
New York..................	March 31	17,557	17,648	180,646	10,260	48.5
North Carolina	June 30	5,874	5,606	46,043	7,819	73.2
North Dakota	June 30	653	657	5,723	8,747	67.3
Ohio	June 30	10,797	10,731	102,410	9,462	54.5
Oklahoma	June 30	3,025	2,892	27,645	9,116	71.0
Oregon	June 30	2,633	2,527	24,587	9,317	56.5
Pennsylvania	June 30	11,867	11,731	112,220	9,434	62.4
Rhode Island	June 30	947	929	8,975	9,444	58.6
South Carolina	June 30	3,119	2,932	22,726	7,266	76.0
South Dakota	June 30	690	689	5,408	7,806	49.7
Tennessee...................	June 30	4,591	4,380	35,525	7,720	62.6
Texas......................	August 31	14,228	13,380	136,146	9,545	58.9
Utah	June 30	1,461	1,367	11,203	7,649	64.1
Vermont....................	June 30	511	493	4,013	7,827	57.9
Virginia....................	June 30	5,346	5,197	50,333	9,392	60.0
Washington	June 30	4,130	3,926	42,677	10,309	71.4
West Virginia...............	June 30	1,950	1,878	15,243	7,800	78.6
Wisconsin	June 30	4,705	4,720	44,095	9,348	67.4
Wyoming	June 30	471	450	5,152	10,898	58.9

Source: U.S. Bureau of the Census, State Government Tax Collections in 1981.
Note: Because of rounding, detail may not add to totals.
(a) U.S. Department of Commerce, 1980 Census of Population and Housing, Advance Reports—U.S. Summary, April 1981.
(b) U.S. Department of Commerce, Survey of Current Business, July 1981.
(c) Bureau of the Census, Governmental Finances in 1979-80, September 1981.

416

TAX AND EXPENDITURE LIMITATIONS

By J. Ward Wright

"TAX AND EXPENDITURE LIMITATIONS" is a term which has made "TELs" an acronym familiar to all state executives and legislators, and it is doubtful that any legislative session since 1978 has failed to address several such proposals. The Council of State Governments (CSG) has sought to keep its members abreast of the developments on TELs, especially in state governments, by reporting on proposed and adopted legislation and explaining the implications of each type of limitation. There is a long history of the use of TELs in the United States, especially at the local level, and it is difficult to assess how successful they have been. Financial administration at the state and local levels is an extremely complex process, which has been complicated in modern times by the ever-increasing scope of governmental activities and the steady integration of federal, state and local concerns for a wide variety of socioeconomic problems.

As a consequence of these developments, modern attempts to limit the collection and use of taxes and other revenues is extraordinarily difficult. Fund structures, the vagaries of fiscal periods, and the variety of intergovernmental fiscal flows all have served to make the application of limitations a very hazardous undertaking. In addition, state officials are faced with perplexing problems when trying to limit spending for "normal" periods while providing for a wide variety of possible emergencies.

In the post-World War II period, demands on the part of the public and special interest groups (including organized public employees) have constantly escalated and appear to be unremitting. "Excess" revenues are quickly claimed by many groups and are very seldom carried forward as "savings" to the taxpayer. Given the wide variety of interests members of a state legislature necessarily represent, it is difficult for any government as a whole to exercise self-restraint. While the governor and legislature in every state have the power to cut back spending and limit needs for revenue, such group discipline is often impossible as a practical matter. Many espouse the desirability of prescribed limitations on taxes and revenues as the only reasonable, effective way of curtailing governmental costs—regardless of how imperfect the various features of these controls may be.

This review highlights those aspects of TELs that should be considered when drafting this type of legislation. It should be noted that a TEL has definite shortcomings. In any reform effort, these types of limitations are not substitutes for the development of equitable systems of taxation, improved productivity in government, or the development of responsive and effective bureaucracies—to mention only some of the pressing issues included in the public's demand for economical and effective government. Properly developed as an integral part of a larger overall effort of governmental reform, a TEL may well play an effective role in finding a balance between the vital need for effective governmental services and the limitations faced by every citizen in attempting to pay the associated costs.

J. Ward Wright is a private attorney and government consultant.

Methods of State Control

As of January 1982, 18 states had placed limitations on their own expenditures or revenues. A listing of these states, together with a brief explanation of the various provisions employed by each, is set forth in Table 1. Many approaches have been used; however, most of them are directed toward relating increases in state (and also local, in some instances) costs and revenue collections to the growth in the economy or to the apparent ability of people to pay.

Of the 18 states with limitations on their own revenues or expenditures, eight have constitutional provisions. Of these, seven imposed limitations by popular initiative and referendum. In these latter instances, the decision on adopting a limitation was not lodged with the state legislatures. On the other hand, 10 of the states imposed the limitations by statute, and it is likely that the majority of the remaining states in the nation considering such actions will have to make a conscious legislative decision about whether to impose such fiscal strictures on themselves.

Every state has taken its own approach to the development of a formula for tying costs to ability of its citizens to pay taxes. Any categorization of these approaches is a risky matter since the classifications are largely in the eye of the beholder. However, the 18 states appear to fall into six categories:

- Growth in expenditures is related to increases (or the rate of increases) in personal income in New Jersey, Tennessee, Hawaii, Texas, Oregon, Utah, Idaho, South Carolina and Missouri.
- Expenditures are limited to 7 percent of state personal income in Arizona.
- Revenues are limited by the level of personal income in Louisiana, Michigan and Washington.
- Formulas combining increases in the cost of living with changes in population are used in Nevada and California.
- Expenditures are limited to 98 percent of estimated general fund revenue in Delaware.
- Expenditures are limited to a flat percentage over the previous year's expenditures in Colorado and Rhode Island (though the latter is only a suggested limitation that is not binding on the legislature).

As can be seen from the table at the conclusion of this report, the actual formulas in use are more complicated than the above comments indicate, and there are usually exceptions to the prescribed limitations. In fact, no two states have adopted the same methods; however, the net results, for most practical purposes, are probably the same in all states except Nevada, California, Delaware, Colorado and Rhode Island. Nevada and California are properly very concerned about continuing growth. Delaware and Colorado seemed determined to tie themselves tightly to current levels of expenditure. Rhode Island has not actually committed itself to any limitation, though an 8 percent increase in the budget was given to the governor as a guideline.

These states have come to realize that there are difficulties involved in determining and applying these types of indices. Thus, different procedures are being used to develop these data:

- In Arizona, a three-member Economic Estimates Commission ascertains personal income.
- In Tennessee, state personal income is derived from an econometric model maintained by the University of Tennessee.

- In Texas, projections of growth in the state's economy will be taken from an econometric model developed by the state comptroller's office.

No comment can be made here about specific models proposed or in use. Presumably they take the most important factors into account. They certainly represent a new level of sophistication in state use of economic data.

Provisions for Emergencies

States all recognize the need for provisions for exceptional circumstances. Every state that has its TEL embodied in its constitution has an explicit arrangement for an emergency override. Most of the statutory states (Colorado, Idaho, Louisiana, Nevada, Oregon, Rhode Island and South Carolina) do not make such provisions; however, their limitations clearly can be changed in the course of the normal legislative process. Presumably, the same perceived pressures that lead to the development of limitations tend to prompt the imposition of conditions that make escape from these conditions more difficult than the passage of the average piece of legislation. Thus, Arizona, Hawaii, Missouri, Michigan, Utah and Washington all require a two-thirds vote of both houses of the legislature (though some additional conditions must also be met in several instances) to override the limitation, and New Jersey requires exceptions to be approved by a majority of the voters in a referendum.

While the governors of Michigan and Missouri and the legislatures of Utah and Washington must "declare" an emergency as a condition of override, many states leave the entire process up to whatever circumstances arise. It does not appear that any state with a TEL has attempted to specify what an emergency is for these purposes.

Exceptions to Limitations

It has also been found that neither *all* revenues nor expenditures can be limited as a practical matter. Any simplistic attempt to limit all expenditures or revenues of any general purpose government is certain to fail for many legal and practical reasons. Overwhelmingly, most of the limitations apply only to the general fund, and exceptions are usually made even from that. A complete list of these exceptions for state TELs is presented in Table 1, but the following are some of the sources of revenue that pose special problems to the framers of TEL legislation:

- *Federal Assistance.* Few states want to discourage the receipt and use of these funds, and the matching requirements and associated mandates require types and levels of disbursements the state might not ordinarily undertake during a period of austerity. Arizona, Louisiana and New Jersey are examples of states that exclude these funds from the limitations.
- *Dedicated Funds.* Receipts from fuel taxes (usually dedicated to highway maintenance), tolls or similarly earmarked receipts obviously are already limited in application.
- *Self-Supporting Enterprises.* For those services that are supported entirely by fees, as is the case with most government-owned public utilities, a spending limit is simply denying people a service for which they are willing to pay.
- *Pensions.* Most state and local pension funds are in such bad actuarial shape that their conditions have sometimes been regarded as little less than a national emergency. Any overall limitation that ignores this continuing condition in a state with this problem may well be fiscally irresponsible.

- *Debt Service.* Debt that has been properly approved constitutes an obligation which must be met, both from a legal and moral standpoint. Inclusion of these expenditures within the limitations can have repercussions on the bond market and can also act to encourage a government to delay undertaking necessary capital maintenance and beginning important projects during periods in which such delays can be extremely costly.
- *Bond Funds.* Directly related to debt service is the question of whether receipts from the sales of bonds should be excluded from the limit. Again, steps that discourage building of necessary facilities or adequate maintenance of existing facilities can be very costly in the long run.
- *Local Assistance.* Where state-collected taxes are distributed to local units of government (including schools), the question arises where the limitations (if any) should be imposed. Especially where the state collects the funds on behalf of the local governments, as with proportions of the sales or income taxes in some states, state-imposed limits are of dubious propriety unless the entire basis of the arrangement is reexamined.

Conclusion

None of the state TELs have been in use for long, and economic conditions have been such that many state governments have fallen short of their revenue estimates. Consequently, it has been impossible to determine how successful TELs have been in achieving their purpose.

Missouri's constitutional provision approved by the people in the fall of 1980 was the last state TEL adopted. Whether the movement will pick up again when economic conditions improve remains to be seen.

Table 1

LIMITS ON STATE EXPENDITURES AND REVENUES: A REVIEW OF THE GENERAL PROVISIONS AS OF JANUARY 1982

State year-basis application	Method of control	Scope	Provisions for waiver
Arizona .... 1978—C Expenditures	Limits state expenditures to 7 percent of the personal income of residents. A committee establishes the level of income to be used as the index.	Includes all tax funds appropriated by legislature.	To override provisions requires two-thirds approval of both houses of the legislature.
California .... 1979—C Expenditures	Limits increases in state appropriations to changes in cost of living and the level of population. Revenues exceeding this amount must be offset by changes in the tax schedules over the ensuing two years.	Excludes approximately 60 percent of state expenditures—debt service, federal court mandates, tax refunds, various insurance funds.	An override permitted; however, extra costs must be compensated for by reduced expenditures in the three ensuing years. Voters also can vote an increase, but this approval is operative for only four years.
Colorado .... 1977—S Expenditures	Limits General Fund spending to 7 percent of the preceding year. Any receipts exceeding this limit by 4 percent must be used for tax relief.	Applies to all General Fund appropriations.	No special provisions; however, statute can be amended at any time.
Delaware .... 1980—C Expenditures	Limits General Fund appropriations to a maximum of 98 percent of estimated revenue for that year. Excess revenue goes to a reserve account which cannot accumulate to more than 5 percent of estimated General Fund revenue.	Applies to all General Fund appropriations.	Upon approval of 60 percent of each house voting, the additional 2 percent may be used in an emergency, or the reserve fund balance may be so utilized.
Hawaii .... 1978—C Expenditures	Limits increases in General Fund expenditures to the estimated rate of growth of the state's economy [in practice, state personal income is the index]. If General Fund surplus exceeds 5 percent of revenue two consecutive years, tax refunds or credits must be provided.	Applies to all General Fund expenditures except those using federal funds.	Upon the governor recommending a definite amount required, a two-thirds vote of each house may approve.
Idaho .... 1980—S Expenditures	Limits General Fund expenditures to 5-1/3 percent of total state personal income.	Applies to all General Fund expenditures.	Statute can be amended at any time.
Louisiana .... 1979—S Revenues	Limits state revenues to a percentage applied to current state personal income. The percentage is derived by dividing FY 78-79 revenues by 1977 state personal income. Excess revenues are deposited in a surplus fund which can only be used for tax refunds.	There are numerous exclusions, including federal funds, severance taxes, utility income.	No special provisions; however, statute can be amended at any time.
Michigan .... 1978—C Revenues	Limits state revenues to a ratio (derived by dividing state revenue received in the prior fiscal year by state personal income the year before that) applied to state personal income reported during the prior year. [Note: In deriving the ratio, a three-year average of personal income may be substituted for the prior year if it will result in a higher percentage.]	Federal funds are not included in the calculations of state revenues. In addition, the cost of general obligation debt service and loans to school districts are excluded.	Upon declaration of an emergency by the governor, and designation of amount required and method of funding, may be approved by a two-thirds vote of each house.
Missouri .... 1980—C Revenues	Limits state revenues to a ratio (derived by dividing state revenues in FY 81 by state personal income in calendar year 1979) applied to personal income in the calendar year prior to the year of appropriations. [Note: In determining personal income, a three-year average may be substituted if it results in a greater amount than the one-year level.]	Neither federal funds nor revenues raised to retire voter-approved debt are included in the revenue limitation.	Governor must request legislature declare an emergency and indicate the reasons and the amount required to meet it. In 1981-82, a simple majority of both houses is required. In subsequent years, a two-thirds vote of each house will be required. If revenues exceed limit by 1 percent or more, they must be used as refunds to income taxpayers.

421

LIMITS ON STATE EXPENDITURES AND REVENUES:
A REVIEW OF THE GENERAL PROVISIONS AS OF JANUARY 1982—Continued

State year-basis application	Methods of control	Scope	Provisions for waiver
Nevada .... 1979—S Expenditures	Limits executive budgetary requests (not legislative action) to the rate of inflation and population growth using the biennium 1975-77 as the base fiscal period.	Applies to all appropriations included in the budget request.	Legislature is not limited.
New Jersey .... 1976—S Expenditures	Limits expenditures for state operations and capital outlays to increases in state per capita income as measured between the second quarters of the preceding two years.	Excluded are appropriations supported by state aid to local governments, federal assistance and retirement of debt authorized by referendums.	Limit can be exceeded only if approved by the majority of voters in a statewide referendum.
Oregon .... 1979—S Expenditures	Limits expenditures to the rate of growth of state personal income for the preceding two years. If revenues exceed limit by more than 2 percent, they must be used as refunds to corporate and personal income taxpayers.	Excluded are debt service and appropriations for tax relief.	Statute may be amended at any time.
Rhode Island .... 1977—S Expenditures	Suggests that the governor limit his budget request to an 8 percent increase over the preceding year's appropriations.	Applies to all General Fund appropriations.	Statute can be amended at any time.
South Carolina .... 1980—S Expenditures	Limits increases in state expenditures over the preceding year to the growth of personal income averaged over the preceding three years.	Applies to all state expenditures.	Statute can be amended at any time.
Tennessee .... 1978—C Expenditures	Limits the growth of appropriations financed by tax revenues to the growth in the state's economy. In practice, the increase in personal income is used as the index.	Applies only to appropriations funded by tax revenues.	Legislature can approve a specific act by majority vote delineating exact amount required.
Texas .... 1978—C Expenditures	Limits growth in state appropriations to the growth of the state's economy. In practice, growth in state personal income is used as the index.	Excludes revenues dedicated by the state constitution.	Legislature may find an emergency and authorize a specific amount by majority vote.
Utah .... 1979—S Expenditures	Limits increases in appropriations to 85 percent of the increase in state personal income.	Exclusions include federal funds, debt service and user charges.	Upon declaration of an emergency by the legislature, the limit can be overridden by a two-thirds vote of each house.
Washington .... 1979—S Revenues	Limits tax revenues to the rate of increase in state personal income as averaged over the preceding three years. Any excess receipts become part of the tax revenue for the next year.	Applies to all state tax revenues.	Upon declaration of an emergency by the legislature, a specified amount may be approved by a two-thirds vote of each house.

Key:
C—Constitutional limitation.
S—Statutory limitation.

3.   State Financial Administration

STATE FINANCIAL ADMINISTRATION

By Kay T. Pohlmann

STATE GOVERNMENT financial management is a topic of increasing importance because of the challenges of the 1980s. Resources must be used more efficiently because of inflation, taxpayer uneasiness over the size of government spending, the weak economy and reduced federal aid. For instance, new federal block grants, for the most part, do not provide the flexibility that the states had sought or the Reagan administration had proposed. In addition, the states must absorb a 25 percent cutback in federal aid since the block grants amount to only 75 percent of funding for the previous year.

With pressure on state government to provide improved and expanded public services during inflationary times, managers must have timely and reliable financial information in order to make sound fiscal policy decisions. Financial management tools include the budget process, the accounting system, the cash management system, the financial reporting system and audits.

Cash Management

Cash management is the collection, processing, disbursement and investment of cash funds. The actions in each of these areas have an effect on available cash resources. Improved cash management can partially compensate for inflation and increase revenue by streamlining the collection procedures, taking advantage of the highest interest rates and reducing "float" time.

States are becoming increasingly aware of the importance of good cash management as evidenced by several states improving their collection process through the use of lock boxes and the selection of banks by competitive bids. Investment policies vary among the states as well as who is responsible for the investment decisions. The investment goal is the same, however, and that is to maximize interest earned. For example, Texas reported that an average of 98.4 percent of available funds was invested for the month of September 1981. This high percentage of investment would not have been possible without a good cash management system.

Several states have conducted cash management studies. For example, Oregon recently instituted several cash management measures as a result of a cash management project. In addition to investment policies, electronic funds transfers have been used to improve cash management. North Dakota recently implemented a direct deposit system for state checks after the state treasurer indicated that most of the state transactions could be handled by computer.

Accounting and Reporting

Accounting and reporting systems are the basic components of financial management.

Kay T. Pohlmann is the Staff Director of the National Association of State Auditors, Comptrollers and Treasurers, The Council of State Governments.

The National Council on Governmental Accounting in *Governmental Accounting and Financial Reporting Principles* indicated that, "A governmental accounting system must make it possible both: (a) to present fairly and with full disclosure the financial position and results of financial operations of the funds and account groups of the governmental unit in conformity with generally accepted accounting principles; and (b) to determine and demonstrate compliance with finance-related legal and contractual provisions."

Several states have converted or are in the process of converting to generally accepted accounting principles (GAAP). Tennessee and Maryland have GAAP financial statements, and approximately 15 other states are in varying stages of implementing GAAP.

In addition to providing a more accurate measure of fiscal condition, GAAP financial statements will also affect the states' bond ratings. Standard & Poor's indicated that the quality of reporting and accounting standards being used by the issuers under review is taken into account in its rating process. Standard & Poor's said in a 1980 policy statement that financial statements should be prepared in accordance with GAAP and that these statements should be independently audited either by a certified public accounting firm or by a qualified independent state or local agency, on a timely basis, i.e, no later than six months after the fiscal year end. Maryland, one of the first states to adopt GAAP, has maintained a Triple A rating on general obligation bonds, and Comptroller Louis V. Goldstein has indicated that the savings in interest has paid for the cost of the new accounting system, plus independent audits for 1979 and 1980.

Auditing

Auditing is an important management tool. The increase in government programs, both federal and state, brought with it an increased demand for full accountability by those administering the programs, and auditing is an integral part of that accountability.

Several years ago the major concern was financial audits; however, today auditors are also interested in the economy, efficiency and effectiveness of government operations. Legislators, investors, public officials and citizens want to know not only whether government funds are handled properly and in accordance with laws and regulations, but also whether the programs are achieving the purposes intended and whether they are doing so economically and efficiently. This type of audit function is often called "post audit" to distinguish it from the activities of some auditors who approve expenditures before payment is made—the pre-audit.

Over the past several years, there has been an effort by state post auditors to improve the operations of their offices and the quality of their audits. Most state auditors are independent and are responsible for auditing all state agencies. Several state auditors are also responsible for auditing local government units and prescribing the scope and nature of audits of local governments by others.

Table 1
STATE CASH MANAGEMENT

State	Investment policy governed by	Determines investment policy	Responsible for investing funds	Restrictions on investing funds	Investment counseling	Bank selection policy	Responsible for selecting banks for demand deposits	Bank selection method for demand deposits	No. of banks used for demand deposits
Alabama	S	State Treas.—E	State Treas.	Yes	SE	S,A	State Treas.—E	All banks used	319
Alaska	N/R	N/R	N/R	N/R	N/R	N/R	N/R	N/R	N/R
Arizona	C,S	State Treas.—E	Investment Officer—Treas. Office	Yes	SE,IC,IF	N/R	Bd. of Deposit/State Treas.—G,E	Competitive bid	1
Arkansas	S	State Bd. of Fin.—E,G	State Treas.	Yes	SE	C,S	State Treas.—E	Size/location	15
California	S	Money Investment Bd.—E,G	Chief of Investments—Treas. Office	Yes	SE	A	State Treas.—E	Geographic coverage of the state with requirement of a Sacramento branch	8
Colorado	S	State Treas.—E	Chief Investment Officer—Treas. Dept.	Yes	SE	T	State Treas.—E	Competitive bid	1
Connecticut	S,A	State Treas.—E	Dep. State Treas.	Yes	SE,IC	A	State Treas.—E	Combination(a)	35
Delaware	S	Cash Mgt. Policy Bd.—G	State Treas.	No(b)	SE,IC,IF	S	Cash Mgt. Policy Bd.—G	Competitive bid	1
Florida	S	S	State Treas.	Yes	SE	(c)	State Treas.—E	Competitive bid	4
Georgia	S	State Depository Bd.—E,G	Dir., Fiscal Div., Dept. of Adm. Services	Yes	SE	(d)	State Depository Bd.—E,G	Location/size	50
Hawaii	S,A	Dir. of Finance—G	Chief, Fin. Div., Dept. of Budget & Finance	Yes	SE	S,A	State Dir. of Finance—G	Competitiveness for int. rates; depository's size; ability to fully collateralize state deposits	8
Idaho	S,A	State Treas.—E	State Treas. & Senior Deputy Treas.	Yes	SE	S	S	S(e)	26 plus branches
Illinois	C,S,A	State Treas.—E	Chief Fiscal Officer, Treas. Office	Yes	(f)	A	State Treas.—E	Size	3
Indiana	S	State Treas.—E	State Treas. & Investment Mgr., Treas. Office	Yes	SE	T	State Treas.—E	Discretion of State Treas.	15
Iowa	S	State Treas.—E(g)	State Treas., Dept. of Investment	Yes	IC	S,A	State Treas.—E	All Federal Reserve Banks in Des Moines	6
Kansas	S(h)	Money Investment Bd.—E,G	Money Investment Bd.	Yes	N/R	(i)	Money Investment Bd.—G,E	Competitive bid	1
Kentucky	S	State Invest. Comm.—E,G	State Treas.	Yes	SE	S	State Treas.—E	Negotiated agreement	1(j)
Louisiana	S	State Treas.—E	Asst. State Treas. & Office of Depository & Investment, Dept. of Treas.	Yes	IC	A	State Treas.—E	Interim Emergency Bd.(k)	1
Maine	S	Deputy State Treas.—CS	State Treas.	Yes	SE	S,A	State Treas.—L	Competitive bid	3
Maryland	S	State Treas.—L	State Treas.	Yes	SE	S	State Treas.—L	Competitive bid/negotiation	1
Massachusetts	S	State Treas.—E	First Deputy, Treas. Dept., Investment Div.	Yes	IC	A	State Treas.—E	Competitive bid/lowest responsible bidder	5
Michigan	S,A	State Treas.—G	State Treas./Deputy Treas./Dir. of Investments	Yes	SE	A	State Treas.—G	Location/convenience	254
Minnesota	A	State Bd. of Investment—E	State Bd. of Investment	Yes	(l)	A	Commr., Dept. of Fin.—G	Competitive bid	225
Mississippi	S,A	State Depository Commission & State Treas.—E	State Depository Commission & State Treas.	Yes	N/A	S	State Auditor—E	State Auditor(m)	6
Missouri	C,S,A	State Treas.—E	State Treas.	Yes	SE	C,S,A	State Treas.	Competitive bid/convenience & rotation on collection accts.	270
Montana	S	Bd. of Investments	Bd. of Investments, Dept. of Admin.	Yes	SE,IC,IF	S,A	Admin., Treas. Div.—CS	All banks used	161
Nebraska	S	Investment Council—G	Dir., Investment Council	Yes	SE,IC,IF	A	State Treas.—E	The six major correspondent banks utilized (clearing accts.)	49
Nevada	C,S,A	State Treas.—E	State Treas. & staff	Yes	SE	S	State Treas.—E	Competitive bid/level of services available	2
New Hampshire	S	State Treas.—E	State Treas.	Yes	SE	A	State Treas.—E	Size/geographic location	12
New Jersey	N/R	N/R	N/R	N/R	N/R	N/R	N/R	N/R	N/R

STATE CASH MANAGEMENT—Continued

State	Investment policy governed by	Determines investment policy	Responsible for investing funds	Restrictions on investing funds	Investment counseling	Bank selection policy	Responsible for selecting banks for demand deposits	Bank selection method for demand deposits	No. of banks used for demand deposits
New Mexico	C,S,A	State Legislature—E	State Treas.	Yes	N/R	S	Secretary, Dept. of Finance & Admin.—G	N/R	60
New York	S	Comptroller—E	Dir., Office of State Comptroller, Investment & Cash Mgt. Div.	Yes	SE	S	Comptroller—E	Competitive bid/convenience/ quality & price of services	145
North Carolina	S	State Treas.—E	State Treas., Investment & Banking Div.	Yes	IC	C,S	State Treas.—E	Convenience & safety in receiving & disbursing state monies/ all banks eligible	200
North Dakota	S	State Investment Bd.—E,G	State Treas., Invest. Dept.	Yes	(n)	S	(o)	(o)	1
Ohio	S	State Bd. of Deposit—E	Dir. of Investment, Treas. Office	Yes	IF	A	State Treas.—E	All banks used	3
Oklahoma	N/R	N/R	N/R	N/R	N/R	N/R	N/R	N/R	N/R
Oregon	S	Investment Council—E,G	Treas. Dept.—Invest. Div.	Yes	SE	(p)	State Treas.—E	All banks used	16
Pennsylvania	S	State Treas.—E	Dir., Treas. Dept., Bureau of Cash Mgt. & Investment	Yes	SE	S	Bd. of Fin. & Rev.—E,G	Size/geography	28
Rhode Island	S,A	Investment Commission—E,G,L,CS	Gen. Treas./Deputy Gen. Treas., Treas. Dept.	No	(Q)	A	Gen. Treas.—E	All banks used	13
South Carolina	S	State Treas.—E	State Treas.	Yes	IC	A	State Treas.—E	All banks used	N/R
South Dakota	S	Investment Office—L	Investment Office, Treas. Dept., Investment Div.	No	IC	A	State Treas.—E	Competitive bid	N/R
Tennessee	C,S,A	State Treas.—L	State Treas.	Yes	SE	S	Treas./Commr. of Fin. & Admin./Governor—E,G,L,(z)	State requirement(s)	360
Texas	N/R	N/R	N/R	N/R	N/R	N/R	N/R	N/R	N/R
Utah	S	State Treas.—E	State Investment Officer, Treas. Office	Yes	N/A	A	State Treas.—E	Competitive bid	165
Vermont	S	State Treas.—E	State Treas.	Yes	SE,IC,IF	T	State Treas.—E	Divided among largest state banks with Montpelier offices	3
Virginia	S	State Treas.—G	Investment Officer, Dept. of Treas.	Yes	SE	A	State Treas.—G	Service capability(t)	177
Washington	C,S	State Treas.—E	Investment Officer, Treas. Office	Yes	SE	A	State Treas.—E	Competitive bid	1
West Virginia	C,S,A	State Bd. of Investment—E	Dir. of Invest., Treas. Office	Yes	SE,IF	S	Bd. of Investment—E	All banks used	6
Wisconsin	S	Investment Bd.—G	State Investment Bd. staff	Yes	IC	S	Depository Selection Bd.—E,G	Competitive bid	2
Wyoming	S,A	State Treas.—E	Dep. State Treas., Treas. Office	Yes	SE	A	State Treas.—E	Banks are invited to make proposals for the state acct.	1

Source: Questionnaire survey conducted by CSG for the National Association of State Auditors, Treasurers and Comptrollers, October 1981.

Key:
N/A—Not applicable
N/R—No response
S—Statute
C—Constitution
A—Administrative practice
E—Elected
G—Appointed by governor
L—Appointed by legislature
CS—Civil service
SE—State employee
IC—Investment council
IF—Investment firm

(a) Competitive bid for disbursing accounts (3); convenience for deposit and various economic and service criteria for others (32).
(b) Some restrictions will likely be established during 1982.
(c) Not limited.
(d) State Depository Board.
(e) Law requires that all banks requesting deposits receive them in proportion to their capital and surplus, with amount covered by federal insurance excluded from apportionment by this formula.

(f) Chief fiscal officer.
(g) Treasurer of state for all but retirement funds.
(h) Statute, State Investment Board.
(i) Statute, Money Investment Board.
(j) Does not include imprest cash and temporary depository receipt accounts.
(k) Banks must be approved fiscal agents of state in order to have state funds. Approval is secured from the Interim Emergency Board.
(l) Representation from the local financial community.
(m) Selection by state auditor's approval of agency request. State treasurer rotates clearing account among capital city banks.
(n) Bank of North Dakota.
(o) All held in Bank of North Dakota.
(p) Agencies have choice of bank deposit location based on convenience.
(q) Advised by major banking firm.
(r) The state does not maintain demand deposit accounts as operating accounts. Rather, taxpayers are permitted to deposit tax payments to local banks. These depository accounts are drawn down on a scheduled basis to concentrate state cash for subsequent investment. Accounts in three banks are utilized as clearing accounts through which state warrants are redeemed.
(s) Request by bank, meeting statute requirements, authorized by governor, treasurer and commissioner of finance and administration.
(t) Established and in operation for three or more years/competitive bidding.

Table 2
STATE ACCOUNTING AND REPORTING

	Who establishes state accounting principles	Responsible for statewide general purpose financial statements	Accounting function centralized	If centralized, who is responsible	Pre-audit function	Method of payment for goods & services	Who issues check or warrant	If checks are used, are warrants used in internal processing	If yes, who is responsible for issuing warrants
Alabama	Legislature—E	Comptroller—CS	Yes	Comptroller	Comptroller—CS	Warrant	Comptroller—CS	...	N/R
Alaska	N/R	N/R	N/R	N/R	N/R	N/R	N/R	...	N/R
Arizona	Asst. Dir. for Fin.—G	Asst. Dir. for Fin.—G	Yes	Asst. Dir. for Fin.	Asst. Dir.—G	Warrant	Asst. Dir. for Fin.—G	...	...
Arkansas	Chief fiscal officer—G	Adm. Office of Acctg. (chief fiscal officer)	Yes	Adm. Office of Acctg.	Dept. of Fin. & Admin. (chief fiscal officer)	Warrant	State auditor—E	...	...
California	Dir. of Fin.—G	State Controller—E	Yes	State Controller	State Controller—E	Warrant	State Controller—E	...	...
Colorado	State Controller—CS	State Controller—CS	Yes	State Controller	State Controller—CS	Warrant	State Controller—E	...	...
Connecticut	State Comptroller—E	State Comptroller—E	Yes	State Comptroller	State Comptroller—E	Check	State Comptroller—E	Yes	State Comptr.
Delaware	Budget Director—G	Budget Director—G	Yes	Dir., Div. of Acctg.	Dir., Div. of Acctg.	Check	Dir., Div. of Acctg. (Appt., Secy. of Fin.)—CS	No	...
Florida	State Comptroller—E	State Comptroller—E	Yes	State Comptroller	State Comptroller—E	Warrant	State Comptroller—E	...	...
Georgia	State Auditor—L	State Auditor—L	...	...	Dir., Office of Planning & Bud.	Check	Fiscal Officer (various depts.)—CS	Yes	Dir., Office of Planning & Bud.
Hawaii	Comptroller—G	Comptroller—G	Yes	Comptroller	Comptroller—G	Warrant	Comptroller—G	...	...
Idaho	State Auditor—E	Financial Mgt.—G	Yes	State Auditor	State Auditor—E	Warrant	State Auditor—E	...	...
Illinois	State Comptroller—E	State Comptroller—E	Yes(a)	State Comptroller	State Comptroller—E	Warrant	State Comptroller—E	...	...
Indiana	State Auditor—E	State Auditor—E	Yes	State Auditor	State Auditor—E	Warrant	State auditor—E	...	...
Iowa	State Comptroller—G	State Comptroller—G	Yes	State Comptroller	State Comptroller—G	Warrant	State Comptroller—G	...	...
Kansas	Dir., Div. of Accts. & Reports—CS	Dir., Div. of Accts. & Reports—CS	Yes	Dir., Div. of Accts. & Reports	Dir., Div. of Accts. & Reports—CS	Warrant	Dir., Div. of Accts. & Reports—CS	...	...
Kentucky	Dir., Div. of Accts.—G	Dir., Div. of Accts.—G	Yes	Dir., Div. of Accts.	Div. of Accts., Pre-Aud. Section—G	Check	State Treasurer—E	Yes	Dir., Div. of Accts.
Louisiana	Commr. of Admin.—G	Commr. of Admin.—G	Yes(b)	Commissioner of Admin.	Legislative Auditor—L	Check	State Treasurer—E	Yes	State Treas.
Maine	State Controller (Fin. Commission)	State Controller (Fin. Commission)	Yes	State Controller	State Controller (Fin. Commission)	Check	State Treasurer—L	Yes	State Contr.
Maryland	Comptroller—E	Comptroller—E	Yes(c)	Comptroller	Comptroller—E	Check	State Treasurer—L	Yes	Comptroller
Massachusetts	State Comptroller—G	State Comptroller—G	Yes	State Comptroller	State Comptroller—G	Check	State Treasurer—E	Yes	State Comptroller
Michigan	Dir. of Acctg.—CS	Dir. of Acctg.—CS	Yes	Dir. of Acctg.	Delegated to agencies—CS	Warrant	State Treasurer—G	...	...
Minnesota	Commr. of Fin.—	Commr. of Fin.—	Yes	Commr. of Fin.	Commr. of Fin.—G	Warrant	Commr. of Fin.—G	...	...
Mississippi	State Aud. of Pub. Accts.—E	State Aud. of Pub. Accts.—E	Yes(d)	State Aud. of Pub. Accts.	Dept. of Pub. Accts.—E	Warrant	State Aud. of Pub. Accts.—E	...	...
Missouri	Commr. of Admin.—G	Dir. of Acctg.—G	Yes	Dir. of Acctg.	Dir. of Acctg.—G	Check	State Treasurer—E	Yes	Dir. of Acctg.
Montana	Dir., Dept. of Admin.—G	Dir., Dept. of Admin.—G	Yes	Dir., Dept. of Admin.	Dir., Dept. of Admin.—G	Warrant	State Auditor—E	...	...
Nebraska	Dir. of Adm. Serv.—G	Dir. of Adm. Serv.—G	Yes	Dir. of Acctg. Admin.	State Acctg. Admin. (Dir. of Adm. Serv.)	Warrant	Dir. of Adm. Serv.—G	...	...
Nevada	State Controller—E	State Controller—E	Combination	State Controller	State Bud. Offr.—G	Check	State Controller—E	Yes	State Contr.
New Hampshire	Dir. of Accts.—G	Dir. of Accts.—G	Yes	Dir. of Accts.	Dir. of Accts.—G	Check	State Treasurer—L	Yes	Gov. & council

STATE ACCOUNTING AND REPORTING—Continued

	Who establishes state accounting principles	Responsible for statewide general purpose financial statements	Accounting function centralized	If centralized, who is responsible	Pre-audit function	Method of payment for goods & services	Who issues check or warrant	If checks are used, are warrants used in internal processing	If yes, who is responsible for issuing warrants
New Jersey	State Comptroller—CS	Asst. State Comp.—CS	Yes	State Comptroller	Agency Approval Officers & Account-ants in Treas. Bureau—CS	Check	Dir., Div. of Bud. & Acctg. and State Treasurer—G	No	...
New Mexico	Dir., Fin. Control Div.—G	Dir., Fin. Control Div.—G	Yes	Dir., Fin. Control Div.	Dir., Fin. Control Div.—G	Warrant	Dir., Fin. Control Div.—G	...	...
New York	Comptroller—E	Comptroller—E	Yes	Comptroller	Comptroller—E	Check	Comptroller & State Treas., jointly—E,G	Yes	Comptroller
North Carolina	State Auditor—E	State Auditor—E	...	...	Each Departmental Controller—CS	Check	Departmental Controllers—CS	Yes	Office of State Budget
North Dakota	Dir., Off. of Mgt. & Budget—G	Dir., Off. of Mgt. & Budget—G	Yes	Dir., Off. of Mgt. & Budget	Dir., Off. of Mgt. & Budget—G	Check	State Treasurer—E	No	...
Ohio	N/R	N/R	N/R	N/R	N/R	N/R	N/R	N/R	N/R
Oklahoma	Dir. of State Fin.—G	Chief Analyst, Budget Div.—CS	Yes	State Comptroller	Chief, Pre-Audit Div.—CS	Warrant	State Treasurer—E	...	...
Oregon	Adminstr., Accounting Div. (Appt., Dir. of Exec. Dept.)	Adminstr., Accounting Div. (Appt., Dir. of Exec. Dept.)	...	...	Agency level	Check	Agency level	Yes	Adminstr., Acctg. Div.
Pennsylvania	Secy. of Budget & Admin.—G	Dep. Secy. for Comptr. Operations—G	Yes(e)	Dir., Bureau of Fin. Mgt.	Comptroller—G State Treasurer	Check	State Treasurer—E	Yes	State Treas.
Rhode Island	Dir. of Admin.—G	State Controller—CS	Yes	State Controller	State Controller—CS	Check	State Controller—CS	Yes	State Contr.
South Carolina	Comptroller Gen.—E	Comptroller Gen.—E	Yes	Comptroller Gen.	Comptroller Gen.—E	Check	State Treasurer—E	Yes	Comptr. Gen
South Dakota	Commr., Bureau of Fin. & Mgt.—G	Chief Accountant, Bur. of Fin. & Mgt.—CS	Yes	Commr., Bureau of Fin. & Mgt.	State Auditor—E	Warrant	State Auditor—E	...	...
Tennessee	Commr., Fin. & Admin.—G, Comptr. of the Treas.—L	Commr., Fin. & Admin.—G	Yes	Asst. Commr. for Acctg.	Dir. of Accts.—CS	Warrant	Commr., Fin. & Admin.—G	...	...
Texas	Comptr. of Pub. Accts.—E, State Aud.—L	Comptr. of Pub. Accts.—E	Yes	Comptr. of Pub. Accts.	Comptr. of Pub. Accts.—E	Warrant	Comptr. of Pub. Accts.—E	...	...
Utah	Dir. of Fin. (Appt. by Dir. of Adm. Serv.)	Dir. of Fin. (Appt. by Adm. Serv.)	Yes	Dir. of Fin.	Dir. of Fin. (Appt. by Dir. of Adm. Serv.)	Warrant	Dir. of Fin. (Appt. by Dir. of Adm. Serv.)	...	...
Vermont	Commr., Dept. of Fin.—G	Commr., Dept. of Fin.—G	Yes	Commr., Dept. of Fin.	Commr., Dept. of Fin.—G	Check	State Treasurer—E	Yes	Commr., Dept. of Fin.
Virginia	Comptroller—G	Comptroller—G	Yes	Comptroller	N/R	Warrant	State Treasurer—G	...	...
Washington	Dir., Office of Fin. Mgt.—G	Dir., Office of Fin. Mgt.—G	...	...	Each agency	Warrant	State Treasurer—E	...	...
West Virginia	State Auditor—E	State Auditor—E	Yes	State Auditor	State Auditor—E	Warrant	State Auditor—E	...	...
Wisconsin	State Fin. Dir. (Appt. by Secy. of Admin.)	State Fin. Dir. by Secy. of Admin.	Yes	State Fin. Dir.	State Fin. Dir. (Appt. by Secy. of Admin.)	Check	State Fin. Dir. (Appt. by Secy. of Admin.)	N/R	N/R
Wyoming	State Auditor—E	State Auditor—E	Yes	State Auditor	State Auditor—E	Warant	State Auditor—E	...	...

Source: Questionnaire survey conducted by CSG for the National Association of State Auditors, Treasurers and Comptrollers, October 1981.

Key:
N/R—No response
E—Elected
G—Appointed by governor.
L—Appointed by legislature.
CS—Civil service.

(a) Treasury held funds are centralized. Non-Treasury held funds are decentralized. Certain information is obtained from an annual form prepared by agencies and sent to the comptroller for inclusion in statewide general purpose financial statements.

(b) Approximately 65 percent centralized, 35 percent decentralized by agencies.

(c) Centralized—however, basic financial data is obtained from decentralized agency accounting offices. Centralized accounting and reporting systems and year-end closing packages. Separate financial reports are prepared by proprietary organizations (higher education funds and other enterprise funds) and certain Trust Funds. These reports are folded in with data from the centralized systems and year-end closing packages to produce the Statewide GPFS.

(d) Large departments maintain detailed accounts. Statements are obtained from colleges and universities and from Employment Security Commission (for FY 1981, for the first time) and combined with amounts handled through State Treasury which are recorded by Department of Public Accounts.

(e) General Fund is centralized; Special Funds decentralized but consolidated centrally. For financial statement preparation, agency comptrollers submit individual fund trial balances to the Bureau of Financial Management. These are then compiled and summarized by the Bureau. For management reports computer tape output is interfaced with Central Accounting System for Major Funds.

Table 3
STATE AUDITING

State/Agency	Audit all state agencies	State agencies permitted to arrange for own audits	Regulation of local govt. acctg., auditing & reporting practices	Audit local governments	Types of local government audits	Prescribe scope & nature for other auditors	Types of audits performed State	Local
Alabama								
State Auditor	Yes	No	Yes	Yes	CI	No	. . .	F,C
Chief Examiner	Yes(a)	No	Yes	Yes	CO,SD,OT	Yes	F,C,E,P	F,C
Alaska								
Legislative Auditor	Yes	Yes	Yes	Yes	OT	No	F,C,E,P	. . .
Internal Auditor	Yes	Yes	No	No	N/A	N/R	. . .	. . .
Arizona								
Auditor General	No	Yes	Yes	Yes	CO,SD	Yes	F,C,E,P	F
Arkansas								
Legislative Auditor	No	Yes	Yes	Yes	CI,CO,SD	No	F,E	F
State Auditor	Yes(b)	No	Yes	No	N/A	N/R	. . .	. . .
California								
Auditor General	Yes	Yes	Yes	Yes	CI,CO,SD	No	F,C,E	E
Dept. of Finance	Yes	No	Yes	Yes	CO,SD	Yes	F,C(c),E	. . .
State Controller	Yes	Yes	Yes	Yes	CO,OT	No	F,C	F,C
Colorado								
State Auditor	Yes	No	Yes	No	N/A	No	F,C(c)	. . .
Connecticut								
Auditors of Accounts	Yes	No	Yes	No	N/A	N/R	F(d)	. . .
Delaware								
Auditor of Accounts	Yes	No	Yes	Yes	CI,CO,SD	No	F(d)	F
Florida								
Auditor General	Yes	No	Yes	Yes	SD,OT	Yes	F,C,E,P	F,C
Georgia								
State Auditor	No	No	Yes	Yes	SD	No	F,C,E,P	F,C
Hawaii								
State Comptroller	No	Yes	No	No	N/A	No	F,C	. . .
Idaho								
Legislative Auditor	No	Yes	Yes	No	N/A	No	F,C(c)	. . .
Illinois								
Auditor General	Yes	No	No	Yes	OT	No	F,C,E,P	. . .
State Comptroller	No	N/A	No	No	N/A	No	. . .	. . .
Indiana								
State Examiner	Yes	No	Yes	Yes	CI,CO,SD,OT	N/A	F,C	F,C
Iowa								
State Auditor	Yes	No	Yes	Yes	CI,CO,SD	Yes	F,C(c)	F,C
Kansas								
Legislative Auditor	Yes	No	Yes	No	N/A	No	F,C(c),P(e)	. . .
Kentucky								
Aud. of Public Accts.	No	Yes	Yes	Yes	CO	Yes	F,C	F,C
Louisiana								
Legislative Auditor	Yes	Yes	Yes	Yes	(f)	Yes	F,C	F,C
Maine								
State Auditor	Yes	Yes	Yes	Yes	CI,CO,SD,OT	Yes	F,C	F,C
Maryland								
Legislative Auditor	Yes	No	Yes	No	N/A	Yes	F,C	. . .
Massachusetts								
Aud. of the Commonwealth .	Yes	Yes	Yes	Yes	OT	No	F,C(c)	. . .
Legislative Auditor	No	Yes	Yes	No	N/A	No	E,P	. . .
Michigan								
Legislative Auditor General .	Yes	No	Yes	No	N/A	No	F,C(c)	. . .
Local Govt. Audit Div.	N/A	N/A	Yes	Yes	CI,CO,SD,OT	Yes	. . .	F,C(g)
Minnesota								
Legislative Auditor	Yes	No	Yes	No	N/A	No	. . .	. . .
Mississippi								
State Auditor	Yes	No	Yes	Yes	CI,CO,SD	Yes	F,C(c)	F,C(e)
Perf. & Expend. Review	Yes	Yes	Yes	Yes	CI,CO,SD	No	E,P	. . .
Missouri								
State Auditor	Yes	Yes	No	Yes	CO	No	F,C(c),E	F,C(c),E
Montana								
Legislative Auditor	Yes	No	Yes	No	N/A	No	F,C(c),E,P(h)	. . .
Nebraska								
Aud. of Public Accts.	Yes	No	Yes	Yes	CO	Yes	F,C,E	F,C,E
Nevada								
Legislative Auditor	Yes	Yes	Yes	No	N/A	No	F,C(c),E	. . .
New Hampshire								
Legislative Budget	No	Yes	No	No	N/A	No	F,C,E,P	. . .
New Jersey								
State Auditing	Yes	Yes	Yes	No	N/A	No	F,C	. . .
New Mexico								
State Auditor	Yes	Yes	Yes	Yes	CI,CO,SD,OT	Yes	F,C	C

State/Agency	Audit all state agaencies	State agencies permitted to arrange for own audits	Regulation of local govt. acctg., auditing & reporting practices	Audit local governments	Types of local government audits	Prescribe scope & nature for other auditors	Types of audits performed State	Local
New York								
Dept. of Audit & Control ...	Yes	No	Yes	Yes	CI,CO,SD,OT	Yes(i)	F,C,E,P(h)	F,C
Leg. Comm. on Exp. Review	No	Yes	Yes	Yes	CI,CO,SD	No	E,P	E,P
North Carolina								
State Auditor.............	Yes	Yes	Yes	No	N/A	No	F,C(c),E	...
North Dakota								
State Auditor.............	Yes	No	Yes	Yes	CI,CO,SD	Yes	F,C	F,C
Leg. Bud. Anal. & Aud.	No	No	N/R	No	N/A	N/R	C,E,P	...
Ohio								
Auditor of State	Yes	Yes	Yes	Yes	CI,CO,SD	Yes	F,C(c)	F,C
Oklahoma								
State Aud. & Inspector	Yes	Yes	Yes	Yes	CI,CO,SD	Yes	F	F,C
Oregon								
Div. of Audits	Yes	No	Yes(j)	Yes	CI,CO,SD,OT	Yes	F,C,P	F,C
Pennsylvania								
Auditor General	No	Yes	No	Yes	CI,CO,SD,OT	No	F,C,E,P	F,C,E,P
Leg. Bud./Fin. Cmte.	No	N/A	N/R	No	N/A	No	E,P	...
Rhode Island								
Bureau of Audits	Yes	No	Yes	Yes	CI,SD,OT	No	F,C	F,C
Auditor General	No	Yes	Yes	No	N/A	Yes	F,C(c),E(k),P	...
South Carolina								
State Auditor..............	Yes	Yes	No	No	N/A	No	F	...
Leg. Audit Council.........	Yes	Yes	No	Yes	SD,OT	N/R	F,C,E,P	...
South Dakota								
Auditor General	Yes	Yes	Yes	Yes	CI,CO,SD,OT	Yes	F,C(c)	F,C
Tennessee								
Div. of State Audit	Yes	No	Yes	Yes	CI(l),CO,SD(l),OT(l)	Yes	F,C(c),E,P(h)	F,C
Texas								
State Auditor..............	Yes	No	Yes	No	N/A	No	F,C,E	...
Utah								
Legis. Aud. General	Yes	No	Yes	No(m)	N/A	No	E,P(h)	...
State Auditor..............	Yes	No	Yes	No	N/A	Yes	F,C(c)	...
Vermont								
Auditor of Accts.	Yes	No	No	No	N/A	No	...	...
Virginia								
Aud. of Public Accts.	Yes	Yes(n)	Yes	Yes	CI,CO,OT	Yes	F,C	F,C
Jt. Legis. Aud. & Review....	Yes	N/A	Yes	No	N/A	No	P	...
Washington								
State Auditor..............	Yes	Yes	Yes	Yes	CI,CO,SD,OT	No	F,C	F,C
Legislative Auditor.........	Yes	No	Yes	Yes	CI,CO,SD	No	P	...
West Virginia								
Legislative Auditor.........	Yes	No	Yes	No	N/A	No	F,C,E,P	...
State Tax Dept.............	No	N/A	Yes	Yes	CI,CO,SD,OT	Yes	...	...
Wisconsin								
State Auditor..............	Yes	Yes	Yes	No	N/A	N/R	F,C,E,P	...
Wyoming								
State Auditor..............	No	Yes	Yes	Yes	CI,CO,OT	No	F,C,E,P	...
Leg. Services Office	(o)	No	Yes	No	N/A	No	P	...

Legend:
N/A—Not applicable
N/R—No response
CI—City
CO—County
SD—School districts
OT—Other
F—Financial audits
C—Compliance audits
E—Efficiency/economy audits
P—Program results audits
  (a) Except other legislative agencies.
  (b) All Treasury funds of state agencies.
  (c) Financial and compliance audits combined.

(d) Have elements of all types.
(e) Includes sunset audits.
(f) All units except municipalities.
(g) Also fraud investigations.
(h) Efficiency and economy and program results combined.
(i) For school districts only.
(j) Budgeting, auditing and reporting only.
(k) Financial, compliance, and economy and efficiency combined.
(l) Monitor.
(m) Has the authority.
(n) Grant audits.
(o) At present, sunset audits only.

Section VIII MAJOR STATE SERVICES
1. Education

STATE PUBLIC SCHOOL SYSTEMS

DECLINING ENROLLMENTS, reductions in force, increasingly scarce resources, a continuing decline in Scholastic Aptitude Test scores and increased interest in vouchers and tuition tax credits, coupled with inflation and a recessionary trend, continued to plague the nation's public schools during the last biennium.

Consolidation of federal aid into block grants to be used largely at the discretion of the states appeared to be the attainment of a long-sought goal on the part of the states. However, the victory was diminished by an accompanying reduction in monies available from the federal government. State monies are also in short supply as budget caps passed in a number of states during the last biennium begin to take effect. In nearly all the states, policy-makers will be faced with hard decisions as they attempt either to continue the programs started by the federal government, making up the deficit with state resources, or risking the wrath of special interest groups whose programs may have to be cut.

The traditional oversupply of teaching candidates began to weaken as spot shortages started to appear. Rural schools had difficulty in attracting teachers, while shortages occurred in special education, vocational education, science and math. Science and math majors were being absorbed by industry at salaries far more attractive than could be offered by the public schools. Despite these problems, the 13th annual Gallup poll of the public's attitudes toward the public schools provided evidence that the decline in the ratings given by the public to the public schools in their communities has apparently come to a halt. On the other hand, there is no evidence that an upturn in the ratings is imminent.

Table A
PUBLIC SATISFACTION WITH THE SCHOOLS: 1974-81
National Totals (in percentages)

Ratings given public schools	1981	1980	1979	1978	1977	1976	1975	1974
A rating	9	10	8	9	11	13	13	18
B rating	27	25	26	27	26	29	30	30
C rating	34	29	30	30	28	28	28	21
D rating	13	12	11	11	11	10	9	6
FAIL	7	6	7	8	5	6	7	5
Don't know	10	18	18	15	19	14	13	20

Analysis of the poll indicates that residents of cities with fewer than 50,000 inhabitants have a much higher opinion of their schools than persons living in cities with populations of more than 1 million. In addition, persons living in the West rate their schools lower than

Prepared by Russell B. Vlaanderen, John Augenblick and Chris Pipho of the Education Commission of the States.

431

persons who live in other sections of the nation. Southerners give their schools the highest grades.

Consolidation

The major problem to be faced by state education policy-makers in the next biennium will be implementing the block grants passed by Congress in the summer of 1981. The law consolidates over 20 previously funded programs and eight previously unfunded programs that can now be funded at state and local discretion. Not included in the block grants are the education of disadvantaged children (formerly ESEA, Title I), bilingual education, education of the handicapped, rehabilitation services, vocational and adult education, the Women's Educational Equity Act (ESEA, Title IX), and training and advisory services (CRA 4). Eighty percent of the funds appropriated must pass through to local education agencies, while 20 percent may be reserved for state-initiated programs. The governor must appoint an advisory committee including persons representative of public and private elementary and secondary schoolchildren, classroom teachers, parents of and secondary schoolchildren, local boards of education, local and regional school administrators, institutions of higher education and the state legislature. The advisory committee shall advise the state educational agency on the use of the funds reserved for the state and on the formula for the allocation of funds to local education agencies. In addition, they will advise the agency on the planning, development, support, implementation and evaluation of state programs assisted under the law. Because of the requirement for assistance to private elementary and secondary schools, many states will have difficulty with the restrictive constitutional clauses. If a local education agency is prohibited by law from providing, or has substantially failed to provide, services on an equitable basis for private schoolchildren, the secretary, under the bypass provision, is authorized to use part of the funds allocated to the local education agency to provide those services. There can be no doubt this will be a trial-and-error effort on the part of the states to administer federally initiated programs. The end result could be increased centralization of control in Washington, D.C.

Teacher Certification

Widespread publicity has appeared concerning the supposed incompetence of the nation's teachers. In an effort to counter this publicity and to increase the quality of education, state policy-makers have turned to, among other things, the screening of teacher candidates, reflecting in part a lack of confidence in teacher preparation institutions. Policy-makers in 17 states have mandated that a test be given to applicants for teaching certificates. In nine states, this has been accomplished by legislative action, while in seven others, the state board of education has taken action. One state, Texas, has seen action by both the state board of education and the legislature. Six states have adopted the National Teacher Examinations as the test to be given. Eight states are developing their own tests. Two states have a combination of state-developed tests and the National Teacher Examinations, while one state, California, the latest to pass legislation, has not yet made a choice.

Creationism

The controversy over providing equal time for the teaching of evolution and creation in the public schools first appeared in the 1920s. Many states enacted anti-evolution laws and the issue reached a peak in public concern with the John T. Scopes "monkey trial." In subsequent years, many of these state laws were invalidated in the courts or were removed by state legislatures.

In the late 1960s, the issue reappeared. This time it was pushed along by national efforts to re-emphasize evolution in biology textbooks and by fundamentalist groups who coined the term "scientific creationism." By the mid-1970s, an equal-time law had been enacted by the Tennessee Legislature and was invalidated by the federal courts, while the state of California became involved in a heated debate over state guidelines calling for creationism to be included in science textbooks.

In the 1980s, increasing pressure to alter what schools teach about man's origins is being applied by vocal groups of citizens who are asking that schools give equal time to evolution and creation in classroom lectures, textbooks and library materials. By using scientific evidence and terminology, these single-interest groups claim that the theory of evolution has become a tenet of a pseudo-religious doctrine called secular humanism. They assert that when evolution theory is taught as fact, the First and Fourteenth Amendment guarantees of separation of church and state and of equal protection under the law are violated. The materials and documents proposed by the creationists for use in classrooms are devoid of Biblical reference, presumably to avoid adverse court rulings.

Interest groups are lobbying local school boards and legislatures to create policy that would require equal time for teaching both creationism and evolution.

While more than 50 groups are known to have an interest in this subject, five organizations have prime visibility: the Institute for Creation Research, a part of Heritage College in San Diego; the Creation Science Research Center, headed by the Segraves family of San Diego; the Creation Research Society, Ann Arbor, Michigan; the Creation of Social Science and Humanity Society, Wichita, Kansas; and the Bible Science Association, Minneapolis, Minnesota.

Scientific creationism received additional attention in 1981 when Arkansas and Louisiana enacted laws calling for the balanced treatment of "creation science" and "evolution science" in the public schools. The Arkansas law specifies that equal time "as a whole" be given in "lectures, textbooks, library materials, or educational programs" that deal " in any way with the subject of the origin of man, life, the earth or the universe." (In early January 1982, a federal judge ruled as unconstitutional the Arkansas "balanced treatment of creation science" law. The state planned to appeal.)

The movement is alive in many states. In 1980, 10 bills were introduced in eight states. In 1981, there were 23 proposed laws in 15 states. Citizens for Fairness in Education, Anderson, South Carolina, one of the groups behind legislative proposals on scientific creationism, has said they expect additional states to consider legislation in 1982.

Quality Education

Increasing the quality of public elementary, secondary and postsecondary schools appears to be a force on the move. During the late 1970s, the idea of minimum competency testing was adopted by more than 35 states. While this movement emphasized the establishment of minimum standards for grade promotion, graduation and remediation programs, it appears to have carried with it the seeds of reform for improving education programs across-the-board.

Secretary of Education T. H. Bell, in a speech before state legislators late in the summer of 1981, called for states and local districts to introduce maximum competency testing in addition to minimum competency testing for all school programs. He asked that academic expectations be raised at all levels so that education would serve not just the minimum needs of students but the maximum needs as well. He pointed out that citizenship education was in obvious need of reform because a majority of the 18 year olds who are eligible to vote have not registered. He also decried the lack of foreign language teaching and the need to strengthen math and science instruction. In order to give these demands more attention, the Department of Education established the National Commission on Excellence in Education, with an 18-month charge to examine U.S. schools for programs that work and "make practical recommendations for action" to the public school officials, educators, parents and others who set school policy.

The call for quality also is evident in education circles, with no less than 10 major studies, commissions or blue-ribbon panels investigating a need for higher quality standards and making recommendations for improving education in the United States. In Florida, this has taken the form of a commission on secondary education to look at the expectations of secondary schools in the areas of science and math. The College Board, sponsor of the Scholastic Aptitude Test (SAT), announced a 10-year program to improve both quality and equality in schools and colleges. The emphasis of the program will be to better improve the quality of high school students entering college and to enhance academic opportunities for minority students. College Board officials said the program was in response to a 14-year drop in SAT scores.

Elementary and Secondary School Finance

As the decade of the 1980s unfolds, a new set of school finance issues is emerging. While many of the concerns of the 1970s continue to be discussed, most notably fiscal equity among school districts, the context of school finance decision-making is changing to reflect fundamental shifts in the social, economic and political structure of the country. Symbolic perhaps of this shift is that the most important issue in education today is the quality of the public school system. While some states have made progress in assessing pupil achievement levels, only slight improvements have been made in analyzing the relationship between the "outputs" of the education process and the "inputs" required to produce them. This is an important exercise if the concern for quality is to be linked to the financing of education. In most states, policy-makers focus on per pupil expenditure levels, pupil-teacher ratios, teacher training and experience and teacher salary levels as indicators of quality.

An issue related to quality is the adequacy of the resources available to schools. In the face of continued inflation and declining enrollments, new problems such as reduced federal support and the cost of maintaining facilities have made it increasingly difficult to assure past levels of funding. Adequate funding requires a recognition that different pupils require different levels of educational resources. Adequacy is also seen by some as a reflection of local rather than state standards, necessitating the state to provide equal opportunities for all districts to set education spending at levels they choose.

The goal of an adequate, high-quality education program for all students may be achieved at the expense of some of the improvements in fiscal equity that have been accomplished during the last 15 years. Many policy-makers feel that in order to promote quality, increased local control must be given to school districts. At least some of the strides in interdistrict fiscal equity resulted from reducing school district control over tax rates or annual budget increases. In 1980, two thirds of the states constrained school district fiscal behavior in some manner. The future of school finance hinges on the tradeoffs that states will make between adequacy, quality, equity and local control. These decisions will be made in an environment characterized more often than not by poorly performing revenue systems, increased competition between education and other public services, and a declining proportion of the population with children enrolled in public schools.

While the concern for quality and adequacy remains solely in the hands of policy-makers, the concern for equity in school finance continues to receive scrutiny from the courts. Following on the heels of lower court decisions in New York and Colorado in 1978 and 1979, courts in Wyoming, Georgia and Maryland have declared state school aid systems unconstitutional. West Virginia is in the midst of a case challenging its school finance system, and cases are pending in Wisconsin and New Jersey. A major concern in much of this litigation is the treatment of urban school districts. Many of the cases originate in the largest city of the state, and the courts appear to be sympathetic to the argument that cities face extraordinary problems related to higher proportions of students with special needs, higher costs of doing business and difficulties in providing support for education, given all the other demands on them.

In general, the courts have moved away from the expectation that every school district must spend the same amount per pupil in order to meet constitutional requirements of equal protection. Rather, the courts have made it clear that there are legitimate reasons for spending to vary across school districts related to characteristics of pupils and characteristics of school districts.

Many states have implemented pupil-weighted approaches to account for such spending differences. By assigning a higher weight to students in different grades or to students with different handicaps or by assigning such weights to all pupils in very small school districts, the state aid systems recognize the expenditure differences associated with providing educational services to different pupils in different school districts. The pupil-weighted approach differs from categorical funding systems in that all districts receive similar recognition for the additional expenditures attributable to specific types of pupils but each district's ability to support such expenditures is also assessed. In this way, pupil-weighted systems promote both equity and efficiency.

States such as Florida, Utah, New Mexico and Oklahoma are notable for their weighting systems. A major difference among these states is the extent to which each requires that money allocated for a special purpose be spent for that purpose. Florida requires that most of the funds received due to extra weighting be spent in the category for which it was received. Oklahoma, however, has no such requirement.

In 1980, Arizona implemented a pupil-weighted approach with little or no requirements about how such money be used, although the state retained an interest in the progress of pupils identified as needing the extra resources. In effect, Arizona anticipated the kind of "block grant" approach that the federal government will be putting into effect in 1982. Arizona's block grant system was not accompanied by a reduction in available resources, however.

The federal block grant program will have a large impact on states because it also reduces federal support for those populations of students that have been identified as being in need of additional resources. At the very time when the states have identified such pupils and begun to create equitable ways of providing supplementary support, the federal government has reduced its funding and placed the burden on the states of assuring an adequate education for all pupils. While the initial approach to federal block grants did not include aid for pupils in need of compensatory education, bilingual pupils or handicapped pupils, it is possible that later modifications will include funds targeted for these groups. The states will face difficult political problems in allocating limited state and federal funds among the special interest groups seeking support.

Future Issues in School Finance

Since 1968, nearly 30 states have reviewed their school finance systems and modified them in fundamental ways. In general, greater strides were made in reducing tax-related inequities than in alleviating variations in per pupil expenditure levels across school districts. Numerous problems now face the states as they attempt to deal with court mandates, adapt to changes in the federal role, modify their revenue generation systems and continue to limit education spending while promoting an adequate and equitable education system.

The states will continue to increase the sensitivity of their school aid systems to school districts with special characteristics. Important among the factors that will be considered are size and municipal overburden. It is generally recognized that small school districts incur higher than average per pupil costs. In the past, much effort has been expended to consolidate small districts to make them more efficient. The conventional wisdom concerning consolidation has generally been abandoned, however, due to offsetting increases in transportation costs and to an interest in preserving local social institutions. States that have numerous small districts, such as Oklahoma, Nebraska or Texas, must now determine how much additional support small districts need to receive in order to operate adequate school programs. It is also believed (and the courts may require) that urban school districts should receive additional state support. Not that long ago, city schools typically offered outstanding education programs. As the fiscal condition of many cities has changed, with decreasing tax bases and increasing public service demands, support for education has deteriorated. In order to assure the adequacy of education programs, additional state education support may need to be allocated to cities.

Another issue that has begun to receive attention in the states is alternative sources of local school district revenue. Most school districts rely almost completely on the property tax base as the source of local support. Fiscally dependent school districts often derive revenues from sales and other taxes imposed by the jurisdictions of which they are a part. In Iowa, school districts have the authority to impose an income tax, although few take advantage of the opportunity. In other states, such as Pennsylvania, a head tax can be imposed. In a few states, a portion of the income tax revenues collected by the state are returned to the school districts although such revenue may then be deducted from state aid. Many districts have considered the imposition of fees for particular services. The reorganization of the intergovernmental fiscal structure of the country is not likely to result in a definitive relationship between functions to be performed by governments and sources of revenue that they, and they alone, can use. Given the unpopularity of the property tax and the continued decline in reliance upon it, it is crucial that local school districts have access to other tax bases if they are to provide a significant share of education support.

A problem that is likely to be exacerbated in the 1980s is the variation among states in the adequacy of their education systems. In the 1970s, there was some discussion of a federal role in helping to equalize educational programs around the country for all pupils, not just those with special needs. Given the changing federal role, this is an unlikely possibility in the future. What is becoming clear, however, is that some states face extreme economic difficulty, including Massachusetts, Michigan and Oregon, and some states enjoy economic prosperity, including Wyoming, Colorado, Texas, Oklahoma and North Dakota. It is likely that these differences will translate into relatively weak or relatively strong support for education. While education is a function of the states, the growing differences in the adequacy of education programs, reversing an opposite trend over the last two decades, may spark interest in using federal aid as a remedy.

A major policy concern in the next few years will be public support for privately sponsored education. Tax credit legislation was strongly supported at the federal level although implementation may depend on the achievement of a balanced budget. Vouchers will be on the ballot in Washington, D.C., and they continue to receive support in California. The resolution of this issue will have an important long-term impact on the governance and financing of public education. This is another area in which the issues of quality and local control will be balanced against equity.

Finally, an important education finance issue looming on the horizon is teacher salary levels. During the past decade, gains have been made in raising teachers' salaries although such gains did not go far beyond the impact of inflation. At the same time, new job opportunities have opened for those who traditionally chose teaching as a profession. The teaching profession may not be capable of attracting well-trained individuals unless the incentives offered are modified in fundamental ways. This is a complex issue because while it may not be necessary to offer windfall bonuses to currently practicing educators, it may be necessary to offer high salaries to new professionals or to the very best practitioners. Any approach that undertakes this differentiation flies in the face of current practice; approaches that do not differentiate may be extremely costly.

The resolution of the salary issue may be the single most important one of the next 10 years. Given the political power attributed to teacher organizations, this issue will keep education finance in the forefront of state fiscal concerns. Resolving the salary problem in conjunction with balancing quality, equity and local control is likely to demand the continued attention of state policy-makers well into the 1980s.

Table 1

AVERAGE ANNUAL SALARY OF INSTRUCTIONAL STAFF IN PUBLIC ELEMENTARY AND SECONDARY DAY SCHOOLS, BY STATE: 1972-73, 1975-76 and 1980-81

State	1972-73	1975-76	1980-81	State	1972-73	1975-76	1980-81
Alabama	$ 8,262	$10,803	$15,472	Montana	$ 8,908	$11,560	$15,980
Alaska	15,176(a)	20,573 (b)	30,292	Nebraska	9,080	10,418	15,659
Arizona	10,863	12,807	17,800	Nevada	11,472	14,000	18,190
Arkansas	7,613	9,986	13,670	New Hampshire	9,913	10,560	13,434
California	12,700	15,600	20,477	New Jersey	11,750	13,941	20,025
Colorado	10,280	12,600	18,009	New Mexico	8,600	13,500	16,269
Connecticut	11,200	13,349	18,100	New York	13,450(c)	16,511 (c)	21,000
Delaware	11,100	13,120	18,052	North Carolina	9,314	11,312	16,175
Florida	9,740	10,996	16,360	North Dakota	8,362	10,112	14,356
Georgia	8,644	10,847	16,218	Ohio	9,800	11,950	17,100
Hawaii	10,900	15,638 (b)	22,107	Oklahoma	8,200	9,800	15,040
Idaho	8,058	10,564	15,650	Oregon	9,949	12,627	18,389
Illinois	11,564	14,419	20,149	Pennsylvania	11,000	12,900	18,120
Indiana	10,300	12,311	18,795	Rhode Island	10,800	13,754	19,807
Iowa	10,564	12,101	16,610	South Carolina	8,310	9,821	14,630
Kansas	8,839	11,115	15,964	South Dakota	8,034	9,363	14,370
Kentucky	8,150	10,135	16,630	Tennessee	8,450	10,470	15,239
Louisiana	9,388	10,422	15,000	Texas	9,029	11,818	15,755
Maine	9,277	10,665	19,052	Utah	8,990	11,800	17,414
Maryland	11,787	14,445	19,863	Vermont	9,110	10,300	13,654
Massachusetts	11,200	12,600	24,973	Virginia	9,842	11,970	15,490
Michigan	12,400	16,030	21,012	Washington	11,100	14,450	21,709
Minnesota	11,115	14,065	18,753	West Virginia	8,505	10,764	16,073
Mississippi	7,145	9,649	13,400	Wisconsin	10,812	12,816	17,086
Missouri	9,329	10,843	16,143	Wyoming	9,900	11,600	19,290

Source: National Education Association, *Estimates of School Statistics, 1973, 1976 and 1981.* (Washington, D.C.)
(a) Reduce 30 percent to make purchasing power comparable to the figures for other areas of the United States.

(b) Reduce 25 percent to make purchasing power comparable to the figures for other areas of the United States.
(c) Median salary.

Table 2
FALL ENROLLMENT IN PUBLIC ELEMENTARY AND
SECONDARY DAY SCHOOLS: 1978-79 and 1980-81

State or other jurisdiction	1978-79 fall enrollment			1980-81 estimated fall enrollment			Percentage change 1978-79 to 1980-81
	Elementary	Secondary	Total	Elementary	Secondary	Total	
United States	24,402,967	18,475,339	42,878,306	24,224,449	16,684,925	40,909,374	-4.3
Alabama	369,100	384,100	753,200	389,984	354,687	744,671	-1.1
Alaska	49,286	40,105	89,391	49,107	38,490	87,597	-2.1
Arizona	386,700	173,300	560,000	356,000	157,000	513,000	-8.4
Arkansas	241,178	215,520	456,698	240,399	207,301	447,700	-2.0
California(a)	2,742,117	1,328,825	4,070,942	2,689,396	1,365,852	4,055,248	0.4
Colorado	300,500	259,500	560,000	311,000	235,000	546,000	-2.5
Connecticut	396,250	196,900	593,150	362,684	184,578	547,262	-7.7
Delaware	53,041	57,993	111,034	48,612	50,791	99,403	-10.5
Florida	771,991	853,549	1,625,540	1,052,000	470,000	1,522,000	-0.2
Georgia	649,748	438,088	1,087,836	655,900	412,800	1,068,700	-1.8
Hawaii	89,336	80,760	170,096	87,669	77,112	164,781	-3.1
Idaho(b)	108,744	94,278	203,022	113,034	90,213	203,247	-0.1
Illinois	1,410,426	696,889	2,107,315	1,335,569	644,952	1,980,521	-6.0
Indiana.............	575,345 (c)	555,319	1,130,664	551,493	502,008	1,053,501	-6.8
Iowa	296,150	272,983	569,133	281,565	252,973	534,538	-6.1
Kansas	261,414	176,466	437,880	237,455	175,108	412,563	-5.8
Kentucky	441,712	251,287	692,999	431,500	238,500	670,000	-3.3
Louisiana	447,000	381,000	828,000	550,000	240,000	790,000	-4.6
Maine	162,550	75,730	238,280	151,200	71,000	222,200	-6.7
Maryland	403,630	408,480	812,110	364,188	386,000	750,188	-7.6
Massachusetts	565,000 (b)	570,000 (b)	1,135,000 (b)	716,360	302,417	1,018,777	-10.2
Michigan	1,016,784	961,336	1,978,120	963,912	907,000	1,870,912	-5.4
Minnesota	388,375	416,460	804,835	370,742	380,455	751,197	-6.7
Mississippi	271,899	219,537	491,436	262,819	209,481	472,300	-3.9
Missouri............	593,923	306,079	900,002	567,198	277,450	844,648	-6.2
Montana	110,500	55,800	166,300	103,600	51,400	155,000	-6.8
Nebraska	155,120	143,180	298,300	154,389	126,317	280,706	-5.9
Nevada	73,222	73,059	146,281	78,300	71,200	149,500	2.0
New Hampshire	102,500	72,150	174,650	99,864	69,720	169,584	-2.9
New Jersey	834,500	511,500	1,346,000	744,380	474,620	1,249,000	-7.2
New Mexico(d).......	144,019	135,322	279,341	146,004	125,327	271,331	-2.9
New York	1,524,700	1,602,900	3,127,600	1,404,960	1,450,790	2,855,750	-8.7
North Carolina	807,470	370,502	1,177,972	792,686	349,013	1,141,699	-3.1
North Dakota	57,570	64,119	121,689	76,318	40,098	116,416	-4.3
Ohio	1,228,150	878,450	2,106,600	1,169,500	802,500	1,972,000	-6.4
Oklahoma(e)........	318,000	274,000	592,000	328,000	250,000	578,000	-2.4
Oregon	273,800	199,700	473,500	283,267	182,223	465,490	-1.7
Pennsylvania	1,012,100	1,045,900	2,058,000	941,700	968,100	1,909,800	-7.2
Rhode Island	79,104	81,274	160,378	73,311	71,515	144,826	-9.7
South Carolina	428,682	196,249	624,931 (d)	423,029	191,601	614,630	-1.6
South Dakota	90,437	47,791	138,228	86,100	42,252	128,352	-7.1
Tennessee	526,318	344,500	870,818	516,013	336,901	852,914	-2.1
Texas	1,532,500	1,337,500	2,870,000	1,591,500	1,301,500	2,893,000	0.8
Utah	182,366	142,102	324,468	201,340	141,545	342,885	5.6
Vermont	60,790	40,760	101,550	50,460	44,928	95,388	-6.1
Virginia	642,590	412,648	1,055,238	622,217	388,154	1,010,371	-4.3
Washington	394,855	372,597	767,452	397,245	359,338	756,583	-1.4
West Virginia(f)	233,518	162,204	395,722	230,973	153,025	383,998	-3.0
Wisconsin	484,417	402,002	886,419	458,355	374,489	832,844	-6.0
Wyoming(f)	51,441	42,887	94,328	55,919	42,385	98,304	4.2
Dist. of Col.	62,099	51,759	113,858	55,233	44,816	100,049	-12.1

Source: Adapted from National Education Association, *Estimates of School Statistics, 1978-79* and *1980-81.* Unless otherwise specified, enrollment data is based on organizational level, i.e., kindergarten and grades 1-6 as elementary, and junior and senior high school, grades 7-12, as secondary.

(a) Junior high school students are counted as elementary students.
(b) NEA estimates.

(c) Includes 555 enrolled in nursery school programs.
(d) Does not collect fall enrollment data; average daily membership is substituted.
(e) Fall enrollment is actually fall membership.
(f) Seventh and eighth graders in middle schools are counted as elementary students.

Table 3
ESTIMATED SCHOOL-AGE POPULATION: 1979

State or other jurisdiction	School-age population (5-17), 1979 (in thousands)	Total state population, 1979 (in thousands)	School-age population as percentage of total population, 1979	Percentage change in total population, 1977 to 1979	Percentage change in school-age population, 1977 to 1979
Alabama	841	3,769	22	2.1	-2.9
Alaska	103	406	25	-0.2	-8.8
Arizona	538	2,450	22	6.7	-5.3
Arkansas	471	2,180	22	1.7	-2.9
California	4,583	22,694	20	3.6	-1.7
Colorado	583	2,772	21	5.8	-1.4
Connecticut	645	3,115	21	0.2	-7.1
Delaware	125	582	22	0.0	-7.4
Florida	1,660	8,860	19	4.8	-1.6
Georgia	1,160	5,117	23	1.4	-3.3
Hawaii	198	915	22	2.2	-3.4
Idaho	203	905	22	5.6	-0.5
Illinois	2,426	11,229	22	-0.1	-5.6
Indiana	1,201	5,400	22	1.3	-3.9
Iowa	619	2,902	21	0.8	-6.5
Kansas	475	2,369	20	1.9	-5.4
Kentucky	770	3,527	22	2.0	-3.1
Louisiana	952	4,018	24	2.5	-3.4
Maine	241	1,097	22	1.1	-4.7
Maryland	893	4,148	22	0.2	-7.4
Massachusetts	1,193	5,769	21	-0.2	-7.2
Michigan	2,086	9,207	23	0.9	-5.7
Minnesota	883	4,060	22	2.1	-6.1
Mississippi	591	2,429	24	1.7	-2.2
Missouri	1,009	4,867	21	1.4	-4.6
Montana	173	786	22	3.3	-0.6
Nebraska	333	1,574	21	0.8	-5.7
Nevada	152	702	22	11	3.4
New Hampshire	193	887	22	4.5	-2.5
New Jersey	1,548	7,332	21	0.0	-6.2
New Mexico	294	1,241	24	4.3	-2.6
New York	3,663	17,648	21	-1.5	-6.8
North Carolina	1,214	5,606	22	1.5	-3.4
North Dakota	144	657	22	0.6	-6.5
Ohio	2,339	10,731	22	0.3	-5.2
Oklahoma	594	2,892	21	2.9	-2.3
Oregon	509	2,527	20	6.4	-0.8
Pennsylvania	2,395	11,731	20	-0.5	-8.2
Rhode Island	193	929	21	-0.1	-6.8
South Carolina	672	2,932	23	1.9	-2.6
South Dakota	150	689	22	0.0	-6.8
Tennessee	933	4,380	21	2.0	-3.1
Texas	2,971	13,380	22	4.3	-1.0
Utah	331	1,367	24	7.8	3.8
Vermont	109	493	22	1.7	-4.4
Virginia	1,097	5,197	21	1.2	-5.4
Washington	815	3,926	21	7.3	-0.6
West Virginia	397	1,878	21	0.1	-3.0
Wisconsin	1,027	4,720	22	1.5	-6.4
Wyoming	97	450	22	10.8	3.2

Source: National Education Association, *Rankings of the States, 1981.*

Table 4
ESTIMATED REVENUE RECEIPTS, PUBLIC SCHOOLS, 1979-80, AND STATE AND LOCAL TAX COLLECTION AS A PERCENTAGE OF PERSONAL INCOME, 1979

State	Total receipts (in thousands) of dollars	Receipts by source, percent			Total state and local tax collections as a percentage of personal income
		Federal	State	Local	
All states	$95,537,323	9.2	48.9	42.0	4.47
Alabama	1,143,324	12.6	69.0	18.4	3.81
Alaska	429,143	13.0	70.2	16.9	8.20
Arizona	1,110,744	11.1	41.6	47.3	4.79
Arkansas	738,961	14.5	53.0	32.5	4.18
California	9,300,000	9.7	71.2	19.1	3.68
Colorado	1,356,656	6.1	41.0	52.9	5.04
Connecticut	1,440,000	6.1	31.5	62.5	4.29
Delaware	305,093	13.0	64.7	22.3	4.89
Florida	3,260,000	11.0	55.2	33.7	3.83
Georgia	1,914,739	11.8	57.6	30.6	4.33
Hawaii	414,576	12.5	85.2	2.4	4.34
Idaho	365,659	9.5	55.0	35.5	4.83
Illinois	5,075,482	12.8	41.2	46.0	4.02
Indiana	2,080,009	6.9	56.1	37.0	4.19
Iowa	1,330,404	6.7	42.2	51.0	4.88
Kansas	1,839,600	6.9	43.3	49.8	4.42
Kentucky	1,217,600	12.5	69.7	17.8	4.09
Louisiana	1,460,900	14.8	54.4	30.8	4.09
Maine	436,284	9.6	48.9	41.5	5.11
Maryland	1,995,514	8.0	40.2	51.8	4.74
Massachusetts	2,970,000	6.5	36.3	57.2	5.41
Michigan	4,914,730	7.4	42.7	49.9	5.26
Minnesota	2,138,200	6.1	56.6	37.3	5.58
Mississippi	780,518	24.1	53.1	22.8	3.95
Missouri	1,752,677	9.7	36.7	53.6	3.94
Montana	379,000	8.4	49.3	42.2	5.75
Nebraska	604,082	7.9	18.2	73.9	4.07
Nevada	273,400	8.6	58.5	32.9	3.38
New Hampshire	339,620	5.1	6.8	88.1	4.35
New Jersey	3,702,700	4.1	40.4	55.5	4.97
New Mexico	626,202	16.6	63.4	20.0	5.57
New York	8,866,000	5.0	40.6	54.4	5.24
North Carolina	2,059,457	15.2	62.4	22.3	4.22
North Dakota	247,100	7.7	46.5	45.7	4.22
Ohio	3,966,100	7.7	40.6	51.6	3.91
Oklahoma	1,221,587	11.5	57.7	30.9	4.39
Oregon	1,266,000	9.9	35.5	54.6	5.05
Pennsylvania	5,301,100	8.5	45.0	46.5	4.83
Rhode Island	372,100	5.9	38.8	55.4	4.43
South Carolina	1,088,757	14.9	56.8	28.3	4.48
South Dakota	258,400	13.9	20.8	65.3	4.33
Tennessee	1,431,907	14.0	48.3	37.7	3.83
Texas(a)	5,876,596	11.0	50.1	38.9	4.45
Utah	630,921	7.8	54.0	38.2	5.91
Vermont	206,800	7.7	28.0	64.2	5.28
Virginia	2,109,836	9.5	40.9	49.6	4.28
Washington	1,802,884	8.6	70.8	20.6	4.39
West Virginia	746,261	10.6	60.1	29.3	4.82
Wisconsin	2,138,514	5.5	37.6	56.8	5.04
Wyoming	251,266	6.6	29.6	63.8	5.26

Source: National Education Association, *Estimates of School Statistics, 1980-81* and *Rankings of the States, 1981*.

(a) Includes expenditures of regular school districts but does not include expenditure data of state school and other districts without taxing authority.

Table 5
ESTIMATED EXPENDITURES FOR PUBLIC ELEMENTARY
AND SECONDARY SCHOOLS: 1980-81

State or other jurisdiction	Total current expenditures (in thousands of dollars)	Per pupil in ADA(a)	Capital outlay (in thousands of dollars)	Total current expenditure, capital outlay and interest (in thousands of dollars)
United States...............	$91,960,346	$2,445	$6,314,521	$102,017,206
Alabama....................	1,118,900	1,593	92,000	1,225,600
Alaska.....................	404,679	5,220	43,050	477,995
Arizona	1,170,672	2,444	62,389	1,267,344
Arkansas	673,371	1,609	93,406	786,510
California	9,708,390	2,513	396,900	10,285,290
Colorado	1,193,840	2,348	74,376	1,306,373
Connecticut................	1,481,500	2,934	25,500	1,543,600
Delaware	282,300	3,142	4,600	302,300
Florida	3,200,000	2,237	260,000	3,510,000
Georgia...................	1,870,200	1,901	46,500	1,967,000
Hawaii	381,935	2,575	31,000	427,852
Idaho	337,900	1,780	46,000	392,165
Illinois....................	4,821,417	2,803	396,396	5,410,401
Indiana	1,976,092	2,031	116,510	2,176,196
Iowa	1,289,543	2,593	107,925	1,415,103
Kansas	974,200	2,693	78,500	1,116,200
Kentucky	1,223,380	1,996	45,444	1,308,496
Louisiana	1,400,000	1,972	92,300	1,525,100
Maine	446,575	2,138	20,000	487,075
Maryland	1,935,988	2,846	92,814	2,081,048
Massachusetts	2,858,375	3,186	289,572	3,293,461
Michigan	5,091,967	2,958	215,000	5,539,070
Minnesota	1,935,600	2,745	132,600	2,169,100
Mississippi	795,271	1,771	72,741	880,477
Missouri	1,595,683	2,101	90,000	1,738,083
Montana...................	358,850	2,550	37,000	404,000
Nebraska	621,502	2,353	55,725	698,662
Nevada	281,520	2,059	52,150	360,530
New Hampshire	313,662	1,882	23,272	348,916
New Jersey	3,802,600	3,325	41,400	3,996,400
New Mexico	554,974	2,153	121,970	745,443
New York..................	8,762,000	3,467	330,000	9,492,000
North Carolina	2,139,948	2,030	115,200	2,424,948
North Dakota	215,000	1,934	20,500	248,400
Ohio	3,867,400	2,143	93,100	4,095,800
Oklahoma	1,200,000	2,202	130,000	1,359,500
Oregon	1,245,000	2,981	128,219	1,406,219
Pennsylvania	4,621,700	2,659	170,800	5,175,500
Rhode Island	389,600	2,919	3,600	403,500
South Carolina	1,014,319	1,773	127,663	1,186,003
South Dakota	239,400	1,995	28,900	273,500
Tennessee.................	1,458,130	1,825	59,310	1,624,288
Texas(b)..................	4,739,638	1,798	918,301	5,890,257
Utah	572,860	1,777	198,438	802,860
Vermont...................	179,172	1,969	4,626	193,484
Virginia...................	1,971,352	2,115	197,528	2,261,124
Washington	1,927,480	2,737	302,956	2,317,185
West Virginia..............	715,079	2,026	73,133	812,590
Wisconsin.................	2,052,940	2,686	112,835	2,255,343
Wyoming	223,026	2,437	35,032	264,715
Dist. of Col.................	325,416	3,785	7,340	344,200

Source: National Education Association, *Estimates of School Statistics, 1980-81.*
(a) Average daily attendance.

(b) Includes expenditures of regular school districts but does not include expenditure data of state school and other districts without taxing authority.

Table 6
MANDATORY COLLECTIVE BARGAINING LAWS
COVERING ELEMENTARY/SECONDARY PUBLIC SCHOOL PERSONNEL

State	Coverage of personnel(a)		Strikes permitted	Provisions for binding arbitration of contract disputes; permissive or mandatory; partial or total
	Professional(b)	Classified(c)		
Alabama	...	...	...	...
Alaska	★	...	...	...
Arizona	...	...	...	...
Arkansas	...	...	...	...
California	★	★	...	...
Colorado	...	...	...	...
Connecticut	★	★	...	★
Delaware	●	●	...	...
Florida	★	★	...	...
Georgia	...	...	...	...
Hawaii	★	★	★	★
Idaho	●	...	...	...
Illinois	●	...	...	...
Indiana	★	...	...	...
Iowa	★	★	...	★
Kansas	★	★	...	...
Kentucky	...	...	...	...
Louisiana	...	...	...	...
Maine	★	★	...	★(e)
Maryland	★	★(d)	...	...
Massachusetts	★	★	...	★
Michigan	★	★	...	...
Minnesota	★	★	★	★
Mississippi	...	...	...	...
Missouri	...	●	...	...
Montana	★	★	★(f)	★
Nebraska	●	★	...	★
Nevada	★	★	...	...
New Hampshire	★	★	...	...
New Jersey	★	★	...	★
New Mexico	...	...	...	...
New York	★	★	...	★
North Carolina	...	...	...	...
North Dakota	★	...	...	...
Ohio	...	...	...	...
Oklahoma	★	★	...	...
Oregon	★	★	★	★
Pennsylvania	★	★	★	★(g)
Rhode Island	★	★	...	★(e)
South Carolina	...	...	...	...
South Dakota	★	★	...	★
Tennessee	★	...	...	...
Texas	...	...	...	...
Utah	...	...	...	...
Vermont	★	★	★(h)	★(i)
Virginia	...	...	...	...
Washington	★	★	...	...
West Virginia	...	...	...	...
Wisconsin	★	★	★	★
Wyoming	...	...	...	...

Source: ECS Clearinghouse, Education Commission of the States.

(a) In these columns only, ★—collective bargaining; ●—meet and confer law.

(b) Generally, a certified teacher or one with similar or higher status.

(c) Generally, one below the rank of a certified teacher; i.e., clerk, food employee, bus driver, custodian, paraprofessional, etc.

(d) Covers 17 of 23 counties; Baltimore has separate procedures.

(e) Non-fund matters only.

(f) Court ruling.

(g) Not binding if legislative action required.

(h) Provisions unclear.

(i) Classified personnel only.

Table 7
NUMBER OF SCHOOL DISTRICTS

State or other jurisdiction	Number of school districts		Percentage change, 1951-52 to 1980-81	Number of non-operating districts, 1980-81
	1951-52	1980-81		
United States	71,117	15,987	-77.5	278
Alabama	108	127	17.6	0
Alaska........................	27	52	92.6	0
Arizona.......................	329	231	-29.8	2
Arkansas	425	370	-12.9	0
California.....................	2,044	1,043	-49.0	0
Colorado	1,333	181	-86.4	0
Connecticut	172	174	1.2	6
Delaware	115	16	-86.1	0
Florida	67	67	0	0
Georgia.......................	204	187	-8.3	0
Hawaii	1	1	0	0
Idaho	281	115	-59.1	0
Illinois.......................	3,413	1,013	-70.3	2
Indiana	1,115	306	-72.5	1
Iowa	4,649	443	-90.5	0
Kansas........................	3,704	307	-91.7	0
Kentucky	231	181	-21.6	0
Louisiana	67	66	-1.5	0
Maine	492	284	-43.3	55
Maryland	24	24	0	0
Massachusetts	351	436	24.2	59
Michigan	4,736	575	-87.8	1
Minnesota	6,018	436	-92.7	2
Mississippi	1,987	153	-92.3	0
Missouri	4,573	550	-87.9	4
Montana.......................	1,386	567	-59.1	14
Nebraska	6,499	1,065	-83.6	55
Nevada	177	17	-90.4	0
New Hampshire................	238	169	-29.0	11
New Jersey	555	617	11.2	21
New Mexico	107	89	-16.8	0
New York	3,175	737	-76.8	6
North Carolina	172	144	-16.3	0
North Dakota	2,135	327	-84.7	34
Ohio	1,429	615	-56.8	0
Oklahoma	2,066	618	-70.1	0
Oregon	995	310	-68.8	1
Pennsylvania	2,514	505	-79.9	1
Rhode Island	39	40	2.6	0
South Carolina	521	92	-82.3	0
South Dakota	3,390	196	-94.2	0
Tennessee.....................	150	147	-2.0	0
Texas.........................	2,281	1,102	-51.7	3
Utah	40	40	0	0
Vermont	263	274	4.2	0
Virginia.......................	127	140	10.2	0
Washington	560	300	-46.2	0
West Virginia.................	55	55	0	0
Wisconsin.....................	5,463	433	-92.1	0
Wyoming	313	49	-84.3	0
Dist. of Col.	1	1	0	0

Source: U.S. Department of Health, Education and Welfare, Office of Education, *Statistics of State School Systems: Organization, Staff, Pupils and Finances, 1951-52.* National Education Association, *Estimates of School Statistics, 1980-81.*

Table 8
STATE BOARDS OF EDUCATION AND CHIEF STATE SCHOOL OFFICERS:
1947 and 1981

State	Chief method of selecting state board						Chief method of selecting chief state school officer					
	Elected by people		Appointed by governor		Other		Elected by people		Appointed by state board		Appointed by governor	
	1947	1981	1947	1981	1947	1981	1947	1981	1947	1981	1947	1981
All states	3	14	30	30	8	5	31	18	11	28	8	4
Alabama	...	★	★	...	...	...	★	...	...	★	...	...
Alaska	...	...	★	★	...	...	...	...	★	★	...	...
Arizona	...	...	...	★	★	...	★	★	...	...	...	...
Arkansas	...	...	★	★	...	...	...	...	★	★	...	...
California	...	...	★	★	...	...	★	★	...	...	...	...
Colorado	...	★	...	...	★	...	★	...	...	★	...	...
Connecticut	...	...	★	★	...	...	...	...	★	★	...	...
Delaware	...	...	★	★	...	...	...	...	★	★	...	...
Florida	...	...	...	...	★	★(a)	★	★	...	...	...	...
Georgia	...	...	★	★	...	...	★	★	...	...	...	...
Hawaii	...	★	★	...	...	...	...	...	...	★	★	...
Idaho	...	★	★	...	...	...	★	★	...	...	...	...
Illinois	(b)	...	...	★	...	...	★	...	...	★	...	...
Indiana	...	...	★	★	...	...	★	...	...	★	...	...
Iowa	(b)	...	...	★	...	...	★	...	...	★(c)	...	...
Kansas	...	★	★	...	...	...	★	★	...	...	...	...
Kentucky	...	...	★	★	...	...	★	★(d)	...	...	...	...
Louisiana	★	★(e)	...	...	...	...	★	★	...	...	...	...
Maine	(b)	...	...	★	...	...	...	...	...	...	★	★
Maryland	...	...	★	★	...	...	...	...	★	★	...	...
Massachusetts	...	★	★	...	...	...	...	...	★	★	...	...
Michigan	★	★	...	...	...	...	★	...	...	★	...	...
Minnesota	...	...	★	★	...	...	...	...	★	★(c)	...	...
Mississippi	...	...	...	...	★	★(f)	★	★	...	...	...	...
Missouri	...	...	★	★	...	...	...	...	★	★	...	...
Montana	...	...	★	★	...	...	★	★	...	...	...	...
Nebraska	(b)	★	...	...	...	...	★	...	...	★	...	...
Nevada	★	★	...	...	...	...	★	...	...	★	...	...
New Hampshire	...	...	★	★	...	...	...	...	★	★(g)	...	...
New Jersey	...	...	★	★	...	...	...	...	...	...	★	★
New Mexico	...	★	★	...	...	...	★	...	...	★(j)	...	...
New York	...	...	★	★	★	★(h)	...	...	★	★(i)	...	...
North Carolina	...	...	★	★	...	...	★	★	...	...	...	...
North Dakota	(b)	...	...	★	...	...	★	★	...	...	...	...
Ohio	(b)	★	...	...	...	...	...	...	★	★	...	...
Oklahoma	...	...	★	★	...	...	★	★	...	...	...	...
Oregon	...	...	★	★	...	...	★	★	...	...	...	...
Pennsylvania	...	...	★	★(j)	...	...	...	...	...	...	★	★(k)
Rhode Island	(b)	...	...	★	...	...	...	...	...	★(i)	★	...
South Carolina	...	...	★	...	...	★(l)	★	★	...	...	...	...
South Dakota	(b)	...	...	★	...	...	★	...	...	★(d)	...	...
Tennessee	...	...	★	★	...	...	...	...	★	★	...	...
Texas	...	★	★	...	...	...	★	...	...	★	...	...
Utah	...	★	★	...	...	...	★	...	...	★	...	...
Vermont	...	...	★	★	...	...	...	...	★	★(g)	...	...
Virginia	...	...	★	★	...	...	...	...	...	...	★	★(m)
Washington	...	...	...	...	★	★(n)	★	★	...	...	...	...
West Virginia	...	...	★	★	...	...	...	...	★	★	...	...
Wisconsin	——————— No state board ———————						★	★	...	...	...	...
Wyoming	...	...	...	★	★	...	★	★	...	...	...	...

Sources: Adapted from The Council of State Governments, *The Forty-eight State School Systems*, 1949, Tables 11 and 12 (Alaska and Hawaii added since). 1981 information from the National Association of State Boards of Education.

(a) State commissioner of education, governor, attorney general, secretary of state, commissioner of agriculture, insurance commissioner, state treasurer and comptroller.

(b) No state board in 1947.

(c) Senate confirms appointment.

(d) State also has gubernatorially appointed secretary of education.

(e) Eight are elected; 3 appointed at large by governor with senate confirmation.

(f) State superintendent of education, secretary of state and attorney general.

(g) Governor confirms appointment.

(h) Board governs all education; selected by legislature.

(i) Chief administers all education; appointed by state board of regents.

(j) Chief is secretary of education with postsecondary responsibilities as well.

(k) Board is subdivided for elementary/secondary education and postsecondary education.

(l) Selected by legislative committee.

(m) State also has gubernatorially appointed secretary of education; General Assembly confirms appointment.

(n) Selected by local school boards.

POSTSECONDARY EDUCATION

By Nancy M. Berve (with Janet Clarke Johnson)

AFTER MORE THAN TWO decades of growth and expansion, American education in the 1980s entered on a new tone. The 1980 presidential election brought a conservative administration to Washington, changed the U.S. House of Representatives to a coalition of Republicans and conservative Democrats, and created a Republican majority in the U.S. Senate. New words became part of the American vocabulary—Reaganomics, rescission, reconciliation and the "New Federalism."

States faced the first reductions in federal funds in 1980, and state policy leaders realized budget pressures and competition for state monies were going to get worse, not better. Early in the 1981 legislative sessions, it became very apparent that public colleges and universities, which count on state funds for approximately 45 cents of every dollar, faced considerable financial difficulties. According to the governor of Indiana, "Few people seem aware that the fiscal problems of many states are more serious than those of the federal government."[1] It was predicted that at least half of the states would face extremely precarious financial straits.

The predictions came true, not only for the states, but also for the federal government, and in some states the problems were worse than predicted. Those who believed in federal support for higher education awaited the actions of the 1981 Congress with fear and trepidation, and their fears were more than realized. In the face of rising costs of higher education and a recent history of expanding federal support of equal opportunity in education through student aid, every federal student aid program was reduced. Even Social Security benefits to dependent college students were targeted for phase-out, and federal support for research at colleges and universities was decreased in terms of constant dollars. Further cuts in many programs were mandated by the Omnibus Reconciliation Act of 1981, and the president recommended in his 1983 budget new cuts below 1982's final appropriations.

The New Federalism and Higher Education in the 1980s

Fiscal Constraints and Crises in the States. The fiscal constraints and their impact on postsecondary education that began emerging in the late 1970s have continued to worsen in the early 1980s. In fiscal 1981, at least 19 states reduced spending to below the amounts originally appropriated; in 21 states, revenues in the first six months of the 1982 fiscal year fell below official forecasts; and in 24 states public payrolls were cut. To quote the *Chronicle of Higher Education*: "For most states, and for the public colleges and universities that depend on state funds for the largest part of their income, hard times are here."[2]

According to a nationwide survey conducted by the National Conference of State Legislatures (NCSL) in late 1981, budget deliberations in the next few years will be more

Nancy M. Berve is Coordinator of Postsecondary Education of the State Services Division, and Janet Clarke Johnson was Associate Director of the Advanced Leadership Program Services project, for the Education Commission of the States.

"excruciating" than usual. In many states, tax collections are lower and slower than fiscal 1981 because of higher unemployment, lower farm prices and general recession. At the same time, the states are faced with considerably fewer federal funds. Although the cuts in federal assistance were not the primary cause of the states' financial distress, they exacerbated it, according to the NCSL. For example, three years ago funds from the federal government to Utah amounted to 25 percent of the budget; by 1981, these funds had declined to 20 percent.

Of the states facing severe budget problems in 1982, Minnesota perhaps is the most critical. By late 1981, the state's projected deficit had grown to $768 million and the state was considering a 12 percent across-the-board cut in aid for education for the biennium. Other states facing large deficits and considerable reductions in higher education support by December 1981 included Washington ($600-$700 million), California ($500 million plus), Oregon ($250 million) and Michigan (about $270 million). According to the NCSL survey, 23 states anticipated ending the 1981-82 fiscal year with deficits or zero balances. The Southern Regional Education Board estimates that in the two years ending June 1982, between two-thirds and three-fourths of the Southern states will have made mid-year adjustments in their budgets, and in each case those adjustments mean budget cuts for state colleges and universities.[3]

Student Assistance. One of the hardest-hit programs affecting postsecondary education during the federal budget and reconciliation process in late 1980 and 1981 were student assistance programs. The outgoing administration had recommended not only cuts in campus-based student aid programs, but also a major revision in the Guaranteed Student Loan Program. Under the Middle Income Student Assistance Act of 1978, guaranteed loans were made available to all students regardless of income. Under the Omnibus Reconciliation Act of 1981, loans were restricted to students from families earning $30,000 a year or less. The Reconciliation Act retains an important element of flexibility for middle-income students in allowing students from families over the $30,000 income ceiling to receive loans if they pass a financial-need test. The 1981 act also requires that students pay a 5 percent fee on their guaranteed loans, to be deducted from the loan when it is granted.

The administration has proposed that, beginning in academic year 1982-83, graduate students be eliminated from the Guaranteed Student Loan Program. However, these students will be included in a new loan program initiated by Congress in 1980. The Parent Loans to Undergraduate Students (PLUS) was expanded in 1981 to include graduate students and renamed the Auxiliary Loans to Assist Students (ALAS). Although the U.S. Department of Education indicated in late 1981 that the program was operating in 23 states, little interest in the new program has been evidenced by lender banks, and the interest rate—14 percent compared to 9 percent on student loans—is expected to deter many graduate students.

The largest federal student grant program, the Pell Grants (formerly called the Basic Educational Opportunity Grant Program), also received much discussion and debate during the 1981 congressional sessions. In fiscal 1981, $2,159 billion was approved for the Pell Grants with the maximum award per student set at $1,750, with an additional $661 million provided by Congress to cover what was needed for the year. Under the continuing resolution for fiscal 1982 passed in December 1981, total funding for 1981-82 was reduced to $2,279 billion with the maximum award reduced to $1,670.

In addition to barring graduate students from the Guaranteed Student Loan Program and curtailing interest subsidies provided to other recipients of the loans, further deep reductions in student aid are predicted for fiscal 1983 including: decreasing the Pell Grant program to $1.4 billion; providing no funds for the Supplemental Educational Opportunity Grant Program, the National Direct Student Loans and the State Student Incentive Grant Program; and eliminating the graduate fellowships administered by the Department of Education under a $10.6 million program that primarily aids women and members of minority groups.

At the state level, 57 states and U.S. territories will provide an estimated $963.6 million in state-funded need-based scholarship and grant programs to undergraduate students in 1981-82. According to the annual survey conducted by the National Association of State Scholarship and Grant Programs (NASSGP), this is an increase of 10.3 percent over fiscal 1980 and a significant difference from 1980-81 when the state programs increased by only 1.6 percent over 1979. It is doubtful the increase reflected the decrease in federal support for student aid, since most state budgets were set before the extent of the federal cuts was clear. The survey also indicated that 31 states expected to increase state support of student aid in 1981-82 and only seven states expected reductions. In 1980-81, 19 states reduced programs.

Although the federal government set up the State Student Incentive Grant Program in 1974 to encourage states to begin new student aid programs, the latest NASSGP survey found that such support was still heavily concentrated in a few large states. Many states with smaller programs depend heavily on the federal funds provided under the SSIG program, and in 15 states the federal matching funds made up half the money spent in 1980-81. Although the program received $73.68 million in fiscal 1982, it is anticipated that zero federal funding will be proposed in fiscal 1983. This could lead to elimination of the program in the smaller states that depend on matching federal funds to continue their need-based programs.[4]

Private Higher Education. Reduced federal support of student financial aid programs is the primary cause of an overall decrease in enrollments at private colleges and universities which had been projected for fall of 1981 by the National Institute of Independent Colleges and Universities. Although the private institutions received more applications for admission to freshman classes than in 1980, the institute's survey suggested that "the uncertainty of federal student assistance has led entering freshmen to either apply to more colleges or to put off making a decision to enroll at college in 1981." The survey predicted a decrease of 2.2 percent in the number of first-year students, causing total enrollment to decline by 0.6 percent. The heaviest enrollment losses were projected to occur in the mid-Atlantic and Northeast regions where combined student aid cuts and increased tuition caused higher levels of expected family contributions to cover the increasing student costs.

Even with a projected enrollment decline, private postsecondary education continued to hold its own share of the state dollar. Legislatures in over 20 states increased funding for private college students for 1981-82, according to another report by the National Institute of Independent Colleges and Universities. In 16 of the states reporting such increases, the increases outpaced rising prices, assuming an annual inflation rate of 10 percent. Even in Michigan, a state with highly publicized economic problems, the legislature approved a 75 percent increase over 1980-81 spending for grants to private college students. In a recent analysis of long-term needs in state student aid, the National Association of State Scholarship and Grant Programs noted a gradual increase in the share of state need-based program funds for students at private institutions. Such students are expected to receive 58 percent of all state aid in 1981-82, compared with 54 percent in 1976-77.[5]

Other state programs that provide assistance to private higher education continue to be maintained, at least at the current level, and in some states the legislatures have provided increased funds. How private higher education fares in the decade of the 1980s will depend on the impact of the federal budget cuts in the states and the states' reaction and ability to assist in the maintenance of the private sector.

The Diminishing Federal Role. Historically and constitutionally, the states have always had the responsibility for the education of their citizens. Much activity and concern has been occasioned by the Reagan administration's total acceptance of this concept, and its continuing withdrawal of federal support for education, including higher education. At the beginning of the second year of his term, the president announced a plan that called for a major shift of federal social programs to the states. However, most programs aiding higher education would remain the federal government's responsibility under the "New Federalism" proposed by the president. While federal funds for all of education make up about 3 percent of the federal budget, these represent about 20 percent of all support for colleges, universities and students.[6]

As noted earlier, the major federal cutbacks in postsecondary education funding that had an impact on the states have been in student assistance. During the 1981 and 1982 budget debates and conferences between the Congress and administration, other areas of diminished funding affected the states. These include reduction in support for the National Science Foundation, the National Institutes of Health and the National Endowments and reduction of programs for the handicapped and vocational and adult education. Even veterans' assistance programs failed to escape the ax.

By January 1982, a federal budget for the Department of Education, as well as other agencies, had not been completed and spending for fiscal 1982 was subject to a third continuing congressional resolution. Although this third resolution would provide for spending in the current fiscal year only through March 1982, it has been predicted that Congress will continue the resolution through the end of 1981-82 and concentrate its efforts on the fiscal 1983 budget. A major piece of federal legislation in 1979 was the creation of a cabinet-level Department of Education. A Reagan campaign promise, one that he re-emphasized in his 1982 state of the union speech, was to dismantle the department and convert it to a sub-cabinet-level education foundation. A number of education groups have formed coalitions to oppose the department's abolition. In light of the fact that 1982 is a major election year, there is little expectation that the president's recommendation will be acted upon before 1983.

Planning and Coordinating for Quality. Statewide planning will persist during the decade of the 1980s, not because of the nicety of coordinating planning for institutions of higher education, but because it is an imperative. It is an imperative for a number of reasons, one of which is the severity of current budget problems at both federal and state levels. Notwithstanding the federal reductions, at the state level competing priorities are battling for a shrinking pool of real dollars. In addition, earlier budgeting attempts to restrain expenditures has for the most part failed in the higher education world. The on-going threat of declining enrollments continues the shift away from only reviewing new programs toward the evaluation and elimination of existing duplicative and low-enrollment programs. Statewide planning bodies will be held even more strictly accountable by state officials for the development of efficient and effective quality planning mechanisms. Indeed, state agencies in the 1980s will be subjected more than ever to close scrutiny.

In 1981, Rhode Island and Massachusetts changed the structures of governance of higher education in attempts by their respective legislatures to make the systems more responsive to the needs of the state. In addition, special studies authorized by the executive or legislative branches of government and executed by a special commission or consultant continue to be conducted across the country on coordination and governance structures, policy-making and programs. These studies increasingly look to the relationship between higher education and the economy of the state as well as the financial costs and potential alternatives to providing educational services. States recently conducting special studies include Connecticut, Kentucky, North Dakota, Pennsylvania and Maryland.

Inherent within any discussion of statewide planning and coordination is the implicit concern for quality, at all levels of education. Any discussion of quality ranges far and wide and can include admission requirements, student performance, basic skills, remediation, accreditation, vocational education, consumer expectations, postsecondary oversight and resource allocation. Concern for standards and the quality of postsecondary education will in no way diminish in the years ahead.

Emerging Issues of the 1980s. In a survey conducted in the fall of 1981 by the Education Commission of the States, to be published in the spring of 1982, state-level policy leaders in each state were asked to identify what they considered to be the emerging issues in postsecondary education for the next few years. The overall impressions created by the response from governors and state legislators and their staffs as well as state education policy leaders were that education quality will be the leading issue for the next few years, funding for higher education is losing ground to inflation, and families will be expected to shoulder an increasing proportion of college costs. All around the country, state and national higher education leaders are forming groups and identifying those issues of primary importance and in all cases, two emerged—financing and quality. It may well be that the 1980s will be an exercise in answering the questions "who pays and for what?" and "how do you set standards of quality in a time of fiscal crises?"

Campus Developments

Student Enrollments. Despite a declining number of 18-year-olds, rising tuition and fees, budget cuts at both state and federal levels and, in some states, enrollment limitations, total enrollments in institutions of higher education continue to increase. According to a preliminary report by the National Center for Education Statistics (NCES), enrollments were expected to increase by 1.9 percent in the fall of 1981, although a smaller increase than 1979 (2.6 percent) and much smaller than 1980's 4.5 percent rise. The number of students enrolled in higher education in the fall of 1981 totaled 12.3 million and set a record according to the NCES.

The increase over fall 1980 was due almost entirely to a substantial gain in enrollment at two-year colleges. Increases at public and private two-year colleges accounted for all but 520 of the estimated 225,574 additional students enrolled. Enrollments at public community colleges increased 4.7 percent, and private two-year college enrollment increased dramatically by 12 percent.

In the four-year institutions, private colleges were estimated to show a net loss in enrollment in fall 1981 of 0.2 percent, while public institutions increased slightly by 0.7 percent. However, four-year public colleges other than doctoral degree-granting universities had a net enrollment loss of 0.6 percent. Some of the declines most likely are the result of state policies aimed at reducing enrollments to fit limited funds and facilities, as in Ohio and California. The effects of the two-year college enrollments on the national total are most evident in California where state officials predicted a statewide increase of 3.9 percent in community college enrollment (despite a legislative mandate authorizing funds for only a 2.5 percent increase). About one of every 10 college students in the United States in 1981 was enrolled in a California community college.

NCES reports that for the sixth consecutive year the enrollment of women in postsecondary education had grown at a faster rate than that of men. The number of women enrolled in the fall of 1981 increased by 3.15 percent over 1980, and women now outnumber men on American campuses by nearly half a million. Fifty-two percent of the total enrollment were women in 1981 compared with 45 percent in 1976.

More than a third of all students enrolled in colleges and universities now are 25 years of age or older, according to a study by the U.S. Census Bureau. Between 1974 and 1979, enrollment of students over age 25 grew about 24 percent, while the enrollment of students under 25 rose by only 10 percent. It is predicted by the bureau that colleges and universities concerned about maintaining enrollment levels in the 1980s will be looking to the older groups to offset a decline in the population of 18-year-olds.[7]

Degrees. Although the percentage change in the number of bachelor's and advanced degrees varied little between 1975-76 and 1978-79, these percentages showed the first significant change in 1979-80. In 1977-78, the number of bachelor's degrees increased by only 0.2 percent; in 1979-80, the number increased by 2.5 percent. After several years of steadily decreasing, the rate of decrease for the number of master's degrees steadied. In 1977-78, the decrease was 1.7 percent and in 1979-80 was 1.3 percent. After showing decreases for several years, doctoral degrees conferred in 1979-80 increased slightly by 0.3 percent, after having a decrease of 3.3 percent in 1977-78. First professional degree output in 1979-80 was 70,442, an increase of 2.7 percent over 1978-79.

The changing sex and racial/ethnic composition of enrollment is reflected in changes in the number of degrees awarded to women and minorities. Within the two-year period between 1976-77 and 1978-79 these changes were significant. The number of men awarded the bachelor's degree dropped by nearly 4 percent, while the increase for women was nearly 5 percent. The number of whites dropped by 1 percent and the increase for minorities ranged between 2 and 14 percent. The largest decrease was recorded for white males, while the largest increases were found in Hispanic and Asian or Pacific Islander women.

Predicting the number of degrees to be conferred in the 1980s will continue to be difficult. The number of students over the age of 25 now entering college has complicated degree data by including more part-time and non-degree credit participants in enrollment totals. Other factors include greater flexibility of programs and time allowed to complete programs and elimination of the distinction between degree credit and non-degree credit students.[8]

Faculty. From 1970 to 1976, the total number of staff in institutions of higher education grew from 573,000 to 793,000, a 38 percent increase. In the next six-year period, 1976 to 1982, the total instructional staff is predicted to increase only 4 percent, from 793,000 to 824,000. Based on projections by the National Center for Education Statistics, this total is expected to decrease beginning in 1981, falling to approximately 759,000 in 1988. Part-time faculty increased at a faster rate than full-time faculty. Between 1970 and 1978, part-time staff doubled, in contrast to full-time staff which increased by 21 percent, and by 1978, 31 percent of all instructional staff were employed on a part-time basis. It has been observed that this ratio may increase during the 1980s as institutions find that part-time faculty involve lower costs and reduced commitment in a time of stabilizing or declining enrollments and reduced fiscal support.

Faculty tenure is also associated with predicted declining enrollments. In 1978-79, 56 percent of the full-time salaried faculty were tenured. As the number of faculty declines in the 1980s, those already tenured may block access of new entrants to the teaching profession, and higher education may find itself without a generation of doctoral recipients in the 1980s, who will seek employment elsewhere.

NCES predicts a gloomy outlook for women employed and seeking tenure in the higher education faculty ranks. In 1978-79, 74 percent of the total faculty number were men, and men held 81 percent of the tenured positions. Although women have been earning doctorates at an increased rate, their chances of increased representation on college and university faculty are small, at least through the 1980s.[9]

In June 1981, an annual salary study by the American Association of University Professors (AAUP) indicated that increases in faculty pay in 1980-81 came closer to matching the increases in consumer prices than was indicated in the previous four years. The average faculty salary for 1980-81 was 8.7 percent higher than in 1979-80, while during the approximate same period, the Labor Department's Consumer Price Index rose at an annual rate of 9.3 percent. However, in November 1981, a survey by the *Chronicle of Higher Education* indicated that this was not to be a trend. The survey showed that faculty salaries in the fall of 1981 for the academic year 1981-82 increased by 8.9 percent over 1980-81, while the Consumer Price Index rose at a seasonally adjusted annual rate of 13.5 percent. That rate contrasted with the price trend from January through June 1981, when institutions and legislatures were making decisions about faculty salary increases.

Although institutions of higher education provided larger pay increases for women than men in 1980-81, the women's average pay still remained lower than men's. Women faculty members received an average of $20,106, compared with $24,402 for men, for full-time faculty on 9- or 10-month contracts in 1980-81. The average salary for fall 1980 was 9.6 percent higher for women and 8.8 percent higher for men.[10]

Student Costs. The increased average total cost (tuition and fees, room and board and other expenses) of attending an institution of higher education in the fall of 1981 ranged from 3.4 percent (public two-year colleges) to 22.0 percent (private two-year colleges). Total costs at public four-year institutions for resident students rose from $3,409 to $3,873, or 13.6 percent, while costs at private four-year institutions increased from $6,082 to $6,885, or 13.2 percent, for resident students.

Average tuition rates in the fall of 1981 for public four-year colleges and universities increased 16 percent, four times the increase reported for fall 1980. In contrast, private four-year institutions increased tuition and fees by 13 percent, compared with 12 percent the previous year. A survey conducted by the College Scholarship Service, the financial aid division of the College Board, indicates these increases for 1980-81 represent the largest rise in tuition and fees in over a decade.

With the sharp decline in federal support, particularly in student assistance, a number of states began discussions during the summer of 1981 on consideration of still more increases in tuition for the 1981-82 academic year. As a consequence, actual tuition rates at public colleges and universities may increase significantly more than the 16 percent reflected in the College Board survey. With fiscal crises and budget deficits appearing in a number of states by late 1981, appropriations received close scrutiny in these states with the result that some institutions received fewer funds than anticipated and in a number of states, including

Washington, Michigan, Minnesota and Oregon, authorized appropriations were reduced after the beginning of the fiscal year. By late fall 1981, legislatures were already considering increasing student charges, particularly for non-resident students, by greater percentages than in past years.[11]

Expenditures and Income. Financial growth for the 3,152 institutions of higher education in the country outpaced inflation in fiscal 1980, according to preliminary data reported by NCES. Total spending for the institutions was $56.8 billion, an 11.9 percent increase over fiscal 1979 expenditures of $50.7 billion. Colleges received $58.3 billion in current funds revenues in 1979-80, an increase of 12.5 percent over 1979. The Higher Education Price Index, which measures inflation in higher education, rose 9.9 percent for fiscal 1980. However, the growth in real terms (constant dollar expenditures) from 1979 to 1980 remained at 1.8 percent.

The financial growth reflected in 1979-80 occurred concurrently with a 2.8 percent enrollment increase. Although per-student revenues increased in 1980, the combined effects of inflation and enrollment increases resulted in a slight decrease in constant dollar revenues per student (0.4 percent).

Total expenditures for public institutions of higher education in fiscal 1980 were $38.7 billion, or 66.4 percent of the total for all institutions. The largest expenditures were for instruction for which $18.4 billion, or 32.5 percent of the total, was spent. The second largest was auxiliary enterprises at $6.4 billion, and third and fourth were research and institutional support, totaling about $5 billion each. Private institutions spent an average of $9,106 per full-time-equivalent student in fiscal 1980, while public institutions averaged $5,894.

Of the total of $58.3 billion in current fund revenues received by institutions in 1979-80, revenues from tuition and fees provided $11.9 billion or 20.4 percent, and federal, state and local governments provided 49.5 percent or $28.9 billion. The smallest income, $2.8 billion or 4.8 percent, came from private gifts, grants and contracts. Of the $28.9 billion in the three levels of government revenues, the states contributed the most, $18.3 billion; the federal government was second, almost $9 billion; and local governments last.[12]

Voluntary Support. Voluntary support for colleges and universities continued to outpace the rate of inflation and the institutions' modest growth in enrollment in 1979-80, according to an annual survey conducted by the Council for Financial Aid to Education. Total voluntary support from all sources for higher education in fiscal 1980 was estimated at $3.8 billion, a 17.6 percent increase over 1979. U.S. corporations increased their support by 25 percent, but no such increase is anticipated in the coming years because of a slowdown in corporate growth.

Institutions of higher education have turned more and more to corporations for support to offset some of the reductions in federal support proposed by the administration. A survey of 427 major corporations in the late fall of 1981 indicated that few corporations will be answering the president's call for private philanthropy to make up for some of the federal reductions in education, welfare and cultural programs. The survey, conducted by the Conference Board of New York, found that only 6 percent planned to increase giving in 1982 to replace lost federal funds. A new federal law—the Economic Recovery Act of 1981—is expected to have little effect on corporate giving and is expected to discourage individual giving to non-profit institutions, including colleges and universities, because the tax incentives will be greatly reduced for those individuals in the higher-income brackets who provide the largest proportion of support.

Gifts from individuals accounted for 46 percent of the total voluntary support received by colleges and universities in 1979-80. Alumni gave an estimated $910 million, an increase of 16 percent over the previous year, and non-alumni gave $847 million, an increase of 15 percent. In the five years ending with fiscal 1980, it was reported that total voluntary support increased by 75.9 percent.

The 10 institutions receiving the most voluntary support in 1979-80 follow (numbers in parentheses indicate top 10 ranking in 1977-78):

1.	Emory University (-)	$115,592,443
2.	Harvard University (2)	76,179,576
3.	University of California System (1)	74,972,959
4.	University of Texas System (-)	60,722,404
5.	Stanford University (3)	60,122,303
6.	Yale University (5)	59,649,269
7.	University of Pennsylvania (10)	49,129,330
8.	Cornell University (8)	47,288,245
9.	University of Southern California (9)	42,234,069
10.	University of Minnesota (6)	40,568,067

The two institutions that dropped from the top 10 since 1977-78 were Columbia University and the Massachusetts Institute of Technology.[13]

Notes

1. *The Chronicle of Higher Education*, February 17, 1981, p. 1.

2. *The Chronicle of Higher Education*, February 10, 1982, pp. 1, 6.

3. Ibid.

4. National Association of State Scholarship and Grant Programs, *13th Annual Survey, 1981-82 Academic Year* (Harrisburg, Pa.: Pennsylvania Higher Education Assistance Agency, 1981).

5. *The Chronicle of Higher Education*, July 27, 1981, p. 1; September 2, 1981, p. 12; November 18, 1981, p. 16.

6. Education Commission of the States, *Issuegram*, February 1982.

7. *The Chronicle of Higher Education*, May 4, 1981, p. 3; December 9, 1981, pp. 1, 19.

8. *The Condition of Education*, 1981 edition (Washington, D.C.: National Center for Education Statistics, 1981), pp. 122, 154, 156; *The Chronicle of Higher Education*, October 14, 1981, p. 10.

9. *The Condition of Education*, 1980 edition, pp. 98, 99, 120.

10. *The Chronicle of Higher Education*, December 8, 1980, p. 1; June 15, 1981, pp. 1, 5; November 11, 1981, pp. 1, 12, 13.

11. *The Chronicle of Higher Education*, September 2, 1981, p. 12.

12. "Current Funds Revenues and Expenditures for Colleges and Universities Fiscal Year 1980 Preliminary Data," *National Center for Education Statistics Bulletin*, December 1981.

13. *The Chronicle of Higher Education*, May 18, 1981, pp. 1, 9; February 3, 1982, p. 2.

Table 1
TOTAL ENROLLMENTS IN HIGHER EDUCATION: 1980
(Including degree credit and non-degree credit students)

State or or other jurisdiction	Total enrollment		Public institutions		Private institutions	
	Number of students, 1980	Percentage change, 1978-80	Number of students, 1980	Percentage change, 1978-80	Number of students, 1980	Percentage change, 1978-80
Total...............	12,234,644	7.4	9,518,086	7.6	2,716,558	6.7
Alabama	164,306	1.7	143,674	2.1	20,632	-1.3
Alaska	21,296	-19.2	20,561	-20.5	735	+49.1
Arizona	202,716	14.8	194,034	13.1	8,682	71.8
Arkansas	77,607	7.3	66,068	6.4	11,539	13.3
California	1,790,993	8.5	1,599,838	9.0	191,155	4.7
Colorado	162,916	6.9	145,598	5.7	17,318	18.4
Connecticut...........	159,632	4.7	97,788	4.8	61,844	4.6
Delaware	32,939	6.5	28,325	7.1	4,614	3.0
Florida	411,891	9.2	334,349	7.5	77,542	17.4
Georgia	184,159	5.3	140,158	1.1	44,001	21.3
Hawaii	47,181	-0.8	43,269	-0.6	3,912	-2.8
Idaho	43,018	9.6	34,491	12.3	8,527	-0.2
Illinois	644,245	5.4	491,274	5.7	152,971	4.5
Indiana..............	247,253	11.0	189,224	12.3	58,029	6.8
Iowa	140,449	8.7	97,454	9.9	42,995	6.2
Kansas	136,605	7.3	121,987	7.4	14,618	6.7
Kentucky.............	143,066	7.8	114,884	6.5	28,182	13.6
Louisiana.............	160,058	5.2	136,703	5.1	23,355	5.5
Maine	43,264	4.4	31,878	5.8	11,386	0.6
Maryland	225,526	5.0	195,051	4.6	30,475	8.2
Massachusetts	418,415	8.8	183,765	8.8	234,650	8.8
Michigan	520,131	7.2	454,147	7.4	65,984	5.4
Minnesota	206,691	9.3	162,379	9.0	44,312	10.6
Mississippi	102,364	4.9	90,661	4.8	11,703	6.2
Missouri.............	234,421	5.9	165,179	8.5	69,242	0.3
Montana	35,177	13.1	31,178	12.4	3,999	18.8
Nebraska	89,488	9.6	73,509	9.6	15,979	9.2
Nevada..............	40,455	20.6	40,280	20.1	175	-29.7
New Hampshire	46,794	12.6	24,119	4.4	22,675	22.9
New Jersey...........	321,610	4.3	247,028	4.4	74,582	3.9
New Mexico	58,283	4.6	55,077	6.0	3,206	-14.6
New York	992,237	3.8	563,251	4.0	428,986	3.7
North Carolina	287,537	9.4	228,154	11.2	59,383	3.1
North Dakota	34,069	5.4	31,709	5.0	2,360	10.8
Ohio	489,145	8.6	381,765	8.9	107,380	7.4
Oklahoma	160,295	7.3	137,188	6.9	23,107	9.8
Oregon	157,458	7.6	140,102	8.0	17,356	4.5
Pennsylvania...........	507,716	7.4	292,499	4.3	215,217	12.1
Rhode Island	66,869	5.2	35,052	5.3	31,817	5.1
South Carolina	132,476	1.9	107,683	5.4	24,793	-11.3
South Dakota	32,761	5.9	24,328	7.5	8,433	1.6
Tennessee	204,581	5.1	156,835	5.6	47,746	3.6
Texas	701,391	6.9	613,552	6.4	87,839	11.0
Utah	93,987	5.6	59,598	7.9	34,389	1.8
Vermont..............	30,628	3.6	17,984	2.5	12,644	5.1
Virginia	280,504	8.6	246,500	9.0	34,004	5.4
Washington...........	303,603	10.3	276,028	10.7	27,575	6.3
West Virginia	81,973	3.8	71,228	4.2	10,745	1.1
Wisconsin	269,086	11.5	235,179	12.4	33,907	5.5
Wyoming.............	21,147	6.1	21,121	6.0	26	100.0
Dist. of Col.	86,675	5.9	13,900	1.7	72,775	6.8
U.S. Service Schools...............	49,808	176.9	49,808	176.9	...	...
Territories(a)..........	137,749	4.5	60,692	5.9	77,057	3.4

Source: Fall Enrollment in Higher Education, 1978 (Washington, D.C.: U.S. Department of Health, Education, and Welfare, National Center for Education Statistics, 1978); Fall Enrollment in Higher Education, 1980 (Washington, D.C.: U.S. Department of Education, National Center for Education Statistics, unpublished).

(a) Includes American Samoa, Canal Zone, Guam, Puerto Rico, Trust Territory of the Pacific Islands and Virgin Islands; 1980 figures do not include Canal Zone.

Table 2
APPROPRIATIONS OF STATE TAX FUNDS
FOR OPERATING EXPENSES OF HIGHER EDUCATION
(In thousands)

State	Fiscal year			1980-82		1972-82	
	1971-72	*1979-80*	*1981-82*	*2-year gain*	*Percentage*	*10-year gain*	*Percentage*
All states	$7,713,709	$19,143,057	$22,925,150	$3,782,093	19.8	$15,211,441	197.2
Alabama..................	106,807	377,135	417,757	40,622	10.8	310,950	291.1
Alaska	19,500	72,492	122,439	49,947	68.9	102,939	527.9
Arizona	97,514	232,707	306,801	74,094	31.8	209,287	214.6
Arkansas	52,177	169,664	183,980	14,316	8.4	131,803	252.6
California	853,623	2,814,321	3,328,706	514,385	18.3	2,475,083	290.0
Colorado	113,463	246,866	305,791	58,925	23.9	192,328	169.5
Connecticut	111,695	226,372	259,971	33,599	14.9	148,276	132.8
Delaware	23,091	53,273	72,125	18,852	35.4	49,034	212.4
Florida	247,540	650,334	802,316	151,982	23.4	554,776	224.1
Georgia..................	162,953	385,132	498,919	113,787	29.6	335,966	206.2
Hawaii	59,866	119,073	154,755	35,682	30.0	94,889	158.5
Idaho	34,167	85,028	95,100	10,072	11.9	60,933	178.3
Illinois...................	475,179	885,201	996,810	111,609	12.6	521,631	109.8
Indiana	201,345	411,198	482,494	71,296	17.3	281,149	139.6
Iowa	119,881	303,631	341,938	38,307	12.6	222,057	185.2
Kansas	84,313	238,839	278,662	39,823	16.7	194,349	230.5
Kentucky	108,661	299,918	355,291	55,373	18.5	246,630	227.0
Louisiana	139,916	330,008	454,754	124,746	37.8	314,838	225.0
Maine	30,741	57,336	66,871	9,535	16.6	36,130	117.5
Maryland	141,913	323,732	385,949	62,217	19.2	244,036	172.0
Massachusetts	130,212	314,929	364,500 (a)	49,571 (a)	15.7 (a)	234,288 (a)	179.9 (a)
Michigan	379,409	808,320	848,532	40,212	5.0	469,123	123.7
Minnesota	164,566	460,783	515,000 (a)	54,217 (a)	11.8 (a)	350,434 (a)	213.0 (a)
Mississippi	84,112	233,738	300,524	66,786	28.6	216,412	257.3
Missouri	149,109	314,807	352,770	37,963	12.1	203,661	136.6
Montana	30,635	60,494	83,693	23,199	38.4	53,058	173.2
Nebraska	51,915	150,940	187,190	36,250	24.0	135,275	260.6
Nevada..................	18,642	56,896	65,851	8,955	15.7	47,209	253.2
New Hampshire	12,419	29,806	39,323	9,517	31.9	26,904	216.6
New Jersey...............	184,679	400,366	464,787	64,421	16.1	280,108	151.7
New Mexico...............	45,307	125,731	171,576	45,845	36.5	126,269	278.7
New York................	803,913	1,543,416	1,855,429	312,013	20.2	1,051,516	130.8
North Carolina	223,486	580,189	736,882	156,693	27.0	513,396	229.7
North Dakota	26,998	75,660	108,538	32,878	43.5	81,540	302.0
Ohio	285,677	669,197	698,350 (a)	29,153 (a)	4.4 (a)	412,673 (a)	144.5 (a)
Oklahoma	79,331	228,827	325,553	96,726	42.3	246,222	310.4
Oregon	103,000	229,013	252,602	23,589	10.3	149,602	145.3
Pennsylvania	347,483	738,686	825,491	86,805	11.8	478,008	137.6
Rhode Island	30,443	71,833	85,257	13,424	18.7	54,814	180.1
South Carolina	99,496	320,412	361,171	40,759	12.7	261,675	263.0
South Dakota	21,844	49,872	52,143	2,271	4.6	30,299	138.7
Tennessee.................	114,034	318,173	357,016	38,843	12.2	242,982	213.1
Texas	418,369	1,315,526	1,905,008	589,482	44.8	1,486,639	355.4
Utah	50,422	145,384	174,139	28,755	19.8	123,717	245.4
Vermont..................	15,856	27,062	33,876	6,814	25.2	18,020	113.7
Virginia..................	153,433	444,054	543,961	99,907	22.5	390,528	254.5
Washington	190,467	467,717	497,821	30,104	6.4	307,354	161.4
West Virginia.............	69,388	158,684	192,092	33,408	21.1	122,704	176.8
Wisconsin	226,403	468,618	532,002	63,384	13.5	305,599	135.0
Wyoming	18,316	51,664	82,644	30,980	60.0	64,328	315.2

Source: M. M. Chambers, *Appropriations of State Tax Funds for Operating Expenses of Higher Education, 1981-1982* (Washington, D.C.: National Association of State Universities and Land-Grant Colleges, December 1981).

(a) Estimated in absence of actual appropriations.

Table 3
PROGRAMS OF STUDENT FINANCIAL AID, BASED UPON NEED, FOR STATE RESIDENTS TO ATTEND EITHER PUBLIC OR NON-PUBLIC COLLEGES OR UNIVERSITIES: 1979-80 TO 1981-82*

State or other jurisdiction	Number of monetary awards		2-year percentage change, 1979-80 to 1981-82	Payout of dollars (thousands)		2-year percentage change 1979-80 to 1981-82	Average award amount	
	1979-80	1981-82		1979-80	1981-82		1979-80	1981-82
Total...............	1,184,636	1,228,957	3.8	$830,897	$924,681	11.3	$ 701	$ 752
Alabama	7,413	1,342	-81.9	2,131	403	-81.1	288	300
Alaska	160	360	125.0	240	339	41.2	1,500	942
Arizona	2,473	3,325	34.5	1,643	2,483	51.1	664	747
Arkansas	4,666	9,871	111.6	1,174	2,732	132.7	252	277
California............	61,576	62,641	1.7	78,812	89,035	13.0	1,280	1,421
Colorado	15,437	17,200 (a)	11.4 (a)	9,755	7,290	-25.3	632	424
Connecticut...........	8,014	8,172	2.0	6,690	7,148	6.9	835	875
Delaware	921	674	-26.8	456	457	0.2	495	678
Florida	10,508	14,000	33.2	9,847	12,302	24.9	937	879
Georgia	9,694	12,000	23.8	2,641	3,750	42.0	272	313
Hawaii	1,923	1,900	-1.2	452	736	62.8	235	387
Idaho	803	890	10.8	507	514	1.4	631	578
Illinois	87,886	95,000	8.1	83,052	91,696	10.4	945	965
Indiana	48,554	40,488	-16.6	27,674	21,288	-23.1	570	526
Iowa	13,990	13,720	-1.9	15,196	15,660	3.1	1,086	1,141
Kansas	6,516	5,450	-16.4	4,613	5,100	10.6	708	936
Kentucky	13,838	15,712	13.6	4,991	6,580	31.8	361	419
Louisiana	1,954	3,974	103.4	823	2,186	165.6	421	550
Maine	5,000	800	-84.0	1,360	400	-70.1	272	500
Maryland	12,371	12,130	-2.0	5,552	5,873	5.8	449	484
Massachusetts	27,257	27,000	-1.0	13,650	16,500	20.9	501	611
Michigan	30,756	30,567	-0.6	30,531	30,772	0.8	993	1,007
Minnesota	27,965	51,000	82.4	18,400	32,000	73.9	658	627
Mississippi	1,800	2,000	11.1	2,516	1,299	-48.4	1,398	650
Missouri	23,330	13,420	-42.5	8,144	9,178	12.7	349	684
Montana	917	900	-1.9	392	389	-0.8	427	432
Nebraska	2,010	2,150	7.0	1,074	1,101	2.5	534	512
Nevada..............	395	450	13.9	291	150	-48.5	738	333
New Hampshire	1,250	1,623 (a)	29.8 (a)	526	575	9.3	421	354
New Jersey	68,577	73,599	7.3	41,213	44,784	8.7	601	608
New Mexico............	1,229	1,500	22.1	646	720	11.5	526	480
New York	329,000	329,000	0.0	252,200	276,450	9.6	767	840
North Carolina..........	6,334	5,254	-17.1	3,504	3,684	5.1	553	701
North Dakota	1,416	1,628	15.0	496	702	41.5	350	431
Ohio	56,000	68,011	21.5	28,100	40,812	45.2	502	600
Oklahoma	10,205	8,500	-16.7	2,265	2,067	-8.8	222	243
Oregon	17,374	15,442	-11.1	7,090	8,015	13.1	408	519
Pennsylvania...........	126,373	131,255	3.9	78,100	82,226	5.3	618	626
Rhode Island	4,746	9,000	89.6	3,792	6,500	71.4	799	722
South Carolina	7,649	8,000	4.6	10,930	13,388	22.5	1,429	1,674
South Dakota	862	470	-45.5	221	431	95.0	256	917
Tennessee.............	11,098	8,500	-23.4	5,978	7,169	19.9	539	843
Texas	23,305	23,480	0.8	13,851	18,962	36.9	594	808
Utah	3,000	3,000 (a)	0.0	1,504	1,504 (a)	0.0	501	501 (a)
Vermont..............	6,069	7,840	29.2	4,168	5,537	32.9	687	706
Virginia	24,118	17,861	-26.0	9,698	3,800	-60.8	402	213
Washington	9,531	13,134	37.8	4,501	7,768	72.6	472	591
West Virginia...........	5,111	6,058	18.5	3,022	4,422	46.3	591	730
Wisconsin	37,871	43,978	16.1	21,631	23,065	6.6	571	524
Wyoming	500	250	-50.0	251	100	-60.2	502	400
Dist. of Col.	943	850	-9.9	1,073	1,118	4.2	1,138	1,315
American Samoa	223	162	-27.4	618	719	16.4	2,769	4,438
Guam	70	60 (a)	-14.3	235	235 (a)	0.0	3,917	3,917 (a)
Northern Marianas........	360	360 (a)	0.0	500	500 (a)	0.0	1,389	1,389 (a)
Puerto Rico	1,940	1,940 (a)	0.0	1,458	1,458 (a)	0.0	752	752 (a)
Trust Territory	1,000	1,000 (a)	0.0	505	505 (a)	0.0	505	505 (a)
Virgin Islands	355	66 (a)	-81.4	214	104 (a)	-51.4	603	1,576

*Comprehensive undergraduate state competitive and non-competitive programs. All figures include both state and federal State Student Incentive Grant Program funds; 1981-82 figures are estimates of the states at November 1981.

Source: *12th Annual Survey, 1980-81 Academic Year and 13th Annual Survey, 1981-82 Academic Year,* National Association of State Scholarship and Grant Programs (Harrisburg, Pa.: Pennsylvania Higher Education Assistance Agency, 1980, 1981).
(a) 1980-81 data; 1981-82 data not available.

Table 4
FEDERAL FUNDS FOR HIGHER EDUCATION
DISTRIBUTED THROUGH STATE AGENCIES: 1978-81*

State or other jurisdiction	1978	1979	1980	1981	4-year total	3-year percentage change 1978-81	2-year percentage change 1979-81	1-year percentage change 1980-81
Total	$84,879,877	$97,281,939	$91,759,490	$78,909,996	$352,831,312	-7.0	-18.9	-14.0
Alabama	1,251,908	1,444,315	1,404,897	1,182,018	5,283,138	-5.6	-18.2	-15.8
Alaska	269,596	319,595	322,411	161,915	1,073,517	-40.0	-49.3	-49.8
Arizona	1,218,733	1,435,550	1,469,469	1,346,623	5,470,375	-10.5	-6.2	-8.4
Arkansas	640,906	738,712	707,907	525,585	2,613,110	-19.1	-28.9	-25.8
California	11,886,815	13,627,231	12,084,589	11,831,954	49,430,589	-0.5	-13.2	-2.1
Colorado	1,121,051	1,306,039	1,256,050	1,088,031	4,771,171	-3.0	-16.7	-13.4
Connecticut	1,126,253	1,286,401	1,256,633	1,039,477	4,708,764	-7.7	-19.2	-17.3
Delaware	376,167	410,261	358,169	244,759	1,389,356	-34.9	-40.3	-31.7
Florida	2,101,439	2,941,370	2,976,669	2,442,086	10,461,564	-16.2	-17.0	-18.0
Georgia	1,524,104	1,696,453	1,621,697	1,372,817	6,215,071	-9.9	-19.1	-15.4
Hawaii	465,021	526,741	478,133	355,368	1,825,263	-23.6	-32.5	-25.7
Idaho	374,727	465,685	421,944	297,018	1,559,374	-20.7	-36.2	-29.6
Illinois	4,052,164	4,808,879	4,623,054	4,188,258	17,672,355	-3.4	-12.9	-9.4
Indiana	1,682,697	1,937,137	1,814,973	1,574,882	7,009,689	-6.4	-18.7	-13.2
Iowa	968,685	1,113,090	1,085,859	865,153	4,032,789	-10.7	-22.3	-20.3
Kansas	925,685	1,135,575	1,023,909	890,464	3,975,633	-3.8	-21.6	-3.8
Kentucky	1,088,118	1,278,124	1,180,528	977,363	4,524,133	-10.2	-23.5	-17.2
Louisiana	1,224,170	1,409,770	1,307,007	1,132,775	5,073,722	-7.5	-19.7	-13.3
Maine	744,274	505,652	454,772	315,089	2,019,787	-57.7	-37.7	-30.7
Maryland	1,482,776	1,728,054	1,660,579	1,439,836	6,311,245	-2.9	-16.7	-13.3
Massachusetts	2,673,024	2,936,216	2,882,937	2,507,767	10,999,944	-6.2	-14.6	-13.0
Michigan	3,461,051	3,796,394	3,658,108	3,212,452	14,128,005	-7.2	-15.4	-12.2
Minnesota	1,537,730	1,787,902	1,726,236	1,524,256	6,576,124	-0.9	-14.8	-11.7
Mississippi	834,440	945,616	842,792	689,646	3,312,494	-17.4	-27.1	-18.2
Missouri	1,632,319	1,904,570	1,759,777	1,556,791	6,853,457	-4.6	-18.3	-11.5
Montana	387,328	422,906	379,809	251,592	1,441,635	-35.1	-42.5	-33.8
Nebraska	667,793	780,113	765,312	590,269	2,803,487	-11.6	-24.3	-22.9
Nevada	362,082	405,415	386,441	249,336	1,403,274	-31.1	-38.5	-35.5
New Hampshire	435,627	362,774	447,905	307,542	1,553,848	-29.4	-15.2	-31.3
New Jersey	2,256,742	2,500,583	2,464,794	2,052,861	9,274,980	-9.0	-17.9	-16.7
New Mexico	526,982	612,946	563,687	429,612	2,133,227	-18.5	-29.9	-23.8
New York	7,689,062	8,411,067	7,266,708	6,478,890	29,845,727	-15.7	-23.0	-10.9
North Carolina	1,785,561	2,013,292	1,962,054	1,706,761	7,467,668	-4.4	-15.2	-13.0
North Dakota	371,628	414,732	376,221	245,605	1,408,186	-33.9	-40.8	-34.7
Ohio	3,251,988	3,734,897	3,539,453	3,082,861	13,609,199	-5.2	-17.5	-12.9
Oklahoma	1,234,013	1,434,379	1,251,626	1,073,514	4,993,532	-13.0	-25.2	-14.2
Oregon	1,066,511	1,249,188	1,173,201	1,025,852	4,514,752	-3.8	-17.9	-12.6
Pennsylvania	3,604,571	4,103,457	3,871,666	3,413,014	14,992,708	-5.3	-16.8	-11.9
Rhode Island	569,708	618,836	592,217	445,040	2,225,811	-21.9	-28.1	-24.9
South Carolina	1,075,980	1,176,626	1,087,893	870,289	4,210,788	-19.2	-26.0	-20.0
South Dakota	383,228	425,050	380,591	257,867	1,446,736	-32.7	-39.3	-32.3
Tennessee	1,407,072	1,606,219	1,562,609	1,282,732	5,858,632	-8.8	-20.1	-17.9
Texas	4,363,337	5,008,867	4,941,979	4,226,616	18,540,799	-3.1	-15.6	-14.5
Utah	697,459	793,527	754,477	610,229	2,855,692	-12.5	-23.1	-19.1
Vermont	354,780	394,620	346,522	232,760	1,328,682	-34.4	-41.0	-32.8
Virginia	1,756,731	1,996,353	1,976,807	1,674,619	7,404,510	-4.7	-16.1	-15.3
Washington	1,589,987	1,992,841	2,118,847	1,781,471	7,483,146	-12.1	-10.6	-15.9
West Virginia	675,814	789,828	733,443	597,416	2,796,501	-11.6	-24.4	-18.6
Wisconsin	1,708,132	1,918,785	1,900,559	1,640,615	7,168,091	-4.0	-14.5	-13.7
Wyoming	256,664	320,777	284,176	168,732	1,030,349	-34.3	-47.4	-40.6
Dist. of Col.	677,918	759,160	720,396	599,036	2,756,510	-11.6	-21.1	-16.9
Puerto Rico	787,299	1,009,005	1,023,945	726,116	3,546,365	-7.8	-28.0	-29.1
Virgin Islands	69,065	121,732	109,452	53,914	354,163	-21.9	-55.7	-50.8
Outlying areas(a)	202,962	418,632	397,601	72,450	1,091,645	-64.3	-82.7	-81.8

*Obligations not funded directly to institutions or students; distributed in accordance with plans submitted and approved by a state agency.
Source: The Office of Institutional Support Programs, Office of Postsecondary Education, U.S. Department of Education.

(a) American Samoa, Guam, Northern Mariana Islands, Micronesia and Trust Territory of the Pacific Islands.

Table 5
NUMBER OF INSTITUTIONS OF HIGHER EDUCATION AND BRANCHES: 1980-81

State or other jurisdiction	All institutions			Publicly controlled institutions			Privately controlled institutions		
	4-year	2-year	Total	4-year	2-year	Total	4-year	2-year	Total
United States	1,948	1,273	3,221	543	944	1,487	1,405	329	1,734
Alabama	29	28	57	16	21	37	13	7	20
Alaska	6	9	15	3	9	12	3	0	3
Arizona	11	17	28	3	16	19	8	1	9
Arkansas	20	15	35	10	9	19	10	6	16
California	151	117	268	30	105	135	121	12	133
Colorado	28	16	44	13	14	27	15	2	17
Connecticut	26	21	47	7	17	24	19	4	23
Delaware	5	5	10	2	4	6	3	1	4
Florida	42	37	79	9	28	37	33	9	42
Georgia	45	31	76	18	16	34	27	15	42
Hawaii	6	6	12	3	6	9	3	0	3
Idaho	6	3	9	4	2	6	2	1	3
Illinois	95	62	157	13	50	63	82	12	94
Indiana	50	24	74	13	15	28	37	9	46
Iowa	38	23	61	3	18	21	35	5	40
Kansas	27	25	52	8	21	29	19	4	23
Kentucky	30	27	57	8	13	21	22	14	36
Louisiana.........	25	7	32	14	6	20	11	1	12
Maine............	20	8	28	7	5	12	13	3	16
Maryland	35	22	57	13	19	32	22	3	25
Massachusetts.....	78	38	116	15	18	33	63	20	83
Michigan	57	36	93	15	30	45	42	6	48
Minnesota	42	28	70	10	20	30	32	8	40
Mississippi	20	22	42	9	16	25	11	6	17
Missouri..........	65	21	86	13	15	28	52	6	58
Montana	10	6	16	6	3	9	4	3	7
Nebraska	20	10	30	7	9	16	13	1	14
Nevada...........	3	4	7	2	4	6	1	0	1
New Hampshire	14	11	25	3	7	10	11	4	15
New Jersey	40	22	62	14	17	31	26	5	31
New Mexico	9	10	19	6	10	16	3	0	3
New York	207	86	293	40	46	86	167	40	207
North Carolina	50	76	126	16	57	73	34	19	53
North Dakota......	10	6	16	6	5	11	4	1	5
Ohio	77	58	135	14	46	60	63	12	75
Oklahoma	26	19	45	14	15	29	12	4	16
Oregon...........	29	16	45	8	13	21	21	3	24
Pennsylvania......	130	70	200	24	37	61	126	33	139
Rhode Island......	11	2	13	2	1	3	9	1	10
South Carolina	31	30	61	12	21	33	19	9	28
South Dakota......	16	4	20	7	1	8	9	3	12
Tennessee	49	28	77	10	13	23	39	15	54
Texas	87	66	153	37	59	96	50	7	57
Utah.............	7	7	14	4	5	9	3	2	5
Vermont	18	3	21	4	2	6	14	1	15
Virginia	43	26	69	15	24	39	28	2	30
Washington........	22	27	49	6	27	33	16	0	16
West Virginia	20	8	28	12	4	16	8	4	12
Wisconsin	43	22	65	13	18	31	30	4	34
Wyoming..........	1	8	9	1	7	8	0	1	1
Dist. of Col.	18	0	18	1	0	1	17	0	17

Source: National Center for Education Statistics. Unpublished data.

Table 6
AVERAGE SALARIES OF FULL TIME INSTRUCTIONAL FACULTY ON 9-MONTH CONTRACTS, IN INSTITUTIONAL UNITS OF HIGHER EDUCATION: 1980-81

State or other jurisdiction	All institutional units				All public institutional units				All private institutional units			
	Professors	Associate professors	Assistant professors	Instructors	Professors	Associate professors	Assistant professors	Instructors	Professors	Associate professors	Assistant professors	Instructors
United States	$30,753	$23,214	$18,901	$15,178	$31,077	$23,772	$19,431	$15,613	$29,994	$21,833	$17,767	$14,192
Alabama	27,524	22,170	18,373	14,989	28,639	22,780	18,839	15,489	22,114	17,778	15,717	13,283
Alaska	44,899	36,876	29,662	24,536	44,899	36,876	29,662	24,536	. . .	. . .	. . .	. . .
Arizona	34,409	25,994	21,087	16,332	34,736	26,365	21,217	16,787	23,717	20,355	16,404	12,160
Arkansas	25,441	20,317	17,372	14,287	26,232	20,830	17,738	14,361	21,428	17,801	15,478	13,879
California	34,490	25,662	20,855	18,716	34,677	26,162	21,609	20,280	33,563	23,880	19,232	16,186
Colorado	28,652	22,208	18,636	15,007	28,654	22,413	18,838	15,910	28,637	21,277	17,810	13,230
Connecticut	33,168	23,491	19,395	16,291	32,299	23,920	19,979	16,499	34,088	22,872	18,699	15,955
Delaware	34,522	24,086	18,810	15,622	35,492	24,623	19,300	16,430	19,967	19,038	15,601	13,353
Florida	29,637	22,010	18,135	14,360	30,559	22,528	18,785	14,971	26,739	20,380	16,729	13,304
Georgia	29,271	22,540	18,488	14,657	30,583	23,447	19,055	15,320	26,112	19,708	16,428	13,087
Hawaii	32,919	23,726	18,945	15,028	33,226	24,256	19,237	15,680	22,344	17,601	15,385	12,766
Idaho	25,699	21,114	17,716	15,806	26,083	21,264	17,778	16,290	20,544	17,529	15,483	12,664
Illinois	31,158	23,379	19,512	16,061	30,755	23,769	20,041	16,360	31,854	22,650	18,545	15,358
Indiana	29,220	22,501	18,181	13,835	30,570	23,464	18,789	13,932	25,967	20,487	17,011	13,690
Iowa	27,868	21,489	17,381	14,639	30,408	23,290	18,981	14,932	24,059	19,054	16,564	14,213
Kansas	27,374	21,238	17,523	14,119	28,641	22,210	18,485	14,851	19,147	16,610	14,234	12,633
Kentucky	26,662	20,922	17,518	14,498	27,731	21,615	18,143	15,004	21,637	17,564	15,011	12,891
Louisiana	27,907	22,857	19,065	15,241	26,119	23,286	19,421	15,501	27,079	21,175	17,268	13,250
Maine	27,106	20,772	16,631	14,492	26,215	20,702	16,793	14,212	28,810	21,037	16,446	14,943
Maryland	30,712	24,374	19,817	15,523	31,162	24,772	20,287	15,669	29,407	21,775	17,370	14,069
Massachusetts	32,541	23,283	18,960	14,899	28,234	22,525	18,577	14,720	34,993	23,784	19,167	15,062
Michigan	31,443	23,840	19,665	16,062	32,252	24,197	20,044	16,552	26,412	22,078	18,083	14,591
Minnesota	29,609	22,308	18,614	15,316	30,539	23,096	19,196	15,971	26,889	21,079	17,694	14,467
Mississippi	26,265	21,531	17,590	14,000	27,040	22,119	18,197	14,367	19,853	16,015	13,441	11,540
Missouri	28,452	22,421	18,276	14,603	28,957	23,438	19,101	15,013	27,427	20,072	16,399	13,224
Montana	24,866	20,554	17,339	15,107	25,139	20,821	17,700	15,700	20,268	17,363	15,047	12,479
Nebraska	27,170	21,363	17,655	14,303	27,955	22,094	18,295	14,787	23,546	19,445	16,172	13,387
Nevada	31,068	24,513	20,425	17,672	31,068	24,513	20,425	17,672	. . .	. . .	. . .	. . .
New Hampshire ...	27,674	20,930	17,737	14,315	25,780	21,210	17,640	14,752	29,939	20,514	17,841	13,940
New Jersey	33,772	25,074	19,752	15,480	34,595	25,948	20,236	15,861	32,323	22,314	18,183	14,343
New Mexico	30,472	23,171	19,099	15,812	30,510	23,441	19,190	15,875	N.A.	18,161	15,925	14,140
New York	32,367	24,586	19,432	15,154	32,282	25,233	20,127	15,446	32,455	23,766	18,750	14,867
North Carolina	29,398	22,677	18,773	14,709	31,878	24,110	19,981	15,992	22,400	18,723	15,306	12,862
North Dakota	25,706	21,612	18,265	15,226	25,747	21,661	18,252	15,437	23,400	20,498	18,481	13,349
Ohio	30,294	23,207	18,740	15,331	32,080	24,230	19,613	15,796	26,528	20,261	16,706	13,931
Oklahoma	27,602	22,619	19,290	15,642	28,079	23,115	19,936	16,024	25,451	20,824	16,866	13,686
Oregon	27,759	21,986	18,286	15,377	28,081	22,281	18,723	15,744	26,409	21,041	17,274	12,807
Pennsylvania	30,933	23,683	18,985	15,233	31,384	24,737	19,742	15,868	30,404	22,212	18,223	14,335
Rhode Island	31,237	23,294	19,170	15,494	29,801	23,161	19,672	14,369	32,761	23,574	18,466	16,038
South Carolina	28,632	22,201	17,975	14,132	31,428	23,527	19,021	14,992	21,524	17,688	14,679	12,286
South Dakota	23,699	19,737	16,812	14,222	24,609	20,293	17,413	14,804	20,635	17,912	15,297	12,820
Tennessee	27,507	21,573	17,535	14,524	26,357	22,227	18,171	14,980	25,633	19,652	15,556	13,247
Texas	28,594	22,291	18,537	15,131	29,003	22,717	18,865	15,491	27,326	20,727	17,210	13,518
Utah	30,535	23,203	19,206	15,842	30,816	23,323	19,416	15,925	19,141	17,803	14,946	14,059
Vermont	26,851	20,109	16,804	14,178	27,140	20,129	16,829	13,871	26,424	20,077	16,777	14,406
Virginia	29,008	22,174	18,188	14,499	30,057	22,691	18,520	14,724	25,268	19,547	16,322	13,289
Washington	29,300	22,437	18,688	14,878	30,206	23,197	19,433	15,409	24,782	20,414	17,245	14,646
West Virginia	24,553	20,402	17,095	14,324	25,279	20,931	17,559	14,458	20,300	17,602	14,981	13,988
Wisconsin	30,231	22,839	19,190	15,909	30,763	23,303	19,715	17,040	26,792	21,042	17,477	13,712
Wyoming	32,966	25,772	20,764	17,514	32,966	25,772	20,764	17,514	. . .	. . .	. . .	. . .
Dist. of Col.	32,808	24,603	19,522	16,279	32,638	25,892	21,078	17,778	32,844	24,248	19,045	15,933

Source: National Center for Education Statistics, U.S. Dept. of Education.

N.A.—Not available.

Table 7
AVERAGE SALARIES OF FULL TIME INSTRUCTIONAL FACULTY ON 12-MONTH CONTRACTS, IN INSTITUTIONAL UNITS OF HIGHER EDUCATION: 1980-81

State or other jurisdiction	All institutional units				All public institutional units				All private institutional units			
	Professors	Associate professors	Assistant professors	Instructors	Professors	Associate professors	Assistant professors	Instructors	Professors	Associate professors	Assistant professors	Instructors
United States	$37,874	$29,431	$24,277	$18,567	$39,092	$30,308	$25,027	$19,127	$33,201	$26,391	$22,066	$17,273
Alabama	35,953	29,396	23,165	18,132	36,646	29,664	23,891	18,602	22,280	15,241	15,861	14,692
Alaska	60,023	49,601	38,967	30,780	60,023	49,601	38,967	30,780	...	...	...	...
Arizona	40,151	32,116	25,788	19,315	40,752	32,116	25,788	19,315	16,026	...	...	...
Arkansas	31,459	26,113	22,564	16,566	32,822	27,413	23,143	16,807	24,107	21,618	20,326	13,729
California	37,849	27,070	23,489	18,906	41,609	30,346	25,249	24,681	35,433	25,639	22,670	18,304
Colorado	36,517	30,981	27,160	19,791	36,553	31,286	27,540	19,635	36,290	29,537	25,764	N.A.
Connecticut	47,365	34,125	28,883	18,187	57,933	42,592	35,170	...	36,796	28,128	23,079	18,187
Delaware	38,706	30,060	22,954	17,236	40,660	30,658	23,176	N.A.	23,564	18,500	21,044	N.A.
Florida	35,928	27,739	24,496	16,535	36,448	28,294	25,266	18,304	32,781	22,553	17,797	14,307
Georgia	41,917	32,146	25,808	18,947	42,858	32,586	26,300	18,999	30,642	28,081	22,406	18,158
Hawaii	39,484	27,576	23,424	17,823	39,693	27,945	23,883	17,687	N.A.	N.A.	N.A.	18,500
Idaho	28,299	24,739	20,241	20,225	33,373	28,071	21,766	20,392	18,573	16,410	15,919	N.A.
Illinois	38,756	29,828	25,314	19,302	39,758	31,023	25,535	20,059	35,808	27,366	24,672	18,081
Indiana	40,851	30,155	23,978	16,457	42,655	31,212	24,788	16,999	28,913	22,981	19,117	15,193
Iowa	38,106	29,050	25,103	18,046	39,213	31,006	25,583	20,291	31,170	24,372	24,380	17,002
Kansas	35,153	28,814	25,627	18,833	36,053	29,759	23,704	19,236	21,991	19,004	17,163	14,515
Kentucky	35,130	29,136	24,704	17,147	35,581	29,364	24,850	17,389	23,396	21,623	18,315	15,596
Louisiana	36,803	32,025	26,068	19,800	37,948	32,796	26,251	19,918	23,059	19,689	22,846	17,666
Maine	28,581	22,618	19,650	13,251	31,982	24,186	21,101	16,962	21,354	19,982	18,406	11,395
Maryland	41,250	31,511	25,480	20,082	40,488	31,476	25,722	20,455	42,682	31,612	24,825	18,297
Massachusetts	34,062	25,941	20,745	18,542	28,536	21,283	17,116	15,096	36,796	29,319	22,913	19,413
Michigan	41,191	31,000	25,552	17,700	41,813	31,941	27,110	19,732	32,506	23,950	18,073	14,894
Minnesota	34,066	29,384	25,100	20,427	39,518	31,202	26,588	21,679	18,511	21,839	18,966	16,392
Mississippi	34,914	29,923	25,120	20,507	35,228	30,143	25,225	20,914	23,903	21,419	19,926	14,976
Missouri	34,464	27,868	23,336	18,840	37,707	30,614	25,708	20,298	29,918	24,790	20,802	17,527
Montana	32,161	25,548	22,490	19,903	32,351	26,276	22,490	19,903	24,762	19,479	...	...
Nebraska	37,442	30,120	23,246	18,245	37,451	29,796	24,615	18,059	37,304	31,374	21,181	20,348
Nevada	35,648	27,819	23,505	17,581	35,648	27,819	23,505	17,581	...	...	...	...
New Hampshire	30,544	23,194	17,548	14,704	29,117	22,872	18,761	14,619	32,417	23,946	14,880	14,840
New Jersey	44,225	33,728	24,872	19,004	45,842	34,514	25,334	19,269	20,966	21,146	17,790	13,259
New Mexico	39,714	29,558	22,610	19,213	39,714	29,558	22,610	19,213	...	...	...	...
New York	39,084	28,556	22,608	18,623	39,016	29,256	23,491	18,962	39,162	27,680	21,841	17,801
North Carolina	40,539	30,384	24,821	17,888	43,198	32,321	26,038	18,418	23,383	20,246	16,466	14,376
North Dakota	32,682	27,222	22,616	17,414	32,682	27,738	22,890	17,401	...	...	...	...
Ohio	38,339	30,342	25,801	19,713	40,577	31,476	26,449	20,802	30,758	27,985	23,560	18,191
Oklahoma	36,596	29,241	26,083	18,131	36,804	29,573	26,280	18,154	25,605	21,383	20,108	N.A.
Oregon	36,168	28,277	23,268	18,309	37,598	29,463	24,537	19,786	29,556	25,211	18,569	15,530
Pennsylvania	39,869	30,548	24,250	17,853	41,727	31,724	24,885	18,489	30,110	24,679	22,286	16,499
Rhode Island	37,850	28,125	21,347	14,704	36,195	28,261	22,278	16,234	42,306	27,171	19,670	15,770
South Carolina	38,618	30,658	24,709	18,969	39,892	31,496	25,447	19,612	22,824	19,092	16,957	13,304
South Dakota	30,482	25,038	21,124	17,861	30,924	25,087	21,685	17,983	24,195	N.A.	18,460	N.A.
Tennessee	33,306	26,607	22,705	17,936	33,087	26,686	22,120	17,449	33,609	26,489	23,461	19,065
Texas	37,827	28,983	23,895	19,098	38,944	29,400	24,223	20,049	32,258	26,301	21,035	16,398
Utah	37,359	29,366	22,660	17,803	37,502	29,491	22,660	N.A.	N.A.	N.A.	...	N.A.
Vermont	32,192	26,833	22,591	15,969	32,192	26,955	22,591	N.A.	...	N.A.	...	N.A.
Virginia	38,096	31,229	25,195	18,645	40,655	31,805	25,580	19,434	24,024	21,744	18,500	13,847
Washington........	42,359	31,777	26,715	19,236	42,664	32,050	26,881	19,133	32,789	26,832	22,179	N.A.
West Virginia	33,256	26,254	21,554	17,259	34,015	26,847	22,128	17,888	19,369	19,198	17,706	14,801
Wisconsin	37,946	31,479	25,462	16,759	38,177	30,468	25,144	20,018	36,655	32,747	25,629	15,619
Wyoming	37,768	31,861	25,960	23,038	37,768	31,861	25,960	23,038	...	...	...	...
Dist. of Col.	41,346	31,942	26,190	19,999	...	...	...	...	41,346	31,942	26,190	19,999

Source: National Center for Education Statistics, U.S. Dept. of Education.

N.A.—Not available.

Table 8
RANK OF STATES IN SELECTED EDUCATION CATEGORIES

State or other jurisdiction	Enrollment per 1,000 population (a)		Percent of U.S. average tax effort (b)		Tax revenue per capita (c)		Revenue spent on higher education (d)		Appropriations per student (e)	
	Number	Rank	Percent	Rank	Amount	Rank	Percent	Rank	Amount	Rank
United States..........	29.1	...	100.0	...	$ 986.50	...	10.7	...	$3,646	...
Alabama	30.8	20	82.8	36	612.90	51	16.1	6	3,205	37
Alaska	24.1	40	166.4	2	3,692.80	1	8.3	42	12,712	1
Arizona	43.5	2	103.3	13	978.20	16	14.2	12	3,193	38
Arkansas	23.4	41	84.4	33	641.50	48	12.6	24	3,441	27
California..............	39.0	4	95.7	20	1,104.30	8	14.4	10	4,087	12
Colorado	37.8	6	87.6	28	968.30	18	11.2	31	2,874	45
Connecticut	21.7	48	102.3	14	1,059.20	11	7.9	44	3,862	16
Delaware	38.7	5	87.4	29	939.50	21	12.9	20	3,129	40
Florida	23.0	43	69.0	49	708.30	44	11.5	30	3,547	25
Georgia	20.5	49	92.8	21	750.40	38	12.3	26	4,492	6
Hawaii	34.4	11	122.9	4	1,261.20	4	12.7	23	4,662	5
Idaho	28.2	27	81.0	37	735.10	41	14.0	15	3,643	21
Illinois	27.3	30	95.8	19	1,049.00	12	9.6	37	3,676	20
Indiana	26.0	35	78.0	42	738.80	40	11.9	28	3,377	30
Iowa	28.4	26	90.7	23	957.60	19	12.2	27	4,101	11
Kansas	37.2	8	86.1	31	909.30	24	14.7	9	3,587	24
Kentucky	24.4	39	80.4	39	689.60	45	14.1	13	3,975	14
Louisiana	26.7	31	74.5	45	808.80	31	13.3	19	4,017	13
Maine	21.7	46	108.5	9	845.60	27	7.4	47	2,886	44
Maryland	30.1	23	106.0	10	1,024.60	14	9.9	36	3,383	29
Massachusetts	22.4	44	137.1	3	1,230.50	6	5.0	51	2,764	46
Michigan	33.7	12	105.4	11	1,060.80	10	9.5	38	2,993	43
Minnesota	29.8	24	105.2	12	1,079.80	9	9.2	40	3,330	31
Mississippi	30.3	22	90.9	22	637.00	49	18.3	2	3,842	17
Missouri	25.4	38	79.3	41	742.90	39	10.3	33	3,008	42
Montana	33.4	13	88.3	27	984.60	15	11.1	32	3,257	34
Nebraska	34.8	10	100.4	17	940.90	20	14.0	14	3,773	18
Nevada	26.2	33	49.6	51	812.60	30	10.2	34	3,154	39
New Hampshire	22.0	45	72.7	47	688.60	46	6.2	49	1,943	51
New Jersey	21.7	47	113.3	7	1,118.10	7	6.2	48	3,207	36
New Mexico	31.5	17	80.9	38	845.70	26	16.1	7	4,320	8
New York	23.3	42	170.8	1	1,432.50	2	7.8	45	4,795	4
North Carolina	30.5	21	89.6	26	725.10	43	17.5	4	4,156	9
North Dakota	43.0	3	76.0	44	809.30	32	20.7	1	3,890	15
Ohio	25.7	36	83.3	35	797.00	33	8.9	41	2,745	47
Oklahoma	32.0	15	70.0	48	794.60	34	13.7	16	3,406	28
Oregon	36.1	9	90.1	24	933.10	22	12.9	21	3,613	22
Pennsylvania	19.1	50	101.7	15	912.60	23	7.6	46	3,458	26
Rhode Island	26.1	34	119.1	6	975.20	17	9.2	39	3,458	26
South Carolina	27.8	29	89.9	25	682.80	47	16.7	5	4,112	10
South Dakota	29.7	25	83.6	34	758.40	37	10.0	35	2,545	49
Tennessee..............	25.4	37	80.0	40	631.60	50	12.3	25	3,059	41
Texas	31.7	16	62.4	50	763.00	36	18.1	3	4,354	7
Utah	33.0	14	96.4	18	827.30	29	14.4	11	3,609	23
Vermont................	27.8	28	101.1	16	838.00	28	8.0	43	2,403	50
Virginia	31.4	18	85.5	32	792.90	35	12.8	22	3,237	35
Washington	44.5	1	86.9	30	891.80	25	13.5	18	2,710	48
West Virginia...........	26.3	32	76.2	43	728.90	42	13.5	17	3,742	19
Wisconsin	37.4	7	110.7	8	1,048.20	13	11.8	29	3,314	33
Wyoming...............	30.9	19	74.0	46	1,387.90	3	14.7	8	6,608	2
Dist. of Col.	12.6	51	120.0	5	1,247.30	5	6.1	50	6,072	3

Source: Halstead, D. Kent, How States Compare in Financial Support of Higher Education, 1981-82, National Institute of Education (Washington, D.C.: U.S. Department of Education, February 1982).
(a) Number of full-time-equivalent students enrolled in public colleges and universities per 1,000 population in the fall of 1980.
(b) State and local tax revenue in 1980 as a percentage of the revenue that would be collected if the state's wealth were taxed at national average rates.

(c) State and local tax revenue per capita in 1980.
(d) Percent of total state and local tax revenue appropriated for current operating expenses of public higher education in 1981-82. Appropriations data from M. M. Chambers, Illinois State University.
(e) Appropriations of state and local tax revenue for current operating expenses of public higher education per actual full-time-equivalent student in 1981-82.

2.   Transportation

TRANSPORTATION AT THE CROSSROADS

By Raymond L. Kassel

"Would you tell me, please, which way I ought to go from here?"
"That depends a good deal on where you want to get to," said the Cat.
"I don't much care where . . .," said Alice.
"Then it doesn't matter which way you go," said the Cat.
Alice in Wonderland, Lewis Carroll

TRANSPORTATION IN THE STATES, like Lewis Carroll's Alice, faces a fork in the road. Transportation is the lifeline of our nation's economy, our society, our standard of living and our lifestyle. But transportation faces some very serious decisions:
  • How large a transportation system is necessary to meet today's transportation needs?
  • How large a transportation system will be necessary to meet tomorrow's transportation needs?
  • How important is it to keep all our transportation options open?
  • Who pays?
  • Who benefits?
The manner in which we face these decisions will determine transportation's role in improving national productivity. Without clear, positive and forthright objectives and policy, we are in danger of destroying our transportation system and all its promise.

How important is transportation to us? Transportation is the key to the accessibility of our resources. Transportation consumes approximately 3.5 percent of our most precious resource—land—yet transportation makes possible the use of other resources, by overcoming problems of distance. Transportation links raw materials to processing and markets and, so, is the catalyst of productivity.

Transporation is crucial to our economic life. Transportation represents 20 percent of our national economy, and in a typical state it is more important than agriculture, business and trade or manufacturing. It has been said that improving the efficiency and productivity of transportation will return larger benefits to the national economy than improvements in industrial productivity alone. Many economists today identify transportation as the largest untapped source of reducing costs, improving services, combating inflation and increasing national productivity.

Transportation is crucial to our economic life. Transportation represents 20 percent of our national economy, and in a typical state it is more important than agriculture, business percent of the world's population, we produce 13 percent of the world's wheat, 29 percent of its coarse grains (mainly corn), 62 percent of its soybeans and 20 percent of its cotton. But, even more importantly, we account for 43 percent of the world's trade in wheat, 63 percent of the trade in coarse grain, 82 percent of the trade in soybeans and 30 percent of the trade in cotton. Even for rice, the basic world foodstuff we consume little of, we ac-

Raymond L. Kassel is the recently retired Director of the Iowa Department of Transportation.

count for 22 percent of the world trade. These agricultural exports earn us currently over $40 billion, offsetting our import bills on everything from radios and televisions to oil. It is largely because the United States can meet this demand better than any other nation that we have become an overwhelmingly important factor in world agricultural trade. One out of every three acres in this country produces commodities for export.

Transportation is also the key to our future energy balance. Transportation consumes approximately one-half of our liquid fuels and represents the largest demand on our increasingly expensive and diminishing energy resources. Improved productivity is already having a major impact on our energy problems. Further changes in the national use of energy for transportation present one of the best potentials for improving our economy's health and the nation's productivity, if energy can be consumed more efficiently in making raw materials and products accessible.

Without transportion our products have no value, no market—our industry has no outlet, our people no income or employment. Yet our transportation problems today are characterized not only by a lack of understanding and lack of recognition, but most importantly, by a lack of support. Without reinvestment, without revitalization, our transportation system will surely self-destruct.

Reinvestment and revitalization will save money in the long run, but we must recognize the changing transportation environment. Today's transportation needs are not the same as those at the turn of the century. In 1910, we had 250,000 miles of railroad track, but only one mile of hard-surfaced roads. Today we have less than 200,000 miles of railroad track, but two million miles of hard-surfaced roads out of a total public road system of 3.9 million miles. Railroad lines are being abandoned. Some highways may need to be abandoned in future years. The responsibility for maintaining existing highways is likely to move toward the local and county levels. Public reinvestment and revitalization under current limited funding capabilities will have to aim at maximum public benefits.

So where are we today?

- We fail to understand the importance of transportation.
- We fail to recognize the role of transportation in our economy and lives.

And we know these facts to be true because:

- We fail to support our transportation system with reinvestment.

Where are we going? Lewis Carroll was right. If we don't care where we're going, it doesn't matter which way we go. If we don't care what our future holds, it doesn't matter what steps we take today to enhance our economy and lives and avoid disasters.

Today we face a national transportation crisis with no national transportation policy—no purposeful pursuit. It remains for state and federal officials and public and private transportation decision-makers to clarify the role of transportation, the significant contribution that transportation can and must make to our national economic survival. The challenge is before us—we must develop a clear and single national transportation policy and we must sell our message:

- Transportation is the moving force behind our nation's economy.
- Transportation service levels must keep pace with economic demand.
- Transportation is potentially the largest single contributor to improving national productivity and taming inflation.
- Transportation determines our standard of living and our lifestyles.

- Having transportation costs less than not having transportation.
- Transportation must be supported with reinvestment.

We do know where we want to go. The challenge will be to get there.

Highways

The 1980s have brought a new emphasis to the nation's highway programs. After several decades of development and expansion, highway administrators have begun to concentrate on system maintenance and preservation. A number of economic reasons lie behind this shift. The extensive network of highways built during the 1930s and 1940s and the heavily traveled Interstate System of the 1950s and 1960s are reaching the end of their useful lives. Major reconstruction and renovation are necessary to preserve the investment the nation has in these systems. Some sections of the Interstate System remain to be completed and some urban highway projects continue to be an important facet of urban renewal, but throughout the country, pavement restoration has become a more urgent priority than the creation of new highway corridors. The present system is further limited by the large number of structurally inadequate or functionally obsolete bridges. In recent years, an increasing portion of highway resources has been spent on these existing systems, and this trend will likely continue.

Even shifting resources from the development of new highways to the restoration of old ones has not been enough to reverse the deterioration of the nation's vital highway network. Revenues from traditional highway sources have not kept pace with the increasing needs. Fuel shortages in the mid-1970s created an incentive for fuel conservation that has been far-reaching in its impact. Travel growth trends declined and even reversed for a time. The fuel economy of new cars improved considerably. Most states depend on motor fuel taxes for a substantial part of their highway budgets. In 1981 alone, 23 states and the District of Columbia found it necessary to raise fuel taxes. At least eight states now levy fuel taxes as a percentage of the sale price in an attempt to increase revenue as the price of fuel increases. Resistance to tax increases in some parts of the country has made it difficult to raise these highway-user fees enough to cover the cost of the highway service provided. Inevitably, then, the extent and quality of that service have begun to decline.

While revenues have declined in relation to needs, highway maintenance and construction costs have increased dramatically. The same high fuel prices that have restrained consumption and limited revenues are also a significant factor in the cost of operating, maintaining and improving highways. The cost of oil-derived paving materials has also increased rapidly. The Federal Highway Administration's composite index of construction costs increased by 250 percent during the 1970s. Faced with that kind of inflation, states have been forced to drastically reduce the rate at which they are rebuilding their roads and bridges.

The role of the federal government in the highway programs of the 1980s remains to be defined. Two aspects of that role seem to be emerging, however. First, the emphasis of federal programs is also moving toward system preservation. The restoration of the Interstate System will be a major concern of the federal government as well as the states. Second, the federal concern is likely to focus on those highway systems most readily identified with national interest. Direct support for local systems of cities and counties may give way to an increasing local and state responsibility for those systems.

As these changes emerged, states have begun to develop appropriate administrative and financial responses. Administrators face the difficult questions of where to limit service, how to raise revenues and how to distribute both the burden of the revenues and the benefits that can be derived from them. The answers to these questions that are forthcoming in this decade will shape the nation's highway system for many years to come.

Mass Transit

The decade of the 1970s closed on a note of change for public transportation. Interest in public transportation is high, and interest in ridesharing (carpools, commuter vans, shared-ride taxis, subscription buses) is growing. Fuel costs tripled during the decade, and people became concerned about the sprawling patterns of urban development. The last decade also brought a better awareness of the important relationship transportation has to the attainment of many national goals: moving the public, improving the economy, providing for the social well-being of the nation, attaining a cleaner environment, conserving and efficiently using our energy resources and providing for our national defense. The federal government support during the 1970s for public transportation, as an integral part of the total surface transportation system, was in sharp contrast to decades of previous disinterest.

No single form of public transportation can adequately serve the national interest and the diverse needs of the nation. Cities require mixtures of conventional and unconventional transit, services that can be designed or shaped to fit market needs of a particular portion of the community. All regions, whether urban or rural, should have a full family of services available from which to choose the most efficient and cost-effective. Densely populated areas, which can support capital-intensive transit services, may use several forms of transportation, including rail services (commuter, rapid or light rail), buses (local, express and feeder services), and, in certain situations, ferries, to link major activity centers as well as to provide services within such centers. In areas of lower population densities, bus systems with complementary services provided by the several forms of ridesharing may be dominant. Low-density residential and rural areas may find that carpools, vanpools and other shared-ride systems are most effective and cost-efficient in providing necessary transportation services in coordination with established public transportation wherever possible.

There is a need to tailor the many forms of public transportation and ridesharing to fit the diverse development patterns of these United States, in order to reduce congestion in the movement of goods and people; supply mobility for the young, the elderly, the disadvantaged and those choosing not to drive; provide alternative transportation during periods of petroleum shortages; and improve the environment.

Financial support for public transportation and ridesharing should be based on the principle that those sharing in the benefits should share in the costs. These beneficiaries include: the users; the community that is both shaped and served by its transportation facilities; industries, other businesses and institutions accommodated; the urban area, region or state that benefits by lower costs and improved economic development; and the federal government.

The federal government, in recognition of the critical link between transportation and national goals, plays a vital role in making the nation's total transportation system work well. Previous federal administrations recognized the benefits of good public transportation to the well-being of the country and established national goals for transportation accompanied by multi-billion dollar funding programs.

While some philosophy is changing, the federal role must support and complement the decision-making of local and state officials. Federal involvement should be directed toward the preservation and maintenance of the nation's investments in public transportation, the assurance of alternative transportation during periods of national emergency and other periods when petroleum is in short supply, and the achievement of related national goals in economic, social and environmental areas.

Railroads

The nation's rail system is currently undergoing its greatest period of change since its initial construction in the late 1800s. This change has caused concern among industries dependent upon good rail transportation, the general public, all levels of government and the railroad industry itself.

Since 1950, the railroad industry has faced financial difficulties with the rate of earnings on capital investment substantially less than the cost to acquire investment capital. The rate of return for the rail industry reached 4.2 percent in 1980, its highest level in 25 years; however, this rate of return on net investment remains inadequate. It was this bleak financial picture which played a major role in the 1970s in the bankruptcy of railroads in the Northeast and the creation of Conrail, the reevaluation of the nation's rail passenger system and the bankruptcies of the Rock Island and Milwaukee Road. Government increased its financial involvement in an attempt to avert a national collapse of the rail transportation system during the last decade, but the current economic position of the nation has altered this situation. Conrail, which received over $3 billion in federal government assistance, is scheduled to be dismantled or sold to other rail systems if it cannot prove its financial independence. Amtrak, which has received over $4 billion, must trim its expenditures and continue to scale down operations.

The U.S. Congress and the administration are steering a new course in revolving the Midwest restructuring. The direction is toward a private solution. It is clear that the bankruptcies of the Rock Island and Milwaukee Road will not result in a "Conrail West." Federal financial assistance to railroads through grants, low-interest loans and loan guarantees is decreasing and being considered for eventual elimination.

While the federal role in providing financial assistance to the rail industry is diminishing, other events are providing the rail industry with opportunities. The energy crisis and increased fuel prices may regain lost traffic for the rail industry. Revenue freight traffic measured in ton miles continues to increase, and the railroad share of U.S. intercity freight traffic took an upswing for the first time in 30 years, to 37.3 percent in 1980 from 35.7 percent in 1979.

Deregulation of the rail industry is making the federal industry much more competitive with the other forms of transportation. Railroads are beginning to enjoy greater flexibility in setting rates, discontinuing service or markets and entering into mergers and consolidations. This new flexibility has resulted in increased rail line abandonments and the establishment of long-term contracts between the carrier and rail user for rates and service, thus increasing the efficiency of the industry.

During 1981, two large railroad mergers became final, and two other applications were pending before the ICC in early 1982. This process is resulting in the creation of regional systems which are expected to result in transcontinental carriers. The smaller residual carriers are being forced into evaluating their future and competitive position in relation to these super systems.

While the trend toward large, super systems continues, the restructuring of the rail system through bankruptcies, liquidations and abandonments has increased local activity in rail service preservation and short-line operations. The states and local communities are faced with hard decisions related to their responsibility, need and financial capability to preserve rail service.

Although many problems need to be addressed and resolved by the rail industry, there is a growing optimism that the industry will face better times ahead. The railroad's inherent energy efficiency on long-haul movements, continued deregulation, improvements in operating efficiencies and the ability to react to market and economic changes all indicate that the prospects of a revitalized rail industry are better than they have been for many years.

Aviation

The aviation industry has already lived through some of the experiences forecast for the trucking and railroad industries during the 1980s. The airline industry has been through deregulation in many facets of its operations. The aviation safety record, practices and procedures are under serious question, as well as the environmental problem of aircraft noise pollution. Beyond these issues is the question of government's role in providing financial assistance for airport construction, rehabilitation, maintenance and operations. Finally, Congress is to examine the results of deregulation in 1982 and decide which roles and powers of the Civil Aeronautics Board should be retained.

The airline industry is now operating under a new regulatory structure that resulted from several years of national debate. The airline industry was deregulated by an act of Congress in 1978. The enactment removed many of the former barriers to entering existing markets of other carriers. At the same time, numerous restrictions on pricing services, i.e., fares, were removed. These two actions, operating in combination, were to inject competition into existing markets, reduce fares, provide a greater selection in the decision of when and where to travel and for how long, and offer new routes and services.

Air service to some small- and medium-sized cities has been reduced, eliminated and, in some cases, improved. Initial fare reductions and special fare plans did reduce the cost to the consumer. The trend is toward steadily increasing fares, but this situation is partially due to fuel cost increases. There was an increase in the number of carriers serving given routes and cities, but after the initial high demand to begin services to existing markets or other carriers, the number of applications has significantly tapered off. It cannot be determined if this is a long-term situation or a static condition after the initial requests. Therefore, deregulation will have to be continuously examined for the next few years to determine its overall effects and benefits to the public.

A continuing problem has been noise pollution. Previous proposals to aid the industry to abate its environmental noise pollution problem have come under growing criticism. Past sessions of Congress had considered partial government funding to retrofit engines or replace aircraft that could not meet the Federal Aviation Administration noise regulations scheduled for complete implementation by 1984. This would affect nearly 80 percent of the existing fleet at a projected price tag, by the industry, of $7 billion. Obviously, noise abatement is a must, but whether the government should assist in the cost is a sensitive issue.

Another issue for the new decade is government's role in overall aviation safety and airport finance. In the past, the Airport Development and Assistance Program has financed about one-third of the safety and construction programs at airports, with the remaining two-thirds being derived from general funds, landing fees and operations. Serious questions have been raised about the use of general funds. Recent proposals suggest the air traveler should support airport construction and safety through usage taxes. Advocates of this position point to the $2.9 billion surplus that exists in the Air Trust Fund which supports the Airport Development and Assistance Program.

The 1980s present an interesting set of aviation issues for government. Safety and service are primary concerns. The resolution of these issues will significantly affect the ability of the industry to meet capital needs while supplying the public with adequate air service in the future.

Table 1
RESPONSIBILITIES OF STATE DEPARTMENTS OF TRANSPORTATION: 1981

State	High-ways	Avia-tion	Mass transit	Rail-roads	Water trans-port	Pipe-lines	Motor vehicles	Highway or trans-porta-tion safety	Highway Patrol	Trans-porta-tion regula-tion
Alaska	★	★	★	★	★	...	...	★	...	★
Arizona	★	★	★	★	...	...	★	...	...	...
Arkansas	★	★	★	★	★	...	...	★	...	★
California	★	★	★	★	...	...	...	★	...	...
Connecticut	★	★	★	★	★	...	...	★	...	...
Delaware	★	★	★	★	...	...	...	...	...	...
Florida	★	★	★	★	★	...	...	...	...	...
Georgia	★	★	★	★	★	...	...	...	...	★
Hawaii	★	★	★	★	★	...	★	★	...	...
Idaho	★	★	★	★	...	...	...	★	...	★
Illinois	★	★	★	★	★	...	...	★	...	...
Iowa	★	★	★	★	★	...	★	...	...	★
Kansas	★	★	★	★	★	★	...	★	...	...
Kentucky	★	★	★	★	★	...	★	...	...	★
Louisiana	★	★	★	★	★	...	...	...	...	★
Maine	★	★	★	★	★	...	...	...	...	...
Maryland	★	★	★	★	★	...	★	★	...	★
Massachusetts	★	★	★	★	★	...	...	...	...	...
Michigan	★	★	★	★	★	...	...	...	...	★
Minnesota	★	★	★	★	★	★	...	...	...	★
Mississippi	...	...	★	★	★	...	...	...	...	★
Missouri	★	★	★	★	★	★	...	...	...	★
Nevada	★	★	★	★	...	...	...	...	...	★
New Jersey	★	★	★	★	...	...	...	★	...	...
New Mexico	...	★	★	...	...	...	★	...	...	★
New York	★	★	★	★	★	...	...	★	...	★
North Carolina	★	★	★	★	...	...	★	★	★	★
Ohio	★	★	★	★	★	...	...	★	...	★
Oklahoma	★	★	★	★	★	...	★	★	...	...
Oregon	★	★	★	★	★	...	★	...	★	...
Pennsylvania	★	★	★	★	★	...	★	★	★	★
Rhode Island	★	★	★	★	...	...	★	★	...	★
South Dakota	★	★	★	★	...	...	...	...	★	★
Tennessee	★	★	★	★	★	...	...	...	...	...
Texas	★	★	★	...	★	...	★	...	★	...
Utah	★	★	★	...	...	...	...	★	...	★
Vermont	★	★	★	★	★	...	★	★	...	★
Virginia	★	...	★	★	...	...	★	★	...	...
Washington	★	★	★	★	...	...	...	★	...	★
Wisconsin	★	★	★	★	★	...	★	...	★	★

Source: Iowa Department of Transportation, *State Transportation Functions*, May 1981.

Table 2
TOTAL ROAD AND STREET MILEAGE: 1980
(Classified by jurisdiction)

	Rural mileage				Urban mileage			Total rural and urban mileage
	Under state control(a,b)	Under local control(c)	Under federal control(d)	Total rural roads	Under state control(a,b)	Under local control(c)	Total urban mileage	
United States	701,846	2,269,770	262,010	3,233,626	79,359	543,120	622,479	3,856,105
Alabama(e)	11,672	62,143	326	74,141	1,575	11,444	13,019	87,160
Alaska(e)	5,227	1,947	1,948	9,122	231	521	752	9,874
Arizona	5,685	26,260	34,985	66,930	321	7,932	8,253	75,183
Arkansas(e)	15,142	51,543	1,795	68,480	1,237	5,731	6,968	75,448
California(e)	14,145	66,105	35,969	116,519	2,934	59,253	62,187	178,706
Colorado(e).................	7,079	57,692	1,008	65,779	649	8,496	9,145	74,924
Connecticut(e)	2,459	6,913	. . .	9,372	1,725	8,284	10,009	19,381
Delaware	3,657	228	3	3,888	981	364	1,345	5,233
Florida(e)..................	9,104	54,548	1,138	64,790	2,192	26,600	28,792	93,582
Georgia(e)..................	16,172	72,516	. . .	88,688	2,535	13,108	15,643	104,331
Hawaii	936	1,967	77	2,980	187	1,242	1,429	4,409
Idaho	4,905	25,804	34,320	65,029	225	2,002	2,227	67,256
Illinois(e)...................	14,192	92,053	304	106,549	3,693	24,707	28,400	134,949
Indiana(e)	9,854	63,752	1	73,607	1,590	16,272	17,862	91,469
Iowa	9,282	94,744	116	104,142	861	7,064	7,925	112,067
Kansas(e)..................	10,439	116,961	21	127,421	507	7,420	7,927	135,348
Kentucky	23,398	37,950	316	61,664	1,574	4,815	6,389	68,053
Louisiana	15,086	30,465	535	46,086	1,171	8,801	9,972	56,058
Maine	11,338	8,194	167	19,699	352	1,842	2,194	21,893
Maryland(e)................	4,342	13,600	337	18,279	904	9,356	10,260	28,539
Massachusetts(e)............	1,856	12,139	33	14,028	1,620	18,129	19,749	33,777
Michigan	7,739	84,240	. . .	91,979	1,779	23,478	25,257	117,236
Minnesota(e)...............	12,072	103,913	1,689	117,674	1,293	11,005	12,298	129,972
Mississippi(e)...............	9,605	53,512	966	64,083	793	5,014	5,807	69,890
Missouri(e).................	31,328	72,568	738	104,634	1,750	11,852	13,602	118,237
Montana...................	6,205	53,615	9,498	69,318	282	2,075	2,357	71,675
Nebraska	10,092	81,937	113	92,142	321	3,847	4,168	96,310
Nevada	4,949	23,258	13,216	41,423	168	1,793	1,961	43,384
New Hampshire	3,961	8,195	141	12,297	489	1,558	2,047	14,344
New Jersey	1,196	11,440	. . .	12,636	1,466	19,336	20,802	33,438
New Mexico(e)	8,838	35,608	5,467	49,913	877	3,400	4,277	54,190
New York..................	12,453	60,860	. . .	73,313	3,888	32,205	36,093	109,406
North Carolina	70,802	3,345	3,434	77,581	5,704	8,949	14,653	92,233
North Dakota	6,993	76,789	635	84,417	183	1,177	1,360	85,777
Ohio(e)....................	16,218	65,554	27	81,799	3,749	25,179	28,928	110,727
Oklahoma	12,245	86,100	. . .	98,345	771	10,659	11,430	109,775
Oregon(e)..................	9,443	34,898	69,327	113,668	765	7,032	7,797	121,465
Pennsylvania	41,460	45,960	738	88,158	5,947	23,318	29,265	117,423
Rhode Island(e)	630	2,138	. . .	2,768	529	3,099	3,628	6,396
South Carolina(e)...........	34,326	20,353	606	55,285	5,247	1,928	7,175	62,460
South Dakota	8,925	61,148	1,651	71,724	162	1,228	1,390	73,114
Tennessee..................	8,872	62,210	1,134	72,216	1,373	10,044	11,417	83,633
Texas(e)...................	66,136	143,970	1,006	211,112	6,829	49,181	56,010	267,122
Utah	5,045	21,699	15,563	42,307	511	3,705	4,216	46,523
Vermont(e)	2,754	10,363	256	13,373	84	609	693	14,066
Virginia....................	49,944	778	2,698	53,420	4,124	7,756	11,880	65,300
Washington(e)	15,891	39,041	15,146	70,078	971	13,839	14,810	84,888
West Virginia(e)	30,890	. . .	1,070	31,960	761	2,451	3,212	35,172
Wisconsin..................	10,752	83,403	64	94,219	1,223	11,609	12,832	107,051
Wyoming	6,112	25,051	3,428	34,591	256	1,387	1,643	36,234
Dist. of Col.(e)	. . .	. . .	. . .	. . .	. . .	1,024	1,024	1,024

Source: Federal Highway Administration, U.S. Department of Transportation. Compiled for calendar year ending December 31, 1980, from reports of state authorities.

Note: This table does not include mileage of non-public roads, or urban mileage under federal control.

(a) Includes local roads under state control in Alabama, Alaska, Delaware, Maryland, Nebraska, New Mexico, Oklahoma and Virginia.

(b) Includes mileage of state park, forest, institutional, toll and other state roads that are not a part of the state highway system.

(c) Includes mileage not identified by administrative authority.

(d) Mileage in federal parks, forests and reservations that are not a part of the state and local highway system.

(e) Incomplete 1980 data submitted for these states. Areawide data used for totals and available data from previous submittals included and factored to 1980 level.

Table 3
STATE RECEIPTS FOR HIGHWAYS: 1980
(In thousands of dollars)

State or other jurisdiction	State highway user tax revenues	Roads and crossing tolls(a)	Other state imposts, general fund revenues	Miscellaneous income	Federal funds — Federal Highway Administration	Other agencies	Transfers from local governments	Bond proceeds (b)	Total receipts
United States	$14,110,543	$1,343,946	$1,858,752	$1,003,036	$9,581,743	$465,560	$248,092	$1,112,166	$29,723,838
Alabama	236,068	. . .	8,228	16,944	223,211	4,457	206	. . .	489,114
Alaska	27,282	19,129	122,555	. . .	102,577	2,730	. . .	. . .	274,273
Arizona	191,340	. . .	11,432	7,929	134,805	5,388	1,769	50,005	402,668
Arkansas	208,166	. . .	6,925	10,257	160,773	30,319	1,814	. . .	418,254
California	1,231,447	52,342	. . .	115,921	499,603	30,567	10,414	. . .	1,940,294
Colorado	167,810	. . .	54,330	10,476	136,803	18,669	7,235	. . .	395,323
Connecticut	195,893	42,078	. . .	6,546	95,152	2,716	. . .	75,223	417,608
Delaware	50,148	23,592	8,069	3,539	32,445	1,126	. . .	42,757	161,676
Florida	522,548	86,784	. . .	32,980	444,195	9,214	1,867	10,989	1,108,577
Georgia	289,673	. . .	151,296	46,313	483,485	5,040	4,674	. . .	980,481
Hawaii	45,357	. . .	10,938	6,047	59,417	886	. . .	15,196	137,841
Idaho	86,876	. . .	. . .	1,194	48,291	6,815	1,643	. . .	144,819
Illinois	647,994	95,453	128,906	24.656	575,840	17,191	38,874	120,007	1,648,921
Indiana	335,916	29,642	31,667	12,957	186,917	4,787	5,470	238,688	846,044
Iowa	283,263	2,285	64,123	14,240	135,930	3,342	3,480	. . .	506,663
Kansas	176,786	21,570	1,697	36,699	145,623	2,820	3,601	. . .	388,796
Kentucky	330,847	18,776	64,449	98,505	232,404	4,858	1,176	. . .	751,015
Louisiana	240,023	. . .	176,450	1,890	174,017	14,183	105	73,771	680,439
Maine	80,311	14,083	1,161	3,596	45,346	1,484	4,584	13,000	163,565
Maryland	277,871	57,191	17,860	35,063	250,936	2,945	. . .	58,836	700,702
Massachusetts	247,269	69,971	71,928	9,406	171,360	4,687	. . .	43,300	617,921
Michigan	682,172	7,201	80,154	19,075	181,528	8,434	7,493	. . .	986,057
Minnesota	332,733	. . .	3,620	36,727	196,626	5,096	14,958	26,000	615,760
Mississippi	163,661	. . .	99,248	46,285	106,387	4,568	3,551	21,998	445,698
Missouri	288,531	. . .	34,716	2,476	210,105	12,550	5,893	. . .	554,271
Montana	72,636	. . .	1,787	2,427	143,421	8,521	. . .	. . .	228,792
Nebraska	135,804	. . .	41,109	4,882	82,165	2,337	7,426	. . .	273,723
Nevada	50,289	. . .	. . .	2,268	102,606	1,095	8,350	. . .	164,608
New Hampshire	67,523	12,738	. . .	2,134	38,804	1,165	2,866	. . .	125,230
New Jersey	217,662	206,854	. . .	38,056	148,629	5,451	. . .	72,500	689,152
New Mexico	119,004	. . .	24,625	4,800	61,313	2,783	803	. . .	213,328
New York	548,844	259,034	231,325	66,590	543,184	17,202	1,753	. . .	1,667,932
North Carolina	407,384	453	. . .	19,275	250,468	6,082	2,228	60,227	746,117
North Dakota	57,554	. . .	10,500	380	62,409	2,950	7,677	. . .	141,470
Ohio	648,950	42,858	. . .	38,863	275,495	12,407	15,763	100,387	1,134,723
Oklahoma	262,792	34,719	124,033	12,686	105,145	5,265	5,951	. . .	550,591
Oregon	183,353	1,351	34,470	10,016	165,744	46,558	4,948	15,009	461,449
Pennsylvania	975,401	137,811	41,000	58,818	323,897	13,977	9,540	. . .	1,560,444
Rhode Island	37,057	4,760	. . .	873	30,420	814	. . .	. . .	73,924
South Carolina	200,899	. . .	. . .	460	102,339	3,895	1,186	. . .	308,779
South Dakota	71,443	. . .	14,080	2,892	50,050	1,626	2,061	. . .	142,152
Tennessee	314,383	. . .	3,987	5,804	225,497	7,157	4,972	. . .	561,800
Texas	957,366	7,117	13,504	67,178	547,745	16,920	18,257	. . .	1,628,087
Utah	82,267	. . .	4,502	480	141,015	1,863	2,436	. . .	232,563
Vermont	51,177	. . .	. . .	872	25,633	992	. . .	10,803	89,477
Virginia	407,468	45,627	59,457	5,599	334,003	5,145	10,372	. . .	867,671
Washington	333,076	36,916	. . .	18,410	292,084	32,325	2,778	. . .	715,589
West Virginia	194,185	13,611	76,805	8,441	269,247	14,175	. . .	50,033	626,497
Wisconsin	281,871	. . .	11,455	919	163,804	5,151	18,230	7,909	489,339
Wyoming	72,505	. . .	16,361	6,651	57,350	42,080	1,688	. . .	196,635
Dist. of Col.	19,665	. . .	. . .	23,541	5,500	2,752	. . .	5,528	56,986

Source: Federal Highway Administration, U.S. Department of Transportation. Compiled for calendar year ending Dec. 31, 1980, from reports of state authorities.

(a) Toll receipts allocated for non-highway purposes are excluded.
(b) Par value of bonds issued and redeemed by refunding is excluded.

STATE DISBURSEMENTS FOR HIGHWAYS: 1980
(In thousands of dollars)

State or other jurisdiction	Capital outlay — State administered highways	Capital outlay — County and township roads	Capital outlay — Local municipal streets	Capital outlay — Total	Maintenance and traffic services	Administration and highway police	Bond interest	Grants-in-aid to local governments	Bond retirement (b)	Total disbursements
United States	$14,013,207	$833,092	$540,070	$15,386,369	$4,645,881	$3,856,728	$1,055,966	$4,113,085	$991,319	$30,049,348
Alabama	263,318	22,456	157	285,931	54,293	41,539	14,386	96,877	23,750	516,776
Alaska	121,966	. . .	7,299	129,265	83,344	42,883	7,809	3,883	7,149	274,333
Arizona	181,707	6,389	9,615	197,711	30,910	63,086	1,634	72,004	. . .	365,345
Arkansas	245,553	7,155	3,057	255,765	68,448	38,468	. . .	62,727	. . .	425,408
California	587,423	46,543	144,731	778,697	208,876	516,550	6,612	413,616	5,636	1,929,987
Colorado	171,809	1,301	19,340	192,450	80,733	47,370	. . .	90,911	. . .	411,464
Connecticut	157,044	3,207	. . .	160,251	54,354	56,379	34,093	22,075	66,373	393,525
Delaware	69,550	. . .	. . .	69,550	18,678	24,545	15,066	2,000	21,767	151,606
Florida	789.694	22,119	. . .	811,813	106,741	85,295	49,991	159,642	47,449	1,260,931
Georgia	446,658	103,030	14,837	564,525	72,709	69,444	22,018	9,688	24,064	762,448
Hawaii	79,095	4,325	. . .	83,420	13,465	7,229	6,466	14,757	8,596	133,944
Idaho	51,003	13,272	. . .	64,275	33,671	24,600	. . .	30,920	. . .	153,466
Illinois	867,121	101,767	4,731	973,619	183,173	147,697	59,303	246,640	41,860	1,652,236
Indiana	147,664	17,630	27,160	192,454	205,163	131,568	4,044	140,078	14,501	687,808
Iowa	190,960	55,145	744	246,849	56,547	56,618	380	142,835	560	503,789
Kansas	211,385	30,206	15,814	257,405	74,625	39,208	18,612	33,905	16,155	439,910
Kentucky	504,649	20,003	16,387	541,039	129,321	68,640	102,747	41,167	29,731	912,645
Louisiana	465,476	. . .	1,620	467,096	50,472	83,468	37,761	6,023	36,989	681,809
Maine	68,973	513	. . .	69,486	54,645	25,447	3,464	2,906	8,330	164,278
Maryland	134,572	12,722	. . .	147,294	65,278	85,678	42,533	321,154	1,610	663,547
Massachusetts	306,084	. . .	. . .	306,084	70,159	116,254	56,193	79,100	76,081	703,871
Michigan	305,287	19,237	4,606	329,130	105,997	157,292	7,207	366,232	30,791	996,649
Minnesota	317,192	21,045	5,496	343,733	79,458	39,940	6,802	127,407	13,908	611,248
Mississippi	228,969	56,997	4,693	290,659	33,040	34,307	52,799	52,552	4,326	467,683
Missouri	236,763	928	3,161	240,852	125,196	99,913	. . .	88,925	. . .	554,886
Montana	146,704	7,493	10	154,207	30,498	21,657	. . .	17,761	. . .	224,123
Nebraska	104,411	17,741	14,663	136,815	30,324	29,263	. . .	76,191	1,000	274,174
Nevada..........	108,723	142	340	109,205	24,126	27,960	. . .	7,380	. . .	168,671
New Hampshire ...	53,546	. . .	. . .	53,546	32,234	42,898	5,069	10,011	8,430	152,188
New Jersey	163,949	28,358	5,175	197,482	190,377	122,778	92,031	4,818	54,049	661,535
New Mexico	99,545	. . .	. . .	99,545	32,120	52,389	263	12,091	1,000	197,408
New York	702,139	42,853	86,715	831,707	242,179	256,052	75,623	117,089	127,018	1,649,668
North Carolina	411,667	. . .	87	411,754	186,178	144,940	8,565	32,817	23,000	807,254
North Dakota	60,059	17,367	5,618	83,044	20,578	13,254	. . .	26,245	. . .	143,121
Ohio	311,283	20,541	55,519	387,343	117,753	147,354	27,886	298,120	53,137	1,031,593
Oklahoma	198,590	6,534	. . .	205,124	73,993	53,655	13,200	107,952	7,214	461,138
Oregon	228,191	9,984	17,271	255,446	68,861	50,402	2,934	100,646	3,301	481,590
Pennsylvania......	469,724	. . .	. . .	469,724	515,545	170,851	143,950	154,969	102,299	1,557,338
Rhode Island	27,417	. . .	. . .	27,417	18,510	8,396	7,306	387	10,478	72,494
South Carolina	164,738	. . .	. . .	164,738	74,567	39,642	4,001	16,529	9,500	308,977
South Dakota	76,602	9,991	4,437	91,030	23,411	19,946	. . .	16,428	. . .	150,815
Tennessee	341,812	42,621	3,459	387,892	60,503	45,688	7,073	91,669	15,720	608,545
Texas	1,461,144	. . .	2,312	1,463,456	229,015	133,603	8,755	44,515	3,107	1,882,451
Utah	157,000	9,846	5,782	172,628	27,019	23,216	. . .	17,911	. . .	240,774
Vermont	28,317	3,177	. . .	31,494	18,944	16,353	3,135	8,120	8,495	86,541
Virginia	511,914	. . .	. . .	511,914	199,345	100,070	15,768	53,653	12,848	893,598
Washington.......	362,107	21,077	23,805	406,989	120,773	98,527	23,022	122,213	15,175	786,699
West Virginia	388,989	. . .	. . .	388,989	126,841	67,982	47,818	. . .	40,172	671,802
Wisconsin	156,063	22,835	19,133	198,031	72,823	37,517	9,066	137,866	12,650	467,953
Wyoming.........	128,658	6,542	433	135,643	30,121	16,876	. . .	9,680	. . .	921,320
Dist. of Col.	. . .	. . .	11,853	11,853	19,992	12,041	10,000	. . .	3,100	56,986

Source: Federal Highway Administration, U.S. Department of Transportation. Compiled for calendar year ending Dec. 31, 1980, from reports of state authorities.

(a) Toll receipts allocated for non-highway purposes are excluded.
(b) Par value of bonds issued and redeemed by refunding is excluded.

Table 4
APPORTIONMENT OF FEDERAL-AID HIGHWAY FUNDS: FISCAL 1982
(In thousands of dollars)

State or other jurisdiction	Consolidated primary(a)	Rural secondary (a)	Urban system (a)	Interstate (b)	Interstate resurfacing (b)	Forest highway funds(c)	Highway safety funds(a,d)	Other program funds(a,e)	Total (f)
Total	$1,337,650	$390,040	$780,080	$3,519,979	$268,153	$32,010	$488,964	$761,258	$7,578,134
Alabama	24,823	8,275	10,057	71,465	4,800	92	9,028	10,932	139,472
Alaska	49,436	21,330	3,900	17,064	...	2,790	4,393	4,537	103,450
Arizona	20,091	6,200	10,084	55,015	6,617	1,802	5,828	2,892	108,529
Arkansas	19,040	7,102	4,765	18,122	3,564	435	6,493	12,393	71,914
California	91,805	14,822	98,858	299,546	23,620	4,584	37,601	24,065	594,901
Colorado	21,592	6,761	10,456	53,343	5,791	2,299	6,787	4,474	111,503
Connecticut	12,303	2,511	11,200	92,181	3,313	...	4,545	7,088	129,141
Delaware	6,688	1,950	3,900	17,064	178	...	2,096	2,101	33,977
Florida	41,616	8,667	37,201	164,499	7,433	186	16,855	26,424	302,885
Georgia	32,674	10,480	14,849	135,593	7,668	113	12,355	19,765	233,497
Hawaii	6,688	1,950	3,900	69,110	348	...	1,985	2,894	86,875
Idaho	12,307	4,860	3,900	17,064	3,311	3,259	3,941	4,892	53,534
Illinois	51,407	11,575	42,559	41,261	10,491	37	23,274	57,740	238,344
Indiana	30,172	9,217	15,508	50,271	7,046	21	13,387	7,858	133,480
Iowa	24,379	8,838	7,098	44,367	4,372	...	10,244	17,606	116,904
Kansas	22,543	8,154	6,636	31,194	3,762	...	10,278	19,467	102,034
Kentucky	22,358	8,177	7,937	63,957	4,728	66	7,839	29,538	145,600
Louisiana	22,642	6,658	12,649	113,614	3,983	74	8,738	41,785	210,147
Maine	9,215	3,492	3,900	17,064	1,459	12	2,648	5,410	43,200
Maryland	17,327	3,643	15,353	175,284	3,560	...	6,357	13,808	235,332
Massachusetts	21,527	3,839	21,763	86,004	3,757	...	8,431	15,991	161,312
Michigan	44,919	12,104	29,412	85,594	8,989	343	17,889	12,546	211,796
Minnesota	29,892	10,044	11,801	67,438	5,353	443	11,525	24,535	161,031
Mississippi	19,446	7,225	4,977	25,289	3,926	151	6,458	6,105	73,577
Missouri	32,927	10,651	14,614	61,670	8,044	164	11,927	11,395	151,392
Montana	17,732	7,314	3,900	26,532	5,375	2,552	4,161	4,319	71,905
Nebraska	17,304	6,463	4,296	17,064	3,044	30	6,642	12,237	67,080
Nevada	12,404	4,647	3,900	30,682	2,785	574	2,534	2,442	59,968
New Hampshire	6,688	1,950	3,900	17,064	1,136	171	2,267	7,553	40,729
New Jersey	25,466	3,458	29,975	95,492	3,157	...	10,860	13,450	181,858
New Mexico	16,622	6,215	4,103	50,476	5,729	1,283	3,620	3,885	91,933
New York	67,680	12,294	67,539	152,589	6,612	...	26,338	58,896	391,948
North Carolina	35,022	12,211	12,094	65,527	5,074	197	11,950	17,927	160,002
North Dakota	12,167	4,956	3,900	17,064	2,969	...	5,558	5,257	51,871
Ohio	49,074	12,327	35,636	75,902	11,150	18	20,376	18,507	222,990
Oklahoma	23,055	7,854	8,685	20,341	4,321	22	8,921	5,579	78,778
Oregon	19,999	6,755	7,759	43,138	4,773	4,410	7,330	7,841	102,005
Pennsylvania	55,950	15,078	36,630	188,287	7,993	85	20,494	42,670	367,187
Rhode Island	6,688	1,950	3,900	43,173	798	...	2,043	4,547	63,099
South Carolina	18,338	6,184	7,155	45,425	4,395	105	7,247	11,964	100,813
South Dakota	12,761	5,253	3,900	17,064	3,297	251	4,284	3,920	50,730
Tennessee	27,814	9,035	12,197	76,209	7,484	107	9,595	24,345	166,786
Texas	85,155	24,316	50,409	164,158	22,106	101	30,936	32,968	410,149
Utah	12,730	4,160	5,487	54,879	4,528	1,063	3,702	2,451	89,000
Vermont	6,688	1,950	3,900	17,064	1,689	57	2,240	8,020	41,608
Virginia	29,280	8,750	15,813	124,330	6,835	208	9,565	27,876	222,657
Washington	23,040	6,612	13,512	130,951	5,775	2,225	9,007	20,746	211,868
West Virginia	13,408	5,145	3,900	71,875	2,328	126	4,431	10,929	112,142
Wisconsin	28,964	9,296	13,141	27,712	3,993	179	11,446	17,769	112,500
Wyoming	11,539	4,719	3,900	28,668	4,516	1,366	2,583	2,466	59,757
Dist. of Col.	1,775	...	3,900	45,220	178	...	1,771	7,569	60,413
American Samoa	...	...	...	...	...	...	1,011	...	1,011
Guam	...	...	...	...	...	...	1,011	...	1,011
No. Mariana Is.	...	...	...	...	...	...	1,011	...	1,011
Puerto Rico	11,490	2,623	9,372	...	...	9	4,113	2,880	30,487
Virgin Islands	...	...	...	...	...	...	1,011	...	1,011

Source: Federal Highway Administration, U.S. Department of Transportation.

(a) Apportioned Oct. 1, 1981.

(b) Apportioned Oct. 1, 1980. Interstate funds are made available one year earlier than other federal-aid funds.

(c) Apportioned Oct. 1, 1980. These funds are limited to those forest highways which are on a federal-aid system as provided in Section 141 of the 1970 Federal-Aid Highway Act.

(d) Includes funds for road hazard elimination, for elimination of hazards at railway crossings, and highway safety programs. Also includes $97 million administered by the National Highway Traffic Safety Administration, including $2.5 million for school bus driver training and $20 million for enforcement of the national maximum speed limit and $9.8 million administered by the Federal Highway Administration.

(e) Includes funds for metropolitan planning, economic growth centers and bridge replacement and rehabilitation.

(f) Amounts in this column are paid from the Highway Trust Fund, but they do not include funds for the following programs: urban high density, discretionary priority primary, emergency relief, discretionary bridges, public lands, bridges over dams, great river road and other special programs authorized under the 1978 Surface Transportation Assistance Act.

Table 5
MOTOR VEHICLE LAWS(a)
(As of June 1981)

State or other jurisdiction	Age for driver's license		Driver's license renewal (in years)	Financial responsi- bility law(b)	No-fault insurance law	Safety inspection	Transfer of plates to another owner
	Regular	Restrictive					
Alabama	16	14(c)	4	★	...	(d)	★
Alaska	18	16(e)	5	★	...	Spot	★
Arizona	18	16(e)	3	★	...	(f)	★
Arkansas	18	14(e)	2 or 4	★	★	★	...
California	18	16(g)	4	★(h)	...	...	★
Colorado	21	18, 16(i)	4	★	★(j)	★	...
Connecticut	18	16(g)	2 or 4	★	★(j)	Spot	★
Delaware	18	16(g)	4	★	★(j)	★	★
Florida	18	15(e)	4	★	★(j)	★	...
Georgia	18	16(e)	4	★(h)	★(j)	★	★
Hawaii	18	15(e)	2 or 4(k)	★	★(j)	★	★
Idaho	16	14(g)	3	★	...	...	...
Illinois	18	16(e,g)	3	★	...	Trucks, buses only	...
Indiana	16½	16 + 1 mo.(g)	4	★	...	...	...
Iowa	18	16(g)	2 or 4(l)	★	...	Spot(m)	...
Kansas	16	14	4	...	★(j)	★(m)	...
Kentucky	18	16(e)	4	★	★(j)	...	★
Louisiana	17	15	4	★	...	★	★
Maine	17	15(g)	2 or 4(n)	★	...	★	...
Maryland	18	16(e,g)	4	★(h)	★(j)	★(m)	...
Massachusetts	18	16½(e,g)	4	★(h)	★(j)	★	...
Michigan	18	16(g)	2 or 4	...	★(j)	Spot	...
Minnesota	18	16(g)	4	...	★	Spot(d)	★
Mississippi	15	...	2	★	...	★	★
Missouri	16	15(g)	3	★	...	★	...
Montana	18	15(e,g)	4	★	...	...	...
Nebraska	16	14	4	★	...	★	...
Nevada	18	16(e)	4	★	...	...	...
New Hampshire	18	16(g)	4	★	...	★	...
New Jersey	17	16	3	★	★(j)	★	...
New Mexico	16	15(e,g)	4	★(o)	...	...	...
New York	18	17(e,g)	4	★(h,o)	★(j)	★	...
North Carolina	18	16(e,g)	4	★	...	★	...
North Dakota	16	14(e,g)	4	★	★(j)	Spot	★
Ohio	18	14(g)	4	★	...	Spot	...
Oklahoma	16	15½(g)	2	★	...	★	★
Oregon	16	14	4	★	★(j)	Spot	★
Pennsylvania	18	16(e,g)	4	...	★(j)	★	...
Rhode Island	18	16(g)	2	★	...	★	...
South Carolina	16	15	4	★(h)	★(j)	★	★
South Dakota	16	14	4	★	★	...	★
Tennessee	16	15	2	★	...	Spot(d)	...
Texas	18	16(g)	4	★(o)	...	★	★
Utah	16	...	4	★	★(j)	★	...
Vermont	18	15	2	★	...	★	...
Virginia	18	16(e,g)	4	★	★	★	...
Washington	18	16(g)	4	★	...	Spot	★
West Virginia	18	16	4	★(h)	...	★	...
Wisconsin	18	16(g)	2	★	...	Spot	...
Wyoming	18	16(e)	4	★	...	...	...
Dist. of Col.	18	16(e)	4	★	...	★	...
American Samoa	18	16(e,g)	2 or 3	★	...	★	★
Guam	18	16(e)	3	★	...	★	...
Puerto Rico	18	16(e)	4	★	...	★	★
Virgin Islands	18	...	3	★(h)	...	★	...

Source: American Automobile Association, *Digest of Motor Laws, 1981/1982.*

(a) All jurisdictions except Guam have laws providing for chemical test for intoxication. All except District of Columbia have implied consent provision; in Maryland, express consent for residents, implied consent for non-residents.

(b) Security and/or future proof requirements.

(c) Restricted to motor-driven cycle, 5 h.p., 200 lb. maximum.

(d) Not required, but cities have authority to maintain inspection stations. State troopers at their discretion.

(e) Must have written consent of parent or guardian.

(f) Emission inspection required in Maricopa and Pima counties.

(g) Must have completed an approved driver education and training course.

(h) Compulsory.

(i) 18-provisional; 16-minor.

(j) Insurance is compulsory whether no-fault or not.

(k) Two-year license issued to persons 15-24 and over 65; four-year license for persons 25-64.

(l) Two-year license issued to persons under 18 and over 70; all others four years.

(m) Iowa: required prior to first registration and on all transfers. Kansas: required upon resale, accident and new title vehicle. Maryland: used passenger cars, trucks, camping and travel trailers and tractors, upon resale or transfer.

(n) Two-year license issued to persons over 65.

(o) Mandatory uninsured motorist coverage.

Table 6
URBAN MASS TRANSPORTATION ADMINISTRATION: DISTRIBUTION OF FUNDS
(Specified fiscal years)

State or other jurisdiction	Capital improvement: Section 3		Capital and operating assistance: Section 5		Interstate transfer:	Urban systems:	Total	Technical studies: Section 8	
	Fiscal 1965-79	Fiscal 1980	Fiscal 1965-79	Fiscal 1980	Fiscal 1965-80	Fiscal 1965-80		Fiscal 1980	Fiscal 1981
Alabama	$ 6,023,568	$ 1,080,880	$ 5,340,722	$ 5,301,822			$ 17,746,992	$ 330,600	$ 324,800
Alaska	4,139,654	2,862,052	205,824	205,824		$ 500,000	7,913,354	80,000	
Arizona	23,872,493	6,980,044	4,133,413	7,663,775	$ 1,133,883		43,783,608	450,000	418,000
Arkansas	3,399,313		250,296	318,696			3,968,305	198,000	171,000
California	952,934,016	145,104,933	43,022,922	51,000,554		14,764,928	1,206,827,353	8,137,000	6,022,470
Colorado	94,495,357	19,115,600	22,308,957	9,551,416	18,419,993		163,891,323	727,640	683,600
Connecticut	181,889,557	22,888,952	3,652,089	2,022,772	5,907,568		216,360,938	506,290	1,090,104
Delaware	6,440,275			927,756			7,368,031	96,000	70,000
Florida	322,789,981	185,517,363	16,010,713	16,288,324			540,606,381	1,635,511	1,285,246
Georgia	889,325,041	30,800,000	4,879,494	4,090,785			929,095,320	1,440,072	1,363,220
Hawaii	37,034,270	3,000,000					40,034,270	244,500	150,000
Idaho	1,108,648	531,020	704,260	180,980			2,524,908	25,000	26,700
Illinois	972,120,692	125,299,948	14,858,944	18,318,048	53,049,486	8,880,651	1,192,527,769	2,531,640	2,059,600
Indiana	26,495,398	18,129,160	11,031,784	7,268,044			62,924,386	829,124	662,700
Iowa	16,340,613	4,638,372	5,527,999	2,539,319		120,000	29,166,303	288,592	209,668
Kansas	2,548,071	1,008,000	4,122,340	1,832,528			9,510,939	138,800	116,900
Kentucky	38,448,581	1,080,880	2,399,756	3,212,895			45,142,112	313,500	328,300
Louisiana	55,781,196	6,146,276	4,880,805	3,941,664			70,749,941	957,000	760,000
Maine	3,300,746	923,420	1,234,760	120,000			5,578,926	95,000	96,200
Maryland	603,282,457	67,883,376	4,651,175	4,429,820			680,248,828	701,700	707,060
Massachusetts	595,855,747	87,389,540	12,984,428	9,633,440	861,913,441		1,567,776,596	1,479,264	1,439,197
Michigan	145,852,594	18,483,912	22,752,909	20,379,115			207,468,530	2,418,824	1,752,332
Minnesota	103,382,649	7,023,916	3,845,064	5,395,600		3,296,639	122,943,868	399,660	878,884
Mississippi	2,826,544		163,968	1,844,849			4,835,361	83,500	104,500
Missouri	18,017,366	13,813,628	1,126,484	12,256,260			45,213,738	1,406,016	1,457,100
Montana	1,652,020	500,000	1,432,568				3,584,588	60,788	63,380
Nebraska	19,459,754	1,240,000	361,888	3,804,184			24,865,826	179,700	173,432
Nevada			779,088	3,545,860			4,324,948	88,000	110,000
New Hampshire	2,746,112						2,746,112	96,400	105,600
New Jersey	405,198,045	123,636,348	10,693,172	12,038,428	30,000,002	1,310,701	582,876,696	647,520	657,072
New Mexico	6,187,742		544,196				6,731,938	84,000	194,000
New York	1,984,640,099	397,261,760	49,637,690	46,636,148	51,194,956	147,193,480	2,676,564,133	8,389,912	5,841,820
North Carolina	19,554,010	1,080,880	3,380,669	3,361,768			27,377,327	382,363	435,860
North Dakota	1,727,788	1,200,000	618,564	1,170,000		30,800	4,747,152	41,000	40,000
Ohio	288,571,170	58,326,408	18,105,803	29,554,496		1,249,000	395,806,877	3,519,162	2,298,940

476

State								
Oklahoma	5,799,733	1,578,361	3,843,960	4,546,060	...	...	15,768,114	212,000	226,000
Oregon	57,797,638	11,600,652	3,176,964	1,939,552	10,691,657	2,524,780	87,731,243	787,500	411,500
Pennsylvania	670,405,714	172,799,532	21,064,860	20,500,448	285,942,228	8,651,405	1,179,364,187	3,808,156	2,839,476
Rhode Island	8,082,745	87,040	3,117,044	4,000,000	...	...	15,286,829	180,000	172,994
South Carolina	322,120	...	...	...	...	...	322,120	89,200	90,600
South Dakota	...	2,044,400	...	1,518,560	...	...	3,562,960	33,332	36,396
Tennessee	35,639,237	6,336,560	2,488,156	4,621,939	...	...	49,085,892	469,500	500,500
Texas	140,910,116	10,617,563	39,142,387	63,436,875	...	1,093,400	255,200,341	3,251,408	2,787,800
Utah	25,626,018	14,940,000	...	2,544,288	...	...	43,110,306	351,456	289,200
Vermont	3,313,390	3,500,000	...	...	...	...	6,813,390	55,000	50,800
Virginia	34,053,930	1,600,000	8,464,326	5,186,380	...	...	49,304,636	656,268	509,904
Washington	140,125,603	27,529,732	12,399,256	6,050,560	...	3,000,000	189,105,151	1,091,962	886,963
West Virginia	77,243,181	3,256,464	842,950	1,061,960	...	...	82,404,555	166,000	106,000
Wisconsin	77,804,724	7,392,772	5,934,435	6,165,389	...	...	97,297,320	1,118,374	1,470,244
Wyoming	...	...	...	...	...	...	...	...	...
Dist. of Col.	8,637,250	7,516,000	...	13,786,534	...	...	29,939,784	2,186,422	1,292,890
Puerto Rico	29,437,901	...	6,835,320	6,961,820	...	364,000	43,599,041	160,240	220,000
Virgin Islands	115,000	1,330,000	...	...	...	...	1,445,000	50,000	100,000

Source: Urban Mass Transportation Administration, U.S. Department of Transportation. Information refers to sections in the Urban Mass Transportation Act of 1964, as amended:

Section 3—*Capital Improvement Grants* are made to public agencies and provide 80 percent of the cost of new system equipment, property acquisition, construction and modernization of transit facilities.

Section 5—*Operating Assistance Grants* are made to public agencies and cover up to 50 percent of the operating deficits involved in providing transit service and 80 percent of the cost for annual routine bus and related equipment replacements.

Section 8 (formerly Section 9)—*Technical Studies Grants* are made to public agencies and provide 80 percent of the cost of transportation planning, engineering surveys, and designing and evaluation of urban transportation projects.

. . . Represents zero. Grants may cover more than one year's program activities; therefore, some states may not have funds in specific grant categories.

Table 7
STATE NO-FAULT MOTOR VEHICLE INSURANCE LAWS

State	Purchase of first-party benefits	Minimum tort liability threshold(a)	Maximum first-party (no-fault) benefits			
			Medical	Income loss	Replacement services	Survivors/funeral benefits
Arkansas	O	None	$5,000 if incurred within 2 yrs.	70% of lost income up to $140/wk. beginning 8 days after accident, for up to 52 wks.	Up to $70/wk. beginning 8 days after accident, for up to 52 wks.	$5,000
Colorado	M	$500	$25,000 if incurred within 3 yrs. (additional $25,000 for rehabilitation)	Up to $125/wk. for up to 52 wks.	Up to $15/day for up to 52 wks.	$1,000
Connecticut	M	$400	Limited only by total benefits limit	85% of actual loss for income loss & replacement services up to $200/wk.		85% of actual loss for income & replacement services up to $200/wk. Funeral benefit: $2,000.
			————— $5,000 overall max. on first-party benefits —————			
Delaware	M	None; but amt. of no-fault benefits received cannot be used as evidence in suits for general damages	Limited only by total benefit limit, but must be incurred within 2 yrs.	$100 of loss; no weekly max.	Limited only by total benefits limit	Funeral benefit: $2,000
			——— $10,000 per person, $20,000 per accident overall max. on first-party benefits ———			
Florida	M	No dollar threshold(b)	80% of all costs	60% of loss; no weekly max.	Limited only by total benefits limit	Funeral benefit: $1,000
			————— $10,000 overall max. on first-party benefits —————			
Georgia	M	$500	$2,500	85% of lost income up to $200/wk.	$20/day	Max. wage loss & replacement services amounts. Funeral benefit: $1,000
			————— $5,000 overall max. on first-party benefits —————			
Hawaii	M	Floating threshold set annually by insurance commissioner	Limited only by total benefits limit(c)	Up to $800/month for income loss and replacement services(c)		Up to $800/mo. for income loss & replacement services. Funeral benefit: $1,500
			————— $15,000 overall max. on first-party benefits —————			
Kansas	M	$500	$2,000 (additional $2,000 for rehab.)	85% of lost income up to $650 a month for 1 yr.	$12/day for 1 yr.	Up to $650/mo. for lost income & $12/day for replacement services, less disability payments received, for up to 1 yr. Funeral benefit: $1,000
Kentucky	(d)	$1,000	Limited only by total benefits limit	85% of lost income (more if tax advantage is less than 15%) up to $200/wk.	Up to $200/wk.	Up to $200/wk. each for survivors' economic loss & survivors' replacement services loss. Funeral benefit: $1,000.
			————— $10,000 overall max. on first-party benefits —————			
Maryland	M	None	Limited only by total benefits limit, but must be incurred within 3 yrs.	100% of loss; no weekly max.	Limited only by total benefits limit; only for services usually performed by nonincome-earners	Funeral benefit: limited only by total benefits limit
			— $2,500 overall max. on first-party benefits for expenses incurred within 3 yrs of accident —			
Massachusetts(e)	M	$500	Limited only by total benefits limit, if incurred within 2 yrs.	Up to 75% of actual loss	Limited only by total benefits limit; payments made to nonfamily members	Funeral benefit: limited only by total benefits limit
			————— $2,000 overall max. on first-party benefits —————			
Michigan(e)	M	No dollar threshold(f)	Unlimited	85% of lost income up to $1,475/30-day period for up to 3 yrs.; max. amt. adjusted annually for cost of living	$20/day for 3 yrs.	Up to $1,000/30-day period for lost income & $20/day for replacement services, for up to 3 yrs. Funeral benefit: $1,000.

Source: National Conference of State Legislatures. Updated by State Farm Insurance Companies.

Key: O—Optional; M—Mandatory.

(a) Refers to minimum amount of medical expenses necessary before victim can sue for general damages ("pain and suffering"). Lawsuits allowed in all states for injuries resulting in death and permanent disability.

Some states allow lawsuits for one or more of the following: serious and permanent disfigurement, certain temporary disabilities, loss of body member, loss of certain bodily functions, certain fractures, or economic losses (other than medical) which exceed stated limits.

(b) Victim cannot sue for general damages unless injury results in significant and permanent loss of important body function, permanent injury, signficant and permanent scarring or disfigurement, or death.

478

State	Purchase of first-party benefits	Minimum tort liability threshold(a)	Maximum first-party (no-fault) benefits			
			Medical	Income loss	Replacement services	Survivors/funeral benefits
Minnesota	M	$4,000	$20,000	85% of lost income up to $200/wk.	$15/day, beginning 8 days after accident	Up to $200/wk. ea. for income loss & replacement services. Funeral benefit: $1,250.
			————— $10,000 max. for first-party benefits other than medical —————			
New Jersey	M	$200	Unlimited	100% of lost income up to $100/wk. for 1 yr.	Up to $12/day to a max. of $4,380/person	100% of lost income up to $100/wk. & $12/day for replacement services. Up to difference between aggregate amt. payable & amt. received by victim. Funeral benefit: $1,000.
New York	M	No dollar threshold(g)	Limited only by total benefits limit	80% of lost income up to $1,000/mo. for 3 yrs.	$25/day for 1 yr.	$2,000 in addition to other benefits
			————— $50,000 overall max. on first-party benefits —————			
North Dakota	M	$1,000	Limited only by total benefits limit	85% of lost income up to $150/wk.	$15/day	85% of lost income up to $150/wk. & $15/day for replacement services. Funeral benefit: $1,000.
			————— $15,000 overall max. on first-party benefits —————			
Oregon	M	None	$5,000, if incurred within 1 yr.	70% of lost income up to $750/mo. for up to 52 wks., only if victim is disabled at least 14 days	Up to $18/day for up to 52 wks., only if victim is disabled at least 14 days	Funeral benefit: $1,000
Pennsylvania	M	$750	Unlimited	Up to $15,000(h)	Up to $25/day for 1 yr.	Income loss & replacement services benefits up to $5,000. Funeral benefit: $1,500.
South Carolina ...	O	None	Limited only by total benefits limit if incurred within 3 yrs.	100% of lost income. No weekly limit	Limited only by total benefits limit	Funeral benefit: limited only by total benefits limit
			————— $1,000 overall max. on first-party benefits —————			
South Dakota	O	None	$2,000 if incurred within 2 yrs.	$60/wk. for up to 52 wks., only if victim is disabled at least 14 days	$30/wk. for up to 52 wks., only if victim is disabled at least 14 days. Benefits to non-wage-earning named insureds only	$10,000 death benefit if death occurs within 90 days of accident
Texas	O	None	Limited only by total benefits limit if incurred within 3 yrs.	100% of lost income; no weekly limit	Limited only by total benefits limit. Payable only to nonwage-earners.	Limited only by total benefits limit
			————— $2,500 overall max. on first-party benefits —————			
Utah	M	$500	$2,000	85% of lost income up to $150/wk. for up to 52 wks. 3-day waiting period which does not apply if disability lasts longer than 14 days	$12/day for up to 365 days. 3-day waiting period which does not apply if disability lasts longer than 14 days	$2,000 death benefit. Funeral benefit: $1,000
Virginia	O	None	$2,000 if incurred within 1 yr.	100% of lost income up to $100/wk. for up to 52 wks.	None	Funeral benefit; included in medical benefit

(c) Income loss not payable to public assistance recipients receiving free insurance.

(d) Accident victim is not bound by tort restriction if (1) he has rejected the tort limitation in writing or (2) he is injured by a driver who has rejected the tort limitation in writing. Rejection bars recovery of first-party benefits.

(e) Liability for property damage for all states with no-fault insurance is under the state tort system. Michigan and Massachusetts have no tort liability for vehicle damage.

(f) Victim cannot sue for general damages unless injuries result in death, serious impairment of bodily function, or serious permanent disfigurement.

(g) Victim cannot recover general damages unless injury results in inability to perform usual daily activities for at least 90 days during the 180 days following the accident; dismemberment; significant disfigurement; fracture; permanent loss of use of a body organ, member, function, or system; permanent consequential limitation of use of a body organ or member; significant limitation of use of a body function or system; or death.

(h) Maximum monthly income loss benefit of $1,000 times the relationship of the average Pennsylvania per capita income to the average U.S. per capita income; or 100% of income loss if income is disclosed prior to accident.

Table 8
STATE MOTOR VEHICLE REGISTRATIONS: 1980

State or other jurisdiction	Automobiles(a)	Motorcycles(a)	Buses(a,b)	Trucks(a)	Comparison of total motor vehicle registrations 1979	1980	Percentage change
United States	121,723,650	5,724,602	528,801	33,637,241	157,291,431	161,614,294	2.7
Alabama	2,105,546	75,990	8,716	823,846	2,915,141	3,014,098	3.4
Alaska(c)	156,000	8,000	1,457	97,543	258,970	263,000	1.6
Arizona	1,372,742	89,129	3,879	540,132	1,845,247	2,005,882	8.7
Arkansas	1,036,456	34,153	5,536	531,726	1,544,287	1,607,871	4.1
California	13,268,006	745,691	24,277	3,580,834	16,990,478	17,618,808	3.7
Colorado	1,739,718	112,890	5,709	596,866	2,472,349	2,455,183	-0.7
Connecticut	1,984,064	72,864	8,293	155,138 (d)	2,280,165	2,220,359	-2.6
Delaware	321,644	11,305	1,577	73,906	404,608	408,432	0.9
Florida	6,196,637	219,485	29,260	1,387,642	7,519,427	7,833,024	4.2
Georgia	2,932,464	109,033	12,554	873,420	3,851,267	3,927,471	2.0
Hawaii	514,509	6,880	3,232	52,061	566,980	576,682	1.7
Idaho	513,256	56,444	2,805	318,007	833,083	890,512	6.9
Illinois	6,240,460	304,255	23,484	1,212,888	7,564,912	7,781,087	2.9
Indiana	2,872,006	180,782	17,308	936,538	3,955,890	4,006,634	1.3
Iowa	1,678,976	219,466	8,038	642,451	2,555,582	2,548,931	-0.3
Kansas	1,387,847	103,790	3,915	615,106	2,074,197	2,110,658	1.8
Kentucky	1,807,358	63,574	8,078	777,278	2,667,629	2,656,288	-0.4
Louisiana	1,968,041	78,531	19,788	791,628	2,754,862	2,857,988	3.7
Maine	518,079	47,721	2,556	202,977	756,596	771,333	1.9
Maryland	2,345,047	81,864	10,042	447,807	2,844,490	2,884,760	1.4
Massachusetts	3,289,836	100,615	11,618	447,789	3,822,193	3,849,858	0.7
Michigan	5,246,057	255,040	18,871	1,223,142	6,592,051	6,743,110	2.3
Minnesota	2,314,444	169,734	17,093	759,589	3,183,376	3,260,860	2.4
Mississippi	1,219,147	28,459	8,552	349,075	1,509,914	1,605,233	6.3
Missouri	2,432,407	105,846	9,889	828,990	3,343,064	3,377,132	1.0
Montana	419,700	34,636	2,075	257,757	695,565	714,168	2.7
Nebraska	835,644	83,743	3,522	414,929	1,284,613	1,337,838	4.1
Nevada	471,593	19,896	1,526	181,548	659,089	674,563	2.3
New Hampshire	593,996	42,347	1,412	108,859 (d)	689,273	746,614	8.3
New Jersey	4,256,753	106,082	12,929	491,675 (d)	4,816,808	3,867,439	1.1
New Mexico	686,626	50,727	3,714	377,395	1,077,800	1,118,462	3.8
New York	6,994,316	196,247	32,806	974,424 (d)	8,171,915	8,197,793	0.3
North Carolina	3,395,784	115,185	26,398	1,109,666	4,550,316	4,647,033	2.1
North Dakota	364,909	29,672	1,911	260,112	644,658	656,604	1.9
Ohio	6,415,046	276,080	27,114	1,329,076	7,957,131	8,047,316	1.1
Oklahoma	1,807,643	129,745	10,474	864,882	2,717,802	2,812,744	3.5
Oregon	1,538,556	91,191	8,503	533,548	2,089,190	2,171,798	4.0
Pennsylvania	5,821,025	213,923	26,773	1,078,057 (d)	6,974,241	7,139,778	2.4
Rhode Island	542,462	24,951	1,617	78,849 (d)	608,427	647,879	6.5
South Carolina	1,533,081	38,994	11,024	451,888	2,011,792	2,034,987	1.2
South Dakota	369,549	35,122	3,002	228,690	629,262	636,363	1.1
Tennessee	2,564,551	84,248	10,374	696,420	3,080,556	3,355,593	8.9
Texas	7,484,817	316,318	31,531	2,958,468	10,292,456	10,791,134	4.8
Utah	678,027	63,322	1,152	313,316	1,045,975	1,055,817	0.9
Vermont	270,287	24,455	1,264	75,772	369,990	371,778	0.5
Virginia	3,071,878	85,439	13,274	541,128	3,589,654	3,711,719	3.4
Washington	2,293,521	140,661	9,912	921,829	3,262,552	3,365,923	3.2
West Virginia	928,962	39,518	3,640	387,313	1,301,631	1,359,433	4.4
Wisconsin	2,399,134	175,267	11,034	530,743	2,934,563	3,116,178	6.2
Wyoming	277,906	21,282	2,494	186,889	477,012	488,571	2.4
Dist. of Col.	247,137 (e)	4,010	2,799	17,629	253,202	271,575	7.3

Source: Federal Highway Administration, U.S. Department of Transportation. Compiled for the calendar year ending Dec. 31, 1980, from reports of state authorities. Where the registration year is not more than one month removed from the calendar year, registration-year data are given. Where the registration year is more than one month removed, registrations are given for the calendar year.

(a) Includes federal, state, county and municipal vehicles. Vehicles owned by the military services are not included.

(b) The numbers of private and commercial buses included in the figures are estimates by the Federal Highway Administration of the numbers in operation, rather than the registration counts of the states.

(c) The state was unable to provide motor vehicle registration data for 1980. The figures shown here are estimates by the Federal Highway Administration.

(d) The following farm trucks, registered at a nominal fee and restricted to use in the vicinity of the owner's farm, are not included in this table: Connecticut—4,995; New Hampshire—5,346; New Jersey—6,681; New York—15,884; Pennsylvania—2,476; and Rhode Island—1,425.

(e) Includes 3,633 automobiles of the diplomatic corps.

Table 9
MOTOR VEHICLE OPERATORS AND CHAUFFEURS LICENSES: 1980

State or other jurisdiction	Operators licenses			Chauffeurs licenses			Estimated total licenses in force during 1980 (in thousands)
	Years for which issued	Renewal date	Amount of fees	Years for which issued	Renewal date	Amount of fees	
Alabama	4	Issuance	$15.00	...	...	...	2,271
Alaska	5	Birthday	5.00	...	...	...	221
Arizona	3	Birthday	5.00	3	Birthday	$ 7.50	1,933
Arkansas	2 or 4(a)	Birth month	6.00 or 12.00	2 or 4(a)	Birth month	11.00 or 21.00	1,469
California	4	Birthday	3.25	...	...	...	15,669
Colorado	4	Birthday	5.50	...	...	...	2,048
Connecticut	2 or 4	Birth month	21.00(b)	1	April 30	5.00(b)	2,174
Delaware	4	Birthday	10.00	...	...	...	417
Florida	4	Birthday	6.50(b)	4	Birthday	10.50(b)	7,268
Georgia	4	Birthday	4.50	...	...	...	3,424
Hawaii	2 or 4(c)	Birthday	5.50 or 8.50(c)	...	...	...	542
Idaho	3	Birthday	7.00	3	Birthday	9.00	631
Illinois	3	Birthday	8.00(d)	...	...	...	7,003
Indiana	4	Birth month	6.00(d)	2	Birth month	4.00	3,631
Iowa	2 or 4(e)	Birthday	5.00 or 10.00	2 or 4(e)	Birthday	10.00 or 20.00	2,107
Kansas	4	Birthday	6.50(b)	...	...	...	1,675
Kentucky	4	Birth month	8.00	2	Birth month	4.00	2,055
Louisiana.........	4	Birthday	7.00	4	Birthday	18.00(f)	2,259
Maine............	2 or 4	Birthday	8.00 or 16.00(d)	...	...	...	730
Maryland	4	Birthday	6.00	...	...	...	2,722
Massachusetts.....	4	Birthday	20.00(b)	...	...	...	3,640
Michigan	2 or 4	Birthday	7.50	4	Birthday	14.50	6,400
Minnesota	4	Birthday	15.50	...	...	...	2,336
Mississippi	2	Birth month	5.00	2	Birth month	9.00	1,587
Missouri..........	3	Issuance	3.00	3	Issuance	10.00	3,245
Montana	4	Birthday	8.00	4	Birthday	8.00	599
Nebraska	4	Birthday	7.00	*...	...	...	1,093
Nevada...........	4	Birthday	6.00(d)	...	...	...	626
New Hampshire	4	Birthday	12.00	...	...	...	652
New Jersey	3	Issuance	12.00	...	...	...	4,928
New Mexico	4	Birth month	8.00	1	Birth month	3.25	855
New York	4	Birthday	8.00	...	...	...	9,240
North Carolina....	4	Birthday	4.00	4	Birthday	10.00	3,777
North Dakota......	4	Birthday	8.00	...	...	...	419
Ohio.............	4	Birthday	5.00	4	Birthday	5.00	7,031
Oklahoma	2	Birth month	7.00	2	Birth month	11.00	1,965
Oregon...........	4	Birthday	9.00	4	Birthday	5.00	1,991
Pennsylvania......	4	Birth month	21.50	...	...	...	7,056
Rhode Island......	2	Birthday	8.00	...	...	...	587
South Carolina....	4	Birthday	4.00	...	...	...	1,953
South Dakota......	4	Birthday	6.00	...	...	...	481
Tennessee	2	Birthday	6.00	2	Birthday	8.00	2,810
Texas	4	Birthday	7.00	2	Birthday	13.00	9,288
Utah.............	4	Birthday	5.00(d)	4	Birthday	5.00(d)	845
Vermont	2	Birthday	8.00	...	...	...	344
Virginia	4	Birth month	9.00	2	Birth month	12.00	3,461
Washington.......	4	Birthday	14.00	...	...	...	2,663
West Virginia	4	Issuance	5.00	1	Issuance	3.00	1,506
Wisconsin	2	Birthday	4.00	1	Birthday	4.00	2,982
Wyoming	4	Birthday	2.50	...	...	...	346
Dist. of Col.	4	Issuance	12.00	...	...	...	344
American Samoa ...	2 or 3	Issuance	5.00 or 7.00	N.A.	N.A.	N.A.	N.A.
Guam.............	3	Birthday	5.00	N.A.	N.A.	N.A.	N.A.
Puerto Rico	4	Issuance	10.00	N.A.	N.A.	N.A.	N.A.
Virgin Islands	3	Birthday	9.00	N.A.	N.A.	N.A.	N.A.

Sources: Federal Highway Administration, U.S. Department of Transportation, *Drivers Licenses—1980*, and *1980 Driver License: Administration Requirements and Fees*; and American Automobile Association, *Digest of Motor Laws, 1981/1982.*

N.A.—Not available.

(a) At licensee's option.

(b) The following examination fees are in addition to the fee shown for original license: Connecticut—$6.50 for operators and $2.50 for public service (chauffeurs) license; Florida—$3; Kansas—$6; and Massachusetts—$5.

(c) Cost varies depending on place where issued. Issued for two years to persons 65 years and over and 15-24 years.

(d) Illinois—69 years and over, $4; Indiana—renewal license for 75 years and over, $3 for two years; Maine—65 years and over, $8 for two years; Nevada—over 70 years, $3 for four years; and Utah—renewal license for 63 years and over, $3.

(e) Two-year operators and chauffeurs licenses at $5 and $10 issued to persons under 18 and over 70 years old.

(f) $22 in New Orleans Parish and municipalities over 300,000 population.

Table 10
CAR POOL AND FRINGE PARKING PROJECTS
FINANCED WITH FEDERAL AID
(Authorized from January 1, 1974 to August 31, 1981)

State or other jurisdiction	Fringe parking(a)	Car pool facilities(b)	Van pool acquisition(c)	Computerized programs(d)	Total(e)
United States	$54,643,643	$20,592,321	$9,072,340	$24,673,742	$108,982,046
Alabama	...	...	...	512,477	512,477
Alaska	...	18,000	...	143,480	161,480
Arizona	...	...	...	...	...
Arkansas	...	...	230,000	...	230,000
California	9,245,720	420,955	...	6,038,908	15,705,583
Colorado	433,072	36,900	...	472,178	942,150
Connecticut	3,486,097	2,692,465	180,000	862,120	7,220,682
Delaware	418,200	17,226	...	...	435,426
Florida	240,577	1,206,000	...	383,349	1,829,926
Georgia	410,702	...	72,602	83,957	567,261
Hawaii	...	...	...	21,470	21,470
Idaho	...	175,742	...	9,318	185,060
Illinois	5,371,161	...	9,022	...	5,386,183
Indiana	...	...	...	179,958	179,958
Iowa	43,852	...	...	31,384	75,236
Kansas	...	...	...	12,231	12,231
Kentucky	13,500	629,565	...	1,424,371	2,067,436
Louisiana	396,450	...	...	301,768	698,218
Maine	...	...	54,000	14,400	68,400
Maryland	552,865	1,173,097	1,594,875	...	3,320,837
Massachusetts	322,877	549,352	...	791,070	1,663,299
Michigan	212,850	1,495,347	...	13,124	1,721,321
Minnesota	348,798	...	...	1,702,337	2,051,135
Mississippi	...	...	...	2,841	2,841
Missouri	...	...	330,551	...	330,551
Montana	...	...	...	5,697	5,697
Nebraska	...	...	...	620,990	620,990
Nevada	...	...	...	21,470	21,470
New Hampshire	...	73,251	...	142,992	216,243
New Jersey	7,073,124	862,260	31,561	582,000	8,548,945
New Mexico	...	...	576,169	41,100	617,269
New York	11,822,107	1,638,346	...	117,000	13,577,453
North Carolina	...	...	...	90,000	90,000
North Dakota	...	541,000	...	3,921	544,921
Ohio	104,004	...	37,500	404,492	545,996
Oklahoma	...	...	...	...	...
Oregon	289,646	373,589	...	975,330	1,638,565
Pennsylvania	3,130,573	373,376	192,327	1,670,572	5,366,848
Rhode Island	154,218	...	294,632	577,410	1,026,260
South Carolina	...	...	30,000	...	30,000
South Dakota	...	20,310	...	...	20,310
Tennessee	...	...	...	344,550	344,550
Texas	1,100,460	48,820	...	2,536,443	3,685,723
Utah	96,740	276,713	650,000	...	1,023,453
Vermont	...	153,438	...	269,191	422,629
Virginia	3,333,050	...	...	...	3,333,050
Washington	4,042,270	7,170,233	4,490,500	2,739,296	18,422,299
West Virginia	...	...	...	...	...
Wisconsin	1,951,433	127,646	298,600	183,729	2,561,408
Wyoming	...	...	...	...	...
Dist. of Col.	43,296	...	...	219,302	262,598

Source: Federal Highway Administration, U.S. Department of Transportation.

(a) Includes all change of mode transportation facilities involving public transportation facilities.

(b) Projects not involving public transportation modes, e.g., designation of car pool only lanes, car pool only parking, van pool demonstration, etc.

(c) Projects for acquiring or providing "abort" protection for vehicles used in a van pool project.

(d) Projects for locating and informing potential car pool riders of ride-sharing opportunities.

(e) Columns may not add to totals due to rounding.

3. Health and Human Services

STATE HEALTH AGENCY PROGRAMS

By Margo L. Rosenbach and Ronald E. Whorton

THE NATION'S PUBLIC HEALTH agencies provide services aimed at protecting and improving the health and well-being of the entire U.S. population. In addition, many public health programs are directed at people who do not receive adequate care or who are at special risk of disease. Since the establishment of the first health departments at the turn of the 19th century, public health agencies have established a unique and important role for themselves. Unlike private medicine, which provides primarily acute and long-term curative care, the public health agencies focus on preventive community health services.

The American public health system is a partnership of federal, state and local health agencies. At the state level, there is one state health agency (SHA) in every state, the District of Columbia, and the six U.S. territories. This chapter presents a brief summary of the organization, responsibilities, services, expenditures and sources of funds of the nation's 57 SHAs. It does not report public health activities of other state agencies. In addition, since Medicaid is primarily a payment program, it is treated here as public welfare rather than public health. Information is based on data collected by the Association of State and Territorial Health Officials (ASTHO) through its National Public Health Program Reporting System (NPHPRS).[1]

State Health Agency Organization and Responsibilities

Each state health agency is headed by a health commissioner or director, appointed by the governor, state legislature or a board of health. The organization of public health services in a state affects *how* services are delivered and, to an extent, *which* services are provided. While some generalizations about public health organizations are possible, there is considerable variation from state to state.

SHA organization may be characterized by two models: (1) a freestanding, independent agency responsible directly to the governor or a board of health; or (2) one component of a superagency structure. Thirty-five of the 57 SHAs follow the first model, while 22 SHAs are characterized by the second.

In addition to variation in their organizational structure, SHAs vary in their range of designated responsibilities. For example, in fiscal 1980:

- 45 SHAs were the designated state crippled children's agency (Title V, SSA).
- 15 SHAs were the designated state mental health authority (Public Law 94-63).
- 10 SHAs were the designated Medicaid single state agency (Title XIX, SSA).

Margo L. Rosenbach is Analyst, and Ronald E. Whorton is Project Director, National Public Health Program Reporting System of the Association of State and Territorial Health Officials. This chapter is based upon work performed pursuant to Contract No. 200-80-0532 with the Centers for Disease Control, the Department of Health and Human Services.

- 33 SHAs were the designated State Health Planning and Development Agency (Public Law 93-641).
- 17 SHAs acted as the lead environmental agency in their states.
- 24 SHAs operated hospitals or other health care institutions.

State Health Agency Services

Despite the differences in structure and responsibilities, there are some common features among SHAs. All, or almost all, SHAs offer services related to maternal and child health, communicable disease control (including venereal diseases, immunization, epidemiology and tuberculosis control), chronic diseases (such as cancer and hypertension), dental health, public health nursing (including home visits), nutrition, health education, consumer protection and sanitation, water quality, health statistics and diagnostic laboratory tests.

In fiscal 1980, the nation's 57 SHAs provided direct public health services to 74 million people—one in every three in the U.S. Table 2 displays the number of persons receiving direct services from SHAs. The SHAs demonstrated their strong commitment to health promotion and disease prevention during fiscal 1980 by:

- Preventing communicable diseases among preschool and school age children and influenza among the elderly and other high risk populations by immunizing over 17 million people.
- Using low-cost, quick and effective techniques to detect and prevent disease, by screening 47 million people, including 14 million for venereal diseases; 10 million for visual acuity; 8 million for hearing acuity; 6 million for dental disease; and 4 million for tuberculosis.
- Inspecting restaurants and other food-related facilities to prevent food poisoning and unsanitary conditions (1.4 million inspections in fiscal 1980).
- Preventing potential solid and hazardous waste disasters by making more than 60,000 inspections.
- Collecting vital records and health statistics to provide essential population-based information on the health and demographic characteristics of communities and states.
- Fluoridating community water supplies to prevent tooth decay.
- Preventing and responding to disease outbreaks using epidemiological methods and surveillance mechanisms.
- Training 2,200 persons to respond to environmental emergencies caused by contaminated air, water and food; pesticide poisoning; and radiation exposure.
- Analyzing nearly 44 million laboratory samples and specimens to prevent and detect disease and environmental hazards.
- Detecting and promoting control of hypertension through extensive health education campaigns and mass screening. About 7 million people were screened and over 110,000 were newly diagnosed as hypertensive. Public health agencies often provided nutrition counseling and follow-up services to those requiring treatment.

Expenditures

The nation's state health agencies spent $4.45 billion for their public health programs in fiscal 1980 (including direct SHA expenditures and intergovernmental transfers to local health departments but excluding Medicaid single-state agency expenditures). SHA expenditures ranged from $2.6 million in the Northern Mariana Islands to $369.6 million in

California. The differences in public health expenditures among the SHAs arise from a number of factors, including variation in state populations and differences in the responsibilities of these agencies. Some SHAs have responsibility only for such traditional public health services as communicable disease control, general sanitation, maternal and child health and vital statistics. In contrast, others have such additional responsibilities as the provision of mental health services and the operation of hospitals. Furthermore, the balance of responsibility for public health services between state and local governments varies greatly among the states.

Of the $4.45 billion in SHA expenditures, 71 percent ($3.18 billion) was spent for personal health programs, including $847 million for the SHA-operated institutions in 24 states. Expenditures for health resources programs were $358 million, 8 percent of the total; expenditures for environmental health programs were $299 million, 7 percent; and expenditures for laboratory programs were $161 million, 4 percent. Funds reported as general administration amounted to $253 million—6 percent of the total expenditures for public health programs. The remaining $204 million was reported as "funds to local health departments not allocated to program areas."

NPHPRS estimates that SHAs spent over $987 million for hospital and other institutional inpatient services. This amount includes $194 million of purchased inpatient care services in institutions other than those operated by the SHAs, as well as $793 million for inpatient care in SHA-operated institutions. The $987 million in purchased and direct inpatient care accounts for almost one-third of all personal health expenditures.

Sources of Funds

State health agencies are funded primarily by state, federal and local governments. Additional funding is collected from fees and reimbursements for services, and other sources such as grants from foundations. Typically, state funds include both the required match for federal grants and general revenue support of state programs. This funding provides the core of support for public health programs. Until recently, federal grants and contracts were primarily categorical, directed at specific health problems of national significance. In addition to the many federal categorical health grants and contracts, public health agencies received Health Incentive Grant funds. These grants were important to SHAs because they were not tied to any categorical programs and could be used to meet varying state and local health priorities.

Of the $4.45 billion in SHA expenditures, $2.54 billion (57 percent of the total) came from state funds. Federal grants and contracts (excluding federal direct assistance in lieu of cash) accounted for $1.6 billion (35 percent), and funds from local sources, fees, reimbursements and other sources accounted for the remaining $368 million (8 percent).

More than half ($798 million) of the federal funds were from the Department of Health and Human Services (DHHS). The following agencies within DHHS provided substantial funding for SHA public health programs: Health Services Administration, $448.2 million; Centers for Disease Control, $109.5 million; Health Care Financing Administration, $86 million; and Alcohol, Drug Abuse and Mental Health Administration, $60 million.

Of the $1.6 billion in federal grant and contract funds spent by the SHAs, 48 percent was from agencies other than DHHS, including 42 percent from the Department of Agriculture (USDA), the Environmental Protection Agency (3 percent) and the Departments of Education, Labor, and Transportation and Regional Commissions (2 percent combined).

Nearly all the USDA grants to SHAs were under the Special Supplemental Food Program for Women, Infants, and Children (WIC)—$642 million or 14 percent of total SHA expenditures. When USDA funds are excluded, the percent distribution of funding sources for SHA programs changes considerably. The federal share decreases from 35 percent to 24 percent, while state funds, fees and reimbursements, and other sources increase.

Local Health Departments

In 47 states and Puerto Rico, there are more than 3,000 local health departments (LHDs) to provide direct community health services. In the nine states and territories with no LHDs, the SHA usually is the primary provider of community services.[2] The nation's LHDs provide such preventive health services as childhood immunizations, restaurant inspections, food-borne and water-borne disease investigation, lead-based paint poisoning prevention and urban rat control.

The structures of LHDs vary—some serve rural populations of a few thousand people, while others are located in urban areas, serving millions of people. Some have only a few employees, such as a public health nurse, a sanitarian and a clerical worker. On the other end of the scale, some LHDs have multi-million dollar budgets and hundreds of employees. Most LHDs, however, lie somewhere between these extremes.

In fiscal 1980, the SHAs granted more than $1 billion to LHDs in their states. About four-fifths (82 percent) of the funds were reported as personal health expenditures, 9 percent as environmental health, 4 percent as health resources, 4 percent as LHD administration and 2 percent as laboratory. Over half (57 percent) came from state revenues, while federal grants and contracts accounted for one-third (32 percent). The remaining 12 percent came from local sources, fees and reimbursements and other sources.

In addition to receiving funds from SHAs, LHDs received funds directly from local governments, federal grants and contracts and other sources. An additional $1.4 billion was spent by LHDs from sources other than the SHA, with three-fourths of this amount from local governments. Altogether, LHDs spent an estimated $2.4 billion in fiscal 1980, including funds from the SHAs and other sources.

Medicaid

Title XIX of the Social Security Act requires the designation of a single state agency to administer the state plan for the medical assistance program (Medicaid) in each state. Ten SHAs were the Medicaid single state agencies (MSSAs) for their states in fiscal 1980; their MSSA expenditures are entirely separate from the public health expenditures discussed in this article. Together these SHAs spent $5.4 billion for their Medicaid programs, an amount that is greater than the total spent by all SHAs for all public health programs. This $5.4 billion represents about one-fifth of the $24.6 billion in total Medicaid expenditures for all states in fiscal 1980.[3]

Notes

1. ASTHO/NPHPRS, *Public Health Agencies 1980: A Report on Their Expenditures and Activities* (Washington, D.C.: August 1981).

2. The nine states and territories without LHDs were Delaware, the District of Columbia, Rhode Island, Vermont, American Samoa, Guam, the Northern Mariana Islands, the Trust Territory and the Virgin Islands.

3. Health Care Financing Administration, Personal Communication, 1981.

Figure 1
STATE HEALTH AGENCIES: 1980
Program Area Expenditures

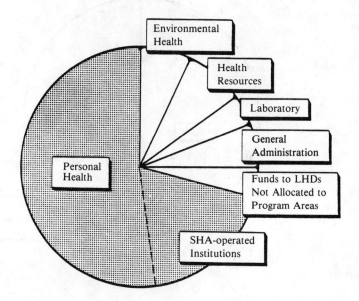

Total: $4.453 billion

Figure 2
STATE HEALTH AGENCIES: 1980
Source of Funds

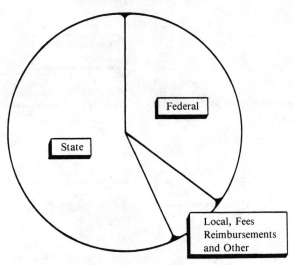

Total: $4.453 billion

Table 1
ORGANIZATIONAL CHARACTERISTICS AND RESPONSIBILITIES DELEGATED TO STATE HEALTH AGENCIES: FISCAL 1980

State or other jurisdiction	SHA organizational structure		SHA designated as:					
	Free-standing independent agency	Component of super agency	State crippled children's agency (Title V, SSA)	Mental health authority (P.L. 94-63)	Medicaid single state (Title XIX, SSA)	State health planning and development agency (P.L. 93-641)	Lead environmental agency	SHA operates institutions
Alabama	★						★	
Alaska		★	★					
Arizona	★		★	★		★	★	★
Arkansas	★							
California		★	★		★			
Colorado	★		★			★	★	
Connecticut	★		★			★		★
Delaware		★	★				★	★
Florida		★						★
Georgia		★	★					
Hawaii	★		★	★		★		★
Idaho		★	★					
Illinois	★					★		
Indiana	★					★	★	
Iowa	★					★		
Kansas	★		★			★	★	
Kentucky		★	★	★		★		★
Louisiana		★	★					
Maine		★	★		★			
Maryland	★		★	★		★	★	
Massachusetts		★	★			★		★
Michigan	★		★					★
Minnesota	★		★					
Mississippi	★		★					
Missouri		★	★					★
Montana	★		★			★	★	
Nebraska	★			★		★		
Nevada		★	★					
New Hampshire		★	★					
New Jersey	★		★			★		
New Mexico	★		★	★		★	★	★
New York	★		★			★		★
North Carolina		★	★					★
North Dakota	★			★		★	★	★
Ohio			★			★		
Oklahoma	★						★	
Oregon		★						
Pennsylvania	★					★		★
Rhode Island	★		★			★		
South Carolina	★		★			★	★	★
South Dakota	★		★			★		
Tennessee	★		★				★	
Texas	★		★			★		★
Utah	★		★		★	★	★	★
Vermont		★	★					
Virginia	★		★		★			
Washington		★	★			★		
West Virginia	★			★				★
Wisconsin		★			★	★		
Wyoming		★	★	★	★	★	★	
Dist. of Col.		★	★	★				★
American Samoa	★		★	★				★
Guam		★	★		★			
No. Mariana Is.	★		★			★	★	★
Puerto Rico	★		★	★	★	★	★	★
Virgin Islands	★		★	★	★	★		★

Source: The Association of State and Territorial Health Officials.

Table 2
PERSONS RECEIVING SELECTED PERSONAL HEALTH SERVICES
FROM STATE HEALTH AGENCIES: FISCAL 1980
(In thousands)

State or other jurisdiction	Receiving any services	Health screening	Immuniza-tion	Maternity services	Infant and child health ambulatory services	WIC nutrition services	Family planning	Genetic counseling	Dental services
United States	74,251	46,696	17,063	631	2,195	3,370	3,360	77	9,142
Alabama	1,372	487	719	16	44	95	72	...	59
Alaska	331E	160E	165	★	25E	3	7	★	1
Arizona	1,385E	960	220	16	27	79	26	★	9
Arkansas	1,220E	753E	422E	14	44	33	69	...	5
California	3,516E	1,870	1,412E	1E	30E	299C	4,306	U	112
Colorado	937E	684E	113E	9	38	49	26	4	10
Connecticut	697E	283E	320	2	17	50	2	1	4
Delaware	177E	122E	33C	1	8C	7	19	U	9C
Florida	1,977E	1,490E	334	39	238	80E	149	1E	42
Georgia	2,040	1,107	630	40	2	68	146	★	174E
Hawaii	759E	483	124E	2	14	29	18	★	65
Idaho	303E	82	89	1	7E	22	17	...	38
Illinois	6,306E	5,543	678	20	22	200	11	U	81
Indiana	556	425	21E	3	15	50	30	U	164
Iowa	420E	236E	96E	6E	11E	34E	47	2	38
Kansas	1,891E	851E	170E	4	22	33E	75E	4E	222E
Kentucky	4,779E	1,554E	147	25	5	94	87	★	2,869
Louisiana	1,690E	1,157E	296	7	20	65E	★	★E	7
Maine	192E	104	52	U	2	U	U	1	U
Maryland	446E	195	109	21E	64	79E	93E	...	35
Massachusetts.....	1,627E	491	970	...	...	38	3	U	2E
Michigan	3,088E	2,349	1,678	U	U	50	70	1	21
Minnesota	1,989E	991E	300E	19	11	52E	31E	★	24
Mississippi	1,240E	851E	190	39	88	60	147	...	135
Missouri..........	1,096	775	187	5	23	45	35	★	21
Montana	280E	243	29E	★	12	30	18	U	88
Nebraska.........	385	319	58	3	U	22	49	1	9
Nevada...........	269E	171	60	1E	5E	18E	8E	...	5
New Hampshire	207E	115	57	1E	★E	8	16	★	23
New Jersey	982E	1,325E	212	11	73	60	130	U	5
New Mexico	315E	167	67E	5	13	21E	14	★	26E
New York	1,389E	978	376	25	114	124	161	1	13E
North Carolina	2,111E	1,275E	227	26	197	136	126	7	363E
North Dakota	342E	224	78	★	★	13	11E	★	14
Ohio.............	1,646	1,072E	495	10	64	183	111	3	33
Oklahoma	966E	748E	201E	2	9E	29	72	★	2
Oregon	429E	229E	155E	...	...	36E	42	...	6
Pennsylvania......	6,967E	5,450	436	17E	118E	203	208E	U	3,222
Rhode Island......	174E	96E	41E	1	14E	14	9	1	7
South Carolina	1,252E	473	458	25	110	78	79	★	295
South Dakota	283E	249E	75	2	5	8	11	...	★
Tennessee	1,198E	783E	338E	30	46	54	152	32	201
Texas	6,666	4,345E	1,158	46	243	324	133	10	98
Utah	453E	277	146E	3	18E	20	12	★	2
Vermont	282E	135	104E	...	3	22	13	...	22
Virginia	1,532	1,016	192	1	3	94	86	U	51
Washington.......	1,151	443	500	8	51	55	96	2	99
West Virginia	923E	542E	188E	4	16	41	69E	★	79
Wisconsin	917E	417E	1,051E	★	15	115E	34	1	10
Wyoming..........	462E	392E	71E	1	6	U	1	★	3
Dist. of Col.	487E	399E	36E	U	16	...	15	...	23
American Samoa ...	82E	21E	5E	1	...	...	3E	...	7
Guam	41	14	7	1	★	...	1	...	8
No. Mariana Is.	34E	17	3	2	1	...	76	★	11
Puerto Rico	1,687E	743E	655E	111	249	45	76	...	212
TTPI	260E	11	100	4	13	...	3	...	56
Virgin Islands	51E	3	9	3	3	7	2	...	5

Source: The Association of State and Territorial Health Officials.
Key:
★—Less than 500.
E—Estimated.
C—Data combined with reporting of another service or program.
U—Data unobtainable.

Table 2—Continued
PERSONS RECEIVING SELECTED PERSONAL HEALTH SERVICES FROM STATE HEALTH AGENCIES: FISCAL 1980
(In thousands)

State or other jurisdiction	Handicapped children's ambulatory services	Communicable disease services			Chronic disease ambulatory services				
		Venereal disease	Tubercu-losis	Other	Cancer	Hyper-tension	Cardio-vascular diseases	Renal dialysis	Other
United States	423	1,806	455	89	50	332	174	22	210
Alabama	...	66	9	...	★	2	...	...	...
Alaska	7	5	1	1	U	U	...	...	...
Arizona	14	12	3	3	U	U	1	★	...
Arkansas	...	32	3	2	...	...	...	...	...
California	51	195	7	U	U	9	U	1	U
Colorado	6	18	1	...	...	3	...	...	...
Connecticut	4	19E	2	...	...	U	...	...	★
Delaware	3	6	1	...	★	★	...	★	★
Florida	...	114	14	17	4	23	15	★	14
Georgia	19	77	6	...	2	26	...	1	10
Hawaii	5	6	29	1	★	...	1	...	1
Idaho	2	4	1	...	...	...	...	...	...
Illinois	...	57	1	...	...	20	...	3E	6
Indiana	...	15E	15	...	...	6	...	★	★
Iowa	...	6	1E	U	...	...	...	★	...
Kansas	4	10	8	2	1	★	10	★	11
Kentucky	13	17	19	49	U	11	3	...	50
Louisiana.........	16	90E	12	...	U	2	U	...	★
Maine............	1	U	1	...	...	...	...	...	9
Maryland	U	8	25	...	2	★	...	3E	U
Massachusetts.....	1	42	17	U	★	★	3	3	★
Michigan	8	90E	7	...	U	27	...	...	..
Minnesota	11	35	1E	2	3	U	10	U	7
Mississippi........	5	26	12	...	1E	14	2	...	4
Missouri..........	7	49	4	...	2	5	★	...	★
Montana	1	4	5	...	1	10	1	...	4
Nebraska	...	3	1	...	...	...	...	★	...
Nevada...........	2	27	2	U	...	U	★	★	...
New Hampshire ...	3	1	★	...	U	U	★E	★	★
New Jersey	13E	38	3	...	...	U	...	1	★
New Mexico	4	18	12	...	★	...	1	...	★
New York	11E	32	5	U	11	U	...	...	...
North Carolina	31E	65	2	...	2E	19	U	...	★
North Dakota	★	3	7	...	★	...	2	★	1
Ohio	25	75	5	...	1	6	1	★	1
Oklahoma	...	46E	8E	1	2	1	1	...	U
Oregon...........	...	40	★E	...	...	U	...	...	..
Pennsylvania......	55E	21	47	5	★	57	63E	3	75
Rhode Island......	1	8	10	...	1	1	1	...	...
South Carolina	8	50	7	...	6	4	1	★	...
South Dakota	2	4	2	...	★	U	3	...	...
Tennessee	7E	118	5	...	U	U	★	1	5
Texas	21	101	99	...	...	...	...	4	...
Utah.............	5	7	5	...	3	3	2	...	2
Vermont	5	2	2	...	...	...	...	...	...
Virginia	23	27	5	U	...	...	...	...	U
Washington........	5	57E	3	...	...	...	...	★	1
West Virginia	1	4E	5	...	7	★	1	...	2
Wisconsin	...	28	8	U	U	60	U	2	★
Wyoming..........	2	4	★	...	★	...	...	★	...
Dist. of Col.	4	21E	8	...	U	U	U	...	...
American Samoa ...	U	★	...	6	...	...	...	...	...
Guam............	1	★	1	★	...	★	...	★	1E
No. Mariana Is. ...	★	★	1	★	...	★E	...	...	...
Puerto Rico........	8	★	★	...	U	22	45	...	★
TTPI	★	★	★	★	...	...	...	★	...
Virgin Islands	6	2	★	...	★	1	★	...	2

Table 2—Concluded
PERSONS RECEIVING SELECTED PERSONAL HEALTH SERVICES FROM STATE HEALTH AGENCIES: FISCAL 1980
(In thousands)

State or other jurisdiction	Mental health and related services				General ambulatory care	Home health care	Inpatient care
	Mental health	Mental retardation	Alcohol abuse	Drug abuse			
United States	249	49	221	84	1,911	243	595
Alabama	...	1	...	...	...	20	1
Alaska	★E	★E	U	U	U	1E	★
Arizona	31	1	20	5C	8	U	34
Arkansas	★	...	...	...	...	3	1E
California	1	...	...	...	U	U	14
Colorado	★	2	8	3	30	...	17
Connecticut	...	1	...	...	20	★	1
Delaware	★	...	...	...	★C	3	1
Florida	7	2	2	1	61	3	3
Georgia	★	1	★	...	70	★	19
Hawaii	11	5	5	1	2	★	103
Idaho	...	...	3	1	...	...	5
Illinois	★	★	...	...	24	...	1
Indiana	...	...	...	...	51	16	★
Iowa	...	...	...	...	...	18	1E
Kansas	17E	★E	★	★	35E	5	1
Kentucky	20	15	18	5	5	4	26
Louisiana	★E	...	U	1	U	1	1
Maine	...	★	...	...	U	...	1E
Maryland	42E	★E	U	15	...	5E	19
Massachusetts	...	★	33	...	25	★	54
Michigan	...	U	43	25	28	★	23
Minnesota	3	1	★	★	340	18	1
Mississippi	...	...	...	...	3E	5	3
Missouri	★	...	...	...	...	★	10
Montana	★	U	...	...	U	...	1
Nebraska	U	★	...	...	12	11	★
Nevada	★E	2E	U	...	★	1	3
New Hampshire	1E	★E	...	...	31	★E	★
New Jersey	U	...	7	15	...	26E	11E
New Mexico	27	2E	7	3	★	...	10E
New York	★	★	...	...	U	U	7E
North Carolina	...	3	60	...	44	18	7E
North Dakota	★	★	★	★	...	3	4
Ohio	U	U	6	U	...	...	1E
Oklahoma	★	1	★	★	★	3	★
Oregon	...	...	...	...	349	...	...
Pennsylvania	★	★	★	U	8	U	1
Rhode Island	...	1	...	...	2	15	3
South Carolina	...	★	...	...	...	...	...
South Dakota	★	...	...	★	6	2	★
Tennessee	★	1	...	...	64	19	4E
Texas	2	★	U	U	1	U	6
Utah	1	...	...	...	★	...	1
Vermont	★	U	...	...	10E	...	★
Virginia	...	4	...	...	259	11	4
Washington	...	★	...	...	...	U	1
West Virginia	2E	4	2	1	7	7	7
Wisconsin	★E	U	...	...	73	...	★
Wyoming	...	2	...	...	14	9	1
Dist. of Col.	15E	...	6	9	53	9	4E
American Samoa	★	...	★	...	16E	...	4E
Guam	...	...	...	...	1	★	★
No. Mariana Is.	★	★E	★E	★E	33	1	3
Puerto Rico	65	...	...	...	99	U	133
TTPI	★	★	★	★	109	...	20
Virgin Islands	1	1E	★	★	18	4	14

Table 3
PUBLIC HEALTH PROGRAM EXPENDITURES
OF STATE HEALTH AGENCIES, BY PROGRAM: FISCAL 1980
(In thousands)

State or or other jurisdiction	Total	Personal health	Environ- mental health	Health resources	Labora- tory	General Adminis- tration	Funds to LHDs not allocated to programs
United States.............	$4,453,378	$3,178,466	$298,936	$357,694	$161,086	$253,407	$203,789
Alabama..................	58,844	34,293	3,572	3,433	3,652	3,885	6,010
Alaska	16,041	10,960	1,531	1,144	1,592	815	...
Arizona	89,384	71,913	10,076	2,053	1,997	3,345	...
Arkansas	38,257	24,239	5,958	2,045	1,937	4,078	...
California................	369,568	150,092	16,385	25,889	13,871	29,302	134,030
Colorado	49,030	32,182	6,105	2,927	1,641	3,273	2,903
Connecticut..............	44,998	30,017	1,296	7,130	3,761	1,787	1,006
Delaware	29,145	26,683	908	433	575	546	...
Florida	129,905	82,001	24,460	8,221	5,067	10,155	...
Georgia..................	87,211	64,035	755	2,516	2,706	677	16,523
Hawaii	112,351	96,550	4,658	7,434	1,181	2,527	...
Idaho	20,195	11,179	3,359	2,028	1,932	1,697	...
Illinois..................	76,725	46,659	5,594	9,581	3,163	6,692	5,035
Indiana	42,623	21,547	15,096	2,448	3,531	...	...
Iowa	23,516	17,847	405	4,260	...	1,001	4
Kansas	25,510	13,105	5,059	4,436	1,523	1,388	...
Kentucky	144,985	121,162	2,976	5,178	2,172	5,616	7,882
Louisiana	66,902	51,813	8,338	1,754	3,117	1,879	...
Maine	20,228	15,793	1,325	2,997	...	113	...
Maryland	341,152	386,907	19,457	8,058	5,028	21,702	...
Massachusetts	126,000	107,875	2,303	5,437	4,399	5,986	...
Michigan	181,688	139,742	12,578	11,461	11,455	6,452	...
Minnesota	46,890	8,688	2,710	6,496	2,825	4,210	21,961
Mississippi	52,690	43,506	4,385	1,414	1,065	2,318	...
Missouri.................	64,203	50,776	2,045	8,221	1,657	1,157	348
Montana	17,753	9,368	4,795	2,012	630	842	105
Nebraska	15,686	9,536	1,180	3,962	561	446	...
Nevada..................	13,387	8,950	863	1,917	714	318	625
New Hampshire	9,162	6,106	841	896	440	880	...
New Jersey...............	97,444	72,181	3,991	11,329	4,979	4,965	...
New Mexico..............	83,359	67,323	6,989	3,588	2,056	3,403	...
New York................	340,818	210,202	8,015	76,736	28,257	17,608	...
North Carolina	104,422	91,547	4,523	1,344	4,541	2,467	...
North Dakota	26,467	21,113	2,251	1,551	396	1,156	...
Ohio	110,738	82,666	3,522	12,671	5,086	6,794	...
Oklahoma	41,761	26,789	8,071	3,102	1,093	2,707	...
Oregon	22,121	12,891	1,551	3,959	1,886	1,216	618
Pennsylvania.............	137,651	102,944	6,111	18,502	3,535	6,081	478
Rhode Island	21,362	9,602	3,311	4,408	2,916	1,124	...
South Carolina	100,296	67,723	18,185	4,425	2,686	7,277	...
South Dakota	12,035	8,820	811	1,461	601	343	...
Tennessee................	96,894	71,944	12,578	4,579	3,473	4,320	...
Texas	177,218	130,808	12,981	18,257	4,483	10,689	...
Utah	25,987	16,975	3,906	1,957	2,167	982	...
Vermont.................	14,381	11,093	763	1,376	690	459	...
Virginia	114,754	71,836	16,663	4,470	998	17,330	3,457
Washington	37,406	27,774	2,698	4,220	2,029	686	...
West Virginia.............	87,905	77,530	1,243	5,489	1,407	1,630	2,605
Wisconsin	37,739	21,976	3,464	9,633	1,515	951	200
Wyoming	14,762	12,573	287	1,376	345	181	...
Dist. of Col...............	103,473	95,836	...	1,374	961	5,301	...
American Samoa	7,154	6,569	196	211	46	131	...
Guam	4,350	2,394	699	103	205	949	...
No. Mariana Is.............	2,613	2,098	353	161	...	...	...
Puerto Rico	266,100	226,144	5,455	12,644	904	20,952	...
TTPI....................	10,255	8,432	594	1,022	...	207	...
Virgin Islands	41,888	27,158	713	1,963	1,641	10,412	...

Source: The Association of State and Territorial Health Officials.

Table 4

PUBLIC HEALTH EXPENDITURES OF STATE HEALTH AGENCIES, BY SOURCE OF FUNDS: FISCAL 1980
(In millions of dollars)

Source of funds	Total	Personal health — Noninstitutional	Personal health — SHA-operated institutions	Environmental health	Health resources	Laboratory	General administration	Funds to LHDs not allocated to program areas
Total	$4,453.4	$2,331.8	$846.6	$298.9	$357.7	$161.1	$253.4	$203.8
Subtotal, excluding federal grants and contracts	2,903.3	1,111.6	818.6	220.7	233.8	132.4	205.3	181.0
State	2,534.9	964.6	719.0	178.0	198.2	119.4	176.5	179.1
Local	114.0	68.4	(a)	23.7	3.9	1.2	16.8	0.1
Fees and reimbursements	200.2	56.7	95.3	17.5	17.3	6.8	4.8	1.8
Patient fees & reimbursements from Medicaid	75.0	26.6	47.7	(a)	…	0.4	0.3	…
Patient fees & reimbursements from other sources	78.9	25.2	47.6	1.3	2.1	0.3	0.8	1.8
Other fees	46.2	4.9	(a)	16.2	15.2	6.1	3.8	…
Other	54.2	21.9	4.3	1.5	14.4	4.9	7.1	…
Subtotal, federal grants and contracts	1,550.0	1,220.3	28.0	78.2	123.9	28.7	48.1	22.8
Department of Health and Human Services	798.0	581.2	23.5	19.1	116.9	21.7	22.3	13.7
Public Health Service	673.0	534.9	13.1	19.1	59.0	20.8	12.4	13.7
Alcohol, Drug Abuse & Mental Health Administration	60.0	58.0	…	(a)	1.5	0.1	0.4	…
Centers for Disease Control	109.5	62.4	…	15.8	2.1	16.0	4.4	8.7
Fluoridation (PHSA Sec. 317)	0.5	0.5	…	(a)	…	…	(a)	…
Health Education/Risk Reduction (PHSA Title XVII, P.L. 95-626 Sec. 402)	0.9	0.8	…	…	0.1	…	(a)	…
Health Incentive Grant (PHSA Sec. 314(d))	64.0	25.2	…	10.2	1.8	14.2	3.9	8.7
Immunization (PHSA Section 317)	14.2	13.9	…	(a)	(a)	0.1	0.2	…
Venereal Disease (PHSA Section 318)	19.2	18.3	…	(a)	…	0.7	0.1	…
Other CDC	10.7	3.7	…	5.5	0.2	1.2	0.1	…
Food & Drug Administration	2.0	(a)	…	1.7	…	0.1	(a)	…
Health Resources Administration	25.5	0.3	(a)	(a)	24.7	(a)	0.5	…
National Health Planning & Resources Development Act (P.L. 93-641)	22.6	0.1	…	(a)	22.1	…	0.5	…
Other HRA	2.9	0.2	…	…	2.6	…	…	…
Health Services Administration	448.2	407.0	(a)	1.2	23.5	(a)	6.2	5.0
Community Health Centers (PHSA Section 330)	4.5	4.4	…	…	…	3.9	…	0.1
Crippled Children (SSA Title V)	73.6	69.3	1.5	…	0.3	0.4	2.3	(a)
Emergency Medical Services (PHSA Title XII)	22.3	(a)	1.2	0.6	21.6	…	0.1	…
Family Planning (PHSA Title X)	70.6	70.0	0.1	…	0.1	0.1	0.4	…
Hypertension (PHSA Section 317(a)(1))	12.0	11.8	0.2	…	…	0.1	0.1	…
Maternal and Child Health (SSA Title V)	245.6	234.0	11.5	0.3	1.4	2.4	2.8	4.8
Migrant Health (PHSA Section 329)	2.5	2.3	0.2	0.2	…	…	(a)	…
Services for Blind/Disabled Children (SSI, Sec. 1615(b) SSA)	7.8	7.7	0.1	0.1	0.2	0.9	0.1	…
Other HSA	9.4	7.4	…	0.4	0.6	0.7	0.5	…
National Institutes of Health	20.4	7.0	…	…	…	…	0.5	…
National Center for Health Statistics	7.3	0.1	…	…	6.5	0.5	0.2	…
Health Care Financing Administration	86.0	10.4	9.6	(a)	56.1	0.5	9.4	…
Medicaid grants and contracts (SSA Title XIX)	52.9	6.9	2.3	(a)	37.5	(a)	6.1	…
Medicare grants and contracts (SSA Title XVIII)	30.3	3.0	7.3	(a)	16.3	0.4	3.3	…
Other HCFA	2.8	0.4	…	…	2.3	…	(a)	…
Social Security Administration	2.8	1.7	…	(a)	1.1	…	0.4	…
Office of Human Development Services	33.9	32.9	0.2	(a)	0.3	(a)	0.4	…
Developmental Disabilities (P.L. 91-517, P.L. 94-103)	5.1	4.3	0.1	…	0.3	(a)	0.4	…
Grants for Services (SSA Title XX)	28.3	28.2	…	…	0.1	(a)	(a)	…
Other OHDS	0.5	0.4	…	(a)	…	…	(a)	…
Other DHHS	2.1	1.1	0.4	(a)	0.2	0.3	(a)	…

494

Other Federal Agencies	743.3	638.9	4.6	58.5	7.1	6.9	18.4	8.8
Department of Agriculture	649.1	632.7	0.4	5.2	(a)	0.2	1.7	8.8
WIC	641.8	631.3	...	(a)	(a)	(a)	1.7	8.8
Other	7.2	1.4	0.4	5.2	...	0.2	0.1	...
Department of Education	3.4	1.7	1.6	...	...	1.0	13.2	...
Department of Labor	19.7	0.8	0.2	4.4	0.1	0.8	0.1	...
Department of Transportation	6.2	0.4	...	(a)	4.9	4.0	1.4	...
Environmental Protection Agency	52.9	0.1	...	47.4	(a)	...	(a)	...
Regional Commissions	1.4	0.2	...	0.1	1.1	...	...	...
Other	10.6	3.0	2.4	1.4	1.0	0.9	1.9	...
Unidentified federal	8.9	0.3	...	0.6	0.1	0.2	7.5	0.3

Source: Association of State and Territorial Health Officials, National Public Health Program Reporting System.

(a) Represents dollar amounts less than $50,000.

Table 5
SELECTED STATE HEALTH STATUTES

State or other jurisdiction	Certificate of need*	Death with dignity*	Brain death†	Physician's assistant—role recognized*	Home health care‡	Treatment of alcoholism‡	Health maintenance organizations*	Clinical laboratories*	Hospices‡	Home health care agencies‡	Medical use of marijuana allowed§	Generic drug substitution allowed*	Statutory right to treatment in mental health facilities*	Emergency medical system organization created by statute*
					(Health insurers must provide coverage for)		*(Licensing/regulation of)*							
Alabama	★	★	★	★		★					★		★	★
Alaska	★		★	★	★		★	★			★	★	★	
Arizona	★		★	★			★	★		★	★	★	★	
Arkansas	★	★	★	★	★	★	★	★		★	★	★	★	
California	★	★	★	★		★	★				★	★		★
Colorado	★			★(a)		★	★				★	★	★	★
Connecticut	★			★			★				★	★		
Delaware	★		★	★			★	★	★		★	★	★	★
Florida	★		★	★	★	★	★	★	★	★	★	★	★	★
Georgia	★(b)		★	★								★	★	★
Hawaii	★	★	★	★		★	★	★		★	★	★		★
Idaho	★	★	★	★			★	★		★	★	★	★	★
Illinois	★			★				★			★	★		
Indiana				★				★						
Iowa	★		★	★							★	★		
Kansas	★		★	★			★	★			★	★	★	★
Kentucky	★			★			★	★			★	★	★	★
Louisiana	★		★	★				★			★	★	★	★
Maine	★			★				★				★		
Maryland	★			★			★	★				★	★	★
Massachusetts	★					★	★	★	★		★	★	★	★
Michigan	★			★		★	★	★			★	★		★
Minnesota	★		★	★			★					★		★
Mississippi	★			★							★	★		
Missouri	★											★	★	
Montana	★		★	★			★			★		★	★	★
Nebraska	★	★	★	★			★	★		★		★	★	★
Nevada	★			★			★	★		★		★	★	★
New Hampshire	★						★	★			★	★		★
New Jersey	★						★					★		
New Mexico	★	★	★	★	★					★	★	★	★	★
New York	★	★	★	★	★						★	★		
North Carolina	★	★	★	★		★					★	★	★	
North Dakota	★		★	★		★					★	★		★
Ohio	★			★			★				★	★		
Oklahoma	★			★			★	★			★	★	★	★
Oregon	★			★			★	★	★		★	★	★	★
Pennsylvania	★			★		★	★	★			★	★	★	★
Rhode Island	★			★		★	★	★		★		★	★	★
South Carolina	★						★					★		
South Dakota	★			★		★	★	★			★	★	★	★
Tennessee	★		★	★			★	★			★	★	★	★
Texas	★	★	★	★(c)			★	★			★	★	★	★
Utah	★			★			★	★			★	★	★	★
Vermont	★			★			★				★	★	★	★
Virginia	★		★	★		★	★				★	★	★	★
Washington	★	★	★	★			★	★		★	★	★	★	
West Virginia	★		★	★		★	★		★		★	★	★	
Wisconsin	★			★		★	★				★	★	★	
Wyoming	★		★	★										
Dist. of Col.	★		N.A.		N.A.	N.A.				N.A.	N.A.	N.A.	★	★
Guam	★		N.A.	★	N.A.	N.A.				N.A.	N.A.	N.A.		★

* From survey of states, July-August 1981.
† Society for the Right to Die, 1981.
‡ American Medical Association, *State Health Legislation Handbook*, April 1981.
§ Alliance for Cannabis Therapeutics, as of August 1981.
N.A.—Not available.

(a) Specifically for assistants working under supervision of pediatrician.
(b) Only for long-term care facilities.
(c) Regulated under rules of Board of Medical Examiners—no statutory provisions.

Table 6

PROVISIONS UNDER "GOOD SAMARITAN" STATUTES

State or other jurisdiction	Who is protected under good samaritan statutes		Statute defines emergency situations	Statute requires(a)			Separate protections for paramedics or EMT personnel
	Any person who renders emergency aid	Medical or licensed personnel		Aid to be given gratuitously	Aid to be rendered only at the scene of the emergency	Person giving aid to have acted in "good faith"	
Alabama	...	★	...	★	★	•	...
Alaska	★	...	★	...	...	•	★
Arizona	★	...	...	★	★	★	...
Arkansas	★	...	...	★	★	★	...
California	★	★	...	(b)	•	★	★
Colorado	★	...	...	★	★	★	...
Connecticut	...	★(c)	...	•	...	★	(d)
Delaware	★	...	...	•	★	★	...
Florida	★	...	...	★	•	★	...
Georgia	★	...	...	★	•	★	...
Hawaii	★	...	★	•	★	★	★
Idaho	★	...	★	...	•	★	★
Illinois	...	★	...	★	•	...	★
Indiana	★	...	...	•	•	...	★
Iowa	★	...	...	★	★	★	★
Kansas	...	★	...	...	•	★	...
Kentucky	...	★	...	...	•	•	...
Louisiana	...	★	★	★	•	•	★
Maine	★	...	★	•	•	...	...
Maryland	★	...	...	★	...	...	...
Massachusetts	★	★	★	•	...	...	★
Michigan	...	★	★	...	★	★	★
Minnesota	★	...	...	•	•	★	...
Mississippi	★	★	★	...	•	★	...
Missouri	...	★	...	...	★	...	...
Montana	★	...	...	★	★	...	...
Nebraska	...	★	...	★	★	★	...
Nevada	★	...	...	★	★	...	★
New Hampshire	★	...	★	★	★	•	...
New Jersey	★	...	...	...	...	★	★
New Mexico	★	...	...	•	•	★	...
New York	...	★	★	•	•	...	...
North Carolina	★	...	★	•	•	...	...
North Dakota	★	...	...	★	★	★	...
Ohio	★	...	...	...	...	...	...
Oklahoma	★	...	★	•	★	•	★
Oregon	...	★	★	•	•	...	...
Pennsylvania	...	★	...	...	...	★	...
Rhode Island	...	★	...	•	★	...	★
South Carolina	★	...	★	★	★	★	★
South Dakota	★	...	★	...	•	•	...
Tennessee	★	...	...	•	★	★	...
Texas	★	...	...	•	•	★	...
Utah	...	★	★	★	★	•	★
Vermont	★	...	...	•	•	...	★
Virginia	★	...	★	•	•	★	★
Washington	★	...	★	•	•	★	★
West Virginia	★	...	...	•	•	★	...
Wisconsin	★	...	★	...	•	•	...
Wyoming	★	...	...	...	★	...	...
Dist. of Col.	...	★	...	...	•	★	...
Guam	★	...	...	...	★	...	...
Virgin Islands	...	★	★	•	...	...	...

Source: Adapted from Miles J. Zaremski, "Good Samaritan Statutes," *Medicolegal News,* vol. 7 (Spring 1979); updated by The Council of State Governments.

(a) ★—The statutory provision applies. •—Not only does the statutory provision apply, but the statute goes on to define the terms used in that provision.

(b) Depends on class of person rendering aid.

(c) Also, certain named individuals who have completed certain first aid courses.

(d) Part of general protection under statute.

PUBLIC WELFARE

PUBLIC WELFARE is undergoing dramatic change, owing to large cuts in the federal budget and the worsening financial situation of many states and localities. The restrictions and reductions in basic programs mark a major turning point in the history of public welfare, which had grown steadily during the 1960s and 1970s.

The most significant revisions in public welfare policy stem from the Omnibus Budget Reconciliation Act (P.L. 97-35), which Congress passed in 1981 as part of President Reagan's economic recovery program. Among other things, this law cut federal spending on basic welfare programs by more than 10 percent, using two principal methods: first, current and potential beneficiaries of these programs are either encouraged or required to make a greater effort to support themselves by working more and relying on financial sources other than federal aid; second, state and local responsibility for funding, as well as administering public welfare, was substantially expanded. Put simply, the reconciliation act aimed at reducing both the number of people assisted by public welfare and the federal role in providing it.

The programs constituting public welfare and the recent changes that have been made in them by the federal government are described in the following sections. Tables 1-6 provide current national statistics for these programs.

Income Assistance

Aid to Families with Dependent Children (AFDC). Title IV-A of the Social Security Act established the AFDC program, which provides financial assistance to the dependent children of indigent families in which a parent has died, is continuously absent from the home or is permanently incapacitated. Section 407 of the act authorizes payment of AFDC benefits to poor, two-parent families on the basis of one parent's unemployment (AFDC-U). Currently, 25 states, the District of Columbia and Guam participate in the AFDC-U program. At the federal level, AFDC is administered by the Office of Family Assistance in the Social Security Administration.

The Omnibus Reconciliation Act made comprehensive changes in the AFDC program that are designed to reduce welfare expenditures through a number of administrative and eligibility revisions limiting benefits to those who are most needy and to encourage employable AFDC recipients to find work. Among the new administrative requirements are systems for retrospective budgeting (i.e., determining a family's benefit based on income in the prior month) and monthly reporting (i.e., requiring recipients to file monthly reports on their circumstances with the welfare office). Recovery of overpayments and compensation for underpayments are also required. States are given new authority to require recipients to work, and limits are placed on the amount of a recipient's earnings that may be deducted

Prepared by the Department of Government Affairs and Social Policy, American Public Welfare Association.

for work and child care expenses in determining eligibility and benefits. (Previously, actual expenses for these items were allowed). In addition, the law establishes a new limit of $1,000 on family resources, restricts AFDC payments to families in which the "principal" earner is the one unemployed, and requires that a portion of the income of a child's stepparent or an alien's sponsor be deemed available to that child or alien in determining AFDC eligibility and benefits. All of these changes went into effect on October 1, 1981.

In fiscal 1980, AFDC served an average monthly caseload of 3.6 million families, representing 10.5 million individuals. The total cost of the program—to all levels of government—was $12.7 billion, of which $11.3 billion (roughly 54 percent of it federal money) went toward benefits and $1.4 billion (50 percent federal money) for administration. By comparison, in fiscal 1979 the AFDC program served an average of 10.3 million persons a month, at a total annual cost of about $12.1 billion. The federal government expects the changes made by the Reconciliation Act to reduce AFDC expenditures in fiscal 1982 by $2 billion ($1 billion in federal funds) and to cut back or eliminate benefits to more than 600,000 families. If these savings are realized, fiscal 1982 AFDC costs will total roughly $13.4 billion.

AFDC costs are funded through a combination of federal, state and, in some cases, local revenue. All states are reimbursed by the federal government at the rate of 50 percent for the program's administrative costs. However, federal reimbursement of AFDC benefit expenditures varies according to a state's per capita income and, in fiscal 1982, will range from a low of 50 percent to a high of 77.36 percent.

Although broad federal guidelines govern the AFDC program, states and their political subdivisions are primarily responsibile for the program's daily administration. States determine AFDC benefit levels and many of the eligibility requirements. Consequently, access to the program and AFDC payment levels differ from one state to the next. For example, in December 1980, the average monthly payment per AFDC recipient ranged from a low of $16.57 in Puerto Rico to a high of $162.61 in Alaska; for the country the average monthly payment per recipient was $99.61. The average annual payment at that time was $3,453—approximately 55 percent of the poverty line for a non-farm family of three (the size of the typical AFDC family).

Both the disparity between high- and low-benefit states and the gap between AFDC benefits and the poverty line have been narrowed somewhat by the availability of food stamps. These benefits are inversely related to AFDC and other household income; that is, they increase as other sources of income decline. For example, in March 1979, the average AFDC payment per family in Alaska equaled $317 a month, and in Puerto Rico, $43, a ratio of about seven to one. When added to AFDC, food stamp benefits gave the Alaska household $442 a month and the Puerto Rico household $215, a ratio of two to one.

Child Support Enforcement. The Child Support Enforcement program began in 1975 as Title IV-D of the Social Security Act to help establish paternity for and secure parental support of AFDC children. AFDC applicants and recipients are required, as a condition of eligibility, to cooperate with the state in determining paternity and obtaining child support from absent parents. States are required to make child support enforcement services available to persons not receiving AFDC as well as to those who are. The Office of Child Support Enforcement within the Department of Health and Human Services oversees the program and operates the Federal Parent Locator Service, which helps states find absent parents. The federal government also pays 75 percent of the state's administrative cost. In addition, to encourage active participation in the child support enforcement program, certain federal incentives are paid to states and localities based on the level of child support they collect.

The Omnibus Reconciliation Act made substantial revisions in the child support enforcement program in order to increase opportunities for collecting child support obligations from absent parents. One change allows the Internal Revenue Service, upon referral from a state, to withhold delinquent child support from the income tax refund that would be otherwise due an absent parent. Another lets states intercept a portion of the owing parent's unemployment compensation benefits to meet the child support obligation. Other changes permit states to collect both spousal and child support and require that a collection fee be charged for child support services provided to non-AFDC families.

Total federal expenditures for administration of the program in fiscal 1980 were $451 million. Child support collections equaled $1.5 billion—$603.2 million obtained on behalf of AFDC recipients and $874.5 million on behalf of persons not on the AFDC rolls. Thus, the program collected approximately $3.30 for each dollar that was spent on administering it.

Supplemental Security Income (SSI). The SSI program, established by Title XVI of the Social Security Act, began providing cash assistance in 1974 to indigent persons who are 65 or older, legally blind, or permanently or totally disabled. Previously, public assistance for the aged, blind and disabled was administered by the states as the adult counterpart of AFDC. The federalization of the adult categories was designed, among other things, to reduce the variation in benefit levels among the states by providing a uniform national minimum benefit, streamline administration by lodging it in the Social Security system and assure that benefits would keep pace with inflation by indexing the basic federal payment to the cost-of-living. States were mandated to supplement the federal minimum up to the level of assistance they were providing in December 1973 and could provide optional income supplements to higher levels.

SSI is administered by the federal government within the Social Security Administration. As of July 1980, an eligible person could receive a basic monthly cash grant of up to $238, and an eligible couple could get up to $357. In fiscal 1980, an average of 4.2 million people drew SSI benefits each month, at a total annual cost of $7.94 billion. State supplements accounted for $2.07 billion that year.

With the exception of Texas, all states and the District of Columbia are providing either mandatory or optional state supplements. When the SSI program began, states were given the option to either administer their supplementary benefits themselves or turn this responsibility over to the federal government. Currently, 26 states and the District of Columbia contract with the Social Security Administration to administer their optional or mandatory supplements. Four states contract with the federal government for administration of their mandatory supplements but manage their optional supplements themselves. Twenty-three state supplement programs are administered by the states that pay for them.

One SSI administrative issue continues to be of concern to the states. This is the federal government's fiscal liability for erroneously spending state supplement funds as a result of poor federal administration of the program. Under the terms of the contract by which states authorize the Social Security Administration to administer their supplements, the federal government is obligated to reimburse states for supplementary payments made in error due to a wrongful determination of SSI eligibility. However, the federal government does not currently recognize its liability for the state share of Medicaid funds paid in the form of services to individuals the Social Security Administration has incorrectly found eligible for

SSI. To resolve this problem, states have been involved since 1978 in re-negotiating their contracts with the federal government. When final, the re-negotiated agreement is expected to provide for federal fiscal liability for such errors but may also waive such liability whenever a state requests and receives a waiver of its liability for AFDC and Medicaid errors.

Low-Income Energy Assistance. The federal low-income energy assistance program, operated by the federal Office of Family Assistance, allows states to help needy people with their heating and cooling bills. Under the terms of the Reconciliation Act, states must target aid to persons with the lowest income and highest energy costs, may reserve a reasonable amount for energy crisis assistance and may use up to 15 percent of their allotment for economical weatherization. As much as 25 percent of the state's annual allocation for energy assistance may be held for use in the following fiscal year; 10 percent of the allocation may be transferred by the state to other federal block grants for health, social services and community services.

Eligibility for low-income energy assistance is limited to households in which one or more persons receives AFDC, food stamps, SSI or certain veterans' benefits or to households with incomes that do not exceed 150 percent of the state poverty level or 60 percent of the state median income, whichever is higher. The state must publicize the program, with special emphasis on notifying elderly and handicapped persons. Direct payments to home energy suppliers on behalf of eligible persons is a state option, as are payments to the operators of buildings in which program participants live. A state can spend no more than 10 percent of its federal allotment for administering the program; any administrative costs above this level must be entirely at the state's expense. In fiscal 1981, Congress appropriated $1.85 billion for the low-income energy assistance program.

General Assistance. In addition to the various federal-state forms of income assistance, most states and many localities operate programs of general assistance. These programs are funded and run exclusively by state and local governments and vary greatly in terms of eligibility standards, benefits and administration. By and large, general assistance is used to aid persons who do not qualify for AFDC and SSI. In 1980, according to estimates by the Department of Health and Human Services, general assistance was provided to around 760,000 cases per month, representing 945,000 individuals, at an annual cost of $1.4 billion in state and local funds.

Food Stamps

In 1961, the Food Stamp program was a limited pilot project assisting fewer than 400,000 poor people with their food purchases. In 1964, Congress passed the Food Stamp Act, and the program became national in scope, enabling indigent persons to purchase food stamps at a discount. The Food Stamp program is unique in that it is the only federally funded welfare program extending benefits to essentially all poor people—not just the categories of people served by AFDC and SSI. In fiscal 1981, the program helped an average of 22 million beneficiaries a month, at a total cost of $11.4 billion.

Benefits are funded completely by the federal government, and administrative costs are split evenly between the federal government and the states. The states administer the program according to regulations issued by the U.S. Department of Agriculture.

Rapid growth of the Food Stamp program in the first half of the 1970s triggered a two-year study that culminated in enactment of the Food Stamp Act of 1977. Through this act, Congress sought to eliminate non-needy persons from the program, improve administration and reduce fraud, make the program more accessible to the poorest people and control program spending. Perhaps the most significant changes it made were the elimination of the purchase requirement and the imposition of a statutory ceiling on program spending. The former provision was intended to make it easier for destitute people, who in the past had difficulty coming up with the cash to purchase stamps, to obtain benefits. The latter measure was designed to give Congress better control over the program's escalating costs. Generally, the expenditure ceilings Congress has placed on food stamps since then have been inadequate, owing to higher than expected inflation of food prices and unemployment making more people eligible. Consequently, each year it has chosen to raise the ceiling and has thereby prevented the Department of Agriculture from reducing benefits as the law requires when funds are expected to run out.

The 1981 Reconciliation Act makes a number of changes to stem the growth of the Food Stamp program. Its primary emphasis is on tightening eligibility by: (1) disqualifying any household with gross income above 130 percent of the federal poverty line, except for those with elderly members whose eligibility is determined using a "net income" (i.e., after certain income deductions have been taken) test; (2) prohibiting boarders and children living with their parents under age 60 from qualifying as separate households; and (3) excluding strikers from participation in the program. The new law also reduces the sensitivity of benefit levels to increases in inflation, requires states to determine benefits based on a household's prior income and recipients to file monthly reports on their circumstances, and calculates the initial benefit to a household based on the time remaining in the month (instead of for the whole month). Additionally, stiffer penalties are to be imposed on people who defraud or abuse the program.

Further changes in food stamp policy—the most significant of which expands the states' authority to set up work programs for recipients—are contained in legislation to reauthorize the program, passed by Congress at the end of 1981 as part of the 1981 farm bill. The reauthorization is for only one year, meaning that the program is likely to be the subject of more revision in 1982, as the federal government continues to look for ways to curtail its cost.

Medicaid Program

Medicaid, enacted in 1965 as Title XIX of the Social Security Act, is a federal-state vendor payment program which is the main source of health care coverage for the nation's poor. Every state (except Arizona), the District of Columbia and the U.S. territories operate such a program to provide medical assistance to all AFDC and SSI recipients. (Arizona will begin a demonstration program of Medicaid in fiscal 1982). In addition, 33 states extend coverage to the "medically needy," those whose income exceeds eligibility standards for AFDC or SSI but is insufficient to meet their medical expenses. Currently, approximately 23 million individuals receive Medicaid benefits, including 11 million children, 5.4 million AFDC adults and 6.6 million SSI recipients. Medicaid is administered at the federal level by the Health Care Financing Administration.

Medicaid funds are used to reimburse health care providers for a wide variety of medical services. Federal law requires that state programs offer certain basic services: inpatient and outpatient care, laboratory and X-ray services, skilled nursing and home health care for certain individuals, physician services, family planning, rural health clinics and health screening for children. States may also receive funds for other services they wish to cover, such as eyeglasses, dental care and intermediate care facility services.

In addition, the Reconciliation Act provides for a waiver process that allows states, with the permission of the Department of Health and Human Services, to make use of home and community-based health care for long-term care patients, and to set up new, non-traditional health care delivery systems such as primary care networks in which a recipient is assigned to a single physician who determines what care is needed and who will provide it. Among other things, the act also allows states more discretion in: restricting a recipient's freedom in choosing providers to those who deliver services economically and effectively; setting reimbursement rates for hospitals to encourage efficient service delivery; and limiting Medicaid coverage for those who qualify for the program because they are medically needy. As an incentive for states to employ these and other cost-saving options, the new law reduces federal reimbursement to states during fiscal years 1982-84, by an increasing amount each year. A state can avoid all or part of the reduction by meeting certain federally established performance standards related to cost containment.

Medicaid expenditures for services were about $30.5 billion in fiscal 1981. Overall, the state portion of these costs was $13.4 billion, with individual state contributions ranging from 22 to 50 percent of the cost of their programs. While nearly half of all Medicaid recipients are AFDC children, this group accounts for only one-sixth of total expenditures. By contrast, SSI recipients, who represent one-fourth of the recipient population, are responsible for roughly 60 percent of all expenditures, the bulk going to hospital and institutional long-term care which tends to be the most expensive service.

Congress will in the near future be considering many proposals to instill competition in the health care sector of the economy. It is not yet clear to what extent the Medicaid program will be part of these proposals. The current trend at the federal level is to give states more flexibility to operate cost-effective Medicaid programs—in a way, letting each state decide how much competition among health care providers it wants in the program.

Social Services

The term "social services" is used to describe a broad array of activities. These services differ from income assistance programs such as AFDC in that help is available in the form of a service rather than a cash payment. The most commonly provided social services are day care, counseling, family planning, protective services and homemaker services.

Social Services Block Grant (Title XX). Congress enacted Title XX of the Social Security Act in 1975, for the first time officially separating social services from the cash assistance programs (e.g., AFDC) that had spawned them. At the time, Title XX was envisioned as a form of special revenue sharing with the states to help organize, finance and administer a broad range of social services. In 1981, in response to President Reagan's policy of increasing state and local control over human services, the Reconciliation Act transformed Title XX into a pure block grant, with only minimal federal strings attached. Federal administration of Title XX is lodged within the Office of Human Development Services of the Department of Health and Human Services.

Since its inception, Title XX has had some aspects of a block grant. The role of the federal government has been, from the outset, limited, with states free to select the number and types of services provided, the manner of delivery, the social problems addressed and the eligibility criteria. States have also been free to determine whether to provide the services directly or to purchase them by contract with other public and private agencies.

Even though under the 1975 law states had a great deal of flexibility, federal regulations interpreting the law often specified in detail how the states were to develop and administer their programs. To be eligible for the 75 percent federal matching, each state had to develop in accordance with federal rules a comprehensive annual services plan for public review and comment. The law also put an annual ceiling on federal Title XX expenditures of $2.5 billion. In 1977 and again in 1978, Congress temporarily increased the ceiling by $200 million to allow 100 percent federal funding of child day care, the single largest service financed by the program. An additional unrestricted $200 million in 1979 raised the cap to $2.9 billion, and with passage of the Adoption Assistance and Child Welfare Act of 1980 (P.L. 96-272), the Title XX law was changed to provide for automatic annual increases in the ceiling to at least partially offset the effect of inflation on the program. Also in 1980, Congress for the first time set a limit on the amount of federal funds available to states for staff training under Title XX; before this, funds for training were open-ended.

In 1981, the Reagan administration sought a social services block grant which would have consolidated 12 programs and reduced their funding by 25 percent below 1981 levels. However, in acting on the reconciliation legislation, Congress decided to include only the Title XX programs (i.e., social services, day care and training) and to pare spending by 20 percent in fiscal 1982, to $2.4 billion, with provision for funding increases until 1986, when the ceiling will reach $2.7 billion.

Adoption of the block grant has not changed the purposes of Title XX, although most of the statutory and regulatory prescriptions that had been governing the programs are removed. States no longer have to match federal funds with money from their own treasuries, and they are not restricted in terms of the people they may serve. An annual report on how the state plans to spend the money is required, and at least every two years another report must describe the activities funded and the extent to which funds were expended in a manner consistent with the pre-expenditure report. Every two years states must also arrange for an independent audit of their Title XX expenditures.

Community Services Block Grant. The 1981 Reconciliation Act also included a new community services block grant to states, thereby abolishing the federal Community Services Administration (CSA). Established in 1975 to replace the Office of Economic Opportunity, CSA was one of the last vestiges of President Lyndon Johnson's "Great Society." Authorized in place of the various CSA federal grant programs, the new block grant turns over to states most of what remains of the federal anti-poverty effort of the 1960s and 1970s. Responsibility for disbursing the funds to the states lies with the Office of Community Services in the Department of Health and Human Services.

As with the social services block grant, states are given substantial latitude in administering the community services block grant. Funds are to be used to ameliorate the causes of poverty in communities within each state. A state's acceptance of the block grant is optional in fiscal 1982, and those states that choose to participate must pass on 90 percent of the funds they receive to local agencies that were supported by CSA in 1981. A total of 39 states have opted to administer the block grant; the Department of Health and Human Services will, in fiscal 1982 only, run the program in the other 12 states. Funding for the community services block grant is authorized at $389 million each year, from fiscal years 1982 through 1986. This represents a cut of 25 percent below the fiscal 1981 level.

Child Welfare Services. The Adoption Assistance and Child Welfare Act of 1980 (P.L. 96-272) was probably the most significant piece of social legislation enacted during the administration of President Jimmy Carter. Signed into law June 17, 1980, P.L. 96-272 sought to change federal policy toward homeless, dependent and neglected children primarily through administrative reforms in state child welfare systems. The impetus for reform had come from studies showing that states were often unable to account for the number and location of children in their care and that children often entered the child welfare system and then drifted for years from one placement to the next, without ever being given a permanent home.

The new law created Title IV-E of the Social Security Act, which authorizes funds to states for maintaining children in foster care and, for the first time, offers a federal adoption subsidy for hard-to-place children. It also established a number of "good practice" requirements which states must meet to receive enhanced funding under the Social Security Act's Title IV-B (child welfare services). Included among these requirements are: completing an inventory of all children in foster care longer than six months; implementing a foster care case review system; setting up an information system to track children in foster care; and developing services to help children return to their own homes. In 1981, 34 states met these requirements.

Work Incentive Program (WIN). WIN is authorized under Title IV (Parts A and C) of the Social Security Act. It is administered at the federal level jointly by the Employment and Training Administration of the Department of Labor and the Department of Health and Human Services, and at the local level by state welfare and employment service agencies. The purpose of WIN is to provide a wide range of employment, training and social services to help recipients of AFDC become self-supporting wage earners. All applicants and recipients of AFDC must register for the program, except children under 16 and full-time students under 18; ill, elderly and incapacitated persons; people who live too far from WIN project sites to participate; persons needed at home to care for others; parents or other relatives caring for a child under 6; and a parent or other relative providing full-time care for a child on a continual basis, if the other adult relative in the home is signed up for WIN. AFDC recipients not required to register may do so voluntarily.

WIN services include job referral, instruction in job search and job retention, job development, classroom and on-the-job training, job placement in public or private non-profit agencies and various support services such as day care, transportation and counseling. Payments of $30 a month plus up to $3 a day (for transportation and meals) are available to WIN registrants as an incentive for them to participate in institutional training or unpaid work experiences. Employable recipients who refuse WIN training or jobs meeting WIN standards may cause the denial of AFDC benefits to the entire family.

Under the Reconciliation Act, states have the option to conduct a three-year demonstration in which the WIN program would be administered solely by the state welfare agency, which could then contract for needed services with the state employment services agency. In these projects, states may demonstrate the use of job-finding clubs, job training and diversion of AFDC grants to wages, and they may vary the components of the projects from one geographic area of the state to another.

Programs for the Elderly

The economic needs of older people are met through various sources. The bulk of their income is derived from earnings, private pensions and Social Security payments. The largest public income support program, Social Security, in 1980 paid out $121 billion in benefits to around 35.6 million people (including disabled persons and survivors). When income from Social Security and these other sources is inadequate, the elderly may obtain assistance through the SSI, Medicaid and Food Stamp programs discussed earlier. Limited support is also available from assorted federal, state and local tax benefits and housing programs.

In passing the Reconciliation Act, Congress revised the Social Security program in four ways designed to curb costs through tightened eligibility: (1) the minimum benefit was eliminated, although Congress has since reinstated it for people who were receiving it in 1981 and for certain future beneficiaries; (2) benefits for students over age 18 were dropped; (3) the lump sum death benefit was deleted for cases in which there is no surviving beneficiary; and (4) benefits for a surviving spouse were terminated in cases where the youngest child is 16 or older.

A number of other major programs target their benefits specifically to the elderly. The Medicare program, established in 1965 as Title XVIII of the Social Security Act, provides acute-care health insurance coverage for nearly all citizens 65 years of age and over. Part A of Medicare covers hospital services, and Part B (Supplemental Medical Insurance) covers a substantial portion of physicians' services. Medicare is an entitlement program financed mainly by Social Security tax revenues, although eligible persons are required to pay a deductible for hospital services and a 20 percent co-payment on physicians' services. In fiscal 1982, Medicare expenditures are expected to approach $50 billion. Medicare is operated by the Health Care Financing Administration.

Indigent older people who are unable to pay the out-of-pocket expenses of Medicare may also be eligible for Medicaid, either as recipients of SSI or as "medically needy" individuals. In this case, the state Medicaid program pays the Medicare co-payment and deductible, in addition to financing a number of services not covered by Medicare such as nursing home care.

The provision of social services to the elderly is facilitated by activities carried out under the Older Americans Act. The act's overriding purpose is to stimulate the provision of needed services and assistance specifically for older people, with the long-term aim of developing a comprehensive, coordinated services system in all parts of the country. Leadership for this is lodged in the federal Administration on Aging within the Department of Health and Human Services, and implementation is the responsibility of state and area agencies on aging.

The 1978 amendments to the Older Americans Act consolidated previously separate provisions for development of social services and multipurpose senior centers. These provisions furnish partial funding for the states to plan, coordinate, evaluate and administer aging programs and, through them, to develop local area agencies responsible for guiding the creation of local service systems. In 1981, there were 665 area agencies and more than 2,100 senior centers funded under the act.

One of the largest and most successful activities financed under the act has been its nutrition program, the goal of which is to enhance the nutritional status of the elderly. The program funds congregate nutrition service projects (which provide at least one hot meal a day at least five days a week in congregate settings) and home-delivered nutrition service projects (which furnish at least one home-delivered meal per day to the elderly). In 1980, more than 372,200 congregate meals and 59,300 home-delivered meals were served daily across the country.

Table 1
GENERAL ASSISTANCE: RECIPIENTS OF PAYMENTS
AND AMOUNTS BY STATE*
(As of December 1980)

| State or other jurisdiction | Number of | | Payments to recipients | | | Percentage change from | | | |
| | | | | Average per | | November 1980 in | | December 1979 in | |
	Cases	Recipients	Total	Case	Recipient	Number of recipients	Amount	Number of recipients	amount
41 states	795,915	986,392	$128,075,145	$160.92	$129.84	-0.4	3.8	11.5	17.4
Arizona	2,666	2,666	286,564	107.49	107.49	2.5	2.7	14.3	18.8
California	26,445	27,717	4,738,726	179.19	170.97	2.7	8.1	-1.3	17.6
Colorado	409	865	42,358	103.56	48.97	1.9	12.3	7.7	-16.9
Connecticut(a)	14,905	22,488	1,983,807	133.10	88.22	0.0	0.0	0.0	0.0
Delaware	2,051	2,898	238,659	116.36	82.35	-2.3	-1.5	21.9	28.6
Georgia	1,682	2,691	113,717	67.61	42.26	4.5	-3.3	-10.2	-22.2
Hawaii	6,035	9,699	1,703,471	282.27	175.63	2.4	3.7	-4.0	3.9
Illinois	84,827	99,715	13,688,070	161.36	137.27	4.2	7.9	19.6	23.9
Indiana	38,043	83,694	1,901,764	49.99	22.72	-25.8	23.5	-12.9	6.4
Kansas	5,931	6,636	951,255	160.39	143.35	1.8	14.3	52.6	59.1
Louisiana	4,046	4,264	312,208	77.16	73.22	3.5	2.1	26.5	37.3
Maine	2,588	6,672	244,570	94.50	36.66	-17.5	-10.6	-2.6	15.4
Maryland	24,364	26,020	2,940,968	120.71	113.03	3.4	3.0	11.5	20.7
Massachusetts	22,598	23,846	3,448,921	152.62	144.63	0.9	-16.3	5.2	4.3
Michigan	105,825	123,456	19,144,550	180.91	155.07	2.0	3.1	47.5	41.8
Minnesota	15,357	17,276	2,743,139	178.62	158.78	8.2	8.0	41.9	69.1
Mississippi	596	734	9,242	15.51	12.59	-19.6	-18.9	-23.2	-31.9
Missouri	6,285	6,809	439,019	69.85	64.48	2.6	1.2	27.5	29.7
Montana(a)	689	1,020	62,999	91.44	61.76	3.9	2.0	13.2	28.2
New Hampshire	1,490	3,250	263,842	177.08	81.18	9.7	28.2	-5.6	14.2
New Jersey	28,085	37,631	4,677,451	166.55	124.30	2.4	10.7	15.2	9.9
New Mexico	647	663	74,600	115.30	112.52	4.4	4.2	23.2	30.1
New York	140,346	171,779	28,606,870	203.83	166.53	3.1	3.2	3.5	5.5
North Dakota	125	282	15,258	122.06	54.11	-4.7	5.4	58.4	59.5
Ohio	55,683	59,482	6,038,066	108.44	101.51	4.7	5.3	44.3	53.7
Oklahoma	839	2,070	29,435	35.08	14.22	-10.7	-7.3	-73.2	-73.7
Oregon	4,068	4,177	456,704	112.27	109.34	0.7	1.2	-8.0	-26.4
Pennsylvania	153,840	181,043	26,208,465	170.36	144.76	-0.6	0.2	9.6	12.1
Rhode Island(a)	3,463	4,784	633,299	182.88	132.38	0.0	0.0	-20.2	-20.7
South Carolina	837	878	54,871	65.56	62.50	2.7	29.2	-6.1	16.3
South Dakota	425	900	32,875	77.35	36.53	-11.8	34.8	33.5	83.7
Utah	1,100	1,314	202,204	183.82	153.88	-0.2	2.5	-28.8	-6.9
Virginia	8,047	11,027	1,051,100	130.62	95.32	36.02	14.6	2.0	13.3
Washington	15,183	16,933	2,319,641	152.78	136.99	22.6	12.8	38.1	30.4
West Virginia	2,938	5,881	79,364	27.01	13.49	40.4	61.9	23.0	10.1
Wisconsin	5,816	6,881	1,103,385	189.72	160.35	22.7	58.3	36.2	40.4
Wyoming	257	625	18,019	70.11	28.83	32.7	12.5	-5.2	2.1
Dist. of Col.	6,558	6,754	1,158,775	176.70	171.57	-1.8	-1.1	-6.1	-9.8
Guam	93	99	7,933	85.30	80.13	(b)	(b)	(b)	(b)
Puerto Rico	368	368	10,449	28.39	28.39	6.1	40.2	15.4	85.3
Virgin Islands	365	405	38,526	105.55	95.13	7.1	17.2	6.0	57.9

Source: Public Assistance Statistics, U.S. Department of Health and Human Services, Social Security Administration, Office of Research and Statistics, December 1980.
*Includes non-medical vendor payments.

(a) Estimated data.
(b) Average payment not computed on base of fewer than 50 cases or recipients; percentage change on fewer than 100 recipients.

Table 2
AID TO FAMILIES WITH DEPENDENT CHILDREN: RECIPIENTS OF CASH PAYMENTS AND AMOUNT BY STATE*
(As of December 1981)

State or other jurisdiction	Number of families	Number of recipients		Payments to recipients			Percentage change from			
					Average per		November 1980 in		December 1979 in	
		Total	Children	Total amount	Family	Recipient	No. of recipients	amount	No. of recipients	Amount
Total	3,842,534	11,101,149	7,599,376	$1,105,776,662	$287.77	$99.61	0.8	1.5	7.0	14.7
Alabama	63,246	178,322	127,684	6,967,928	110.17	39.07	-0.4	-0.2	-0.4	0.9
Alaska	6,606	15,931	10,882	2,590,514	392.15	162.61	0.4	4.1	5.5	31.3
Arizona	21,573	59,809	43,589	3,809,666	176.59	63.70	1.1	1.9	19.7	26.8
Arkansas	29,822	85,008	61,667	4,360,856	146.23	51.30	1.1	2.3	0.4	3.1
California	511,486	1,498,216	996,054	220,451,580	431.00	147.14	1.0	1.0	10.1	27.8
Colorado	29,467	81,031	55,415	7,591,646	257.63	93.69	1.4	8.6	8.9	17.8
Connecticut	49,407	139,685	96,240	18,308,524	370.57	131.07	-0.3	-0.3	2.9	14.7
Delaware	12,404	34,243	23,555	2,817,520	227.15	82.28	3.0	3.6	5.1	5.9
Florida	103,315	279,392	199,015	18,229,236	176.44	65.25	1.8	2.7	12.8	16.0
Georgia	89,912	233,730	168,813	12,591,009	140.04	53.87	0.6	0.5	8.5	23.4
Hawaii	20,046	61,342	40,802	7,731,955	385.71	126.05	0.7	1.2	2.2	3.7
Idaho	7,503	20,326	13,845	2,064,949	275.22	101.59	0.8	1.4	-0.9	3.0
Illinois	222,937	691,434	482,773	62,903,873	282.16	90.98	1.2	4.3	4.6	8.4
Indiana	60,229	170,239	119,431	12,351,154	205.07	72.55	0.3	0.2	11.8	23.5
Iowa	40,476	111,287	73,907	12,553,542	310.15	112.80	0.6	0.5	13.6	15.3
Kansas	27,720	71,956	50,828	7,817,479	282.02	108.64	(a)	5.4	11.3	19.3
Kentucky	67,159	175,071	122,437	12,478,662	185.81	71.28	0.9	1.4	6.7	22.5
Louisiana	72,163	218,966	160,212	11,254,465	155.96	51.40	0.7	0.3	4.1	19.1
Maine	21,466	57,700	39,504	4,954,190	230.79	85.86	(a)	-0.6	5.1	-0.9
Maryland	80,823	220,316	148,989	19,304,624	238.85	87.62	0.6	0.5	5.0	17.5
Massachusetts	125,232	347,830	226,570	43,793,572	349.70	125.91	0.1	1.0	-1.2	7.2
Michigan	246,648	752,578	494,459	96,243,119	390.20	127.88	0.9	1.2	16.4	21.3
Minnesota	53,856	145,634	96,383	18,582,462	345.04	127.60	0.5	-0.8	11.9	20.0
Mississippi	59,814	176,253	129,704	5,257,257	87.89	29.83	0.4	0.5	2.8	5.8
Missouri	73,506	215,682	144,865	16,795,310	228.49	77.87	1.1	2.5	12.9	24.1
Montana	7,136	19,883	13,621	1,646,790	230.77	82.82	-0.8	1.9	8.7	12.0
Nebraska	13,573	37,541	25,900	3,890,757	286.65	103.64	0.4	0.8	10.6	24.8
Nevada	5,114	13,827	9,524	1,096,034	214.32	79.27	6.0	7.3	23.9	35.7
New Hampshire	8,647	23,648	15,636	2,377,068	274.90	100.52	1.4	2.1	9.7	17.2
New Jersey	153,709	468,603	320,955	49,028,742	318.97	104.63	-0.4	-0.6	2.8	11.1

New Mexico	19,550	56,157	38,657	3,705,145	189.52	65.98	0.5	0.5	7.8	21.9
New York	367,628	1,109,601	762,672	136,745,976	371.97	123.24	0.8	0.8	1.3	1.9
North Carolina	80,074	201,828	142,638	13,014,235	162.53	64.48	0.3	0.4	4.3	5.5
North Dakota	4,859	13,111	9,045	1,413,489	290.90	107.81	-1.0	-2.4	3.2	9.9
Ohio	200,243	572,347	380,365	50,348,940	251.44	87.97	1.9	2.4	16.9	16.9
Oklahoma	31,543	91,984	66,752	7,880,651	249.84	85.67	1.1	2.5	5.5	6.4
Oregon	35,440	93,993	60,731	9,315,930	262.86	99.11	-1.4	-1.2	-4.3	-23.5
Pennsylvania(b)	218,713	637,387	435,408	64,712,837	295.88	101.53	0.5	-0.3	2.6	9.1
Rhode Island	18,772	53,950	36,563	7,613,825	405.59	141.13	1.2	38.3	7.3	8.7
South Carolina	57,643	156,080	110,573	6,685,505	115.98	42.83	1.2	2.0	4.5	21.8
South Dakota	6,946	18,753	13,120	1,555,186	223.90	82.93	-0.8	0.6	-7.1	-1.8
Tennessee	65,958	173,854	122,637	7,448,916	112.93	42.85	0.9	0.5	10.2	10.7
Texas	106,104	320,002	232,384	11,490,205	108.29	35.91	0.4	0.9	4.5	4.6
Utah	13,954	43,710	27,335	4,504,653	322.82	103.06	(a)	0.4	25.9	33.8
Vermont	8,129	24,251	15,379	2,839,074	349.25	117.07	0.1	0.3	14.7	21.2
Virginia	65,272	175,927	121,821	14,487,213	221.95	82.35	1.4	1.5	7.8	19.1
Washington	61,639	173,339	108,234	23,443,682	380.19	135.20	2.3	4.1	20.9	27.2
West Virginia	28,026	79,970	60,820	4,970,373	177.35	62.15	3.0	2.5	3.8	5.6
Wisconsin	85,129	231,979	154,465	32,026,663	376.21	138.06	1.1	1.9	15.2	26.7
Wyoming	2,737	7,008	4,996	720,012	263.07	102.74	-0.3	-0.9	6.5	8.3
Dist. of Col.	30,278	81,985	56,556	7,661,257	253.03	93.45	0.1	1.5	-5.1	-4.4
Guam	1,492	5,311	3,877	316,333	212.02	59.56	-1.0	0.2	12.4	15.6
Puerto Rico	46,245	169,697	118,368	2,812,545	60.82	16.57	1.9	24.3	-2.9	14.9
Virgin Islands	1,165	3,441	2,721	228,534	196.17	66.41	4.0	10.6	13.3	57.6

Source: *Public Assistance Statistics*, U.S. Department of Health and Human Services, Social Security Administration, Office of Research and Statistics, December 1980.

*Includes non-medical vendor payments, unemployed parent segment and AFDC-Foster Care data.

(a) Increase or decrease of less than 0.05 percent.

(b) Estimated data.

Table 3

SUPPLEMENTAL SECURITY INCOME FOR AGED, BLIND AND DISABLED PERSONS RECEIVING FEDERALLY ADMINISTERED PENSIONS

State or other jurisdiction	Number of persons receiving federally administered payments				Payment (in thousands)			Average monthly amount of combined federal and state payments in states with federally administered state supplements			
	Total	Aged	Blind	Disabled	Total federal payments	Federal SSI	Federally administered state supplementation	Total	Aged	Blind	Disabled
United States(a)	4,037,881	1,701,964	78,371	2,257,546	$736,244	$580,048	$156,195	...	...	...	...
Alabama(b)	131,124	71,917	1,920	57,287	19,126	19,126	...	...	...	...	...
Alaska(b)	3,079	1,158	55	1,866	544	544	...	...	...	...	...
Arizona(b)	29,212	10,968	586	17,658	5,246	5,246	...	...	...	...	...
Arkansas	75,473	40,299	1,474	33,700	10,203	10,197	6	$135.18	$106.09	$180.46	$167.99
California	698,612	304,202	18,077	376,333	180,685	73,251	107,434	258.63	205.96	315.58	298.48
Colorado(b)	29,543	12,074	363	17,106	4,525	4,525	...	...	...	...	...
Connecticut(b)	23,453	7,020	379	16,054	3,976	3,976	...	...	...	...	...
Delaware	6,996	2,398	153	4,445	1,093	1,055	38	156.22	99.78	175.22	186.02
Florida	172,422	83,195	2,765	86,462	29,959	29,958	1	173.75	150.72	199.46	195.09
Georgia	151,206	67,458	2,933	80,815	22,826	22,817	8	150.96	114.41	189.82	180.05
Hawaii	10,073	4,780	161	5,132	2,011	1,630	381	199.66	169.51	226.81	226.89
Idaho(b)	7,450	2,423	112	4,915	1,131	1,131	...	...	...	...	...
Illinois(b)	122,111	33,479	1,860	86,772	20,757	20,757	...	...	...	...	...
Indiana(b)	41,018	13,728	1,137	26,153	6,128	6,128	...	...	...	...	...
Iowa	25,174	10,028	1,033	14,113	3,466	3,375	91	137.69	90.94	176.51	168.07
Kansas	20,049	7,314	303	12,432	2,806	2,800	6	139.98	100.72	164.64	162.47
Kentucky(b)	93,259	39,660	2,041	51,558	15,161	15,161	...	...	...	...	...
Louisiana	132,167	60,441	2,150	69,576	21,175	21,161	14	160.21	124.85	197.10	189.79
Maine	20,915	8,933	292	11,690	2,790	2,422	368	133.40	77.43	177.23	175.08
Maryland	47,515	15,219	667	31,629	8,181	8,164	17	172.17	113.00	198.24	200.09
Massachusetts	111,539	55,835	5,013	50,691	20,629	11,793	8,836	184.95	135.71	246.98	233.05
Michigan	111,897	35,022	1,884	74,991	21,965	16,812	5,153	196.29	132.43	222.10	225.47
Minnesota(b)	30,982	11,908	639	18,435	4,147	4,147	...	...	...	...	...
Mississippi	111,081	58,890	1,817	50,374	16,728	16,721	6	150.59	115.67	197.16	189.74
Missouri(b)	81,420	36,620	1,335	43,465	12,463	12,463	...	...	...	...	...
Montana	6,834	2,153	137	4,544	1,081	1,020	61	158.12	97.06	180.96	186.36
Nebraska(b)	13,294	4,908	231	8,155	1,920	1,920	...	...	...	...	...
Nevada	6,706	3,431	451	2,824	1,112	884	228	165.75	139.34	217.16	189.64
New Hampshire(b)	5,296	1,896	130	3,270	802	802	...	...	...	...	...
New Jersey	84,192	30,910	1,131	52,151	15,530	13,195	2,336	184.46	147.01	204.54	206.23

New Mexico(b)	25,075	9,972	453	14,650	4,089	4,089	...	...	...	...	...
New York	355,616	127,911	4,086	223,619	75,616	56,019	19,597	212.63	160.57	229.59	242.10
North Carolina(b)	137,416	60,734	3,048	73,634	20,635	20,635	...	...	...	...	...
North Dakota(b)	6,130	2,993	75	3,062	845	845	...	...	...	...	...
Ohio	116,988	32,106	2,314	82,568	19,850	19,839	11	169.68	110.07	187.63	192.35
Oklahoma(b)	64,170	31,300	987	31,883	9,381	9,381	...	...	...	...	...
Oregon(b)	22,066	6,930	492	14,644	3,484	3,484	...	...	...	...	...
Pennsylvania	158,788	53,342	3,162	102,284	29,564	24,647	4,916	186.18	125.45	242.57	216.11
Rhode Island	14,826	5,666	204	8,956	2,454	1,851	603	165.53	116.39	203.86	195.75
South Carolina(b)	82,280	36,372	1,882	44,026	12,273	12,273	...	...	...	...	...
South Dakota	7,940	3,587	140	4,231	1,077	1,073	4	135.66	97.53	201.47	165.94
Tennessee	127,665	57,245	1,977	68,443	19,397	19,396	1	151.94	108.94	199.99	186.51
Texas(c)	255,951	139,607	4,225	112,119	35,829	35,829	...	...	...	...	...
Utah(b)	7,613	2,275	156	5,182	1,168	1,168	...	...	...	...	...
Vermont	8,725	3,400	121	5,204	1,526	1,092	434	174.86	117.65	218.12	211.24
Virginia(b)	79,761	33,051	1,390	45,320	12,123	12,123	...	...	...	...	...
Washington	43,825	14,214	563	29,048	7,988	6,605	1,382	182.26	126.03	212.04	209.20
West Virginia(b)	40,336	12,691	659	26,986	7,177	7,177	...	...	...	...	...
Wisconsin	61,153	25,158	947	35,048	10,191	6,271	3,920	166.65	111.34	212.19	205.12
Wyoming(b)	1,736	685	36	1,015	251	251	...	...	...	...	...
Dist. of Col.	15,080	4,094	206	10,780	3,007	2,665	342	199.39	135.64	212.47	223.35
No. Mariana Is.(c)	602	347	19	236	131	131	...	...	...	...	...
Unknown	47	17	...	30	26	26	...	...	...	...	...

Source: Supplemental Security Income Monthly Statistics, Department of Health and Human Services, Social Security Administration, Office of Policy, September 1981.

(a) Includes persons with federal SSI payments and/or federally administered state supplementation, unless otherwise indicated.

(b) Data for federal SSI payments only. State has state-administered supplementation.

(c) Data for federal SSI payments only; state supplementary payments not made.

Table 4
FOOD STAMP PROGRAM
(As of March 1981)

State or other jurisdiction	Monthly household recipients	Monthly individual recipients	Monthly total value of coupons issued	Monthly average value per person	Monthly average value per household
United States........	8,336,316	22,807,162	$962,423,832	$41.73	$114.00
Alabama	214,371	610,970	26,623,612	43.35	124.19
Alaska	13,450	39,681	2,693,001	69.22	200.22
Arizona	73,599	204,786	10,715,766	50.45	145.59
Arkansas	110,430	315,418	12,644,646	39.96	114.50
California	610,482	1,615,981	36,016,957	34.05	91.75
Colorado	70,177	184,174	8,079,349	44.16	115.12
Connecticut..........	69,794	175,732	6,685,269	37.45	95.78
Delaware	23,385	56,650	2,557,664	43.93	109.37
Florida	385,959	969,970	45,035,219	45.94	116.68
Georgia	235,506	674,531	28,030,446	41.39	119.02
Hawaii	40,450	102,643	6,029,884	58.29	149.07
Idaho	25,191	69,311	3,266,269	47.19	129.66
Illinois..............	388,302	981,927	46,457,965	46.16	119.64
Indiana..............	145,669	425,004	18,733,053	44.01	128.60
Iowa	66,078	167,890	6,738,806	39.65	101.98
Kansas	44,556	108,616	4,703,165	42.18	105.55
Kentucky	179,522	530,736	24,421,112	45.16	136.03
Louisiana............	204,676	587,254	24,415,939	41.69	119.29
Maine	58,446	151,445	6,501,432	43.51	111.24
Maryland	104,021	354,014	15,422,607	43.30	103.49
Massachusetts.........	170,978	449,710	17,347,544	38.29	101.46
Michigan	397,733	950,161	35,903,593	37.05	90.27
Minnesota(a)..........	80,453	204,529	7,674,935	37.13	95.39
Mississippi	167,801	528,054	21,138,277	40.05	125.97
Missouri.............	143,397	387,161	16,677,059	42.46	116.30
Montana	18,627	49,198	2,079,813	41.75	111.65
Nebraska	29,706	79,326	2,874,786	36.33	96.77
Nevada..............	16,998	41,206	1,903,402	46.80	111.97
New Hampshire	23,490	57,026	2,555,365	44.10	108.78
New Jersey...........	211,100	632,900	24,000,000	38.97	113.69
New Mexico	63,712	189,941	8,200,801	43.12	128.71
New York(a)..........	767,437	1,853,418	79,348,081	41.95	103.39
North Carolina........	223,098	635,802	25,213,487	39.61	113.02
North Dakota	10,741	29,970	1,121,926	36.61	104.45
Ohio(a)	373,642	977,195	44,761,773	45.47	119.75
Oklahoma	84,416	215,338	7,529,776	35.39	89.19
Oregon(a)	96,529	232,936	11,951,941	50.07	123.81
Pennsylvania..........	465,378	1,075,467	42,986,601	39.78	92.36
Rhode Island	33,845	88,535	3,475,032	42.17	102.67
South Carolina(a)	152,621	454,194	18,796,889	41.66	123.16
South Dakota	16,257	47,074	1,912,894	40.85	117.67
Tennessee	268,118	705,065	30,790,856	43.60	114.84
Texas	390,225	1,251,235	54,241,275	43.44	139.00
Utah(a)	19,908	62,502	2,620,492	40.86	131.63
Vermont(a)	15,852	46,162	1,816,792	39.71	114.61
Virginia(a)...........	167,938	444,280	18,263,541	40.68	108.75
Washington...........	118,567	281,619	13,961,288	49.36	117.75
West Virginia	79,348	237,481	10,067,776	41.65	126.88
Wisconsin	103,101	271,321	9,389,165	33.72	91.06
Wyoming..............	6,119	15,558	677,442	42.54	110.71
Dist. of Col.	43,190	102,682	4,315,894	41.65	99.92
Guam	5,572	25,380	1,579,224	61.22	283.42
Puerto Rico...........	497,855	1,823,236	75,673,951	41.87	152.00
Virgin Islands	8,500	34,767	1,800,800	51.72	211.76

Source: Food and Nutrition Service, U.S. Department of Agriculture.
(a) State totals exclude SSI/Elderly Cash-Out Demonstration Project.

Table 5
MEDICAID VENDOR PAYMENTS: FISCAL 1979

State or other jurisdiction	Total payment computable for federal funding(a) (in millions)	Percent federal share	Adjusted federal share (in millions)	State share (in millions)	Local share (in millions)
Total	$21,421.1	...	$11,385.5	$8,449.5	$812.6
Alabama	237.3	71.32	174.1	64.9	0
Alaska	28.5	50.00	15.3	13.6	0
Arizona(b)	...	...	...	...	...
Arkansas	200.5	72.82	146.2	55.9	0
California	2,618.6	50.00	1,294.2	1,306.2	0
Colorado	163.7	53.16	88.0	73.6	0
Connecticut	296.5	50.00	146.7	147.8	0
Delaware	39.0	50.00	21.0	18.2	0
Florida	364.6	58.94	203.9	158.1	0
Georgia	400.5	66.76	257.4	136.5	0
Hawaii	83.9	50.00	41.8	41.7	0
Idaho	46.4	65.70	30.4	16.9	0
Illinois	957.4	50.00	471.7	477.4	0
Indiana	318.1	57.86	181.1	137.0	0
Iowa	205.5	56.57	106.0	75.5	22.7
Kansas	171.3	53.52	89.1	81.4	0
Kentucky	258.7	68.07	179.1	78.0	0
Louisiana	344.6	68.82	247.1	101.9	0
Maine	125.1	69.53	87.0	37.7	0
Maryland	338.1	50.00	170.3	168.4	0
Massachusetts	963.8	51.75	490.7	465.7	0
Michigan	1,070.6	50.00	541.6	532.1	0
Minnesota	488.5	55.64	267.4	197.5	20.4
Mississippi	203.7	77.55	161.9	44.4	0
Missouri	235.7	60.36	148.7	92.4	0
Montana	54.4	64.28	33.2	21.1	0
Nebraska	95.3	57.62	53.7	28.7	15.6
Nevada	32.8	50.00	16.1	16.3	0
New Hampshire	61.5	61.11	38.4	22.8	0
New Jersey	684.3	50.00	343.5	340.8	0
New Mexico	60.8	69.03	43.9	16.9	0
New York	3,630.4	50.00	1,757.4	1,116.5	693.8
North Carolina	347.6	67.64	241.4	88.1	23.4
North Dakota	42.6	61.44	21.5	18.7	2.3
Ohio	681.7	55.10	382.9	303.3	0
Oklahoma	261.9	63.64	173.8	90.4	0
Oregon	166.4	55.66	96.6	69.6	1.0
Pennsylvania	1,141.4	55.14	623.2	487.9	23.5
Rhode Island	134.9	57.81	79.7	57.9	0
South Carolina	196.2	70.97	135.9	54.9	0
South Dakota	49.9	68.74	31.7	17.7	0
Tennessee	322.7	68.88	222.3	100.4	0
Texas	937.1	58.35	566.8	367.8	0
Utah	74.7	68.07	57.3	22.9	0.2
Vermont	53.6	68.40	36.7	17.1	0
Virginia	302.4	56.54	181.0	129.6	0
Washington	302.0	50.00	156.1	145.4	0
West Virginia	94.1	67.35	65.7	28.1	0
Wisconsin	629.7	57.95	360.0	260.4	0
Wyoming	11.3	50.00	6.0	5.2	0
Dist. of Col.	142.0	50.00	70.0	70.4	0.3
Guam	2.2	50.00	0.9	0	1.1
Puerto Rico	60.2	50.00	28.3	24.5	7.4
Virgin Islands	1.5	50.00	0.8	(c)	0.8

Source: Expenditures for Public Assistance Programs, Fiscal Year 1979, Office of Research and Statistics, SSA, Department of Health and Human Services.

(a) Represents only those payments for which FFP is allowed. Thus, these numbers differ from "Total Payments" found in other tables.
(b) No Title XIX program in effect.
(c) Less than .05.

Table 6
TOTAL ESTIMATED TITLE XX EXPENDITURES: FISCAL 1980

State or other jurisdiction	Total Title XX expenditure estimates FY 1979 (in thousands)	Total Title XX expenditure estimates FY 1980 (in thousands)	Change in total expenditure estimates FY 1979-80 (in thousands)	Percentage change in estimated expenditures FY 1979-80
Total...................	$39,600	$42,000	+240	+6.1
Alabama.................	65,980	65,960	-20	0.0
Alaska..................	6,140	6,300	+160	+2.6
Arizona	41,500	60,070	+18,570	+44.7
Arkansas	32,770	33,610	+840	+2.6
California..............	447,760	498,920	+51,160	+11.4
Colorado	44,010	46,800	+2,790	+6.3
Connecticut.............	77,700	61,000	-16,700	-21.5
Delaware	9,740	9,700	-40	-0.4
Florida	139,640	149,250	+9,610	+6.9
Georgia.................	86,170	91,480	+5,310	+6.2
Hawaii	13,600	14,720	+1,120	+8.2
Idaho	12,900	13,230	+330	+2.6
Illinois................	278,500	270,120	-8,380	-3.0
Indiana	86,470	90,500	+4,030	+4.7
Iowa	47,450	50,540	+3,090	+6.5
Kansas	35,730	36,560	+830	+2.3
Kentucky	53,910	55,020	+1,110	+2.1
Louisiana	62,670	61,450	-1,220	-2.0
Maine	19,100	20,910	+1,810	+9.5
Maryland	65,340	74,890	+9,550	+14.6
Massachusetts	157,920	182,830	+24,910	+15.8
Michigan	163,990	163,160	-830	-0.5
Minnesota	61,520	72,070	+10,550	+17.1
Mississippi	40,010	36,700	-3,310	-8.3
Missouri	79,980	86,850	+6,870	+8.6
Montana	15,320	17,840	+2,520	+16.4
Nebraska	24,330	27,900	+3,570	+14.7
Nevada	9,580	10,010	+430	+4.5
New Hampshire	13,420	14,730	+1,310	+9.8
New Jersey..............	126,810	128,110	+1,300	+1.0
New Mexico	18,000	20,580	+2,580	+14.3
New York................	280,810	316,870	+36,060	+12.8
North Carolina	84,270	84,470	+200	+0.2
North Dakota	10,310	10,380	+70	+0.7
Ohio	166,480	164,480	-2,000	-1.2
Oklahoma	43,430	44,610	-1,180	-2.7
Oregon	49,540	59,470	+9,930	+20.0
Pennsylvania	244,540	213,760	-30,780	-12.6
Rhode Island	16,960	18,540	+1,580	+9.3
South Carolina	49,920	54,090	+4,170	+8.3
South Dakota	11,440	12,250	+810	+7.1
Tennessee...............	68,190	71,870	+3,680	+5.4
Texas	215,510	249,240	+33,730	+15.7
Utah	19,000	20,030	+1,030	+5.4
Vermont.................	7,350	7,350	0	0.0
Virginia................	86,280	92,080	+5,800	+6.7
Washington	75,280	105,510	+30,230	+40.2
West Virginia...........	38,120	38,910	+790	+2.1
Wisconsin	106,900	116,230	+9,330	+8.7
Wyoming	6,010	6,940	+930	+15.5
Dist. of Col............	41,760	40,860	-900	-2.2

Source: Technical Notes: Summaries and Characteristics of States' Title XX Social Services Plans for Fiscal Year 1980, U.S. Department of Health and Human Services, Office of the Assistant Secretary for Planning and Evaluation.

MENTAL HEALTH AND DEVELOPMENTAL DISABILITIES

By William J. Page Jr.

GREAT UNCERTAINTIES were in prospect for state and local mental health and developmental service organizations as they faced calendar year 1982. Radical changes in public policy, recently made or proposed, made dismal the prospects for public financial support.

Mental health and developmental disabilities were among the most innovative and active components of a generally lively human services sector in the 1960s and 1970s. Public policies developed and implemented during these two decades reflected increased public awareness and governmental willingness to engage social problems. New treatment styles were developed and applied widely, and more resources—physical, human and fiscal—expanded services; however, threats to these trends in the 1980s produced anxiety about possible reversal of recent gains and consequent waste of human potential.

Mental Health

Mental illness is among the most frequent and widely distributed health problems in the United States. Although incidence and prevalence are not precisely established, estimates indicate that 15 percent of the population are affected by a mental disorder each year. Approximately 3 million are severely affected. Twenty-four million persons are moderately to severely disabled as a consequence. More than half of the severely disordered persons, or about 1.7 million, experience severe and prolonged disability and are classified as chronically mentally ill.[1]

It is unknown whether incidence and severity have declined, increased or remained fairly constant over the centuries. One thing is certain: the problem has been part of this nation's history from the beginning. Provision was made in colonial Williamsburg, Virginia, in the 18th century for a public residential facility for the mentally disordered.

Social isolation, neglect, mistreatment and earnest efforts to care for mentally ill persons were concurrent historical patterns. Occasionally, these actions overlapped because of the mystical aura that surrounded mental illness and produced misconceptions of the sources of disease and appropriate treatment. Signs of such disorders were widely believed to indicate flawed moral character, manifestation of divine punishment or manipulation by demonic forces. It probably seemed logical to impose rigid discipline, physical punishment, strict religious practices and forceful restraints.

Society had learned enough by the mid-19th century to support a movement led by Dorothea Dix to revise old practices and provide better care. The U.S. Congress responded through passage of a bill in 1854 which would have provided federal resources to support improved care. President Franklin Pierce, apparently inept in health policy, vetoed the bill, asserting that mental health was not a proper concern of national government and

William J. Page Jr. is Professor of Public Administration and Social Work at Florida State University, Tallahassee, Florida.

that it should be handled by the states. His negative decision established federal policy respecting mental health for nearly a century.

Meanwhile, state and local governments built and operated "mental hospitals." These facilities frequently were located on sites far removed from population centers. The labor-intensive, mainly custodial character of care in these institutions made them particularly attractive as income producers in economically depressed areas. Long hospital stays meant steady jobs and a socially acceptable alternative to home care of mentally disturbed persons. The homeless, aged and mentally retarded were usually included with mental patients. Overloaded facilities were in part the result of institutional compassion, political accommodations and lack of alternative arrangements.

Experiences during and after World War II wrought changes in mental health policy. The high rates of draft deferrals and mental illness among medical dischargees focused national attention on mental health. The issues were lack of manpower and a social commitment to care for veterans of the recent war. Public policy was expressed in the National Mental Health Act of 1946.

The landmark legislation provided grants to states (with dollar matching arrangements), planning for community mental health programs, educational and consultative activities, expansion of clinical capacity, rehabilitation of former patients, and intensification of preventive work in alcoholism and drug addiction. The peak of state mental hospitalization was reached in 1955, when 559,000 persons were in residental care.[2]

Pharmacotherapy and psychosocial therapeutic techniques were important factors in reducing the populations of state mental hospitals after 1955. Even more important was the emergence of the community mental health services ideology. Many mental health professionals and public policy-makers believed that the large mental hospitals, which they frequently labeled "human warehouses," should be closed and public resources used to support locally controlled, community-based, comprehensive services. Ascendance of this ideology over the politically entrenched state hospitals produced the Community Mental Health Centers Construction Act of 1963 (P.L. 88-164).

This policy caused major changes. Federal funds appropriated for mental health were given directly to local community mental health centers without passing through the state government. The state mental health authorities were encouraged to review the local and private centers' applications for funds and reduce state hospital populations. Thus, a two-tiered system of mental health services was established, one in which privately controlled centers provided the bulk of local services while states provided hospital care. Extensions of and amendments to the Community Mental Health Centers Construction Act in 1965, 1967 and 1970 provided authority and expanded resources for an increasingly dichotomous arrangement.

Two additional pieces of legislation reinforced the new strategy—Titles XVIII (Medicare) and XIX (Medicaid), added to the Social Security Act in 1965. A series of amendments to the Social Security Act in 1962, 1967 and 1974 also increased resources for social services in mental health programs. These programs provided financial incentives for private care of persons formerly treated in public hospitals. New energy was added to the idea that deinstitutionalization was an unmitigated good and that communities could and would provide services of better quality than care in large state hospitals.

Experience did not always square with the ideal. Ideological commitment to community mental health services displaced careful planning. Persons who were discharged from state mental hospitals too frequently returned to local communities which did not welcome them and were not prepared to serve them. They congregated in cities, often drifting aimlessly and not using local services that might have been available. Communication between state hospitals and local, privately controlled mental health centers frequently was inadequate or non-existent. Mass media and scholarly literature raised doubts about the efficacy of fragmented, disparate service.[3]

Other problems influenced the expected transition from dependence on large inpatient facilities to community services. Some of the more significant difficulties were:

- State mental hospitals received strong political support from their surrounding communities and other sources; resistance to rapid change often was sufficiently effective to protect their budgets.

- The expectation that community mental health centers would be able to coordinate local services was inadequately realized.

- Resources for local services were uncertain because of determinate federal statutory authorities for staffing and other essentials; last-minute renewals produced lurches and halts in local program development.

The institutional durability of state and local mental hospitals is a function of politics, social utility and adaptation. Reasons for political support were economic, personal and local, and utility was due partly to the shortage or absence of alternative services and partly to traditional values. In any case, the high hospital census of 559,000 in 1959 declined to 370,000 in 1969 and 216,000 in 1974. Adaptation by hospitals is evidenced by three factors: number of institutions, dispersion and shorter average lengths of stay. The increase in number from 275 in 1955 to 313 in 1976 and dispersion improved accessibility to patients. The increase of admissions from 180,000 in 1955 to 400,000 in 1976 was possible because of improved therapeutic techniques and use of nursing homes and other types of facilities for long-term, less intensive care.

The overall effect is one of failure to design and implement a system of mental health services under changing and often conflicting policies. None of the participating entities is free of blame in this debacle. Elected and appointed federal officials, ideologically aligned with community mental health interest groups, distrusted the states and by-passed them with direct support for local private entities. States, given opportunity for planning change and minor federal support for their obsolescent clinical facilities, failed to provide resources adequate to assure high quality of services and maximize their influence in integration of public and private systems. Community mental health centers, constantly anxious about the possibility of state control, failed to coordinate local programs and cooperate with states in establishing systematic local service arrangements.

Evaluation might have been institutionalized and used to improve systems, but political, technical and ideological factors prevented appropriate evaluation. Although the 1975 Amendments to the Mental Health Centers Act (P.L. 94-63) specifically required evaluation, several deterrents to effective evaluation were apparent. Information was even scarcer than the will to perform rigorous, standardized evaluation of national and state operations. In fact, goals and their relative priority varied among national, state and local policy-makers and administrators. Evaluation of systems reflected this variance as well as differing competence in the technology of evaluation. In an effort to solve some of these problems, performance contracting was developed and first applied on state initiative to state-local fiscal transfers in the latter half of the 1970s. By this time, Congress (through its own committees and the work of the General Accounting Office), a succession of presidents, governors and local officials had registered sufficient dissatisfaction to assure another round of change.

President Jimmy Carter established the President's Commission on Mental Health in February 1977 to review the mental health situation and recommend policy revision. The commission's report in 1978 significantly influenced formation of the "Partnership for Mental Health Act" which was offered by state officials as a substitute for the federal government's draft, "The Mental Health Systems Act." Different values related to the state role were reflected in the two policy proposals. When the congressional political dust settled, a typical compromise was enacted. The Mental Health Systems Act of 1980 (P.L. 96-398) was signed by President Carter on October 7, 1980. The act and its legislative history preserved an element of the "partnership" doctrine of the states, authorizing the states to plan and oversee mental health services that used funds under the new legislation. The performance contracting concept did not survive as a major feature of the revised policy. The net effect of this sequence of events was a policy base which could be used to unify state and local programs into mental health service systems. The states, whose expenditures for mental health services are nearly ten times as great as the federal government's, had regained influence over system development and operations.

Mental Health Situation and Prospects for the 1980s

Any expectations of stable policy, a less turbulent environment and more resources were dispelled by two national developments: severe economic recession and radical national policy change respecting human services.

Sharp and extensive economic recession in 1981 had two results. State and local revenues from sales taxes and other sources dropped sharply. Unemployment, which increased from 7 to 8.9 percent in the period July-December 1981, signaled increased service demands. A survey by the National Conference of State Legislatures indicated that the fiscal prospects for 1982 were even gloomier than recent adversities.[4] Half of the states had begun to reduce their work forces.

Economic recession was exacerbated by federal policy changes with long-range implications. National defense gained higher priority than human services. Recisions of funds appropriated for fiscal 1981 began early in calendar year 1981, causing abrupt changes in service programs. Block grants, long advocated by state policy-makers, were legislated with sharp reductions in planned expenditures for fiscal 1982. The National Governors' Association reported the bad news: ". . . appropriations for major programs of interest to state governments will be 15.6% lower in FY 1982 than in FY 1980 and 17.5% lower than in FY 1981. In terms of constant dollars . . . appropriations are 36.7% lower in FY 1982 than in 1980 and 26.5% lower than in FY 1981."[5] The nine block grants enacted in 1981 apparently were slated for a 22.7 percent reduction in fiscal 1982, taking inflation into account.

Uncertainty compounded state anxieties. Only 10 of 13 fiscal 1982 appropriation bills had been enacted by the Congress at the end of 1981. The remaining programs were covered by the third in a series of continuing resolutions for the period ending March 31, 1982. Most of the human services were in this state of fiscal limbo. "Health, Income Security, and Social Services," the federal budgetary entity which includes intergovernmental assistance through the Department of Health and Human Services, apparently would be reduced (in constant dollars) 17.3 percent and 15.9 percent compared to fiscal 1981, respectively.[6]

The cutback in the block grant for alcohol, drug abuse and mental health was considerably more than for some other "blocked" items. The actual appropriation for these three programs was $624.8 million. Compared to $548.7 million (the amount available after recisions) in fiscal 1981, the continuing resolution for fiscal 1982 promised only $432 million, or a reduction of 21.3 percent in constant dollars. None of the nine block grants gained an increase in purchasing power, compared to fiscal 1981.[7]

Making it clear that the federal government intends to minimize its involvement in human service programs, President Reagan reported in January 1982 that he would propose federal withdrawal from most grant-aided human service programs in the future, concurrently rescinding all or portions of certain federal excise taxes in favor of state taxation.

The most optimistic outlook for mental health services is one which includes further reductions of federal financing, increases in state taxation to compensate partially, and dramatic reductions in the federal role. This would return states and local communities to their pre-1946 status, which vested total responsibility in states and localities.

Developmental Services

The high incidence and prevalence of mental retardation distinguish this condition from epilepsy, cerebral palsy, autism and other developmental disabilities. Mental retardation occurs more frequently and outnumbers the other handicaps. Because the criteria for designation of persons as mentally retarded vary from place to place and over time, historical data may be invalid and unreliable. Unlike some congenital anomalies, which are always apparent at birth, mental retardation sometimes cannot be identified, even by professionals, in the first weeks, months or years after the birth of a child. Professionals may disagree whether symptoms and degree of severity warrant a classification of "mentally retarded" and whether the cause is genetic, environmental or both.

The President's Committee on Mental Retardation estimated incidence and prevalence. The incidence of mental retardation is estimated at 3 percent of births each year, of which 89.0 percent are mildly retarded, 6.0 percent are moderately retarded, 3.5 percent are severely retarded and 1.5 percent are profoundly retarded.[8] The prevalence of all developmental disabilities is probably 10 million in the population of the United States. Experts who make such estimates are among the first to qualify the numbers, calling attention to many uncertainties in the data.

The history of public services for mentally retarded persons indicates that the first organized efforts to educate mentally retarded children began in several states in the 1850s. Between 1850 and 1900 the model of public service to this group was the "colony." In the first half of the 20th century, programs were designed to identify, segregate and sterilize mentally retarded persons—and in some states this approach lasted beyond 1950.[9]

Initial programs were developed and operated by state and local governments and private organizations. Federal policy did not develop until 1912, when the Children's Bureau was established in the Department of Labor. The bureau immediately began studies of mental retardation in Washington, D.C., and Delaware. The first significant policy for education of the handicapped came in 1963, when the Division for Handicapped Children and Youth was established in the U.S. Office of Education and funds provided for planning, services and construction assistance to the states (P.L. 88-164).

The 1960s and 1970s produced legislation, program innovations and great expansion of services to developmentally disabled citizens. From a historical pattern of custodial care, program designs moved through a treatment model to the present developmental model. Modern delivery of services in the states follows one or more of the following patterns:

- The specialized mental retardation or developmental disabilities service center, which emphasizes alternatives to long-term institutionalization.
- Existing residential institutions as administrative foci of regional service systems.
- Substate regional administrative arrangements, within a "comprehensive" human services agency or limited to mental retardation or all developmental disabilities.
- Regional human service centers, which include all or most human service organizations operating in the area.

The most significant changes have been in program philosophy and design and in expansion of community-based, public and private systems. Large residential institutions were the mainstay in earlier years. In the period 1965-1974, the average size of such institutions dropped dramatically from approximately 950 beds to 240 beds. The number of patients in 176 public residential facilities declined from a peak of 155,000 in 1970 to 141,000 in 1974.[10] Few of the mental retardation institutions have been disestablished, but most have changed. Some switched from custodial to intensive service methods, and some reduced the number of clients. More residents are in the severely and profoundly retarded categories, and thus cannot be treated by many local communities. The trend definitely is toward smaller, residential facilities, group homes and other less restrictive environments.

Changes toward normalization of living arrangements did not come spontaneously. The greatest single influence probably has been a coalition of tens of thousands of advocates, organized into interest groups such as the National Association for Retarded Citizens. These organizations, nationally and in hundreds of local chapters, have influenced public policy and its implementation through lobbying, service on public advisory councils, program monitoring and advocacy of individuals. Activism is not limited to mental retardation. Public agencies have changed names and functions from mental retardation to developmental disabilities, in part because of advocates of persons with cerebral palsy, epilepsy, autism and other developmental handicaps.

The public policy changed in other ways favorable to developmental service. Medicaid, Medicare, Supplemental Security Income, social services and disability benefits were made available through additions to the Social Security program. Hospitalization, intermediate care, training and rehabilitative services expanded. Specific federal legislation provided token support to state and local school systems for education of the handicapped. In education, as in most service areas, state and local governments continued to provide the great majority (more than three-fourths) of financial support and other resources.

Developmental services display the usual characteristics of special interests. The overall strategy is to get maximum services and other benefits for a particular group. Advocates, policy-makers and administrators alike have difficulty coordinating programs and service delivery. Federal organizations tend to operate separately and a similar tendency is apparent in state and local realms. The advocacy organizations themselves occasionally show signs of competitiveness and refraction of efforts. This general tendency toward multiple centers has encouraged a majority of the states to consolidate administrative arrangements of their human service systems. The resultant organizational forms, which vary widely in degrees of unification, are known as "umbrella agencies."

Two federal legislative initiatives had major influences on developmental services between 1975 and 1980. The first of these was the Developmentally Disabled Assistance and Bill of Rights Act of 1975 (P.L. 94-103). This act, in addition to providing improved coordination and adding programs, expanded the domain of developmental services to include autism and dyslexia. The second major legislative action involved amendments to the

Developmental Disabilities and Facilities Construction Act (P.L. 95-602) in 1978, which redefined developmental disabilities functionally, rather than categorically, and made other improvements in national program design and resource authorization. This policy expansion covered more than 3 million persons who previously might not have been served. These legislative changes were significant, but they appear miniscule in comparison to the Reagan administration's sweeping proposals—and initial congressional actions—to overhaul the entire federal system.

The developmental disability programs had been aggregated, maintaining certain program distinctions, before the block grant legislation of 1981 (Omnibus Budget Reconciliation Act of 1981, P.L. 97-35). The only substantive amendment to the developmental disabilities statute was deletion of evaluation requirements. The appropriations outlook was the major dimension of intergovernmental policy change for developmental services.

As of December 1981, the outlook for resources in developmental services included the following actual or prospective changes:

- Actual dollar reductions in the pending appropriations bill, from $59.4 million in fiscal 1982. (The president's revised budget request would have provided only $33.7 million.)
- Actual reductions in the social services block grant (formerly Title XX of the Social Security Act).
- Adverse fiscal effects of changes in Medicaid, Supplemental Security Income and other programs.
- President Reagan's proposal for radical revision and eventual phase-out of federal assistance for many current intergovernmental programs serving developmentally disabled persons.

Scarcely any other human service programs would experience as many long-range effects as developmental services.

Conclusion

Mental health and developmental services have much in common. Learning was necessary to counteract misinformation, and that learning was pushed by activists and advocates in cooperation with political leadership. Policy-making and administration were slow to develop and remain only partially successful. Both sets of programs receive most of their financial support from state and local public agencies, but the federal partner's resources have stimulated innovation and service improvements. Service models and facilities in both program areas have changed substantially, though not at a revolutionary pace, during the past three decades. Prevention is highly desirable and underachieved in both areas. Difficulties are encountered in evaluating results in each program area, especially in demonstrating systematic capability for evaluation. Both depend on other major programs, such as Medicaid, for substantial resources in meeting the needs of their clientele. Their similarities do not end with these examples.

Perhaps the most significant common factor is an uncertain future. This uncertainty derives not only from direct reductions of federal funds but from being placed behind national defense and private enterprise on the list of national priorities.

The most optimistic prospect for state mental health and developmental services is minimum damage from radical public policy changes.

Notes

1. National Institute of Mental Health, Division of Mental Health Service Programs, "State Mental Health Service Trends" (Bethesda, Md.: The Institute, December 15, 1981).

2. Ibid.

3. As an example, the chaos which occurred in California in the wake of radical deinstitutionalization is reported by James E. Cameron, "Ideology and Policy Termination: Restructuring California's Mental Health System," in Judith V. May and Aaron B. Wildavsky (eds.), *The Policy Cycle* (Beverly Hills, Calif.: Sage Publications, 1978).

4. Steven D. Gold and Karen Benker, "State Fiscal Conditions as States Entered 1982," National Conference of State Legislatures, Denver, Colorado, January 1982.

5. National Governors' Association, "FY 1982 Appropriations Update," *Infoletter*, December 22, 1981, p. 3.

6. Ibid., p. 4, Table 1.

7. Ibid., p. 5, Table 2.

8. President's Committee on Mental Retardation, *Mental Retardation: Past and Present* (Washington, D.C.: U.S. Government Printing Office, January 1977).

9. Ibid.

10. President's Committee on Mental Retardation, *Report to the President: Mental Retardation: Century of Decision* (Washington, D.C.: U.S. Government Printing Office, March 1976), p. 23.

4. Public Protection

THE STATES AND THE CRIMINAL JUSTICE SYSTEM

By Jack D. Foster

CRIME AND THE ADMINISTRATION of justice continued to interest the states throughout the 1970s, and much attention was given to improving courts and corrections—the two areas of primary state responsibility. Criminal codes were revised in a majority of states, with special attention given to reforming the sentencing structure. As the 1970s came to a close, the federal role in state criminal justice assistance had all but disappeared. The controversial Omnibus Crime Control and Safe Streets Act of 1968, which created the Law Enforcement Assistance Administration (LEAA) through which millions of dollars in federal aid was distributed to state and local governments, ended in 1980 when the Congress, at the urging of the Carter administration, did not fund LEAA for fiscal 1981. Federal funds for criminal justice improvements through the LEAA never represented more than 5 percent of state and local criminal justice expenditures; however, they financed many innovations and programs which probably would never have been supported with state and local funds alone.

The summary below covers major criminal justice activity in the states between 1978 and 1982.

Corrections

Prison conditions continued to be a problem for many states as the 1970s came to a close. Overcrowding was a major source of many problems. The number of state and federal prisoners had reached an all-time high of 314,083 by 1979, with the largest growth occurring in Texas and California.

Major Court Cases

Inmate lawsuits contesting conditions of confinement resulted in several major court orders affecting state correctional systems. In 1979, a federal district judge declared the maximum security Colorado State Penitentiary at Canon City, Colorado, "unfit for human habitation" (*Ramons* v. *Lamm*) and ordered the state to improve conditions in the aging facility. The state already had under construction a replacement facility. Colorado appealed the case, but proceeded to make changes in many of the areas addressed in the lawsuit.

In February 1979, a U.S. District Court judge placed the Alabama state prison system in the receivership control of Governor Fob James for at least one year, declaring that the State Board of Corrections had failed to carry out a prison reform court order issued in January 1976.

Kentucky, in response to a lawsuit, agreed in 1980 to spend $42 million to alleviate over-

Jack D. Foster is former Research Director for The Council of State Governments and is now in private consulting work with State Research Associates, Lexington, Kentucky.

crowding and to make various other changes involving food, fire safety, visiting rights and parole. Maryland was placed under court order to reduce prison overcrowding.

In 1981, a federal District Court ordered Texas, inmate plaintiffs and the U.S. Department of Justice to devise a plan to bring living and working conditions in the state prisons up to "health and safety standards." The court ordered major changes in management, architectural design, and prison locations to correct what the court considered "constitutional violations." Texas appealed the decision.

Prison Disorders

Over the weekend of February 1, 1980, the New Mexico State Prison at Santa Fe was the scene of the most serious prison disorder since the Attica (N.Y.) prison riot in 1971. The three-day uprising resulted in the brutal killing of 33 inmates by other prisoners. A major reason given for the disaster was overcrowding. In a special session, the New Mexico legislature authorized $60 million in bonds for a new prison and $27.9 million in appropriations to make emergency funds available to pay for the out-of-state housing of inmates from the devastated prison, reimbursement of the National Guard, to cover the cost of medical care for those injured in the riot, and to finance the salaries of additional prison personnel.

In May 1981, disorders occurred at three Michigan prisons involving large numbers of inmates but resulting in no deaths. Following the uprising, Governor William G. Milliken noted that the Michigan state prisons were designed to hold 12,874 inmates, but were overcrowded with a current population of 13,111 inmates. Some two years earlier the governor had proposed a major $404 million corrections improvement program for the state, which would have made many changes in the system including the construction of eight new prisoner facilities and a prototype regional jail. A bond issue to finance the program was defeated by Michigan voters in November 1980. However, since then, the Michigan legislature has approved general fund financing for two new facilities to be completed in 1982 and 1983.

Accreditation

In 1974, the Commission on Accreditation for Corrections was created to develop comprehensive, operational standards for corrections and to implement a voluntary national accreditation program. Sponsored by the American Correctional Association with support from the Law Enforcement Assistance Administration, the commission has published 10 volumes of standards for adult and juvenile residential facilities, prisons and jails, and probation and parole services. These standards were developed by corrections professionals for correctional agencies in an effort to maximize use of resources and to improve conditions of confinement. Each standard addresses a specific agency function or activity. Through the implementation of these standards, correctional administrators are able to:

- Minimize the potential for costly, time-consuming litigation.
- Assess strengths and the need for change.
- Approach funding sources with well-documented budget requests.
- Protect the life, health and safety of staff and offenders.
- Improve the overall atmosphere of the agency, including the morale of staff and offenders.

• Enhance the credibility of corrections with the courts and the general public by requiring minimum levels of decency, humane treatment and professional accountability.

The second major function of the commission is accreditation, which is the quality control process for measuring acceptable performance in corrections agencies based on compliance with the standards. The commission began the accreditation process in 1978 and in 1979 became an independent, private, non-profit organization. Accreditation is a three-step process: self-evaluation, independent audit and formal approval/denial of accreditation. During the self-evaluation, an agency documents its compliance with each standard. For those standards with which the agency does not comply, it must prepare a plan indicating how and when the standard will be met. To verify standards compliance, a team of consultant-examiners with a minimum of five years experience audits the agency. During the audit, they review standards documentation, interview staff and offenders, and tour the facility. A report is prepared which describes the agency and the results of the audit.

The panel of the Board of Commissioners elected by the American Correctional Association membership, with three additional members appointed to represent the American Bar Association, the American Institute of Architects and Canada, has sole responsibility for granting or denying accreditation. When granted, accreditation is awarded for a three-year period. During this period, the agency may receive a monitoring visit to ensure compliance maintenance. As of November 1981, 208 agencies had been awarded accreditation, and nearly 700 were in applicant status.

Sentencing

The last few years of the 1970s saw a general toughening of the penalties for more serious crimes in the states. Violent crimes were made subject of greater penalties in California, Idaho, Massachusetts, Michigan, Nebraska, New York, North Carolina, Oklahoma and Tennessee. Colorado, Illinois and Nevada increased the penalty for crimes against the aged. Use of guns in the commission of crimes was accorded stiffer penalties in California, Idaho, Nevada, New Mexico, West Virginia and Wisconsin.

The trend away from indeterminate sentencing which began in the mid-1970s continued on into the early 1980s. Colorado, Connecticut, Hawaii, New Mexico and North Carolina were the latest states to adopt fixed or presumptive sentences for felonies. By 1980, 24 states had adopted some form of mandatory imprisonment or determinate sentence laws, especially for high-fear crimes.

Alaska Attorney General Avrum Gross ordered in 1975 a ban on criminal case plea bargaining in the state. The move was considered innovative, since no other state had totally abolished plea bargaining in all cases. The Alaska Judicial Council, in a study released in 1980, determined that the ban had not inundated the courts with criminal trials or diminished the number of cases in which defendants plead guilty as some opponents had contended. It also found the stiffness of sentences being handed down by judges had increased during the period.

Insanity Plea

Statutory provisions for insanity pleas in criminal cases were revised over the last two years in Florida, Indiana, Iowa, Kansas, Maryland, New York and Oklahoma. Indiana now allows a verdict of ''guilty but mentally ill'' when a defendant enters a plea of insanity. Kansas and Oklahoma adopted similar laws. New York made the courts responsible for custody of persons acquitted of crimes due to insanity and requires hospitals to inform police and potential victims of the pending release of those found incompetent to stand trial. Maryland required defendants who claim insanity or incompetence to stand trial to be held in jail rather than a hospital until evaluation.

Death Penalty

Controversy over the use of death as a penalty for certain crimes was revived in 1972 when the U.S. Supreme Court in *Furman* v. *Georgia* ruled that existing death penalty laws constituted "cruel and unusual punishment." In response to the *Furman* decision, Georgia and other states enacted new capital punishment laws which made death a mandatory penalty for certain offenses. The implication of the *Furman* decision was that the laws were inherently discriminatory because they could be applied differentially for persons convicted of similar offenses. The Supreme Court clarified its position in 1976 when in *Woodson* v. *North Carolina* it struck down mandatory death penalties which do not take into account "aggravating or mitigating" circumstances, but in a later decision that same year it upheld the constitutionality of using death as a penalty (*Gregg* v. *Georgia*.) In the *Gregg* decision the Court upheld the Georgia, Florida and Texas death penalty statutes which contained provision for withholding the death penalty in capital offenses under certain circumstances.

States moved quickly after *Gregg* to enact laws patterned after the Georgia, Florida and Texas statutes, with 20 states making such revisions over the next several years. The first execution to occur following *Gregg* was the death of Gary Gilmore before a firing squad in Utah in 1977 after he refused to seek appeals for his murder conviction. Gilmore's death was followed two years later by the execution of John A. Spenkelink, a convicted murderer in Florida. Spenkelink's execution was carried out in 1979 after the First Circuit Court of Appeals in New Orleans denied a stay of execution, concluding that he had waited too long to raise the compliant that his 1973 trial counsel was incompetent. Steven Judy, confessed killer of a young mother and her three children, was executed in 1981 becoming the fourth convicted murderer to be executed since 1976, as Indiana enforced its death penalty.

The issue has not been entirely settled as yet. South Dakota and New Mexico both reinstated the death penalty in 1979. Governor Hugh L. Carey of New York vetoed death penalty legislation for the fourth consecutive year in 1980, arguing for mandatory life imprisonment without parole as preferable to death. Governor John Carlin of Kansas vetoed a death penalty bill three times. On the other side of the issue, Governor Charles Thone of Nebraska vetoed in 1979 a bill that would have substituted a mandatory minimum 30-year prison sentence for first-degree murder while eliminating the death penalty.

Nor is the litigation ended. The Rhode Island Supreme Court ruled in 1979 that the state's death penalty law was unconstitutional. It said the 1973 law did not allow judicial discretion in sentencing. The Massachusetts Supreme Court struck down that state's death penalty in 1980 saying that its 1979 statute could be arbitrarily applied. In 1980, a federal appeals court ruled against an Alabama death penalty law because it failed to meet the constitutionality test set forth in *Gregg* v. *Georgia*. The Alabama legislature passed a new law in 1981 patterned after the Georgia and Florida statutes. Death penalty statutes in California, Illinois, Indiana, Maryland, Tennessee and Virginia were upheld by their highest courts after legal challenges based upon *Gregg*.

Criminal Justice Planning in the States

A principal purpose of the Omnibus Crime Control and Safe Streets Act of 1968 was to encourage states and their local units of government to plan a criminal justice system and to allocate resources to the interrelated parts of that system.

With the phase-out of the federal assistance authorized by the Crime Control Act and administered through the Law Enforcement Assistance Administration, which followed closely on the heels of the 1979 reauthorization of that act, states were forced to decide whether to assume the costs of criminal justice planning from within their own resources and to consider whether criminal justice planning should be institutionalized as an ongoing function of state government. For many states this was a decision to be faced not only in consideration of the withdrawal of federal support to criminal justice planning but amid extreme fiscal constraints at the state level.

In the majority of states, action is under way to permanently install in their state governmental structures a planning process dedicated to the oversight of program development and resource allocation activities within the criminal justice system. Most states are retaining one or more of the characteristics of the planning portion of the LEAA program: legislative development activities; advice to the executive branch of state government on criminal justice matters; review and advice on the allocation of state resources for criminal justice activities; the delivery of technical assistance to operational agencies of that system; and the management of criminal justice data collection and analytical capabilities. Operationally, many of these functions have been attached to the office of the governor, the department of management and budget, a department of law or justice, or a multi-purpose state planning or development agency.

Those states which have been most successful to date in preserving some aspect of systematic planning or interagency coordination are those which anticipated the ultimate phase-out of federal resources and began the institutionalization process some years ago.

Drug Abuse

From 1979 to 1981, nearly one-third of the states passed some form of legislation prohibiting drug paraphernalia sales. The Federal Drug Enforcement Administration (FDEA) estimated that as many as 30,000 "head shops," which specialized in drug-related accessories, were operating in the country. The legal sale of drug accessories was regarded by legislators and others as a blatant endorsement and glamorization of the illegal drug trade. They feared that the open sale of such items would encourage children and young people to experiment with marijuana, cocaine and other drugs. A model act for banning drug paraphernalia was drafted by the FDEA. Indiana enacted the first drug paraphernalia statute in 1976. North Dakota followed with its law in 1979. Thirteen more states enacted similar laws in 1980: Idaho, Virginia, West Virginia, Indiana, Maryland, Connecticut, Delaware, Florida, Nebraska, Colorado, Louisiana, California and New York.

Some states modeled their statutes after the FDEA model act which makes possession of paraphernalia, when accompanied by an intent to use it with illicit drugs, a crime. Manufacturing and delivering paraphernalia under circumstances that clearly indicate it will be used with illicit drugs is also a crime. The delivery of paraphernalia to a child by an adult is made a special offense. The publication of commercial advertisements promoting sale of paraphernalia is made unlawful. A civil forfeiture section provides for seizure and condemnation of inventories of paraphernalia dealers. The model act defines drug paraphernalia as equipment, products, and material used, intended for use, or designed for use, essentially to produce, package, store, test or use illicit drugs. To ensure that innocent objects are not classified as drug paraphernalia, criminal intent of the person is a key element in the definition. The object must be used, intended for use, or designed for use in connection with illicit drugs. The act also includes a detailed description of common forms of property that can be defined as drug paraphernalia.

Some of these statutes met almost immediate challenge in the courts. The accessories trade association of drug paraphernalia manufacturers challenged the first law passed by Indiana in 1976. A three-judge federal panel struck down the Indiana statute in February 1980 on grounds that the law defined paraphernalia too broadly and vaguely. The court felt that the definition could apply to common objects such as paper clips, baggies or envelopes. Indiana enacted a new statute in 1980, but rejected the FDEA model act on the basis that it was too similar to the voided 1976 statute. The 1980 Indiana law does not attempt to define drug paraphernalia, but makes it a crime to manufacture, deliver, or possess an object which is intended to be used for introducing into the body, testing, or enhancing the effect of a controlled drug.

Although legislatures seem anxious to enact some kind of legislation to control "head shops," the question of the constitutionality of these laws was a major element of the legislative debate. The governors of three states (New Jersey, Tennessee and Delaware) vetoed similar legislation in 1979. However, the Delaware legislature passed a revised bill in 1980 which was signed by the governor. A drug paraphernalia bill passed by the 1980 Tennessee legislature was vetoed by Governor Lamar Alexander after Attorney General William Leech said it was "unconstitutionally vague." The bill was designed to outlaw the sale of hash pipes, cocaine spoons, bongs and other related items.

In 1980, a federal judge declared West Virginia's 1980 drug paraphernalia law unconstitutional, stating that the law permitted police to "level arbitrary and discriminatory charges" and declared the prohibition against the sale of water pipes, rolling paper and other items was "vague and unenforceable." A similar law enacted in Maryland in 1980 was restrained in court after an action of head shop owners. A permanent injunction was granted later in the year. Nebraska agreed not to attempt to enforce its ban on drug paraphernalia until after a federal court trial determined its legality.

In the midst of this flurry of legislative activity to control head shops, New York in 1979 revised its tough drug law which Governor Carey regarded as unenforceable and impractical. A mandatory life sentence for possession or possession for sale of certain drugs was repealed. The drug law revision was designed to establish a more rational relationship between the seriousness of offenses and sentences in drug cases.

Six states (Arizona, Georgia, New York, Rhode Island, South Carolina and Washington) enacted laws permitting the use of marijuana under medical supervision for some cancer and glaucoma patients. Florida, Illinois, Louisiana and New Mexico had enacted similar laws prior to 1979. Under court challenge, the Florida Supreme Court ruled in 1980 that the Florida legislature, in permitting research into the possible medical uses of marijuana, did not authorize general use of the drug, even by physicians in their everyday practice.

Gun Control

State legislators continued to struggle with the issue of gun control as the 1970s ended. As many as 17 states and the District of Columbia legislated stricter sentences for crimes committed with a firearm. These laws range from a broad mandate that an additional sentence be added (Tennessee) to the imposition of a sentence of no less than five years, with no suspension and no probation, for use of a handgun in the commission of a felony (Maryland).

In 1979, Idaho passed a law which provided mandatory minimum sentences for offenders who commit felonies while using a deadly weapon or instrument and had been convicted of a previous felony within 10 years. West Virginia passed a law in which persons convicted of crimes involving the use of a firearm may not be granted parole, probation or suspension of sentence. Nevada also adopted a "use a gun—go to jail" law that year. In 1980, the Wisconsin legislature increased penalties for persons convicted of using dangerous weapons to commit crimes and provided that judges sentencing persons convicted of crimes involving the use of weapons to less than a minimum sentence must give public reasons for the lesser sentence. The Wisconsin law also added an additional six-month to five-year penalty to the basic sentence for a crime committed with a dangerous weapon. New Jersey Governor Brendan T. Byrne in 1981 signed a bill forcing judges to send gun-wielding criminals to prison. A first offender who uses a gun to commit a serious crime must serve three years in addition to the sentence imposed for the crime itself, with longer additional sentences for repeat offenders.

Laws like those just described provide for "enhancement" of penalties for felonies when a gun is used in the commission of a crime. Such laws have been popular as a method of deterring the use of guns by criminals. However, there have been some challenges to these laws. In December 1978, the California Supreme Court in the *Tanner* case overturned a 1975 law mandating prison sentences for persons who use guns to commit crimes. However, early the next year the California Supreme Court decided to reconsider its December decision striking down the state's "use a gun—go to prison" law. Soon after the court's decision was announced, the state senate voted unanimously to reinstate the law. The California Supreme Court then reversed its own December decision and ruled that prisoners who used a gun in the commission of a crime shall not be granted probation.

The application of Michigan's additional two-year sentence for felons committing crimes with firearms was restricted by the Michigan Supreme Court in 1981. The court said that the prosecution must prove that an unarmed accomplice to the crime helped obtain the gun or encouraged its use to be subject to the extra penalty. The U.S. Supreme Court ruled the same year that multiple penalties do not constitute double jeopardy in an affirmation of Missouri's mandatory sentencing statute for felony convictions involving a dangerous weapon. As a result, five reversed convictions were returned to the Missouri Court of Appeals. The challenged state law sets a three-year mandatory sentence and prohibits suspended sentences, parole or conditional release.

Gun Registration

According to the National Rifle Association, illegal possession of specific firearms is a felony in eight states (Arkansas, Iowa, Kansas, Missouri, Ohio, South Dakota, Virginia and Washington), as well as Guam and Puerto Rico. Mandatory sentences for the illegal possession of specific firearms in certain circumstances are imposed in eight states (Idaho, Massachusetts, Minnesota, Missouri, Montana, Nebraska, Nevada and Tennessee).

A permit to purchase a handgun is required in eight states (Hawaii, Massachusetts, Michigan, Missouri, New Jersey, New York, North Carolina and South Dakota). Illinois requires a firearms owner identification card for the purchase of any firearm. Applications to purchase handguns and a waiting period are imposed in a dozen states, giving law enforcement officials time to check the criminal background of applicants. The longest wait—two weeks—is required by California, Connecticut and Tennessee. Most of these states also require that law enforcement officials keep records of handgun sales by dealers.

Registration of handguns is required in Hawaii, Michigan, Mississippi and New York. A license to carry a handgun is required in Massachusetts, New Jersey and New York. Permits to carry a handgun or a concealed handgun, or bans on concealed weapons, are imposed in most states.

The most stringent gun restrictions are imposed by Massachusetts, New York, New York City and the District of Columbia. Massachusetts requires a permit to buy or a license to carry a handgun and mandates a one-year jail sentence for violations. New York, which advertises its 1980 law as the toughest in America, also mandates a year in jail for violations and requires a license to own or carry, a permit to buy, and registration of a handgun. Using a somewhat different approach, Rhode Island enacted a law that requires Rhode Islanders who want to buy handguns to take a safety course offered by the state Department of Environmental Management.

The U.S. Supreme Court, in a major test of New York's illegal possession law, ruled in June 1979 that it was not unconstitutional for a jury to presume that an illegal weapon found in an automobile belongs to all occupants in the car, unless the car is stolen, or unless the weapon is found upon the person of one of the occupants.

Sex Offenses

States were active in defining obscenity and pornography, especially when it involved children; revising rape statutes to make them gender-neutral; and providing treatment and other services to victims of sexual assault. Reported here are the more significant legislation and judicial decisions affecting the states in these areas since 1977.

Pornography and Obscenity

Legislators have attempted for many years to regulate sexually offensive materials, but state "obscenity and pornography" statutes are repeatedly challenged in the courts and declared unconstitutional. In 1979, the Michigan Supreme Court wrote its own anti-obscenity regulations revising a 22-year-old state law that failed the U.S. Supreme Court tests. The state court said its rules are enforceable even though the rules have not been before the legislature. Five justices in the majority opinion said they were acting with some reluctance, but "in view of previously expressed legislative public policy, we refuse to leave Michigan without a valid criminal obscenity statute."

In a suit against the state's attorney general and two sheriffs, the Rhode Island Supreme Court ruled the state's obscenity law unconstitutional. In a May 14, 1979, decision, the court said that the law is too broad because the legislature included in the definition of obscenity the phrase "patently offensive sexual conduct." The Tennessee Supreme Court has also declared unconstitutional the state's 1978 anti-obscenity law which outlawed everything from topless waitresses to written articles about sex. The court said the law violated state and federal constitutional guarantees of free speech and free press.

The United States Supreme Court has let stand a Missouri Supreme Court ruling that the state's obscenity law is unconstitutional. In a 1980 ruling, the court said the law constitutes prior restraint, because it bars distribution of questionable material before it is declared obscene in a court. In a related case the same year, the U.S. Supreme Court declared Texas' obscenity law unconstitutional because it constitutes prior restraint of an indefinite duration. The law permitted the state to obtain an injunction to prevent the showing of potentially obscene materials. One theater had already been found guilty of showing obscene movies. Sections of the Arkansas obscenity law were declared unconstitutional by a federal judge in a lower court ruling. The judge ruled October 17, 1980, that the language of the law was so broad that a jury could find that constitutionally permissible material violated state law.

Recent legislation focused on a specific aspect of pornography—the depicting of minors in obscene acts. Over a two-year period (1978-79), 16 states (Alabama, Arizona, Georgia, Hawaii, Indiana, Iowa, Kansas, Kentucky, Maine, Michigan, Nevada, New Mexico, South Carolina, Utah, West Virginia and Wisconsin) enacted child pornography laws. About two-thirds of the states now have such a law.

Sexual Assault

A number of states modified other sexual offense laws. Gender designations in rape statutes were removed in Utah, Nevada, Virginia, Alaska and Hawaii. In a related matter, the Alaska Supreme Court ruled in 1979 that the state's prostitution law was unconstitutional because it defines the crime in terms of women. The court said that if the statute were made gender-neutral, it would be legal.

Missouri increased the penalties for rape to a minimum of five years and a maximum of life imprisonment. Rape-murder is punishable by the death penalty. The law also provides for a rehabilitation program for sex offenders. The state must pay the examination costs of rape victims not covered by private health insurance if the evidence will be turned over to the prosecutor.

Nevada enacted legislation that requires counties to provide up to $1,000 free medical treatment and psychological counseling for sexual assault victims and their spouses. To be eligible for free treatment, victims must file a report of the crime within three days of the attack. California in 1980 repealed its law granting judges authority to order rape victims to undergo psychiatric examinations before being allowed to testify in court. Such examinations had been upheld by the state's Supreme Court in a 1966 decision as a test of the victim's "credibility."

Arson

The crime of arson received considerable attention in the states in the late 1970s. State concern is reflected in new laws enacted in 36 states since 1976, which provide civil immunity for insurance companies that share information with state law enforcement authorities in suspected arson cases. In the other 14 states, insurance companies must substantiate the facts first to avoid being sued for libel. The immunity legislation varies from state to state with only four states incorporating all major provisions of a model bill proposed by the insurance industry.

Early in 1979, New Jersey's insurance commissioner approved a plan to quickly cancel insurance on insurance-subsidized buildings that are not properly maintained by their owners. A 2 percent surcharge on New Jersey fire insurance policies subsidizes insurance on the high-risk properties. Claims on those properties have exceeded by $42 million the amount of premiums paid on the same buildings since 1968. New York Governor Hugh Carey proposed legislation to develop a $2 million statewide arson control program. New York arson damages were $175 million in 1977, and arson-related deaths in the state are estimated to be 200 annually. In 1980, the Illinois legislature attacked the problem of arson-for-profit by removing financial incentives for arson and providing for better arson enforcement and prevention. Three of the new laws tightened the Illinois Fair Access to Insurance Requirements (FAIR) plans, set up a task force to prevent FAIR-insured buildings from being over-insured, and gave tax incentives for competition among insurers participating in the program.

Ironically, federal and state programs to assist owners of property in deteriorating neighborhoods, such as the Federal Riot Insurance Program, have unwittingly proven to be an incentive to arson-for-profit, and are discussed in a General Accounting Office (GAO) study released in 1978 titled *Arson-For-Profit: More Could Be Done to Reduce It*. The GAO proposed how to reduce the incentives for arson in the Fair Access to Insurance Requirements plans.

Although arson-for-profit is a major concern, there is evidence that most arsons are committed by juveniles as acts of vandalism. A number of large cities have conducted anti-arson campaigns in an effort to reduce vandalism-related arsons. Before its demise, the LEAA provided grants for the improvement of arson investigations, prosecution, and evidence collection and analysis. In December 1979, the LEAA announced $9 million in grants to support programs to improve investigation and prosecution of arson, data collection, analysis of evidence, and arson prevention and public education. Funds went to nine states (Arizona, Connecticut, Delaware, Florida, Illinois, Maryland, Massachusetts, New Jersey and Rhode Island) and 26 regional, county and local jurisdictions.

The most significant change in recent efforts to combat arson was congressional action in 1978, making arson a Part 1 offense, thereby requiring reporting of arson to the Federal Bureau of Investigation. By classifying arson as a Part 1 crime, more detailed statistics will be kept, and law enforcement agencies will probably give it more attention.

Perhaps the most aggressive state-level action to control arson-for-profit occurred in Massachusetts. A series of suspicious fires led the Massachusetts attorney general to create an arson task force to coordinate prosecutorial efforts with police and fire and local arson squad members in the city of Boston. Investigations of 35 Boston fires, which caused $6 million in property losses, resulted in 33 persons being indicted for arson conspiracy. Of 27 brought to trial, all but one pled guilty or had been found guilty as a result of the investigation. The Massachusetts attorney general's office had earlier aided in the indictment of 20 persons for arson in another city. The attorney general's office had received a $600,000 grant from the LEAA to fund its arson task force, establish a comprehensive arson prevention and enforcement system, and encourage community anti-arson efforts.

Other Legislation

A major criminal activity associated with auto theft is the stealing of automobiles for their parts. These activities have been dubbed "chop shop" operations. Several states have attempted to deal with this problem. The Illinois secretary of state attempted to stop "chop shop" operations in that state by requiring junkyards to record auto parts they acquire and sell, contending that a 50-state system for recording parts as well as automobiles was needed. The secretary's authority to impose a recording requirement was upheld by the Illinois Supreme Court in 1979. There are approximately 14,000 parts in an automobile, but only the major elements enter the stolen parts market, according to the secretary of state. In that same year, the Michigan legislature passed laws designed to reduce stolen car problems. One law requires auto wrecking firms and insurance companies to surrender titles of totally damaged late model cars to the state in exchange for a salvage title. The other law makes it a felony to potentially mislead a buyer by changing the engine or serial number of a vehicle. The Committee on the Office of Attorney General (COAG) studied the problem of chop shops and in a 1979 report suggested ways in which states can become more active and effective in combating the problem.

Several states also enacted laws defining certain misuses of computers as crimes. Michigan passed a law in 1979 which defines fraudulent computer uses and prohibits intentional or unauthorized access to computers for the purposes of altering, damaging or destroying the computer, a computer system, or any computer software. That same year the National Association for State Information Systems (NASIS) released a report on guidelines for development of computer crime legislation with a sample computer crime bill.

In 1980, Illinois passed a law which made it a criminal offense to use a computer or alter or destroy a computer program or data without the owner's consent. The same year, New Mexico passed its Computer Crimes Act which prohibited computer fraud, making the intent to carry out a scheme to defraud a felony.

Several states enacted what were called "Son of Sam" laws which prohibit criminals from receiving profits from publications or other promotions regarding details of their crimes. Minnesota enacted a law in 1979 which required that the profits from such writings or promotions go to the crime victims reparations board. South Carolina passed a similar law which would prevent convicted criminals from profiting by re-enacting, talking or writing about their crimes. Money from such activities would be deposited in an interest-bearing escrow account which the victim may sue to receive within five years if the accused is convicted of the crime.

Table 1
CRIMINAL JUSTICE STATUTES IN SPECIFIED AREAS

State or other jurisdiction	Victim compensation programs(a)			Domestic violence(b)			Decriminalization of marijuana		Public intoxication uniform act which includes decriminalization
	Beneficiaries(c)	Minimum-maximum award(d)	Source of revenue(e)	Provides injunctive relief(f)	Shelter services legislation	Criminal laws(g)	Amount that can be legally possessed(h)	Fine for exceeding amount specified	
Alabama	A,B,C,D	(d)	GTR	★	★		1 oz. in public	Up to $100	★
Alaska				★	★				★
Arizona					★	★(i)			
Arkansas	A,B,C,D	$100-23,000	PA	★	★	★	1 oz.	Up to $100	★
California	A,B,C,D			★			1 oz.	Up to $100	★
Colorado	A,C,D	$25-1,500	PA	★	★		1 oz.	Up to $100	★
Connecticut	A,B,C	$100-10,000	PA	★	★				★
Delaware	A,C,D	$25-10,000	PA	★	★				★
Florida	A,B,C	Up to $10,000	GTR, PA	★	★				
Georgia	A,B,C,D	Up to victims' damages	PA	★	★				
Hawaii	A,B,C,D,E	Up to $10,000	GTR	★	★	★			★
Idaho	A,B,C,D	$200-15,000	GTR		★				★
Illinois	A,B,C,D	$100-10,000	GTR, PA	★	★				★
Indiana	A,B,C,F		GTR, PA	★	★				
Iowa				★	★				
Kansas	A,B,C,G	$100-10,000	GTR	★	★				★
Kentucky	A,B,C	$100-15,000	GTR	★	★				★
Louisiana									
Maine				★	★		1.5 ozs.	Up to $200	★
Maryland	A,B,C	$100-45,000	GTR, PA	★	★				★
Massachusetts	A,C	$100-10,000	GTR	★	★	★			
Michigan	A,B,C	$100-15,000	GTR		★		1.5 ozs.	Up to $100	★
Minnesota	A,B,C,D,H	$100-25,000	GTR	★	★		1 oz.	$100-250	★
Mississippi				★					
Missouri(a)		$200-10,000	PA	★	★				
Montana	A,B,C	Up to $25,000	PA	★	★		1 oz.	Up to $100	★
Nebraska	A,B,C,D	Up to $10,000	GTR	★	★				★
Nevada	B,C,D	$100-5,000	PA	★	★				★
New Hampshire				★	★	★			★
New Jersey	A,B,C,D	$100-10,000	GTR, PA	★	★				★
New Mexico	A,C,D	Up to $12,500	GTR	★	★		25 gms.	Up to $100	★
New York	A,C	(d)	GTR	★	★		1 oz.	Up to $100	★
North Carolina				★	★				★
North Dakota	A,B,C	$100-25,000	GTR	★	★	★	100 gms.		★
Ohio	A,B,C,G	Up to $50,000	PA	★	★	★		Up to $100	

534

	(c)	Award limits(d)	(e)											
Oklahoma	A,C,D	Up to $10,000	PA			...	...	★	...	...	...	...		
Oregon	A,B,C	$250-23,000	GTR	★	★	★	★	...	...	★	Up to $100		
Pennsylvania	A,B,C	$100-25,000	PA	★	★	...	★	...	...	★	★		
Rhode Island(a)	A,C,D	...		★	...	★	...	...	...	★	...		
South Carolina	...	...		...	...	...	...	...	...	...	...		
South Dakota	A,B,C,D	$100-10,000	PA	...	...	...	...	...	...	...	...		
Tennessee	A,B,C	Up to $50,000	PA	★	★	★	★	...	...	★	...	1 oz.	
Texas	A,B,C	...	PA	★	★	★	★	★	...	★	★		
Utah	...	...		...	...	...	...	...	...	...	...		
Vermont	...	$100-10,000	PA	★	★	★	★	...	...	★	★		
Virginia	A,B,C	...	PA	...	...	...	...	...	...	...	...		
Washington	A,C,D	Up to $20,000	PA	★	★	★	★	...	...	★	★		
West Virginia	A,C,D	Up to $12,000	PA	★	★	★	★	...	...	★	★		
Wisconsin	A,B,C,D		GTR	★	★	★	★	★	...	★	...		
Wyoming	...	...		...	...	...	...	...	...	...	...		
Dist. of Col.	...	...		★	...	★	...	...	...	★	...		

Sources: Crime Victim Compensation—Charles L. Schafer, *Summary of State Statutes on Victim Compensation and Related Federal Legislation* (Washington, D.C.: National Retired Teachers Association/American Association of Retired Persons) and Mindy Gaynes, "Compensating the Victim," *State Legislatures* (Nov./Dec. 1981): 12; Domestic Violence—Center for Women Policy Studies, *Response to Violence in the Family*, 4, 7 (Sept./Oct. 1981); Marijuana—National Organization for the Reform of Marijuana Laws; and Public Intoxication—National Coalition for Jail Reform.

(a) The victim compensation program columns reflect legislation enacted as of December 31, 1981. In Missouri, victims may apply for compensation beginning January 1, 1983, if funds are on hand from collection of $26 judgments against convicted offenders. In Rhode Island, the statute will not become effective until passage of federal victim compensation legislation.

(b) Legislation enacted as of September 1981.

(c) A—Victims; B—Intervenors; C—Dependents; D—Persons or relatives who assume costs, maintenance or responsibility for injured party or victim; E—Persons who assume costs for in-tervenors; F—Law and fire officers injured in performance of duties; G—Other third persons; H—Victims' estates.

(d) Includes medical expenses, lost earnings and funeral expenses. In Alaska, $25,000 per victim; $40,000 if there are two or more surviving dependents. In New York, $20,000 plus unlimited medical expenses.

(e) GTR—General tax revenue; PA—Penalty assessment.

(f) Civil order to prevent violence by one member of a household against another. Decision to file for injunctive relief lies solely with victim.

(g) Statute makes domestic violence a separate criminal offense. Decision to file charge rests solely with the prosecutor.

(h) For comparative purposes: one ounce=28.35 grams.

(i) Applies to abuse of wives only.

Table 2
STATE DEATH PENALTY
(As of December 1981)

State	Method of execution	No. of women on death row	Persons on death row	State	Method of execution	No. of women on death row	Persons on death row
Alabama	Electrocution	0	55	Montana	Hanging	0	3
Alaska	...	...	...	Nebraska	Electrocution	0	12
Arizona	Gas chamber	0	37	Nevada...........	Gas chamber	0	12
Arkansas	Electrocution	0	23	New Hampshire	Hanging	0	0
California	Gas chamber	0	80	New Jersey	...	...	...
Colorado	Gas chamber	0	1	New Mexico	Lethal injection	0	3
Connecticut	Electrocution	0	0	New York(a).......	Electrocution	0	0
Delaware	Hanging	0	4	North Carolina	Gas chamber	1	17
Florida	Electrocution	0	162	North Dakota	...	...	...
Georgia	Electrocution	4	109	Ohio	Electrocution	0	0
Hawaii	...	...	...	Oklahoma	Lethal injection	1	37
Idaho	Lethal injection	0	0	Oregon............	...	...	...
Illinois	Electrocution	0	40	Pennsylvania.......	Electrocution	0	23
Indiana	Electrocution	0	10	Rhode Island	...	...	...
Iowa..............	...	...	...	South Carolina	Electrocution	0	21
Kansas	...	...	...	South Dakota	Electrocution	0	0
Kentucky	Electrocution	1	10	Tennessee	Electrocution	0	26
Louisiana.........	Electrocution	0	30	Texas	Lethal injection	2	144
Maine.............	...	...	...	Utah	Firing squad	0	3
Maryland	Gas chamber	1	7	Vermont(b)........	Electrocution	0	0
Massachusetts	...	...	...	Virginia	Electrocution	0	17
Michigan	...	...	...	Washington........	Hanging or lethal injection(c)	0	0
Minnesota	...	...	...				
Mississippi	Gas chamber	0	23	West Virginia	...	...	...
Missouri...........	Gas chamber	0	14	Wisconsin	...	...	...
				Wyoming..........	Gas chamber	0	1

Source: American Civil Liberties Union.
(a) Applicable only to inmates convicted of murder while serving a life sentence.
(b) The statute is unconstitutional on its face, but there has been no occasion for a court to strike it down.
(c) Defendant may choose lethal injection.

Table 3
TRENDS IN STATE PRISON POPULATION

State or other jurisdiction	Total population			Population by maximum length of sentence					
				More than a year			Year or less and unsentenced		
	1980	1979	Percentage change	1980	1979	Percentage change	1980	1979	Percentage change
United States	304,332	288,086	5.6	293,661	278,882	5.3	10,671	9,201	16.0
Alabama	5,961	5,464	9.1	5,786	5,464	5.9	175	0	...
Alaska(a)	822	760	8.2	571	532	7.3	251	228	10.1
Arizona	4,372	3,749	16.6	4,360	3,737	16.7	12	12	0.0
Arkansas	2,925	3,042	-3.8	2,925	2,980	-1.8	0	62	-100.0
California(b)	24,569	22,632	8.6	23,264	21,260	9.4	1,305	1,372	-4.9
Colorado	2,792	2,668	4.6	2,772	2,658	4.3	20	10	100.0
Connecticut(a)	4,308	4,061	6.1	2,116	2,139	-1.1	2,192	1,922	14.0
Delaware(a)	1,474	1,419	3.9	1,087	1,088	-0.1	387	331	16.9
Florida	20,735	19,748	5.0	20,211	19,407	4.1	524	341	53.7
Georgia	12,210	12,106	0.9	11,954	11,666	2.5	256	440	-41.8
Hawaii(a)	985	856	15.1	624	539	15.8	361	317	13.9
Idaho	817	830	-1.6	817	830	-1.6	0	0	...
Illinois	11,899	11,935	-0.3	10,724	11,361	-5.6	1,175	574	104.7
Indiana	6,683	5,667	17.9	6,281	5,270	19.2	402	397	1.3
Iowa	2,513	2,272	10.6	2,511	2,261	11.1	2	11	-81.8
Kansas	2,494	2,290	8.9	2,494	2,290	8.9	0	0	...
Kentucky	3,608	3,691	-2.2	3,608	3,691	-2.2	0	0	...
Louisiana	8,889	7,618	16.7	8,889	7,618	16.7	0	0	...
Maine	829	776	6.8	686	641	7.0	143	135	5.9
Maryland	7,731	7,860	-1.6	7,731	7,860	-1.6	0	0	...
Massachusetts	3,268	2,924	11.8	3,233	2,877	12.4	35	47	-25.5
Michigan	15,124	15,002	0.8	15,124	15,002	0.8	0	0	...
Minnesota	2,001	2,094	-4.4	2,001	2,094	-4.4	0	0	...
Mississippi	3,374	3,508	-3.8	3,339	3,425	-2.5	35	83	-57.8
Missouri	5,524	5,279	4.6	5,524	5,279	4.6	0	0	...
Montana	738	715	3.2	737	712	3.5	1	3	-66.7
Nebraska	1,446	1,291	12.0	1,402	1,193	17.5	44	98	-55.1
Nevada	1,839	1,566	17.4	1,839	1,566	17.4	0	0	...
New Hampshire	326	316	3.2	326	316	3.2	0	0	...
New Jersey(c)	5,884	5,852	0.5	5.564	5.539	0.5	320	313	2.2
New Mexico	1,461	1,556	-6.1	1,381	1,466	-5.8	80	90	-11.1
New York	21,829	20,856	4.7	21,653	20,856	3.8	176	0	...
North Carolina	15,382	14,255	7.9	14,325	13,461	6.4	1,057	794	33.1
North Dakota	253	186	36.0	185	136	36.0	68	50	36.0
Ohio	13,489	13,360	1.0	13,489	13,360	1.0	0	0	...
Oklahoma	4,571	4,250	7.6	4,571	4,250	7.6	0	0	...
Oregon	3,170	3,179	-0.3	3,165	3,168	-0.1	5	11	-54.5
Pennsylvania	8,182	7,772	5.3	8,107	7,685	5.5	75	87	-13.8
Rhode Island(a)	814	738	10.3	612	559	9.5	202	179	12.8
South Carolina	7,862	7,643	2.9	7,427	7,115	4.4	435	528	-17.6
South Dakota	635	562	13.0	609	539	13.0	26	23	13.0
Tennessee	7,022	6,629	5.9	7,022	6,629	5.9	0	0	...
Texas(d)	29,892	26,522	12.7	29,892	26,522	12.7	0	0	...
Utah	932	960	-2.9	928	957	-3.0	4	3	33.3
Vermont(a)	480	431	11.4	342	311	10.0	138	120	15.0
Virginia	8,920	8,449(c)	5.6	8,581	8,200	4.6	339	249	36.1
Washington	4,382	4,342	0.9	4,382	4,342	0.9	0	0	...
West Virginia	1,257	1,251	0.5	1,257	1,251	0.5	0	0	...
Wisconsin	3,980	3,677	8.2	3,980	3,677	8.2	0	0	...
Wyoming	534	504	6.0	534	504	6.0			
Dist. of Col. (a)	3,145	2,973	5.8	2,719	2,599	4.6	426	374	13.9

Sources: Bureau of Justice Statistics, U.S. Department of Justice; and Bureau of the Census, U.S. Department of Commerce unpublished data.
(a) Figures include both jail and prison inmates; jails and prisons are combined into one system.
(b) All figures exclude adult inmates under the jurisdiction of the California Youth Authority.

(c) Official prison population count excludes state prisoners held in local jails.
(d) Figures for inmates under state jurisdiction but not in state custody are not available.

Table 4

CRIMINAL JUSTICE SYSTEM DIRECT EXPENDITURES: FISCAL 1979

State or other jurisdiction	Total criminal justice system — Amount (in thousands of dollars) State	Local	Percentage of total direct expenditure(a) State	Local	Expenditures for specified programs as a percentage of total criminal justice system — Police protection(b) State	Local	Judicial(c) State	Local	Legal services & prosecution(d) State	Local	Public defense(e) State	Local	Corrections(f) State	Local	Other criminal justice(g) State	Local
United States	$7,392,554	$15,256,613	5.9	13.0	26.9	64.7	16.2	11.9	5.8	6.2	1.6	1.6	47.8	14.1	1.7	1.5
Alabama	105,569	146,848	4.7	14.0	27.2	72.1	26.7	8.8	6.9	3.8	1.4	0.3	34.6	13.7	3.1	1.3
Alaska	77,704	32,688	7.4	4.1	33.6	83.1	21.3	0.2	12.7	14.2	3.4		28.1	2.2	0.9	0.4
Arizona	99,084	227,209	7.9	18.7	42.3	63.2	5.5	13.8	5.2	7.6		2.7	45.9	12.6	1.1	0.2
Arkansas	44,731	64,847	3.7	11.6	36.1	65.6	8.9	14.7	2.5	6.2	*	1.2	48.7	10.9	3.8	1.4
California	716,973	2,354,590	6.2	16.5	37.3	52.8	5.7	13.4	5.6	9.3	0.7	3.2	49.1	20.1	1.5	1.3
Colorado	108,945	169,939	7.3	13.0	20.6	71.6	21.6	6.5	4.2	10.8	4.2	*	48.0	9.4	1.3	1.6
Connecticut	140,309	147,256	7.1	6.4	23.9	94.7	21.6	1.2	6.8	2.9	2.6	0.2	43.5	0.3	1.6	0.8
Delaware	49,689	22,660	9.6	14.0	29.0	86.0	21.3	9.5	4.4	4.1	2.1	0.3	41.0		2.2	0.1
Florida	378,842	605,798	10.6	15.0	17.3	70.5	10.9	14.0	9.1	2.8	4.0	0.7	56.1	10.4	2.6	1.6
Georgia	149,494	259,353	5.5	16.9	27.5	60.8	7.4	17.7	4.3	4.6	0.2	1.1	57.9	15.3	2.7	0.5
Hawaii	45,615	57,282	3.3	16.4	3.8	90.2	33.5		5.3	8.0	3.2		50.9	1.3	3.3	0.5
Idaho	30,433	37,649	5.6	15.0	33.0	69.2	15.9	12.2	8.5	8.7		2.8	34.8	6.3	7.8	0.8
Illinois	313,737	935,356	5.0	23.1	27.3	70.8	16.0	8.5	4.2	5.0	0.6	1.4	50.8	10.7	1.0	3.5
Indiana	124,284	217,161	5.4	11.7	37.5	65.0	6.9	15.6	3.8	5.8	0.5	1.3	49.0	11.4	1.1	1.0
Iowa	81,709	127,982	4.8	10.1	33.9	61.3	10.3	16.7	3.8	7.2	0.1	2.9	50.9	11.5	1.0	0.4
Kansas	71,067	104,863	5.2	11.3	19.3	65.9	22.0	14.8	7.1	7.6	3.1	0.2	47.7	8.6	0.8	2.8
Kentucky	154,841	120,274	5.7	13.7	29.1	73.4	25.9	3.9	9.8	3.9	1.2	0.6	32.2	14.4	1.8	3.9
Louisiana	147,620	239,372	5.7	15.6	30.3	64.3	9.5	15.7	5.5	5.2		0.9	53.7	13.3	0.9	0.6
Maine	34,219	31,553	4.7	6.1	30.1	80.0	19.1	4.5	7.0	4.6	2.3	*	37.6	10.8	3.9	*
Maryland	220,254	284,398	7.3	7.7	26.0	70.0	11.9	12.6	1.2	6.3	3.3	*	56.6	10.7	1.0	0.3
Massachusetts	166,127	460,526	4.2	8.9	27.4	67.7	9.9	15.6	7.4	3.5	2.2	1.1	51.2	10.9	2.0	1.1
Michigan	304,563	747,992	5.1	15.4	31.2	62.1	8.7	15.7	4.9	5.6	0.5	2.0	54.1	14.4	0.7	0.3
Minnesota	96,144	246,844	3.9	11.2	34.6	56.0	13.9	13.0	5.9	8.6	1.0	2.6	42.9	19.2	1.9	0.7
Mississippi	59,186	72,886	4.2	9.1	37.0	67.9	8.0	15.1	6.0	3.7		1.3	47.0	11.8	2.0	0.3
Missouri	112,995	280,991	5.1	18.8	32.6	70.4	17.0	11.5	2.5	5.5	2.4	0.1	45.0	12.0	0.5	0.5
Montana	24,382	35,739	4.5	10.8	31.9	63.4	8.4	14.4	5.2	8.2	0.3	1.7	50.1	11.2	4.1	1.2
Nebraska	52,316	69,904	6.3	11.4	27.4	64.9	14.5	11.3	2.3	9.2		1.8	55.0	12.2	0.7	0.7
Nevada	32,519	86,968	7.2	17.4	24.2	56.0	7.4	15.1	5.7	8.7	0.8	2.2	60.7	17.4	1.2	0.7
New Hampshire	23,258	40,261	4.5	11.3	38.6	70.2	9.3	12.7	5.7	3.7	2.7	0.1	41.0	12.6	2.7	0.7
New Jersey	226,799	671,401	6.0	14.4	32.7	64.9	14.3	13.1	5.8	7.8	8.2	0.1	38.8	13.5	0.2	0.7
New Mexico	63,981	57,734	6.5	13.6	22.5	76.0	16.6	3.9	11.5	3.7	4.2	0.1	40.1	15.4	5.1	0.8
New York	981,158	2,112,870	10.8	10.7	12.5	74.4	42.5	3.2	5.0	6.4	1.0	1.5	36.6	13.4	2.3	1.1
North Carolina	276,395	185,132	9.1	5.0	16.7	81.1	14.6	5.6	7.8	2.2	2.2	*	57.4	9.4	1.2	1.6
North Dakota	13,220	26,449	2.5	11.2	28.0	66.5	15.7	16.9	8.1	8.0		1.3	37.0	7.3	2.7	0.7
Ohio	212,299	659,358	4.3	14.6	26.1	59.7	7.2	18.0	6.2	5.6	0.5	1.6	59.2	12.8	0.2	0.7
Oklahoma	100,932	102,514	5.8	11.3	24.8	73.0	9.1	13.0	6.7	4.7	4.2	1.1	58.7	7.9	0.7	0.8
Oregon	102,416	179,830	5.7	16.8	29.1	54.7	8.7	14.2	12.8	7.9	1.0	3.2	47.5	19.2	1.5	0.8
Pennsylvania	292,914	763,065	4.6	19.3	40.2	58.6	12.9	16.3	7.8	2.2	2.2	1.6	39.5	18.2	2.1	1.6
Rhode Island	53,306	40,131	6.4	6.5	20.0	96.7	23.4	0.8	5.3	8.0		*	49.7	7.3	2.0	*
South Carolina	104,178	108,004	5.8	14.8	35.0	65.0	7.1	21.0	5.3	3.6	0.8	0.9	50.5	8.7	1.3	0.7

538

State															
South Dakota	23,310	22,188	4.5	10.4	29.1	77.2	25.5	5.1	7.7	9.7	‥	2.2	36.4	5.6	1.3	0.1
Tennessee	118,916	222,641	5.3	8.1	18.8	61.2	9.2	14.5	8.6	2.1	1.9	0.7	60.4	11.9	1.0	9.6
Texas	234,421	734,986	3.8	17.7	36.7	61.5	8.0	16.2	4.8	6.2	0.1	1.2	49.6	11.9	0.8	3.0
Utah	46,610	65,950	5.1	17.2	38.2	66.9	11.4	14.1	5.0	8.2	‥	1.5	43.0	7.0	2.4	2.2
Vermont	28,781	9,534	6.4	8.7	25.6	88.6	17.5	6.5	6.4	4.4	4.2	★	43.2	0.6	3.2	★
Virginia	211,017	255,892	6.3	7.2	24.2	61.7	13.0	10.8	1.5	5.8	3.3	0.1	56.6	19.2	1.4	2.4
Washington	129,315	243,536	4.6	17.1	29.6	58.5	5.9	14.7	7.3	6.9	0.5	3.3	55.6	14.7	1.1	1.9
West Virginia	53,779	48,808	3.5	13.0	39.4	68.6	22.4	11.7	5.1	8.1	2.9	0.1	28.0	11.3	2.3	0.2
Wisconsin	128,147	279,529	4.9	8.5	19.3	68.6	11.0	11.8	8.4	6.3	3.2	1.6	55.3	8.8	2.8	2.8
Wyoming	24,051	26,733	6.7	11.4	21.7	72.7	8.4	11.5	4.9	8.2	2.4	0.5	60.6	7.1	2.0	
Dist. of Col.		216,136		12.1		47.6		10.5		3.0		2.8	35.9			0.2

Source: U.S. Department of Justice, Law Enforcement Assistance Administration, and U.S. Department of Commerce, Bureau of the Census, unpublished data.

Key: ‥ Represents zero or rounds to zero.

★ Represents less than one-half of one-tenth of a percent.

(a) The relation of criminal justice direct expenditure to total direct expenditure is based on data for general purpose governments only and does not include data for independent school districts or special districts.

(b) Police protection is the function of enforcing the law, preserving order and apprehending those who violate the law, whether these activities are performed by a police department, a sheriff's department, or a special police force maintained by an agency whose prime responsibility is outside the criminal justice system.

(c) Judicial activities encompass all civil and criminal courts and activities associated with courts such as law libraries, grand juries, petit juries and the like.

(d) Legal services and prosecution includes the civil and criminal justice activities of the attorneys general, district attorneys, state's attorneys and their variously named equivalents; corporation counsels, solicitors and legal departments with various names.

(e) Public defense includes legal counsel and representation in either criminal or civil proceedings as provided by public defenders, and other government programs that pay the fees of court-appointed counsel.

(f) Corrections is that function of government involving the confinement and rehabilitation of adults and juveniles convicted of offenses against the law and the confinement of persons suspected of a crime and awaiting adjudication.

(g) Other criminal justice activities includes expenditure data that is not else where classified, that cuts across more than one category or that is not allocable to separate categories.

CONSUMER PROTECTION

By Louis S. Meyer

AS THE UNITED STATES moves into the decade of the 1980s, the legislative, regulatory and judicial activities of 1980-81 in the area of consumer protection may well be a turning point. The election of Ronald Reagan and the implementation of massive cuts in a large number of social programs have had a serious impact on both state and local government budgets. In addition, high interest rates and the effect of inflation on the American economy have created serious problems both for consumers and state governments. In particular, the high cost of energy and money have placed heavy demands upon state governments to resolve the many problems bearing on high interest rates, the cost of energy and energy assistance programs, and other issues that have a spinoff effect on various levels of government following both program reductions and budget cuts at the federal level.

A further complication that will limit the ability of the states to provide adequate consumer protection is federal legislation deregulating certain industries, including airlines, aspects of telecommunications and possibly others. Incorporated in the Airline Deregulation Act and proposals for telecommunications deregulation are provisions to remove various regulatory responsibilities from state jurisdiction and place them under federal regulatory control. Such actions will limit state consumer protection responsibilities, particularly in the utility arena, and prevent consumers from using state agencies in the complaint process. With continuing federal preemption of regulatory authority, consumer participation in regulatory proceedings will diminish at the state level.

One further action by the new federal administration that will adversely affect various consumer protection activities is the elimination or cutback of many grants-in-aid to the states. Such grants have often been intended for redistribution for intrastate local and regional consumer protection programs.

Irrespective of deteriorating budgets at all levels of government, the commitment of many states to consumer protection did not relax during 1980-81. Instead, state legislators enacted or amended many state laws which productively addressed consumer concerns. At the same time, it should be noted that many important statutory proposals were rejected. Among these was the Warranty of Auto Merchantability (California), otherwise known as the "Lemon Bill."

While consumer protection legislation covered a broad range of topics during the 1980-81 period, certain issues dominated legislative action:

• *Landlord-Tenant and Housing.* This area of consumer protection continues to receive considerable attention, but in recent years the conversion of apartments to condominiums has added another issue of concern—what are the rights of tenants in the conversion process? States are implementing legislation that provides the "right to remain" for so many days (180 days, for example, in Maryland) and gives existing tenants a certain time option to

Louis S. Meyer is Professor of Political Science and Director, Institute for Community Services, Edinboro State College, Edinboro, Pennsylvania.

buy (30 days in Illinois). No doubt many additional states will be examining this area of concern, particularly in terms of how conversions affect senior citizens and the handicapped (Michigan).

Of equal concern in housing issues has been the establishment of various rights to tenants of mobile home parks. Past evidence has shown that park operators exerted considerable pressure on tenants regarding what they could or could not do. Tenants were compelled to buy gasoline and groceries from park operators, rental fees were arbitrarily set, and quite often tenants could not sell their mobile home without going through the park operator as the seller. In recent years things have changed. Mobile home park tenant rights have been drawn up in many states. During 1980-81 the trend continued. Colorado passed rights legislation; park operators are prohibited from charging rental fees according to family size and from requiring tenants to purchase landscaping services from any particular company (California); similarly, in New York, operators may not require mobile home dwellers to purchase any commodities or services from the operator.

In addition, other issues such as interest on security deposits (Virginia), individual metering of premises (Delaware), and wrongful exclusion and inspection of premises (Virginia) were acted upon. With housing costs escalating at a rapid rate, many people are building their own homes; however, North Carolina has enacted legislation requiring any person building a structure for more than $30,000 to be licensed as a general contractor.

In a directly related area, several states established regulations affecting home contractors (Louisiana).

• *Licensing.* Another area that received considerable attention during 1980-81 was licensing, particularly of occupations and professions. Rarely does a legislative session end without new groups being licensed in various states. During the 1970s, the idea of "sunset" began to take hold, and legislators commenced reviewing the need for agencies. While sunset has been accepted in many areas, its objective of reducing regulatory agencies that have outlived their usefulness has met with limited success. During the past two years, numerous states moved to both extend and restrict licensure. New licensure boards were established for opticians and social workers in Arkansas and for electrolysis in Hawaii. In North Carolina, discount buying clubs and rental referral agencies came under regulation, while in West Virginia, legislation was passed to license wine sellers. During this same period, Hawaii extended the sunset date for the Boards of Hearing Aid Dealers and Fitters, Psychologists, Opticians and Nursing Home Administrators, while repealing the Mortuary and Cemetery Board. Delaware abolished its Drug Board, while Missouri implemented a wide range of provisions in its regulatory boards legislation.

• *Insurance.* Again, as in past years, several states have given attention to consumer issues related to insurance. During the 1980-81 period, further concern was evidenced for the readability and understanding of policies—a matter that is drawing increasing consideration not only in the legislative branch such as enacted in West Virginia, but also in the regulatory process as promulgated in Massachusetts. Whether it is life, property, health or other insurance, consumers are pushing for policies that are understandable to the general public. In addition, in insurance, as in other areas, there is increasing frustration over the use of terms that are understood only by those in the industry. As a result, it is safe to predict that, whether through the legislative or regulatory process, there will be a continued call for agents to provide a better understanding of policies to the consumer. It should be pointed out that some insurance industry efforts are being made to address these issues. In addition, there appears to be an increased interest on the part of some companies and associations to discuss the issues through consumer-industry panels and roundtables—mechanisms that are used quite extensively in the telecommunications industry.

• *Interest Rates.* The impact of inflation on our society has led to various actions that are having serious repercussions in the marketplace. In the consumer protection sector, no issue has caused greater concern than the raising of interest rates on the purchase of consumer goods. No longer can one scan the state annual percentage rates and find a fairly consistent listing of 15-18 percent. Instead, interest rates for credit card purchases, automobiles, revolving credit plans, second mortgages and other purchases have been raised from a few percentage points to a doubling of the rates. In some states, rates for some commodity purchases have reached extreme proportions.

Blame for such escalation of rates is placed on the high cost of money. Merchants are reluctant to loan money at 15 percent when it costs the merchant 20 percent. Yet, to raise the rates to the 20, 30 and even 40 percent levels drives many would-be buyers away—regardless of the state involved.

In recent months, action has been taken by many states, from sparsely populated South Dakota to heavily populated California. From Arizona and Texas to West Virginia and Delaware, maximum interest rates have been raised.

But the efforts have not all met with success. Pennsylvania's House of Representatives decided not to call SB 409 up for a vote (after Senate passage) due to heavy opposition to the bill. However, it is certain that further attempts will be made to raise rates in the Keystone State just as further efforts will be made in other states. It is equally certain that public interest coalitions will be mobilized to do whatever possible to thwart efforts to increase interest rates.

• *Special Issues.* Several state actions bear mention in view of their significance in the marketplace.

Alabama has passed a deceptive trade practices act, the last state to do so. Thus, all 50 states, Puerto Rico and the Virgin Islands now have such acts.

Alaska has amended its statutes in an area of consumer protection that is a continual marketplace issue among consumers: price comparison. Advertisements are full of phrases such as "regularly priced at," "compare at," "nationally advertised value" and other phrases or terms. In most cases, these terms mean very little; comparisons between discount, catalogue and normal retail operations may be significant. Thus, when a catalogue operation that has a reduced price on an item advertises it as "regularly priced at" the term means something different than a normal retail sale that used the same term.

Alaska's action has made it unlawful to advertise price comparisons based on a price other than the regular price, based on catchwords such as "wholesale" unless the price is, in fact, no greater than normal wholesale including actual freight cost if paid by seller or based on comparison of price with price of merchandise if materially different in composition.

In an area that promises to attract attention in other states, New York has addressed the interrelationship of food and transportation energy costs to bring food into the state from various parts of the country. Throughout the Northeast, state officials are becoming increasingly aware of the cost consumers must pay for food and the high percentage of food imported into the region. In particular, New York passed legislation to develop and implement programs to facilitate the sale of farm and food products directly from producers to consumers and amended its direct purchasing law to expand the list of food commodities that local boards of education may directly purchase from local growers for school meals programs. The state also amended and reviewed its item pricing law for another three years.

This issue (item pricing) is another area that will probably see considerable state and local action in the months to come.

• *Judicial Action.* Consumer protection in the several states transcends action of the legislative branch through decisions by the judicial branch.

In several cases, litigation involved violations of statutes concerning deceptive trade practices, consumer protection, restraints of trade, consumer sales protection and merchandising practices. Part of these cases stemmed from violations of the law; others were challenges against the laws themselves. The Ohio statutes prohibiting deceptive acts or practices and the rule-making authority of the director of commerce both survived court challenges. In Alaska, the courts ruled in favor of the state concerning investigative demands pursuant to the Unfair Trade Practices, Consumer Protection and Restraint of Trade Acts. Likewise, cases involving unfair trade in real estate, advertising and other issues were litigated in Oregon, Nebraska, North Carolina, Missouri, Maryland and Mississippi.

Further cases of consumer protection that found their way into the state court systems include, but are not limited to: building contractors' responsibility in designating proper and safe home sites (Wyoming), product liability (Nebraska), implied warranty (West Virginia), tenants' rights (North Carolina and Illinois), telephone solicitation sales (Ohio), pyramid sales (Missouri) and contract language (West Virginia).

• *Legislation vs. Regulation.* As consumer protection is analyzed in the several states and the following table is examined, it should be noted that legislative action is not the sole source of such protection. In many cases, states have not passed consumer protection laws in various areas. However, to determine what action states have taken, an examination of regulations that have been promulgated by various state agencies should also be made. Thus, state action must be a compilation of legislative, regulatory and judicial action to determine the direction of consumer protection.

STATE LAWS ON MAJOR CONSUMER ISSUES
(As of 1981)

	Auto repair/ dealer regulation	Consumer education compulsory—secondary	Holder in due course	Home solicitation sales— cooling-off period	Landlord-tenant rights/ responsibilities set	Landlord-tenant rent escrow deposits	Mobile home park tenants' rights	Pyramid sales regulated	Open dating required for foods	Item pricing required for foods	Private remedies provided	Private remedies: class actions	Private remedies: attorneys' fees	Private remedies: treble damages	Prescription drug advertising permitted	Hearing aid sales regulations	Private business and trade schools regulated	Small claims courts	TV/radio repair/dealer registration/licensing	Unit pricing of foods required	Unfair and deceptive trade practices law	Home building/repair contractors regulated	Generic drug law
Alabama								★															
Alaska	★		★		★	★	★	★			★	★			★	★		★			★		
Arizona	★			★		★	★	★			★	★			★		★	★			★	★	
Arkansas			★					★									★				★	★	★
California	★		★	★	★		★	★	★	★	★	★	★	★	★	★	★	★	★		★	★	★
Colorado	★		★	★	★		★	★			★	★	★	★		★					★		★
Connecticut	★	★	★	★	★	★	★	★			★	★	★	★		★	★	★	★		★		★
Delaware	★		★	★	★	★	★	★			★			★	★		★	★			★	★	★
Florida	★	★	★	★	★		★	★			★	★	★		★	★	★	★			★	★	★
Georgia			★		★		★	★	★	★	★		★		★	★	★	★			★		
Hawaii	★			★	★						★		★			★		★		★	★		★
Idaho			★	★	★						★	★		★			★	★			★		
Illinois			★	★	★						★					★	★	★			★		
Indiana			★	★	★			★			★	★		★		★	★	★			★		
Iowa			★	★	★	★	★	★			★					★	★	★			★		
Kansas			★	★	★			★			★	★	★	★		★	★	★			★		
Kentucky		★	★	★	★		★		★		★	★	★	★	★	★	★	★			★		★
Louisiana	★	★	★	★	★		★				★	★	★	★		★	★	★			★		★
Maine	★	★	★	★	★		★		★		★		★			★	★	★		★	★		★
Maryland	★	★	★	★	★		★				★	★				★	★	★		★	★		★
Massachusetts	★	★	★	★	★	★	★	★	★	★	★	★	★	★		★	★	★	★	★	★		★
Michigan	★		★	★	★	★	★	★			★	★	★	★		★	★	★		★	★	★	★
Minnesota	★		★	★	★	★	★	★	★		★	★	★			★	★	★		★	★	★	★
Mississippi	★		★	★							★					★	★	★			★		
Missouri			★	★				★			★	★	★	★	★	★	★				★		★
Montana				★	★						★	★	★	★		★		★			★		★
Nebraska	★		★	★	★						★		★			★	★	★			★		★
Nevada	★		★	★	★		★				★					★	★	★			★	★	
New Hampshire	★		★	★	★	★	★				★	★	★	★		★	★	★		★	★		★
New Jersey	★		★	★	★		★	★			★	★	★	★		★	★	★			★	★	★
New Mexico					★						★					★		★			★		
New York	★		★	★	★						★	★				★	★	★		★	★		
North Carolina				★	★			★			★	★				★	★	★			★	★	★
North Dakota			★	★	★		★	★			★	★				★	★	★			★		
Ohio	★	★	★	★	★		★	★			★	★	★	★		★	★	★	★		★		★

State																				
Oklahoma	★	★	★	★			★	★		★		★			★			★			★
Oregon		★					★					★			★			★	★		
Pennsylvania	★	★	★	★	★		★	★	★	★	★	★	★	★	★			★	★	★	
Rhode Island		★		★							★		★					★			
South Carolina	★										★	★						★			
South Dakota	★	★	★	★			★	★	★	★	★	★	★	★	★			★	★	★	
Tennessee	★	★	★	★	★			★	★	★	★		★	★		★			★		
Texas	★	★	★	★			★			★		★			★		★				
Utah	★	★	★	★	★			★	★	★	★			★			★			★	★
Vermont			★	★	★			★	★	★	★			★		★			★		

★ indicates yes.   .... indicates no.

Note: Many states have only partial legislation in different categories of legislation. To be certain of state legislation in a particular area a check should be made with the attorney general's office of the state in question.

545

STATE REGULATION OF
OCCUPATIONS AND PROFESSIONS

By Frances Stokes Berry and Doug Roederer

OCCUPATIONAL LICENSING is a common form of state regulation that affects most businesses and professions. It is an exercise of the state's inherent police power to protect the health, safety and welfare of its citizens. Generally accepted criteria for the appropriate exercise of licensure authority are:

(1) Unqualified practice poses a serious risk to a consumer's life, health, safety or economic well-being.
(2) Such risks are likely to occur.
(3) The public cannot accurately judge a practitioner's qualifications.
(4) Benefits to the public clearly outweigh potential harmful effects of licensure (such as a decrease in the supply of practitioners).

Failure to meet these criteria, in general, indicates that licensure is not justified, or that some alternative form of regulation such as registration or certification, may be appropriate.

Before 1900, most states granted licensure to attorneys, dentists, pharmacists, physicians and teachers. By 1950, frequently licensed occupations included veterinarians, accountants, nurses, architects, engineers, barbers, cosmetologists and funeral directors. In the last 30 years, the list has expanded rapidly with the addition of such groups as physical therapists, psychologists, social workers, radiologic technicians, emergency medical personnel, physicians' assistants and many others.

State officials and others concerned with occupational and professional licensing today face at least five major issues: (1) sharp increases in the number of groups requesting licensure; (2) questions about the organization, structure and composition of licensure boards; (3) evaluation of the performance of licensure boards; (4) ways to assure the public of the continuing competence of licensed practitioners; and (5) creation of mechanism for exchanging information.

Requests for Licensure

Occupational and professional groups seek licensure for many reasons. It offers an opportunity for increased status for the practitioners, it is sometimes a prerequisite for third-party reimbursement, and it offers mechanisms for keeping unqualified or unscrupulous practitioners from engaging in the occupation or profession. Professional groups usually draft legislation providing for regulation of the profession and then attempt to convince legislators of the utility of that regulation.

The benefits of protecting the public from incompetent practitioners are not without negative side effects, however. Several pitfalls of occupational regulation are now recognized. Licensure laws frequently place restrictions on advertising and on various business

Frances Stokes Berry is Project Director for Licensure and Regulation, and Doug Roederer is Director, Office of Research and Management Services, The Council of State Governments.

structures and practices. By restricting the number of people entering a profession and the ability of new professions to work independently, licensure may increase the cost to consumers of some professional services. The mobility of practitioners has been hampered and in many fields, auxiliaries have been underused. Licensure often focuses on testing applicants for the initial license and is less concerned about the competence and performance of practitioners after the initial license is granted.

Several states have instituted formal processes for evaluating requests for regulation in an attempt to restrict licensure only to those occupations that meet the generally accepted criteria. These processes are referred to as sunrise processes and usually call for the requesting group to submit information to an executive branch office or legislative committee which reviews the information against a set of standards or criteria.

In Virginia, a commission within the Department of Commerce reviews such requests and makes a recommendation to the legislature. In Michigan, this responsibility is vested in the Health Occupations Council within the Department of Health. Illinois' legislature has a Select Joint Committee on Regulatory Reform, which reviews requests for regulating new professions.

The New York legislature has established a similar review process in the Assembly's Committee on Higher Education. A group requesting licensure must fill out an 18-item questionnaire before a bill to license a profession may be considered. The information received through the questionnaire is a basis for the committee decision regarding licensure. The process ensures that certain standardized information will be available to the committee.

Organization of Licensure Boards

Historically, in most states, licensure boards have been autonomous. Roughly half the states have now established a central agency for most or all licensure boards. The central agencies differ widely in terms of the authority exercised over board decisions. In many states, the central agency is responsible for receiving applications, issuing licenses, recordkeeping, fee collection and routine correspondence, while each board continues to regulate practitioners by conducting examinations and exercising disciplinary authority.

In Virginia, the central licensure agency (Department of Commerce) has authority over board staff and budgets. In Illinois, the central agency (Department of Registration and Education) appoints board members and receives and investigates complaints against licensees. In New York, the central agency (Department of Education) has authority for appointing board staff, allocating budgets, conducting investigations of practitioners and promulgating rules and regulations. Florida enacted legislation in 1979 to increase the central agency's (Department of Professional Regulation) authority over board personnel, budgets, investigations and consumer complaints. In addition, the central agency may challenge board rules. In Connecticut, the central agency has authority to issue and review licenses, receive and investigate complaints, administer exams, appoint staff and allocate board budgets. The 1980 legislation consolidating these administrative functions within the Department of Health Services also precludes the department or the various boards or commissions from regulating any aspect of the professions' business practices.

The composition of licensure boards is changing as well. Traditionally, boards have been comprised exclusively of members of the regulated profession. Most states now tend to place one or more public or lay members on licensure boards. The California Public Member Act requires that boards be made up of a majority of lay members except for health and accountancy boards which are to have one-third lay members. Michigan requires one-third of the board members to represent the general public. A related trend involves adding to board membership practitioners who are specialists or auxiliaries to the profession regulated by the board.

Opponents of the trend toward centralization of licensure functions contend that it adds to bureaucracy and red tape and reduces the responsiveness of the licensure authority to both licensee needs and citizen complaints. Further, they argue that individual licensure boards with professional members best understand the issues of examinations, professional practice and discipline.

States that have moved toward centralization have done so in part on the assumption that numerous autonomous boards duplicate expensive administrative procedures. In addition to these perceived cost efficiencies, some states have sought to devise a mechanism for co-ordination of board policy and procedures.

Evaluation of Licensing Boards and Commissions

In general, there has been little evaluation of the performance of boards or their continuing need for existence, unless a state enacts a sunset law. Almost all of the 36 states that have sunset laws apply them to occupational and professional licensure boards. These laws either focus exclusively on licensure boards or include them in the agencies to be reviewed under sunset.

The sunset movement has made several contributions to an improved state licensure system. Sunset has introduced the idea or "mortality" to regulatory boards; the automatic termination clause forces the legislature to take positive action if it wishes to retain regulatory boards. Sunset reviews and hearings have opened the boards to greater public scrutiny, increased the boards' and professions' awareness of public needs, and emphasized that boards are governmental agencies. Sunset presents an opportunity for administrative practices to be reviewed and improved. It focuses legislative attention on the effects of board and agency rule-making and administrative decision-making. Legislators are then better able to assess the need for legislation.

Sunset reviews are usually conducted by a legislative audit staff. Colorado, however, requires an executive branch agency to conduct the sunset review. Review findings or recommendations are then submitted to a standing or special legislative committee.

Criteria used for sunset evaluations of boards fall into two categories: (1) the need for regulating the profession, and (2) the performance of the board or agency, regardless of the need for regulation. In part because the burden of proof for regulation has usually been placed on legislative committee staff rather than on the board under review, the dominant change resulting from sunset has been to reform board practices rather than take more radical action. Few boards have been terminated under sunset.

Specific changes in health regulatory laws resulting from sunset reviews include the following:[1] (1) the composition of boards was altered, to include lay members and auxiliary health practitioners; (2) board meetings were opened to the public; (3) scopes of practice were expanded or changed to accommodate emerging health care practitioners; (4) specialists and auxiliary health care practitioners were granted broader scopes of practice to perform functions independently or with less supervision; (5) licensing examination guidelines were strengthened or clarified; (6) reciprocal licensure arrangements with other states were encouraged; (7) grounds for disciplinary action were expanded with new definitions of negligence, incompetence, malpractice and others; and (8) mechanisms were created and strengthened for receiving and processing complaints.

Sunset has also paved the way in some states for systemwide reforms. Attention to several independent boards has revealed common problems and pointed up the need for general changes in policy and structure. Some states, such as Florida and Connecticut, have used sunset to adopt proposals to coordinate certain groups of boards, such as health boards. Sunset also offers an opportunity to examine some of the allied health or auxiliary occupations and their relationship to the "parent" occupational board.

Unexpected changes have occurred. In some cases, licensure boards and members improved their performance in anticipation of sunset reviews. In other cases, previously unregulated professions, such as denturists and midwives, used the sunset process as an opportunity to present their case for licensure.

On the other hand, sunset has not been without its shortcomings where licensure boards are concerned. Some sunset evaluations have focused extensively on how well the board did what it was charged to do rather than whether or not the function was needed in the first place. In addition, sunset has presented substantial scheduling and staffing problems in some states. These problems are exacerbated for those states undertaking reviews for large numbers of licensure boards. Indiana, in response to the workload dilemma, assigned staff to research certain common issues, such as public members, discipline, reciprocal licensure, etc., for all boards rather than to review each board separately.

The cost of performance audit reviews can be enormous. The average seems to be $10,000 to $20,000 per board reviewed. Some have compared this cost with the actual budgets of boards and agencies under scrutiny in an attempt to prove the negative cost-benefit of sunset. Where regulation is concerned, the greatest potential cost savings are in indirect costs of regulation, such as the artificial scarcity of certain practitioners or higher prices resulting from advertising restrictions. However, the cost of the review process cannot be overlooked.

Sunset invites lobbying, political bartering and other attempts to circumvent the evaluation process. Many professional groups are politically experienced and have been able to take their case to the legislature and overturn sunset committee recommendations. Some boards have essentially begun public relations campaigns, rather than justifying their need or performance.

Continuing Competence

There is a growing recognition that the state government regulatory system that attempts to ensure beginning practitioners' competence should also attempt to ensure the public that practitioners continue to practice above minimum levels. In recent years, various groups have advocated mandatory continuing education as a vehicle for ensuring competent practice. There is, however, more and more debate about the utility of this mechanism.

Critics argue that when states mandate continuing education, they place confidence in an unproven device. Course content varies widely and practitioner learning is often not assessed. While continuing education may address practitioner knowledge and skills, it may or may not have an impact on the manner in which the practitioner deals with the public in practice. States are concerned with more than the ability of the practitioner to appropriately apply knowledge and skills; they must also be concerned with actual performance of the practitioners.

Strong and effective disciplinary and enforcement procedures may do more to protect the public from practitioners performing below minimum levels. Using this approach, state governments' efforts are directed at the small percentage of practitioners who do practice below minimum levels rather than toward the substantially larger group of competent practitioners.

States continue to mandate continuing education. (See the following table on Mandatory Continuing Education for Selected Professions.) Forty-six states require continuing education for nursing home administrators and optometrists. Since 1979, the number of states with mandatory continuing education for certified public accountants, psychologists and real estate agents has increased by over 30 percent.

Exchanging Information

Responding to the expressed need for a forum to share information and discuss common problems, state licensing officials formed the Clearinghouse on Licensure, Enforcement and Regulation in 1980. Clearinghouse members include board members and staff, central agency administrators, legislators, and staff from sunset commissions, attorneys general's offices and consumer protection agencies.

The clearinghouse, with staff support from The Council of State Governments, has state information concerning professional disciplinary procedures, public membership on boards, sunset performance audits and the organization of state licensure functions, as well as bibliographies on sunset, oversight and occupational licensing. Annual meetings and regular information exchange hold promise for keeping board members and administrative staff informed about innovative actions in other states.

Conclusion

While regulation of occupations and professions has come under some criticism, regulation of certain practitioners will certainly continue. Changes will likely occur, such as reducing boards' autonomous powers by centralizing administrative functions and eliminating some board functions. Other areas, such as continuing competence assurance and reduction of conflicts between the boundaries of practitioner groups, will continue to be important and will likely receive increased attention from state officials.

Note

1. Doug Roederer and Patsy Palmer, *Sunset: Expectation and Experience* (Lexington, Ky.: The Council of State Governments, 1980).

Table 1

OCCUPATIONS REGULATED IN THE STATES

State or other jurisdiction	Abstractor	Acupuncturist	Aerial duster/ pesticide sprayer	Ambulance attendant/EMT	Auctioneer	Audiologist/ speech pathologist	Boiler inspector	Chauffeur	Collection agency operator	Contractor, general/ building	Contractor, specialty	Contractor, well drilling	Driver training instructor	Electrician	Elevator inspector	Embalmer/funeral director
Alabama	...	...	...	...	★	★	...	...	...	★	...	...	★	...	...	★
Alaska	...	★	...	★	...	...	...	★	★	★	★	...	★	...	...	★
Arizona	...	...	...	★	...	...	...	★	★	★	★	★	★	★	...	★
Arkansas	★	...	...	...	★	★	...	★	★	★	...	...	★	...	★	★
California	...	★	...	...	...	★	...	...	★	...	★	★	★	...	...	★
Colorado	★	...	...	...	...	★	...	...	★	...	...	★	★	★	...	...
Connecticut	...	...	★	★	...	★	★	...	★	...	...	★	★	★	...	★
Delaware	...	...	...	...	...	★	★	...	★	...	...	★	★	★	...	★
Florida	...	...	...	★	...	★	★	...	★	...	...	★	★	★	★	...
Georgia	...	...	...	★	★	★	★	...	★	...	...	★	★	...	...	★
Hawaii	★	★	...	...	...	★	...	...	...	★	★	...	★	...	...	★
Idaho	★	...	★	...	...	...	...	★	★	...	...	★	★	...	...	★
Illinois	...	★	...	...	...	★	★	★	★	★	...	★	★	...	★	★
Indiana	...	...	★	★	★	★	★	★	★	...	...	★	★	...	...	★
Iowa	...	...	...	★	★	★	★	...	★	...	...	★	★	...	...	★
Kansas	★	...	...	★	...	★	★	★	★	...	...	★	★	...	...	★
Kentucky	...	...	★	★	★	★	★	★	★	...	...	★	★	...	...	★
Louisiana	...	★	...	★	★	★	★	★	★	★	★	...	★	...	...	★
Maine	...	...	★	★	★	★	★	...	★	...	...	...	★	★	★	★
Maryland	...	...	...	...	★	★	★	...	★	...	...	...	★	★	...	★
Massachusetts	...	...	...	★	...	...	...	...	★	...	...	★	★	★	★	★
Michigan	...	...	...	★	...	★	★	★	...	...	...	★	★	★	★	...
Minnesota	★	...	★	★	★	★	★	...	★	...	...	★	★	★	★	★
Mississippi	...	...	★	★	...	★	★	...	...	★	...	★	★	...	...	...
Missouri	...	...	★	...	★	★	...	★	...	...	...	...	★	...	...	...
Montana	★	★	...	★	★	★	★	...	★	...	...	★	★	...	★	★
Nebraska	★	...	★	★	★	★	★	...	★	...	...	★	★	...	★	★
Nevada	...	★	★	★	...	★	★	★	★	★	★	★	★	...	★	★
New Hampshire	...	...	★	★	★	★	★	★	★	...	...	★	★	★	★	★
New Jersey	...	...	...	...	...	★	★	...	★	...	...	...	★	★	...	...
New Mexico	...	...	...	...	...	★	...	★	★	★	...	...	★	...	...	★
New York	...	★	...	★	...	★	...	★	★	...	...	...	★	...	...	★
North Carolina	...	★	★	★	★	★	★	...	★	★	★	★	★	...	★	★
North Dakota	★	...	★	★	★	★	★	★	★	★	...	★	★	★	★	★
Ohio	...	...	...	★	★	★	★	...	★	...	...	...	★	...	★	★
Oklahoma	...	...	...	...	...	★	...	...	★	...	...	...	★	...	...	...
Oregon	...	★	...	★	★	★	★	★	★	★	★	...	★	★	...	★
Pennsylvania	...	...	...	★	★	...	★	...	★	...	...	...	★	★	★	...
Rhode Island	...	★	...	★	★	★	★	★	...	...	...	...	★	★	...	...
South Carolina	...	...	...	★	★	★	...	...	...	★	...	...	★	...	...	...
South Dakota	★	...	...	★	...	...	...	...	...	...	...	★	★	...	★	...
Tennessee	...	...	★	★	★	★	★	★	★	★	...	★	★	...	★	★
Texas	...	...	★	★	...	★	...	★	...	...	...	...	★	...	...	★
Utah	★	...	...	★	...	★	...	...	★	★	★	★	★	★	...	★
Vermont	...	...	...	...	★	...	...	...	...	...	...	...	★	★	...	...
Virginia	...	★	...	★	...	★	★	★	★	★	...	...	★	...	...	★
Washington	...	★	...	★	...	★	★	★	★	★	...	★	★	★	★	...
West Virginia	...	...	★	★	★	...	...	...	★	...	...	...	★	...	★	★
Wisconsin	...	...	★	★	...	...	★	★	★	★	...	...	★	...	...	★
Wyoming	★	...	★	★	...	...	★	★	★	★	...	...	★	★	★	★
Dist. of Col.	...	...	...	★	...	...	★	...	...	...	...	...	★	...	...	...

Source: U.S. Department of Labor, Office of Research and Development, Employment and Training Administration, *Directory of State-Regulated Occupations*, 1980.

Note: In addition to the occupations listed in the table, the following are regulated in all jurisdictions: Accountant, Architect, Attorney, Barber, Chiropractor, Cosmetologist, Dental Hygienist, Dentist, Insurance Agent, Licensed Practical Nurse, Registered Nurse, Optometrist, Osteopath, Pharmacist, Physical Therapist, Physician/Surgeon, Podiatrist, Real Estate Agent, Primary School Teacher, Secondary School Teacher.

★—Surveys returned from the states indicated these occupations were either licensed, certified or regulated.

OCCUPATIONS REGULATED IN THE STATES—Continued

State or other jurisdiction	Employment agency operator	Engineer, professional	Forester	Geologist	Guide	Hearing aid dealer	Landscape architect	Librarian	Marriage counselor (marriage/family)	Masseur/masseuse	Medical laboratory technician	Medical laboratory director (clinical)	Midwife	Milk and/or cream sampler	Mine foreman	Moving picture projectionist
Alabama	★	★	★			★	★				★		★		★	
Alaska	★	★			★										★	
Arizona	★	★			★	★	★				★		★	★	★	
Arkansas	★	★	★		★	★	★	★		★				★	★	
California	★	★	★	★	★	★	★	★	★		★	★	★	★		
Colorado	★	★			★	★							★	★	★	★
Connecticut	★	★				★	★	★		★			★	★		
Delaware	★	★		★		★	★		★		★		★			★
Florida	★	★			★	★	★		★		★					★
Georgia	★	★	★	★		★	★	★	★	★						
Hawaii	★	★				★	★			★	★	★				★
Idaho	★	★		★	★	★	★					★	★	★		
Illinois	★	★					★		★			★	★	★		
Indiana	★	★				★	★									
Iowa	★	★				★	★									
Kansas	★	★				★	★							★		
Kentucky	★	★			★	★	★	★				★		★	★	
Louisiana	★	★				★	★	★				★		★	★	
Maine	★	★	★	★	★	★	★	★				★		★	★	
Maryland	★		★		★	★	★	★				★		★		★
Massachusetts	★	★				★	★	★				★		★		★
Michigan	★	★	★			★	★	★	★	★	★	★		★		
Minnesota	★	★	★				★	★				★		★		
Mississippi	★	★	★				★	★				★		★		
Missouri	★	★				★							★			
Montana	★	★			★	★	★	★		★			★	★	★	
Nebraska	★	★				★	★	★					★	★		
Nevada	★	★			★	★	★			★		★			★	
New Hampshire	★	★	★		★		★		★	★		★	★	★		
New Jersey	★	★				★		★	★			★	★			
New Mexico	★		★				★			★				★		
New York	★	★			★	★	★	★			★		★	★		
North Carolina	★	★		★	★	★	★			★				★	★	
North Dakota	★	★				★	★	★					★		★	
Ohio	★	★				★	★	★	★				★		★	
Oklahoma	★	★	★			★						★		★	★	
Oregon	★	★		★	★	★	★	★				★		★	★	
Pennsylvania	★	★				★	★	★					★	★	★	★
Rhode Island	★	★				★	★	★			★		★	★		
South Carolina	★	★	★	★		★	★	★		★		★	★			
South Dakota	★	★				★					★			★		
Tennessee	★	★			★	★	★				★	★	★	★		
Texas	★	★				★	★	★	★				★			
Utah	★	★			★		★		★				★			
Vermont	★	★														
Virginia	★	★				★		★					★	★	★	
Washington	★	★			★	★	★	★		★			★	★	★	
West Virginia	★	★	★		★	★	★						★	★	★	
Wisconsin	★	★			★	★									★	
Wyoming	★	★				★							★			
Dist. of Col.	★	★											★			

OCCUPATIONS REGULATED IN THE STATES—Continued

State or other jurisdiction	Naturopath	Nursing home administrator	Occupational therapist	Occupational therapy assistant	Optician (ophthalmic dispenser)	Outfitter	Pest control applicator, commercial	Pesticide applicator	Pharmacist assistant	Physical therapist assistant	Physician's assistant	Plumber	Polygraph examiner	Private detective	Private patrol agency operator	Psychologist
Alabama		★										★	★			★
Alaska		★			★					★	★	★				★
Arizona	★	★			★				★	★				★	★	★
Arkansas		★	★	★			★	★		★	★	★	★	★	★	★
California		★	★		★					★				★	★	★
Colorado		★				★	★		★			★		★		★
Connecticut	★	★					★	★	★			★		★	★	★
Delaware		★					★	★	★			★		★		★
Florida	★	★			★		★				★	★	★	★	★	★
Georgia	★	★	★						★	★	★	★	★	★		★
Hawaii	★	★			★							★		★	★	★
Idaho		★				★	★					★	★	★	★	★
Illinois		★									★	★	★	★	★	★
Indiana		★						★	★	★	★	★		★		★
Iowa		★						★						★		★
Kansas		★						★				★		★		★
Kentucky		★			★			★	★	★	★	★	★			★
Louisiana		★					★	★				★	★	★		★
Maine		★					★	★				★	★	★		★
Maryland		★								★		★		★		★
Massachusetts		★			★		★					★	★	★	★	★
Michigan		★					★		★	★	★	★	★	★	★	★
Minnesota		★					★				★	★		★		★
Mississippi		★					★		★					★		★
Missouri		★														★
Montana		★				★	★					★		★		★
Nebraska		★									★	★		★		★
Nevada		★			★		★			★	★	★		★	★	★
New Hampshire		★	★	★				★			★	★		★	★	★
New Jersey		★			★					★	★	★		★	★	★
New Mexico		★						★	★			★		★	★	★
New York		★	★	★	★						★		★	★	★	★
North Carolina	★	★			★				★		★		★	★	★	★
North Dakota		★	★	★								★		★		★
Ohio		★	★	★				★				★		★		★
Oklahoma		★							★	★	★	★	★			★
Oregon	★	★	★	★			★		★	★	★	★				★
Pennsylvania		★									★	★		★		★
Rhode Island		★			★							★	★		★	★
South Carolina		★	★		★						★	★		★		★
South Dakota	★	★					★	★	★	★	★	★				★
Tennessee		★			★		★	★	★			★				★
Texas	★	★					★	★	★			★	★	★	★	★
Utah	★	★	★	★						★	★	★	★	★	★	★
Vermont		★			★			★			★	★	★	★		★
Virginia	★	★			★		★					★	★	★	★	★
Washington	★	★			★		★		★		★		★	★	★	★
West Virginia		★				★	★		★		★			★	★	★
Wisconsin		★					★							★	★	★
Wyoming		★					★									★
Dist. of Col.												★		★		★

OCCUPATIONS REGULATED IN THE STATES—Concluded

State or other jurisdiction	Radio & TV technician	Radiologic technologist	Sanitarian	School bus driver	Securities agent	Ship harbor/river pilot	Shorthand reporter	Social worker	Soil tester	Surveyor, land	Tree expert or surgeon	Veterinarian, animal technician	Watchmaker	Watchman/guard agency owner/operator	Weather modifier	Weighmaster
Alabama			★		★	★		★	★	★	★					★
Alaska				★	★	★				★					★	★
Arizona		★			★					★				★		
Arkansas			★		★			★	★	★						
California		★	★		★	★		★		★		★			★	★
Colorado					★			★		★		★			★	★
Connecticut			★		★	★				★	★			★	★	★
Delaware					★	★				★					★	★
Florida			★	★	★	★				★					★	★
Georgia			★		★	★	★		★	★						★
Hawaii		★	★		★					★						★
Idaho			★		★		★	★		★					★	★
Illinois			★		★		★	★		★	★	★				
Indiana	★		★		★	★	★			★		★	★			
Iowa					★	★	★			★		★	★			
Kansas				★	★			★		★			★		★	
Kentucky		★	★		★			★		★		★				
Louisiana	★		★		★	★	★	★		★	★	★		★	★	
Maine				★	★	★	★	★	★	★	★					★
Maryland			★	★	★	★		★		★						★
Massachusetts	★		★	★	★			★		★						
Michigan		★			★	★		★		★		★	★	★	★	
Minnesota					★	★		★		★		★	★			
Mississippi		★			★			★		★						
Missouri					★					★						
Montana		★	★		★					★		★		★	★	
Nebraska			★		★					★		★		★	★	★
Nevada			★		★		★			★		★		★	★	★
New Hampshire					★	★	★			★	★	★				
New Jersey		★			★	★	★					★	★			
New Mexico			★		★		★			★		★		★	★	★
New York		★	★			★	★	★		★		★		★	★	★
North Carolina			★		★					★				★		★
North Dakota			★			★			★	★						★
Ohio			★		★	★				★						
Oklahoma			★		★		★	★		★					★	
Oregon		★	★		★		★			★		★	★		★	★
Pennsylvania			★		★	★				★					★	
Rhode Island			★	★	★	★		★		★				★		★
South Carolina			★		★			★	★	★				★		★
South Dakota			★		★			★		★		★			★	
Tennessee			★	★	★					★					★	★
Texas					★					★					★	★
Utah			★		★		★	★		★						★
Vermont	★	★		★	★					★						
Virginia			★		★	★	★			★						★
Washington			★		★	★	★			★					★	
West Virginia		★	★		★					★					★	
Wisconsin			★		★				★	★				★	★	
Wyoming					★					★						
Dist. of Col.					★											

Table 2
MANDATORY CONTINUING EDUCATION
FOR SELECTED PROFESSIONS
(As of January 1981)

State or other jurisdiction	Architects	Certified public accountants	Dentists	Engineers	Lawyers	Nurses	Nursing home administrators	Optometrists	Psychologists	Pharmacists	Physical therapists	Physicians	Real estate agents	Social workers	Licensed practical nurses	Veterinarians
Alabama	...	★	...	...	...	...	★	★	...	★	...	...	...	★	...	★
Alaska	...	★	...	...	...	...	...	...	...	...	...	...	...	...	...	...
Arizona	...	★	...	...	S	...	★	★	★	...	...	★	★	...	...	★
Arkansas	...	★	...	...	...	...	★	★	...	★	...	•	...	...	...	★
California	...	★	★	...	S	★	★	...	★	★	...	★	★	...	★	★
Colorado	...	★	...	...	★	•	★	...	★	...	...	...	...	★	...	★
Connecticut	...	★	...	...	...	...	★	★	...	...	...	...	...	...	...	...
Delaware	...	★	...	...	...	...	★	★	...	...	...	...	...	★	★	...
Florida	•	★	★	...	S	...	★	★	★	★	...	★	...	★	★	★
Georgia	...	★	...	...	S	...	★	★	...	★	...	...	...	...	...	...
Hawaii	...	★	...	...	...	...	★	...	...	...	...	★	...	...	...	...
Idaho	...	★	...	...	★	...	★	★	...	...	...	...	...	...	...	...
Illinois	...	★	...	...	...	...	★	...	...	★	...	...	★	...	...	★
Indiana	...	★	...	...	...	...	★	...	...	★	...	...	...	...	...	★
Iowa	★	★	★	★	★S	★	★	★	★	★	★	★	★	★	★	★
Kansas	...	★	★	...	...	★	★	★	★	•	★	★	★	★	★	★
Kentucky	...	★	...	...	...	...	★	★	...	★	...	•	S	★	★	★
Louisiana	...	★	...	...	...	•	★	★	★	★	...	★	★	★	★	...
Maine	...	★	...	...	...	...	★	★	★	★	...	...	★	★	★	...
Maryland	...	★	...	...	...	...	★	★	★	...	★	★	★	★	...	...
Massachusetts	...	★	•	...	...	★	★	★	...	...	...	★	★	...	★	★
Michigan	...	★	...	...	...	...	★	★	★	•	...	★	★	...	...	★
Minnesota	•	★	★	★	•	★	★	★	★	•	★	★	★	...	...	...
Mississippi	...	★	...	...	...	S	★	★	★	...	...	...	...	...	...	•
Missouri	...	★	...	...	...	...	★	★	...	...	...	...	...	...	...	...
Montana	...	★	...	...	...	...	★	...	...	...	...	...	...	...	...	★
Nebraska	...	★	...	...	...	...	★	...	...	...	...	...	...	...	★	★
Nevada	...	★	...	...	...	★	★	★	...	★	...	•	...	...	★	•
New Hampshire	...	...	...	...	...	S	★	★	...	★	...	•	...	...	...	★
New Jersey	...	...	★	...	S	...	★	...	...	...	...	...	...	...	...	...
New Mexico	...	★	★	...	S	★	★	★	★	★	...	★	★	...	★	★
New York	...	...	...	...	...	...	...	...	...	...	...	...	★	...	...	...
North Carolina	...	★	•	...	...	...	★	★	•	...	...	...	...	...	...	★
North Dakota	...	★	★	...	★	...	★	★	...	...	...	...	...	...	...	★
Ohio	...	★	...	...	...	...	★	★	...	...	...	★	...	...	...	★
Oklahoma	...	★	...	...	...	...	★	...	...	...	...	...	★	★	...	...
Oregon	...	★	★	...	S	...	★	★	★	★	...	...	★	...	...	★
Pennsylvania	...	★	...	...	...	...	★	★	...	...	...	S	...	...	...	★
Rhode Island	...	★	...	...	...	...	★	...	...	...	...	★	...	...	...	...
South Carolina	...	★	...	...	★S	...	★	★	...	...	...	...	...	...	...	...
South Dakota	...	★	★	...	...	...	★	★	★	★	...	...	★	★	...	★
Tennessee	...	★	...	...	...	...	★	★	...	...	...	...	★	...	★	★
Texas	...	•	...	...	S	...	★	★	...	★	...	★	...	...	...	...
Utah	...	...	...	...	...	...	★	★	★	•	...	...	★	★	...	...
Vermont	...	★	...	...	...	...	★	★	•	...	...	...	...	...	...	...
Virginia	...	...	...	...	...	...	★	...	...	...	...	...	...	...	...	...
Washington	...	★	...	...	★	•	★	★	★	★	★	...	★	...	...	★
West Virginia	...	...	...	...	...	...	★	★	★	...	...	...	...	...	...	...
Wisconsin	...	...	...	...	★	...	★	★	...	...	...	...	★	★	...	...
Wyoming	...	★	...	...	...	...	★	★	...	•	...	...	...	...	...	...
Dist. of Col.	...	★	...	...	...	...	...	...	...	...	...	...	...	...	...	...

Source: Louis E. Phillips, Associate Director for Managerial Services, Center for Continuing Education, The University of Georgia, Athens, Georgia. Information obtained from national professional associations.

Key: ★—Required by statute or regulation.
•—Enabling legislation passed.
S—Required under certain circumstances.
...—No requirement.

STATE POLICE AND HIGHWAY PATROLS

By R. H. Sostkowski

Historic Development

WHEN OUR NATION was in its infancy and composed of widely separated municipalities, local enforcement of state laws was the most acceptable and reliable method. However, as society grew larger and more mobile, crime began to expand past municipal boundaries, rendering local enforcement inadequate. This, combined with factors such as the reluctance of local sheriffs to enforce unpopular state laws, dissimilarity in enforcement techniques by various local agencies and lack of coordination of enforcement activities in an area of mobile crime, called for a centralized mechanism to ensure the preservation of law and order among the municipalities within the states. Early state-level enforcement agencies emerged to meet this need.

There has always been debate among the states concerning the first "true" state police agency. The initial state-level law enforcement agencies were specialized forces with narrowly defined responsibilities, such as the Texas Rangers, founded in 1835 principally to patrol the Mexican border. Arizona and New Mexico formed border patrols in the early 1900s, which existed for only a few years before they were disbanded. Some police historians believe that the first true state police force (or constabulary as it was initially termed) was formed in Massachusetts in 1865. This agency was created primarily to suppress vice, but was granted the ability to use *general* police powers throughout the state. In 1879, the agency was absorbed into the Massachusetts District Police, a state detective unit, broadening its scope to include fire investigations, enforcement of fish and game laws and building inspections, and was incorporated into the Department of Public Safety in 1920. This final merger included the granting of *full* police authority throughout the state and has resulted in some police historians considering 1920 as the actual beginning of the Massachusetts State Police. The next state to create a state police force was Connecticut (1903), which was patterned after the Massachusetts District Police and was primarily concerned with the enforcement of vice and liquor laws. Again, because of its narrow scope, it is argued that this was not the first "true" state police agency.

In 1905, the Pennsylvania "State Constabulary" was organized, marking the beginning of a new era in rural police administration and becoming the model for most police forces established thereafter. From its inception, it operated as a mounted and uniformed body with a widely distributed system of troop headquarters and substations. In addition, the superintendent of the state agency, who was made responsible to the governor alone, had broad administrative powers. Because of these characteristics, the Pennsylvania State Police is most often credited as being the first "true" state police agency. It was 12 years before New York created the next state law enforcement agency in 1917, and by 1929, 20 states had implemented such agencies. After the following decade, 26 more had done so.

R. H. Sostkowski is Director of the Division of State and Provincial Police of the International Association of Chiefs of Police.

As the number of motor vehicles and highways grew after World War I, a new priority emerged—the uniform enforcement of state motor vehicle codes and regulations. Highway Patrols were created to meet this need and advocated as a solution to the problem of too ardent enforcement of vehicle regulations at the local level. A second purpose was to spread the increased cost of highway policing to a state-level tax base, including revenues earned through state licensing and taxing of motor vehicles.

Although today one generally equates state-level law enforcement as being embodied as either a state police force or highway patrol, in reality, there are a variety of state enforcement agencies. In some instances, state law enforcement functions are fractionalized and the responsibility of separate and distinct units which operate only within their sphere of expertise. In other instances, almost complete state law enforcement responsibility rests with the organization operating the large and most visible uniform field force. For example, narcotics, organized crime, intelligence, identification and communications systems, state crime laboratory, etc., could in one state fall within the purview of the state police agency, while in another be independent agencies or units within other state-level departments.

Categories of State Law Enforcement

Although these differences exist among the 49 state agencies[1], there is one feature distinguishing the state police or highway patrol from all other state-level enforcement agencies—their operation of a uniform field patrol on highways throughout the state, as opposed to patrol by uniformed officers within narrowly restricted areas. Currently, the Division of State and Provincial Police of the International Association of Chiefs of Police categorizes state-level law enforcement agencies as follows:

1. Highway patrol—a state law enforcement agency which:
   * Operates a uniformed field patrol force and concentrates its police services on traffic, vehicle and highway-related activities.
2. State police—a state law enforcement agency which:
   * Operates a uniformed field patrol force and non-uniformed investigative units.
   * Conducts criminal law investigations generally, rather than concentrating on a specialized category of offenses or specifically assigned sensitive cases.
   * Is responsible for providing general police services and activities.
3. Department of law enforcement—a state law enforcement investigative agency which:
   * Does not operate a uniformed field patrol force.
   * Is responsible for criminal investigations generally, rather than concentrating on a specialized category of offenses or specifically assigned sensitive cases.
4. Law enforcement unit—a state law enforcement unit which is only:
   * Responsible for investigations of specialized categories of offenses or specifically assigned sensitive cases and does not operate a uniformed field patrol force.
   * Responsible for providing security or general police services in a limited geographical area, such as that encompassed by state institutions, buildings or parks, and employs uniformed or non-uniformed personnel.
   * Responsible for enforcement of state wildlife, conservation or game laws by uniformed or non-uniformed personnel.

Departmental Responsibilities

The major distinguishing factor between the state police and highway patrols is that the former are responsible for providing full police services, while the latter direct their primary efforts to the enforcement of highway and motor vehicle regulations and traffic safety programs. In California, for example, the highway patrol is responsible for all traffic matters while the sheriff's departments are responsible for all criminal offenses and providing services to unincorporated areas. In other states, jurisdictional boundaries are not clear-cut, and the agency first responding to a call may have primary jurisdiction. In Michigan, for example, the state police and county sheriffs respond to the same calls for service in unincorporated areas, with the authority for handling the call given to the agency first responding.

State law enforcement agencies seldom pursue investigations within incorporated cities. In some states they may have the authority to do so, but as a matter of policy do not. In other states, they are prohibited from conducting investigations or patrols unless requested to do so by municipal officials or directed to by the governor in especially sensitive cases. In some states, state officers provide traffic services on state and interstate highways within cities, while in others they do not. A trend is beginning to emerge, however, whereby state law enforcement agencies assist incorporated areas at the request of a governmental entity, as evidenced in Miami, where highway patrol forces were delegated the responsibility of patrolling the expressways in the city during the 1981 riots, thereby freeing city personnel for crowd and riot control. Similar cases were New Orleans, where state police patrolled the city during Mardi Gras when municipal officers were on strike, and California, where highway patrol officers provided crowd control at the Diablo Canyon nuclear energy facility during extended demonstrations.

In recent years, state "departments of public safety" have increased, but depending on the particular state, this may not have changed responsibilities. In some instances, the change was in name only, while in others, previously independent investigative and uniformed forces were combined under one executive. Further, there are agencies with a uniformed field patrol force (in reality a "highway patrol") organized within a "state police" agency designated as a "department of public safety." Such is the case in both Arizona and Texas.

Defining the duties and responsibilities of a state law enforcement agency by its title alone is no longer possible, nor by the same token, is it possible to compare the state agencies by grouping them according to title.

Redefinition of the State Law Enforcement Mission

Today's state law enforcement agencies are shifting priorities. As with other parts of government, state law enforcement agencies feel the inflationary pinch and realize their inability to provide a full range of services with reduced budgets and with fewer people. The energy shortage further affects the state law enforcement mission, forcing agencies to conserve fuel. And, this is compounded when states are required, by federal law, to enforce the 55 mph speed limit under the threat of financial sanctions against the states if compliance falls short of the mandated limit for any given year.[2] State law enforcement agencies, often with fewer personnel, are now required to devote a greater percentage of time to speed limit enforcement in order to ensure the continuation of federal funding. This alone has led state law enforcement administrators to rethink their mission.

The recent trend toward giving assistance to incorporated areas has led to an increase in "Mutual Aid Agreements," which are formal compacts for assistance defining the roles of all parties to ensure responsiveness and cooperation, as well as to minimize the potential liability of all agencies or individuals operating under the agreement. In addition, the compacts delineate any equity, both real and in-kind compensation. The use of such agreements has expedited state/county/local law enforcement cooperation.

The Future

The following issues are of particular concern to those involved in the planning and operation of state law enforcement agencies:

- *Statewide Motor Vehicle Theft Units.* Theft of motor vehicles has become a multimillion-dollar-a-year industry through the development of "chop-shop" operations whereby vehicles are stolen for their parts, which are then recycled. In addition, the exportation of stolen vehicles to other countries has become a growth industry. Because of the magnitude of the problem, both financially and geographically, statewide units are beginning to emerge, designed to assist both municipalities within the state and other state units in the investigation and recovery of stolen vehicles.

- *Minority/Female Recruitment.* State law enforcement agencies are actively recruiting female and minority candidates. Entry-level requirements are undergoing validation studies to ensure their applicability to the position, and in the next few years, the number of minorities and females inducted into state law enforcement agencies should show a marked increase.

- *Pursuit Policies.* The issue of high-speed pursuit has long been of importance to state law enforcement and remains a key issue due to the liability of the agency for any mishap resulting from the pursuit. In addition, in keeping with federal requirements, automobile manufacturers have found it necessary to reduce the size of police vehicles, and doing so reduces their performance. This has often resulted in longer pursuits with an increased risk of mishap to an innocent party. Because of the liability of the agency for damages occurring as a result of police pursuits, state law enforcement administrators are rethinking the departmental policies on high-speed chases, usually limiting them to only the most extreme circumstances.

Notes

1. Hawaii is the only state having neither a state police nor highway patrol.
2. See, Norman Darwick, "State Police and Highway Patrols," *The Book of the States, 1980-81* (Lexington, Ky.: The Council of State Governments, 1980), pp. 452-53.

NUMBER OF STATE LAW ENFORCEMENT PERSONNEL: 1980

State	Number of law enforcement employees					State	Number of law enforcement employees				
		Sworn		Civilians				Sworn		Civilians	
	Total	Male	Female	Male	Female		Total	Male	Female	Male	Female
Alabama	1,165	675	4	200	286	Montana	303	195	4	19	85
Alaska	391	265	9	20	97	Nebraska	505	382	3	62	58
Arizona	1,425	872	7	277	269	Nevada	255	177	3	20	55
Arkansas	642	485	19	59	79	New Hampshire	290	222	...	37	31
California	6,925	4,960	73	756	1,136	New Jersey	3,294	2,058	36	683	517
Colorado	768	527	8	97	136	New Mexico	585	334	5	89	157
Connecticut	1,297	851	23	208	215	New York	4,030	3,418	39	203	370
Delaware	576	430	5	77	64	North Carolina	1,442	1,136	1	210	95
Florida	1,704	1,155	8	238	303	North Dakota	120	96	1	2	21
Georgia(a)	1,441	...	...	...	...	Ohio	1,979	1,143	7	418	411
Hawaii(b)	...	...	...	...	...	Oklahoma	1,184	620	4	238	322
Idaho	190	161	1	7	21	Oregon	1,057	887	21	21	128
Illinois	2,067	1,441	25	318	283	Pennsylvania	4,598	3,640	32	391	535
Indiana	1,732	1,120	13	279	320	Rhode Island	205	165	...	32	8
Iowa	785	543	14	117	111	South Carolina	907	761	4	65	77
Kansas	557	404	...	87	66	South Dakota	168	138	...	16	14
Kentucky	1,925	1,253	7	348	317	Tennessee	1,031	628	3	153	247
Louisiana	1,095	814	10	172	99	Texas	4,387	2,469	24	620	1,274
Maine	403	293	1	55	54	Utah	488	419	1	8	60
Maryland	2,146	1,516	43	219	368	Vermont	371	251	4	48	68
Massachusetts	1,144	954	12	127	51	Virginia	1,839	1,280	9	155	395
Michigan	3,037	2,080	50	445	462	Washington	1,343	815	8	328	192
Minnesota	659	495	6	85	73	West Virginia	841	559	6	84	192
Mississippi(a)	821	...	...	...	...	Wisconsin	593	428	10	89	66
Missouri	1,678	842	2	555	279	Wyoming	197	157	...	9	31

(a) Male and female breakdowns not available for police officers and civilians.

(b) No state law enforcement agency.

DEVELOPMENTS IN PUBLIC UTILITY REGULATION

By James E. Suelflow

"THE MORE THINGS CHANGE the more they are the same" is an appropriate motto to characterize recent developments in public utility regulation. The New Deal era saw significant reforms in public utility regulation; likewise, the 1980s are a time of similar significant changes.

Demands for energy conservation, cost-based pricing, protection of the environment, competitive forms of communications and consumerism are reaching new heights. To paraphrase Governor Richard A. Snelling of Vermont, it will no longer be possible for regulators to regard themselves merely as umpires or protectors of those they regulate. Regulators will have to be more accountable to both the public and the utilities. If we are to have efficient public utilities, we must have regulators who are willing to reward good management with rate increases and increased stability, and to penalize poorly run utilities by denying requests for rate increases and letting them fail. Well-managed utilities should thrive; poorly managed utilities should wither and eventually be taken over by their stronger, more efficient rivals. Whether one agrees or not with this evaluation, the increased role of regulators is evident.

The term "public utility" generally refers to suppliers of electricity, natural gas firms (including production, transmission and distribution), telephone and telegraph companies and, in some instances, water and sewerage operations as well as cable television companies. Regulation takes place at one or more governmental levels. In the case of water and sewage utilities most regulation is at a local level. However, the final distribution of the more traditional energy and communications utilities is usually overseen by state regulatory commissions. Any activities involving interstate commerce, of necessity, must be controlled by the federal regulators. In some instances, various aspects of a utility's operations simultaneously come under all three forms of control.

State regulatory agencies are known by different titles including: public service commission, public utility commission, state corporation commission, commerce commission, and even railroad commission (see Table 1). Table 2 gives some idea of the scope of their regulatory authority over the traditional public utility firms, and Table 3 shows some results of regulation with average monthly bills by customer class for electricity and gas.

To give some insight into the magnitude of nationwide state regulatory activities, these agencies are responsible for the oversight of approximately 1,843 telephone companies; 390 investor-owned (private) electric companies; 646 rural electric cooperatives; 706 municipal, regional and other publicly (governmentally) owned electric systems; 856 investor-owned gas distribution utilities; and 405 publicly owned gas systems which operate facilities and lie within the jurisdictional bounds of state commissions. In addition, these agencies regulate a significant portion of over 6,826 water utilities, public and private.

James E. Suelflow is Professor of Business Administration, Department of Public Utilities and Transportation, Graduate School of Business, Indiana University, Bloomington.

The scope of the regulation includes the determination of total revenue requirements and individual rates as well as entry and exit, safety and territorial market limits. In order to accomplish these tasks, among other things, commissions prescribe uniform accounting systems and procedures, perform accounting audits, control financial practices, and provide safety regulations and oversee both quantity and quality of services rendered.

Increased Federal Regulatory Dominance

Although state commissions provide the principal control in the ultimate distribution of utility services to final consumers, Congress and federal commissions in recent years have taken the initiative in pursuing regulatory changes and reforms. The 1980s continue to reflect the increased implementation of congressional legislation and court decisions over intrastate aspects of utilities which may ultimately result in usurping significant state authority over public utility operations. Among those areas in which federal forces affect state administrative law include: (1) attempts to apply antitrust law to the actions of state administrative agencies; (2) federal pre-emption of regulatory authority traditionally exercised by state administrative agencies; and (3) impacts of the 1st and 10th Amendments upon actions of state agencies.

For over 30 years, public utilities were essentially sealed from antitrust view. Immunity, however, has deteriorated substantially since 1975. In 1978, the U.S. Supreme Court ruled that municipally owned utilities are not automatically immune from suit under federal antitrust laws. In a Louisiana case involving restrictive competition, a city-owned electric company agreed to sell water to customers outside the city limits only if the customer purchased electric power from the city utility rather than the private company generally servicing the area. The Court ruled that governmental entities, whether state agencies or subdivisions of the state, are not exempt from antitrust laws simply by reason of their status. In another case the same year, the Court set forth a three-part test for antitrust exemption. They ruled that a defendant must show: (1) an independent state regulatory interest in the subject of the antitrust controversy; (2) a clear and affirmative articulation of state policy with regard to the interest; and (3) an act of state supervision. Thus, if a utility seeks to avoid antritrust liabilities it must abide by these tests.

Several states are challenging the legality of recently enacted congressional utility regulatory reform laws. The states have used as their defense the 10th Amendment to the U.S. Constitution, which is designed to protect state sovereignty from interference by the federal government. Challenges have centered around the Public Utility Regulatory Policies Act (PURPA) and the National Gas Policy Act (NGPA) of 1978. In one case the Court ruled in favor of the state (Mississippi), saying that certain aspects of the PURPA resulted in an intrusion on state sovereignty. In a similar case involving the NGPA, the decision was in favor of the Federal Energy Regulatory Commission, holding that federal authority takes precedence over state sovereignty if interstate commerce is involved. In a related case involving the Commerce Clause and its effects on interstate commerce, the Supreme Court ruled that Louisiana's "first use" tax was an interference with interstate commerce in favor of purely local interest. In a Montana severance tax case, the Court ruled that the tax did not violate the terms of either the Commerce Clause or the Supremacy Clause. Additionally, the Supreme Court ruled against New Hampshire in a case involving its ban on wholesale sales of hydro-electric energy across state lines.

The National Energy Conservation Policy Act of 1978 (NECPA) was specifically intended to regulate interstate commerce in order to reduce the growth of energy demand and to conserve non-renewable energy resources without inhibiting beneficial economic growth. The NECPA requires electric utilities to offer to inspect customers' residences in a kind of "energy audit," looking for such things as insulation and weather stripping, and to determine energy-saving steps and aid in the financing of these steps if the customer cannot afford them. In the past several years, states have viewed conservation measures in somewhat different light. For example, Arkansas ruled that natural gas utilities should not be forced to finance residential conservation under the state residential conservation service program required by federal regulations, because such conservation measures did not permanently reduce demands for natural gas or future exploration. In Idaho, the commission found no economic justification for a natural gas utility to provide proposed low-interest loans on conservation-related home weather additions. The state of California approved the creation of a wholly owned utility subsidiary to coordinate federal conservation measures.

The PURPA and the NGPA have also been active in retail rate-making. Through newly established federal procedures and standards for rate design, utilities have been forced into rate data filings. These filings require consideration of federal requirements for lifeline rates, class rates based on cost of service, declining block rates, time of day rates, seasonal rates, interruptable rates, load management techniques, prohibition of master metering, restriction on use of automatic adjustment clauses, provision for consumer information and termination procedures, restrictions on advertising and curtailment plans.

Recent developments in natural gas price regulation have primarily centered around producer rates set under the Natural Gas Act and the NGPA. The controversy involves the NGPA's congressional enactment of "maximum lawful prices."

The NGPA also increases federal jurisdiction by setting certain prices for both inter- and intrastate gas sales by reducing or limiting price controls on new gas and deregulating certain interstate gas by 1985 or before. Other jurisdictional conflicts, which were recently resolved, found that the FERC held jurisdiction over state-mandated deliveries of natural gas from well heads to local customers. In another ruling, Minnesota held that the state commission had jurisdiction to regulate retail sales of gas made directly from a pipeline.

In a different issue related to jurisdictional boundaries, an interesting aspect has recently arisen regarding funding for energy research and development. While a number of federal jurisdictional utilities have engaged in a gas and energy research institute funded both by the FERC and surcharges assessed against rate payers, control of expenditures for research projects generally come under states' jurisdiction. A number of states have issued various opinions for sponsored research projects. Some have allowed such expenditures while others have disallowed them.

Finally, a federal appeals court delineated federal-state jurisdiction in a nuclear power siting ruling in California. The decision specified that the state statute was directed more toward economic issues, whereas federal authority was directed more toward safety.

The Industries-Regulatory Update

Energy. While shortages and curtailments in the supply of electric energy have eased somewhat, rate increases have been on the rise. Reductions, abandonments and curtailments of construction programs of many utilities, especially those building nuclear plants, continue at a high rate.

Innovative rate-making at the state level continues, since rates must still be based on revenue requirements and test-year expenses. An Ohio ruling on post-test-year expenses found that wage increases were improperly included in spite of the fact that the wages would be in effect during the rate period. The Indiana Public Service Commission ruled that just because a utility saved money by filing a consolidated tax return, it was not justified in flowing through the tax savings to rate payers.

Time-of-day or peak-load pricing tests continue. A number of states (New York, Virginia, Wisconsin and Kansas, among others), following the PURPA requirements, conducted generic hearings on such rate schedules. In accordance with the option presented in the PURPA, several states including Montana and New York, have ruled that time-of-day pricing is an acceptable option. However, the Idaho commission has rejected time-of-day rates when the energy is generated by hydro-based facilities.

Seasonal rates are being scrutinized on a case-by-case basis or in generic hearings. In one case in New York, the state ruled that seasonal rates are confusing and accomplish little. In Wyoming, the commission ordered the Utah Power and Light Company to file seasonal rates that comply with the PURPA requirements, specifically for seasonal irrigation purposes. In the same vein, several states like Michigan and Montana, have questioned marginal cost pricing since marginal costs are difficult to determine.

The continued pressures of inflation and economic recession have given fresh emphasis to lifeline rates as concessions to the poor and fixed income members of society. Although the utility industry believes they should be classed as a welfare problem, the federal government has encouraged such rates, and the states have responded. Lifeline rate structures offer a low uniform kilowatt hour (KWH) charge for the first several hundred KWHs consumed. California and Michigan have mandated such rates, but other states, such as Pennsylvania, have questioned whether or not it is legal under state statute since lifeline rates give unreasonable preference or advantage to certain individuals. These economic issues as well as welfare considerations and energy conservation will be debated for some years to come.

In other cost-related matters, in spite of a California Supreme Court pronouncement to the contrary, the California commission awarded the reimbursement of attorney's fees to an intervenor participating in a "quasi-legislative" plant siting case.

Another pressing issue is how to deal with the costs of abandoned plants. In general, commissions have included plant cancellation costs as part of the cost of service, as in an Ohio case where the decision was made that the costs of the abandoned plant initially were prudent, but had since become excessive. The Ohio commission, however, was overruled by the courts which stated, in effect, that cost of service could be nothing more than current *test period* costs, and abandoned plant costs were essentially extraordinary losses not recoverable from rate payers.

Finally, a new intrastate jurisdictional problem has been raised with regards to setting rates for *electric* utilities that purchase coal from wholly owned subsidiaries. The issues basically center around the profit motive and incentives for competitive pricing of such sales. Idaho, California and Montana have ruled to some extent on this issue.

Communications. The Federal Communications Commission (FCC) adopted a rule allowing telephone companies to account for new station installation costs as current expenses rather than capital investment, but left the final decision up to the state commissions in applying what have become known as "flash cut" options. In 1981, Connecticut, Utah and California adopted such procedures.

In a related matter, the state courts in Ohio ruled that telephone common carriers are not required to provide free use of interior wire and cable initially supplied by the telephone company to a subscriber who wishes to terminate existing telephone service and install a privately owned telephone system connected to the inside wiring.

In spring 1980, the FCC issued its long-awaited Second Computer Inquiry decision, which has been cited as perhaps the most momentous case impacting the industry, regulation and public interest since the original 1934 Communications Act. The Second Inquiry adopted regulations on "basic" and "enhanced" communication services. Basic communication services include only the offering of transmission capacity and switching features designed to facilitate transmission, while enhanced communication service incorporates all other telecommunications activities. As a result of the Second Computer Inquiry decision, enhanced services and customer premises equipment were deregulated. AT&T and General Telephone Electronics were asked to create separate subsidiaries for such services. In a "final, final" decision, GTE was excused from the separate subsidiaries requirement. In the main, however, this decision will undoubtedly be affected by the Justice Department's most recent antitrust settlement. While Congress was debating in committee one of its many recent proposed bills to update the communications industry, on January 1, 1982 AT&T, in a surprise move, entered into a consent decree to divest itself of 22 wholly owned local telephone operating companies. In exchange, AT&T will be freed from a 1956 decree and be allowed to enter the computer field. Particulars on the agreement must still be worked out.

With the increased competitive pressure, state commissions must take a much closer look at local-measured telephone service. Additionally, directory assistance charges are becoming more common as well as requirements for the telephone companies to allow multiple listings at no additional costs.

Community Antenna Television (CATV). Cable television experienced regulation that might affect the industry during a period of growth. The FCC and the courts have been concerned about regulating program content and about charges by electric and telephone companies for CATV cable attachment and rate-setting. In *Home Box Office, Inc., et al.* v. *FCC and U.S.* (40 RR2d 283, March 25, 1977), the District of Columbia Court of Appeals struck down what had become known as anti-siphoning rules as they apply to cable casters, specifically to pay cable suppliers. The anti-siphoning rules are designated to prevent the movement of programs from commercial to pay television. The court found that lack of proper evidence made the rule arbitrary and of doubtful validity with respect to 1st Amendment requirements. Other issues center around regulation and changes for utility pole attachments and actual rate regulation by the companies themselves. As regards CATV pole attachments, P.L. 95-234, effective March 1978, required action by each state that desires to assume jurisdiction over pole contract rentals. If a state takes no action, the FCC assumes jurisdiction.

Other Recent Regulatory Developments. In recent years, several state commissions have attempted to assess the management efficiency of public utilities under their jurisdiction. Some commissions, including Michigan and Massachusetts, have awarded higher rates of return to companies found to be efficient in operations and providing improved services. In several instances, utilities have been given reduced rates of return in order to coerce better service. Ohio, Florida and Virginia are examples of such negative adjustments.

In a pair of precedent-setting decisions, involving advertising as a 1st Amendment right, the U.S. Supreme Court allowed advertising expenditures by energy-short utilities on politically controversial topics even though they have insufficient energy for sale. Other decisions have focused on whether advertising was beneficial to the customer and could be included as an expense only if it showed clear consumer benefits. This was the case in both Indiana and Ohio. New Jersey banned advertising entirely as part of the cost of service, and Maryland has a similar rule regarding charitable contributions.

"Surplus" deferred tax reserves have become an issue in some states. The federal income tax rate was changed in 1978 from 48 percent to 46 percent for corporations. Utilities that followed the normalization procedures for deferred income tax suddenly found themselves with a deferred surplus. The question, three years later, is how the surpluses should be treated. New York, California, Pennsylvania and Virginia have ordered utilities with surplus deferred taxes to refund them to rate payers over periods of from one to 10 years. Other states including Kansas, Michigan, Missouri and North Carolina, as well as the Federal Energy Regulatory Commission, have allowed the 48 percent normalized reserve to be amortized over the life of the asset.

The Economic Recovery Act of 1981 provided through its Accelerated Cost Recovery System (ACRS) mandatory rules for calculating depreciation on tangible property acquired after December 31, 1980. Tax savings *must* be normalized to be realized, so in effect, the flow-through method of accounting for accelerated depreciation was repealed.

The New York State Public Service Commission amended its rules to eliminate fuel adjustment clauses unless a utility can definitely show that fuel costs are not susceptible to reasonable estimation. New Jersey has also reached a similar conclusion with respect to automatic adjustment clauses.

In an unprecedented decision in Pennsylvania affecting rate bases, the court held that the commission had the prerogative of interpreting its fair value rule to mean original cost *only*. Other recent advocates of an original cost rate base, based on "physical facility investment" include Minnesota, North Carolina and Ohio.

Another pressing regulatory issue faced by many state commissions as well as the FERC involves construction work in progress (CWIP). In a federal case, the FERC denied a Texas electric utility the right to include CWIP in the rate base on the basis of "severe financial difficulty." In a state-related decision, Wisconsin ruled that any CWIP costs added to the rate base would be decided on a case-by-case basis. In the past, Wisconsin had a rule that allowed such inclusion to the extent of 10 percent of the utilities net investment rate base. A novel approach by the Michigan commission allowed CWIP in the rate base but then ruled that the return paid on CWIP by rate payers would in turn represent interest payments for tax purposes to benefit rate payers.

Additionally, the Government Accounting Office reports that the Securities and Exchange Commission has failed to live up to its mandate in the oversight of public utility holding companies and has called for more forceful action.

The Financial Accounting Standards Board (FASB) is reviewing its position to revise its addendum on accounting principles affecting regulated industries. This addendum emphasizes exceptions to generally accepted accounting definitions and procedures as related to rate-making.

Aid for State Commissions. Over the last several years and particularly since the passage of the National Energy Act, many more state commissions have held generic hearings rather than hearings on a case-by-case approach. A number of organizations have continued to provide assistance, including the National Association of Regulatory Utility Commissioners. Additionally, Electric Power Research Institute (EPRI) and the Edison Electric Institute (EEI) have jointly engaged in massive rate design projects. EEI members have available to them a computerized data bank known as "URAP" to help utility companies become acquainted with useful rate-case information. Finally, in order to meet the research needs of state regulators as well as to provide on-site technical assistance and conduct workshops, the National Regulatory Research Institute (NRRI) was organized. While NRRI continues to be funded through federal sources, state grants are expected to become the predominant resource base in the future. NRRI studies have produced information to aid commissions on electric rate reforms, conservation, operating efficiencies and fuel clause adustments. A series of publications on regulatory information exchange are issued quarterly.

Table 1
STATE PUBLIC UTILITY COMMISSIONS

State or other jurisdiction	Regulatory authority	Members Number	Members Selection	Selection of chairman	Length of commissioners' terms (in years)	Number of full-time employees
Alabama	Public Service Commission	3	E	E	4	81
Alaska	Public Utilities Commission	5	GL	G	6	37
Arizona	Corporation Commission	3	E	C	6	194
Arkansas	Public Service Commission	3	GS	G	6	53
California	Public Utilities Commission	5	GS	C	6	979
Colorado	Public Utilities Commission	3	GS	G	6	95
Connecticut	Public Utilities Control Authority	5	GS	C	4	107
Delaware	Public Service Commission	5	GS	G	5	18
Florida	Public Service Commission	5	G	C	4	354
Georgia	Public Service Commission	5	E	C	6	108
Hawaii	Public Utilities Commission	3	GS	G	6	17
Idaho	Public Utilities Commission	3	GS	C	6	56
Illinois	Commerce Commission	5	G	G	5	269
Indiana	Public Service Commission	3	G	G	4	103
Iowa	State Commerce Commission	3	GS	G	6	129
Kansas	State Corporation Commission	3	GS	C	4	192.5
Kentucky	Public Service Commission	5	G	G	4	52
Louisiana	Public Service Commission	5	E	C	9	99
Maine	Public Utilities Commission	3	GE	G	7	76
Maryland	Public Service Commission	5(a)	GS	G	6	107
Massachusetts	Dept. of Public Utilities	3	G	G	4	122
Michigan	Public Service Commission	3	GS	G	6	315
Minnesota	Public Utilities Commission	5	GS	C	6	133
Mississippi	Public Service Commission	3	E	C	4	89
Missouri	Public Service Commission	5	GS	G	6	254
Montana	Public Service Commission	5	E	C	4	44
Nebraska	Public Service Commission	5	E	C	6	56
Nevada	Public Service Commission	3	G	G	4	72
New Hampshire	Public Utilities Commission	3	G	G	6	45
New Jersey	Board of Public Utilities	3	GS	G	6	227
New Mexico	Public Service Commission	3	GS	G	6	29
New York	Public Service Commission	7	GS	G	6(b)	640
North Carolina	Utilities Commission	7	GL	G	8	168
North Dakota	Public Service Commission	3	E	C	6	50
Ohio	Public Utilities Commission	3	GS	G	6	332
Oklahoma	Corporation Commission	3	E	C	6	223
Oregon	Public Utility Commissioner	1	G	...	4	351
Pennsylvania	Public Utility Commission	5	GS	G	10	538
Rhode Island	Public Utilities Commission	3	GS	G	6	35
South Carolina	Public Service Commission	7	GS	(c)	4	145
South Dakota	Public Utilities Commission	3	E	C	6	34
Tennessee	Public Service Commission	3	E	C	6	142
Texas	Public Utility Commission	3	GS	C	6	110
	Railroad Commission	3	E	C	6	610
Utah	Public Service Commission	3	GS	G	6	26
Vermont	Public Service Board	3	GS	G	6(d)	26
Virginia	State Corporation Commission	3	L	C	6	456
Washington	Utilities and Transportation Commission	3	GS	G	6	203
West Virginia	Public Service Commission	3	G	G	6(e)	151
Wisconsin	Public Service Commission	3	GS	G	6	146
Wyoming	Public Service Commission	3	GS	C	6	37
Dist. of Col.	Public Service Commission	3	M	C	3	31
Puerto Rico	Public Service Commission	3	GS	GS	4	256

Source: National Association of Regulatory Utility Commissioners, *Annual Report on Utility and Carrier Regulation,* 1977 and 1979 (Washington, D.C.: 1978, 1980).

Key:

G— Appointed by governor.
GS— Appointed by governor, with confirmation by senate.
GE— Appointed by governor, confirmed by executive council.
GL— Appointed by governor, approved by joint session of legislature.
E— Elected.
C— Elected by commission.
L— Appointed by legislature.
P— Appointed by president of the United States.
M— Appointed by mayor.

(a) Two are part-time.
(b) Chairman designated by and serves at pleasure of governor.
(c) Rotates annually.
(d) Chairman appointed by governor for two years.
(e) Chairman appointed by governor for one year.
(f) One commissioner.
(g) Chairman and vice chairman.

Table 2
CERTAIN REGULATORY FUNCTIONS OF
STATE PUBLIC UTILITIES COMMISSIONS

State or other jurisdiction†	Controls rates of privately owned utilities on sales to ultimate consumers of				Prescribe temporary rates, pending investigation			Require prior authorization of rate changes			Suspend proposed rate changes			Initiate rate investigations on its own motion		
	Electric	Gas	Telephone	CATV	Electric	Gas	Telephone	Electric	Gas	Telephone	Electric	Gas	Telephone	Electric	Gas	Telephone
Alabama PSC	★	★	★	...	★	★	...	★	★	...	★	★	★	★	★	★
Alaska PUC	★	★	★	★	★	★	★	★	★	★	★	★	★	★	★	★
Arizona CC	★	★	★	...	★	★	★	★	★	★	...	...	...	★	★	★
Arkansas PSC	★	★	★	...	★	★	★	★	★	★	★	★	★	★	★	★
California PUC	★	★	★	★	★(a)	★(a)	★(a)	★	★	★	★	★	★	★	★	★
Colorado	★	★	★	...	★(b)	★(b)	★(b)	★	★	★	★	★	★	★	★	★
Connecticut PUCA	★	★	★	★	★	★	★	★	★	★	★	★	★	★	★	★
Delaware PSC	★	★	★	★	★	★	★	★	★	★	★	★	★	★	★	★
Florida PSC	★	★	★	...	★	★	★	★	★	★	★	★	★	★	★	★
Georgia PSC	★	★	★	...	★	★	★	★	★	★	★	★	★	★	★	★
Hawaii PUC	★	★	★	...	★	★	★	★	★	★	(c)	(c)	(c)	★	★	★
Idaho PUC	★	★	★	★	★	★	★	★	★	★	★	★	★	★	★	★
Illinois CC	★	★	★	★	★	★	★	★	★	★	★	★	★	★	★	★
Indiana PSC	★	★	★	...	...	...	...	★	★	★	★	★	★	★	★	★
Iowa SCC	★	★	★(d)	...	★(e)	★(e)	★(e)	★	★	★	★	★	★(d)	★	★	★(d)
Kansas SCC	★	★	★	...	★	★	★	★	★	★	★	★	★	★	★	★
Kentucky PSC	★	★	★	...	★	★	★	★	★	★	★	★	★	★	★	★
Louisiana PSC	★	★(f)	★	★	★	★	★	★	★	★	★	★	★	★	★	★
Maine PUC	★	★	★	...	★	★	...	★	★	★	★	★	★	★	★	★
Maryland PSC	★	★	★	...	★	★	★	★	★	★	★	★	★	★	★	★
Massachusetts DPU	★	★	★	★	★	★	★	★	★	★	★	★	★	★	★	★
Michigan PSC	★	★	★	...	★(g)	★(g)	★(g)	★	★	★	(h)	(h)	(h)	★	★	★
Minnesota DPS	★	★	★	...	★	★	★	★	★	★	★	★	★	★	★	★
Mississippi PSC	★	★	★	...	...	...	...	★	★	★	★	★	★	★	★	★
Missouri PSC	★	★	★	...	★	★	★	★	★	★	★	★	★	★	★	★
Montana PSC	★	★	★	...	★	★	★	★	★	★	★	★	★	★	★	★
Nebraska PSC(i)	...	...	★	...	...	...	★	...	...	★	...	...	★	...	...	★
Nevada PSC	★	★	★	★	★	★	★	★	★	★	★	★	★	★	★	★
New Hampshire PUC	★	★	★	...	★	★	★	★	★	★	★	★	★	★	★	★
New Jersey BPU	★	★	★	...	★	★	★	★	★	★	★	★	★	★	★	★
New Mexico PSC	★	★	★	...	★	★	★	★	★	...	★	★	...	★	★	(j)
New York PSC	★	★	★	★	★	★	★	★	★	★	★	★	★	★	★	★
North Carolina UC	★	★	★	...	★	★	★	★	★	★	★	★	★	★	★	★
North Dakota PSC	★	★	★	...	★	★	★	★	★	★	★	★	★	★	★	★
Ohio PUC	★	★	★	...	★	★	★	★	★	★	(h)	(h)	(h)	★	★	★
Oklahoma CC	★	★	★	...	★	★	★	★	★	★	★	★	★	★	★	★
Oregon PUC	★	★	★	★	★	★	★	★	★	★	★	★	★	★	★	★
Pennsylvania PUC	★	★	★	★	★	★	★	★	★	★	★	★	★	★	★	★
Rhode Island PUC	★	★	★	...	★	★	★	★	★	★	★	★	★	★	★	★
South Carolina PSC	★	★	★	...	★	★	★	★	★	★	★	★	★	★	★	★
South Dakota PUC	★	★	★	...	★	★	★	★	★	★	★	★	★	★	★	★
Tennessee PSC	★	★	★	...	★	★	★	★	★	★	★	★	★	★	★	★
Texas PUC	★	...	★	...	★	...	★	★	...	★	★	...	★	★	...	★
RC	...	★(k)	...	...	...	★	...	...	★	...	...	★	...	...	★	...
Utah PSC	★	★	★	★	★	★	★	★	★	★	★	★	★	★	★	★
Vermont PSB	★	★	★	★	★	★	★	★	★	★	★	★	★	★	★	★
Virginia SCC	★	★	★	...	★	★	★	★	★	★	★	★	★	★	★	★
Washington UTC	★	★	★	★	★	★	★	★	★	★	★	★	★	★	★	★
West Virginia PSC	★	★	★	...	★	★	★	★	★	★	★	★	★	★	★	★
Wisconsin PSC	★	★	★	...	★	★	★	★	★	★	(h)	(h)	(h)	(h)	(h)	(h)
Wyoming PSC	★	★	★	...	★	★	★	★	★	★	★	★	★	★	★	★
Dist. of Col. PSC	★	★	★	...	...	...	...	★	...	★	★	★	...	★	...	★
Puerto Rico PSC	...	★	(l)	★	...	...	(l)	...	...	(l)	...	...	(l)	...	★	(l)

Source: National Association of Regulatory Commissioners, *1980 Annual Report on Utility and Carrier Regulation* (Washington, D.C.: 1981).

†Full names of commissions on preceding table.

(a) May fix temporary rates, but practice is not followed.

(b) No specific statutory authority.

(c) Rate increases may not go into effect until approved by the commission.

(d) Not for companies with less than 2,000 stations.

(e) Application rates are temporary and are collected under bond, subject to refund from one to 90 days after suspension.

(f) Except no authority over rates charged to industrial customers by any gas company.

(g) Commission has authority to grant partial and immediate rate relief during pendency of final order, after statutory requirements are met.

(h) Specific authority required to change rates. Rates do not become effective after a specified period; consequently, no suspension is required.

(i) Telephone is the only regulated utility.

(j) Regulated by New Mexico State Corporation Commission.

(k) The commission has original jurisdiction over companies in unincorporated areas, and appellate jurisdiction over companies in cities. Cities have original jurisdiction over companies operating within their limits.

(l) The Puerto Rico Telephone Authority, a state public corporation, purchased the Puerto Rico Telephone Company.

Table 3
AVERAGE MONTHLY BILLS, BY CUSTOMER CLASS,
FOR ELECTRICITY AND GAS: 1979

State or other jurisdiction	Electricity			Gas(a)		
	Residential(b)	Commercial(c)	Industrial(d)	Residential	Commercial	Industrial
U.S. average	$48.76	$385.46	$3,431	$28.86	$161.27	$7,462.54
Alabama...................	44.34	331.78	3,271	24.68	127.45	13,544.92
Alaska	42.78	318.25	2,759	31.45	149.37	N.A.
Arizona	51.64	405.19	3,522	18.28	108.76	6,726.41
Arkansas	37.00	268.69	2,245	17.52	80.33	8,962.15
California................	47.65	334.71	3,131	18.19	155.26	5,360.86
Colorado	43.27	312.72	2,621	27.99	165.05	7,591.30
Connecticut...............	57.95	465.97	3,635	34.53	187.32	2,393.26
Delaware	63.23	542.18	4,285	31.15	209.04	9,981.25
Florida	48.37	358.51	3,203	14.42	193.76	34,273.75
Georgia..................	38.42	402.24	3,247	27.25	149.99	11,846.82
Hawaii	69.60	512.34	4,206	23.55	301.46	831.67
Idaho	23.28	180.94	1,566	28.93	181.83	32,551.25
Illinois..................	44.94	416.70	3,396	42.49	132.98	4,461.74
Indiana...................	44.83	324.48	2,530	34.27	146.33	10,022.02
Iowa	48.44	360.62	3,166	32.83	147.74	10,106.36
Kansas	44.58	322.06	3,041	22.54	109.89	6,893.19
Kentucky	35.27	267.93	2,223	27.59	122.22	9,231.53
Louisiana	35.04	298.00	2,070	18.23	83.64	28,526.97
Maine....................	45.91	314.61	2,813	19.02	174.40	N.A.
Maryland	46.44	271.14	2,425	30.73	131.36	2,308.09
Massachusetts	58.69	452.73	3,599	33.40	227.58	2,023.73
Michigan	45.85	341.25	3,284	38.63	257.63	6,426.16
Minnesota	43.97	273.78	2,596	37.56	175.40	2,946.77
Mississippi	42.20	356.87	3,001	20.63	90.82	15,607.22
Missouri	44.45	356.30	2,904	33.28	226.05	16,339.48
Montana	27.41	213.73	1,321	28.64	141.85	7,469.33
Nebraska	37.26	239.45	2,043	29.65	114.64	4,857.02
Nevada	46.64	334.25	3,241	23.73	421.07	97,342.50
New Hampshire	59.02	413.64	3,393	26.83	143.92	5,465.83
New Jersey................	60.02	485.93	4,321	30.09	110.58	3,758.74
New Mexico................	55.71	398.86	3,806	23.99	109.04	3,737.48
New York.................	69.48	606.03	5,594	29.93	138.10	2,450.64
North Carolina	41.83	227.66	2,332	28.46	139.70	8,294.95
North Dakota	40.67	229.24	2,692	38.11	246.10	2,147.08
Ohio	51.11	370.72	3,279	38.75	192.04	11,420.67
Oklahoma	36.72	250.45	2,159	20.18	105.22	13,223.86
Oregon	28.92	172.40	1,768	372.84	157.83	22,235.00
Pennsylvania	53.89	438.95	3,624	35.10	184.19	9,969.30
Rhode Island	58.57	411.19	3,503	31.65	140.39	1,494.89
South Carolina	44.38	313.69	2,594	22.46	125.96	11,976.81
South Dakota	42.85	317.51	2,632	30.77	148.01	1,525.00
Tennessee.................	30.16	221.07	2,419	21.39	131.91	9,326.98
Texas	43.87	314.55	2,838	21.22	128.08	14,689.71
Utah	42.76	381.12	2,447	26.99	105.62	12,530.42
Vermont..................	46.80	390.11	2,507	35.15	222.35	N.A.
Virginia..................	58.92	392.06	3,846	30.47	176.96	4,074.72
Washington	16.44	119.31	983	33.57	216.92	16,186.94
West Virginia.............	39.41	308.01	2,437	33.08	159.37	32,264.79
Wisconsin	39.42	280.98	2,747	34.46	184.78	4,219.40
Wyoming.................	28.32	183.58	1,365	31.17	164.66	20,027.08
Dist. of Col...............	36.39	373.77	3,320	31.71	191.58	N.A.

(a) *Gas Facts, 1979 Data* (Arlington, Va.: American Gas Association, 1980), pp. 74 and 104.

(b) 1,000 kwhs. *Typical Electric Bills—January 1, 1980* (Washington, D.C.: U.S. Department of Energy, Energy Information Administration, December 31, 1980).

(c) 30 KW-6,000 KWH.

(d) 300 KW-60,000 KWH.

5.   Housing and Development

HOUSING AND COMMUNITY DEVELOPMENT

By Dana A. Cohoon

THE PICTURE FOR HOUSING and community development has darkened over the biennium, as the housing and construction industries entered 1982 in the worst slump in decades. In Washington, the Reagan administration put the Section 8 Housing Assistance Payments Program, the Community Development Block Grant Program (CDBG) and the Urban Development Action Grant Program (UDAG) on the chopping block, along with other domestic programs, as the president attempted to cut the federal deficit. Congress entered the final month of 1981 unable to resolve the dilemmas in the federal budget, and departments operated under stop-gap resolutions. Further cuts in these subsidy programs are promised for fiscal 1983.

The cut in federal programs left few alternatives for the states as the private sector was unable to fill the gap. Interest rates fluctuated widely during 1981, but always in the high range. New housing construction starts fell to low levels. The lending industry tightened its belt as more and more lenders opted or were forced by regulatory agencies into mergers to supplement their assets. The long-term, fixed-rate mortgage became harder and harder to find as lenders experimented with variable rate mortgages, graduated payment mortgages, graduated equity mortgages and other short-term devices which will vary with the market conditions. In the past, states would have been able to partially alleviate this crisis, but even this ability was restricted by Congress.

While the short-term picture for the federal subsidy programs, which had grown and matured into useable, operative programs, is bleak, innovations and revised ideas from the past are beginning to find their way to the forefront. Housing vouchers and enterprise zones may be the Section 8 and CDBG programs of 1982 and future years.

Housing

States play a significant role in providing decent and afforable housing for all Americans. As the economy declined and a recession developed in sectors of the housing industry, government assistance became crucial, especially for low- and moderate-income families.

Specifically, states have had to re-evaluate usury ceiling laws, as interest rates hit and exceeded established ceilings. States are also developing methods of assisting homeowners and renters to meet rising costs and are attempting to cope with the rapid conversion of rental housing to condominium ownership, which, combined with the lack of new rental development, has caused a reduction in the available rental units.

One of the key elements of a strong state housing program is the establishment of a statewide agency with the ability to finance housing. Proceeds from the sale of tax-exempt bonds provide construction and permanent financing for both rental developments and single-family homes in over 47 states, the District of Columbia and Puerto Rico.

Dana A. Cohoon is Director of Property Improvement Programs, New Jersey Mortgage Finance Agency.

In the rental housing area, state housing finance agencies (HFAs) have traditionally financed approximately one-third of the Section 8 new construction/substantial rehabilitation units each year, or approximately 50,000 units. This has not been as true in recent months, as HFA interest rates have increased because of the poor conditions in the bond market throughout 1981. During the period of July 1980 through June 1981, HFAs financed approximately 38,000 units subsidized through the Section 8 program. Much time and energy was spent during the year developing the "Financing Adjustment Factor" (FAF) to allow project costs to include the high cost of financing within the project rents. In addition to their participation in the Section 8 new construction/substantial rehabilitation programs, state HFAs have been developing financing mechanisms for the Section 8 Moderate Rehabilitation Program.

State HFAs have also concentrated some of their energies on providing resources to make older developments built under the Section 236 program financially viable again. These are basically sound projects, but their income has not been keeping pace with operating and energy cost increases. State HFAs are using their own resources for this purpose and also worked to have their projects included under the federal Flexible Subsidy Program.

Through the use of the tax-exempt bond financing capacities of the housing finance agencies, states have been providing low-interest mortgage financing to assist low- and moderate-income residents to purchase or improve a home and to aid in the rehabilitation of the nation's urban areas.

In mid-1978, cities and counties began to establish similar programs. However, many of these local programs did not provide for a qualified staff or targeting the funding to those families that could not own homes under conventional terms.

In 1979, Congressman Al Ullman, then chairman of the Housing Ways and Means Committee, and his colleagues put a temporary halt to all such programs. Legislation was debated for 18 months, and in December 1980, the Mortgage Subsidy Bond Tax Act of 1980 was adopted and signed into law. In July 1981, the U.S. Treasury Department promulgated regulations to implement that law.

The law seriously limits the states' ability to meet a growing need for mortgage financing. Because of the restrictions of the statute, no bond issues have been sold without some infusion of funds. This further depletes already limited resources. The restrictive nature of the bill and the high interest rates in the bond marketplace throughout 1981 resulted in housing finance agencies selling only a handful of bond issues for both mortgage and home improvement financing during the year. State HFAs worked through their congressional delegations and with the federal agencies to have the law amended to provide reasonably structured financing programs with public purposes. This process will continue and grow more critical as the 1983 "sunset" approaches.

While working to change the law, state HFAs also began to explore other types of financing. The Alaska Housing Corporation sold taxable bonds, and the Hawaii Housing Authority experimented with growing equity mortgages. In addition, states looked at the possibility of tapping the large reserves in pension funds to provide mortgage financing. Such programs have already begun in New York and Connecticut, and use of these funds is a primary recommendation of the President's Housing Commission.

Community Development

The emphasis on the conservation and rehabilitation of housing is evident in state community development programs. State programs for development and housing rehabilitation co-exist with new legislative initiatives to attract private investment to core areas. This leveraging effort has been duplicated and built upon by the federal government in many of its programs, such as HUD's Urban Development Action Grant Program and Neighborhood Strategy Area Program.

In many ways, community development has been encompassed within overall urban or economic development strategies. California and Massachusetts led the way in forming comprehensive state urban policies, and others have followed. For example, Connecticut, Illinois and Michigan developed urban strategies, and Colorado put together a "human settlement policy," including urban needs, energy development and rural development.

In 1981, Congress passed legislation that could change significantly federal community development policy. The new legislation, developing from the administration's new federalism emphasis, gives states the option of managing a state community development block grant program for non-entitlement areas.

The problem of development financing continues to plague local government efforts at community revitalization. States help alleviate the financial burden of local governments with programs of state-funded revenue sharing or state assistance in the local match requirement for federal grant programs. State technical assistance has also aided local governments in channeling funds from numerous sources into one project. Twenty-five states have received funds from HUD for technical assistance as part of the CDBG program.

In addition to forming comprehensive development plans with a strong housing element, state departments of community affairs (DCAs) have active housing programs. DCAs and HFAs administer statewide rental housing programs under the federal Section 8 Existing Housing Program and have administered and financed units under the Section 8 Moderate Rehabilitation Program.

A successful vehicle for state and local cooperation has been built around the Neighborhood Housing Services Program, now under the Neighborhood Reinvestment Corporation. Participating lenders generally provide capital for mortgages and home improvements in targeted areas, while the local government supplements the private funding with municipal improvements. States often assist the local government with additional subsidies, and state HFAs have targeted mortgage funds into the designated areas. Citizen participation in this process is a requirement. Programs in Massachusetts, New Jersey and Pennsylvania are excellent examples.

Special Housing Programs

Anti-redlining. Efforts to remove barriers to mortgage lending in urban neighborhoods continue. California, Colorado, Connecticut, Michigan, Missouri, New Jersey, New York and Utah followed Illinois' example in adopting mortgage disclosure measures by statute or regulation. California, Michigan, New Jersey and Utah prohibit lending discrimination on racial or ethnic grounds and encourage affirmative lending by regulation or by selective deposit of state funds. Michigan's law, which requires disclosure of average down payments and average annual interest rates, also permits the levying of fines and legal action for damages suffered. Missouri extended anti-redlining prohibitions to fire and homeowners insurance programs. In addition, state HFA mortgage funds are often used in areas not generally served by conventional lending institutions. HFA mortgage programs allow lenders to operate in a broader area with little risk to themselves. State efforts to increase the availability of mortgage funds in urban neighborhoods are complemented by federal measures laid out in the Community Reinvestment Act of 1977.

Energy Conservation. Residential and commercial buildings became prime targets for state energy conservation efforts. Over half the states have adopted policies or programs to encourage efficient energy use in buildings. Common is the adoption of tax incentives (property tax exemptions, income tax credits) to encourage greater use of non-fossil fuel or solar heating and cooling in buildings. For example, in Arkansas, buyers and builders of passive-solar design homes in the Housing Development Agency's program receive a 1 percent rebate. A growing number of states require or encourage adoption of energy conservation measures in state and local building codes.

States also acted to assist low- and moderate-income persons to finance energy conservation in the home. While federal winterization funds are generally administered by state energy or community affairs agencies, state HFAs in Alaska, Colorado, Idaho, Illinois, Maryland, Michigan, Minnesota, New Jersey, Oregon, Pennsylvania, Tennessee, Vermont, Virginia and Wisconsin provide energy conservation loans for low- and moderate-income families. Federal and state insurance programs are used to back the energy conservation loan program.

Housing and Development

Building Codes. The trend toward adoption of statewide building codes continued. While this trend created some local concern about state intrusion into local affairs, statewide uniform codes can address a problem cited by builders—conflicting codes and standards that contribute to increased housing costs through delays and confusion.

Utah adopted legislation calling for an energy conservation building code with voluntary compliance. Montana's building code now applies consistently to cities and counties, with provision for either local or state administration. In Oregon, the pre-emptive state building code was upheld by the court, even though a local government might prefer a more stringent code.

Minnesota moved beyond building codes to establish a program of statutory warranties to protect buyers of new residential buildings. The warranty deals with defects due to faulty workmanship and non-compliance with building codes, faulty installation of utility systems and major construction defects.

New Initiatives. The outlook for federally funded housing and community development programs is not as rosy as it was in the late 1970s. The private lending industry has several problems as a result of the large growth during the past decade. The ideal of a single-family detached house for all Americans may no longer be a reality as the first-time homebuyer has trouble entering the market. Condominiums are accepted as an alternative in all areas of the country, and states and localities are wrestling with the problems of condominium regulation.

Housing vouchers, an outgrowth from the Section 8 Existing Housing Program, may replace all assisted housing programs. At the same time, some states such as Maryland are identifying enterprise zones in anticipation of this new federal initiative. Within these zones, businesses would receive tax benefits to encourage economic growth and development. Finally, the President's Housing Commission has been studying the overall housing crisis and its final report is due during the first half of 1982.

STATE HOUSING FINANCE AGENCY FUNCTIONS

State or other jurisdiction	Agency name	Year established	Single family				Multifamily			
			Direct construction loans	*Direct permanent loans*	*Mortgage purchases*	*Loans to lenders*	*Direct construction loans*	*Direct permanent loans*	*Mortgage purchases*	*Loans to lenders*
Alabama	...	...								
Alaska	Housing Finance Corporation	1971	●	●	★	●	●	●	●	●
Arizona	...	...								
Arkansas	Housing Development Agency	1977	●	●	★	●	★	●	●	
California	Housing Finance Agency	1975	...	...	★	...	★	★	...	★
Colorado	Housing Finance Authority	1973	●	●	●	★	★	★	●	...
Connecticut	Housing Finance Authority	1969	★	●	●	...	★	★	●	...
Delaware	Housing Authority	1968	★	●	●	★	★	★	●	●
Florida	Housing Finance Agency	1980	●	●	★	●	●	●	●	●
Georgia	Residential Finance Authority	1974	●	●	★	●	●	●	●	●
Hawaii	Housing Authority	1979	...	...	★	...	●	●	●	●
Idaho	Housing Agency	1972	...	...	★	●	★	★		
Illinois	Housing Development Authority	1967	...	...	●	●	★	★		
Indiana	Housing Finance Authority	1978	...	...	★	●	...	...	●	●
Iowa	Housing Finance Authority	1975	...	...	★	●	...	●	★	●
Kansas	...	...								
Kentucky	Housing Corporation	1972	●	●	★	★	★	★	★	●
Louisiana	Housing Finance Agency	1980	●	●	★	●	●	●	●	●
Maine	Housing Authority	1969	●	●	★	●	●	●	★	●
Maryland	Community Development Administration	1970	★	★	★	●	★	★	●	●
Massachusetts	Home Mortgage Finance Agency	1974	●	●	★	●				
	Housing Finance Agency	1968	...	...	...	...	★	★		
Michigan	Housing Development Authority	1966	●	★	...	...	★	★		
Minnesota	Housing Finance Agency	1971	●	●	★	●	★	★	●	
Mississippi	Housing Finance Corporation	1980	...	...	★	●	...	...		
Missouri	Housing Development Commission	1969	...	●	★	...	★	★	●	●
Montana	Board of Housing	1975	●	●	★	●	★	●	★	●
Nebraska	Mortgage Finance Fund	1978	●	●	★	★	★	●	★	●
Nevada	Housing Division	1975	●	●	★	★	★	★	●	●
New Hampshire	Housing Finance Authority	1975	...	●	●	★	★	●	●	●
New Jersey	Housing Finance Agency	1967	...	...	★	●	★	★	●	●
	Mortgage Finance Agency	1970	...	...	★	●	...	...	...	...
New Mexico	Mortgage Finance Authority	1975	...	...	★	★	...	...	...	...
New York	City Housing Development Corporation	1971	...	...	...	...	★	★(a)	...	...
	Housing Finance Agency	1960	...	...	...	...	★	★	...	●
	Mortgage Agency	1970	...	...	★	●	...	...	●	
North Carolina	Housing Finance Agency	1973	●	●	★	●	●	...	★	●
North Dakota	Finance Agency	1980	...	...	●	●	●	●	●	●
Ohio	...	...								
Oklahoma	Housing Finance Agency	1975	●	●	★	●	★	★	●	★
Oregon	Housing Division	1971	●	●	★	●	★	★	●	●
Pennsylvania	Housing Finance Agency	1972	...	...	★	●	★	★	●	●
Rhode Island	Housing and Mortgage Finance Corp.	1973	●	●	★	●	★	★	●	●
South Carolina	Housing Authority	1971	●	●	★	●	★	●		
South Dakota	Housing Development Authority	1973	...	●	★	●	★	★	●	●
Tennessee	Housing Development Agency	1973	●	★	★	●	★	★	●	●
Texas	Housing Agency	1979	●	●	★	●	●	●	★	...
Utah	Housing Finance Agency	1975	●	●	★	...	★	●	★	...
Vermont	Housing Finance Agency	1974	...	●	★	★	★	★	●	●
Virginia	Housing Development Authority	1972	★	★	★	●	●	●	★	●
Washington	...	...								
West Virginia	Housing Development Fund	1968	...	...	★	●	★	★		
Wisconsin	Housing Finance Authority	1972	●	●	★	●	★	★	★	●
Wyoming	Community Development Authority	1975	...	...	★	...	...	...		
Dist. of Col.	Housing Finance Agency	1979	●	●	●	●	●	●	●	●
Puerto Rico	Housing Finance Corporation	1977	...	...	...	...	★	★	●	●

Source: Council of State Housing Agencies, 1981 Survey of Housing Finance Agencies.
(a) Also multifamily refinancing.

Key:
★ —Agency presently performing function.
● —Statutory authority but not implemented.

BUSINESS AND INDUSTRIAL DEVELOPMENT

A SLUGGISH NATIONAL ECONOMY, the first round of Reagan administration budget cuts and a lingering desire for more tax relief pressured state legislatures during the biennium to get the most out of already-austere budgets. Overall, the pressures resulted in a trend of shifting tax liabilities to improve the climate for business and industry in most states around the nation.

Nevada legislators, for example, approved a significant increase in the state's sales and use taxes—from 3.5 to 5.75 percent—in order to slash property taxes levied on businesses and individuals. North Dakota cut corporate income taxes and taxes on businesses under out-of-state ownership, while raising the state's oil extraction tax. New Mexico cut taxes on sales and on corporate and personal income and got out of the business of collecting property taxes altogether. To help make up any revenue shortfalls, counties were authorized to raise property taxes.

Other states followed a similar pattern by cutting taxes in some categories and increasing them in others. Twenty-six states hiked taxes on motor fuels; 15 raised taxes on alcoholic beverages; nine increased sales and use taxes; and six hiked tobacco taxes. Nine states cut taxes on personal income, and five lowered corporate income taxes. Only three states—Alabama, New Mexico and Oklahoma—cut sales taxes.[1]

The apparent shift away from heavy reliance on property and income taxes—both personal and corporate—also reflected continuing state activity to attract more industry and increase expansion of existing factories in the face of an uncertain national economic future.

Several states either enacted wide-ranging economic improvement programs or modified existing programs. West Virginia tightened requirements for unemployment benefits, broadened the investment tax credit and increased bonding authority to benefit industries, water projects and housing. Colorado passed a $136 million tax cut on corporate and personal incomes, while Montana authorized reductions in corporate property taxes and eliminated a 10 percent surtax on personal income. Minnesota approved property tax reforms which reduce assessments on commercial and industrial property. Florida, prompted by a series of tax incentives passed by the state's voters during 1980, took a different approach by allocating direct aid for the road needs of new and expanding plants ($11 million) and for support of advanced engineering education ($3.4 million).

Some states joined West Virginia in making qualifications for unemployment benefits more stringent. Increased demands for benefits due to higher rates of joblessness led Georgia, Illinois and South Dakota to change eligibility rules. Other states, including Michigan and Utah, were expecting similar action in 1982. On the other hand, states with low unemployment rates, like Oklahoma, maintained ample cash in their unemployment funds.

This article was prepared by Conway Publications, Inc., Atlanta, Georgia, based on data from *Industrial Development*, Jan./Feb. 1982, copyright Conway Publications, Inc. 1982.

States continued to assist in securing new plants and plant expansion by issuing industrial revenue bonds (IRBs) during 1981, even though congressional action to limit or even phase-out IRBs by 1983 was pending.

Representative Charles Rangel (D.—N.Y.) chaired hearings in April by the Oversight Subcommittee of the House Ways and Means Committee to investigate charges that the use of IRBs has grown "out of control" since the last IRB restrictions were passed in 1968. However, on July 9, the subcommittee's recommendation (called the "Rangel Amendment") that the use of IRBs be eliminated by December 31, 1983, was not taken up by the full Ways and Means Committee for possible inclusion in President Reagan's tax package. The future of IRBs remained uncertain later in the year, as the Treasury Department continued work on drafting restrictive legislation of its own.

Against the threatening backdrop in Washington, state activity in IRB financing continued apace. During 1981, Pennsylvania issued 1,490 IRBs totaling $2.2 billion. New Hampshire and Utah enacted modifications to allow more entities to qualify for the bonds, and Kansas gave counties authority to issue them. Oregon removed its interest rate restrictions. In November, voters in Washington State passed a constitutional amendment to allow industrial revenue bonds, leaving Idaho the only state without such a program.

Activity also focused on other types of bond assistance for business. Mississippi approved a law allowing cities and counties to issue bonds for industrial construction even before industries have been secured to occupy the buildings. Maryland authorized the issuance of "umbrella" bonds to provide assistance to more than one business in a single bond issue, and voters in New York approved an increase in the bonding limit for the Jobs Development Authority. In Kentucky, officials offered to provide $4.1 million from economic development bonds to help reopen two steel plants.

Most state legislatures appeared cool during 1981 to the establishment of "enterprise zones," which would allow tax breaks to stimulate business investment and jobs in depressed areas and which are a keystone of President Reagan's urban policy. Although more than 70 enterprise zone measures were introduced in state legislatures around the country, only Connecticut, Delaware, Florida, Illinois, Indiana, Louisiana, Maryland, North Dakota, Oregon and Pennsylvania enacted the program which, to succeed, will require major state involvement, according to Reagan.

Connecticut, the first state to pass enterprise zone legislation, will offer corporation tax credits, a temporary freeze on tax increases on renovated property, sales tax breaks and a grant for each new employee of industries locating in the state's zones. The state will also allow for bonding to finance loans for new small businesses and will pay for any job training needed for residents of the zone.

Louisiana has similar legislation but with a new twist: the law allows the establishment of enterprise zones in both rural and urban areas.

The Illinois legislature approved enterprise zone legislation, but Governor James Thompson vetoed it as too vague and in need of clarification before enactment. Passage in Illinois is considered a possibility in 1982, and Massachusetts and Kentucky are also expected to take up the issue.

Illinois was one of many states passing significant legislation dealing with hazardous wastes during 1981. The Illinois legislature approved a government-industry cooperative effort to recycle hazardous materials by setting up the Industrial Material Exchange Service. It offers producers of such wastes a method to market them to other industries.

Georgia and North Carolina set up state boards to oversee the location and operation of hazardous waste landfill sites, and Hawaii will join other Western states in putting together a compact for disposal of low-level radioactive wastes. Texas banned the disposal of out-of-state waste unless an interstate compact or reciprocal agreement is in effect, and Colorado required approval of waste disposal sites by the affected locality.

Overall, the legislation in most states favored industrial development interests. Even so, considering the likelihood that the Reagan administration will try to cut more social spending and turn over control of (and responsibility for) many programs to the states in the near future, one wonders how much more tax revenue the states can afford to lose by way of industrial and business incentives. Currently, though, the race for industrial development continues, and industrial site planners can look forward to increased development incentives created by recent legislation.

Note

1. Tabulations are based on 1981 legislation only.

Table 1

SPECIAL SERVICES FOR INDUSTRIAL DEVELOPMENT

Column key:

1. State financed speculative building
2. City and/or county financed speculative building
3. Cities and/or counties provide free land for industry(a)
4. City and/or county-owned industrial park sites(b)
5. State funds for city and/or county development-related public works projects
6. State funds for city and/or county master plans
7. State funds for city and/or county recreational projects
8. State funds for private recreational projects
9. State program to promote research and development
10. State program to increase export of products
11. University R&D facilities available to industry
12. State and/or universities conduct feasibility studies to attract or assist new industry
13. State supported training of industrial employees(c)
14. State re-training of industrial employees
15. State supported training of "hard-core" unemployed
16. State incentive to industry to train "hard-core" unemployed
17. State help in bidding on federal procurement contracts
18. State science and/or technology advisory council

State or other jurisdiction	1	2	3	4	5	6	7	8	9	10	11	12	13	14	15	16	17	18
Alabama		★	★(d)	★	★	★	★		★	★	★	★	★	★	★	★		★
Alaska		★(d)		★			★	★		★	★	★	★	★	★			
Arizona	★		★(d)	★	★	★	★		★	★	★	★	★	★	★	★		★
Arkansas		★(d)	★(d)	★	★	★	★		★	★	★	★	★	★	★	★		★
California			★(d)	★	★		★		★	★	★	★	★	★	★		★	★
Colorado	★(d)	★(d)	★(d)	★	★	★	★	★		★	★	★	★	★	★	★	★	★
Connecticut	★			★	★	★(e)	★	★		★	★	★	★	★	★	★	★	★
Delaware				★	★	★	★			★	★(j)	★	★	★	★(g)		★	★
Florida	★	★		★	★	★	★			★	★	★	★	★	★(g)	★	★	★
Georgia				★	★	★	★			★	★	★	★	★	★	★	★	★
Hawaii			★(d)	★	★	★	★			★	★	★	★	★	★	★	★	★
Idaho				★	★	★	★			★	★	★	★	★	★		★	★
Illinois		★		★	★	★	★			★	★	★	★	★	★	★	★	★
Indiana	★(i)			★	★	★	★	★(h)		★	★	★	★	★	★	★	★	★
Iowa	★(i)			★	★	★	★			★	★	★	★	★	★		★	★
Kansas		★(j)	★(d)	★	★	★	★			★	★(k)	★	★	★	★		★	★
Kentucky			★(m)	★	★	★	★		★	★	★(l)	★	★	★	★	★	★	★
Louisiana	★(l)		★(n)	★	★		★			★	★	★	★	★	★		★	★
Maine	★			★	★	★	★		★	★	★	★	★	★	★	★	★	★
Maryland				★	★		★		★	★	★	★	★	★	★		★	★
Massachusetts		★(i)		★	★	★	★		★	★	★	★	★	★	★		★	★
Michigan				★	★	★	★		★	★	★	★	★	★	★	★	★	★
Minnesota			★(m)	★	★	★	★		★	★	★	★	★	★	★		★	★
Mississippi	★			★	★	★	★			★	★	★	★	★	★	★	★	★
Missouri	★			★	★		★	★		★	★	★	★	★	★		★	★
Montana				★	★(q)	★(q)	★		★	★	★	★	★	★	★		★	★
Nebraska				★					★	★	★	★	★	★	★		★	★
Nevada			★(d)	★		★	★	★(o)	★	★	★	★	★	★	★		★	★
New Hampshire	★			★			★	★(p)	★	★	★	★	★	★	★	★(r)	★	★
New Jersey				★			★		★	★	★	★	★	★	★		★	★
New Mexico			★	★					★	★	★	★	★	★	★		★	★
New York				★	★	★	★		★	★	★	★	★	★	★	★	★	★
North Carolina	★		★	★	★	★	★		★	★	★	★	★	★	★		★	★
North Dakota				★	★			★	★	★	★	★	★	★	★		★	★
Ohio				★	★		★		★	★	★	★	★	★	★		★	★
Oklahoma		★	★	★	★	★	★		★	★	★	★	★	★	★	★	★	★
Oregon		★		★	★	★	★		★	★	★	★	★	★	★		★	★
Pennsylvania				★	★	★	★	★	★	★	★	★	★	★	★	★	★	★
Rhode Island		★		★	★	★	★		★	★	★	★	★	★	★	★	★	★
South Carolina			★(d)	★			★		★	★	★	★	★	★	★	★		★
South Dakota				★	★(s)	★(t)	★		★	★	★	★	★	★	★		★	★
Tennessee		★		★	★	★	★		★	★	★	★	★	★	★	★	★	★
Texas				★	★	★	★		★	★	★	★	★	★	★	★	★	★
Utah				★			★			★	★	★	★	★	★			★
Vermont	★			★	★	★	★		★	★	★	★	★	★	★	★	★	★

State or other jurisdiction	State financed speculative building	City and/or county financed speculative building	Cities and/or counties provide free land for industry(a)	City and/or county-owned industrial park sites(b)	State funds for city and/or county development-related public works projects	State funds for city and/or county master plans	State funds for city and/or county recreational projects	State funds for private recreational projects	State program to promote research and development	State program to increase export of products	University R&D facilities available to industry	State and/or universities conduct feasibility studies to attract or assist new industry	State supported training of industrial employees(c)	State re-training of industrial employees	State supported training of "hard-core" unemployed	State incentive to industry to train "hard-core" unemployed	State help in bidding on federal procurement contracts	State science and/or technology advisory council
Virginia		★(i)		★	★					★	★	★	★	★				★
Washington	★(i)			★(j)	★		★			★	★	★	★	★	★	★	★	★
West Virginia				★(u)	★	★	★	★	★	★	★	★	★	★	★	★	★	
Wisconsin				★	★				★	★	★	★	★	★				★
Wyoming																		
Puerto Rico	★				★	★	★	★	★	★	★	★	★	★	★	★	★	★

Source: Adapted from copyrighted data supplied by Conway Publications, Inc., Atlanta, Ga. 30341, U.S.A.

(a) No state provides free land for industry.
(b) State-owned industrial park sites in Alabama, Hawaii, Maryland, Mississippi, New Hampshire, New Jersey, Oklahoma, Rhode Island, Tennessee and Puerto Rico.
(c) All states but New Mexico provide for recruiting and screening of industrial employees.
(d) Provided only in rare instances. In California, a few cities and counties will lease land they own at nominal rates.
(e) Limited to technical assistance.
(f) Facilities available on a contractual basis.
(g) State vocational education program keyed to federally funded program.
(h) State matching funds for private non-profit organizations.
(i) State pays interest on speculative buildings until they have been sold or leased.
(j) Carried out through local development corporations.
(k) Available to industry on a contract and/or consulting basis.
(l) Authorized but not active.
(m) Activity limited to certain units.
(n) City-owned land only. Cities may not purchase land for purpose of providing free land to industry.
(o) Highway Commission will build first two miles of road into new ski areas.
(p) Industrial Development Financing Authority will guarantee up to 80 percent of the mortgages for land and 70 percent for equipment.
(q) A coal tax fund is available to areas directly affected by coal development.
(r) Under the New York Job Incentive Program, a corporate franchise or unincorporated business tax credit is allowed to firms locating, expanding or improving facilities in the state.
(s) Funds are from public health for solid waste disposal projects.
(t) State matches funds from U.S. Department of Housing and Urban Development.
(u) Port districts only.

Table 2

TAX INCENTIVES FOR INDUSTRY AND OTHER PERTINENT LAWS

State or other jurisdiction	Corporate income tax exemption	Personal income tax exemption	Excise tax exemption	Tax exemption or moratorium on land capital improvements	Tax exemption or moratorium on equipment/machinery	Inventory tax exemption on goods in transit (free port)	Tax exemption on manufacturers' inventories	Sales/use tax exemption on new equipment	Tax exemptions on raw materials used in manufacturing	Tax incentive for creation of jobs	Tax incentive for industrial investment	Tax credits for use of specified state products	Tax stabilization agreements for specified industries	Tax exemption to encourage research and development	Accelerated depreciation of industrial equipment	State right to work law	State minimum wage law	State fair employment practice code	Statewide uniform property tax evaluation law	Statewide industrial noise abatement law*
Alabama	★	★	★	★	★	★	★	★	★					★	(a)	★	★		★	
Alaska															★		★	★	★	
Arizona						★	★		★						★	★	★	★	★	★
Arkansas				★	★	★	★	★	★			(c)			(e)				★	★
California		(f)	★	★					★			★			★		★	★	★	
Colorado	★			(b)	(b)	(g)	(g)		(g)	(d)	(j)				(a)			★	★	
Connecticut	★ (f)	(h)			★ (i)			★		★ (i)	★				★		★	★	★	★
Delaware	★ (e)		(k)								★	(n)			★		★	★		★
Florida	★		(k)	★ (l)	★ (l)			★	★	(m)	★ (m)				(a)	★		★		
Georgia	★	(h)							★	(m)	★ (m)	(n)			(a)	★			★	
Hawaii																	★	★	★	★
Idaho			★	★	★			★	★						★	★			★	
Illinois				(p)	(q)		(r)	(o)	(w)		(p)				(a)		★	★	★	★
Indiana					(u)	(r)	(v)								(a)	★	★	★	★	
Iowa	(s)							★	★						★					★
Kansas	★ (f)		★	(x)	(x)		(y)	(x)	(z)	(aa)	(m)				(a)	★	★	★	★	
Kentucky			★	(ac)	(l)		(l)	(ab)	(l)	(aa)	★ (aa)		★		★ (a)	★	★	★	★	★
Louisiana	★ (ab)			(l)	(l)				(z)	(ad)	★			(af)	(a)	★		★	★	★
Maine									(ae)					★		★	★	★	★	
Maryland									★					★	★		★	★	★	
Massachusetts																	★	★	★	
Michigan				(ag)				(ah)			★						★	★	★	
Minnesota				(e)		★	★										★	★	★	★
Mississippi						★	★	★	★						★	★		★	★	★
Missouri						★	★	★	★						★	★		★	★	
Montana	★ (ai)						(aj)	(ak)		(ai)					(a)		★	★	★	
Nebraska	★ (ai)	(h)	(k)	★	★	★	★	★	★				★			★	★		★	★
Nevada	★	★ (h)				★	★		★							★	★	★	★	★
New Hampshire						(al)		(ak)	★						(u)		★	★	★	★
New Jersey					(u)		★		★						(u)		★	★	★	★

TAX INCENTIVES FOR INDUSTRY AND OTHER PERTINENT LAWS—Continued

State	Corporate income tax exemption	Personal income tax exemption	Excise tax exemption	Tax exemption or moratorium on land capital improvements	Tax exemption or moratorium on equipment/machinery	Inventory tax exemption on goods in transit (free port)	Tax exemption on manufacturers' inventories	Sales/use tax exemption on new equipment	Tax exemptions on raw materials used in manufacturing	Tax incentive for creation of jobs	Tax incentive for industrial investment	Tax credits for use of specified state products	Tax stabilization agreements for specified industries	Tax exemption to encourage research and development	Accelerated depreciation of industrial equipment	State right to work law	State minimum wage law	State fair employment practice code	Statewide uniform property tax evaluation law	Statewide industrial noise abatement law*
New Mexico	★(am)	★(am)	(k)	★(am)	★(an)	★(an)	★(an)	★(ao)	★	★(am)	★(am)			★(am)	★(a)		★	★		★
New York	★		★(k)	★(am)	★(an)	★(al)	★(an)	★	★								★	★	★	
North Carolina	★	★		★(aq)	★(an)	★(an)	★(an)	★	★(ap)						★	★	★	★	★	★
North Dakota								★	★	★						★	★	★	★	
Ohio								★	★								★	★	★	
Oklahoma			★(as)	★(aq,as)		★(at)		★	★				★(ar)	★(af)	★(a)		★	★		★
Oregon									★						★(c)		★	★	★	
Pennsylvania						★(av)	★(av)	★(au)	★(au)						★		★	★	★	
Rhode Island									★						★		★	★		
South Carolina									★				★		★	★			★	
South Dakota	★(h)	★(h)	★	★(l)		★	★	★(aw)	★(ax)	★★	★(ay)					★		★	★	
Tennessee	★(h)	★(h)		★(az)	★(aw)	★	★		★			(n)				★			★	
Utah					★(az)	★			★			★				★	★	★		
Vermont			★(k)			★★	★★	★	★					★★			★		★	★
Virginia	★(h)	★(h)		★(l)	★(l)	★(ba)	★(ba)	★	★(bb)	★	★★		★		★(a)	★			★	
Washington	★(h)	★(h)	★★	★★	★★				★								★	★	★	★
West Virginia	★(bd)							★★	★					★(bc)	★		★	★		
Wisconsin	★(h)	★(h)	★						★								★	★	★	
Wyoming				★					★		★				★	★	★	★	★	★
Puerto Rico	★	★	★			★	★	★	★		★			★	★		★		★	★

582

Source: Adapted from copyrighted data supplied by Conway Publications, Inc., Atlanta, Ga. 30341, U.S.A.

*All states have statewide air and water pollution control laws.
(a) Allowable depreciation is similar to that permitted under federal laws.
(b) Exempt using Act 9 in some cities.
(c) Seven-year ad valorem tax exemption on textile plants.
(d) Targeted jobs tax credit program.
(e) Applies only to pollution control equipment.
(f) An income tax credit is allowed for a period of 10 years against the income taxes generated by the operation of a new business activity. The credit is based on the number of new jobs created as well as the capital investment involved.
(g) Law allows reduction in taxes but not exemption. Goods in transit, inventories and raw materials are assessed at 5 percent.
(h) Connecticut, Florida and New Hampshire do not tax personal income. Nevada, South Dakota, Texas, Washington and Wyoming do not tax corporate or personal income.
(i) Equipment and machinery acquired after the 1973 assessment date is exempt from local property tax.
(j) Connecticut Urban Jobs Program, available in 18 "distressed" and 29 "high unemployment" communities.
(k) State does not collect an excise tax.
(l) In Florida, the exemption is a local option, and school and special district taxes are excluded from the exemption. In Kentucky, the exemption is applicable at the local level only. In Maryland, the exemption may be applicable at the county or local level. In Tennessee, the exemption is applicable to plants financed with industrial revenue bonds. In Virginia, localities have the option of totally or partially exempting certified pollution control facilities and equipment, certified solar energy equipment and facilities and energy conversion equipment of manufacturers from taxation.
(m) Corporate income tax credit equal to 25 percent of wages paid by business employing residents from designated areas and a corporate income tax credit for investment in new or expanded business in designated areas.
(n) In Florida, applies only to alcoholic beverages produced from specified Florida-grown agricultural products. In Tennessee, allowed for products of state soil.
(o) Phased exemption; fully exempt by 1984.
(p) Ten-year partial property tax abatement in designated areas of all cities and towns for renovation or construction of new facilities.
(q) Five-year partial exemption on installed new manufacturing equipment.
(r) Finished goods stored in public or private warehouses destined for out-of-state shipment are exempt.
(s) 50 percent of federal tax paid is exempt from corporate income tax on profits from sales outside Iowa. Corporate income tax is figured only on profits from sales in Iowa.
(t) Five-year tax abatement on building, equipment and machinery. Can also apply to expansions.
(u) The business personal property tax on machinery, equipment and other tangible property is 1.3 percent of 50 percent of original cost or cost at acquisition. This tax has been repealed for equipment purchased after January 1, 1977.
(v) Personal property taxes are being phased out. First $145,000 of assessed taxable value of personal property is exempt. An additional exemption is added by the county, and the amount varies by county.
(w) Inventory, goods in process and finished goods are taxed only the value of raw materials.
(x) Applicable to industrial-revenue bond financed property only. A ten-year exemption is allowed.
(y) Applicable to goods stored in licensed and bonded warehouse, provided that 35 percent or more of the previous year's sales or shipments from the storage area were shipped in interstate commerce to a point outside the state.
(z) Sales/use tax exemption.
(aa) Limited to fuel alcohol production facilities.
(ab) Applicable under the tax equalization law, Enterprise Zone Act, and Flood, Fire and Famine Act.
(ac) Exemption applicable to capital improvements only.
(ad) $100/job created by any business enterprise. However, in high unemployment areas, $225/job can be credited. The Rural Enterprise Zone Act allows a tax credit of $2,500/job.
(ae) Allowed except for sales/use tax when purchased for use as an ingredient in tangible personal property for sale.
(af) R&D equipment is classified as manufacturer's machinery and equipment and, as such, is eligible for tax exemptions.
(ag) Local option in designated redevelopment areas.
(ah) Exemption is allowed on separate, detachable accessory tools and equipment which have a useful life of less than 12 months.
(ai) A 1 percent tax credit, based on wages paid, is allowed for the first three years to new and expanding industry engaged in the mechanical or chemical transformation of materials or substances into new products. "Expanding" means to expand a present operation so as to increase total permanent jobs by 30 percent.
(aj) Five-year partial exemption on installed new manufacturing equipment.
(ak) State does not collect sales/use tax.
(al) Applicable to goods stored in bonded warehouses.
(am) Tax credit or exemption allowed for specified items or operations, usually for specified time under certain conditions.
(an) Tangible and intangible personal property is not subject to ad valorem taxes.
(ao) New equipment is allowed a preferential rate of 1 percent, with a minimum tax of $80/article.
(ap) Leaf tobacco is allowed an exemption of 60 percent of tax rate; bales of cotton 50 percent; and peanuts 20 percent.
(aq) In North Dakota, exemption extends only to new construction. In Oregon, exemption is allowed while facility is under construction only.
(ar) A gross production tax on textile mills in lieu of property tax.
(as) Tax credits allowed to manufacturers and processors for property taxes paid on goods in process.
(at) In city of Portland and in Coos, Curry and Douglas Counties from EDA revolving loan fund.
(au) Exclusion from sales and use tax on industrial purchases used directly in industrial production and research.
(av) Exclusion of tangible personal property from taxation at local level. State has no inventory tax.
(aw) State tax rate of 1 percent will be phased out by July 1, 1983.
(ax) Raw materials for processing are exempt from sales and use taxes. However, a personal property inventory tax is levied at the local level on raw materials a manufacturer has on hand January 1. Finished goods are exempt from taxation.
(ay) One percent of investment in industrial machinery against corporate excise tax. Fully effective July 1, 1984.
(az) Seven-year annexation or de-annexation exemption.
(ba) Applies to imported goods if they have not lost their status as imports.
(bb) Exempt from sales/use tax, but not from business capital tax.
(bc) Local governments may classify separately the tangible personal property of research and development firms from that of other taxpayers and tax it at different rates.
(bd) A credit allowed for sales tax paid on energy.

Table 3
FINANCIAL ASSISTANCE FOR INDUSTRY

State or other jurisdiction	State-sponsored industrial development authority	Privately sponsored Development Credit Corporation	State authority or agency revenue bond financing	City and/or county revenue bond financing	State authority or agency general obligation bond financing	City and/or county general obligation bond financing	State loans for building construction	City and/or county loans for building construction	State loans for equipment/machinery	City and/or county loans for equipment/machinery	State loan guarantees for building construction	State loans guarantees for equipment/machinery	State financing aid for existing plant expansions	State matching funds for city and/or county industrial financing programs	State incentive for establishing industrial plants in areas of high unemployment	City and/or county incentive for establishing industrial plants in areas of high unemployment
Alabama	★(a)	★	...	★		★(b)	...		...				★(c)	...		
Alaska	★	★	★	★	★	★(i)	★		★				★	...		
Arizona	...	(d)	★	★												
Arkansas	★	★	...	★		★					★(e)	★(e)	...			
California	...	★(f)	★(g)	★	★	★	★	★(b)	★	★(b)	...	...	★	...	★	★
Colorado	...		...	★												
Connecticut	★	★	★	★	★		★	★	★	★	★	★	★	★	★	★
Delaware	★	...	★	★	★	★	★	★	★	★	★	★	★	★	...	★
Florida	...	★	★	★											★(h)	
Georgia	...	★	★	★												
Hawaii	★	...	★	★	★	★			★				★			
Idaho	...	★	...													
Illinois	★	★	★	★		★							★			★
Indiana	★	★	...	★									★			
Iowa	...	★	...	★												
Kansas	...	★	...	★		★										
Kentucky	★	★	★	★	★	★							★			
Louisiana	...	(d)	★(c)	★	★	★	★		★		★	★	★		★	
Maine	★	★	★	★	★	★	★	★	★	★	★	★	★			
Maryland	★	★	★	★		★	★	★(j)	★		★	★	★	★(k)		
Massachusetts	...	★	★	★		★			★		★	★	★	...	★	★
Michigan	★	(d)	★	★		★		★			★	★	★		★	
Minnesota	...	★	...	★		★	★	★(l)	★	★(l)	...	...	★	★	★	★
Mississippi	...	★	...	★		★								★(c)	...	★
Missouri	...	★	...	★		★							★			
Montana	...	★	...	★			★(m)							★(c)		
Nebraska	...	★	...	★										★(c)		
Nevada	...		...	...												
New Hampshire	★	★	★	...		★					★	★	★			
New Jersey	★	...	★(g)	★		★(g)	★(g)	★	★(g)		★	★	★			
New Mexico	★	(d)	...	★												
New York	★	★	★	★	★	★	★	★	★	★	★	★	★	...	★(n)	★(n)
North Carolina	...	★	★	★												
North Dakota	...	★	★	★	★	★			★		★	★			★	★
Ohio	★	★	★	★							★	★	★		★	★
Oklahoma	★	★	★	★	★	★	★	★	★	★	★		★			
Oregon	★	★	★(i)	★(g)	★	★	★	★	★	...	★		★	★	★	★
Pennsylvania	★	★	★	★				★(o)	★(o)	★(p)			★		★	★
Rhode Island	★	★	★	★							★	★	★		★	★
South Carolina	★	★	★	★												
South Dakota	★		★													
Tennessee	...	...	★	★	★	★		★					★	★(q)		★(r)
Texas	★		★			★		★								
Utah	★		★													
Vermont	★	★	★	★							★	★	★			
Virginia	★		★													
Washington	★	★	...	★(i)		★(i)				★(i)			★		★	★
West Virginia	★	★	★	★	★	★	★	★			★		★	★	★	★
Wisconsin	...	(d)	...			★(s)										
Wyoming	...		★	★												
Puerto Rico	★	★	★	★	★	★	★		★		★	★	★	★	★	★

Source: Adapted from copyrighted data supplied by Conway Publications, Inc., Atlanta, Ga. 30341, U.S.A.

(a) State grants to assist in industrial site preparation.

(b) Permitted only in specified municipalities.

(c) State allows cities or counties to offer financial aid for existing plant expansions. In Louisiana, state financing aid is directly involved only in the case of those port authorities whose obligations are backed by the state's full faith and credit.

(d) Authorized but not active.

(e) Guarantee applies to Act 9 industrial revenue bonds up to $1 million.

(f) State-sponsored but privately operated non-profit Regional Job Development Corporations may be established in low-income areas to provide loans to small businesses.

(g) Applies only to pollution control equipment.

(h) Corporate income tax credits of 50 percent of contributions to eligible community development projects, 25 percent of wages of employees hired from designated areas, and an economic revitalization tax incentive credit to new or expanding business located in designated areas.

(i) Activity is limited to Ports Authority in Georgia and to port districts in Oregon and Washington.

(j) Has been used in city of Baltimore.

(k) Limited to EDA-designated areas.

(l) For proceessing products of agriculture, forestry and timber production.

(m) Authorized if a one-mill, multi-purpose tax levy is approved by local voters.

(n) Under the New York Job Incentive Program, a corporate franchise or unincorporated business tax credit is allowed to firms locating, expanding or improving facilities in the state.

(o) State and local program of participation in building construction.

(p) Available through the Minority Business Development Agency.

(q) Loan guarantee of up to 90 percent of the project amount, not to exceed $250,000.

(r) Priority given to companies applying for assistance under the Tennessee Industrial Development Authority program, which is a loan guarantee only at present.

(s) For acquiring and developing sites.

6. Natural Resources

ENVIRONMENTAL MANAGEMENT

By Anne Stubbs and Leslie Cole

Introduction

AS THE 1970s drew to a close, states looked back on major accomplishments, abrupt changes and major challenges in their efforts to protect and manage the environmental and natural resources. The decade witnessed a revolution in national commitment to protecting and enhancing basic land, water and air resources. Partially in response to federal mandates and financial assistance, states strengthened and expanded laws and programs for water quality, water resources management, air quality, coastal resources management, and solid and hazardous waste. A "cooperative federalism" evolved with states implementing programs, with federal assistance, to meet national goals and standards.

By 1980, the terms of the partnership began to change. With the basic legislative and program structures in place, federal attention turned to other pressing national concerns of energy, economic development and federal budget deficits. Responsibility for environmental management increasingly devolved to states as federal policy changes and budget reductions diminished the federal role in designing, managing and enforcing environmental programs.

As states prepare to assume these new responsibilities, a review of their capability to plan, manage and finance the environmental programs offers signs of both encouragement and caution. The basic laws enabling states to manage and protect air, water and land resources are in place, with hazardous waste management authority being the most recent addition to states' legal powers. The laws, standards and administrative procedures continue to be refined as states gain experience in management and as new problems emerge. While less dramatic than the institution of new laws and programs, this quiet "fine tuning" is an important step marking the maturity and emergence of effective, efficient programs.

Water Resources

The states' long-stated claim to primary authority and responsibility for the development, management and protection of water resources moved a step closer to realization in 1980 and 1981. The rhetoric of a federal-state partnership took on new meaning as the Reagan administration offered new terms for the partnership: greater federal recognition of state water rights, expanded state responsibilities for planning, development and management of water resources—but at the cost of severely reduced federal funding. The administration proposed to end funding of such programs as coastal resources management, water quality management planning, and state and regional water resources planning. Washington also

Anne Stubbs is Program Manager of The Council of State Governments' Environmental Resources and Development Program. Leslie Cole is a Research Assistant with the Council.

wanted increased cost sharing in water projects, and revision of water project evaluation criteria to favor national economic needs at the expense of regional and non-economic needs.

Adequate legislative authority; strong planning, management and enforcement programs; and adequate financial resources will be needed in order for states to assume greater responsibility for water resources management. By 1981, states were fine tuning their administrative programs in water quality and assessing existing water resources management efforts. Whether states can fund expanded water resource programs remained an open question.

Water Quality. Water quality has long been the centerpiece of state water programs. Traditional state concerns with public health were strengthened and vastly expanded by federal water quality initiatives and the infusion of federal planning, management and construction financial assistance. The Federal Water Pollution Control Act of 1972, amended by the Clean Water Act of 1977, and the Safe Drinking Water Act of 1974 involved the states in implementation of a complex and fragmented array of programs. These include water quality standard setting, stream classification, water quality management (Section 208), National Pollutant Discharge Elimination System (NPDES), wastewater facilities construction grants (Section 201), safe drinking water, underground injection control (UIC), and dredge and fill management (Section 404).

After a decade of intensive federal-state water quality management initiatives, all states have legislation for promulgation and implementation of water quality planning, quality standards and program administration. In spite of criticisms levied against the federal program, progress has been made in upgrading or preventing degradation of the nation's surface water.

States accepted increasing responsibility for program management and administration as they gained experience in the federal water quality programs. However, state involvement in these programs is not uniform. The NPDES program to control effluent discharges and the wastewater treatment construction grants programs are the heart of most states' involvement in water quality management. As of late 1981, 32 states and the Virgin Islands had assumed primary responsibility for the NPDES program for monitoring and regulation of point source discharges.[1] Eight states assumed responsibility for monitoring industrial discharges into municipal treatment facilities. Forty-one states and Puerto Rico have delegated responsibility to manage the construction grants program (Sec. 205[g]).[2] Thirty-five states assist local governments in financing the 25 percent non-federal share. Through a variety of grant and loan programs, these states provide from 5 percent to the full 25 percent of the non-federal share. Forty-four states and three territories have primacy for regulating the quality of deliverable drinking water under the Safe Drinking Water Act. By early 1981, five states (Alabama, California, New Mexico, Oklahoma and Texas) had submitted programs to control the injection of waste materials into groundwater under the UIC program. A majority of states requested an extension on program submittal. Since no state has applied for primacy under Section 404 to regulate the discharge of dredged or fill material into navigable waters, the Corps of Engineers and the Environmental Protection Agency (EPA) continue to administer this program.

The state commitment to administering the federal water quality management programs faces new challenges in the 1980s. As inflation and federal budget reductions cut into the level of support for managing the Clean Water Act programs, state officials voice increasing concern over state and federal roles and the need for flexibility in administering the programs. Total state budget support for the Section 106 management program of the Clean Water Act doubled during the life of the program, from approximately $40 million dollars in fiscal 1972 to slightly over $80 milion in fiscal 1980.[3] As combined state and federal funding support stabilized and federal program requirements increased, state officials called for greater flexibility in administering the program and for setting priorities among programs. More ominously, reduced real support raised concerns over the ability to maintain effective programs. Two states, California and Iowa, responded to their financial and administrative problems by returning delegated responsibilities to the Environmental Protection Agency for the Safe Drinking Water program (Iowa) and construction grants (California).

The water quality management program authorized under Section 208 of the federal law continued its troubled history. Originally designed to integrate areawide wastewater treatment planning with management of point and non-point sources of pollution, the program has undergone major changes. The goal of integrating point and non-point sources of pollution was an ambitious one. In its implementation, the program suffered from too short a planning period, changing priorities, uncertain funding, an inadequate data base and the difficulty of bringing together diverse state and local jurisdictions into a coherent planning effort. In most states, the program for substate, areawide planning was accorded lower priority than the NPDES or construction grants program. Over 225 local and state water quality management plans document the significant impact of non-point sources of water quality. By 1981, 31 states had approved 208 plans; but the elimination of federal funds to implement the programs and the lower state interest in the program will affect the implementation of these plans.

Water Resources Management. The federal mandates of the Clean Water Act give consistency to the programs for water quality among the 50 states. The same cannot be said for water resources management. The diverse physical characteristics of water resources and the types and levels of demand for use determine the problems and solutions to protection, management and development. Providing adequate municipal water supply in the water-rich East involves a different set of issues and programs than does developing water supplies in the West. How water is developed and allocated for irrigation or energy development is a major public issue in the Western states, but receives less attention in the East. Water management for navigation and flood control has been a central concern to the Midwestern states. As a consequence of these differences in resource problems, state water laws and institutional systems for management vary widely.

While state water resource problems and management vary, growing competition for use of the nation's available supplies of fresh water has become a common concern among most state water resource managers. Across the country, water resources are being recognized as a significant factor in the economic development of the states. The availability and price of water has long been crucial to economic development and growth in the West; the Eastern and Great Lakes states are coming to recognize the importance of water to their urban centers and industrial bases. Quality issues concerned federal and state water officials in the 1970s; conflict over resource uses is emerging as the dominant issue of the 1980s. With diminished expectations of effective federal action to resolve use conflicts, states are likely to bear greater responsibility for anticipating and managing water resource problems. Effective solution of these problems will depend in part upon states' ability to develop and implement programs which recognize the interdependency of the water resource and the interrelationship among competing uses.

Water Problems. In spite of progress in controlling point source discharges, water quality in a number of states is threatened by excessive withdrawals and use. In the Mid-Atlantic and Northeastern states, droughts in 1980 drew attention to the inadequacy of distribution systems and management programs.

The protection and management of groundwater, which supports 50 percent of the nation's drinking water supplies, is becoming a major concern in all areas of the country. In Northeastern and Mid-Atlantic states, concentrated populations and municipal and industrial wastes threaten contamination of public drinking water sources. In the Midwestern and Western states, where groundwater is an important source of irrigation for agriculture and a potential source for energy development, depletion and associated contamination from minerals and saltwater intrusion are the issues. Groundwater mining—withdrawals at a rate in excess of natural recharge—is a problem in the Great Plains where the Ogallala aquifer, which supports irrigated agriculture in the area from Texas to Nebraska, is threatened.

Imbalances and scarcity of water give rise to management and political problems. Interbasin transfers, a long-standing subject of management and political disputes, are gaining renewed interest and controversy in both Eastern and Western states. The 1980 drought renewed interest in interbasin transfer to supply municipal water systems. In the West, proposals for slurry pipelines to use water from the Oahe reservoir in South Dakota or the Great Lakes raised both interest and alarm. Finally, with greater pressures on the finite water resource, state water managers are recognizing that quantity and quality and surface and groundwater management cannot be addressed separately. State water laws and management systems began to come under close scrutiny as the task of water resources management devolved to the states.

State Responses. The diversity of water problems in the states is mirrored in the varied legal and institutional approaches to managing water resources. The legislative basis of state water resources programs provides some insight to states' capability to undertake comprehensive planning and management; however, the existence of authorizing legislation does not automatically translate into effective programs. The picture is mixed on how states approach the planning and management of water quality and quantity.[4]

Planning is frequently separate from management, and water quality and water quantity are often addressed by different agencies, acting under different legislative mandates. Comprehensive legislative authority for integrated planning and management of water and related land resources exists in only three states: Delaware, Florida and Washington. Eight states have created comprehensive water quality planning and management agencies.[5] In 13 states,[6] both water quality and water quantity planning are legislatively integrated in a single agency, while 11 states[7] have a lead agency authorized to undertake water quality planning. In 12 states, no legislation expressly mandates comprehensive water resources planning and management.

The variations between states are significant, yet, there are some similarities in management techniques. In the Western states, water has long been managed through a prior appropriation system which allocates water among various users. As demands from municipalities, energy companies and agriculture intensify, existing water management systems come under examination. Montana has begun the process of reserving water rights for future use in the Yellowstone basin. In Arizona, where groundwater is being rapidly depleted, the state adopted in 1980 a new groundwater law which replaces reasonable use with an active management program that restricts uses in the largest consumption areas.

The water-rich Eastern states are looking hardest at existing institutional systems for water management. The effectiveness of the established riparian/common law system of water rights, which allows reasonable use by adjoining landowners, is coming into question. Concerns for current and potential water shortages, the costs of developing new sources and delivery systems, and proposals for interbasin transfers have resulted in a number of state initiatives to review state water systems and to establish greater oversight and management water uses.

At least 11 states now put a permit system on top of the surface-water riparian system by requiring prior authorization for special uses.[8] North Carolina has established "capacity use areas" and regulates the largest groundwater and surface water users in these areas. Connecticut continues to develop a strong groundwater quality management program with development of a statewide water management plan based upon the mapping and water quality classification of ground and surface water. New Jersey in 1981 adopted legislation requiring large-use withdrawal permits. It completed a state water master plan, which calls for legislative action to change the relationship among all authorities, agencies and water companies dealing with water resources. The master plan deals with water supply sources, distribution systems and protection of recharge aquifers through permit requirements on waste disposal sites and discharges to groundwater. In response to supply problems aggravated by the 1980 drought, New Jersey and Pennsylvania authorized bond authority ($350 and $300 million respectively) to finance water resource projects.

A number of states have begun the difficult task of assessing existing state water law and management systems. Virginia continued its extensive examination of water law and systems governing ground and surface water management and interbasin transfers. In Pennsylvania, a comprehensive water management code was introduced in the 1981 legislative session, providing for a state water plan, reform of the public water supply allocation program, establishment of a protected area program and a state water resources emergency plan. Arkansas, Connecticut, Florida, Illinois, South Carolina and Wisconsin were among other states initiating reviews of state water law or state plans for water resources.

Interstate Cooperation. In 1981, many states began a new experience in regional water resources planning and management. With the demise of the six state-federal Title II river basin commissions authorized by the Water Resources Planning Act of 1965, the member states continued interstate coordination in water resources management.* Supported by carryover federal funds, the states reorganized as non-profit organizations (Missouri Basin States Associations), associations of states (Ohio River Basin Commission, Upper Mississippi River Basin Commission, Pacific Northwest River Basin Commission), and as adjuncts to existing multistate organizations (Great Lakes Commission, New England Governors' Conference).

Originally designed to coordinate state and federal plans for the development of water and related land resources and to study regional water resource problems, the new organizations will take on new roles. Federal agencies are no longer members, but states express interest in informal coordination with federal agencies. The states view these state associations as a means to coordinate and cooperate informally on interstate concerns and to develop and promote positions on water resource issues of interest to the region. Communication and cooperation on issues of mutual interest replace planning, research and interstate programs. None of the new organizations have authority to implement or enforce policies

---

*The Title II Commissions include the New England, Ohio, Great Lakes, Missouri, Upper Mississippi and Pacific Northwest River Basin Commissions. Unaffected by the executive order were the Delaware and Susquehanna interstate compact commissions.

or programs or to allocate water among the states. The challenge facing each organization is to develop a program which will serve the member states and win their continued support.

Coastal Zone Management

In response to the need for balancing preservation and development in the nation's coastal areas, Congress passed in 1972 and amended in 1976 the Coastal Zone Management Act (CZMA). The act authorized a federal grant-in-aid program to be administered by the National Oceanic and Atmospheric Administration's (NOAA) Office of Coastal Zone Management (OCZM). In 1980, Congress further amended the act and reauthorized the program through 1985.

The act provides financial and technical assistance to coastal states to prepare and implement their coastal management programs (Section 306). In addition, the act provides grants, loans and loan guarantees to help communities plan for services and public facilities to accommodate growth caused by energy development (Section 308) and assists states in the preservation and management of valuable estuarine sanctuaries (Section 315). Between 1974 and September 1979, $70 million was distributed to the 35 CZM states and territories to assist in developing coastal management programs. As development grants were phased out and implementation grants phased in, Congress made $32.72 million available in grants during fiscal 1980 and $36.44 million in fiscal 1981. Congress voted to make $33 million available for coastal zone management for the next three years beginning in fiscal 1982.

State management programs must respond to the policy objectives of the act including protection of valuable natural coastal resources, better management of development in coastal areas, enhanced recreational access to the coasts and improved coordination and simplification of government decision-making. With the approval of the Florida Coastal Management Program on September 24, 1981, 83,046 miles or 87 percent of the nation's shorelines are now managed by 25 states under the CZMA.

The work undertaken by states varies greatly and reflects differing degrees of public concern about coastal management problems. Many states, some without federal program approval, have new or strengthened regulations designed to protect critical coastal resources. To date, 25 states, the Virgin Islands and Puerto Rico have federal approval for their coastal management plans and are receiving implementation grants on a cost-sharing basis. New York expects program approval sometime in 1982.

States are providing an increasing level of protection to crucial resource areas. Many of these initiatives have been in direct response to CZMA requirements. Thirty-five of the eligible states and territories have either adopted new statutes and regulations protecting wetlands or improved implementation of existing laws as part of state coastal zone management programs. Because wetlands are prime floral and faunal habitats, most wetlands statutes provide habitat protection as well. In addition, 29 states have special management programs that deal with unique plant and animal species protection.

States have already made considerable progress in providing public access to the coast. Twelve states now mandate shoreline access as a condition for permits to build new structures in the coastal zone. Seventeen jurisdictions have open beach laws that provide the public with the right to use all beaches within the state's defined "beach" boundaries.

Protecting crucial resources requires proper management of coastal development. Federal and state agencies have for some time been particularly concerned about controlling development in hazardous areas. Twenty-four jurisdictions control development in erosion-prone shoreline areas, primarily through setback requirements or beach and dune preservation laws. Many states have also sought better floodplain management by coordinating coastal zone program requirements with those of the National Flood Insurance Program. Fourteen states currently provide some form of protection of barrier islands. The 1981 Omnibus Reconciliation Act prohibits federal flood insurance on undeveloped barrier islands and beaches after October 1, 1983. In addition a proposed barrier islands bill, supported by the Department of the Interior, would further prohibit federal expenditures that foster commercial and residential growth on undeveloped barrier islands and beaches.

Regulation of certain economically important but potentially environmentally damaging activities is also a part of coastal management. Exploiting valuable offshore mineral reserves—sand and gravel, and oil and gas—can threaten other coastal resources. Twenty-eight jurisdictions have measures regulating offshore sand and gravel minining and/or oil and gas extraction.

Problems with siting of energy facilities in the coastal zone have focused attention on the many land-use conflicts whose resolution is delayed in the absence of coordinated management. Coordinated and effective review of proposed energy facilities requires effective state as well as federal siting procedures. Twenty-five jurisdictions have adopted programs to improve siting procedures. These programs include expedited permit processing, advance industrial site designations, advance purchase programs and state preemption of local decisions in siting energy facilities in the coastal zone. In addition, amendments to the CZMA have provided funds for states to alleviate the impact of new energy facilities. The Coastal Energy Impact Program (CEIP), added to the CZMA by amendments in 1976, gives federal assistance to coastal states and local governments to meet community and environmental needs resulting from coastal energy development. The Outer Continental Shelf Lands Act Amendments of 1978 significantly amended the CEIP. Whereas the original program emphasized loans from a revolving fund, the amendments provided a much larger amount for grants—$200 million a year. In 1981, the CEIP funded over 200 projects and expended $29 million in grants and loans. Among the programs receiving CEIP financing were Massachusetts' oil spill program, the purchase and development of recreational parks in South Carolina, the development of state policy regarding 16 Outer Continental Shelf (OCS) lease sales in Alaska and energy facility planning in Maine.

The sanctuary programs added six new sanctuaries during fiscal 1981, bringing the total of marine sanctuaries to six.[9] The National Estuarine Program now boasts 12 sanctuaries with the addition of the Tijuana River area in California, Jobos Bay in Puerto Rico and two sites in Chesapeake Bay, Maryland.[10]

Outer Continental Shelf. The continental shelf is a broad, gently sloping area extending from the shore to the shelf edge or "continental slope." The federal government generally owns the portion of the OCS beyond the states' three-mile jurisdictional limit, with rights to offshore oil and gas development beyond the three-mile mark obtainable under a lease from the U.S. Department of the Interior (DOI). Before issuing a lease, DOI solicits information from the oil industry and from affected states concerning the size of the area to be offered for lease and the environmental, social and economic costs and benefits of such a lease sale. The process involves 11 steps that take place over two to three years. However, the recent DOI plan to lease 29 tracts in California's offshore waters, previously removed by the former administration for environmental reasons, has challenged the states' role in the OCS decision-making process. California, concerned that environmental dangers associated with leasing in the four northern basins of lease sale number 53 significantly outweigh the potential for oil and gas recovery, sued DOI for removal of the tracts. The state was joined in its suit by several environmental groups. An injunction was granted against the sale of the tracts, with a ruling that the DOI violated the provisions of the Outer Continental Shelf Lands Act which gave a directly affected state the power to prevent offshore drilling found to be inconsistent with the state's federally approved coastal zone management program. The Federal Consistency Regulations of CZMA (Section 307[c][1]) had been challenged by the states and were withdrawn pending a new definition. Specifically at issue is the question of whether OCS lease sales are activities which "directly affect" the coastal zone.

Air Quality*

After almost 30 years of uneven state and federal efforts to improve air quality, Congress passed the Clean Air Act in 1970, establishing a dominant federal role in air quality control. The act provided states and localities with primary responsibility for developing and implementing plans, programs, standards and regulatory programs to control air pollution. The Clean Air Act of 1970, as amended in 1977, expired September 30, 1981. Changes made in the requirements of the very complex act will affect all the states as air quality considerations involve trade-offs between environmental protection, energy production and economic development.

One of the chief instruments of the Clean Air Act and its 1977 Amendments are the National Ambient Air Quality Standards (NAAQS), which establish the permissible level of regulated pollutants. In areas where emission levels exceed NAAQS for one or more pollutants, states must develop and implement a federally approved State Implementation Plan (SIP). For areas that currently meet the NAAQS, air quality is to be protected by the Prevention of Significant Deterioration (PSD) program.

A number of issues face Congress in the reauthorization of the Clean Air Act. These include the SIP process, mobile sources, PSD requirements, long-range transport of pollutants, and state-federal roles.

State Implementation Plans. Attainment and maintenance of air quality standards are primary responsibilities of the states. The CAA mandated that each state submit a SIP to the Environmental Protection Agency (EPA) for its approval. The plan must set forth the state's strategy for attaining and maintaining the NAAQS. As of September 2, 1980, all 50 states and Washington, D.C., whose plans were due July 1, 1979, had officially submitted their SIPs.

In 1981, EPA formally proposed easing federal air pollution regulations. The proposal would incorporate the "bubble" concept by redefining a pollution source. Under the rewritten regulations, a total plant, factory or refinery complex would be considered a "pollution source" rather than individual emission source within the complex. Specific pollutants could increase within the facility as long as total pollution from the entire complex does not. Construction or modification of plants in non-attainment areas would be allowed as long as the pollution emitted from the entire area was not made significantly worse.

Inspection and Maintenance. Responsibilities for standard-setting, implementation and enforcement of the mobile sources program are centralized in the EPA. States have no responsibilities under the program with the exception of inspection and maintenance (I/M) programs for vehicles. The I/M programs are required under the act in areas which cannot

---

*This section was modified from the "Clean Air Reporter," a continuing series appearing in *State Government News.*

attain the automotive exhaust emission standards by the end of 1982. States can receive extensions to 1987 if they establish an annual exhaust emission test program for autos in the non-attainment areas. States failing to enact such I/M programs are subject to EPA-imposed sanctions which include withdrawal of federal highway funds and federal grants for sewage treatment plants and air pollution control, as well as bans on new industrial construction. At least 29 states have passed or are considering enactment of I/M programs, but the program remains controversial.

Several states have questioned the air quality benefits derived from I/M programs, and are not confident that the potential benefits have any correlation to the costs incurred in operating the programs. Many states feel they have little say in how the programs are implemented and little or no choice in whether to enact the programs. Some officials view the I/M programs as an inequitable policy enforcement tool and argue that a more appropriate target for enforcement of emission standards would be at the point of production.

California and Kentucky are two states in which EPA has initiated sanctions for failure to enact I/M programs. Because California failed to meet EPA's deadline for the inspection and maintenance program, EPA in late 1980 froze $850 million in federal funds. Colorado faced similar sanctions—the withholding of $300 million in federal highway and sewer monies—but the freeze was lifted in May 1980 when the legislature approved a plan acceptable to EPA.

Prevention of Significant Deterioration. The most complex feature of the Clean Air Act of 1970 is the Prevention of Significant Deterioration (PSD) program, which provides for control technology and a complicated classification system to limit pollution increments in areas meeting national ambient air quality standards.

Among the controversial issues are how to streamline PSD procedures, selection of technology-based requirements for Best Available Control Technology (BACT), and modeling and monitoring requirements.

At issue in the West, where the PSD program is alleged to restrain energy development, is extension of strict air quality protection afforded federal Class I areas (international parks, certain national parks and wilderness areas) beyond the boundaries of those areas.

In the 11 Western states, more than 140 million acres have special land use classifications which control development. The classifications include lands in the National Park System, National Forest System, Indian reservations, National Wildlife Refuges, military reservations, and the Bureau of Land Management Wilderness System.

The Four Corners region of Arizona, Colorado, New Mexico and Utah exemplifies the competing energy and environmental values and difficult implementation problems at issue in the Clean Air Act renewal. The region, which covers 145,000 square miles, is sparsely populated, and its air is the cleanest in the United States, with visibility exceeding 100 miles in some places. No other part of the country contains so many primitive and wilderness areas, national parks, monuments and forests, but beneath these vistas lie vast reserves of oil, oil shale, uranium, natural gas and high-quality, low-sulfur coal.

The Four Corners region is adjacent to or contains 14 mandatory Class I areas. Not only do PSD provisions apply, but so do visibility protection regulations. Visibility is affected by plume blight, regional haze and layered discoloration. The regulations protect "integral vistas"—defined as views from within a mandatory Class I area that extend beyond its boundaries and which are "important to the visitor's experience of the area or the fundamental purpose for which the area was designated and preserved." Integral vistas often cover more than 50 miles.

Implementation of the Clean Air Act in this region raises difficult political questions. The Four Corners region comprises almost 40 counties. Twelve Indian tribes and five major federal agencies have jurisdiction over various portions of the land. The region's low population and high proportion of federally owned land means that local development decisions may be subordinated to national ones.

Long-Range Transport. * In recent years, air pollutants transported long distances from emitting sources have been recognized to have effects that are not mitigated adequately by air quality standards in the vicinity of the emitting source. The pollution control programs established under the Clean Air Act were designed primarily to solve ground-level air quality problems caused by high ambient concentrations relatively near the pollution sources. Those programs generally have required only limited consideration of effects of emissions dispersed into areas far downwind. However, the long-range transport and chemical transformation of some air pollutants cause emissions to have important effects much farther from the source than was previously believed.

Several problems have been found to be associated with long-range pollutant transport. Among the most serious are acid deposition (including acid rain and dry deposition of acid), the deterioration of visibility on a regional scale, the transport of ozone and ozone precursors between neighboring areas, and the increasing amount of interstate air pollution. All of these effects can hinder efforts to improve air quality through existing state and local regulatory programs.

Acid Rain. The long-range transport of air pollutants, particularly of pollutants contributing to acid deposition, has become an interstate, interregional and international concern. Approximately one-half of the sulfur emissions deposited in Eastern Canada purportedly originate in the United States' Ohio Valley. Acid deposition in the Sierra Nevadas is blamed on emissions from the urban areas of Los Angeles and San Francisco; those affecting the western slope of the Colorado Rockies are thought to be produced by the coal-powered generating plants in the Four Corners region. In August 1979, President Carter commissioned a 10-year, $10 million federal study by the Acid Rain Coordination Committee into the causes and effects of acid rain. Congress created an Acid Precipitation Task Force in 1980.

The Clean Air Act does not directly address the problem of acid rain. Section 126 of the act does empower EPA to disapprove a State Implementation Plan if it allows a source within a state to prevent or interfere with the attainment or maintenance of NAAQS in another state. Two problems undermine the effectiveness of the present statute. First, because ambient air quality is measured close to the ground in areas near the source, the true levels of emissions are not always detected. Second, the possibility of long-range transport makes identification of the source difficult.

The acid rain issue affects Midwestern states in two ways. Acid rain affects Midwestern soil and lakes, while other states blame the industrialized Midwestern cities for their acid rain problem. New York, Pennsylvania and Maine recently petitioned EPA under Section 126 of the act that 38 Midwestern sources contribute heavily to pollution levels in those states. This issue has put the urban industrial Midwestern interests at odds both with Eastern states and with agricultural interests within the region.

Positions as to what should be done about acid rain range from amending the Clean Air Act so as to require national standards to assertions that too little is known to attempt

---

*Adapted from *To Breathe Clean Air*, National Commission on Air Quality, March 1981.

regulation. The National Commission on Air Quality, which recently completed its three-year independent study of the Clean Air Act, agreed that Congress should continue to provide adequate funds for acid rain research and a national atmospheric deposition monitoring program. More importantly, the commission recommended that the interstate abatement provisions of the act be strengthened to reduce emissions in one state that affect other states, that Congress consider regional uses of secondary ambient air quality standards to get at the acid rain problem, and that existing sulfur dioxide emissions limitations contained in State Implementation Plans not be relaxed unless undue economic or other hardships would result.

State-Federal Roles. As Congress began the difficult task of reauthorizing the Clean Air Act in 1981, states expressed concerns over the appropriate balance of state and federal responsibilities in implementing and funding an essentially national program.

The primary responsibility for carrying out the Clean Air Act falls on state air pollution control agencies. With the increased emphasis on enforcement in the 1977 amendments and EPA's increased role, many states feel there is too much duplication of effort and even federal preemption of state prerogatives. States want a clear delineation of roles. Issues include how much discretion states have in developing a SIP within the federal framework, revising specific elements of an approved SIP and determining an effective enforcement and compliance strategy. Another major issue facing the states with respect to the review of the Clean Air Act is the level of funding provided, especially Section 105 program management funds. EPA program management grants (Section 105) represent from 20 percent (for smaller states) to 60 percent (for larger states) of state and local air control agencies' budgets. Frustration with federal requirements and the level of federal funding prompted the Idaho Legislature to end funds for the air program in 1981. As a result, responsibility for administering the air program returned to EPA until the legislature appropriated funds in 1982 for continued state support. States are also concerned with possible changes in assistance provided through the assigning of personnel to states under the Intergovernmental Personnel Act and the provision of technical assistance and specialized equipment.

Waste Management

Begining with the enactment of the Solid Waste Disposal Act and continuing with the Resource Recovery Act of 1970 and the Resource Conservation and Recovery Act (RCRA), Congress has recognized the need to develop and encourage the use of better systems for the disposal of solid and hazardous wastes. The national program encourages states to implement solid waste, resource recovery, resource conservation and hazardous waste programs through a cooperative effort among state, federal, substate and private enterprise.

Solid Waste/Resource Recovery. Subtitle D of the RCRA established a broad-based national program to improve solid waste management through the development of state and regional solid waste management plans. The act offered federal financial assistance to states interested in developing and implementing a solid waste management plan. The state plans, under federal guidelines, identify respective responsibilities of local, state and regional authorities, encourage resource recovery and conservation and the application and enforcement of environmentally sound disposal practices. By November 16, 1981, 34 states had submitted their adopted state plans to EPA for approval. One state plan, Iowa's, has received federal approval. Thirteen other states and four U.S. territories are in the process of developing or adopting a state plan, with one state, New Mexico, choosing not to participate under the Subtitle D program.

Another major element of RCRA's Subtitle D program is the open dump inventory. The inventory is designed to inform Congress and the public of the extent of the open dump problem and also provide states with a listing of problem sites that need correction. The first national listing in 1981 identified 1,029 existing dumps.

Although the federal government has, under RCRA, provided grants to states for their solid waste management programs, federal support has been reduced from $14 million in fiscal 1980 to $8 million in fiscal 1981. All federal Subtitle D funds have been eliminated for fiscal 1982. Many of these cutbacks can be attributed to the shifting of federal and state programs from solid waste to hazardous waste management. This will confront many state solid waste programs with severe financial problems. As a result, some states will assume a minimum level of effort and activity in their solid waste management programs. Many other states are seeking increased legislative appropriations as an alternative source of program funds. Other funding sources now under consideration in several states are license or permit fees, disposal surcharges and taxes, inspection fees and increased fines.

States which have implemented quasi-public solid waste/resource recovery authorities have been affected less by the loss of federal funds. The solid waste facilities are generally self-supporting through service charges and user fees. Regional or multi-county solid waste authorities exist in Texas, Georgia and Vermont. State authorities exist in Louisiana, Connecticut, Puerto Rico, Delaware, Rhode Island and Wisconsin. Other states, such as New York, Maryland and Ohio, have state authorities whose scope also encompasses other areas of environmental concern. Many of the authorities are also active in resource recovery facility development.

Although resource recovery is not a new idea, technological advances and the rising costs of land disposal have made the concept economically feasible. Faced with increasing environmental, economic and energy pressures, states are considering resource recovery as one of today's most workable solutions to the high costs and physical limitations of landfills and the establishment of new open dump sites.

State resource recovery efforts range from high technology recovery projects to much simpler source separation and waste reduction and waste exchange programs. Source separation first become popular in the 1970s, and according to EPA, there are now over 1,000 community recycling centers. One of the most successful source separation programs, Arizona's Beverage Industry Recycling Program (BIRP), was established in 1971 and now operates 14 centers around the state. Similar Beverage Industry Recycling Programs now operate in New Mexico, Maryland and Kentucky. Another litter reduction program which has encountered wide success in over 200 communities is the Clean Community System, a program which involves teaching the public not to litter. Other state approaches to promote and encourage recycling include the development of state recycling associations in Nebraska and Colorado and the popular use of state and regional waste exchanges. The general purpose of a waste exchange is to put waste users in touch with waste producers in order to minimize disposal expense and recover as much value from waste as possible. Twenty-three states currently participate in some form of state or regional waste exchange.

Many of these state litter reduction efforts were alternatives to a mandatory beverage container deposit law. The first deposit law was enacted by Oregon in 1972. As of November 19, 1981, nine states—Connecticut, Delaware, Iowa, Maine, Michigan, Oregon, Rhode Island, Vermont and Massachusetts—had passed mandatory deposit laws. Delaware's bottle bill has not yet gone into effect pending appropriations, and the Virgin Islands has similar legislation pending. Two states, Nebraska and Washington, have enacted legislation which levies a tax on litter-prone goods. The revenue generated from the tax is used for litter programs and grants to local communities developing recycling programs. California and Connecticut repealed similar legislation, and Connecticut allowed its litter material tax to expire.

Additional state resource recovery efforts include tax incentives and loan and grant programs. North Carolina provides tax incentives to individuals or corporations who purchase resource recovery or recycling equipment or construct resource recovery facilities. Oregon offers tax credits, 5 percent per year for 10 years, to eligible resource recovery projects. Connecticut, Washington, Nebraska, Pennsylvania, Minnesota, California and New Jersey all provide some form of loan or grant for resource recovery activities, including city and county waste-to-energy systems. According to the American Iron and Steel Institute, there are over 100 cities and counties operating, building or developing waste-to-energy facilities. Although some of these facilities have been eligible for state grants and loans, a majority have been financed by public means, usually tax-emempt, long-term bonds. The Connecticut Solid Waste/Resource Recovery Authority has four waste-to-energy projects in various stages of development. Delaware, Rhode Island, Louisiana and Wisconsin authorities are also in the process of constructing or developing city and regional systems. Oregon, Tennessee, Washington, Illinois, New Jersey, New York, Ohio and Maine provide state financial assistance for the construction and operation of resource recovery facilities through the issuance of bonds.

Although a few state resource recovery programs are self-supporting, most have relied on federal financial support ($4 million in 1981). Recent cutbacks have also eliminated federal funding for state resource recovery programs for fiscal 1982. In light of this, many states are considering funding alternatives for their resource recovery programs. Maine recently passed a bond issue in support of resource recovery activities and facility development, while West Virginia and the Virgin Islands are exploring bonding alternatives. Many states are prepared to request additional state legislative appropriations for program funding. New Jersey recently passed a landfill tax which will be used to develop, over a long period, a $30 million resource recovery program. Other states are considering similar taxes and fees in an effort to protect and preserve their resource recovery programs.

Hazardous Wastes. Under Subtitle C of the RCRA, EPA was directed to establish a national program to regulate hazardous wastes from the "cradle to grave." EPA approves state hazardous waste management (HWM) programs in two phases. Phase I authorization gives states the right to control transportation and generation of hazardous wastes within their borders and to regulate existing Treatment, Storage and Disposal (TSD) facilities. Phase II authorization grants states the authority to issue permits to hazardous waste facilities. As of January 26, 1982, 28 states had received EPA authorization for Phase I of their hazardous waste management programs, and five states had applied for final authorization. Where states have not established HWM programs, or the programs do not meet federal standards, EPA is required to assume regulatory control. Federal monies were made available to encourage state participation. Federal funding for state programs under Subtitle C of RCRA rose from $30 million in fiscal 1981 to $41.7 million in fiscal 1982.

States seeking Phase I interim authorization have incorporated, with slight modification, EPA's identification standards of hazardous wastes into their state's HWM program (at least eight states have indicated their substances list is more stringent than the federal list). Other states, such as Washington and California, have adopted an alternative approach that defines hazardous wastes on the basis of "degree of hazard" by specifying, in their respective programs, different standards of control for different hazardous wastes. EPA has begun to analyze whether the hazardous waste regulations under RCRA can be adjusted to control specific wastes based on waste type, the usual management technology, and the surrounding environment. The EPA "degree of hazard" analysis is expected in 1982.

Another major element of Phase I authorization is the development of a manifest system for tracking a waste shipment to its destination. Currently, 35 states provide a manifest system in their HWM programs. EPA plans to make final, by April 1982, a prescribed, uniform manifest form to achieve standardization and efficiency in the manifest system. The New England states were the first to implement a regional manifest system in 1980 to provide uniformity and improve the overall management of hazardous wastes between the states. This regional manifest has allowed states in the New England region to track shipments of waste through their states.

The Phase I interim status regulations also require creation of closure and postclosure plans as well as financial responsibilities. EPA is now considering a proposal to suspend permanently federal requirements for liability insurance and has deferred the financial regulations effective date to April 13, 1982, pending a decision. A majority of the states require proof of financial responsibility and hold an owner or operator of an HWM facility liable for damages. However, since some state statutes, as in Texas and Massachusetts, have incorporated RCRA's financial regulations by reference, their status is also pending the EPA decision.

In January 1981, Phase I regulations were supplemented by more technical Phase II standards. Phase II standards include technical and environmental performance criteria designated to guide EPA in issuing permits. Of the five states seeking Phase II authorization to issue permits for storage and treatment facilities and incinerators, Texas and Georgia are also seeking authority to write land disposal permits although EPA regulations do not currently allow for that.

Phase III standards or final authorization will resolve complex technical issues and establish detailed requirements for design, construction and operation of facilities. For states seeking final authorization, RCRA regulations require the administration of a strict enforcement program. It generally includes within a compliance evaluation program reports and notices, an independent inspection and surveillance program, entry, inspection and monitoring authority, and proper evidence gathering procedures. Most states provide for civil and criminal fines; however, many states have moved toward classifying hazardous waste violations as felonies. Twenty states have amended their statutes to provide for felony status.

In addition to meeting the minimum requirements under Subtitle C of RCRA, many states are also active in facility siting, comprehensive planning and emergency response. One of the major issues related to siting is permitting authority. In most states, an existing department issues the permit; however, in several cases, a state board, consisting often of state agency heads, issues the permit. Five states have developed a state siting board specifically for hazardous waste facilities. The way siting legislation deals with local governments varies significantly among the states. Seventeen states provide state preemption of local zoning ordinances while eight states specifically give local governing bodies approval over hazardous waste land disposal facilities. In some cases, states provide for mediation and arbitration to resolve siting conflicts. Florida, for example, has an appeals procedure set up for dealing with conflicts.

Fourteen states currently provide for public involvement in the ownership and operation of hazardous waste facilities. Virginia, under its HWM program, allows the state to own and operate an HWM facility, while states such as Georgia and Texas have established quasi-public state authorities to own, operate and lease HWM facilities.

Several states are also active in comprehensive planning in order to assess and evaluate hazardous waste issues and problems and to develop, in general, state siting, resource recovery, funding policies and program strategies. A majority of the states have undertaken waste surveys to determine the scope of the hazardous waste problem.

Although RCRA and additional state actions have made great progress in establishing comprehensive safeguards against the release of hazardous wastes into the environment, they have not dealt with the problems of past waste disposal practices. Many inactive and abandoned hazardous waste disposal sites have proven to be serious threats to public health and the environment.

In December 1980, Congress enacted the Comprehensive Environmental Response, Compensation and Liability Act (CERCLA). This law, known as Superfund, created a five-year, $1.6 billion fund which will be used to clean up about 400 sites nationwide. The fund will be paid for by a tax on generators (87.5 percent) and federal appropriations (12.5 percent). EPA has identified 115 of the worst dump sites and targeted the locations for clean-up under Superfund. The sites are located in 45 states and territories, with 16 sites in Florida, 12 in New Jersey, and eight in New York and Pennsylvania. Twenty-six states and territories have one site on the list.

Thirty states have some type of state spill or trust fund to provide funding for an assortment of hazardous waste management activities. A major concern to some states is whether the federal Superfund preempts states' collection of fees and taxes to support state funds. New Jersey's spill compensation and control fund surcharge collection is currently being challenged by five petrochemical companies. The outcome of the New Jersey case leaves the legal status of many state funds in question. Florida has reacted by adding language to its state fund indicating that it will not be used in a manner inconsistent with CERCLA. State laws authorizing the establishment of trust funds often spell out the funding source. California recently enacted Superfund legislation in response to a 1980 state survey which identified 67 hazardous waste sites in need of clean-up. The $100 million fund, to be collected over the next 10 years, will be supported entirely on industry-paid fees on hazardous waste disposal. Several states can activate their funds to provide for emergency response and clean-up. Other funds, such as Kentucky's and Massachusetts', have been set up to also encourage volume reduction and alternatives to land disposal of hazardous wastes.

Although most states encourage the recycling of all wastes and many require alternatives to be considered before land disposal, few actually provide incentives to recycle hazardous wastes. Utah, Montana, South Carolina, Washington and Michigan exempt or partially exempt generators from regulation under the state hazardous waste management program if the wastes are recycled. Florida and Missouri provide fee and tax exemptions for generators who recycle. Oregon provides a 100 percent tax credit on capital costs for projects recovering usable material or energy from wastes, and New Jersey funds low-interest, state-subsidized loans for equipment and other capital expenditures related to recycling residentially generated waste oils. New Jersey municipalities which recycle residential waste oils receive a separate state rebate derived from a tax on landfillls. Many states have also become involved in state and regional solid and hazardous waste exchanges in an effort to recycle wastes. The New York Waste Exchange Law authorized the New York State Environmental Facilities Corporation (a public benefit corporation) to study and establish a statewide effort in order to reduce the quantities of hazardous wastes that need ultimate disposal.

Other state recycling efforts include research and development. Illinois has earmarked 25 percent of its Hazardous Waste Fund to be used for research in order to reduce, recycle or detoxify hazardous wastes in the state, and Oklahoma has set up a separate Resource Recovery Division to research and encourage recycling.

Low-Level Nuclear Waste. Before 1954, the management and use of atomic energy and radioactive materials were largely confined to the federal government; however, the Atomic Energy Act of 1954 enabled private entities to operate nuclear facilities and use radioactive materials. Although the Atomic Energy Commission (AEC) was charged to carry out the regulations of the act, many states voiced concern over public health and safety and expressed an interest in state regulation of atomic energy and radioactive materials. In response to the states' concern, Section 274 of the Atomic Energy Act was passed in 1959 and gave a governor the right to enter into an agreement program with the AEC and later the Nuclear Regulatory Commission (NRC) and to assume certain regulatory authority over radioactive by-products, source materials and small quantities of special nuclear materials. Low-level waste would fall under the regulatory purview of the states participating in the program (low-level wastes are defined as industrial, medical or research waste contaminated with small amounts of radioactive material). To join the program, a state is required to pass enabling legislation authorizing the governor to enter into such an agreement and have a state radiation control program compatible with regulations and standards set by the NRC.

Between 1962 and 1971, six commercial low-level waste burial sites opened: Maxey Flats, Kentucky; West Valley, New York; Sheffield, Illinois; Barnewell, South Carolina; Richland, Washington; and Beatty, Nevada. Government facilities which generate and dispose of low-level waste on site are: Oak Ridge National Laboratory, Tennessee; Los Alamos National Laboratory, New Mexico; Idaho National Engineering Laboratory; Hanford Reservation, Washington; and Savannah River Plan, South Carolina. There are also government disposal facilities in Texas, New Mexico, Ohio, New York, Kentucky, Tennessee and Missouri.

Under the state agreements with the NRC, state authorities have regulated five of the six disposal sites under the federal-state agreement program. As of November 15, 1981, 26 states had agreement status and 18 others had enabling legislation. The non-agreement states have also developed radiation control programs in an effort to protect the public health and safety of their citizens, regarding those radiation sources which are not controlled by the federal government. By 1979, three of the six low-level waste commercial sites had closed. The three states in which commercial facilities are currently operating—Nevada, South Carolina and Washington—have since exerted considerable pressure on the states which send waste to their respective commercial sites by limiting the types and amounts of out-of-state wastes to be acccepted. Furthermore, over the past five years, at least 25 states have placed restrictions on the disposal of radioactive wastes within their borders.

Recognizing the nation's needs for developing additional low-level disposal sites, Congress passed the Low-Level Radioactive Waste Policy Act of 1980. Under the act, states are responsible for providing low-level radioactive waste disposal capacity for wastes generated in their states, except for wastes generated by the military or federal research and development activities. To carry that responsibility, the act authorizes states to enter into regional compacts to establish and operate regional disposal facilities for low-level radioactive wastes.

To date, more than 20 states have completed or are conducting studies of their low-level waste management requirements. During 1981, groups of states in each region of the country met to discuss regional management of low-level wastes. The Northwestern states are the first to seek federal approval of a regional low-level waste compact.

The Southern states expected to have a draft low-level waste compact ready for submission to state legislatures by January 1982. Other meetings concerning the regional siting of low-level facilities have been held in the Midwest and New England.

Other areas of state regulation of low-level materials include transportation and emergency response. While some states have left radioactive material transportation regulation to the federal government, others have been active in providing regulatory authority in areas such as pre-notification, financial responsibility, and surveillance, monitoring and inspection. Twenty states have adopted pre-notification requirements, 12 states have defined financial responsibility limits of transporters, and 24 states have enacted some form of transporter monitoring, surveillance and inspection program. The most frequent transportation actions by states are the adoption of federal Department of Transportation regulations and requiring some form of registration, fee payment, permit or license.

The Three Mile Island incident and recent experiences of improper disposal and storage of hazardous wastes at Love Canal (New York) and the Valley of the Drums (Kentucky) accelerated state concern regarding emergency response planning. Many state emergency response programs are directed at nuclear reactor incidents, but several states have developed or expanded their emergency response to consider all radioactive and hazardous materials incidents. Currently, 45 states provide some kind of state emergency response program.

Organizational and Administrative Reform

Efficient administration and management of environmental programs has gained increased state attention in recent years. As the number of federal, state and local laws and regulations governing environmental protection increases, duplication and conflict make good management difficult if not impossible. Neither state officials nor those subject to regulations can easily determine what is required and how effectively the environment is being protected. The pressure for regulatory reform and tight state budgets fuel state efforts to streamline regulatory and administrative programs. These efforts include both organizational and administrative changes.

Reorganization. The major initiative to reorganize state programs for environmental protection and resource management came in the early 1970s. In many states, environmental protection agencies and environmental superagencies took over responsibility for environmental programs from health departments. In the latter half of the decade, the trend slowed as states fine-tuned earlier reorganizations. Through reorganization and realignments within environmental programs, states sought an organizational structure for effective program management. By 1981, 12 states had environmental protection agencies, while 19 had created an environmental superagency. In 15 states, environmental protection programs remained in state health departments. Louisiana, Mississippi, Rhode Island and South Dakota most recently created superagencies, while Nevada and New Hampshire reorganized as environmental protection agencies. New Mexico went against the tide, moving its program back into the health department.

Formal reorganization of environmental programs among state agencies is only one state effort at effective management. Through internal realignment, many related programs were consolidated, and duties and responsibilities were expanded and upgraded. Internal realignments occurred in 25 states, with the greatest number in solid and hazardous waste programs. Responsibilities for solid waste were transferred from health programs to natural resources programs or newly created in health or natural resources programs in 14 states. The other major internal realignment occurred in water resources. Alabama, Hawaii, Kentucky and Kansas consolidated water quality and quantity into one division.

Administrative Reform. As structural reorganization of the 1970s takes effect, state officials anticipate that improved administrative procedures will provide additional efficiencies in implementing regulatory programs. The highly visible one-stop permit approach instituted in Washington has given way to quiet internal efforts to streamline the permit review process. All states are currently trying to improve the management and administration of environmental permit programs. In some states, the effort is informal and relies on personal contacts; in others, highly structured and automated data information systems are being examined. States facing rapid growth, particularly in energy development, are most interested in reform of permit and licensing procedures.

One way to streamline permit reviews is consolidation, including pre-application conferences, permit coordination, deadlines for permit decisions, one-stop permitting, concurrent reviews and joint hearings, and consolidated applications. In some states with consolidated environmental protection or superagency organizations, coordinated review is more easily achieved on an informal basis. Designation of a permit coordinator to serve as a lead contact is fairly common. Alaska, Florida, Illinois, Michigan, Minnesota and New Jersey are among the states with a formal coordination procedure. Several states have instituted a form of one-stop permitting, including New York, Oregon, Pennsylvania (substate regional level) and Washington. Permit simplification is being examined by state task forces in Alabama, Hawaii, Maine, Massachusetts and New Mexico.

A second aid to more efficient management and administration of permits and licenses is permit-tracking systems. The purpose of such manual or automated monitoring and tracking of permit requirements and permit status is the development of early communication between the applicant and the agency, evaluation of the interrelated regulatory requirements, and early detection of management issues in permit administration. Kentucky, Pennsylvania and North Carolina are among several states investigating the feasibility of permit-tracking systems.

A third means to improve the management of environmental programs is the Joint Review Process (JRP). The process, pioneered by Colorado in 1978, has been adopted by Illinois, Tennessee and Utah for major energy developments. The JRP is designed to organize complex sets of federal, state and local regulatory requirements associated with major development. Through the formal but voluntary process, the various regulatory and administrative reviews can be identified and coordinated, and participation by industry and the public can occur in a timely manner. Colorado has continued to refine its process as it gains experience in working with six major energy projects.

Summary

States, chafing under federal requirements on standards and administration, have long argued for a greater state voice and flexibility in design and implementation of environmental programs. The expanded responsibilities thrust upon the states provide a test of their capability to plan, manage and finance environmental programs. States have the potential to assume an expanded role in environmental policy development and problem-solving.

They have demonstrated a capacity to deal with environmental and natural resource problems with realism and moderation. Many pioneered innovations later adopted for national use. With immediate knowledge of particular environmental problems, they can implement programs and target investments far more effectively than federal programs and agencies.

Less optimism can be voiced over states' capability to support environmental management activities at levels commensurate with federal programs. Even with savings through more efficient program administration, individual states are unlikely to have the financial resources to substitute for federal funds. Federal money has supported technical staff, planning and research activities, and basic environmental management programs. States have depended upon federal agencies and federally sponsored research for data gathering, issue analyses and technical assistance. Reductions in federal direct and indirect assistance, combined with revenue and spending limitations in the states, cast a note of uncertainty on the ease with which states can assume expanded responsibilities to manage and enforce environmental programs.

As the states take on expanded responsibilities for environmental programs, several issues continue to cloud the state-federal partnership. States remain concerned over terms and speed with which federal programs incorporating national objectives are being transferred. The prospective size and timing of reduced federal support create problems for an orderly transfer and stable management of programs. The degree of administrative flexibility and the access to new funding sources remain unknown. Redefining the federal-state partnership in environmental management will be a major task confronting the states in the upcoming years.

Notes

1. States without primacy include: Alaska, Arizona, Arkansas, Florida, Idaho, Kentucky, Louisiana, Maine, Massachusetts, New Hampshire, New Jersey, New Mexico, Oklahoma, Rhode Island, South Dakota, Texas, Utah.

2. Those without delegated authority for 205[g] include: Arkansas, Florida, Hawaii, Indiana, Kansas, Louisiana, New Mexico, Oregon and Virginia. California returned responsibility to EPA.

3. Association of State and Interstate Water Pollution Control Admnistrators. "Assessment of the National Water Quality Management Program." 1 (August 1981): ii-2.

4. U.S. Water Resources Council. *State of the States Water Resources Planning and Management, FY 1981 Update.* (Washington, D.C.: U.S. Water Resources Council, September 1981).

5. Idaho, Iowa, Maryland, Minnesota, Montana, Oklahoma, Oregon, Texas.

6. Arizona, Connecticut, Georgia, Kansas, Mississippi, Nevada, New York, Pennsylvania, Texas, Vermont, Virginia, West Virginia, Wisconsin.

7. Arkansas, California, Colorado, Hawaii, Massachusetts, Nebraska, South Carolina, Tennessee, Utah, Wyoming.

8. Delaware, Florida, Georgia, Iowa, Kentucky, Maryland, Minnesota, New Jersey, New York, North Carolina, Wisconsin.

9. Pt. Reyes-Farallon Islands, California; Gray's Reef, Georgia; Looe Key, Florida; U.S.S. Monitor, North Carolina; Channel Islands, California; Key Largo Coral Reef, Florida.

10. South Slough, Oregon; Sapelo Islands, Georgia; Waimanu, Hawaii; Old Women Creek, Ohio; Rookery Bay, Florida; Apalachicola River/Bay, Florida; Elkhorn Slough, California; Padella Bay, Washington; Narragansett Bay, Rhode Island.

Table 1
STATUS OF STATE WATER, MINING, AIR PRIMACY

State or other jurisdiction	Air PSD primacy	Water NPDES primacy	State pretreat-ment program	Drinking water primacy	Section 404 primacy	Surface mining Coal mining primacy
Alabama	F	★	★	★	...	R
Alaska	O	...	...	★	...	O
Arizona	(P,pdg,'82)	...	...	★	...	...
Arkansas	(F,pdg,'81-82)	...	...	★	...	X
California	...	★	...	★	...	...
Colorado	...	★	...	★	...	...
Connecticut	...	★	★	★	...	...
Delaware	F	★	...	★	...	...
Florida	P	...	...	★	...	...
Georgia	Fs	★	★	★	...	...
Hawaii	...	★	...	★	...	...
Idaho	...	...	...	★	...	...
Illinois	F	★	...	★	...	R
Indiana	F	★	...	...	...	Re
Iowa	pdg	★	★	RP	...	X
Kansas	...	★	...	★	...	X
Kentucky	F	...	...	★	...	X,D
Louisiana	P	...	...	★	...	X,C
Maine	Fs	...	...	★	...	X,D
Maryland	pdg.	★	...	★	...	X,D
Massachusetts	...	...	...	★	...	O,B
Michigan	F	★	...	★	...	O,A
Minnesota	F	★	★	★	...	...
Mississippi	F	★	...	★	...	X,C
Missouri	F	★	★	★	...	X
Montana	(P,pdg,'82)	★	...	★	...	X
Nebraska	...	★	...	★	...	...
Nevada	...	★	...	★	...	...
New Hampshire	...	...	...	★	...	...
New Jersey	...	...	...	★	...	...
New Mexico	(P,pdg,'82)	...	...	★	...	X
New York	...	★	pdg	★	...	...
North Carolina	P	★	...	★	...	...
North Dakota	Fs	★	...	★	...	X
Ohio	F	★	...	★	...	R
Oklahoma	P	...	...	★	...	X,E
Oregon	pdg	★	★	...	...	O,B
Pennsylvania	P	★	...	...	...	R
Rhode Island	...	...	...	★	...	O,A
South Carolina	F	★	...	★	...	...
South Dakota	...	...	...	...	...	...
Tennessee	F	★	...	★	...	R
Texas	P	...	...	★	...	X
Utah	P	...	...	★	...	X
Vermont	Fs	★	...	★	...	...
Virginia	F	★	...	★	...	Re
Washington	...	★	...	★	...	O
West Virginia	P	pdg	pdg	★	...	X,D
Wisconsin	P	★	★	★	...	...
Wyoming	Fs	★	...	...	...	X
Dist. of Col.	P	...	...	...	...	...
American Samoa	...	...	...	...	...	...
Guam	...	pdg	...	★	...	...
Puerto Rico	...	pdg	pdg	★	...	...

Key:
P—Partial delegation; does not write permits, does review and comment, writes SIP.
F—Full delegation; issues permits, not incorporated into SIP.
Fs—Full delegation; issues permits, incorporated into SIP.
★—Full primacy.
pdg—Pending
RP—Returned primacy to EPA.
O—State currently working on rules for program.
R—State expected to resubmit program to OSM for review and approval.
A—Submitted draft legislation to OSM for review.
B—Coal deposits never mined.
C—Not currently producing coal.
D—State injunction.
E—State legislature rescinded regulations, to repromulgate and resubmit to OSM for review and approval.
X—OSM awarded surface mining primacy.
Re—Resubmitted program to OSM for review and approval.
Air:
   PSD Primary—States which have been delegated full or partial authority to carry out the 1978 Prevention of Significant Deterioration Regulations of the Clean Air Act Amendments, 1977.

Water:
   NPDES(National Pollution Discharge Elimination System)
   Primacy—States which have been delegated authority to issue permits for the discharge of any pollutant into navigable waters under Section 402 of the Federal Water Pollution Control Act.
   State Pretreatment Program—States which have assumed responsibility in ensuring that industrial discharges into publicly owned treatment works meet national pretreatment standards promulgated under the Clean Water Act.
   Drinking Water Primacy—States which have assumed primary enforcement responsibility for drinking water programs under the Safe Drinking Water Act of 1977.
   Section 404 Primacy—States which have been delegated authority to administer their own individual and general permit program for the discharge of dredged or fill materials into navigable waters.
Mining:
   Surface Mining Primacy—States which have assumed authority for the administration, regulation and enforcement of surface mining operations under the Surface Mining Control and Reclamation Act.

Table 2
CLASSIFICATION OF STATE ENVIRONMENTAL ORGANIZATIONS

State or other jurisdiction	Date of re-organization	Health department	Little EPA	Environmental superagency	Partially consolidated or unconsolidated agency	Citizen environmental council/commission
Alabama		★				
Alaska	1971			★		
Arizona		★				★
Arkansas	1971		★			
California	1975				★	
Colorado		★				
Connecticut	1971			★		
Delaware	1970			★		
Florida	1969		★			
Georgia	1972			★		
Hawaii		★				★
Idaho	1972	★				
Illinois	1970		★			
Indiana		★				
Iowa	1972		★			
Kansas	1974	★				★
Kentucky	1973			★		★
Louisiana	1979			★		★
Maine	1971		★			
Maryland	1969	★				
Massachusetts	1969			★		
Michigan	1973			★		
Minnesota	1967		★			
Mississippi	1979			★		
Missouri	1974			★		★
Montana	1971	★				★
Nebraska	1971		★			★
Nevada	1975		★			★
New Hampshire	1980		★			★
New Jersey	1970			★		
New Mexico	1971	★				
New York	1970			★		
North Carolina	1977			★		★
North Dakota		★				
Ohio	1972		★			
Oklahoma		★				
Oregon	1969		★			
Pennsylvania	1970			★		
Rhode Island	1977			★		★
South Carolina	1973	★				
South Dakota	1981			★		
Tennessee		★				★
Texas					★	
Utah		★				
Vermont	1970			★		
Virginia					★	
Washington	1971			★	★	
West Virginia					★	
Wisconsin	1967			★		
Wyoming	1973		★			★
American Samoa						
Guam						
No. Mariana Is.						
Puerto Rico	1970					
Virgin Islands						

Key:

Health Department Model: Fifteen states currently include their pollution control programs within their state health or health and human resources department. While a few states have chosen explicitly to consolidate their previously fragmented pollution control programs within a reorganized health department, in most states this model represents the historical relationship between environmental protection programs and public health considerations.

Little EPA Model: Twelve states currently have what might be called little EPAs because they mirror the U.S. Environmental Protection Agency in their program responsibilities.

Environmental Superagency Model: Nineteen states consolidate their pollution control functions in what this study calls an environmental superagency. It is difficult to define precisely what constitutes a superagency. The minimum definition is the inclusion of the three major pollution control programs with at least one other state conservation or development program.

Table 3
SUMMARY OF STATE PROTECTION OF HISTORIC
AND CULTURAL RESOURCES UNDER CZMA

State or other jurisdiction	Actual or estimated federal approval date by fiscal year(a)	Summary of state protection of historic and cultural resources under CZMA				Summary of state protection of significant natural resources under CZMA					
		Required dedication of access	Open beach laws or court action	Protection/restoration of historic & cultural resources	Protection of scenic areas/provision of visual access	Wetlands	Floral & faunal habitats	Beaches & dunes	Barrier islands	Reefs	Offshore oil & gas; sand & gravel extraction
Alabama	1979	●	...	★	★	★	★	★	...	...	★
Alaska	1979	★	...	★	...	★	★	...	★	...	★
California	1978	★	★	★	★	★	★	★	...	★	★
Connecticut	1980	...	★	★	●	★	★	●	●	N.A.	★
Delaware	1979	...	★	★	★	★	★	★	...	...	★
Florida	1981	...	...	...	...	★	★	★	★	★	...
Georgia	(b)	...	(c)	(c)	(c)	(c)	(c)	(c)	(c)	(c)	(c)
Hawaii	1978	★	★	★	★	...	★	★	...	★	★
Illinois	N.A.	...	...	★	★	★	...	★	...	★	★
Indiana	N.A.	...	...	...	...	★	...	...	...	...	...
Louisiana	1980	...	★	★	★	★	★	★	★	...	★
Maine	1978	...	...	...	★	★	★	★	★	...	★
Maryland	1978	★	★	★	...	★	★	★	★	...	★
Massachusetts	1978	...	...	★	★	★	★	★	★	...	★
Michigan	1978	...	...	★	★	★	★	★	...	★	★
Minnesota	N.A.	...	...	★	...	★	...	...	...	★	★
Mississippi	1980	...	★	★	★	...	★	★	★	★	★
New Hampshire	1980	★	★	★	...	★	★	★	...	...	★
New Jersey	1980	★	★	★	...	★	★	★	...	...	★
New York	1982	...	...	●	★	★	★	...	...	...	★
North Carolina	1978	...	★	★	★	★	★	★	...	...	★
Ohio	N.A.	...	...	★	...	★	★	★	★	★	★
Oregon	1977	...	★	★	★	★	★	★	...	★	★
Pennsylvania	1980	●	...	●	...	★	●	...	...	...	★
Rhode Island	1978	...	★	★	...	★	★	★	★	...	★
South Carolina	1979	★	★	★	...	★	★	★	★	...	★
Texas	...	...	(d)	(d)	...	...	...	(d)	...	...	(d)
Virginia	(b)	...	...	...	...	(c)	...	(c)	...	...	(c)
Washington	1976	...	...	★	★	★	★	★	...	★	★
Wisconsin	1978	★	...	★	★	★	★	★	...	★	★
American Samoa	1980	●	...	★	★	...	★	...	...	★	...
Guam	1979	...	★	★	...	★	★	★	...	★	★
No. Mariana Is.	1980	...	...	★	...	★	★	★	...	★	★
Puerto Rico	1978	★	...	★	...	★	★	★	...	●	...
Virgin Islands	1979	★	★	★	★	★	★	★	★	★	★

Source: National Oceanic and Atmospheric Administration, Office of Coastal Zone Management, *The First Five Years of Coastal Zone Management* (Washington, D.C.: U.S. Department of Commerce, 1979), Tables II and V, pages 20 and 39. Updated by The Council of State Governments, November 1981.

●—Proposed law or program to be part of Coastal Management Program.

★—Pre-existing law or program incorporated into CMP or new or expanded law or program directly attributable to CZM partipation.

(a) These are the states as defined in the Coastal Zone Management Act.

(b) State law of its own design and currently not participating in federal CZMP.

(c) Pre-existing law or program or new or expanded program directly attributable to state coastal zone law.

(d) Pre-existing law or program within various state agencies.

Table 4
STATE LAWS AFFECTING MANAGEMENT OF COASTAL DEVELOPMENT, BY TYPE OF ACTIVITY OR AREA AFFECTED

	Erosion-prone areas	Floodplains	Subsidence and/or saltwater intrusion	Energy facility siting	Priority to water dept. uses	Locating dredge disposal sites	Offshore oil and gas sand & gravel extraction
Alabama	...	★	★	...	★	...	★
Alaska	★	★	★	★	★	...	★
California	★	★	★	★	★	★	★
Connecticut	★	★	N.A.	★	●	★	
Delaware	★	...	...	...	★	...	★
Florida	★	...	...	★	...	★	...
Georgia	(a)	...	(a)	(a)	(a)	(a)	(a)
Hawaii	★	★	★	...	★	...	★
Illinois	...	★	...	...	...	★	★
Indiana	...	★	...	...	...	★	★
Louisiana	★	★	★	★	★	★	★
Maine	★	★	...	★	★	...	★
Maryland	★	★	★	★	★	...	...
Massachusetts	★	★	...	★	★	★	★
Michigan	★	★	...	●	★	★	★
Minnesota	...	★	...	★	...	★	★
Mississippi	...	★	...	★	●	●	★
New Hampshire	...	★	...	★	★	★	★
New Jersey	★	...	...	★	...	...	★
New York	★	●	...	★	★	★	★
North Carolina	★	★	★	●	★	★	★
Ohio	...	...	...	★	...	★	★
Oregon	★	★	...	★	★	★	★
Pennsylvania	★	★	...	●	...	...	★
Rhode Island	★	★	...	★	...	★	★
South Carolina	★	...	...	★	★	★	★
Texas	...	...	...	...	...	...	(b)
Virginia	(a)	(a)	...	...	...	...	(a)
Washington	★	★	...	★	★	★	★
Wisconsin	★	★	...	★	★	★	★
American Samoa	★	★	...	★	★	...	...
Guam	...	★	...	...	...	...	...
No. Mariana Is.	...	...	...	★	...	...	...
Puerto Rico	★	★	...	...	★	...	...
Virgin Islands	★	★	★	★	★	★	★

Source: National Oceanic and Atmospheric Administration, Office of Coastal Zone Management, *The First Five Years of Coastal Zone Management* (Washington, D.C.: U.S. Department of Commerce, 1979), Table IV, page 31. Updated by The Council of State Governments, November 1981.

●—Proposed law or program to be part of Coastal Management Program.

★—Pre-existing law or program incorporated into Coastal Management Program or new or expanded law or program directly attributable to Coastal Zone Management participation.

(a) Pre-existing law or program incorporated into state coastal zone management program or new or expanded law or program directly attributable to state coastal zone management law.

(b) Pre-existing law or program within various state agencies.

Table 5
SUMMARY OF SOLID WASTE AND RESOURCE RECOVERY PROGRAMS
(As of November 1981)

State or other jurisdiction	Solid waste		Resource recovery				
				Industrial waste exchange programs			
	State solid waste management plans	State solid waste/ resource recovery authorities	State used oil recycling programs	State operated	Industry/ private operated	Bottle bill legislation enacted	State litter control program
Alabama	F,C	...	A	...	IE	I	A
Alaska	D	...	A	...	...	...	A
Arizona	F	...	...	...	P	...	...
Arkansas	C,FA	...	...	...	...	...	A,L,TR
California	C	...	A	...	ME	...	A,L,TE
Colorado	F,C	...	...	...	IE	...	A,L,TE
Connecticut	F,C	A	...	...	...	A	A,L,TR
Delaware	D	A	...	...	...	P	...
Florida	F,C	...	I	...	IE	...	...
Georgia	C,FA	A	...	...	IE	...	A
Hawaii	CW	...	A	...	...	...	A
Idaho	D	...	...	...	...	...	A
Illinois	F,C	...	A	IE	...	...	A
Indiana	F,C	...	A	IE	...	...	A
Iowa	C,FA	...	...	...	IE	A	...
Kansas	F,C	...	A	IE	...	...	...
Kentucky	F,C	...	A	...	...	...	...
Louisiana	F,C	A	...	...	...	...	...
Maine	F,C	...	A	...	...	A	...
Maryland	D	A	A	...	IE	...	...
Massachusetts	F,C	...	A	...	...	A	...
Michigan	F,C	...	A	...	ME	A	...
Minnesota	F,C	...	A	...	IE	...	...
Mississippi	F,C	...	...	...	...	...	...
Missouri	F,C	...	A	...	IE	...	...
Montana	F	...	A	...	...	...	...
Nebraska	D	...	...	...	IE	...	A,L
Nevada	D	...	...	...	...	...	...
New Hampshire	CW	...	A	...	...	...	...
New Jersey	D	...	A	...	IE	...	A
New Mexico	N	...	...	...	...	...	...
New York	D	A	A	IE	...	...	...
North Carolina	F,C	...	...	...	IE	...	...
North Dakota	F,C	...	...	...	...	...	...
Ohio	F,C	A	P	IE	ME	...	A
Oklahoma	F,C	...	...	...	IE	...	...
Oregon	F,C	...	A	IE	IE	A	...
Pennsylvania	F,C	...	A	IE	ME	...	...
Rhode Island	F,C	A	A	...	...	A	...
South Carolina	D	...	...	...	...	...	...
South Dakota	F,C	...	...	...	...	...	A
Tennessee	F,C	...	P	IE	IE	...	A
Texas	F,C	A	...	...	IE	...	...
Utah	F	...	A	...	...	...	...
Vermont	F,C	A	...	...	IE	A	...
Virginia	C	A	...	...	...	...	A
Washington	F,C	...	...	...	IE	...	A,L
West Virginia	D	...	...	...	...	...	...
Wisconsin	F,C	...	I	...	...	...	...
Wyoming	D	A	...	...	...	...	...
American Samoa	F,C	...	...	...	...	...	...
Guam	D	...	...	...	...	...	...
No. Mariana Is.	D	...	...	...	...	...	...
Puerto Rico	D	A	...	...	...	...	...
Virgin Islands	D	A	...	...	...	P	...

Key:
F—Completed plans awaiting federal approval.
C—Completed plan adopted by state.
D—Plan in draft stages.
N—No subtitle D program.
A—Active program.
I—Inactive program.
P—Pending.

IE—Information exchange.
ME—Material exchange.
FA—Federal approval.
L—State litter materials tax.
CW—Completed plan awaiting state adoption.
TR—Tax repealed.
TE—Tax legislation expired, not renewed.

Table 6
HAZARDOUS WASTE FUNDS

State or other jurisdiction	State hazardous waste trust and spill funds	Source of fund	Major scope of fund
Alabama	Hazardous Waste Management Fund	FO	Administrative costs.
	Perpetual Care Fund	FO	Monitoring beyond the active use of the site.
Alaska	...	...	...
Arizona	Hazardous Waste Trust Fund	FO	Operation, maintenance, perpetual care.
Arkansas	...	...	...
California	Hazardous Substances Account	TG	Match federal superfund monies, cleanup, incident contingency fund, victim compensation fund, health studies, emergency equipment.
Colorado	Hazardous Waste Disposal Fund	L,P	...
	Emergency Response Cash Fund	L	Emergency response.
Connecticut	Emergency Spill Response Fund	L,R	Oil and hazardous spills.
Delaware	...	...	...
Florida	Hazardous Waste Management Trust Fund	L,T,FO,R,P	Reduce hazard at abandoned sites.
Georgia	Hazardous Waste Trust Fund	FO,B	Maintenance of abandoned sites.
Hawaii	...	...	...
Idaho	...	...	...
Illinois	Hazardous Waste Fund	FO	Take action against long-term danger, research and development of recycling.
Indiana	Hazardous Substances Emergency Trust Fund	TG	Emergency response, match under superfund.
	Environmental Management Special Fund	F,P	Multipurpose environmental response.
Iowa	...	...	...
Kansas	Perpetual Care Trust Fund	FO,L	Cleanup and monitoring.
Kentucky	Hazardous Waste Management Fund	FGO,R	Emergency response, postclosure, monitoring and maintenance.
Louisiana	Hazardous Waste Protection Fund	B,L	Perpetual care, assure financial responsibility.
	Abandoned Hazardous Waste Site Fund	Excess $, L	Match federal funds, cleanup at abandoned sites.
	Environmental Emergency Response Fund	R,L,P	Environmental emergency responses, match federal funds.
Maine	Hazardous Waste Fund	FG,OT	Emergency response.
Maryland	Oil Disaster Containment Cleanup & Ctgy. Fund	F O	Oil and petroleum products spills.
	Hazardous Substance Control Fund	FO,L	Hazardous substances in water cleanup.
Massachusetts	...	...	...
Michigan	Disposal Facility Trust Fund	FO	Long-term care of closed facilities.
	Hazardous Waste Service Fund	L,R	Emergency response.
Minnesota	...	...	...
Mississippi	...	...	...
Missouri	Hazardous Waste Fund	FG,TO,L	Administrative costs, cleanup.
Montana	...	...	...
Nebraska	...	...	...
Nevada	State Emergency Fund	L	Emergency response.
New Hampshire	Hazardous Waste Cleanup Fund	F,P,L	Cleanup.
New Jersey	Spill Compensation Fund	TO,L	Cleanup of spills.
New Mexico	Hazardous Waste Emergency Fund	L,R,P	Cleanup, disposal, containment.
New York	Hazardous Waste Remedial Fund	L	Emergency response.
	Environmental Protection & Spill Comp. Fund	P	Oil spills only.
North Carolina	...	...	...
North Dakota	...	...	...
Ohio	Hazardous Waste Facility Mgt. Special Account	FG	Administration, closure, abatement, grants.
	Emergency Response Spill Fund	L,P	Emergency response to spills.
Oklahoma	...	...	...
Oregon	Hazardous Waste Account	FG	Perpetual care.
Pennsylvania	Solid Waste Abatement Fund	P,R,B	Emergency situations, spills.
Rhode Island	Hazardous Waste Substance Emergency Fund	L,BS	Abandoned site spills.
South Carolina	Hazardous Waste Contingency Fund	F,G	Emergencies at permitted landfills.
South Dakota	...	...	...
Tennessee	Hazardous Waste Trust Fund	B	Cleanup, perpetual care.
	Perpetual Care Trust Fund	FO	Containment of abandoned site.
Texas	Disposal Facility Response Fund	L	Match federal superfund monies.
Utah	...	...	...
Vermont	Oil & Hazardous Spill Contingency Fund	L,R	Response to spills, hazardous substances
Virginia	...	...	...
Washington	...	...	...
West Virginia	...	...	...
Wisconsin	Hazardous Waste Fund	FO	Closing and long-term care.
	Hazardous Substances Spill Fund	L,R	Cleanup and disposal.
Wyoming	...	...	...
Dist. of Col.	Pending	...	...
American Samoa	...	...	...
Guam	...	...	...
No. Mariana Is.	...	...	...
Puerto Rico	...	...	...
Virgin Islands	...	...	...

Key:
F—Fees.
L—Legislative appropriations.
P—Penalties.
R—Reimbursements.
B—Bond forfeiture.
T—Taxes.
BS—Bond supported.
O—Operator.
G—Generator.
OT—Out-of-state transporters.

Table 7
HAZARDOUS WASTE MANAGEMENT IN THE STATES
(As of November 1981)

State or other jurisdiction	State hazardous waste management programs(a)	State hazardous waste management plans	Permitting/approval authority		Siting Hazardous Waste Facilities		Siting provisions		Transportation	Enforcement
			State level department	State level board	State level siting board	State ownership/ operation	State preemption	Local veto	State manifest system	Felony status
Alabama	E	pdg	...	A	...	...	...	...	A	A
Alaska	D	...	A	...	...	...	...	...	...	A
Arizona	S	...	A	...	...	A	A	...	...	...
Arkansas	E	A	A	...	...	...	...	...	A	...
California	E	A	A	...	...	...	...	A	A	A
Colorado	S	A	A	...	...	...	A	A	...	...
Connecticut	E, pdg	...	A	...	A	...	A	...	A	A
Delaware	E	A	...	...	...	...	A	...	A	...
Florida	E, pdg	A	...	...	...	A	A	...	...	A
Georgia	E	A	A	...	...	A	A	...	A	A
Hawaii	S	...	...	...	...	...	...	...	...	...
Idaho	E, pdg	pdg	A	...	...	...	...	A	A	A
Illinois	A	A	A	...	...	...	A	A	A	A
Indiana	E	...	A	A	...	...	A	...	A	A
Iowa	E	A	A	...	A	A	A	...	A	A
Kansas	E	pdg	A	A	...	A	A	...	A	A
Kentucky	E	A	A	A	...	...	...	A	A	A
Louisiana	E	...	A	A	...	...	...	...	A	...
Maine	E	A	A	...	...	...	A	A	A	A
Maryland	E	A	A	A	A	A	A	...	A	A
Massachusetts	E	A	A	...	...	...	A	A	A	A
Michigan	S	A	A	...	A	A	A	...	A	A
Minnesota	S	A	A	...	A	A	...	...	A	...
Mississippi	E	A	...	A	...	A	...	...	A	A
Missouri	S	A	A	...	...	...	...	A	A	...
Montana	E	A	A	...	...	A	...	...	A	A
Nebraska	C	A	A	...	...	A	...	A	...	...
Nevada	S	pdg	pdg	...	...	A	...	...	A	A
New Hampshire	E	pdg	A	...	...	...	pdg	...	A	A
New Jersey	E, pdg	...	A	...	pdg	...	pdg	...	A	A,M

612

State							
New Mexico	S				A,ED	··	A
New York	E,pdg	pdg			A,ED	··	pdg
North Carolina	E	A,W					
North Dakota	E,pdg				··	··	A
Ohio		A		A	A	··	A
Oklahoma	E	A		A	A		A
Oregon	E	A					A
Pennsylvania	E						A
Rhode Island	E	pdg					
South Carolina	E						
South Dakota	S	A	A				A
Tennessee	E		A				
Texas	E		A				A
Utah	E						
Vermont	E	A					
Virginia	E	A,W	A	A	A	A	A
Washington	S	A	A		A		pdg
West Virginia	C	A	A		A		A
Wisconsin	E	A					
Wyoming	A						
Dist. of Col.	pdg	A		A	A	A	A
American Samoa							pdg
Guam	S	pdg	pdg				A
Puerto Rico	E,pdg	pdg			pdg	pdg	pdg
Virgin Islands							

Key:
E—EPA interim authorization (Phase I).
A—Active state program.
I—Inactive.
S—Adopted state regulations.
D—State regulations in development and draft stages.
W—Under state solid waste plan.
ED—Under state eminent domain statutes.
pdg—Pending
M—Some regulations are enforced under misdemeanor status, some under felony status.
C—State regulations completed and pending adoption.
  (a) Updated January 26, 1982.

Table 8
RADIOACTIVE MATERIAL MANAGEMENT IN THE STATES

State or other jurisdiction	State radiation control program	State emergency resource programs		Transportation		Regulation	
		Nuclear reactor specific	All radioactive materials incidents	Federal source of transportation requirements adopted by states	Requires registration fees, permits, licensing, certificates	Commercial low level waste disposal facilities	Regulation of radioactive waste disposal
Alabama	A,FS	A	A	DOT	L	...	BO
Alaska	A	...	...	DOT	R	...	CC
Arizona	A,FS	A	A	DOT	L	pdg	pdg
Arkansas	A,FS	A	A	DOT	P	...	...
California	A,FS	A	A	NRC, DOT	R	...	...
Colorado	A,FS	A	A	DOT	L	...	(a)
Connecticut	A	A	...	ICC	P,F	...	B L
Delaware	A	A	A	DOT,S	P	...	L A
Florida	A,FS	A	A	DOT,S	F	...	O
Georgia	A,FS	A	A	DOT,S	P,L	...	...
Hawaii	A	...	...	...	...	...	LA
Idaho	A,FS	...	...	DOT,S	L	...	...
Illinois	A	A	A	DOT,S	P,C	pdg	B
Indiana	A	...	A	...	...	...	...
Iowa	A	...	A	DOT	...	...	...
Kansas	A,FS	...	A	DOT,S	R	...	LA
Kentucky	A,FS	A	A	DOT,S,NRC,S	L	I	LA
Louisiana	A,FS	A	A	DOT	L	...	H
Maine	A	A	I	DOT,S	P	...	LA
Maryland	A,FS	...	A	DOT,S	...	...	...
Massachusetts	A	A	A	DOT,S	...	...	...
Michigan	A	A	A	DOT,S	R,F	...	BO
Minnesota	A	...	A	DOT,S	...	...	LA
Mississippi	A,FS	A	A	...	...	...	LA
Missouri	A	A	A	...	...	...	...
Montana	A	...	A	...	L	...	B
Nebraska	A,FS	...	A	DOT	L	...	...
Nevada	A,FS	...	A	DOT,S	P , L	C D	L,F
New Hampshire	A,FS	...	...	DOT	...	...	BL
New Jersey	A	A	A	...	C	...	...
New Mexico	A,FS	...	A	DOT		...	CC
New York	A,FS	A	A	DOT,S	P	I	CC
North Carolina	A,FS	A	A	DOT,NRC	...	...	...
North Dakota	A,FS	...	A	DOT	L	...	LA
Ohio	A	...	A	DOT,S	...	...	...
Oklahoma	A	...	A	...	...	...	CC
Oregon	A,FS	A	A	DOT	L	...	BR
Pennsylvania	A	A	A	DOT,S	P	...	...
Rhode Island	A,FS	...	...	DOT,NRC	P	...	...
South Carolina	A,FS	A	A	...	P	C D	L
South Dakota	A	...	A	DOT,pdg	...	...	B,G
Tennessee	A,FS	...	A	DOT	...	...	...
Texas	A,FS	...	A	DOT,NRC	F,L	pdg	B,BO
Utah	A	...	A	DOT	...	...	...
Vermont	A	A	A	DOT,S	R	...	BO
Virginia	A	A	A	DOT	R,C	...	BL
Washington	A,FS	A	A	DOT,NRC	L	C D	P,F,C
West Virginia	A	...	A	DOT,NRC	...	...	BO
Wisconsin	A	A	A	DOT	...	...	...
Wyoming	A	...	...	DOT,S	L	...	...
Dist. of Col.	A	...	A	...	...	...	...

Key:
FS—Federal/state agreement
DOT—Department of Transportation
NRC—Nuclear Regulatory Commission
ICC—Interstate Commerce Commission
S—Specific titles
F—Fees
P—Permits
L—Licensing
R—Registration
C—Certificates
A—Active state program
I—Inactive
BO—Bans disposal of all radioactive waste generated outside state

B—Bans disposal of high-level waste
LA—Requires legislative approval prior to disposal of radioactive waste
CC—Requires consultation and concurence before disposal is permitted
O—Requires disposal operator to meet specific technical and environmental criteria
G—Requires governor's approval prior to disposal
BR—Bans all radioactive waste disposal within the state
CD—Commercial disposal site
H—Requires Assistant Secretary of Office of Environmental Affairs approval prior to disposal
BL—Bans disposal of high-level waste; low-level radioactive waste disposal requires prior legislative approval.
(a) Disposal of foreign, high-level or transuranic wastes, unless site is approved by governor and legislature.

STATE PARKS AND OUTDOOR RECREATION

By Ney C. Landrum

AS LONG AS an appreciation of nature and a desire for wholesome outdoor recreation remain important to Americans, state parks will play a major role in the satisfaction of these public needs. Bridging the considerable gap between the grandiose, but generally more remote, areas of the national park system on the one hand, and the numerous, usually smaller and more formalized local parks on the other, the nation's state parks are uniquely suited to offer the American people a wide array of recreational opportunities in the broadest possible choice of natural and man-made settings. The public has demonstrated its approval of the state park approach to balanced, diversified recreation by turning out in ever-increasing numbers.

Although the concept of state parks has been around for well over a century, the real boom in development did not occur until the mid-1930s, when widespread federal assistance became available under the Civilian Conservation Corps (CCC) program. Today, on the eve of the CCC's golden anniversary, all 50 states have thriving park systems, characterized by continuing innovation and growth. It is interesting to note, however, that no state is the readily acknowledged leader in this field, because all state park systems differ substantially, each seeking in its own way to respond to the important needs of its state. Thus, some state park systems may place maximum emphasis on preservation of natural areas and historic sites while others seek to stimulate economic growth through operation of large and luxurious "resort" parks. All, however, share the one overriding goal of providing to the public a wide variety of high quality outdoor recreation experiences.

Growth and Use Trends

Although the trend over the years has been one of steady growth in the numbers and use of state parks, a precise measurement of progress in this field is difficult because of varying and imperfect methods of reporting data. Until it was undertaken as a project of the National Association of State Park Directors in 1978, there was no standard annual statistical survey of the nation's state park systems. Even now, attempts to compile and compare state parks data are complicated by inconsistent terminology and lack of uniformity in agency responsibility for park functions among the states. Areas loosely grouped under the generic term "state park," for instance, might be more specifically identified as recreation areas, preserves, reserves, wilderness areas, natural areas, waysides, beaches, historic sites and memorials—to mention a few—depending on the state. Similarly, certain functions or types of areas assigned to the state parks agency in some states might be administered spearately in other states (by wildlife, forest or highway agencies, for instance) and thus not treated the

---

Ney C. Landrum is Director of the Division of Recreation and Parks for the Florida Department of Natural Resources.

same for reporting purposes. These problems are fully recognized within the state parks profession, however, and real progress is now being made in the effort to collect and report state parks statistical data in a meaningful way.

In mid-1981, the 50 states reported a total of 4,068 state park units in their systems, up 436 from 1979. Illinois alone reported an increase of 102 units, while New Jersey added 77, Ohio 55, Montana 51, and California 48. Some of these increases are due to inconsistent reporting procedures, but some reflect true expansion. While the number of units increased over the biennium, the aggregate acreage in state parks declined slightly during the same period, from 9,692,176 acres in 1979 to 9,200,814 acres in 1981. Again, some of this is attributable to reporting procedures, especially in the case of decreases: e.g., Wisconsin down 413,282 acres, Arkansas down 379,968, Montana down 53,231. States showing significant gains in acreage were California up 83,302 acres, South Dakota up 72,000, Alaska up 58,757 and Texas up 55,010. State park systems vary in acreage from Delaware with 8,900 acres to Alaska with 3 million acres.

State park visitation figures are subject to the same reporting limitations as other data, but nonetheless evidence a growing popularity of the state parks through a strong upward trend over the years. For a variety of reasons, however, growth slowed over the 1979-81 biennium, as the combined attendance of 629,335,930 reported in 1981 was up only 3 percent from that reported two years ago. Even so, the state parks collectively drew almost three times as many recreational visitors as did the national park system during its last year of record (1980), further attesting to their immense popularity. It is interesting to note that exactly half the states reported decreases in state park visitation over the biennium and the other half reported increases. In the former category, Oklahoma showed the greatest loss with 15,564,581 fewer visitors, followed by Montana (down 4,895,000) and Kansas (down 3,212,545). Among those gaining most in attendance were New Mexico (up 20,020,125), Hawaii (up 16,617,398) and California (up 6,019, 398).

Diversity—A State Parks Characteristic

Diversity has always been the hallmark of the state parks, and this diversity is evident not only from state to state but within state park systems. The immense variety available among the state parks has resulted first from the vast differences in locations and natural landscapes and second from the ingenuity and creativity man has applied to these natural assets over the years. While most of the earlier parks were simply scenic natural areas set aside for passive enjoyment and appreciation, parks today owe much of their distinction to the type of development undertaken, usually in response to a perceived public need or desire. This change might be regarded as either good or bad, depending on the philosophical viewpoint, but it is generally conceded today that a well-balanced state park system should provide a wide variety of outdoor recreation settings and activities. A few examples will serve to illustrate the lengths to which the state parks have pursued this objective.

A number of states—such as Kentucky, West Virginia, Tennessee and Alabama—have directed much of their state park efforts into the development of full-fledged vacation resorts, containing lodges, restaurants, swimming pools, golf courses and in some cases even landing facilities for private aircraft. These resort parks might be regarded as the ultimate in park development—one end of the state park spectrum. Good examples of this type are Joe Wheeler State Park Resort in Alabama and Canaan Valley Resort park in West Virginia. In a completely different direction, some of the more urban states are focusing attention on neglected inner-city areas. New Jersey, for example, is developing its Liberty

State Park right in the heart of the Hoboken-Jersey City commercial waterfront area, overlooking Ellis Island and the Statue of Liberty.

Many state parks are characterized by emphasis on a single feature or activity. Kentucky has a whole park devoted to the horse; California has recently opened a new state park facility showcasing trains and railroad memorabilia; and skiing is king at New Hampshire's Cannon Mountain, where a visitor can attend ski school and learn to ski one of the 25 trails and slopes available. Some state parks are built around complete country estates developed by notable people. Rhode Island has Colt State Park, a former home of firearms manufacturer Samuel P. Colt, while Ohio operates Malabar Farm State Park in the spirit of its former owner, Pulitzer Prize-winning author Louis Bromfield. Historic villages are being brought to life by Utah at Old Deseret and by Illinois at New Salem.

With all the emphasis on innovative park development features and themes, however, the traditional state park purpose of preserving wilderness and natural areas has certainly not been abandoned. Many state parks still are maintained primarily for the nature-lover and the backwoodsman. Two highly diverse examples of this type are Michigan's Porcupine Mountains Wilderness State Park, a 58,000-acre expanse of rugged north woods in the Upper Peninsula, and Florida's Fakahatchee Strand, a 45,000-acre tropical swamp forest whose spectacular beauty can best be appreciated only by a hike through its interior in waist-deep water.

Truly, the rich diversity of America itself is preserved for all time in the myriad landscapes of its state parks.

The Impact of Reduced Funding

After years of steady growth and expansion, the nation's state park systems now find themselves faced with a major financial crisis brought on by a sluggish national economy and the retrenchment policies of the Reagan administration. The severity of the problem is reflected by the measures various states are taking to operate within their reduced means. In mid-1981, well over half of the states reported having to curtail state park operations to some extent. Sixteen parks in six states had been closed altogether, and 66 other parks in 11 states had been partially closed. Thirteen states reported having to institute shorter operating hours for some or all of their parks.

State park personnel have been an early target of budget-cutting activity in many states. During 1980-81, 594 full-time park employees were laid off, or their positions not filled, in 24 states. Part-time and seasonal employment was even more severely affected, as 1,694 positions in 18 states were lost through terminations or a slow-down in hiring.

Much of the curtailment in state park operations was directly attributable to elimination or reduction in federal programs. Through mid-1981, 25 states reported a combined loss of almost 3,000 employees from the Youth Conservation Corps (YCC), Young Adult Conservation Corps (YACC) and Comprehensive Employment and Training Assistance (CETA) programs. Moreover, the impact of federal budget cuts on state park capital outlay programs is expected to be substantial. Thirty-three states report that their park acquisition and development efforts will be reduced by almost 35 percent (unweighted average) through permanent loss of Land and Water Conservation Fund program assistance.

The Outlook

As state park administrators look to the future, they are at the same time heartened by the increasingly important public service role the parks have to play and concerned by a

617

growing array of problems affecting state park operations. As park systems expand and facilities get older, costs for routine operation and maintenance as well as major repairs and renovations greatly increase. Changing visitation patterns brought about by rising travel costs are subjecting more accessible parks to intense pressures, while leaving more remote parks underused. As pressures increase, particularly in urban and near-urban state parks, problems of resource management, maintenance and law enforcement are intensified. None of these problems can be fully resolved without adequate funding.

Still, in the face of formidable challenges, the states remain optimistic about state park prospects in the years ahead. Many are already adjusting fees, contracting for more services from private concessionaires and exploring new ways to cut costs and generate revenues. Whatever the circumstances, the important place of the state parks in the lives of the American people will remain assured.

Table 1

STATE PARK AREAS, ACREAGE AND ATTENDANCE: 1981

State	Administrative agency	Total units	Total acreage	Total attendance(a)
Alabama	Dept. of Conservation & Natural Resources, Div. of State Parks	23	48,027	3,967,725 (b)
Alaska	Dept. of Natural Resources, Div. of Parks	96	3,000,000	3,000,000
Arizona	State Parks Board	18	26,314	2,322,124
Arkansas	Dept. of Parks & Tourism, State Parks Div.	43	42,210	5,133,182
California	Dept. of Parks & Recreation	277	1,045,050	62,376,690
Colorado	Dept. of Natural Resources, Div. of Parks & Outdoor Recreation	27	159,693	6,900,000
Connecticut	Dept. of Environmental Protection, Office of Parks & Recreation	88	30,316	7,277,037 (c)
Delaware	Dept. of Natural Resources & Environmental Control, Div. of Parks & Recreation	11	8,900	2,500,000
Florida	Dept. of Natural Resources, Div. of Recreation & Parks	125	288,283	11,506,599
Georgia	Dept. of Natural Resources, Div. of Parks, Recreation & Historic Sites	54	51,679	9,809,083
Hawaii	Dept. of Lands & Natural Res., Div. of State Parks, Outdoor Rec. & Hist. Sites	69	20,836	17,169,000 (d)
Idaho	Dept. of Parks & Recreation	26	41,700	2,052,934
Illinois	Dept. of Conservation, Bureau of Land & Historic Sites	283	336,403	33,455,360 (d)
Indiana	Dept. of Natural Resources, Div. of State Parks	19	54,126	7,612,554
Iowa	State Conservation Commission, Park Section	66	50,537	14,533,926
Kansas	Park & Resources Authority	24	31,316	1,641,675
Kentucky	Dept. of Parks	44	43,336	26,677,360 (c)
Louisiana	Dept. of Culture, Recreation & Tourism, Office of State Parks	54	31,406	3,885,759
Maine	Dept. of Conservation, Bureau of Parks & Recreation	105	70,657	2,037,173 (c)
Maryland	Dept. of Natural Resources, Forest/Park Service	49	83,756	5,344,806
Massachusetts	Dept. of Environmental Management Div. of Forests & Parks	169	251,782	10,587,552
Michigan	Dept. of Natural Resources, Parks Div.	93	245,595	20,784,290 (c)
Minnesota	Dept. of Natural Resources, Div. of Parks & Recreation	65	180,514	6,083,722 (c)
Mississippi	Dept. of Natural Resources, Bureau of Recreation & Parks	27	21,500	4,171,275
Missouri	Dept. of Natural Resources, Div. of Parks & Historic Preservation	71	97,450	8,656,670
Montana	Dept. of Fish, Wildlife & Parks, Parks Div.	287	44,769	3,270,000 (b)
Nebraska	Game & Parks Commission	91	133,335	8,143,850 (c)
Nevada	Dept. of Conservation & Natural Resources	20	151,202	3,498,193 (c)
New Hampshire	Dept. of Resources & Economic Development, Div. of Parks & Recreation	48	70,541	4,206,645 (c)
New Jersey	Dept. of Environmental Protection, Div. of Parks & Forestry	114	272,238	7,914,062
New Mexico	Dept. of Natural Resources, State Park & Recreation Div.	36	105,303	23,683,682
New York	Office of Parks, Recreation & Historic Preservation	178	249,396	47,377,000 (e)
North Carolina	Dept. of Natural Resources & Community Dev., Div. of Parks & Recreation	38	118,478	5,374,225
North Dakota	Parks & Recreation Dept.	23	16,209	997,000 (c)
Ohio	Dept. of Natural Resources, Div. of Parks & Recreation	71	198,027	47,422,975
Oklahoma	Tourism & Recreation Dept., Div. of State Parks	73	71,368	2,386,833 (c)
Oregon	Dept. of Transportation, State Parks & Recreation Div.	240	89,838	35,000,000
Pennsylvania	Dept. of Environmental Resources, Bureau of State Parks	112	274,641	38,132,818
Rhode Island	Dept. of Environmental Management, Div. of Parks & Recreation	80	12,000	7,500,000
South Carolina	Dept. of Parks, Recreation & Tourism, Div. of State Parks	64	70,729	11,217,279 (c)
South Dakota	Dept. of Game, Fish & Parks, Div. of Parks & Recreation	62	89,106	5,202,000 (c)
Tennessee	Dept. of Conservation, Div. of Parks & Recreation	51	139,163	17,346,946
Texas	Dept. of Parks & Wildlife, Parks Div.	111	187,189	14,503,337
Utah	Dept. of Natural Resources, Div. of Parks & Recreation	44	87,962	6,536,572
Vermont	Dept. of Forests, Parks & Recreation, Div. of Parks	45	31,824	783,179 (c)
Virginia	Dept. of Conservation & Economic Dev., Div. of Parks	23	53,770	3,322,892
Washington	State Parks & Recreation Commission	202	87,038	37,384,065 (c)
West Virginia	Dept. of Natural Resources, Div. of Parks & Recreation	50	148,542	7,750,903
Wisconsin	Dept. of Natural Resources, Bureau of Parks & Recreation	70	114,853	10,531,353 (c)
Wyoming	Recreation Commission	9	121,907	1,083,625 (f)

Source: Division of Recreation and Parks, Florida Department of Natural Resources.

(a) For year ending June 30, 1981, unless otherwise noted.
(b) October 1979-September 1980.
(c) Calendar year 1980.
(d) July 1979-June 1980.
(e) April 1979-March 1980.
(f) May 1980-September 1980.

STATE AGRICULTURE

By Edward H. Glade Jr. and Keith J. Collins

THE MAJOR FORCES of the past 50 years continue to influence agriculture today. The technologically based increase in farm productivity has caused substantial adjustments in farm organization and land use and has affected all other sectors of the economy. In addition, agricultural policy, regulation, inflation and export growth will occupy state agriculture departments in the years ahead.

Changing Nature of Production

The nation's supply of food and fiber continues to depend on fewer and fewer producers. While total land in farms has changed relatively little in the past decades, the number of individual farms has dropped sharply. Historically, farms of under 500 acres have declined, but those of 500 acres or more have increased in number. Currently, over 48 percent of U.S. farmland is owned by only 5 percent of farm operators. Contrary to frequent assertion, most farms, although larger, continue to be family-operated. Corporations have a small role in farm production and in farmland ownership. Based on the latest Census of Agriculture, less than 3 percent of the number of farms and about 12 percent of total acreage are controlled by corporations.

The concern of state agriculture departments over increased concentration of farm production and loss of control over land involves more than numbers. Larger farms are becoming more vertically integrated and entering greater and more complex contracts. These changes suggest farm management could gradually become more controlled by the non-farmers. Moreover, rising production expenses, unstable product prices and greatly increased capital needs encourage farm consolidations and restrict entry into farming. Many small farms continue to incur high debt-to-income ratios and consequent credit and cash flow problems. These problems have encouraged state and federal efforts to promote balanced growth of state agriculture.

State departments of agriculture also continue to deal with such broad agricultural issues as water policy and the preservation of prime lands. In many areas, declining groundwater levels, inadequate surface water, pollution and more stringent federal regulations for water projects have required states to take a strong stand on water policy. Solutions to these water problems may well determine the direction of future agricultural development for many states. The preservation of prime farmlands is an increasing concern of state agriculture departments and the federal government. In the future, land use alternatives and priorities for development projects that take prime land out of agricultural production may need to be closely examined to ensure the public interest is served. Programs for the preservation of farmland are increasingly important functions of state departments of agriculture.

Edward H. Glade Jr. and Keith J. Collins are Economists of the U.S. Department of Agriculture, Economic Research Service, National Economics Division.

Agricultural Programs

Farm policy and the administration of agricultural commodity programs have generally been the responsibility of the federal government. Recent trends, however, suggest that states will play a more important role in carrying out farm program goals.

U.S. farm policy no longer relies on strict control of production and income through acreage allotments, marketing quotas and high loan rates. The more flexible current programs allow market prices to vary in relation to supply and demand. Producers are free to determine production levels, production practices and marketing plans. Since 1974, price and income support has been provided through a target price and loan rate system. The price support loan rate is set at or below market-clearing levels and provides a price floor and interim financing for producers. A direct payment is made if market price falls below the target price. In contrast to a system of artificially high loan rates serving as market prices, target price deficiency payments are made outside the market so as not to disrupt prices established by supply and demand.

As a result of these market-oriented programs, producers are also more vulnerable to wide swings in prices and farm income.

State departments of agriculture, therefore, must work closely with producers and provide information and services which aid in sound production and marketing decisions. These decisions are increasingly important in determining farm returns and require that producers have timely market news and analysis. Traditional state programs such as grading and inspection, market reporting, testing services and producer education programs are crucial. Increased emphasis is also being placed on domestic and foreign market development and product promotion. Problems of farm credit and rapidly rising production costs are also being addressed by state departments of agriculture as they work through state extension agents, land grant colleges and local financial institutions.

Inflation and Farming

A fundamental concern of state departments of agriculture is inflation, as well as the problems it creates in the farm sector. Inflation often encourages farmers to purchase larger equipment and buildings sooner than they can be fully used, which drives up the cost of production and creates pressure for government action to raise farm returns. Inflation also increases the wealth of farmland owners, giving many of them a competitive advantage in bidding for available land. Potential farmers are restricted as high interest rates and land prices preclude many from qualifying for loans.

The trend toward fewer but larger farms is accelerated by these conditions, increasing the incentives for conversion of prime farmlands to commercial or residential uses in many states.

State departments of agriculture are called upon to take the lead in ensuring the structural and financial soundness of the agricultural sector and promoting equitable distribution of the impact of inflation on farming.

Export Market Development

U.S. farm exports in 1980 totaled $40.5 billion, creating a surplus agricultural trade balance of about $20.4 billion, and greatly aiding the overall U.S. trade deficit. While exports vary by state, it is clear that to maintain farm income and prices, farmers in every state need foreign markets, and in turn, foreign countries depend on U.S. exports.

The agriculture departments of most states regard assistance to exporters as basic and help farmers and exporters to improve marketing techniques and expand markets. Most states employ staff marketing specialists who deal directly with the export trade. Some states may have a single international trade specialist, while others have established international trade sections within the department's overall structure.

To encourage new export enterprises and to provide existing exporters with the latest information, a number of seminars and workshops are sponsored each year covering production, marketing, finance, shipment modes and export trends. State departments of agriculture, acting individually or together, also take part in domestic food exhibits for foreign food buying teams held in key cities across the United States and in foreign countries.

Moreover, to promote export market development, 44 state agriculture departments have formed regional trade associations. These groups include the Eastern U.S. Agricultural and Food and Export Council, the Mid-America International Agri-Trade Council, the Southern U.S. Trade Association and the Western U.S. Agricultural Trade Association.

With prospects for continued expansion of world trade in the 1980s, state departments of agriculture will be strengthening efforts to provide their farmers an opportunity to share in this growth.

Foreign Ownership

Monitoring of foreign ownership of U.S. farmland and the control of foreign land investments continue to receive careful attention by the states. The Agricultural Foreign Disclosure Act of 1978 (P.L. 95-460) requires foreigners to report current holdings to the secretary of agriculture and any new purchases within 90 days. In addition, the secretary of agriculture must report these holdings to the states.

As of December 31, 1980, less than 1 percent of U.S. agricultural land was owned or controlled by foreign interests. But, distribution is not even among states and not all land is of equal value, thus foreign ownership has greater significance in certain states.

Maine reported the largest number of acres owned by foreign persons. Foreign holdings and acquisitions account for over 5 percent of total privately owned agricultural land in Maine. Foreign holdings and acquisitions are primarily concentrated in the South and West. Alabama, Florida, Georgia, North Carolina, South Carolina, Tennessee and Texas reported 32 percent of all foreign holdings and acquisitions. Arizona, California, Colorado, Montana, Nevada, New Mexico and Utah reported 29 percent. Rhode Island is the only state with no reported foreign-owned agricultural land.

Future foreign acquisition of U.S. farmlands will be closely watched by both states and the U.S. Department of Agriculture (USDA) for the extent of purchases and the effects on land prices, family farms and local communities.

State/USDA Programs

The traditional cooperation between the states and the USDA in agricultural production, marketing and the conservation of resources is the cornerstone of state agriculture and USDA relations.

Cooperative market news programs are conducted in 43 states covered by 62 individual agreements. Commodities include fruits and vegetables, dairy and poultry, livestock, grain, cotton and tobacco. In addition, the USDA and departments of agriculture in 45 states assist each other in enforcement of livestock and poultry licensing, registration and bonding laws.

Programs covering the collection and dissemination of agricultural statistics are conducted with the USDA in 47 states. All agreements provide for operation of a joint office under the supervision of the state statistician who is a federal employee. The cooperative state agency in most cases is a state department of agriculture. Regulatory programs are conducted in animal health and plant pest control including cooperative programs with all states, Puerto Rico and the Virgin Islands to prevent, control and eradicate diseases and plant pests.

State conservation districts blanket the nation. Some 3,000 districts are organized by local people under state law. The USDA's Soil Conservation Service receives appropriations from Congress earmarked for assistance to local conservation work within its boundaries.

These programs, along with others, will help serve as a foundation for continued progress in state agriculture in the coming decade.

Table 1

FARM INCOME: 1980

(In thousands of dollars)

State	Cash receipts from farming				Farm income			
	Total	Livestock & products	Crops	Government payments	Total net income	Realized gross farm income	Farm production expense	Net change in farm inventories
All states..................	$137,636,998	$67,405,497	$69,025,823	$1,205,678	$19,859,547	$152,512,253	$130,656,031	$-1,996,675
Alabama.....................	1,859,346	1,140,519	695,798	23,029	256,718	2,133,878	1,915,655	38,495
Alaska......................	11,728	4,076	7,458	194	1,732	13,386	15,169	51
Arizona	1,725,285	782,704	937,500	5,081	393,263	1,832,268	1,534,839	95,834
Arkansas	3,022,692	1,457,023	1,531,155	34,514	513,096	3,332,086	2,810,336	-8,654
California..................	13,553,070	4,148,593	9,390,368	14,109	3,386,760	14,230,483	11,143,892	300,169
Colorado	3,203,138	2,219,922	965,204	18,012	405,514	3,412,401	3,063,389	56,502
Connecticut.................	297,170	172,410	123,819	941	42,207	329,042	282,525	-4,310
Delaware	334,160	236,505	96,620	1,035	47,979	355,195	304,532	-2,684
Florida	3,811,318	955,937	2,848,338	7,043	1,116,811	4,064,618	3,003,503	55,696
Georgia.....................	2,705,581	1,503,310	1,173,405	28,866	41,618	3,021,378	2,954,836	-24,924
Hawaii	440,054	81,320	358,023	711	143,755	484,580	343,973	3,148
Idaho	2,015,326	851,513	1,155,912	7,901	452,598	2,217,992	1,870,833	105,439
Illinois....................	7,926,930	2,312,430	5,578,766	35,734	208,727	8,977,355	7,627,877	-1,140,751
Indiana	4,523,049	1,661,756	2,846,269	15,024	559,269	5,379,359	4,563,794	-256,296
Iowa	10,084,537	5,487,358	4,552,616	44,563	554,427	11,001,553	10,272,808	-174,318
Kansas	5,899,941	3,361,761	2,524,929	13,251	537,344	6,389,266	5,651,606	-200,316
Kentucky	2,687,680	1,344,850	1,332,073	10,757	761,143	3,140,685	2,219,142	-160,400
Louisiana	1,672,097	458,079	1,194,789	19,229	311,344	1,870,883	1,569,178	9,639
Maine	428,011	299,914	124,654	3,443	13,096	471,778	455,168	-3,514
Maryland	906,272	614,612	288,146	3,514	98,586	1,059,545	961,849	890
Massachusetts	309,267	125,572	182,952	743	59,069	345,984	281,425	-5,490
Michigan	2,704,234	1,118,819	1,574,749	10,666	515,446	3,086,453	2,611,888	40,881
Minnesota	6,361,917	3,303,966	2,988,358	69,593	1,156,494	7,120,720	5,918,822	-45,404
Mississippi	2,163,507	891,797	1,252,940	18,770	271,362	2,432,684	2,097,726	-63,596
Missouri	4,184,371	2,181,302	1,924,162	78,907	306,334	4,696,630	4,018,608	-371,688
Montana.....................	1,465,774	746,840	660,450	58,484	109,359	1,647,698	1,545,574	7,235
Nebraska	6,157,607	3,570,282	2,504,407	82,918	129,183	6,505,741	6,281,001	-95-557
Nevada	234,407	157,701	75,276	1,340	41,371	261,834	240,846	20,383
New Hampshire	99,158	72,344	26,112	702	2,101	122,156	118,581	-1,474
New Jersey..................	432,555	122,311	309,375	869	34,160	491,829	450,918	-6,751
New Mexico..................	1,165,437	875,878	268,671	20,888	163,852	1,267,898	1,043,806	-60,240
New York....................	2,423,478	1,703,910	713,747	5,821	379,609	2,697,883	2,376,026	57,752
North Carolina	3,634,506	1,436,249	2,185,070	13,187	1,038,839	4,117,112	3,057,046	-21,227
North Dakota	2,503,017	781,422	1,604,961	116,634	88,601	2,750,793	2,343,686	-318,506
Ohio	3,746,732	1,356,110	2,381,219	9,403	451,754	4,495,766	4,003,047	-40,965
Oklahoma	3,265,882	2,147,030	1,083,962	34,890	359,230	3,568,970	3,055,421	-154,319
Oregon	1,617,711	537,334	1,074,480	5,897	254,053	1,861,754	1,724,436	116,735
Pennsylvania	2,674,827	1,919,557	746,937	8,333	570,667	3,075,718	2,528,677	23,626
Rhode Island	32,604	13,318	19,191	95	3,888	37,434	33,748	202
South Carolina	1,082,000	413,215	655,354	13,431	38,398	1,233,194	1,123,497	-71,299
South Dakota	2,610,890	1,790,038	755,580	65,272	191,713	2,800,698	2,521,604	-87,381
Tennessee...................	1,755,815	884,681	852,453	18,681	92,895	2,098,674	1,978,966	-26,813
Texas.......................	9,186,265	5,188,052	2,766,373	231,840	1,248,374	9,934,535	8,843,340	157,179
Utah........................	529,103	383,946	140,067	5,090	68,458	613,727	567,330	22,061
Vermont.....................	379,799	352,885	25,592	1,322	94,616	424,017	329,752	351
Virginia....................	1,472,765	949,459	510,004	13,302	217,522	1,762,312	1,525,023	-19,767
Washington	2,714,839	846,883	1,858,498	9,458	727,579	2,973,625	2,263,432	17,386
West Virginia...............	239,233	172,371	64,373	2,489	28,795	334,254	323,773	18,314
Wisconsin	4,723,896	3,743,216	968,307	12,373	1,353,491	5,304,360	4,168,597	217,728
Wyoming	658,011	524,327	126,361	7,323	19,811	730,069	714,531	4,273

Source: Economic Research Service, U.S. Department of Agriculture.

Table 2
FARM ACREAGE AND INCOME PER FARM: 1980

State	Farms — Number of farms	Farms — Total acreage (in thousands)	Realized gross income per farm	Realized net income per farm(a)	Total net income per farm(b)	Value of farm real estate (in millions)
All states.................	2,727,830	1,042,245	$ 62,818	$ 9,002	$ 8,180	$756,172
Alabama....................	58,000	12,700	36,791	3,762	4,426	10,058
Alaska.....................	370	1,520	36,178	-4,818	-4,680	107
Arizona	7,000	38,900	261,753	42,490	56,180	10,270
Arkansas	59,000	16,500	56,476	8,843	8,697	15,197
California.................	380,000	33,900	177,881	38,582	42,335	48,341
Colorado	26,500	36,500	128,770	13,170	15,302	13,724
Connecticut................	4,200	490	78,343	11,075	10,049	1,174
Delaware	3,500	650	101,484	14,475	13,708	1,141
Florida	39,000	13,400	104,221	27,208	28,636	18,117
Georgia....................	59,000	15,500	51,210	1,128	705	13,454
Hawaii	4,300	1,970	112,693	32,699	33,431	2,384
Idaho	24,100	15,400	92,033	14,405	18,780	10,303
Illinois...................	107,000	28,800	83,901	12,612	1,951	57,974
Indiana	88,000	16,800	61,129	9,268	6,355	30,794
Iowa	119,000	33,800	92,450	6,124	4,659	61,212
Kansas	75,000	48,300	85,190	9,835	7,165	27,676
Kentucky	102,000	14,600	30,791	9,035	7,462	13,943
Louisiana	37,000	10,100	50,564	8,154	8,415	13,009
Maine	8,300	1,615	56,841	2,001	1,578	935
Maryland	17,500	2,750	60,545	5,583	5,633	6,190
Massachusetts	5,900	680	58,641	10,942	10,012	1,055
Michigan	66,000	11,400	46,764	7,190	7,810	12,335
Minnesota	104,000	30,000	68,468	11,557	11,120	31,830
Mississippi	55,000	14,600	44,231	6,090	4,934	12,045
Missouri	120,000	31,500	39,139	5,650	2,553	27,657
Montana....................	23,800	62,100	69,231	4,291	4,595	14,221
Nebraska	65,000	47,700	100,088	3,458	1,987	28,620
Nevada	2,900	8,990	90,288	7,237	14,266	2,274
New Hampshire	3,400	545	35,928	1,051	618	538
New Jersey	9,400	1,020	52,322	4,352	3,634	2,985
New Mexico.................	13,500	46,800	93,918	16,599	12,137	8,892
New York....................	48,000	9,400	56,206	6,705	7,909	6,655
North Carolina	93,000	11,700	44,270	11,399	11,170	14,216
North Dakota	40,000	41,700	68,770	10,178	2,215	16,638
Ohio	95,000	16,300	47,324	5,187	4,755	27,351
Oklahoma	72,000	34,600	49,569	7,133	4,989	20,898
Oregon	35,000	18,100	53,193	3,923	7,259	10,064
Pennsylvania	62,000	9,000	49,608	8,823	9,204	12,636
Rhode Island	860	75	43,528	4,286	4,521	191
South Carolina	35,000	6,400	35,234	3,134	1,097	5,626
South Dakota	38,500	45,000	72,745	7,249	4,980	12,285
Tennessee..................	96,000	13,600	21,861	1,247	968	12,961
Texas......................	186,000	138,800	53,411	5,867	6,712	62,182
Utah	13,000	12,600	47,210	3,569	5,266	6,678
Vermont....................	7,700	1,740	55,067	12,242	12,288	1,235
Virginia...................	58,000	9,800	30,385	4,091	3,750	9,888
Washington	38,000	16,100	78,253	18,689	19,147	11,673
West Virginia..............	20,000	4,200	16,713	524	1,440	2,957
Wisconsin..................	93,000	18,600	57,036	12,213	14,554	18,228
Wyoming	9,100	35,000	80,227	1,707	2,177	5,355

Source: Economic Research Service and Statistical Reporting Service,
U.S. Department of Agriculture.

(a) Excludes net inventory changes.
(b) Includes net inventory changes.

Table 3
PRODUCTION OF MAJOR GRAINS, BY STATE: 1980*

State	Feed grains				Food grains			
	Corn	Oats	Barley	Sorghum	Wheat	Rye	Rice	Soybean
All states	6,647,534	457,953	358,544	577,272	2,369,666	15,532	145,063	1,817,097
Alabama	14,580	1,260	...	1,122	5,758	...	...	31,500
Alaska	...	...	...	...	...	...	...	...
Arizona	4,000	...	3,950	1,950	17,200	...	...	...
Arkansas	1,036	2,079	...	5,887	31,160	...	52,615	69,600
California	36,450	4,340	44,144	11,096	85,500	...	35,301	...
Colorado	89,680	1,683	15,925	12,250	109,900	120	...	...
Connecticut	...	...	...	...	...	...	...	...
Delaware	12,744	...	1,225	...	1,080	87	...	5,200
Florida	15,416	...	...	...	...	...	...	10,120
Georgia	54,600	3,445	...	1,968	19,800	1,995	...	25,680
Hawaii	...	...	...	...	...	...	...	...
Idaho	4,700	2,990	58,960	...	96,030	...	...	...
Illinois	1,065,780	14,030	258	3,658	75,360	368	...	309,875
Indiana	602,880	5,850	...	416	53,900	182	...	157,680
Iowa	1,463,000	62,000	...	1,330	3,496	150	...	322,530
Kansas	116,560	4,560	2,419	156,520	420,000	210	...	23,925
Kentucky	103,600	240	1,595	1,300	13,825	72	...	36,800
Louisiana	1,380	...	...	476	1,876	...	20,768	70,350
Maine	...	2,436	...	...	...	...	...	...
Maryland	46,080	1,121	3,640	...	3,686	216	...	9,360
Massachusetts	...	...	...	...	...	...	...	...
Michigan	247,000	20,100	1,113	...	35,200	504	...	30,400
Minnesota	610,130	82,650	34,638	...	102,556	1,900	...	152,320
Mississippi	2,464	...	...	1,330	7,750	...	9,226	61,600
Missouri	109,710	1,978	...	43,200	89,010	115	2,341	138,250
Montana	592	3,212	44,100	...	119,800	...	...	...
Nebraska	603,500	15,170	950	121,800	112,100	468	...	53,100
Nevada	...	...	1,960	...	1,800	...	...	...
New Hampshire	...	...	...	...	...	...	...	...
New Jersey	7,725	275	795	...	1,849	216	...	3,492
New Mexico	7,225	...	1,995	10,280	10,500	...	...	...
New York	67,890	17,920	517	...	6,000	288	...	456
North Carolina	103,800	3,900	2,880	2,232	10,500	400	...	35,705
North Dakota	16,820	13,500	48,000	...	179,650	1,470	...	3,500
Ohio	440,700	19,430	416	...	67,130	231	...	135,360
Oklahoma	5,250	3,900	1,650	16,320	195,000	816	...	3,000
Oregon	1,166	4,140	10,075	...	77,400	150	...	...
Pennsylvania	96,000	19,040	3,750	250	9,250	434	...	2,524
Rhode Island	...	...	...	...	...	...	...	...
South Carolina	24,720	1,960	1,012	330	6,912	616	...	22,400
South Dakota	121,900	66,000	13,860	...	62,425	4,030	...	20,020
Tennessee	28,800	552	168	1,470	13,300	...	...	48,450
Texas	117,000	12,580	1,080	181,700	130,000	494	24,812	13,860
Utah	1,500	915	10,804	...	8,942	...	...	...
Vermont	...	...	...	...	...	...	...	...
Virginia	32,725	900	4,590	387	10,582	...	...	9,150
Washington	11,280	1,860	31,500	...	160,220	...	...	...
West Virginia	5,162	539	396	...	342	...	...	...
Wisconsin	348,400	58,743	1,534	...	4,365	...	...	10,890
Wyoming	3,589	2,295	8,645	...	8,512	...	...	...

Source: Economic Research Service, U.S. Department of Agriculture.
*Amounts in 1,000 bushels, except rice which is in 1000 cwt.

Table 4
LIVESTOCK ON U.S. FARMS, BY STATE: 1980
(In thousands)

	Cattle and calves		Other livestock		Poultry	
	Total	Milk cows	Hogs and pigs	Sheep and lambs	Chicken	Turkeys
All states..................	110,961	10,810	67,059	12,686	399,676	156,529
Alabama.....................	1,730	76	880	...	22,000	...
Alaska.......................	8	1	110	4	25	...
Arizona	1,050	72	149	385	469	...
Arkansas	2,000	88	600	...	27,000	13,340
California...................	4,550	878	180	1,175	45,510	18,855
Colorado	2,975	72	430	870	2,300	3,885
Connecticut..................	104	49	11	5	5,871	46
Delaware	30	12	50	...	850	348
Florida	2,300	184	425	...	18,543	...
Georgia.....................	1,600	127	2,280	...	36,200	2,516
Hawaii	213	13	53	...	1,306	...
Idaho	1,860	142	110	468	1,023	...
Illinois......................	2,700	235	6,950	173	6,950	516
Indiana	1,850	200	4,900	120	20,500	5,640
Iowa	7,150	372	16,200	408	9,600	6,160
Kansas	6,100	122	2,070	235	2,470	184
Kentucky	2,700	244	1,400	21	3,501	...
Louisiana	1,300	116	150	12	3,500	...
Maine	131	57	13	13	11,250	...
Maryland	380	130	235	20	2,150	118
Massachusetts	103	44	60	7	1,726	140
Michigan	1,310	400	960	132	8,000	1,200
Minnesota	3,750	860	4,900	264	12,500	24,666
Mississippi	1,810	99	440	...	10,550	...
Missouri	5,350	270	4,550	123	7,720	10,950
Montana.....................	2,645	28	209	574	890	...
Nebraska	6,400	120	4,150	210	3,930	654
Nevada	580	15	9	122	13	...
New Hampshire	70	30	10	7	1,277	36
New Jersey..................	100	41	57	9	1,555	59
New Mexico..................	1,600	35	87	660	2,190	...
New York....................	1,780	912	139	65	10,200	227
North Carolina	1,080	141	2,600	8	20,800	23,100
North Dakota	2,000	93	370	236	430	1,020
Ohio........................	1,925	380	2,070	320	11,600	2,350
Oklahoma	5,500	110	370	93	4,400	1,890
Oregon	1,510	94	115	495	3,200	1,265
Pennsylvania	1,900	712	840	105	20,930	4,740
Rhode Island	8	4	10	...	332	...
South Carolina	625	50	650	...	9,770	2,998
South Dakota	4,010	165	2,000	783	2,850	1,253
Tennessee...................	2,300	214	1,400	12	5,400	...
Texas.......................	13,200	315	910	2,400	17,500	8,000
Utah	840	75	55	625	2,000	2,921
Vermont.....................	340	187	8	8	570	...
Virginia.....................	1,750	170	850	160	5,882	9,174
Washington..................	1,579	195	126	83	6,033	...
West Virginia................	545	37	56	113	940	2,633
Wisconsin...................	4,280	1,813	1,830	113	5,400	5,645
Wyoming....................	1,340	11	32	1,050	70	...

Source: Economic Research Service, U.S. Department of Agriculture.

Table 5
AGRICULTURAL PRODUCTION, BY COMMODITY, FOR SELECTED ITEMS, BY STATE: 1980
(In thousands)

State	Vegetables		Fruits		Other crops			
	Fresh (tons)	Processed (tons)	Citrus (tons)	Non-citrus (tons)	Potatoes (cwt.)	Cotton (bales)	Tobacco (lbs.)	Hay (tons)
All states	264,592	10,783,170	16,491	14,020	301,006	11,126	1,772,001	131,070
Alabama	1,301	4,890	...	10	1,105	275	816	1,031
Alaska	...	...	...	...	...	...	...	...
Arizona	11,900	1,600	371	14	1,276	1,413	...	1,260
Arkansas	321	12,210	...	38	...	450	...	1,221
California	118,730	5,746,730	3,215	7,503	18,692	3,150	...	7,736
Colorado	4,681	32,150	...	57	12,545	...	...	3,276
Connecticut	396	...	...	25	405	...	5,475	168
Delaware	325	55,730	...	8	969	...	...	40
Florida	42,914	65,040	12,418	47	5,304	8	20,291	552
Georgia	3,432	7,880	...	85	...	86	110,550	736
Hawaii	369	...	...	704	...	...	...	4,395
Idaho	2,453	172,120	...	78	78,455	...	...	3,558
Illinois	600	248,640	...	63	414	...	...	3,558
Indiana	1,617	136,510	...	35	966	...	15,300	2,208
Iowa	1	24,680	...	6	322	...	...	8,037
Kansas	...	...	...	10	...	...	...	4,230
Kentucky	223	4,350	...	18	...	...	409,222	2,970
Louisiana	73	100	...	6	119	455	56	612
Maine	...	8,380	...	52	24,960	...	...	362
Maryland	1,057	107,220	...	53	306	...	22,575	564
Massachusetts	1,020	8,020	...	102	748	...	2,058	258
Michigan	7,276	234,720	...	541	9,022	...	...	3,844
Minnesota	723	647,100	...	8	11,486	...	...	7,115
Mississippi	735	2,630	...	2	...	1,150	...	1,040
Missouri	288	2,070	...	46	...	178	5,125	4,470
Montana	...	...	...	3	1,725	...	...	4,170
Nebraska	...	1,750	...	...	2,136	...	...	7,083
Nevada	...	...	...	...	4,420	1	...	1,095
New Hampshire	...	...	...	29	...	...	...	187
New Jersey	4,278	92,170	...	126	1,968	...	...	255
New Mexico	1,775	4,000	...	7	540	110	...	1,144
New York	11,581	380,750	...	726	10,668	...	...	5,787
North Carolina	3,011	95,280	...	218	2,227	51	763,665	592
North Dakota	...	...	...	...	15,680	...	...	2,519
Ohio	2,327	343,140	...	71	2,234	...	20,510	3,588
Oklahoma	210	19,670	...	6	...	216	...	2,315
Oregon	6,055	569,680	...	406	19,745	...	...	2,893
Pennsylvania	1,711	66,150	...	372	4,180	...	22,750	4,182
Rhode Island	...	...	...	3	736	...	...	18
South Carolina	2,818	22,550	...	193	...	76	125,125	354
South Dakota	...	170	...	...	1,072	...	...	5,359
Tennessee	563	21,580	...	9	196	200	112,544	1,764
Texas	21,182	98,100	487	11	2,306	3,305	...	5,115
Utah	656	19,900	...	49	1,144	...	...	2,058
Vermont	...	...	...	25	120	...	...	886
Virginia	1,266	33,170	...	251	1,540	2	108,919	1,626
Washington	4,639	411,090	...	1,783	43,935	...	...	2,625
West Virginia	...	160	...	142	...	...	2,720	977
Wisconsin	2,085	1,081,090	...	79	16,000	...	24,300	12,545
Wyoming	...	...	...	...	1,340	...	...	1,850

Source: Economic Research Service, U.S. Department of Agriculture.

Table 6
U.S. AGRICULTURAL LANDHOLDINGS OF FOREIGN OWNERS,
BY STATE, AS OF FEBRUARY 1, 1979

State or other jurisdiction	1,000 acres			Percent of foreign-owned agricultural land
	Total area of state	Privately owned agricultural land(a)	Foreign-owned agricultural land	
Total.................	2,263,597	1,290,217	6,657,629	0.5
Alabama	32,452	29,467	180,955	0.6
Alaska	362,516	400	337	0.1
Arizona	72,587	10,983	154,501	1.4
Arkansas	33,245	28,834	54,165	0.2
California..............	100,071	47,353	418,478	0.9
Colorado	66,410	37,527	232,620	0.6
Connecticut.............	3,112	2,267	303	N
Delaware	1,268	1,064	6,627	0.6
Florida	34,618	26,529	316,399	1.2
Georgia	37,167	33,253	325,311	1.0
Hawaii	4,112	1,992	47,938	2.4
Idaho	52,913	15,166	12,900	0.1
Illinois	35,679	32,326	109,808	0.3
Indiana	23,102	20,909	92,573	0.4
Iowa	35,802	33,912	27,408	0.1
Kansas	52,344	49,911	43,661	0.1
Kentucky	25,376	22,915	22,638	0.1
Louisiana	28,755	26,463	115,172	0.4
Maine	19,789	18,829	960,677	5.1
Maryland	6,330	5,146	22,530	0.4
Massachusetts...........	5,009	3,322	438	N
Michigan	36,363	26,117	43,412	0.2
Minnesota	50,745	36,204	28,272	0.1
Mississippi	30,269	26,629	89,566	0.3
Missouri	44,157	40,025	60,456	0.2
Montana	93,176	54,189	272,768	0.5
Nebraska	48,949	45,397	79,994	0.2
Nevada	70,328	7,586	155,847	2.1
New Hampshire	5,777	4,682	30,973	0.7
New Jersey.............	4,813	2,894	19,868	0.7
New Mexico.............	77,703	34,451	313,220	0.9
New York	30,612	24,257	211,806	0.9
North Carolina	31,231	27,321	177,276	0.6
North Dakota	44,339	39,617	17,727	N
Ohio	26,224	22,979	25,677	0.1
Oklahoma	44,020	38,875	24,849	0.1
Oregon	61,557	25,685	169,691	0.7
Pennsylvania	28,778	22,380	154,561	0.7
Rhode Island............	671	439	0	0
South Carolina	19,344	15,932	289,531	1.8
South Dakota	48,611	38,241	18,694	N
Tennessee..............	26,450	22,901	296,484	1.3
Texas	167,766	156,768	440,431	0.3
Utah	52,541	10,779	222,908	2.1
Vermont................	5,931	5,251	50,971	1.0
Virginia	25,459	21,499	59,132	0.3
Washington	42,605	23,028	99,925	0.4
West Virginia...........	15,405	13,744	21,393	0.2
Wisconsin	34,857	27,637	13,620	N
Wyoming	62,210	26,142	122,022	0.5
Guam	135	85	336	N
Puerto Rico	N.A.	N.A.	780	N

Source: Economic Research Service, U.S. Department of Agriculture.
Key:
N—Negligible
N.A.—Not available.

(a) Privately held land based on unpublished data; T. Frey, Economic Research Service, U.S. Department of Agriculture, 1979. Estimate of total land less public, Indian, transportation and urban lands. Includes forest, pasture, crop, range and miscellaneous lands.

Table 7
FOREIGN INVESTMENT IN U.S. CROPLAND AND FARMLAND:
FEBRUARY 1, 1979 TO DECEMBER 31, 1980

State	Ownership transfers (acres)(a)	Foreign investment		
		Total owners (numbers)	Cropland (acres)	Farmland (acres)
All states..................	185,119	6,746	1,000,768	1,747,801
Alabama.....................	3,862	27	2,811	830
Alaska.......................	...	2	204	46
Arizona	714	153	8,536	79,913
Arkansas	4,159	63	43,891	5,722
California...................	8,224	641	210,945	103,428
Colorado	2,523	131	62,465	139,588
Connecticut	(b)	8	60	197
Delaware	301	7	1,200	81
Florida.....................	,227	738	47,812	105,738
Georgia.....................	5,062	203	36,232	17,443
Hawaii	...	40	256	8,450
Idaho.......................	2,021	36	2,113	6,392
Illinois.....................	8,330	130	35,139	2,788
Indiana.....................	6,239	58	8,272	2,173
Iowa	8,459	90	26,113	2,961
Kansas	5,546	60	13,504	7,330
Kentucky	8,459	50	4,037	6,342
Louisiana...................	2,079	58	48,192	18,442
Maine	(b)	30	84	636
Maryland...................	1,454	82	13,533	5,456
Massachusetts	2,196	11	31	15
Michigan	6,133	71	6,581	720
Minnesota	5,226	44	11,371	5,500
Mississippi	4,615	96	56,552	7,987
Missouri....................	8,688	73	24,289	9,523
Montana....................	1,999	102	32,550	181,468
Nebraska	4,813	39	31,339	34,060
Nevada	(c)	20	5,608	192,570
New Hampshire	(b)	18	480	165
New Jersey	820	41	9,261	6,891
New Mexico.................	1,196	43	8,067	180,098
New York...................	4,843	468	4,144	7,120
North Carolina	7,681	75	22,301	5,285
North Dakota	2,096	49	11,871	2,726
Ohio	7,877	52	4,489	2,864
Oklahoma	4,226	33	7,043	7,967
Oregon	3,437	45	7,857	152,661
Pennsylvania	4,662	43	1,209	942
Rhode Island	(b)	...	...	...
South Carolina	2,330	63	7,322	6,357
South Dakota	2,985	38	29,623	6,223
Tennessee...................	7,124	56	1,965	1,758
Texas.......................	14,378	718	109,032	334,175
Utah	1,152	316	186	31,852
Vermont....................	(b)	708	8,278	7,276
Virginia	3,845	164	11,231	16,471
Washington	3,273	666	9,740	17,420
West Virginia...............	1,610	23	111	369
Wisconsin...................	7,496	52	10,804	1,424
Wyoming	759	12	2,034	11,958

Source: Economic Research Service, U.S. Department of Agriculture.
(a) Data shown reflects March 1, 1979 through March 1, 1981.

(b) To avoid disclosure, ownership transfers for these states have been included in total for Massachusetts.
(c) Insufficient data.

STATE FORESTRY ADMINISTRATION

By H. Mike Miller

THE NATION'S FORESTS have played a major role in the development of this country. At first, these forests were obstacles in the way of settlements and farms. Eventually, through the work of far-sighted individuals, forests came to be viewed as a renewable natural resource.

Today, the United States has 75 percent as much forest land as when the pilgrims landed. The growing population has placed increased demands on these forests for lumber, paper, plywood and many other by-products. With proper management of all forests, public and private, these lands are capable of producing the wood that we need, now and in the future.

Nearly one-third of our nation's land is forested, about 750 million acres. Of these forests, some two-thirds are in timber production. The balance is managed as wilderness, watersheds or recreational areas.

About 58 percent of the forests are in non-industrial private ownership. Another 12 percent are owned by large private forest industries. National forests comprise about 18 percent, with other public forests, including state, county and city forests, totaling some 9 percent.

Organization

All states have a state forestry organization. Usually this organization is part of a cabinet-level state department that reports directly to the governor. Some forestry agencies are part of a land grant university extension system. In a few states, the forestry organization operates as an independent agency under a state commission.

The primary responsibility of each state forestry organization is to conduct forestry work for the public good and encourage good forestry on privately owned forest land. In addition, these agencies work in cooperation with private, federal and other state agencies, organizations and individuals to direct and strengthen all forestry programs within their state.

In 1920, state foresters organized the National Association of State Foresters (NASF). This organization has supported federal legislation to meet national goals for forests and served as a forum for exchanging forestry information and providing opportunities for cooperation among the various states in meeting their own state goals.

Goals of Forestry

The Resources Planning Act Assessment for 1980 shows that if current practices are continued unchanged, by 2000 we will have serious shortages of timber, outdoor recreation opportunities, clean water, wildlife habitat and many other benefits currently provided by

H. Mike Miller is State Forester in Oregon.

631

forests. These shortages will be caused both by the increasing population and increased demands for resources. Meeting this demand for more forest services, more diverse recreation opportunities, cleaner water and a generally high-quality environment are the goals of forestry.

Recent findings of the Forest Industries Council Forest Productivity Project show that there are opportunities to increase productivity, with the greatest on private non-industrial forest land. If these opportunities are realized, the United States can grow sufficient timber to hold down consumer costs and to build the potential for an international net trade surplus of forest products, while supplying domestic markets adequately.

Three-quarters of the opportunities for increasing future timber production lie within the borders of non-industrial private ownerships. However, the present trend is for the private landowner to harvest timber without making necessary investments to reforest the cutover area, except in those states where reforestation following harvest is required by law or where natural reforestation is adequate. Because of economic factors, many private, non-industrial landowners are unwilling or unable to make the investment in reforestation without incentives to reduce the costs or provide an adequate return on investment.

State and private cooperative programs authorized by the Cooperative Forestry Assistance Act of 1978 are aimed at providing those incentives. Through state forestry organizations, the federal government can aid the private landowner with financial and technical assistance in protection from fire, insects and disease. However, to be effective in meeting long-term future needs, these programs require sustained and increased funding levels. Through the strong cooperative effort of the U.S. Forest Service, state forestry organizations and private forest landowners, America can meet its future needs for renewable resources.

Forest Management Assistance

Upon request, technical forestry assistance is available to private landowners through various state forestry agencies. The U.S. Forest Service provides additional technical and financial assistance to the states through their Rural Forestry Assistance Program. Advice is available to landowners, loggers and processors on tree planting, timber stand improvement, more efficient harvesting, improved sawmilling methods, forest management inventories and forest management plans. Once management plans have been prepared, landowners are encouraged to secure the services of private forestry consultants to complete the work for them or to offer continuing advice as work progresses.

Two federal funding programs provide financial assistance to non-industrial private landowners. The Forestry Incentives Program is a production-oriented program that provides up to 65 percent of cost for tree planting and timber stand improvement work. The Agricultural Conservation Program also provides funds for planting and forest improvement, as well as for other benefits, including watershed and wildlife protection.

In 1972, cooperative state and federal urban forestry assistance began when the Cooperative Forest Management Act of 1950 was amended to include urban forestry. That act, in turn, was superseded by the Cooperative Forestry Assistance Act of 1978 which authorizes the secretary of agriculture to provide financial, technical and related assistance to state foresters who, in turn, provide information and technical assistance to local government units and others who promote urban forestry through services of consultants, vendors and businesses.

NATURAL RESOURCES

Forest Fire Control

Many state forestry agencies were created because of the need for forest fire control services. All states are now involved in the protection of state and private lands from wildfires.

The federal government encouraged fire control by passage of the Week's Law of 1911. Under this law, cooperating states had to provide a system of fire protection to which the federal government could contribute up to one-half the cost. In 1924, the Clarke-McNary Act was passed that gave financial assistance to state forestry agencies to provide manpower and organization to do the job within each state. Today, the U.S. Forest Service continues support through financial assistance, coordination, review and audit. The federal agency also provides services, including the training of personnel, development and procurement of fire equipment, radio communications and direction of the nationwide forest fire prevention program.

The Cooperative Forest Fire Prevention Program is a joint effort of the U.S. Forest Service, the National Association of State Foresters and the Advertising Council. It provides leadership for the Smokey Bear fire prevention program throughout the nation. Some 90 percent of all wildfires are still man-caused. Of this total, incendiary and debris burning cause over one-half of the 125,646 man-caused fires that burn annually.

A number of states assist rural fire departments to obtain fire fighting equipment and to train department personnel in wildfire fighting techniques. Fire prevention programs are conducted to reduce the annual incidence of fire and to maintain a high level of awareness on the problems of uncontrolled burning. Some states have interstate compacts to provide assistance or personnel and equipment during catastrophic situations. The U.S. Forest Service, the federal Bureau of Land Management and other public agencies also cooperate in exchanging manpower and equipment for large fires.

The National Wildfire Coordinating Group (NWCG) coordinates state and federal efforts in all areas of fire management. Based in Boise, Idaho, NWCG has encouraged the development of improved standards for fire prevention and fire control efforts, cooperative training for fire managers and other services to fire agencies in federal and state governments.

State Forests

Most state forestry organizations administer state-owned forest lands under the multiple-use concept. These forests produce wood fiber to local wood-using industries, provide watershed for public water supply and offer other public benefits, including outdoor classrooms, research areas and recreation areas.

Revenues from the sale of these forest products help the local economy, and in some cases, provide a source of revenue for local governments.

Because of the large land base of state forests and their proximity to population centers, many of these areas are experiencing an increased use in forest recreation, including camping, hiking, hunting, fishing, cross-country skiing and horseback riding. With increased costs of transportation, these lands will likely feel continued pressures as the public seeks recreation closer to home.

The largest state forests are in Alaska, Michigan, Minnesota, New York, Pennsylvania and Washington. The greatest volume of timber harvesting and revenues occur in the Western United States.

633

Reforestation

Most states grow tree and shrub seedlings for reforesting state forests and to sell to private owners to reforest their lands. In addition, seedlings are sold for establishing windbreaks, shelterbelts and reforesting eroded lands. These seedlings are sometimes supplied to private landowners with cost subsidized by state and federal government.

Some states have forest practices law that requires successful reforestation after harvesting. Seedlings are sold to private landowners for this effort. Some states work cooperatively with private forest nurseries to encourage an adequate supply of nursery stock to meet all needs. Most states operate their own nurseries in growing trees for state forests as well as to sell to private landowners. This work has become highly specialized in recent years as more has been learned about growing seedlings.

Many state forestry agencies have genetic tree improvement programs, designed to improve the quality of nursery stock. Forest genetics identify high-quality individual trees growing in natural conditions and use seed from these trees to establish seed orchards. Eventually, these seed orchards produce the seed used by forest nurseries to grow the next crop of forest seedlings.

Use and Marketing

An important element of many state forestry programs is technical assistance offered to wood-using industries, with the goal of assuring the best use of the raw material from each state's forest resource. Assistance is provided in all phases from logging, to processing, to marketing. Specialists work with loggers to help identify improvements in logging techniques and what new equipment might be employed to increase the amount of usable wood taken from the forest. Processors are given assistance in sawing, planing and resawing roundwood into secondary products, as well as in wood-drying technology. Other industries are assisted with marketing information to help assure a stable demand for wood products.

Wood fuel for energy and increased use of residues are two areas that have received increased attention in recent years. State forestry agencies have been heavily involved in responding to these issues. Agencies are looking for ways to meet the demand for increased wood fuel without degrading the forest resource base and affecting forest management plans for other resources.

Forest Pest Control

Nationwide, insect and disease attacks produce greater losses to the nation's timber resource than all other causes. Protection of the forests from uncontrolled insect and disease attacks requires combining all forces to prevent, detect and suppress pests.

Increased public concern on the use of toxic chemicals, such as pesticides, has led forestry agencies to establish an integrated pest management approach to controlling insects. This approach includes understanding the biology of the insect and the type of damage it does, then using the best combination of management methods, including bacterial spray, natural predators and pesticides. Foresters do not attempt to eradicate a pest. Rather, efforts are geared to holding the pests at acceptable levels so that damage stays within limits that can be tolerated. Research is under way by many states on symbiotic relationships between organisms to learn more about how to control pest populations naturally.

Forest Resource Planning

Many state agencies and the National Association of State Foresters have become increasingly active in the total planning of forest resources at state and national levels. Within each state, state forestry agencies are reviewing federal land use plans and goals, as well as supporting improved forest management on all other public and private lands. Nationally, NASF has established national and state goals, as well as specific federal land goals addressing all issues of forestry.

With the philosophy of shared responsibility and cooperation among state, federal and private forest landowners, state forestry organizations are hoping to meet the future needs of the nation for renewable forest resources. Specific information on each state's forestry program is available from the state forestry organization.

Table 1
FOREST RESOURCES*
(In thousands of acres)

State	Total land area	Total forest area	Private forest area	State forest area	Federal forest area
All states	2,285,172	719,332	372,823	30,722	175,166
Alabama	33,030	21,330	20,310	158	733
Alaska	375,000	110,000	5,000	500	24,000
Arizona	72,688	13,500	600	350	11,500
Arkansas	33,470	16,600	13,700	237	2,349
California	100,300	40,200	7,600	79	8,500
Colorado	66,430	22,580	7,300	570	14,710
Connecticut	3,170	1,860	1,600	180	2
Delaware	1,000	400	300	13	6
Florida	35,180	17,930	14,090	310	1,650
Georgia	37,300	25,300	23,110	140	1,800
Hawaii	4,110	1,990	1,010	960	20
Idaho	53,000	21,000	3,154	992	16,490
Illinois	36,000	3,789	3,412	14	256
Indiana	20,000	3,900	3,500	141	213
Iowa	35,870	1,560	1,350	240	0
Kansas	52,500	1,500	1,150	8	26
Kentucky	25,500	12,300	11,500	70	800
Louisiana	31,060	14,530	13,510	443	579
Maine	19,000	17,000	16,600	400	200
Maryland	6,380	2,520	2,280	185	24
Massachusetts	5,013	3,500	3,251	240	96
Michigan	36,300	19,200	12,200	3,800	2,400
Minnesota	51,210	19,000	8,100	6,900	4,000
Mississippi	30,309	16,504	14,829	426	1,122
Missouri	44,000	12,400	10,400	280	1,300
Montana	93,174	23,189	6,564	491	16,150
Nebraska	50,000	1,000	876	68	56
Nevada	70,260	134	65	10	59
New Hampshire	5,770	4,960	3,140	99	501
New Jersey	4,820	1,860	1,540	250	30
New Mexico	77,703	18,580	5,580	924	11,576
New York	30,640	17,170	13,390	800	57
North Carolina	31,300	19,600	17,400	320	336
North Dakota	44,900	410	200	108	30
Ohio	26,251	6,873	6,323	175	170
Oklahoma	44,750	8,580	8,340	0	240
Oregon	61,574	29,980	9,868	785	19,337
Pennsylvania	28,820	16,830	13,170	2,040	490
Rhode Island	670	570	359	211	0
South Carolina	19,350	12,503	11,412	167	900
South Dakota	47,130	1,700	560	78	1,060
Tennessee	27,000	13,100	11,500	150	1,200
Texas	174,000	25,000	9,000	60	634
Utah	53,000	16,600	3,000	3,000	10,600
Vermont	5,900	4,400	4,000	200	200
Virginia	25,000	16,500	14,500	500	1,500
Washington	42,600	23,180	8,730	1,790	6,930
West Virginia	15,400	11,630	10,300	330	1,000
Wisconsin	35,000	14,500	9,790	418	1,266
Wyoming	62,340	10,090	1,820	202	8,068

*These do not reflect all resources, since some ownerships are not reported.

Table 2
FOREST FIRE CONTROL PROGRAM

State or other jurisdiction	State & private lands protected (thousands of acres)*	Federal & state fire control expenditures (thousands of dollars)	Average number of fires per year 1974-78	Average acreage burned per year 1974-78
All states.................	736,141	$246,878	123,267	1,672,648
Alabama.....................	25,030	4,095	6,906	183,117
Alaska......................	30,000	4,000	212	10,294
Arizona	18,000	267	184	7,986
Arkansas	14,267	5,500	3,638	63,028
California	33,300	93,810	10,386	146,838
Colorado	14,450	2,900	746	6,598
Connecticut	2,300	300	1,066	2,394
Delaware	400	1,320	50	292
Florida	26,100	16,080	8,907	238,694
Georgia.....................	27,300	12,168	12,855	55,453
Hawaii	1,990	250	287	7,552
Idaho	1,815	5,228	512	12,067
Illinois....................	8,000	500	175	3,433
Indiana	7,500	337	234	2,679
Iowa	1,560	243	2,196	10,896
Kansas	19,800	2,100	1,837	76,041
Kentucky	11,500	4,000	2,693	65,019
Louisiana	14,530	7,600	6,494	69,857
Maine	17,000	400	901	4,793
Maryland	3,650	1,140	782	2,820
Massachusetts	3,500	1,460	8,551	9,196
Michigan	19,700	5,500	1,007	12,624
Minnesota	22,800	2,789	1,720	86,653
Mississippi	17,000	5,650	7,265	90,123
Missouri	11,000	1,056	4,068	26,897
Montana.....................	25,866	2,137	343	2,343
Nebraska	27,00	373	2,034	29,406
Nevada	8,000	1,500	222	2,963
New Hampshire	4,660	883	946	482
New Jersey	2,705	2,600	1,936	14,070
New Mexico..................	40,200	590	279	38,925
New York....................	17,000	3,300	709	5,139
North Carolina	17,500	7,731	4,351	39,655
North Dakota	18,000	172	78	2,194
Ohio	5,800	1,058	625	2,106
Oklahoma	6,000	1,764	1,607	59,163
Oregon	15,700	8,262	1,088	4,071
Pennsylvania	16,830	2,940	1,463	8,865
Rhode Island	512	424	841	922
South Carolina	12,000	6,378	7,338	40,095
South Dakota	25,816	1,000	694	27,788
Tennessee...................	15,000	5,300	4,502	45,487
Texas.......................	25,000	3,600	2,535	34,914
Utah	15,000	1,170	498	24,755
Vermont.....................	4,400	200	209	569
Virginia	14,000	3,933	3,688	9,618
Washington	12,060	6,250	1,060	7,061
West Virginia...............	12,600	1,000	2,005	42,142
Wisconsin...................	17,000	5,250	2,309	18,944
Wyoming	25,000	1,000	544	15,630

*Acres protected do not equal total forest lands (Table 1) because areas with other classifications are also included.

Table 3
SUMMARY OF FORESTRY INCENTIVE PROGRAMS
AND RURAL FORESTRY ASSISTANCE EXPENDITURES

State	FP-1, Planting trees (fiscal 1979)		FP-2, Improving a stand of trees (fiscal 1979)		Rural forestry assistance expenditures (fiscal 1980)		
	Acres planted	Total cost share	Acres improved	Total cost share	Federal	State	Total
All states	211,977	$11,536,926	117,585	$2,847,356	$8,011,181	$35,636,117	$43,682,398
Alabama	42,733	2,045,812	2,310	30,111	330,848	1,134,300	1,465,148
Alaska	...	...	...	...	68,180	68,180	136,360
Arizona	...	...	227	8,286	60,800	60,800	121,600
Arkansas	10,213	549,723	8,831	234,035	207,590	1,592,072	1,799,662
California	1,992	201,610	975	92,031	264,164	1,054,833	1,318,997
Colorado	10	800	346	19,707	154,020	530,922	684,942
Connecticut	71	3,550	637	20,338	44,500	229,616	274,116
Delaware	266	21,462	...	...	45,000	97,000	142,000
Florida	14,957	759,451	1,415	12,361	282,673	1,879,327	2,162,000
Georgia	18,115	1,202,092	585	11,138	340,000	1,773,961	2,113,961
Hawaii	60	9,693	...	...	81,300	379,323	460,623
Idaho	...	...	96	6,868	86,900	333,350	420,250
Illinois	127	12,535	2,063	56,319	67,000	67,000	134,000
Indiana	324	17,510	7,547	136,759	163,000	860,197	1,023,197
Iowa	216	12,118	390	10,381	68,000	239,148	307,148
Kansas	28	4,797	368	13,653	83,000	417,490	500,490
Kentucky	250	15,149	4,073	101,127	228,000	635,757	863,757
Louisiana	12,056	570,438	4,692	137,980	155,117	547,556	702,673
Maine	832	51,313	2,174	67,010	160,000	426,800	586,800
Maryland	1,114	67,198	1,222	33,171	164,700	716,589	881,289
Massachusetts	30	2,487	3,406	96,447	83,000	205,335	288,335
Michigan	2,464	93,696	4,592	106,601	239,000	325,200	564,200
Minnesota	988	69,051	2,436	41,633	222,000	222,000	444,000
Mississippi	17,239	915,246	2,891	62,005	241,000	2,855,637	3,096,637
Missouri	1,283	73,428	9,414	152,502	237,000	518,000	755,000
Montana	2	100	923	65,807	119,150	314,189	433,339
Nebraska	18	1,452	187	6,019	54,100	58,142	112,242
Nevada	...	...	...	...	56,250	510,724	566,974
New Hampshire	...	...	2,979	107,175	143,150	235,810	378,960
New Jersey	43	2,408	1,905	29,941	132,750	384,460	517,210
New Mexico	...	...	870	22,064	111,800	111,800	223,600
New York	375	21,183	7,618	193,308	275,000	336,000	611,000
North Carolina	22,872	1,215,506	2,743	63,139	382,681	3,543,003	3,925,684
North Dakota	...	...	10	825	55,550	71,000	126,550
Ohio	730	34,929	6,888	221,527	140,000	630,000	770,000
Oklahoma	1,759	74,288	967	22,366	59,110	450,900	510,010
Oregon	3,893	341,897	1,378	42,212	138,000	1,624,000	1,762,000
Pennsylvania	372	16,923	3,927	155,784	245,400	1,477,994	1,723,394
Rhode Island	16	344	306	9,166	38,600	49,500	88,100
South Carolina	18,808	1,157,999	112	3,270	205,830	205,830	411,660
South Dakota	...	...	200	11,256	63,200	189,531	252,731
Tennessee	1,260	70,135	1,318	24,726	261,876	1,187,100	1,448,976
Texas	9,998	563,251	4,973	109,961	214,800	1,240,922	1,455,722
Utah	...	...	...	...	63,000	268,868	331,868
Vermont	29	1,806	2,752	55,271	171,000	274,393	445,393
Virginia	22,083	980,414	647	9,827	342,928	2,413,550	2,756,478
Washington	1,741	214,082	2,108	42,834	249,000	460,000	709,000
West Virginia	394	19,512	10,371	121,049	169,000	557,782	726,782
Wisconsin	2,216	121,538	3,561	72,954	244,000	1,810,103	2,054,103
Wyoming	...	...	152	6,412	43,214	60,123	103,337

Table 4
INSECT AND DISEASE MANAGEMENT EXPENDITURES, PROFESSIONAL FORESTRY PERSONNEL, STATE FOREST LAND AND STATE NURSERY PROGRAMS

| | Insect and disease management expenditures | | | Profes-sional state forestry personnel | State nursery programs | | |
| | | | | | Acreage of state-owned forest land (in thousands) | Number of tree seedlings produced by state nurseries (in thousands) | Acres of seed orchard |
	Federal	State	Total				
All states	$11,008,900	$29,601,900	$40,755,900	3,291	61,735	697,196	13,689
Alabama	729,600	824,50	1,554,100	74	155	61,000	1,006
Alaska	...	...	...	...	20,900	386	...
Arizona	17,600	17,600	35,200	17	2,600	...	...
Arkansas	65,900	98,800	164,700	70	19	17,952	552
California..............	406,200	529,000	935,200	119	70	5,533	262
Colorado	616,400	761,900	1,378,300	60	570	2,045	...
Connecticut............	...	...	...	...	180	2,358	9
Delaware	...	...	...	8	6	330	6
Florida	62,100	110,400	172,500	126	310	43,762	2,271
Georgia	666,000	352,700	1,018,700	115	13	61,785	1,459
Hawaii	17,600	33,400	51,000	35	960	351	...
Idaho	33,600	334,500	368,100	...	881	885	376
Illinois	...	...	...	45	11	5,800	89
Indiana	31,200	31,500	62,700	44	140	6,100	37
Iowa	35,200	35,200	70,400	23	24	2,501	14
Kansas	20,800	20,800	41,600	20	...	959	37
Kentucky	44,100	44,100	88,200	70	42	12,200	46
Louisiana	144,300	68,000	212,300	75	443	82,600	949
Maine	1,401,000	9,053,000	10,454,000	56	250	2,210	6
Maryland	42,300	29,800	72,100	51	185,000	2,707	25
Massachusetts	18,200	56,100	74,300	...	240,000	...	...
Michigan	67,800	76,800	144,600	98	3,800	6,800	80
Minnesota	60,500	90,500	151,000	...	3,700	2,986	33
Mississippi	582,500	374,800	957,300	134	460	77,437	734
Missouri	50,600	101,200	151,800	74	350	11,040	29
Montana	38,100	80,100	118,200	58	491	1,110	38
Nebraska	15,600	15,600	31,200	10	68	3,403	20
Nevada	6,000	...	6,000	12	6	207	...
New Hampshire	33,500	119,300	152,800	23	112	300	19
New Jersey.............	513,000	535,900	1,048,900	87	250	842	49
New Mexico............	34,900	58,800	93,700	...	900	...	...
New York	416,200	416,200	832,400	126	3,300	7,789	175
North Carolina	313,600	100,500	414,100	113	398	47,140	807
North Dakota	...	...	...	9	22	1,198	22
Ohio	25,000	39,100	64,100	64	170	8,180	105
Oklahoma	28,400	30,900	59,300	30	...	4,633	190
Oregon	59,100	163,000	222,100	246	785	22,500	984
Pennsylvania...........	279,600	1,179,000	1,458,600	164	2,000	4,062	106
Rhode Island	18,300	18,300	36,600	12	30	...	...
South Carolina	337,700	250,800	588,500	91	167	44,878	796
South Dakota	233,400	281,500	514,900	31	78	950	...
Tennessee..............	43,000	43,000	86,000	78	150	20,874	405
Texas	168,000	232,600	400,600	68	49	26,250	652
Utah	...	...	...	18	1,000	130	...
Vermont................	30,800	177,500	208,300	40	200	285	21
Virginia	169,800	122,900	292,700	121	12,500	53,399	636
Washington	62,000	141,600	203,600	510	1,800	19,700	396
West Virginia..........	49,100	196,400	245,500	54	330	5,043	18
Wisconsin	3,127,600	12,290,300	15,417,900	...	418	14,313	230
Wyoming	37,000	64,800	101,800	12	202	383	...

SOIL AND WATER CONSERVATION

By Neil Sampson

EVEN THOUGH people have expressed concern for the fate of America's topsoil since early Colonial days, it took the Dust Bowl of the 1930s to elicit action from the federal government. In 1928, Hugh Hammond Bennett, a scientist with the federal Bureau of Chemistry and Soils, published a circular entitled "Soil Erosion, A National Menace," which led, in 1929, to the first federal appropriations for soil conservation work. The money—$160,000—was used to set up 10 soil erosion measurement stations, and the information that began flowing from those efforts was widely publicized by Bennett and his co-workers.

In 1933, President Franklin D. Roosevelt named Bennett director of the Soil Erosion Service in the U.S. Department of the Interior and gave him $5 million to employ people on erosion control projects. The Civilian Conservation Corps (CCC) eventually put 3 million idle young men to work on America's farms, forests and streambanks.

That early work was largely done in demonstration projects, although the word "demonstration" was somewhat a misnomer, since it implied some knowledge about what would be "demonstrated." Often these first workers didn't really know what to do or what would result. Through these projects came the confidence that soil erosion could be stopped and the beginning knowledge of how to do it. People who had worked on the early efforts became articulate advocates of soil conservation and effective teachers who could show others the needed skills.

USDA Takes Over, Turns to States

Bennett's call for a "coordinated program" resulted in 1935 in the Soil Conservation Act (Public Law 74-46) which created the Soil Conservation Service (SCS) as a permanent agency within the Department of Agriculture (USDA) to develop and execute a continuing program of soil and water conservation. In order to carry out the new program, it was decided within the USDA that soil conservation districts should be established as independent units of special-purpose government at the local level to take major responsibility for planning and operating the program. These districts would handle soil and water conservation as their only mission, much like a school district operates only schools or a sewer district sewers. USDA lawyers drafted a suggested state law that contained the legal details worked out in the department and, after much review within the administration, President Roosevelt sent a letter in February 1937 to all the state governors, enclosing the "standard" enabling act and suggesting that each state adopt such a law as part of an effective national effort to conserve the soil.

Arkansas and Oklahoma were the first, but by the end of 1937 a total of 22 states had enacted the soil district law. Within a decade, every state, Puerto Rico and the Virgin

Neil Sampson is Executive Vice President, National Association of Conservation Districts, Washington, D.C.

Islands had established the legal framework for landowners to create soil conservation districts. The final state laws varied somewhat, but generally included provisions for establishing a state soil conservation agency (called a committee, commission or board in the various states) to oversee the formation and operation of districts; a petition and referendum procedure for creating local districts; and a statement of the authorities that would be granted to the new units of special-purpose government.

At the local level, the districts entered into a memorandum of understanding with the Secretary of Agriculture, and the Soil Conservation Service agreed to provide technical assistance to the district and its cooperating land users. This assistance was in the form of federal technicians who would live in the district and help farmers solve soil and water problems.

Evolution of Conservation Districts

In the early 1960s, rapid shifts in land use away from agriculture, excessive soil and sedimentation from construction of housing and other developments, and growing public concern for environmental quality presented new challenges for conservation districts.

In many cases, this meant entering into activities that districts were not authorized to do in their state enabling legislation. To help meet that need, over 200 amendments to state soil and water conservation district laws were adopted between the late 1960s and 1975.

Some of the needed changes included broadening the scope of the law in 30 states to include issues such as flood prevention, drainage, irrigation, water pollution and storm water runoff; including urban areas within district boundaries; providing for urban or non-farm representation on district governing bodies; authorizing the levying of taxes or assessments; the exercise of eminent domain; and allowing districts to receive funds from counties.

In the early 1970s, a new sense of urgency was added to the conservation effort by the passage of Section 208 of the Federal Water Pollution Control Act Amendments of 1972. This brought the threat of federal regulation over farm activities if, as the law proposed, the Environmental Protection Agency (EPA) enforced its authority to stop pollution at whatever source it originated. Farmers and their organizations were adamantly opposed to such federal regulation.

Erosion and Sediment Control Laws

In a cooperative effort with The Council of State Governments, USDA and EPA, the National Association of Conservation Districts (NACD) worked out a model state erosion and sediment control act. The Council of State Governments included the model act in its *Suggested State Legislation* for 1973, and NACD carried out 42 state sediment control conferences to increase awareness of erosion and sediment control, explain the provisions of the model act and encourage state action to meet the challenges posed by water pollution.

As a result of these efforts, 20 states, the District of Columbia and the Virgin Islands adopted legislation to establish sediment and erosion control programs. Most of these laws prohibit local governments from issuing subdivision approvals or building permits without an erosion and sediment control plan approved by the conservation districts.

State Agencies Expand Roles

For most of the 1940-1960 period, the role of the state soil conservation agencies was largely limited to helping form local districts and providing some guidance in their operation. As district programs became more independent and active, state appropriations to support their operations became more common. These funds were used to hire district employees and pay for other district programs, so the state soil conservation agency has become more active in monitoring district programs, understanding their needs and telling state legislators what those state funds are buying and why new appropriations are needed.

In some states, the state agency hires technicians on the state's payroll and stations them in district field offices to assist with the local program, but the more common pattern is for the state agency to transfer funds to the district, where district officials are responsible for hiring and managing the staff. These employees, no matter who pays their salaries, are integrated with the federal staff provided by SCS into one local office that provides a broad range of technical services to the public.

The concept of a long-range program to guide these state investments and coordinate them with all the other conservation activities was not needed for many years, but as states took a more active part in funding district efforts, a need grew for the state government to develop its own soil and water program. When the Soil and Water Resources Conservation Act of 1977 (RCA) required SCS to develop a national report on conservation program needs, SCS in turn encouraged each state to conduct an inventory and appraisal of its soil and water resources. From this base, most state soil conservation agencies are developing a state long-range program to set out a strategy for solving resource problems.

State Programs

State long-range plans follow several different formats, according to the particular authorities and responsibilities delegated to the state soil conservation agency. Common features include an assessment of the overall condition of the state's soil and water resource base and a program to guide the state agency's actions in coordinating the activities of the local conservation districts. Data used in developing the state plan comes from district long-range programs, state water quality plans and other sources such as the National Resource Inventories conducted by USDA's Soil Conservation Service. The state plan provides a forum around which the policies and activities of the state agency, as well as the local districts, can address major land and water conservation issues.

An important outcome of the development of state long-range plans has been a more widespread recognition of the soil conservation problem within state government, as well as wider recognition of the constructive roles that the states can and must play in a truly intergovernmental effort. Many states, for example, have used the program as a basis for new state legislation and budget priorities, including state-funded technical and financial assistance for land users, resource data gathering, watershed management and public education.

This type of expansion in state and local activity has increased their financial contribution to conservation work. In the early years of the conservation effort in the United States, practically all of the financing for soil and water conservation programs came from the federal government. Today, substantial contributions are being made by state and local governments and private interests. Table A demonstrates the rapid growth in state and local funds for soil and water conservation programs. (By comparison, the federal soil conservation effort in 1980 totaled about $900 million.)

Table A
GROWTH OF STATE AND LOCAL GOVERNMENTAL FUNDS
IN SOIL CONSERVATION DISTRICT PROGRAMS,
1957-1979, IN ACTUAL DOLLARS
(In millions)

Source of funds	1979	1973	1968	1963	1957
State..............	$ 65	$42	$30	$14	$ 4
County and local ...	87	44	33	17	9
Total	$152	$86	$63	$31	$13

Source: NACD, *RCA Note Number 7,* July 25, 1980.

Of the approximately 6,000 employees working for the 2,925 conservation districts in 1980, over two-thirds are employed by state and local funds. From 1979 to 1980 the total number of district employees hired with state and local funds increased by 8 percent, and included a 15 percent increase in full-time positions and a 31 percent increase in full-time technicians. This indicates the tremendous movement on the part of districts in the past few years to strengthen their contribution to the on-the-land assistance available to farmers—a service formerly provided almost entirely by federally paid technicians.

The early state funding efforts were aimed almost entirely at helping districts provide technical assistance or develop resource information, but recently there have been several new programs that provide funds to help farmers actually apply conservation measures. Iowa, Wisconsin, Illinois, Kansas, Missouri and Minnesota all have cost-sharing programs that supplement the funds available through similar programs in USDA; Montana and Utah have revolving loan funds to help ranchers improve grasslands. These programs are administered by the state soil conservation agencies and the conservation districts, giving them an active assistance program to offer farmers. In addition, some of the new state laws permit cost sharing in urban areas, a feature not available in USDA programs.

In the decade of the 1980s, most observers of the conservation scene forecast a continuation of the trend toward growing state and local involvement in the soil and water conservation effort, as states and localities discover that investments in protecting the productivity of the resource base are essential to the continued environmental and economic health of their jurisdictions.

Selected References

Environmental Protection Agency, *Conservation Districts and 208 Water Quality Management.* Washington, D.C., 1977.

National Association of Conservation Districts. *Conservation Districts Program Authorities.* Washington, D.C., 1978.

National Association of Conservation Districts. *Erosion and Sediment Control Programs: Six Case Studies.* Washington, D.C., 1976.

National Association of Conservation Districts. *Inventory of Private Recreation Facilities.* Washington, D.C., 1977.

Sampson, R. Neil. *Farmland or Wasteland: A Time to Choose.* Rodale Press, Emmaus, Pa., 1981.

Soil Conservation Society of America. *Soil Conservation Policies: An Assessment.* Ankeny, Iowa, 1979.

United States Department of Agriculture. *Compilation of Statutes Relating to Soil Conservation, etc.* Agriculture Handbook No. 476, Washington, D.C., 1981.

United States Department of Agriculture. *Statutory Authorities for the Activities of the Soil Conservation Service.* Agriculture Handbook No. 588, Washington, D.C., 1981.

Table 1
STATUS OF WATERSHED APPLICATIONS
(Under Public Law 83-566)
Cumulative to September 1, 1981

	Applications		Planning		Operations	
	Number	Acres (1,000)	Number	Acres (1,000)	Number	Acres (1,000)
Total	764	66,023	168	16,686	1,236	78,947
Alabama	9	434	4	245	35	2,146
Alaska	2	205	. . .	. . .	. . .	. . .
Arizona	9	998	5	615	13	1,136
Arkansas	15	813	7	1,088	55	3,143
California	33	2,576	3	192	22	931
Colorado	4	482	. . .	. . .	18	1,066
Connecticut	9	93	2	74	10	142
Delaware	. . .	. . .	1	70	4	282
Florida	5	288	2	91	20	1,231
Georgia	21	1,708	6	555	62	3,861
Hawaii	2	24	1	6	8	475
Idaho	2	212	6	470	7	339
Illinois	20	1,460	3	389	20	992
Indiana	26	2,100	2	156	36	2,288
Iowa	36	2,006	6	233	45	880
Kansas	29	3,892	9	802	50	5,010
Kentucky	16	915	1	5	32	2,142
Louisiana	10	1,240	5	769	38	4,543
Maine	11	776	1	81	11	528
Maryland	9	391	5	422	17	276
Massachusetts	3	153	1	41	11	459
Michigan	2	224	. . .	. . .	20	864
Minnesota	19	1,794	3	414	16	1,195
Mississippi	20	1,283	7	909	53	3,946
Missouri	48	4,880	8	830	20	986
Montana	22	1,512	6	678	14	633
Nebraska	25	3,127	8	1,027	44	2,667
Nevada	14	1,825	. . .	. . .	5	388
New Hampshire	1	18	. . .	. . .	7	457
New Jersey	5	29	1	12	12	253
New Mexico	29	3,081	1	158	28	1,682
New York	11	743	3	54	17	819
North Carolina	22	1,608	3	199	47	2,052
North Dakota	8	1,289	. . .	. . .	18	2,518
Ohio	16	2,271	4	628	15	1,026
Oklahoma	35	3,957	10	1,462	66	6,442
Oregon	10	1,757	3	368	15	967
Pennsylvania	13	452	4	215	23	1,141
Rhode Island	. . .	. . .	. . .	. . .	. . .	. . .
South Carolina	3	145	4	325	38	1,679
South Dakota	5	792	3	527	14	525
Tennessee	36	1,779	5	263	36	1,544
Texas	28	2,550	8	1,396	88	8,886
Utah	16	1,963	2	231	13	1,313
Vermont	4	304	1	68	5	100
Virginia	25	1,089	2	152	30	1,615
Washington	26	1,854	1	6	14	308
West Virginia	13	732	6	245	23	822
Wisconsin	12	533	2	108	26	1,419
Wyoming	24	3,591	2	95	12	578
Caribbean Area	1	75	1	12	3	252

Source: Soil Conservation Service, U.S. Department of Agriculture.

Table 2
MAJOR PROVISIONS OF STATE SOIL CONSERVATION PROGRAMS
(As of December 1981)

State or other jurisdiction	Status of long-range plan	Major resource concerns								Major program needs				
		Soil erosion	Food/fiber production	Water Quality	Loss of ag. lands	Forestry	Water quantity	Flooding	Prime farmland	Water management	Technical assistance	Cost-share	Clerical assistance	Information/education
Alabama	…			★	★		★		★		★		★	
Alaska	Complete	★	★	★		★		★	★	★	★			
Arizona	Complete	★	★	★	★	★	★	★	★	★	★			★
Arkansas	Draft	★	★	★	★	★	★	★		★				
California	January 1983													
Colorado	Complete	★		★			★			★	★		★	★
Connecticut(a)	January 1982			★							★		★	
Delaware	Complete	★	★	★	★	★	★	★			★			
Florida	January 1982									★	★		★	★
Georgia	January 1982										★			
Hawaii	Complete	★	★	★	★	★	★	★	★	★	★			
Idaho	Complete	★	★	★	★	★	★			★	★			
Illinois(a)	January 1982			★							★			
Indiana	Complete	★	★	★	★	★				★	★		★	★
Iowa	Complete	★	★	★	★	★	★	★	★	★	★	★		★
Kansas	Complete	★	★				★				★	★		
Kentucky	October 1981										★	★		
Louisiana	Complete	★	★	★	★	★	★	★		★	★		★	
Maine	Complete	★	★	★	★	★	★	★	★	★	★		★	
Maryland	Complete	★	★	★	★		★		★	★	★		★	
Massachusetts	Complete													★
Michigan	Complete			★	★		★				★	★		
Minnesota	Complete	★		★		★	★	★	★		★	★		
Mississippi(a)	January 1982										★			
Missouri	Complete	★	★	★	★	★	★							
Montana	Complete													
Nebraska	Complete	★		★	★	★	★	★						
Nevada(a)	January 1982													
New Hampshire(a)	January 1982												★	
New Jersey	December 1981										★		★	
New Mexico	Draft	★	★	★	★	★	★	★	★	★	★			
New York	Complete			★	★						★		★	
North Carolina	Complete	★		★	★	★	★	★		★	★	★		
North Dakota	Complete	★	★	★	★	★	★			★	★			
Ohio	Draft	★	★	★	★	★	★	★	★	★	★			
Oklahoma	Draft										★	★		
Oregon	Complete	★	★	★	★	★	★	★		★	★			★
Pennsylvania	Complete	★	★	★	★	★	★	★	★	★	★			
Rhode Island(a)	January 1982										★		★	
South Carolina(a)	January 1982										★		★	
South Dakota	Complete										★			
Tennessee	Complete	★	★	★	★	★	★	★			★			★
Texas	Complete	★		★		★				★	★			★
Utah	January 1982										★			
Vermont(a)	January 1982										★		★	
Virginia	Complete	★		★	★		★	★	★	★	★			★
Washington(a)	January 1982									★	★			★
West Virginia(a)	January 1982									★	★		★	★
Wisconsin	Complete	★				★		★	★		★			
Wyoming(a)	January 1982									★				
Puerto Rico	Complete													
Virgin Islands	…										★			★

(a) Estimated completion date.

Table 3
CONSERVATION DISTRICTS
As of September 30, 1980

State or other jurisdiction	Date district law became effective	Districts organized(a) (number)	Approximate area and farms within organized districts			Districts having memoranda of understanding with USDA(b) (number)
			Total area (1,000 acres)	Farms (thousands)	Land in farms (1,000 acres)	
Total.................	...	2,921	2,200,808	2,348	1,048,049	2,906
Alabama	March 18, 1939	64	33,030	54	13,100	64
Alaska	March 25, 1947	1	375,304	1	1,700	1
Arizona	June 16, 1941	31	60,378	6	40,400	30
Arkansas	July 1, 1937	76	33,826	57	16,800	76
California.............	June 26, 1938	127	75,201	60	32,300	126
Colorado	May 6, 1937	83	61,432	26	37,700	83
Connecticut............	July 18, 1945	8	3,132	4	450	8
Delaware	April 2, 1943	3	1,266	3	620	3
Florida	June 10, 1937	60	33,866	35	13,800	60
Georgia	March 23, 1937	34	37,959	54	16,000	26
Hawaii	May 19, 1947	15	4,089	4	2,290	15
Idaho	March 9, 1939	51	52,285	24	15,500	51
Illinois	July 9, 1937	98	29,095	105	28,600	98
Indiana................	March 11, 1937	92	23,102	88	16,900	92
Iowa	July 4, 1939	100	36,012	119	34,000	100
Kansas	April 10, 1937	105	52,649	72	48,200	105
Kentucky	June 11, 1940	121	25,377	94	14,300	121
Louisiana..............	July 27, 1938	38	28,214	35	10,200	38
Maine	March 25, 1941	16	17,539	8	1,640	16
Maryland	June 1, 1937	24	6,282	16	2,780	24
Massachusetts...........	June 28, 1945	15	4,973	5	650	15
Michigan	July 23, 1937	84	37,241	63	10,500	84
Minnesota	April 26, 1937	92	50,659	104	30,300	92
Mississippi	April 4, 1938	82	30,269	48	14,500	82
Missouri...............	July 23, 1943	110	42,154	117	32,300	110
Montana	February 28, 1939	59	89,724	22	62,000	59
Nebraska	May 18, 1937	24	48,982	63	47,800	24
Nevada................	March 30, 1937	30	70,605	2	8,990	30
New Hampshire	May 10, 1945	10	5,955	8	580	10
New Jersey.............	July 1, 1937	16	4,813	8	990	16
New Mexico.............	March 17, 1937	47	62,415	11	46,700	47
New York	July 20, 1940	57	30,489	44	9,800	57
North Carolina..........	March 22, 1937	93	31,229	98	12,300	93
North Dakota...........	March 16, 1937	62	45,148	40	41,690	62
Ohio	June 5, 1941	88	26,383	96	16,200	88
Oklahoma	April 15, 1937	88	43,726	71	34,500	88
Oregon	April 7, 1939	47	60,603	31	18,600	47
Pennsylvania...........	July 2, 1937	66	29,352	61	9,000	66
Rhode Island	April 26, 1943	3	677	1	63	3
South Carolina	April 17, 1937	46	19,345	35	6,500	46
South Dakota	July 1, 1937	69	49,309	41	45,450	69
Tennessee...............	March 10, 1939	95	26,450	92	13,600	95
Texas	April 24, 1939	201	169,890	159	138,400	198
Utah	March 23, 1937	40	49,229	12	12,600	40
Vermont................	April 18, 1939	14	5,935	6	1,740	14
Virginia	April 1, 1938	42	25,630	60	9,700	42
Washington.............	March 17, 1939	52	37,073	34	16,100	50
West Virginia...........	June 12, 1939	14	15,411	20	4,180	14
Wisconsin	July 1, 1937	72	34,858	94	18,600	72
Wyoming...............	May 22, 1941	38	59,944	7	35,100	38
Puerto Rico	July 1, 1946	17	2,189	30	1,336	17
Virgin Islands	June 1946	1	110	...	...	1

Source: Soil Conservation Service, U.S. Department of Agriculture. The term conservation district may be prefixed by resource, soil, water, natural resource, or other descriptive names due to variance in individual state laws.

(a) For specific procedure on organization of soil conservation districts, reference should be made to each of the respective state soil conservation districts' laws.

(b) Upon request, the U.S. Department of Agriculture enters into memoranda of understanding with districts for such assistance from the departmental agencies as may be available.

ENERGY

By Russell Barnett and Brian Weberg

OVER THE PAST DECADE, energy shortages and accelerating prices have made us realize the need for effective management of our energy resources. World petroleum production peaked in 1970 and has been declining ever since. U.S. dependence on imported oil now costs the country $80 billion annually. Electric rates have increased 50 percent in the last five years, and natural gas rates may increase 40 to 60 percent as domestic production is deregulated. The federal government has been unable to develop a comprehensive national policy, and most national programs adopted to date depend upon state implementation.

We must find state, local and regional solutions for national energy problems. The states have passed their own energy-related legislation, and while the states have limited resources or legal authority to influence energy prices and supply, they are uniquely suited to assume leadership in many areas of energy policy. This is especially true in areas such as conservation, utility regulation, taxation policies to encourage alternative energy development, industrial development activities and the provision of public infrastructures to support energy development.

In the absence of a comprehensive national policy, the states have assumed increased responsibility for assuring the adequate supply and availability of energy, and for promoting the development of indigenous resources to meet national energy needs. With its own markets and geographic, economic, social, climatic and political conditions, each state has developed individual techniques to meet its energy needs. Energy issues will continue to remain important nationally; however, financial problems are forcing many states to reevaluate their roles in energy management.

State Energy Offices

Since 1973, every state has created a state organization responsible for energy issues. Following the Arab oil embargo, the federal government delegated authority to the states under the Emergency Petroleum Allocation Act to operate state set-aside programs. Most states established temporary offices to run them; however, as the states and the federal government began to realize the broad scope of energy problems, legislative and executive programs were developed. State energy offices increased in size to carry out growing responsibilities and to receive federal grants.

By 1981, 30 of the state energy offices had been established by statute, while the others operated under executive order of the governor. Four alternative organizational structures have emerged. Energy responsibilities are assigned either to a cabinet-level department or agency, to the governor's office, to a commission or council or to a division of an already existing agency with related functions, such as the department of natural resources or commerce. Agencies independent of the governor's office frequently are given greater statutory

Russell Barnett is Staff Professional for The Council of State Governments. Brian Weberg is Senior Research Analyst for the National Conference of State Legislatures.

responsibilities. The duties and authority of energy agencies vary, and the decision to organize along any particular line is affected by specific factors within each state. The trend has been toward expanding the purview and responsibilities of state energy offices and toward administrative consolidation. Staffing patterns vary by state and type of organizational structure. Fourteen states have formed departments of energy responsible for comprehensive energy planning and management. Staff size ranges from 13 to 182, with an average of 74. As federal funding has decreased, energy functions have tended to fall within divisions of cabinet-level departments, where staff size ranges from 20 to 67, with an average of 34.

Funding levels vary considerably from state to state, ranging from $750,000 to over $30 million per year. Reliance on federal funding is common. Fifteen states depend on federal aid to finance over 85 percent of the cost of their state energy offices. Only 14 states provide more than half the cost of running their offices. As federal funding has decreased, the great dependency on federal support has created problems in the continuation of office operations. A few states have dedicated revenue to support their energy offices, commonly through utility surcharges or severance taxes. California, for example, finances 70 percent of its $30 million energy commission budget through a surcharge on utilities. Nebraska, Montana and New Mexico fund over 60 percent of their energy programs through severance taxes.

Energy Planning

Comprehensive state energy plans are being developed in many states. The purposes of the plans are to evaluate the state's energy characteristics and to begin to develop policies and strategies to ensure adequate energy supplies for the future. Statutes establishing state energy offices often contain references to energy planning responsibilities. New York's energy office, for example, must prepare a state energy master plan to include: (a) 15-year energy forecasts; (b) a summary of the plans of major energy suppliers for meeting forecasted energy requirements; (c) identification and analysis of emerging trends related to energy supply, price and demand; and (d) a statement of specific energy policies, rationale for them and recommendations for desired administrative and legislative actions.

States not preparing comprehensive plans conduct a variety of strategic planning activities concerning specific energy issues or problems. Most states prepare State Energy Conservation Plans as required for federal assistance.

Energy Emergency Plans have been or are being developed in 30 states. Interruptions of the energy supply created by oil embargoes, labor disputes, natural disasters or accidents have caused serious economic dislocations and threatened public health and safety. The Emergency Energy Conservation Act of 1979 (EECA) requires states to create standby emergency energy conservation plans, and they have developed a variety of statutes, plans and regulations to address short-term energy disruptions.

Energy emergency legislation has been adopted in 33 states. Statutes often include broad statements that grant authority for necessary and appropriate steps to protect the "health, safety and welfare of the people." Some states operate under poorly defined authorities that require war or natural disaster emergencies. Ten states have amended their disaster acts to define energy interruption as a disaster, and a few rely upon implied authorities supported by attorneys general's opinions.

The definition of an energy interruption varies by state. Declaration of a federal emergency is the basis for most state action; however, in half the states, the governor may declare an emergency on the basis of some quantitative indicator (length of lines at service stations, percentage of shortfall), a qualitative determination or a combination of both. The degree of shortage may trigger progressively stronger powers. Typically, an energy alert requesting voluntary conservation is issued first. If that is insufficient, mandatory restrictions are imposed.

Governors typically are empowered to implement plans, programs or controls through executive order to deal with emergencies. In 17 states, the governor's declaration is subject to legislative review. In half the states, management powers are delegated to special committees (comprised of legislators, state agency heads, industry and public representatives), the state energy office, local governments and public utility commissions.

Although a few states will try to increase energy production during an emergency, the basic response will be to enforce conservation through broad authority to allocate, ration and distribute scarce fuels; reduce lines at service stations through imposition of regulations (odd/even or minimum purchase); relax specific regulatory standards (air quality); curtail public/private transportation use; encourage or mandate energy conservation; close specific industries or shorten workweeks; or curtail energy use by other means. Violations are misdemeanors with fines ranging from $100 to $1,000. Oregon provides for energy supplies to be cut off to recalcitrant individuals or groups.

Energy Data Collection and Education Programs

A major role of each state energy office is to collect and analyze data on energy resources and demand in the state. State officials, as well as the general public, must have access to accurate information in order to develop energy policies and programs and to respond to energy emergencies. Energy data is collected and analyzed for the governor and legislature in order to assess the impact of alternative energy policies, identify future problems, track federal energy initiatives and programs, and assess the availability and desirability of alternative resources.

Most collection is based on national aggregate data, compiled according to broad economic sector. Fuel supply information, for example, is often compiled from bulk distribution reports submitted to the U.S. Energy Information Administration. The states vary in their ability to use information for policy analysis. Several states, including California, Minnesota, Ohio, Texas and Wisconsin, have sophisticated data systems capable of assessing production and consumption trends; energy pricing policies; alternative contingency plans; social, economic and environmental consequences of energy policies; and other policy issues.

A major need is for reliable energy demand forecasts. In 16 states, energy forecasts are submitted to the state by energy companies. Commonly, state public service commissions review forecasts prepared by utilities seeking certification to construct new generating or transmission facilities. Such a case-by-case approach is often inadequate as a basis for state policy. Independent mid- to long-range independent forecasts are developed in 25 states. These forecasts are used in policy and regulatory analysis, impact assessment and ascertaining the need for proposed energy facilities.

Forecasts may range in complexity from intuitive judgments to very sophisticated energy models. Energy forecasts may be made by type of fuel (e.g., electricity or natural gas) or by economic sector (e.g., industrial, residential, transportation). States update forecasts annually or biennially.

A major role of state energy offices or, in some cases, state universities is to offer educational programs on alternative energy sources and conservation practices. Programs are directed primarily toward small energy consumers (individuals, small businesses, schools, hospitals and local government) and take a variety of forms: newsletters, publications, hotlines, workshops, seminars, public school programs or consultant services.

In New York and Georgia, state energy offices provide trained advisors to industries at no cost to conduct on-site energy efficiency surveys. Michigan has an Elderly Outreach Program to provide information on the availability of energy assistance programs to the elderly. A number of states, including Louisiana, Indiana and Nevada, have educational programs in public elementary and high schools. Most states conduct boiler efficiency seminars. To promote transfer of innovative education programs, the Department of Energy, Region V, has developed a Midwest Energy Education Consortium to aid states in sharing energy education programs.

A major source of funding for state energy education programs has been the Energy Extension Service authorized by the national Energy Extension Act of 1977.

Conservation

Energy conservation is the most efficient way to solve short-term energy problems. Conservation may mean actual reduction of energy consumption or more efficient energy use. A slower rate of growth in energy demand can soften the economic effects of higher energy prices and reduce environmental impacts associated with increased production. A reduced energy demand can also extend the time available for solving energy supply problems. Current studies suggest that energy savings of 40 percent may be achieved through conservation without disruption.

The states are in the best position to affect energy conservation and still respond to unique state needs and conditions. The states and the federal government initially viewed conservation as a stop-gap measure to deal with energy crises, but current legislation emphasizes conservation as a major long-range policy and planning tool. A range of options is available to state policy-makers, including regulation of public and private activities, economic incentives or disincentives, public education and suasion, and research. Most state policies include a blend of options.

The basis of most state energy conservation programs may be found in a number of federal laws, including the Energy Policy and Conservation Act, Energy Conservation and Production Act, Natural Energy Act, and National Energy Conservation Act. These laws mandate specific program areas but also provide a basis for state-initiated conservation programs and policies. Each law provides a model for the states, but the future of the federal laws is uncertain due to the Reagan administration's cutbacks in conservation program funding and its reliance on the free market to determine conservation practices.

State conservation programs have been directed toward a variety of objectives: buildings, utilities, transportation and others.

Conservation in Buildings. Heating, cooling and lighting residential and commercial buildings consumes 18 quadrillion Btu's, or nearly a third of all energy used in the U.S. New structures designed for conservation could reduce energy use by 40 to 50 percent. The states have initiated a number of programs to reduce residential and commercial energy demands through building codes, incentives to retrofit existing structures, establishment of conservation material standards, grants for weatherization of low-income households, and energy audits for hospitals and schools.

The Energy Policy and Conservation Act stipulates that as a prerequisite for federal assistance a state must require that all new construction meet thermal and lighting efficiency standards. Forty-six states to date have adopted energy efficiency standards. Most are based

on standards adopted by the American Society of Heating, Refrigeration and Air Condi-
tioning Engineers. Building codes adopted are adaptations of the National Conference of
States of Building Codes and Standards, Building Officials and Code Administrator's International, Inc., or were developed by the states themselves. In many states, standards apply
not only to new construction but to existing state and public buildings.

Only 22 states have state building codes to implement energy standards. The other states
rely on local building codes or voluntary implementation of standards. Kansas, Maryland,
New Mexico, New York, North Carolina and Wisconsin enforce standards by prohibiting
utility hookups to buildings not meeting state requirements.

Although prescriptive standards are easy to implement, problems of enforcement, possible inhibition of innovative energy-efficient techniques, and inertia may limit the effectiveness of building codes. Also, building codes alone may not be sufficient to reduce demand significantly. New construction replaces existing buildings at the rate of only 2 to 3
percent a year. Even when codes are enforced, a state would still have many energy-
inefficient buildings.

Some states have bonding programs to retrofit publically owned buildings. Massachusetts
authorized a $20 million bond program to retrofit public buildings; Maine passed a $25
million bond for local government buildings. States match federal funds available under the
Institutional Buildings Grant Program to finance energy audits in schools, hospitals and
local government buildings, and to carry out needed conservation improvements. In 1980,
$200 million was used to modify furnaces and to install insulation, solar heating/cooling
and weatherstripping in 21,000 buildings.

Mandatory retrofitting of private buildings has been largely rejected by the states because
of the hardship it would place on lower-income homeowners. Minnesota has a Home
Energy Disclosure Program requiring sellers to disclose energy use characteristics to potential buyers at or before the time of sale. The program is designed to encourage retrofits.

Owners or builders deciding whether to invest in energy-efficient improvements consider
the initial capital outlay and the length of the payback period; thus most states provide incentives based on those factors. States have largely opted for tax incentives to encourage
retrofitting of existing buildings. Seven states offer income tax credits for conservation
practices such as installation of insulation, weather stripping, and storm windows and
doors. These credits are in addition to those offered by the federal government, and range
up to 40 percent of the cost of the conservation measure. Arkansas allows conservation
measures to be fully deducted from state income tax. It is not known how much these incentives have contributed to voluntary retrofitting, or to what extent they have simply
reduced the tax bills of those persons who would have retrofitted anyway.

To overcome the problem of obtaining initial capital outlays, 12 states make low- or no-
interest loans available to low- and moderate-income households, often through state housing authorities. Minnesota's loan program for low- and moderate-income families is funded
by revenue bond sales and general appropriations, and is part of the state housing program.
Almost 25 percent of the program's home improvement loans were for energy-saving
measures.

Some states coordinate their loan programs with private companies. Incentives are provided to lending institutions in a few states to encourage loans for conservation retrofits.
Missouri encourages conservation loans by depositing state funds with cooperative financial
institutions. California was the first state to pass legislation permitting its utilities to begin a
home insulation and financing program. This served as a model for the 1978 National

Energy Act, which mandates the states to implement a Residential Conservation Service (RCS). The RCS program requires public utilities to provide consumer education and information on conservation; to perform residential energy audits; to help customers arrange for installation; and to assist homeowners in financing energy-efficient improvements. Forty-five states have begun residential energy conservation programs, with some states exceeding minimum requirements. Massachusetts has expanded its RCS program by allowing public utilities to create a corporation to conduct the programs. Fifty-three utilities are currently financing the program through an energy surcharge. Similar programs have been developed in Rhode Island and Vermont. Some states include provisions for utility zero- or low-interest loan programs. Zero-interest conservation loans are now offered in Arkansas, California, Michigan, Montana and Oregon. In some other states, utilities are required to provide low-interest (6.5-8 percent) conservation loans.

Financial incentives that promote conservation are not applicable in all cases. Rental property is a particularly difficult area. Where energy costs are passed on to the renter, the landowner has little incentive to conserve and the renter is not willing to make major financial commitments to the property. In Minnesota and Wisconsin, residential landlords will be required to make specified improvements such as installation of weather stripping, storm windows and attic insulation. Rhode Island offers a 20 percent tax credit with a $1,000 limit to landlords who make conservation improvements to rental property.

Low-income families seldom respond to tax credits or loan programs, but the Energy Conservation and Production Act and the National Energy Conservation Act provide federal funds for low-income housing weatherization assistance. Over 860,000 homes have been weatherized to date, conserving the equivalent of almost two million barrels of oil annually. In most cases, weatherization programs are administered by state housing or local community development agencies. Often the programs are supplemented by state funds.

Utilities. The regulation of public utilities offers many avenues for energy conservation. Electric consumption accounts for 27 percent of the U.S. energy demand and thus is of prime concern in state energy conservation efforts. The use of energy is inversely proportional to its cost, and traditional rate structures have often encouraged use of electricity.

The Public Utilities Regulatory Policies Act mandates that state public utility commissions examine the appropriateness of 12 rate-making and regulatory standards designed to conserve energy. As a result, some standards are to take effect immediately, while others are to be imposed only for the duration of rate increase hearings or while states are experimenting with alternative standards for select consumer groups. Major rate standards being implemented include cost of service (16 states), peak-load pricing (30), interruptible service (28), inverted rates (6), and prohibition of declining block rates (16 states).

Florida's Energy Efficiency and Conservation program requires the state public service commission (PSC) to set statewide conservation goals for electric and gas utilities in order to reduce the rate of growth of energy consumption, seasonal peak demand and dependence on oil-fired generation, and to increase efficiency in the end-use of natural gas. Each utility develops its own plans to meet these goals and recovers the cost of implementing them through a cost-recovery clause in the approved rate base.

Other utility actions for energy conservation include allowing energy conservation advertisement expenses and the costs of load management and conservation to be treated as rate-base expenses.

Transportation. Transportation accounts for more than 25 percent of America's energy use. The states promote conservation in transportation by encouraging vanpools, carpools and mass transit. Kansas pays for mass transit fares for state employees, and a ridesharing program in Knoxville, Tennessee, saved over a million gallons of gasoline in 1980 alone. Improving the energy efficiency of existing transportation modes has been the focus of uniform legislation allowing right turns on red lights, 55-mph speed limits and automobile maintenance programs.

Other. Energy-efficient purchasing by state and local governments is encouraged by the Energy Policy and Conservation Act. Most states have altered their procurement practices so that life-cycle costs (i.e., the total cost of purchasing and operating a building or equipment) and energy conservation are taken into account when purchasing decisions are made.

Recovery of resources offers states opportunities to save energy. Resource recovery programs in many states recycle paper, beverage containers, solid waste and waste oil. California, Maryland, Minnesota, New York and Ohio require all state agencies to favor suppliers of recycled paper. Georgia requires that all state waste paper be recycled. Forty states have oil recovery programs. North Carolina owns and operates its own waste oil recovery plant where all used oil from the state transportation pool is recycled.

Thirteen states have and are enforcing energy-efficiency standards for certain home appliances. Prohibition of pilot lights in gas appliances is the most common standard.

Incentives for Resource Development

Although conservation is important for short-range energy supply problems, long-range energy needs must be met through development of new energy sources. Many states have increased their commitments to promote development and use of indigenous resources to meet their particular needs. Accelerating energy costs in some energy-deficient states threaten their economic stability by causing a flow of capital to other states.

States with non-renewable energy resources (coal, oil shale, oil, gas or uranium) are concerned with state policies and programs to encourage development of under-used resources. Programs include financial incentives such as tax credits; technical research and development or technologies to mine or use new energy resources such as oil shale, or traditional resources such as coal; and provision of direct assistance, such as that for geologic surveys or small coal operators.

Some of the ways states can facilitate resource development include removing institutional barriers, streamlining permits, sponsoring research on means of mining and utilizing energy resources in an environmentally compatible manner, and assuring the availability of adequate transportation systems.

Development of renewable energy sources (wind, solar, hydroelectric, geothermal and biomass) entails great initial cost and small short-term investment return. These drawbacks must be overcome. State policies have been directed at removing institutional and legal barriers that impede renewable energy development. Potential investors in renewable energy systems can be discouraged by uncertainties about a system's quality and reliability; thus 14 states have developed standards for solar equipment or conservation materials. Because many renewable energy sources still depend on traditional sources, such as electricity, for backup power, public utility management and rate-making authorities may require adjustment to encourage renewable energy development while protecting established energy system investments and ensuring reliability.

Non-renewable Resource Incentives. States enact incentives for investment in indigenous resources such as oil, gas or coal to stimulate economic development and help reduce reliance on imported energy supplies. Montana has exempted half of its net proceeds tax and, for three years, all severance tax on new indigenous gas production that the state consumes. Texas allows individuals the same interest rate as corporations on loans for oil or gas exploration or recovery. Eligible coal gasification and liquefaction projects in West Virginia can qualify for an exemption from the business and occupation tax on gross income. Through its Coal Development Bond Act, Illinois has created a fund to support and assist both public and private coal-related energy projects. Such actions indicate the range of state financial incentives that promote non-renewable energy resources.

Renewable Energy Incentives. State incentives for renewable energy fall into two broad categories: *tax incentives* and *non-tax incentives*. Within each category, incentives vary widely from state to state in scope, complexity and purpose. All of the incentives were enacted during a time of ferment and change, when diverse constituencies were actively altering traditional patterns of energy supply and demand, and when states were only beginning to find out what incentives are most effective.

State tax incentives involve four basic types of tax: sales tax, property tax, income tax, and franchise and license taxes. States frequently offer partial or total exemptions from sales tax to encourage renewable energy development. Ethanol is usually exempted from both sales and excise taxes. California exempts raw biomass products from both sales and use taxes. In 10 states, solar energy devices are exempted from sales taxes.

Because equipment that uses renewable energy often costs more than equipment that does not, many states have lessened the burden that high property taxes would otherwise impose on users of renewable energy. Thirty-six states provide incentives ranging from reduction or elimination of property taxes to credits for equipment value. Most property tax incentives benefit end-users of renewable energy rather than producers. Colorado and Oregon, however, reduce property taxes for producers of alcohol fuel.

Property taxes are particularly burdensome to hydroelectric and geothermal projects due to their high equipment and facility costs. States such as Massachusetts, Indiana, Oregon and Washington exempt geothermal and hydroelectric systems from property tax. Such exemptions can, however, provide a revenue shortfall for the affected locality. New Hampshire requires small, exempt power producers to pay part of their revenues to the city in lieu of property taxes.

Income tax credits, which directly reduce liability, are a popular state financial incentive. Half the states offer income tax credits to residential consumers of renewable energy technologies. California's provision for a 55 percent credit to a maximum of $3,000 is perhaps the most liberal. Several states grant investment tax credits to industries that produce renewable energy systems. In Oregon, specific alternative energy development investments can qualify for a 35 percent credit distributed over three years to a maximum of $350,000.

Less common incentives are tax deductions, which reduce the income against which taxes are assessed. Commercial investors in Massachusetts can receive a 100 percent deduction on the purchase of renewable energy systems. Alabama allows a 100 percent deduction for the cost of converting residences from gas or electricity to wood heating systems. The actual benefit to a taxpayer of a 100 percent deduction of the cost of renewable energy equipment is roughly equivalent to the benefits of a 10 percent tax credit, because state income taxes average about 10 percent of net income.

If businesses can deduct expenses at unusually fast rates, they can temporarily lower their tax liabilities. Some states, therefore, allow shortened amortization schedules or accelerated depreciation to businesses that invest in equipment that uses renewable energy. Accelerated depreciation in Arizona and California for solar device costs allows a 36-month amortization in lieu of any other tax credits.

States have also used other incentives to promote renewable energy development. Kansas, California and Washington allow regulated utilities a higher rate of return on investments in renewable energy facilities. State procurement programs that require renewable resources or renewable energy systems can demonstrate a state's commitment to a new industry. Most such procurement programs require alcohol fuel for state vehicles. Michigan has required its Park Commission and Department of Highways to use solar-heated water in park and highway facilities. New state buildings in Connecticut must employ some form of alternative energy to heat and cool half of the new space.

Since research in new technologies is costly and time-consuming, some states offer financial incentives for research or demonstration and development of renewable energy systems. Research funds may be allocated by state legislatures for specific projects or by state agencies with bonding capability.

Far fewer states offer grants than income tax credits or deductions; thus nationwide patterns are much less apparent. Montana's Renewable Energy Program uses on-going funding set at 2.25 percent of the state's coal severance tax to offer grants in four broad categories: Resource and Technology Development, Human Services, Incentive, and Standards and Practices. Alaska limits its grants for the development of "small-scale technologies appropriate to Alaska" to $5,000. Indiana, on the other hand, provides grants through the Indiana Energy Development Board that are intended primarily to encourage large-scale projects.

States employ a variety of loan programs to promote renewable energy. Connecticut lends money to individuals or businesses (3,350 to date) that adopt conservation measures or install solar equipment. Some states have limited eligibility for direct loans to designated groups. Tennessee, for example, makes loans to people with low or moderate incomes who install solar hot water heating systems in their residences; California makes loans to veterans who install solar heating.

There are many less direct ways for states to see that loans are available to finance use of renewable energy. New Mexico has appropriated $500,000 to a solar power loan fund deposited in lending institutions that loan money at 7 percent interest to homeowners who invest in solar equipment. Financial institutions in Oregon that make loans for solar systems at 6.5 percent receive state corporate excise tax credits for the difference between 6.5 percent and the prevailing interest rate. The Alaska Renewable Resource Corporation guarantees loans and revenue bonds. An attractive feature of loan guarantees is that state financial liability is limited, because state money is spent only if a borrower defaults. The North Carolina Alternative Energy Corporation, a quasi-public, tax-exempt corporation chartered in 1979 to finance energy projects that reduce electricity demand, collects funds from private utilities and electric cooperatives and is accountable to the Utilities Commission.

Other Energy Policy Concerns

Energy policy questions are not restricted to those of supply and demand, but are integrated with a variety of state activities, including environmental protection, social equity, economic development, intergovernmental relations and transportation.

The extraction, development, transportation, use and disposal of energy resources may create a range of undesirable environmental consequences. State policy leaders must evaluate the trade-offs inherent in assuring that sufficient energy supplies are available both now and in the future, and not minimize environmental concern. State environmental programs imposed on major energy facilities, such as mining and reclamation regulations of air and water emissions standards, affect the cost and availability of energy.

Major environmental factors associated with energy development that concern the states include acid rain, availability of water to support energy development, implementation of surface mine reclamation regulations, use of public lands for energy development and location of energy facilities.

The location of a major energy facility largely determines its environmental impact. Thirty-three states exercise energy facility placement legislation to examine the need for and suitability of proposed projects. While most of the legislation focuses on electric generating facilities, recent acts expand areas of concern to synthetic fuel plants, petroleum refineries, geothermal plants and major transmission lines. Twenty-eight states regulate placement of electric transmission lines, and 23 regulate the location of gas transmission lines.

The location of major facilities can create negative social and economic effects. Basic public and social services such as roads, schools, water treatment facilities, police and fire departments, and housing and health facilities may become overburdened. Local communities often cannot respond to the demands of rapid growth caused by construction of major energy facilities. Their resources may be limited, or they may be unwilling to make financial commitments until assured tht the project will be completed—which is often impossible, due to economic and regulatory uncertainties, until just before construction begins. A few states (Colorado, Montana, New Mexico, North Dakota, South Dakota and Wyoming) dedicate a portion of their coal severance tax for grants to local communities affected by energy development. In Montana and Utah, industries may prepay property and sales taxes to fund needed local developments in exchange for lower assessments.

The labyrinth of environmental regulations sometimes has been cited as an unnecessary hindrance to energy development. The need to streamline regulatory processes to balance demands for energy and for environmental protection has become a high priority in most states. Colorado has streamlined permit processes by allowing all stakeholders—the state, industry, local governments and the public—to enter into contracts concerning energy development issues. The procedure has also been adopted in Utah, Tennessee and Illinois.

Substantial increases in energy costs have severely affected elderly and low-income people, who have historically paid a high percentage of their income (18 percent in 1978) for heat. Often, meeting high energy costs is a matter of nothing less than survival. The states and the federal government recognize the severity of this problem and have enacted a variety of assistance programs. The federal government in 1981 funded a Low-Income Energy Assistance Program (LIEAP) administered by state social service and welfare agencies. The states were given several options for distribution of funds, but most chose to transfer them to their Community Service Administration-Energy Crisis Assistance Programs to be awarded to applicants on a first come, first served basis. Recipients received an average of $158, or about 25 percent of typical home energy costs. The program, however, reached only 29 percent of all eligible households in 1981, and federal cutbacks are proposed for the future.

The states have helped fill gaps in the federal program. Connecticut, New York, Maine and Minnesota have programs to provide additional assistance. New York's Energy Crisis Assistance Program, for example, enables families facing utility cut-offs to receive $100 to $200 grants.

A major criticism of LIEAP in the past has been its exclusive focus on minimizing effects of high energy prices. In 1981, changes in the LIEAP program allow up to 15 percent of state grants to be used for making low-income households more energy-efficient. State programs have attempted to bridge the gap by providing weatherization assistance to low-income families. Some states have initiated state weatherization programs. Rhode Island uses computer lists of LIEAP recipients to identify possible candidates, and Massachusetts distributes free low-cost weatherization kits. Other state actions to assist low-income families have been directed at utility companies to cause them to restrict termination of service during winter, provide lifeline rates and refrain from imposing fuel adjustment costs.

Production and consumption of energy resources often require transportation of energy over great distances. The states are addressing environmental issues associated with such transport, as well as working to ensure that adequate networks are available.

One of the obstacles to increasing use of coal is an inadequate transportation network. Railroads, the major coal haulers, are not always able to expand service to meet the needs of the coal industry. Some states provide tax incentives as well as direct loans and grants to help railroads upgrade their service. Kentucky uses part of its severance tax to improve coal-haul roads. Recent attention has also been focused on use of slurry pipelines to transport coal. South Dakota recently reached an agreement with a private developer to sell water from its Oahe Reservoir for a coal slurry pipeline to be run from Wyoming to Arkansas.

Some states have enacted legislation to regulate transportation of radioactive materials. Under federal law, states along the route of a shipment of spent fuel or large quantities of nuclear waste must be notified before the shipment is made. Some states also impose license, packaging, insurance, placarding and reporting requirements, as well as route restrictions, on the transportation of radioactive materials. At least three states (Illinois, Louisiana and Washington) have tried to ban transport of high-level radioactive waste for disposal or storage in their state, but such laws have been overturned by courts in both Illinois and Washington. Regulations adopted by the U.S. Department of Transportation, which would override local bans, have recently been enjoined by a U.S. district court.

The disparity between energy demands and the location of energy resources creates economic and social tensions among states. Only 12 states produce more fossil fuel than they consume, while 19 states have no indigenous fossil fuel and are totally dependent upon imported fuels. States unable to produce sufficient energy are more vulnerable to energy shortfalls and face economic problems as increasing capital becomes necessary for meeting energy demands. Consumers may pay other states as much as 30 cents per million Btu's of energy used. Meanwhile, severance taxes, royalties and other fees on energy development are producing windfall revenues for energy-producing states. The largest fiscal beneficiaries are Texas, Alaska, Oklahoma, Louisiana and New Mexico, where from 27 to 50 percent of state revenue is derived from severance taxes. Revenues from severance taxes vary from state to state, but increases in energy prices will, in each case, increase state revenues from severance taxes. State income taxes have been eliminated in Alaska, Texas and Wyoming, partly because of the ability of severance taxes to generate sufficient revenues.

Usually, most of the severance tax burden is shifted to other states in the form of higher energy prices that create tension between the states. In 1981, the Supreme Court was asked to rule on two interstate energy issues. In *The State of Maryland et al.* v. *The State of Louisiana*, the Court ruled that Louisiana's "first-use" tax on the processing of offshore gas was unconstitutional. A decision in *Commonwealth Edison et al.* v. *The State of Montana et al.* upheld Montana's 30 percent coal severance tax. Sectional rivalry over energy has also been channeled through regional organizations, several of which are growing in strength and influence. Final resolution of severance tax issues will be difficult, however, and will require cooperation among the states.

Table 1
STATE ENERGY AGENCIES

State	Organizational categories† Department/ agency	Commission/ council	Office	Division	Basis of establishment Statute	Executive Order
Alabama	★	...	...	...	Act 80-449 of 1980	...
Alaska	...	...	...	★	...	21
Arizona	...	...	★	...	...	77-10
Arkansas	...	...	...	★	Act 7 of 1981	...
California	...	★	...	...	Pub. Res. Code 25000 et seq.	...
Colorado	...	...	★	...	...	Issued 7/1/81
Connecticut	...	...	...	★	Title 16a	...
Delaware	...	...	...	★	63 Del. Law C80, Sec. 56(b)	...
Florida	...	...	★	...	377.601-703 F.S.	...
Georgia	...	...	★	...	Ga. law 1976, P.1740	...
Hawaii	...	...	★	...	Act 237, 1974	...
Idaho	...	...	★	...	...	76-4
Illinois	★	...	...	...	Chap. 96½, Sec. 7401 et seq.	...
Indiana	...	...	...	★	...	1973 Ex. order
Iowa	...	★	...	...	93.1-93.16	...
Kansas	★	...	...	...	74-6801 et seq.	...
Kentucky	★	...	...	...	S.B. 307	...
Louisiana	...	...	...	★	LRS 30.501 et seq.	...
Maine	...	...	★	...	Title 5, Chap. 338 MRS	...
Maryland	...	...	...	★	...	1973 Ex. order
Massachusetts	★	...	...	...	Chap. 25A	...
Michigan	...	...	★	...	...	1976-2
Minnesota	★	...	...	...	Chap. 116H, 116J	...
Mississippi	...	★	...	...	...	No. 151, 164, 177 & 270
Missouri	...	...	...	★	...	1977 Ex. order
Montana	...	...	...	★	...	1979 Ex. order
Nebraska	★	...	...	...	L.B. 954, 1980	1980 Ex. order
Nevada	★	...	...	...	NRS 523, all et seq.	...
New Hampshire	...	★	...	...	...	73-12
New Jersey	★	...	...	...	N.J.S.A. title 14, Sec. 1.1, Chap. 146	...
New Mexico	★	...	...	...	Chap. 239	...
New York	...	...	★	...	Chap. 819 & 707, L. 1978	...
North Carolina	...	...	...	★	Chap. 113B	...
North Dakota	...	...	★	...	...	1974-1
Ohio	★	...	...	...	H.B. 415	...
Oklahoma	...	★	...	...	740 S. 1981, Sec. 34.1	...
Oregon	★	...	...	...	Rev. Stat. 469.010 et seq.	...
Pennsylvania	...	★	...	...	...	Issued 7/19/79
Rhode Island	...	...	...	★	...	E.O. 81-4
South Carolina	...	...	★	...	...	Issued 9/11/78
South Dakota	...	...	★	...	...	77-7
Tennessee	★	...	...	...	TCA 4-28-101 et seq.	...
Texas	...	★	...	...	...	...
Utah	...	...	...	★	43 272-77	...
Vermont	...	...	★	...	T3, Chap. 41, Sec. 2286 VSA	...
Virginia	...	...	...	★	...	No. 5-1978
Washington	★	...	...	...	Chap. 295, L81	...
West Virginia	...	...	...	★	...	...
Wisconsin	...	...	...	★	Chap. 16, 1977	...
Wyoming	...	...	★	...	...	...

†*Key:* Department/agency—line item agency in state budget, cabinet-level status; Commission/council—governing body composed of gubernatorial appointees (public agency heads, legislators) with executive director retained to carry out governing body's policies; Office—functional unit of executive office (governor or lieutenant governor); Division—energy agency under the direction of a cabinet-level department.

Table 2
STATE ENERGY FORECASTING ACTIVITIES

State	Forecasts prepared for				Legal basis for forecasts	
	Electricity	Natural gas	Refined petroleum products	Other	Law	Regulation
Alabama	★	...	...	...	★(a)	★(a)
Alaska	★	...	★	Heating Btu's regardless of source	★	★
Arizona	...	...	...	...	...	...
Arkansas	...	...	...	...	...	...
California	★	★	...	...	★(a)	...
Colorado	★	★	★	General energy demand	...	...
Connecticut	...	...	...	Price and fuel mix	...	...
Delaware	...	...	...		...	...
Florida	★	★	★	General energy demand	★	...
Georgia	...	...	...	...	...	...
Hawaii	...	...	...		...	...
Idaho	...	...	...		...	...
Illinois	★	...	...	...	...	★(a)
Indiana	...	...	...		...	...
Iowa	...	...	...		...	...
Kansas	★(b)	...	...	General supply and demand	...	...
Kentucky	...	...	...	...	...	...
Louisiana	★	★	...	...	...	★
Maine	★	★	★	...	★	...
Maryland	★	...	...		...	...
Massachusetts	★	★	...		★	★
Michigan	★	★	...	General energy demand	...	★(a)
Minnesota	★	★	★	Coal, LPG, conservation	★	...
Mississippi	...	...	...		...	...
Missouri	★	★	...		...	★
Montana	★(b)	...	...	Coal conversion, transmission lines	★	...
Nebraska	★	★	★	General energy demand	★	...
Nevada	★(b)	...	...		...	...
New Hampshire	...	...	...		...	...
New Jersey	★	★	★		★	...
New Mexico	...	...	...	General energy demand	...	...
New York	★	★	★		★	★
North Carolina	★	★	...	Nuclear, hydropower coal	★	...
North Dakota	...	...	...		...	...
Ohio	★	...	...		★(a)	...
Oklahoma	...	...	...		...	...
Oregon	★	★	★	Solar, geothermal, hydroelectric, biomass, conservation	★	...
Pennsylvania	...	...	...	...	...	...
Rhode Island	...	...	...		...	...
South Carolina	...	...	...		...	...
South Dakota	★	...	...		(a)	...
Tennessee	★	★	...	...	...	★
Texas	...	★	...	...	...	...
Utah	...	...	...		...	...
Vermont	★	...	...		★	...
Virginia	...	...	...		...	...
Washington	...	...	...		...	...
West Virginia	...	...	...		...	...
Wisconsin	★	★	★	★	★(c)	★(c)
Wyoming	...	...	...		...	...

(a) Utilities required to submit long-range energy demand forecasts.
(b) Only on a facility-by-facility basis.
(c) Electrical forecasts only.

Table 3
STATE ENERGY TAX EXEMPTIONS

State	Excise or fuel use (gasohol only)	Sales	Property	Other	Qualified energy systems
Alabama	3¢	...	...	...	...
Alaska	8¢	★	...	...	E
Arizona	...	★	★	Accelerated depreciation	S
Arkansas	9.5¢	...	...	...	...
California	...	★ (5¢/gal. E only)	★ (S only)	Accelerated depreciation	S,H,G,Co
Colorado	5¢	...	★	Electric cars exempt from sales, use, registration & ownership taxes	S,W,G
Connecticut	...	★	★(a)	Franchise fee	S,W
Delaware	...	...	...	...	...
Florida	4¢	★	★	Transaction tax (E only), franchise tax	S
Georgia	...	★	★(a)	...	S
Hawaii	...	...	★	Gross proceeds (E only)	A
Idaho	4¢	...	★	...	E
Illinois	...	★ (E only)	★	...	S
Indiana	...	★ (E only)	★	...	S,W, oil shale, G, H
Iowa	10¢	...	★	...	S
Kansas	4¢	...	★	Accelerated depreciation	S,W
Kentucky	...	...	...	...	...
Louisiana	8¢	★	★	...	E
Maine	...	★	★(a)	...	S
Maryland	4¢	...	★(a)	...	S,W
Massachusetts	...	★ (Wood stove only)	★	...	S
Michigan	...	★	★(a)	...	S
Minnesota	4¢	...	★	...	S
Mississippi	...	★	...	...	...
Missouri	...	...	...	...	...
Montana	2¢	...	★(b)	...	S,W,H,B(excludes wood stoves)
Nebraska	5¢	★	★	...	A
Nevada	...	...	★	...	S,W,G,H,B
New Hampshire	5¢	...	★(a)	...	S
New Jersey	...	★	★	...	S,W
New Mexico	9¢	...	...	Gross receipts	E
New York	...	...	★	...	S,W
North Carolina	3¢	...	★	...	...
North Dakota	4¢	★ (E only)	★	...	S,W,G
Ohio	...	★	★	Franchise tax (10%)	S,W,H
Oklahoma	6.5¢	...	...	...	...
Oregon	...	...	★	...	S,G,W,H
Pennsylvania	...	...	...	License fee	E
Rhode Island	...	★	★	...	S,W,C
South Carolina	4¢	...	...	...	...
South Dakota	60¢	...	★	...	S,W
Tennessee	9¢	...	★(a)	...	S,W
Texas	...	★	★	Franchise tax	...
Utah	5¢	...	...	Franchise tax (10%)	S,W
Vermont	...	...	★(a)	...	...
Virginia	...	...	★(a)	...	...
Washington	1.2¢	★ (E only)	★	Personal property tax for cogeneration, business & occupation tax	...
West Virginia	...	...	...	...	...
Wisconsin	...	...	★	Permit fee	E
Wyoming	4¢	★	...	...	E

Key:
A—Alterantive energy systems
C—Conservation/weatherization
S—Solar
H—Water power, hydroelectric
W—Wind

G—Geothermal
B—Biomass conversion, wood burning stoves
Co—Cogeneration
E—Ethanol, gasohol
 (a) Local government has authority to exempt.
 (b) For first ten years after installation.

Table 4
BONDING AUTHORITIES FOR ALTERNATIVE ENERGY/CONSERVATION

State or other jurisdiction	Dollar amount (in millions)	Qualified energy systems	Purposes
Alabama	18	C	State facilities
Alaska	35	A	Projects approved by legislature
Arizona	...	...	...
Arkansas	...		
California	200/750	A/C,S	Revenue bonds to finance loan fund; bonds for home loans to veteran
Colorado	...	...	...
Connecticut	3	C,A	Finance loan fund
Delaware	...	...	...
Florida	...	...	...
Georgia	...	...	...
Hawaii	...	...	...
Idaho	...	...	
Illinois	5/65	...	R&D & capital development of non-coal, non-nuclear energy; R&D & capital development of coal resources
Indiana	...	...	...
Iowa	50	S,A	Low/medium income households
Kansas	...	...	...
Kentucky	...	...	
Louisiana	...	...	...
Maine	7	C	Public schools
Maryland	2	C	Municipal bonds for loans & loan guarantees to improve residential buildings (Baltimore only)
Massachusetts	5	C	Public buildings
Michigan	...	...	
Minnesota	...	S,W,G,Co,C	Municipalities authorized to issue bonds
Mississippi	...	...	...
Missouri	...	...	...
Montana	...	...	...
Nebraska	10	A	Residential modifications
Nevada	...	...	...
New Hampshire	...	...	...
New Jersey	50	C	State buildings
New Mexico	...	...	...
New York	...	...	...
North Carolina	...	...	...
North Dakota	...	...	...
Ohio	...	...	...
Oklahoma	...	...	...
Oregon	300	A	Finance loan fund
Pennsylvania	...	...	...
Rhode Island	...	...	...
South Carolina	...	...	...
South Dakota	...	...	...
Tennessee	...	...	...
Texas	...	...	...
Utah	...	...	...
Vermont	...	...	...
Virginia	...	...	...
Washington	...	...	...
West Virginia	...	...	...
Wisconsin	75/15	...	Housing and Neighborhood Conservation Program; state buildings
Wyoming	...	...	...

Key:
A—Alternative energy systems
C—Conservation/weatherization
S—Solar
W—Wind
G—Geothermal
Co—Cogeneration

Table 5

STATE INCOME TAX CREDITS AND DEDUCTIONS
FOR ENERGY CONSERVATION AND ALTERNATIVE ENERGY

State	Credit (percent)	Maximum amount (dollars)	Qualified energy systems	Time limits of statue	Deductions (percent)	Qualified systems
Alabama	25 12.5	1,000 1,000	S (active) S (passive)	1985	100	B
Alaska			No income tax			
Arizona	35 25	1,000 100	S C	1989	... ...	...
Arkansas	... ...	... ...	...	... ...	100	A,C,S,H,W,G,B
California	55 40	3,000 15,000	S C	1983 1983	... ...	... ...
Colorado	30 20	3,000 400	S,G,W C	1986 1986	... ...	... ...
Connecticut			No income tax			
Delaware	100	200	S	...	...	...
Florida			No income tax			
Georgia	... ...	... ...		... ...	... ...	... ...
Hawaii	10	... ...	S	1985	...	...
Idaho	... ...	... ...	...	... ...	40% 1st yr., 20% next 3 yrs. up to $5,000	S,G,W,B,C
Illinois	... ...			... ...	... ...	... ...
Indiana	25	3,000(residential) 10,000 (other)	S,W G,H	1985	...	...
Iowa	... ...	... ...		... ...	... ...	... ...
Kansas	30	1,500	S,W	1983	...	...
Kentucky	... ...	... ...		... ...	... ...	... ...
Louisiana	... ...	... ...		... ...	... ...	... ...
Maine	20	100	S,W,B	... ...	... ...	... ...
Maryland	... ...	... ...	A	... ...	... ...	... ...
Massachusetts	35	1,000	A	1983	100(corporations only)	S
Michigan	20	1,200	S	1985	...	...
Minnesota	20	2,000	S	1982	...	...
Mississippi	... ...	... ...	...	... ...	... ...	... ...
Missouri	... ...	... ...			... ...	... ...
Montana	5(1st $1,000), 2.5(next $3,000) 5 5	125 150 300	S,W,H,B (excl. wood stoves) C(residential) C(commercial)	1982	...	...
Nebraska	... ...	...		... ...	... ...	... ...
Nevada			No income tax			
New Hampshire			No income tax			
New Jersey	... ...	... ...	...	... ...	... ...	... ...

State	Percent	Maximum amount	Systems	Year / Note
New Mexico	25	10,000	S	1985
	100	25,000	S (irrigation pumps)	
New York	55	2,750	S	1986
North Carolina	25	1,000	S (passive and active)	...
	20	1,000	Photovoltaic or olvine branch product	
	15	1,000	Conversion to wood heat	
	20	1,000	E	
	10	1,000	Co,W	
	10	2,500	Methane gas	
	20	8,000	Solar process	
	10	5,000	H	
North Dakota	15	(5% for 3 yrs.)	S,W,G	5%
Ohio	10	1,000	S,W,G	1985
Oklahoma	25	3,200	S,W	1987
Oregon	25	1,000	S,G,H	1985
	25	125	C	
	35		Co,A,C(commercial)	
Pennsylvania	...	...	...	...
Rhode Island	10	1,000	S,A(residential)	1985
	10	50,000	H	
	20	1,000	C(rental unit)	
	10	1,500	S,A	
	10	5,000	C(commercial)	
South Carolina	25	1,000	S	1983
South Dakota	— No income tax —			
Tennessee	— No income tax —			
Texas	— No income tax —			
Utah	10	1,000	S,W,H	1985
	10	3,000	S,W,H(commercial)	
Vermont	25	1,000	S,W,H,B	1983
	25	3,000	S,W,H,B(commercial)	
Virginia	...	...	...	...
Washington	— No income tax —			
West Virginia	...	...	...	...
Wyoming	24	2,400	S,W,B	Direct refund

Key:
A—Alternative energy systems
C—Conservation/weatherization
S—Solar
H—Water power/hydroelectric

W—Wind
G—Geothermal
B—Biomass conversion, wood burning stoves
Co—Cogeneration
E—Ethanol, gasohol

Table 6
STATE LOAN PROGRAMS FOR ENERGY CONSERVATION
AND ALTERNATIVE ENERGY DEVELOPMENT

State	Program
Alabama	. . .
Alaska	Renewable Resource Corp. established, funded with 2.5% of oil & gas revenue loans up to $10,000 at 5% interest (A); $5,000 (C).
Arizona	. . .
Arkansas	. . .
California	Business & Industrial Dev. Corp. $2.5 million program. Interest-free loans up to $2,000 available. Loans to veterans for home cons. & solar at 10%. Energy Conservation Assistance Loans to schools, hospitals & local government for (C) & (A), $28 million.
Colorado	. . .
Connecticut	$400-$3,000 (A,C) from Housing Finance Authority.
Delaware	. . .
Florida	. . .
Georgia	. . .
Hawaii	. . .
Idaho	. . .
Illinois	. . .
Indiana	Loans and grants available through the Indiana Energy Development Board for the development of indigenous energy resources.
Iowa	Low income families eligible for renewable energy systems ($50 million total).
Kansas	. . .
Kentucky	. . .
Louisiana	. . .
Maine	. . .
Maryland	. . .
Massachusetts	Financial institutions can make loans with extended maturation period.
Michigan	Utilities make interest-free loans to qualified customers.
Minnesota	Municipalities authorized (C,S,W,G, Co) to provide loans. Home finance authority provides for low/moderate income persons (C).
Mississippi	. . .
Missouri	Loan fund established to lend money to financial institutions.
Montana	Financial institutions & public utilities authorized to make public low or no interest loans for conservation and alternative energy. Interest foregone may be credited to corporate tax rate. DNR may make loans through financial institutes for commercialization or renewable energy systems.
Nebraska	Mortgage Finance Fund available for residential property up to $1,500.
Nevada	. . .
New Hampshire	. . .
New Jersey	. . .
New Mexico	Solar Power Loan Fund established to lend money to financial institutions for 7% loans (S) up to $2,500.
New York	Utilities required to finance loans up to $3,000 (C), payback through utility bills.
North Carolina	. . .
North Dakota	. . .
Ohio	Utilities required to make loans up to $750 (C).
Oklahoma	. . .
Oregon	$10,000 loans at 6½% interest from financial institution. Corporate excise credit awarded for difference between average rate & 6½%. Loan fund for alternate energy from available DOE & veterans eligible for loans (S).
Pennsylvania	. . .
Rhode Island	. . .
South Carolina	. . .
South Dakota	. . .
Tennessee	Housing Development Authority provides for low/moderate income persons (C,S)
Texas	. . .
Utah	. . .
Vermont	Car pool van loans available interest-free.
Virginia	Housing Development Authority provides loans for low/moderate incolme persons (C,S,A).
Washington	Utilities can conduct energy audits, recommend improvements, arrange housing (C).
West Virginia	State Housing Finance Agency provides low interest loans to low/moderate income persons.
Wisconsin	. . .
Wyoming	. . .

Key:
A—Alternative energy systems W—Wind
C—Conservation/weatherization G—Geothermal
S—Solar Co—Cogeneration

Table 7
STATE GRANT PROGRAMS FOR ALTERNATIVE ENERGY/CONSERVATION

State	Program
Alabama	Appropriate Technology Small Grants Program.
Alaska	Renewable Resource Corp., funded by oil & gas lease revenues (2½%), extends grants for alternative energy development. Division of Energy & Power Development offers grants up to $300 for energy conservation measures.
Arizona	. . .
Arkansas	. . .
California	. . .
Colorado	Dept. of Local Affairs extends grants to low income households for weatherization.
Connecticut	Dept. of Housing extends grants to make energy conservation improvements in housing under their authority.
Delaware	. . .
Florida	PSC administers $3 million trust fund for energy R&D.
Georgia	. . .
Hawaii	. . .
Idaho	. . .
Illinois	Dept. of Energy & Natural Resources administers $5 million research, development & demonstration project for non-coal, non-nuclear energy. Also administers a $56 million trust fund for coal conversion projects.
Indiana	. . .
Iowa	Low income families eligible for renewable energy system, $50 million total.
Kansas	. . .
Kentucky	Has a trust fund of $55 million for coal conversion demonstration projects.
Louisiana	. . .
Maine	Division of Community Services extends grants to low income households for weatherization.
Maryland	. . .
Massachusetts	State & local institutions.
Michigan	Energy Administration provides financial assistance for commercial development & demonstration of renewable energy resources & energy conservation technologies.
Minnesota	. . .
Mississippi	. . .
Missouri	. . .
Montana	Dept. of Natural Resources & Conservation can participate in commercial & demonstration projects for renewable energy development. Funded by 2.25% of coal severance tax revenues.
Nebraska	. . .
Nevada	. . .
New Hampshire	. . .
New Jersey	. . .
New Mexico	Division of Human Resources provides up to $200 for weatherization of low income & elderly households.
New York	. . .
North Carolina	N.C. Energy Institute & Alternative Energy Corp. sponsor grants for energy R&D.
North Dakota	. . .
Ohio	. . .
Oklahoma	. . .
Oregon	Dept. of Revenue provides up to $300 for weatherization of low income & elderly households.
Pennsylvania	. . .
Rhode Island	Provides one-time grant up to 50% of cost of weatherization, maximum of $200, to elderly.
South Carolina	. . .
South Dakota	. . .
Tennessee	. . .
Texas	Energy & Natural Resources Advisory Council funds projects demonstrating alternative energy & energy conservation technologies.
Utah	. . .
Vermont	. . .
Virginia	. . .
Washington	. . .
West Virginia	. . .
Wisconsin	Division of Energy has a $225,000 Energy Development & Demonstration Program.
Wyoming	. . .

Table 8
ENERGY EFFICIENCY STANDARDS

State	Standards for solar equipment	Standards for conservation materials and installation	Standards for appliance efficiency
Alabama	★	★	. . .
Alaska	. . .	. . .	
Arizona	★ (a)	. . .	Gas appliances(b)
Arkansas	. . .	. . .	. . .
California	. . .	★	Gas appliances(b)
Colorado	. . .	. . .	. . .
Connecticut	★	. . .	
Delaware	. . .	★	HVAC
Florida	★	. . .	Air conditioners
Georgia	. . .	. . .	. . .
Hawaii	. . .	. . .	Gas appliances(b)
Idaho	. . .	. . .	. . .
Illinois	. . .	. . .	. . .
Indiana	★	★	. . .
Iowa	. . .	. . .	Gas appliances(b)
Kansas	. . .	★	Air conditioners, heat pumps
Kentucky	. . .	. . .	. . .
Louisiana	★	. . .	. . .
Maine	. . .	★	
Maryland	. . .	. . .	Gas appliances(b)
Massachusetts	. . .	. . .	. . .
Michigan	★	. . .	
Minnesota	★	★	Air conditioners, gas appliances(b), display lighting, commercial heated garages
Mississippi	. . .	. . .	
Missouri	. . .	. . .	. . .
Montana	. . .	. . .	. . .
Nebraska	. . .	. . .	. . .
Nevada	★	★	Gas appliances(b)
New Hampshire	. . .	. . .	. . .
New Jersey	. . .	. . .	. . .
New Mexico	★	. . .	. . .
New York	★	★	TV, gas appliances, air conditioner, refrigerator, freezer, dishwasher, hot water heater
North Carolina	. . .	★	. . .
North Dakota	. . .	. . .	. . .
Ohio	. . .	★	. . .
Oklahoma	. . .	★	. . .
Oregon	★	★	Gas appliances(b)
Pennsylvania	. . .	. . .	. . .
Rhode Island	. . .	★	. . .
South Carolina	. . .	. . .	. . .
South Dakota	. . .	. . .	. . .
Tennessee	. . .	. . .	. . .
Texas	. . .	. . .	. . .
Utah	. . .	. . .	. . .
Vermont	. . .	. . .	. . .
Virginia	. . .	. . .	. . .
Washington	. . .	. . .	. . .
West Virginia	. . .	. . .	
Wisconsin	. . .	. . .	Gas appliances(b)
Wyoming	★	. . .	. . .

(a) No single family dwelling shall be constructed unless it is designed to facilitate future installation of solar heating equipment.

(b) Requires intermittent ignition devices in lieu of pilot lights.

Table 9
ENERGY RESOURCE DEVELOPMENT AND CONSUMPTION

State or other jurisdiction	Coal		Crude petroleum		Natural gas		Fossil fuel produced as percentage of consumption(c)
	Production (thousands of short tons, 1980)	Consumption(a) (thousands of short tons, 1980)	Production (thousands of barrels, 1979)	Consumption (thousands of barrels, 1979)	Production(b) (million cubic feet, 1979)	Consumption (million cubic feet, 1979)	
United States..........	829,700	724,810	3,104,110	6,757,082	20,452,760	19,315,853	79
Alabama	26,403	25,980	19,161	130,266	85,815	283,435	51
Alaska	791	754	511,335	22,942	220,754	157,236	1,057
Arizona	10,905	13,165	472	66,762	247	172,738	26
Arkansas	319	3,756	18,869	70,324	109,452	250,747	31
California...............	...	3,128	352,268	637,997	248,206	1,810,381	42
Colorado	18,846	13,422	32,324	68,492	191,239	292,272	84
Connecticut..............	...	16	...	100,677	...	67,957	0
Delaware	...	1,336	...	28,592	...	24,981	0
Florida	...	7,778	47,168	301,782	50,190	344,177	15
Georgia	3	20,314	...	143,142	...	312,299	(d)
Hawaii	...	...	...	45,203	...	...	0
Idaho	...	525	...	26,880	...	54,237	0
Illinois	62,543	42,106	21,793	324,882	1,585	1,142,732	40
Indiana.................	30,873	50,618	4,715	159,879	350	504,185	29
Iowa	559	12,568	...	97,877	...	291,521	1
Kansas	842	12,840	56,995	81,389	797,762	584,236	88
Kentucky	150,144	27,927	5,514	95,283	59,520	218,689	262
Louisiana...............	...	2,934	489,687	222,817	7,266,271	1,978,382	310
Maine	...	130	...	45,704	...	(e)	0
Maryland	3,760	9,982	...	110,761	28	201,584	(d)
Massachusetts	...	510	...	179,508	...	156,459	0
Michigan	...	31,206	34,682	195,424	159,731	875,726	13
Minnesota	...	13,275	...	107,249	...	334,202	0
Mississippi	...	3,624	37,327	112,970	144,077	254,366	42
Missouri	5,503	23,933	91	128,228	...	347,257	8
Montana	29,872	3,658	29,957	35,028	53,888	69,805	267
Nebraska	...	5,029	6,068	48,306	3,208	170,013	7
Nevada.................	...	4,638	1,235	25,347	...	84,433	2
New Hampshire	...	1,148	...	25,632	...	14,881	0
New Jersey	...	2,805	...	241,737	...	260,579	0
New Mexico.............	18,425	11,032	79,649	41,844	1,181,363	211,182	305
New York	...	12,121	855	439,879	15,468	623,891	(d)
North Carolina	...	24,496	...	147,027	...	130,844	0
North Dakota	16,975	12,986	30,914	26,938	...	29,236	123
Ohio	39,394	67,300	11,953	275,824	123,431	898,029	28
Oklahoma	5,358	8,455	143,642	84,859	1,835,366	824,980	189
Oregon	...	1,334	...	68,316	2	93,707	(d)
Pennsylvania	93,125	64,455	2,874	298,187	96,313	740,818	59
Rhode Island	...	7	...	21,327	...	27,219	0
South Carolina	...	9,435	...	77,224	...	119,319	0
South Dakota	...	2,939	846	25,738	914	25,724	3
Tennessee...............	9,850	26,237	614	105,968	941	226,477	16
Texas	29,354	50,899	1,018,094	740,727	7,174,623	4,001,355	150
Utah	13,236	7,352	27,728	38,430	58,605	126,047	108
Vermont.................	...	13	...	13,592	...	(e)	0
Virginia	41,009	9,374	4	161,685	8,544	134,088	77
Washington	5,140	5,652	...	103,763	...	158,515	(d)
West Virginia............	121,584	36,514	2,406	42,267	150,505	148,538	251
Wisconsin	...	16,658	...	112,491	...	367,517	0
Wyoming................	94,887	18,313	131,890	39,441	414,416	93,797	473
Dist. of Col.	...	133	...	10,475	...	(f)	0

Source: U.S. Department of Energy, Energy Information Administration, U.S. Geological Survey.
(a) Domestic distribution.
(b) Marked production represents gross withdrawals of natural gas from gas and oil wells less gas used for repressuring and quantities vented and flared.

(c) Percentage shows Btu's of oil, natural gas and coal produced divided by Btu's consumed. 100 percent would mean equal balance of production and consumption. More than 100 means production exceeds consumption.
(d) Less than 1 percent.
(e) Included with New Hampshire.
(f) Included with Maryland.

Table 10
ENERGY RESEARCH AND DEVELOPMENT ACTIVITIES

State	R&D function	Conducted by	May participate in demonstration projects
Alabama	...	Dept. of Energy, State Universities	...
Alaska	★	Div. of Energy and Power Development	★
Arizona	...		...
Arkansas	...	...	...
California	★	California Energy Commission	★
Colorado	★	Energy Research Institute	...
Connecticut	...	...	...
Delaware	...	...	...
Florida	★	State Universities, Public Service Commission, Solar Energy Center	★
Georgia	...	...	...
Hawaii	★	National Energy Institute	...
Idaho	...	...	
Illinois	★	Dept. of Energy and Natural Resources	★
Indiana	★	Energy Development Board	★
Iowa	★	Energy Policy Council	...
Kansas	★	Energy Office	★
Kentucky	★	Institute of Mines and Minerals	★
Louisiana	...	...	...
Maine	★	State Universities, State Agencies	...
Maryland	...	...	...
Massachusetts	...	...	...
Michigan	...	...	...
Minnesota	...	Energy agency, state universities	...
Mississippi	★	Solar Research Center	...
Missouri	...		...
Montana	★	Division of Energy	★
Nebraska	...	...	...
Nevada	...	...	...
New Hampshire	...	...	...
New Jersey	...	...	...
New Mexico	★	Energy R&D Institute	...
New York	★	Energy R&D Authority	...
North Carolina	★	Alternative Energy Corporation, Energy Institute	★
North Dakota	...	...	...
Ohio	★	Dept. of Energy	...
Oklahoma	...	...	...
Oregon	★	Dept. of Energy	...
Pennsylvania	★	Science and Engineering Foundation	...
Rhode Island	...	...	...
South Carolina	...	Energy Research Center	...
South Dakota	...	...	...
Tennessee	★	State universities	...
Texas	★	State universities	...
Utah	...	...	...
Vermont	...	...	...
Virginia	...	...	...
Washington	...	Office of Energy	★
West Virginia	...	...	...
Wisconsin	★	Div. of Energy	...
Wyoming	...	...	...

7. Labor Relations

LABOR LEGISLATION: 1980-81

By Richard R. Nelson

The 1980-81 biennium was marked by legislative interest in a wide variety of both new and traditional labor law subjects. Several states adopted major new pieces of worker protection legislation including California and New York which passed laws to protect garment industry workers, Connecticut and West Virginia with new laws regulating the use of hazardous chemicals in the workplace, and Texas which passed a comprehensive new child labor law. Oregon made significant revisions in its minimum wage, prevailing wage, farm labor contractor and child labor laws. Michigan prohibited sexual harassment, enacted a "whistleblowers protection act" and made an important change in its workers' compensation law. During the biennium, which included a year designated as the International Year of Disabled Persons, several states enacted legislation to enhance the employment opportunities of the handicapped.

Wages and Hours

Minimum Wages. During 1980 and 1981, minimum wage rates were increased in 29 of the 45 jurisdictions with minimum wage laws.[1] While most of these increases resulted from wage escalation schedules adopted in previous years, new amendments or wage orders were responsible for increases in eight states[2] and the District of Columbia.

As of January 1, 1982, 15 jurisdictions had a minimum rate for some or all occupations equal to the $3.35 per hour federal standard that took effect January 1, 1981, the last of four scheduled increases provided for in the 1977 amendments to the Fair Labor Standards Act (FLSA). The $3.35 federal standard will be reached by Rhode Island on July 1, 1982, and by North Carolina on January 1, 1983, through previously scheduled rate increases. In addition, Alaska, Connecticut and certain industries in the District of Columbia continued with minimums higher than the federal rate.

The extent to which employers may offset employees' tips against the minimum wage was reduced under federal law on January 1, 1980, from 45 percent to 40 percent of the minimum rate. An identical reduction was made in the Pennsylvania law. The tip credit in Connecticut was increased for hotel and restaurant industry employees from 60 cents per hour to 23 percent of the minimum wage rate. Overall under state law, employers in 17 jurisdictions are obligated to pay a higher minimum cash wage to tipped employees than the $2.01 per hour requirement under federal law. Nine of them do not allow any tip credit and, in the other eight, the credit is lower than the 40 percent federal allowance.

In other wage developments, the labor commissioner in New York was given authority to order payment of a civil penalty of up to 25 percent of the total amount due under violations of the minimum wage and wage payment laws. Additional workers gained minimum

Richard R. Nelson is a Labor Standards Adviser in the Division of State Employment Standards, Employment Standards Administration, U.S. Department of Labor.

wage protection in North Carolina where coverage was extended to employers of three or more rather than four or more as before. In Oregon, persons over age 65 were removed from a list of those for whom a subminimum hourly wage rate may be set. (A 1979 amendment had eliminated Wage and Hour Commission authority to set subminimum wage rates for minors under age 18.)

Wage Garnishment and Assignment. Twenty-six jurisdictions enacted legislation during 1980 and 1981 concerning the use of wage garnishment or assignment to require payment under a court order for support of an employee's dependents.[3] Most of these laws involved delinquent child support payments, many by authorizing garnishment or assignment for the first time or by setting or increasing limits on the amount of earnings subject to either type of action.

Employees in Alaska, Illinois, Iowa, Louisiana, Nevada, Rhode Island, Tennessee and Wyoming were protected from employer disciplinary action because of the garnishment or assignment, and existing protections were expanded in Hawaii and North Dakota.

Wage garnishment provisions previously applicable to private sector employees in Nebraska and Rhode Island will now apply to public employees as well, as will provisions in Wisconsin for court-ordered assignment for maintenance or support payments. Also in Rhode Island, assignments for support payments now have priority over any other attachments and are not subject to any statutory dollar limit. In Guam, a new Child Support Employment Office was established in the Department of Public Health and Social Services, and the courts were authorized to order garnishment of wages or pensions for child support.

Prevailing Wages. Prevailing wage laws which specify wage rates paid on publicly funded contracts be not less than those prevailing in the locality have continued to be of particular interest and controversy at both the state and federal levels.

There are currently 37 states with prevailing wage laws. One or more amendments were introduced in most of these states during the last two years. Some of these bills were to strengthen or extend coverage of existing laws, but the vast majority were to repeal them or reduce coverage.

Repealer bills were introduced in 18 states[4] in 1980 or 1981. All failed except in Alabama in 1980 where the law was repealed when the legislature failed to continue it as required by a delayed repealer enacted in 1979, and in Utah in 1981 where the law fell when the governor's veto was overridden. Repealers passed both houses in the Colorado and New Mexico legislatures in 1981 but were vetoed.

Bills to repeal the comparable Federal Davis-Bacon Act or eliminate coverage program-by-program from various authorization bills were unsuccessful. Proposed regulatory changes in administration of the federal act have been published but final decisions not yet made at press time.

On another front, the constitutionality of state laws or rate determination methodology was challenged in the courts of Arizona, Michigan, Missouri and New Jersey. The Arizona law became inoperative in 1980 as the result of the state Supreme Court declining to review a lower court decision holding unconstitutional the section of the law establishing the method for rate determination (use of collectively bargained rates). On the other hand, the same method of rate determination was upheld in three other states—New Jersey in 1980 and Michigan and Missouri in 1981.

The prevailing wage picture was balanced by several laws enacted to improve worker protection. Prevailing wage payment was extended in New Jersey to construction projects funded through the state's Economic Development Authority or undertaken by the New Jersey Building Authority. Rhode Island made violators subject to an 18-month ban on bidding for or being awarded a public contract. The labor department in Montana was given subpoena power to compel the production of payroll records, and the prevailing wage rate is to be included in bid specifications and contracts. In Oregon, changes include authorizing the labor commissioner to seek an injunction against employers to prevent future failure to pay prevailing rates.

The Oklahoma law was amended to require use of federal Davis-Bacon rates where available and to require payment of prevailing fringes. In Washington, wage rates must now be posted at the job site, and new laws in Connecticut and Washington prohibit wage kickbacks on public construction projects.

Equal Employment Opportunity

Legislation addressing various forms of employment discrimination was enacted in a majority of the jurisdictions during the biennium. The largest number reflected state interest in furthering equal employment opportunity for handicapped individuals by expanding job rights or opportunities. Some of this activity may have been sparked by the designation of 1981 as the International Year of Disabled Persons. Among the more significant laws were a new civil rights act for the handicapped in Louisiana and a comprehensive new law to provide equal employment for the handicapped in Georgia, applicable to both the public and private sectors. Discrimination because of handicap was added to the list of prohibited practices in existing Oklahoma and Vermont laws.

Tennessee and Texas provided for alternate forms of testing handicapped job applicants including removal of time limits, oral or visual testing, and work-test periods on the job. In Maryland at grievance proceedings, deaf employees are now entitled to an interpreter paid for by the employer and union. Other states extended protection from discrimination to additional classifications of handicapped individuals including the mentally handicapped and those with impaired hearing.

The subject of age discrimination in employment, especially the practice of compulsory retirement based solely on age, did not receive as much attention in 1980 and 1981 as it had in the recent past. Mandatory retirement was addressed only in Vermont where the anti-discrimination law was amended to prohibit age discrimination and to prohibit mandatory retirement. The upper age limit in the ban on age discrimination in employment was raised from 65 to 70 for all employees in Georgia, Kentucky and Oregon; for public employees in Mississippi; and for state employees and teachers in Virginia. This matches the minimum mandatory retirement age set by the 1978 amendments to the Federal Age Discrimination in Employment Act for employees of private industry and state and local governments. Arizona and Tennessee enacted new provisions prohibiting age-based employment discrimination against persons age 40 to 70. Nevada, which formerly had no age limits, reduced coverage of its ban on age discrimination to those between age 40 and 69.

Extensions of job bias protection to the public sector were enacted in Alaska and Hawaii. Coverage extensions were also made in Michigan where the fair employment practices law now applies to all employers, rather than only those having four or more workers, and in Kentucky where the ban on sex-biased wage discrimination now applies to employers of two or more rather than eight or more as before. A new law in Alaska prohibits sex discrimination in employment in public education, and a New York law made domestics, farmworkers and employees of non-profit organizations subject to the equal pay law through repeal of a previous exemption.

Among other new enactments dealing with protection from sex discrimination in employment, sexual harassment, an area of new interest, was prohibited in Connecticut and Michigan. California and Connecticut made it unlawful to require sterilization as a condition of employment.

Equal pay for jobs of comparable worth is a new issue that has received widespread attention. It was the central issue in a San Jose city worker strike in July 1981 and in publicized disputes in other jurisdictions. The concept of equal pay for comparable work applies to job classifications that are not the same in content but are of comparable worth to the employer. This differs from equal pay for equal work requirements that men and women doing the same job receive the same pay. California, in September 1981, passed a law establishing a policy of comparable worth in setting salaries in state government in jobs dominated by women, on the basis of the work performed. Also, in Hawaii, resolutions were adopted urging all employers to adopt the comparable worth concept.

Other new enactments dealt with protection from discrimination for ex-criminal offenders and for veterans.

Industrial Relations

Little in the way of comprehensive new labor relations legislation was enacted during the last two years. Most new activity involved changes in coverage or refinements in existing legislation as in Maine where collective bargaining rights were extended to county employees and in North Carolina where strikes by public employees were prohibited. The Virgin Islands, however, did pass a new public employee collective bargaining law.

In what may prove to be an emerging trend, California, Michigan, Ohio and Wisconsin prohibited awarding of state contracts to persons or firms found to be in violation of the National Labor Relations Act. A similar law was enacted in Connecticut in 1979.

In other labor relations activity, local public employees in California and all public employees in New Jersey were authorized to negotiate agency shop agreements, a new department of employee relations was created in Minnesota, the use of strikebreakers was barred in Wisconsin, and in Oklahoma and one county in Alabama prison inmates on work release programs may not be used to replace strikers.

Again in 1980 and 1981 many unsuccessful attempts were made to pass "right-to-work" legislation barring compulsory union membership. The only measures that passed one or both houses of the legislature were a New Mexico bill which was vetoed by the governor and an Idaho bill that passed the House but was tabled by the Senate. As in earlier years, several of these bills were introduced in states where efforts were also being made to repeal or reduce coverage of prevailing wage legislation.

Occupational Safety and Health

Occupational safety and health legislation was enacted in several jurisdictions covering a wide variety of concerns including boiler, elevator and amusement ride inspection, mine safety and the handling and transportation of hazardous materials and nuclear waste. Among the new laws, a comprehensive railroad safety and health law was enacted in Maryland, to be administered and enforced by the labor commissioner. The commissioner of labor in West Virginia is to establish and maintain a list of up to 600 chemical substances and materials which have been proven or are suspected of being injurious to the health of employees, and employers of 10 or more are to notify employees where any such substance is used. Workers in Connecticut are to be warned of the presence and dangers of carcinogens in the workplace, and foundry workers are to be given lung function tests every two years. Employers in Oregon with higher than average worker injury rates may be required to establish and administer safety committees.

Of the 24 state plans approved under the Federal Occupational Safety and Health Act,[5] 18 were certified as of December 1981—eight of these within the last two years. Certification indicates that a state has successfully completed its developmental commitments and meets federal requirements. State performance continues to be monitored for at least one year following certification before final approval is given and federal jurisdiction removed. No state has yet received this final approval.

Workers' Compensation*

State legislatures were less active in the area of workers' compensation during this biennium than in previous years. Legislative changes mainly affected benefits, coverage and administration.

Michigan enacted one of the most significant amendments. It became the second state (Iowa was the first) to establish maximum weekly benefit levels for disability and death at 80 percent of spendable earnings effective January 1, 1982. Spendable earnings are defined as the employee's gross wage less federal and state income taxes and Social Security. Previously, maximum weekly benefits were 66-2/3 percent of the employee's average weekly wage before taxes. Forty-eight states and the District of Columbia increased their maximum weekly benefit levels for temporary total disability (see Table 1). Most of the increases were a result of automatic benefit adjustments based on increases in the state average weekly wage.

Twenty-seven legislatures revised coverage, and 20 of these extended coverage to include such groups as off-duty or volunteer police officers and fire fighters, certain volunteers, some apprentices and students, specific public employees, and prisoners. Twelve of the 27 states exempted such groups as participants in some athletic events, certain volunteers, corporate officers, sole proprietors, partners, domestic employees, real estate brokers on commission, and prisoners.

Several states broadened insurance options for private employers. Kansas, Rhode Island and Tennessee joined 44 other states that allow employers to self-insure. In Georgia, Missouri and Oregon, employers can now form groups of self-insurers. Previously, 20 states had permitted group self-insurance.[6]

Administrative changes included extensions in the statute of limitations for filing injury claims in three states and for filing occupational disease claims in five other states.[7] Ten states stiffened penalties for carriers and employers who do not make timely compensation payments or fail to submit required reports.[8] Study committees were established in seven states to recommend improvements in the workers' compensation law.

At the federal level, amendments to the Black Lung Benefits Act and the Black Lung Benefits Revenue Act were passed and signed into law during the 97th Congress. Under the new amendments, tax rates paid by coal operators into the Black Lung Trust Fund are in-

---

*This section was prepared by Anne Giese, Workers' Compensation Specialist, Division of State Workers' Compensation Standards, Employment Standards Administration, U.S. Department of Labor.

creased from 25 cents to 50 cents per ton for surface mining and from 50 cents to $1 for underground mining. The doubled tax rates will revert to current levels no later than 1995, and sooner if the trust fund becomes solvent. In addition, the amendments tightened eligibility and evidence standards for newly filed claims.

Private Employment Agencies

Protection for workers who use commercial employment agencies continues to interest legislatures, with many of their actions reflecting the conflict between industry support for self-regulation and those urging greater worker protection. Forty-four states currently have regulatory laws, and 30 of these are administered by state labor departments.

Seventeen states enacted legislation during the biennium affecting the regulation of these agencies. Regulation ended in Florida as the result of previous sunset legislation and in South Dakota where the law was repealed. In other developments, Montana will no longer set by statute the maximum placement fees charged by agencies, and in Hawaii, regulation was transferred out of the Department of Labor and Industrial Relations and administrative authority to set placement fees was repealed. South Carolina removed licensing and enforcement authority from the Department of Labor, and rule-making, investigatory and penalty provisions were deleted from the law. Licenses in South Carolina will now be issued by the secretary of state, and enforcement will be by court action.

Among other provisions, Arizona made the law applicable only to agencies charging a fee to job applicants, Maryland exempted private employment agencies whose fees are all employer-paid and do not require job applicants to sign a contract, and temporary help firms were exempted in New Jersey. Also, services which place medical doctors exclusively were exempted in Minnesota as were placement services of the University of Wyoming, and Montana exempted agents for professional athletes (California now requires such agents to be licensed and regulated by the labor commissioner).

Several amendments were made in the Ohio law to strengthen applicant protection, including a ban on registration fees, tightened restrictions on misleading advertising, and requirements that applicant contracts be in writing and placement fees refunded in certain circumstances. Maximum placement fees for jobs paying less than $13,000 a year are now established by statute.

Child Labor

As has been the trend for the past several years, many states continued to ease employment restrictions for youth, particularly with respect to hours of work, permitted nightwork, and certificate requirements, while at the same time other states amended their laws to provide greater protection.

Nightwork restrictions were eased for minors of 16 and 17, whose work hours are not federally regulated, in Connecticut, Florida, New Jersey and Rhode Island. Nightwork limitations were also eased for children under 16 in a number of other states, making the provisions more lenient than federal restrictions (see Table 2).

Alabama deleted requirements for both physical examinations and personal appearances by parents for granting employment certificates. Certificates were also either made easier to obtain or eliminated for some or all minors in Delaware, Florida, Georgia, Louisiana and Ohio. Florida and Texas joined those states which may approve variances for individual minors on a case-by-case basis. The change in Texas was part of a comprehensive new law setting 14 as the basic minimum age for employment and requiring the labor commissioner to determine hazardous occupations for workers under age 18. The law also prescribes hours of work restrictions and provides for age certificates. In other developments, hazardous occupation provisions were amended to cover more youths in Alabama, and minors in Michigan may not work, without an adult present, after sunset or 8 p.m. (whichever is earlier), in a job that involves a cash transaction.

New Jersey and West Virginia passed laws permitting minors to participate in activities of volunteer fire departments, and Virginia exempted from the child labor law those participating in volunteer rescue squads.

Agricultural Workers

While only a few states passed legislation on the employment problems of migrant and other farmworkers, important new protection was provided in states where heavy use is made of such labor. Among these new enactments, Minnesota requires employers who use agents to recruit out-of-state migrant workers to give each worker, when recruited, a written statement specifying the minimum duration of employment, working conditions, wages, and housing provision if any. Workers must receive at least 70 hours pay, at no less than the federal minimum wage, for any two consecutive week period, unless work is unavailable due to weather conditions, and must receive a written pay statement itemizing wage deductions. Similarly, changes in the Oregon law require that migrant workers be given the names and addresses of their employers and be provided with notification of any labor dispute at the work site as well as statements of hours of work and rates of pay. Texas prohibited the use of short-handled hoes in most agricultural labor, and also discontinued state licensing of farm labor contractors who are registered under the Federal Farm Labor Contractor Registration Act. School districts in Florida were authorized to adjust the school day and school year to help children of migrants in the farm labor and fish industries complete their education.

Other Laws

Garment Industry. Violations of wage, hour, child labor and safety standards by some garment industry employers have received considerable attention in recent years at both the federal and state levels. The U.S. Department of Labor has supplemented regular enforcement efforts with special task forces concentrating efforts for short time periods in cities where such abuses are considered to be prevalent. At the state level, California passed a law requiring all garment industry manufacturers, jobbers and contractors to register annually with the state labor commissioner and to keep certain hour, wage, production and contract price records. Failure to register or doing business with an unregistered contractor may result in penalties, including fines and garment confiscation. A Garment Industry Job Retention Act was passed in New York, directing the industrial commissioner to study the garment manufacturing industry and the feasibility of registration or licensing and bonding of employers. The study is also to deal with labor standards practices and violations and the adequacy of health and safety conditions.

In a related development, following an intensive review of existing rules on industrial homework which had applied to seven industries, the U.S. Department of Labor issued regulations lifting restrictions in the knitted outerwear industry when it found that the restrictions reduced job opportunities and earning power, particularly in rural areas. Federal restrictions were retained on homework in six other industries (women's apparel, jewelry, gloves and mittens, buttons and buckles, handkerchiefs, and embroideries).

Whistleblowers. In an area of new concern, six states[9] amended individual statutes to protect from employer retaliation an employee who reports the possible violation of certain laws or who participates in an enforcement proceeding. The Illinois change additionally provides protection for any employee who reports mismanagement, waste of funds or abuse of authority. Michigan adopted a separate Whistleblowers' Protection Act to afford protection from retaliation to all employees in both the private and public sectors.

Plant Closings. In what may signal an area of future worker protection measures, legislators in many states introduced bills in 1980 and 1981 designed to lessen the impact of plant closings on workers and communities. Although the proposals are not identical, they share one or more common features, such as advance notice, severance pay, retirement benefit protection, creation of a community assistance fund and, in some instances, granting employees an opportunity to purchase and operate the plant. The only laws enacted to date are a 1975 Wisconsin statute requiring that the labor department be notified in advance of any closings and a Maine law, expanded in 1981, requiring severance pay and advance notice of a plant closing to the labor department, the employees and the municipality. Connecticut created a committee in 1981 to conduct a comprehensive study of plant relocation and mass layoffs and to make legislative recommendations to the 1982 General Assembly.

Resident Contractor Preference. Several states have had laws for some time granting preference to in-state contractors. Most of these laws were enacted in the smaller population states, although a few industrial states, including New York, have also adopted such legislation. During 1980 and 1981, Maine and Oklahoma amended existing laws by increasing to 5 percent the amount of the previous preference. A new law in Maryland, applicable to public construction contracts, and one in Louisiana, applicable to non-construction contracts, give preference to in-sate contractors in those instances where they are bidding against contractors from states that give preference to their own resident contractors. Public works construction contractors were already protected by a similar law in Louisiana. A California law was passed permitting state-based companies up to a 9 percent preference on state contracts provided the work is performed in areas considered "distressed" and if workers with a high risk of unemployment are hired.

Jury Duty. Legislation was enacted in seven states[10] protecting workers from discharge or other retaliation because of required jury service. In addition to protection from discharge, employees in Ohio are not to be required to use sick leave or vacation time. The law in Louisiana, applicable to school board employees, specifically states that there is to be no loss of pay, leave or benefits. Employees in Florida and Kentucky, absent because of active service in the National Guard, now have similar protection from adverse actions.

Employee Privacy. Several measures were enacted to protect workplace privacy, including those regulating the use of polygraph or stress evaluation tests as conditions of employment, restricting employer access to criminal history and medical records and guaranteeing workers the right to review their personnel files. New laws regulating the use of polygraph and related examinations were enacted in Mississippi, Nebraska, Nevada, Texas, Utah and Wisconsin.[11] In addition, the California law was amended to require employers to notify employees that they may not be required to take such tests, and the law in Oregon was amended to restrict the use of breathalyzer tests to detect the presence of alcohol.

Five states amended laws regulating the release of criminal history data to ease restrictions and permit disclosure of information in specific instances, such as with employee approval or for employment in nuclear-related businesses.

Flexible Hours. The recent movement continued toward creating flexibility in employee working hours with the goals of enhanced service to the public, greater employee efficiency and expanded job opportunities for those whose personal responsibilities make it difficult to work full-time or during the traditional hours of employment. New laws were enacted in Maine and North Carolina, permitting state government employees to work alternative work schedules, including use of flexible hours, part-time work and job-sharing. An existing pilot project in Hawaii testing the feasibility of job-sharing was extended for two years.

Notes

1. Minimum wage rates were increased in Alaska, Arkansas, California, Connecticut, Hawaii, Maine, Maryland, Massachusetts, Michigan, Minnesota, New Hampshire, New Jersey, New Mexico, New York, North Carolina, North Dakota, Oklahoma, Oregon, Pennsylvania, Rhode Island, Utah, Vermont, Virginia, West Virginia, Wisconsin, District of Columbia, Guam and the Virgin Islands.

2. Arkansas, California, Montana, New Jersey, North Carolina, Oklahoma, Virginia and West Virginia.

3. Alabama, Alaska, Arizona, California, Colorado, Florida, Georgia, Hawaii, Illinois, Iowa, Louisiana, Maryland, Mississippi, Nebraska, Nevada, New York, North Dakota, Ohio, Rhode Island, South Dakota, Tennessee, Virginia, Washington, Wisconsin, Wyoming and Guam.

4. Arizona, Arkansas, California, Colorado, Connecticut, Idaho, Illinois, Kansas, Louisiana, Minnesota, Nevada, New Mexico, Ohio, Oklahoma, Pennsylvania, Texas, Utah and Wisconsin.

5. As of November 20, 1981, the 24 jurisdictions with approved plans were Alaska, Arizona, California, Connecticut, Hawaii, Indiana, Iowa, Kentucky, Maryland, Michigan, Minnesota, Nevada, New Mexico, North Carolina, Oregon, South Carolina, Tennessee, Utah, Vermont, Virginia, Washington, Wyoming, Puerto Rico and the Virgin Islands.

6. Alabama, Arkansas, Connecticut, Delaware, Florida, Illinois, Indiana, Iowa, Kentucky, Louisiana, Maine, Maryland, Massachusetts, Michigan, Minnesota, New Hampshire, New York, North Carolina, South Carolina and Virginia.

7. Injury claims: Arizona, Missouri, North Dakota. Occupational disease claims: Louisiana, Maryland, New Jersey, New York, North Carolina.

8. Alaska, Arkansas, Idaho, Maine, Massachusetts, Missouri, North Carolina, South Carolina, Virginia and Wisconsin.

9. Connecticut, Illinois, Louisiana, Maryland, Ohio and Oregon.

10. Alabama, Connecticut, Louisiana, Ohio, Virginia, West Virginia and Wisconsin.

11. Previous laws are in effect in Alaska, California, Connecticut, Delaware, Hawaii, Idaho, Maine, Maryland, Massachusetts, Michigan, Minnesota, Montana, New Jersey, New York, Oregon, Pennsylvania, Rhode Island, Virginia, Washington and the District of Columbia.

Table 1
MAXIMUM BENEFITS FOR TEMPORARY TOTAL DISABILITY
PROVIDED BY WORKERS' COMPENSATION STATUTES
(As of November 1981)

State or other jurisdiction	Maximum percentage of wages	Maximum payment per week		Maximum period		Total maximum stated in law
		Amount	Based on*	Duration of disability	Number of weeks	
Federal (FECA)(a)..	75	$722.78	75% of specific grade level in federal civil service	★	...	...
(LS/HWCA)(a)..	66-2/3	496.70	200% of NAWW	★	...	...
Alabama	66-2/3	$161.00	66-2/3% of SAWW	...	300	...
Alaska	66-2/3	858(b)	200% of SAWW	★	...	...
Arizona	66-2/3	203.86	...	★	...	...
Arkansas	66-2/3	140.00(c)	...	...	450	$63,000(c)
California	66-2/3	175.00	...	★	...	...
Colorado	66-2/3	261.80(b)	80% of SAWW	★	...	...
Connecticut	66-2/3	310.00(d)	100% of SAWW	★	...	...
Delaware	66-2/3	175.28	66-2/3% of SAWW	★	...	...
Florida	66-2/3	228.00(b)	100% of SAWW	...	350	...
Georgia	66-2/3	115.00	...	★	...	...
Hawaii	66-2/3	235.00	100% of SAWW	★	...	...
Idaho	90	198.00 to 275.00(e)	90% to 125% of SAWW(e)	★(f)	52(f)	...
Illinois	66-2/3	394.19	133-1/3% of SAWW	★	...	...
Indiana	66-2/3	140.00	...	...	500	70,000
Iowa	80(g)	501.00	200% of SAWW	★	...	...
Kansas	66-2/3	187.00	75% of SAWW	★	...	75,000
Kentucky	66-2/3	233.26	100% of SAWW	★	...	...
Louisiana	66-2/3	183.00	66-2/3% of SAWW	★	...	...
Maine	66-2/3	367.25	166-2/3% of SAWW	★	...	...
Maryland	66-2/3	248.00	100% of SAWW	★	...	...
Massachusetts	66-2/3	269.93(h)	100% of SAWW	★	...	45,000
Michigan	66-2/3	181.00 to 210.00(i)	...	★	...	...
Minnesota	66-2/3	267.00	100% of SAWW	★	...	...
Mississippi	66-2/3	112.00	...	...	450	50,400
Missouri	66-2/3	174.00	...	...	400	...
Montana	66-2/3	219.00(b)	100% of SAWW	★	...	...
Nebraska	66-2/3	180.00	...	★	...	...
Nevada	66-2/3	270.20	150% of SAWW	★	...	...
New Hampshire	(j)	234.00	100% of SAWW	★	...	...
New Jersey	70	199.00	75% of SAWW	...	400	...
New Mexico	66-2/3	221.50	100% of SAWW	...	600	(k)
New York	66-2/3	215.00	...	★	...	...
North Carolina	66-2/3	210.00	100% of SAWW	★	...	...
North Dakota	66-2/3	233.00(l)	100% of SAWW	★	...	...
Ohio	72 to 66-2/3(m)	275.00	100% of SAWW	★	...	...
Oklahoma	66-2/3	175.00	66-2/3% of SAWW	...	300	...
Oregon	66-2/3	286.00	100% of SAWW	★	...	...
Pennsylvania	66-2/3	262.00	100% of SAWW	★	...	...
Rhode Island	66-2/3	238.00(n)	100% of SAWW	★	...	...
South Carolina	66-2/3	216.00	100% of SAWW	★	500	...
South Dakota	66-2/3	191.00	100% of SAWW	★	...	...
Tennessee	66-2/3	126.00	...	★	...	50,400
Texas	66-2/3	154.00(o)	...	...	401	...
Utah	66-2/3	256.00(p)	100% of SAWW	...	312	...
Vermont	66-2/3	225.00(q)	100% of SAWW	★	...	...
Virginia	66-2/3	231.00	100% of SAWW	...	500	...
Washington	75	223.34(b)	75% of SAMW	★	...	...
West Virginia	70	276.26	100% of SAWW	...	208	...
Wisconsin	66-2/3	249.00	100% of SAWW	★	...	...
Wyoming	66-2/3	411.21	100% of SAMW	★	...	...
Dist. of Col.	66-2/3	496.70	200% of NAWW(r)	★	...	...
Puerto Rico	66-2/3	45.00	...	...	312	...

Source: Division of State Workers' Compensation Standards, Office of Workers' Compension Programs, Employment Standards Administration, U.S. Department of Labor.

*SAWW—State's average weekly wage; SAMW—State's average monthly wage; NAWW—National average weekly wage.

(a) Federal Employees' Compensation Act and the Longshoremen's/Harbor Workers' Compensation Act. LS/HWCA benefits are for private-sector maritime employees (not seamen) who work on navigable waters of the U.S. including dry docks.

(b) Payments are subject to Social Security offsets.

(c) Effective March 1, 1982, the weekly maximum will increase to $154 and total to $69,300.

(d) Additional $10 weekly for each dependent child under 18 years of age, up to 50 percent of basic benefit, not to exceed 75 percent of worker's wage.

(e) Benefits vary according to number of dependents. Additional 7 percent ($15.40) of SAWW payable for each child up to five children, beginning week 53.

(f) 60 percent of SAWW for duration of disability after 52 weeks.

(g) Maximum benefits are based on 80 percent of the worker's spendable earnings, rather than a percentage of the worker's average weekly wage.

(h) Additional $6 weekly for each dependent, not to exceed worker's average weekly wage or $150.

(i) Benefits vary according to number of dependents. Maximum payment is adjusted annually based on changes in SAWW. Effective January 1, 1982, the percentage of the worker's wage will be 80 percent of spendable earnings. Maximum weekly benefit will be 90 percent of SAWW.

(j) Benefits set by a "wage and compensation schedule" up to average weekly wage of $138 (maximum benefit $92). If worker's average weekly wage is over $138, benefits shall be 66-2/3 percent of average weekly wage, not to exceeed 100 percent of SAWW.

(k) Benefits for disability and death shall not exceed an amount equal to 600 multiplied by the maximum weekly compensation payable at the time of injury.

(l) Additional $5 weekly for each dependent child, but not to exceed worker's net wage. Workers' compensation benefits shall be reduced by 50 percent of Social Security benefits.

(m) 72 percent for first 12 weeks; thereafter 66-2/3 percent.

(n) Additional $6 weekly for each dependent, aggregate not to exceed 80 percent of worker's average weekly wage.

(o) Each cumulative $10 increase in average weekly wage for manufacturing production workers will increase the maximum weekly payment by $7.

(p) Additional $5 weekly for dependent spouse and each dependent child up to four, but not to exceed 100 percent of SAWW.

(q) Additional $5 weekly for each dependent child who is unmarried and under 21 years of age.

(r) NAWW ($228.12) as determined by U.S. Department of Labor.

Table 2
SELECTED STATE CHILD LABOR STANDARDS AFFECTING MINORS UNDER 18
(As of November 1981)
(Occupational coverage, exemptions and deviations usually omitted)

State or other jurisdiction	Documentary proof of age required up to age indicated(a)	Maximum daily and weekly hours and days per week for minors under 16 unless other age indicated(b)	Nightwork prohibited for minors under 16 unless other age indicated(b)	Minimum age for agricultural employment outside school hours(c)
Federal (FLSA) ..	(d)	8-40, non-school period. Schoolday/week: 3-18(e).	7 p.m. (9 p.m. June 1 through Labor Day) to 7 a.m.	14 (12 with written parental consent or on farms where their parents are working). (f) No minimum on parents' farm, or with written parental consent on farm of an employer who did not use more than 500 man-days of agricultural labor in any quarter of preceding calendar year.
Alabama	17; 19 in mines and quarries.	8-40-6. Schoolday/week: 4-28.	8 p.m. to 7 a.m.	...
Alaska	18	6-day week, under 18. Schoolday/week: 9(h)-23.	9 p.m. to 5 a.m.	14
Arizona	(g)	8-40. Schoolday/week: 3-18.	9:30 p.m. to 6 a.m.	...
Arkansas	16	8-48-6. 10-54-6, 16 and 17.	7 p.m. (9 p.m. before non-schoolday) to 6 a.m. 11 p.m. before schoolday to 6 a.m., 16 and 17.	14
California	18	8-48-6, under 18. Schoolday: 4, under 18, except 8 before non-schoolday, 16 and 17.	10 p.m. (12:30 a.m. before non-schoolday) to 5 a.m., under 18.	14 (12 during vacation and on regular school holidays).
Colorado	16	8-40, under 18. Schoolday: 6.	9:30 p.m. to 5 a.m., before schoolday.	12
Connecticut	18	9-48, under 18. 8-48-6, under 18 in stores, and under 16 in agriculture. (Overtime permitted in certain industries.)	10 p.m. to 6 a.m., under 18. 11 p.m. (midnight before non-schoolday or if not attending school) to 6 a.m., 16 and 17 in restaurants or as usher in non-profit theater.	14 (no minimum in weeks when average number of employees is 15 or fewer).
Delaware	18	8-48-6.	7 p.m. (9 p.m. in stores on Friday, Saturday and vacation) to 6.a.m.	...
Florida	18	10-40-6. Schoolday: 4 when followed by schoolday, except if enrolled in vocational program.	9 p.m. (11 p.m before non-schoolday) to 6:30 a.m. 1 a.m. to 5 a.m., 16 and 17.	12
Georgia	18	8-40. 60-hour week, 16 and over in cotton and woolen manufacturing. Schoolday: 4.	9 p.m. to 6 a.m.	...
Hawaii	18	8-40-6. Schoolday/week: 10(h).	7 p.m. to 7 a.m. (9 p.m. to 6 a.m. June 1 through day before Labor Day).	12 (10 in coffee harvesting on non-schooldays under direct parental supervision, with specified hours standards).
Idaho	(g)	9-54.	9 p.m. to 6 a.m.	...

State				
Illinois	16	8-48-6. Schoolday: 3 [8(h)].	7 p.m. (9 p.m. June 1-Labor Day) to 7 a.m.	10
Indiana	17	8-40-6, under 17, except minors of 16 not enrolled in school. 9-48 during summer vacation, minors of 16 enrolled in school. Schoolday/week: 3-23.	7 p.m. (9 p.m. before non-schoolday) to 6 a.m. 10 p.m. (midnight before non-schoolday) to 6 a.m., minors of 16 enrolled in school.	12
Iowa	16	8-40. Schoolday/week: 4-28.	7 p.m. (9 p.m. June 1 through Labor Day) to 7 a.m.	14 (for migrants: 14 before schoolday in available school, 12 at other times. No minimum for part-time work by non-migrants.)
Kansas	16(g)	8-40.	10 p.m. before schoolday to 7 a.m.	...
Kentucky	18	8-40 for under 16, 8-48 for 16 and 17 if attending school. 10-60, 16 and 17 not attending school. Schoolday/week: 3-18, under 16. 4 (8 on Friday)-32, 16 and 17 if attending school.	7 p.m. (9 p.m. June 1 through Labor Day) to 7 a.m. 10 p.m. (midnight on Friday, Saturday and during vacation) to 6 a.m., 16 and 17 if attending school.	
Louisiana	18	8-44-6. Schoolday: 3.	10 p.m. to 6 a.m.	
Maine	16	8-48-6. Schoolday/week: 4-28.	9 p.m. to 7 a.m., under 15. 10 p.m. to 7 a.m., 15.	
Maryland	18	8-40. Schoolday: 4, under 16. 12(h), under 18. Schoolweek: 23 when school in session 5 days.	8 p.m. (9 p.m. Memorial Day-Labor Day) to 7 a.m. 8 hours of non-work, non-school time required in each 24-hour day, 16 and 17.	...
Massachusetts	18	8-48-6. 4-24 in farmwork, under 14. 9-48-6, 16 and 17.	6 p.m. to 6:30 a.m. 10 p.m. (midnight in restaurants on Friday, Saturday and vacation) to 6 a.m., 16 and 17.	
Michigan	18	10-48-6, under 18. Schoolweek: 48(h), under 18.	9 p.m. to 7 a.m. 10:30 p.m. to 6 a.m., 16 and 17 if attending school. 11:30 p.m. to 6 a.m., 16 and 17 if not attending school.	
Minnesota	18	8-40.	9:30 p.m. to 7 a.m.	14
Mississippi	(g)	8-44 in factory, mill, cannery or workshop.	7 p.m. to 6 a.m. in factory, mill, cannery or workshop.	
Missouri	16	8-40-6.	7 p.m. (10 p.m. before non-schoolday and for minors not enrolled in school) to 7 a.m.	14 (no minimum for occasional work with parental consent).
Montana	18	...	...	...
Nebraska	16	8-48.	8 p.m. to 6 a.m. under 14. 10 p.m. (beyond 10 p.m. before non-schoolday with special permit) to 6 a.m., 14 and 15.	...
Nevada	17(g)	8-48.	...	...
New Hampshire	18	8 on non-schoolday, 48-hour week during vacation, if enrolled in school. 10-48 at manual or mechanical labor in manufacturing. 10½-54 at such labor in other employment, under 16 if not enrolled in school, and 16 and 17. Schoolday/week: 3-23 if enrolled in school.	9 p.m. to 7 a.m. if enrolled in school.	12

Table 2—Concluded

SELECTED STATE CHILD LABOR STANDARDS AFFECTING MINORS UNDER 18

State or other jurisdiction	Documentary proof of age required up to age indicated(a)	Maximum daily and weekly hours and days per week for minors under 16 unless other age indicated(b)	Nightwork prohibited for minors under 16 unless other age indicated(b)	Minimum age for agricultural employment outside school hours(c)
New Jersey	18	8-40-6, under 18. 10-hour day, 6-day week in agriculture. Schoolday: 8(h).	6 p.m. to 7 a.m. 11 p.m. to 6 a.m., 16 and 17 during school term, with specified variations.	12
New Mexico	16	8-44 (48 in special cases), under 14.	9 p.m. to 7 a.m., under 14.	. . .
New York	18	8-40-6. 8-48-6, 16 and 17. Schoolday/week: 3-23, under 16. 4-28, 16 if attending school.	7 p.m. to 7 a.m. Midnight to 6 a.m., 16 and 17.	14 (12 on home farm for parents, and in hand harvest of berries, fruits and vegetables with parental consent under specified hours standards).
North Carolina	18	8-40. Schoolday/week: 3-18.	7 p.m. (9 p.m. before non-schoolday) to 7 a.m.	. . .
North Dakota	16	8-48-6, under 18. Schoolday/week: 3-24 if not exempted from school attendance.	7 p.m. (9 p.m. June 1 through Labor Day) to 7 a.m.	. . .
Ohio	18	8-40. Schoolday/week: 3-18.	7 p.m. (9 p.m. June 1 through September 1 or during school holidays of 5 days or more) to 7 a.m.	. . .
Oklahoma	16	8-48.	6 p.m. to 7 a.m.	. . .
Oregon	18	10-44 (emergency overtime with permit)-6. 44-hour week (emergency overtime with permit), 16 and 17.	6 p.m. to 7 a.m., except with special permit.	(i)
Pennsylvania	18	8-44-6, under 18. Schoolday/week: 4-18, under 16. 28 in schoolweek, 16 and 17 if enrolled in regular day school.	7 p.m. (10 p.m. during vacation from June to Labor Day) to 7 a.m. 11 p.m. (midnight before non-schoolday) to 6 a.m., 16 and 17 if enrolled in regular day school.	. . .
Rhode Island	16	8-40. 9-48, 16 and 17.	7 p.m. to 6 a.m. 11:30 p.m. (1:30 a.m. before non-schoolday) to 6 a.m., 16 and 17 if regularly attending school.	. . .
South Carolina	(g)	10-55, 16 and over in cotton and woolen manufacturing establishments. (Limited emergency overtime permitted.)	8 p.m. (11 p.m. before non-schoolday in stores, domestic service, farmwork) to 5 a.m.	. . .
South Dakota	16	8-40.	After 7 p.m. in mercantile establishments, under 14.	. . .
Tennessee	18	8-40. Schoolday/week: 3-18.	7 p.m. to 7 a.m. (9 p.m. to 6 a.m. before non-schooldays).	. . .
Texas (j)	18(g)	8-48.	10 p.m. (midnight before non-school day or in summer if not enrolled in summer school) to 5 a.m.	. . .
Utah	(g)	8-40 Schoolday: 4.	9:30 p.m. to 5 a.m. before schoolday.	12 (no minimum if with parental consent).

State	Age under which certificate required	Maximum daily and weekly hours and days per week	Nightwork prohibited	Minimum age for employment
Vermont	16(g)	8-48-6. 9-50, 16 and 17.	7 p.m. to 6 a.m.	...
Virginia	16	8-40-6.	6 p.m. (10 p.m. before non-schoolday and June 1 to September 1 or with special permit) to 7 a.m. (minors of 15 may begin at 5 a.m.)	14 (no minimum if with parental consent).
Washington..........	18	8-hour day, 5-day week, under 18. Schoolday/week: 3-18.	7 p.m. (9 p.m. during summer vacation) to 7 a.m. After 9 p.m. on consecutive nights preceding schoolday, 16 and 17.	(i)
West Virginia	16	8-40-6	8 p.m. to 5 a.m.	...
Wisconsin	18	8-24-6 when school in session and 8-40-6 in non-schoolweek. 8-40-6 when school in session and 8-48-6 in non-schoolweek (voluntary overtime per day and week permitted in non-schoolweek up to 50-hour week), 16 and 17 if required to attend school.	8 p.m. (9:30 p.m. before non-schoolday) to 7 a.m. 12:30 a.m. to 6 a.m., except where under direct adult supervision, and with 8 hours rest between end of work and schoolday, 16 and 17 if required to attend school.	12
Wyoming..........	16	8-hour day.	10 p.m. (midnight before non-schoolday and for minors not enrolled in school) to 5 a.m. Midnight to 5 a.m., girls 16 and 17.	...
Dist. of Col.	18	8-48-6, under 18.	7 p.m. (9 p.m. June 1 through Labor Day) to 7 a.m. 10 p.m. to 6 a.m., 16 and 17.	14
Guam	16	8-40-6, under 18. Schoolday: 9(h), under 18.	After 7 p.m. on schoolday, under 18.	...
Puerto Rico........	18	8-40-6, under 18. Schoolday: 8(h).	6 p.m. to 8 a.m. 10 p.m. to 6 a.m., 16 and 17.	14

Source: Division of State Employment Standards, Employment Standards Administration, U.S. Department of Labor.

(a) Many states require an employment certificate for minors under 16 and an age certificate for 16 and 17 year olds; in a few states other types of evidence are acceptable as proof of age. In most states the law provides that age certificates may be issued upon request for persons above the age indicated, or although not specified in the law, such certificates are issued in practice.

(b) State hours limitations on a schoolday and in a schoolweek usually apply only to those enrolled in school. Several states exempt high school graduates from the hours and/or nightwork or other provisions, or have less restrictive provisions for minors participating in various school-work programs. Separate nightwork standards in messenger service and street trades are common, but are not displayed in table.

(c) Under federal law and in the laws of most states, there is a specific parental exemption for employment by a parent or on a farm owned or controlled by parents.

(d) Not required. State age or employment certificates which show that the minor has attained the minimum age for the job are accepted under the Fair Labor Standards Act.

(e) Students of 14 and 15 enrolled in approved Work Experience and Career Exploration programs may work during school hours up to three hours on a schoolday and 23 hours in a schoolweek.

(f) Local minors 10 and 11 years of age may work for no more than eight weeks between June 1 and October 15 for employers who receive approval from the Secretary of Labor. This work must be confined to hand-harvesting short-season crops outside school hours under very limited and specified circumstances prescribed by the Secretary of Labor.

(g) Proof of age is not mandatory under state law in Arizona, Idaho, Mississippi, South Carolina, Texas and Utah; or in Kansas for minors enrolled in secondary schools, and in Nevada and Vermont for employment outside school hours. For purposes of the Fair Labor Standards Act, federal age certificates are issued upon request by the State Department of Labor in South Carolina and by Wage and Hour Offices in Mississippi and Texas. In Utah, state law directs schools to issue age certificates upon request.

(h) Combined hours of work and school.

(i) Oregon. There is no minimum age for agricultural employment outside school hours, except for a nine-year minimum in harvesting berries and beans for intrastate commerce under specified circumstances; applicable only to employment subject to FLSA.

Washington. The child labor law exempts all agricultural employment from its coverage. However, a separate provision in the statute relating to agriculture generally, expressly permits outside-school-hour employment of minors under 12 in harvesting berries for intrastate commerce under specified circumstances; applicable only to employment subject to FLSA.

(j) Texas. New law, as displayed in table, took effect January 1, 1982.

Table 3
CHANGES IN BASIC MINIMUM WAGES IN NON-FARM EMPLOYMENT
UNDER STATE LAW: SELECTED YEARS
1965 TO 1982

State or other jurisdiction	1965(a)	1968(a)	1970(a)	1972	1976(a)	1979	1980	1981	1982
Federal (FLSA)	$1.15 & $1.25	$1.15 & $1.60	$1.30 & $1.60	$1.60	$2.20 & $2.30	$2.90	$3.10	$3.35	$3.35
Alabama									
Alaska	1.75	2.10	2.10	2.10	2.80	3.40	3.60	3.85	3.85
Arizona	18.72-26.40/wk. (b)	18.72-26.40/wk. (b)	18.72-26.40/wk. (b)	18.72-26.40/wk. (b)					
Arkansas	1.25/day(b)	1.25/day(b)	1.10	1.20	1.90	2.30	2.55	2.70	2.80
California	1.30(b)	1.65(b)	1.65(b)	1.65(b)	2.00	2.90	2.90	3.35	3.35
Colorado	.60-1.00(b)	1.00-1.25(b)	1.00-1.25(b)	1.00-1.25(b)	1.00-1.25(b)	1.90	1.90	1.90	1.90
Connecticut	1.25	1.40	1.60	1.85	2.21 & 2.31	2.91	3.12	3.37	3.37
Delaware	...	1.25	1.25	1.60	2.00	2.00	2.00	2.00	2.00
Florida									
Georgia	...	...	...	1.25	1.25	1.25	1.25	1.25	1.25
Hawaii	1.25	1.25	1.60	1.60	2.40	2.65	2.90	3.10	3.35
Idaho	1.00	1.15	1.25	1.40	1.60	2.30	2.30	2.30	2.30
Illinois	...	...	...	1.40	2.10	2.30	2.30	2.30	2.30
Indiana	...	1.15	1.25	1.25	1.25	2.00	2.00	2.00	2.00
Iowa	...	...	...	...	...	...	...	...	...
Kansas	.65-.75(b)	.65-.75(b)	.65-.75(b)	.65-.75(b)	...	1.60	1.60	1.60	1.60
Kentucky	...	...	...	...	1.60	2.00	2.15	2.15	2.15
Louisiana									
Maine	1.00	1.40	1.60	1.40-1.80	2.30	2.90	3.10	3.35	3.35
Maryland	...	1.00 & 1.15	1.30	1.60	2.20 & 2.30	2.90	3.10	3.35	3.35
Massachusetts	1.25	1.60	1.60	1.75	2.10	2.90	3.10	3.35	3.35
Michigan	1.00	1.25	1.25	1.60	2.20	2.90	3.10	3.35	3.35
Minnesota	.70-1.15(b)	.70-1.15(b)	.70-1.15(b)	.75-1.60	1.80	2.30	2.90	3.10	3.35
Mississippi	...	...	...	...	...	...	...	...	...
Missouri	...	...	...	...	...	...	...	...	...
Montana	...	1.00	1.00	1.60	1.80	2.00	2.00	2.00	2.50
Nebraska	1.15(b)	1.25	1.30	1.00	1.60	1.60	1.60	1.60	1.60
Nevada	1.25	1.40	1.45-1.60	1.60	2.20 & 2.30	2.75	2.75	2.75	2.75
New Hampshire	1.00-1.50(b)	1.40	1.50	1.60	2.20-2.30	2.90	3.10	3.35	3.35
New Jersey	1.00-1.50(b)	1.40	1.50	1.50	2.20	2.50	3.10	3.35	3.35

State									
New Mexico	.70–.80	1.15–1.40	1.30–1.60	1.30–1.60	2.00	2.30	2.65	2.90	3.35
New York	1.25	1.60	1.60	1.85	2.30	2.90	3.10	3.35	3.35
North Carolina	.85	1.00	1.25	1.45	2.00	2.50	2.75	2.90	3.10
North Dakota	.75–.85(b)	.75–1.25(b)	1.00–1.45	1.00–1.45	2.00–2.20	2.10–2.30	2.60–3.10	2.80–3.10	2.80–3.10
Ohio	.70–1.00(b)	.70–1.00(b)	.75–1.25(b)	.75–1.25(b)	1.60	2.30	2.30	2.30	2.30
Oklahoma	1.00	1.00	1.40	1.40	1.80	2.00	2.00	3.10	3.10
Oregon	.75–1.00	1.25	1.40	1.40	2.00	2.30	2.90	3.10	3.10
Pennsylvania	1.00	1.15	1.25	1.30	2.20	2.90	3.10	3.35	3.35
Rhode Island	1.25	1.40	1.60	1.60	2.30	2.30	2.65	2.90	3.10
South Carolina	...	...	...	...	...	...	...	...	...
South Dakota	17.00–20.00/wk.(b)	17.00–20.00/wk.(b)	1.00	1.00	2.00	2.30	2.30	2.30	2.30
Tennessee	...	...	...	...	...	...	...	...	...
Texas	.95–1.10(b)	1.00–1.15(b)	1.00–1.15(b)	1.40	1.40	1.40	1.40	1.40	1.40
Utah	1.00	1.20–1.35(b)	1.20–1.35(b)	1.55–1.70(b)	2.20–2.45(b)	2.20–2.45(b)	2.35–2.60(b)	2.50–2.75(b)	2.50–2.75(b)
Vermont	1.40	1.40	1.60	1.60	2.30	2.90	3.10	3.35	3.35
Virginia	...	1.25	1.60	1.60	2.00	2.20–2.30	2.35	2.65	2.65
Washington	1.25	1.25	1.60	1.60	2.00	2.20–2.30	2.30	2.30	2.30
West Virginia	1.00	1.00	1.20	1.20	2.00	2.20	2.20	2.75	3.05
Wisconsin	1.00–1.10(b)	1.25(b)	1.30(b)	1.45(b)	2.10	2.20	2.80	3.00	3.25
Wyoming	.75	1.20	1.30	1.50	1.60	1.60	1.60	1.60	1.60
Dist. of Col.	40.00–46.00/wk.(b)	1.25–1.40	1.60–2.00	1.60–2.25	2.25–2.75	2.46–3.00	2.50–3.50	2.50–3.75	2.50–3.90
Puerto Rico	.35–1.25	.43–1.60	.43–1.60	.65–1.60	.76–2.50	1.20–2.50	1.20–2.50	1.20–3.10	1.20–3.35

Source: Prepared by the Division of State Employment Standards, Employment Standards Administration, U.S. Department of Labor.

Note: Rates are for January 1 of each year, except in 1968 and 1972 which show rates as of February. The rates are per hour unless otherwise indicated. A range of rates, as in North Dakota and a few other states, reflects rates which differ by industry, occupation, geographic zone or other factors, as established under wage-board type laws or by statute.

(a) Under the federal Fair Labor Standards Act (FLSA), the two rates shown in 1965, 1968, 1970 and 1976 reflect the former multiple-track minimum wage system in effect from 1961 to 1978. The lower rate applied to newly covered persons brought under the act by amendments, whose rates were gradually phased in. A similar dual-track system was also in effect in certain years under the laws in Connecticut, Maryland and Nevada.

(b) The law applies only to women and minors.

EMPLOYMENT SECURITY ADMINISTRATION IN THE STATES

Employment Service

THE PUBLIC EMPLOYMENT service was authorized by the Wagner-Peyser Act during the Depression, when unemployment had reached an estimated 13 million. It was established as a nationwide, federal-state system of local employment offices, assisting workers at no fee to find employment.

Responsibility for the employment service system is shared by the U.S. Department of Labor and its state partners, with the department assisting in the establishment and maintenance of the system of public employment offices, including a veterans employment service, in the states. The department also establishes the procedures, standards and guidelines for the operation of the system, while states prepare plans and carry out the actual operation of the service.

The Social Security Act of 1935, which established the federal-state Unemployment Insurance Program, greatly expanded the role of the public employment service. Unemployment insurance laws stipulate that availability and ability to work are conditions of eligibility for unemployment compensation. This requirement to be "able and available" for work has come to be known as the "work test" or "work requirement." The public employment service participates in the administration of the work test by providing labor exchange services to claimants and reporting the results of those services to the Unemployment Insurance Service.

In addition to performing its statutory role of a labor exchange under the Wagner-Peyser Act of 1933 and the Social Security Act of 1935, the federal-state employment service is now affected by 25 other laws and 17 executive orders that directly or indirectly require work with specific target groups such as Vietnam-era veterans, handicapped individuals, recipients of Aid to Families with Dependent Children, Food Stamp recipients, and Comprehensive Employment and Training Act trainees.

Labor exchange involves a variety of activities, depending upon the needs of the applicant, including:

- Interviewing applicants to determine their skills, knowledge and interests.
- Soliciting job openings from employers and ascertaining their job requirements.
- Matching and referring applicants to openings.
- Counseling, testing and providing placement assistance to applicants who want or need to make an occupational change, choice or adjustment.

Applicant Clientele

In fiscal 1981, approximately 16.5 million job seekers with a wide variety of backgrounds and needs filed new or renewal applications with the nearly 2,400 local employment service

---

This chapter was prepared by the U.S. Employment Service and the Unemployment Insurance Service.

offices. (Most states now use "Job Service" to identify local offices of the public employment service.) Four out of ten applicants had high school diplomas, and two were educated beyond high school. The applicants included veterans, minorities, youth, older workers, handicapped workers, women, poor people, people with limited skills, and people with diverse skills and experience.

Of all applicants, approximately 13 percent were veterans, 32 percent were minority group members, and 30 percent were youth under age 22. About 13 percent were older workers, age 45 and over. About 4 percent were handicapped individuals who often excel if placed in appropriate employment. Approximately 45 percent were women, many seeking to re-enter the labor force. About 37 percent had limited education and few job skills.

Employer Services

The employer services program aims to establish and maintain an effective and productive relationship with employers. Its primary objective is to create a sufficient volume and diversity of jobs in order to satisfy the needs of applicants.

The program includes several basic elements. It is the central point of communication between job service local offices and employers, and through employer technical assistance, employers are helped to recruit, use and retain employees. Through the Job Service Improvement Project (JSIP), employers help to improve the overall operations of the local job service. The objective of JSIP is to bring in a larger volume and broader mix of job openings. It is oriented toward the local offices, around which employer committees are organized as a way to directly involve employers. In fiscal 1981, there were approximately 1,075 committees in 50 states, representing more than 22,000 employers.

Employment Service Performance

The economic conditions in fiscal 1981 resulted in fewer registered job-seekers and fewer job listings and placements than in fiscal 1980. New and renewal applicants decreased 2 percent, from 16.8 million in fiscal 1980 to 16.5 million in fiscal 1981. The number of individuals placed in jobs declined 8.8 percent, from 4.1 million in fiscal 1980 to 3.7 million in 1981. Of those individuals placed, over 3.5 million were in jobs expected to last over 150 days—a decrease of 11 percent from fiscal 1980. On the average, the placement wage rate was $4.26 per hour—up 7 percent over the year.

In fiscal 1981, 7 million job openings were received from non-agricultural industries, compared to 7.7 million in fiscal 1980. Of the non-agricultural job openings received in 1981, .7 million were subsidized and 6.6 million were unsubsidized.

Targeted Jobs Tax Credit. The Economic Recovery Tax Act of 1981 amended and extended until January 1, 1983, the Targeted Jobs Tax Credit, which was established by the Revenue Act of 1978. The Targeted Jobs Tax Credit (TJTC) is an elective tax credit that applies to wage costs incurred by employers for employees in specific target groups. The job service is responsible for managing the program and providing the necessary certification for the employer to be eligible for the credit.

The target groups established by the Economic Recovery Tax Act are:
- Recipients of Aid to Families with Dependent Children (AFDC)
- Registrants in the Work Incentive (WIN) program
- Public Service Employment (PSE) employees under the Comprehensive Employment and Training Act (CETA) who were involuntarily terminated after January 31, 1980.
- Individuals 18 to 24 who are economically disadvantaged.

- Economically disadvantaged Vietnam-era veterans.
- Recipients of Supplemental Security Income (SSI).
- Persons who have received general assistance for 30 or more days.
- Youth 16 through 18 participating in cooperative education programs (after December 30, 1981, they must be economically disadvantaged).
- Handicapped persons referred from vocational rehabilitation programs or the Veterans Administration.
- Ex-offenders (felons) who are economically disadvantaged and are hired within five years after conviction or prison release.

Unemployment Insurance

The Unemployment Insurance Program is a federal-state system which has been in operation for over 40 years. Under the system the federal government sets general standards, provides all administrative financing, and cooperates with the states in all aspects of the program. The states are responsible for the enactment of pertinent state laws and are primarily responsible for administration of the program.

Unemployment insurance benefits are given as a matter of right with no means test and with the level of benefits related to the individual's wages. It is by far the most important income maintenance program for the unemployed and has successfully provided benefits for the unemployed and acted as an economic stabilizer. The unemployment insurance system covers approximately 97 percent of all wage and salary workers.

Extended Benefits

The basic objective of the Unemployment Insurance Program is to provide individuals and the economy with partial replacement of wages and purchasing power lost during short periods of involuntary unemployment. Most state laws limit benefits to a maximum of 26 weeks, but during periods of high unemployment, an additional 13 weeks may be provided in an individual state under an extended benefits program, with costs shared between the federal and state governments. During recessions, Congress on several occasions has enacted temporary programs to lengthen the period of benefits.

New Developments

Major 1981 developments include federal legislation to improve the mechanisms for loan repayment by states and to encourage future state solvency. Requirements for payment of benefits to ex-service members were tightened, as were requirements for payment of extended benefits. Currently, the primary emphasis is on improving the integrity of the unemployment insurance system. Two improvements are now under way in 10 states—the random audit process and an internal security component. The random audit process selects claimants at random for in-depth investigation of their eligibility. It identifies the rates of improper payments and the specific causes and provides information for state use in designing systems and procedures to significantly reduce the level of overpayments. The internal security component provides, for the first time, resources to all states for a planned effort to detect and prevent fraud.

Trade Adjustment Assistance

Trade adjustment assistance is a federal program administered by the U.S. Department of Labor and cooperating state employment security agencies under provisions of the Trade Act of 1974, as amended by the Omnibus Budget Reconciliation Act of 1981. Established to help workers who become totally or partially unemployed as a result of increased imports, the program provides re-employment services (such as testing, counseling and job placement) designed to assist workers in returning as quickly as possible to productive employment. Such benefits as training, job search allowances and relocation allowances are available to those who meet specific qualifying requirements. Workers who qualify are paid trade readjustment allowances for weeks of unemployment after exhaustion of all rights to unemployment insurance.

Redwood Employee Protection Program. The Redwood Employee Protection Program is an employment, training and benefits program administered by the California Employment Development Department as an agent of the Secretary of Labor. It aids workers adversely affected by the 1978 amendments to the Redwood National Park Act of 1968, which expanded the Redwood National Park by 48,000 acres and, in so doing, caused the layoff or downgrading of workers engaged in sawmill, plywood and wood processing operations. The program aids eligible persons through weekly layoff benefits, vacation replacement benefits, continuation of health and welfare benefits, accrual of pension rights and credits, retraining, job search allowance, relocation allowance, or severance payment.

Airline Employee Protection Program. The Airline Employee Protection Program has been designed as a federal program to be administered by the U.S. Department of Labor and cooperating state employment security agencies, after final regulations have been issued by the department and approved by Congress. The Airline Deregulation Act of 1978 provides protected employees with the first right of hire with other air carriers hiring additional employees, as well as seniority and recall protection with the former air carrier. (A protected employee is one whose employer has suffered a major contraction and qualifying dislocation or bankruptcy as determined by the Civil Aeronautics Board.) Further, the act requires the Secretary of Labor to publish a comprehensive list of job vacancies in the airline industry and provides protected employees with full employment services. In addition, the act provides eligible protected employees with monthly assistance payments for months of reduced wages and unemployment and relocation assistance to move outside the employee's commuting area to accept employment. The employee protection program is still awaiting release of final regulations before implementation.

Table 1
SELECTED DATA ON STATE UNEMPLOYMENT INSURANCE OPERATIONS, BY STATE: CALENDAR 1979

State or other jurisdiction	Employers subject to state law	Initial claims	Beneficiaries	Avg. weekly benefit amount paid for total unemployment	Average duration of benefits (weeks)	Total benefit payments (in thousands)	Actual avg. employer contribution rate during year	Funds available for benefits at end of year (in thousands)
Total..................	4,619,476	20,160,148	8,077,727	$ 87.36	12.6	$8,578,614	2.5	$8,390,025
Alabama................	67,558	410,044	174,604	73.38	10.8	125,463	2.2	118,116
Alaska.................	10,510	64,093	38,999	82.52	16.8	56,346	4.0	75,383
Arizona	49,335	123,336	42,638	76.44	10.8	31,402	2.2	226,248
Arkansas	49,402	218,829	85,494	77.53	11.5	60,675	2.1	491
California.............	536,256	2,487,464	976,520	77.82	13.6	862,318	3.4	2,738,865
Colorado	69,247	142,031	51,645	102.65	10.5	52,710	1.4	136,585
Connecticut	77,189	280,664	125,276	94.50	11.1	114,926	2.6	-267,349
Delaware	13,436	57,632	26,916	100.25	12.3	30,546	2.8	-29,929
Florida	194,486	359,637	153,016	66.53	12.1	112,809	2.0	665,144
Georgia................	96,611	483,526	191,176	76.28	9.2	122,395	1.9	447,377
Hawaii	20,371	73,420	29,183	95.38	13.3	30,789	2.8	79,395
Idaho	22,621	98,219	38,870	90.07	10.8	33,823	2.1	93,242
Illinois...............	238,081	815,812	412,404	106.12	16.1	665,180	3.3	-459,583
Indiana	91,686	529,981	203,694	79.41	9.6	143,051	1.6	419,654
Iowa	65,395	166,335	81,362	110.71	12.7	106,095	2.8	155,484
Kansas	53,634	102,632	58,423	94.91	11.2	57,631	1.3	238,442
Kentucky	64,698	343,320	135,149	92.31	12.4	144,555	2.2	159,031
Louisiana	73,689	231,682	107,849	98.64	13.9	140,057	3.3	237,975
Maine	28,101	164,446	65,009	77.98	10.3	42,668	3.1	44
Maryland	75,231	274,008	125,257	85.30	11.8	115,864	3.7	41,507
Massachusetts	119,641	518,550	216,622	89.47	15.1	253,072	3.4	363,652
Michigan	158,775	1,488,702	558,244	99.03	11.4	595,577	4.0	112,224
Minnesota	84,137	203,738	110,855	105.38	13.1	134,506	2.2	70,262
Mississippi	41,848	171,303	67,579	63.81	11.5	44,816	2.1	230,732
Missouri	109,273	551,860	189,700	77.82	10.8	148,396	2.3	295,904
Montana	22,318	62,825	28,386	88.29	13.0	29,877	3.2	16,084
Nebraska	36,329	55,600	28,396	83.93	10.6	23,793	1.3	81,305
Nevada	18,705	71,839	32,134	90.87	11.7	33,719	3.0	95,197
New Hampshire	21,527	56,316	30,480	78.76	7.1	26,190	2.0	81,544
New Jersey.............	161,616	843,370	400,665	93.39	16.1	550,876	3.6	-507,378
New Mexico.............	27,391	64,378	21,476	75.49	14.7	22,204	2.0	79,982
New York...............	392,419	1,725,854	598,960	89.19	19.2	898,280	3.9	402,613
North Carolina	125,170	578,564	190,040	76.45	8.4	112,149	2.1	564,465
North Dakota	18,228	37,839	18,002	94.65	14.2	21,868	2.5	20,807
Ohio	195,669	1,033,679	391,294	114.59	11.8	494,397	2.4	513,167
Oklahoma	57,517	120,522	45,512	88.30	11.4	41,748	1.7	176,977
Oregon	64,849	312,852	107,268	88.05	12.5	115,542	3.4	320,240
Pennsylvania	207,311	1,659,999	648,603	102.78	13.5	809,265	3.1	-1,091,115
Rhode Island	24,105	166,216	63,371	83.62	13.8	59,742	2.9	-96,297
South Carolina	51,509	228,465	84,756	74.85	11.2	65,645	2.1	195,216
South Dakota	17,561	27,086	13,056	85.80	10.5	9,956	1.2	16,179
Tennessee..............	72,767	574,330	186,093	70.45	11.4	139,879	1.8	264,409
Texas	250,000	438,458	196,197	75.23	12.1	163,186	0.7	396,604
Utah	28,379	72,829	36,530	95.28	12.5	38,443	1.7	67,431
Vermont................	14,126	47,106	20,641	82.30	13.4	19,152	3.2	-21,096
Virginia...............	92,973	277,271	106,668	87.32	11.5	92,461	1.1	103,123
Washington	91,987	382,945	141,263	98.05	12.4	139,227	3.3	72,888
West Virginia..........	34,327	168,898	109,286	92.08	10.3	100,936	2.6	38,945
Wisconsin	91,626	422,437	198,239	103.39	11.5	217,339	3.3	465,374
Wyoming	14,394	14,817	7,359	95.30	9.7	8,039	1.2	68,949
Dist. of Col...........	17,897	38,644	25,317	114.49	19.7	44,295	2.4	-43,999
Puerto Rico	55,492	310,546	77,975	46.71	26.0	72,223	3.0	-32,870
Virgin Islands	2,073	5,199	3,276	66.06	15.6	2,513	3.7	-6,635

Source: U.S. Employment Service, U.S. Department of Labor.

Table 2
TOTAL UNEMPLOYMENT AND UNEMPLOYMENT RATES, BY STATE
ANNUAL AVERAGES: 1975-1980

State or other jurisdiction	Unemployment (in thousands)						Unemployment rates					
	1975	1976	1977	1978	1979	1980	1975	1976	1977	1978	1979	1980
Alabama	111.0	100	114	101	116	144	7.7	6.8	7.4	6.3	7.1	8.8
Alaska	10.8	14	16	20	17	18	6.9	8.0	9.4	11.2	9.2	9.6
Arizona	111.9	92	80	61	53	75	12.1	9.8	8.2	6.1	5.1	6.7
Arkansas	81.0	62	60	58	59	74	9.5	7.1	6.6	6.3	6.2	7.6
California	925.0	888	834	755	683	760	9.9	9.2	8.2	7.1	6.2	6.8
Colorado	80.0	71	78	71	66	82	6.9	5.9	6.2	5.5	4.8	5.6
Connecticut	133.0	138	106	79	81	95	9.1	9.5	7.0	5.2	5.1	5.9
Delaware	25.1	23	23	21	22	22	9.8	8.9	8.4	7.6	8.0	7.7
Florida	365.0	311	289	245	230	234	10.7	9.0	8.2	6.6	6.0	6.0
Georgia	185.0	179	156	131	119	154	8.6	8.1	6.9	5.7	5.1	6.4
Hawaii	31.8	39	30	31	25	20	8.3	9.8	7.3	7.7	6.3	5.0
Idaho	23.0	21	23	23	24	33	6.6	5.7	5.9	5.7	5.7	7.9
Illinois	356.0	331	321	323	293	454	7.1	6.5	6.2	6.1	5.5	8.3
Indiana	206.0	148	141	146	167	253	8.6	6.1	5.7	5.7	6.4	9.6
Iowa	55.8	53	56	57	59	83	4.3	4.0	4.0	4.0	4.1	5.7
Kansas	48.2	46	45	35	40	53	4.6	4.2	4.1	3.1	3.4	4.4
Kentucky	103.0	81	70	82	87	131	7.3	5.6	4.7	5.2	5.6	8.1
Louisiana	106.0	102	109	113	112	115	7.4	6.8	7.0	7.0	6.7	6.7
Maine	47.2	42	39	29	35	39	10.3	8.9	8.4	6.1	7.2	7.7
Maryland	128.0	127	118	114	124	137	6.9	6.8	6.1	5.6	5.9	6.4
Massachusetts	303.0	262	225	173	160	163	11.2	9.5	8.1	6.1	5.5	5.6
Michigan	487.0	374	337	289	335	541	12.5	9.4	8.2	6.9	7.8	12.6
Minnesota	107.0	110	98	76	86	120	5.9	5.9	5.1	3.8	4.2	5.7
Mississippi	76.6	62	71	68	57	76	8.3	6.6	7.4	7.1	5.8	7.5
Missouri	142.0	133	131	114	104	161	6.9	6.2	5.9	5.0	4.5	7.0
Montana	20.6	20	22	22	19	22	6.4	6.1	6.4	6.0	5.1	6.0
Nebraska	27.7	24	28	23	25	31	3.9	3.3	3.7	2.9	3.2	4.0
Nevada	28.0	27	23	15	18	23	9.7	9.0	7.0	4.4	5.1	6.2
New Hampshire	34.0	25	24	16	14	22	9.1	6.4	5.9	3.8	3.1	4.7
New Jersey	333.0	345	316	246	245	258	10.2	10.4	9.4	7.2	6.9	7.2
New Mexico	44.6	43	39	30	35	40	10.0	9.1	7.8	5.8	6.6	7.4
New York	729.0	792	708	603	571	603	9.5	10.3	9.1	7.7	7.1	7.6
North Carolina	217.0	159	155	116	129	180	8.6	6.2	5.9	4.3	4.8	6.6
North Dakota	9.7	10	14	14	11	15	3.6	3.6	4.8	4.6	3.7	4.9
Ohio	428.0	369	311	267	297	426	9.1	7.8	6.5	5.4	5.9	8.4
Oklahoma	83.0	65	61	49	44	64	7.2	5.6	5.0	3.9	3.4	4.8
Oregon	110.0	102	83	72	83	105	10.6	9.5	7.4	6.0	6.8	8.2
Pennsylvania	421.0	404	398	364	366	417	8.3	7.9	7.7	6.9	6.9	7.8
Rhode Island	47.9	35	38	29	30	33	11.1	8.1	8.6	6.6	6.6	7.2
South Carolina	130.0	87	92	74	65	90	8.7	6.9	7.2	5.7	5.0	6.9
South Dakota	11.5	11	10	10	12	16	3.7	3.4	3.3	3.1	3.5	4.7
Tennessee	151.0	110	120	110	115	145	8.3	6.0	6.3	5.8	5.8	7.2
Texas	296.0	320	310	288	263	337	5.6	5.7	5.3	4.8	4.2	5.3
Utah	32.3	29	28	21	25	38	6.5	5.7	5.3	3.8	4.3	6.2
Vermont	20.0	19	16	14	12	16	9.4	8.7	7.0	5.7	5.1	6.4
Virginia	145.0	136	127	130	117	129	6.4	5.9	5.3	5.4	4.7	5.1
Washington	147.0	137	144	120	120	143	9.5	8.7	8.8	6.8	6.8	7.5
West Virginia	57.0	51	49	46	51	72	8.5	7.5	7.1	6.3	6.7	9.4
Wisconsin	148.0	122	109	118	108	169	6.9	5.6	4.9	5.1	4.5	7.0
Wyoming	7.0	7	7	7	6	9	4.2	4.1	3.6	3.3	2.8	3.9
Dist. of Col.	26.0	30	32	28	24	23	7.6	9.1	9.7	8.5	7.5	7.2

Source: U.S. Employment Service, U.S. Department of Labor.

Table 3
SELECTED EMPLOYMENT SERVICE ACTIVITIES BY STATE: FISCAL 1980

State or other jurisdiction	New applicants and renewals	Individuals counseled	Individuals tested	Individuals placed nonag.	Placement transactions nonag.
Total....................	16,632,460	1,106,287	826,674	3,827,263	5,605,207
Alabama...................	392,019	26,327	32,596	84,316	99,048
Alaska	68,040	3,261	4,163	22,697	31,421
Arizona	292,430	18,769	5,280	68,110	96,899
Arkansas	305,904	13,667	9,371	74,078	106,909
California................	1,466,435	46,505	29,932	296,367	435,644
Colorado	243,168	14,569	13,367	53,847	83,035
Connecticut	189,994	15,615	5,663	42,890	49,812
Delaware	41,360	3,185	2,273	7,698	9,121
Florida	626,670	26,498	42,839	175,671	228,379
Georgia...................	440,256	47,428	15,514	105,297	133,855
Hawaii	83,962	5,183	2,751	21,319	24,596
Idaho	109,294	10,132	7,680	31,026	41,905
Illinois	697,764	55,084	19,017	165,915	201,444
Indiana	513,377	16,163	18,989	66,000	80,855
Iowa	291,587	12,259	21,968	95,033	138,541
Kansas	195,481	11,040	7,548	54,039	76,840
Kentucky	309,448	33,932	21,177	58,670	67,502
Louisiana	268,946	17,261	15,870	73,479	87,779
Maine	77,967	5,419	1,806	25,366	29,621
Maryland	206,506	12,653	9,019	30,475	34,073
Massachusetts	302,956	28,713	6,726	79,379	112,368
Michigan	822,571	38,523	20,866	105,569	144,381
Minnesota	292,354	12,772	17,838	73,078	99,290
Mississippi	288,946	45,408	26,953	81,255	103,016
Missouri	490,600	24,381	28,720	106,619	136,572
Montana	100,520	11,124	6,698	32,194	49,399
Nebraska	113,472	8,556	7,322	37,175	53,506
Nevada	101,663	5,813	5,741	22,182	37,826
New Hampshire	69,555	3,519	1,165	13,724	16,018
New Jersey................	324,911	23,377	6,791	90,610	163,233
New Mexico................	162,694	13,407	6,856	39,558	53,966
New York..................	713,831	63,038	41,643	216,119	661,920
North Carolina	492,320	36,520	39,973	100,943	118,804
North Dakota	76,405	5,705	6,371	30,449	43,820
Ohio	754,251	37,832	27,199	96,816	127,622
Oklahoma	304,123	28,155	27,003	91,778	159,160
Oregon	274,373	25,919	11,401	59,245	79,187
Pennsylvania	595,575	33,013	29,695	154,289	209,319
Rhode Island	64,075	9,277	1,563	20,537	24,461
South Carolina	270,713	18,834	22,491	68,593	97,910
South Dakota	73,342	7,989	7,103	29,840	50,841
Tennessee.................	296,473	23,693	20,063	89,859	110,311
Texas	1,180,620	76,915	82,195	275,383	421,661
Utah	157,778	16,533	13,048	50,894	76,066
Vermont...................	61,452	5,407	2,429	12,368	14,967
Virginia..................	393,064	25,098	28,468	73,636	88,263
Washington	305,547	21,048	12,444	71,516	103,699
West Virginia.............	171,929	13,709	4,787	26,052	30,959
Wisconsin	405,290	30,607	13,071	75,635	87,540
Wyoming	51,812	5,821	5,697	21,410	31,114
Dist. of Col...............	98,637	10,631	7,531	28,265	40,729

Source: U.S. Employment Service, U.S. Department of Labor.

Section IX
THE STATE PAGES

THE FOLLOWING section presents information on all the states of the United States and the District of Columbia; the commonwealths of Puerto Rico and the Northern Mariana Islands; the territories of American Samoa, Guam and the Virgin Islands; and the United Nations trusteeships of the Federated States of Micronesia, the Marshall Islands and the Republic of Belau.*

Included are listings of various executive officials, the justices of the supreme courts and officers of the legislatures. Lists of all officials are as of late 1981 or early 1982. Comprehensive listings of state legislators and other state officials appear in other publications of The Council of State Governments. Concluding each state listing are population figures and other statistics provided by the U.S. Bureau of the Census, based on the 1980 enumeration.

Preceding the state pages are three tables. The first lists the official names of states, the state capitols with zip codes and the telephone numbers of state central switchboards. The second table presents historical data on all the states, commonwealths and territories. The third presents a compilation of selected state statistics from the state pages.

---

*The Northern Mariana Islands, the Federated States of Micronesia, the Marshall Islands and the Republic of Belau (formerly Palau) have been administered by the United States since July 18, 1947, as part of the Trust Territory of the Pacific Islands (TTPI), a trusteeship of the United Nations. The Northern Mariana Islands separated themselves from TTPI in March 1976 and now operate under a constitutional government instituted January 9, 1978. The Federated States of Micronesia approved a constitution on July 12, 1978, which became effective May 10, 1979. The Marshall Islands approved a constitution on March 1, 1979, which became effective May 1, 1979. The Republic of Belau adopted a constitution on July 9, 1980, which became effective January 1, 1981, and changed the name from Palau to Belau.

Table 1
OFFICIAL NAMES OF STATES AND JURISDICTIONS, CAPITOLS, ZIP CODES AND CENTRAL SWITCHBOARDS

State or other jurisdiction	Name of state capitol(a)	Capital	Zip code	Area code	Central switchboard
Alabama, State of	State Capitol	Montgomery	36130	205	832-6011
Alaska, State of	State Capitol	Juneau	99811	907	465-2111
Arizona, State of	State Capitol	Phoenix	85007	602	255-4900
Arkansas, State of	State Capitol	Little Rock	72201	501	371-3000
California, State of	State Capitol	Sacramento	95814	916	322-9900
Colorado, State of	State Capitol	Denver	80203	303	866-5000
Connecticut, State of	State Capitol	Hartford	06115	203	566-2211
Delaware, State of	Legislative Hall	Dover	19901	302	736-4000
Florida, State of	State Capitol	Tallahassee	32301	904	488-1234
Georgia, State of	State Capitol	Atlanta	30334	404	656-2000
Hawaii, State of	State Capitol	Honolulu	96813	808	548-2211
Idaho, State of	State Capitol	Boise	83720	208	334-2411
Illinois, State of	State House	Springfield	62706	217	782-2000
Indiana, State of	State House	Indianapolis	46204	317	232-3140
Iowa, State of	State Capitol	Des Moines	50319	515	281-5011
Kansas, State of	State House	Topeka	66612	913	296-0111
Kentucky, Commonwealth of	State Capitol	Frankfort	40601	502	564-2500
Louisiana, State of	State Capitol	Baton Rouge	70804	504	342-2000
Maine, State of	State House	Augusta	04333	207	289-1110
Maryland, State of	State House	Annapolis	21401	301	269-6200
Massachusetts, Commonwealth of	State House	Boston	02133	617	727-2121
Michigan, State of	State Capitol	Lansing	48909	517	373-1837
Minnesota, State of	State Capitol	St. Paul	55515	612	296-6013
Mississippi, State of	New Capitol	Jackson	39201	601	354-7011
Missouri, State of	State Capitol	Jefferson City	65101	314	751-2151
Montana, State of	State Capitol	Helena	59620	406	449-2511
Nebraska, State of	State Capitol	Lincoln	68509	402	471-2311
Nevada, State of	State Capitol	Carson City	89710	702	885-5000
New Hampshire, State of	State House	Concord	03301	603	271-1110
New Jersey, State of	State House	Trenton	08625	609	292-2121
New Mexico, State of	State Capitol	Santa Fe	87503	505	827-4011
New York, State of	State Capitol	Albany	12224	518	474-2121
North Carolina, State of	State Capitol	Raleigh	27611	919	733-1110
North Dakota, State of	State Capitol	Bismarck	58505	701	224-2000
Ohio, State of	State House	Columbus	43215	614	466-2000
Oklahoma, State of	State Capitol	Oklahoma City	73105	405	521-1601
Oregon, State of	State Capitol	Salem	97310	503	378-3131
Pennsylvania, Commonwealth of	The Capitol	Harrisburg	17120	717	787-2121
Rhode Island and Providence Plantations, State of	State House	Providence	02903	401	277-2000
South Carolina, State of	State House	Columbia	29211	803	758-0221
South Dakota, State of	State Capitol	Pierre	57501	605	773-3011
Tennessee, State of	State Capitol	Nashville	37219	615	741-3011
Texas, State of	State Capitol	Austin	78701	512	475-2323
Utah, State of	State Capitol	Salt Lake City	84114	801	533-4000
Vermont, State of	State House	Montpelier	05602	802	828-1110
Virginia, Commonwealth of	State Capitol	Richmond	23219	804	786-0000
Washington, State of	Legislative Building	Olympia	98504	206	753-5000
West Virginia, State of	State Capitol	Charleston	25305	304	348-3456
Wisconsin, State of	State Capitol	Madison	53702	608	266-2211
Wyoming, State of	State Capitol	Cheyenne	82002	307	777-7011
District of Columbia	District Building	Washington	20004	202	727-1000
American Samoa, Territory of	Maota Fono	Pago Pago	96799	. . .	633-4116
Federated States of Micronesia	. . .	Kolonia	96941	. . .	NCS
Guam, Territory of	Congress Building	Agana	96910	. . .	477-7821
Marshall Islands	. . .	Majuro	96960	. . .	NCS
Northern Mariana Is., Commonwealth of	Civic Center	Saipan	96950	. . .	NCS
Puerto Rico, Commonwealth of	The Capitol	San Juan	00904	809	721-2100
Republic of Beleau	. . .	Koror	96940	. . .	NCS
Virgin Islands, Territory of	Government House	Charlotte Amalie	00801	809	774-0001

NCS—No central switchboard.
(a) In some instances the name is not official.

Table 2
THE STATES OF THE UNION—HISTORICAL DATA

State or other jurisdiction	Capitol	Source of state lands	Date organized as territory	Date admitted to Union	Chronological order of admission to Union
Alabama	Montgomery	Mississippi Territory, 1798(a)	March 3, 1817	Dec. 14, 1819	22
Alaska	Juneau	Purchased from Russia, 1867	Aug. 24, 1912	Jan. 3, 1959	49
Arizona	Phoenix	Ceded by Mexico, 1848(b)	Feb. 24, 1863	Feb. 14, 1912	48
Arkansas	Little Rock	Louisiana Purchase, 1803	March 2, 1819	June 15, 1836	25
California	Sacramento	Ceded by Mexico, 1848	(c)	Sept. 9, 1850	31
Colorado	Denver	Louisiana Purchase, 1803(d)	Feb. 28, 1861	Aug. 1, 1876	38
Connecticut	Hartford	Fundamental Orders, Jan. 14, 1638; Royal charter, April 23, 1662(e)	. . .	Jan. 9, 1788(f)	5
Delaware	Dover	Swedish charter, 1638; English charter, 1683(e)	. . .	Dec. 7, 1787(f)	1
Florida	Tallahassee	Ceded by Spain, 1819	March 30, 1822	March 3, 1845	27
Georgia	Atlanta	Charter, 1732, from George II to Trustees for Establishing the Colony of Georgia(e)	. . .	Jan. 2, 1788(f)	4
Hawaii	Honolulu	Annexed, 1898	June 14, 1900	Aug. 21, 1959	50
Idaho	Boise	Treaty with Britain, 1846	March 4, 1863	July 3, 1890	43
Illinois	Springfield	Northwest Territory, 1787	Feb. 3, 1809	Dec. 3, 1818	21
Indiana	Indianapolis	Northwest Territory, 1787	May 7, 1800	Dec. 11, 1816	19
Iowa	Des Moines	Louisiana Purchase, 1803	June 12, 1838	Dec. 28, 1846	29
Kansas	Topeka	Louisiana Purchase, 1803(d)	May 30, 1854	Jan. 29, 1861	34
Kentucky	Frankfort	Part of Virginia until admitted as state	(c)	June 1, 1792	15
Louisiana	Baton Rouge	Louisiana Purchase, 1803(g)	March 26, 1804	April 30, 1812	18
Maine	Augusta	Part of Massachusetts until admitted as state	(c)	March 15, 1820	23
Maryland	Annapolis	Charter, 1632, from Charles I to Calvert(e)	. . .	April 28, 1788(f)	7
Massachusetts	Boston	Charter to Massachusetts Bay Company, 1629(e)	. . .	Feb. 6, 1788(f)	6
Michigan	Lansing	Northwest Territory, 1787	Jan. 11, 1805	Jan. 26, 1837	26
Minnesota	St. Paul	Northwest Territory, 1787(h)	March 3, 1849	May 11, 1858	32
Mississippi	Jackson	Mississippi Territory(i)	April 7, 1798	Dec. 10, 1817	20
Missouri	Jefferson City	Louisiana Purchase, 1803	June 4, 1812	Aug. 10, 1821	24
Montana	Helena	Louisiana Purchase, 1803(j)	May 26, 1864	Nov. 8, 1889	41
Nebraska	Lincoln	Louisiana Purchase, 1803	May 30, 1854	March 1, 1867	37
Nevada	Carson City	Ceded by Mexico, 1848	March 2, 1861	Oct. 31, 1864	36
New Hampshire	Concord	Grants from Council for New England, 1622 and 1629. Made royal province, 1679(e)	. . .	June 21, 1788(f)	9
New Jersey	Trenton	Dutch settlement, 1618; English charter, 1664(e)	. . .	Dec. 18, 1787(f)	3
New Mexico	Santa Fe	Ceded by Mexico, 1848(b)	Sept. 9, 1850	Jan. 6, 1912	47
New York	Albany	Dutch settlement, 1623; English control, 1664(e)	. . .	July 26, 1788(f)	11
North Carolina	Raleigh	Charter, 1663, from Charles II(e)	. . .	Nov. 21, 1789(f)	12
North Dakota	Bismarck	Louisiana Purchase, 1803(k)	March 2, 1861	Nov. 2, 1889	39
Ohio	Columbus	Northwest Territory, 1787	May 7, 1800	March 1, 1803	17
Oklahoma	Oklahoma City	Louisiana Purchase, 1803	May 2, 1890	Nov. 16, 1907	46
Oregon	Salem	Settlement and treaty with Britain, 1846	Aug. 14, 1848	Feb. 14, 1859	33
Pennsylvania	Harrisburg	Grant from Charles II to William Penn, 1681(e)	. . .	Dec. 12, 1787(f)	2
Rhode Island	Providence	Charter, 1663, from Charles II(e)	. . .	May 29, 1790(f)	13
South Carolina	Columbia	Charter, 1663, from Charles II(e)	. . .	May 23, 1788(f)	8
South Dakota	Pierre	Louisiana Purchase, 1803	March 2, 1861	Nov. 2, 1889	40
Tennessee	Nashville	Part of North Carolina until land ceded to U.S. in 1789	June 8, 1790(l)	June 1, 1796	16
Texas	Austin	Republic of Texas, 1845	(c)	Dec. 29, 1845	28
Utah	Salt Lake City	Ceded by Mexico, 1848	Sept. 9, 1850	Jan. 4, 1896	45
Vermont	Montpelier	From lands of New Hampshire and New York	(c)	March 4, 1791	14
Virginia	Richmond	Charter, 1609, from James I to London Company(e)	. . .	June 25, 1788(f)	10
Washington	Olympia	Oregon Territory, 1848	March 2, 1853	Nov. 11, 1889	42
West Virginia	Charleston	Part of Virginia until admitted as state	(c)	June 20, 1863	35
Wisconsin	Madison	Northwest Territory, 1787	April 20, 1836	May 29, 1848	30
Wyoming	Cheyenne	Louisiana Purchase, 1803(d,j)	July 25, 1868	July 10, 1890	44
Dist. of Col.	. . .	Maryland(m)		. . .	. . . .
American Samoa	Pago Pago	———————————— Became a territory, 1900 ————————————			
Federated States of Micronesia	Kolonia	. . .	May 10, 1979	. . .	. . .
Guam	Agana	Ceded by Spain, 1898	Aug. 1, 1950	. . .	. . .
Marshall Islands	Majuro	. . .	May 1, 1979	. . .	. . .
No. Mariana Is.	Saipan	. . .	March 24, 1976	. . .	. . .
Puerto Rico	San Juan	Ceded by Spain, 1898	. . .	July 25, 1952(n)	. . .
Republic of Belau	Koror	. . .	Jan. 1, 1981	. . .	. . .
Virgin Islands	Charlotte Amalie	———————————— Purchased from Denmark, March 31, 1917 ————————————			

(a) By the Treaty of Paris, 1783, England gave up claim to the 13 original Colonies, and to all land within an area extending along the present Canadian border to the Lake of the Woods, down the Mississippi River to the 31st parallel, east to the Chattahoochie, down that river to the mouth of the Flint, east to the source of the St. Mary's, down that river to the ocean. The major part of Alabama was acquired by the Treaty of Paris, and the lower portion from Spain in 1813.

(b) Portion of land obtained by Gadsden Purchase, 1853.

(c) No territorial status before admission to Union.

(d) Portion of land ceded by Mexico, 1848.

(e) One of the original 13 Colonies.

(f) Date of ratification of U.S. Constitution.

(g) West Feliciana District (Baton Rouge) acquired from Spain, 1810; added to Louisiana, 1812.

(h) Portion of land obtained by Louisiana Purchase, 1803.

(i) See footnote (a). The lower portion of Mississippi was also acquired from Spain in 1813.

(j) Portion of land obtained from Oregon Territory, 1848.

(k) The northern portion and the Red River Valley were acquired by treaty with Great Britain in 1818.

(l) Date Southwest Territory (identical boundary as Tennessee's) was created.

(m) Area was originally 100 square miles, taken from Virginia and Maryland. Virginia's portion south of the Potomac was given back to that state in 1846. Site chosen in 1790, city incorporated 1802.

(n) On this date, Puerto Rico became a self-governing commonwealth by compact approved by the U.S. Congress and the voters of Puerto Rico as provided in U.S. Public Law 600 of 1950.

Table 3
STATE STATISTICS*

State or other jurisdiction	Land area in square miles	Rank in nation	Population	Rank in nation	Percentage change 1970 to 1980	Density per square mile	No. of representatives in Congress	Capital	Population	Rank in state	Largest city	Population
Alabama	50,708	28	3,890,061	22	12.9	76.7	7	Montgomery	178,157	3	Birmingham	284,413
Alaska	566,432	1	400,481	50	32.4	.7	1	Juneau	19,528	3	Anchorage	173,017
Arizona	113,417	6	2,717,866	29	53.1	24.0	5	Phoenix	764,911	1	Phoenix	764,911
Arkansas	51,945	27	2,285,513	33	18.8	44.0	4	Little Rock	158,461	1	Little Rock	158,461
California	156,361	3	23,668,562	1	18.5	151.4	45	Sacramento	275,741	7	Los Angeles	2,966,763
Colorado	103,766	8	2,888,834	28	30.7	27.8	6	Denver	491,396	1	Denver	491,396
Connecticut	4,862	48	3,107,576	25	2.5	639.2	6	Hartford	136,392	2	Bridgeport	142,546
Delaware	1,982	49	595,225	47	8.6	300.3	1	Dover	23,512	3	Wilmington	70,195
Florida	54,090	26	9,739,992	7	43.4	180.1	19	Tallahassee	81,548	10	Jacksonville	540,898
Georgia	58,073	21	5,464,265	13	19.1	94.1	10	Atlanta	425,022	1	Atlanta	425,022
Hawaii	6,425	47	965,000	39	25.3	150.2	2	Honolulu(a)	762,874	1	Hololulu(a)	762,874
Idaho	82,677	11	943,935	41	32.4	11.4	2	Boise	102,451	1	Boise	102,451
Illinois	55,748	24	11,418,461	5	2.8	204.8	22	Springfield	99,637	4	Chicago	3,005,072
Indiana	36,097	38	5,490,179	12	5.7	152.1	10	Indianapolis	700,807	1	Indianapolis	700,807
Iowa	55,941	23	2,913,387	27	3.1	52.1	6	Des Moines	191,003	1	Des Moines	191,003
Kansas	81,787	13	2,363,208	32	5.1	28.9	5	Topeka	115,266	3	Wichita	279,272
Kentucky	39,650	37	3,661,433	23	13.7	92.3	7	Frankfort	25,973	9	Louisville	298,451
Louisiana	44,930	33	4,203,972	19	15.3	93.6	8	Baton Rouge	219,486	2	New Orleans	557,482
Maine	30,920	39	1,124,660	38	13.2	36.4	2	Augusta	21,819	6	Portland	61,572
Maryland	9,891	42	4,216,446	18	7.5	426.3	8	Annapolis	31,740	5	Baltimore	786,775
Massachusetts	7,826	45	5,737,037	11	0.8	733.1	11	Boston	562,994	1	Boston	562,994
Michigan	56,817	22	9,258,344	8	4.2	163.0	18	Lansing	130,414	5	Detroit	1,203,339
Minnesota	79,289	14	4,077,148	21	7.1	51.4	8	St. Paul	270,230	2	Minneapolis	370,951
Mississippi	47,296	31	2,520,638	31	13.7	53.3	5	Jackson	202,895	1	Jackson	202,895
Missouri	68,995	18	4,917,444	15	5.1	71.3	9	Jefferson City	33,619	10	St. Louis	453,085
Montana	145,587	4	786,690	44	13.3	5.4	2	Helena	23,938	5	Billings	66,798
Nebraska	76,483	15	1,570,006	35	5.7	20.5	3	Lincoln	171,932	2	Omaha	311,681
Nevada	109,889	7	799,184	43	63.5	7.3	2	Carson City	32,022	5	Las Vegas	164,674
New Hampshire	9,027	44	920,610	42	24.8	102.0	2	Concord	30,400	3	Manchester	90,936
New Jersey	7,521	46	7,364,158	9	2.7	979.1	14	Trenton	92,124	5	Newark	329,248
New Mexico	121,412	5	1,299,968	37	27.8	10.7	3	Santa Fe	48,899	2	Albuquerque	331,767
New York	47,831	30	17,557,288	2	-3.8	367.1	34	Albany	101,727	6	New York	7,071,030
North Carolina	48,798	29	5,874,429	10	15.5	120.4	11	Raleigh	149,771	3	Charlotte	314,447
North Dakota	69,273	17	652,695	46	5.6	9.4	1	Bismarck	44,485	2	Fargo	61,308
Ohio	40,975	35	10,797,419	6	1.3	263.5	21	Columbus	564,871	2	Cleveland	573,822

State or other jurisdiction	Land area in square miles	Rank in nation	Population	Rank in nation	Percentage change 1970 to 1980	Density per square mile	No. of representatives in Congress	Capital	Population	Rank in state	Largest city	Population
Oklahoma	68,782	19	3,025,266	26	18.2	44.0	6	Oklahoma City	403,213	1	Oklahoma City	403,213
Oregon	96,184	10	2,632,663	30	25.9	27.4	5	Salem	89,233	3	Portland	366,383
Pennsylvania	44,966	32	11,866,728	4	0.6	263.9	23	Harrisburg	53,264	10	Philadelphia	1,688,210
Rhode Island	1,049	50	947,154	40	-0.3	902.9	2	Providence	156,804	1	Providence	156,804
South Carolina	30,225	40	3,119,208	24	20.4	103.2	6	Columbia	99,296	1	Columbia	99,296
South Dakota	75,955	16	690,178	45	3.6	9.1	1	Pierre	11,973	9	Sioux Falls	81,343
Tennessee	41,328	34	4,590,750	17	16.9	111.1	9	Nashville	455,651	2	Memphis	646,356
Texas	262,134	2	14,228,383	3	27.1	54.3	27	Austin	345,496	6	Houston	1,594,086
Utah	82,096	12	1,461,037	36	37.9	17.8	3	Salt Lake City	163,033	1	Salt Lake City	163,033
Vermont	9,267	43	511,456	48	15.0	55.2	1	Montpelier	8,241	5	Burlington	37,712
Virginia	39,780	36	5,346,279	14	14.9	134.4	10	Richmond	219,214	3	Norfolk	266,979
Washington	66,570	20	4,130,163	20	21.0	62.0	8	Olympia	27,447	15	Seattle	493,846
West Virginia	24,070	41	1,949,644	34	11.8	81.0	4	Charleston	63,968	1	Charleston	63,968
Wisconsin	54,464	25	4,705,335	16	6.5	86.4	9	Madison	170,616	2	Milwaukee	636,212
Wyoming	97,203	9	470,816	49	41.6	4.8	1	Cheyenne	47,283	2	Casper	51,016
Dist. of Col.	61	...	637,651	...	-15.7	10,453.3	1(b)		637,651	...		
American Samoa	76	...	32,395	...	19.3(c)	426.3	...	Pago Pago	3,058	...	Pago Pago	3,058
Federated States of Micronesia	271	...	73,755	...	(d)	272.2	...	Kolonia	7,633	...	Moen, Truk	9,679
Guam	209	...	105,816	...	24.5(c)	506.3	1(b)	Agana	881	...	Dededo	23,659
Marshall Islands	70	...	31,042	...	35.6(c)	443.5	...	Majuro	8,667	...	Majuro	8,667
No. Mariana Is.	184	...	16,758	...	73.8(c)	91.1	1(b)	Saipan	14,585	...	Saipan	14,585
Puerto Rico	3,421	...	3,187,570	...	17.5(c)	931.8	1(b)	San Juan	1,083,114	...	San Juan	1,083,114
Republic of Belau	192	...	12,177	...	8.6(c)	63.4	...	Koror	7,643	...	Koror	7,643
Virgin Islands	132	...	95,591	...	53.0(c)	724.2	1(b)	Charlotte Amalie, St. Thomas	11,756	...	Charlotte Amalie, St. Thomas	11,756

*Bureau of the Census population figures indicate final April 1, 1980 population counts for all states and the District of Columbia. Other population figures are based on a preliminary 1980 count by the Bureau of the Census.
 (a) Honolulu County.
 (b) Delegate with committee voting privileges only.
 (c) Unofficial.
 (d) Not available.

Alabama

Nickname	The Heart of Dixie
Motto	*We Dare Defend Our Rights*
Flower	Camellia
Bird	Yellowhammer
Tree	Southern (Longleaf) Pine
Song	*Alabama*
Stone	Marble
Mineral	Hematite
Fish	Tarpon
Entered the Union	December 14, 1819
Capital	Montgomery

SELECTED OFFICIALS

Governor	Forrest H. James Jr.
Lieutenant Governor	George D. H. McMillan Jr.
Secretary of State	Don E. Siegelman
Attorney General	Charles Graddick

SUPREME COURT

C. C. Torbert Jr., Chief Justice
Oscar W. Adams Jr.
Reneau P. Almon
Samuel A. Beatty
T. Eric Embry
James H. Faulkner
Richard L. Jones
Hugh Maddox
Janie L. Shores

LEGISLATURE

President of the Senate
...... George D. H. McMillan Jr.
President Pro Tem of the Senate
...... Finis E. St. John III
Secretary of the Senate ...... McDowell Lee

Speaker of the House ..... Joe C. McCorquodale Jr.
Speaker Pro Tem of the House ... Richard S. Manley
Clerk of the House ...... John W. Pemberton

STATISTICS

Land Area (square miles)	50,708
Rank in Nation	28th
Population	3,890,061
Rank in Nation	22nd
Density per square mile	76.7
Number of Representatives in Congress	7
Capital City	Montgomery
Population	178,157
Rank in State	3rd
Largest City	Birmingham
Population	284,413
Number of Cities over 10,000 Population	44

Alaska

Motto	*North to the Future*
Flower	Forget-me-not
Bird	Willow Ptarmigan
Tree	Sitka Spruce
Song	*Alaska's Flag*
Gem	Jade
Fish	King Salmon
Purchased from Russia by the United States	March 30, 1867
Entered the Union	January 3, 1959
Capital	Juneau

SELECTED OFFICIALS

Governor	Jay S. Hammond
Lieutenant Governor	Terry Miller
Attorney General	Wilson L. Condon

SUPREME COURT

Jay A. Rabinowitz, Chief Justice
Edmond W. Burke
Allen Compton
Roger G. Connor
Warren Matthews

LEGISLATURE

President of the Senate	Jalmar Kerttula
Majority Leader	Tim Kelly
Secretary of the Senate	Peggy Mulligan
Speaker of the House	Joe Hayes
Majority Leader	Rick Halford
Chief Clerk of the House	Irene Cashen

STATISTICS

Land Area (square miles)	566,432
Rank in Nation	1st
Population	400,481
Rank in Nation	50th
Density per square mile	0.7
Number of Representatives in Congress	1
Capital City	Juneau
Population	19,528
Rank in State	3rd
Largest City	Anchorage
Population	173,017
Number of Cities over 10,000 Population	3

Arizona

Nickname . . . . The Grand Canyon State
Motto . . . . *Ditat Deus* (God Enriches)
Flower . . . . Blossom of the Saguaro Cactus
Bird . . . . Cactus Wren
Tree . . . . Palo Verde
Song . . . . *Arizona*
Gemstone . . . . Turquoise
Entered the Union . . . . February 14, 1912
Capital . . . . Phoenix

SELECTED OFFICIALS

Governor . . . . Bruce E. Babbitt
Secretary of State . . . . Rose Mofford
Attorney General . . . . Robert K. Corbin

SUPREME COURT

Fred C. Struckmeyer Jr., Chief Justice
William A. Holohan, Vice Chief Justice
James Duke Cameron
Frank X. Gordon Jr.
Jack D. H. Hays

LEGISLATURE

President of the Senate . . . . Leo Corbet
President Pro Tem of the Senate . . . . James Mack
Secretary of the Senate . . . . Shirley Wheaton

Speaker of the House . . . . Frank Kelley
Speaker Pro Tem of the House
. . . . Sam A. McConnell Jr.
Chief Clerk of the House . . . . Jane Richards

STATISTICS

Land Area (square miles) 113,417
   Rank in Nation 6th
Population 2,717,866
   Rank in Nation 29th
   Density per square mile 24
Number of Representatives in Congress 5
Capital City . . . . Phoenix
   Population 764,911
   Rank in State 1st
Largest City . . . . Phoenix
Number of Cities over 10,000 Population 17

Arkansas

Nickname . . . . The Land of Opportunity
Motto . . . . *Regnat Populus* (The People Rule)
Flower . . . . Apple Blossom
Bird . . . . Mockingbird
Tree . . . . Pine
Song . . . . *Arkansas*
Stone . . . . Diamond
Entered the Union . . . . June 15, 1836
Capital . . . . Little Rock

SELECTED OFFICIALS

Governor . . . . Frank White
Lieutenant Governor . . . . Winston Bryant
Secretary of State . . . . Paul Riviere
Attorney General . . . . John Steven Clark

SUPREME COURT

Richard B. Adkisson, Chief Justice
Robert H. Dudley
Steele Hays
Darrell Hickman
Frank Holt
John I. Purtle
George Rose Smith

GENERAL ASSEMBLY

President of the Senate . . . . Winston Bryant
President Pro Tem of the Senate . . . . Ben Allen
Secretary of the Senate . . . . Lee Reaves

Speaker of the House . . . . Lloyd McCuiston
Speaker Pro Tem of the House . . . . . Charles Stewart
Chief Clerk of the House . . . . Mrs. Jim Childers

STATISTICS

Land Area (square miles) 51,945
   Rank in Nation 27th
Population 2,285,513
   Rank in Nation 33rd
   Density per square mile 44
Number of Representatives in Congress 4
Capital City . . . . Little Rock
   Population 158,461
   Rank in State 1st
Largest City . . . . Little Rock
Number of Cities over 10,000 Population 30

California

Nickname . . . . The Golden State
Motto . . . . *Eureka* (I Have Found It)
Flower . . . . Golden Poppy
Bird . . . . California Valley Quail
Tree . . . . California Redwood
Reptile . . . . California Desert Tortoise
Song . . . . *I Love You, California*
Stone . . . . Serpentine
Mineral . . . . Native Gold
Animal . . . . California Grizzly Bear
Fish . . . . California Golden Trout
Insect . . . . California Dog-Face Butterfly
Marine Mammal . . . . California Gray Whale
Fossil . . . . Saber-Toothed Cat
Entered the Union . . . . September 9, 1850
Capital . . . . Sacramento

SELECTED OFFICIALS

Governor . . . . Edmund G. Brown Jr.
Lieutenant Governor . . . . Mike Curb
Secretary of State . . . . March Fong Eu
Attorney General . . . . George Deukmejian

SUPREME COURT

Rose Elizabeth Bird, Chief Justice
Allen E. Broussard
Otto M. Kraus
Stanley Mosk
Frank C. Newman
Cruz Reynoso
Frank K. Richardson

LEGISLATURE

President of the Senate . . . . Mike Curb
President Pro Tem of the Senate . . . . . David Roberti
Secretary of the Senate . . . . Darryl White

Speaker of the Assembly . . . . Willie L. Brown Jr.
Speaker Pro Tem of the Assembly . . . . Tom Bane
Chief Clerk of the Assembly . . . . . . James D. Driscoll

STATISTICS

Land Area (square miles) 156,361
   Rank in Nation 3rd
Population 23,668,562
   Rank in Nation 1st
   Density per square mile 151.4
Number of Representatives in Congress 45
Capital City . . . . Sacramento
   Population 275,741
   Rank in State 7th
Largest City . . . . Los Angeles
   Population 2,966,763
Number of Cities over 10,000 Population 255

Colorado

Nickname . . . . The Centennial State
Motto . . . . *Nil Sine Numine*
   (Nothing Without Providence)
Flower . . . . Rocky Mountain Columbine
Bird . . . . Lark Bunting
Tree . . . . Colorado Blue Spruce
Song . . . . *Where the Columbines Grow*
Stone . . . . Aquamarine
Animal . . . . Rocky Mountain Bighorn Sheep
Entered the Union . . . . August 1, 1876
Capital . . . . Denver

SELECTED OFFICIALS

Governor . . . . Richard D. Lamm
Lieutenant Governor . . . . Nancy Dick
Secretary of State . . . . Mary E. Buchanan
Attorney General . . . . John D. MacFarlane

SUPREME COURT

Paul V. Hodges, Chief Justice
Jean Dubofsky
William H. Erickson
Robert B. Lee
George E. Lohr
Joseph R. Quinn
Luis D. Rovira

GENERAL ASSEMBLY

President of the Senate . . . . Fred E. Anderson
President Pro Tem of the Senate . . . . . . Dan Schaefer
Secretary of the Senate . . . . . Marjorie L. Rutenbeck

Speaker of the House . . . . Carl Bledsoe
Chief Clerk of the House . . . . . Lorraine F. Lombardi

STATISTICS

Land Area (square miles) 103,766
   Rank in Nation 8th
Population 2,888,834
   Rank in Nation 28th
   Density per square mile 27.8
Number of Representatives in Congress 6
Capital City . . . . Denver
   Population 491,396
   Rank in State 1st
Largest City . . . . Denver
Number of Cities over 10,000 Population 33

Connecticut

Nickname . . . . The Constitution State
Motto . . . . *Qui Transtulit Sustinet*
       (He Who Transplanted Still Sustains)
Animal . . . . Sperm Whale
Flower . . . . Mountain Laurel
Bird . . . . American Robin
Tree . . . . White Oak
Song . . . . *Yankee Doodle*
Mineral . . . . Garnet
Insect . . . . Praying Mantis
Entered the Union . . . . January 9, 1788
Capital . . . . Hartford

SELECTED OFFICIALS

Governor . . . . William A. O'Neill
Lieutenant Governor . . . . Joseph J. Fauliso
Secretary of State . . . . Maura L. Melley
Attorney General . . . . Carl R. Ajello

SUPREME COURT

John A. Speziale, Chief Justice
Maurice J. Sponzo, Chief Court Administrator
Anthony J. Armentano
Arthur H. Healey
Leo Parskey
Ellen A. Peters
David M. Shea

GENERAL ASSEMBLY

President of the Senate . . . . Joseph J. Fauliso
President Pro Tem of the Senate
      . . . . James J. Murphy Jr.
Clerk of the Senate . . . . Donald Cassin

Speaker of the House . . . . Ernest N. Abate
Deputy Speaker of the House . . . . Robert F. Frankel
Clerk of the House . . . . Thomas P. Sheridan

STATISTICS

Land Area (square miles) 4,862
    Rank in Nation 48th
Population 3,107,576
    Rank in Nation 25th
    Density per square mile 639.2
Number of Representatives in Congress 6
Capital City . . . . Hartford
    Population 136,392
    Rank in State 2nd
Largest City . . . . Bridgeport
    Population 142,546
Number of Cities and Towns over 10,000
    Population 85

Delaware

Nickname . . . . The First State
Motto . . . . *Liberty and Independence*
Flower . . . . Peach Blossom
Bird . . . . Blue Hen Chicken
Tree . . . . American Holly
Song . . . . *Our Delaware*
Entered the Union . . . . December 7, 1787
Capital . . . . Dover

SELECTED OFFICIALS

Governor . . . . Pierre S. du Pont IV
Lieutenant Governor . . . . Michael N. Castle
Secretary of State . . . . Glenn Kenton
Attorney General . . . . Richard S. Gebelein

SUPREME COURT

Daniel L. Herrmann, Chief Justice
William Duffy Jr.
Henry R. Horsey
John J. McNeilly
William T. Quillen

GENERAL ASSEMBLY

President of the Senate . . . . Michael N. Castle
President Pro Tem of the Senate
    . . . . Richard S. Cordrey
Secretary of the Senate . . . . Betty Jean Caniford

Speaker of the House . . . . Charles L. Hebner
Chief Clerk of the House . . . . Janice Donovan

STATISTICS

Land Area (square miles) 1,982
    Rank in Nation 49th
Population 595,225
    Rank in Nation 47th
    Density per square mile 300.3
Number of Representatives in Congress 1
Capital City . . . . Dover
    Population 23,512
    Rank in State 3rd
Largest City . . . . Wilmington
    Population 70,195
Number of Cities over 10,000 Population 3

Florida

Nickname . . . . The Sunshine State
Motto . . . . *In God We Trust*
Flower . . . . Orange Blossom
Bird. . . . . Mockingbird
Tree . . . . Sabal Palmetto Palm
Song . . . . *Old Folks at Home*
Gem . . . . Agatized Coral
Saltwater Mammal . . . . Dolphin
Saltwater Fish . . . . Atlantic Sailfish
Shell . . . . Horse Conch
Beverage. . . . . .Orange Juice
Entered the Union . . . . March 3, 1845
Capital . . . . Tallahassee

SELECTED OFFICIALS

Governor . . . . D. Robert Graham
Lieutenant Governor . . . . Wayne Mixson
Secretary of State. . . . . George Firestone
Attorney General. .Jim Smith

SUPREME COURT

Alan Carl Sundberg, Chief Justice
James C. Adkins Jr.
James E. Alderman
Joseph A. Boyd Jr.
Raymond Ehrlich
Parker Lee McDonald
Ben F. Overton

LEGISLATURE

President of the Senate . . . . W. D. Childers
President Pro Tem of the Senate . . . . Curtis Peterson
Secretary of the Senate . . . . Joe Brown

Speaker of the House. . . . . Ralph H. Haben Jr.
Speaker Pro Tem of the House . . . . Barry Kutun
Clerk of the House . . . . Allen Morris

STATISTICS

Land Area (square miles) 54,090
  Rank in Nation 26th
Population. 9,739,992
  Rank in Nation 7th
  Density per square mile 180.1
Number of Representatives in Congress 19
Capital City . . . . Tallahassee
  Population 81,548
  Rank in State 10th
Largest City . . . . Jacksonville
  Population 540,898
Number of Cities over 10,000 Population 96

Georgia

Nickname . . . . The Empire State of the South
Motto . . . . *Wisdom, Justice and Moderation*
Flower. . . . . .Cherokee Rose
Bird. . . . . Brown Thrasher
Tree . . . . Live Oak
Song . . . . *Georgia on My Mind*
Fish . . . . Largemouth Bass
Entered the Union . . . . January 2, 1788
Capital. . . . . .Atlanta

SELECTED OFFICIALS

Governor. .George D. Busbee
Lieutenant Governor . . . . Zell B. Miller
Secretary of State. . . . . .David B. Poythress
Attorney General. . . . . .Michael J. Bowers

SUPREME COURT

Robert H. Jordan, Chief Justice
Harold N. Hill Jr., Presiding Justice
Harold G. Clarke
Hardy Gregory Jr.
Thomas O. Marshall
George T. Smith
Charles L. Weltner

GENERAL ASSEMBLY

President of the Senate . . . . Zell B. Miller
President Pro Tem of the Senate . . . . . . Al Holloway
Secretary of the Senate . . . . Hamilton McWhorter Jr.

Speaker of the House . . . . Thomas B. Murphy
Speaker Pro Tem of the House. . . . . . . .Jack Connell
Clerk of the House . . . . Glenn W. Ellard

STATISTICS

Land Area (square miles) 58,073
  Rank in Nation 21st
Population. 5,464,265
  Rank in Nation 13th
  Density per square mile 94.1
Number of Representatives in Congress 10
Capital City. . . . . Atlanta
  Population 425,022
  Rank in State. 1st
Largest City . . . . Atlanta
Number of Cities over 10,000 Population 44

Hawaii

Nickname . . . . The Aloha State
Motto . . . . *Ua Mau Ke Ea O Ka Aina I Ka Pono*
(The Life of the Land Is Perpetuated
in Righteousness)
Flower . . . . Hibiscus
Bird . . . . Hawaiian Goose
Tree . . . . Candlenut
Song . . . . *Hawaii Ponoi*
Entered the Union . . . . August 21, 1959
Capital . . . . Honolulu

SELECTED OFFICIALS

Governor . . . . George R. Ariyoshi
Lieutenant Governor . . . . Jean Sadako King
Attorney General . . . . Tany Hong

SUPREME COURT

William S. Richardson, Chief Justice
Herman T. F. Lum
Benjamin Menor
Edward Nakamura
Thomas S. Ogata

LEGISLATURE

President of the Senate . . . . Richard S. H. Wong
Vice President of the Senate . . . . . Duke T. Kawasaki
Clerk of the Senate . . . . Seichi Hirai

Speaker of the House . . . . Henry Haalilio Peters
Vice Speaker of the House . . . . Daniel J. Kihano
Clerk of the House . . . . George M. Takane

STATISTICS

Land Area (square miles) 6,425
    Rank in Nation 47th
Population 965,000
    Rank in Nation 39th
    Density per square mile 150.2
Number of Representatives in Congress 2
Capital City . . . . Honolulu
    Population (county & city) 762,874
    Rank in State 1st
Largest City . . . . Honolulu
Number of Cities over 10,000 Population 12

Idaho

Nickname . . . . The Gem State
Motto . . . . *Esto Perpetua* (Let It Be Perpetual)
Flower . . . . Syringa
Bird . . . . Mountain Bluebird
Tree . . . . Western White Pine
Song . . . . *Here We Have Idaho*
Gemstone . . . . Idaho Star Garnet
Horse . . . . Appaloosa
Entered the Union . . . . July 3, 1890
Capital . . . . Boise

SELECTED OFFICIALS

Governor . . . . John V. Evans
Lieutenant Governor . . . . Philip E. Batt
Secretary of State . . . . Pete T. Cenarrusa
Attorney General . . . . David H. Leroy

SUPREME COURT

Robert E. Bakes, Chief Justice
Stephen Bistline
Charles R. Donaldson
Joseph J. McFadden
Allan G. Shepard

LEGISLATURE

President of the Senate . . . . Philip E. Batt
President Pro Tem of the Senate . . . . Reed W. Budge
Secretary of the Senate . . . . Dorthea Baxter

Speaker of the House . . . . Ralph Olmstead
Chief Clerk of the House . . . . Phyllis Watson

STATISTICS

Land Area (square miles) 82,677
    Rank in Nation 11th
Population 943,935
    Rank in Nation 41st
    Density per square mile 11.4
Number of Representatives in Congress 2
Capital City . . . . Boise
    Population 102,451
    Rank in State 1st
Largest City . . . . Boise
Number of Cities over 10,000 Population 11

Illinois

Nickname . . . . The Prairie State
Motto . . . . *State Sovereignty-National Union*
Flower . . . . Native Violet
Bird . . . . Cardinal
Tree . . . . White Oak
Song . . . . *Illinois*
Mineral . . . . Fluorite
Animal . . . . White-tailed deer
Insect . . . . Monarch Butterfly
Entered the Union . . . . December 3, 1818
Capital . . . . Springfield

SELECTED OFFICIALS

Governor . . . . James R. Thompson
Lieutenant Governor . . . . (Vacancy)
Secretary of State . . . . James Edgar
Attorney General . . . . Tyrone Fahner

SUPREME COURT

Joseph H. Goldenhersh, Chief Justice
William G. Clark
Thomas J. Moran
Howard C. Ryan
Seymour Simon
Robert C. Underwood
Daniel P. Ward

GENERAL ASSEMBLY

President of the Senate . . . . Philip J. Rock
Secretary of the Senate . . . . Kenneth A. Wright

Speaker of the House . . . . George H. Ryan
Chief Clerk of the House . . . . Tony Leone

STATISTICS

Land Area (square miles) 55,748
   Rank in Nation 24th
Population 11,418,461
   Rank in Nation 5th
   Density per square mile 204.8
Number of Representatives in Congress 22
Capital City . . . . Springfield
   Population 99,637
   Rank in State 4th
Largest City . . . . Chicago
   Population 3,005,072
Number of Cities over 10,000 Population 175

Indiana

Nickname . . . . The Hoosier State
Motto . . . . *Crossroads of America*
Flower . . . . Peony
Bird . . . . Cardinal
Tree . . . . Tulip Poplar
Song . . . . *On the Banks of the Wabash, Far Away*
Stone . . . . Limestone
Entered the Union . . . . December 11, 1816
Capital . . . . Indianapolis

SELECTED OFFICIALS

Governor . . . . Robert D. Orr
Lieutenant Governor . . . . John M. Mutz
Secretary of State . . . . Edwin J. Simcox
Attorney General . . . . Linley E. Pearson

SUPREME COURT

Richard M. Givan, Chief Justice
Roger O. DeBruler
Donald H. Hunter
Alfred J. Pivarnik
Dixon W. Prentice

GENERAL ASSEMBLY

President of the Senate . . . . John M. Mutz
President Pro Tem of the Senate
. . . . Robert F. Garton
Secretary of the Senate . . . . Sandra B. Culp

Speaker of the House . . . . J. Roberts Dailey
Speaker Pro Tem of the House . . . . Nelson J. Becker
Principal Clerk of the House
. . . . Sharon Cummins Thuma

STATISTICS

Land Area (square miles) 36,097
   Rank in Nation 38th
Population 5,490,179
   Rank in Nation 12th
   Density per square mile 152.1
Number of Representatives in Congress 10
Capital City . . . . Indianapolis
   Population 700,807
   Rank in State 1st
Largest City . . . . Indianapolis
Number of Cities over 10,000 Population 61

Iowa

Nickname . . . . The Hawkeye State
Motto . . . . *Our Liberties We Prize and Our Rights We Will Maintain*
Flower . . . . Wild Rose
Bird . . . . Eastern Goldfinch
Tree . . . . Oak
Song . . . . *The Song of Iowa*
Stone . . . . Geode
Entered the Union . . . . December 28, 1846
Capital . . . . Des Moines

SELECTED OFFICIALS

Governor . . . . Robert D. Ray
Lieutenant Governor . . . . Terry E. Branstad
Secretary of State . . . . Mary Jane Odell
Attorney General . . . . Thomas J. Miller

SUPREME COURT

W. Ward Reynoldson, Chief Justice
Robert G. Albee
K. David Harris
Jerry L. Larson
Clay LeGrand
Mark McCormick
A. A. McGiverin
Louis W. Schultz
Harvey Uhlenhopp

GENERAL ASSEMBLY

President of the Senate . . . . Terry E. Branstad
President Pro Tem of the Senate
. . . . Richard R. Ramsey
Secretary of the Senate . . . . . Linda Howarth MacKay

Speaker of the House . . . . Delwyn Stromer
Speaker Pro Tem of the House . . . . Lester D. Menke
Chief Clerk of the House . . . . Elizabeth Isaacson

STATISTICS

Land Area (square miles) 55,941
   Rank in Nation 23rd
Population 2,913,387
   Rank in Nation 27th
   Density per square mile 52.1
Number of Representatives in Congress 6
Capital City . . . . Des Moines
   Population 191,003
   Rank in State 1st
Largest City . . . . Des Moines
Number of Cities over 10,000 Population 29

Kansas

Nickname . . . . The Sunflower State
Motto . . . . *Ad Astra per Aspera*
(To the Stars through Difficulties)
Flower . . . . Native Sunflower
Bird . . . . Western Meadowlark
Tree . . . . Cottonwood
Song . . . . *Home on the Range*
Animal . . . . American Buffalo
Insect . . . . Honeybee
Entered the Union . . . . January 29, 1861
Capital . . . . Topeka

SELECTED OFFICIALS

Governor . . . . John W. Carlin
Lieutenant Governor . . . . Paul V. Dugan
Secretary of State . . . . Jack H. Brier
Attorney General . . . . Robert T. Stephan

SUPREME COURT

Alfred G. Schroeder, Chief Justice
Alex M. Fromme
Harold Herd
Richard W. Holmes
Kay McFarland
Robert H. Miller
David Prager

LEGISLATURE

President of the Senate . . . . Ross O. Doyen
Vice President of the Senate . . . . . . Charlie L. Angell
Secretary of the Senate . . . . Lu Kenney

Speaker of the House . . . . Wendell Lady
Speaker Pro Tem of the House . . . . Ben Foster
Chief Clerk of the House . . . . Geneva Seward

STATISTICS

Land Area (square miles) 81,787
   Rank in Nation 13th
Population 2,363,208
   Rank in Nation 32nd
   Density per square mile 28.9
Number of Representatives in Congress 5
Capital City . . . . Topeka
   Population 115,266
   Rank in State 3rd
Largest City . . . . Wichita
   Population 279,272
Number of Cities over 10,000 Population 34

Kentucky

Nickname . . . . The Bluegrass State
Motto . . . . *United We Stand, Divided We Fall*
Flower . . . . Goldenrod
Bird . . . . Cardinal
Tree . . . . Coffee Tree
Song . . . . *My Old Kentucky Home*
Entered the Union . . . . June 1, 1792
Capital . . . . Frankfort

SELECTED OFFICIALS

Governor . . . . John Y. Brown Jr.
Lieutenant Governor . . . . Martha Layne Collins
Secretary of State . . . . Frances Jones Mills
Attorney General . . . . Steven L. Beshear

SUPREME COURT

John S. Palmore, Chief Justice
J. Calvin Aker
Boyce G. Clayton
Robert F. Stephens
James B. Stephenson
Marvin J. Sternberg
(Vacancy)

GENERAL ASSEMBLY

President of the Senate . . . . . . Martha Layne Collins
President Pro Tem of the Senate
. . . . Joseph W. Prather
Chief Clerk of the Senate . . . . Marjorie Wagoner

Speaker of the House . . . . Bobby Richardson
Speaker Pro Tem of the House . . . . David Thomason
Chief Clerk of the House . . . . Evelyn Marston

STATISTICS

Land Area (square miles) 39,650
   Rank in Nation 37th
Population 3,661,433
   Rank in Nation 23rd
   Density per square mile 92.3
Number of Representatives in Congress 7
Capital City . . . . Frankfort
   Population 25,973
   Rank in State 9th
Largest City . . . . Louisville
   Population 298,451
Number of Cities over 10,000 Population 30

Louisiana

Nickname . . . . The Pelican State
Motto . . . . *Union, Justice and Confidence*
Flower . . . . Magnolia
Bird . . . . Eastern Brown Pelican
Tree . . . . Bald Cypress
Songs . . . . *Give Me Louisiana* and
You Are My Sunshine
Entered the Union . . . . April 30, 1812
Capital . . . . Baton Rouge

SELECTED OFFICIALS

Governor . . . . David C. Treen
Lieutenant Governor . . . . Robert L. Freeman
Secretary of State . . . . James H. Brown
Attorney General . . . . William J. Guste Jr.

SUPREME COURT

John A. Dixon Jr., Chief Justice
Fred S. Blanche Jr.
Pascal F. Calogero Jr.
James L. Dennis
Harry T. Lemmon
Walter F. Marcus Jr.
Jack C. Watson

LEGISLATURE

President of the Senate . . . . . Michael H. O'Keefe Jr.
President Pro Tem of the Senate
. . . . Samuel B. Nunez Jr.
Secretary of the Senate . . . . Michael S. Baer III
Speaker of the House . . . . John J. Hainkel Jr.
Speaker Pro Tem of the House
. . . . Frank P. Simoneaux
Clerk of the House . . . . David R. Poynter

STATISTICS

Land Area (square miles) 44,930
   Rank in Nation 33rd
Population 4,203,972
   Rank in Nation 19th
   Density per square mile 93.6
Number of Representatives in Congress 8
Capital City . . . . Baton Rouge
   Population 219,486
   Rank in State 2nd
Largest City . . . . New Orleans
   Population 557,482
Number of Cities over 10,000 Population 34

Maine

Nickname	The Pine Tree State
Motto	*Dirigo* (I Direct)
Flower	White Pine Cone and Tassel
Bird	Chickadee
Tree	Eastern White Pine
Song	*State of Maine Song*
Mineral	Tourmaline
Fish	Landlocked Salmon
Insect	Honeybee
Animal	Moose
Entered the Union	March 15, 1820
Capital	Augusta

SELECTED OFFICIALS

Governor	Joseph E. Brennan
Secretary of State	Rodney S. Quinn
Attorney General	James E. Tierney

SUPREME JUDICIAL COURT

Vincent L. McKusick, Chief Justice
Gene Carter
Edward S. Godfrey
David A. Nichols
David G. Roberts
Elmer H. Violette
Daniel E. Wathen

LEGISLATURE

President of the Senate	Joseph Sewall
Secretary of the Senate	May M. Ross
Speaker of the House	John L. Martin
Clerk of the House	Edwin H. Pert

STATISTICS

Land Area (square miles)	30,920
Rank in Nation	39th
Population	1,124,660
Rank in Nation	38th
Density per square mile	36.4
Number of Representatives in Congress	2
Capital City	Augusta
Population	21,819
Rank in State	6th
Largest City	Portland
Population	61,572
Number of Cities and Towns over 10,000 Population	17

Maryland

Nickname	The Old Line State
Motto	*Fatti Maschii, Parole Femine* (Manly Deeds, Womanly Words)
Flower	Black-eyed Susan
Bird	Baltimore Oriole
Tree	White Oak
Song	*Maryland, My Maryland*
Animal	Chesapeake Bay Retriever
Fish	Striped Bass
Entered the Union	April 28, 1788
Capital	Annapolis

SELECTED OFFICIALS

Governor	Harry R. Hughes
Lieutenant Governor	Samuel W. Bogley III
Secretary of State	Fred L. Wineland
Attorney General	Stephen H. Sachs

COURT OF APPEALS

Robert C. Murphy, Chief Judge
Harry A. Cole
Rita C. Davidson
J. Dudley Digges
John C. Eldridge
Laurence Rodowsky
Marvin H. Smith

GENERAL ASSEMBLY

President of the Senate	James Clark Jr.
President Pro Tem of the Senate	Frederick C. Malkus Jr.
Secretary of the Senate	Oden Bowie
Speaker of the House	Benjamin L. Cardin
Speaker Pro Tem of the House	Daniel J. Minnick Jr.
Chief Clerk of the House	Jacqueline M. Spell

STATISTICS

Land Area (square miles)	9,891
Rank in Nation	42nd
Population	4,216,446
Rank in Nation	18th
Density per square mile	426.3
Number of Representatives in Congress	8
Capital City	Annapolis
Population	31,740
Rank in State	5th
Largest City	Baltimore
Population	786,775
Number of Cities over 10,000 Population	18

Massachusetts

Nickname . . . . The Bay State
Motto . . *Ense Petit Placidam Sub Libertate Quietem*
(By the Sword We Seek Peace,
but Peace Only under Liberty)
Flower . . . . Mayflower
Bird . . . . Chickadee
Tree . . . . American Elm
Song . . . . *All Hail to Massachusetts*
Fish . . . . Cod
Insect . . . . Ladybug
Horse . . . . Morgan
Dog . . . . Boston Terrier
Beverage . . . . Cranberry Juice
Mineral . . . . Babingtonite
Entered the Union . . . . February 6, 1788
Capital . . . . Boston

SELECTED OFFICIALS

Governor . . . . Edward J. King
Lieutenant Governor . . . . Thomas P. O'Neill III
Secretary of the Commonwealth
. . . . Michael J. Connolly
Attorney General . . . . Francis X. Bellotti

SUPREME JUDICIAL COURT

Edward F. Hennessey, Chief Justice
Ruth Abrams
Robert Braucher
Benjamin Kaplan
Paul J. Liacos
Francis J. Quirico
Herbert P. Wilkins

GENERAL COURT

President of the Senate . . . . William M. Bulger
Clerk of the Senate . . . . Edward B. O'Neill

Speaker of the House . . . . Thomas W. McGee
Clerk of the House . . . . Wallace C. Mills

STATISTICS

Land Area (square miles) 7,826
   Rank in Nation 45th
Population 5,737,037
   Rank in Nation 11th
   Density per square mile 733.1
Number of Representatives in Congress 11
Capital City . . . . Boston
   Population 562,994
   Rank in State 1st
Largest City . . . . Boston
Number of Cities and Towns over 10,000
   Population 149

Michigan

Nickname . . . . The Wolverine State
Motto . . . . *Si Quaeris Peninsulam Amoenam
Circumspice* (If You Seek a Pleasant Peninsula,
Look About You)
Flower . . . . Apple Blossom
Bird . . . . Robin
Tree . . . . White Pine
Song . . . . *Michigan, My Michigan*
Stone . . . . Petoskey Stone
Gem . . . . Chlorastrolite
Fish . . . . Trout
Entered the Union . . . . January 26, 1837
Capital . . . . Lansing

SELECTED OFFICIALS

Governor . . . . William G. Milliken
Lieutenant Governor . . . . James H. Brickley
Secretary of State . . . . Richard H. Austin
Attorney General . . . . Frank J. Kelley

SUPREME COURT

Mary S. Coleman, Chief Justice
John W. Fitzgerald
Thomas G. Kavanagh
Charles L. Levin
Blair Moody Jr.
James L. Ryan
G. Mennen Williams

LEGISLATURE

President of the Senate . . . . James H. Brickley
President Pro Tem of the Senate . . . . Jack Faxon
Secretary of the Senate . . . . William C. Kandler

Speaker of the House . . . . Bobby D. Crim
Speaker Pro Tem of the House . . . Matthew McNeely
Clerk of the House . . . . Thomas S. Husband

STATISTICS

Land Area (square miles) 56,817
   Rank in Nation 22nd
Population 9,258,344
   Rank in Nation 8th
   Density per square mile 163
Number of Representatives in Congress 18
Capital City . . . . Lansing
   Population 130,414
   Rank in State 5th
Largest City . . . . Detroit
   Population 1,203,339
Number of Cities over 10,000 Population 89

Minnesota

Nickname . . . . The North Star State
Motto . . . . . *L'Etoile du Nord* (The Star of the North)
Flower . . . . Pink and White Lady's-Slipper
Bird . . . . Common Loon
Tree . . . . Red Pine
Song . . . . *Hail! Minnesota*
Gemstone . . . . Lake Superior Agate
Fish . . . . Walleye
Grain . . . . Wild Rice
Entered the Union . . . . May 11, 1858
Capital . . . . St. Paul

SELECTED OFFICIALS

Governor . . . . Albert H. Quie
Lieutenant Governor . . . . Lou Wangberg
Secretary of State . . . . Joan A. Growe
Attorney General . . . . Warren R. Spannaus

SUPREME COURT

Robert J. Sheran, Chief Justice
Douglas Amdahl
James C. Otis
C. Donald Peterson
George M. Scott
John Simonett
John J. Todd
Rosalie Wahl
Lawrence R. Yetka

LEGISLATURE

President of the Senate . . . . Jack Davies
Secretary of the Senate . . . . Patrick E. Flahaven

Speaker of the House . . . . Harry A. Sieben Jr.
Chief Clerk of the House . . . . Edward A. Burdick

STATISTICS

Land Area (square miles) 79,289
    Rank in Nation 14th
Population 4,077,148
    Rank in Nation 21st
    Density per square mile 51.4
Number of Representatives in Congress 8
Capital City . . . . St. Paul
    Population 270,230
    Rank in State 2nd
Largest City . . . . Minneapolis
    Population 370,951
Number of Cities over 10,000 Population 65

Mississippi

Nickname . . . . The Magnolia State
Motto . . . . *Virtute et Armis* (By Valor and Arms)
Flower . . . . Magnolia
Bird . . . . Mockingbird
Tree . . . . Magnolia
Song . . . . *Go, Mississippi*
Entered the Union . . . . December 10, 1817
Capital . . . . Jackson

SELECTED OFFICIALS

Governor . . . . William F. Winter
Lieutenant Governor . . . . Brad Dye
Secretary of State . . . . Edwin L. Pittman
Attorney General . . . . William A. Allain

SUPREME COURT

Neville Patterson, Chief Justice
L. A. Smith Jr., Presiding Justice
Stokes V. Robertson Jr., Presiding Justice
Francis S. Bowling
Vernon Broom
Armis E. Hawkins
Roy Noble Lee
R. P. Sugg
Harry G. Walker

LEGISLATURE

President of the Senate . . . . Brad Dye
President Pro Tem of the Senate
    . . . . William B. Alexander
Secretary of the Senate . . . . Charles H. Griffin

Speaker of the House . . . . C. B. Newman
Clerk of the House . . . . Charles J. Jackson Jr.

STATISTICS

Land Area (square miles) 47,296
    Rank in Nation 31st
Population 2,520,638
    Rank in Nation 31st
    Density per square mile 53.3
Number of Representatives in Congress 5
Capital City . . . . Jackson
    Population 202,895
    Rank in State 1st
Largest City . . . . Jackson
Number of Cities over 10,000 Population 27

Missouri

Nickname .... The Show Me State
Motto .... *Salus Populi Suprema Lex Esto*
(The Welfare of the People Shall Be
the Supreme Law)
Flower .... Hawthorn
Bird .... Bluebird
Tree .... Dogwood
Song .... *Missouri Waltz*
Stone .... Mozarkite
Entered the Union .... August 10, 1821
Capital .... Jefferson City

SELECTED OFFICIALS

Governor .... Christopher S. Bond
Lieutenant Governor .... Kenneth J. Rothman
Secretary of State .... James C. Kirkpatrick
Attorney General .... John D. Ashcroft

SUPREME COURT

Robert T. Donnelly, Chief Justice
John E. Bardgett
Andrew J. Higgins
J. P. Morgan
Albert L. Rendlen
Robert E. Seiler
Warren D. Welliver

GENERAL ASSEMBLY

President of the Senate .... Kenneth J. Rothman
President Pro Tem of the Senate
.... Norman L. Merrell
Secretary of the Senate .... Vinita Ramsey

Speaker of the House .... Robert F. Griffin
Speaker Pro Tem of the House .... Patrick J. Hickey
Chief Clerk of the House ...... Douglas W. Burnett

STATISTICS

Land Area (square miles) 68,995
   Rank in Nation 18th
Population 4,917,444
   Rank in Nation 15th
   Density per square mile 71.3
Number of Representatives in Congress 9
Capital City .... Jefferson City
   Population 33,619
   Rank in State 10th
Largest City .... St. Louis
   Population 453,085
Number of Cities over 10,000 Population 51

Montana

Nickname .... The Treasure State
Motto .... *Oro y Plata* (Gold and Silver)
Flower .... Bitterroot
Bird .... Western Meadowlark
Tree .... Ponderosa Pine
Song .... *Montana*
Stones .... Sapphire and Agate
Fish .... Blackspotted Cutthroat Trout
Grass .... Bluebunch Wheatgrass
Entered the Union .... November 8, 1889
Capital .... Helena

SELECTED OFFICIALS

Governor .... Ted Schwinden
Lieutenant Governor .... George Turman
Secretary of State .... Jim Waltermire
Attorney General .... Michael T. Greely

SUPREME COURT

Frank I. Haswell, Chief Justice
Gene B. Daly
John C. Harrison
Frank Morrison
Daniel J. Shea
John Sheehy
Fred Weber

LEGISLATURE

President of the Senate .... Jean A. Turnage
President Pro Tem of the Senate ... Allen C. Kolstad
Secretary of the Senate .... John W. Larson

Speaker of the House .... Bob Marks
Speaker Pro Tem of the House .... Art Lund
Chief Clerk of the House .... Don Byrd

STATISTICS

Land Area (square miles) 145,587
   Rank in Nation 4th
Population 786,690
   Rank in Nation 44th
   Density per square mile 5.4
Number of Representatives in Congress 2
Capital City .... Helena
   Population 23,938
   Rank in State 5th
Largest City .... Billings
   Population 66,798
Number of Cities over 10,000 Population 9

Nebraska

Nickname.................The Cornhusker State
Motto..................*Equality Before the Law*
Flower............................Goldenrod
Bird......................Western Meadowlark
Tree..............................Cottonwood
Song......................*Beautiful Nebraska*
Gemstone..........................Blue Agate
Fossil.............................Mammoth
Grass.......................Little Blue Stem
Insect.............................Honeybee
Rock..............................Prairie Agate
Entered the Union................March 1, 1867
Capital................................Lincoln

SELECTED OFFICIALS

Governor........................Charles Thone
Lieutenant Governor..........Roland A. Luedtke
Secretary of State..............Allen J. Beermann
Attorney General................Paul L. Douglas

SUPREME COURT

Norman Krivosha, Chief Justice
Leslie Boslaugh
Donald Brodkey
Lawrence M. Clinton
William C. Hastings
Hale McCown
C. Thomas White

LEGISLATURE

President of the Legislature.....Roland A. Luedtke
Speaker of the Legislature.......Richard D. Marvel
Chairman of Executive Board,
    Legislative Council..............Howard Lamb
Vice Chairman of Executive Board,
    Legislative Council...............Don Dworak
Clerk of the Legislature.......Patrick J. O'Donnell

STATISTICS

Land Area (square miles)..................76,483
    Rank in Nation........................15th
Population...........................1,570,006
    Rank in Nation........................35th
    Density per square mile....................20.5
Number of Representatives in Congress..........3
Capital City...........................Lincoln
    Population..........................171,932
    Rank in State...........................2nd
Largest City............................Omaha
    Population..........................311,681
Number of Cities over 10,000 Population........12

Nevada

Nickname.....................The Silver State
Motto......................*All for Our Country*
Flower............................Sagebrush
Bird........................Mountain Bluebird
Tree.....................Single-leaf Pinon
Song.....................*Home Means Nevada*
Animal...................Desert Bighorn Sheep
Metal................................Silver
Grass.......................Indian Rice Grass
Fossil............................Ichthyosaur
Entered the Union..............October 31, 1864
Capital..........................Carson City

SELECTED OFFICIALS

Governor........................Robert F. List
Lieutenant Governor...........Myron E. Leavitt
Secretary of State........William D. Swackhamer
Attorney General...............Richard H. Bryan

SUPREME COURT

E. M. Gunderson, Chief Justice
Noel E. Manoukian
John C. Mowbray
Charles E. Springer
(Vacancy)

LEGISLATURE

President of the Senate..........Myron E. Leavitt
President Pro Tem of the Senate
    ....Melvin D. Close Jr.
Secretary of the Senate........Leola H. Armstrong

Speaker of the Assembly............Paul W. May
Speaker Pro Tem of the Assembly
    ....Robert R. Barengo
Chief Clerk of the Assembly...Mouryne B. Landing

STATISTICS

Land Area (square miles)................109,889
    Rank in Nation.........................7th
Population............................799,184
    Rank in Nation........................43rd
    Density per square mile....................7.3
Number of Representatives in Congress..........2
Capital City.......................Carson City
    Population...........................32,022
    Rank in State............................5th
Largest City........................Las Vegas
    Population..........................164,674
Number of Cities over 10,000 Population.........6

New Hampshire

Nickname . . . . The Granite State
Motto . . . . *Live Free or Die*
Flower . . . . Purple Lilac
Bird . . . . Purple Finch
Tree . . . . White Birch
Song . . . . *Old New Hampshire*
Insect . . . . Ladybug
Entered the Union . . . . June 21, 1788
Capital . . . . Concord

SELECTED OFFICIALS

Governor . . . . Hugh J. Gallen
Secretary of State . . . . William M. Gardner
Attorney General . . . . Gregory H. Smith

SUPREME COURT

John W. King, Chief Justice
William F. Batchelder
Maurice P. Bois
David A. Brock
Charles G. Douglas III

GENERAL COURT

President of the Senate . . . . Robert B. Monier
Vice President of the Senate
. . . . Louis E. Bergeron
Clerk of the Senate . . . . Wilmont S. White

Speaker of the House . . . . John B. Tucker
Clerk of the House . . . . James A. Chandler

STATISTICS

Land Area (square miles) 9,027
   Rank in Nation 44th
Population 920,610
   Rank in Nation 42nd
   Density per square mile 102
Number of Representatives in Congress 2
Capital City . . . . Concord
   Population 30,400
   Rank in State 3rd
Largest City . . . . Manchester
   Population 90,936
Number of Cities and Towns over 10,000
   Population 21

New Jersey

Nickname . . . . The Garden State
Motto . . . . *Liberty and Prosperity*
Flower . . . . Purple Violet
Bird . . . . Eastern Goldfinch
Tree . . . . Red Oak
Insect . . . . Honeybee
Animal . . . . Horse
Entered the Union . . . . December 18, 1787
Capital . . . . Trenton

SELECTED OFFICIALS

Governor . . . . Thomas H. Kean
Secretary of State . . . . Donald P. Lan
Attorney General . . . . Irwin I. Kimmelman

SUPREME COURT

Robert N. Wilentz, Chief Justice
Robert L. Clifford
Alan B. Handler
Daniel J. O'Hern
Morris Pashman
Stewart G. Pollock
Sidney M. Schreiber

LEGISLATURE

President of the Senate . . . . Carmen A. Orechio
President Pro Tem of the Senate
. . . . Matthew Feldman
Secretary of the Senate . . . . Robert E. Gladden

Speaker of the Assembly . . . . Alan J. Karcher
Speaker Pro Tem of the Assembly
. . . . Thomas J. Deverin
Clerk of the Assembly . . . . John J. Miller, Jr.

STATISTICS

Land Area (square miles) 7,521
   Rank in Nation 46th
Population 7,364,158
   Rank in Nation 9th
   Density per square mile 979.1
Number of Representatives in Congress 14
Capital City . . . . Trenton
   Population 92,124
   Rank in State 5th
Largest City . . . . Newark
   Population 329,248
Number of Cities and Townships over
   10,000 Population 210

New Mexico

Nickname . . . . The Land of Enchantment
Motto . . . . *Crescit Eundo* (It Grows As It Goes)
Flower . . . . Yucca
Bird . . . . Roadrunner
Tree . . . . Pinon
Songs . . . . *Asi es Nuevo Mexico* and
O, Fair New Mexico
Gem . . . . Turquoise
Animal . . . . Black Bear
Fish . . . . Cutthroat Trout
Entered the Union . . . . January 6, 1912
Capital . . . . Santa Fe

SELECTED OFFICIALS

Governor . . . . Bruce King
Lieutenant Governor . . . . . . Roberto A. Mondragon
Secretary of State . . . . Shirley Hooper
Attorney General . . . . Jeff Bingaman

SUPREME COURT

Mack Easley, Chief Justice
Dan Sosa Jr., Senior Justice
William R. Federici
H. Vern Payne
William F. Riordan

LEGISLATURE

President of the Senate . . . . . Roberto A. Mondragon
President Pro Tem of the Senate . . . . . I. M. Smalley
Chief Clerk of the Senate . . . . Juanita M. Pino

Speaker of the House . . . . C. Gene Samberson
Chief Clerk of the House . . . . Albert R. Romero

STATISTICS

Land Area (square miles) 121,412
Rank in Nation 5th
Population 1,299,968
Rank in Nation 37th
Density per square mile 10.7
Number of Representatives in Congress 3
Capital City . . . . Santa Fe
Population 48,899
Rank in State 2nd
Largest City . . . . Albuquerque
Population 331,767
Number of Cities over 10,000 Population 13

New York

Nickname . . . . The Empire State
Motto . . . . *Excelsior* (Ever Upward)
Flower . . . . Rose
Bird . . . . Bluebird
Tree . . . . Sugar Maple
Fruit . . . . Apple
Gem . . . . Garnet
Animal . . . . American Beaver
Fish . . . . Brook Trout
Beverage . . . . Milk
Entered the Union . . . . July 26, 1788
Capital . . . . Albany

SELECTED OFFICIALS

Governor . . . . Hugh L. Carey
Lieutenant Governor . . . . Mario M. Cuomo
Secretary of State . . . . Basil A. Paterson
Attorney General . . . . Robert Abrams

COURT OF APPEALS

Lawrence H. Cooke, Chief Judge
Jacob D. Fuchsberg
Domenick L. Gabrielli
Matthew J. Jasen
Hugh R. Jones
Bernard S. Meyer
Sol Wachtler

LEGISLATURE

President of the Senate . . . . Mario M. Cuomo
President Pro Tem of the Senate
. . . . Warren M. Anderson
Secretary of the Senate . . . . Roger C. Thompson

Speaker of the Assembly . . . . Stanley Fink
Speaker Pro Tem of the Assembly
. . . . William F. Passannante
Clerk of the Assembly . . . . Catherine A. Carey

STATISTICS

Land Area (square miles) 47,831
Rank in Nation 30th
Population 17,557,288
Rank in Nation 2nd
Density per square mile 367.1
Number of Representatives in Congress 34
Capital City . . . . Albany
Population 101,727
Rank in State 6th
Largest City . . . . New York
Population 7,071,030
Number of Cities over 10,000 Population 87

North Carolina

Nickname . . . . The Tar Heel State
Motto . . . . *Esse Quam Videri*
(To Be Rather Than to Seem)
Flower . . . . Dogwood
Bird . . . . Cardinal
Tree . . . . Long Leaf Pine
Song . . . . *The Old North State*
Mammal . . . . Gray Squirrel
Gem . . . . Emerald
Fish . . . . Channel Bass
Insect . . . . Honey Bee
Reptile . . . . Turtle
Rock . . . . Granite
Entered the Union . . . . November 21, 1789
Capital . . . . Raleigh

SELECTED OFFICIALS

Governor . . . . James B. Hunt Jr.
Lieutenant Governor . . . . James C. Green
Secretary of State . . . . Thad Eure
Attorney General . . . . Rufus L. Edmisten

SUPREME COURT

Joseph Branch, Chief Justice
David M. Britt
H. Phil Carlton
J. William Copeland
James G. Exum Jr.
J. Frank Huskins
Louis B. Meyer

GENERAL ASSEMBLY

President of the Senate . . . . James C. Green
President Pro Tem of the Senate . . . W. Craig Lawing
Principal Clerk of the Senate . . . . Sylvia Fink

Speaker of the House . . . . Liston B. Ramsey
Speaker Pro Tem of the House
. . . . Allan C. Barbee
Principal Clerk of the House . . . . Grace Collins

STATISTICS

Land Area (square miles) 48,798
   Rank in Nation 29th
Population 5,874,429
   Rank in Nation 10th
   Density per square mile 120.4
Number of Representatives in Congress 11
Capital City . . . . Raleigh
   Population 149,771
   Rank in State 3rd
Largest City . . . . Charlotte
   Population 314,447
Number of Cities over 10,000 Population 43

North Dakota

Nicknames . . . . The Flickertail State and
The Sioux State
Motto . . . . *Liberty and Union, Now and*
Forever, One and Inseparable
Flower . . . . Wild Prairie Rose
Bird . . . . Western Meadowlark
Tree . . . . American Elm
Song . . . . *North Dakota Hymn*
March . . . . *Spirit of the Land*
Stone . . . . Teredo Petrified Wood
Fish . . . . Northern Pike
Grass . . . . Western Wheatgrass
Entered the Union . . . . November 2, 1889
Capital . . . . Bismarck

SELECTED OFFICIALS

Governor . . . . Allen I. Olson
Lieutenant Governor . . . . Ernest M. Sands
Secretary of State . . . . Ben Meier
Attorney General . . . . Robert O. Wefald

SUPREME COURT

Ralph J. Erickstad, Chief Justice
William L. Paulson
Vernon R. Pederson
Paul Sand
Gerald W. VandeWalle

LEGISLATIVE ASSEMBLY

President of the Senate . . . . Ernest M. Sands
President Pro Tem of the Senate
. . . . Stanley Wright
Secretary of the Senate . . . . Leo Leidholm

Speaker of the House . . . . James A. Peterson
Chief Clerk of the House . . . . G. Roy Gilbreath

STATISTICS

Land Area (square miles) 69,273
   Rank in Nation 17th
Population 652,695
   Rank in Nation 46th
   Density per square mile 9.4
Number of Representatives in Congress 1
Capital City . . . . Bismarck
   Population 44,485
   Rank in State 2nd
Largest City . . . . Fargo
   Population 61,308
Number of Cities over 10,000 Population 9

Ohio

Nickname . . . . The Buckeye State
Motto . . . . *With God, All Things Are Possible*
Flower . . . . Scarlet Carnation
Bird . . . . Cardinal
Tree . . . . Buckeye
Song . . . . *Beautiful Ohio*
Stone . . . . Ohio Flint
Insect . . . . Ladybug
Beverage . . . . Tomato Juice
Entered the Union . . . . March 1, 1803
Capital . . . . Columbus

SELECTED OFFICIALS

Governor . . . . James A. Rhodes
Lieutenant Governor . . . . (Vacancy)
Secretary of State . . . . Anthony J. Celebrezze Jr.
Attorney General . . . . William J. Brown

SUPREME COURT

Frank D. Celebrezze, Chief Justice
Clifford F. Brown
William B. Brown
Robert E. Holmes
Blanche E. Krupansky
Ralph S. Locher
A. William Sweeney

GENERAL ASSEMBLY

President of the Senate . . . . Paul E. Gillmor
President Pro Tem of the Senate
. . . . Thomas A. Van Meter
Clerk of the Senate . . . . James R. Tilling

Speaker of the House . . . . Vernon G. Riffe Jr.
Speaker Pro Tem of the House . . . . . . Barney Quilter
Legislative Clerk of the House . . . . . . Richard Murray
Executive Secretary of the House
. . . . Catherine Ashley

STATISTICS

Land Area (square miles) 40,975
   Rank in Nation 35th
Population 10,797,419
   Rank in Nation 6th
   Density per square mile 263.5
Number of Representatives in Congress 21
Capital City . . . . Columbus
   Population 564,871
   Rank in State 2nd
Largest City . . . . Cleveland
   Population 573,822
Number of Cities over 10,000 Population 149

Oklahoma

Nickname . . . . The Sooner State
Motto . . . . *Labor Omnia Vincit*
           (Labor Conquers All Things)
Flower . . . . Mistletoe
Bird . . . . Scissor-tailed Flycatcher
Tree . . . . Redbud
Grass . . . . Indian Grass
Song . . . . *Oklahoma*
Poem . . . . "Howdy Folks"
Stone . . . . Barite Rose (Rose Rock)
Animal . . . . American Buffalo
Reptile . . . . Mountain Boomer Lizard
Fish . . . . White Bass
Entered the Union . . . . November 16, 1907
Capital . . . . Oklahoma City

SELECTED OFFICIALS

Governor . . . . George Nigh
Lieutenant Governor . . . . Spencer Bernard
Secretary of State . . . . Jeannette B. Edmondson
Attorney General . . . . Jan Eric Cartwright

SUPREME COURT

Pat Irwin, Chief Justice
Don Barnes, Vice Chief Justice

John B. Doolin   Marian P. Opala
Rudolph Hargrave   Robert D. Simms
Ralph B. Hodges   (Vacancy)
Robert E. Lavender

COURT OF CRIMINAL APPEALS

Tom Brett, Presiding Judge
Hez Bussey
Thomas R. Cornish

LEGISLATURE

President of the Senate . . . . Spencer Bernard
President Pro Tem of the Senate . . . . . . Marvin York
Secretary of the Senate . . . . Lee Slater

Speaker of the House . . . . Daniel D. Draper Jr.
Speaker Pro Tem of the House . . . . Mike Murphy
Chief Clerk of the House/Administrator
. . . . Richard Huddleston

STATISTICS

Land Area (square miles) 68,782
   Rank in Nation 19th
Population 3,025,266
   Rank in Nation 26th
   Density per square mile 44
Number of Representatives in Congress 6
Capital City . . . . Oklahoma City
   Population 403,213
   Rank in State 1st
Largest City . . . . Oklahoma City
Number of Cities over 10,000 Population 33

Oregon

Nickname . . . . The Beaver State
Motto . . . . *The Union*
Flower . . . . Oregon Grape
Bird . . . . Western Meadowlark
Tree . . . . Douglas Fir
Song . . . . *Oregon, My Oregon*
Stone . . . . Thunderegg
Animal . . . . Beaver
Fish . . . . Chinook Salmon
Insect . . . . Swallowtail Butterfly
Entered the Union . . . . February 14, 1859
Capital . . . . Salem

SELECTED OFFICIALS

Governor . . . . Victor Atiyeh
Secretary of State . . . . Norma Paulus
Attorney General . . . . David B. Frohnmayer

SUPREME COURT

Arno H. Denecke, Chief Justice
J. R. Campbell
Berkeley Lent
Hans A. Linde
Edward J. Peterson
Jacob Tanzer
Thomas H. Tongue

LEGISLATIVE ASSEMBLY

President of the Senate . . . . Fred W. Heard
President Pro Tem of the Senate
. . . . Clifford W. Trow
Secretary of the Senate . . . . Maribel Cadmus

Speaker of the House . . . . Hardy Myers
Speaker Pro Tem of the House . . . . Vera Katz
Chief Clerk of the House . . . . Winton J. Hunt

STATISTICS

Land Area (square miles) 96,184
   Rank in Nation 10th
Population 2,632,663
   Rank in Nation 30th
   Density per square mile 27.4
Number of Representatives in Congress 5
Capital City . . . . Salem
   Population 89,233
   Rank in State 3rd
Largest City . . . . Portland
   Population 366,383
Number of Cities over 10,000 Population 29

Pennsylvania

Nickname . . . . The Keystone State
Motto . . . . *Virtue, Liberty and Independence*
Flower . . . . Mountain Laurel
Game Bird . . . . Ruffed Grouse
Tree . . . . Hemlock
Dog . . . . Great Dane
Animal . . . . Whitetail Deer
Insect . . . . Firefly
Fish . . . . Brook Trout
Entered the Union . . . . December 12, 1787
Capital . . . . Harrisburg

SELECTED OFFICIALS

Governor . . . . Richard L. Thornburgh
Lieutenant Governor . . . . . . William W. Scranton III
Secretary of the Commonwealth . . . William R. Davis
Attorney General . . . . LeRoy S. Zimmerman

SUPREME COURT

Henry X. O'Brien, Chief Justice
John P. Flaherty Jr.
William D. Hutchinson
Rolf Larsen
James T. McDermott
Robert N. C. Nix Jr.
Samuel J. Roberts

GENERAL ASSEMBLY

President of the Senate . . . . William W. Scranton III
President Pro Tem of the Senate
. . . . Henry G. Hager
Secretary of the Senate . . . . Thomas Andrews

Speaker of the House . . . . Matthew J. Ryan
Chief Clerk of the House . . . . John J. Zubeck

STATISTICS

Land Area (square miles) 44,966
   Rank in Nation 32nd
Population 11,866,728
   Rank in Nation 4th
   Density per square mile 263.9
Number of Representatives in Congress 23
Capital City . . . . Harrisburg
   Population 53,264
   Rank in State 10th
Largest City . . . . Philadelphia
   Population 1,688,210
Number of Cities over 10,000 Population 83

Rhode Island

Nickname .... Little Rhody
Motto .... *Hope*
Flower .... Violet
Bird .... Rhode Island Red
Tree .... Red Maple
Song .... *Rhode Island*
Rock .... Cumberlandite
Mineral .... Bowenite
Entered the Union .... May 29, 1790
Capital .... Providence

SELECTED OFFICIALS

Governor .... J. Joseph Garrahy
Lieutenant Governor .... Thomas R. DiLuglio
Secretary of State .... Robert F. Burns
Attorney General .... Dennis J. Roberts II

SUPREME COURT

Joseph A. Bevilacqua, Chief Justice
Thomas F. Kelleher
Florence K. Murray
Donald F. Shea
Joseph R. Weisberger

GENERAL ASSEMBLY

President of the Senate .... Thomas R. DiLuglio
President Pro Tem of the Senate
.... William A. Castro
Secretary of the Senate .... Robert F. Burns

Speaker of the House .... Matthew J. Smith
First Deputy Speaker of the House
.... Maureen E. Maigret
Reading Clerk of the House
.... Eugene J. McMahon

STATISTICS

Land Area (square miles) 1,049
    Rank in Nation 50th
Population 947,154
    Rank in Nation 40th
    Density per square mile 902.9
Number of Representatives in Congress 2
Capital City .... Providence
    Population 156,804
    Rank in State 1st
Largest City .... Providence
Number of Cities and Towns over 10,000
    Population 27

South Carolina

Nickname .... The Palmetto State
Mottos .... *Animis Opibusque Parati*
    (Prepared in Mind and Resources) and
    Dum Spiro Spero (While I Breathe, I Hope)
Flower .... Carolina Jessamine
Bird .... Carolina Wren
Tree .... Palmetto
Song .... *Carolina*
Stone .... Blue Granite
Entered the Union .... May 23, 1788
Capital .... Columbia

SELECTED OFFICIALS

Governor .... Richard W. Riley
Lieutenant Governor .... Nancy Stevenson
Secretary of State .... John T. Campbell
Attorney General .... Daniel R. McLeod

SUPREME COURT

James Woodrow Lewis, Chief Justice
George Tillman Gregory Jr.
David W. Harwell
Bruce Littlejohn
Julius B. Ness

GENERAL ASSEMBLY

President of the Senate .... Nancy Stevenson
President Pro Tem of the Senate
.... L. Marion Gressette
Clerk of the Senate .... James P. Fields Jr.

Speaker of the House .... Ramon Schwartz Jr.
Speaker Pro Tem of the House
.... Michael R. Daniel
Clerk of the House .... Lois T. Shealy

STATISTICS

Land Area (square miles) 30,225
    Rank in Nation 40th
Population 3,119,208
    Rank in Nation 24th
    Density per square mile 103.2
Number of Representatives in Congress 6
Capital City .... Columbia
    Population 99,296
    Rank in State 1st
Largest City .... Columbia
Number of Cities over 10,000 Population 26

South Dakota

Nickname . . . . The Coyote State
Motto . . . . *Under God the People Rule*
Flower . . . . Pasque Flower
Bird . . . . Ringnecked Pheasant
Tree . . . . Black Hills Spruce
Song . . . . *Hail, South Dakota*
Mineral . . . . Rose Quartz
Gem . . . . Fairburn Agate
Animal . . . . Coyote
Entered the Union . . . . November 2, 1889
Capital . . . . Pierre

SELECTED OFFICIALS

Governor . . . . William J. Janklow
Lieutenant Governor . . . . Lowell C. Hansen II
Secretary of State . . . . Alice Kundert
Attorney General . . . . Mark Meierhenry

SUPREME COURT

Roger L. Wollman, Chief Justice
Francis G. Dunn
Jon Fosheim
Frank E. Henderson
Robert E. Morgan

LEGISLATURE

President of the Senate . . . . Lowell C. Hansen II
President Pro Tem of the Senate . . Mary A. McClure
Secretary of the Senate . . . . Joyce Hazeltine

Speaker of the House . . . . Walter D. Miller
Speaker Pro Tem of the House

. . . . Jerome B. Lammers
Chief Clerk of the House . . . . Paul Inman

STATISTICS

Land Area (square miles) 75,955
   Rank in Nation 16th
Population 690,178
   Rank in Nation 45th
   Density per square mile 9.1
Number of Representatives in Congress 1
Capital City . . . . Pierre
   Population 11,973
   Rank in State 9th
Largest City . . . . Sioux Falls
   Population 81,343
Number of Cities over 10,000 Population 9

Tennessee

Nickname . . . . The Volunteer State
Motto . . . . *Agriculture and Commerce*
Flower . . . . Iris
Bird . . . . Mockingbird
Tree . . . . Tulip Poplar
Wildflower . . . . Passion Flower
Songs . . . . *When It's Iris Time in Tennessee;*
   The Tennessee Waltz; My Homeland, Tennessee;
                 and *My Tennessee*
Stone . . . . Agate
Animal . . . . Raccoon
Insects . . . . Ladybug and Firefly
Gem . . . . Tennessee Pearl
Rock . . . . Limestone
Slogan . . . . Tennessee—America at Its Best
Entered the Union . . . . June 1, 1796
Capital . . . . Nashville

SELECTED OFFICIALS

Governor . . . . Lamar Alexander
Lieutenant Governor . . . . John S. Wilder
Secretary of State . . . . Gentry Crowell
Attorney General . . . . William M. Leech Jr.

SUPREME COURT

Ray L. Brock Jr., Chief Justice
Robert E. Cooper
Frank F. Drowota III
William H. D. Fones
William J. Harbison

GENERAL ASSEMBLY

Speaker of the Senate . . . . John S. Wilder
Chief Clerk of the Senate

. . . . Clyde W. McCullough Jr.

Speaker of the House . . . . Ned R. McWherter
Speaker Pro Tem of the House

. . . . Harper Brewer Jr.
Chief Clerk of the House . . . . David Welles

STATISTICS

Land Area (square miles) 41,328
   Rank in Nation 34th
Population 4,590,750
   Rank in Nation 17th
   Density per square mile 111.1
Number of Representatives in Congress 9
Capital City . . . . Nashville
   Population 455,651
   Rank in State 2nd
Largest City . . . . Memphis
   Population 646,356
Number of Cities over 10,000 Population 36

Texas

Nickname .... The Lone Star State
Motto .... *Friendship*
Flower .... Bluebonnet
Bird .... Mockingbird
Tree .... Pecan
Song .... *Texas, Our Texas*
Stone .... Palmwood
Gem .... Topaz
Grass .... Sideoats Grama
Dish .... Chili
Entered the Union .... December 29, 1845
Capital .... Austin

SELECTED OFFICIALS

Governor .... William P. Clements
Lieutenant Governor .... William P. Hobby
Secretary of State .... David A. Dean
Attorney General .... Mark W. White

SUPREME COURT

Joe R. Greenhill, Chief Justice

Charles W. Barrow	Jack Pope
Robert M. Campbell	C. L. Ray
James G. Denton	Franklin S. Spears
Sears McGee	James P. Wallace

COURT OF CRIMINAL APPEALS

John F. Onion Jr., Presiding Judge

Sam H. Clinton	Leon Douglas
Carl E. F. Dally	Wendell Odom
Tom G. Davis	W. T. Phillips
W. C. Davis	Truman Roberts

LEGISLATURE

President of the Senate .... William P. Hobby
President Pro Tem of the Senate
.... Walter H. Mendgen Jr.
Secretary of the Senate .... Betty King

Speaker of the House .... Bill Clayton
Speaker Pro Tem of the House ... Craig Washington
Chief Clerk of the House .... Betty Murray

STATISTICS

Land Area (square miles) 262,134
  Rank in Nation 2nd
Population 14,228,383
  Rank in Nation 3rd
  Density per square mile 54.3
Number of Representatives in Congress......... 27
Capital City .... Austin
  Population 345,496
  Rank in State 6th
Largest City .... Houston
  Population 1,594,086
Number of Cities over 10,000 Population 151

Utah

Nickname .... The Beehive State
Motto .... *Industry*
Flower .... Sego Lily
Bird .... Seagull
Tree .... Blue Spruce
Song .... *Utah, We Love Thee*
Gem .... Topaz
Entered the Union .... January 4, 1896
Capital .... Salt Lake City

SELECTED OFFICIALS

Governor .... Scott M. Matheson
Lieutenant Governor/Secretary of State
.... David S. Monson
Attorney General .... David L. Wilkinson

SUPREME COURT

Gordon R. Hall, Chief Justice
Christine M. Durham
Richard C. Howe
Dallin H. Oaks
I. Daniel Stewart

LEGISLATURE

President of the Senate .... Miles Ferry
Secretary of the Senate .... Sophia C. Buckmiller

Speaker of the House .... Norman H. Bangerter
Chief Clerk of the House .... Allan M. Acomb

STATISTICS

Land Area (square miles) 82,096
  Rank in Nation 12th
Population 1,461,037
  Rank in Nation 36th
  Density per square mile 17.8
Number of Representatives in Congress........... 3
Capital City .... Salt Lake City
  Population 163,022
  Rank in State 1st
Largest City .... Salt Lake City
Number of Cities over 10,000 Population 22

Vermont

Nickname . . . . The Green Mountain State
Motto . . . . *Freedom and Unity*
Flower . . . . Red Clover
Bird . . . . Hermit Thrush
Tree . . . . Sugar Maple
Song . . . . *Hail, Vermont!*
Animal . . . . Morgan Horse
Insect . . . . Honeybee
Entered the Union . . . . March 4, 1791
Capital . . . . Montpelier

SELECTED OFFICIALS

Governor . . . . Richard A. Snelling
Lieutenant Governor . . . . Madeleine M. Kunin
Secretary of State . . . . James H. Douglas
Attorney General . . . . John J. Easton Jr.

SUPREME COURT

Albert W. Barney Jr., Chief Justice
Franklin S. Billings Jr.
William C. Hill
Louis P. Peck
Wynn Underwood

GENERAL ASSEMBLY

President of the Senate . . . . Madeleine M. Kunin
President Pro Tem of the Senate
. . . . Robert A. Bloomer
Secretary of the Senate . . . . Robert H. Gibson

Speaker of the House . . . . Stephan A. Morse
Clerk of the House . . . . Robert L. Picher

STATISTICS

Land Area (square miles) 9,267
  Rank in Nation 43rd
Population 511,456
  Rank in Nation 48th
  Density per square mile 55.2
Number of Representatives in Congress 1
Capital City . . . . Montpelier
  Population 8,241
  Rank in State 5th
Largest City . . . . Burlington
  Population 37,712
Number of Cities and Towns over 10,000
  Population 8

Virginia

Nickname . . . . The Old Dominion
Motto . . . . *Sic Semper Tyrannis*
(Thus Always to Tyrants)
Flower . . . . Dogwood
Bird . . . . Cardinal
Tree . . . . Dogwood
Song . . . . *Carry Me Back to Old Virginia*
Animal . . . . Foxhound
Shell . . . . Oyster
Entered the Union . . . . June 25, 1788
Capital . . . . Richmond

SELECTED OFFICIALS

Governor . . . . Charles S. Robb
Lieutenant Governor . . . . Richard J. Davis
Secretary of the Commonwealth
. . . . Frederick T. Gray III
Attorney General . . . . Gerald L. Baliles

SUPREME COURT

Harry Lee Carrico, Chief Justice
George M. Cochran
A. Christian Compton
Richard H. Poff
Roscoe B. Stephenson Jr.
W. Carrington Thompson
(Vacancy)

GENERAL ASSEMBLY

President of the Senate . . . . Richard J. Davis
President Pro Tem of the Senate
. . . . Edward E. Willey
Clerk of the Senate . . . . Jay T. Shropshire

Speaker of the House . . . . A. L. Philpott
Clerk of the House . . . . Joseph H. Holleman Jr.

STATISTICS

Land Area (square miles) 39,780
  Rank in Nation 36th
Population 5,346,279
  Rank in Nation 14th
  Density per square mile 134.4
Number of Representatives in Congress 10
Capital City . . . . Richmond
  Population 219,214
  Rank in State 3rd
Largest City . . . . Norfolk
  Population 266,979
Number of Cities over 10,000 Population 33

Washington

Nickname . . . . The Evergreen State
Motto . . . . *Alki* (By and By)
Flower . . . . Western Rhododendron
Bird . . . . Willow Goldfinch
Tree . . . . Western Hemlock
Song . . . . *Washington, My Home*
Dance . . . . Square Dance
Gem . . . . Petrified Wood
Fish . . . . Steelhead Trout
Entered the Union . . . . November 11, 1889
Capital . . . . Olympia

SELECTED OFFICIALS

Governor . . . . John D. Spellman
Lieutenant Governor . . . . John A. Cherberg
Secretary of State . . . . Ralph Munro
Attorney General . . . . Kenneth O. Eikenberry

SUPREME COURT

Robert F. Brachtenbach, Chief Justice

Carolyn R. Dimmick	Hugh R. Rosellini
James M. Dolliver	Charles F. Stafford
Fred H. Dore	Robert F. Utter
Floyd V. Hicks	William H. Williams

LEGISLATURE

President of the Senate . . . . John A. Cherberg
President Pro Tem of the Senate . . . . . Sam C. Guess
Secretary of the Senate . . . . Sidney R. Snyder

Speaker of the House . . . . William M. Polk
Speaker Pro Tem of the House . . . . Otto Amen
Chief Clerk of the House . . . . Vito T. Chiechi

STATISTICS

Land Area (square miles) 66,570
   Rank in Nation 20th
Population 4,130,163
   Rank in Nation 20th
   Density per square mile 62.0
Number of Representatives in Congress 8
Capital City . . . . Olympia
   Population 27,447
   Rank in State 15th
Largest City . . . . Seattle
   Population 493,846
Number of Cities over 10,000 Population 36

West Virginia

Nickname . . . . The Mountain State
Motto . . . . *Montani Semper Liberi*
            (Mountaineers Are Always Free)
Flower . . . . Big Rhododendron
Bird . . . . Cardinal
Tree . . . . Sugar Maple
Songs . . . . *West Virginia, My Home Sweet Home;*
                The West Virginia Hills; and
              This Is My West Virginia
Animal . . . . Black Bear
Fish . . . . Brook Trout
Entered the Union . . . . June 20, 1863
Capital . . . . Charleston

SELECTED OFFICIALS

Governor . . . . John D. Rockefeller IV
Secretary of State . . . . A. James Manchin
Attorney General . . . . Chauncey H. Browning

SUPREME COURT OF APPEALS

Thomas B. Miller, Chief Justice
Sam R. Harshbarger
Darrell V. McGraw Jr.
Thomas E. McHugh
Richard Neely

LEGISLATURE

President of the Senate . . . . Warren R. McGraw
President Pro Tem of the Senate . . . . . Robert Nelson
Clerk of the Senate . . . . Todd C. Willis

Speaker of the House . . . . Clyde M. See Jr.
Clerk of the House . . . . C. A. Blankenship

STATISTICS

Land Area (square miles) 24,070
   Rank in Nation 41st
Population 1,949,644
   Rank in Nation 34th
   Density per square mile 81
Number of Representatives in Congress 4
Capital City . . . . Charleston
   Population 63,968
   Rank in State 1st
Largest City . . . . Charleston
Number of Cities over 10,000 Population 15

Wisconsin

Nickname . . . . The Badger State
Motto . . . . *Forward*
Flower . . . . Wood Violet
Bird . . . . Robin
Tree . . . . Sugar Maple
Song . . . . *On, Wisconsin!*
Rock . . . . Red Granite
Mineral . . . . Galena
Animal . . . . Badger
Wildlife Animal . . . . White-tailed Deer
Domestic Animal . . . . Dairy Cow
Fish . . . . Muskellunge
Symbol of Peace . . . . Mourning Dove
Entered the Union . . . . May 29, 1848
Capital . . . . Madison

SELECTED OFFICIALS

Governor . . . . Lee Sherman Dreyfus
Lieutenant Governor . . . . Russell A. Olson
Secretary of State . . . . Vel R. Phillips
Attorney General . . . . Bronson C. La Follette

SUPREME COURT

Bruce F. Beilfuss, Chief Justice
Shirley S. Abrahamson
William G. Callow
John L. Coffey
Roland B. Day
Nathan S. Heffernan
Donald W. Steinmetz

LEGISLATURE

President of the Senate . . . . Fred A. Risser
Chief Clerk of the Senate . . . . . . Donald J. Schneider

Speaker of the Assembly . . . . Edward G. Jackamonis
Deputy Speaker of the Assembly
. . . . Louise M. Tesmer
Chief Clerk of the Assembly . . . . David R. Kedrowski

STATISTICS

Land Area (square miles) 54,464
    Rank in Nation 25th
Population 4,705,335
    Rank in Nation 16th
    Density per square mile 86.4
Number of Representatives in Congress 9
Capital City . . . . Madison
    Population 170,616
    Rank in State 2nd
Largest City . . . . Milwaukee
    Population 636,212
Number of Cities over 10,000 Population 55

Wyoming

Nickname . . . . The Equality State
Motto . . . . *Equal Rights*
Flower . . . . Indian Paintbrush
Bird . . . . Meadowlark
Tree . . . . Cottonwood
Song . . . . *Wyoming*
Stone . . . . Jade
Entered the Union . . . . July 10, 1890
Capital . . . . Cheyenne

SELECTED OFFICIALS

Governor . . . . Ed Herschler
Secretary of State . . . . Thyra Thomson
Attorney General . . . . Steven F. Freudenthal

SUPREME COURT

Robert R. Rose Jr., Chief Justice
Charles Stuart Brown
John F. Raper
John J. Rooney
Richard V. Thomas

LEGISLATURE

President of the Senate . . . . Donald R. Cundall
Vice President of the Senate . . . . Gerald E. Geis
Chief Clerk of the Senate . . . . . . Nelson E. Wren Jr.

Speaker of the House . . . . Bob J. Burnett
Speaker Pro Tem of the House . . . . Russ Donley
Chief Clerk of the House . . . . . . Herbert D. Pownall

STATISTICS

Land Area (square miles) 97,203
    Rank in Nation 9th
Population 470,816
    Rank in Nation 49th
    Density per square mile 4.8
Number of Representatives in Congress 1
Capital City . . . . Cheyenne
    Population 47,283
    Rank in State 2nd
Largest City . . . . Casper
    Population 51,016
Number of Cities over 10,000 Population 8

District of Columbia

Motto .... *Justitia Omnibus* (Justice for All)
Flower .... American Beauty Rose
Bird .... Wood Thrush
Tree .... Scarlet Oak
Became U.S. Capital .... December 1, 1800

OFFICERS

Mayor .... Marion S. Barry, Jr.
City Administrator .... Elijah B. Rogers
Executive Secretary .... Dwight Cropp
Corporation Counsel .... Judith Rogers

U.S. COURT OF APPEALS FOR THE
DISTRICT OF COLUMBIA

Chief Judge .... J. Skelly Wright

DISTRICT OF COLUMBIA
COURT OF APPEALS

Chief Judge .... Theodore R. Newman, Jr.

U. S. DISTRICT COURT FOR THE
DISTRICT OF COLUMBIA

Chief Judge .... William B. Bryant
U.S. Attorney .... Carl S. Rauh

THE SUPERIOR COURT OF THE
DISTRICT OF COLUMBIA

Chief Judge .... H. Carl Moultrie

DISTRICT OF COLUMBIA COUNCIL

Chairman .... Arrington Dixon
Chairman Pro Tem .... Nadine P. Winter

STATISTICS

Land Area (square miles) 61
Population 637,651
   Density per square mile 10,453.3
Delegate to Congress† 1

---

†Committee voting privileges only.

American Samoa

Motto .... *Samoa-Muamua le Atua*
(Samoa, God Is First)
Flower .... *Paogo*
Plant .... *Ava*
Song .... *Amerika Samoa*
Became a Territory of the United States 1900
Capital .... Pago Pago

SELECTED OFFICIALS

Governor .... Peter T. Coleman
Lieutenant Governor .... Li'a Tufele
Attorney General .... Aviata Fa'alevao

HIGH COURT

Richard Miyamoto, Chief Justice
Thomas W. Murphy, Associate Judge
Ta'iau Mamea, Chief Judge
Itumalo A'au
Mageafaiga Faoa
Ape Poutoa
Faisiota Tauanu'u

LEGISLATURE

President of the Senate .... Galea'i P. Poumele
President Pro Tem of the Senate
.... Mulitauaopele Tamotu
Secretary of the Senate .... Mrs. Salilo K. Levi

Speaker of the House .... Tuanaitau F. Tuia
Speaker Pro Tem of the House
.... Muasau S. Savali
Chief Clerk of the House .... Malaetia Tufele

STATISTICS

Land Area (square miles) 76
Population 32,395
   Density per square mile 426.3
Capital City .... Pago Pago
   Population 3,058
Largest City .... Pago Pago
Number of Villages 76

Guam

Nickname . . . . Pearl of the Pacific
Flower . . . . *Puti Tai Nobio* (Bougainvillea)
Bird . . . . *Toto* (Fruit Dove)
Tree . . . . *Ifit* (Intsiabijuga)
Song . . . . *Stand Ye Guamanians*
Stone . . . . Latte
Slogan . . . . Where America's Day Begins
Animal . . . . Iguana
Ceded to the United States by Spain
. . . . December 10, 1898
Created a Territory . . . . August 1, 1950
Capital . . . . Agana

SELECTED OFFICIALS

Governor . . . . Paul M. Calvo
Lieutenant Governor . . . . Joseph F. Ada
Attorney General . . . , ... Jack Avery

DISTRICT COURT OF GUAM

Judge . . . . Cristobal C. Duenas

SUPERIOR COURT OF GUAM

Presiding Judge . . . . Paul J. Abbate

LEGISLATURE

Speaker . . . . Thomas V. C. Tanaka
Vice Speaker . . . . Frank F. Blas
Legislative Secretary . . . . Thomas C. Crisostomo
Executive Director . . . . Jose Nededog

STATISTICS

Land Area (square miles) 209
Population 105,816
   Density per square mile 506.3
Delegate to Congress† 1
Capital City . . . . Agana
   Population 881
Largest City . . . . Dededo
   Population 23,659

---

†Committee voting privileges only.

Puerto Rico

Nickname . . . . Island of Enchantment
Motto . . . . *Joannes Est Nomen Ejus*
(John Is Thy Name)
Song . . . . *La Borinquena*
Animal . . . . Coqui
Became a territory of the United States
. . . . December 10, 1898
Became a self-governing commonwealth
. . . . July 25, 1952
Capital . . . . San Juan

SELECTED OFFICIALS

Governor . . . . Carlos Romero-Barcelo
Secretary of State . . . . Carlos S. Quiros
Attorney General . . . . . Hector Reichard de Cardona

SUPREME COURT

Jose Trias Monge, Chief Justice
Hiram Torres Rigual
Angel M. Martin
Carlos V. Davila
Antonio Negron Garcia
Jorge Diaz Cruz
Carlos J. Irizarry-Yunque

LEGISLATIVE ASSEMBLY

President of the Senate . . . Miguel Hernandez Agosto
Vice President of the Senate . . . . Sergio Pena Clos
Secretary of the Senate . . . . Hipolito Marcano
Speaker of the House . . . . Angel Viera Martinez
Vice President of the House . . . . Severo Colberg
Secretary of the House . . . . Cristino Bernazard

STATISTICS

Land Area (square miles) 3,421
Population 3,187,570
   Density per square mile 931.8
Delegate to Congress† 1
Capital City . . . . San Juan
   Population 1,083,114
Largest City . . . . San Juan
Number of Places over 10,000 Population 29

---

†Committee voting privileges only.

Virgin Islands

Flower .... Yellow Elder or Ginger Thomas
Bird .... Yellow Breast or Bananaquit
Song .... *Virgin Islands March*
Purchased from Denmark .... March 31, 1917
Capital .... Charlotte Amalie

SELECTED OFFICIALS

Governor .... Juan F. Luis
Lieutenant Governor .... Henry Millin
Attorney General (Acting) ...... Donald M. Bouton

DISTRICT COURT

Chief Judge .... Almeric L. Christian
Judge .... David O'Brien
United States Attorney .... Ishmael Meyers

LEGISLATURE

President .... Ruby M. Rouss
Vice President .... Gilbert Sprauve
Legislative Secretary .... Ruby Simmonds
Executive Secretary .... Mary Innis

STATISTICS

Land Area (square miles) 132
   St. Croix (square miles) 80
   St. John (square miles) 20
   St. Thomas (square miles) 32
Population 95,591
   St. Croix 49,013
   St. John 2,360
   St. Thomas 44,218
Density per square mile 724.2
Delegate to Congress† 1
Capital City .... Charlotte Amalie, St. Thomas
   Population 11,756

---

†Committee voting privileges only.

Northern Mariana Islands

Tree .... Flame Tree
Flower .... Plumeria
Administered by the United States as a trusteeship
   for the United Nations .... July 18, 1947
Voters approved a proposed constitution
   .... June 1975
U.S. President signed covenant agreeing to com-
   monwealth status for the islands ...... March 1976
Became a self-governing commonwealth
   .... January 9, 1978
Capital .... Saipan

SELECTED OFFICIALS

Governor .... Pedro P. Tenorio
Lieutenant Governor .... Pedro A. Tenorio

U.S. DISTRICT COURT

Judge .... Alfred Laureta

COMMONWEALTH TRIAL COURT

Chief Justice .... Robert A. Hefner

LEGISLATURE

President of the Senate .... Olympia T. Borja
Vice President of the Senate
   .... Benjamin T. Manglona

Speaker of the House .... Benigno R. Fitial
Vice Speaker of the House .... Francisco T. Cabrera

STATISTICS

Land Area (square miles) 184
Population 16,758
   Density per square mile 91.1
Capital City .... Saipan
   Population 14,585
Largest City .... Saipan

Trust Territory of the Pacific Islands

Federated States of Micronesia

Administered by the United States as a trusteeship for the United Nations.............July 18, 1947
Voters approved a proposed constitution ....July 12, 1978
Effective date of constitution.........May 10, 1979
Capital........................Kolonia, Ponape

SELECTED OFFICIALS

President† ....Tosiwo Nakayama
Vice President† ....Petrus Tun
Attorney General.....................Fred Ramp

CONGRESS

Speaker..........................Bethwel Henry
Vice Speaker ....Joab Sigrah
Chief Clerk ....Nishima Siron

STATISTICS

Land Area (square miles).....................271
    Kosrae District............................42
    Ponape District...........................134
    Truk District 49
    Yap District 46
Population 73,755
    Kosrae District 5,522
    Ponape District 22,319
    Truk District.........................37,742
    Yap District 8,172
    Density per square mile..................272.2
Capital City ....Kolonia, Ponape
    Population 7,633
Largest City ....Moen, Truk
    Population 9,679

†Selected by the elected unicameral congress from among its own members.

Marshall Islands

Administered by the United States as a trusteeship for the United Nations.............July 18, 1947
Voters approved a proposed constitution ....March 1, 1979
Effective date of constitution.........May 1, 1979
Capital................................Majuro

SELECTED OFFICIALS

President ....Amata Kabua

MARSHALL ISLANDS HIGH COURT

John C. Lanham, Chief Justice

LEGISLATURE
(Nitijela)

Speaker...........................Atlan Anien
Vice Speaker ....Henry Samuel

STATISTICS

Land Area (square miles)......................70
Population 31,042
    Density per square mile...................443.5
Capital City............................Majuro
    Population 8,667
Largest City ....Majuro

Republic of Belau

Administered by the United States as a trusteeship
for the United Nations . . . . July 18, 1947
Voters approved a proposed constitution
. . . . July 9, 1980
Effective date of constitution . . . . January 1981

SELECTED OFFICIALS

President . . . . Haruo I. Remeliik
Vice President . . . . Alfonso R. Oiterong

SUPREME COURT

Mamoru Nakamura, Chief Justice
Kevin Kirk, District Attorney

SENATE

President . . . . Kaleb Udui

STATISTICS

Land Area (square miles) 192
Population 12,177
   Density per square mile 63.4
Capital City . . . . Koror
   Population 7,643
Largest City . . . . Koror

AUTHOR INDEX

INDEX

Numbers in bold face indicate tables.

INDEX